ACPL ITEM
DISCARDED

OVERSIZE

ENCYCLOPEDIA
OF EMERGING
INDUSTRIES

THIRD EDITION

HIGHLIGHTS

The third edition of *Encyclopedia of Emerging Industries* details the inception, emergence, and current status of 118 newly flourishing U.S. industries and industry segments.

EEI's focused essays unearth for users a wealth of relevant, current, factual data previously accessible only through a diverse variety of sources. This volume provides broad-based, highly readable industry information under such headings as Industry Snapshot, Organization and Structure, Background and Development, Industry Leaders, Current Conditions, America and the World, Pioneers, and Research and Technology.

WHAT'S NEW FOR THIS EDITION

The essays in this edition have been completely revised, with updated statistics and the most current information on industry trends and developments. In addition, we have added essays on 19 of the most interesting and influential upcoming new industries including:

- Alternative Fuels
- Cross-Marketing
- Elder Day Care
- Liquid Metals
- Outlet Centers
- Telephone Services and Accessories
- Virtual Communities

INCLUDES GRAPHS, PHOTOS, AND SIDEBARS

Enhancing the text are nearly 200 visual elements. Graphs, charts, and tables detail sales figures, market share, industry growth rates, and historical trends. Specially selected photographs—of people, places, products, and procedures—lend context to the data featured within the essays. Sidebars provide a unique addition to the information found in *EEI*, focusing on anecdotal statistics, unusual incidents, trends, and the histories of integral individuals.

ADDITIONAL FEATURES

- Contents are arranged alphabetically

- General Index lists company names, people, legislation, court cases, significant business terms, and provides broad subject access via cross-referencing

- Industry Index offers access to essays via Standard Industrial Classification (SIC) codes

- Two Conversion Tables function as keys to SIC codes and to North American Industry Classification System (NAICS) codes

- Further Reading sections suggest avenues for continued study

A valuable addition to Gale's business resource collection, *EEI* is the only annual publication of its type that zeroes in on emerging industries while they are still well in the spotlight.

ENCYCLOPEDIA OF EMERGING INDUSTRIES

THIRD EDITION

SUSAN J. CINDRIC, EDITOR

Detroit
San Francisco
London
Boston
Woodbridge, CT

ENCYCLOPEDIA OF EMERGING INDUSTRIES

Susan J. Cindric, *Editor*

Donna Craft, Sheila Dow, Rebecca Marlow-Ferguson, Terrance W. Peck, Amanda C. Quick, Brian Rabold, *Contributing Editors*

Erin Braun, *Managing Editor*

Synapse, the Knowledge Link Corporation, *Indexer*

Mary Beth Trimper, *Production Director*
Evi Seoud, *Assistant Production Manager*

Cynthia Baldwin, *Product Design Manager*
Pamela A. E. Galbreath, *Senior Art Director*

Barbara J. Yarrow, *Graphic Services Manager*
Randy Bassett, *Image Database Supervisor*
Pamela A. Reed, *Image Coordinator*
Mike Logusz, *Imaging Specialist*

Nick Sternberg, Frontline Design, Ltd., *Graphic Designer*

Maria Franklin, *Permissions Manager*
Kimberly F. Smilay, *Permissions Assistant*

TABLE OF CONTENTS

INTRODUCTION

Welcome to the third edition of the *Encyclopedia of Emerging Industries (EEI)*. In this volume readers will find essays covering specific businesses, as well as broad business sectors that have, for the most part, shown evidence of significant growth in the recent past or potential for exemplary growth in the near future. In some cases, these areas of commerce fall within older, well-established industries—prominent examples include bottled beverages, coffee, and microwaves. More commonly, the essays focus on offshoots of relatively new industries, such as developments in push technology, electronic commerce, molecular modeling, and photonics. Students, entrepreneurs, investors, and job seekers alike will find information on technical subjects as arcane as telephony or XML, and on topics as commonplace as health spas and anti-aging products and services.

CONTENT AND ARRANGEMENT

Arranged alphabetically within the book, essay titles are cross-referenced in the General Index. So, while *Advanced Ceramics* falls as the first essay, it is also accessible via the General Index under the term *Ceramics, Advanced*. Within essays, readers may encounter statements referring them to related areas of potential interest, such as: "Also see the essay in this book on Home Health Care Services."

Supplementing the text are photographs, charts, graphs, and sidebars. In each essay, readers may expect to find some or all of the following aspects discussed:

- **Industry Snapshot.** Provides a brief overview of the topic and identifies key issues.

- **Organization and Structure.** Discusses the configuration and functional aspects of the business, including sub-industry divisions.

- **Background and Development.** Relates the genesis and history of the industry to date, including major technological advances, scandals, pioneering companies, major products, important legislation, and other shaping factors.

- **Pioneers.** Discusses individuals who have made significant contributions to the development of the industry.

- **Current Conditions.** Provides information on the status of the industry in the mid- to late 1990s, with an eye to industry challenges on the horizon.

- **Industry Leaders.** Profiles major companies, along with discussion of financial performance.

- **Work Force.** May contain information on the size, diversity, and characteristics of the industry's labor force, as well as discussion of skills needed by employees.

- **America and the World.** Contains information on the global marketplace in relation to the topic discussed.

- **Research and Technology.** Furnishes information on cutting edge developments, areas of research, and their potential to impact the industry.

- **Further Reading.** Provides users with further reading on the industry. These sources, many of which were also used to compile the essays, are from publicly accessible materials such as magazines, general and academic periodicals, books, annual reports, and government sources, as well as material supplied by industry associations. Also included are references to numerous Internet sources; when available, the URL address of these sources are included.

INDEXES AND CONVERSION TABLES

The General Index contains alphabetic references to companies, trade and professional associations, significant business trends, government agencies, prominent individuals, significant court cases, key legislation, and cross-referenced essay titles.

The Industry Index contains a listing of the essay topics along with *suggested* 1987 Standard Industrial Classification (SIC) references.

Two industry classification tables allow cross-referencing of SIC categories used in the Industry Index with the 1997 North American Industry Classification System (NAICS) codes.

TOPIC SELECTION AND INCLUSION CRITERIA

In determining topic selection, the editors found it best to rely upon several means, a portion of which were decidedly subjective. (Users will note that we have chosen to employ the term "emerging industries" rather loosely, often referring not only to entire *industries,* but to specific industrial and business *sectors,* discrete types of business *enterprises,* and sometimes simply to describe a particular *range of products or services.*) In considering inclusion, the questions we repeatedly asked ourselves revolved around these central points:

- Is the industry experiencing a period of significant growth, either financial or otherwise?

- Has the business been the recent focus of much public attention and, if so, why?

- Is the product or service being newly marketed in a particularly innovative way?

- Is the business involved in the use or production of cutting edge technologies?

Ideas for topics were culled, in part, from a wide assortment of variously ranked lists detailing the recent accomplishments of promising or well-established companies. Assorted content experts, along with our team of advisors, also provided myriad suggestions and assisted in refining the coverage within *EEI.* Finally, we relied to a certain degree on hunch, experience, and intuition, predicting to the best of our ability which emerging business areas our users would want and need to know more about.

The *EEI* series will be published annually. Chapters in future volumes will be comprised of fresh updates to selected existing topics, and will explore new industries that have entered the spotlight. Enhancements in essay comprehensiveness will be a focus.

ACKNOWLEDGEMENTS AND ADVISORS

The editors would like to sincerely thank the members of the *EEI* advisory board for their valuable assistance:

- **Joanne Kosanke,** Librarian, Business Department, Toledo Public Library, Toledo, Ohio.

- **Dr. Susan G. Neuman,** Librarian, Katz Graduate School of Business Library, University of Pittsburgh, Pittsburgh, Pennsylvania.

- **Judith M. Nixon,** Librarian, Management and Economics Library, Purdue University, West Lafayette, Indiana.

- **Ruth A. Vondracek,** Librarian, Research Library, Hewlett-Packard Corporation, Corvallis, Oregon.

COMMENTS AND SUGGESTIONS

Comments and suggestions, including ideas for future essays, are most welcome. We invite readers to send us their thoughts at:

Editors/Encyclopedia of Emerging Industries

Gale Group, Inc.
27500 Drake Rd.
Farmington Hills, MI 48331-3535

Toll-free phone: 1-800-347-GALE
Toll-free fax: 1-800-339-3374
E-mail Susan J. Cindric: Sue.Cindric@gale.com

ADULT AND RETIREMENT COMMUNITIES

The adult and retirement communities industry includes adult communities that cater to the needs of people 55 and older. These communities offer residences and, at times, special care for their occupants. According to the National Investment Center based in Annapolis, Maryland, which monitors the growth in the senior housing industry, the four categories of senior living include senior apartments, active adult communities, and owner-occupied housing; congregate care facilities, independent living units in CCRCs, and board and care living facilities; assisted living in congregate and CCRCs and board and care facilities; and nursing homes and skilled nursing units in congregate, CCRCs, and hospitals. CCRCs often evolve around a certain theme, such as a resort community offering recreational activities or a health care community offering nursing care.

The senior housing market was surging in the 1990s, spurred on by what is often referred to as the "graying of America." America's elderly population is rapidly expanding—with women aged 80 and older as one of the fastest growing segments of the U.S. population. The trend is expected to continue as baby boomers, approximately 77 million of them, come into their retirement years, beginning in 2010. The Administration on Aging estimated that by the year 2030, the United States will have more than 85 million people over the age of 60. Further, the U.S. Census Bureau's projections reflect the increasingly aged population as well. In the year 2000 there will be an anticipated 72,000 people 100 years of age or older. By 2050, the calculated projection for the population

of that same age group was over 834,000. By that same year, the over-65 population is expected to exceed 78 million, up from over 34 million in the year 2000.

These retirees will be looking for a diverse array of housing options, depending on activity level and health. Planned retirement, resort, and senior communities are available for those able to provide their own care. Others needing some assistance look for facilities that provide assisted living or full-time nursing care. In addition, seniors have greater wealth than in the past, which will enable them to shop around for quality services.

Assisted living communities are the fastest growing segment of the senior housing market, while the entire industry experienced significant growth in the late 1990s. Occupancy in the mid-1990s reached an all-time high across the board, with congregate facilities having the highest rates at 98 percent. According to Leslie Alan Horvitz in a December 1997 article for *Insight*, "More than 1 million Americans lived in 30,000 assisted living communities, some of which specialized in certain populations—Alzheimer's patients, for example." Assisted living and continuing care residences both had approximately 95 percent occupancy rates. Horvitz quoted David Schless, executive director of American Seniors Housing Association (ASHA), in that same article, "Assisted living has captured the fancy of the consumer and Wall Street." Horvitz went on to note that the 16 assisted living companies that had gone public had impressive stock performance. By the year 2000 the industry, valued at $12 billion in the late 1990s, was expected to double.

ORGANIZATION AND STRUCTURE

The senior housing market consists of a variety of facility options. According to a 1996 Development Survey by ASHA, assisted living facilities made up 54 percent of the total market. Congregate housing constituted 25 percent, continuing care retirement communities comprised 12 percent, and senior apartments accounted for 9 percent of the total adult housing market. By the end of the 1990s, the options had expanded to include single-family dwellings, geared by builders in communities across the United States to cater to the maturing home buyer.

Since 1992 ASHA has followed and reported on the adult housing industry. The association was started by the National Housing Council and, along with Coopers & Lybrand, L.L.P, has published annually the leading 25 managers and owners of senior housing in the United States. ASHA also serves as a membership organization for companies involved in senior housing. They noted how volatile the market was and how many new companies entered the field at rapid speed. Their 1996 review of the industry reported that, "Nearly a quarter, (24 percent) of the organizations appearing on the 1996 ASHA 25 ownership and management rosters were companies that had not been previously ranked. The top owners list included six newcomers, as did the top managers list." In 1998 the association had more than 300 firms as members.

The industry also appeared to be headed toward some type of government involvement. In the mid-1990s, the majority of all senior housing was private pay, but some states had begun to allow Medicaid waivers for assisted living residences. William E. Colson, president of Colson & Colson/Holiday Retirement Corporation, the largest owner and manager of senior housing for several years through 1998, remarked that, "The whole assisted living business is going to end up being under government control and will become semi-skilled nursing care." ASHA's 1998 survey of the 25 largest senior housing owners included congregate living, assisted living skilled nursing facilities, and rental or condominium living for seniors. Colson's corporation, based in Salem, Oregon, owned 23,706 housing units with ownership interest. Government involvement was expected to come mainly by way of regulations imposed as a condition of state and federal reimbursements. Many in the industry did not see the government as a positive influence. A few, such as Marriott's Senior Living Services' Phil Downer, did believe that it could help more people move into assisted living who otherwise would need to move to a nursing home.

BACKGROUND AND DEVELOPMENT

Adult and retirement communities first began as simple housing options for people entering their retirement years. According to Laura Ochipinti Zaner, author of *Assisted Living Fuels Much of the Heat in a Hot Seniors Housing Market,* the basic focus of these communities was to lure those seniors who were able to remain independent and who were willing to give up their homes in favor of a residential area with other people their age. Unfortunately, throughout the 1980s the industry was not able to attract the number of seniors it had anticipated. What leaders in the senior housing market discovered was that seniors were not interested in giving up their homes unless the new adult communities could provide them with value-added services as they grew older. Once builders and managers realized what it took to attract seniors, the industry, especially assisted living facilities, took off, increasing by 24 percent during the 1980s.

A major resource and forecaster in the senior housing industry is the National Investment Conference, which changed its name to the National Investment Center (NIC) in 1998. NIC held its first conference in 1991. According to Ben Johnston, writing for *National Real Estate Investor,* in January 1998, Robert Kramer, executive director of NIC said that, "NIC was started as an 'information bridge' between the lender/investor community and the owner/operator community. The primary focus was on educating the financial community about the seniors housing industry and what the opportunities are. Initially the focus was more on stimulating capital flows to the industry. In fact, that was in our initial mission statement." NIC conducts research independently and along with other major senior resource organizations, including ASHA and the American Health Care Association. NIC hosts an annual conference that provides industry information. Among the members of the research projects committee are leaders in the field of real estate investment in housing for seniors. According to Kramer, "The key to this industry growing and maturing was getting good date, good research, good information." NIC's research publications, available for sale through their Web site include *Lender and Investor Survey Results: Preferences and Trends in Financing Long Term Care and Senior Living Projects* and *National Survey of Assisted Living Residents: Who is the Customer?*

Johnston's article also traced what was deemed the "turn-around" in the seniors housing market from the 1980s into the late 1990s. Johnston said that the assisted living industry began to turn upward in the mid-1990s due to, "some heavy hitters sitting in New

York City in late 1994 and early 1995 who recognized the possibilities of taking this segment into the public markets, along with much of the rest of the commercial real estate industry."

PIONEERS IN THE FIELD

The person considered the true pioneer of American retirement living is Del Webb. In the late 1950s Webb started to develop the idea. He would end up, a few years later, successful in finding retirees who were healthy enough to live independently in their own homes and luring them to the desert outside of Phoenix. In 1960 his Sun City, Arizona, development opened; Webb created the model of what would constitute America's notion of retirement communities. By the end of the 1970s that idea had been successfully transformed on 8,900 acres when the first development was completed to fruition. Retirees fleeing the cold of the East Coast and Great Lakes, flocked to the age-segregated, planned community. Until that time, many Northern retirees went only to Florida. The Del Webb Corporation led the way to the future of comfortable living for people on fixed incomes—many of whom suffered the Great Depression, fought in World War II, and worked hard in factories to save for a time of leisure as they aged. Other Sun City retirement communities grew up elsewhere, including Tucson, Arizona; Hilton Head, South Carolina; and Roseville, California.

At the end of the 1990s, the corporation that still bore the name of the deceased founder was at work on eight more Sun Cities. Dirk Johnson reported on March 4, 1999 in the *The New York Times,* that the Sun City concept had evolved again. Sun City was moving North, to the cold, bleak farmland of northern Illinois, about 50 miles northwest of Chicago. The Del Webb Corporation, following years of market research, decided there was a market for their resort-like living in the nation's heartland. Sun Cities are built around an 18-hole golf course and include an indoor recreation lodge, artificial lakes, and tennis courts. At least one of the spouses had to be 55 or older. That plan was not altered when moving North. The difference in this community was that natives were tied to the land—and their grandchildren. The idea of living closer to the family they loved and the countryside that was familiar, not far from the city that might nurture them for many years was seen as the crucial element in the expected success of Sun City in the "Frost Belt."

CURRENT CONDITIONS

As the "graying of America" increases, the senior housing industry is expected to continue to grow and thrive. More than 6,000 Americans were turning 65 each day by the end of the 1990s. That figure does not include the crop of baby boomers who would start retiring in 2010. According to a report by Timothy Boyce, a member of the Real Property Division's I-2 Committee of the American Bar Association, by the year 2003, 21 percent of the U.S. population will be over 65 years old, compared with only 11 percent in 1997.

The industry realized its greatest growth in the mid-1990s. By 1996 the National Real Estate Investor (NREI) reported that senior housing was one of the real estate industry's six major commercial property types. *Fortune* magazine listed assisted living as one of 1997's most promising industries. The growth in senior housing is fueled additionally due to an industry more inclined to listen to the consumer—the retirees who have very specific requirements for a retirement residence. A 1997 study by ASHA found that 85 percent of the residents surveyed were satisfied with their accommodations and the services that were offered in their community.

The year 1997 gave witness to more gains in the number of units being built and managed. ASHA reported that the top 10 firms in 1996 realized a 10.9-percent increase in their portfolios. In addition, the industry witnessed more mergers in 1997. According to Irving Levin Associates, six mergers totaling more than $100 million each occurred in 1996. By contrast, during the first three quarters of 1997, eight acquisitions were in place, with the top three deals valued at more than $1 billion each. The top 10 transactions in 1996 totaled $1.5 billion and included 30,000 units. In 1997 the top 10 were valued at more than $6.3 billion with more than 90,000 units involved. By 1998 figures revealed that the top three companies—Colson & Colson, Prometheus Senior Quarters of New York City, and Alternative Living Services of Brookfield, Wisconsin—operated nearly 50,000 units.

As Americans grow older and health care prolongs the lives of people suffering from chronic diseases, assisted living and continuing care facilities began experiencing residents who required additional care. Mel Gamzon wrote that many operators were, "witnessing unexpectedly large numbers of frail residents requiring complex chronic care not considered in the initial pro forma." He went on to say, "The reality that 30 percent to 40 percent of assisted living residents suffered from various degrees of Alzheimer's, or other forms of dementia," overwhelmed staff and had an impact on the bottom line financial results.

The senior housing market remained an excellent investment even with concerns about additional operating and health care expenses. NREI reports that an increasing number of commercial banks, life insurance companies, credit companies, and real estate investment trusts were getting into the field. The AFL-CIO Housing Investment Trust financed over $1.4 million in an assisted living facility. Companies such as Cambridge Realty Capital, Ltd., a HUD lender, focused their attention on senior housing investments.

The changes on the horizon of the twenty-first century were expected to alter senior lifestyles further. For baby boomers retiring at younger ages and leading more active lives than their parents, retirement housing was different, too. In addition to self-contained retirement communities, or assisted living centers, the housing market began designing homes for the leisure of retirement. As an example of this branching out, Christine Schuyler and Susan Bradford Barror focused on five communities across the country in the July 1997 issue of *Builder* magazine. These communities were located in Oceanside, California; Niantic, Connecticut; Jamesburg, New Jersey; Mill Creek, Washington; and Mt. Kisco, New York. Three of the featured communities had age restrictions, and the other two were age-diverse. "Early evidence shows that today's 50- and 60- somethings have very different requirements from the Depression generation that precedes them. The boomers plan to continue their active lifestyles in retirement," the authors noted. According to Ben Orvedal, a Connecticut builder who established his first senior-oriented community in Niantic, Connecticut, in the summer of 1996, "Some of the features they want are so simple, but our industry is not set up to cater to this market." That was expected to change, too. The advantage that builders who had been a part of a community was clear. They often saved the expense of research because they understood the people who had always been their customers. In an ever-evolving market due to the vastly diverse population of aging adults, sometimes the best investment was directed by the intimate knowledge of developers of the local level.

In addition, retirement communities operating within the focus of health care continued to alter their perspective by the end of the 1990s. Typical of some of these changes was The Washington House (TWH) in Alexandria, Virginia, which operates as a non-profit

corporation. TWH offers an array of options for living within the community. A companion program called "Community Washington House" was created to assist older adults in their own homes, as well as the caregiver. This program was a modification of what was predicted as a possible "wave of the future," long-term care "without walls." Membership, according to Washington House president and CEO, Judith Braun, R.N., Ph.D., offers senior citizens the option of staying in their own homes longer. Community Washington House was unique as late as 1999 because it did not include an insurance component for payment of services, as did other similar programs. As past president and as a fellow of the National Gerontological Nursing Association, Braun witnessed the changing landscape of retirement living beginning in the late 1970s. Programs such as this one reflected the knowledge and commitment to ongoing care. Comprehensive membership in Community Washington House includes use of the fitness center, which is also offered for memberships separately; monthly wellness seminars; utilization of a personal liaison to coordinate home chores through the use of local service providers; and the benefit of social activities at the retirement community. Washington House gives seniors exercising this option the additional reassurance of priority placement on a waiting list. "We started Community Washington House," said Braun, "not only for the obvious business reason to spread our name among seniors, but also because as a nonprofit we believed in giving back to the community in which we lived." This model was certain to be followed and modified to serve public and business interests.

Decision making as people age and require additional care is a burden that many similar communities alleviated. Such arrangements encompassed three levels of care on the site, thus providing the security from upheavals at the times when illnesses made such moves unduly traumatic. The options of either living independently at home or retiring to a nursing home when a person could no longer deal with increasing frailty due to illness and age had been nudged aside by the end of the twentieth century. Braun noted that CCRCs and nursing home facilities of the late 1990s looked very much like hospitals of the early 1980s. Length of stay was measured in weeks, rather than years. "Demographics and morbidity figures seem to indicate that will always have the old and the sick with us," noted Braun. "Consequently, I think there will always be a need for nursing homes of some sort. Perhaps, however, only for the very, very ill and for short periods of time." Many industry observers were looking to CCRCs, such as Washington House, as the "potential sleeper" that was likely to surge within the early years of the twenty-first century.

A major development in the future of retirement living occurred on March 2, 1999. Residents of the Leisure World retirement community in Laguna Hills, California, voted to incorporate as a city. According to Don Terry, in *The New York Times,* "The residents of the Leisure World retirement community here voted . . . to transform their gated niche of 'God's Country', into California's newest city." With an average age of 77, the 18,000 residents proved that aging Americans exercised political clout, in addition to their increasing economic influence. Other unincorporated communities, including the Sun City developments continue to enjoy their status.

Government on the federal level, too, took note of this vastly diverse market. Concerns about truth in advertising to older adults, especially as regarded assisted living centers, were being addressed by the General Accounting Office (GAO), one of the key investigative offices for the United States Congress. By early spring 1999, the GAO reported that "Providers do not always give consumers information sufficient to determine whether a particular assisted living facility can meet their needs, for how long and under what circumstances." Due to the predictions that by the early years of the twenty-first century assisted living homes would eventually care for more elderly Americans than would nursing homes; Congress was expected to take these findings into serious consideration. Nursing homes are subject to federal standards. Assisted living homes are overseen by states, who have varying regulations. Consumer advocates for the elderly population are expected to rise along with the rise of care facilities." In that same article for the Associated Press, writer Alice Ann Love also reported that the GAO "reviewed state records on 753 homes in the four states, [California, Florida, Ohio, and Oregon] and found that 27 percent were cited for consumer protection problems in 1996 and 1997." The possibility of changes in the marketplace due to government regulations, along with independent voter strength, was imminent.

In addition to other government issues relating to senior housing, Congress passed the Housing for Older Persons Act of 1995, along with a final rule in 1999. This allowed for housing limited to the over-55 age market to be exempt from any anti-age discrimination provisions under the Civil Rights Act of 1964. The ruling specified that as long as housing was provided with the intention of housing older persons, at least 80 percent of the residents in any living facility

was 55 or older, and adherence to policies and procedures was confirmed, it could qualify as senior housing. In fact, most retirement communities required that at least one spouse in houses or other living units be 55 or older. This allowed for younger spouses who would not meet the age requirement.

INDUSTRY LEADERS

In 1998, ASHA released a list of the top five senior housing owners: Colson & Colson/Holiday Retirement Corp. based in Salem, Oregon; Prometheus Senior Quarters located in New York City; Alternative Living Services of Brookfield, Wisconsin; Health Care REIT of Toledo, Ohio; and Emeritus Corporation of Seattle, Washington. The market continued to change quickly through the end of the 1990s.

Colson & Colson/Holiday Retirement Corporation, had estimated sales of $600 million in 1997, the last figure available. One hundred percent of their sales come from private pay, a fact that William Colson, the firm's president, considered to be a source of pride; he insists that they do not want to work with the government in any capacity. In 1996, the company owned 57 residences with more than 19,000 units and managed 159 congregate residences with 19,300 units in North America. By 1998, the number of owned residences climbed to 193 with more than 23,000 units. They also held approximately 23,000 leaseholds in Europe and Canada. Colson had not moved aggressively into building assisted living residents, instead preferring to acquire those that had undergone bankruptcy.

The changes were reflected as well with early industry leaders such as Living Centers of America who had joined forces with GranCare, Paragon Health Network, and Mariner Health Group and formed a new company called Mariner Post-Acute Network, Inc. between 1997 and 1998. Headquartered in Atlanta, Georgia, the company boasted sales of $2.03 billion in 1998. The company operates approximately 450 inpatient and assisted living centers in about 40 states and is also involved in other health care services and hospitals.

Another company long listed in the top 10 but moved down to number 11 by 1998, Marriott Senior Living Services, sold 7 of its assisted living communities to Prime Care Two LLC and sold even more before the end of 1998. The company still retains the operating rights of the facilities in each instance. These include 81 full-service and assisted living communities. Marriott planned to continue expanding and hoped to have more than 200 communities by the year 2000. The company achieved sales of more than $7.9 billion in 1998 by attracting those seniors in the upper-third income bracket; this total did include their combined business interests, including hotels and food services.

Other key leaders in the list of the top 25 owners, as designated by ASHA included ARV Assisted Living, Inc., which was founded in 1980 and headquartered in Costa Mesa, California. In 1998, they operated approximately 65 assisted living communities in 10 states with approximately 7,900 units. Company sales for 1998 were $128.6 million, a growth of 66.4 percent over the previous year.

Life Care Service Corporation (LCS), a non-profit corporation, was first established in 1961 as part of Weitz Company. In 1979 it offered fee management services to other developers and owners and began acquiring existing facilities, as well as developing new ones. By 1998 it was the fifth largest provider of long-term care for the elderly in the United States. In 1999 LCS was involved in the planning, developing, or managing of more than 70 senior residences—an increase of more than 30 percent since 1996.

Adult Communities Total Service, Inc. (ACTS) has been a leader in lifecare since 1971. It operates from West Point, Pennsylvania, and houses 6,000 residents in 15 communities throughout Pennsylvania, North Carolina, and Florida.

AMERICA AND THE WORLD

By 1998, Colson & Colson was one of the few companies that had expanded into Europe. The company held approximately 23,000 European senior housing leaseholds by the end of the 1990s. As the U.S. market hits the saturation point, more companies will be taking a serious look at moving into more international markets.

FURTHER READING

"1996 American Senior Housing Association 25 Owners." *National Real Estate Investor,* October 1996.

American Seniors Housing Association. "1996 American Senior Housing Association 25 Managers." *National Real Estate Investor,* October 1996.

American Seniors Housing Association. "1998 Company Profiles," May 1999. Available from http://www.asha.nmhc.org.

"ARV Assisted Living," 1998. Available from http://arvi.com/ARV.html.

"ARV Assisted Living, Inc." *Hoover's Online,* May 1999. Available from http://www.hoovers.com.

"ASHA 1996 Company Profiles." *National Real Estate Investor,* October 1996.

Binzen, Peter. "From Ad Agency and Seminary to Chief of ACTS Inc." *Philadelphia Money and Business,* 4 November 1997. Available from http://business.phillynews.com/retirement/retire97/binz10.asp.

Boyce, Timothy J. "Financing Senior Living Facilities." *American Bar Association,* 1997. Available from http://www.abanet.org/rppt/srliving.html.

Braun, Judith V., R.N., Ph.D. An Interview with Jane E. Spear. "Washington House, Alexandria, Virginia," April 1999.

"Colson & Colson Construction Company." *Hoover's Online,* May 1999. Available from http://www.hoovers.com.

Gamzon, Mel. "Seniors Housing Forecast: If We Build It, Will They Come?" *National Real Estate Investor,* February 1997.

Henry, Randy. "Cambridge Realty Launches First Web Site For Seniors Housing." *National Real Estate Investor,* March 1998.

———. "Seniors Housing Market Surpasses 1996 Pricing Records." *National Real Estate Investor,* November 1997.

Horvitz, Leslie Ann. "Aging America is Big Business." *Insight,* 8 December 1997.

Johnson, Dirk. "In the Frost Belt, a Place in the Sun." *The New York Times,* 8 February 1999.

Johnston, Ben. "NIC Charts the Changes for Seniors Housing Industry." *National Real Estate Investor,* January 1998. Available from http://www.internetreview.com/pubs/nrei/nrei.html.

Life Care Services Corporation. "About LCS." Iowa: Life Care Services, 1998. Available from http://www.csnet.com/about.html.

"Living Centers of America and GranCare Announce Appointment of President of Rehab Division." *PR Newswire,* 29 October 1997. Available from http://www.prnewswire.com/cgi-bin/stories.

Love, Alice Ann. "Elderly Are Warned on Choosing Assisted living Center." *Associated Press,* 27 April 1999.

Marriott International. "Marriott International Announces Sale of Seven Senior Living Communities to Prime Care Two LLC, Retains Long-Term Management Agreements," 15 September 1997. Available from http://www.marriott.com/news/saleof7.asp.

"Marriott International, Inc." *Hoover's Online,* May 1999. Available from http://www.hoovers.com.

"Paragon Health Network, Inc." *Hoover's Online,* May 1999. Available from http://www.hoovers.com.

Shelter, Kim. "Sun City Holds On." *Planning,* January 1996.

Schless, David S. "1996: A Year of Rapid Growth in the ASHA 25." *National Real Estate Investor,* October 1996.

Schuyler, Christine, and Susan Bradford Barror. "Modern Maturity." *Builder,* July 1997.

Terry, Don. "In This Brand-New City, No Shortage of Elders." *The New York Times,* 4 March 1999.

Zaner, Laura Ochipinti. "Assisted Living Fuels Much of the Heat in a Hot Seniors Housing Market." *National Real Estate Investor,* October 1996.

—Nancy Hatch Woodward, updated by Jane E. Spear

ADVANCED CERAMICS

At the end of the 1990s, the U.S. advanced ceramics industry encompassed a diverse applications market in which ultimately the ceramic process was the largest—and in some cases the only—common denominator. Many of the markets were industries in themselves. In the area of cutting tool inserts, four major producers had 75 percent of the market. Bioceramics and wear-resistant parts also had clear market leaders while leadership in other markets was less defined.

Business Communications Company (BCC) in Norwalk, Connecticut, has studied the advanced ceramics market since the early 1980s. According to BCC, market researchers in the early 1980s predicted rapid growth for advanced ceramics through the end of the twentieth century, especially in the area of structural ceramics. Such growth failed to occur, however, and some portions of the industry actually declined. For example, large cuts in military spending decreased the demand for ceramic coatings used for military engines, and the development of ceramic armor for military vehicles was reduced. Additionally, technological advances in some applications areas resulted in ceramics no longer being used in those products.

In spite of these military industrial cuts, demand for advanced ceramics continued to grow slowly but steadily as the twentieth century drew to a close, with particular growth coming from consumer applications in telecommunications and computer equipment. Structural ceramics appeared to be one of the most promising growth markets for the early twenty-first century, due mostly to the material's increasing applications, and wear resistance. Some segments of the industry have seen continuous growth, including elec-tronics, cutting tools and wear-resistant parts, and bioceramics.

According to BCC, company mergers, acquisitions, and joint ventures increased through the first half of the 1980s when "ceramics fever" was at its peak. Such activities declined by half in 1987 and 1988, rose again in 1989, then decreased in the early 1990s. The mid-1990s saw an overall increase in the number of U.S. ceramics companies and foreign-owned U.S. subsidiaries; Japanese and European companies especially have become more active in the U.S. market through acquisitions, joint ventures, and subsidiaries. Conversely, company mergers and acquisitions continued to consolidate efforts in some markets because of the technological sophistication needed to manufacture advanced ceramics and the finite amount of business available.

Foreign competition came mainly from Japan, which dominated the world's integrated circuit market. Japanese companies import finished or semi-finished products for their U.S. plants. The United States imported 20 to 30 percent of its ceramic magnets, capacitors, and piezoelectric components at the end of the 1990s, but was still the leader in technology. Many high-performance electronic components were manufactured only in this country because of military requirements. Foreign competition was seen in areas where components can be mass-produced more inexpensively overseas because of lower labor costs.

Companies in the advanced ceramics industry ranged in size from small job shops to large multi-national corporations. Small companies provided limited quantities of specific products that large companies did not want to pursue. A large degree of variation existed in manufacturing integration: most industry suppliers used a mix of horizontal and vertical systems of integration. An increasing trend toward using the systems approach resulted in new relationships between companies.

The systems approach includes all activities needed to produce a product: from production of raw materials through design, manufacturing, and integration of parts into a final assembly. Companies that take the systems approach also may depend on outside sources to fulfill some of the materials-to-part functions.

Large companies typically were more heavily involved in research and development activity, but some small start-up companies were also involved in such activities as well. At the end of the 1990s more than 500 advanced ceramic companies (including foreign-owned companies) operated in the United States as research entities, producers and suppliers of raw materials, and developers and manufacturers of components. These included 100 involved in structural ceramics and 150 in electrical and electronic ceramics.

MATERIALS AND PROCESSING

The materials most commonly used to create advanced ceramics are alumina, silicon carbide, silicon nitride, zirconia, ferrites, titanates, and sialon (silicon-aluminum-oxygen-nitrogen). Minerals and rocks found naturally must undergo initial processing to create uniform particle size, distribution, and purity. Materials not naturally occurring are chemically created. Greater control is possible with synthetic materials, which can provide powders having precise chemical compositions. After processing, raw materials are formed into a desired shape. Water and other additives are combined with the raw materials, which are then formed using methods such as extrusion, slip casting, pressing, tape casting, and injection molding. After forming, ceramics are heat-treated (fired or sintered) to produce a rigid, finished product.

Glass products are processed differently. Raw materials such as silica, lime, and soda ash are melted in a furnace, then formed while molten and cooled into solid shapes. Additional processing steps such as cutting, etching, grinding, decorating, or heat-treating (tempering) may be performed.

APPLICATIONS

Advanced ceramics applications can be divided into the following categories:

- electrical/electronic (including capacitors, insulators, substrates and integrated circuit (IC) packages, ferrite magnetic materials, high temperature superconductors, and piezoelectrics)

- structural (including aerospace and defense, bioceramics, cutting tool and wear-resistant parts, and high-temperature and energy-related components)

- high-performance coatings (including coatings for all types of engines, heat exchangers, high-temperature wear parts, and cutting tool inserts)

- environmentally related products (including filters, membranes, catalysts, and catalyst supports)

Mature market segments for electrical/electronic ceramics include capacitors, insulators, substrates, magnetic ferrites, integrated circuit packages, and piezoelectric ceramics. Portions of the electrical/electronics also are the fastest-growing segment overall. Ceramic superconductors allow the flow of electricity with little or no resistance or heat loss. Other applications are sensors, actuators, electro-optic materials, semiconductors and multi-layer capacitors. Ceramic coatings are also used to protect or lubricate metal materials. The ceramic coatings can prevent electronic shutdowns, component failure, and excessive wear and tear in computers or other electronic devices. Elec-

PROJECTED ADVANCED CERAMICS MARKET SEGMENT SALES, 2002	
Market segment	Value in 2002
Electronic ceramics	$6.8 billion
Chemical processing and environmental-related ceramics	$1.7 billion
Tool inserts, wear-resistant and other industrial applications	$805 million
Structural ceramics	$585 million
Source: Business Communications Co., 30 April 1998	

3 1833 03748 5346

tronic ceramics are also chemically inert, capable of withstanding high temperatures and less susceptible to corrosion.

Wear-resistant parts are the largest segment of the structural ceramics market. Applications include: bearings, dies, components for the pulp and paper industry, grinding media, guides and pulleys, liners, mechanical seals and valves, and nozzles. Energy applications include reticulated ceramics for molten metal filters, heat exchangers, and heating chambers and other high-temperature applications. Aerospace and defense applications include air, ground, and personal armor; thermal insulation for aircraft and space shuttles; antenna windows; nozzles; radomes; and exhaust ducts. Bioceramic materials are used to repair and replace human hips, knees, shoulders, elbows, wrists, and fingers. They also are used to repair and replace teeth, and research is being done on a ceramic replacement gum.

Coatings for aircraft engines and aerospace applications, along with cutting tool applications, make up 90 percent of the coatings market.

Chemical processing and environmental-related ceramic products include catalytic converters for vehicle applications, as well as ceramic membranes and catalysts. Ceramic membranes have the largest growth rate of any commercial market segment.

BACKGROUND AND DEVELOPMENT

Ceramics comprise one of the three largest classes of solid materials: the other two classes are polymers and metals. Ceramics are inorganic, crystalline compounds that are formed by combining metallic ele-

ments such as silicon and aluminum with non-metallic elements such as carbon, oxygen, and nitrogen. Glass is sometimes considered a subset of ceramics; however, glass is different from ceramic in that its structure is amorphous rather than crystalline.

Ceramic materials are divided into two categories: traditional and advanced. Materials in both categories possess qualities of strength, hardness and resistance to deformation by chemicals, heat, and water. Traditional ceramics have been used in some form for centuries. Archaeologists have discovered human-made ceramics in Czechoslovakia that date back to 24,000 B.C. These ceramic figures were made of animal fat and bone mixed with bone ash and fine clay. Ceramic vessels were used by the Egyptians in 9000 B.C., and glass was first produced independently of ceramics in 1500 B.C. Traditional or classical ceramic substances are still used in sanitary, thermal, and construction applications such as brick, sewer tile, floor and wall tile, and dinnerware.

Also called technical, engineering, high-tech, or fine ceramics, advanced ceramics are made from finer, purer versions of raw materials than their traditional counterparts, and their microstructure is different from that of traditional ceramics. As a result, advanced ceramics have superior properties that make them useful in biological, chemical, electrical, magnetic, mechanical, optical, and nuclear applications. Examples include electrical/electronic and engine components, replacement parts for the human body such as artificial bones and teeth, space shuttle insulation tile, and—in the case of glass—fiber optics.

Ceramics have evolved into an important component of human life. Today, sophisticated refractory (heat-resistant) ceramics make high-temperature steel and non-ferrous metal production possible. Refractory

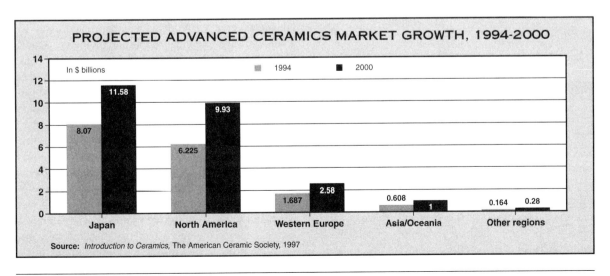

Precision machined, alumina, zirconia advanced ceramic components. (Courtesy Astro Met, Inc.)

materials are also essential in the petroleum, chemical, and energy-conversion industries. The electronics industry could not exist without ceramics, which are used as insulators in a wide variety of applications. For example, high-voltage insulators make it possible to transmit electricity to homes and businesses. In 1986, it was discovered that ceramics could also be used as superconductors of electricity: a superconductor can transmit electrical current without power loss or resistance. Additionally, fiber optics has revolutionized telecommunications and reduced negative environmental impacts caused by mining and processing copper.

CURRENT CONDITIONS

Advanced ceramics continue to play an important role in the U.S. economy by improving the performance of existing products and creating opportunities for the emergence of new technologies. A 1998 report by the Freedonia Group, a technical marketing research group, estimated the global market for advanced ceramics at $17-20 billion and projected it to reach $25 billion by 2000, a growth of 7.0 percent. A report by Business Communications Co. (BCC) pre-

dicted the U.S. market would grow 7.9 percent by the year 2001 to $9.24 billion. This same study projected the world market for electronics ceramics at $6.29 billion in 2001, for structural ceramics at $540 million, ceramic coatings at $750 million, and chemicals processing ceramics at $1.66 billion. In the U.S. market, electronics ceramics was expected to account for 68.1 percent of the total advanced ceramics market. In a separate report, BCC projected the growth of the U.S. market for advanced ceramic powders to be 9.0 percent per year through the year 2003, led again by electronics applications.

A number of significant obstacles to growth exist in the industry. William H. Werst, Jr., executive director of the United States Advanced Ceramics Association (USACA), identified these obstacles: high production costs because of high raw material and finished machining costs, expensive prototypes, and the lack of awareness of advanced ceramics properties and performance in the general industrial marketplace. A forum organized by Gorham Advanced Materials, Inc., identified the lack of industry standards and a long product development cycle as additional barriers to growth. In the United States growth may also be slowed by increasing pressure on the federal government to reduce spending on research in advanced materials by the Department of Defense and NASA.

Steps were being taken in various quarters to overcome some of these obstacles. USACA produced a report on the opportunities for advanced ceramics in the Department of Energy's "Industries of the Future" program, which focuses on the industries that use 70-80 percent of the energy used by manufacturing. The report identified the contributions already being made by advanced ceramics and pointed to possibilities for the future such as gas turbines in transportation and improved electrodes in aluminum smelting.

The high cost and long development cycle for new advanced ceramics products was being addressed by a collaborative research program involving the Sandia and Los Alamos National Laboratories and five commercial ceramics manufacturers. The program is being carried out under a Cooperative Research and Development Agreement (CRADA). The traditional path for the development of new ceramics parts was largely a matter of trial and error, guided by the designer/manufacturer's experience. A preliminary design was developed, a prototype was made and tested, problems were discovered, refinements were made, a new prototype was designed and produced, more testing was done, and so on. Building the prototype was a key cost factor, because of the cost of material and the considerable time needed for the machining of ceramics.

The CRADA group reported in June 1999 the achievement of one of its primary goals: modeling the forming of a ceramic part on a computer and using the computer model to test the design for flaws. Ultimately, such computer modeling could greatly simplify and accelerate the development process.

A group of researchers at Oklahoma State University reported the development of a faster and cheaper way to polish ceramic ball bearings and roller bearings. Properly polished, ceramic bearings provide higher performance than steel for many demanding applications, but the time required to polish them, measured in weeks, using traditional processes and diamond abrasives, has inhibited their use. Dr. Ranga Komanduri and a group of colleagues developed a process using a magnetic field that could polish ceramic ball bearings to an excellent finish in less that 24 hours. A similar process was described for roller bearings. Dr. Komanduri was looking for a business enterprise to come forward to commercialize the process.

INDUSTRY LEADERS

The largest companies in the advanced ceramics industry at the end of the 1990s were somewhat diversified manufacturing companies. The Japanese company Kyocera, the largest in advanced ceramics worldwide, also manufactured non-ceramics electronic components and optical instruments. In 1998 its ceramic products generated $3.6 billion, 66 percent of the total. Once the world's largest manufacturer of ceramic semiconductor packaging, with 60 percent of the market, Kyocera suffered when that industry shifted to plastic casing. Twenty-one percent of 1998 sales came from the United States.

Coors Ceramics, a subsidiary of ACX Technologies, which in turn is a spin-off from Coors Brewing, is probably the largest U.S. company in the advanced ceramics industry. In 1998 ACX posted sales of $988 million, an increase of 35 percent over 1997. Ceramics accounted for 30 percent of the total, or $296 million. Coors Ceramics sells its products to the automotive, beverage, telecommunications, semiconductor, power generation, oil, and paper industries. In early 1998, Coors Ceramics formed a joint venture with Pall Corporation to license U.S. Department of Energy (DOE) technology to make next-generation membrane tube filters. These filters will produce ultra-clean water for use in the pharmaceutical and semiconductor industries.

Carpenter Technology Corporation, based in Reading, Pennsylvania, is primarily a producer of stainless steel and other specialty metal alloys, but ceramics and other products accounted for about 5.0 percent of 1998 sales, or $69.2 million. Overall, the company experienced 25.3-percent growth in 1998. Fifteen percent of Carpenter's sales came from outside the United States.

American Technical Ceramics Corp. (ATC) and Ceradyne, Inc. are U.S. companies that focus on advanced ceramics. ATC makes ceramic capacitors and thin-film products that are used in applications such as mobile phones, aircraft radar and navigation systems, missiles, and broadcast satellites. It reported 1998 sales of $40.4 million. Ceradyne produces ceramics that are used in applications such as armor for military helicopters, personal armor for soldiers, internal engine components, microwave tubes, and orthodontic brackets. It reported 1998 sales of $26.3 million.

RESEARCH AND TECHNOLOGY

Leading-edge research in advanced ceramics focused on smart materials systems. Smart materials are capable of sensing and responding to environmental stimuli. They can transform strain into an electric charge and can convert an applied electric field into stress. For example, piezoelectric ceramics, the most widely used smart materials, expand and contract when electric current is applied. Smart materials are useful for monitoring structural integrity, reducing noise, and suppressing vibration. U.S. government agencies provide approximately $40 million and industry contributes another $12 million annually for smart materials research.

Nanostructured materials are another focus of research. Such materials have extremely small (nano-sized) crystals: a nanocrystal typically has a diameter of a millionth of a centimeter. Although nanostructured materials were synthesized in 1857 and have been in commercial use for 30 years or more, the 1990s have seen a resurgence of interest in these infinitesimal structures. Nanocrystals often exhibit properties that are vastly different from those of conventional materials. Since 1991 the U.S. government has spent more than $20 million funding research into commercial uses for nanostructured materials, and more than 300 patents have been awarded to individuals and corporations.

In 1996 the U.S. market for nanostructured particles and coatings was $42.3 million and was expected

More On THE DEVELOPMENT OF SMART MATERIALS

The aerospace and defense industries are primary developers and markets for smart technology. Defense applications include controlling the twist and vibration of helicopter rotor blades and suppressing the acoustic, vibrational signature of submarine hulls. In the computer industry, smart read/write head micropositioners are being developed for data storage devices. The medical and health care markets are predicted to be longer-term developers of smart systems, although ultrasonically assisted surgical tools are already on the market. Other potential medical uses for smart materials are drug-delivery devices such as insulin pumps.

Smart packs or patches that can be integrated into various kinds of products are key to many of the emerging commercial markets. Active Control Experts, Inc., in Cambridge, Massachusetts, produces a smart pack that is used in skis to improve control on downhill runs. A piezoelectric plate in the ski converts mechanical energy to electricity and dissipates it, which in turn controls vibration, allowing the skier to turn more easily and reducing pressure on his or her legs and back. Other applications for the smart packs include self-diagnostic computer disk drives and hand guns that can only be fired by a user who is wearing a special ring.

engine that can withstand temperatures of 1,800 degrees, it cannot yet be cost-effectively produced in large quantities. Kyocera has been marketing the engine's components to companies such as Detroit Diesel Corporation, which builds heavy engines for trucks and buses. However, ceramics continued to play an important role in automobile component parts including turbocharger rotors, piston rings, valves, bearing, catalytic converters, and glass fiber components used in tires, body panels, windshields and headlights.

Ten years after their discovery in 1986, superconducting materials began to be used in commercial applications such as cellular phone systems. Superconducting ceramics conduct electricity with extremely low losses of heat, but the materials are brittle, which makes them difficult to form and even more difficult to use. Conductus, a company in Sunnyvale, California, has developed the superconducting cellular phone technology and is also developing superconducting probes for nuclear magnetic resonance spectrometers. The spectrometers will be used by scientists to study the structure of proteins such as those found in HIV. Other applications for superconductive materials include magnetic resonance for medical diagnosis and ultra-high-speed switches for the telecommunications industry.

to reach $154.6 million by 2001. Products expected to appear on the market in the near term include nanocrystalline barium titanate multi-layer capacitors and nanostructured cobalt tungsten carbide precision microdrills.

Ceramics are becoming increasingly popular in the medical arena. Surgeons are using bioceramic materials for the repair and replacement of human joints such as hips, knees, shoulders, elbows, fingers, and wrists. Ceramics are also being used to replace diseased heart valves. Dentists are using ceramics for tooth replacement implants and braces. When used as implants or as coatings to metal replacements, ceramic materials can stimulate bone growth, encourage tissue formation, and provide protection from the immune system.

Predictions that a ceramic automobile engine would be on the market by the end of the 1990s failed to materialize. Ceramic-based automobile engines could withstand much higher temperatures than metal engines and could theoretically burn less fuel. Although Kyocera Corporation has developed a ceramic

FURTHER READING

Abbe, Mary. "Wonder Dirt." *Minneapolis Star Tribune,* 10 April 1996.

Abraham, Thomas. "Electronics and Environmental-Related Ceramics Push Overall Use."

———. *U.S. Advanced Ceramics Industry—Status and Market Projections.* Paper delivered at the World Ceramics Industry Conference 1998. Norwalk, Connecticut.

"Advanced Ceramics." *Ceramic Industry,* August 1998.

"Advanced Ceramics: An Industry and Market Overview." *Chemical Business NewsBase: Industrial Ceramics,* 18 February 1999.

"Advanced Ceramics for the New Millennium." *Ceramic Industry,* June 1998.

"Advanced Ceramics Market Struggles to Maintain Growth." *Ceramic Industry,* August 1998.

"Advanced Ceramics: The World View." *Ceramic Industry,* August 1998.

The American Ceramic Society. *Ceramic Facts,* Westerville, OH: American Ceramic Society.

——. Ceramic Information Center. Available from http://www.acers.org.

Bradby, Tanya. "Ceramic Fiber Papers Solve Transportation Challenges." *Industrial Heating,* August 1996.

"Ceramic Bearing Demands Point to Magnetic Answers." *PR Newswire,* 14 December 1998.

"Ceramics Proving Durable in High-Pressure, Deepwater Situations." *Offshore,* March 1997.

"Ceramics WebBook." National Institute for Standards and Technology. Available from http://www.ceramics.nist.gov/webbook/webbook.htm.

"Collaborative Research Programme Aims for Predictable Production and Design Processes." *Advanced Ceramics Report,* 1 June 1999.

"Digital Technology, Other Developments Drive Consumer Electronic Industry." *Ceramic Industry,* December 1996.

Frost & Sullivan. "Miniaturization and Intensified R&D Efforts Result in Drop in Electronic Ceramic Prices." Mountain View, CA: Frost & Sullivan.

Geiger, Gregory R. *Introduction to Ceramics: A Beginner's Guide.* Westerville, OH: The American Ceramic Society.

Gottschalk, Mark. "Tough Problems? Tougher Ceramics!" *Design News,* 2 December 1996.

Iannotta, Ben. "Breaking the Heat Barrier." *New Scientist,* August 1997, 28.

"Markets Thrive Despite Challenges." *Ceramic Industry,* August 1997.

Marshall, Jonathan. "Hot Start for Icy Material." *San Francisco Chronicle,* 13 March 1997.

Metals and Ceramics Lab, Oak Ridge National Laboratory. Available from http://www.ms.ornl.gov/ctnl/ctnhp.htm.

"Nano-powders Lead Growth n USA." *Advanced Ceramics Report,* 1 June 1999.

National Institute for Standards and Technology Materials and Science Lab. Available from http://www.msel.nist.gov.

Ouelette, Jennifer. "How Smart are Smart Materials?" *The Industrial Physicist,* December 1996.

Parmet, Sharon. "Ceramic Bones." *Popular Science,* January 1998, 30.

Rittner, Mindy N. and Thomas Abraham. "The Nanostructured Materials Industry." *American Ceramic Society Bulletin,* June 1997.

Robinson, Gail. "Breakthrough Ceramics Can Take the Heat." *Electronic Engineering Times,* 20 May 1996.

Sheppard, Laurel M. "Incubator Center Spurs Growth of Ceramics Businesses." *Ceramics Industry,* April 1997.

Strock, Harold B. "Emerging Smart Materials Systems." *American Ceramic Society Bulletin,* 4 April 1996.

—Joanne Wolfe, updated by Janet Whittle and Howard Distelzweig

AIDS Testing, Treatment, and Services

INDUSTRY SNAPSHOT

Acquired Immunodeficiency Syndrome (AIDS) is a range of diseases and medical conditions (the result of HIV or the Human Immunodeficiency Virus) that attacks the body's immunological system and, currently, always results in death. Humans who are HIV-positive (and who eventually develop AIDS) have contracted the virus through unprotected sexual contact with an infected individual, through intravenous drug use, by receiving a blood transfusion from an infected individual, or prenatally from an infected mother to her unborn child. Considerable press has been given to the famous people such as former professional basketball player Earvin "Magic" Johnson and former Olympic diver Greg Louganis who are currently HIV-positive, as well as to the individuals who have died of AIDS, including actors Rock Hudson, Anthony Perkins, and Amanda Blake, dancer Rudolph Nureyev, fashion designer Roy Halston, and tennis great Arthur Ashe.

AIDS is one of the most significant phenomena to affect life in the late twentieth century. On its most basic level, it is a debilitating and ultimately fatal disease; its potency derives from the effect of its viral components on the body's immune system. It has been called an epidemic that has affected all nations on Earth: as of December 1998, an estimated 33.4 *million* people were living with HIV/AIDS worldwide. In 1998 alone a sad 2.5 million had lost their lives to HIV-associated illnesses. By 1999 over 16,000 people were becoming infected with HIV *every day.*

From the beginning, AIDS has been difficult to categorize using only one classification. AIDS involves political, charitable, social, and economic con-

siderations in addition to the health concerns of infected individuals and their families. Because of the way AIDS is spread, and because of the time- and money-intensive nature of AIDS treatment and research, AIDS engenders significant political, social, religious, and emotional responses. But the production and the research involved in the development of medicines to manage and, hopefully, arrest or cure AIDS, along with the provision of services to AIDS-infected individuals and such related areas as AIDS fundraising and education and outreach efforts, make AIDS a multibillion dollar industry that continues to grow.

ORGANIZATION AND STRUCTURE

AIDS is a vast subject, and discussing it in dollar terms is somewhat problematic. Figures that might assist in the understanding of AIDS as a public health problem and as an industry are usually outdated by the time they become available to the general public. The National Insurance Association of America has estimated that insurance costs in 1994 for treating an HIV-positive patient throughout his or her lifetime averaged $119,000. Those figures have continued to rise. Multiplying that number by the Centers for Disease Control's (CDC) numbers of identified AIDS cases, the estimated cost of treating all HIV-infected individuals during their lifetimes rises to in excess of $79 billion.

One way to define the scope and impact of the domestic AIDS-related industry is to look at infection and mortality rates. As of June 30, 1998, the CDC, based in Atlanta, Georgia, indicated a total of 665,357

AIDS cases have been reported in the United States since these statistics have been kept. Of that number, 553,048 were males and 104,028 were females. In that same time period, 8,280 children under the age of 13 at the time of diagnosis also were classified as having AIDS. AIDS deaths totaled 401,028 by June 1998. The causes of AIDS transmission, in the 84 percent of cases where a cause had been clearly identified, were broken down as follows: 51 percent were men who had sex with men, 25 percent originated with injected drug users, and 8 percent of the cases were the result of heterosexual contact (chiefly by sexual contact with an injecting drug user). Of the AIDS cases reported between 1981 and mid-1996 alone, 63 percent, or approximately 330,000 persons, had died.

Several elements of AIDS-related industries are more visible than others. Possibly the most visible of these industries involves pharmaceutical companies. Research and development is the hub of the AIDS industry and accounts for the most spending, in part because this area carries with it the promise of finding a cure for AIDS.

A second major arm of the AIDS-related industry is not a business, but rather, government agencies. In the United States, much of the focus of AIDS policy, as well as the source of research funding, has rested with two agencies: the National Institutes of Health (NIH) and the Centers for Disease Control (CDC). These agencies are part of the Department of Health and Human Services (HHS), which contributes to the underwriting of research at drug companies and at educational institutions throughout the country. NIH is the principal biomedical research arm of the federal government. The CDC, part of the U.S. Public Health Service's efforts to control infectious diseases, works with state health officials and is a repository of statistical information about AIDS and other diseases. This country's general AIDS policy is formulated through the Presidential Commission on AIDS, established under the administration of President Ronald Reagan in 1987. This commission has been a source of controversy since its inception. High-profile members, such as basketball great Magic Johnson, have resigned from the commission, complaining the body was not serious about addressing all AIDS-related issues, including directing enough funding to research and development. At a time when President Reagan was citing government funding of research efforts, AIDS activists offered substantial criticism of the funding level and suggested the Reagan administration was not really committed to finding a cure for AIDS.

The third major arm of AIDS-related industry involves the private and quasi-private, locally funded, service-oriented, and/or foundation-based enterprises classified as AIDS service organizations, or ASOs. Some of the largest ASOs generate and distribute millions of dollars for research and education and prevention efforts. Smaller ASOs may be involved in work at the community level, such as distributing condoms or assisting individuals to find medical testing or housing. While dwarfed by government agencies and the large pharmaceutical companies, ASOs generate funds used in research, provide direct services, and are beneficiaries of funding from government sources. Related businesses, such as condom manufacturers, medical supply companies, health food stores, and home health care aides, are also impacted by AIDS, but they have not broken down the impact the disease has on their financial operations.

The CDC issues a handbook each year listing national organizations providing HIV and AIDS services. Virtually all of these are either governmental or nonprofit. Some are funded by significant private donors, such as the Rockefeller Archive Center (which is involved in epidemiology). Others are funded by religious organizations, such as the Presbyterian AIDS Network. Many are community-based, such as the Gay Men's Health Crisis Center in New York, the San Francisco AIDS Foundation—two of the largest—and the Madison, Wisconsin-AIDS Network. Although it is inaccurate to characterize AIDS as only a homosexual disease, many ASOs are based in communities where substantial gay populations are located. In 1998, the National Prevention Information Network (formerly the National AIDS Clearinghouse) reported there were more than 19,000 ASOs, many of which had sprung up in the years 1982 to 1986, when the general public's awareness of AIDS also increased. Writer Robert Searles Walker suggested in his book, *AIDS Today, Tomorrow: An Introduction to the HIV Epidemic in America,* that the proliferation of AIDS-related organizations had a tendency to divert money from services and research into salaries and organization-based expenses.

Foundations, ASOs, and the federal government have sometimes endured criticism, particularly from the populations hardest hit by HIV and AIDS. But those criticisms are no worse than those directed against the private enterprise element of AIDS-related industry.

Federal funds directed toward AIDS research, treatment, prevention, and education (other major elements of the AIDS industry) are the result of passage by the U.S. Congress of the Ryan White Act of 1990. Named for a teenager from Indiana who died as a result of receiving an HIV-contaminated blood transfusion, the Act authorized $4.5 billion in federal spending for five years (from 1991 through 1996). Though the funding was authorized, the appropriation did not begin until 1994. The vast majority of the funding was directed toward research and development and treatment, although a portion was also directed toward education programs in schools and prisons and toward minorities. In December 1998 President Bill Clinton announced the release of an additional $479 million in new Ryan White funding money. This time, most of the money went to primary health care and supportive services for people living with HIV/AIDS. Since that time, AIDS organizations have continued their private fundraising and continued to pressure the federal government to budget additional money to eradicate AIDS.

As part of his 1998 budget message, Democratic President Bill Clinton requested $14.8 billion for NIH, the bulk of which would go for biomedical research in 1999. Republican congressional leaders pushed to increase that figure to nearly $16 billion. While the NIH budget represents an increase in spending, AIDS activists have contended that the amount of money devoted to AIDS research has always been too small, given the nature of the epidemic in this country and worldwide—the same criticism leveled at Republican Presidents Reagan and George Bush.

Insurance companies also comprise a major part of AIDS-related industry. While initial reports of HIV and AIDS generated considerable confusion and concern over possible impacts on the insurance industry, those concerns have not materialized. It was presumed that insurers would take a financial hit as the number of HIV-infected individuals and persons with AIDS grew. However, *Life Association News* has reported that AIDS has not had a significant negative impact on the insurance business. The debate is less over how much of the cost of HIV/AIDS treatments is covered (although that is a concern given the high cost of medications and care) than over what some have called the "buying off" of persons with AIDS. This area, where insurance companies have found themselves in an unwanted spotlight, involves something called viaticals. The word is from the Latin *viaticum,* which refers either to the rites administered to dying persons in the Roman Catholic Church, or to the provisions for a journey. It has come to mean a new growth segment of the AIDS-related insurance industry.

A small number of companies—usually not an individual's life insurer—have entered into Living Benefits arrangements with AIDS patients. These individuals tend to be unable to find employment and may have to rely on assistance programs such as Social Security disability payments or public relief payments. The viatical companies agree to "buy" the life insurance policy of an AIDS sufferer for between 50 and 80 percent of its face value. The policyholder gets access to needed money; the viatical company collects on the life insurance policy when the individual with AIDS dies. This approach has both supporters and detractors. Although someone with AIDS may not be able to work (either because of health considerations or because of de facto job discrimination), living expenses continue. Added to daily living costs are increasing costs for medicines and health-related services. Additionally, the ability to pay off student loans, make automobile payments, or be responsible for any kind of debt, means the cost of having AIDS quickly mounts. The viatical approach has been viewed as a way for needed funding to get into the hands of those suffering from AIDS at a time when they really need the money—while they are still alive. The viatical insurance industry was generating an estimated $300 million in annual receipts in the mid-1990s. However, by early 1999, the industry had decidedly slacked off, not only because of the increased life span of AIDS patients due to medical advances, but also because of negative media attention directed at the industry.

Yet another element in the AIDS-related industry is equipment, ranging from extremely expensive machines used in the treatment of blood and blood-related products to disposable plastic gloves and condoms. Prior to the 1980s, condoms were rarely seen in public and were not widely marketed. With the coming of AIDS and public education campaigns that suggested condom use was one way to minimize exposure to HIV, condoms became a product for mass marketing. With considerable fanfare (and inevitable controversy), condoms were advertised on television, with their regular use endorsed by sex therapist Dr. Ruth Westheimer. After basketball star Magic Johnson's November 1991 announcement that he was HIV-positive, stock in condom companies soared. John Silverman of LifeStyles condoms was roundly criticized in 1987 when he said AIDS was "a condom manufacturer's dream," but he may have been expressing a regrettably insensitive sentiment shared by others in the industry.

There have been other, sometimes questionable, products and services resulting from AIDS. Author

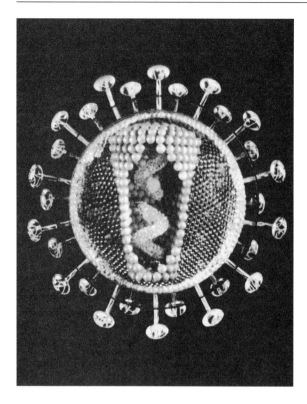

A three-dimensional model of the HIV virus. (Corbis Corporation.)

Elinor Burkett, who coined the phrase "AIDS Industrial Complex" in her book *The Gravest Show on Earth,* listed a wide array of activities ranging from well-meaning failures to tasteless exploitation to outright scams. There were health food stores that claimed certain vitamins could cure AIDS and a Texas company that peddled what it also claimed was an AIDS cure. There was an advertisement in a national magazine for Lasting Impression cards (sold for $19.95) for terminally ill patients to send to loved ones, and a $15 red rhinestone version of the AIDS ribbon often seen at entertainment events.

Virtually all of these arms of the AIDS industry have come under criticism at one time or another for their failure to eradicate AIDS. A common theme has involved the amount of money devoted to AIDS services and research. The cost of hospital care for AIDS patients in the United States has totaled more than $1.4 billion since the disease was first diagnosed six years ago, and the stories about advances seem to be balanced by stories of failures and rising death rates; therefore, it is unclear whether anything short of total eradication of HIV and AIDS would satisfy critics. Given the nature of the disease, that is not likely to happen in the near future.

BACKGROUND AND DEVELOPMENT

As chronicled in Randy Shilts' book *And the Band Played On,* it is generally accepted that AIDS originated in Africa. While a subsequent examination of medical records suggests that persons may have died of AIDS-like diseases throughout history, awareness of AIDS as an identifiable condition was first observed in the late 1970s. At that time, there were large population shifts in countries such as Zaire, with thousands of rural dwellers moving to the cities, resulting in increased overcrowding and increased prostitution, which led to the spread of the disease. There had been plagues earlier in history, such as the Black Death that ravaged Europe in the Middle Ages and the worldwide influenza epidemic of 1918 to 1920, which killed more people than all who had died in World War I. But the causes of those plagues had long before been identified. That was not the case with AIDS.

Initially, it was believed this disease was spread only by inoculation, that the virus must somehow be injected into an individual's bloodstream. That thinking made intravenous drug users (who often shared needles while shooting up) prime candidates for the syndrome. But in the early 1980s, medical personnel began noticing a high death rate among gay males from such opportunistic diseases as Kaposi's sarcoma, a form of cancer. Medical personnel also noticed that individuals who had exceptionally low T-cell counts were virtually unable to fight off even simple infections. Initially, causes of death among this group of people were attributed to the infections. The reporting of Randy Shilts (who eventually died of AIDS) suggested that the disease may have been brought to this country as a result of a sexually profligate gay male airline steward.

AIDS was formally identified as a syndrome, or series of diseases, opportunistic infections, and conditions, in 1981. It was believed AIDS originated in Africa as a result of human-animal sexual activity and/or bites from infected animals, then spread to Western countries primarily through homosexual activity. While some theorize that people may have died of AIDS throughout history, cases of the syndrome have been traced to the 1960s. In 1983, scientists identified HIV as the cause of AIDS. Initially thought to be a gay male's or drug user's disease, AIDS deaths began to multiply among persons (young and old) who received blood transfusions from HIV-positive individuals, as well as those who engaged only in heterosexual practices.

AIDS quickly became a sensitive political and social issue. President Ronald Reagan's administration was viewed as largely unresponsive to AIDS, prompting considerable protest and rhetoric. While President George Bush gave more attention to the problem, AIDS surfaced as a campaign issue in 1992 when Bush was challenged for the presidency by Arkansas Governor Bill Clinton. Since he became president, Clinton has greatly expanded government's role in research, treatment, education, and prevention—with a substantial amount of money and effort still devoted to educating people about how AIDS is contracted and what should be done to minimize exposure to the disease. During this same period of time, the American Red Cross took extraordinary precautions to prevent the spread of AIDS through the blood supply.

In the mid-1990s there was an increase in AIDS-related lawsuits. One of the more significant lawsuits pitted Jackson National Life against Mrs. Frank Deramus, whose husband had died of AIDS. Mrs. Deramus sued the insurance company for not informing her husband that he had AIDS. A court ruled that insurers had no responsibility to notify those they insured of medical information to which the company had access. Another significant set of cases involved a Japanese government AIDS researcher, Takeshi Abe, who in 1983 received donations from five different blood product manufacturers that were accused of having sold HIV-tainted products. Similar cases involving HIV-tainted blood also surfaced (and have been settled) in Canada and France.

CURRENT CONDITIONS

In February 1999, scientists were finally able to confirm *scientifically* their long-held belief that the AIDS virus (HIV-1) epidemic/pandemic came from chimpanzees in Africa. Dr. Beatrice Hahn of the University of Alabama at Birmingham, along with her research team, made the startling discovery by perchance, examining frozen tissue of the only monkey to have tested positive for HIV from a colony of chimpanzees used by the Air Force in the 1970s and 1980s for space travel study. Hahn has further posited that the leap from chimp to man may have occurred as the result of hunting and butchering chimps for food, a common practice in Africa. The origin of the infected chimpanzees was in a region southeast of Nigeria, to include Cameroon, Gabon and Equatorial Guinea. Interestingly, the first documented case of AIDS was in 1959, across the Congo River from Gabon.

At the same time this news was released, a prominent coalition of AIDS researchers, animal conserva-

tionists and academic primatologists (including famed Jane Goodall) had unitedly urged vaccine developers not to inject chimpanzees with virulent strains of HIV. Sadly, vaccine efforts had failed to the point that vaccinated chimps in the study were dying more than living. The vaccines had sickened or killed all the infant monkeys, and most of the adults. None were warding off the disease, the main objective of vaccination. This prompted many to consider the future of vaccine research to be tenuous at best, unless the current approach was drastically changed.

Notwithstanding, in 1998 the VaxGen, Inc. company of Brisbane, California, began human test trials of their own developed vaccine, AIDSVAX, and the Joint United Nations Programme on HIV/AIDS (UNAIDS) concurred in a decision by the government of Thailand to proceed with human testing (2500 volunteers) of AIDS vaccines to address the different strains of HIV that exist in that country.

Other news in early 1999 was the positive result of a multi-year study showing that shorter-term medication for HIV-infected babies born to infected women was nonetheless effective. While results were hopeful for developing countries, the study was not without controversy. One concern was the trial testing, which gave real medicine to only half the study's infected mothers, thus building into the study model a mortality statistic that was considered by many as unethical. Simply put, the study might have saved many more otherwise doomed infants, but those that have survived now may be orphaned because of untreated mothers. The alternative, argued scientists from the U.N. AIDS program, was to let the babies die.

It is hard to determine whether AIDS cases are actually going down or are increasing, based on news reports. A study by Philip S. Rosenberg and Dr. Robert J. Biggar of the National Cancer Institute indicates a drop in the spread of HIV infection in young men through homosexual contact and injection drug use. This same study concludes that there is a dramatic increase in HIV infection by heterosexual transmission to young women, particularly young black women. In 1996, the Department of Health and Human Services (HHS) reported that the number of African Americans in the United States diagnosed with AIDS exceeded the number of whites and that the number of AIDS cases among males who had sex with other males continued to decline.

Again in 1998, the Center for Disease Control (CDC) published new data through its National Center for Health Statistics, indicating a 47 percent de-

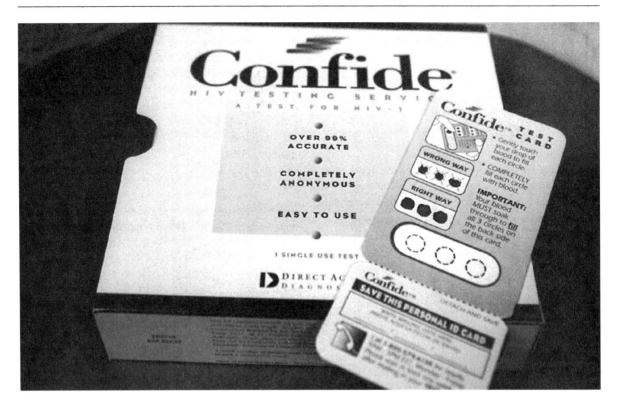

The Confide HIV testing kit allows users to test themselves for HIV at home. (AP Photo/Ron Edmonds.)

cline in HIV-related deaths in the United States for the period of 1996 to 1997. According to the CDC, both AIDS deaths and reported AIDS cases dropped, for the first time. These figures resulted in HIV infections falling from eighth to fourteenth place among leading causes of death in the United States for the year 1997. Another report released in early 1999 indicated a "substantial reduction" in AIDS-related deaths from 1995 to 1998 in the New York State prison population. Notwithstanding, over 60,000 new cases of AIDS were reported in 1997, 40,000 with HIV infections: a figure considered more stable than dynamic, according to CDC. This was attributed to medical advances that have lengthened the lifespan of an increasing number of HIV-infected people. Concomitantly, the number of people *living* with HIV was increasing, somewhere between 700,000 and 900,000 in the late 1990s in the United States.

But the increase in lifespan of AIDS patients and the steady or increasing incidence of HIV infections has outpaced the available funds for AIDS research and treatment. In an April 1999 press release, UN-AIDS published statistics indicating that, while the number of people living with HIV more than tripled between 1990 and 1997, HIV/AIDS funding had not even doubled for the correlative period. But still, the

United States is the largest funder of international AIDS efforts, in 1997 alone contributing $135.2 million of the total $273 million. Reported AIDS cases in the United States constitute about 0.1 percent of the national population in the late 1990s. The worldwide AIDS and HIV cases total approximately 0.3 percent of the global population during the same period.

In 1998, the Clinton Administration launched a new initiative on World AIDS Day, directed toward helping AIDS orphans and the international AIDS crisis. The initiative was to boost research funds by 12 percent, HIV vaccine research by 33 percent, and $10 million specifically earmarked for AIDS orphans in developing countries.

Another alarming finding was the three-year study reported in the February 1999 Journal of the American Medical Association (JAMA), which showed an increase in unsafe sex and rectal gonorrhea among gay males in the San Francisco area from 1994-1997. There was reported an increase from 23.6 to 33.3 percent of men having *unprotected* anal sex with *multiple* sex partners. Moreover, male rectal gonorrhea, which had been on the decline prior to 1993, suddenly increased during the study period from 21 to 38 percent. These figures represent a dangerous increase in risk for HIV infection and transmission.

INDUSTRY LEADERS

While a number of companies are involved in the development and testing of the wide array of expensive drugs used to treat persons with HIV and AIDS, the first name that comes to the minds of medical practitioners and their patients is Glaxo Wellcome, the company that developed AZT. Glaxo is also the manufacturer of the new protease inhibitor Agenerase, approved by the FDA in April 1999 for treatment of HIV infections.

The 342 pharmaceutical firms listed in the 1997 *Ward's Business Directory of U.S. Private and Public Companies* together constituted $138 billion in annual sales. The largest among these, Glaxo Wellcome and Abbot Laboratories, produced AIDS treatments that were among the most expensive types of medicine on the market. It can be assumed that AIDS-related sales constituted a significant portion of the drug sales for these companies, as well as a significant portion of total pharmaceutical sales. British-based Glaxo Wellcome (formerly Burroughs Wellcome) has likely profited in the range of $1 billion from its development of AZT. The three leading producers of protease inhibitors, a major pharmaceutical component of AIDS treatment, are Merck & Co., Abbott Laboratories, and Hoffman-La Roche. Serono Laboratories has produced a drug called serostim, which is designed to address AIDS-wasting syndrome. Another significant AIDS product, Confide—the first home HIV test—was introduced by Johnson & Johnson. The test has since been pulled from the market due to insufficient sales. In late 1996, Home Access Health Company introduced its own home test with a $20-million ad campaign.

AIDS-related health care services also appear to have emerged as a multi-billion-dollar industry, although *Nursing Homes* magazine reported in April 1997 that the AIDS market in the late 1990s is largely untapped by long-term health care providers. One leading AIDS-related health care provider is Coram Healthcare, which in 1996 entered into a management venture with Johns Hopkins Medical Institutions. *Health Industry Today* has predicted that home care in particular will grow through the year 2000.

Among the major health insurers involved in AIDS-related activities are State Farm, Allstate, and Prudential. Government-provided health insurance also pays for AIDS-related medicines and services.

WORK FORCE

The frontline workers in the AIDS battle are clinical physicians, related clinic- and hospital-based professionals, and home health care workers. Also part of the army of AIDS industry workers are the research scientists, pharmacists, related direct-care providers, and the educators, outreach workers, and fundraisers who help keep the issue of AIDS in the public consciousness.

Biomedical researchers are the behind-the-scenes workers who rarely come into direct contact with AIDS patients. Many of them work for the National Institutes of Health, the Food and Drug Administration, and the Centers for Disease Control. A substantial number of university-based researchers and individuals working for private pharmaceutical manufacturers also contribute to the $11.79 billion research industry.

A number of other occupations are also a part of AIDS-related industries, particularly significant are manufacturing jobs. These include those involved in the production of treatment equipment and items for prevention, such as condoms and latex gloves. Except for doctors and other health care workers treating AIDS patients, very few persons in the AIDS industry run any risk of infection through their jobs.

Initially, there was dramatic fear that HIV and AIDS could be spread through casual contact with an infected individual; a number of medical workers became infected as a result of being stabbed by instruments that had touched virus-infected blood. While there are still some personnel who refuse to provide treatment to or come in contact with an HIV-positive/AIDS-infected individual—something the American Medical Association has condemned as a violation of its code of ethics—precautions in all areas of medical practice have improved to the point where the risk of accidental infection is minimal.

AMERICA AND THE WORLD

AIDS knows no political, social, or racial boundaries; it is a global phenomenon. While the relatively rich United States has undertaken efforts on all fronts to deal with all aspects of HIV and AIDS, other countries are only beginning to come to grips with the disease and the magnitude of its destruction.

In December 1998, the Joint United Nations Programme on HIV/AIDS (UNAIDS) updated its basic statistics, evincing a pandemic rather than epidemic crisis. More than 13.9 million people had died world-wide since the epidemic began—10.7 million of them were adults; 3.2 million were children under age 15. There was also an increase in the number of women affected, reaching 43 percent, or 13.8 million.

Internationally, UNAIDS reports what they call an alarming increase in HIV and AIDS worldwide among persons aged 13 to 24. Rates in foreign countries are also rising dramatically. A study by Louis Harris & Associates indicates that 25 percent of HIV/AIDS patients in the United States do not follow treatment guidelines developed by the U.S. Department of Health and Human Services, even when they have AIDS-related symptoms.

Figures from UNAIDS conclude that more than half of all new HIV infections acquired after infancy occur among young people between the ages of 10 and 24. Of the estimated 33 million people worldwide living with HIV, at least a third are young people; by the year 2020, there will be more than 40 million orphans under the age of 15 in the 23 countries most affected by HIV, one third of them under the age of 5. These children will have lost their parents to AIDS.

More than 1.7 million young people aged 13 to 24 are infected with HIV every year in Africa. South of the Sahara Desert, nearly 21 million Africans are living with HIV, and countries of that region account for the 21 highest HIV prevalence rates in the world. India has an estimated 4 million people living with HIV. And more than 700,000 young people in Asia and the Pacific contract HIV each year. The totality of these staggering figures shows that more than 95 percent of all HIV-infected people now live in the developing world, with a correlative 95 percent of all AIDS related deaths.

At one time, it was believed infection rates in eastern European countries were relatively small. That has changed. By the end of 1997, more than 190,000 people in the region were living with HIV, a six-fold increase from the previous year. Uganda and Thailand are the only developing countries studied by Dr. David Heymann with the World Health Organization that have declining HIV rates.

While many developing countries have embarked on strong prevention programs, their HIV and AIDS rates have not dropped, and these countries have neither the infrastructure nor the funding capabilities to make strong inroads without outside financial assistance.

France, whose researchers narrowly edged out Robert Gallo of the National Cancer Institute in Bethesda, Maryland, for credit in isolating HIV as the cause of AIDS in 1983, has had its own problems with public perceptions. Researchers in the United States and abroad have suggested that France's hierarchical research system has stunted the ability of researchers to effectively continue AIDS-related research. And France's problems worsened in 1999. Former French Prime Minister Laurent Fabius and two administration members were on trial for manslaughter for failing to act on available tests to detect HIV-infected blood back in the mid-1980s. The result, said prosecutors, was the AIDS infection of more than 4000 people, from tainted blood transfusions, 40 percent of whom have since died. (The defendants were acquitted in March 1999.)

The United States, which itself has been the target of substantial worldwide criticism for its AIDS policies, has begun to question the effectiveness of UNAIDS. A General Accounting Office (GAO) analysis of UNAIDS has concluded this United Nations agency has had little success in its two years of operation. According to the GAO report, the United Nations has not increased AIDS spending, despite its goal of expanding the fight against the disease, particularly in the developing world. The report also said United Nations' efforts to coordinate its AIDS and health activities in various countries have gotten off to a slow start. The report did praise UNAIDS for research it has sponsored to identify which programs work to curb the spread of AIDS.

RESEARCH AND TECHNOLOGY

AZT, also known as azido-deoxythymidine, as zidovudine (ZDV), or by its trademarked name Ritrovir, was the first and probably the best known of the battery of drugs used to keep AIDS at bay. Most doctors still start anti-viral therapy (when a person has some symptoms of HIV) with this drug. As the first HIV drug to receive U.S. Food and Drug Administration approval, it has been widely studied. Since there is no generic version of this drug, and since only one company manufactures it, Glaxo Wellcome has been in the forefront of AIDS-related industries.

While AZT is still considered the first-line treatment of HIV, it brings with it a wide array of negative side effects, and the drug may produce a harsh interaction with other drugs used as part of the drug "cocktail" approach now used to stave off HIV and to treat AIDS. In 1999, it was shown that AZT and 3TC together could substantially reduce risk to newborns, even when given during a smaller window period during the mother's pregnancy and post-partem days. New treatments involving anti-viral protease inhibitor drugs have had mixed reviews, although mostly positive. More alarming than mixed treatment prognoses are the financial aspects of AIDS. Many patients cannot get the costly medicines needed to keep their conditions under control because of restrictions imposed on them by their HMOs and state programs set up to assist low-income persons. The kinds of drug combinations recommended by doctors treating AIDS patients can easily cost $10,000 to $15,000 a year—a cost likely to continue for as long as the individual is being treated for AIDS. A total of 35 of 52 state-administered AIDS programs have curbed patient access to protease inhibitors because of costs.

The nature of the HIV virus has served to spur the development of other drugs used to treat infected individuals. The virus has a way of "changing" when it reproduces in an individual's blood cells. Consequently, an individual's ability to fight off a wide range of infections is substantially compromised, and it means a drug or combination of drugs may work for one person but not for another. That has kept a number of pharmaceutical companies continuing research to find either a cure or a way to substantially prolong the lives of AIDS-infected persons.

In 1997, anti-viral protease inhibitors were among the most promising of the new drugs in the developing HIV/AIDS arsenal. These drugs interrupt the way HIV uses a healthy cell to make more viruses. Protease inhibitors and AZT continue to be among the first drugs prescribed by doctors. And in April 1999, the FDA approved Agenerase, generically known as amprenavir, the first new protease inhibitor approved since 1997.

A new combination of drugs, referred to as a drug "cocktail" appears to be capable of eliminating all detectable levels of HIV in the body tissues where the virus is known to reside. Previous studies have shown that these drugs can reduce the level of HIV in the bloodstream. But the virus is known to hide in the tonsils, lymph nodes, spinal fluid, and semen. Canadian scientists have found that drug cocktails have been most effective with individuals who have not been ill with HIV for a long period of time.

One set of cocktail drugs is produced by Glaxo Wellcome and Abbott Laboratories and utilizes the drugs AZT, 3TC, and Norvir. A separate study has found that the combination of AZT, 3TC, and Viramune (manufactured by Boehringer Ingelheim) had a similar effect. This approach, known as HIV thera-

peutics, was welcomed at the twelfth International Conference on AIDS held June 28 through July 3, 1998 in Geneva, Switzerland, and has generated optimism within the research community.

While drug cocktails in combination with other anti-HIV treatments is becoming the standard of care, it has not yet been determined which of the anti-HIV drug combinations are the most effective and consistent. What is clear is that the stronger the anti-HIV effects of a drug combination, the less likely it is that HIV will become resistant to the effects of the drugs. This will keep the world's drug manufacturers involved in research for the near future.

Another viable research area remains in the biochip industry. Also known as DNA arrays, biochips are microscopic devices studded with a kind of molecular "tweezer" that grips human DNA, the genetic code carried in all cells of a person's body. These chips allow medical researchers to study thousands of genes at once. By mapping genes, scientists may learn how cells mutate and may eventually be able to stop HIV before it takes over a human organism. Gene mapping may also open the door to immune reconstitution following successful suppression of HIV replication. Pathogenic events surrounding primary HIV infection are being actively studied by several groups throughout the world.

What may be the most welcome news to drug companies and AIDS researchers is a finding by Dr. Beryl Koblin and colleagues of the New York Blood Center that a large percentage of individuals—77 percent—who are at high risk of HIV infection say they are willing to participate in HIV vaccine trials. The study included responses from homosexual men, intravenous drug users, and women at risk of HIV infection from heterosexual sex. An HIV vaccine, as well as a "day-after" pill or medicine, remains the goal of researchers grappling with this frustrating disease.

FURTHER READING

"AIDS Falls from Top Ten Causes of Death . . ." *NCHA News Release,* 7 October 1998. Available from http://www.cdc.gov.nchswww/releases.

"AIDS from Chimps." *Maclean's,* 15 February 1999.

Altman, Lawrence K. "H.I.V. Is Linked to a Subspecies of Chimpanzee." *New York Times,* 1 February 1999, A1.

———. "Spare AIDS Regime Found to Reduce Risk to Newborns." *New York Times,* 2 February 1999.

"An Asymptomatic 41-Year Old Man With HIV Infection." *JAMA,* 24 February 1999.

Balter, Michael. "French AIDS Research Pioneers to Testify in Trial of Ministers." *Science,* 12 February 1999.

———. "Has French AIDS Research Stumbled?" *Science,* 16 January 1998.

Burkett, Elino. *The Gravest Show on Earth: America in the Age of AIDS.* Boston: Houghton Mifflin, 1995.

Centers for Disease Control and Prevention. "Basic Statistics," 26 April 1999. Available from http://www.cdc.gov.

———. "Decline in AIDS Deaths Indicates Continued Success of New HIV Treatments: And Suggests Continued Increase in HIV Prevalence." 1 October 1998.

———. *National Organizations Providing HIV/AIDS Services: A Directory for Community-Based Organizations,* October 1996.

Christensen, D. "AIDS Virus Jumped From Chimps." *Science News,* 6 February 1999.

Cohen, Jon. "AIDS Virus Traced to Chimp Subspecies." *Science,* 5 February 1999.

———. "Cheap Treatment Cuts HIV Transmission." *Science,* 12 February 1999.

———. "Researchers Urged Not to Inject Virulent HIV Strain into Chimps." *Science,* 19 February 1999.

Cohen, Oren J., and Anthony Fauchi. "HIV/AIDS in 1998—Gaining the Upper Hand?" *The Journal of the American Medical Association,* 1 July 1998.

Couzin, Jennifer. "Small Steps Against AIDS." *US News & World Report,* 15 February 1999.

Cue, Eduardo. "A Battle Over French Blood." *US News & World Report,* 22 February 1999.

Gay Stolberg, Sheryl. "U.S. AIDS Research in Poor Nations Raises an Outcry." *The New York Times on the Web,* 18 September 1997.

Golden, Frederic. "The First Chimpanzee." *Time,* 8 February 1999.

Gorman, Christine. "If the Condom Breaks: A Morning-After Treatment for Exposure to HIV Might Protect You from AIDS, but Don't Count on It." *Time,* 23 June 1997.

"Health Tips: Grants Given to Develop an AIDS Vaccine." *United Press International,* 26 April 1999.

"HIV Testing-United States, 1996." *Journal of American Medical Association (JAMA),* 24 February 1999.

"Increases in Unsafe Sex and Rectal Gonorrhea among Men Who Have Sex With Men-San Francisco, California, 1994-1997." *JAMA,* 24 February 1999.

Ireland, Doug. "Silence Kills Blacks." *The Nation,* 20 April 1998.

Irlanda, Iria, and Harold Kessler. "New Media." *JAMA,* 3 February 1999.

Jerome, Richard, and Giovanna Breu. "Ryan White." *People,* 22 March 1999.

Lankford, Kimberly, and Margaret Ringer. "Death Watch." *Kiplinger's Personal Finance Magazine,* March 1999.

Lemonick, Michael D. "Good News At a Price." *Time,* 15 February 1999.

N.S. "AZT Shows No Ill Effects on Babies." *Science News,* 6 February 1999.

Nichols, Mark. "Hope, not Miracles; in Some Cases, a Promising AIDS Drug Is Failing." *Macleans,* 22 September 1997.

Pear, Robert. "Budget Urges Increases for Child Care, Medicare, Medical Research." *The New York Times on the Web,* 3 February 1998.

Pedersen, Daniel, and Eric Larson. "Too Poor to Treat: States Are Balking at Paying for Pricey AIDS Drugs." *Newsweek,* 28 July 1997.

"President Clinton and Vice President Gore: Leading the Fight Against HIV/AIDS," 18 December 1999. Available from http://www.whitehouse.gov.

———. "Government Ready to Boost Spending for Biomedicine." *The New York Times on the Web,* 3 January 1998.

Schindehette, Susan, and Joanne Fowler, et al. "Best on the Block." *People,* 8 March 1999.

Seppa, Nathan. "HIV Not Eradicated by Drug Cocktail." *Science News,* 6 December 1997.

———. "Prospects Dim for Live AIDS Vaccine." *Science News,* 13 February 1999.

"A Tainted Blood Trial in France." *Maclean's,* 22 February 1999.

Walker, Robert Searles. *AIDS Today, Tomorrow: An Introduction to the HIV Epidemic in America,* 2nd Ed. New Jersey: Humanities Press, 1994.

Werner, Curt. "Big Three Producers Still Dominate IV Solutions Market." *Health Industry Today,* August 1996.

Whitney, Craig R. "Top French Officials Cleared Over Blood With AIDS Virus." *New York Times,* 10 March 1999.

Wright, L.N., and P.F. Smith, et al. "Decrease in AIDS-Related Mortality in a State Correctional System-New York, 1995-1998." *JAMA,* 10 February 1999.

—Judson Knight, updated by Virginia Black and Lauri R. Harding

ALTERNATIVE ADULT EDUCATION

Alternative adult education, as the term "alternative" implies, encompasses many educational opportunities for adults whose needs vary from the traditional on-site, degree-granting methods of schooling. The emergence and growth of this industry has capitalized on three important factors for its continued success: inability or hardship in attending regularly-scheduled classes, time and financial difficulties, and the continued need for exposure to new learning experiences, dubbed "andragogy" by one of the early leaders in this field, Malcolm Shepherd Knowles (1913-1997).

The industry is not limited in its success to the proffering of "higher" education in the traditional sense. The number of adults completing high-school equivalency classes and examinations in the United States and Canada reached an all-time high (in the 57 years of the testing program's history) of more than 750,000 in 1996 alone. Moreover, as it is anticipated that the adult elderly population will double by the year 2050, more and more senior citizens are joining the ranks of "students" to fill their leisurely retirement hours with stimulating learning experiences. The result of the industry's ability to tap into these expanding markets is that adults now have ever-increasing opportunities to enhance job skills and expand employment options. They can attain higher levels of formal education and develop personal interests through enrichment and leisure classes.

Vocational education is another example of substantive alternative education. Often incorporated at job sites, vocational education is alternatively combined with off-site home-study and/or company-spon-sored classroom or conference training. The purpose of this training is to provide an opportunity to enhance earning potential in a learning structure that is compatible with adult students' time, interest, and capacity. Another development in the adult education arena is the evolution of electronic methods of teaching and learning for higher education, often called on-line education, distance instruction, or the virtual university. Distance instruction is used by degree-granting colleges and universities, vocational educators, and corporate trainers in an ongoing effort to offer more options to adult students.

Adult enrichment classes and programs, vocational education, and distance instruction are likely to play large roles in future educational efforts. As the new century approaches, adults will increasingly turn to distance instruction and satellite campuses that make the combination of work and education possible. With these new developments, students can improve their career skills by earning a college degree in on-line classrooms or, more commonly, with a combination of classroom work and technological methods. Institutions providing new and reliable developments in this area lead the industry of adult learning.

ORGANIZATION AND STRUCTURE

VOCATIONAL EDUCATION
The 1990 Perkins Act defines vocational education as "organized educational programs offering a sequence of courses which are directly related to the preparation of individuals in paid or unpaid employ-

ment in current or emerging occupations requiring other than a baccalaureate or advanced degree." Post-secondary level occupational curricula typically offer programs falling into the following categories: agriculture; business and office; marketing and distribution; health; home economics; technical education, including protective services, computers, and data processing; engineering, science, and communication technologies; and trade and industry. Vocational education is also provided at the secondary level.

The National Assessment of Vocational Education found that 5.8 million students were enrolled in post-secondary vocational education in 1990, making up about 35 percent of all undergraduate post-secondary enrollment. Vocational enrollment represented an even larger share of the non-baccalaureate undergraduate population, approximately 50 percent of which reported majoring in a vocational program area.

DISTANCE INSTRUCTION

While the historical basis of distance instruction lies in correspondence education, essentially two forms of distance instruction existed in the late 1990s: traditional correspondence-based instruction, which is oriented for independent study, and telecommunications-based instruction, which offers the teaching and learning experience simultaneously. Some scholars distinguish between distance learning and distance education, instead of using the term "instruction." Distance learning is exemplified by programs designed to encourage self-directed learning, such as do-it-yourself books, while distance education requires formal evaluation and two-way communication with an institution, as well as independent study.

Distance instruction is delivered through media such as audiotape, videotape, radio and television broadcasting, and satellite transmission. Microcomputers, the Internet, and the World Wide Web are shaping the current generation of distance learning. The next generation may be built on virtual reality, artificial intelligence, and knowledge systems. Although broadcast television was often used for distance instruction in the mid- to late 1990s, it may be used more rarely in the future, as media such as print, audiocassette, and telephone access prove to be more convenient.

There are two primary forms of communication utilized to deliver distance instruction—asynchronous and synchronous. The main distinction between the two is whether teachers and learners are participating at the same time. Asynchronous methods use recorded instructional materials that allow participants to be separated in time and distance from the instruction. Thus, telecommunications systems such as television, or electronically stored media such as video, audio, and computer software, are among the technologies used. Synchronous programs, however, use technologies offering live, interactive instruction. Instructional Television Fixed Service and point-to-point microwave are among the most common live interactive systems that link classrooms within the regional area surrounding an institution; the students are able to see and hear one another, as well as the instructor. Other examples of synchronous communications include audio conferencing and real-time computer communications. Synchronous programs are also being used increasingly by elementary and secondary schools.

The organization and administration of distance instruction in the late 1990s varied according to the type of institution offering the learning opportunity. The transmission of learning over distance is the sole responsibility and purpose of some universities, while others offer distance instruction as one of a number of programs. One of the fastest growing segments of distance education in the late 1990s was a consortium of institutions devoted to distance instruction. This approach was exemplified by an on-line learning environment called Mind Extension University (MEU), a privately owned distance learning company. MEU developed tele-courses and offered them in conjunction with other colleges and universities, and even expanded into courses offered on the World Wide Web through its global electronic International Community College.

Another consortium in the late 1990s was the National Universities Degree Consortium (NUDC). The NUDC is a consortium of 13 accredited U.S. universities offering over 1,000 courses, 11 bachelor's degrees, and 24 graduate degrees through distance instruction. Course presentations include videotape and print-based independent study and correspondence study courses.

Accreditation of distance instruction establishments vary by state and region. Institutions that also maintain a traditional campus often have the distance instruction component accredited as part of the main institution. One accrediting body specific to the industry is the Distance Education and Training Council (DETC)—formerly the National Home Study Council—founded in 1926 in Washington, D.C. The DETC is an association of distance learning and correspondence schools recognized by the U.S. Department of Education and the Commission on Recognition of Post-Secondary Accreditation.

BACKGROUND AND DEVELOPMENT

INCREASED ENROLLMENT IN VOCATIONAL EDUCATION

For well over a century, a debate was fought in the United States over how to prepare students to become adult workers. Until the country's economy was transformed from an agricultural to a manufacturing base, children received a common core curriculum of academic subjects, and most left school before the end of the eighth grade. In 1900, approximately 6.5 percent of students graduated from high school, as compared to about 72 percent in the mid-1990s. As the modern manufacturing economy took hold, changes in vocational education were required for both children and adults.

In response to the growing economy, some policy makers proposed setting up separate vocational education programs to prepare young people for work. Others, especially John Dewey, urged the integration of academic and vocational instruction so that all students could learn the same academic material, but in the context of occupations and adult experiences. The federal government, however, created distinct programs of vocational instruction when it passed the Smith-Hughes Act of 1917. Eventually, most schools divided students into "academic" and "vocational" tracks, and in the 1920s, many schools added a general track to give students a sampling of both. Although commissions and studies throughout the twentieth century have suggested that this approach to vocational education is needed, many schools and school districts still designated vocational education as a separate track designed primarily to prepare students for work.

As high school graduates were increasingly seen as under-qualified to perform the technical jobs for which vocational education supposedly had trained them, adult vocational training took on added importance. In addition, improvements were sought in secondary school vocational training, notably in the Carl Perkins Vocational and Applied Technology Education Act of 1990, which promoted the integration of academic and vocational learning. The Perkins Act required each state to use academic achievement as a measure of success, and it encourages linkages between secondary and post-secondary course work through tech-prep education. Another statute designed to improve vocational education was the School-to-Work Opportunities Act of 1994, which sought to raise educational standards and prepare students for post-secondary education.

In the early 1990s, the most popular post-secondary vocational program of study was business, with about 17 percent of all non-baccalaureate students declaring a major in that area. This was followed in popularity by health, with 11 percent, and trade and industry, with 8 percent. The combined technical fields—computers and data processing, engineering and science technologies, protective services, and communications technologies—accounted for 12 percent of all non-baccalaureate majors.

At the post-secondary level in the 1990s, community and technical colleges served a broad range of students, including those still in high school, recent high school graduates, college graduates returning for specific technical skills, adult workers returning for retraining, welfare recipients, and adults with limited basic skills. Community colleges and private proprietary schools redesigned curricula to deal with a changing student body and the added burdens on adult education.

Public two- to three-year institutions, including community colleges, enrolled 60 percent of all non-baccalaureate post-secondary students reporting a vocational major. The second-largest providers were private proprietary institutions, which educated about 22 percent of non-baccalaureate vocational students.

THE GROWTH OF DISTANCE INSTRUCTION

As early as 1728, advertisements appeared in the Boston *Gazette* soliciting students for shorthand lessons by mail. Early detailed accounts of distance instruction indicate that, like today, the process appealed to adults seeking new methods of learning that did not interfere with the workday. In 1840, Isaac Pitman offered shorthand courses by mail in Bath, England.

The 1880s saw the founding of private British correspondence colleges. Schools such as Skerry's College and University Correspondence College, established by the University of London, prepared students for post-secondary examinations. Correspondence schools also found fertile soil on the European continent. In Berlin, Germany, a modern language correspondence school was established by Charles Toussaint and Gustav Langenscheidt in 1856; this school still published instructional materials in the late 1990s. In 1894, another correspondence school was founded to aid students in preparation for university entrance examinations.

American academic distance learning began in 1874 at Illinois' Wesley University, which offered

Pioneer WILLIAM RAINEY
HARPER, 1856-1906
EDUCATING AMERICA

William Rainey Harper was one of America's great pioneers in education, most notably by helping to establish, and serving as the first president of, the University of Chicago.

Harper was born in New Concord, Ohio, to Ellen Rainey and Samuel Harper, a grocery store keeper. As a boy, William supported his father's business by purchasing and selling wool and by helping dam a local stream to produce and sell ice. He entered the Muskingum College preparatory department when he was 8 years old, and at 10 became a freshman at the "college on the hill." At 16 he attended Yale University, and within three years had earned a doctorate. His first teaching job was at Dennison University. A year later he took a teaching position at the Baptist Theological Seminary in Chicago.

In the fall of 1891, John D. Rockefeller called on 35-year-old Harper to help organize and run a new private, nondenominational, coeducational university—a "Harvard of the Midwest." On October 1, 1892 classes began at the University of Chicago. So great was the university's promise that eight college and university presidents resigned their posts in order to teach there. Harper was the University's first president, and he envisioned a modern research university, combining an English-style undergraduate college and a German-style graduate research institute.

Largely eschewing the areas of established excellence, Harper encouraged early administrators to seek new disciplines and ambitious faculty. The University of Chicago quickly became a national leader in higher education and research, despite the fact that Harper was outspoken and scorned tradition. For example, seizing an opportunity generated by academic unrest at another institution, he visited Clark University and recruited two-thirds of the faculty and half of the graduate students, generating a solid core upon which to build his vision.

By the end of its first century, the University had an enrollment of more than 10,700, a faculty of 1,200, and more than 60 Nobel Prize-winners. It included an undergraduate college, four graduate divisions, six graduate professional schools, the Office of Continuing Education, the University of Chicago Press, and the "Chicago Research Schools."

Harper was an innovative force in education throughout his career. Some of his greatest accomplishments included:

- Establishing the first Department of Sociology in the world.

- Establishing the first University extension program in the United States.

- Establishing a *core curriculum,* which became the model for colleges throughout the United States for more than 60 years.

- Establishing programs for the admittance of women and minorities in all academic programs.

both undergraduate and graduate degrees by correspondence. In 1883, the Correspondence University was established in Ithaca, New York. Study outside the traditional classroom was furthered by Anna Eliot York, who founded The Society to Encourage Study at Home in 1873. Home reading circles for adults were created by John Vincent, who became a founder of the Chautauqua movement. The aim of this popular education society was to extend educational access to all Americans, and the movement has been called "the first significant distance education effort in America."

Chautauqua continued to play a role in distance instruction when William Harper, called by many the father of American correspondence study, established a correspondence program for his students. Chautauqua later became an accredited university in New York State, and Harper became the first president of the University of Chicago and founder of the first university-level correspondence study division in the United States.

The growth of distance instruction centers spawned growth in other media. The first federally licensed radio station devoted to educational broadcasting, WHA, evolved from an amateur wireless station started by University of Wisconsin professors in 1919. The birth of educational television broadcasts occurred at the University of Iowa between 1932 and 1937.

A remarkable example of the potential for adult distance instruction can be seen in the Open University of the United Kingdom, established in 1971. In its first 10 years, the school enrolled 60,000 to 70,000 students per year. By the mid-1980s, more than 70,000 students had earned a bachelor's degree from the university. American attempts to emulate the Open University met with limited success. In 1974, the University of Mid-America was founded, aiming to create distance education in seven Midwestern states. The university, despite large enrollments over the years, closed its doors in 1982. Other consortia have done

Students working with pottery in an alternative adult education class. (AP/Wide World Photos.)

well, however, enrolling large numbers of students while allowing the member institutions control over the programs.

Since the 1980s, distance instruction has been characterized by technologies such as television, teleconferencing, video and audiotapes, satellite, and computer and other forms of on-line education. These methods have been the staple of government, military, and corporate training, continuing education, and telemedicine. Before the 1980s, those courses were available electronically, but few degree programs existed.

By the early 1990s, however, distance education had established itself with massive numbers of students. From 1981 to 1988, the Public Broadcasting Service (PBS) broadcast telecourses through its Adult Learning Service, and over 1 million learners enrolled. Over 100,000 Americans still enroll in higher education telecourses each year.

In the last two decades, colleges and universities in many locales introduced some kind of Internet-based program, offering both courses and full degree programs. Grants and sponsors to outfit libraries, senior centers, and cybercafes with Internet-ready computers were becoming more commonplace in the late

1990s, which helped communities gain access to distance courses.

Of concern, however, is the potential growth of "bogus" degrees from "diploma mills," especially on the Internet and World Wide Web. Since accreditation is largely non-regulated and confusing at best, many on-line colleges and universities can offer advanced degrees and diplomas, costing thousands of dollars to the unknowing consumer, and offering little, if any, substantive education, without breaking any laws. This poses a potential danger not only to the general public, but also to the reputation and continued health of those legitimately accredited educational institutions offering adult education. Many members of the public assume that the United States government regulates the industry and they are misled by advertisements boasting of full accreditation from an important-sounding accrediting entity, especially ones that contain the words, "U.S." or "American." As Michael P. Lambert, executive director of the Distance Education and Training Council (which offers information about legitimate distance-learning programs and institutions) advised Lisa Guernsey of *The Chronicle of Higher Education,* "The Internet has given new life to this [diploma mill] movement." As of 1998, the only nationally recognized accrediting agency that evaluates distance-education programs is the Accrediting Commission of the Distance Education and Training Council.

John Bear, co-author of *Bears' Guide to Earning College Degrees Nontraditionally,* created an informational Web site to dispense information about dubious adult education institutions, including "Columbia State University," which advertised that one could earn a college degree in as few as 27 days. Emir Mohammed, a Canadian student who was fortunate enough to save his money by investigating before investing, created a Web site entitled "Distance Ed for Dummies" to help others save money from false or misleading institutional claims. Mohammed even created a fictitious Web site to illustrate the ease with which an unwitting student might engage in transactions or communications with less-than-meritorious institutions of higher education.

CURRENT CONDITIONS

OUTLOOK AND COMMITMENT

During President William Clinton's 1997 inaugural address, he postulated that "education will be every citizen's most prized possession." True to that statement, Congress, in 1998, continued to hammer out the details of a massive piece of legislation, then-referred-to as the Workforce Investment Partnership Act. Under its umbrella were numerous provisions for the consolidation of federal job training, vocational education, and adult education programs, in the form of block grants directly to states and school districts. Another provision created the Twenty-First Century Workforce Commission to study ways and means to address the anticipated overwhelming need for workers in the information-technology field.

VOCATIONAL EDUCATION

The 1990s saw a continued increase in vocational school enrollment by adult learners. As almost 6 million students sought to improve career-related skills, vocational education in the United States was on track to surpass traditional academic post-secondary education in enrollment, especially among students in non-baccalaureate programs.

DISTANCE INSTRUCTION

The 1990s saw a continued boom in distance instruction. In the early part of the decade, the International Council for Distance Education

estimated at least 10 million people worldwide studied at a distance every year. A survey of 52 countries found 142 associate or bachelor's degree programs and 61 postgraduate degree programs offered by distance methods.

In the late 1990s, approximately 6,000 colleges and universities offered 31,000 courses delivered over the Internet at the same costs as courses taught with traditional methods, ranging from $400 to more than $1,000 each. With interest in easily accessible coursework growing, some analysts predicted on-line courses could surpass traditional classrooms as the primary vehicle for higher education.

Adult learners have always been the majority group in distance instruction and extension courses. However, the type of student using on-line and distance instruction in the late 1990s was broad-based. The most rapidly growing sector is the pre-university age group—kindergarten through twelfth grade. The usual provider in this area is universities, which offer advanced course programs with curriculum supplements and telecommunications for middle-school students.

One dilemma facing the large numbers of traditional colleges and universities seeking to enter the on-line education market is the strain of managing a business enterprise necessary to a successful distance education program. Another difficulty is the great cost associated with the technology that is necessary to establish effective distance instruction. On the student level, access to education for those who do not attend classes on campus could be a question of their access to technology—the higher or more exotic the technology, the fewer students with the means to use it. Some critics wonder whether this could lead to a divide between the "technology rich" and the "technology poor." Finally, most universities seek to integrate distance and traditional education, but studies suggest that there are often institutional barriers to the convergence of distance and mainstream education.

The May 1999 issue of *Yahoo! Internet Life* offers a look at distance learning, as well as a general look at how universities and colleges use the Internet, from the perspective of students. In it's third year, the survey seeks to rate university and college use of the Internet as an educational means. The magazine, with the help of publisher Peterson's, e-mailed interview questions to 571 four-year institutions in the U.S. about Internet and computer usage on campus. The result, as published, is a listing of the "America's 100 Most Wired Colleges." Of note in the 1999 survey is the ranking of 200 schools for the Internet edition only, as opposed to only 100 in the two previous years and in the printed version. Findings reported diverse online offerings, as well as a new trend of instructors integrating distance-learning techniques into traditional classrooms, such as use of the Internet and chat environments.

The survey also reports significant growth in how universities and colleges use the Internet. For example, according to survey findings 82 percent of the listed schools reported that students could register on-line for classes, compared with only 64 percent in 1998; and 54 percent of schools offered distance-learning courses through the Internet in 1999, as opposed to 31 percent in the previous year.

INDUSTRY LEADERS

Alternative education industry leaders in the late 1990s were as diverse as the field itself. The market included providers of vocational, career, and leisure/enrichment education for adults, traditional universities offering courses and degrees on-line, and institutions existing solely on-line. Distance instruction caused some overlap. For example, providers of vocational education often provide coursework on-line or in some other distance environment, and traditional universities offering on-line courses may also teach career courses.

An industry leader in alternative, specifically vocational, education in the late 1990s was DeVry, Inc., of Oakbrook Terrace, Illinois. One of the largest publicly owned international education companies in North America, DeVry owns and operates DeVry Institutes, Keller Graduate School of Management, Becker CPA Review, and Corporate Educational Services. DeVry Institutes have offered technology-based career training to high school graduates for more than 65 years, and the Institutes are located on 16 campuses in the United States and Canada, with more than 33,000 full- and part-time students. DeVry's 1998 fiscal year revenues were $353.5 million, up 14.6 percent from the $308.3 million reported for fiscal year 1997. In July 1997, 29,510 students were enrolled at DeVry Institutes, while enrollment increased 12.1 percent for a total of 33,088 students in 1998. New student enrollment for 1998's summer term reached 9,038, compared with 8,255 for 1997's summer term. DeVry's Keller Graduate School of Management (KGSM) is one of the nation's largest part-time graduate schools for working adults, and operates 27 sites in major metropolitan areas with attendance by more than 5,300 students. Offerings at KGSM include asynchronous, web-based courses for students needing greater flexibility than a traditional, on-site classroom offers. In a company news release dated April 20, 1999, DeVry announced the intent to purchase Education Development Corporation, which acts as Denver Technical College. According to the release, the purchase of the 1,700-student institution allows DeVry to enter the Rocky Mountain area more quickly than they could by opening a new DeVry Institute. In the same news release, DeVry chairman Dennis J. Keller credits increased student enrollments and new DeVry and Keller Graduate School sites as fueling the company's record revenues.

Another leader in alternative education was Sylvan Learning Systems, Inc., of Baltimore, Maryland. Sylvan's 1998 revenues were $440.3 million, up 47 percent from 1997. The company is a leading provider of educational services to families, schools, and businesses. The company provides supplemental and remedial educational services and computer-based testing services through several divisions and more than 3,000 educational and testing centers around the world. Sylvan delivers computer-based testing for academic admissions, as well as for professional licensure and certification programs, at testing centers through its Sylvan Prometric division; the company is best known for its Sylvan Learning Centers—the network of over 700 centers providing personalized instructional services to students of all ages and skill levels. Sylvan provides contracted educational services to 120 school districts and training services to 300 corporations through the Sylvan Contract Educational Services division. Professional development programs used in this division are based on products originally developed by the Canter companies, now a recent addition to Sylvan. The Caliber Learning Network, a joint initiative of Sylvan and MCI Communications Corp., provides educational and training programs through videoconferencing and the Internet. Sylvan's network of English language instructional centers offers English-language instruction to professionals in more than 200 centers throughout Europe and South America. Finally, in early 1997 Sylvan formed a not-for-profit foundation to promote high-quality educational practices in the United States. The Sylvan Learning Foundation's assets are currently valued at $11 million. Other Sylvan subsidiaries include corporate consulting and training by the PACE Group; and ASPECT, which provides English language instruction to students.

ICS Learning Systems, a subsidiary of National Education Corporation, and a subsidiary of Harcourt

General, Inc., is another leader in alternative education. In 1997, ICS sought to further cement its leadership by entering into a job placement alliance with Manpower, the world's largest staffing firm. According to ICS, it was the first distance education provider to offer nationwide job placement opportunities to students who looked to improve job skills through distance instruction. ICS' students ranged from those seeking high school diplomas to college graduates seeking continuing education. The company targeted both the degree and professional education markets, offering allied health, accounting, and law courses. In 1999, the ICS student body was made up of more than 350,000 men and women studying in 150 countries; and 2,000 American corporations use ICS training systems with their employees.

A pioneer in education through learning networks is Connection Education, or Connect Ed. Established in 1985, Connect Ed provides an electronic campus that offers courses. On-line students can also find a book order service, a library, counseling information, and even electronic lectures by visiting scholars. Connect Ed offers an on-line master's degree program in media studies, with a concentration in technology and society, as part of the graduate program of the New School for Social Research. Up to 200 students are enrolled on-line each term.

A new field with ever-expanding membership is that of computer education for senior citizens. San Francisco-based SeniorNet is a nonprofit corporation offering classes from basic computer literacy skills to opening e-mail sites and surfing the Internet. In 1995, William Ashkin, then a 94-year-old retired dentist, created Century Club, a Web page and computer forum for adults over the age of 90. As another senior, Mindy Bacey, told *Village Voice's* Randi Glatzer in a 1997 article on seniors and computers, "I thought people would say, 'A senior citizen, what's he doing in school? This guy is passe already. It's a world for the kids.'" He took a five-night introductory class on computers and passed with an "A." Seniors play bridge or exchange recipes over the Internet with others from places like Norway and London, and stimulate interest in other seniors to take basic courses in computer technology.

AMERICA AND THE WORLD

In 1997, the United Nations Educational, Scientific and Cultural Organization (UNESCO) held its fifth International Conference of Adult Education (COFINTEA) in Hamburg, Germany, with over 1,500 attendees from around the world. Previous conferences were held in Elsinore, Denmark (1949), Montreal, Canada (1960), Tokyo, Japan (1972), and Paris, France (1985). The 1997 conference resulted in the publication of a broad policy statement, *Declaration of Adult Learning,* and more detailed proposals in *Agenda for the Future.* The conference's overall theme was to promote democratic understanding through the education processes. This includes the important concept of making education accessible to all. The conference held several key seminars directed toward accessibility technology, women, global minorities, and the physically and developmentally challenged.

As of 1997, it was estimated that 1 billion adults worldwide were unable to read or write, many falling within the above groups, and many of them from rich and/or industrialized nations, including the United States.

One topic that challenged the conference attendees concerned the state-of-the-art transmission of educational knowledge and information, not only from one global community to another, but from one culture or subculture to another. No longer relying on classroom instruction to teach a universal language (written or spoken words) for the transmission of educational information, new technology has employed the introduction and proliferation of international symbols and visual characters through media tools such as video tapes and interactive compact discs (CDs), with or without computer or Internet application. These new devices could have the added advantage of cutting through the barriers of language as well as distance. On the one side, many third-world countries, whose adult populations could best stand to be enriched by alternative education measures, have neither the financial nor technological capability to provide widespread electronic transmission of information. On the other side, there is articulated fear that widespread use of the Internet and other technologies in adult education could jeopardize the inherited values, languages, and cultural norms of industrialized nations to that which is transmitted and/or stored in software programs or communications. One would readily admit that it has been difficult enough to merely get a single-language computer software program to be understood by any given homogenous class. Thus, the popularity of the "user-friendly" term to imply a computer language that does not disconnect a user who does not understand the use of any given command or term. The challenge of electronic transmission of educational materials to diverse adult cultures and peoples remains a global priority into the twenty-first century.

As for the value and legitimacy of international adult education, the Global Alliance for Transnational Education (GATE) was formed in 1995 and remains a respected entity for certifying international institutions, both on-line and off. But accreditation is not everything. England's Labour Party gained wide support in its pre-election speeches addressing the "life-long learning" needs of adults and the unfairness of the fact that adults get neither government financial help nor recognition for many nontraditional or non-degree learning experiences. In 1998, Britain's Department for Education proposed The University for Industry, a vocational and technical initiative comparable to the successful Open University, and complete with governmental financial assistance in the form of "individual learning accounts." These proposals were intended to address the fact that while the majority of existing educational subsidies and post-school education budget funds was spent on universities, only one-fourth of the nation's 5 million post-16 learners attended universities.

FURTHER READING

About DeVry. Oakbrook Terrace, IL: DeVry, Inc., 1999. Available from http://www.devry.com/sub/about.html.

Barker, B.O., et al. "Broadening the Definition of Distance Education in Light of New Technologies." *The American Journal of Distance Education,* 1989.

Brey, R. "U.S. Postsecondary Distance Learning Programs in the 1990s: A Decade of Growth." Washington, DC: American Association of Community and Junior Colleges, Instructional Telecommunications Consortium, 1991.

Brock, R. "Symposium on Telecommunications and the Adult Learner." Washington, DC: American Association of Community and Junior Colleges, Instructional Telecommunications Consortium, 1991.

Commission on Institutions of Higher Education of the North Central Association of Colleges and Schools. *Principles of Good Practice for Electronically Offered Academic Degree and Certificate Programs,* 3 August 1995. Available from http://homepage.interaccess.com/~ghoyle/nca.html.

Dede, C. "Emerging Technologies in Distance Education for Business." *Journal of Education for Business,* March-April 1996.

"DeVry Reports Fiscal Year Earnings Up 27 Percent and Double-Digit Increases in Summer Total Student Enrollments." Oakbrook Terrace, IL: DeVry, Inc., August 1998.

Available from http://www.devry.com/sub/news/nr080598.html.

Elliot, Sergio. *Distance Education Systems.* Rome: Food and Agriculture Organization of the United Nations, 1990.

Frauenfelder, Mark. "Degrees of Separation: Distance Learning." *Yahoo! Internet Life.* Available from http://www.zdnet.com/yil/content/college/colleges99/distance.html.

Glam, Ernie. "Fast Times at Cyber Senior High." *Village Voice,* 14 October 1997.

Glatzer, Randi. "Computer Age." *Village Voice,* 16 April 1997.

Guersney, Lisa. "Is the Internet Becoming a Bonanza for Diploma Mills?" *The Chronicle for Higher Education,* 19 December 1997.

Harasim, Linda, S. R. Hiltz, L. Teles, and M. Turoff. *Learning Networks: A Field Guide to Teaching and Learning Online.* Cambridge, MA: MIT Press, 1995.

Holmberg, Borje. *Growth and Structure of Distance Education.* London: Croom Helm, 1986.

ICS Learning Systems. "ICS Enters Into Agreement with Manpower." 28 May 1997. Available from http://biz.yahoo.com/prnews/97/05/28/nec_1.html.

Ivey, Mark. "Long-Distance Learning Gets an 'A' at Last." *Business Week,* 9 May 1988. Available from http://www.wcc-eun.com/wcc/BsnsWeek.html.

Jeffries, Michael. *Research in Distance Education.* Indiana Higher Education Telecommunication System, 1995. Available from http://www.ihets.org/distance_ed/ipse/fdhandbook/resrch.html.

Kaye, A., and G. Rumble. *Distance Teaching for Higher and Adult Education.* London: Croom Helm, 1981.

Kerka, Sandra. "Distance Learning, the Internet, and the World Wide Web." *ERIC Clearinghouse on Adult, Career, and Vocational Education,* 1996. Available from www.ed.gov/databases/ERIC_Digests/ed395214.html.

Lane, Hilary. "Graduate in Cyberspace." *Boulder County Business Report,* 1996. Available from http://www.bcbr.com/aug96/disted2.htm.

"Malcolm Shepherd Knowles." *Traning & Development,* February 1998.

McIntosh, Christopher. "Adult Education for Tomorrow." *The UNESCO Courier,* July/August 1997.

Mealer, Brian. "Washington Update: Senate Panel Approves Job-Training Measure." *The Chronicle of Higher Education,* 3 October 1997.

Nixon, D.E. "Simulteaching: Access to Learning by Means of Interactive Television." *Community Junior College Quarterly of Research and Practice,* Vol. 16, 1992.

Parrott, Sarah. "Future Learning: Distance Education in Community Colleges." *ERIC Clearinghouse for Commu-*

nity Colleges, 1995. Available from http://www.ed.gov/databases/ERIC_Digests/ed385311.html.

Rumble, G. *The Planning and Management of Distance Education.* London: Croom Helm, 1986.

Spodick, Edward F. "The Evolution of Distance Learning." *Hong Kong University of Science & Technology Library,* August 1995. Available from http://sqzm14.ust.hk/distance/distance-2.html.

Status and Trends of Distance Education. London: Kogan Page, 1986.

Strosnider, Kim. "More Students Pass High-School Equivalency Exam." *The Chronicle of Higher Education,* 13 June 1997.

Stucky, Mark D. "Online U: College Courses by Computer." *PC Novice Magazine,* August 1995. Available from http://www.wcc-eun.com/wcc/PCMagazine.html.

Swedburg, Randy, and Lisa Ostiguy. "Leisure and Lifelong Learning." *Physical Education,* February 1998.

"Sylvan Learning Systems, Inc. Reports Record First Quarter 1999 Financial Results." *Business Wire,* 21 April 1999.

"Sylvan Learning Systems, Inc. Reports Record Fourth Quarter And Year End 1998 Financial Results." *Business Wire,* 25 February 1999.

U.S. Department of Education. "Vocational Education in the United States: The Early 1990s." Available from http://www.ed.gov/NCES/pubs/95024-2.html.

Verduin, John R., Jr., and Thomas A. Clark. *Distance Education: The Foundations of Effective Practice.* San Francisco: Jossey-Bass Publishers, 1991.

Wilberg, Elizabeth. "Cyber Schools Serve Up Virtual College Experience." *Gannett News Service,* 22 July 1997. Available from http://www.usatoday.com/life/cyber/tech/cta913.htm.

Wilby, Peter. "It Hurts the Rich to Teach the Poor." *New Statesman,* 20 February 1998.

—Tim Eigo, updated by Lauri Harding
and by Lisa DeShantz-Cook

ALTERNATIVE FUELS

INDUSTRY SNAPSHOT

The quest for alternative fuels has changed with the tides of the global economy, as well as the volatile relationship between suppliers and recipient nations of traditional gasoline fuel. So tenuously polarized are the relationships between these nations that promises have been broken, treaty terms have been compromised, and budgeted funds have mysteriously moved from one priority to another without question. The ultimate goal, of course, is to convert from gasoline-dependent economies to alternative fuel-based economies without causing a break in service or major conflict.

In the 1990s, more sustained interest in alternative fuels began to take hold. This was partly due to the "yin and yang" of supply and demand, but more importantly, to evolving world attitudes toward environmental, health, and perpetuity issues. Petroleum was not a *renewable* resource, and this reality translated into a global wake-up call that forced heightened efforts to find alternatives. Added to this was the history of petroleum disasters such as Valdez, pressing issues of "global warming," and contemporary medical research linking illnesses and cancers to petroleum by-products or burn-off. Thus, the quest for alternative fuels became but a part of a much broader and universal effort directed toward discovering sources of alternative *energy*. For purposes of this essay, the discussion of alternative fuels will not include other alternative energy sources such as electric "fuel-cells" or "photovoltaic cells," etc., excepting for occasional mention or comparison. Alternative fuels, in the purest form of the term, include but are not limited to ethanol, methanol, natural gas, and the newly developed bio-fuels. The overwhelming use for fuels (all kinds) is to power engines, and the overwhelming application of that use is in the transportation industry, primarily for automobile vehicles; this, then, constitutes the focus of research and data available on the subject.

ORGANIZATION AND STRUCTURE

Because of the interrelationship and interdependency between transportation fuels and national economy, as well as national security, both gasoline and alternative fuel industries are heavily structured, controlled, and regulated by federal and state interests. Control spills over into the user market in that private industry must not only produce alternative fuel vehicles, which can compete with the price and efficiency of traditional gasoline-fueled vehicles, but must also meet strict emissions and other environmental regulation standards.

INDUSTRY REGULATION

To ease the pain of regulation as well as stimulate interest, numerous laws and tax incentives are directed toward both producers *and* users of domestically produced alternative fuels, giving them a chance to compete with the oil industry and its monopolized hold on the global market. By promoting the use of domestic renewable resources, it is anticipated that the United States will decrease its economic dependency on foreign nations. Some of the more important federal legislation supporting biofuels include: the Energy Security Act (1978); the Energy Tax Act (1978); the Gasohol Competition Act (1980); the Crude Oil

Windfall Profit Tax Act (1980); the Energy Security Act (1980); the Surface Transportation Assistance Act (1982); the Tax Reform Act (1984); the Alternative Motor Fuels Act (1988); the Omnibus Budget Reconciliation Act (1990); the Clean Air Act Amendments (1990); the Energy Policy Act (1992); the Building Efficient Surface Transportation and Equity Act (BESTEA) (1998); and the Energy Conservation Reauthorization Act (1998). These acts are administered and overseen by the Department of Energy.

The manner in which these Acts affect and interface with private industry can be summed up in one example, the Alternative Motor Fuels Act of 1988. Its stated objective is to encourage the widespread development and use of methanol, ethanol, and natural gas as transportation fuels. Section 400AA requires the U.S. government to acquire the maximum number of alternative-fueled vehicles in its fleets as is practical. Importantly, the vehicles are to be supplied by original equipment manufacturers (OEMs), thus stimulating private industry. The Act also provides that the Department of Energy must assist state and local governments in developing public transportation buses capable of operating with alternative fuels. These responsibilities are managed by the Department's National Renewable Energy Laboratory (NREL), and data collected from these projects are available through the Alternative Fuels Data Center's on-line site, or through the National Alternative Fuels Hotline.

Concurrently, acts such as the Clean Air Act and its amendments continue to focus on reducing the amount of pollutants emitted from motor vehicles. In January 1999, the Argonne National Laboratory at the Center for Transportation Research released an exhaustive report on the "Effects of Fuel Ethanol Use on Fuel-Cycle Energy and Greenhouse Gas Emissions." The report was made available for public review directly from the Department of Energy and also on-line. The Environmental Protection Agency (EPA) also remains greatly involved in the monitoring of environmental effects caused by vehicular traffic and fuel byproducts.

To monitor progress under the Energy Policy Act of 1992, The Department of Energy reports to Congress annually on the progress of the Act's focus, which is the encouraged use of alternative fuels. Field researchers, OEM markets, and fuel suppliers complete lengthy annual surveys that primarily address the number and type of alternative fueled vehicles available; the number, type, and geographic distribution of these vehicles in use; the amount and distribution of each type of alternative fuel consumed; and informa-

tion about the refueling/recharging facilities. As the data builds from year to year, the DOE paces its monetary funding and program initiatives accordingly.

For the most part, the industry is structured such that governmental interest and money funds most of the research and development of fuel alternatives, and monitors environmental impact, as well. At the same time, private industry works on developing vehicles that can efficiently use these fuels and still remain competitively priced.

A good example of structure and relationship in the government-industry-research coalition was in the area of compressed natural gases (CNG) and liquid petroleum gas (LPG) fuel development, two strong leaders in the alternatives market. In 1997, the EPA announced new certification procedures for converting gasoline-fueled engines to CNG. Shortly thereafter, the San Marino Engineering Company (SME) in New York announced that it was the first to be issued a certificate from the EPA giving permission to install the CNG conversion kits on Ford Crown Victoria sedans equipped with 4.6 liter engines. SME then actively solicited international partners to develop certification kits for other engine families, and also for LPG users. The New York State Energy Research and Development Authority (NYSERDA) then signed a contract with SME to develop a more advanced system architecture for installing certification kits at the time of vehicle manufacture. NYSERDA also sponsored a pilot project to put CNG-using taxis in service in New York. For this, they received a $3.2-million

STATES WITH THE MOST ESTIMATED ALTERNATIVE-FUELED VEHICLES IN USE, 1999	
California	72,016
Texas	44,903
Illinois	20,082
Ohio	19,265
Michigan	18,454
Oklahoma	16,584
New York	15,265
Pennsylvania	14,228
Georgia	11,994
Florida	11,865

Source: Energy Information Administration, Office of Coal, Nuclear, Electric and Alternative Fuels

federal grant. General Motors' Chevrolet Caprice was the taxi vehicle, but when GM stopped making the Caprice, Ford Crown Victorias took over. Meanwhile, in November 1998, Honda unveiled its CNG-version of its popular Civic model with near-zero emissions. Then Thiokol Corporation announced it had developed and produced a more efficient storage tank for LPG and CNG user vans, with a goal to eventually replace the aluminum tanks with injection-molded plastic ones. As things got hot in the CNG/LPG market, the United States and China signed environmental agreements in April 1999 that, among other things, provided for an U.S. investment in an on-shore natural gas pipeline in China. Enron Corporation and China National Petroleum Company were to jointly develop the project.

BACKGROUND AND DEVELOPMENT

It would be remiss not to begin the industry's history by emphasizing the enormous economic influence that gasoline had over both Western and Eastern countries. In the United States for example, a single dollar increase in the price per barrel of crude oil could lead to a $1-billion dollar change in oil imports. In fact, gasoline supply disruptions between 1974 and 1984, such as those surrounding the 1973 Arab Oil Embargo and the 1979 Iranian Oil Embargo, cost Americans $1.5 *trillion* dollars. In the latter 1990s, petroleum imports accounted for nearly half of the U.S. trade deficit, and were expected to rise to 60-70 percent within the next 10 to 20 years, even though Congress voted in 1990 that a dependence on foreign oil of more than 50 percent would constitute a "peril point" for the United States.

The additional cost in terms of military security and protection of foreign oil interests cost the United States an estimated $365 billion between 1980 and 1990. The Persian Gulf War alone cost $61 billion. Factoring in these energy security costs results in the astounding reality that the true financial cost of oil consumption in 1998 was approximately $5 dollars per gallon. Finally, there is always the concern for terrorism: the United States pours billions of dollars every year into distant foreign lands. In the Middle East alone, it was estimated that by 2010 oil revenues would reach $250 billion per year. Many of these countries were strongly anti-Western in sentiment.

These factors helped create the stimulus to continue efforts toward near-total replacement of gasoline fuels with renewable alternative fuels. Henry Ford

himself, back in 1908, well expected his Model T automobile to be fueled by ethanol, the most viable alternative fuel at that time. In fact, an ethanol-gasoline mix (25 percent ethanol) was rather successfully marketed by the Standard Oil Company in the 1920s. When high corn prices, doubled with storage and transportation costs, made ethanol less desirable, federal and state initiatives were undertaken to keep interest alive. Ford again reentered the picture and joined others to establish a fermentation plant in the Corn Belt, capable of producing 38,000 liters per day. But the efforts could not effectively overcome the low petroleum prices, and ethanol production plants closed down in the 1940s.

Interestingly, at about the same time Ford was developing prototype vehicles, Rudolph Diesel was perfecting his diesel engines to run on peanut oil, with the intention that eventually they would be able to operate on several types of vegetable oils. It is unfortunate that both Ford's and Diesel's hopes were relegated to the back burners of a hot petroleum market with which these resourceful fuels could not then compete. It was not until the critical gasoline market in the 1970s that momentum was reestablished. Ethanol-gasoline blends were again reintroduced to the U.S. market in 1979. However, these blends were marketed not as gasoline replacement fuels but as "octane enhancers" or "gasoline extenders." This may have softened any sense of urgency in the public's mind to accelerate conversion of a transportation economy so comfortable with inexpensive gasoline. Further softening the effort was the creation of a Strategic Petroleum Reserve (SPR) established by the U.S. government, to stockpile nearly 6 million barrels of oil (about 75 days's worth of fuel at 1998 consumption rates) in an underground facility in Louisiana. Since 1993, no oil has been added to the reserves and the facility's $200 million annual operating cost ultimately prompted Congress to mandate selling the reserve oil at half price.

But complacency again reverted to a proactive attitude during the 1990s as Americans became more sensitive about environmental issues and economic dependency. The Clean Air Act Amendments of 1990 required that special fuels be sold and used in areas of the country with harmful levels of carbon monoxide. This resulted in the development and promotion of a cleaner-burning and lighter gasoline product known as "reformulated gasoline," and of course, California had its own formula. Again, ethanol blends and other alternative fuel choices caught the public's attention. Concurrently, the federal government continued to infuse money into numerous projects for bio-

Ford's zero emission P2000 Hydrogen Fuel Cell Vehicle. *(Courtesy of Ford Motor Co.)*

fuel development, also giving private industry a stake in the results. By the end of the 1990s, the alternative fuel industry had been resurrected.

CURRENT CONDITIONS

The Clinton Administration's Partnership for a New Generation of Vehicles created an industry-government consortium with the ultimate goal of phasing out gasoline engines over the next 20-30 years. The federal government pledged an annual investment of $500 million dollars (half of which included direct federal funds) to help the industry. In early 1999, The Department of Energy announced a grant of $1 million for new ethanol technologies, to be awarded through NREL to recipients of its "Bridge to the Corn Ethanol Industry" initiative at the National Conference on Ethanol Policy and Marketing. It was estimated that in 1998, the ethanol industry alone had created about 200,000 jobs.

In 1997, both Ford and Chrysler automobile manufacturers committed to produce as many as 225,000 "flexible fuel" vehicles per year, with prices comparable to traditional gasoline models. William Clay Ford, Jr., great-grandson of Henry Ford, openly com-

mitted his company to becoming a "fuel-cell driven enterprise," expressing his concern that public sentiment could turn on the auto industry if it did not provide clean vehicles as part of a socially responsible effort.

Notwithstanding the impressive efforts to increase the market share of alternative fuels, the gasoline companies weren't going to take it lying down. The enormous size of the gasoline industry and its political clout translated into heavy lobbying. In March 1998 two leading trade associations representing gasoline manufacturers appealed to federal regulators to impose stricter limits on sulfur in gasoline. Their objectives were obvious: lower sulfur content means cleaner gasoline. The cleaner burning gasoline will keep competition from alternative fuels at bay. The EPA was to decide on this issue by early 1999.

In general, three major types of gasolines dominated the market in the latter 1990s: conventional (approximately 60 percent of the gasoline market), reformulated (30 percent), and California reformulated (10 percent and gaining). California had the cleanest gasoline of all and, in 1998, it cost residents about 10 cents per gallon more, which they were willing to pay to help fight the infamous urban smog.

But the industry may take another unexpected turn in the future. The burning of *any* kind of fuel may soon be deemed primitive. In 1999, a company in Brignoles, France, known as CQFD Air Solution Sarl, released plans to market a vehicle powered by *compressed air.* Company owner Guy Negre told *Wired* magazine's Heather McCabe that he came up with the idea in the early 1990s, and has worked on it ever since. The vehicle has a two-cylinder engine that uses heated outside air combined with super-compressed air from the car's storage tanks. A fill-up takes three minutes, and the vehicle will go 120 miles on each fill-up. The vehicle was scheduled for international release in 2000. So impressive was the vehicle's idea and promise that the Mexican government has expressed its interest in purchasing 40,000 of them.

AMERICA AND THE WORLD

One of the primary problems facing alternative fuels at the end of the 1990s was the cost. Gasoline remained the cheapest fuel, even cheaper than diesel fuel and blends. Some countries, like Germany, placed high taxes on gasoline, making diesel and other fuels more competitive. (The international newsletter *Energy Detente* reported in March 1998 that gasoline prices in Germany were nearly twice as high as diesel fuel prices because of the tax. Yet, the efforts made less headway than anticipated.) Still, as of 1999, oil exploration was down, and gasoline/oil index stocks were lackluster. Although OPEC announced in early 1999 that it would cut oil production to help boost prices, this was considered a sign of weakness in the marketplace.

Around the world, other countries also increased efforts to develop alternative fuel technologies, not only for their own economic safety, but also to be first at the finish line and cash in on America's needs. In 1999, Alternate Power Products Asia Limited announced its version of an electric vehicle, and selected Agar, Uttar Pradesh, India, as its demonstration project site. Canada introduced its "Bombadier" electric vehicle in 1999, which it calls an NEV, for "neighborhood electric vehicle." And China has focused on the development of hydrogen as a viable transportation fuel source.

A private poll of American voters taken in 1998 showed overwhelming support (close to 83 percent) for continued development of alternative fuels like ethanol. The same voters expressed similar percentages of fear about the vulnerability of the United States in an energy crisis because of foreign dependency on oil and the serious threat it could represent to the economy.

RESEARCH AND TECHNOLOGY

One of the original criticisms for the real potential of alternative fuels was their ostensibly lower "energy density," technical jargon for the formulized relationship between weight or mass of the energy source and the energy it would produce. Historically, gallon for gallon, alternative fuels offered smaller driving ranges, less acceleration capability, and more vulnerability at high speeds or in heavy traffic situations than their gasoline counterpart. But interestingly, most of the energy in gasoline and diesel fuel was burned off as combustible heat and friction, not as locomotive power. Notwithstanding, it was true that gasoline engines were distinguishable for rapid acceleration capability, a desirable quality in a nation with as many freeway systems as the United States. Conversely, alternative fuels such as ethanol and methanol were considered to burn cleaner than gasoline, an important consideration in urban areas plagued with smog. Beginning in the latter 1990s, federal Clean Air laws began to require automobile manufacturers to increase the number of vehicles offered that met the newly mandated Ultra Low Emissions Vehicles (ULEV) standards. Ultimately, vehicles would be required to meet Zero Emissions Vehicle (ZEV) standards, and clearly, alternative fuel vehicles held the competitive edge in this arena. In fact, combustible natural gas was so clean-burning that the only byproducts were carbon dioxide and water vapor. Still, gasolines have been purified and made to burn cleaner over the years and, in 1998, the most desirable choice following gasoline was diesel, not alternative fuel.

The real potential for alternative fuels remains the fact that they are not only renewable resources, but in the late 1990s, were increasingly made of environmental waste, or "biomass." This subcategory of alternative fuels, known as "biofuels," converts agricultural and forestry residue, and even municipal solid and industrial waste, into bioethanol, biodiesel, biomethanol, and pyrolysis oil fuels. Moreover, in the 1990s, researchers developed several forms of "energy crops," terrestrial and aquatic plants grown solely for energy conversion.

In 1998, agricultural waste in the United States amounted to more than 86 million metric tons, and included such residue as corn stover, wheat straw, and orchard trimmings. Corn provides the largest quantity of biomass waste, with a potential stover (leaves, stalks, and cobs) of 120 million dry tons, based on the 1998 estimate of 80 million acres of corn grown by U.S. farmers.

Also high in quantity was forestry waste, accounting for some 90 to 250 million metric tons, mostly comprised of underutilized wood and logging residues, imperfect commercial trees and trees removed in forest-thinning measures intended to enhance the natural health of the forest. The energy density of dry biomass ranges from 7000 BTUs per pound for straw, to 8500 BTUs per pound for wood.

By the year 2000, it was anticipated that 216 million tons of municipal solid waste would be generated in the United States alone. Added to this will be an estimated 12 *billion* tons of industrial waste generated by industry and requiring treatment and disposal. The burden on existing landfills was near capacity, and tighter regulation was forcing many landfills to close. Conversion of this waste matter to biofuel was an extremely attractive concept.

With respect to biocrops specifically grown to generate biofuel, 1998 estimates identified approximately 190 million acres of excess agricultural land that could be used for crop growth. Officially, the U.S. Department of Agriculture estimates approximately 100 million acres available for growing energy crops in the twenty-first century. Energy crops were primarily trees, shrubs, and grasses developed for fast growth, such as hybrid poplars, willows, and switchgrass. Areas such as riverbanks, lakeshores, and areas between farms, otherwise non-harvestable, could be used for biocrop development. One added benefit was that planned growth stimulated the creation of habitat for wildlife and the renewal of depleted soil bases. But another palpable benefit was the increased diversity of marketable agricultural product, thus tempering the income vulnerability of farmers to fluctuations in market demand or unexpected natural disasters. Because energy crops are man-made and cultivated, they were also more disease and pest resistant.

Biofuels are, by composition, alcohols, ethers, esters, and other chemicals made from cellulosic biomass. The U.S. Department of Energy's Office of Fuels Development established the National Biofuels Program, which sponsors research at the NREL and Oak Ridge, Tennessee, laboratories, and works to promote private industry commercialization of this technology.

But the conversion from biomass to biofuel is not without complication. Biomass energy at the plant cellular level is comprised of complex lignocellulosic compositions that include hemicellulose, cellulose, lignin, and extractives; cellulose also has hydrogen bonds that form crystalline structures. These long chains of sugar-like molecules have resistant linkages that inhibit the release of potential energy. In the latter 1990s, the Office of Fuel Development initiated the Bioethanol Project, which had a stated objective of demonstrating commercial production of waste-based bioethanol by the end of the year 2000.

In consort with private companies, the Bioethanol Project focuses on developing four process technologies. The first, concentrated acid cellulose conversion, uses recombinant microorganisms to separate sugars and acids. Basically a hydrolysis process, the technology is being used by Arkenol and the Masada Resource Group in specially located plants in California and New York, respectively. Arkenol, which already holds several patents on acid-based ethanol development, is working with the Department of Energy to establish a commercial facility for the conversion of rice straw to ethanol. Masada, on the other hand, plans to establish a facility to process the lignocellulosic portion of municipal solid waste into ethanol, using concentrated sulfuric acids.

Another technology, and actually the oldest, is dilute acid hydrolysis. This process is expected to be further developed by the BCI Company during the startup phase of its facility in Jennings, Louisiana. The company plans to focus on the use of sugarcane bagasse, indigenous to the area, as feedstock for conversion. A variation of this process, referred to as enzymatic cellulose hydrolysis, is under development in Canada by Iogen/Petro Canada, and is also being considered by BCI for its Gridley project. This technology focuses on the refinement of earlier cellulases to wood hydrolysis, now incorporating simultaneous saccharification and fermentation (SSF). The SSF process combines cellulase with fermenting microbes that convert the produced sugars to ethanol. Finally, a process known as syngas fermentation will be studied and further developed by Bioresource Engineering, Inc. in an effort to successfully commercialize the process. Syngas (synthesis gas) is composed primarily of carbon monoxide, carbon dioxide, and hydrogen that have been converted from biomass. After gasification, anaerobic bacteria are introduced to convert the gases to ethanol.

Ethanol remains the most widely marketed biofuel. Made from brewed starch crops such as corn or, in the case of bioethanol from cellulosic biomass, it was marketed in the latter 1990s as an octane-booster and a cleaner emissions fuel additive. In 1998, more than 1.5 billion gallons were sold as gasoline-blend additives. It could be used in its pure form or, more often, blended as E10 (10 percent ethanol) on up to E85 blends. But ethanol tax incentives will end in 2007; therefore, the Ethanol Project has developed a research plan with a stated goal of reducing the cost of bioethanol technology by a minimum of 40 cents per gallon by 2010. The ethanol industry alone created more than 200,000 jobs, and by the year 2002 will have added $51 billion dollars to the U.S. economy.

Biodiesel fuel is made from soybean, rapeseed, vegetable, or animal oils. Combined with alcohol, it is then chemically altered to form fatty esters in a process referred to as "transesterification." It is typically marketed as a fuel additive in a 20 percent blend. The 1998 amendments to the Energy Policy Act of 1992 allow regulated fleets to use up to 450 gallons of biodiesel per vehicle per year to qualify for EPAct credit. About 30 million gallons of biodiesel fuel was produced domestically in 1998, and that figure is expected to grow annually. Increasingly, it is replacing traditional fuel in work environments that require exposures to diesel exhaust, such as near airports or locomotive systems. Another positive consideration is that biodiesel is made from feedstocks that take carbon dioxide *out* of the atmosphere, thus reducing greenhouse gases and not contributing to global warming trends.

FURTHER READING

"Alternative Fuels Data Center." Washington, D.C.: Office of Transportation Technologies, 1999. Available from http://afdc3.nrel.gov.

Alternative Fuel Data Center Documents, Arlington, VA: National Alternative Fuels Hotline, 1998. Available from http://www.afdc.nrel.gov/search.

"American Business Disc - Full Record Report." American Business Information, Inc., 1998.

Bowen, David. "The Search For A Technological Fix." *World Press Review,* December 1996.

"Canada's Bombardier Introduces NV." *EV World.* Papillon, NE: Digital Revolution, 1999. Available from http://evworld.com.

"China at The Crossroads." *EVWorld,* April 1999. Available from http://evworld.com.

Eaton, John. "In The News-Ford Gives Peek at Electric Vehicle." *The Denver Post,* 4 October 1997.

Hogarty, Thomas. "Why Gasoline Is Superior to Alternatives." *Consumer's Research,* May 1998.

McCabe, Heather. "Running on Empty." *Wired,* May 1999.

Murphy, Kate, and Amy Dunkin. "Fighting Pollution-and Cleaning Up, Too." *Business Week,* 19 January 1998.

"Nation' Public Votes 'Yes' to Ethanol." *Successful Farming,* January 1999.

Office of Fuels Development. *Biofuels Program.* Washington, D.C.: U.S. Department of Energy, 1998. Available from http://www.biofuels.doe.gov/research/html.

"OPEC Talks Tough Again." *Time,* 22 March 1999.

Peters, Eric. "Alternative Fuel Vehicles." *Consumer's Research,* October 1997.

—Lauri R. Harding

ALTERNATIVE MEDICINE

Alternative medicine—also called complementary medicine or non-Western medicine—refers to the practice of over 200 therapies and treatments not used by traditional Western medical practitioners. Alternative medicine includes numerous loosely related techniques or procedures such as acupuncture, aroma therapy, chelation therapy, herbal medicine, homeopathy, hypnotherapy, light and color therapy, massage therapy, and nutritional management. The common denominator of alternative medicine is its holistic focus—the treatment of an illness by considering the role played by both the body and the mind. Demand for alternative medicines in the United States has ballooned in the 1990s; approximately 42 percent of the population has used or continues to use alternative medicine and the industry generated revenues of $21-34 billion in the late 1990s, according to *American Medical News*. Furthermore, alternative medicine received considerable public attention in the 1990s as the cost of health care continued to rise and the public increasingly grew wary of bureaucratic delays in the release of new therapeutic products or systems. The American Medical Association (AMA) announced that alternative medicine was one of the top three subjects addressed by its members in the late 1990s. The leading fields of alternative medicine include mind/body medicine, chiropractic therapy, massage therapy, homeopathy, and acupuncture.

Alternative health care providers operate practices just as conventional doctors do, although these alternative practitioners tend to spend more time getting to know their patients during the initial consulta-

tion. Practitioners of alternative medicine generally ask questions not only about a patient's illness, but also about a patient's mood, general temperament, food likes and dislikes, or if some subtle change seems to alleviate or aggravate their symptoms. After gathering all pertinent patient information, these practitioners devise a course of therapy based on both the symptoms and the information from the diagnostic interview and examination. Providers of alternative medicine believe in a holistic approach to medicine, and they believe that when illness occurs it is because the body is out of balance.

ORGANIZATION AND STRUCTURE

MIND/BODY MEDICINE

Mind/Body medicine is the most popular form of alternative medicine, according to the *New England Journal of Medicine*. While traditional Western medicine focuses on the body, mind/body medicine explores the role the mind plays in healing the body, as well as the role the body plays in healing the mind. Although mind/body medicine is not a treatment in the common sense, it is a method of influencing and controlling the reactions and responses of the body. All forms of mind/body medicine strive to achieve the ultimate goal of relaxation or the reduction of stress, which is considered the catalyst for many kinds of illness. Consequently, mind/body medicine is largely a complementary form of treatment, not a primary form. Standard medical testing procedures demonstrate the power of the mind to overcome poor health. Patients who have been given placebos, such as sugar pills, often report feeling relief from their symptoms.

Mind/Body techniques include meditation; progressive relaxation, which is similar to meditation; autogenic training, which is the use of autosuggestive phrases like "I'm calm"; hypnosis; and biofeedback or amplification of body signals so that patients can hear or see signs of stress and learn how to control stress. All of these techniques seek to counteract the body's reaction to stressful situations. When experiencing stress, the body releases various chemicals that affect the body by causing the heart rate to speed up, blood pressure to rise, and the muscles to become tense. Frequent and long-term stress impairs the immune system and can cause insomnia, high blood pressure, and depression, among other things. Although biofeedback therapy requires special training and a state license, other forms of mind/body medicine do not; yet, practitioners of these other therapies often hold licenses in other fields.

CHIROPRACTIC THERAPY

Chiropractic therapy assumes that the body has an inherent healing mechanism that strives to return the body to a state of balance and, therefore, health. Chiropractic theory holds that the nervous system is responsible for maintaining the body's balance. Subluxations (bones out of alignment within joints) and fixations (motion anomalies) obstruct the flow of nervous impulses and, consequently, the body's natural healing system. By manipulating the bones and their respective joints and muscles—especially the spine—chiropractic therapy seeks to align bones and joints properly and undo motion anomalies. Chiropractic therapy is employed to relieve or alleviate arthritis, asthma, back pain, carpal tunnel syndrome, headaches, premenstrual syndrome, and tendinitis, among other illnesses.

While still considered an alternative form of medicine, chiropractic therapy is widely accepted. Chiropractic services are covered by Medicare and Medicaid in many states, as well as by most of the large private insurers. In addition, the practice is licensed in all 50 states and taught at special chiropractic colleges. Chiropractic licenses are governed by the Council of Chiropractic Education and the Federation of Chiropractic Licensing Boards. Moreover, chiropractors make up the second largest group of primary care providers, behind physicians, with more than 45,000 practitioners, and they receive about 66 percent of all visits for back pain. In the late 1990s, over 10 percent of the population regularly underwent chiropractic therapy. Chiropractic is the second most frequently used form of alternative medicine.

Daniel David Palmer, originally a magnetic healer, founded the practice of chiropractic therapy in 1895. Palmer manipulated a man's ill-aligned vertebra and cured his deafness. He considered this proof that misaligned spines could cause poor health and that manipulation of the spine could restore health by correcting the flow of nervous impulses. In 1897, Palmer established the first chiropractic school, which his son managed.

However, one of the school's instructors, John Howard, disputed Palmer's contention that subluxations caused disease. Consequently, he left Palmer's school and founded his own—the National College of Chiropractic. Howard's school relied on some of Palmer's basic teachings but tempered them with standard scientific and medical thought and evidence. Hence, the split created two camps of modern practitioners: the straights, who follow Palmer, and the mixers, who follow Howard. Straights focus solely on the manipulation of the spine, whereas the mixers integrate other techniques like massage and nutritional therapy.

MASSAGE THERAPY

Massage therapy ranks third as the most frequently used form of alternative medicine. In the mid- to late 1990s, there were over 50,000 practicing massage therapists, and the American Massage Therapy Association was one of the fastest growing associations of health care professionals. Numerous schools or forms of massage therapy exist, including shiatsu (acupressure), deep tissue massage, neuromuscular massage, Swedish massage, and Esalen massage.

The myriad forms of massage therapy are based on a series of common tenets: circulation of blood, release of tension, release of toxins, and reduction of stress. Massage therapy holds that proper blood circulation is essential for health. Tension can impede circulation, thus interfering with the flow of nutrients and the removal of waste and toxins and possibly causing psychological and immune-system problems. Hence, by releasing tension in muscles and other soft tissues, massage therapists strive to improve the circulation of blood, which will bring about the removal of toxins and the reduction of stress, which some believe causes over 80 percent of all illnesses.

Considered by many to be one of the oldest health care techniques, mention of massage use can be found in Chinese records dating back about 3,000 years, but its use probably predates these documents by many years. Physicians and health care practitioners from many cultures and from many eras have practiced massage therapy. In Germany, Japan, and China, for example, massage therapy has continued to be used as it has for centuries, and massage therapists work alongside doctors.

The medical use of massage began to decline in the United States in the early part of the twentieth century as surgical and pharmaceutical approaches to medicine began to blossom. Physicians began to view massage as too time-consuming so they delegated it aides—who evolved into modern day physical therapists. Massage therapy began to turn professional in 1943 when the graduates of massage school decided to found the American Massage Therapy Association.

HOMEOPATHY

Homeopathy represents another one of the largest sectors of the industry. The word homeopathy comes from the Greek *homios,* meaning "like," and *pathos,* meaning "suffering." Thus, the term implies its conceptual underpinnings, to treat "like with like." Contrary to traditional Western (allopathic) medicine, which hastens to suppress, alleviate, or obliterate symptoms, homeopathy works with a patient's symptoms, not against them. Homeopaths view a sick person's symptoms, such as a dry cough or runny nose, as the body's attempt to heal itself. The remedies, therefore, often attempt to stimulate the exacerbation of existing symptoms, thus triggering the sick body's natural healing response to cure the patient.

Because homeopathic remedies are based on inexpensive natural substances like plants, herbs, or minerals, homeopathy is often conflated with other forms of alternative medicine such as aromatherapy, acupuncture, massage, herbal medicine, and chiropractic care. In its purest form, homeopathy is not really aligned with these other forms, many of which are allopathic in approach and methodology. Nonetheless, the association has hardly hurt the industry, as a "back to basics, back to nature" mentality swept across America and the world. Continually barraged with news of oil spills, toxic exposures, hormonal additives in food sources, chemical and often-carcinogenic sprays and herbicides on fresh produce, and untoward side effects of conventional pharmaceutical and prescriptive medications, the public's resurgent interest and search for homeopathic and other natural alternative medicines was all too apparent and predictable. This conveniently combined with a renewed interest in preventive, rather than palliative medicine, as people learned how to prolong their health and life expectancies through natural diet, exercise, and therapy. Health food stores became one of

the hottest industries in the 1990s—with shelves loaded with herbal teas, megavitamins, natural mood enhancers, stimulants, depressants, aphrodisiacs, and purportedly natural cures for everyday ailments. Caught up in the momentum of all this, "homeopathy" became a household term. According to the American Homeopathic Pharmaceutical Association (AHPhA), sales of homeopathic remedies climbed by as much as 25 percent annually from the late 1980s to the late 1990s.

Homeopathic methods have remained popular for more than two centuries, despite criticism from some doctors that these methods rely more on anecdotal than empirical knowledge. Since the 1970s, many people suffering from common chronic ailments found relief through homeopathy, leading some doctors, researchers, lawmakers, and insurance carriers to become more open to sanctioning homeopathy. Led by consumer demand, homeopathy and homeopathic medicine are poised for even greater public acceptance and new growth. In 1997 the American Homeopathic Pharmaceutical Association estimated sales at about $230 million per year and a growth rate of 12 percent. The average homeopathic remedy cost $3 to $7 per bottle. Also, some analysts claimed that there were over 3,000 homeopaths in the United States in the late 1990s.

A recent survey of homeopathic practitioners claimed that those in the industry found homeopathy most effective in treating common ailments such as colds and flu, chronic headaches, arthritis, allergies, asthma, pre-menstrual syndrome, and menopause. Homeopathic treatments have also been used for depression and anxiety, as well as common childhood conditions such as earaches, colic, and teething. Patients can get these remedies from mainstream pharmacies, natural pharmacies, and health food stores or from catalogs featuring alternative health care products. Several catalogs and pharmacies sell home treatment kits that contain 20 or more vials of common homeopathic remedies. Included in these kits are reference materials that can be used to explain which remedy to use to treat specific ailments. Homeopathic remedies typically come in liquid, tablet, or granule form.

To practice homeopathy in the United States, one must be a licensed health care provider. All states have laws that allow medical doctors (MDs) and osteopathic doctors (DOs) to diagnose and treat illnesses. A few states—including Alaska, Arizona, Connecticut, Hawaii, Montana, New Hampshire, Oregon, Utah, and Washington—license naturopathic doctors (NDs) to do the same. An MD or DO can be certified as competent to practice homeopathy through the American Board of Homeotherapeutics, which grants a DHt certification. Naturopathic physicians go through the Homeopathic Academy of Naturopathic Physicians, which grants a DHANP certification. All health care providers can be certified through the Council for Homeopathic Certification (CHC). The Council on Homeopathic Education (CHE) monitors these educational programs. Moreover, the U.S. Food and Drug Administration (FDA), regulates all homeopathic remedies, but because homeopathic products contain little or no active ingredients, many are exempt from the same regulations as other drugs.

ACUPUNCTURE

Acupuncture, like other forms of traditional Chinese medicine, dates back roughly 4,500 years. While its practice in the West has been slow to catch on, it has received steady interest. A 1971 *New York Times* story acted as the catalyst that led to growth of acupuncture in the United States. Acupuncture is based on the concept of *Chi,* which is the life force that circulates through the body within 14 channels called *meridians.* When *chi* flows freely, people experience good health. However, when *chi* is blocked or flows slowly, people experience poor health.

Consequently, the goal of acupuncture is to stimulate proper flow of *chi.* To do so, acupuncturists insert very thin sterilized needles to penetrate the area just under the surface of the skin, where the *chi* passageways, or acupoints, are said to be. Acupuncturists insert the needles less than an inch into the skin in some cases and three to four inches in others. They also rotate the needles and the entire procedure causes little pain. Acupuncture, in Western parlance, builds host resistance, which is the body's natural defenses and its ability to fight illness.

Acupuncture's primary application in the United States has been the alleviation of pain caused by a plethora of illnesses including arthritis, back pain, headache, gout, stress pain, and toothache. Nevertheless, acupuncturists are beginning to use this technique to relieve symptoms of other kinds of illnesses, such as those of addiction and stroke. Of the 12,000 acupuncturists in the country, about 3,000 of them are licensed medical doctors. However, many doctors of traditional Western medicine find it hard to accept the theory of invisible flowing energy and contend that acupuncture produces nothing more than the placebo effect or that the localized pain takes the mind off more global pain— although acupuncture causes little pain when properly employed. Despite the criticism, scientific research

indicates that acupuncture helps to improve health and relieve pain by stimulating the body's production of natural pain killers (endorphins and enkephalins) and a natural anti-inflammatory substance (cortisol).

More On **INDUSTRY ASSOCIATIONS**

Those looking for homeopathic physicians can consult the *Directory of Homeopathic Practitioners,* published by the National Center for Homeopathy (NCH) in Alexandria, Virginia. The NCH serves as both a lobbying and educational organization for homeopathy in the United States. The NCH also encourages home study groups for people who wish to self-treat common ailments after learning about homeopathy. The NCH recognizes 165 self-help homeopathic study groups in North America, and reports that these groups grow at the rate of three per month. Because most homeopathic remedies are non-toxic and sold without a prescription, educated patients can treat themselves relatively safely.

Other related entities include the American Homeopathic Pharmaceutical Association/Homeopathic Pharmacopoeia of the U.S., headquartered in Valley Forge, Pennsylvania, and the American Institute of Homeopathy. The above-mentioned National Center for Homeopathy also provides information regarding the location of facilities offering education in the field.

CURRENT CONDITIONS

In 1997, sales from all forms of alternative medicine in the United States totaled between $21 and $34 billion, up from about $14 billion in the early 1990s. Alternative therapies accounted for about $19.6 billion, herbal medicine for about $5.0 billion, and therapy classes and materials for about $4.7 billion of the industry's overall sales, according to the *Journal of the American Medical Association* (*JAMA*). *JAMA* also reported that the largest growth in the industry came from "herbal medicine, massage, megavitamins, self-help groups, folk remedies, energy healing, and homeopathy." Demand for alternative medicine grew rapidly in the 1990s with about 42 percent of the population using these treatments and therapies by the late 1990s, up from 33 percent in the early 1990s. Moreover, consumers visited practitioners of alternative medicine 628 times during the late 1990s, in contrast to visiting practitioners of traditional medicine only 386 times, according to *JAMA*. The high cost of conventional health care and consumer dissatisfaction help drive the alternative medicine industry. In addition, consumer interest in treatments and therapies that do not cause significant side effects also has spurred demand for alternative medicine. While some of the more than 200 techniques and therapies lumped together in the industry still receive strong criticism, others such as chiropractic therapy, acupuncture, and massage therapy have become accepted or recognized by U.S. physicians and medical organizations. Indeed, many licensed physicians are also licensed practitioners of therapies such as acupuncture and biofeedback.

Many patients of alternative medicine have paid for their treatments out-of-pocket, but many insurers are starting to cover some complementary therapies. For example, Blue Cross of Washington and Alaska offers a plan covering naturopathic and homeopathic physicians and acupuncturists. Other insurance carriers offering some coverage for alternative medicine include: Catholic HealthCare West, Mutual of Omaha, and Oxford Health Plans (an HMO). During the 1990s some states also passed medical freedom bills, which stated that alternative medical providers could not be found incompetent "solely on the basis that a licensee's practice is unconventional or experimental in the absence of demonstrable physical harm to a patient." Medical freedom states include Alaska, Washington, Colorado, South Dakota, Oregon, New York, Oklahoma, and North Carolina. Although not all insurance plans cover homeopathic therapy, many familiar multi-state drug store chains carried over-the-counter homeopathic remedies, which is helpful since 95 percent of homeopathic remedies are available without a prescription.

Another important development in the late 1990s was the introduction of the Access to Medical Treatment Act. The bill would allow consumers to choose any medical treatment that was not proven to be dangerous, had fully disclosed side effects, and fell within the scope of a provider's expertise. It also allowed a new definition of health care providers as "any properly licensed medical doctor, osteopath, chiropractor or naturopath."

INDUSTRY LEADERS

Complete Wellness Centers, Inc. and American HealthChoice, Inc. rank among the leading providers of alternative medicine therapies, offering these therapies along with conventional health care services. Founded in 1994, Complete Wellness Centers establishes and runs over 140 diversified medical centers throughout the country. Complete Wellness Centers offer acupuncture, chiropractic, and massage therapy. In addition to providing services by physicians and alternative medicine practitioners, the company has programs to help patients quit smoking and lose weight. In 1998 the company's sales rose to $19 million, and Complete Wellness Centers had 400 employees.

American HealthChoice, Inc. owns and manages 15 medical centers, including primary care, urgent care, physical therapy, and chiropractic clinics in Georgia, Louisiana, and Texas. While the company owned some unprofitable medical centers, it has sold

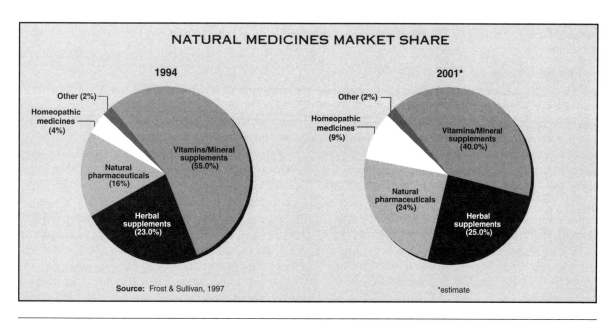

NATURAL MEDICINES MARKET SHARE

1994

Other (2%)
Homeopathic medicines (4%)
Natural pharmaceuticals (16%)
Vitamins/Mineral supplements (55.0%)
Herbal supplements (23.0%)

2001*

Other (2%)
Homeopathic medicines (9%)
Vitamins/Mineral supplements (40.0%)
Natural pharmaceuticals (24%)
Herbal supplements (25.0%)

Source: Frost & Sullivan, 1997

*estimate

them and sought to acquire new, more promising operations. The company posted sales of $7.2 million in 1998 and employed 109 workers.

In the homeopathy sector, two of the highest-grossing remedy makers include The Boiron Group and Dolisos Homeopathic Pharmacology Laboratories. Boiron, based in France, reported worldwide annual sales of $243.0 million and net profits of $13.5 million in 1997. The company's work force totaled 2,200 employees that year. The company has 29 units for production, distribution, and information in France, and it has 18 establishments worldwide. The Boiron Group produces 100 million single and multi-dose tubes of homeopathic medicine each year, covering a range of 200 homeopathic remedies. The company was formed in 1932 by three French homeopathic pharmacists.

While Boiron enjoyed success in its early years, it did not achieve significant growth until 1965 when the French Pharmacopoeia included homeopathy, thus including the medicines they produced in the health care system coverage. Boiron grew steadily from 1968 on and expanded worldwide through the 1990s with establishments in countries such as Italy, India, the United States, Canada, Poland, and Bulgaria. The company was privately held until June 1987 when the Boiron family first listed it on the French stock exchange. In 1988 Boiron merged with Laboratoires Homeopathiques de France (LHF). In 1990 they bought another competitor, Herbaxt. Since the mid-1990s, the company has maintained the Institute Boiron, an independent homeopathic laboratory staffed with more than 100 clinical physicians working on research and development. Their research has developed products for veterinary and medical prescriptions, as well as products and guidelines for pharmacies and home medication.

The other prominent industry leader in the homeopathic sector, Dolisos, also of France, reported annual sales of more than $120 million and employed approximately 200 people in the late 1990s. Dolisos claimed to be the world's biggest investor in homeopathic research, while Boiron claimed the most sales. In 1996, the world's leading seed-producing company, Groupe Limagrain, acquired Dolisos, allowing their new subsidiary to keep its own name. Dolisos was founded in 1937 by Dr. Jean Tetau, a French pharmacist. The company specializes in homeopathic medicines available primarily through prescriptions. Their plant produces active ingredients for pharmacists to blend, or finished products ready for the patient.

In 1978, Dr. Tetau directed the firm to be the first homeopathic laboratory with independent research facilities. Next, the company established links between their industry and university researchers. As of 1997, Dolisos claimed to have "20 teams in 15 medical centers in France, Belgium, Italy, and the United States researching the effectiveness of homeopathic dilutions to better understand their action mechanisms." Anticipating future interest, the company began selling and researching homeopathic veterinary drugs during the mid-1990s. As of 1997, Dolisos had eight worldwide subsidiaries in Belgium, Italy, the United States, Spain, Holland, Canada, and Switzerland.

RESEARCH AND TECHNOLOGY

In 1995 the Office of Alternative Medicine (OAM) appointed a new director, Wayne Jonas, a retired military physician who had run the Medical Research Fellowship program at Walter Reed Army Institute of Research in Washington, D.C. Of interest to proponents of alternative medicine was that Dr. Jonas himself had been trained in bioenergetics, homeopathy, acupuncture, and spiritual healing, and he had used such treatments in his family medical practice. When Jonas addressed the first International Congress on Alternative and Complementary Therapy, he cautioned against self-conclusions about the efficacy of alternative medicine without the support of corroborative data. Shortly thereafter, in October 1995, OAM announced the funding of eight additional centers for alternative medicine research. Of these, at least two were cited for specific research in homeopathy—The University of California at Davis and Harvard Medical School's Beth Israel Deaconess Medical Center in Boston, Massachusetts. As of 1999, study reports and findings were not yet available.

In a comprehensive study reported in the September 20, 1997 edition of the respected medical journal, *The Lancet,* scientists concluded that they could neither endorse nor dispel the critical and stigmatic hypothesis that the clinical effects of various forms of alternative medicine were the result of a "placebo effect." Nor could they conclude one way or the other, having found insufficient evidence, that these remedies were effective for any single clinical condition. However, they enthusiastically supported the need for additional "rigorous and systematic" research in this area. At a minimum, advised George Washington University School of Medicine's Megan A. Johnson (not a member of the above study) in her 1998 JAMA published essay, homeopathy could complement modern medicine as "another tool in the bag."

FURTHER READING

The Alternative Advisor. Alexandria, VA: Time-Life Books, 1997.

Avalon, Bruce B. "Homeopathy for Homesteaders." *Mother Earth News,* April/May 1998.

Boericke & Tafel, Inc., 1997. Available from http://www.hpr .room.net/hprcat1.html.

Collinge, William. *The American Holistic Health Association Complete Guide to Alternative Medicine.* New York: Warner Books, 1996.

Comarow, Avery. "Going Outside the Medical Mainstream." *U.S. News & World Report,* 23 November 1998.

"Dolisos Answers Your Homeopathy Questions," 1997. Available from http://www.lyghtforce.com/Dolisos/ Medicate.htm.

Eisenberg, David M., et al. "Trends in Alternative Medicine Use in the United States, 1990-1997." *Journal of the American Medical Association,* 11 November 1998.

"The History of Dolisos," 1997. Available from http://www.lyghtforce.com/Dolisos/Dolisos.htm.

"Homeopathy Sales Defy Critics." *CQ Researcher,* 14 February 1997.

Jarvis, William. "Health Fraud Leader Speaks Out on Homeopathy." *FDA Consumer,* 6 April 1997.

Johnson, Megan A. "Homeopathy: Another Tool in the Bag." *Journal of the American Medical Association (JAMA),* 4 March 1998.

Linde, Karl, et al. "Are the Clinical Effects of Homeopathy Placebo Effects? A Meta-Analysis of Placebo-Controlled Trials." *The Lancet,* 20 September 1997.

Stapleton, Stephanie. "Alternative Medicine: Time to Talk." *American Medical News,* 14 December 1998

Stehlin, Isadora. "Homeopathy: Real Medicine or Empty Promises?" *FDA Consumer,* December 1996. Available from http://www.fda.gov/.

Wheeler, David L. "From Homeopathy to Herbal Therapy: Researchers Focus on Alternative Medicine." *The Chronicles of Higher Education,* 27 March 1998.

—Dave Fagan, updated by Lauri Harding and Karl Heil

ANTI-AGING PRODUCTS AND SERVICES

Throughout the ages, men and women have made use of cosmetics to enhance appearance and mask signs of aging. In modern societies—particularly in the West—youth is valued over maturation and experience, and individuals often go to great lengths to stave off the appearance of age. The pursuit of youth, coupled with the general aging of Western societies, created an unprecedented demand for anti-aging products and services such as cosmetics, laser surgery, facials, dietary supplements, and hair restoration services.

The market for anti-aging products has never been greater. The Census Bureau predicts that by 2030 the number of Americans over the age of 65 will reach more than 70 million, one-fifth of the population. There will be 9 million people over 85 and, by 2050, 40 percent of Americans will be 50 or older. These older consumers control the majority of wealth and are spending it more freely than any other time in history.

Traditionally, all cosmetic preparations shared a common trait: they were not meant to alter the physiology or function of the body's tissues. Beginning in the mid-1970s, however, cosmetic companies fortified products with hormones, amino acids, antioxidant vitamins, oils, and herbs, some of which had proven therapeutic value. These new products blurred the line between cosmetics and pharmaceuticals, giving rise to the term "cosmeceutical." Furthermore, some companies no longer market new cosmetic preparations as "beauty aids," having found that expanding product descriptions by touting clinically proven health benefits yields more success. Therapeutic cosmetics, such

as the hair-replacement solution minoxidil, dominated the market by the early 1990s. The extremely technical nature of these new formulations created an increasing reliance on research and development within the industry and provided large pharmaceutical companies with a niche in the cosmetics industry.

Anti-aging products were not limited to cosmetics. Customers increasingly turn to dietary supplements containing hormones, such as dehydroepiandrosterone (DHEA), and antioxidant vitamins such as A, C, E, and K. The hormones melatonin, human growth hormone, estrogen, and testosterone all show varying degrees of promise as anti-aging compounds. Small manufacturers proliferated in this market, but larger pharmaceuticals manufacturers have joined as the industry grows. In addition, traditional medicinal preparations like the herbal medicines Echinacea, green tea leaf extract, Gingko biloba, St. John's wort, and Saw palmetto have been recognized by consumers as having anti-aging properties. As is the case with the dietary supplement industry, small manufacturers dominate the herbal medicine market.

The food we consume is also becoming an important part of anti-aging research and development. The USDA Human Nutrition Research Center on Aging at Tufts University in Boston found that eating fruits and vegetables with a high Oxygen Radical Absorbency Capacity helps slow the aging process in both the body and brain. Researchers found that spinach, strawberries, and blueberries raise the antioxidant power of human blood and prevent some loss of memory and learning ability.

With medicine continuing to advance our understanding of the aging process and potential methods for slowing it, the anti-aging products industries must respond to scientific discovery in order to meet consumer expectations. Companies that strengthen extensive scientific development continue to yield stronger returns. For example, in 1997 consumers perceived L'Oreal's L'Oreal, Maybelline, and Lancome cosmetic brands as ineffective in their incorporation of anti-aging substances; however, in 1998 L'Oreal saw sales of its cosmetics line increase 9.4 percent, while its dermatology line increased 21.7 percent. Estee Lauder, owner of Estee Lauder, Clinique, and Aramis cosmetics, also continued to develop new anti-aging delivery systems and helped the company enjoy a steady growth of 7 percent.

About... PROVEN THERAPEUTIC PROPERTIES OF ANTI-AGING SUBSTANCES

Relatively few advantages of anti-aging substances have been scientifically verified. Substances and their purported benefits are as follows:

- Green tea extract: inhibits the growth of tumors.
- Gingko biloba extract: protects nerve tissue by increasing cerebral blood flow.
- Blueberries: improve vision and overall eye health.
- Estrogen: reduces the incidence of heart disease and helps prevent osteoporosis in postmenopausal women.
- Zinc: heightens the sense of taste in older individuals.
- Growth hormone replacement: increases muscle mass, decreases average visceral fat, improves metabolic rate, and lowers high-density lipoprotein levels in the bloodstream.
- Alpha- and beta-hydroxy acids: improve cell function by increasing their ability to retain moisture.
- Retinoids (antioxidant vitamins): reduce fine wrinkles on the skin and reverse mild skin discoloration.

ORGANIZATION AND STRUCTURE

Large pharmaceutical companies and cosmetics manufacturers produce most cosmeceuticals. Many of the largest cosmetics companies are part of multinational personal hygiene and home care product manufacturers. Both the large cosmetics companies and the pharmaceutical manufacturers have access to internal research and development resources, giving

them an inestimable advantage in the ever-evolving anti-aging products market.

Hormonal compounds used for medicinal purposes are manufactured primarily by pharmaceutical companies, and are subject to Food and Drug Administration (FDA) scrutiny and approval. Hormonal preparations used in dietary supplements, such as DHEA, are not subject to governmental regulation at present, and, as such, are manufactured by a wide range of companies.

Amino acids and enzymes, including alpha- and beta-hydroxy acids, are essential components of many cosmeceuticals and dietary supplements. Like cosmeceuticals, these substances are produced primarily by large pharmaceutical and cosmetics manufacturers, although some independent chemical laboratories and a few small firms are also engaged in their production.

Herbal anti-aging preparations and dietary supplements are manufactured primarily by small companies. As is the case with hormones used in dietary supplements, herbal supplements are not subject to governmental regulation, which enables companies to develop new products with far less expenditure on research and development. The trade in herbal remedies and supplements became so lucrative that Warner-Lambert, a large manufacturer of pharmaceuticals and consumer health care products, made plans to enter the market in the late 1990s.

Within the anti-aging products industries, a strict dichotomy exists between those sections of the market that come under federal regulatory scrutiny and those that do not. Under the provisions of the Food, Drug, and Cosmetic Act of 1938, the FDA must approve only pharmaceutical preparations. The distinction between cosmetics and pharmaceuticals was quite clear at the time of the Act's passage, but modern cosmeceuticals have made changes in the Act a possibility. Many countries, including Japan, have amended similar regulatory rules to classify cosmetics that alter physiology as pharmaceuticals subject to regulation. While companies in the anti-aging products industries dread increased regulation, the trend in the United States has not been in this direction. In fact, the Dietary Supplement Health and Education Act of 1994 exempted "natural substances"—including human hormones, herbal compounds, amino acids, and enzymes—from regulation so long as these substances were included in dietary supplements rather than medicines. However, increasing reports of dangerous side effects and drug interactions suffered by people taking herbal and hormonal dietary supplements may trigger increased regulatory scrutiny of these products.

BACKGROUND AND DEVELOPMENT

Medical science has been aware of the therapeutic uses of hormones since the 1930s, but they were not widely used in over-the-counter preparations until the Dietary Supplement Health and Education Act of 1994. While the efficacy of medical hormonal therapies such as estrogen replacement has been demonstrated irrefutably, the effectiveness and safety of hormonal dietary supplements remains questionable. Small manufacturers produce most of these substances. In fact, many local health food stores are able to manufacture their own DHEA, a human hormone synthesized by the adrenal glands. DHEA was one of the first hormones recognized to play a role in the aging process, as its level drops markedly as individuals age. DHEA replacement, however, has not been demonstrated to slow or reverse the aging process, and has caused troubling side effects in those who ingest more than 50 milligrams per day.

During the mid-1970s, the popular solution of alpha-hydroxy acid was first used in cosmetic preparations, but it did not attract widespread consumer attention until the 1992 release of Avon's Anew line of skin care products. The Anew product line achieved sales of over $190 million in 1997, and its phenomenal success led other major cosmetics manufacturers to launch competing compounds. These new products enabled the skin care products industry to grow 12 percent overall in 1993 and 14 percent overall in 1994, reaching a total market size of $5.1 billion in the United States alone by the end of that year. Industry growth has slowed since the initial onslaught of al-

pha-hydroxy products, but new innovations have enabled individual companies to post fabulous growth rates in the mid- to late 1990s.

Anti-oxidants and vitamins, including beta carotene and vitamins A, C, E, and K, have long been observed to protect cells from certain forms of damage caused by environmental factors. As customers became increasingly concerned about the potential effects of environmental degradation on their health, and in particular, the effects of increased ultraviolet radiation on their skin, demand for skin treatment products that incorporated antioxidant vitamins soared. Anti-oxidants are useful in treating far more aging problems than previously thought—research conducted in 1998 finds that antioxidants showed great promise for preventing chronic aging diseases such as Alzheimer's, cataracts, heart disease, and cancer.

Hair restoration services traditionally did not involve medication, but rather physical replacement of hair. The introduction of Rogaine with minoxidil by the Upjohn Company in 1988 revolutionized this portion of the anti-aging industry, enabling individuals suffering hair loss to enjoy some renewed growth through application of the product. Rogaine's limited efficacy allowed hair weave and other services to survive, but the product continued to post steady success into the late 1990s.

The problem of impotence received its first medicated treatment when Pfizer introduced its new impotence drug, Viagra, in the United States in 1998 and received instant phenomenal success, garnering

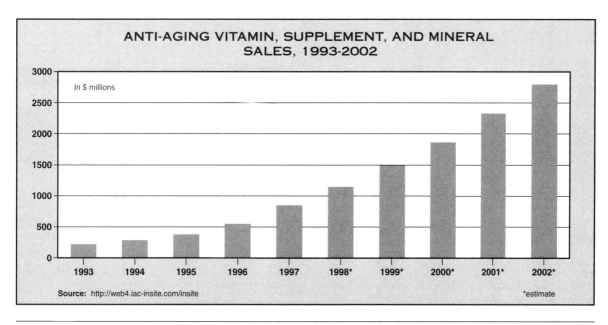

ANTI-AGING VITAMIN, SUPPLEMENT, AND MINERAL SALES, 1993-2002

In $ millions

Source: http://web4.iac-insite.com/insite

*estimate

worldwide sales of $193 million. One in three U.S. doctors have written a prescription for Viagra, and it has recently been approved in 77 countries around the world. Research has shown that while Viagra doesn't increase libido or boost sexual desire, it does enhance normal physiological response.

Passage of the Dietary Supplement Health and Education Act of 1994 provided great impetus to the herbal remedy and dietary supplement industries. Herbs have been used to treat a variety of maladies from prehistoric times. While the therapeutic properties of some herbs, including gingko biloba and aloe vera, were proven, many others were subject to question. Of particular concern were the effects of ingesting high concentrations of the active ingredients present in herbs, as these ingredients often interact harmfully with medications. Such concerns notwithstanding, small manufacturers readily filled the huge public demand for herbal anti-aging remedies, dietary supplements, and skin care products, with global demand for herbal preparations reaching $12 billion by the mid-1990s.

CURRENT CONDITIONS

Although demand for cosmetics containing alpha-hydroxy acids slowed by the mid-1990s, the skin care industry as a whole continued to boom, reaching $25 billion in U.S. sales by 1998. The cosmeceutical portion of the skin care industry was dominated by cosmetic firms Estee Lauder, Procter & Gamble, Cosmair, Maybelline, and Avon Products, Inc., each of which has incorporated anti-aging substances in product lines to some degree.

Increased consumer concern over the effects of ultraviolet radiation on the skin led to a booming market for sunscreens and related products in the mid- to late 1990s. To capitalize on this demand, industry leaders introduced cosmetic products incorporating beta-hydroxy acids and other compounds thought to provide sun protection. Procter & Gamble's Oil of Olay Age Defying Series of products was the most notable of these releases, capturing a facial care market share of 18.3 percent in 1996. Other successes in the facial care market included: L'Oreal's Plenitude, which captured an 11.7 percent market share; Chesebrough Ponds—a division of multinational pharmaceutical, personal hygiene, and household products giant Unilever—whose various brands secured a 12.8 percent market share; and Johnson & Johnson, whose Neutrogena product line accounted for 7.8 percent of facial care product sales. In 1998, the La Roche Posay division of L'Oreal introduced a new sun protection formula, Mexoryl SX, which was the first photostable filter to protect against both harmful UVA and UVB rays.

The market for dietary supplements and skin care products incorporating hormones was mixed in the mid- to late 1990s. The importation of huge quantities of inexpensive DHEA produced in the People's Republic of China caused the price of this hormone to drop from $900 to $350 per kilogram during 1996. The glut on the DHEA market, along with regulatory and liability concerns, allowed small manufacturers to continue to dominate this portion of the anti-aging industries into the late 1990s. ReVive, a brand of skin care product containing the epidermal growth factor hormone, is typical of this type of product. ReVive was created in 1997 by Dr. Greg Brown. Brown, working in conjunction with Chiron, a small, San Francisco-based biotechnology firm, learned to clone epidermal growth factor, making production of a cosmetic containing this hormone economically practical. The resulting ReVive line of products was quickly picked up by the national retail chain Neiman Marcus and was expected to achieve sales in excess of $1 million in its first year of availability.

Pharmacia and Upjohn's domination of the hair restoration medication market was challenged in 1998 with the introduction of Propecia, an orally administered hair restoring pharmaceutical by Merck and Company, Inc. By March 1, 1998, sales of Rogaine had dropped 41.9 percent from the previous year's levels, but increased advertising was expected to mitigate the slump.

INDUSTRY LEADERS

Large cosmetics companies, some of which were owned by multinational pharmaceutical manufacturers, dominated the amino acid-based cosmeceuticals industry. Avon Products, Inc., originator of Anew, the first cosmetic product to include alpha-hydroxy acids, remains a major player in the industry with sales of more than $5 billion for the 1998 fiscal year. Avon's competitive position was enhanced when it added retinol, a vitamin A-based compound said to help protect skin from ultraviolet radiation, to its original Anew formula in 1997. In 1998 Avon introduced Avon Basics worldwide. This line of vitamin-enriched skin care broadened its sun screen formula to encompass all skin types. L'Oreal SA, whose product lines include Maybelline and Lancome, is another leading cosmetics manufacturer, with 1998 sales of more than $17 billion. Corporate subsidiaries operate in medical and pharmaceutical research and development, and support L'Oreal's creation of new cosmeceutical products.

Estee Lauder accounts for nearly 46 percent of over-the-counter sales of women's cosmetics in the United States and showed a net sales of $3.6 billion in 1998. The company expanded into the teen cosmetics and natural cosmetics markets in 1997, acquiring Sassaby and Aveda. Revlon, Inc. has also entered the anti-aging cosmetics market with its Almay and Color Stay product lines. Clarins SA, manufacturer of the Sisley and Helena Rubinstein brands, posted sales of $611.8 million for the 1998 fiscal year.

Large pharmaceutical manufacturers also play a key role in the anti-aging products industry. Procter & Gamble, whose brand names include Cover Girl, Oil of Olay, and Max Factor, is one such corporation, with 1998 sales of more than $37 billion. Unilever NV and Unilever PLC, which trade separately but are run by a single board of directors, produce the Chesebrough Ponds line of cosmetics and toiletries, and enjoyed sales of more than $51 billion for the 1998 fiscal year. Health care product manufacturer Johnson & Johnson, with sales of more than $23 billion in 1998, participates in the cosmeceuticals industry through its Neutrogena product line. LVMH Moet Hennessy Louis Vuitton Inc., owner of the Christian Dior and Givenchy lines of cosmetics, is another major player in the cosmeceuticals industry with sales of $6.9 billion in 1998. Schering-Plough Corporation also participates in the anti-aging products industry through its Coppertone line of sunscreen products.

Small, independent laboratories and other corporations continue to produce the majority of the non-pharmaceutical hormones and hormone-based dietary supplements and cosmeceuticals.

Two companies dominate the hair replacement portion of the anti-aging products industry: Pharmacia and Upjohn, manufacturer of Rogaine with minoxidil; and Merck & Company, Inc., manufacturer of Propecia. Since these were the only proven hair restoration medications on the market, the companies faced no competition apart from each other in the late 1990s. Pharmacia and Upjohn has dominated the hair restoration market since the introduction of Rogaine—and its active ingredient, minoxidil—in 1988.

As is the case with hormonal anti-aging products, herbal-based anti-aging compounds are primarily produced by small, independent concerns. Natrol, a California-based producer of melatonin, and Sunsource International, a Hawaii-based producer of melatonex—melatonin to which vitamin B6 has been added—are typical of these concerns. An exception to this rule is Yamanouchi Pharmaceutical Company, a Tokyo-based corporation that produces herbal remedies and supplements in the United States under the Shaklee Corporation name. Nature Made is another important player in this sector of the anti-aging products industry, having received the endorsement of the American Medical Women's Association for its products in 1998.

The face of this portion of the anti-aging products industry may have been permanently altered in 1997, when multinational pharmaceutical manufacturer Warner-Lambert introduced herbal varieties of its Halls Lozenges and Celestial Seasonings product lines. Another notable newcomer to the herbal remedy and dietary supplement industry is PharmaPrint Inc., an Irvine, California-based company established in 1997. PharmaPrint intended to standardize the potency and dosage of the active ingredients in various herbal preparations, making such preparations amenable to FDA regulation should herbal compounds and supplements come under federal regulatory scrutiny. Standardization of herbal remedies and dietary supplements could also open new markets for such products among individuals who at present avoid them due to fears of side effects and interactions with other medications.

AMERICA AND THE WORLD

Demand for anti-aging products is centered in the West and the economically developed areas of Asia. Manufacturing of anti-aging products is also concentrated in Europe and the United States. Multinational giants Unilever, LVMH, and Procter and Gamble and their subsidiaries play a prominent role in the industry globally. Production of herbal and hormonal cosmetics and dietary supplements is fragmented among small manufacturers, although Europe accounted for approximately one-half of worldwide demand for herbal remedies in the late 1990s. Despite the predominance of the West in the anti-aging products industry, production and exportation of non-pharmaceutical quality hormones, most notably DHEA, by the People's Republic of China led the value of these substances to fall dramatically in 1996.

RESEARCH AND TECHNOLOGY

Research and development has driven the growth of the anti-aging products industry throughout the 1990s. As advances in medical understanding of the aging process reveal the therapeutic properties of new substances, cosmetics and pharmaceutical firms adapt these substances for use in their products. The industry also expends a great deal of effort identifying the exact effects of anti-aging compounds. This is particularly true of the anti-aging hormones and herbs. By 1998, the industry focused on catalysts and biovectors, such as Lipacide PVB and Cosmederm-7, designed to carry anti-aging compounds to the cells and render these compounds—many of which are somewhat acidic—less irritating. Another potentially promising substance is beta-hydroxy, a less irritating amino acid with many of the same anti-aging properties as alpha-hydroxy. Beta-hydroxy was scheduled to replace alpha-hydroxy as the active ingredient in the Oil of Olay Age Defying product line in 1998. Beta-hydroxy also was demonstrated to assist athletes in adding muscle mass when taken as a dietary supplement, and had no known side effects in preliminary studies.

FURTHER READING

Acello, Richard. "Health Care: It's Back to Nature." *San Diego Business Journal,* 3 February 1997.

Born, Pete. "Avon Adding More Anew Ideas." *WWD,* 25 July 1997.

Brookman, Claire. "Oil of Olay Bets on Beta-Hydroxy." *WWD,* 14 March 1997.

Davis, W. Marvin. "Antiaging Products and Tactics." *Drug Topics,* 17 February 1997.

Djerassi, David. "The Role of the Protective Vitamins and Sunscreen in the New High Performance Cosmetics." *Drug & Cosmetic Industry,* September 1997.

"Endless Youth," 14 April 1999. Available from http//:www.endlessyouth.com.

Fine, Jenny B. "ReVive: Skin Care With a Twist." *WWD,* 11 July 1997.

Flanagan, William G., and David Stix. "The Bald Truth: There Really is a Drug That Grows Hair." *Forbes,* 22 July 1991.

Gerry, Roberta. "Ironing Out Wrinkles." *Chemical Market Reporter,* 12 May 1997.

Goldemberg, Robert L. "Believe it or Not." *Drug & Cosmetic Industry,* March 1997.

———. "Raw Materials." *Drug & Cosmetic Industry,* August 1995.

Gorman, Christine. "Can This Pill Really Make You Younger?" *Time,* 23 September 1996.

Hahn, Gary S. "A New Line of Defense Against Aging." *Drug and Cosmetics Industry,* January 1998.

Hearn, Wayne. "New Food Supplement Said to Build Strength—Safely." *American Medical News,* 19 August 1996.

Henderson, Carter. "Affluent Seniors: Industry and the Aging." *Reid Educational Foundation,* 1 February 1999.

Jordan, Peg. "Preventative Measures." *American Fitness,* 5 February 1999.

Klepacki, Laura. "Melatonin: Nightcap of the '90s." *American Druggist,* September 1996.

Lerner, Matthew. "DHEA Follows Melatonin in Demand, But Not in Price." *Chemical Marketing Reporter,* 28 October 1996.

McBride, Judy. "Can Foods Forestall Aging?" *Department of Agriculture,* 19 March 1999.

Michel, Nelly, and Corinne Stoltz. "The Interest of Amino Acid Biovectors." *Drug and Cosmetic Industry,* September 1996.

"Pfizer Inc." *Hoover's Online,* 17 April 1999. Available from http://www.hoovers.com.

Portyansky, Elena. "New Generation Retinoid Rids More Than Just Acne." *Drug Topics,* 7 July 1997.

"The Procter & Gamble Company." *Hoover's Online,* 22 April 1999. Available from http://www.hoovers.com.

Raloff, J. "New Gene Therapy Fights Frailty." *Science News,* 11 January 1999.

Sargissan, Susan. "Capturing Trends in Skin Care and Color Cosmetics." *Drug & Cosmetic Industry,* October 1995.

Snyder, Karen. "Different Groups Working to Standardize Herbal Drugs." *Drug Topics,* 6 January 1997.

Snyder, Susan. "Cosmeceuticals: A New Product Category to Watch." *Drug Topics,* 24 June 1996.

"Soften Wrinkles with All-Natural Skincare." *Better Nutrition,* March 1999.

Stover, Dawn. "Fountain of Youth?" *Popular Science,* 15 February 1999.

"Supplemental UV Prevention." *Industry Week,* 3 February 1997.

"Time Stands Still." *European Cosmetic Markets,* 15 February 1999.

"Universal Network Plans to Launch Anti-Aging Super Site." *Business Wire,* 6 April 1999.

Wilck, Jennifer. "Baby Boomers and Natural Ingredients Lift Personal Care." *Chemical Market Reporter*, 12 May 1997.

Wilke, Michael. "Halls Brand Will Move Into Natural Remedies." *Advertising Age*, 23 June 1997.

———. "Merck Kicks Off $60 Mil DTC Push for Rogaine Rival." *Advertising Age*, 20 April 1996.

Wyandt, Christy M., and John S. Williamson. "An Herbal Update." *Drug Topics*, 1 June 1996.

Yazan, Y., K. Arslan, and M. Seiller. "Formulation and Evaluation of Multiple Emulsion Containing Glycolic Acid." *Drug & Cosmetic Industry*, January 1997.

—Grant Eldridge, updated by Susan Jensen

ANTIBACTERIAL PRODUCTS

INDUSTRY SNAPSHOT

Antibacterial products were born of several different sectors of the health industry, both in traditional medicine and alternative medicine. The four major industries that utilize the knowledge gained from decades of medical experience and research are: the pharmaceutical industry; the household products industry, which produces household cleaning soaps and detergents; the plastics industry, which creates everything from antibacterial swimming pool liners to antibacterial coating for children's toys; and the veterinary and agricultural products industry. In the 1980s, during the height of the AIDS epidemic, manufacturers of soaps and household cleaning products tested a niche in the market. Antibacterial products had been met with some caution by health professionals. Still, a 1998 poll conducted by CBS News indicated that at least 52 percent of U.S. consumers would always choose antimicrobial or antibacterial products whenever possible.

ORGANIZATION AND STRUCTURE

The U.S. Food and Drug Administration (FDA) oversees the production of pharmaceuticals, or any products that include regulated, approved medicinal or health benefits. With such a product as soap, for instance, the FDA has very clear guidelines. According to the FDA Office of Cosmetics Safety, there are two categories of soap: "True" soaps, made up solely of fats and an alkali, and synthetic "detergent products." "True" soaps are regulated by the Consumer Product Safety Commission, not the FDA, so they do not re-

quire labeling. Most synthetic soaps come under the regulation of the FDA. "If a cosmetic claim is made on the label of a 'true' soap or cleanser," the FDA noted in its Facts Sheet in February of 1995, "such as moisturizing or deodorizing, the product must meet all FDA requirements for a cosmetic, and the label must list all ingredients. If a drug claim is made on a cleanser or soap, such as antibacterial, antiperspirant, or anti-acne, then the product is a drug, and the label is required to list all active ingredients, as is required for all drug products." Any antibacterial products pertaining to livestock health or veterinary medical practices are regulated by the FDA as well.

The antibacterial products classified as homeopathic, or alternative medicine, are not regulated by the FDA. In essence, they are "above the law," and could make any claim, valid or questionable, regarding their effectiveness in fighting bacteria. In the area of plastics that utilize antibacterial protections, all industry standards pertaining to their occupational safety, along with consumer protection guidelines, direct production.

BACKGROUND AND DEVELOPMENT

The market for antibacterial products owes its success to the origins of bacterial study and Sir Alexander Fleming, a Scottish researcher who joined the research department of St. Mary's Hospital in London in 1906. Fleming's experiences during World War I as a soldier in France presented him with the terrible reality of infectious wounds. World War I brought horrors that other wars had not due to modern artillery, machine guns, and bombs. Physical disfigurements, infections, and wounds that resulted from the new technology inspired many medical breakthroughs. In addition to Fleming's commitment to finding medicines that would attack infections, much of modern-day plastic surgery underwent its earliest experiments during this time. According to Ted Gottfried, for *Scotsmart Books* in an online biography, "Fleming discovered in 1928 that an unwashed and bacterially infected flask appeared to be disinfected by mould which had grown from airborne spores. Penicillin's use in combating bacterium had been discovered." After World War II, thanks to Fleming's discovery, penicillin began to treat people in their fight against infections.

The onset of the use of antibiotics, such as penicillin and its derivative administered orally or intravenously, remained the focus of medical research and pharmaceutical companies. Products that employed antibacterial safeguards in surgical products like heart catheter tubes were crucial in hospitals and other medical care settings to offset the chance of spreading disease. In alternative medical arenas, various herbal compounds and natural plants were the basis for homeopathic remedies and beauty products. As far back as ancient times, natural poultices, creams, and herbal drinks were taken for the cure of infections. Although the industry had supplied antibacterial items to hospitals and medical supply companies, not until "Safeguard," a soap from the Procter & Gamble Company, was introduced in the early 1970s did most Americans see the term "antibacterial" appearing on any product, even though products such as "Lysol," a disinfectants, and "Listerine," a mouthwash, had been available for decades. Safeguard soap was introduced into hospitals first, then it was advertised to the American consumer. Procter & Gamble kept it on the market due to its well received response for the product in terms of sales.

Despite warnings of the possible harmful aspects of non-traditional practices, the alternative medicine industry managed to grow into an $18-billion market by 1996, as reported by the *Nutrition Business Journal* and as referenced in a series of investigative articles in the *Los Angeles Times*. They reported that even insurance companies began to look at various alternative treatments as viable and offered some reimbursement for certain procedures. The market for homeopathic remedies in California alone enjoyed an income of $3.65 billion, up 100 percent in the period between 1994 and 1998. All of the natural health companies offered some line of antibacterial products, both for personal and household use. The products include soaps, lotions, herbs, teas, vitamins, and household cleaning products, all thought to improve physical health and immunity. The natural products industry vigorously pursued the consumer market that continually sought out products to destroy the harmful effects of bacteria.

CURRENT CONDITIONS

A trip to any grocery store, discount store, or drugstore can yield any number of products labeled as "Antibacterial." Most major manufacturers of household cleaning products, for instance, market at least one antibacterial product. Among these products are some of the oldest and best-known brand names in America. Lysol has an antibacterial spray disinfectant and an antibacterial kitchen cleaner. Other antibacterial products on store shelves include Pro Formula 409, degreaser and all-purpose cleaner; Dow toilet bowl antibacterial and disinfectant cleaner; Palmolive antibacterial dishwashing liquid; Fantastik antibacterial spray cleaner; and Mr. Clean, whose label listed its antibacterial qualities as protecting against salmonella choleraesuis, escherichia coli, and proteus mirabilis.

Advertising for antibacterial products is becoming more prominent. In a four-page promotion in the May 11, 1999 *Woman's Day*, Lysol advertised seven of their key products. In addition to disinfecting and deodorizing, two of the products were antibacterial. In the same issue of that magazine four other antibacterial products were advertised—Tilex "Soap Scum" antibacterial bathroom cleaner; Joy's "Ultra Joy" antibacterial dishwashing liquid; "Soft Scrub" antibacterial cleanser; and "Pine-Sol" cleaner & antibacterial spray. All of these ads were in full color, and three of them were full-page. Such marketing and advertising campaigns were aired on television, too, especially in spring, when large amounts of cleaning occur, and summer, when heat and outdoor activities make people more susceptible to certain bacteria.

In 1999 consumers were not completely satisfied that antibacterial products were effective, and some authorities even suggested that the frequent use of them might create a problem. In the October 1998 issue of the *Tufts University Health & Nutrition Letter,* an article entitled, "Antibacterial Overkill" addressed that issue. In an attempt to ensure themselves against the harmful effects of bacteria, the consumer has been willing to pay more, believing that the antibacterial product is worth the cost for the protection it gives. According to a growing number of medical researchers, says the article, "Using a special antibacterial cleanser when ordinary soap will do the job just as well (and it will) is a form of overkill that can backfire. It can lead to the development of bacteria that will be able to withstand the action of antibacterial agents should they ever really be needed." Similarly, there was growing concern at the end of the twentieth century that antibiotics had been over-prescribed, over-used, and, therefore, increasingly less effective. The article also states that "It's the same with antibacterial compounds used in common household cleaners, researchers say. The more they're used, the more the bacteria that they are supposed to destroy— E. Coli, Salmonella, and other germs that make their way into food—will undergo mutations that only serve to strengthen them by allowing them to 'resist' the antibacterial attacks. The upshot: the germs will thrive on kitchen counters, floors, sinks, dishes, and hands, and more people could potentially be sickened by bacteria contaminated food. Furthermore, the antibacterial compounds that originally could have killed the germs won't be effective anymore in situations where they would truly be called for, say, when someone comes home from the hospital and may still be particularly vulnerable to infection." The real problem, researchers determined, is with triclosan, the major ingredient in antibacterial cleansing agents, soaps, and lotions.

Stuart B. Levy, M.D., director of the Center for Adaptation Genetics and Drug Resistance at the Tufts University School of Medicine, discovered some interesting results in his research of the antibacterial agent triclosan. It was initially believed, reported the university's publication, that triclosan worked simply by "punching holes" in the bacterial membranes, but when Levy published his results in Nature, he reported that his research group determined that the agent destroys E. Coli by simply killing a single gene. If that gene underwent a mutation, the E. Coli bacteria would be able to fight off the force of the triclosan and continue to live and grow. More importantly, the gene similar to the one that mutated in the experiment at Tufts was found in a strain of bacteria that caused tuberculosis. Levy and others noted that such a condition had not yet been observed outside of a laboratory environment. Still, Levy warned that before all of the evidence was examined over a long period, caution should be used. Antibacterial products are sometimes necessary, but not always. He also noted that while bleach and chlorine-containing products are not labeled as antibacterial products, they were still effective in wiping out entire bacteria colonies.

According to Deborah Franklin in an article for *Health,* in the spring of 1998, there were some bene-

fits to some of the antibacterial products and cleansers. In an incident she cited, Franklin reported that "Antibacterial skin cleansers generally contain chemicals that in high concentrations are known to kill bacteria. The lower concentrations found in the new products slow bacterial growth, enough that it sometimes makes a dent in disease transmission. In a hospital nursery several years ago, for example, Staphylococcus aureus sickened 22 newborns over the course of seven weeks, despite control measures. The problem was squelched only after the staff started using antibacterial hand soap—of the same strength as versions found in the supermarket—to wash their hands and bathe their babies." Marsha Koopman, a nurse epidemiologist at UCDavis Medical Center, explained in the university health publication that washing hands remained the best protection against bacteria, at least in the average situation. "It's not just the soap that accomplished this, it's also the friction caused by rubbing your hands together and rinsing them with water," Koopman said.

In the late 1990s, the U.S. Environmental Protection Agency (EPA) publicly reprimanded the toymaker Hasbro and a number of their manufacturers for leading the consumer to believe that a germicide embedded into their plastic products would fight the spread of disease-producing germs. Franklin quoted Brenda Mosley, a microbiologist at the EPA, in her article as saying, "If that evidence exists, we haven't see it." One plastic distributor, Neste Polyester, entered into a licensing agreement with Microban Products Company that was intended to put antibacterial, anti-mold, and anti-mildew protection into polyester gelcoat applications used for surfacing reinforced plastics products in everything from bathroom fixtures to boats. The Microban antibacterial protection was listed on *The Plastic Distributor & Fabricator Magazine* Web site as ". . . a proprietary technology that inhibits the growth of a broad range of bacteria, mold, mildew, and fungus in polymeric products. The protection works by neutralizing the ability of organisms to function or reproduce. Unlike surface coating, the antibacterial protection is incorporated directly into the polymer's molecular structure."

INDUSTRY LEADERS

Some of the major manufacturers of antibacterial products for personal and household use include Procter & Gamble, Johnson & Johnson, Reckitt & Coleman, Dial, and Clorox. Procter & Gamble is one of the biggest consumer goods companies in the world. They manufacture more than 300 brands, including

Bounty, Cheer, Dawn, Pampers, Safeguard, and Tide. In 1998 the company employed more than 110,000 people worldwide and had sales of $37.2 billion.

Johnson & Johnson is a diversified health care products manufacturer with such brands as Tylenol, Band-Aid, and Reach. In 1998 Johnson employed 93,100 people and had sales of $23.6 billion.

Reckitt & Coleman (manufacturer of Lysol, Woolite, and Airwick) had 15,900 employees and sales of $3.7 billion in 1998. The Dial Corporation (maker of Dial, Purex, and Renuzit) had 3,759 employees and sales of $41.5 billion in 1998. The Clorox Corporation (manufacturer of Clorox bleach, Pine-Sol, and Soft Scrub) had 6,600 employees and sales of $2.7 billion in 1998.

WORK FORCE

Decades of research go into producing antibacterial products, requiring a continued supply of medical personnel, including physicians, researchers, nurses, and technologists. Opportunities also exist in factories that are regulated under FDA standards and practices.

AMERICA AND THE WORLD

While the market for antibacterial products is ripe in a germ-conscious culture like America, other countries do not necessarily share in the zeal. As reported by Lynn Payer in *Medicine and Culture,* the French medical establishment has suggested that germs are healthy for people. Some diseases, they argue, such as Hepatitis A, when contracted in childhood through a natural sort of vaccination, are much milder and protect from further dangers in adulthood. American doctors tend to disagree with this medical philosophy, although they do acknowledge that antibacterial artillery might not be as beneficial and that some exposure to bacteria and germs provide a defense rather than an attack.

Drugstores in the United States, often selling many of these antibacterial products, continue to thrive. The boom at the very end of the twentieth century for antibacterial products shows no immediate signs of subsiding. It is an area, however, that calls for close attention. With continuing research on any possible negative effects of such products by medical researchers, scientists, and the FDA, a turn in another direction might possibly affect production and sales.

FURTHER READING

"Antibacteria." *Diddi & Gori's Answers,* 29 April 1999. Available from http://diddigori.it.

"Antibacterial Overkill." *Tufts University Health & Nutrition Letter,* October 1998.

"Antibacterial Protection for Gelcoats." *The Plastics Distributor & Fabricator Magazine,* 29 April 1999. Available from http://pdfm@plasticsmag.com.

"Blacklock Medical Products Ltd.," 29 April 1999. Available from http://www.blacklock.com.

Fayerman, Pamela. "Skin Glue Replaces Stitches for Injured Kids." *The Vancouver Sun,* 21 May 1997.

Franklin, Deborah. "Gel Crazy." *Health,* May/June 1998.

Gottfried, Ted. "Famous Scots: Sir Alexander Fleming," 2 May 1999. Available from http://scotsmart.com.

"History of the Microscope," 29 April 1999. Available from http://www.as-microscope.on.ca/history/history.html.

Monmaney, Terence, and Shari Roan. "Alternative Medicine: The 18 Billion Dollar Experiment." *Los Angeles Times,* 30 August 1998.

United States Food and Drug Administration. "Guideline No. 18 Human Health Safety Criteria," 26 April 1999. Available from http://www.fda.gov.

United States Food and Drug Administration. "Office of Cosmetics Fact Sheet," 3 February 1995. Available from http://www.fda.gov/CFSAN.

—Jane E. Spear

Artificial Intelligence

The artificial intelligence industry has progressed from its once exclusive tenure in academia to a burgeoning multi-billion dollar industry in the late 1990s. With the speed and density of computer chips doubling every two years, artificial intelligence (AI) now rapidly drives most of the software and hardware advances enjoyed by the computer industry. For example, major software producers such as Microsoft Corp, Corel Corp., and Adobe Systems Inc. rely on artificial intelligence tools to make products more functional and user friendly. In 1997, IBM Corp.'s computer, Deep Blue, successfully defeated World Chess Champion Garry Kasparov, thus advancing an exciting new era of artificial intelligence having the capability to imitate human logical thought sequences and processes in a way similar to the activity of brain neurons. In the field of medicine, Multicase, Inc., in conjunction with the University of Pittsburgh, worked on the development of software "virtual animals" loaded with databases on chemical compound toxicity, to improve the odds of successful human trials on new medicines and reduce the need for real animals in pharmaceutical research. The Food and Drug Administration (FDA), which is compiling the toxicity databases, is working with Multicase, Inc. to get the software on the market by the year 2000. Also in the field of medicine, a 1997 comparative study pitted an experienced cardiologist against AI software to read dozens of electrocardiograms (EKGs) and detect and diagnose heart attacks; the computer was correct more often. While it was acknowledged that the computer software was dependent upon human input for the databases used in its conclusions, nonetheless, software developers are confident that ultimately, AI will represent a compilation of the best of the best in human minds and intelligence, thus eliminating inconsistencies inherent with individual human input and analysis.

Large and small companies alike have turned to AI as a means of increasing efficiency and productivity. Large businesses used AI for such programs as training and monitoring applications, while small businesses have taken advantage of labor-saving AI technologies that allow them to keep up with competitors without employing a large staff.

It is clear that one of the most exciting factors in the burst of emerging AI industries in the late 1990s was the development of software that could mimic human logic and reasoning. Researchers at the Massachusetts Institute of Technology (MIT) predicted that the next big breakthrough in AI at the turn of the century would be the imputation of "emotional capacity" as well as logical capacity in the development of AI software designed to mimic human behavior. Another breakthrough during the late 1990s paralleled human genetic and reproductive research. In Switzerland and elsewhere, researchers were developing a self-replicating and self-repairing version of a specialized computer, a successful step toward the development of a self-replicating universal machine.

The artificial intelligence industry has several primary areas of focus: research and development (including expert systems), natural language processing, artificial vision, robotics, training, cognitive model-

Deep Blue's two tower RS/6000 system. *(Courtesy of IBM.)*

ing, knowledge representation and use, and knowledge acquisition. Expert systems are intelligent computer programs that use knowledge and inference to solve problems normally requiring human expertise. Natural language processing is concerned with creating programs that can function with natural language commands and programs that can understand strings of natural language prose without the aid of special made-for-computer languages. Natural language advances using AI resulted in noticeable changes in computer interfaces. Speech recognition technology also figures into this domain of artificial intelligence. Artificial vision systems were integrated into manufacturing systems and robotics, performing tasks such as machine and product inspection, recognition, and guidance. Other applications of this technology included image interpretation as used for military and cartographic purposes. Artificial vision relies on a computer program for analyzing digitized images.

A significant commercial application of AI technology has been Computer Aided Instruction (CAI), which permits a computer to take on the role of educator by interacting with students and providing answers and instruction. Robotics research strives to create mechanical intelligent agents to perform a variety of industrial tasks. Robotics (as well as other sub-

fields of AI) incorporates other areas of AI technology such as language processing and artificial vision. Cognitive modeling, neural networks, knowledge representation, and knowledge acquisition are theoretical AI pursuits that underlie and give rise to the commercial and industrial AI products. These fields seek to develop practical models of how humans gain, store, and use knowledge and thereby create more effectual and precise AI technology.

Software logic known as "fuzzy logic" has also been instrumental in the development of intelligent software that can process patchy or unclear data. In contrast to binary or Boolean logic that only recognizes expressions of truth or falsity, fuzzy logic permits the expressions of partial truth such as: "sort of true," "maybe false," or "okay." This kind of flexibility lets the fuzzy logic software replicate the way the human mind processes real-world, real-time information.

A key association in this industry is the American Association of Artificial Intelligence (AAAI), which promotes continuing research in the industry. Founded in 1979, AAAI hosts conferences and symposia covering all aspects of artificial intelligence and provides technical and general publications. AAAI strives to advance the scientific understanding of thought and intelligent behavior and its realization in AI technology.

BACKGROUND AND DEVELOPMENT

THE EARLY YEARS

It is difficult to say when the science of artificial intelligence began, since that depends in part on the definition of AI. The story of artificial intelligence as it is known in the late 1990s and is used within industries follows the development of computers and software. However, Daniel Crevier, author of *AI,* notes that mechanical calculating devices and crude automata antedate computers by over two to three centuries, tracing back to early pioneers such as Leonardo Da Vinci (painter, architect, and inventor 1452-1519), Blaise Pascal (mathematician and philosopher 1623-1662), and Gottfried Wilhelm Leibniz (philosopher and mathematician 1644-1716). Early stabs at quasi-computer artificial intelligence came from inventors such as Herman Hollerith in 1890, with his tabulating machine used by the U.S. government for processing census data. The machine operated on a punch-card method. This invention led to a kind of calculator with cogged wheels representing numbers. Hollerith called these "digital calculators," for a wheel with 10 positions could represent the digits 0 to 9. Hollerith's company, Tabulating Machines Company, later merged with International Business Machines (IBM).

A major breakthrough in artificial intelligence research and technology came around the time of World War II. Three separate projects in three different countries—the United States, Germany, and England—yielded the first transistor and vacuum tube computers. Crevier points out that unlike its gear-and-cog and electromechanical predecessors, these computing devices contained no moving parts and, hence, could operate substantially faster than the previous calculators, computing 20,000 multiplication problems per minute. The U.S. military first used the machine, electronic numerical integrator and calculator (ENIAC), for figuring artillery tables during the war. The drawback to this device was its size: with 18,000 vacuum tubes, it weighed 30 tons and took up about the space of a gymnasium. In addition, to put the machine to post-war use, engineers could only "reprogram" ENIAC by rewiring hundreds of different connections, which highlighted another crucially inefficient aspect of the machine, according to Crevier in *AI*.

In response to this problem, John von Neumann proposed to store both the computer's instructions and the data it manipulated in the same circuitry, coining the term *memory* to refer to this information storage chamber. Hence, the memory has two parts: one for instructions and one for malleable data. The von Neumann computer operated by first retrieving the instructions or commands, and then by retrieving the data needed for any given operation. This conception still lives on in most post-World War II computers.

THE FIELD OF ARTIFICIAL INTELLIGENCE EMERGES

The post-World War II era and climate also launched AI into a field of its own, independent from—though connected with—computer development. Key scholars in the field included Marvin Minsky, John McCarthy, Allan Newell, and Herbert Simon. Minsky contributed to AI development by exploring brain simulation, and he pioneered the study of neural networks. This kind of research sought to construct artificial intelligent agents or machines by modeling them after brains and neurological networks. In 1951, using a grant from the Office of Naval Research, Minsky and his collaborator Dean Emmonds created a neural net machine out of 300 vacuum tubes and the automatic pilot system from a B-24 bomber, which they named Snarc. This machine simulated the

John McCarthy, a key scholar in artificial intelligence.
(The Library of Congress.)

brain of a rat learning its way through a maze. But Minsky discovered that to push this kind of artificial intelligence further would require an exponentially greater number of tubes and accouterments to replicate the millions of neurons he thought composed the human brain.

McCarthy pursued development of intelligent agents in the other direction. His work at IBM in 1955 inspired him to rely on computers as the medium for creating AI systems, rather than the replication of neural networks. McCarthy also organized a summer workshop on artificial intelligence in 1956 at Dartmouth College, which led to the formation of artificial intelligence as an academic discipline. In 1958, McCarthy created the programming language Lisp, which remains one of the key AI languages. In same year, he also conceived the first general AI program that could solve general problems, instead of being limited to only math problems.

In 1955, Newell and Simon worked on what has been labeled the first AI program: Logic Theorist. This program proved geometry theorems using a " search tree" system where the search was represented in a branching manner that extended from the starting point, or the root node. The proof branched out from

---

Pioneer MARVIN MINSKY,
1927-
DESIGNING A MIND

Marvin Lee Minsky, an educator and computer scholar at Massachusetts Institute of Technology, has devoted his life's work to defining and explaining the thinking process, and making a machine that can duplicate that process.

Minsky was born in 1927, and has been near the scientific field almost his whole life. His father was a surgeon who encouraged his son's interest in science by sending him to private schools where his intellect could be nurtured. And, aside from a brief stint in the Navy for a year, Minsky has been in the academic world ever since.

Always fascinated in a variety of subjects, Minsky studied several fields while a student at Harvard University. He majored in physics, but also studied genetics, mathematics, psychology, and the nature of intelligence. He finally graduated with a degree in mathematics, and immediately began working on his doctoral studies at Princeton, trying to develop a learning machine.

This machine was called the Snarc, which learned how to navigate a maze by a system of reward success and was thus enabled to eventually learn to anticipate outcome, based on past experiences. The Snarc was never sophisticated enough to give Minsky any satisfactory progress. He based his doctoral thesis on his reward concept, and came under fire from critics who argued whether his line of thinking belonged in the world of mathematics. After joining the staff at MIT in 1958, he immediately founded the MIT Artificial Intelligence project with his colleague John McCarthy.

Minsky alienated or angered many of his colleagues with his theories of the human mind. According to Minsky, the mind was merely a collection of semi-autonomous but unintelligent computers that work together cooperatively and unconsciously, and are often mistaken for intelligence. Minsky defended his views against psychological and biological critics by arguing that their research merely failed to "ask the right questions."

Minsky wrote two books, one a detailed explanation of his theories, and the other a science fiction novel based, again, on his theories of the properties of the mind. He has also been published numerously in periodicals such as *Omni* and *Discover*, and received the prestigious Japan award in 1990.

---

the starting point and Logic Theorist used rules of thumb to locate the path most likely to lead to the proof. This project also led to the creation of a new programming language information processing language (IPL), which, unlike its contemporaries, permitted later expansion and the interconnectivity of thoughts (i.e., the activation of one piece of knowledge could also activate an associated piece, as with the human mind). Later on, they developed general problem solver (GPS), which imitated human approaches to problem-solving in the way it considered and pursued subgoals and possible actions.

With the success of these projects, rampant optimism pervaded AI research and discussion. Simon and others began to predict that they would develop infinitely complex machines within a few years and produce computers that could defeat champion chess players. They also attempted to create programs that could communicate and translate. However, these projects never bore the fruits that the developers prophesied.

ARTIFICIAL INTELLIGENCE MATURES

Throughout the 1960s and 1970s, artificial intelligence researchers realized that they had not solved all the problems associated with creating intelligent agents. In addition, artificial intelligence research began to shift away from its narrow focus on math computation, bringing many real-world problems into its purview. When programs failed to accurately translate Russian to English, the U.S. government rescinded its financial support of AI translation projects. This caused researchers in this area to reconsider their assumptions about natural language in order to devise more precise programs. In 1969 researchers experimented with *expert systems*, programs that specialize in different areas of human expertise. A Stanford researcher and student of Herbert Simon's, Ed Feigenbaum, collaborated with philosopher Bruce Buchanan and Nobel laureate geneticist Joshua Lederberg to create DRENDEL, a sophisticated problem-solving program that had theoretical knowledge as well as special rules for solving the problems programmed into it.

Stemming from this endeavor, Feigenbaum and Buchanan teamed up with Dr. Edward Shortliffe to create a medical expert system, MYCIN. MYCIN contained about 450 rules for diagnosing blood infections and could compete with medical experts and outperform junior physicians, according to Russell and Norvig in *Artificial Intelligence.* The technological milestone achieved by MYCIN was its ability to factor in uncertainty. The developers created MYCIN based on interviews with medical experts and formulated it to carry out reasoning processes in the manner of these experts. Many other such applications of artificial intelligence soon followed.

Another key advance of this era, though only slowly picked up by the industry, was the notion of fuzzy logic. With antecedents in the theories of philosophers Bertrand Russell and Jan Lukasiewiez, the idea actually goes back to the 1920s. However, in 1965 the University of California, Berkeley professor Lotfi Zadeh officially brought the notion to bear on contemporary scientific endeavors. He designed a logic system that mirrored the kinds of judgments the human mind makes: "sort of true," "may be false," or "okay," according to Mohsen Attaran in *Journal of Systems Management.* This logic could recognize these natural linguistic expression, whereas Boolean logic could not. As an electrical engineer, Zadeh applied fuzzy logic, for example, to control thermostats where three rules were possible based not on simple truth or falsity but rather on notions such as "sort of," "about," and so forth.

AN INDUSTRY EMERGES

Russell and Norvig argue in *Artificial Intelligence* that the AI industry did not fully emerge until about 1980. Prior to this time, most research took place at universities such as MIT, Stanford, and Carnegie-Mellon, although a few companies such as IBM and RAND also contributed heavily to AI development. Few commercial products were generated, but companies slowly began turning to this new technology. Digital Equipment Communication (DEC) used the first commercial expert system, R1, to keep track of computer system orders. By 1986, the company reported saving some $40 million since the implementation of R1. As of 1988, DEC had 40 expert systems in operation, according to Russell and Norvig. Other companies began to catch on. DuPont Inc. operated 100 expert systems during this period and had 500 more in development. Russell and Norvig contend that almost every key U.S. corporation maintained its own AI staff and used or intended to implement AI technology. Many companies got in on the development of AI applications. Companies like Carnegie Group, Inference, and Teknowledge began creating software tools to facilitate expert system design, while others like Lisp Machines, Inc., Texas Instruments, and Xerox started to build workstations for developing Lisp programs, according to Russell and Norvig. By 1988, the industry soared from earning only a couple million in 1980 to taking in $2 billion.

CURRENT CONDITIONS

In the late 1990s, many branches of artificial intelligence research, development, and application had individual triumphs and disappointments as researchers, developers, and marketers attempted to push the technology even further. The marketable and practical output that emerged from previous decades of research was predominantly a set of AI tools and techniques for performing specific tasks—not a single multifaceted AI unit, capable of performing a variety of tasks and even replacing human beings in the workplace with its diversified proficiencies, as some prophesied. Nonetheless, artificial intelligence has played an understated role in the success of the computer and software industries.

GAMES

For the gaming sector of AI, Herbert Simon's prediction came closer to fruition: the performance of IBM's computer chess agent Deep Blue reverberated through the industry, highlighting the unprecedented ability of a computerized chess player. Deep Blue took on chess champion Garry Kasparov in 1997 and proved to be an outstanding opponent by defeating Kasparov in May. Kasparov commented that his overall strategy has been to make moves that vary slightly from conventional ones so that Deep Blue would not be able to compare the moves with previous patterns and make an informed move in response. This strategy underscores an ongoing problem with computerized chess games: they decide on moves based largely on preprogrammed patterns and moves. However, Deep Blue can calculate over six moves in advance, which made it a challenging opponent for Kasparov. Deep Blue, a 32-node IBM computer with 30 Power Two Super Chip processors, can evaluate about 200 million chess positions each second, whereas Kasparov can consider only three positions at a time. In 1998, the AI gaming challenge continued, as competitors at the World Bridge Championship went up against a PC running bridge-playing software designed by Matthew Ginsberg, a University of Oregon mathematician and AI expert.

NEURAL NETWORKS

Neural network technology, though abandoned at times throughout the development of AI technology, has become an important industrial innovation. Neural networks allow software developers to overcome program-creation obstacles because they learn by exposure to examples so that developers need not ponder every possible scenario. Instead, the neural networks

IBM's Deep Blue Development Team. *(Courtesy of IBM.)*

function in a similar manner as the human brain: they match input to past experiences. Current uses of neural networks include detecting credit card fraud, controlling blast furnaces at Nippon Steel in Japan, forecasting events, and marketing products.

Peter Coffee explains in *PC Week* that unlike procedural based software—software designed using languages such as COBOL, C++, or Java—neural networks do not rely on preprogrammed recipes or algorithms. Instead, they learn from past experiences, considering information in this way: if A occurs, then B should result. Consequently, they can perform tasks more precisely than traditional software. In late 1998, a neural network technology chip developed by NASA's Jet Propulsion Laboratory was adapted by the Ford Motor Co. to diagnose misfiring under the hoods of Ford vehicles; this chip, based on the human mind, was expected to help reduce automobile emission levels.

Neural networks have also aided traditional areas of commerce such as mail-order companies. Neural network technology provided an alternative classification system to ones where customers were pigeonholed in terms of last date of purchase, average amount of money spent per purchase, and frequency

of purchases, according to Sarah Schafer in *Inc.* Neural networks also allowed companies to bypass expenses incurred for employing statisticians to track customers. Instead, neural networks identified the spending habits and interests of customers so that mail-order companies could tailor their catalog campaigns to these different categories of consumers. The advent of neural net use sprouted a host of neural network consultancies to help companies get their software up and running.

FUZZY LOGIC

Besides neural nets, fuzzy logic technology has become a major commercial class of artificial intelligence technology. Mohsen Attaran reported in *Journal of Systems Management* that developers of consumer products, computer systems, software, and support systems have started to integrate fuzzy logic into products. In addition, leading companies such as Ford, United Technologies, General Electric, and Honeywell have invested in the development of their own fuzzy logic programs for use in products and industrial control systems. Furthermore, computer chip makers such as Intel and Motorola rely on fuzzy micro-controllers.

IBM'S DEEP BLUE DEVELOPMENT TEAM

Who are the scientists and researchers behind the marvel chess-playing computer called Deep Blue that beat Garry Kasparov for the best of six matches in 1997? IBM Corporation announced that the six-man development team includes one former U.S. chess champion-turned-computer-scientist, an International Chess Grand Master, a software engineer, a project support engineer, a senior department manager, and the man who developed the prototype computer as a graduate student at Carnegie Mellon University, Feng Hsiung Hsu. Team headquarters are located at the Thomas J. Watson Research Center in Yorktown Heights, New York

Feng Hsiung Hsu developed a rudimentary chess-playing computer, called Chiptest, as a graduate student at Carnegie Mellon University in the mid-1980s. His machine achieved grand master competency and won the Hsu the Fredkin Intermediate Prize in 1988. He received a Ph.D. in Computer Science from the university in 1989 and joined the IBM Deep Blue Development Team that same year. Hsu's computer was the prototype for the original IBM Deep Blue, a machine that failed to defeat Kasparov in 1996. A second-generation machine (an IBM RS/6000), nicknamed "Deeper Blue," ultimately bested the human chess champion in 1997.

Joel Benjamin of New York City is a Yale Graduate and an International Master of Chess. He earned a U.S. Master title at age 13 and was the U.S. Champion in 1987. He was the first recipient of the Samford Chess Fellowship, a 3-time U.S. Junior Champion, a member

of five U.S. Olympic Chess Teams, and a World Team Championship Gold Medalist in 1993. Additionally Benjamin was a defending champion of the Harvard Cup, a competition between Grandmasters and computers. He once met Kasparov in a regulation match in 1994 that ended in a draw.

Murray Campbell, a high school chess player and former chess champion, earned a Ph.D. in Computer Science from Carnegie Mellon University in 1987. Campbell and Hsu met as doctoral candidates, and the two collaborated on Hsu's Chiptest computer project in 1986.

Software engineer, A. Joseph Hoane, Jr., holds an undergraduate degree from the University of Illinois in Urbana and an M.S. in Computer Science from New York's Columbia University. He went to work for IBM and was assigned to the Deep Blue Project Team in 1990.

Jerry Brody, an IBM Researcher since 1978, joined the Deep Blue Project as a support engineer in 1990. Brody's responsibilities included design, inspection, and de-bugging the system.

Chung-Jen Tan has headed the Deep Blue Project since 1992 as project supervisor and spokesperson. He is the senior manager of the Parallel System Platforms Department at IBM and spokesman for the development team. Tan, a member of the Watson research staff since 1969 earned a BSEE from Seattle University and a Ph.D. in Engineering Science from Columbia University in 1969.

OTHER APPLICATIONS

Artificial intelligence also began to refine Internet searching and promises to make the somewhat bewildering and circuitous task much faster and more precise. For example, EchoSearch, an Internet searching tool that scan several traditional search engines, used AI technology to scan texts and locate concepts and meanings, instead of simply detecting search words as traditional search engines do; such products then summarize their findings. These search engines imbued with recent AI technology are installed in computer hard drives. Businesses snapped up AI technology fairly quickly in order to market products to Internet users once the World Wide Web craze began. With the nebulous and perhaps insidious name "cookies," companies monitored the activities and data characteristics of Web site visitors by placing a device on a visitor's hard drive that reports such information. In mid-1998, Neural Applications Corp. released Optimatch, a plug-in for Microsoft's Site Server that applied neural learning, built-in fuzzy logic and advanced statistical analysis to learn the habits of Net

surfers, make neural predictions about their potential Web page visits, and match them with Web content. Aegis, its core technology, employed neural networks, fuzzy logic, genetic algorithms and standard AI technologies.

Furthermore, according to Paul Munger in *Training & Development,* companies invested in artificial intelligence technology for training employees. This method of training allows the knowledge of a company's expert to be conveyed to a company's novice with AI-based training programs. Munger also states that paper mills, for example, implemented such technology so that pulp-press operators could control cost tracking and decision making as needed under the auspices of an AI tutoring program, instead of depending on middle management to make such decision. The switch to AI technology provided the companies with substantial savings.

AI technology also found its way into graphic design software and hardware. For example, scanners used to contain an assortment of knobs and buttons for adjusting the quality of a scan-job, but many companies have let artificially intelligent sensors make the adjustments. Printing and graphic design products also became increasingly automated by artificial intelligence.

However, the industry faced a series of challenges and hindrances. AI technology advanced faster than it could be implemented. Often, by the time a company adopted an AI-based product and adapted to it, a new version arose, fostering an atmosphere of trepidation for purchasing and implementing new technology that only promised a short life. In addition, Jon Kaye of *Computer Weekly* contended that only a few companies took the initial development and marketing risks for new AI products, but, after the risks dissipate, other companies quickly flooded the market with similar products. Furthermore, Kaye argued that companies confronted budgetary conflicts when it came to investing in new technology. They were under pressure to allocate funds for Web sites and data storage archives rather than AI. Companies burned in the past by succumbing to exaggerated claims by AI developers and marketers have also been reluctant to venture into newer artificial intelligence products. Products once lauded as able to perform the tasks of humans failed to live up to lofty expectations, especially for decision-making tasks. Thus, analysts suggested that AI developers and marketers needed to define the niche of AI technology more narrowly, as much of the expert system and neural network products have done.

INDUSTRY LEADERS

Based in Armonk, New York, IBM played a key role in artificial intelligence development from the outset by persistent work in creating computers. Although known largely for its computer systems and software, the company created machines that allowed AI to prosper. IBM also subsidized some of the earliest AI research. IBM created the AI chess agent Deep Blue that has outperformed all other AI chess players to date. In the late 1990s, IBM continued to work toward revamping its image with an emphasis on Internet business. In 1998, Louis V. Gerstner Jr. headed the company as its CEO and IBM reported $81.7 billion in revenues for all its concerns. The company employed 291,067 workers in 1998.

Xerox Corporation, commonly known only for its end product—copiers—contributed to the artificial intelligence industry and continues to integrate AI into its document-related products. In addition, Xerox has

developed artificial intelligence workstations to promote further research in this field. G. Richard Thoman led the Stamford, Connecticut-based company, which posted $19.45 billion in 1998 sales for all its operations. Xerox maintained a staff of 92,700 employees in 1999.

Brightware developed AI products such as BrightResponse and BrightAdvisor, which received the accolades of business and technology periodicals. Brightware has also received numerous awards from the American Association of Artificial Intelligence. Chuck Williams, who leads the company as president and CEO, also founded another AI company, Inference, from which Brightware spun off in 1995.

Lucent Technologies, the spin-off company of AT&T's Bell Laboratories, has worked extensively in various branches of artificial intelligence, including multilingual text-to-speech software, voice processing systems, and security systems. Lucent earned $30.1 billion in 1998 and employed 141,600 workers. Richard A. McGinn served as the company's CEO.

Other key AI companies include Mountain View, California-based IntelliCorp, specializing in object-oriented environments; Novato, California-based Inference providing knowledge management solutions; Oakbrook Terrace, Illinois-based Platinum Technology, Inc., maker of expert systems; and Cambridge, Massachusetts-based Ascent Technology, Inc., offering resource planning, assessment, and control solutions.

AMERICA AND THE WORLD

Though the United States led much of the AI development and research, other major industrial countries also played instrumental roles in the conception and advancement of artificial intelligence and promise to carry the industry further in the coming decades. Countries such as Japan, Germany, and the United Kingdom developed AI technologies on their own. They have collaborated with each other and with the United States.

The German Research Institute for Artificial Intelligence has pioneered a new area of natural-language AI: speech-to-speech translation backed by the German government. Though text-to-speech and voice-recognition technology was being explored for awhile, this project marks one of the first in this field. Designed to translate English to German and vice versa, Verbmobil was slow to translate a simple utterance such as "I am going to the dentist." As world trade and collaboration expands, the need for these translators increases. Verbmobil was one of several translation systems studied by the European Commission research project, DISC, which is meant to establish the first industry standards for speech recognition-based user interfaces. Victor Zue of MIT's Laboratory of Computer Science has predicted that such translators will not achieve true functionality until after the turn of the century.

The United States has lagged behind Japan as far as the development of fuzzy logic technology is concerned, though analysts predict that U.S. production should increase, making fuzzy logic a sizable market force. Japanese companies have integrated fuzzy logic into air conditioners, camcorders, vacuum cleaners, rice cookers, and shower systems. Computer companies have also used fuzzy logic controllers extensively. Japan has been the worldwide industry leader and is predicted to remain a key competitor in fuzzy logic technology.

RESEARCH AND TECHNOLOGY

Microsoft chairman and CEO Bill Gates identified his vision of a new kind of software-user interface in which the software adapts to the user—not the other way around. Gates forecasted that such software would lead the next technology revolution, using natural-language-processing technology to search the Internet and retrieve information all without opening separate programs. He predicted that speech interaction (talking) computers would constitute the next major industry breakthrough. While there would be limited applications like dictation and telephone interfacing, some analysts and researchers expressed concern for the slower processing time for speech interaction than for example, visual displays.

Long awaited and much desired research into the development and refinement of automobiles driven by AI technology has continued. Experimental AI systems have been created that control all aspects of driving—steering, accelerating, braking, etc.—via input from video cameras, sonar, and laser sensors. The system uses the data to give the appropriate commands to the robotic machinery that controls the mechanical aspects of driving. These kinds of systems use sensory data in conjunction with knowledge learned from practice drives.

AI applications do not escape all criticism. Ben Shneiderman, who heads the Human-Computer Inter-

action Laboratory at the University of Maryland at College Park, told *Forbes* interviewers in 1998 that the direction of AI was more amusing and entertaining than useful for the future. He called on the industry to develop more simple computers and software, particularly search engines that would bring to the user specific on-line communities of information. Shneiderman disagreed with Bill Gates as to where the direction of AI should go. He believed that we do not need computers to mimic us, but rather, to serve our needs, e.g., to find information for us and help us communicate it faster. He also predicted that the Web computers of the future would be thin (less than an inch) and have wireless connections to the Web.

Some continue to defend anthropoid aims, foreseeing as fact what science fiction only dreams. As of mid-1998, the Artificial Intelligence Lab at the Massachusetts Institute of Technology had already developed a humanoid robot, designed "to follow the same sorts of developmental paths that humans follow, building new skills upon earlier competencies." Inventor Ray Kurzweil—the man who pioneered the development of machines that recognize voices, read text and turn it into speech—predicts that a $1,000 computer will match the 20-million-billion calculations per second of the human brain by 2019, followed in 2029 by a personal computer equal to 1,000 brains. He told the Christian Science Monitor in 1999 that the construction of artificial humans is inevitable and could occur before the 22nd century. Once the neurological correlates of human thought are understood, he suggested, even spiritual experiences can be replicated. "Twenty-first-century machines - based on the design of human thinking - will do as their human progenitors have done - going to real and virtual houses of worship, meditating, praying, and transcending - to connect with their spiritual dimension."

FURTHER READING

Ascarelli, Silvia. "Goodbye Gutenberg: Germans Tap System To Translate Speech." *The Wall Street Journal*, 20 November 1995, 10.

Attaran, Mohsen. "The Coming Age of Fuzzy Logic in Manufacturing and Services." *Journal of Systems Management*, March-April 1996, 4.

Clark, Don. "Technology: Gates, in Speech, To Outline Strategy for PC Programs That Adapt To Users." *The Wall Street Journal*, 14 November 1995, 12.

Coffee, Peter. "Beyond Programming." *PC Week*, 10 March 1997, 64.

Crevier, Daniel. *AI: The Tumultuous History of the Search for Artificial Intelligence.* New York: BasicBooks, 1993.

Dawson, Jim. "Scientists Take Baby Steps with Humanoid Robot," *Minneapolis Star Tribune,* 20 May 1998, pp. 20A.

Epstein, Jeffrey H. "Technology: Computers with Emotions." *The Futurist,* April 1998.

Gelernter, David. "How Hard Is Chess?" *Time,* 19 May 1997, 72.

Hogan, James P. *Mind Matters: Exploring the World of Artificial Intelligence,* Del Ray, 1997.

Industry Group '99. "JPL Neural Network Chip Paves the Way to a Cleaner America as Ford Signs Licensing Agreement." *Regulatory Intelligence Data,* 10 September 1998.

International Business Machines Corporation. *Hoover's Company Capsules.* Hoover's, Inc.: 1 April 1999.

Johnson, R. Colin. "Neural Applications Tackles Site-presentation—Tools Rotate Web Content." *Electronic Engineering Times,* 18 May 1998, pp. 42.

Journal of Artificial Intelligence Research. Available from http://www.cs.washington.edu/research/jair/home.html

Kaye, Jon. "Systems Fail IQ Test." *Computer Weekly,* 23 January 1997, 36.

Knapschaefer, Johanna. "A Good Day for Lab Rats." *Business Week,* 23 March 1998.

Kurzweil, Ray."Essays on the Millennium/2000: WHEN MACHINES THINK: Computers and humans may be indistinguishable by the end of the next century." *Maclean's,* 1 Mar 1999, 54.

Lucent Technologies Inc. *Hoover's Company Capsules.* Hoover's, Inc.: 1 April 1999.

McCall, William. "Bridge players will compete against a computer at tourney in France." *AP Online,* 19 Aug 1998.

Mitchell, Russ. "A Better Search Engine." *U.S. News & World Report,* 21 March 1998.

Munger, Paul David. "A Guide to High-Tech Training Delivery: Part 1." *Training & Development,* December 1996, 55.

Nartonis, David K. "Mapping the Pace of Artificial Intelligence," *The Christian Science Monitor,* 11 Mar 1999, pp. 17.

Russell, Stuart J. and Peter Norvig. *Artificial Intelligence: A Modern Approach.* Englewood Cliffs, New Jersey: Prentice Hall, 1995.

Schafer, Sarah. "Software That Thinks." *Inc.,* 19 November 1996, 109.

Shook, Carrie. "Banks that Chat, and Other Irrelevancies." *Forbes,* 20 April 1998.

Taubes, Gary. "After 50 Years, Self-Replicating Silicon." *Science,* 26 September 1997.

"Vocalis in EC Project to Create the First Industry Standards for Spoken Dialogue Systems," *M2 PressWIRE,* 20 Aug 1998.

Wilken, Earl. "More AI Set for Product and Systems." *Graphic Arts Monthly,* July 1996, 59.

Xerox Corporation. *Hoover's Company Capsules.* Hoover's, Inc.: 1 May 1999.

Ziegler, Bart. "The Internet: How Can I Find What I'm Looking for?" *The Wall Street Journal,* 9 December 1996, 20.

—Karl Heil, updated by Lauri Harding,
updated by Brett Allan King

ASTRONAUTICS

Humans remain determined to conquer space, the so-called "final frontier." Private and public sectors continue to fund scientific discovery and human space exploration in an effort to unlock the secrets of the universe. Critics still view manned missions as a needless waste of money and an unnecessary risk of lives to appease those who want to go higher, further, and faster. In 1999, government and business leaders held a forum to discuss short-term plans to commercialize near-range space and long-term plans to launch industrial development throughout space. Seeming to imitate science fiction, visionaries still talk of flying laboratories, space colonies, interplanetary travel, and even affordable cruises to Mars for paying space tourists.

Konstantin Tsiolkovsky, a Russian schoolteacher who cracked the theory of rocketry back in 1903, understood the universal draw of astronautics, which is defined as the science and technology of space flight. "The earth is the cradle of mankind—one cannot remain in the cradle forever."

ORGANIZATION AND STRUCTURE

As a part of the aerospace and defense industry, astronautics rides along on the cyclical ups and downs related to politics and economics. The industry experienced widespread consolidation throughout the 1990s as major defense contractors reacted to government spending cutbacks in the post Cold War era. Notable activities included the merger of Lockheed and Martin-Marietta to form the Lockheed Martin

Corporation in 1995 and the $16-billion purchase of McDonnell Douglas Corporation by the Boeing Company in 1997. Wary of the decreasing presence of competitors, the U.S. Department of Justice and the Pentagon protested the proposed purchase of Northrop Grumman Corporation by Lockheed Martin, and the deal fell through in 1998.

The rapid restructuring of the aerospace industry left four prime contractors and a host of suppliers by 1999. The four giants were: Boeing, Lockheed Martin, Raytheon Company, and Northrop Grumman. These four companies commanded 70 percent of the aerospace market in 1999, up from 20 percent just two years earlier. Strong demand for satellites, launchers, and commercial passenger planes bolstered the industry in the late 1990s, but contractors and suppliers both took hits from the ongoing economic turmoil in Asia.

BACKGROUND AND DEVELOPMENT

Written accounts date the use of gunpowder and rockets to Chinese military leaders as far back as 1045 A.D. The Mongols later used smoke screens and rocket-like weapons against Europeans in 1232 A.D. Nevertheless, it would take a few more centuries for astronautics to get off the ground. Historians credit three men whose work spanned three centuries with developing the basic theory of space flight: German physicist Johannes Kepler, who discovered in 1609 that the planets move in ellipses rather than follow a circular path; English mathematician Sir Isaac Newton, who expounded on Kepler's conclusion and published a book in 1687 that laid out the basic laws of force, motion, and gravitation; and Russian schoolteacher Konstantin Tsiolkovsky, who designed rockets on paper, determined the optimum mix of fuels for space travel, and originated the basic equations for rocketry in 1903.

THE ROCKETEERS

It took three rocket scientists to further the cause of space travel and advance rocketry principles in the early twentieth century: American university professor Robert Goddard, now called the father of modern rocketry, who designed, built and launched the world's first liquid fueled rocket in 1926; German scientist Hermann Oberth, who published a book in 1929 that persuaded the world that rockets deserved serious consideration as a space vehicle; and German engineer Wernher Von Braun, who led the development of the German V2, the first ballistic missile capable of reaching space, for the Nazis and later led the development of military and space exploration rockets for the United States.

World War II, the atomic bomb, and a changing world order fueled support for the development of more powerful rockets in the United States and the Soviet Union (now the Russian Republic and its allies) in the name of self-preservation and technological advancement. In 1957, the globally-declared International Geophysical Year (IGY), scientists worldwide pledged to pump up efforts to study the Earth's land, oceans, and atmosphere.

THE RACE TO SPACE

As part of the IGY, America announced upcoming plans to launch a multistage rocket that would put the first satellite in orbit above the Earth. The Soviet Union immediately countered with plans to launch the first satellite using a more powerful multistage rocket, a secret project that had been in the works for years. The Soviets launched *Sputnik* ("satellite" in Russian) in October 1957. One month later they fired up Sputnik 2, which carried the first mammal in space, a dog named Laika, and burned in the atmosphere in April 1958. Americans tried and failed to launch Vanguard in December 1957. The next month Americans successfully launched the Explorer 1, the first satellite to detect the Van Allen radiation belts. Also in 1958, the United States officially established the National Aeronautics and Space Administration (NASA). According to recently declassified material, one of the principle objectives of the civilian agency was "to gain stature for the nation in the general struggle with world communism."

Fueled by the Cold War, both the United States and the Soviet Union continued to launch more than a dozen space probes, spy satellites, and assorted weather and communications devices over the coming years. Humans had clearly cracked the dawning of the space age in the second half of twentieth century.

Astronautics took off in April 1961 when cosmonaut Yuri Gargarin became the first man in space. Three weeks later Alan Shepard became the first American in space. Also in 1961, U.S. President John F. Kennedy voiced America's commitment to put the first man on the moon. Many firsts followed on the way to the moon for both sides. Cosmonaut Gherman Titov made the first multiorbit flight, going around the globe 17 times in 1961. John Glenn made three orbits in 1962, and cosmonaut Valentina Tereshkova became the first woman in space in 1963. The number of orbits and missions increased—as well as the intensity of docking, rendezvous, and extravehicular activities—all in preparation of a lunar landing. Photographs, film, and video footage from Mercury, Gemini, and Apollo missions captured the attention of an eager public. Additionally, the first fatality of the space race occurred in 1967, when cosmonaut Vladimir Komarov died after his parachute failed.

WALK ON THE MOON

In July 1969 the U.S. Apollo 11 touched down on the moon. The world sat glued to its television sets as astronaut Neil Armstrong took "one small step for man" and a "giant leap for mankind." Millions of kids started drinking Tang, the beverage of astronauts.

Many astronauts followed in Armstrong's footsteps—with seemingly only a few hundred pounds of moonrocks to show for all the effort. Public interest waned. The second landing took place in November 1969. The next year Apollo 13 faced fuel cell failure and a loss of pressure in liquid oxygen in its service module, which caused NASA to abandon the third attempt to land on the moon. Further underscoring the danger of space flight, three cosmonauts died during reentry to the Earth's atmosphere after a 1971 mission. Four successful moon landings by the U.S. space program happened in 1971 and 1972.

All totaled, the Apollo space program cost about $25 billion ($95 billion 1990 dollars). Only the construction of the Panama Canal rivals the program's size as the largest U.S. civilian technological endeavor ever undertaken.

CONTINUED DISCOVERY

In the following years, the United States and the Soviet Union launched numerous space stations that conducted countless scientific tests and experiments in astronomy, biology, and medicine. A series of malfunctions plagued the early days of the Skylab space stations. Other nations also started to hop aboard U.S. and U.S.S.R. space vehicles and programs during the 1980s.

In 1981 NASA deployed the Columbia, the first reusable space shuttle, representing a ground-breaking engineering and technological feat. The United States completed 24 successful flights of the space shuttle over the next five years. The greatest disaster to the U.S. space program occurred in 1986 when the Challenger exploded 73 seconds after liftoff, killing all on board—six astronauts and schoolteacher Christa McAuliffe. A short hiatus in shuttle operations followed.

In the 1980s and early 1990s, NASA experienced major economic setbacks. Among them were sensor troubles in a $1.7-billion series of weather satellites, mirror flaws in the $1.5-billion Hubble space telescope, malfunctions in the $25-billion space shuttle fleet, and design defects in the planned $30-billion space station. A return to space by 77-year-old Senator Glenn, 36 years after he became the first American to orbit the Earth, stirred renewed interest in space travel in October 1998. While NASA insisted Glenn's flight answered serious questions about aging in space, even skeptics agreed it served as a much-needed public relations coup for the troubled agency.

CURRENT CONDITIONS

Aerospace engineer Daniel Goldin took the helm at NASA in 1992, after 25 years at TRW Inc. Insiders credit the new NASA administrator with changing the culture of the organization. The agency published a clear policy directive in 1998: "NASA is an investment in America's future. As explorers, pioneers and innovators, we boldly expand frontiers in air and space to inspire and serve America and to benefit the quality of life on Earth."

NASA continues to collect data and push the boundaries on both manned and unmanned missions that go further and longer. Space probes with sophisticated sensors revealed the 900 degree surface of Venus and the frozen wasteland of Pluto. Expanding on Viking probes of Mars in the 1970s, the 1997 $266-million Mars Pathfinder mission beamed back live images for a riveting television broadcast of a barren land with a thin atmosphere and no visible wa-

ter. By 1999 astronomers had reviewed 17,050 images of the red planet, which turned out to be more of a Butterscotch color. The Galileo spacecraft made trips around Jupiter and discovered possible oceans on Europa and Calisto, two of the moons circling the giant planet. As a result of those findings, NASA is planning further investigations of Europa, which closely resembles Earth, to check for signs of life. Other planned missions involve experiments in astronomy, remote sensing, communications, and robotic explorations.

In manned missions of December 1998, astronauts turned on the lights and put up radio and television antennas on the multibillion dollar International Space Station (ISS). It will take five years to completely assemble the space laboratory. The project draws on decades of technological advancements and improvements in space gear, materials, and equipment. Planners estimate 160 space walks will be needed to piece together the modular units. An international crew plans to live aboard ISS in 2000.

In March 1999 the Rotary Rocket Company rolled out a reusable, cargo-carrying spaceship in the Mojave Desert, marking a historic step in astronautics. While Roton's first mission will be deploying small telecommunications satellites, NASA views the low-cost launcher as a forerunner to a much cheaper space age. If all goes according to design, upon reentry into the Earth's atmosphere, helicopter blades on the craft will unfold and rotate, allowing for a gentle touchdown. Pat Dasch, the executive director of the National Space Society (NSS), said, "Today, Rotary Rocket is opening the door to an exciting future in space. This generation of launch vehicles will open space for routine travel—for business and recreation."

Two weeks later, Apollo 11 astronaut Buzz Aldrin spoke at the National Forum on the Future Development of Space. Aldrin serves as chairman of the NSS, which considered the forum an "important opportunity for government and business leaders to identify key issues in the growing commercialization of near-Earth space, as well as the longer term issues in bringing more industrial development to space."

NASA launched the Landsat-7 spacecraft in April 1999. Landsat satellites are part of an ongoing research project that has been recording changes in the Earth's land, oceans, atmosphere, ice, and life since 1972. Applications for the latest mission include agricultural crop planning and information gathering on water quality and population changes. NASA Administrator James Fletcher said in 1975, "If one space age devel-

This artist's concept shows the International Space Station (ISS) in orbit. The ISS is scheduled to be completed by 2003. (Courtesy of NASA.)

opment might save the world, it would be Landsat and its successor satellites."

Also in 1999, NASA reported significant progress in achieving its mission and goals by doing business faster, better, and cheaper without compromising safety. Even so, Congress gave NASA almost equal funding during the 1990s as it did in the moon-driven 1960s, after adjusting for inflation. Ever budget-conscious, administrator Goldin passed on some operations costs and other expenses to private sector partners to further boost research and development.

INDUSTRY LEADERS

The aerospace industry consists of four prime contractors and a host of suppliers. Ranked by revenue, the major players are Boeing, Lockheed Martin, Raytheon, and Northrop Grumman

Boeing blows past the competition as the world's largest maker of commercial jets and military aircraft. The company clinched its title as NASA's leading contractor with the 1996 acquisition of the space and defense unit of Rockwell International Corporation. The

Seattle-based company further unseated all rivals with the 1997 merger of Boeing with McDonnell Douglas. Boeing makes planes, missiles, rockets, helicopters, space-faring vehicles, and advanced communications systems. The company derived 40 percent of its 1997 revenue from its pumped up space and defense unit, with the U.S. government accounting for roughly 70 percent of the unit's total sales. The unit experienced two major defeats in 1998, when its large-payload Delta 3 rocket exploded on the launch pad and the U.S. government imposed a $10-million fine on Boeing for disclosing proprietary information to Russian and Ukrainian partners in its Sea Launch satellite project.

Lockheed Martin builds warplanes, rockets, and satellites and offers a variety of technical and managerial services to military, government, and communications organizations around the world. The Maryland-based company helped develop the Hubble space telescope and the Landsat spacecraft for NASA. Lockheed Martin led the wave of consolidation in the industry when it merged with defense giant Martin Marietta in 1995 and became the world's largest aerospace and defense firm. Citing a concern for a shrinking amount of competition, federal regulators blocked the company's acquisition of Northrop Grumman in 1998. That year, Lockheed Martin derived nearly 70 percent of its revenue from the U.S. government.

Raytheon doubled in size in 1997 when it bought the defense electronics arm of Texas Instruments Inc. for $3 billion and the aerospace and defense division of Hughes Electronics Corporation for $9.5 billion from General Motors Corporation. In 1999, Raytheon signed a $33-million contract with NASA to continue to provide information services at the Goddard Space Flight Center, where the company manages tens of trillions of bytes of information generated by NASA's space science missions. The Massachusetts-based company also makes radar, sonar, surveillance, and missile systems.

Northrop Grumman racked up 80 percent of its sales from high-dollar defense contracts in 1998. Twenty five years earlier, the California-based company started work on the lunar module for Project Apollo, the space program that put a man on the moon. In July 1969, a world audience watched the first lunar landing courtesy of the first hand-held video camera, built by Northrop Grumman engineers.

AMERICA AND THE WORLD

In 1984, U.S. President Ronald Reagan publicly backed and touted an eight-year plan to build an $8-

In all, 16 countries are participating in the creation of the ISS, which will take 5 years and 43 flights to complete. (Courtesy of NASA.)

billion International Space Station (ISS). The flying laboratory, orbiting 200 miles above Earth, promised to help scientists from around the world to invent new materials, conduct pharmaceutical experiments and study the effects of extended periods of weightlessness (a necessary lesson in a proposed mission to Mars).

Twenty billion dollars later, ISS' assembly still hadn't begun in 1998, and the ISS accounted for one-seventh of NASA's total budget. The five-year construction plans called for 43 space flights to haul up—and 160 space walks to fit together—460 tons of modular units—including living quarters, power systems, truss segments, solar arrays, thermal radiators, and assorted hardware.

ISS construction finally began in December 1998. Astronauts completed initial assembly during three space walks totaling 21 hours and 22 minutes. As the pieces come together, an international crew of three Russian and U.S. astronauts is set to live aboard the outpost in January 2000, thereby establishing a known permanent human presence in space for the new millennium. Eventually six permanent residents plan to carry out long-duration research on life science, microgravity, and space science in the nearly gravity-free environment of the state-of-the-art facility.

In the largest cooperative scientific endeavor in world history, 16 nations comprise the ISS Team: Belgium, Brazil, Canada, Denmark, France, Germany, Italy, Japan, the Netherlands, Norway, Russia, Spain, Sweden, Switzerland, the United Kingdom, and the United States. Over the years, more than 100,000 people have worked on the program in space agencies and at hundreds of contracting and subcontracting company sites around the globe.

Boeing serves as the prime contractor for the ISS, while Lockheed Martin heads up development of the eight solar array wings, the rotary mechanical joints, and the advanced air processing and filtering system.

RESEARCH AND TECHNOLOGY

Private and public entities around the world plan to launch a variety of spacecraft in the early part of the twenty-first century. Planned missions involve experiments in astronomy, remote sensing, communications, and crewed and robotic explorations. For true success, space travel must become even faster, better, and cheaper. After all, as NASA Administrator Goldin said in a 1998 Time Magazine article, "Our principle goal is getting to Mars."

On behalf of NASA, the National Research Council (NRC) identified six key technologies that NASA needs to pursue to meet its unique science and exploration goals. NRC calls all six high-risk and high-payoff technologies. First, wideband, high data-rate communication over planetary distances, could enable live transmissions of high-resolution images from robotic rovers, orbiters and astronauts on missions to other planets. NASA will need to take the lead in developing technologies—including high-precision spatial acquisition and tracking systems and high-efficiency lasers—to support such communications over planetary distances. Second, structures in a weightless environment—especially structures that are unique to space—pose difficult control challenges. These challenges must be met to enable the next generation of instruments for space-based astronomy and to support the development of very large antennas for communications and remote sensing. Third, microelectromechanical systems (MEMS) could enable the development of small, relatively low-cost spacecraft devices and subsystems with very low mass, volume, and power consumption. MEMS could be used to enhance conventional spacecraft or

to create miniature spacecraft that could enable a broad range of new space activities. Fourth, advanced space nuclear power systems will probably be required to support deep space missions, lunar, and planetary bases, extended human exploration missions, and high-thrust, high-efficiency propulsion systems. Fifth, radiation in the space environment can damage sensitive electronics, disrupt signals, cause single-event phenomena, and degrade microelectronic devices. Low-cost, high-capacity, low-mass, radiation-resistant memories and electronics are not currently available. NASA's support is needed to lay the groundwork for major improvements in radiation-resistant memories and electronics. Sixth, the capability to extract and utilize space resources can significantly improve the performance and lower the costs of planetary exploration, reduce the cost of constructing and shielding human habitats, and enable and accelerate the development of new generations of in-space capabilities. Virtually no other organization is working in this field, so NASA must support research and technology in certain areas, such as planetary material handling, materials processing technologies, and systems design and engineering to optimize process efficiencies.

NRC also stressed that NASA must work more effectively with industry and academia to develop advanced space technologies.

In 1999, Goldin listed the fundamental questions that have challenged humankind for centuries and renewed NASA's vow to pursue the answers. Some of the questions include:

- How did the universe, galaxies, stars, and planets form and evolve?

- Does life in any form, however simple or complex, carbon-based or other, exist elsewhere than on planet Earth?

- How can we utilize the knowledge of the Sun, Earth, and other planetary bodies to develop predictive environmental, climate, natural disaster, and natural resource models to help ensure sustainable development and improve the quality of life on Earth?

- What is the fundamental role of gravity and cosmic radiation in vital biological, physical, and chemical systems in space, on other planetary bodies, and on Earth?

- How can we enable revolutionary technological advances to provide air and space travel for anyone, anytime, anywhere more safely, more affordably, and with less impact on the environment and improve business opportunities and global security?

- What cutting-edge technologies, processes, techniques, and engineering capabilities must we develop to enable our research agenda in the most productive, economical, and timely manner?

FURTHER READING

"A Brief History of Rocketry." Available from http://www. Mirkwood.ucs.indiana.edu/space/rocketry.htm.

"Changing the Way Humans Use Space." Seattle, WA: Boeing Corporation, 1999. Available from http://www.boeing.com.

"History of Space Travel." New Berlin, WI: ExecPC, 1999. Available from http://www.execpc.com.

Kluger, Jeffrey. "Who Needs This?" *Time Magazine,* 23 November 1998.

"Lockheed Martin Landsat-7 Spacecraft Ready for Launch." Bethesda, MD: Lockheed Martin, 1999. Available from http://www.lmco.com.

Miller, Nick."Aerospace Industry Braces for Lean Years." Scripps Howard News Service, 2 September 1998.

"National Space Society Online," 1999. Available from http://www.nss.org.

Petit, Charles W. "Little Rockets, Cheap." *U.S. News & World Report,* 15 March 1999.

Raeburn, Paul. " How NASA Can Survive Its Midlife Crisis." *Business Week,* 5 October 1998.

"Raytheon Awarded $33 Million NASA Goddard Contract." Available from http://www.raytheon.com.

"Space Technology For the New Century." Available from http://www.nap.edu.

"Spaceflight." Available from http://www.nasa.gov.

Willis, Clint. "Aerospace Stocks Prepare for Takeoff." Available from http://www.moneycentral.msn.com.

—Denise Worhach

BIOMETRICS

In the James Bond movie *Never Say Never Again* (1983), a villain accesses the U.S. nuclear arsenal by foiling what was thought was a foolproof security system—a scan of the President's right eye. In *Mission Impossible* (1996), an espionage agent outwits retinal scanners, voice verifiers, and fingerprint readers. Both of these films showcase biometrics at work. Once used only in high-security government installations, nuclear power plants, and law enforcement agencies, biometrics devices are no longer just for spies—they are, in fact, in the process of becoming mainstream.

Biometrics was originally known as the statistical study of biological variation. In the late 1990s, the term also referred to the use of measurements of unique human traits to recognize or verify identity for security purposes. Biometrics devices measure physical traits, such as fingerprints, retina and iris patterns, voiceprints, hand geometry, and facial features; or behavioral characteristics, such as the dynamics with which a person signs his or her name or types on a keyboard. Biometrics technologies allow for the automated verification or recognition of an individual whose template of unique traits has been previously stored in a computer database.

Biometrics is slowly making its way into businesses worldwide. By 1998 more than 10,000 facilities, including financial institutions, hospitals, prisons, airports, apartment complexes, and day-care centers used biometrics to ensure that people were who they claimed to be. Biometrics have been used to reduce welfare fraud, prevent drivers from obtaining multiple licenses, control access to college dormitories and cafeterias, and monitor immigration. Credit cards may be the biggest consumer application for biometrics, which promise to eliminate billions of dollars in fraud. And the new low-cost biometrics technology promises necessary security that undoubtedly will fuel commercial Internet transactions made from personal computers.

The brave new world of biometrics may facilitate commerce and security, but the technology raises serious concerns. Some groups have argued that biometrics are the mythical "mark of the beast"—a number on the hand or forehead required for commerce. More secular critics argue that widespread use of biometrics will lead to an Orwellian loss of privacy, with consumers offering up a body part for an institution's review in order to access what is rightfully theirs.

Still, people may be willing to forego some of their privacy for the sake of security and convenience. With an ever-increasing number of keys, personal identification numbers (PINs), passwords, and magnetic cards to keep track of, people may opt for a solution that cannot be lost, stolen, or forgotten. Since unique biometrics are encoded in a person's biology and behavior, it is literally impossible to leave home without them.

VERIFICATION AND IDENTIFICATION

Biometric devices record and store a template of unique biological or behavioral features. That template is later matched against features obtained from an individual for purposes of verification or identification.

With the former, a person utilizes two forms of input (for example, a PIN and a biometric), and a computer verifies whether the data match. With the latter, a person provides a biometric (such as a picture taken at a border crossing), and a computer uses that data to identify the person.

Most biometrics systems can only verify. Identification systems have to be more powerful because they don't involve cues from PINs or access cards. The computer has to search its entire database and compare biometric data for all its enrolled users—a time-consuming enterprise—until a match is made or the data is rejected as unidentified

Biometric systems often include safeguards to ensure that a live person is the source of the data. A fingerprint system, for example, may require the detection of body heat before it will validate a fingerprint. Similarly, a voice-recognition system may look for air pressure to prevent the use of a tape recording.

TYPES OF BIOMETRICS

Fingerprints. With as many as 60 variations to analyze and compare, fingerprints are the most widely used biometric employed in forensic and government databases. Once isolated, the trend is toward compiling databases into national, statewide, and regional networks. Technology is becoming available to allow sharing of fingerprint data from dissimilar systems. The Federal Bureau of Investigation (FBI) maintains the world's largest fingerprint database, used by the military and the police. Biometric devices may measure prints, dimensions, patterns, or topography of fingers, thumbs, or palms. At one time fingers were inked and pressed on paper to create a print, but in the late 1990s fingerprint scanners, such as those used by the California Department of Motor Vehicles, required no ink. With a mere touch of a glass plate or silicon chip, details of one's print are recorded and stored in an electronic database.

Fingerprinting is quickly gaining popularity. Many banks now use thumbprints to identify customers. Toronto-based Mytec Technologies Inc. developed a fingerprint scanner used by the Royal Canadian Mounted Police to identify individuals and by the Louvre museum in Paris to control access to secured areas. American Biometric Co. sells a fingerprint scanner that thwarts unauthorized access to computers and protects the transmission of data over the Internet. Fingerprint readers at an Amsterdam airport let frequent flyers avoid long lines at passport control. In addition, many state governments in the United States use fingerprint data to verify eligibility for welfare.

Hand geometry. To measure hand geometry, two infrared photos of a person's hand—one shot from above, one from the side—record more than 90 measurements such as length, width, thickness, surface area, finger shape, and joint positions. First developed for nuclear power plants, hand scanners were used in prisons, universities, airports, and hospitals in the late 1990s. Many manufacturing and construction sites rely on hand scanners to provide a biometric "time card" to verify attendance. (Nicks and dirt do not significantly alter readings.)

National research labs were among the first users of Recognition Systems Inc.'s ID3D HandKey Biometric System. Industry has followed suit, however. For example, HandKey identifies workers at L.L. Bean, parents at a day-care center run by Lotus Development Corp., and people trying to get free food at the University of Georgia's cafeteria. In addition, HandKey controlled the access of more than 65,000 athletes, trainers, and support staff to the Olympic Village in Atlanta, Georgia.

In 1992 the Colombian parliament began requiring hand scanning before voting. The previous voting system required delegates to put white and black balls in a basket, and confusion sometimes arose over who had voted and who had not. When the Colombian people demanded assurances that they were being represented fairly, a company called International Roll-Call installed a hand-geometry system. A similar technology measuring finger geometry grants access to season pass holders at some Walt Disney facilities.

Facial recognition. Individual face patterns are unique, even between identical twins. While some systems evaluate shadow patterns on a face illuminated in a specific way, others use an infrared camera to record multiple heat patterns (thermal images) at points around the cheekbones and eyes. Face recognition is growing in popularity because the hardware is inexpensive: manufacturers are already building camera lenses into computer monitors to accommodate videoconferencing. TrueFace, a system from Miros, Inc. of Wellesley, Massachusetts, makes check cashing safer by comparing images obtained from a security camera with stored images of pre-authorized individuals.

In another venture, the company has teamed with Computer Associates International to store images in database Jasmine. The partnership enables users to search a large database for a live-image match. Applications include identification of missing children and terrorists, as well as registering employees' time and attendance. A Miros system also secures the Pentagon's computer network. Len Polizzotto, corporate vice president for new ventures at Polaroid, uses FaceIt software from Visionics Corp. to control access to his personal computer: a camera takes his photo when he turns on his machine and matches it with a photo stored on the hard drive. If there's no match, the computer will not boot up. Other firms offering face-recognition technologies include Identification Technologies International Inc. of Coral Gables, Florida; Viisage Technology Inc. of Acton, Massachusetts; of Alexandria, Virginia; and Siemens Nixdorf of Pederborn, Germany.

Retinal scans. Retina scanners flash an infrared light into the eye and examine the distinct pattern of blood vessels behind the retina. Retinal-scanning data occupies less memory space in a computer than does fingerprinting data, so it could be useful in decreasing the time necessary to search the large databases used for identification. Retina scanning, however, is perceived as intrusive by some. When military pilots were first subjected to retinal scans, they refused them, thinking the scans might impair their visual acuity (despite the fact that no evidence indicated this would happen). In other cases, users with watery eyes sometimes left retinal scanners moist, causing concerns about eye diseases, transfer of body fluids, and acquired immune deficiency syndrome (AIDS). User concern was so great that the original product was withdrawn from the market and replaced with a new non-contact device. In the late 1990s retinal scanning was being explored for defense, law enforcement, and financial applications.

Iris scans. Both the iris and retina contain more identification points than a fingerprint. At distances up to 12 inches, for instance, iris scans can measure 400 unique characteristics, such as freckles, contraction furrows, rings, and darkened areas, which remain stable from infancy. Even identical twins do not have the same features. Iris scans convert the distinct details of the colored part of the eye into a biological "bar code" that acts as a unique identifier. Positive identification can be made through glasses, contact lenses, and most sunglasses.

Iris scanning made its global debut at the 1998 Winter Olympics in Nagano, Japan, when security officials required biathletes to undergo scans to check out their rifles. By December 1998, three banks in Europe had piloted iris scans in ATMs, joining a British bank that had run a successful trial in the previous six months. NCR Corporation produces the machines equipped with Sensar Inc.'s iris scanning technology. The iris also can be scanned without the knowledge of the subject, which could be useful in applications such as airport security and terrorist detection. Sensar licensed the camera technology from Sarnoff Corp. in Princeton, New Jersey, which originally designed it for taking ground surveillance photos from high-flying military helicopters.

According to Sensar, Inc., the matching probability of their iris scanning process is greater than that of DNA technology. In fact, they continue, iris identification is the only form of personal electronic identification that has never granted a false acceptance.

Voice verification. Although voices may sound similar to the human ear, no two are alike. The unique topography of a person's mouth, teeth, and vocal cords produce inimitable aspects, such as pitch, tone, cadence, and dynamics. Character, expression, and regional dialects also influence voice patterns. Voice systems are an obvious choice for phone-based applications. They are also suitable for use with PCs. Saflink Corporation offers voice-activated software, SafetyLatch, which will scramble files on command.

About... **BREAKING BIOMETRIC SECURITY**

PC Magazine editors and laboratories masqueraded as authorized users in their review of 11 popular biometrics systems for both individual desktop and corporate-level network security systems. They tested the systems' abilities to screen imposters while admitting authorized users. Each of the products were equipped with a sensitivity threshold that had to provide an acceptable level of security while being able to overlook fluctuations such as cold or moist hands for fingerprint scanners, changes in lighting for face recognition, and background noise for voice recognition.

In their attempts to break past security checkpoints, the testers tried several tests on the different devices and had variable degrees of success dependent on the type of biometrics data collected. Fingerprint scanners resisted all attempts including the re-application of latent fingerprints that were lifted from the device itself. In contrast, the testers were able to fool face recognition systems set at low security thresholds by using a mask made from a photograph of an enrollee with an impersonator's nose projecting through a hole in the appropriate spot. Higher confidence settings rejected the masked imposters, but also increased the frequency of false rejections. Voice recognition systems allowed easy and efficient authentication even in noisy environments, but testers were able to crack the system by mimicking an enrollee's voice.

Verivoice in Princeton, New Jersey, is testing a system it hopes to sell to insurance companies and banks that want to offer online services.

Signature dynamics. The speed and style with which a person signs his or her name is a unique behavioral biometric. Signature dynamics measure the pressure, angel of attack, and stroke characteristics with which a person writes. They have been used to verify identity for banking transactions, insurance forms, and electronic filing of tax returns. Chase Manhattan was the first bank to test this technology.

Keystroke dynamics. Individuals are unique in how they work a keyboard, and these differences can be exploited as a means of identification. As of 1997, keystroke dynamics—typing speed and patterns—had not been used as a commercial biometric, mainly due to concerns that employers would monitor the hourly productivity of employees.

The next generation of unique identifiers may include measurements of lip and ear shape, knuckle creases, wrist veins, and even vibrations from major body organs. Soon to hit the market is a British-made device called the Scentinel, which "sniffs" hands and purports to identify people by body odor. DNA testing, the ultimate biometric, is too slow and intrusive to be viable in commercial applications.

APPLICATIONS

Biometric devices were first developed to keep unauthorized persons out of military installations and nuclear power plants. The FBI's Automated Fingerprint Identification System (AFIS) came next, drawing upon technologies developed by defense industries. In 1968 a Wall Street brokerage became the first financial institution to apply biometrics when it used fingerprints to open vaults that stored stock certificates. Biometrics technology is now changing the world by making transactions cheaper, safer, and easier.

Biometrics currently plays a role in security and identification across industry lines. From banks to retail chains, increasingly more businesses worldwide are taking advantage of the ease, accuracy, and decreased expense associated with the use of biometrics.

Finance. In 1995 MasterCard International Inc. lost $1.5 billion to fraud, according to the Public Interest Research Group, and fraud *quadrupled* in 1996. To thwart swindlers, both MasterCard and Visa have been exploring finger imaging. MasterCard's pilot system stores fingerprint data in the credit card itself. When a customer makes a purchase with a credit card,

his or her finger is scanned at the store, and that data is compared to the data encrypted in the credit card. Joel Lisker, MasterCard's senior vice president of security and risk management, says these smart cards could eliminate 80 percent of fraudulent charges. (If the cardholder is not present, as in phone sales, the risk of fraud remains.)

Banks testing or using finger-based biometrics include Bank of America, Citicorp, Mellon Bank, Bankers Trust, and Chevy Chase Savings and Loan Association. Perdue Employees' Federal Credit Union in West Lafayette, Indiana, was the first U.S. bank to implement finger imaging to identify customers. Biometrics are also employed at some U.S. banks to identify people cashing checks or accessing vaults where computer records are stored. Several banks in South America, Asia, and Europe also use biometrics. In Italy, some bank customers must check in at hand-geometry readers before being allowed to enter. In 1996 Chase Manhattan Corp. began using a voice verification system called Xtra Secure to identify customers. Chase's research showed that 95 percent of customers would accept voice verification, whereas only 80 percent would accept fingerprinting.

In the late 1990s Oki Electric, a major ATM vendor, teamed with IriScan and Sensar, both of New Jersey, to put iris scanners in Japanese ATMs. In the United States, Citibank also began testing iris scanning for ATMs. With the new technology, traditional PINs are replaced with iris patterns, which are recorded, digitized, and stored on the ATM card. At the ATM, a scanner then compares the user's iris pattern to that encrypted in the card.

This type of system involving a card encrypted with biometrics data to be verified by the user has become known as SmartCard. Virtually any type of biometrics data can be stored on the card, allowing security systems to verify without storing the information in large databases. In addition to use in banking, SmartCard uses are extending to PC security, regulating medical prescriptions and other human service applications.

The use of biometrics is also replacing passwords in some computers. In 1996 a government supplier, The National Registry Inc., added a finger identification system called NRIdentity to enhance security when logging on to Microsoft Windows. Also in 1996, discount securities broker Charles Schwab & Co. installed finger-imaging systems in its headquarters to increase staff security.

In 1997 Veridicom Inc. of Santa Clara, California, gave biometric sales a major boost by introduc-

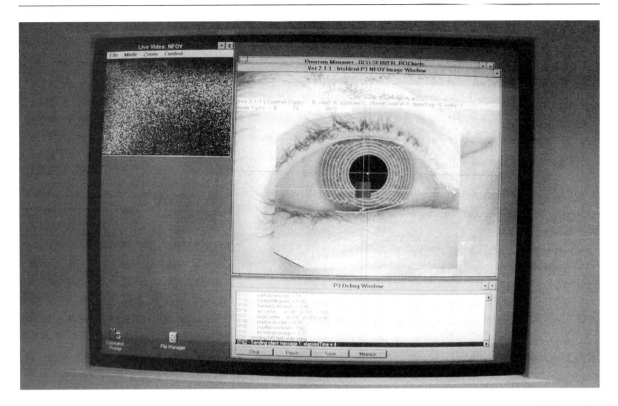

This ATM system machine by Sensar measures the pattern of the iris of the eye and then generates a special bar code.
(AP Photos/Scott Lituchy.)

ing a stamp-sized fingerprint reader on a chip that cost only $100. This inexpensive technology made it easy to build fingerprint verification into computer products. Oracle Corp. of Redwood City, California, secured one of its computer products with a fingerprint system by Identix Inc.

Some 50 shops, eateries, and bars at the Yalta Hotel in Ukraine use HandKey to authorize withdrawals from accounts at Bank Slaviansky, a small bank that wanted to distinguish itself in Ukraine's new, competitive banking environment. HandKey also lets people open accounts anonymously: customers deposit funds in the bank and register their hands. To pay bills, they enter an account number and an amount on the HandKey device. Their hands are scanned, a deduction is made from their account, and a receipt issued. Many in this region reportedly fear crime and do not have credit cards, so they are attracted to cashless transactions.

Hand geometry readers also serve as time clocks and security protection for employees of Oneida Bingo and Casino of Green Bay, Wisconsin. The readers, provided by Recognition Systems, monitor passage at all employee entrances.

Retail. In 1993 catalog sales giant L.L. Bean, which staffs its phones around the clock, began using hand geometry to identify employees and grant access to facilities. For added security, employees also enter an authorization number. A card access system would have been too expensive during the holiday rush, during which the company typically hires about 3,000 temporary workers. Instead, the firm chose the ID3D HandKey Biometric System from Recognition Systems Inc. With the system, L.L. Bean didn't need to buy extra access cards for the holiday season, and it was easy to enter and delete employee records.

Likewise, for several years Australia's largest supermarket chain, Woolworth Ltd., has used a fingerprint identification system by Identix to monitor the attendance of 80,000 workers in 500 stores. Home Depot, a large retail firm, also experimented with the use of signature verification to reduce fraud.

Airports. Airport entryways in San Francisco, New York, and Toronto are equipped with HandKey hand-geometry readers for access control. Authorized personnel swipe access cards, then place their hands into entryway readers to gain access. In 1997 Malaysia's Langkawi Airport installed the first face-recognition technology to increase airport security. The system, by Visionics Corp. and TL Technology, matches a passenger's face with an image encoded in the boarding pass during check-in.

Correctional institutions. In some jails, inmates speak a password into a phone to verify their presence. In the early 1990s, a federal prison in Georgia evaluated a hand-geometry system to verify and control staff comings and goings and inmate releases. The system was judged a success. The first six months' use of fingerprint readers in the Pima County, AZ Jail, exposed 300 inmates who had given false identities.

Moreover, in Great Britain a partnership between the Advanced Fingerprint Recognition system (AFR), the world's largest of its kind, and several technology providers has brought live-scan fingerprinting at low cost to its prisoner handling centers. Processing nearly 83,000 sets of fingerprints has exposed 3,800 prisoners as having given false identities.

Upon release, former inmates can use a biometric system to report to their parole officers without actually meeting in person. At a prearranged time, the parolee goes to a kiosk similar to an ATM, enters an identification number, and is verified by a hand geometry reader. The parolee receives messages from the parole officer on a display terminal. It has been found that the kiosk system has a better attendance rate than personal meetings. If a parolee fails to appear for a check-in, an intense follow-up is initiated.

Colleges and universities. With hand templates encoded in photo identification cards, colleges and universities can better manage physical access for large student populations. At the University of Georgia, hand-geometry readers allow access to the student cafeteria. Since 1992, hand readers have controlled security turnstiles at New York University dormitories. At the University of Montreal, students use a hand scanner to enter an athletic complex.

Housing. In Chicago, the 628-unit Marshall Field Garden Apartments were half abandoned and crime-ridden before the introduction of biometrics. In 1992 Developers Design Corporation bought the complex, renovating it and installing hand ID verifiers at the two entryways for added security. Apartment renters are enrolled in the hand geometry system when they sign their lease, and they can enroll up to 99 guests with the security office. Today, the complex is rented to capacity, with 1,000 applicants on the waiting list. A different type of biometric technology, voiceprints, allows access to some posh California housing estates.

Athletic clubs. YMCA athletic clubs in Ashland and Youngstown, Ohio, use hand geometry to replace membership cards. Hand readers are hooked to turnstiles at entrances, verifying patrons within seconds, denying access to non-payers, and eliminating the need to replace lost or stolen cards. The system also simplifies record keeping of the facilities' more than 3,000 and 5,000 members, respectively, and staffs that turn over fairly rapidly. In Palo Alto, California, Hewlett Packard, Inc. installed a similar device in its corporate athletic facility. The hand-geometry system assures that only employees use the facility and that users have first undergone a physical exam.

Day care centers and hospitals. Lotus Development Corp. uses hand geometry readers in its day care center to verify the identities of people picking up children. When authorized people pick up children, the hand geometry system records the time, date, and identification of the receiver.

In 1998 Scott and White Memorial Hospital in Temple, Texas, began a pilot project to see if fingerprints could replace passwords on hospital computers. A staff member puts his or her finger on a scanner, and the captured image is sent to a computer network, which treats the digitized fingerprint as a password.

CURRENT CONDITIONS

Growth in the biometrics industry has been steady but gradual, with more of the same expected. Approximately 200 biometric products were on the market in 1998, according to the International Computer Security Association. Biometrics earned $103 million in 1996, according to *World Biometrics Identification Markets.* Experts forecast a 7.5 percent annual growth rate for the industry through 2003, with strong growth for fingerprinting; increased growth for hand geometry and face recognition; and steady growth for iris, voice, and signature systems. Slow growth is predicted, however, for retinal products, whose high-security market suffers from government cutbacks.

Past market growth has been limited by high prices, performance problems, and poor user acceptance. As the industry meets these challenges, consumers are responding favorably. Security applications provide a major market with steady growth. Health care organizations are adopting biometric security faster than any other industry. Although still new to the private sector, biometrics equipment and software are predicted to generate $170 million by 2003.

Prices of biometric devices are dropping. As an extreme example, one fingerprint scanner costing $1,000 in 1997 cost less than $100 in 1998. From 1990 to 1997, the cost of biometric devices dropped 70 percent, according to CardTech/SecurTech Inc., sponsors of an industry trade show. Regardless, the devices still cost more than conventional measures. To secure a door with a traditional card system, the 1993 cost was $1,000. To secure that same door with voice verification cost $1,200; hand geometry $2,100; fingerprinting $3,500 to $6,000; and retinal scanning $4,500.

Applications for PC security are now affordable enough for mainstream use. An add-on product to protect confidential files, such as a fingerprint reader and software, sells for under $100. The SafetyLatch voice identification program referred to earlier in this article, requires no additional hardware and costs around $60.

Consumer acceptance of biometrics is increasing as the technology becomes more widespread. A Columbia University survey showed that 83 percent of respondents accepted fingerprint imaging for security purposes. Likewise, the International Biometric Group polled 100 people to see how they would react to a finger scan at a bank. Before they tried it, only 60 percent reacted favorably. After they tried it, however, acceptance rose to 90 percent. The International Biometric Group has taken a big step to educate consumers by opening the first "supermarket" of biometric devices in Manhattan. The Biometric Store gives users a chance to test over two dozen currently available technologies. The devices on display are supplied by a myriad of venders. The Biometrics Store Web

site (www.biometricstore.com) also provides links to information and consultation services.

Organizations including Boeing, Fidelity Investments, the Mayo Clinic, and Polaroid Corp. are now exploring the use of biometrics as well. Still, only 4 percent of the 413 companies surveyed in 1997 used biometric security, and just 6 percent planned to buy the technology in 1998, according to the Computer Security Institute and Zona Research Inc. Regardless, the number of biometric devices sold increased exponentially throughout the 1990s: sales rose from 2,000 units in 1992 to an estimated 50,000 units in 1998.

THE EFFECTS OF REGULATION

Laws dealing with welfare reform, immigration control, and identification of commercial drivers have played important roles in supporting the biometrics industry.

Welfare. In 1998 more than 20 states verified welfare eligibility with fingerprints. The state of Connecticut saved more than $9 million by using fingerprints to reduce welfare fraud. In 1991 the Los Angeles County Department of Public Social Services used fingerprinting on 70,000 aid recipients. Approximately 3,000 clients were dropped either because they refused to be fingerprinted or because the fingerprinting showed that they were receiving duplicate benefits. By 1996 the county had saved approximately $20 million.

Immigration. In the late 1990s, an open-skies agreement between the United States and Canada called for the increased use of biometrics. INSPASS, a large air-travel biometric application, helps speed frequent travelers through immigration lines. It is part of the Immigration and Naturalization Service's future automated screening for travelers (FAST) program. Travelers' passports, nationalities, and security details are verified, and a system encodes their hand-geometry templates into INSPASS cards, which are later used to verify authorization for entry into the host country. The system has processed more than 25,000 entries at major airports in New York, New Jersey, and Toronto. Immigration officials worldwide are now considering encoding biometrics into passports.

The Immigration and Naturalization Service (INS) awarded Digital Biometrics Inc. a contract for 276 TENPRINTER live-scan fingerprint systems valued at in excess of $8.8 million. They agreed to place TENPRINTER systems in 125 INS application support centers throughout the United States by the end of 1999.

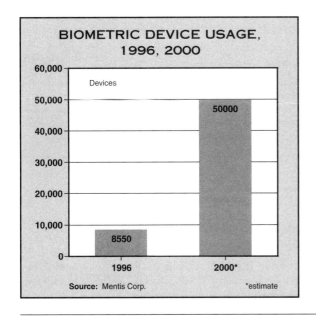

BIOMETRIC DEVICE USAGE, 1996, 2000

Source: Mentis Corp. *estimate

Drivers. Starting in 1992 bus and truck drivers, as well as anyone else seeking a commercial driver's license, were required by law to provide a "unique identifier" such as a fingerprint. The law aimed to prevent truck drivers from obtaining licenses in several states and continuing to drive after one license had been revoked. States having mandatory fingerprinting for all drivers include Texas, California, Colorado, Hawaii, and Georgia. Editor Linda Poltorak of *Biometrics in Human Services User Group's* "Biometric Watch" cites the *Savannah Morning News* report that since implementation in October 1996, the Georgia law has exposed 681 people attempting to obtain fraudulent licenses.

FURTHER READING

"Airport Security to 'Read Faces.' (Visionics Corp. and TL Technology Research Plan Use of Biometric Face-Recognition Technology in Airports)." *Travel Weekly,* 2 June 1997.

Aragon, Lawrence. "Show Me Some ID (Biometrics Software)." *PC Week,* 12 January 1998.

Barancik, Scott. "Multiple Formats Seen Hobbling Biometrics." *American Banker,* 21 May 1998.

Beiser, Vince. "The Keyless Society: New Security Devices Scan Fingerprints, Eyes, Even Body Odors. (Biometrics)." *Maclean's,* 25 August 1997.

"Biomatric Watch." Biometrics in Human Services User Group Newsletter, March 1999. Available from http://www.dss.state.ctus/digital/news13/bhsug13.html.

"Biometrics: The Measures of Man." *The Economist,* 19 September 1992.

Brown, Randy. "The New Measures. (Biometric System Devices)." *Buildings,* September 1997.

"Digital Biometrics Fingerprint System Receives FBI Certification." *PR Newswire,* 13 January 1999.

Digital Biometrics, Inc. "Digital Biometrics Inc. Awarded Contract from Immigration and Naturalization (INS) for Fingerprint Project." *PR Newswire,* 11 January 1999.

Dussalt, Raymond. "AFIS Links Help Corner Crooks." *Government Technology Magazine,* February 1999. Available from http://www.govtech.net/gmag/1999/feb/jandt/jandt.shtm.

"Entrust Software Support for Biometric Devices." *American Banker,* 5 November 1997.

Frink, Sharon. "High Tech 'Toys' Cut Business Costs." *New Mexico Business Journal,* November 1993.

Garfinkle, Simon. "Voice Over." *Wired Magazine,* September 1997.

"Handing It to Biometrics." *Security Management,* February 1998.

"Handling Security. (L.L. Bean's Access Security System)." *Security Management,* November 1993.

Himowitz, Michael J. "Keep Your Secrets Safe with Voice-Activated Software." *Fortune,* 1 March 1999.

———. "Hot Stuff: Keep Your Secrets Safe with Voice-Activated Software." *Fortune,* 1 March 1999.

"Look Me in the Eye." *Discover,* February 1990.

Luhby, Tami. "Bank in Ukraine Using Hand Scanning Device to Identify Customers." *American Banker,* 13 October 1997.

Mintie, Dave, Sally Duncan, Jim Weaver, and Michael Mahoney. "State Updates: CT—NC—TX—PA." *Biometrics in Human Services User Group,* March 1999. Available from http://www.dss.state.ct.us/digital/news13/bhsug.html.

Morrison, Gale. "The $10 Fingerprint Module Arrives. (From Who? Vision)." *Electronic News,* 12 January 1998.

"New Banks Sign Up to Pilot Iris Identification with NCR and Sensar." NCR Press Release, 2 December 1998. Available from http://www.sensar.com/press/press-release-newbanks120298.stm.

"Order for 276 Live Scan Systems—Largest in History." *PR Newswire,* 11 January 1999.

O'Sullivan, Orla. "Biometrics Comes to Life. (Banks May Increase Use of People's Physical Characteristics in Security Systems)." *ABA Banking Journal,* January 1997.

Phillips, Ken. "Biometric Identification Looms on Landscape of Network Log-ins." *PC Week,* 24 March 1997.

——— "Moving to Biometric Standards." *PC Week,* 27 October 1997.

——— "Standards Coming to Biometrics Market." *PC Week,* 25 May 1998.

Pina, Michael. "INS Eyes Fingerprints, Voice Recognition for Entry to U.S. (Immigration and Naturalization Service)." *Travel Weekly,* 13 March 1995.

Poltorak, Linda, ed. "Biometric Watch." *Biometrics in Human Services User Group,* March 1999. Available from http://www.dss.state.ct.us/digital/news13/bhsug.html.

Power, Carol. "Biometric 'Supermarket' Offers an ID Smorgasbord. (International Biometric Group Opens Biometric-Store Identification Technology Shop)." *American Banker,* 8 September 1997.

Purcell, F.J. Bud. "Biometrics for the Uninitiated." *Manage,* February 1998.

Richards, Donald R. "Bioidentification Systems Seen as Future Retail Security Tool. (Loss Prevention)." *Stores,* January 1996.

———. "Rules of Thumb for Biometric Systems." *Security Management,* October 1995.

Ross, Julie Ritzer. "Finger Identification Studied as Weapon Against Credit Fraud." *Stores,* April 1997.

Scott, William B. "Defense Skills Applied to Biometric ID." *Aviation Week & Space Technology,* 17 October 1994.

"Sensar Products." *Sensar Web Site* Available from http://www.sensar.com/products/products.stm.

Stevens, Tim. "Who Goes There? (Biometrics)." *Industry Week,* 16 March 1998.

Woodward, John D. "Biometrics Offers Security—But Legal Worries, Too (Biological Information Used for Identification)." *American Banker,* 23 August 1996.

Wu, Corinna. "Private Eyes: Biometric Identification Is Set to Replace Passwords and PINs." *Science News,* 4 April 1998.

Zunkel, Richard L. "Palm Reading for Protection. (Biometric Technologies)." *Security Management,* November 1994.

—Dawn M. Levy, updated by Sondra E. O'Donnell

Book, Music, and CD Superstores

INDUSTRY SNAPSHOT

For hundreds of years, booksellers sold books to the public from cozy storefronts. Even if a chain owned and operated the store, it was usually an intimate place with limited titles for book buyers to browse and purchase. Around 1990, everything changed when the biggest chains of booksellers created the book and music superstore. Within a short time, these stores transformed the bookselling industry.

Superstores are much larger than traditional bookstores. They carry more titles than can be found in a smaller outlet and offer deep discounts—often up to 30 percent on bestsellers and 10 to 20 percent on most hardcovers. Sometimes they combine extensive offerings of music CDs and tapes with books, creating, in effect, two stores within one. They also offer amenities such as coffee bars, poetry readings, and unlimited no-pressure-to-buy browsing that once were the hallmark of bookstores, but had faded in more modern times. Supported by the price-marking might of the bookstore chains, the superstore concept quickly became the single most important trend in bookselling. The superstore, however, has become the focus of debate as it has managed to squeeze out independent booksellers who have been unable to compete with the mass purchasing power of large chains.

In the 1990s entertainment superstores, such as Media Play (part of the Musicland empire), entered the marketplace. Then came the Internet, with on-line companies such as amazon.com and Music Boulevard, making book and music purchases even easier. The Internet changed buying habits as prospective customers could browse through thousands of available book and music titles, review synopses of those of interest, make selections, complete the financial and delivery arrangements, and receive their purchases without ever leaving home.

Even as independent booksellers fought back in the courts and online shopping expanded its reach, the superstore concept continued to expand. Further competition arose from discount chains, such as Wal-Mart, but the result of this increased competition was growth for bookselling in general. Online book sales rose from $152 million in 1997 to $650 million in 1998. Book sales in stores also increased—from $11.95 billion in 1997 to $12.37 billion in 1998.

BACKGROUND AND DEVELOPMENT

The book superstore dates back to 1990 when industry leader, New York-based Barnes & Noble, opened stores that incorporated concepts that other retailers had successfully used. Barnes' chief rival, Borders, headquartered in Ann Arbor, Michigan, already had perfected the state-of-the-art computerized inventory system that would become a necessary element in the superstore's success. Another rival, Crown, had developed the idea of strict inventory control, which allowed them to cater to niche tastes such as mystery or science fiction. Additionally, the idea of oversized warehouse-type retail outlets had been tested and proven successful in other segments of the retailing industry before the book superstore emerged.

In the 1990s, the industry leaders—Barnes and Borders—opened superstores at an astonishing rate. In early 1996 Steve Riggio, chief operating officer of Barnes & Noble, told writer Michael Hartnett of *Stores* magazine that his company expected to open 90 new superstores a year for the next couple of years although he later scaled that prediction back to 70 new openings a year. "We are about halfway through what we believe is our rollout," Riggio told Hartnett. "Most of the stores in our current base are in terrific pre-preemptive locations, and we still see opportunities to put superstores in hundreds of other locations."

Within a few short years, superstores were contributing to the bottom line of the big chains. Superstore revenue contributed 76 percent of Barnes & Noble's total sales in 1996, up from 68 percent in 1995 and 59 percent in 1994. Conversely, revenues from the company's traditional mall bookstores declined 1 percent in 1996. In late 1997 Barnes & Noble announced the opening of three new superstores in the United States—complete with books, music, and café—and a new superstore in Singapore. By January 1998, Borders was operating 206 superstores worldwide.

The superstore concept goes beyond being just bigger, but size is a good place to start. A traditional bookstore outlet in a mall or in a small town might occupy 3,000 to 5,000 square feet and may stock anywhere from a few thousand to 20,000 or 30,000 titles. By contrast, the superstores measure from 10,000 to 60,000 square feet and stock up to 150,000 titles or more. Barnes & Noble's 1998 opening of its Arlington Heights, Illinois, superstore boasted 175,000 book titles and 20,000 CDs, along with a cafe. Superstores operate extensive coffee bars featuring exotic blends and baked goods. Stores sometimes employ special events coordinators who organize events such as live readings by authors. Couches and lounge areas are everywhere so people can read. There are no high-pressure sales tactics; in fact, people don't have to buy. Instead, the store wants to create an atmosphere where people will want to return and spend their money.

In some areas, the superstore has meant the demise of smaller booksellers, including other stores owned by the chain. For example, Barnes & Noble closes about 1 smaller mall outlet of its own for each 2 or 3 superstores it opens. Also, the superstore has been blamed for the loss of independent bookstores. The American Booksellers Association (ABA), which is made up of independents and small chain stores, has seen its membership decline from 5,200 in 1991 to 3,300 in 1999. Independent U.S. booksellers, such as Shakespeare & Co. on Manhattan's upper west side and the Doubleday Book Shop on 5th Avenue and 56th Street in New York, closed their doors in the 1990s. The number of bookstores that closed each year rose from 25 per year in 1992 and 1993 to 175 per year in the mid-1990s. Meanwhile, the market share of independent bookstores fell steadily from more than 32 percent in 1991 to about 18 percent in 1996.

Some people see the superstores as Goliath, using their muscle to overpower small independents, but others believe that superstores are a retail success and offer a better product. In a May 27, 1996 article in *The Weekly Standard* titled "Five Ways America Keeps Getting Better," writer Christopher Caldwell listed the growth of Borders as number one, citing its vast collection of titles. In a commentary on June 20, 1997 in the *The New York Times,* Victor Navasky wrote that "while giving lip service to the idea of independent shops like Shakespeare & Company, I have been buying most of my books from Barnes & Noble; this is partly because, my romantic notions aside, too often Shakespeare & Company didn't have the book I needed and wasn't sufficiently solicitous about getting it quickly. Barnes & Noble, on the other hand, usually had a copy or could, by calling one of its other stores, miraculously make one appear in time for deadline or vacation reading."

The intellectual debate over the impact of the superstore on U.S. culture may sometimes obscure the question of how a superstore actually goes about the business of making money. As Doreen Carvajal, writing about book publishing for *The New York Times,* asked in a 1997 article in the *Times Sunday Magazine:* "How do you turn a profit while running a parlor overrun by literary lounge lizards?" Just to break even, Carvajal pointed out, a 25,000 square foot store needs sales of $11,000, or roughly 400 hardcover books, a day. Despite the unhurried pace at a typical superstore, the cash registers seldom stop whirring. "Their basic strategy is that the superstores are the third place between home and work," said Craig Bibb, an analyst with Paine Webber quoted in Carvajal's article. "People are not just hanging out there and having a warm feeling. They are buying." Approximately 90 percent of Barnes & Noble's superstore revenues come from books, according to Bibb, and the remainder comes from coffee, magazines, and novelty items like bookmarks and reading lights. On average, a superstore costs about $2 million to create but generates about $6 million in total revenue the first year.

Indeed, a chain of superstores known as Media Play, operated by the Musicland Stores Corp., demonstrated just how tricky it can be to get the ambiance and product mix of the superstore just right. The Media Play stores were designed to provide consumers with one-stop shopping for all of their media needs, including books, music, movies, specialty videos, computer software, computer games, personal electronics, and licensed movie, music, and sports apparel. A typical Media Play store features 45,000 square feet of sales floor and a vast inventory. During 1996 the corporate parent halted its rollout of new stores and closed 32 unprofitable ones in a major retrenchment. As of early 1997, there were 68 Media Play superstores across the United States. In 1997 Media Play closed 19 more of its outlets, yet maintained a modest increase in sales, 3.4 percent, in its remaining stores.

Even the more successful chains are feeling the pinch of competition from new Internet services such as amazon.com and Music Boulevard. In May 1997, Barnes & Noble sued the Seattle-based Amazon over the cyberstore's claim to be "Earth's Biggest Bookstore." Barnes & Noble asked for unspecified damages and asked Amazon to issue "corrective ads." Barnes & Noble maintains that it is the world's largest bookseller and that Amazon, which keeps only a few hundred titles in stock and operates as a broker or clearinghouse for orders, isn't really a bookstore at all. In what many perceived to be a deliberate slap, Barnes & Noble filed its suit the day before Amazon's stock started trading on Wall Street. The effect on Amazon's stock price seemed to be negligible. It was priced at $18.00 but began trading at $29.95 on May 15, 1997. The initial public offering thus raised some $54 million. During the same month it filed suit, Barnes & Noble started its own bookselling site on the World Wide Web—using that adage that if you can't beat them, join them—billing it as "The World's Largest Bookseller Online."

CURRENT CONDITIONS

Independent booksellers believe that the large chains have used unethical business practices that have resulted in small retailers going out of business. To combat this problem, in 1998 the ABA and 26 independent bookstores filed an antitrust lawsuit against Barnes & Noble and Borders. Among other things, the ABA alleged in its complaint that defendants were advising employees that their success would be measured by whether or not they put their small-town competitors out of business. It was also alleged that Borders and Barnes & Noble forced publishers into secret and illegal deals that put nonchain competitors at a disadvantage. Similar lawsuits filed by the ABA and independents in 1994 and 1996 resulted in a $25 million settlement from publisher Penguin USA. However, a spokesperson for the ABA said in a February 6, 1999 article that the ABA decided that the prob-

lems involving unfair competition are from the retail chains and not the publishers' side.

In 1999 the ABA and independents were fighting Barnes & Noble's plans to acquire Ingram Books, the number one U.S. book wholesaler. As reported by Valerie Fields in an April 17, 1999 article in *The Arlington Morning News,* Tariq Jabari, owner of Afro Awakenings Books in Dallas, said that 80 percent of the books he purchases are through Ingram. The ABA alleges that because nearly every small independent buys books from Ingram, owning the distributor would give Barnes & Noble an advantage. In effect, independents would then be buying books from their competitor.

The number of bookstores in the United States is a matter of some debate. *The New York Times* cites a figure of 30,000, but other sources place the number of establishments that include books among their merchandise at nearly 70,000. Indeed, the traditional "bookstore," whether independent or chain owned, offering new books or used, accounts for only about 50 percent of all books sold in the United States. Mail order operations, including clubs like the famous Book of the Month Club and the newer amazon.com operation on the Internet, as well as mail order operations run by traditional bookstore chains like Barnes & Noble, account for roughly 24 percent of the total sold. The remaining market share is divided among a vast array of drug stores and supermarkets, price clubs, discount outlets, card and gift stores, hobby craft stores, and others. As important as the superstore concept has become, Americans buy their books from a variety of sources, not just one.

In the late 1990s, superstore chains extended their reach to the online community. While amazon.com dominated online book sales in 1999—with sales of $610 million—it is receiving competition from Borders, Barnes & Noble, and Chapters, as well as smaller specialty book sellers. It is estimated that online book sales will reach $3.6 billion by 2002. On the music end, Musicland began selling online in 1999 to squelch online rivals, such as CDNow, from taking sales away from its 1,350 stores. It will face competition from NzK Entertainment's Music Boulevard, which was the fastest-growing online music seller in 1998, according to Media Metrix. Other online music retailers include Sony Music Entertainment, JAMTV Corporation, and Best Buy. Total online music sales were $135 million in 1998 and are expected to reach $1.6 billion in 2002.

In 1998, a new merchant, Third Place Books, entered the superstore arena, with plans to open 2 to 4 stores in the Pacific Northwest. Its marketing strategy emphasized ambiance, complete with live music, meeting rooms, and plenty of lounge space to read or listen to music. "The focus is on making community happen," founder Ron Sher told *Publishers Weekly*'s Steven Zeitchik.

In the late 1990s, another type of music superstore appeared selling musical instruments. Traditionally, musical instrument retailers have been small, family-owned businesses catering to a specific niche in the market. Janet Moore reported in a February 1999 *Minneapolis Star Tribune* article that the musical instrument business is a $6 billion-a-year industry, with approximately 8,400 music stores across the United States. Two superstore chains hoping to cash in on that market are Guitar Center, Inc. and MARS. Guitar Center was able to show a 12.4 percent same-store sales growth in 1997, with new stores turning profits within three months of opening. The chain had 38 stores in 1998, 17 of which opened after 1995. Guitar Center went public in March 1997. Privately owned MARS boasted opening 9 new stores in 1997 and 1998, with a goal of operating 60 superstores ranging in size from 35,000 to 40,000 square feet. The existing stores have demonstration rooms, recording studios, and stages.

INDUSTRY LEADERS

BARNES & NOBLE

Barnes & Noble traces its corporate roots to the 1870s, but many people date its modern era from a single store in lower Manhattan opened in 1932. From that time, Barnes & Noble has grown into the nation's largest bookstore company. By 1999 New York-based Barnes & Noble Inc. operated 1,000 stores, including over 500 superstores under the Barnes & Noble, Bookstop, and Bookstar names, and slightly fewer than 500 mall stores with the trademark names B. Dalton Bookseller, Doubleday Book Shops, and Scribner's Bookstore. Barnes & Noble publishes books under its own imprint for exclusive sale through its retail store and nationwide mail-order catalog. Sales revenue for the fiscal year ended January 1999 topped $3 billion, a 7.5 percent increase from 1998. The company employed nearly 30,000 full and part-time employees in 1998.

BORDERS GROUP INC.

Borders, an Ann Arbor, Michigan-based bookstore, was established in 1971 as an 800-square-foot used book shop near the University of Michigan campus. It was founded by two brothers, Tom and Louis Borders, who saw a niche for a serious book store in the academic community. By 1974 Borders had moved several times, each store larger, and began selling new books instead of used. As it grew, Borders became known as one of the nation's finest book stores. The company tests all prospective sales clerks on their knowledge of literature and music before hiring them. Typical questions include: "Who wrote 'Death of a Salesman'?" and "Who composed 'Four Seasons'?" Borders is the number two bookstore in the United States, accomplished through its computerized inventory control system. Invented by Louis Borders in 1974, this system revolutionized the bookselling business and paved the way for handling the enormous inventory now carried in Borders and other superstores.

In 1992 Borders was acquired by K-mart, an affiliation that lasted three years. As of 1999, the company had more than 1,100 retail stores—250 Borders superstores, 900 Waldenbooks mall stores, and UK-based Books etc.—in all 50 states, the United Kingdom, Australia, and Singapore. In addition to more than 150,000 book titles in a typical store, a Borders Books and Music superstore also features more than 50,000 titles on compact discs and cassettes. The company has hosted in-store appearances by musical artists including Bruce Hornsby, Linda Ronstadt, and Tony Bennett. Revenue for the fiscal year ended January 26, 1999 reached $2.6 billion, representing a 15 percent increase over the previous year. The company employed 24,300 workers in 1998.

CHAPTERS, INC.

Chapters, Inc., based in Etobicoke, Ontario, is Canada's largest bookseller. Barnes & Noble owns 20 percent of Chapters, which operated 300 bookstores by 1999. As of 1998, superstores represented about 35.6 percent of Chapter's total revenues. For the fiscal year ended March 1998, Chapters reported revenue of $321 million, a 14-percent growth over 1997. The company employed over 4,200 people in 1998.

GUITAR CENTER, INC.

Guitar Center, Inc., based in Agoura Hills, California, caters to the musical needs of garage bands, offering guitars, amplifiers, drums, keyboards, and audio equipment. The company operates about 50 superstores, which range in size from 12,000 square feet to 15,000 square feet. Revenues for 1998 reached $392 million, an increase of 32 percent from the previous year. The company employed over 1,720 people in 1998.

MARS

MARS: The Musician's Plant was founded in 1977 by Mark Begelman. Prior to entering the musical instrument superstore business, Begelman had been president and chief operating officer at Office Depot Inc., an office supply chain. In 1999 Florida-based MARS had grown to 22 stores with plans to open another 30 within a year or two. The company is privately held.

MUSICLAND STORES CORPORATION

Minnetonka, Minnesota-based Musicland Stores Corporation is the number one music retailer in the United States. After struggling financially the company rebounded, in part because of the movie soundtrack for *Titanic*. By 1999 the company operated 1,350 stores, including its Media Play superstores. Sales revenue for 1998 reached $1.8 billion, and the company employed 15,600 people.

WORK FORCE

The American Booksellers Association estimates that about 100,000 people are employed in bookstores in America; approximately two-thirds of them are women. However, this figure doesn't include the number of people who, in various types of stores, sell books along with other merchandise. As with many retailing outlets, book and music superstores tend to do a significant portion of their trade during the holiday season. Borders Group Inc., for example, reports that all operating profit during 1996 came during the fourth quarter, which includes the gift-buying Christmas season.

AMERICA AND THE WORLD

In the late 1990s Britain experienced the "American invasion" of superstore expansion into the conservative British book and music world. First came Borders, which opened its first superstore on London's Oxford Street in 1998. In October 1997, Borders had acquired Books, Inc., a chain if 17 London bookstores, for a reported $65 million and made no secret of its future intentions. "We plan on opening superstores [in Britain] ultimately similar to the U.S. format," advised Vice President of planning and finance, Rick Vanzura, to *Billboard* magazine's Jeff Clark-Meads. Next came offers from Barnes & Noble and online merchants, such as amazon.com. Within its

own borders, Britain's Waterstones chain merged with Dillons under the new corporate name of EMI, which represented approximately 20 percent of the 1998 quality book market, in addition to sales of music and other merchandise.

Japan's Sony Corporation reported in January 1998 that its third-quarter earnings (ending December 31, 1997) rose 46 percent to $883 million in U.S. dollars. Sony attributed this to both the strong dollar and its successful box-office and music sales. However, Japan's music superstores were beginning to slump in compact disc sales, particularly in the singles market. As of 1998, Japan had almost doubled its sales from previous years of blank MiniDisc (MD) hardware and software products. This coincided with the decrease in sales of pre-recorded singles, which could be passed from person to person for individual recording on blank MDs at their convenience. The United States did not yet have that concern in 1998, since the MD market was still a minor one. Moreover, intellectual property laws in the United States, which protect copyrights and prohibit unauthorized copying, have helped control illegal "bootlegged" copies.

In the Philippines, the country's only music superstore, MusicOne, adopted the Western practice of purchased rather than consigned labels for its retail establishments. The megastore opened in Cavite City, Philippines, in August 1997 and far outsized its competitors, both in floor space and available titles.

FURTHER READING

Baker, John F. "All Change Here!" *Publishers Weekly,* 9 March 1998.

Barnes & Noble Inc. *1996 Annual Report.* New York: Barnes & Noble Inc., 1997.

Borders Group Inc. *1996 Annual Report.* Ann Arbor, MI: Borders Group Inc., 1997.

Carvajal, Doreen. "Falling Sales Hit Publishers for Second Year." *The New York Times,* 7 July 1997.

Clark-Meads, Jeffrey. "Borders Enters Crowded U.K. Market." *Billboard,* 27 December 1997.

———. "Reading the Bottom Line." *The New York Times Magazine,* 1997.

"The Endangered Bookshop." *The New York Times,* 19 June 1997.

Fields, Valerie. "City's Only Black Bookstore to Close; Chains Flooding Market." *The Arlington Morning News,* 17 April 1999.

Freund, Charles Paul. "Literature in Chains: Are Superstore Databases Turning Books Into Pretzels?" *Reason,* November 1997.

Gardner, James. "In Defense of Chain Stores." *National Review,* 20 May 1996.

Gonzales, David. "Filipino Biz Challenged By Music One." *Billboard,* 14 March 1998.

Gregory, Diona. "Book Wars." *Independent on Sunday,* 2 August 1998.

Halkias, Maria. "Taylors Among Plaintiffs Suing Superstore Chains, Publishers." *The Dallas Morning News,* 6 February 1999.

Hartnett, Michael. "Barnes & Noble Reshapes Book Market with Superstore Success." *Stores Magazine,* April 1996.

Linsmayer, Ann. "The Big Box Comes to Music." *Forbes,* 9 March 1998.

Marks, John. "How Borders Reads the Book Market." *U.S. News & World Report,* 30 October 1995.

"Media Play/On Cue Sales Fall 8 Percent." *Publishers Weekly,* 9 February 1998.

Moore, Janet. "MARS Has Opened Its First Superstore in Twin Cities." *Minneapolis Star Tribune,* 21 February 1999.

"Music Business Makes Waves on the Internet." *Advertising Age,* 16 February 1998.

Navasky, Victor. "Buying Books: Theory Vs. Practice." *The New York Times,* 20 June 1997.

Noah, Timothy. "Big Bookstores: Octopi in Tweed?" *U.S. News & World Report,* 30 March 1998.

Roiphe, Anne. "A Vanishing Luxury: Buying Books from the Readers of Books." *The New York Times,* 30 May 1997.

"Sales and Earnings Rise at Chapters." *Publishers Weekly,* 9 February 1998.

Theobald, Steven. "Chapters Mum on Net Sales Revenue." *The Toronto Star,* 30 January 1999.

"Three New B&N Superstores Planned." *Publishers Weekly,* 8 December 1997.

Townsend, Alair. "The Superstores' New Approach to Books Fills Void Left by Libraries." *Crain's New York Business,* 24 June 1996.

"Travelfest Hikes to Houston." *Publishers Weekly,* 1 September 1997.

Wieffering, Eric. "Musicland Readies Belated Entrance to Online Retailing." *Minneapolis Star Tribune,* 12 January 1999.

Zeitchik, Steven. "Washington Entrepreneur Starts Superstore Chain." *Publishers Weekly,* 22 December 1997.

—John Gallagher, updated by Lauri Harding and
Katherine Wagner

CHARTER SCHOOLS

In 1991, Minnesota was the first state to pass legislation allowing for the formation of charter schools. By 1999, nearly all states had passed legislation allowing charter schools and there were 1,128 such schools in existence. This phenomenal growth rate prompted President Bill Clinton in his 1997 State of the Union Address to call for federal assistance in advancing these types of schools in all states.

Charter schools are basically independent public schools that are publicly funded. They also tend to be free from many of the regulations and restrictions that other public schools must adhere to. Most charter schools are run by parent or education groups, but several for-profit companies have become involved in this arena, hoping to start what experts have dubbed "charter chains." Even the National Education Association (NEA) came out with limited support and a pledge of more than $1.5 million to help in the development of charter schools.

ORGANIZATION AND STRUCTURE

As of March 1998, 32 states as well as Washington, D.C., had passed legislation allowing for charter schools. Only 24 states, however, had any such schools actually running or approved to run. By July 1998, there were approximately 800 charter schools with more than 165,000 students in the United States.

There is no one formula for setting up a charter school, in particular because each state has its own set of regulations on how the school may be set up, receive funding, and demonstrate student performance. In addition, some states only allow state-accredited teachers, while other states are more lax on qualifications. Some proposed schools must win support in their local communities, while others are not required to; and some states allow only public schools or public school personnel to set up such schools, as well as allowing only a set a number of charter schools in the state. All of these differences make it hard to determine an overall financial analysis for this field.

Perhaps one of the most important and unclear aspects of charter schools is how they receive their funding. Some districts give charter schools 100 percent of the per-pupil funding that the other public schools receive, while other school systems allow for only a certain portion of that amount. In addition, charters may or may not be permitted or eligible for monies for special education students or other entitlement programs. Minnesota totally funds its charter schools, while Louisiana state-approved charter schools do not receive any district funding. Each state has its own formula for deciding upon funding, and each company seems to negotiate individual contracts with each state system.

Most charter schools are relatively small, and start-up capital has been one of the greatest problems facing those companies and groups interested in creating such schools. The federal and state governments are pledging low-interest or even no-interest loans to combat this problem. In addition, several companies and foundations also pledged start-up money for charter schools.

BACKGROUND AND DEVELOPMENT

Experimentation in the privatization of public schools began in 1969 in Texarkana, Texas. In an *Education Week* article, author Mark Walsh reported that a private company was given permission "to provide remedial instruction in the district's schools. By the 1971-72 school year, more than 200 school districts had entered into performance contracts for remedial instruction." The results were not promising. The company was accused of teaching to the tests, instead of providing a well-balanced curriculum.

Then in 1988, a new "school choice" battle ensued. Politicians, as well as some private citizens, started calling for more choice in public education: vouchers, waivers, and alternative schools. In 1991, Minnesota passed legislation allowing for the formation of charter schools, and numerous other states soon followed. According to the North Central Regional Educational Laboratory (NCREL), the vast majority of these schools have been set up in eight states: Arizona, California, Colorado, Massachusetts, Michigan, Minnesota, Texas, and Wisconsin.

Support for charter schools has come from very diverse sources. Reasons for supporting charters range from a desire for public school options to a belief that such competition will strengthen all public schools. Proponents also hope that these schools will initiate reform not possible at other public schools and that education will improve because these schools are held accountable for student performance.

Critics are just as vocal and diverse. They raise concerns that charter schools will destroy standard public education, are too limited in scope, and will not serve the needs of children needing special attention. In addition, these critics believe that because charter schools do not face the same scrutiny public schools face, they will not be held as accountable as they should be.

By 1992, private companies were eyeing the charter school field as a possible business proposition. That year, the Baltimore board of education signed an agreement with Education Alternatives, Inc. (EAI) to run nine of the district's schools for a period of five years; however, in just three short years, the board ended its relationship with EAI, citing several on-going problems with the company, including continued antagonism between EAI and the Baltimore's teachers union and EAI's failure to disclose financial information to the Baltimore city council. Student scores had also not shown the improvement that had been originally anticipated.

Even the Edison Project, started by Chris Whittle of Whittle Communications, found that its ambitious plans were going to have to be cut back. While Whittle initially wanted to set up 1,000 schools, that plan was scaled back. In fact, by 1999, after four years of operation, the Edison Project was only operating 51 public schools.

PIONEERS IN THE FIELD

Most charter schools are started by parent or education groups. Some are started by small businesses, but a few private companies have come to the field with the idea of for-profit corporate involvement on a wide-scale basis. The three most notable ones have been EAI (which later changed its name to The TesseracT Group, Inc.), Edison Project, and Alternative Public Schools, Inc. (which later became Beacon Education Management, LLC).

EAI began operating schools in 1987, with one school in Miami, Florida, though its involvement with charter schools began in 1992 with its contract with the Baltimore school district. The company also signed on with the school board in Hartford, Connecticut, to manage the entire city's school system. By 1996, both boards had voted to end their contracts with EAI. Baltimore cited several problems with the company, including decreases in standardized test scores for the elementary schools; cuts in staff, which increased class size; reductions in services for special education students, as well as the company's inability to account for certain Chapter 1 funds during its first year of operation; and its ongoing dispute with the teachers' union. A National Education Association report on charter schools stated that Hartford discontinued its association with the company over financial disputes, and Miami did not renew its contract because student scores were not improving as expected. By 1996, EAI did not have a single contract with any schools. At that time, the company announced that it would work with suburban schools, instead of city schools, in hopes that their methods would be more appropriate in those locations.

In 1995 the Edison Project began managing four elementary schools, located in Michigan, Massachusetts, Texas, and Kansas. In 1996, the company added eight more schools. According to Dr. F. Howard Nelson, the Edison Project took a different approach than EAI had. First, Edison worked more closely with the teachers' unions. It also kept its cost down by using

This charter school is utilizing notebook computers to enhance their students' learning abilities. (Courtesy of NEC USA, Inc.)

less-experienced teachers. In fact, many of their teachers were first-year teachers. Edison also initiated longer school days and school years. In addition, many of Edison's schools are magnet schools, which because of their popularity ensure optimal enrollment levels. Class sizes also run higher for Edison schools (29 versus 24 national average). Edison invested more than $1.5 million in each school it opened the first year.

In 1995, Alternative Public Schools, Inc. (APS) began managing one elementary school in Wilkinsburg, Pennsylvania, just outside Pittsburgh, as well as another one in Chelmsford, Massachusetts. Consistently challenged by teacher union opposition and court challenges, APS staffed its schools with nonunion teachers and counselors, who were APS employees, not employees of the school district. The company's policy of tying teachers' salaries to student achievement was a concern for teachers when first-year standardized test results at Turner Elementary were lower than they had been before APS began managing the school. In 1997, the company changed its name to Beacon Education Management, LLC, and began moving into other states.

CURRENT CONDITIONS

Parents and politicians are clamoring for new innovations in education as well as new funding possibilities. Amid calls for vouchers and waivers, the movement has been steadily growing since 1991, when Minnesota opened the first charter school in the nation.

Many charter schools have found a niche serving at-risk students, those students who often fall through the cracks in a traditional school setting. Charter schools can be more responsive to these students because the schools have greater flexibility and can accommodate individual student needs. In 1998, more than half of Texas' 60 charter schools catered to special-needs children. To encourage this trend, the Texas legislature amended the education code in 1997 to make it easier for schools that provide services for at-risk students to obtain a charter. Many of the Dallas charter schools are conversion schools, rather than start-up institutions. Conversion schools often find that receiving a state charter provides additional financial resources. One Texas school, Dallas Can! Academy, serves as a dropout recovery program for young people in Dallas and was established as a private institution in 1985. After receiving its charter in 1998, Dallas Can! saw the number of students it serves rise from 896 to 1,600.

SCHOOL CLOSING

Sometimes institutions that provide much-needed services for at-risk children can find themselves at risk. In January 1999, the Chicago Preparatory Charter High School was shut down after being in operation for two and half years. The school served teenagers with alcohol or drug abuse problems and had been founded through the Mayor's Office on Substance Abuse Policy. The school did not keep attendance records or transcripts and, as a consequence, the 45 students who were enrolled at the time of the closing were not awarded academic credit. The school's failure raised the issue of the need to monitor charter schools. Following the Chicago Prep woes, the Illinois State Board of Education asked for legislation that would require charter schools to report information, such as test scores and graduation rates, the same as all other public schools. In Washington, D.C., charter schools are already required to submit such data. In addition, volunteer monitors make regular visits to the schools. The purpose of these visits is to allow the monitors to examine files and financial statements. These actions are part of the D.C. Public Charter School Board's accountability plan for charter schools. In 1999 the board was responsible for 8 of the area's 18 charter schools.

Even as charter schools make inroads in addressing special-needs children, it is unclear if they will prosper in more affluent areas where good public school systems are already in place. While charter schools in the city of Chicago have waiting lists, the outlying suburban areas have been less enthusiastic to the charter concept. One proposed charter school in the northwest suburbs of Chicago has had an uphill battle since organizers announced their intentions to create the Jefferson Charter School. Despite opposition from the local Elk Grove Township Elementary District 59, Jefferson School finally received its charter from the state of Illinois after three years of legal wrangling. However, when Jefferson School finally opened enrollment for the 1999-2000 school year, the response was lukewarm. During the two-day advance registrations in January 1999, 50 students signed up, far short of the 96 needed to satisfy state requirements, and much less than the 220 that Jefferson School officials had hope for.

In 1998, according to the Reason Public Policy Institute and John M. McLaughlin, head of the Education Industry Group (EIG), charter schools had become the fastest-growing portion of the approximately $310 billion spent annually on public K-12 education. EIG reports that only about 10 percent of these charter schools are managed by larger private companies intent on making a profit from running them.

Increased student enrollment across the country has spurred the growth of new schools. Lisa Snell's article, "Chartering Classes," in *Reason* magazine, noted that in 1997 enrollment reached 51.7 million nationwide and that figure could climb to 54.6 million by 2006. To accommodate all of these students, new schools were being built across the nation. To address this issue, President Clinton announced in his 1997 State of the Union Address that he wanted more than $51.0 million to be made available to states working to implement such schools. Lori Mulholland with the

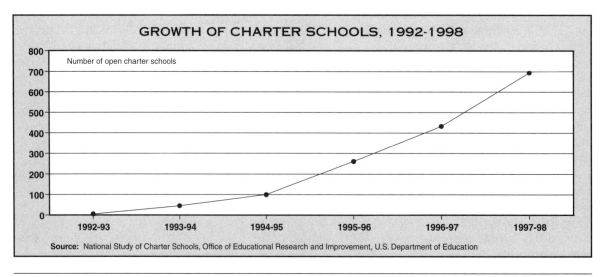

GROWTH OF CHARTER SCHOOLS, 1992-1998

Number of open charter schools

Source: National Study of Charter Schools, Office of Educational Research and Improvement, U.S. Department of Education

Students at a Boston charter school document the results of a hands on experiment. (Photograph by Peter Hamblin.)

Morrison Institute for Public Policy noted that this amount was almost a 10-fold increase over the amount of money ($5.4 million) that Congress had allocated for the federal Charter Schools Program through Title X of the Improving America's Schools Act in 1995. By 1998 Congress had upped the ante even more, allocating $80.0 million for assistance to states working on setting up charter schools.

FUNDING SOURCES

Funding is crucial for a charter school. The U.S. Department of Education acknowledged that one of the most difficult tasks facing proponents of charter schools was raising the needed capital. Some schools became extremely innovative with ways to cut initial start-up costs by holding classes in churches, local YMCA facilities, and other spaces. In addition to finding federal support, new charters were also finding by 1998 that several states and private foundations were more than willing to help them with the start-up costs of opening these schools. Several states, including Louisiana, Minnesota, Pennsylvania, and Ohio have all allocated either low- or no-interest loans available to charters, and Arizona and Minnesota have found new ways to help schools find and pay for adequate facilities.

Several major foundations assisted charter schools in the 1990s. *U.S. News Online* stated that Donald and Doris Fisher, founders of Gap, Inc. decided to put their money into educational choice projects. The Fishers pledged $25 million to help San Francisco schools bring in The Edison Project, while A. Alfred Taubman, chairman of Sotheby's, put up $680 million to launch his own for-profit charter school management company, the Leona Group. Moreover, the Walton family members offered $350,000 of their Wal-Mart fortune to promote charter schools.

Companies were also looking at other ways to fund and support these schools. In 1998, one Florida community had plans to establish the nation's first municipally run open-enrollment charter school. Octavio Visiedo, vice president of Haskell Education Services and former superintendent of Florida's Dade County schools, put forth the idea that his company, which designed and built the school, could also operate the charter elementary.

EAI, on the other hand, was granted a charter by the state of Arizona in 1997 to partner with home developers to build schools in newly established neighborhoods. The company expected to build and oper-

---

Pioneer CHRIS WHITTLE
EDUCATING AMERICA

Beginning with his bid for student government president at the University of Tennessee in 1968, Chris Whittle saw a need to reform education. His platform centered on reforming the university. It was the first step leading toward Whittle's national school reform plans that shook up the world of education.

After graduation, Whittle signed on to teach at a private school in Connecticut but instead began publishing magazines for schools and later health magazines as founder and chairman of Whittle Communications. From 1979 to 1986, he was also the chairman and publisher of *Esquire* magazine. After 19 years of publishing, Whittle branched out into electronics to begin his next venture, Channel One, in 1989. Channel One was an electronic news system that provided thousands of students with free video equipment and news programs in classrooms. The project was supported through commercial advertisements that played between the news segments. Channel One was controversial from the start, and many people wondered if the project simply used children to garner a profit.

Two years later, Whittle again challenged the educational status quo when he founded the Edison Project.

The idea behind the project was to create public schools run by the private sector. Under Whittle's plan, school districts that voted to adopt the Edison Project school system would turn over tax money designated for each student's education. The Edison system would then be contracted to teach those students. The draw, according to Whittle, was that students in the Edison Project would receive a high-level, more global and technology-oriented instruction that resembled the education primarily taught to children in elite schools. After several years of research and $75 million in fundraising, the first of the Edison Schools opened in 1995.

The trail of Whittle's success was not always a smooth ride, however. Whittle had to sell Channel One in September of 1994 to account for losses of two other ventures under Whittle Communications: *Medical News Network* and *Special Report*. But he charged ahead with Edison. As of 1998, 51 schools had joined the Edison National Network. By May 1998, the company expected its revenues to grow from $68 million that year to $126 million in 1999. Yet just as with Channel One, the Edison Project remains controversial as people question the concept of making a profit from public education.

---

ate 12 such schools by the year 2000. Other companies were looking to do the same thing in not only Arizona, but also in other states such as Texas and California.

Finally, one of the most innovative charter school possibilities in the late 1990s was the home learning/distance learning model. Theodore Rebarber, author of the Reason Public Policy Institute's study on charter schools, noted that this model has great potential, because of the growing interest in home-schooling. Recent technological advances make home learning a reasonable and affordable idea, allowing charter schools the ease of starting the school without having to invest a great deal of money in facilities.

Even Lehman Brothers is betting on charter schools. As early as 1996, the company held an education-industry convention to promote investment in this field for its clients. The company likened the trend in school choice to that of the health care industry, intimating that the education industry will continue to grow into a formidable market. In addition, they see companies such as EAI, APS, and the Edison Project as the future large-scale HMO's of the education field.

INDUSTRY LEADERS

The Edison Project, founded in 1991 and based in New York, New York, is probably the most widely known for-profit company involved in the charter school movement. This recognition has a great deal to do with its founder, Chris Whittle, of Whittle Communications. Even though Edison did not take off as quickly as Whittle had hoped, the company is expanding each year. At the end of their fiscal year in June 1997, The Edison Project showed $37 million in sales. The company has continued expanding, growing from 4 schools and 3,000 students in 1995 to 51 schools and 24,000 students in the 1998-99 school year. Edison has invested over $161 million in these schools, which has helped to supply computers for home use by their students and telephones and televisions in the classrooms. Edison has been shifting its focus from charter schools to operating public schools by contract with local school districts. In November 1998, Edison initiated a stock-option plan for its staff in Miami Dade County, Florida. In a move backed by the Miami teachers' union, Edison's Dade County employees were given the opportunity to buy shares valued from $1,000 to $10,500, which they can redeem, hopefully at a profit, when the company is traded pub-

---

licly. Edison plans to expand its stock-option program nationwide and to go public sometime in 2000.

TesseracT Group, formerly EAI, moved its headquarters from Minneapolis, Minnesota, to Scottsdale, Arizona, in May 1999. The company reported sales of $15.3 million for the fiscal year ended June 1998, a figure that represented a substantial increase over 1997 sales of $4.8 million. The company employed nearly 1,000 workers in 1998, an increase of 716 percent from the previous year. In 1998 the company acquired Sunrise Educational Services, which operated 16 charter schools in Arizona. During the 1998-99 school year, TesseracT operated over 40 schools serving 9,000 students in 6 states.

Alternative Public Schools also changed its name, becoming Beacon Education Management, LLC in 1997. Beacon is headquartered in Westborough, Massachusetts, and, in 1999, provided services, such as total school management, for seven schools in four states; Rochester Hills, Michigan-based JCR & Associates, a Beacon affiliate, provided services for nine schools in Michigan as of November 1998.

In November 1998 there were a dozen for-profit companies in the industry, including Philadelphia, Pennsylvania-based Aramark Corp., a leader in institutional food service. Aramark opened 28 private, for-profit elementary schools in 8 states in 1997. Other names in the field include Boston-based Advantage Schools, Inc., which operates 8 schools in 7 states, and Educational Development Corp., headquartered in Grand Rapids, Michigan.

FURTHER READING

American Federation of Teachers. "An Analysis of the EAI Experience in Baltimore." Baltimore, MD: AFT, 1996. Available from http://www.aft.org/research/reports/private/eai1/eai1.htm.

Applebome, Peter. "For-Profit Education Venture to Expand." *New York Times,* 2 June 1997. Available from http://www.public-policy.org/~ncpalpi/edu/pdedu/48.html.

Ascher, Carol, Norm Fruchter, and Robert Berne. "Hard Lessons: Public Schools and Privatization." New York: Twentieth Century Fund, September 1996. Available from http://epn.org/tcf/schlch7c.html.

Beacon Educational Management. "Beacon and ABS Collaborate to Develop Arizona Charter Schools." *Beacon News,* March 1998. Available from http://www.beaconedu.com/release3-98.html.

———. "Beacon History," 1998. Available from http://www.beaconedu.com/history.html.

Boney, Brian. "Change of Plans: Charter Schools Taking on Most Challenging Students." *The Dallas Morning News,* 14 April 1998.

Center for Education Reform. "Answers to Frequently Asked Questions About Charter Schools." CER, 1998. Available from http://edreform.com/faq/faqcs.htm.

———. *Charter School Workbook: Your Roadmap to the Charter School Movement.* CER,1997. Available from http://edreform.com.

Cohen, Warren. "The New Education Bazaar." *USNews Online,* 27 April 1998. Available from http://www.usnews.com/usnews/issue/980427/27char.htm.

DeFotis, Dimitra. "Charter School Registration at a Crawl." *Chicago Tribune,* 21 January 1999.

Edison Project. "Annual Report on School Performance." Edison Project, 1998. Available from http://www.edison-project.com/annualframe.html.

"The Edison Project." *Hoover's Capsules.* Available from http://www.hoovers.com.

Education Information Center. "Private Companies in Public School Classrooms." *Ohio School Board Association Journal,* August 1996. Available from http://www.osba-ohio.org/August-96/8-96EIC.html.

ENR. "Builder Teams with Municipality to Provide All School Services." *ENR,* 6 April 1998.

Ferrechio, Susan. "Verdict Not in on Charter Schools' Performance; Oversight Panels Reserve Judgement." *The Washington Times,* 23 March 1999.

Fulford, Nancy, Lenaya Raack, and Gail Sunderman. "Charter Schools in Our Midst: Charter Schools as Change Agents: Will They Deliver?" North Central Regional Educational Laboratories, January 1998. Available from http://www.ncrel.org/sdrs/pbriefs/97/97-1chg.htm.

———. "Charters in Our Midst: An Overview." North Central Regional Educational Laboratories, January 1998. Available from http://www.ncrel.org/sdrs/pbriefs/97/97-1over.htm.

Guthrie, James. W. "Reinventing Education Finance: Alternatives for Allocating Resources to Individual Schools." Washington, DC: National Center for Educational Statistics, 1998. Available from http://nces.edu.gov/pubs98/finance/98217.5.html#note12.

Lewin, Tamar. "Edison Group Say Students Gain." *The New York Times,* 7 April 1999.

Martinez, Michael. "Charter School's Failure Reverberates." *Chicago Tribune,* 1 April 1999.

Mulholland, Lori. "Charter Schools: The Reform and The Research." Center for Education Reform, March 1996. Available from http://edreform.com/pubs.morrison.htm.

National Conference of State Legislatures. "Charter Schools." NCSL, 24 March 1998. Available from http://www.uscharterschools.org.

National Educational Association. "For-Profit Management of Public Schools." NEA, November 1996. Available from http://www.nea.org/info/corp.html.

Nelson, F. Howard, Ph.D. "How Private Management Firms Seek to Make Money in Public Schools." Washington, D.C.: American Federation of Teachers, January 1997. Available from http://www.aft.org/research/reports/private/jsbm/jsbm.htm.

Reason Public Policy Institute. "Charter School Innovations: Keys to Effective Reform." *Spectrum: The Journal of State Government,* Fall 1997.

Schnaiberg, Lynn. "Firms Hoping to Turn Profit From Charters." *Education Week,* 10 December 1997. Available from http://www.edweek.org/ew/vol-17/16profit.h17.

Snell, Lisa. "Chartering Classes." *Reason,* September 1997. Available from http://www.reason.mag.com/index.htm.

Strobel, Warren P., Marci McDonald, Mike Tharp, Joseph L. Galloway, and Thomas Toch. "Aramark Looks to Join Charter-School Market." *U.S. News & World Report,* 16 November 1998.

The TesseracT Group. "The TesseracT Group Completes First Phase of $20 Million Sale-leaseback of Five School Properties." *Money,* 16 June 1998. Available from http://www.pathfinder.com/money/latest/press/pw/1998Jun16/1272.html.

"The TesseracT Group, Inc." *Hoovers's Online.* Available from http://www.hoovers.com.

Toch, Thomas. "A Carrot for the Teacher." *U.S. News & World Report,* 2 November 1998.

Walsh, Mark. "Brokers Pitch Education as Hot Investment." *Education Week,* 21 February 1996. Available from http://www.edweek.org/ew/vol-15/22biz.h15.

———. "Privatization Found to Fall Short of Billing." *Education Week,* 6 November 1996. Available from http://www.edweek.org/ew/vol-16/10piv.h16.

—Nancy Hatch Woodward, updated by Katherine Wagner

COMPUTER ANIMATION ENTERTAINMENT

Animation, the art of producing the illusion of movement from a sequence of two-dimensional drawings or three-dimensional objects, has long been a staple of the entertainment industry. Animation can take on many shapes, ranging from primitive drawings in television cartoons such as the "Flintstones," to complex, dinosaur-sized creatures in *Jurassic Park.* The animation industry flourished from the 1930s to the 1950s, largely through the efforts of pioneer Walt Disney, who produced such full-length animated movies as *Dumbo, Bambi,* and *Snow White and the Seven Dwarfs.* By the 1970s, however, animation had nearly died out. It would take the advent of computers, and the eventual combination of technology and artistry in the 1980s, to revive the public's interest.

The 1990s saw an animation renaissance and, during this period, the animation studios and production companies that were able to find the right combination of creative talent and technical wizardry found a burgeoning marketplace for their products. As reported by Cindy Waxer in a December 1998 article in *The Globe and Mail,* "According to the 1997 Roncarelli Report, an annual market analysis, the computer animation field is a $15.8 billion [U.S.] industry that will double in size by 2000. From 1996 to 1997, the worldwide value of commercial computer animation rose by 35 percent." In 1992 there were a half-dozen computer animation studios in California. By 1998 several dozen firms had emerged to produce computer-generated imaging (CGI). Because of the high cost of making a full-length animated feature—upwards from $12 million—Hollywood studios started forming partnerships to split the costs of pro-

ducing a movie. For instance, the 1998 box-office hit, *A Bug's Life,* was created by Pixar Animation Studio and distributed by The Walt Disney Company.

Animation projects are generally collaborative efforts and include the talent of animators, technical directors, producers, artists, and engineers. Because of the high level of technical sophistication required, many of these workers have advanced degrees and come from disciplines such as math or computer programming. In the past, the animation field was divided into two segments. From the very beginning, studios employed animation artists—people who could painstakingly draw quirky animated characters by hand. The arrival of computers in the 1980s, however, marshaled in other workers (namely scientists, engineers, and programmers) who were capable of developing complex animation software. As the 1990s drew to a close, animation firms, wanting to reduce costs and decrease production cycles, started hiring individuals who possessed both technical know-how and artistic flair. This practice resulted in a shortage of qualified animators and left some companies spending considerable energy recruiting candidates or employing overseas workers. In response, colleges and universities began offering programs to teach both the artistry and technical side of the animation process.

While cartoons and movie special effects are among the most visible uses for computer animation, computer-generated three-dimensional (3-D) modeling also has applications in the fields of interior decoration, architecture, engineering, medical science, and forensics. Until 1999 most sophisticated graphics could only be produced on costly supercomputers. In March 1999, though, Sony unveiled its Playstation II, an interactive video game with a $500 price tag, armed with powerful graphic capabilities. If low-cost machines such as the Playstation II become state-of-the-art technology, high-quality computerized animation would be put within the reach and pocketbooks of everyday consumers.

ORGANIZATION AND STRUCTURE

Animation has always been a labor-intensive process and, as a consequence, most animation projects are accomplished through a team effort. Even though computer animation is technology driven, the workflow for an animated feature movie is still essentially the same as it was in the earliest days of animation. While the computer has replaced some hand drawings, it has not entirely eliminated pen-and-ink sketches. An animation project begins with the creation of a storyboard, a series of sketches outlining the important points of the story and some of the dialogue. When animation was strictly done by hand, the workload would then be distributed between senior artists, who sketched the frames where the most action was occurring and junior artists, who filled in the in-between frames. When computers are being used, artists use the storyboard sketches to create clay figures that are made into digitalized 3-D characters, which are then manipulated by animation artists who also create the background fill. Altogether, an animated feature is the collective work of many people, including animators, lighting experts, story writers, and sound technicians.

BACKGROUND AND DEVELOPMENT

Before the arrival of computers, animation was created entirely by hand. By producing a series of successive images in frames, animation simulates movement. In order to trick the eye into seeing motion, each second of animated sequence for film requires 24 frames. In the earliest cartoons, each one of the frames was drawn by hand. This resulted in a great deal of work just to create a short cartoon. For instance, the 1910 cartoon *Gertie the Trained Dinosaur,* which was primitive compared to later animation, required 10,000 drawings. In 1915 Earl Hurd streamlined the process by developing a time-saving method known as cel animation. In cel animation, each individual character is drawn on a separate piece of transparent paper. Then, the background is drawn on a piece of

opaque paper. When the animation is shot, the transparent paper is overlaid on the opaque. With this method, the background was drawn once, and only the parts that needed to be changed had to be redrawn instead of the entire frame.

For many decades, hand-drawn animation was the industry standard. Filmmaker John Whitney began to change that in the late 1950s and early 1960s; Whitney pioneered motion graphics using equipment that he purchased at a government war surplus auction. These precise instruments allowed Whitney to develop motion control of the camera, zoom, and artwork. Later these techniques would be used to create the star-gate slit-scan sequence in Stanley Kubrick's movie *2001: A Space Odyssey* (1968). In 1986 Whitney received an Academy of Motion Pictures Arts and Sciences "Medal of Commendation for Cinematic Pioneering" in recognition of his contribution.

The 1960s saw another development that led to the eventual rise of computer animation. In 1963 Ken Knowlton, who worked at Bell Laboratories, authored a programming language that could generate computer-produced movies. It wouldn't be until 1982, though, with the release of Disney's *TRON,* that computer graphics would be explored as a serious movie-making technique.

PIONEERS IN THE FIELD

There is perhaps no name more well-known in the field of animation than that of Walt Disney, the cartoon artist who founded the mega-entertainment empire that bears his name. Disney, who was born in Chicago in 1901, left school at 16 and later studied briefly at art schools in Chicago and Kansas City, Missouri. Disney's 1928 cartoon *Steamboat Willie* was a first on two accounts. It was the first cartoon that was synchronized with sound, and it also introduced Mickey Mouse, his enduringly popular cartoon character. Disney would go on to many other firsts in the field of animation. In 1932 he used full color in a cartoon for the first time in the film *Flowers and Trees.* He also created the first full-length animated feature with his 1937 *Snow White and the Seven Dwarfs,* which was produced with 400,000 sketches. Disney's production company ushered in the golden age of animation with film classics such as *Pinocchio* (1940), *Fantasia* (1941), and *Bambi* (1942). At that time, all animation work was done by hand with Disney overseeing the productions. Before he died in 1966, Disney had expanded his enterprise to include the Disneyland Theme Park in Anaheim, California; numerous syndicated comic strips featuring his cartoon characters; and television programs such as "The Mickey Mouse Club" and "Walt Disney's Wonderful World of Color." Disney received 32 Academy Awards.

CURRENT CONDITIONS

While the roots of computer animation date back to animated movies early in the 1900s, computer-generated imaging (CGI) is a relatively new technique. The popularized idea of combining the power of computer processing and the originality of animated artistry as a movie art form began in the 1980s. Computers revolutionized the animation process, supplementing traditional animation methods with hardware and software capable of creating realistic on-screen characters. Advancements in the computer animation field swept the entertainment industry in the 1990s. In 1991 George Lucas's special effects firm Industrial Light & Magic (ILM) created an oozing cyborg (at a cost of $6.4 million) that had five minutes of screen time in the film *Terminator 2: Judgment Day*. Developments were happening so quickly, though, that Dennis Muren, a senior visual-effects supervisor at ILM, was quoted in an April 13, 1992, Time magazine article as saying, "Movie effects have been the same for a hundred years, and they're changing this year."

State-of-the-art technology in the animation field is ever changing and seems to have no end in sight. Elaborate computer-generated movie special effects have become the industry's standard. One result of this is that movie production costs have soared. In 1996 two films each cost more than $100 million to produce. Just one year later, 10 movies had budgets greater than $100 million. The possibilities for computer special effects are endless, ranging from lava flowing down an exploding volcano in *Dante's Peak* to virtual people aboard the Titanic in the movie of the same name. Even George Lucas, founder of ILM, spent $10 million for special effects refurbishment of his 1975 blockbuster *Star Wars* on the movie's twentieth anniversary reissue.

Before 1995, conventional wisdom was that computer-generated imaging was too inexact a science to replace hand-drawn animation, which many felt was the only way to capture small, quirky facial and body movements. In 1995, however, Pixar Animation Studios and its partner, The Walt Disney Company, showed that computer animation wasn't just an ancil-

lary technique with the release of *Toy Story*, the first fully computer animated feature-length movie. The success of *Toy Story*, which grossed $350 million in worldwide box-office sales in 1995, proved that computer animation is a viable movie-making art form—one that requires constant research and development (R&D). As an example, Pixar has an annual R&D budget of $10 million, which it uses to develop proprietary software that allows for greater control of characters' body movements. After *Toy Story*, the company had already greatly advanced its computer animation techniques by the time it began work on its next project, *A Bug's Life*, which was released in 1998. In *Toy Story*, it took 700 software controls to manipulate the features of Woody, the film's most intricate character. By contrast, Pixar used 3,942 controls to animate Hopper, the most complex character in *A Bug's Life*. Riding on the success of *Toy Story* and *A Bug's Life*, Pixar has ambitious plans to produce full-length feature films. In 1998 Steve Jobs, Pixar's CEO, announced that the company intends to release a new movie every year.

Computer animation is an important component of video games. Phoenix, Arizona-based Rainbow Studios had 15 employees spend two years to create the 3-D animation for Microsoft's video game, "Motocross Madness."

Computer animation does go beyond entertainment value though, and it can even save people's lives. Surgeons use 3-D animation to simulate a procedure before they enter the operating room. In the area of forensics, police and the FBI trace missing persons with the aid of computer-aged photos.

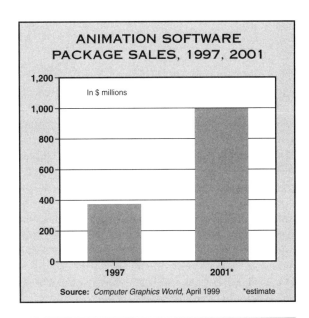

ANIMATION SOFTWARE PACKAGE SALES, 1997, 2001

In $ millions

Source: *Computer Graphics World*, April 1999   *estimate

INDUSTRY LEADERS

Many of the leading animation firms bring together powerhouse names from the entertainment and computer fields. The co-founders of Microsoft and Apple Computers have both paired up with influential filmmakers to produce animated movies. The results of these ventures have generally been financial successes and, as a consequence, new animation studios and production companies have started to form around the world.

DREAMWORKS SKG

DreamWorks SKG, based in Universal City, California, co-produced the highly successful 1998 animated feature *Antz*. DreamWorks produces films, television shows, software, and records. It represents the collaborative effort of three founding partners—movie producer Steven Spielberg, former Disney executive Jeffrey Katzenberg, and music industry whiz David Geffen, who each received a 22-percent share of the company for individual investments of $33 million. The main shareholder, at 24 percent, is Paul Allen, the co-founder of computer software giant Microsoft.

INDUSTRIAL LIGHT & MAGIC

Filmmaker George Lucas's Industrial Light & Magic (ILM), part of Lucas Digital, is an outgrowth of the special effects team that worked on the box-office smash *Star Wars*. The San Rafael, California-based company has been supplying special effects in Hollywood since the mid-1970s. ILM was responsible for creating dinosaurs in Steven Spielberg's *The Lost World*, rampaging fire in *Backdraft*, and water for *The Abyss*.

PACIFIC DATA IMAGES

Located in Palo Alto, California, Pacific Data Images (PDI) produces high-end animation and visual effects for feature films and projects in the commercial and entertainment industries. PDI, along with partner DreamWorks SKG, produced the 1998 full-length animation feature *Antz*. It took a team of 27 PDI animators 18 months to create the film. PDI has developed software that controls precise movements of body parts and facial features, such as the eyes or mouth. The software allows animators to create complex expressions without having to memorize facial musculature. In the television arena, PDI created the animated lead-in to *Entertainment Tonight* and the 3-D episode of *The Simpsons*. PDI was started in 1980 and employed over 300 people in 1998.

PIXAR ANIMATION STUDIOS

Steve Jobs, cofounder of Apple Computers, put up $50 million of his own money to purchase Richmond, California-based Pixar Animation Studios from George Lucas. Under Jobs' leadership, Pixar went on to create *Toy Story*, the first fully computer-animated movie, in partnership with The Walt Disney Company. *Toy Story*, created by a team of 60 Pixar animators, was the highest grossing film released in 1995. Pixar has developed proprietary software in the areas of modeling, animating, lighting, production management, and image rendering. Its RenderMan software was used to create dinosaurs in *Jurassic Park*. Pixar licenses its software to other production companies. In 1997 Pixar and Disney announced a five-movie deal. As part of the agreement, Disney will handle marketing and distribution of the movie with Pixar having creative control. As part of the agreement, the two companies produced *A Bug's Life*, which was released in 1998. Much of Pixar's success is credited to John Lasseter, who worked for Disney and at George Lucas's special effects company and now oversees creative development at Pixar. Sales in 1998 reached $14.3 billion, an increase of nearly 60 percent over the previous year. The firm employed 430 people in 1999, a sizable expansion over the company's six employees in 1986.

THE WALT DISNEY COMPANY

The Walt Disney Company, headquartered in Burbank, California, was an early pioneer in full-length animated feature movies and continued its dominance in the 1990s. Disney produced two of the top grossing animated features of all time—*The Lion King*, which had grossed $313 in domestic box office receipts by 1998; and *Aladdin*, which had recorded domestic box office sales of $219 million by 1998. In 1991 Disney entered into a three-movie deal with Pixar Animation Studios, which resulted in the 1995 animated feature *Toy Story*, a film that earned $1 billion dollars in box office, video, and licensing sales. After renegotiating their deal in 1997, Pixar and Disney signed a five-picture agreement that will allow Disney to buy up to five percent of Pixar. *A Bug's Life*, co-produced by Disney and Pixar, opened in 1998 and took in $45.7 million over the 1998 Thanksgiving weekend. Disney is the second-largest media company in the world and includes theme parks, television and film studios, publishing companies, a cruise line, and professional sports teams. For the fiscal year ended September 1998, Disney's total operation had sales of $22 billion and employed 117,000 people.

WORK FORCE

The computer animation industry is characterized by a well-educated work force, populated with people who combine computer expertise and creative ability. While there is some on-the-job training, to learn an individual company's proprietary software programs for instance, production studios generally do not train employees in technical areas such as creating special effects or programming languages. These skills, in addition to basic animation drawing, are learned in specialized computer animation programs offered in colleges, universities, and art schools. A typical computer animation program includes the following classes: life drawing, character animation, color and design, character design, animation layout, storytelling, 3-D character computers, and background painting. Most animators enter the job market with degrees in computer animation. Quite often, these programs work closely with companies in the industry and tailor their curriculum to meet the marketplace's needs. For instance, in addition to funding an animation program at the California Institute of the Arts (CalArts), Disney Studios hires graduates of the program. Alumni of the CalArts program include filmmaker Tim Burton and Pixar's John Lasseter.

According to the Bureau of Labor Statistics, the outlook for computer graphic artists, which include computer animators, is better than average through 2006. The 1990s saw a hot job market for qualified computer animators. In 1996, according to P.J. Huffstutter as reported in *The Dallas Morning News,* salaries ranged from $40,000 for those with no experience to $150,000 after two years of hands-on training. That same year, graduates of Texas A&M University's Master's degree program in visualization sciences were receiving offers of $45,000 to $55,000, mainly for jobs as technical directors. It seems likely that salaries will continue to increase as employers compete for highly skilled workers who have both creative vision and the expertise to handle the industry's technical demands. In a December 1998 article in the *South China Morning Post,* Steve Jobs was quoted as saying that part of his job as CEO of Pixar was being a talent scout. Jobs went on to say that in order to attract and retain employees, he pays his employees well and offers benefits such as stock options.

Because of an increasing demand for computer animators and not enough qualified U.S. applicants, some studios have turned to workers from outside the United States, recruiting candidates from countries such as Canada, France, and India. In 1996 U.S. firms reported that between 26 and 50 percent of the digital artists they employed were working in the United States with a visa. Even that approach has failed to keep up with the demand for experienced computer animators, though. Huffstutter quoted Gail Currey, director of digital production operations at ILM, as saying that an estimated 3,000 workers in 1996 weren't enough to fill the growing need in films, games, the Internet, and commercial work.

AMERICA AND THE WORLD

While U.S. companies, such as Pixar and Disney, dominate the computer animation field, it is a truly global industry. Canadian companies, for instance, are leading-edge innovators in animation technology. In 1998 Toronto-based Nelvana Ltd. and Vancouver-based Mainframe Entertainment Inc. have both created 3-D computer-generated television shows for children. In order to make 3-D animation viable for television, both firms had to invest in new software and hardware. For Mainframe, this multimillion dollar capital outlay produced decreased financial results in the first half of 1998 and dropped the company's share from $9.75 in June 1997 to $5 in June of 1998. Nevertheless, Mainframe believes that its investment will pay off. Mainframe representatives told Gayle MacDonald in a June 15, 1998 article in *The Globe and Mail* that Mainframe had streamlined their operations to the point where they were able to produce a half-hour 3-D animation show at nearly the same cost as a 2-D program—somewhere between $300,000 to $500,000 per half hour. Nelvana is not quite so optimistic about their production costs. In the same article, Nelvana's co-founder and co-chief executive estimated the cost to produce a half-hour 3-D animated program at 15 to 30 percent higher than 2-D. Nelvana created, along with partner French MediaLab, "Donkey King Country," a 3-D cartoon series. Nelvana also partnered with another French company, Sparx, to create a series of half-hour 3-D television shows called "Rolie Polie Olie." It took a team of 20 employees one year to complete the show's 13 episodes.

Hollywood has often sent animation work overseas, especially to companies in the Far East. In Korea though, one firm has made its own bid into the market. Graphic Animatio Visual and Multimedia (GAV), owned by Shon Dong-soo, is the only Korean company to produce CD-ROMs, computer games, television shows, music videos, Internet sites, stop-motion clay animation, and video magazines. Shon, who was the first person in his country to use computer animation, began experimenting with the process in 1993 after a tour of NHK studios in Japan. By 1999 Shon had created an award-winning educational CD-ROM featuring Ricky and Ralph, a small boy and his fuzzy yellow friend. Shon's long-term goals include producing a full-length animated movie.

RESEARCH AND TECHNOLOGY

Creating animated characters out of thin air is a long, laborious process. While computers play a large role in animation, hand drawings are still the first step. Artists' sketches develop the story line and characters. As an example, it took 27,000 such sketches to define the plot and personalities of the characters in *A Bug's Life*. The design department then used these sketches to model clay figures of the insects. These clay figures gave the animators an idea of how the characters moved. From there, the clay figures were transformed onto a computer screen as 3-D wire-frame model. Technical directors put opaque-surfaced polygons over the wire-frame models. The purpose of the opaque surfaces was to show the animators how light would reflect off the figures. Following that, animators brought the 3-D images to life and technical artists filled in the background and applied the final touches to the characters. When animators want to create animated human figures, they use a motion capture booth, which records a person's movements and translates them into 3-D images. Rainbow Studios has an 800-square-foot motion capture booth that it uses in the development of animated video games for Microsoft.

The computer can transform or alter an on-screen image. For instance, morphing, a popular special effect technique that blends one image into another and was first used in the movie Willow in 1988, is created by technicians providing the computer with the first frame in the transformation sequence and the last frame. The computer then automatically generates the fill-in frames segueing from one image to the other. While computers can add images to the screen, they also can erase what is there. This technique was used to digitally remove the cable that helped Julia Roberts to fly as Tinkerbell in *Hook*.

Many computer software developers are working to create realistic animated human facial expression, which has been difficult to accomplish because of the complexity of human behavior. In 1998 Brian Guenter of Microsoft Research offered two scenarios on how to construct photorealistic computer-generated humans. One was through video compression, where fa-

cial expressions would be captured in a studio and delivered to the user over the Internet in a virtual 3-D environment. The user would then choose the desired face position using a virtual camera. In addition, Guenter said that morphing could be used to blend one facial expression into the next.

FURTHER READING

Booth, Cathy. "The Wizard of Pixar." *Time,* 14 December 1998.

Cohen, David. "Jobs Uses Midas Touch on Filmmaker Pixar." *South China Morning Post,* 22 December 1998.

Corliss, Richard. "They Put the ILM in Film at George Lucas' Oscar-hoarding Industrial Light & Magic." *Time,* 13 April 1992.

Craven, Delia. "Pixar Reveals Some of the Secrets Behind Its New Movie." *Red Herring,* January 1999. Available from http://www.redherring.com/mag/issue62/out.html.

DeMocker, Judy. "Making Antz No Picnic." *Wired News,* 29 September 1998. Available from http://www.wired.com.

"GAV Media Pioneers Digital Animation in Korea." *The Korea Times,* 20 January 1999.

Goddard, Connie. "Technology Brings 'Drawing Board' to Life." *Chicago Tribune,* 20 November 1998.

Huffstutter, P.J. "Animation Studios Vying to Draw Digital Artists: Small Pool of Workers Makes for Hot Job Market." *The Dallas Morning News,* 2 December 1996.

Kilday, Gregg. "Magic Behind The Fantastic Realism of 'T2' Lies an Array of Visual Artists Stretching Their Craft into New Limits." *Entertainment Weekly,* 30 August 1991.

Kunde, Diana. "Aggies in Wonderland: A&M Grads Snapped up as Computer Animators." *The Dallas Morning News,* 3 July 1996.

MacDonald, Gayle. "Canadian Animators Leading 3-D Revolution." *The Globe and Mail,* 15 June 1998.

"Making Games Come to Life\Rainbow Studios' Animation Realistic." *The Arizona Republic,* 1999.

Markoff, John. "Silicon Valley's Awesome Look at New Sony Toy." *The New York Times,* 19 March 1999.

Sherrid, Pamela. "Is 'A Bug's Life' Good for an Investor's Life?" *U.S. News & World Report,* 23 November 1998.

Tanner, Mike. "Pixar Keeps Creative Control in Disney Deal." *Wired News,* 26 February 1997. Available from http://www.wired.com.

Waxer, Cindy. "Animation Artists Brush up on Computer Skills." *The Globe and Mail,* 31 December 1998.

Wolfe, Alexander. "News: Unix-level Quality Sought for PCs—Wintel Duo Readies 3-D Graphics Push," *Electronic Engineering Times,* 27 July 1998.

Zeidler, Sue. "Special Effects Invade U.S. Movie Industry in 1997." *Reuters,* 1 February 1997.

Zoglin, Richard. "What's Up, Doc? Animation! The Cartoon Boom in TV and Movies is Reviving a Neglected Craft." *Time,* 6 August 1990.

—Katherine Wagner

COMPUTER NETWORK SUPPORT SERVICES

INDUSTRY SNAPSHOT

The care and feeding of networks is a major focus for businesses of all sizes. Surveys conducted by Computer Reseller News have indicated that networking and service/support were two of the fastest-growing areas of business information technology spending in the late 1990s.

Computer network support services rely on increasingly complex business operations and a strong growth rate in network implementation, which are both due in part to advances in computing, as well as business trends in outsourcing and a shortage of in-house technical expertise. By providing necessary assistance in operating and maintaining computer networks, participants in this emerging industry engage in profitable and growing markcts.

As the 1990s drew to a close, California-based market research firm Dataquest Inc. reported $262 billion worth of sales and 14.5 percent growth in yearly revenues for the information technology services market. Annual services growth is expected to continue at 13 to 15 percent—reaching more than $516 billion by the year 2001.

ORGANIZATION AND STRUCTURE

In a typical network support agreement, the service provider may assume daily responsibility of the LAN or WAN (local-access network or wide area network, respectively) and guarantee a specified response time to all problems and difficulties. Additional services may include 24 hour, 7 days a week support; planning for optimal capacity; and preventive mainte-

nance activities like scheduled upgrades. Help desk services include handling trouble calls, resolving problems, and staging or coordinating inventories. Often the network support services provider becomes the liaison contact with other computer vendors involved with the contracting company including software, hardware, and telecommunications providers. Profit comes only with experienced personnel and volume—additional customers are incremental costs to a support operation.

Companies supplying computer network support services range in size from large vendors, such as IBM Global Services Division and Compaq Computer Corporation, down to much smaller resellers. The resellers, or VARs (value-added resellers), are often "business partners" with larger corporations; that is, the VAR enters into a reseller agreement with the large corporation, and the giant wholesales its hardware and/or software to the reseller. VARs like CompuCom Systems and Entex Information Services, Inc. customize products channeled from the vendor, bundle them with network and other services, and add value in other ways. VARs serve as the distribution channel for vendors and are often the primary source of computer purchases for companies.

Due to growing client demand for support services and escalating hardware and software complexity, the interaction between large vendors and VARs is not always clearly defined. There is money to be made in services, and it seems everybody wants to take advantage of the opportunity. In response to the demand, and in an effort to boost revenues, vendors like Hewlett-Packard and IBM run integration, consulting, and service units or divisions that often compete with their channel partners for customers.

In reaction to the forced competition, a VAR can concentrate on available niche opportunities that are more appropriate for their smaller, more tightly focused organizations, or the reseller can work in a joint-venture or subcontract mode with a large services provider. The third option, which allows the reseller firm to be acquired by the giant, nets a nice profit for the business owner at the cost of the VAR's independent existence.

Because of the shortage of qualified information technology personnel, the large corporations often cooperate with smaller firms in an attempt to provide enough quality consultants to implement the services that have been marketed. For example, during the 1990s Hewlett-Packard partnered with other large consulting firms, other information technology firms that maintain high staffing levels, and VARs who had specialized expertise not available internally at Hewlett-Packard. Intra-channel competition and cooperation work most smoothly for both parties when the large vendor operates under a set of consistent guidelines so that the VARs know when and where they will need to compete.

Telephone companies and their subsidiaries, such as Bell Atlantic Network Integration, perform network support and systems integration without a direct stake as reseller or vendor channel. Telecommunications companies, such as MCI Communications Corporation and AT&T Corporation, have become active in providing network support services and systems integration. In early 1997 AT&T expanded its network management services to offer a variety of benchmarking, design, and implementation services through an $80 million management platform called Managed Network Solutions. In 1998 the company introduced new Service Level Agreements (SLAs) supported by powerful new network management tools for its customers. That same year, AT&T also introduced Interactive Advantage, a suite of extranet-based network management tools that could be accessed through a single interface.

Finally, consultants, such as Arthur Andersen, and staffing service firms, such as MacTemps, provide network support services from a large pool of technical personnel.

BACKGROUND AND DEVELOPMENT

In the 1980s and early 1990s, network was a simple noun referring to "a group of computers and associated devices that are connected by communications facilities." It was easy to define and easy to visualize. A network's activities, which consisted mostly of making shared files and printers available to network members, were coordinated by a network operating system installed on a server. The network's activities were fairly limited and routine; a few information technology professionals could tame, control, and manage it.

In the mid-1990s, hardware and software advances gradually expanded the basic network. Two advances included a local-area network (LAN) that connects computers within a building or a wide-area network (WAN) that connects computers over a large geographic area. Networks became the infrastructure for a client/server computing environment. Networks were systems that consisted of a number of personal computers (clients) connected to and working with larger computers that stored and retrieved shared data and managed shared resources (servers). Early on, the network was still circumscribed; it covered specified territory for a specified purpose.

Technological advancement during the late 1990s has changed how a network can be defined and understood. Businesses have to deal with inter-networks, intranets, and the Internet. Networks have become harder to define and extremely difficult to manage, while, ironically, information technology staffs have become smaller. Stretched to the limit, companies have turned to vendors or third-party companies for help in installing, configuring, managing, maintaining, and troubleshooting their increasingly more complex networks. By 1996, according to a *PC Week* feature, all Fortune 1000 companies had implemented outsourcing contracts with third-party companies for network support services.

Computer network support services became a rapidly growing, highly profitable industry niche. In 1996 the U.S. market for network management services ranged from $1.3 to $3.0 billion. The average annual growth rate in 1996 was 20 to 30 percent. For example, at Comdisk Network Services, earnings in three months of 1996 were equal to all earnings in 1995.

Outsourcing was a hot trend in 1997; almost 73 percent of surveyed information technology managers responded that they had outsourced. The top function outsourced was network maintenance (46.6 percent), followed by software development (42.5 percent), mainframe/legacy migrations (37.0 percent), software maintenance (32.9 percent), and Internet Web site hosting (24.7 percent). According to one study, 27 percent of surveyed companies were considering outsourcing remote network management services as well.

The foremost problem with external service and support, according to a 1996 survey, was cost. Outsourcing expenses depended on the services required and the system's complexity. One company, NetSolve, offered a service called ProWatch Exchange for $5,500 per month for a 30-site network. Other companies offered more configurable pricing arrangements. AT&T Managed Network Solutions used a base rate of $225 per site per month for a managed router contract, but it added $50 for each additional LAN or WAN connection. Additional problems identified in the same survey were poor responsiveness and lack of multivendor expertise.

The network computer (NC) was an unpredictable factor in the future of network support services. Touted as a solution to the complexities of the personal computer, network computers did not contain the complex bundle of software, hardware, and interconnectivity, thereby alleviating some support problems. Instead, NCs retrieved necessary information and files from a central computer, thus simplifying their own internal operating systems, configurations, and attendant problems. However, industry reaction was mixed. While 69 percent of Fortune 1000 chief information officers anticipated purchasing an NC by 2001, other predictions foresaw a robust future for the desktop computer and network support services.

CURRENT CONDITIONS

As the twenty-first century begins, the nature of computer networks is changing with breathtaking speed. Several trends have emerged that will impact the industry significantly. For example, industry experts predict that wireless LANs will steadily become more commonplace for both business and home network users. This development carries considerable implications for the network support service providers. In addition to wireless connectivity, other important trends include the rise of electronic commerce, gigantic increases in bandwidth, and the movement away from PC-centered computing to the use of portable, handheld computers and miniature devices that can be worn by the user.

In the world of WANs, meanwhile, a number of acquisitions in 1999 further consolidated a shifting market. Three major developments were the acquisition of Sentient Networks by Cisco Systems; Ericsson Communication's acquisition of routing pioneer Torrent Networking Technologies; and Nortel's purchase of Shasta Networks.

Another interesting development is the advent of "self-curing" networks that can diagnose and fix weak spots in the system. According to Patrick Taylor, Vice President of strategic marketing at Internet Security Systems, Inc. (ISS), "networks will be equipped with sensors that will interact with smart programs to enable the network to dynamically make decisions and change configurations." These developments, along with other technological advances, promise to present new challenges for companies that provide network support services.

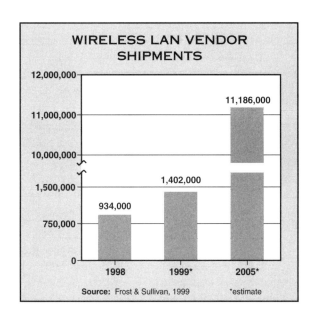

WIRELESS LAN VENDOR SHIPMENTS

Source: Frost & Sullivan, 1999   *estimate

INDUSTRY LEADERS

In the late 1990s, large companies—such as IBM, Hewlett-Packard, and Compaq, which in 1998 acquired Digital Equipment Corporation—dominated the computer network support services industry.

IBM GLOBAL SERVICES DIVISION

IBM's Global Services division posted 1998 revenues of $28.9 billion. IBM Global Services made headlines that year when it introduced high-speed asymmetric digital subscriber line (ADSL) services designed to boost customers' access to IBM's data services and the Internet 15-fold.

HEWLETT-PACKARD

In 1998 Hewlett-Packard restructured its services division, creating a larger "computer products, service and support" group. In addition to networking products, consulting and integration services, and support and maintenance services, this business unit of Hewlett-Packard also encompassed hardware and software, printers and scanners, and calculators and photography products. Net revenues for the entire division in 1998 were $39.4 billion.

In 1999 Hewlett-Packard acquired Transoft Networks, a Santa Barbara, California, company that developed storage area networking (SAN) management software. The acquisition marked Hewlett-Packard's first foray into SANs.

COMPAQ COMPUTER CORPORATION

Compaq emerged as a major network support services player after its purchase of Digital Equipment Corporation in 1998. According to an article in *Network World,* the acquisition bestowed upon Compaq was "a large base of enterprise customers; a world-class, worldwide service organization; and a slew of NT developers." Compaq also formed strategic partnerships with Computer Associates, Tivoli, and BMC Software to provide customers with next-generation Web-based enterprise management (WBEM) tools. The company's services revenues in 1998 were $3.7 billion, a $3.3 billion increase over the previous year due to the acquisition of Digital.

OTHER MAJOR VENDORS

Lucent Technologies Inc. was another prominent network support services provider in the late 1990s. In 1997 the company formed Lucent NetCare Services, which offered clients consulting, management, and maintenance services for enterprise voice, data, and video networks. By 1999 Lucent had expanded its NetCare support capabilities to customers in 55 countries.

WORK FORCE

At the end of the twentieth century, the United States was experiencing a dramatic shortage of information technology workers. The Information Technology Association of America (ITAA) estimated that there were 346,000 unfilled IT positions at U.S. firms in 1999. Demand for IT workers showed no sign of flagging either. The U.S. Bureau of Labor Statistics (BLS) predicted in 1998 that computer scientists, computer engineers, and systems analysts would be the three fastest-growing occupations through 2006. The forces cited by BLS as driving the demand for sys-

tems analysts included the expansion of client/server environments and increasing demand for networking to share information.

Computer network support services rely on highly trained and technologically proficient employees to garner contracts and produce profits. The Bureau of Labor Statistics projected that the number of jobs nationwide for database administrators, computer support specialists, and other computer scientists would grow from 212,000 in 1996 to 461,000 by 2006, a 118 percent increase. In one month alone (June 1998), computer service employment offerings grew by 21,000 jobs nationwide.

Starting salaries for network administrators in the late 1990s ranged from $36,000 to $55,000. For help desk support technicians, starting salaries ranged from $25,000 to $36,500. The starting salaries for systems analysts at companies with more than 50 staff members varied from $46,000 to $57,500. For analysts at small firms, the range was $38,000 to $48,000.

AMERICA AND THE WORLD

Because of the Internet, global opportunities become more realistic every day. The need to access mission-critical information—whether on products, production status, or policies—from any company site is the reason businesses need to invest in global networking technology. Information technology managers do not have the staff to manage the complicated networks with global reach; therefore, the market is ripe for international providers of network support services.

GLOBAL MARKET SIZE AND OPPORTUNITIES

Lucent Technologies estimated the global market for network support services to be worth approximately $100 billion in 1998, with an annual growth rate of 16 percent.

In the late 1990s Australia was an estimated $2.4 billion per year market for computer services, and it was expected to grow as systems became more complex and technical requirements for staff expertise became more rigorous. Services in demand included systems management, consulting, and education, which included training and help desk services.

Latin America also presented a growing market opportunity for computer services with its information services market estimated at $6.3 billion. Of that market opportunity, Brazil had the largest share ($3.3 billion). With markets emerging for online databases and electronic data interchange at the century's end, network support services were expected to make up a significant percentage of the overall market for services.

FURTHER READING

Aragon, Lawrence. "In Pursuit of Service." *VARBusiness,* 6 July 1998. Available from http://www.techweb.com/se/directlink.cgi?VAR19980706S0020.

"AT&T Offers Integrated Suite of Web-based Network Management Tools," 27 January 1998. Available from http://www.att.com/press/0198.

"AT&T Raises the Bar on Data Networking Guarantees." 27 January 1998. Available from http://www.att.com/press/0198.

"Bank of America. Australia: Leading Sectors for U.S. Export and Investment." Available from http://www.tradeport.org/ts/countries/australia/sectors.shtml.

Bliss, Jeff. "Deathwatch for Desktops?" *Computer Reseller News,* 10 March 1997.

Briere, Daniel. "Network Integrators Can Be Lifesavers." *Network World,* 24 February 1997.

"A Call to Action: ITAA's Efforts to Address the Information Technology Skills Gap," 9 May 1999. Available from http://www.itaa.org/workforce/resources.

Compaq Corporation 1998 Annual Report, 9 May 1999. Available from http://www.compaq.com/corporate/1998ar.

"Computer Scientists, Computer Engineers, and Systems Analysts." *U.S. Bureau of Labor Statistics 1998-99 Occupational Outlook Handbook,* 9 May 1999. Available from http://www.bls.gov/oco.

Connor, Deni. "HP Makes SAN Strides." *Network World Fusion,* 4 May 1999. Available from http://www.nwfusion.com/news/1999.

Dash, Julekha. "Care and Feeding for Desktops." *Software Management,* December 1996.

"Discussion Papers on Services, Information Technology and Electronic Commerce." *Free Trade Area of the Americas,* August 1997. Available from http://www.alcs-ftaa.oas.org/EnglishVersion/Services/its.htm.

Dix, John. "NW 200: Bigger and Better." *Network World,* 20 April 1998. Available from http://www.nwfusion.com/news/nw200.

"Fastest Growing Occupations, 1996-2006." U.S. Bureau of Labor Statistics Employment Projections, 9 May 1999. Available from http://www.bls.gov/emptab1.htm

Gallant, John. "Handing Off Your Net Management Burden." *Network World,* 7 April 1997.

"Giant Appetites for Little Bites." *Dataquest Alert,* 16 April 1999. Available from http://gartner6.gartnerweb.com/dq/static/whatsnew.

Greene, Tim. "Paying the Price for Good Network Service and Support." *Network World,* 25 March 1996.

Hewlett-Packard 1998 Annual Report, 9 May 1999. Available from http://www.hp.com/financials/98annrep.

Horwitt, Elisabeth. "Go Boldly: Leading-Edge Corporate Users Recommend an Aggressive Approach Toward Adopting New Technologies." *Network World,* 3 May 1999. Available from http://www.nwfusion.com/news/1999.

IBM 1998 Annual Report, 9 May 1999. Available from http://www.ibm.com/annualreport/1998.

Jacobs, April. "Start-ups Lead the Way." *Network World,* 3 May 1999. Available from http://www.nwfusion.com/news/1999.

Lieberman, Lenny. "Going Global." *Internet Week,* 29 June 1998. Available from http://www.techweb.com/se/directlink.cgi?INW19980629S0065.

Lucent Technologies 1998 Annual Report, 9 May 1999. Available from http://www.lucent.com/annual98.

"Lucent Technologies Announces NetCare Business: Will Seek Growth Opportunities in Network Support Services." *Business Wire,* 28 April 1997.

Marion, Larry. "At Your Service; Expanding Services Industry." *PC Week,* 15 January 1996.

Merrill, Kevin. "Entex Beefs Up Network Integration Business." *Computer Reseller News,* 24 June 1996.

"Network Support Contract Spending Projected at $6 Billion by 2001." *EDP Weekly,* 26 March 1997.

Pappalardo, Denise. "IBM Global Services Testing ADSL Service." *Network World,* 5 October 1998. Available from http://www.nwfusion.com/archive/1998.

Radcliffe, Deborah. "Hot On the Asset Trail." *Software Magazine,* December 1996.

Roberts, John. "Network Spending Will Continue to Surge." *Computer Reseller News,* 22 December 1997.

Rohde, David. "Managed Net Costs Add Up." *Network World,* 21 April 1997.

Rosa, Jerry. "Forecast for 97: Continued Growth." *Computer Reseller News,* 13 January 1997.

Thyfault, Mary E. "AT&T's Network Menu." *Informationweek,* 17 February 1997.

Weil, Nancy. "Wireless LANs Take Flight." *PC World Online,* 20 April 1999. Available from http://www.pcworld.com/shared/printable_articles.

Weinberg, Neil. "Networks of the Future." *CNN Interactive,* 5 May 1999. Available from http://www.cnn.com/TECH/computing/9905/netpredict.ent.idg.

Weston, Rusty. "Why Fight IT? Outsourcing Impacts IT Professionals; Industry Trend or Event?" *PC Week,* 22 July 1996.

Wolfenberger, Mark. "Close-Up: Computer Services." *Upside,* March 1997.

"World of Service, Support Opportunity." *Computer Reseller News,* 23 December 1996.

Wright, John W. *The American Almanac of Jobs and Salaries.* New York: Avon Books, 1996.

Zarley, Craig. "The New Face of Client/Server: Channel Conflict Looms, But So Does Opportunity." *Computer Reseller News,* 1 January 1996.

—Tona Henderson, updated by Judith Harper and Marinell James

Computer Security

The need for people to protect computer hardware, software, databases, and files from being compromised has given rise to a burgeoning security industry that comprises large numbers of small businesses and some large ones. The business of information security—safeguarding data; locking down the processors and disk arrays that generate, massage, analyze and store it; and insulating the networks that transmit and disseminate it—is forecast to increase from a $5.2 billion market in the mid-1990s to $13.1 billion by the year 2000.

The computer security business does not always lend itself to large businesses since many corporations employ their own experts on staff. With such a large amount of security work performed by consultants or contract workers, industry experts find it difficult to pinpoint the exact number of firms engaged in computer security or to estimate financial earnings. The *Computer Security Institute's Buyer's Guide* lists more than 200 companies of all sizes offering computer security products. Even industry giants International Business Machines Corp. (IBM) and Hewlett-Packard Co. produce security products. As society becomes more reliant on computers, the need for computer security specialists will continue to grow.

ORGANIZATION AND STRUCTURE

The field of computer security is diverse and one in which opportunities are abundant for those with a wide range of skills. It has three main levels—physical, software, and administrative controls. Each level is addressed by a different specialist using different skills.

Physical security addresses problems such as fire, theft, sabotage, and malicious pranks. Systems analysts and security officers can address these types of problems.

Software security involves factors like accidental disclosures caused by partially debugged or poorly designed programs, and active or passive infiltration of computer systems. Active infiltration includes activities like using legitimate access to a system to obtain unauthorized information, obtaining identification to gain access through improper means, or getting into systems via unauthorized physical access. Passive infiltration includes activities like wiretapping on data communications lines or databases and using concealed transmitters to send or retrieve data in central processing units, databases, or data communications lines. People involved in software security include analysts, network administrators, programmers, auditors, and security officers.

Administrative controls involve issues such as controls on personnel for fraud protection, controls on sensitive programs, security of remote terminal access, software security, and file reconstruction capability. Auditors, programmers, systems analysts, security officers, and network administrators are involved in addressing the development and implementation of administrative controls.

While different specialists often address all of these security issues, the need for multi-level controls is increasing as the number of computers grow—one more indication that additional computer security is a continuing demand. The industry will no doubt grow to accommodate the problem.

BACKGROUND AND DEVELOPMENT

Computers for commercial use date back to the 1940s. Since that time, computers have evolved from gigantic board-wired, cathode-ray tube, card deck-operated machines that literally filled climate-controlled glass houses into desk top machines that are many more times powerful than their larger predecessors.

As of the 1990s, people in every walk of life were using computers to perform a variety of tasks ranging from mixing recipe ingredients to desktop publishing. In many cases, they were tied into networks such as wide-area networks (WANs), local-area networks (LANs), and the Internet. The increasing reliance on networks has created a greater demand for security since networks allow for more opportunities to compromise files and databases.

Businesses in particular have been utilizing more powerful computers for every function possible. Naturally, the almost infinite growth in data processing has led to computer-related problems such as crime, terrorism, and harassment from hackers who break into computer systems; and crackers who deliberately damage other's computers. The need for protection against hackers and crackers has prompted corporations and individuals to seek the help of security specialists.

The development of computer security procedures paralleled developments in the data processing industry. Each succeeding generation of computers has been accompanied by concomitant developments in security measures. Originally, computer security involved controlling access to computer rooms. It was concentrated in the industrial arena, since computers were rarely found outside the business industry. Computer security specialists were generally senior-level members of a company's data processing staff. In the early days of data processing, computers were generally standalone units that calculated data at an unbelievably slow rate, by 1990's standards. Gradually, manufacturers added components such as tape and disk drives to increase storage capacity, and modems that allowed computers in remote locations to communicate with one another. The development of networking enhanced the need for security measures such as encryption—secretly coding data being moved between computers.

During the 1960s and 1970s, the trend was toward bigger, more powerful computers. Eventually, though, computer manufacturers learned to build smaller systems with escalating storage capacities and processing speeds. This process was enhanced tremendously by the arrival of the microprocessor chip. With the creation of the chip came the desktop and laptop computers, the use of which has been multiplying exponentially throughout businesses and homes. To provide applications for all these new computers, software specialists have developed an array of programs that put spreadsheets, games, and desktop publishing packages at users' fingertips.

HACKERS, CRACKERS, AND THIEVES

Along with developments in the hardware, software, and networking environments, however, hackers and crackers emerged. Computer security accounted for about 2 percent of companies's information technology (IT) expenditures in 1998, according to International Data Corp. (IDC). Some hackers breach computers just for the fun of it, while others hope to gain wealth, information, cause harm, or wreak havoc.

In 1998 IDC said that roughly 70 percent of Fortune 1000 companies had hired an ethical hacker to try and break into their own computer system. Such penetration testing to check firewalls will become a necessary part of every security consulting package in the future, according to the market-research firm.

The increase in computer crime in turn gave rise to a new breed of law enforcement officials who were experts in computer use. There also grew a need for specialists who could help law enforcement officials and others involved in the criminal justice system, such as lawyers and judges, familiarize themselves with security procedures concerning computers. These technical advisers and consultants have been responsible for much of the research and new product development in the industry today.

The Adaptive Network Security Alliance (ANSA), a coalition of 40 hardware and software vendors, tries to promote and enforce industry-wide standards to ensure all security products work well together. With the integration of automated tools, network administrators can plug a breach in a firewall in nanoseconds.

COMPUTER SECURITY AND THE LAW

One of the unique aspects of the computer security industry is its connection to the criminal justice system. Many of the activities in which computer security deals with are illegal. Thus, these activities fall under the broad heading of computer crime.

There are three primary areas of computer crime: data security and integrity, national security threats, and protection of software copyright. Currently, there is a technological gap between the criminal justice system and the enforcement of laws designed to prosecute computer criminals. This lag opens the door for more computer security experts among attorneys, law enforcement agencies, military, and government organizations.

In August 1998 the nation"s top anti-terrorism chief discussed the threat of computer warfare that could cripple the United States. Potential targets include banks, airports, stock markets, telephones, and power suppliers. Richard Clark—the first national coordinator for security, infrastructure protection, and counter terrorism—proposed backup plans and vigilance to foil a systematic, coordinated multi-pronged attack from a foreign military, terrorist, or intelligence group.

CURRENT CONDITIONS

The Computer Security Institute (CSI) and the Federal Bureau of Investigation (FBI) released the results of a joint survey of 520 U.S. universities, corporations, government agencies, and financial institutions in 1998. Sixty-four percent of the respondents reported computer systems security breaches within the previous year, many of which went unreported. They pegged total losses due to security breaches at more than $136 million.

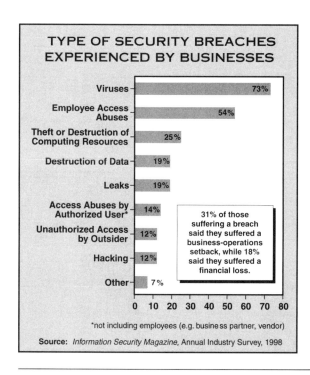

TYPE OF SECURITY BREACHES EXPERIENCED BY BUSINESSES

Viruses 73%
Employee Access Abuses 54%
Theft or Destruction of Computing Resources 25%
Destruction of Data 19%
Leaks 19%
Access Abuses by Authorized User* 14%
Unauthorized Access by Outsider 12%
Hacking 12%
Other 7%

31% of those suffering a breach said they suffered a business-operations setback, while 18% said they suffered a financial loss.

*not including employees (e.g. business partner, vendor)

Source: *Information Security Magazine,* Annual Industry Survey, 1998

The survey found that disgruntled workers represented the most likely source of attacks on computer systems. Independent hackers placed second. For high-tech entities, industry competitors ranked the third most likely source. Fourth and fifth place went to foreign competitors and foreign governments, respectively.

The CSI/FBI survey further found that nearly 50 percent of attacks on computer networks came from inside the organization. (Accordingly, another survey by NetVersant discovered that 83 percent of employees admitted to little or no compliance with their company's network security policies.)

The 1998 survey also cited the Internet connection as a frequent point of attack. In April 1999, the FBI initiated the largest Internet manhunt ever to catch the world's fastest spreading computer virus to date. The virus, known as Melissa, replicated itself through e-mail. All totaled, the FBI estimates that the virus infected more than 100,000 computer systems in commercial, government, and military installations, forcing some administrators to shut down their e-mail systems for a week. Investigators tracked down the originator with the help of a controversial serial ID number—called a Global Unique Identifier or GUID. In the end, authorities charged a 30-year-old computer programmer with creating Melissa. If convicted, the suspected hacker faces a possible 40-year sentence.

SECURITY BREACHES EVERYWHERE

Companies in every type of industry—government agencies, transportation, manufacturing, financial, retail companies, medical, high-tech, and utility firms—were subject to attack and suffered financial loss because of computer crimes during 1997. The types of attack reported ranged from equipment theft to data misappropriation to network sabotage.

PIRACY IN THE COMPUTER ROOM

Illegal software use, sometimes called software piracy, has become a problem for some government agencies. For example, the city of Philadelphia, paid a $120,000 fine in July 1997 because employees in two agencies installed pirated software.

Software piracy is not always intentional, however. In some cases, the laws are vague and potential pirates don't understand relevant copyright laws. The Federal Copyright Act of 1976, for example, allows users to copy their purchased software once and only once, making a single copy for backup. Buyers do not purchase software; they purchase licenses to use the software. Many do not know or understand that distinction.

LOSSES DUE TO COMPUTER CRIME

There are other significant and growing risks associated with the increase in computer usage. A 1985 survey of 1,000 organizations assessed verifiable computer crime-related losses somewhere between $145 to $750 million. More recent figures suggest that in the late 1990s, the cost of computer theft—both hardware and software—ran as high as $8 billion a year. True figures are difficult to determine, however, because computer crime victims are not always willing to divulge actual loss figures in order to protect themselves and to prevent other violators from compromising their systems. Thus, in reality, estimated loss figures are most likely more than those actually reported or surmised.

HARDWARE THEFT

The theft of hardware in particular is becoming more pronounced. The tiny microchips used in computers are extremely valuable. Moreover, many computers do not have serial numbers, which makes them virtually impossible to trace. Based on that fact alone, some experts suggest that the cost of computer theft might reach $200 billion by the year 2000.

A similar poll taken in 1986 by the National Institute of Justice reported that 75 percent of police chiefs and 63 percent of sheriffs surveyed said that computer crime investigations were likely to have a significant impact on their workloads in the future. The proportions were even higher in jurisdictions that had a population of more than 500,000. In these larger areas, 84 percent of the police chiefs and 75 percent of the sheriffs indicated a future problem.

THE ENCRYPTION DILEMMA

Companies often use data-scrambling technology to protect their proprietary data and that of their clients. But the U.S. government insists that special access keys be built into encrypted messages, allowing law enforcement personnel to read them when they need to in order to solve crimes or prevent terrorist activity. The federal government also bans U.S. firms from exporting top-quality encryption products, citing a concern that spies or terrorists may use the stolen software to evade government wiretaps. The U.S. computer industry stands to lose $35 billion in revenues over five years to international firms who sell encryption products, according to a 1998 study by a Washington-based think tank.

Free speech and privacy advocates are pushing for stronger encryption to maintain the confidentiality of corporate records and the privacy of personal data. The existence of built-in loopholes undermines general public confidence in the security of their data. Resolving this issue, strong encryption for privacy versus built-in government access for law enforcement and national security, will be an important step in the development of secure communications over a global network.

DOUBLE-DIGIT GROWTH

Hurwitz Group, Inc. (a Framingham, Massachusetts, consulting firm) claims that the market for risk-assessment and intrusion detection products alone ($65 million in 1997) is exploding at a 50 percent compound annual growth rate.

The market for firewalls—software that protects vital information while allowing interaction with the

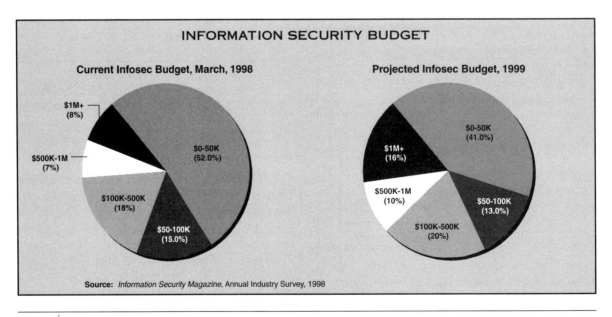

INFORMATION SECURITY BUDGET

Current Infosec Budget, March, 1998

$1M+ (8%)
$500K-1M (7%)
$100K-500K (18%)
$50-100K (15.0%)
$0-50K (52.0%)

Projected Infosec Budget, 1999

$1M+ (16%)
$500K-1M (10%)
$100K-500K (20%)
$50-100K (13.0%)
$0-50K (41.0%)

Source: *Information Security Magazine,* Annual Industry Survey, 1998

Internet and other internal networks known as intranets—was just $48 million annually in the mid-1990s; however, a Boston-based consulting firm estimated it to be more than $250 million in 1997 and more than $700 million by the year 2000.

MERGE AND GROW

Major companies in the security products market went on a merge-and-grow binge in 1997-98. AXENT Technologies, a top supplier of risk-assessment and intrusion detection products with revenues of approximately $101 million in 1998, merged with Raptor Systems, a major firewall supplier.

Network Associates was created in 1997 through the merger of McAfee (makers of virus detection software) and Network General (which was not previously focused on the security market). Early in 1998 Network Associates acquired Trusted Information Systems (TIS). Only a year earlier, in 1997, TIS, which had been mainly a firewall supplier, acquired intrusion-detection software maker Haystack Labs. Network Associates earned about $990 million in revenue across its entire product line in 1998.

WheelGroup, formerly a major player with a respected intrusion detection product and $3 million in 1997 revenues, was acquired by networking company CISCO in 1998. WheelGroup's intrusion detection product analyzes its customer's system by using the same technique computer hackers and crackers use to penetrate corporate data processing systems.

Veritas merged with OpenVision in 1997. The resulting company sold $2 million worth of security products in the year of the merger. Early in 1998, Veritas sold its security product line to PLATINUM Technology.

OTHER MAJOR PLAYERS

The number of companies providing computer security products and methods is a mix of large, medium, and small firms. These companies are scrambling for leadership in a nascent industry. Internet Security Systems (ISS) sold about 35.9 million worth of security products, mainly risk-assessment and intrusion-detection products, in 1998.

WORK FORCE

The computer security industry is a component of the larger computer and data processing industry, and it is only recently that computer security technicians (or their equivalent) have become specialists within the industry. However, the *Career Security Techni-*

cians, published by the U.S. Department of Labor, does acknowledge that security analysts belong to one of the small, rapidly growing specialties within the classification.

As the number of computers in use grows, so will the number of security analysts. Employment in the industry was projected to grow 90 percent between 1990 and 2005, making it the third-fastest growing industry in the economy. One out of every four employees in the industry is a computer programmer or computer systems analyst. Three of every four workers are between the ages of 25 and 44. The average firm in the industry employs only 18 workers.

Computer security specialists are also responsible for detecting illegalities in software copyright and bringing them to the attention of the proper authorities. In some cases, law enforcement agencies offer employment opportunities for security analysts. In other cases, computer security experts act alone to detect illegal or fraudulent activities. The variety of available experiences illustrate the numerous opportunities available to security experts who wish to become consultants in the field.

EMPLOYMENT OPPORTUNITIES

Security staffing levels have increased dramatically in the past 8 years, nearly doubling since a 1989 survey showing only 0.033 percent of total staff devoted to information security issues. Information security staff, including consultants, contractors, and temporary workers, made up about 0.061 percent of total staff head count for North American companies that responded to a survey published in the spring 1998 issue of *Computer Security Journal.*

In firms with national security requirements, such as defense contractors and other government-affiliated organizations, information security staffing levels are higher (0.121 percent) than in firms without national security requirements (0.052 percent). In other statistics resulting from the survey, the responding companies devote 38.9 percent of their information security budget to in-house security staff and outsource 5.8 percent of their information security activities. Overall, as the demand for computers escalates in the coming years, opportunities will abound for people interested in entering the computer security field.

AMERICA AND THE WORLD

Along with the advantages of the growing industry of computers and networks is the disadvantage of the computer crimes becoming universal. People in the 1990s have access to an international network of computers, which makes it more difficult for security experts to detect and prosecute computer criminals. For example, if a New York City Police Department computer security expert detects a computer criminal operating in Thailand or Chad, the security expert is not likely to be able to make an immediate arrest. Even if an arrest were possible, prosecution is often delayed, or even prevented altogether by international extradition treaties and cultural differences in approaches to criminal activity. Examples like this highlight the complexities involved in detecting and halting computer crime and explain why computer security specialists emerge from such a diverse range of backgrounds.

SECURITY IS A WORLDWIDE CONCERN

The CERT Coordination Center (CERT/CC), based in Pittsburgh at the Carnegie Mellon University Software Engineering Institute, is an U.S. government-funded center used to coordinate communication during major computer security breaches. Established in 1988, CERT/CC strives to minimize the threat of future incidents by operating a 24-hour point of contact that can respond to security emergencies anywhere on the global Internet. The organization also facilitates communication among experts around the world who are working to solve security problems.

CERT/CC-developed incident response procedures have become the model for more than 69 incident response teams worldwide, including the Forum of Incident Response and Security teams (FIRST). FIRST consists of individual incident response teams that focus on special national, industrial, and/or academic communities. Each FIRST team establishes contacts within its community, making it possible for FIRST members to meet the community's security needs, collaborate on incidents that cross national boundaries, and post trans-national alerts and advisories on problems with local and/or global relevance. More than 50 FIRST teams work together in this global effort, including groups from Australia, Germany, the United Kingdom, Israel, and France.

RESEARCH AND TECHNOLOGY

Information security consultants and companies use a number of strategies to counter the threat of computer crime. The most commonly used security technologies are: anti-virus software, which detect and nullify the effect of software "viruses" or programs that destroy or garble data when they're run on an unsuspecting victim's computer system; access control procedures, including the use of passwords and other user authentication techniques; physical security such as locked doors, guarded rooms, and other barriers to physical access; firewalls or software programs that restrict incoming and outgoing network traffic; and encryption or coding messages to data illegible without the decoding key.

NEW SECURITY PRODUCTS

There is a constant need for new security-related computer products. International Data Corp. (IDC) estimates the market for security products (firewalls, data-scramblers, etc.) alone reached somewhere between $2.0 billion and $2.5 billion in 1997. The market-research firm says another $2.0 billion went to the corresponding services market, which IDC predicts will grow at 26 percent a year.

One contemporary way of improving computer security is through keystroke analysis. This system, developed by New Mexico State University professor Juris Reinfetds and two associates, allows computer access only to individuals based on their typing styles. The system is relatively simple. It monitors the pace of user's keystrokes. A timing device or box traps keyboard signals before they reach the computer processor. The box then sends out two signals. One goes to the computer, and the second shows how many milliseconds have elapsed since the last keystroke. If the typing patterns do not match, the computer denies further access. The developers say the system detects impersonators 99 percent of the time. Moreover, it detects unauthorized users even after they enter legitimate passwords.

Another high-end line of products by Miros Inc. uses biometrics technology to fend off intruders. True-Face Network, which rolled out in 1998, records the faces of authorized personnel to build a database of users. To log on to a personal computer or workstation, a user must face an attached video camera so the computer can compare the facial image to stored images. Recognition gains appropriate access in seconds. As a further fraud deterrent, TrueFace stores all logon attempts and notifies administrators of unauthorized attempts. Miros also came up with the first facial recognition product used in check-cashing ATMs worldwide.

Also in 1998, Compaq Computer Corp. came out with a low-cost fingerprint ID device that plugs into the home or office computer. To start, authorized users stick a finger inside the device, which takes a picture of the print. Then built-in software turns the print into

---

Trends

SOFTWARE LICENSING LEGISLATION— CRACKDOWN ON SOFTWARE PIRACY

The practice of software licensing was conceived in the 1970s by Seymour Rubinstein. Software licenses allow consumers to use a product, but expressly preclude the outright purchase of the software program. Legislation to protect software from illegal duplication was first enacted in the federal Copyright Act of 1980. Prior to the Act of 1980 and beginning in 1964, the U.S. Patent Office protected software programs under copyright. The Software Rental Amendments Act of 1990, further detailed the illegality of renting, leasing, and lending of software without written permission from the copyright holder. A 1992 amendment to U.S. Code Title 18 established criminal penalties up to five years imprisonment and/or $250,000 in fines for software infringement. Offenders may be further held liable in civil court for offenses committed in violation of the code. Penalties for damages are permissible up to $100,000 for each violation.

To encourage compliance with software copyright legislation, a coalition of software manufacturers was formed consisting of Adobe Systems, Autodesk, Inc., Bentley Systems, Lotus Development Corp., Microsoft Corp., Novell Inc., and Symantec Corp.. The coalition, called the Business Software Alliance (BSA), is a worldwide watchdog, committed to eliminating software piracy, which is increasingly prevalent and reportedly generates losses of billions of dollars for the software industry. Between 1996 and 1999 BSA more than doubled its staffing levels and took increasingly combative measures to halt software piracy. The alliance instituted an aggressive advertising crusade and educational campaigns worldwide to discourage the practice. BSA established a confidential Internet site at http://www.nopiracy.com and anti-piracy hotlines are available worldwide. BSA further recommended the use of specific business software products, called software audit tools, for maintaining control of software product licenses held at a company. BSA publishes a booklet called "Guide to Software Managers," that details recommended methods of ensuring compliance with federal law regarding software usage.

---

a point map, which is stored for future reference. To log on, a user holds up the finger to the camera, and the computer checks the database. A matched print gains access to the hard drive or network.

FIREWALLS

Firewalls are another method of monitoring access to computers. There is some debate as to how effective firewalls can actually be, however. Some experts believe they are easy to get around for hackers and crackers. Even though there is much debate over their effectiveness, this has not prevented firewalls from becoming popular. Different types of firewalls offer different levels of security. The lowest-level firewall uses a technology called *packet filters.* The system examines the address from which data enters a system or the address to which it is going. It decides whether to let the data pass through based on its analysis.

Mid-level firewalls are circuit-level gatekeepers that prevent systems from coming into direct contact with the outside world. More advanced systems go well beyond examining the addresses or prohibiting direct contact. High-level programs look at the content of messages as well as the "to" and "from" addresses. Of course, prices of such packages and ease of installation are based on the level of the firewall, ranging in cost from $3,000 to $100,000. Installation of the more expensive packages can be time consuming and must be performed by security experts.

HARDWARE SECURITY

Researchers are developing security packages for hardware as well as software. Some are applicable to personal computers (PCs) as well as to computers owned by corporations. For example, the CompuTrace security system, developed by Absolute Software, instructs a PC modem to dial the company's toll free number hotline at least once a week. Via the phone call, the modem reports its location through a Caller ID system, and all calls are logged. If the PC has been reported stolen, its new location is monitored and reported to local police.

One important feature of CompuTrace that lends to its success as a security method is that it acts like a computer virus—one of the computer security breaches that experts are defending against. CompuTrace does not show up in a computer's file directory, and it survives the reformatting of the hard disk on which it resides. If the phone line is inaccessible at the regularly scheduled call-in time, or if the connection is broken, the modem makes its check-in phone call when the line is free or when the connection is restored. CompuTrace also turns off the modem speaker before dialing. Perhaps the greatest draw to

---

CompuTrace is its cost, which is under $100 per year for the software and service.

In 1999 a security breakthrough caused a stir amongst privacy advocates. Reacting to a boycott threat, industry giant Intel Corp. agreed to deactivate the ID system imbedded on Pentium III computer chips. With the system activated, online vendors can trace any transaction to a particular machine. The chips use a 96-digit serial number for the trace, similar to caller-ID devices for phones. Although deactivated for shipment, consumers can activate their system any time after purchase. Critics still worry that Web site proprietors and software vendors might make activation a condition of access to popular sites and programs.

Computer technologies change so rapidly that researchers are not always able to keep up. One source of help to deal with technological changes is the Internet. Computer users and security experts can access programs and Web sites designed to facilitate security. There is the Security Analysis Tool for Auditing Networks (SATAN), which helps systems administrators recognize common network security problems. SATAN reports the problems without actually exploiting them. The Conduit is another computer security Web site that provides helpful information and links regarding network security. The concern about computer security is prompting people in diverse fields to develop new products designed to enhance network, individual PC, and standalone integrity. This continued focus guarantees an expansion of computer security efforts to protect owners and users against problems.

FURTHER READING

Bray, Hiawatha. "Encryption Plan Gives Computer Industry Hope Would Allow Software Exports, Ease U.S. Security Concerns." *Boston Globe,* 14 July 1998.

Brister, Kathy. "A Computer Security Firm With Top Secret Clearance." *Scripts Howard News Service,* 5 October 1998.

Career Guide to America's Top Industries. U.S. Department of Labor, JIST Works, 1994.

Clothier, Mark. "Coalition Adopts ISS Group's Computer Security Standards." *The Atlanta Journal and Constitution,* 22 October 1998.

Edelman, Vladimir. "Primed for Crime on the Internet. Inc.," September 1995.

Fielder, Terry. "Secure Goes All Out Turnabout." *Minneapolis Star Tribune,* 24 April 1997.

Folker, Richard, et al. "Cutting Edge: Great Buys in Personal Technology, From Toys to Tools." *U.S. News & World Report,* 16 November 1998.

Hare, Chris. *Internet Firewalls and Network Security.* Indianapolis, IN: New Riders Publishers, 1996.

"How We Invaded a Fortune 500 Company." *Fortune,* 3 February 1997.

Information Security: Assessing Risks and Detecting Intrusions. Framingham, MA: Hurwitz Group, 1998.

Japan MITI to Set Up Rating System for Computer Security. Asia Pulse Pte. Ltd., 20 May 1998.

Lardner, James. "Intel Even Move Inside." *U.S. News & World Report,* 8 February 1999.

MacLachlan, Malcolm. "Companies Big and Small to Profit from Computer Security." *Business Journal Serving San Jose and Silicon Valley,* 2 March 1997.

O'Malley, Chris. "Personality." *Popular Science,* June 1996.

Pethia, Richard. *Testimony Before the Permanent Subcommittee on Investigations, U.S. Senate Committee on Governmental Affairs,* 5 June 1996. Available from http://www.cert .org/Congressional_testimony/testimony_Pethia96.html.

Power, Richard. *Computer Security Issues & Trends.* San Francisco: Computer Security Institute, 1998.

Quittner, Joshua. "Technology: The Netly News." *Time Magazine,* 14 October 1996.

"Rainbow Technologies Internet Security Group Appoints Mitch Simon as Manager of Sales and Marketing." *Business Wire,* 11 March 1997.

Santos, Karen. "Compaq Unveils Fingerprint ID For Computer Users." *Houston Chronicle,* 8 July 1998.

Schafer, Sarah. *Digital Security. Inc.,* November 1996.

Simonds, Fred. *Network Security: Data and Voice Communications.* New York: McGraw-Hill, 1996.

Sutton, Steven A. *Windows NT Security Guide.* MA: Addison-Wesley Developers Press, 1997.

Wallack, Todd. "Computer Security Companies Are Making It Big Business in Massachusetts." *Boston Herald,* 31 August 1998.

Wood, Charles Cresson. *1998 Information Security Staffing Levels and the Standard of Due Care.* San Francisco: Computer Security Institute, 1998.

Young, Jeffrey. "Play to Hack Your Own System." *Forbes,* 4 June 1996.

—Arthur G. Sharp, updated by Judith Harper and Denise Worhach

CRAFT BEER

INDUSTRY SNAPSHOT

Beer has been brewed for thousands of years in numerous parts of the world and the U.S. beer market has been dominated by brewers of light, mass-produced beer for over a century. Nevertheless, a new trend began to emerge in the U.S. beer market about 25 years ago. The beverage industry refers to this trend as the craft beer industry, although it is also known as brewpub beer, microbrew, specialty beer, or simply "good beer" to its fans. Unlike the major brewing companies, such as Anheuser-Busch, Coors Brewing, Stroh's, and Miller—the four companies that account for about 85 percent of U.S. sales and shipping millions of barrels of mass-produced beer—the craft brewers produce small amounts, often measured in mere hundreds or thousands of barrels a year. Mass-produced beers like Budweiser and Miller tend to be lighter, milder, and more uniform in color. Craft beers, on the other hand, are often heavier and more flavorful, with a distinctly "European" taste and hues that range from red to brown to almost black. In comparison to the giant companies that ship products nationwide (and around the world), craft brewers turn out beer mostly for local use, often to be consumed on the same premises where it was brewed. In an affluent America that became accustomed in the 1970s, 1980s, and 1990s to boutique coffee, designer clothing, and fine food and dining, the emergence of a craft beer industry was perhaps inevitable.

While there were no more than half a dozen major American beer companies left by the mid-1990s (Anheuser-Busch, Miller, Coors, Stroh's, and Pabst among these leaders), the small but crowded craft brewing segment of the beer industry was comprised of a total of 1,370 craft breweries in the late 1990s, including 37 regional specialty breweries, 423 microbreweries, and 910 brewpubs in the United States, as reported by the Institute for Brewing Studies (IBS) in Boulder, Colorado. This is in contrast to the two craft breweries operating in all of North America in 1976.

In 1997 the craft beer market expanded by 5 percent to $3.03 billion, even though the overall beer market declined. Nevertheless, the industry shows signs of maturing with craft brewers reporting flat or falling sales and with a sharp drop in the industry's overall growth. Despite the downturn and stagnancy, craft beer seems to have permanently staked out a place in the beer market, appealing to about 6 percent of the country's beer drinkers.

ORGANIZATION AND STRUCTURE

The IBS has identified three major categories within the craft-brewing industry: brewpub, microbrewery, and specialty brewery. The brewpub, the most numerous, is a brewery/restaurant that brews and sells most of its beer at its site. A microbrewery is a brewery that produces fewer than 15,000 barrels of beer each year. It sells to the public either through the traditional three-tier arrangement of brewer to wholesaler to retailer to consumer; the two-tier system, where the brewer serves as wholesaler to retailer to consumer; or directly to the consumer through carryouts, an on-site tap room, or brewery restaurant sales. The IBS described the regional specialty brewery, the third category, as a regional-scale brewery (having the capacity to brew between 15,000 and 2 million barrels) whose flagship brand is an all-malt or "specialty beer." There is a fourth group that is often considered a part of the craft brewing industry: the contract brewer. The contract brewer hires another company to brew and package its beer but handles marketing, sales, and distribution itself. Alongside the craft brewing industry is an army of suppliers offering services, products, and the accouterments required for the brewing of fine beers. The "Real Beer Page" lists almost 40 such suppliers; doubtless many more can be unearthed by surfing the Internet—not to mention the *Yellow Pages.*

In August of 1998, a University of Maryland researcher released a report that indicated about 47 percent of all beer drinkers or 24 percent of all adults have tried a "microbeer" and were able to name a brand they had tried, according to the Institute for Brewing Studies. Initially, the typical craft beer drinker was a young, upscale, white male living on either the East or West Coast. Recently, however, craft beer began showing up in more middle-class households. The major brewers were taking note. Anheuser-Busch now offers "American Originals," a beer based upon recipes used 100 years ago. Miller, Coors, and Stroh's have each come up with their own specialty beer products as well.

While this multiplicity of brews may be good for consumers and fun for the brewers, it holds a downside for the larger craft brewers such as Boston Beer Co., producer of the acclaimed Samuel Adams brand, and Pete's Brewing Co., producer of Pete's Wicked Ale. The smaller craft brewers have swamped the industry to the extent that the larger brewers, like Boston Beer Co., have seen their natural market nibbled away by numerous tiny competitors. To many beer fans, this represents a triumph of economic democracy in action; it also works to hold prices down. To investors, however, especially those on Wall Street, this growth means that the larger craft brewers that have gone public with stock sales are poor risks.

Given the numbers, it appears likely that the fantastic growth rates of recent years may be about to skid to a halt. As reporter Lee Moriwaki wrote in the *Seattle Times,* "The truth is that the specialty-brewing industry here and across the country is bracing for a shakeout following several years of breathless growth."

BACKGROUND AND DEVELOPMENT

Ironically, before the age of refrigerated trucks and modern methods of mass production, all beers in the United States were craft beers. That is, they were all produced and sold locally according to highly distinctive recipes handed down by the various ethnic groups that produced them. This tradition of local brewing all but disappeared for a time as the industry modernized and consolidated from hundreds of brewers in the early twentieth century to no more than a handful of surviving major brewers in the 1990s. The tide appears to have turned. Sara Doersam, writing in an online article titled "The Craft Brewing Renaissance," suggested that the rapid increase of breweries indicates a promising future for craft-beer lovers, but that future begins to look more uncertain as craft brewing becomes big business. "A return to craft brewing's golden era—when the pre-Prohibition total of some 4,000 breweries included a small brewery in nearly every community—is becoming more plausible each year as the American beer renaissance rolls on," she said.

As author Michael Jackson notes in *The New World Guide to Beer,* beer and wine are both as old as civilization. Beer may be the older of these two great fermented beverages and may even pre-date bread. Brew was being made as long as 10,000 years ago, and there is specific evidence of its having been consumed in Mesopotamia as early as 4000 BC. Beer has varied tremendously in taste over time and in different cultures, and Jackson writes that only when the civilizations of modern Europe took shape in the 1700s did beer begin to assume the styles that we know today.

The first beer made with the intention that it be a mass-market product was the American brand Budweiser, first produced more than a century ago. It is still the market leader today. The advent of refrigerated containers and modern production methods led the way for a national market dominated by a few large players.

By the 1960s another trend was running counter to the theme of ever-greater consolidation and mass production. This "small is beautiful" movement reflected other changes in modern life, including growing prosperity, more leisure time, rising expectations, and greater interest in food and drink among the middle class. Against this cultural backdrop, the first microbrews emerged in Britain but spread quickly to the United States. Jackson dates the first opening of a U.S. microbrewery to 1976: the New Albion in Sonoma, California. The movement spread with astonishing rapidity.

According to Christopher Finch and W. Scott Griffiths in their *America's Best Beers* guidebook, there is nothing overly complicated about the basic principles of brewing beer. "A grain substance, classically malted barley, is blended with water and the

CHARLES PAPAZIAN

Charlie Papazian accepted his first taste of beer from a family friend called Uncle Paul in 1954 when he was just five years old. That first taste sparked an interest in beer that lasted a lifetime. For the next 13 years, Papazian did not have another drop of beer but he remembered the taste, Papazian wrote in his book, *The Home Brewer's Companion.*

He graduated from Watchung Hills Regional High School in Warren, New Jersey, with never higher than a C in English and he remembered that an English teacher suggested he go into science. Papazian celebrated his graduation with some beer and a high school buddy named Bob. The two split a 6-pack of "down-right awful" beer and then spent half the night in the parking lot of Union Village Methodist Church. After he and Bob and four other underage drinkers were eventually arrested and had to pay a $240 fine, Papazian decided to modestly indulge in store-bought beer through his first years of nuclear engineering studies at the University of Virginia in Charlottesville.

Throughout college, he maintains, he did not enjoy a sip of beer so satisfying as the Ballantine beer offered to him by Uncle Paul. A friend named George, who worked at his own Arbor Hill Preschool and daycare center, was a beer drinker and one day suggested that Papazian visit his beer-making neighbor. Papazian obliged and became infatuated with the novelty of beer-making, if not the Prohibition-style beer of George's neighbor. They walked home with a recipe. Though Papazian's first three 10-gallon batches of brew only "kept the sewer rats happy" he persisted with beer-making and soon discov-

ered corn sugar and beer yeast. George's preschool basement became the birthplace of many a brew.

Papazian continued his education for five years. During his fourth year, he turned down an invitation to continue with the naval ROTC. However, he achieved a Bachelor of Science degree in 1972. After graduating, whimsy took him to Boulder, Colorado where he abandoned nuclear engineering and became a preschool teacher and home brewer. In the subsequent years as a teacher, he took summers off to travel, testing out home brews and village brews wherever he could.

In 1973, he began to teach a class in brewing at Boulder's Community Free School. From 1973-83, he taught more than 1,000 people, and members of his class inspired the formation of The American Homebrewers Association and its magazine, *zymurgy.* He self-published his first book, *The Joy of Brewing* in 1976, which was revised to 90 pages in 1980. Three years later he signed a contract with Avon Books to write *The Complete Joy of Home Brewing.*

In 1981, Papazian left teaching to take on the one full-time position of AHA, drawing a $300 a month salary. By 1987, the AHA evolved to serve as one division of the Association of Home Brewers still based in Boulder and had more than 30 full-time employees in 1994. Papazian, as the president, traveled, managed, wrote and edited. The AOB has three divisions, including the Institute for Brewing Studies, American Homebrewers Association and Brewers Publications. Papazian still finds time to brew beer and averages about 20 batches a year, he said.

---

mixture is encouraged to ferment, almost always through the agency of a yeast culture added at the appropriate time. Hops are added to flavor the brew, to temper its sweetness, to provide aroma, and to serve as a natural preservative." Traditionally, this is all it took to make beer, and the Bavarian law known as *Reinheitsgebot* requires German brewers to stick to these basics—barley malt, yeast, hops, and water. Indeed, the success of the craft brewing movement in the United States stems in part from a distaste for the practice of national brewers to add a variety of chemicals to their beers. These chemicals are designed to enhance flavor or color, to increase or decrease the size of the "head" or foam, or to act as preservatives. Most, if not all, craft brewers consider themselves purists who are getting back to the true essence of beer by following the traditional recipes. For brewer and consumer alike, this reliance on natural methods and ingredients is probably a major part of the appeal of craft beers.

With hundreds of entrants in the marketplace, craft brewers rely on fanciful, even silly names to win product recognition among consumers. Some names play off geographic points of interest, such as Seismic Ale, Earthquake Porter, and Survivor Stout from the San Andreas Brewing Company, or Honkers Ale from the Goose Island Brewery. Others employ tongue-in-cheek names based upon puns and double entendres such as Voluptuous Blonde Ale and Weisenheimer Wheat Beer. By some estimates, there are as many as 300 specialty brews named after animals or fish. Flavors offered range from pumpkin to strawberry. Shannon Mullen of the *Chicago Sun-Times* reports: "Some of the weaker breweries are being forced out, and a lot of the silliness that's been going on—raspberry mocha pale ale and that sort of thing—is starting to fade, say bar managers."

One offshoot from the growth of the craft beer industry is the multiplicity of books, magazines, and

Internet sites devoted to beer. Whereas someone rhapsodizing on the glories of craft beer would have been dismissed as a wine critic "wannabe" 20 years ago, today it is broadly accepted that beer, too, can enjoy its own language and culture of appreciation. Indeed, the number of styles and the terms used to describe craft beers—stouts, porters, ales, lagers, pilsner, bock, and wheat beers, to name just a handful of the most common terms—can be every bit as bewildering and intimidating to the uninitiated as the world of wine appreciation.

CURRENT CONDITIONS

Craft brewers brought in sales of over $3.03 billion in 1997, representing 6 percent of the nation's $50 billion in beer sales. Demand for craft beer has declined, according to a number of analysts. For example, the industry enjoyed a yearly growth of 50 percent earlier in the decade but watched its growth fall to 27 percent in 1996 and plummet to only 5 percent in 1997, according to the Institute for Brewing Studies. David Edgar, Institute for Brewing Studies director, told *Modern Brewery Age* magazine that he attributed part of the industry's problems to overcapacity because the brewers were producing more craft beer than consumers demanded.

Moreover, because the craft beer industry actually managed to expand in 1997, while the overall beer industry declined, craft brewers believe that market is maturing after experiencing exceptional growth earlier in the decade. Consequently, craft beer has established itself as a permanent sector of the overall beer industry. Nonetheless, since the industry began to mature in the late 1990s, a number of consolidations be-

gan to take place. For example, Gambrinus, a craft brewer and distributor, acquired Peter's Brewing Company in 1998 and Saxer Brewing Co. bought Nor'Wester the same year. Some industry observers expect this trend to continue.

In addition, as the industry shakeout continues, a number of craft brewers have found shelter from the ferocious competition by means of alliances with the larger, mass-market brewers, thus gaining access to distribution and resources otherwise beyond their reach. Such financial partnerships also benefit the majors, giving them access to consumers who are skeptical that macro-brewers can produce a microbrew-quality product. Online author Sara Doersam pointed out that with the major brand beer market remaining flat, "Anheuser-Busch, Miller, and Coors are scrambling to join the growing ranks of 'microbrewers' with microbeer knockoffs, attempted buyouts, and micro-mega mergers." She goes so far as to say that micros are no longer always what they appear to be, stating that "increasingly they are fronts for megabrewers."

Redhook Ale Brewery in Seattle and Widmer Bros. Brewing Co. in Portland, Oregon, have become partly owned by Anheuser-Busch. Anheuser-Busch has also tested the market with several microbrewed "imposters," as Doersam termed them. Another of the big brewers, Miller Brewing, has created American Specialty & Craft Beer Co., comprised of three small brewers: Celis Brewery, Inc. of Austin, Texas; Shipyard Brewing Co. in Portland, Maine; and Leinenkugel Brewing Co. in Wisconsin. Denver-based Coors has a craft brewing division producing Blue Moon Belgian White Ale and other specialty beers.

Another form of alliance is being explored in Oregon. A group of 40 local microbrewers have banded together to form the Oregon Brewers Guild. Their

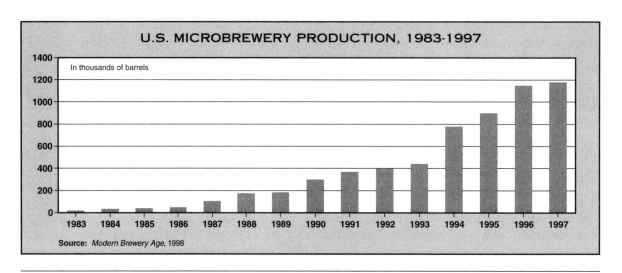

U.S. MICROBREWERY PRODUCTION, 1983-1997

In thousands of barrels

Source: *Modern Brewery Age,* 1998

original aim was to lobby on legislative issues affecting the industry, but they have discovered strength in numbers. To counter what one calls "pseudo craft brews" offered by the larger brewers, the guild developed a common quality-assurance label to help distinguish their brews from "knockoffs." A handful of guild members have started shipping beer together to Japan, where craft brews show signs of catching on.

The effects of the slowdown also could be seen in the number of registrants at the Craft Brewers Conference in Atlanta in April 1998—2,500, down from 3,300 the year before. Tony Forder wrote in *Ale Street News* that most noticeably absent were those looking to enter the industry, who usually make up at least one-third of the attendees, adding, "evidently, the word is out that the category is getting clogged."

A new trend in the industry is the growing popularity of the brewpub, where beer is brewed and sold on-site. The Institute for Brewing Studies (IBS) found that these brewery-restaurants made up 73 percent of all new craft breweries in 1997, up from 66 percent the year before. This trend was in part a response to increased competition on the microbrewery side. The brewpub share grew by 25 percent in 1997, with 215 openings and 50 closings, which put the failure rate at one in seven, much lower than that for restaurants, according to IBS.

The craft beer movement also has benefited beer imports, which have been growing throughout the 1990s. At 6 percent of the U.S. market, specialty beers only amount to half the imports' share of 12 percent. Imports grew 10 percent in 1997, led by brands produced in Mexico. *Beverage World*'s Eric Sfiligoj speculated in 1998 that the reason for the increase in import growth was consumers switching to prestige brands with the decline of the craft beer movement.

The crowded field has 450-plus regional specialty brewers and microbrewers competing for limited amounts of space on trucks and store shelves, making distribution difficult for the smaller players. Moreover, the dominant brewers have been accused of blocking the access of craft brewers to the channels of distribution. For example, four California craft brewers filed separate class action suits in federal courts on behalf of their counterparts in 12 western states in 1997. Their complaint was that Anheuser-Busch violated antitrust laws by persuading its distributors to drop craft beers other than its own brands. However, the market has come up with a solution. The crush on the trucks has given rise to a new breed of distributor, about 20 of whom specialize around the country in getting craft and specialty beers into bars, restaurants, and liquor stores.

INDUSTRY LEADERS

Great debate rages among insiders on just what constitutes a craft beer. For some it is a matter of the recipe. For others, anything bigger than a brewpub is simply too big to qualify. Some of the leading craft brewers, including Boston Beer Co. and Pete's Brewing Co., contract out the brewing of their beers to other breweries around the nation as a cost-saving measure. This alone is enough to push them into the ranks of "major" brewers, according to some purists. Nonetheless, these companies are usually counted among craft brewers when the industry is discussed.

Boston Beer Co., by far the largest of the specialty-beer makers, had sales of $183.5 million in 1998, up 2 percent from the previous year. The company produces more than 17 varieties, with several variations of its highly touted Samuel Adams brand—including lager, bock, ale, porter, pilsner, and stout— shipping nearly 1.2 million barrels throughout the United States and to select international markets. In an effort to maintain interest in its craft beers, Boston Beer introduces new beers frequently. Founded in Boston in 1984 by entrepreneur Jim Koch, one of the leading personalities of the craft beer movement, Boston Beer Co. has breweries in Boston and Cincinnati and contracts with five other breweries to produce its beers. Although Boston Beer is now publicly traded, Jim Koch still owns 27 percent of the company.

Pete's Brewing Co. in Palo Alto, California, is the nation's second-largest craft brewer. It is 10 percent owned by Detroit brewer Stroh's, which produces Pete's beer at its facilities under Pete's supervision. Best known for Pete's Wicked Ale, a dark amber made with chocolate and caramel malts, the company produces eight other beers, distributing them in 49 states and the United Kingdom. As part of the industry's consolidation, the Palo Alto brewer was acquired by San Antonio-based brewer and distributor Gambrinus Co. for $69 million in May 1998. Gambrinus posted sales of over $350 million in 1998. The company produces Shiner Bock and also owns BridgePort Brewing Company of Oregon.

Redhook Ale Brewery, Inc., with breweries at its home base in Seattle, brews its own beer, unlike rivals Boston Beer and Pete's. It produces seven types of beer, including major labels Redhook E.S.B., Blackhook, Wheathook, and Doubleblack Stout, and is distributed nationally. Sales were down 5 percent in 1998, dipping to a total of $32.6 million. Expanding to the East Coast, the Seattle-based company opened a new brewery in Portsouth, New Hampshire, during the final quarter of 1996, only to see the utilization rate of this new brewery slide to low levels due to heightened competition. Redhook serves as the craft beer arm of the industry giant Anheuser-Busch, maker of mass-produced Budweiser beer and 25-percent owner of Redhook. Consequently, some purists are said to have tagged the company with the unflattering nickname of "Budhook."

Also based in Seattle, Pyramid Breweries, Inc. markets about 25 ales and lagers under the Pyramid brand, including fruit-flavored beers and the Thomas Kemper labels, which includes root beers and premium sodas. It is distributed in more than 30 states, but primarily in California, Oregon, and Washington. The company's sales dropped 6 percent in 1998, falling to $25.6 million. Founded in 1984, Pyramid has three breweries with adjoining alehouses in Seattle and Berkeley, California, which can produce about 170,000 barrels annually, and the company plans to expand its brewery/alehouse operations into other metro areas.

Impact, the publication of the wine, beer, and liquor industry, ranked Boston Beer the top specialty brewer in 1997, with an 18 percent market share. Coors was second with 11 percent, Highfalls Brewing (Genesee) had 7 percent, Pete's and Anheuser-Busch tied at 6 percent each, and Sierra Nevada Brewing had 5 percent.

It seems highly probable that craft beer, both as a cultural phenomenon and a consumer preference, will continue to grow in popularity. At the same time, many of the entrepreneurs who brought this good-tasting addition to the market will not be rewarded financially for their troubles. It remains to be seen how much of the market for craft beer is siphoned off by the likes of Anheuser-Busch and other majors with their boutique brews. Yet even with a shakeout among brewpubs and the inevitable winnowing of the field, true craft brewers will continue to influence national beer tastes as long as barriers to entry in the industry remain so low.

FURTHER READING

"Beer Here." *Restaurant Hospitality,* September 1998, 90.

Demetrakakes, Pam. "Getting Crafty." *Food Processing,* February 1997.

Doersam, Sara. "The Craft Brewing Renaissance." 1996. Available from http://www.bpe.com/drinks/beer/craft/index.html.

Dorsch, Jim. "Micros Seek Allies, Regional Crafters Retrench." *Modern Brewery Age,* 23 March 1998.

Emma, Sal. "It Might Just Be an Ideal Job." *Brew Your Own,* September 1997.

Fenn, Donna. "Sleeping with the Enemy." *Inc.,* November 1997.

Finch, Christopher, and W. Scott Griffiths. *America's Best Beers,* New York: Little, Brown, & Co., 1994.

Forder, Tony. "Craft Brewers Conference, Atlanta, April 98." *Ale Street News,* June 1998.

Higgins, Patrick, Maura Kate Kilgore, and Paul Hertlein. *The Homebrewer's Recipe Guide.* New York: Simon & Schuster, 1996.

———. *Michael Jackson's Beer Companion.* Philadelphia: Running Press, 1993.

Institute for Brewing Studies. "Craft-Brewing Fact Sheet." 11 September 1998. Available from http://www.beertown.org/ibsframeset.htm.

Kreck, Dick. "Growth Bubbles Burst for Craft-Brewing Industry." *Denver Post,* 24 June 1998.

Melcher, Richard A. "Those New Brews Have the Blues." *Business Week,* 9 March 1998.

Moriwaki, Lee. "Shakeout Brewing." *Seattle Times,* 3 November 1996.

Mullen, Shannon. "Big Labels, Imports Beat Back Craft Beers." *Chicago Sun-Times,* 15 April 1998.

Nachel, Marty. *Beer Across America.* Pownal, VT: Storey Communications Inc., 1995.

Papazian, Charlie. *The Homebrewer's Companion.* New York: Avon Books, 1994.

Poling, Travis E. "Local Firm Prepares to Purchase Craft Beer Giant Pete's Brewing Co." *San Antonio Express-News,* 23 May 1998.

Rose, Michael. "Portland Brewing Girds Kilts for War." *Business Journal-Portland,* 25 December 1998, 1.

Sfiligoj, Eric. "The Mexican Revolution." *Beverage World,* 15 February 1998.

Steinriede, Kent. "Distribution Is a Rocky Road for Craft Brewers." *Beverage Industry,* October 1997.

Theodore, Sarah. "Still Crazy About Craft Beer." *Beverage Industry,* January 1998, 26.

Wood, Heather, ed. *The Beer Directory.* Pownal, VT: Storey Communications Inc., 1995.

—John Gallagher, updated by Shirley Gray and Karl Heil

CREATIVE DINING

Creative dining in the United States at the end of the twentieth century reflected the ability Americans possessed to continually reinvent themselves and their lifestyles. The business of food, its preparation, and its serving, became the core of American social life. By the end of the 1990s, creative dining encompassed eating out in restaurants, both full service and fast food; grocery stores offering more extensive prepared food options from on-site kitchens for customers to take home; and the heightened interest in gourmet cooking for family and friends in the comfort of private homes. Creative dining refers to both extraordinary cuisine and the exotic settings in which it might be served. On a global level, both Americans and others engage in the pleasurable pastime of eating. According to a report from *Euromonitor International*, and noted in *Prepared Foods*, in November 1998, foodservice became an industry of global proportions. "In Europe," reports *Euromonitor International* in 1998, "the leading 'Eating Out' country was Spain at $55.4 billion, followed by Italy at $47.3 billion; the United Kingdom at $45.2 billion, Germany at $40.4 billion, and France at $27.4 billion." The United States remained the largest foodservice market in the world but ranked third in per capita spending at $936 per person. Japan ranked first at $1,670, and Spain ranked second at $1,410 per person. At the end of the twentieth century the trend toward eating out and gourmet dining was expected to grow. In addition to eating out on a regular basis, Americans, especially, began to enjoy world cruises and tours devoted to experiencing exotic cuisine.

The food industry in the United States is subject to federal, state, and local laws that ensure the safety of the food offered for consumption. At the federal level, the U.S. Department of Agriculture (USDA) and the U.S. Food and Drug Administration (FDA) regulates several aspects of the industry. For meat, poultry, and seafood providers these agencies offer guidelines regarding the gradings of the quality of meat cuts, an example of which are the USDA "Prime" and "Choice" cuts of meat. In the safety of overseeing the seafood industry, protection from harmful bacteria that might lead to serious diseases such as hepatitis or salmonella poisoning in humans provide these government agencies with ongoing inspections. The USDA leads inspections of all imported fruits and vegetables coming into the United States, as well. At the end of the 1990s more exotic varieties of these were becoming desirable as gourmet tastes gave rise to interest in the imported produce from other countries, particularly the tropics.

On the local and state levels, the food and restaurant industry is subject to guidelines that direct sanitary conditions in food preparations for restaurants and grocery stores. All local jurisdictions in the United States, either at a county or city level, require the licensing of restaurants or other food establishments such as pizza shops and bakeries. Environmental engineering standards regarding the actual structures were key factors in constructing and opening food establishments by the end of the twentieth century. Consideration is given to heating and ventilation systems particularly. This accommodates environmental regulations, fire safety regulations, and other health concerns for humans. Unlike most of Europe, the United States by the 1990s had become conscious of the hazards of cigarette and cigar smoke in public establishments where a number of people were congregated in a confined area. In the 1980s many cities began to ban smoking in all public places, including restaurants. As was often the case with similar trends, California led the way with legislation; the city of Berkeley, California, enacted the first such legislation. Eventually, smoking was also banned in San Francisco in public places. Until 1998 smokers could be served food in bars, often sectioned away from the main restaurant. After this time, smoking was prohibited in bars, as well, which changed the dining experience for many, smokers and non-smokers alike.

National and local restaurant associations are the industry's way of monitoring itself. Innovations are spurred most often by customer demand. In brief, as the American consumer becomes more sophisticated to new cuisine, and as families and single, affluent adults are able to better afford the luxury of eating out, the restaurant industry increasingly meets customer demand. As celebrity chefs became a fixture on television, in cookbooks, at trend-setting restaurants, and with novel food products, food took on yet another dimension in the role it played. The creation of *The Food Network* on cable television in the 1990s continued to spark interest in the introduction of foods that might have otherwise been unfamiliar to millions of viewers. The traditional line-up of weekend cooking shows on the Public Broadcasting System (PBS) also played a crucial role in the growth and maintenance of the billion-dollar industry. Every place from McDonald's, which was credited in bringing about an entire fast-food market into prominence in the late 1950s, to Chez Panisse in Berkeley, California, the restaurant acclaimed for introducing "California" or "Nouvelle" (the French word for "new") cuisine took its own spot along the spectrum of dining in America.

BACKGROUND AND DEVELOPMENT

History itself offered reliable clues regarding the path that led to exotic dining experiences. Perhaps the most crucial advances were the voyages of Marco Polo as early as the thirteenth century. These began the modern age's fascination with food and its possibilities. When the Venetian trader and explorer first began his travels to Asia and discovered many of the spices now considered commonplace, he opened up the possibility that food could be something more than

mere sustenance. In an age that lacked refrigeration, the exotic spices of the Far East made inferior meat taste better and last longer. These spices were used as barter that only the wealthy could trade for at first. As the bounty eventually trickled down to the common person, and as settlers ventured to the "New World" of the Americas by the sixteenth century, a whole new world of food was born. People discovered hundreds of foods, and ways of preparation that were different from their own. Travel in those ancient times, as well as modern-day travel experiences taking place in person and through television, was the important ingredient that boosted the food industry from growing and raising various foods to serving travelers at roadside inns whatever the local fare could offer. Once people understood that money could be made from feeding people, the industry of food began to grow.

The experiences of eating out in America began to emerge as people left their small towns and rural farms and moved into industrial-age jobs in cities. That was a gradual process in the United States. Early America enjoyed roadside inns, or the generosity of a hotel owner who might offer a traveler a meal. By the middle of the nineteenth century restaurants were already established on the scene in the large metropolitan areas of New York, Boston, and Washington, D.C. Such famous places as Delmonico's restaurant in New York City, whose name eventually lent itself to a certain cut of steaks, to particular kinds of salt and pepper shakers, and even to a specific style of checkered tablecloth, flourished in that era known as the "Gilded Age" of the 1890s. That was a period of time when wealthy industrialists, such as Cornelius Vanderbilt and others, flaunted their newfound wealth in extravagant ways previously unknown to the Puritanical America.

Americans moved westward to Chicago, for instance, following the Civil War, and by 1900, people there and west of the Mississippi began to regularly enjoy meals away from home in commercial establishments. These might have been restaurants, neighborhood taverns, or hotel and department store dining rooms. Marshall Field placed restaurants of varying styles and price ranges into his famous Chicago department store early in its history as a means of keeping shoppers in his store longer. Still, in late nineteenth century America, restaurant dining rooms were frequented mostly by men. Those restaurants that accommodated women often had separate dining rooms that advertised as "Ladies' Dining Room."

Into the 1920s and 1930s eating out was more of a lunchtime ritual for the average working person and housewife out shopping. The lunch counter and soda fountain at the neighborhood drugstore expanded into lunch counters at the downtown department stores, and 5 and 10 cent stores, also known as "The Five & Dime" to three generations of Americans, into the 1970s. Except for movie stars in Hollywood or those celebrities frequenting such fashionable restaurants and nightclubs as "21" and "Sardi's" in New York City, or the "Coconut Grove" in Los Angeles, eating dinner out was not the common habit of the American people until the 1950s and 1960s. Often, even eating out in elegant restaurants meant variations of meat and potatoes. Only in ethnic restaurants, such as Chinese, Italian, or Greek, or in the Kosher delicatessens could one expect anything out of the ordinary.

Social custom changed as more women entered the job force after World War II, and especially in the 1970s when adulthood for the baby boomers coincided with the surge of the Feminist movement. Eating out until then was something that families might do on vacation or on special occasions. For many middle class Americans, the church supper or Rotary pancake breakfast was as far as dining experiences extended. In the 1950s when drive-in restaurants began to dominate the scene with places such as "Big Boy" restaurant chain, followed closely by McDonald's, affordable prices for the average family began to change the way people ate. The 1950s also witnessed the appearance of Pizza parlors, many of them carryout. Pizza and other fast food were those dining experiences that got more people, especially families, out to eat more often. Fast food was also the area of the food business that started to reflect varying tastes in an increasingly health-conscious America. For some, the first step toward "creative cuisine" was the advent of the salad bar in many fast food chain restaurants. In the 1970s salad bars began to offer the first variety of choices different from the hamburgers, french fries, and fried chicken that had been the basis for most fast food restaurants until that time. Every fast food restaurant from Burger Chef to Burger King eventually introduced salad bars. McDonald's entered into the trend, not with salad bars, but instead with individual, prepared salads.

Other restaurants began to flourish as well. Yet, until 1980, in large and small metropolitan areas, many were still remnants of recently bygone eras. They were the darkened Italian restaurants with velvet-embossed wallpaper and candles melted into emptied Chianti bottles. Or, they might have been the more exotic Middle Eastern restaurants, complete with shish kabobs and belly dancers. An undercurrent was slowly drifting into mainstream America, however. Average Americans were venturing out of their provincial ex-istences. People who might not have had the money to do so even a decade earlier were seeing the world because of a new affluence and affordability. What came to be known as the "Rust Belt" with the decline of the steel and auto businesses moved people to the "Sun Belt" of the United States. The Sun Belt included the South, the Southwest, and most important demographically, California. American taste buds were experiencing the Creole cooking of New Orleans, the spicy Mexican food of the Southwest, and the health-conscious Asian cuisine of San Francisco. What was once considered exotic or creative, had become commonplace. Food went further into new territory because of the demand that was born. By the end of the 1970s strides in food production and packaging made produce available year-round, for instance, that might have otherwise been offered regionally in the summer months. Artichokes and strawberries became as common in Ohio in March as they had been in California. With the opening of trade in China during President Richard Nixon's administration in the early 1970s, as well as the flood of migrating tourists to the West Coast, tastes became acquainted with the variety of Chinese cuisine that included Mandarin and Hunan. Whereas previously Chinese meant only Cantonese to most Americans, the many tastes that absorbed everything from chili garlic paste to Napa cabbage and steamed dumplings were cravings that Americans could not seem to satisfy.

The Vietnam War also helped change American tastes. In addition to the American soldiers who returned, a flood of refugees came to America in 1975 when South Vietnam finally fell to the Communist regime of the North, two years after American troops left and the war for the United States was officially ended. Many Vietnamese refugees who settled in the United States opened restaurants. Because Vietnam had been occupied by the French for many years prior to American involvement, Vietnamese cuisine was often an interesting combination of French and Asian, yet another new taste for Americans. These led the way to American tastes for other Asian cuisine, including Filipino, Korean, and Thai, which became the trendiest cuisine of California by the early 1980s.

The Mongolian Barbeque entered America slowly, first through the West Coast, and Washington, D.C., but stayed popular through the late 1990s. People could pick out the meat and vegetables they wanted to eat, season their selection, then go to the next table where the chef would grill while the patrons watched. In the early 1970s the Benihana restaurant chain popularized this concept with Japanese food. According to their catchy, innovative ads, the tradition of the ancient Japanese Samurai warriors was conjured up for all who wanted to be mesmerized. Knives flew into the air like swords, and all 6 or 8 people seated around the table that surrounded the grill and cutting board surface were entertained by two Japanese chefs who often gave off what sounded more like a war call or karate chops.

As early as the 1970s, another popular aspect of Japanese cuisine was entering the American scene, mostly in New York and California. Sushi, which consists of raw fish in varying sorts of rice and vegetable rolls, was an instant hit with some. The cuisine of India also began to rise in popularity as many Americans turned away from beef and turned toward vegetarian diets. By the early 1980s many restaurants offered vegetarian entrees. Meat substitutes made from soy, Tofu, beans, and grains began sprouting up in the form of hamburgers, chicken salads, and meat loaves. Ice cream could easily be made with tofu and rice in the products known as "Tofuti," and "Rice Dream." A cheesecake might have been made with soy protein as well as with the expensive Italian cheese Mascarpone. What was once available only in gourmet markets in America's larger cities and posh suburbs was becoming commonplace at everybody's regular neighborhood grocery chain. Imports from France and Italy initially scored the biggest when it came to captivating Americans. Before the revolution was over, even the primitive foods of eastern Europe and native America were exulted into the gourmet arena.

In the early 1980s another explosion in food occurred, quietly at first, in Berkeley, California. A simple new restaurant was sweeping restaurant critic raves. That restaurant was Chez Panisse. Its founder, a chef named Alice Waters, offered food in a new way. In what would come to be known as "California cuisine," Waters was taking some traditional food dishes and giving them a twist by filling ravioli dough with pureed pumpkin, wild mushrooms, or lobster, tossing fresh pasta with sun-dried tomatoes; and preparing calamari salads to be served cold. Salads became an adventure with radicchio and arugula alongside fresh herb dressings. In the San Francisco Bay area, Waters pushed the limits even further. Not everybody could afford a meal at her restaurant, but everybody could afford to think what had been previously unthinkable in mixing and matching foods, especially fresh, organically grown produce. Of the many elements that went into the creative dining at the end of the twentieth century, the leap that Alice Waters took was a big step toward opening up American tastes and innovating American restaurants to continually changing environments.

PIONEERS IN THE FIELD

Not many would dispute that it was Julia Child and her "French Chef" program on PBS in the late 1960s that gave the push to a new creative cuisine in America. The success of the television series, still in reruns 30 years later, was unmatched. Child let viewers know that they could do what they thought only Cordon Bleu-trained chefs could do. Child's own two-volume cooking "manual" and cookbook for French cuisine started competing with Betty Crocker, Fanny Farmer, and Rombauer's "Joy of Cooking," the longtime food authorities for the American housewife. James Beard was another well-known chef, being the preeminent leader of American cuisine for several decades. Following his death in the 1980s, his legacy survived to promote young chefs through the James Beard Foundation, an organization that serves up competitions and awards and gives homage to humanitarian efforts in feeding the world.

In 1997 Waters of *Chez Panisse,* was honored by the James Beard Foundation for her own humanitarian efforts, and named "Humanitarian of the Year" for her innovative project called, "The Edible Schoolyard." In an article for *Whole Earth* magazine in the Summer of 1997, Waters talked about that project, and her lifelong relationship to food. In "The Ethics of Eating, [Part ii]" Waters noted that her own ethics probably grew up out of political involvement in the 1960s. She noted that, "When people choose mass-produced food and fast food they are supporting a network of supply and demand that destroys local communities and traditional ways of life all over the world—a system that replaces self-sufficiency with dependence." Waters began conceiving the "Edible Schoolyard," after driving by a run-down schoolyard in her Berkeley, California, community for several years. In 1994, to the delight of the school principal, teachers, parents, and children, the unkempt schoolyard became a garden.

In the age of *The Food Network,* new stars were rising all the time. The chef with enough flair to get nearly anybody to take a chance with the spicy cuisine of Louisiana was Emeril Lagasse. With cookbooks, two television shows, and restaurants in Las Vegas, New Orleans, and Universal Studios in Florida, Lagasse with his exotic French Canadian-Portugese heritage kept television viewers glued to the screen whether he was deep frying a turkey for Thanksgiving, or blending the ingredients for a tropical fruit dessert. Among others who tempted tastes on that network were David Rosengarten with his exploration of American "Taste" exploring such simple dishes as deep-fried onion rings and Jewish knishes, and "Multo Mario" with his Italian cuisine.

CURRENT CONDITIONS

By the end of the twentieth century food was a major industry all around the world. Eating had indeed become a global pastime, but with some twists and turns. A 1996 survey by Zagat's, the restaurant review organization, reported in *ADWEEK,* that New Yorkers ate an average of 4.7 home-cooked lunches or dinners per week. Atlanta followed with 5.0 while the combined market of Portland, Oregon, and Seattle, Washington, indicated that people there cooked an average of 6.6 lunches or dinners. As reported by *The Voice of Foodservice Distribution,* in an article entitled, "Family Dining: Trends in Progress," the move to court families and senior citizens was a move that restaurant owners knew they had to make in order to keep revenues up. Those were the restaurants that were less creative, and big on American fare of pork chops, all-day breakfasts, grilled sandwiches, and fried fish dinners. *Restaurant and Institutions,* reported in February 1998 that, surprisingly, "about 47 percent of those reporting at least some college education" ate fast food at least once a week, as opposed to 38 percent of those with only a high-school diploma.

In addition to the flood of gourmet restaurants and cooking schools that created great interest in more creative dining, supermarkets began to hone in on the competition for challenging tastes. By the late 1990s all sorts of interesting trends were occurring at the grocery store. In the fast-paced society with families that might have had both spouses and teenaged children working, the need for convenience food was still crucial to successful sales in all sectors of American society. What was different by the late 1990s, though, was that those convenience choices likely included freshly prepared dinners from their grocery stores' in-house kitchen, rather than simply a tour of whatever Stouffer's or Swanson's might have had to offer in the frozen food section. On her way home from work, a woman might be able to stop by her local grocery store and choose from a selection at a Sushi bar, piping hot kettles of Crab Bisque, gourmet pizzas topped with sun-dried tomatoes and fresh goat cheese, or steamed mussels or crab legs, to serve to her family a half hour later.

In fact, AFC Sushi, based in Compton, California, was responsible for setting up Sushi sections in mainstream supermarkets and natural food stores all over the United States, 20 years after the concept was introduced to the diners of New York and California. In 1999 Kevin Burton, managing director for AFC Sushi, estimated that the U.S. Sushi industry grossed $50 million a year. Through arrangements with individual store and grocery operators, AFC ran the Sushi bar, and even employed the chefs who worked it. Single people were able to buy a fully cooked Cornish game hen stuffed with wild rice, and other similar dishes they might not have bothered to prepare for themselves. Fresh salads prepared with organic greens were ready to be picked up in the produce section. A stop by the bakery counter might yield a freshly baked Caibiatta (an Italian bread made with unbleached and semolina flour), tomato-basil dinner rolls, or Key Lime pie.

Among interesting trends in food items were the emergence of the "bug" trade. According to Brendan I. Koerner, writing for the *U.S. News and World Report,* "Entomophagy—noshing on bug—is no longer just for playground gross-out contests. Hotlix, a California confectioner known for its tequila-flavored worm-in-the center of lollipops, is doing a brisk business in bug-bearing treats." Among the products available are, "Larvets," beetle larvae in cheddar cheese or Mexican spice flavor, and "Amber InsectNside," toffee candies wrapped around roasted larvae, wings, and cuticles intact. Still, with 80 percent of the rest of the world engaging in some sort of insect delicacies, Americans remained skeptical. Expensive liqueur-filled chocolate truffles and Dove ice cream bars were gourmet items more likely to satisfy American curiosity.

By the end of the twentieth century baby food had evolved, too, into an item of gourmet proportions. Jennifer Smither, Associated Press writer, reported on one such company, The Well Fed Baby Inc., in April 1999. Based in San Marcos, California, an affluent San Francisco suburb of the East Bay, the company expected to earn $1 million in the first year of operation. Company founder O. Robin Sweet developed this organic line of baby food in answer to her own problem. After nursing her six-month old child back to health on a vegetarian diet, Sweet started her own company, which joined a host of other organic baby food producers. Sales of organic baby food rose from $1 million in 1989 to $25 million in 1995, according to the USDA. The organic food market as a whole grew in sales to exceed $3.5 billion in 1996.

INDUSTRY LEADERS

In the competitive food markets at the end of the twentieth century, nearly every food production and packaging company and restaurant tried to undo each other in the edge for creative cuisine. The theme-based restaurants of Disney World and Universal Studios in

Florida were a portrait in varied cuisine, both to suit adult tastes and children's. Whether it was the "Hard Rock Cafe," or "Planet Hollywood," or one small "Nouvelle Cuisine" restaurant that opened in the heart of Ohio's Amish country, all over the United States creative dining became the rule for any eatery. Barbecued pulled pork was considered a unique taste treat in uptown Manhattan. Sushi and Creole cooking often were considered exotic in middle America. The next millionaire, or billionaire, in the food market was the person or company who could come up with yet one more interesting concept to excite diners of all ages, ethnic groups, and tastes.

WORK FORCE

Food workers include wait people, food preparation specialists, expert chefs and cooks, researchers and testers seeking new and safer ways to market food, restaurant managers, and owners. Whereas fast food staff workers might at one time have expected to make no more than minimum wage, at the end of the 1990s, with the competition for workers in a growing economy, it was not unusual for them to earn $7-$10 an hour all around the United States. At the high end of the spectrum, a chef trained at one of the more renowned cooking schools, such as the Culinary Institute of America, in upstate New York, or Johnson & Wales in Providence, Rhode Island, might expect to field a host of offers at some of the country's finest hotels and restaurants, eventually earning a six-figure income. In the restaurant business, where the law was "location, location, location," the quality of food lingered as a key ingredient in a successful operation. Running a restaurant often involves a 7-day week, with a more than 14-hour day commitment, to breed success. Many businesses fail, but, again, restaurants specializing in out-of-the-ordinary dining experiences could prove a lucrative enterprise.

AMERICA AND THE WORLD

One of the most interesting concepts to emerge from the craze for exotic and creative dining was the "food tour" that gained in popularity in the 1990s. One such tour, "Come With Me to the Kasbah," was offered through Carlsbad Travel in southern California, and featured as tour guide, Moroccan-born cookbook author Kitty Morse. By 1999, the twelfth annual 15-day tour of Morocco was offered at a price of $4,150 per person. The focus of this tour, as with many sim-

ilar tours, whether to Paris or the Tuscany region of Italy, is food.

Other than tourists, the most quickly expanding export the United States offers the world is fast food. By 1998, according to the *U.S. Industry and Trade Outlook 1998,* approximately 160 U.S. food service companies were operating abroad. McDonald's boasted the largest number of markets with 5,400 units that generated 43 percent of its sales. Joining together for totals of 1,000 units each were Pizza Hut, Burger King, and Baskin-Robbins Ice Cream franchises. TGI Friday's actually averaged $1 million more a year in sales in it international operations than domestically.

FURTHER READING

Behrens, James Stephen. "If You're Looking for God, Try the Dinner Table." *National Catholic Reporter,* 17 July 1998.

Dulan, Jacqueline. "Changing Tastes: An R & I Survey Examines the Dining Habits of an Increasingly Diverse Foodservice Clientele." *Restaurants & Institutions,* 1 February 1998.

"Eating Out is a Global Pastime." *Prepared Foods,* November 1998.

Heubusch, Kevin. "Getting It to Go." *American Demographics,* April 1997.

Krummert, Bob. "Family Dining: Trends in Progress." *ID: The Voice of Foodservice Distribution,* August 1997.

La Reaux, Sherri. "Setting Up a Sushi Section." *Natural Foods Merchandiser,* July 1998. Available from http://www.Newhope.com/naturalfoods.

Lassell, Michael. "High/low Dining Niche—How to Cook up a Serene Space for Meals—Whether Your Prix-fixe Menu Includes Fine Haute Cuisine or Simpler Market Fare." *Metropolitan Home,* November-December 1998.

"Let's Do Lunch!" *Nation's Restaurant News,* 29 July 1996.

Marcus, Mary Brophy. "Heart Healthy? Restaurant Fare." *U.S. News & World Report,* 28 April 1997.

Raffio, Ralph. "Are They Worth It? RB's Exclusive CEO Compensation Study Determines Not Only Who Made the Most, but Whether They Deserved It." *Restaurant Business,* 1 September 1997.

"Restaurant Business Still Sizzles—No Cooling Off in '97's Hot Concepts." *Nation's Restaurant News,* 12 May 1997.

Salkever, Alex. "The Burger Queens: How Two Southern California Women Turned a Song into a $7 Million-a-year Restaurant Business." *Hawaii Business,* May 1996.

Sheridan, Margaret. "Behind Closed Doors: Operators' Commitment to Private Dining Rooms Sow Seeds for New Customers and Profit During Slack Time." *Restaurants & Institutions,* 1 October 1997.

Smith, Jennifer. "Company Builds Success on a Well Fed Baby." *Associated Press,* 2 May 1999.

Stephenson, Susie. "Seeking out Singles." *Restaurants & Institutions,* 1 April 1996.

Waters, Alice. "The Ethics of Eating {Part II}," *Whole Earth,* Summer 1997.

"What's on the Stove, Ma? Probably Cobwebs." *ADWEEK,* Eastern edition, 9 December 1996.

—Jane E. Spear

CROSS-MARKETING

The cross-marketing industry touts no particular product or service. From the vantage of the consumer, cross-marketing is a convenient one-stop shopping mechanism, sometimes involving a single price tag. From the standpoint of modern high-tech vendors, cross-marketing is a complex maze of databases, data warehouses, and data mining algorithms. The principle of cross-marketing is not new to the advertising industry, although cross-marketing mushroomed into an industry of its own in the wake of increasingly comprehensive and sophisticated digital databases that evolved with the expansion of computerized business applications. Prior to the new age of automation, between 1950 and 2000, cross-marketing promotions were simple processes whereby a radio personality, for example, might endorse a familiar product and remind the public to tune in to his or her upcoming radio show in the process. Similarly name-recognition companies sponsored sporting events, to promote the name-brand product simultaneously with the sporting entertainment. The rapid growth of fast food chains during the 1950s holds testament to cliche, campaigns such as, "Buy a Big-O-Burger, and get a free Coke."

After 1950, the proliferation of database technology in conjunction with the innovation of desktop computers a few years later furnished vendors with new and easy access to a vast repository of previously untapped consumer data. Analytical software enhanced this resource to provide marketing professionals with the capability to venture informed predictions regarding the impact of specific advertising campaigns aimed at pre-defined sectors of the consumer population. Analysts used modern data mining techniques to study consumer buying patterns in depth, and cross-

marketing solutions evolved rapidly from that basic threshold. The addition of a continually expanding and intertwined network of information on the Internet brought the crowning dimension of "virtual" (limitless) cross-indexing to the inherent power and potential of cross-marketing.

The cross-marketing industry is unique because it is most effective when it remains undetectable to the consumer. The best cross-marketing schemes are those that go unnoticed. This inherent transparency of cross-marketing is not achieved by accident. It is entrenched in an environment of automated databases, data warehousing, and data mining systems that essentially tap all available knowledge about consumers and their spending habits, including the arguably private details concerning income, family status, and social and spending habits.

TOP-DOWN VERSUS BOTTOM-UP

Many cross-marketing structures may be obvious, as when a correlation exists between co-sponsored products. This "top-down" structure is easy to perceive, for example, when multiple travel-related industries launch a cooperative effort to promote car rentals, hotel accommodations, and airline reservations through a single convenient outlet. Likewise many Internet links let consumers browse through virtual displays of products that offer some inherent characteristic of commonality. Other top-down structures, while less blatant, are apparent to the consumer nevertheless—for example, when a grocery store offers a one-half price admission ticket to a local theme park, as a premium with every $50 purchase of groceries. The consumer buys groceries eagerly, is more likely to frequent the theme park and appreciates the "family values" message touted by the grocer.

Less obvious, "bottom-up" structures occur in marketing promotions devised from sophisticated data mining applications that contrive more elusive patterns of consumption. A bottom-up correlation evolves from patterns uncovered in automated database structures. Primitive structures exist, for example, when products are marketed to consumers within a particular geographical area, as derived from the address entry in a database listing. The source of the database listing serves as a contributing factor—for example, the commonality of the database entries might be as vague as the entries in a telephone directory, or more specific such as a listing of all credit card holders from a specialty store.

STANDARDS AND STATUTES

While the easy availability of consumer data may serve as a boon to the cross-marketing industry, it spawns an increasingly disgruntled segment of the consumer base, those who fear significant loss of privacy and intrusive marketing techniques. Privacy concerns are most acute under those circumstances where warehoused data from financial institutions is at issue, as more and more financial institutions, banks, and insurance companies merge together to form massive conglomerates. The Financial Information Privacy Act of 1999, proposed in January of 1999 by Democratic Senators Paul S. Sarbanes of Maryland and Christopher J. Dodd of Connecticut; sought to mandate federal legislation limiting the use of consumer data. At that time the House Banking chairman, Jim Leach, proposed less restrictive guidelines, only to prevent information brokers from propagating any type of ruse in order to gain access to the proprietary consumer data of a financial institution. In this regard, the American Bankers Association (ABA) is concerned about restrictions that would bar disclosure of key information such as account balances, maturity dates, and holdings information. ABA also opposes any requirements that would force financial institutions to obtain permission to sell or share information of a confidential nature. The issues addressed by pending legislation concerning shared information have broad implications.

Overall, and not surprisingly, ABA supports self-regulation. Regulatory proposals pending in the U.S. legislature could further curtail the cross-marketing affairs of the banking and finance industries, by prohibiting the growing trend toward consolidation of banking and finance, and insurance industries. The federal legislation would preclude the formation of crossover corporations, those that deal in both securities and savings and loan transactions for certain types of institutions. Regulation of this nature might pose an impediment that would limit the potential advantages of cross-marketing schemes by the financial industry.

CROSS-OWNERSHIP

Corporate subsidiaries, mergers, partnerships, and alliances underscore a vast number of cross-marketing promotions. Large parent corporations with diverse subsidiaries frequently turn to cross-marketing to promote otherwise unrelated products. A discount coupon for a new and improved laundry detergent that is strategically placed on a jar of facial cream is not far fetched when a single parent organization owns each of the companies that produce the two products. It is not uncommon for corporate liaisons to exist between the assorted products on grocery store shelves. Likewise, liaisons are increasingly common between entertainment industries such as television, magazines, and movie production. The interactions between industries and corporations cannot be simply defined. In some cases, competing brands of similar products are manufactured by the same parent organization, resulting in cross-promotion between competing brands of the same item. A package of cough drops, for example, might include a coupon for a discount on the purchase of cough drops marketed under a different brand name by the same parent company.

The Telecommunications Act of 1996 opened a myriad of new pathways to inter-corporate mergers and resulting cross-marketing within the expansive telecommunications industry, through the process of deregulation. The Act suspended older regulatory statutes that prohibited diverse media corporations from cross-ownership. The true potential of the Telecommunications Act cannot be predicted nor realized for years to come, as the competing technologies of telephone, cable television, and Internet services converge under deregulation and new and unimagined technologies emerge.

BACKGROUND AND DEVELOPMENT

Modern cross-marketing is a spin-off of automated database technology. After World War II, direct mass marketing techniques evolved freely from the use of computerized billing applications. These afforded businesses with a cheap and easy method of reaching large groups of consumers through automated mailing lists that printed address labels and envelopes with ease. Direct mail promotions subsequently entered a new era, when mail-merge techniques provided a means of further personalizing direct mail advertising. Through mail-merge programs, an offshoot of word and text processing, direct mail advertisers created the illusion of personalization although they distributed preformatted messages as always. A "personalized" letter that started "Dear Mr. Jones, Congratulations on your recent purchase of a new Mustang Cobra...." might shift abruptly into a mass-produced "boilerplate" text (standardized for all recipients). The personal message at the opening would arouse considerable interest, and the targeted customer could be easily swayed into thinking that he or she was among a limited few to receive the advertised offer. Cliche, homeowners, formerly known to advertisers as "Occupant" and "Resident," were evicted from the residences of modern America. A new wave of advertising addressed recipients by proper name and address. Presorted databanks gave vendors the further convenience of targeting advertisements to consumers according to zip code, income bracket, and other bits of information that accrued into massive databases, until the automated database became a commodity in its own right. Databases, initially called mailing lists, were bought and sold by marketing professionals for ready access to a potential customer base. Database technology expanded rapidly during the 1980s and 1990s, and primitive "flat-file" (linear) mailing lists swelled into "rational," interconnected databases and dynamic "object-based" systems that opened new vistas to marketing professionals. These new systems could be used to "analyze" and "predict" massive amounts of data, including consumer buying patterns. Direct mail and other mass marketing systems offered a fertile environment for vendors to cross-market products, reach a larger customer base, and reduce advertising costs in the process.

State-of-the-art databases correlate information between customer records in order to perceive existing trends and to attempt to predict future trends. The sophistication of cross-marketing promotions increased directly with the sophistication of database technology. Complex computer systems enabled advertisers to appraise customer potential based on factors that were previously too complex for the human mind to correlate. Common sense could readily establish the connection between dollars spent for airline travel, car rental, and hotel accommodations, yet the new rational databases predicted with some accuracy the customer's travel patterns, insurance needs, meal patterns, and even personal consumption patterns at home. The most dramatic impact of database advancement is visible in the ongoing consolidation of the financial industries. Insurance companies, for example, reportedly cut their sales forces by tens of thousands of personnel, in response to a growing trend whereby stockbrokers sell life insurance to investors. Major brokerage firms including Merrill Lynch tout proprietary life insurance as a matter of course. The notion that the information stored in the Merrill Lynch customer database provides keen insight for insurance sales is not far-fetched. The potential for cross-marketing within the highly regulated financial industry assumed such proportions during the 1990s that legislators and institutions embarked on a diligent crusade to further refine existing limitations imposed on the banking and finance industry early in the twentieth century.

CURRENT CONDITIONS

According to U.S. Bancorp, high-volume cross-selling techniques account for 50 percent of sales of some types of investment services and reportedly save 66-75 percent of the cost of sales overhead for many financial corporations. This is possible because cross-marketing of diverse financial services eliminates the overhead associated with recruiting new clientele. Statistics further support the notion that existing customers who are cross-targeted customers are more likely to bring repeat business. It takes a certain length of time and a certain number of purchases before one can establish a reasonable assurance of an ongoing business relationship with a customer. Cross-selling of financial services increases the number of purchases per customer more quickly than waiting for clients to return spontaneously to purchase the additional goods or services.

The travel and recreation industries are among the most visible of cross-marketers, with high stakes corporations including hotels and resorts, common carriers, public media, sports franchise, credit card lenders, and clothing stores among the wide variety of industries that establish cooperative cross-marketing ventures. When Neiman-Marcus Department Stores, Wide World of Golf Tours, and Preferred Hotels and Resorts Worldwide formed a cross-marketing partnership, the cross-marketing program offered premium incentives to travelers such as bargains at the retail store, guaranteed tee times, and accommodation packages at the resorts and hotels. Starwood Hotels & Resorts Worldwide launched a similar $50 million campaign called Starwood Preferred Guest. The Preferred Guest program, geared to frequent travelers, included cross-marketing incentives on car rentals, credit cards, clothing stores, mail-order catalog shopping, and more.

Telecommunication firms are well known for a variety of high-visibility promotional packages as well. Philadelphia-based telephone company, Bell Atlantic, devised a Business-to-Business Frequency Program to cross-market its own telephone services along with the respective services of its business customers. The program, designed to encourage Bell customers to patronize each other's businesses, offered price incentives on calls to "frequently called" numbers between businesses, with the stipulation that all businesses would use Bell Atlantic phone services. The scheme proved advantageous not only for the phone company, but also for all businesses within the frequently called circuit. Bell Atlantic reaped an additional benefit as the communications carrier accumulated large amounts of data concerning the calling habits of all businesses within the calling plan for use in further marketing campaigns.

The movies, television, and other entertainment media cross-market in sometimes subtle ways, as seen by a motion picture promotion for the teleflorist, Sell 1-800-Flowers. The florist received exposure and credits when the name brand appeared in a major feature film, plus the florist reaped the benefits of ongoing publicity from video sales and residual screenings. In another media campaign, network owner Rupert Murdoch teamed with sports entrepreneur Philip Anschutz to create "Fox Sports One," a marketing group designed to cross-market a string of commodities, including Dodgers Stadium and the Los Angeles Dodgers, the National Hockey League's Kings, Major League Soccer games, and the Staples Center sports arena, among others.

WORLD WIDE WEB

For all industries, the World Wide Web comprises a "virtual" cross-marketing oasis, a dynamic and revolutionary concept unrivaled by other media. The unique component of Internet advertising is the perpetual change and unpredictability that stems from random "linking" features intrinsic to Internet browsing software. The paradigm of the World Wide Web is, in essence, "cross-marketing." Companies abound to assist with marketing strategies specifically geared to tap the extraordinary potential of Internet commerce. Companies such as Yahoo! and AltaVista provide easy and efficient linkage for vendors to advertise and do business across the "cyberspace" of the Web. Consulting sites, academic papers, and other information about Internet advertising can be located efficiently through automated search engines and hyperlinks. Specialists in Internet advertising, known as Webmasters, provide a myriad of services to assist customers in utilizing the interactive cross-linking capabilities available on the Web. The growing popularity and convenience of Internet shopping makes the World Wide Web an extraordinary haven for cross-marketing. In December 1998 *Business Week* reported a prediction by Forrester Research Incorporated that "cybershopping" (buying products and services on the Internet) could total $108 billion by the year 2003.

BUNDLING

Bundling is a specialized niche of cross-marketing that relies on the theory that customers willingly gravitate toward the "better value." Consumers further appreciate the convenience of one-stop shopping and consolidated billing. A 1998 Price Waterhouse study upholds these theories—as related by Scott Hample in *Marketing Tools*—55 percent of consumers preferred to purchase telephone (long-distance and local) services from a single provider, and 69 percent agreed that there were advantages to one bill. Conversely, only 29 percent of consumers did not mind paying separate or multiple telephone bills, and only 33 percent were unconcerned about multiple vendors in the telephone industry.

In keeping with this premise, MCI assembled a cross-marketing package that offered customers a complete assortment of services in a single bundle. The bundle featured an 800 number, voice mail, call routing, Internet service, cellular phone service, long distance service, local calling, and paging. Advertised savings were calculated at 20-50 percent for most services and 70 percent for long distance. The plan failed to sell as anticipated because it offered too many services. Outside of a very specialized market of business callers, few customers expressed interest. Additional statistics from the Strategis Group (quoted by Hample) indicated that 32 percent of telephone customers wanted local and long distance calling, but were impervious to the rest of the package, including the cell phone service, which also failed to attract customers as originally anticipated. Only 14 percent of survey respondents indicated that they might consider the purchase of no more than 6 of the multiple features that were offered. Most commonly these included combined local and long-distance telephone service, paging, Internet, cell phone, and cable television. Studies further reveal that customers may be willing to purchase bundled products when the bundle offers a savings of 10-20 percent over separately purchased items. Consumers additionally factor product quality into such decisions of whether to purchase a product bundle, and buyers will defer to individual purchases when quality is an issue. Bundling therefore becomes more attractive when customers can choose between a variety of bundles at different levels of quality. The American Express Card, for example, is available in green, gold, and platinum, which allows a customer to select the bundle of services that best meets his or her needs, and allows customers to pay annual card premiums accordingly. Likewise, food-and-beverage bundles featured at fast food restaurants afford the convenience of speedy selection and a single price to pay, but successful restaurants offer an assortment of meal bundles to suit individual tastes.

In all cases, the prerequisite for any successful cross-marketing liaison between multiple vendors is the potential for mutual and equal advantage for all partners. According to a report by Beth Mattson in *City Business* (Minneapolis, St. Paul), marketer Ron Sackett of Foley Sackett, Incorporated in Minneapolis advised that, "The good promotions are a win-win and literally a 50-50 arrangement."

INDUSTRY LEADERS

In 1998 a record-setting merger between Travelers Group and Citicorp, touted as the largest in history, was appraised at $700 billion. The two groups repeatedly made headlines with the mega-deal that represented a unique and precedent-setting convergence between the insurance industry, commercial banks, and investment banking industry. Far-reaching implications of the merger therefore extended into credit cards, banks, and brokerages. In terms of physical scope, the April 6, 1998, deal that created the combined new organization called Citigroup spans 10 countries and 6 continents.

In the travel and hotel arena, Cendant Corporation emerged in 1997 as one of the largest conglomerates in the hotel industry. Cendant resulted from a merger between CUC International and HFS Incorporated. The formation of Cendant Corporation promised the potential for convenient cross-marketing opportunities between HFS's Avis Rent-a-car, Howard Johnson International Incorporated hotels, Ramada International Hotels and Resorts, and assorted real-estate and mortgage ventures. Intrinsic to the merger was HFS's massive data warehouse, completed in August 1997. Reputedly, the warehouse contains 37 million

records with a projected growth rate of over 3 million entries per year. In 1998 Cendant purchased the American Bankers Insurance Group, a move that gave Cendant entry into the single most lucrative cross-marketing arena in existence, banking and finance.

Among the cutting-edge opportunists of new age technology, the Internet-based retailer Amazon.com, experienced phenomenal growth despite perennial controversy. Amazon.com originated as an Internet-based book dealer but expanded over time to virtually vend anything, including CDs, consumer electronics, videos, and toys. Amazon.com exploits the previously untapped convenience of "point-and-click" Internet shopping. The company brought cross-marketing one step farther into cyberspace and refined the point-and-click concept with unsolicited offerings of selected book titles at every step of the Internet "surfer's" path. Book selections, based on information accessed by the Internet client, proves highly pertinent to the Internet shoppers topic of interest—a traveler planning a Paris itinerary through the Internet might receive an unso-

More On **INDUSTRY GIANTS**

When a 1999 *Fortune* magazine promotion accepted nominees for the "Businessman of the Century," the first published group of finalists included Coca-Cola's Robert Woodruff, Ray Kroc of McDonald's Restaurants, and advertiser Leo Burnett, creator of Kellogg's Tony the Tiger mascot. A common trait among the nominees was a perceived close media association between each entrepreneur and his respective product. Additionally, and perhaps more than mere coincidence, one other point of interest noted by journalist Shelly Branch in her write-up of the contenders was the notion that, "Like charged atomic particles, great brands and their creators have a natural affinity."

Branch went on to remark on the perennial advertising campaigns associating Coca-Cola in tandem with McDonald's Restaurants. Allowing the indisputable success of those promotions, it might come as little surprise that "Businessman of the Century" nominee Leo Burnett headed the agency that handled McDonald's advertising since the early 1980s.

Phil Knight of Nike was another nominee for the top business-person of the 1900s. Knight is credited with bringing the Nike sports apparel logo to the world, and it was he who originated the idea of contracting big-name athletes to endorse Nike products, thus cross-marketing the excitement of the sports arena and superstar athletes with the experience of wearing Nike clothing.

licited prompt from Amazon.com to "click here" for books about Paris. A researcher combing the Internet for information on the rock-and-roll music phenomenon in the United States might receive a similar prompt, to "click here" for "oldies but goodies" and other audio CDs.

In the process of dominating the cybershopping mall of the Internet, Amazon.com eliminated the costly overhead of retail outlets and large stocks of inventory, and it considerably reduced personnel requirements in the process. *Business Week* reported at the end of 1998 that Amazon.com was in command of 4.5 million customers, with sales totals anticipated to top out at $540 million dollars, to comprise a company valued at $11.1 billion.

AMERICA AND THE WORLD

Around the world, as in the United States, financial institutions stand in the forefront of the cross-marketing industry. Prominent financial institutions persevere in establishing global alliances. Through such powerful networks, institutions gain access to consumer data worldwide and realize the potential for massive international cross-marketing endeavors. As in the United States, issues of consumer privacy exist at the forefront of the cross-marketing arena, and the policies and concerns of the European Union (EU) weigh heavily over the entire global community in this regard.

In 1998 the EU embraced a policy to protect the citizens' privacy of member nations, with global implications for electronic commerce (E-commerce) and cross-marketing. Europe, with 350 million people, exists as the largest commercial economy in the world. The EU issued a directive to protect consumer data, effective October 25, 1998, that companies are subject to prosecution for policies and procedures that compromise data privacy. The rigid policy, developed over a six-year period, was defined to protect European citizens from invasion of data privacy, according to European privacy standards. The dictate requires all foreign governments to provide privacy protection equivalent to European standards with respect to all data concerning European citizens.

Organizations that fail to abide by the mandates of Article 29 of the European Union Directive on Data Protection, face the potential jeopardy of losing all rights of commerce with Europe in terms of permanent interruption of data flow. The U.S. federal government in Washington initiated ongoing attempts to

intervene with the EU, to limit the clout of the European directive, although resolution remains forthcoming. Indeed the issues at stake involve the entire non-European community. Internet practices, such as sending transparent "cookies" to trace a consumer's path through the Internet, are virtually outlawed, as are many existing methods of cross-marketing. At best, the European Commission in Brussels agreed to consider alleged privacy violations on an individual basis, a policy that would permit data flow even under the threat of prosecution.

In England an organization called Privacy International, consisting of privacy activists based in London, looms as a watchdog over 25 major corporations including Electronic Data Systems, Microsoft Corporation, United Airlines, and Ford Motor Company. U.S. companies targeted by Privacy International cannot afford to underestimate the threat of prosecution for privacy violations.

In France, the National Association on Data Processing & Liberty (CNIL) in Paris addresses the thousands of formal privacy complaints filed annually. The association dispatches staff to conduct inspections and fields thousands of phone calls every month.

In Germany, the Datenschutz (data police) dispatch operatives worldwide as a matter of course, to insure the rights of German citizens with respect to data privacy. It was necessary for credit card giant, Citigroup, among others, to submit to regular inspection of their data processing center in Sioux City, as a prerequisite to offering credit cards to a lucrative customer base of millions of German citizens.

United States corporations might spend more time in developing systems acceptable to the European Union and its stringent privacy requirements, than in developing products and services to peddle across the Atlantic. U.S. airline companies, in the habit of cross-marketing anything and everything based on privately held databases of executive stature individuals must devise new methods of utilizing the information, or at the very least obtaining approval from every customer affected. Some look to hardware manufacturers such as NCR Corporation to develop new data-storage systems that can address the rigid standards of the European privacy laws. Truly the task is daunting, but not insurmountable, as even British Airways painstakingly works to replace existing questionnaires with carefully worded updates that comply with European privacy mandates. Similarly, Microsoft Corporation, with European headquarters in Paris, hopes to devise a customer-inquiry software to quell the concerns of the European community with respect to privacy invasion through cross-marketing techniques and Internet-based e-commerce (electronic commerce).

In 1999 Standard & Poor's revealed its agreement with Swiss-based international securities service, Telekurs Financial. The two firms indicated their mutual intent to utilize the strategic alliance to share data for cross-marketing of services, and to collaborate in developing new products in the process. Reportedly, Standard & Poor's agreed to represent Telekurs with respect to specific services in the Americas. Telekurs agreed to reciprocate by representing certain Standard & Poor products in Europe. The agreement was an expansion of an ongoing 10-year collaboration between the two companies that cross-marketed the International Securities Identification Directory. Under the alliance the two firms would target Asian nations in cross-marketing of securities information.

RESEARCH AND TECHNOLOGY

DATA MINING

Data mining takes marketing researchers into new and undiscovered territory. Data mining provides market researchers with the tools to fine tune their information base and to re-segment consumers according to previously anticipated groupings and according to unforeseen patterns. "Spelunking" marketers implement new data mining technologies in search of "mother lodes" of data interpretation, as researchers continually refine data mining algorithms. These algorithms, used in conjunction with modern neural networks, create "intelligent" systems. Through neural network technology computing devices are able to learn and retain information, and to simulate the human "thinking" processes for future use in solving new problems. Previous generations of data systems permitted marketing analysts to sort and analyze continually expanding databases according to existing patterns. Data mining techniques use neural networks to build on existing knowledge and to "learn more," thereby continually augmenting what is known about existing data. Ford Motor Company spokespeople tout that company's data mining resource called Power Point, which allows a Ford dealer to pinpoint more than potential car buyers. Based on a series of demographics as tracked by the data mining system, Ford dealers isolate the names of specific people in a specific locale who are likely to purchase a particular model of car manufactured by Ford. Future systems may pinpoint more precisely when a consumer is ready to make the purchase.

The development of impenetrable encryption technology is the panacea to virtual commerce that could revolutionize Internet shopping. Consumers eager to access the convenience of purchasing products and services on-line are often reticent to supply personal information through the Internet. Credit card and phone numbers, addresses, and other personal information passed through the Internet remains vulnerable to computer "hackers" who intercept and decode the information, then re-use it for illegal purposes. Encryption technology involves complex encoding schemes to protect businesses and consumers from unauthorized intrusion into Internet transactions, but while effective encryption schemes are extremely difficult to decipher, none are guaranteed fail-safe.

Software companies and other technology firms announce regularly that the ultimate encryption technology is under development, but the fact remains that Internet thieves take every new encryption method as a challenge, and hackers devote untold hours to deciphering encrypted data. In 1998, RSA Data Security Incorporated, a leader in the field of encryption technology, announced an Optimal Asymmetric Encryption Padding enhancement to the powerful Public Key Cryptography Standard #1. As with many improvements, the enhancement was developed to counteract vulnerability in the earlier systems and came about only after the earlier version was compromised. An observation in *Computer,* a weekly magazine, commented that, "Real-life cryptography is a constant game of cat and mouse."

FURTHER READING

Baker, Stephen, with Marsha Johnston and William Echikson. "The Internet: Europe's Privacy Cops." *Business Week International,* 2 November 1998.

Berry, Michael J.A., and Gordon Linoff, *Data Mining Techniques: for Marketing, Sales, and Customer Support.* John Wiley & Sons, 1997.

Berson, Alex, and Stephen J. Smith. *Data Warehousing, Data Mining, and Olap.* McGraw-Hill, 1997.

Boland, Vincent. "STP Strengthens Telekurs Link." *Financial Times,* 2 February 1999.

"Bundling May Be Operational Hurdle for Incumbent Providers." *Radio Communications Report,* 17 February 1997.

Dalton, Gregory. "Tip of the Week: Pressure for Better Privacy—Business Moves to Fend off Regulation of Internet Data." *Information Week,* 22 June 1998.

"Finding a FORMULA for Success." *Telephony,* 3 February 1997.

Hample, Scott. "Packing It In." *Marketing Tools,* March 1998.

Hargrove, Thomas, and Guido H. Stemple III, "Poll Reveals Public Unease about Big Brother Watching." *Denver Rocky Mountain News,* 10 August 1998.

Hof, Robert D., with Ellen Neuborne and Heather Green. "A Business Week Info Tech 100 Company." *Business Week,* 14 December 1998.

Marshall Martin. "Data Mining: Rich Vein for Market." *Communications Week,* 13 January 1997.

Morgan, Richard. "Radio Biz Stirs in Cross-Promo Fizz." *Variety,* 22 June 1998.

"Optimal Asymmetric Encryption Padding." *Computer Weekly,* 23 July 1998.

Vijayan, Jaikumar. "A Data Warehouse, 18 Months Later Cendant Cross-Markets Brands Using Customer Records." *Computerworld,* 8 March 1999.

Weiss, Sholom M., and Nitin Indurkhya. *Predictive Data Mining: a Practical Guide.* Morgan Kaufman Publishers, 1997.

Whitford, Marty. "Chain Reaction." *Hotel & Motel Management,* 19 October 1998, 1.

—Gloria Cooksey

CRYONICS

Humanity's attempt to preserve itself has a long and well-documented history. We need only look to the funeral rituals and lengthy embalming measures undertaken by early Egyptian and Mediterranean cultures to prepare and preserve their dead for passage into the next life. Whether born of personal interest or concern for our species, this desire was alive and well in the twentieth century. A heightened focus on preserving youth and youthful qualities for the *present* life spawned a plethora of new industries and markets. Catering to a global populace bent on preserving appearance, vitality, and life expectancy, self-enhancement products and services flooded the open market, many without guaranteed results or proven benefit. But in the medical and scientific communities, great strides had been made in the preservation and reproduction of living human tissue. In the general field of cryopreservation (from the Greek *kryos,* meaning icy or cold), the reviving of embryos, spermatozoa, and certain plant species after lengthy frozen suspension was near-routine by the 1990s. The revival or reanimation of *dead* tissue remained beyond scientific grasp. Nonetheless, dedicated professionals in the field of cryonics, the deep-freezing (in liquid nitrogen) of human bodies at death for possible re-animation in the future, entered the third millennium hopeful to achieve that goal. The very contemplation of restoring to life the scientifically preserved body of a deceased person went from sci-fi humor to credible fancy in just a matter of decades.

ORGANIZATION AND STRUCTURE

Coming from all walks of life, cryonicists are fundamentally united by the optimistic belief that the chance of being brought back to life, after having been frozen upon death, is well worth paying for. They funnel interest and money mostly into nonprofit organizations (cryonics "providers"), which guarantee suspension and revival/reanimation when the technology becomes available. These ideas have gained increasing respect due to important advances made in the related fields of cryobiology and nanotechnology (the structural control/repair of matter at the molecular level), which have shed new light and hope on the future. The burgeoning cryonics industry, little more than 30 years old in 1999, and still lacking in scientific legitimization, remained essentially self-structured, self-supported, and self-regulated.

The cryonics field generally breaks down into three major components: research groups, suspension providers, and support industries, such as nitrogen suppliers and storage facilities. These are not mutually exclusive groups, and most major cryonics organizations have sub-organizations with more narrowed missions or functions in each of these three areas. For example, the Cryonics Society of South Florida, through its nonprofit Life Extension Foundation, helps to fund research through its for-profit wing, the Life Extension Buyers Club, which, in turn, sells nutritional supplements and also helps fund the Reanimation Foundation, an international perpetual trust fund set up in Liechtenstein.

As credibility and interest in cryonics grow, so do entrepreneurial spin-offs, such as sales of "afterlife" insurance policies and liquid nitrogen suppliers and capsule manufacturers. Additionally, corollary industries such as those dealing in nutritional supplements have begun to market products specifically intended to physically enhance human bodies in preparation for the afterlife, and some of these companies even donate a portion of all profits to cryogenic research.

MEMBERSHIP

In a 1998 publication for prospective candidates, the Alcor Life Extension Foundation, the largest cryonics organization in the world, described its members as mostly "highly intelligent and highly motivated, with an independent mindset." Like most people who are enthused about their personal interests or beliefs, cryonicists have made information about their work and progress readily available to the general public, but they seldom engage in direct proselytization.

Many members of cryonics organizations prefer to remain anonymous, particularly those in the scientific community, who fear professional consequence for their involvement in a technology not yet embraced by the scientific community. Others are more daring, notably, Ralph Merkle, a research scientist at Xerox in Palo Alto, California, and one of the world's leading experts in nanotechnology. In the mid-1990s, he openly expressed his belief that a human body that had been carefully and correctly preserved by cryosuspension might indeed be resuscitated/reanimated through nanotechnology-based medicine. Another of Alcor's members, Don Laughlin, the founder of Laughlin, Nevada, brought his personal wealth into the organization and publicly spoke about his involvement. And singer Michael Jackson has been interested in the subject for years.

Reasons for becoming members of cryonics organizations are as varied as membership itself, but all prospective members must be able to tolerate the thought of their own eventual death. As cryonicist Charles Platt candidly told *Omni* magazine, "I always used to tell people that I had no illusions about death, and I accepted the finality of it. Yet it took me almost three years to overcome my psychological resistance to cryonics. Even after I had written a will and obtained life insurance, Alcor's legal documents languished on my desk for many months. I avoided signing them in the same way that I might turn away from the sight of an ugly accident. I imagined myself dead, dunked in a vat of liquid nitrogen. It was too vivid, too personal, too real." In the end, Platt decided to go for it. "Cryonics is the ultimate gesture of defiance," he concluded. "Even if it offers only one chance in a hundred thousand, that chance is worth taking. Death is intolerable, and I am seizing the only available opportunity to transcend it."

When Alcor sponsored an essay contest, asking participants why they would like to be frozen, the entries pleaded recurring themes: an appreciation for the value of the human experience and being part of passing on its legacy; an incredible excitement about the future and the unknown possibilities ahead; and the desire to communicate with future generations. Still others felt shortchanged by circumstance in their present lives and hoped for a better tomorrow, waking up healthy and healed, with a chance to live a new life. Many people express the sentiment that they feel they were born too soon and wish they were born 50 or 100 years later; cryonic suspension could afford them this opportunity. Even Ben Franklin, in a time way before cryonics, expressed the desire to be "immersed in a cask of Madeira wine, with a few friends, till that time [when he could] be recalled to life by the solar warmth of [his] dear country."

FUNDING

Since its beginning and on through the 1990s, the cryonics industry has remained financially self-sustained through membership fees and donations. Administrative costs are comparatively low: most organizations are structured as nonprofit entities, engaging in little, if any, advertising or promotional activity. Although the organizations have full-time salaried employees, the lion's share of the money is spent on clinical procedures and research.

The average cost of cryonic suspension in 1999 was more than $125,000 for a whole body suspension, and approximately $60,000 for a "neurosuspension," limited to the brain and supporting blood vessels. While this tidy sum adequately provides for a first-class suspension, it is not always paid for in advance. As a matter of fact, by 1999, an increasing number of members and would-be-members were planning to pay for eventual suspensions by purchasing life insurance policies naming cryogenics organizations as irrevocable beneficiaries. Dubbed "afterlife insurance" by the insurance industry, the issued policies are ordinarily above challenge from family members and heirs-at-law in any probate proceedings. In 1998, insurance broker Mary Naples of San Francisco, California, told *Forbes* magazine that selling such insurance constituted about 10 percent of her total insurance business.

In 1999, initial membership fees in cryonics organizations were generally around $100-200, with annual maintenance fees of approximately $400. The organizations rely on these annual fees to maintain state-of-the-art equipment and full-time salaried employees, including emergency response teams, which might be called upon at any time to appear anywhere in the world following the sudden demise of a member.

The hefty suspension fees usually do *not* cover the costs of personal reanimation, or the continued scientific efforts to make reanimation a reality. For these expenses and costs, the organizations rely almost exclusively on private trust foundations primarily funded by donations and pledges. For example, funds in the Reanimation Foundation in Liechtenstein have been earmarked almost exclusively to pay for reviving suspended persons when the technology becomes available.

INDUSTRY REGULATION

As the cryonics industry relies upon itself for structure and funding, so it remained essentially self-regulated through 1999. Internally, members have to rely upon basic promissory contract law and moral obligation to ensure that the cryonics providers would be there in the future to uphold contractual obligations: cryonically suspend the member upon death and hold him or her in that state for eventual reanimation. In return, members pay often-hefty membership fees. As mentioned earlier, in response to prospective and active members' concerns, some of the organizations set up irrevocable trusts to guarantee payment for the suspension and eventual resuscitation of membership, and financial records are available for review.

Externally, cryonics providers remain vulnerable to, and are impacted by, laws and regulations not specifically legislated or effected for application to cryonics. For example, most of the cryonics industry and membership eagerly followed the 1999 trial and conviction of Dr. Jack Kevorkian, the Michigan pathologist charged with murder for lethally injecting controlled substances into his clients with the stated objective of terminating their lives. The impact of that conviction upon the cryonics industry was palpable: the entire hope for resuscitation of lifeless human tissue is believed to be inversely proportionate to the degree of death/damage the tissue suffers by lack of oxygenation or cell membrane rupture. This is why cryopreservation techniques must be applied as soon as possible following death, to prevent further tissue deterioration and damage. It follows that the "right to die" movement's efforts to control the time for the moment of death would have been an important gain for the cryonics industry: a member could arrange to have at his bedside the entire preservation team, ready to begin efforts upon his exacting calculation and manipulation of the moment of death, thus minimizing the amount of "dead" tissue and improving his chances for reanimation. As of 1999, cryonics preservation remained legally prohibited until clinical death had been established by traditional criteria.

BACKGROUND AND DEVELOPMENT

The field of cryogenic preservation owes its beginning to the research of Sir James Dewar, who liquefied hydrogen in 1898, and H. Kamerlingh Onnes, who liquefied helium in 1908. Both men developed techniques to cool gases down to temperatures near absolute zero (-273.15 degrees Centigrade), then studied the behavior of matter, both animate and inanimate, at those temperatures. Building on these principles, the medical research community eventually branched off into the field of cryobiology, and began using liquefied nitrogen to preserve living matter, including human tissue. The key success of biological cryopreservation is that some forms of living tissue, suspended in a frozen state over a period of time, may be revived and restored to full physiologic capacity when rewarmed to normal temperatures.

In the 1950s, British researcher Audrey Smith was able to revive hamsters whose brains and bodies had been partially frozen. Later research conducted by Isamu Suda of the Department of Physiology at Kobe University in Japan, showed that cat brains, frozen and stored for several months and then rewarmed, resumed electrical brain wave activity spontaneously. In 1997, baby mice born at St. George's Hospital Medical School in London were grown from embryos that had been cryopreserved for 25 years, when the mother mouse died in 1972.

While many of these scientific advances (e.g., progressively impressive reanimations of frozen living tissue, suspended for lengthier periods and at lower temperatures), were directly applicable to cryonics technology, they still required a broad leap of faith to reach the latter's focus on the reanimation of *dead* tissue. Nonetheless, since cryonics researchers believe that human memory and emotion (important considerations in the quality of restored life) are electrochemically stored in brain tissue, the results were encouraging. Even by the latter 1950s, there were enough people interested in the future of cryonics that organization and mobilization of resources became inevitable. One of the oldest organizations, and still the largest provider of cryonics services, is the Alcor Life Extension Foundation.

Alcor's most famous member was also the first cryonically frozen human. Dr. James H. Bedford, a 73-year-old retired psychology professor from Glendale, California, had previously declared his wishes for cryonic preservation prior to his death in 1967 of kidney cancer. His family, though skeptical of the newly developing field, dutifully followed his wishes, having his body iced down until trained personnel from the Cryonics Society of California could arrive and begin the technical process of cryopreservation. His body was then immersed in liquid nitrogen and stored in a "dewar," (named after Sir James Dewar, the scientist mentioned earlier) then transported to a cryonics-related corporation in Phoenix. Two years later, he was transferred to a facility in California, where he was placed in a more efficient dewar. Several relatives began making waves, challenging his suspension and asking courts to order that he be defrosted and given a proper burial. The family successfully defended these challenges, but new problems surfaced when the liability carrier of the storage facility demanded his removal. His son toted him off in a rented U-Haul trailer to another location in California, near Berkeley. Frustrated by less-than-friendly outsiders and price-gouging by opportunist nitrogen providers, Bedford's family then moved him two more times, including once to a self-storage warehouse facility near Burbank in 1982. Nine years later, in 1991, Bedford's dewar began to fail, and Alcor researchers transferred him to a multi-unit dewar housing three other persons. At that time, they noted enthusiastically that he appeared in "good" condition and essentially intact. Ultimately, growing concerns for California's natural earthquakes (as well as regulatory shakers and movers) convinced Alcor to move all its frozen members to Scottsdale, Arizona, in 1994, where they remained through 1999. Bedford's original dewar was mounted for display in Alcor's lobby.

TECHNICAL BACKGROUND

Cryogenic suspension involves not only the preservation of the human body, but also the protection of structural information contained in the mind and body, thus preserving the potential resuscitation of the electro-chemical links between brain cells that result in memory and emotion. Damaged cells can seriously alter or compromise that goal. Damage mostly occurs from death itself, which causes a toxic reaction at the cellular level due to lack of nutrients and oxygen. But cellular and tissue damage can also occur as a result of the freezing process. Therefore, organizations such as Alcor have mobilized emergency response teams worldwide that are capable of recovering, stabilizing, and transporting suspension patients within a minimum amount of time, resulting in minimum damage. While the technical detail that follows may be somewhat unsettling to contemplate, it must be remembered that the process or procedure is no more traumatic than many traditional embalming or autopsy procedures performed every day on deceased persons.

Alcor members wear necktags or bracelets providing instructions for both summoning Alcor staff in a life-threatening situation and stabilizing the member's body until Alcor staff arrive. Upon being pronounced dead by traditional medical standards, the member's body is placed on a heart-lung machine to maintain cerebral-vascular circulation. Simultaneously, external cooling of the body is commenced by packing the body in ice water. Once the body is transported to an Alcor facility, cryoprotective perfusion is performed surgically, which basically involves replacing body fluids with a special glycerol-based "cryoprotectant," to inhibit ice crystal formation at the cellular and tissue level. When this is completed, the body is removed from the heart-lung machine and submerged in a bath of cold silicone oil. The body's temperature is incrementally and evenly lowered over the next 36-48 hours, until it reaches minus 79 degrees Centigrade, at which time the body is transferred to an aluminum pod and lowered into a cooldown vessel. Liquid nitrogen vapor is gradually introduced over the next five days until the body has reached the negative temperature of liquid nitrogen, equivalent to approximately minus 196 degrees Centigrade, or minus 320 degrees Fahrenheit. At this temperature, all metabolic and biochemical activity is suspended, and persons preserved at this temperature can be maintained with very little change for decades or centuries.

The dewars containing suspended patients are stored inside steel-reinforced concrete vaults (to protect against natural disasters such as earthquake, fire, etc.). No electric power is needed for continued refrigeration, but liquid nitrogen must be replenished every 8-10 days to account for "boiloff," (about 13 liters a day for a dewar containing four bodies). Round-the-clock staff protects the storage facilities and performs nitrogen replacement duties. Liquid nitrogen is an inexpensive, non-toxic natural substance that is delivered in steel cylinders much like propane gas.

CURRENT CONDITIONS

Between 1988 and 1993, total membership in cryonics organizations doubled worldwide, and there has been a steady increase ever since. As of 1999, fewer than a dozen formal cryonics organizations existed worldwide, and only half of them were cryonic suspension providers. At that time, less than 100 deceased persons were preserved in a state of cryonic suspension worldwide, but the waiting list was in the hundreds. By far, the majority of membership was in the United States, and the largest provider of cryonics services in the world was the Alcor Life Extension Foundation, based in Riverside, California. As of June 1998, Alcor had 431 suspension members, 488 associate members, and 35 patients in suspension. The largest numbers were concentrated in the United States, Canada, England, and Australia. Other countries represented in the aggregate Alcor membership were Germany, Japan, Spain, and Brazil. Trained emergency response teams were available in New York, Los Angeles and San Jose, California; Indianapolis; Chicago; Miami; Dallas; Fort Collins (Colorado); Oregon; Canada; Australia; and London, England.

Legal battles continue. In the 1990s the State of California brought suit to render cryonics illegal, but lost the case. As of 1999, cryonics was legal in all 50 states and most Canadian provinces, but not legal in British Columbia, Canada. Additionally, cryonics providers have had their facilities inspected by state and federal health officials, coroners, etc. Most states also have anatomical gift acts, which become the legal vehicles facilitating the acquisition and possession of the cryonics providers for members' bodies.

In another legal battle, deceased cryonicist Dora Kent, who elected to have only her brain saved ("neuro-suspension"), caused great legal troubles for her son Saul in 1994, when he left the folds of Alcor to join a rival organization (CryoCare) but was unable to gain legal custody of, or have transferred to him, the dewar containing his mother's suspended skull and brain.

To bridge funding wars between suspension and resuscitation efforts, a few private research foundations and trusts were set up worldwide, notably the Prometheus Project. Initiated in the latter 1990s by a small group of Internet communicators who discovered their common futuristic interests, the Project attracted the attention of major players worldwide. Its ultimate goal was the fully reversible cryo-suspension of humans, first for medical application (to save the lives of the terminally ill until they could be resuscitated and cured), and then on to allow time travel into the future. In 1998 funding for this project came from two specific sources. First, the "Life On Hold Trust" was set up, favored over a business corporate structure because of the lack of foreseeable short-term investment returns. The trust was set up such that contributors owned trust certificate units (TCUs) instead of stock, but the principles were similar to corporations in that TCU holders/beneficiaries would benefit directly upon any distribution of the trust's assets. Monies from this fund were specifically earmarked for research and development. Similarly, a charitable trust

called the "Full Length Life Society" was set up to handle educational and promotional facets of the Project. Contributors had the choice of either making direct donations, or making conditional pledges that were contingent upon the Project collecting at least $1 million annually in either pledges or donations. In 1998, the first research pilot program went into effect, with a goal of achieving the reversible cryopreservation of hippocampal slices, such research being conducted at a major university medical research center. As of 1999, well over $4 million dollars had been received in donations and pledges for the first 10-year project. The project staff had prepared two 10-year budget plans, at $500,000 and $1 million, respectively, to ensure incremental allocation of existing funds for the project without regard to future funding shortages, if necessary. This would permit the luxury of additional or accelerated research from all donations and pledges in excess of the budgeted amounts.

By 1999, Project leaders had raised enough capital to support research toward the 10-year articulated goal of fully reviving the cryo-preserved central nervous system of a mammal. If successful, the Project next hoped to prove full reanimation and restoration to normal of a mammal that had been cryonically suspended for at least six months, using preservation methodology hypothetically applicable to humans.

INDUSTRY LEADERS

The Alcor Life Extension Foundation in Riverside, California, remains the most well-known (and largest) cryonics organization in the world. Other organizations of note include The American Cryonics Society of Mountain View, California; Trans-Time, Inc. of San Leandro, California; the American Cryonics Foundation of Stockton, California; the Cryonics Society of South Florida in Fort Lauderdale; and the Cryonics Institute in Clinton Township, Michigan. The CryoCare Foundation and the New Zealand Cryonics Society maintain information on-line, as well as Alcor and several others. Two additional California companies, Trans Time and CryoSpan, offer suspension for profit, but they netted less than $10,000 in revenues in 1996.

RESEARCH AND TECHNOLOGY

Perhaps the most exciting area of related science, and the one most pertinent to cryonics, is the rapidly developing field of nanotechnology, which involves the scientific control of particulate/matter at the molecular level. At that level, scientists hope to be able to manipulate genetic codes in laboratory models, which would then be programmed to search out and repair and/or replace their damaged counterparts in any given tissue sample. These researchers believe that physical disease, environmental pollution, and toxic chemotherapy for cancer will all someday be things of the past, because eventually abnormal development would be nipped and reversed at an early stage. Unfortunately, the promise of such technology is both exciting and frightening, because of its potential misuse in the wrong hands. In the 1990s, similar concerns surrounded the controversial subject of genetic engineering when scientists successfully cloned sheep and other mammals from their own genetic material.

With respect to cryopreservation in general, the 1998 Lindberg Award in Europe went to researchers who compared glycerol preservation to pure cryopreservation in their abilities to inhibit HIV-1 activity in cadavers. Glycerol was found to be superior in inactivating both extracellular and intracellular HIV activity in human cadaver donor skin. The import of this to the more specific cryonics field is in the strong desire to halt any infectious or disease processes at the time of suspension, not only for the good of the preserved person, but also for the protection of handlers and cryonics workers.

In summary, despite grand efforts and successes in closely related fields, cryonicists need to acknowledge two major considerations that remained as viable industry moderators through 1999: the true feasibility of reanimating cryonically suspended corpses, and the uncomfortableness of the general public when contemplating the handling, surgical manipulation, and storage of dead bodies in a non-traditional manner, perhaps for many, many years.

FURTHER READING

"American Business Disc—Full Record Report." American Business Information, Inc., 1998.

Barton, R.F. *Cryogenic Systems,* 2nd ed. Oxford: Oxford Press, 1985.

"Cold Storage, Happy Returns." *People Weekly,* 12 October 1998.

"Cryonics: Reaching for Tomorrow." Riverside, CA: Alcor Life Extension Foundation, 1994. Available from http://www.alcor.org/crft09.txt.

Drexler, Eric, and Chris Peterson with Gayle Pergamit. *Unbounding the Future: The Nanotechnology Revolution.* New York: William Morrow and Company, Inc., 1991.

Huyghe, Patrick. "Freezer Wars." *Omni,* January 1995.

Kellner, Tomas. "Resurrection Insurance." *Forbes,* 24 August 1998.

"Membership Status." Alcor Life Extension Foundation. Available from http://www.alcor.org/phoenix/may_june98/members.html.

Merkle, Ralph. "The Technical Feasibility of Cryonics." *Medical Hypotheses,* September 1992.

"On Ice." *Economist,* 11 October 1997.

Platt, Charles. "Confessions of a Cryonist." *Omni,* February 1992.

———. "The Omni/Alcor Immortality Contest." *Omni,* January 1993.

———. "Please Freeze Me." *Omni,* January 1994.

"Prometheus Project." Available from http://www.prometheus-project.org/summary.html.

"Still Frozen After All These Years." *New York Times Magazine,* January 1997.

Stuttaford, Andrew. "Frozen Future." *National Review,* 2 September 1996.

"What May Be Next." *Time,* 25 November 1996.

"What We Do: Cryonics and the Alcor Life Extension Foundation." 1997. Available from http://www.alcor.org .01b.html.

"Would You Pay $125,000 to Get Frozen?" *Fortune,* 24 November 1997.

Van Baare, J., P.U. Cameron, N. Vardaxis, J. Pagnon, J. Reece, E. Middelkoop, and S.M. Crow. "The 1998 Lindberg Award. Comparison of Glycerol Preservation with Cryopreservation Methods on HIV-1 Inactivation." *Journal of Burn Care Rehabilitation (HLK),* November-December 1998.

—Lauri R. Harding

CYBERCAFES

As consumer demand for the Internet increased in the mid- to late 1990s, the number of subscribers to Internet service providers also grew—between 14 and 20 million. With approximately twice as many users in 1997, entrepreneurs saw the potential for new Internet-related services. Following the trend of theme-based cafes and bars, entrepreneurs conceived the idea of the cybercafe—a cafe offering computers and computer services. These establishments feature coffeehouse amenities such as gourmet coffee and pastries, as well as computers that can be used to surf the Internet or create documents and spreadsheets. (Also see the essay in this book entitled Specialty Coffee.)

Cybercafes largely appeal to three types of patrons: travelers, business people, and those who do not have home computers. Travelers can use these public computers for sending e-mail, for gathering news and information, and for recreational purposes. Business people who may not want to carry a notebook computer can check on stocks or send e-mail while having coffee or lunch. Finally, people who do not own a computer can frequent cybercafes to learn about general computing and the Internet. Increasingly, cybercafes started offering services whereby patrons may also receive e-mail. Usage fees vary, but cybercafes typically offer rates at $6 to $10 per hour for general use with Web-only use costing about $8 per hour. Monthly e-mail accounts cost extra. Computer time is typically sold by the hour, half hour, or minute, and owners rely on several different methods to monitor usage. Some have staff employees who track the patron's amount of time using a computer, while others issue prepaid debit cards to regulate use. Some cafes utilize coin-operated computers that allow customers to pay for as few as ten minutes at a time.

To attract novice computer users, cybercafes often offer an array of beverages, including exotic coffees, and deluxe bakery goods. To entice experienced computer users, they provide high-speed Internet access and powerful Pentium and Power Macintosh computers. One New York cybercafe owner, however, reported that the cost of high-speed access in mid-1998 was equal to the cafe's rent. Cybercafes obtain Internet access from both large national Internet service providers (ISPs), such as America Online, Inc.(AOL) and smaller regional companies.

The newness of the cybercafe industry leaves room for growth, especially in the area of services offered. Whereas the patrons of the first cybercafes were happy for latte and Web sites, in 1999 cybercafes offered newly expanded services to usher in the second millenium, including video rentals, bookstores, in-house Web sites, and game tournaments. For owners and operators, new software programs addressed and expedited the technicalities of day-to-day business operations associated with cybercafes and *kiosks* (public-access computer sites).

Opening a cybercafe may require a range of investments depending on the number of computers to be installed and the level of the food service to be offered. An Orlando entrepreneur, according to the *Orlando Business Journal*, started a 50-seat Internet coffeehouse replete with eight computers for less than $150,000. The publication also reported that a cafe's location often determined its success, especially in smaller cities and university towns. Most cybercafes are privately owned, but many owners franchise their operations.

Cybercafes draw patrons by providing a user-friendly environment. Many employ staff to help novice computer users and Internet explorers overcome their computer-phobia and be at ease with both the computer and the Web. Some cybercafes provide computer and Internet classes; some even offer one-on-one computer training. Because the industry is in its infancy, cybercafe operators tend not to target any one group of customers exclusively. Instead, they try to place equal emphasis on all aspects of their service in order to appeal to a wide range of patrons, which usually means providing appealing food service and powerful Internet capabilities.

Consumers seeking information concerning the locations and available services of cybercafes may reference a number of Internet sites. Comprehensive listings of cafe locations worldwide appear on the "Cybercafe Guide," for example, which tracks the locations of cybercafes across the globe. In an effort to provide up-to-date service, this site and similar sites, such as "Cybercafe Ring," encourage cafe owners to add and update information about new establishments through a simple online procedure. The "Cybercafe Ring" features links to cybercafe establishments in many cities and countries, plus it includes links to information about cybercafes in general. "Cybercafe Ring" also includes a link to the "Cybercafe Guide." "Cybercafe Search Engine" provides information for curious observers and for serious cybercafe patrons alike. Users may search the site for information about accepted protocol for Internet use, definitions of Internet jargon, and listings of newsgroups related to the cybercafe phenomenon.

BACKGROUND AND DEVELOPMENT

Interest in cybercafes stems from the growing popularity of both the Internet and coffeehouses. The massive computer network known as the Internet was largely underwritten by the U.S. Department of Defense to provide an emergency communications system. That early network soon included the exchange of scholarly information by scientists and academicians. In the Internet's early stages, transmissions and documents were in text form only so the Internet did not resemble its contemporary version. As the Internet grew into a useful tool for scholarly and scientific interchange around the world, it began to attract a busi-

ness following with companies offering online stock reports and business services. With the evolution of graphics software technology, attractive images and animated displays were added to enhance the information; thus, the Internet developed mass appeal.

By the mid-1980s companies emerged that offered Internet access services to the public. A venture between Sears Roebuck & Co. and IBM developed Prodigy in 1984 to compete with CompuServe, which had offered business services since 1969. America Online launched its service in 1985 and amassed nearly 9 million subscribers by 1997. In 1988 and 1989 Netcom On-line Communication Services, Inc. and PSINet Inc. initiated their Internet access campaigns. The Internet audience expanded rapidly in 1993 with the introduction of graphic-based Web browsers and the Internet's World Wide Web pages. Documents came to life as Web site authors added vibrant colors, graphics, and images. Mass interest in the Internet increased exponentially because companies could market the Internet not only as a source for information but also as a vehicle for entertainment and a mechanism for selling advertising space. Heightened interest in the Internet encouraged well-established companies to diversify into the Internet service provider (ISP) industry. Companies such as AT&T and Microsoft offered Internet access in the mid-1990s, and the number of Internet subscribers increased to well over 16 million by the decade's close.

Key demographics of the United States in the 1980s and 1990s contributed to the emergence of the Internet and cybercafes—these factors included suburban expansion, an increase in the number of the home offices, and rising consumer patronage of such informal eateries as cafes and frozen yogurt parlors. Sociologists refer to these informal establishments as "third places" in contrast to home (the first place) and work (the second place). Third places offer venues for socialization and relaxation. Cybercafes sought to integrate the services of two growing trends, specifically the Internet and the cafe. In 1991, the first U.S. Internet cafe, SFNet, opened in San Francisco. SFNet patrons paid a quarter for five minutes of use on the coin-operated computer. A few years later, cybercafes began to appear throughout the country and the world.

CURRENT CONDITIONS

According to *USA Today,* numerous cybercafes operated throughout the world in 1996, with approximately 100 Internet coffeehouses in the United States alone—an increase from just 60 worldwide in 1995.

By October of 1998 there were more than 300 cyber-cafes in existence just in the United States, according to a report by Julie Bollinger of Cincinnati's *Business Courier*.

Cybercafes attract a mix of patrons—Internet novices and veterans, young children and senior citizens, and men and women—although the long-term solvency of cybercafes remains largely undetermined. Robin Frost reported in the *Wall Street Journal* that Internet Cafe of New York merely breaks even by offering coffee house food, potables, and Internet browsing stations. The owner of Cafe Kaldi cybercafe in Sarasota, Florida, maintained that food service sales generate the bulk of the cafe's revenues. Around 1995, a flood of cybercafes opened in many large cities and university towns throughout the United States, including New York, Philadelphia, Princeton, Palo Alto, and San Francisco. A number of those early enterprises ultimately removed their public computers to focus exclusively on food service, or they closed up shop altogether. A few made concessions in the other direction by liquidating the cafe side of the business and restructuring their companies to provide Internet services exclusively, including Web site design and hosting.

While some cybercafe operators experienced "growing pains," others exposed a lucrative industry. Late in 1998, Jim Long of Dayton, Ohio, reported that he anticipated $250,000 in revenues from his Interface Cybercafe that year, and he described his plan to further expand the enterprise. "I want to become all things Internet," Bollinger quoted him as saying. Long indicated that his establishment, which opened in April of 1997, turned a profit within 15 months. Long's cybercafe originally evolved from his computer service outlet and resale shop, but his investments realized fruition only after he expanded into a 1,500 square foot space and offered state-of-the art Internet access as the primary attraction, with food and beverage as a secondary feature. Long's concept is neither unique nor far-fetched. In the face of growing competition, many Internet coffeehouses lure customers by upgrading their computer equipment to offer faster Internet connections and the more powerful computers.

Cybercafes must compete against the home-based Internet market as well. Some cafe owners strike deals with cable providers or telephone companies to install Integrated Services Digital Network (ISDN) connections for state-of-the-art Internet speed. Other cybercafe managers invest in proprietary Web servers, thus assuming the role of ISP in their own right.

In addition to Internet access and cafe fare, some cybercafes expanded their services to include virtual-reality theme games, motion-based simulator rides, alcoholic beverages, and up-scale cuisine. To complete the novelty, some establishments have integrated the technology theme into their menus. Major hotel chains rushed to adapt the cybercafe market to that industry as well. Holiday Inn, a subsidiary of Holiday Hospitality Corporation, and Host Marriott Services Corporation planned to convert a number of their lounges into cybercafes. In 1996, Holiday Inn transformed one lounge at its Heathrow location into a computing and Internet-surfing site, complete with cafe amenities. Marriott, in turn, embarked on a joint venture with CyberFlyer Technologies in 1997 to test cyber lounges in 30 airports throughout the United States. The CyberFlyer hardware includes Intel-based technology, a modem connected to rapid-transmission T1 phone lines, and a flat-screen monitor.

INDUSTRY LEADERS

FRANCHISE INDUSTRY

David Green's Seattle-based Cafe Internet opened in mid-1995 and met with such success that, by March 1998, he had patented the money-making operation into a "cookbook" style formula for sale to franchise investors. In return for a pre-arranged investment sum, potential entrepreneurs may receive formal training sessions, assistance with site selection, facility planning and layout, and use of the Cafe Internet trademark and French cafe motif. Green's enterprise addressed a myriad of details such as providing each franchise with pricing and protocol advice, access to "Allsports Talk Online," a cafe-specific World Wide Web home page, and private stock coffee beans—complete with espresso training videos and manuals. Additionally, Cafe Internet franchises are eligible to receive assistance from the Small Business Administration (SBA).

KIOSK SOFTWARE

Among cybercafes, even the most effectively designed operation has a need for business-specific software. Cyber-Times Software offers *turnkey* (plug-and-play) systems for cybercafes and other computer installations of a kiosk nature. The company's flagship product, called *Cyber-Time* features billing functions, multi-language support, flat-rate and block time accounting, earnings reports, customer interfaces, diagnostics, and security systems. Cyber-Times advertises kiosk management systems to libraries, cruise lines, restaurants, hotels, and schools, in addition to cybercafes.

Simon Media of Austria markets a kiosk package that includes client-server networking software called *Instant NetCafe.* The product addresses the details of the administration of usage fees.

AMERICA AND THE WORLD

Although half the world's cybercafes were located in the United States in the mid-1990s, the European market expanded substantially over time, and large cities around the world—especially those with robust tourism—now provide numerous cybercafes. In 1997, the online directory *CyberCafes of Europe* contained more than 600 Internet cafes with operations in Germany, France, and the United Kingdom, as well as in smaller countries such as Latvia and Malta. Another directory, the *Internet Cafe Guide,* listed more than 1,000 cybercafes in 71 countries. Paris—birthplace of the cafe—had 8 Internet coffeehouses listed in 1999, although the French in general have resisted the Internet. Per every 1,000 people, France has only 4 computers connected to the Internet in contrast to 31 in the United States and 11 in Great Britain. Cities such as Berlin became the targets of many U.S. companies seeking to take their businesses abroad. Tourists in these cities use cybercafes to communicate with friends, relatives, and colleagues; to keep up on local and international news; and to obtain information on the city they are visiting. Moreover, these cities have large, diverse populations that can support new experimental business ventures such as the cybercafe.

WORLDWIDE DISTRIBUTION

The number of cybercafe enterprises has stabilized from an initial surge in the mid-1990s. *The New York Times,* in April 1998, reported a decline in cybercafe business in markets as diverse as New York City, Washington, and Louisville, Kentucky, and even in the cybercafe's birthplace, San Francisco. Only the State of Hawaii showed growth on that front, according to the *Times.* Statistics tallied independently in 1999 revealed that the largest number of existing cybercafes were located in the State of California, which offered 41 such establishments—more than twice as many as New York State, which offered 19. France offered 38 cybercafes altogether, including 10 in the Alpine region, 8 in Paris, and 1 in Alsace. Other concentrations of cybercafes could be found in San Francisco (with 8), and Hawaii (with 14). Although the industry is spread thin, it reaches remote and less industrialized nations; at least one cybercafe was on record in India in 1999. Cybercafes were found in Croatia, Russia, and North Africa as well.

ASIA

Japan experienced strong interest in Internet cafes, and Tokyo hosted a number of cybercafes, which like their U.S. counterparts, offered computer use for about $10 per hour. Some of Japan's cyber coffeehouses catered to teen-agers, bundling Internet use with soft drinks, while others targeted professionals with state-of-the-art Internet technology. An economic crisis that permeated Asia in 1997 left Tokyo with only one cafe listing, according to *Cafe Guide,* but an infusion of capital to that region brought some stability by early 1999, and observers awaited revised economic reports for all industries.

RESEARCH AND TECHNOLOGY

Since Internet coffeehouses generally want to offer the best available Internet access service to their patrons, developments in Internet access technology promise to affect the cybercafe industry. With the increased number of subscribers around the world in the 1990s, the Internet quickly became inundated, and users became frustrated with the slow response times and problems when downloading documents. Largely relying on standard telephone lines, and with an insufficiency of responding modems, the Internet could only transmit information at relatively slow speeds when besieged with users. Because of these issues, researchers and Internet service providers sought technological solutions.

These solutions primarily took the form of new transmission cables or alternative transmission channels. ISDN lines, for example, can send information at a substantially higher rate than ordinary telephone lines. However, companies were hesitant to change because it would cost each consumer between $150 and $300 to install these lines and would carry a monthly service fee and a per-minute charge. T1 lines, on the other hand, can transmit data at 1.5 megabits per second (mbps). Other alternatives include Asymmetrical Digital Subscriber Lines (ADSL), which are faster than both ISDN and T1 lines, sending data at 640 kilobits per second (kbps), and can receive documents from the Internet at 6 mbps.

Along with trying to create faster telephone lines, some Internet service providers have turned to entirely new conveyances, such as coaxial cable or satellites. Cable and cable modems can transmit data 100 times faster than standard telephone lines; however, cable companies would need to replace their one-way cable with two-way cable in order to accommodate the Internet. Furthermore, only about 7 percent of cable companies offered Internet service in 1996. Despite these complications, some cybercafes treated customers to high-speed Internet access via cables in 1997. Satellites constitute a potential alternative to telephones lines, receiving about 400 kbps, or 7 to 11 times faster than even the 56 kbps and 36.6 kbps modems used with standard phone lines. However, satellites send data at a slower rate and, in addition to interface software, users must purchase satellite dishes at a cost of about $1,000.

FURTHER READING

Bollinger, Julie. "Coffee Goes High-tech at Dayton Cybercafe." *Business Courier,* 19 October 1998.

"Cafe Internet—Franchise!" 8 April 1999. Available from http://www.cafe?inet.com/realindex.html.

Cavanaugh, Katherine. "Pioneer New York Cyber-Cafe Is Rewriting Its Digital Menu." *The New York Times,* 17 August 1996.

"Cybercafe Guide," 8 April 1999. Available from http://www.cyber-star.com/cgi-bin/csn.cgi?r=3&f=no.

"CyberCafe Ring," 8 April 1999. Available from http://www.webring.org/cig-bin/webring?ring=cybercafe&list.

"CyberFlyer Turns Host Marriott Services' Lounges into Cyber Cafes." *PR Newswire,* 12 June 1997.

"CYBER-TIME SOFTWARE," 8 April 1999. Available from http://www.cybertimesoftware.com.

Frost, Robin. "Alone Together: A Day in the Life of a Cyber Cafe." *Wall Street Journal,* 8 May 1997.

———. "The Internet: Is Being Online Going to be Easier?" *Wall Street Journal,* 9 December 1996.

Hainer, Cathy. "Surf and Sip at the Cybercafe: Trendy Spots Tie Technology, Coffee Culture." *USA Today,* 1 May 1996.

Harmon, Amy. "Why the French Hate the Internet." *Los Angeles Times,* 27 January 1997.

"Holiday Inn Set to Offer Internet Cafes Hotels." *Travel Trade Gazette UK & Ireland,* 30 October 1996.

Kanaley, Reid. "Cyber Cafe Opens in Princeton, NJ." *Knight-Ridder/Tribune Business News,* 6 April 1997.

Krueger, Jill. "Cyber-Cafe Next Online." *Orlando Business Journal,* 11 August 1995.

Marriott, Michel. "The Ballad Of the Cybercafe." *The New York Times,* 16 April 1998.

"Solutions for Internet of Cyber Cafes—Simon Media," 8 April 1999. Available from http://www.sime.com/netcafe/e/.

Tedesco, Richard. "Coffee, Chips, and Apples: Apple Gets Into Cyber-Cafes." *Broadcasting & Cable,* 18 November 1996.

Urbonas, Stacey. "French Cafes Swap Carafes for Computers." *USA Today,* 8 February 1996.

Williams, Louise. "Not for the Naive, But the Demise of the Internet Cafe Has Been Greatly Exaggerated." *Computergram International,* 1 August 1996.

—Karl Heil, updated by Mike Jackson
and Gloria Cooksey

Desktop Publishing

The world of publishing has been greatly affected by the advent of computer technology and software applications. Chief among these has been the proliferation of desktop publishing. Desktop publishing (DTP) combines words, graphics, and pictures to produce a variety of camera ready documents using a personal computer (PC). Conventional publishing requires writers, designers, typesetters, and artists, but with DTP a single individual can perform all these functions on a PC to produce output for commercial printing. Sophisticated software and hardware provides the ordinary desktop publisher with the same capabilities and resources that previously required a staff of several persons and expensive equipment. DTP equipment costs will continue to decrease, while functionality and productivity per investment will continue to increase. These lowered costs mean that even small publishers can now produce CD-ROMs containing entire books with a modest investment. Books and newsletters sent directly to the consumer via the World Wide Web shift the cost of reproduction—paper, toner, printer wear and tear—to consumers who print or download the product on their own equipment.

Consequently, printing capabilities that were once the exclusive domain of large publishing firms—at a cost of tens or hundreds of thousands of dollars—are now available to any individual for between $3,000 and $10,000.

"Today, there are more than 53,000 publishers in the United States, including 8 large New York companies, 15 companies a step below them, and about 300 mid-sized companies that each generate between $1 and $10 million in sales annually. That leaves more than 52,000 small publishers who publish between one and three books annually. Most of these are self-publishers," according to John Tessitore in a 1996 article in *The Christian Science Monitor.* Some estimates are even higher. The Publishers Marketing Association, for example, estimated that there were 80,000 to 90,000 individual publishers.

In 1995 alone, more than 11,000 new publishing firms were created—a 38 percent increase over the annual average of 8,000. Tom Dial of Book World Marketing, a national book distributor, states "this jump is directly attributable to desktop publishing."

This trend is reflected in the computer software industry as well. For example, retail sales of personal computer software reached $1.3 billion annually in the early 1990s, and desktop publishing software garnered the lion's share of the market—sometimes as much as 68 percent.

Some of the advantages of desktop publishing (DTP) include total control over all phases of production, faster time between conception and production, and greater profit potential. Small desktop publishers are able to produce books faster than major publishers, offer more up-to-date information, and better target their audience through direct mail or specialty stores and magazines. They also serve a unique market need created by ever-increasing specialization and differentiation of topics.

DTP is often associated with a single individual or small group of individuals who produce a book, newsletter, or other types of written communication.

Desktop or electronic publishing can be used by small to medium size publishers to produce an entire book or newsletter in camera-ready, or printable, form. Since the cost of software and equipment is low, large publishers also use DTP in-house for preparation of copy—including typesetting, graphics, layout, and other pre-press activities—instead of outsourcing these tasks. In some cases, the intermediate film or paper copy used to produce a plate has been replaced by a direct computer-to-plate process. In the case of direct computer-to-Web publishing, a printed copy may never come from the publisher.

The small publisher must be concerned with proofreading, editing, production of camera-ready copy for reproduction or printing, marketing, distributing, shipping, and all other aspects of a small business such as accounting and inventory control. The typical and most common publication formats are used by individuals or small businesses to produce flyers, newsletters, books, disk copies to be used by a printer for processing, or CD-ROMs. Regardless of format, however, the publishing process is essentially the same, except for the medium of the final product.

The medium on which a product is printed largely governs the distribution method. Conventional paper books or newsletters are frequently distributed via a third party book or news distributor who acts as a jobber, specialty book stores direct from the publisher, or direct mail order solicitation. A new method of distribution and marketing is via the World Wide Web, on which publications can be conveniently advertised to an estimated 31.3 million users, 27 percent of whom made online purchases in the past 12 months, according to a 1997 American Internet User Survey. Over 55 million people are poised to become Web users, which increases its marketing appeal.

A number of companies print, bind, store, and drop ship final copies for desktop publishers. Seventy percent of books do not earn enough to cover the cost of a major distributing agent, so some distributors also assist small publishers in marketing or distribution to bookstores, providing a channel not otherwise available. Publishers Group, Publishers Group West, Book World, and the National Book Network are some of the distributors who help expand the small publishers market. While these distributors may charge a fee up to $25,000 per book, some vendors have collective exhibits at national conferences by a single distributor that charges a modest one-time fee for display in an exhibit booth. Large book company royalties are between 8 and 10 percent, while self-publishing and marketing via a distributor can yield a 35 to 65 percent return on the retail price. Organizations assisting

small publishers include the Publishers Marketing Association, Small Publishers Association of North America, and Independent Publishers Network. Most marketing is often handled by the individual desktop publisher.

Some of the avenues for the communication and exchange of ideas in the electronic and DTP industry are the semiannual Seybold Conference and Exposition, the annual MacWorld Expo, *Publish* magazine, and the *DTP Journal,* available on the Internet. The 1996 Seybold Conference featured more than 300 exhibitors, was attended by 40,345 visitors, and provided a mix of Internet and digital publishing. The 1999 MacWorld Expo in San Francisco featured more than 460 exhibitors showing products and updates for the Mac publishing environment, and was attended by 69,800 visitors. *Publish* magazine is produced throughout the world, including Asia, Russia, Poland, Australia, and Brazil.

Industry associations also aid in DTP communications. The National Association of Desktop Publishers has 30,000 members and seeks to provide information, buying discounts, and other services to its professional and non-professional desktop publishers. The Publishers Marketing Association, a trade association of 3,100 independent publishers including 200 foreign affiliates, was formed in 1983. Its purpose was advance DTP professional interests, provide cooperative marketing programs, sponsor educational seminars about the industry, and make members' products visible to the trade and to the consumer. Each year it offers around 48 seminars on various facets of publishing.

Tax regulations relating to home businesses will likely affect individual and small desktop publishers. Home businesses must be fully justified, usually separately contained within a home and devoted solely to business functions, to qualify as a home business. New legislation was introduced in Congress in February 1997 to broaden the tax deductibility of home office expenses.

BACKGROUND AND DEVELOPMENT

In the late 1970s, when PCs had capacities of 640 kilobytes (KB) of memory and storage was approximately 120,000 bytes on a 5.25 inch diskette, word processing was available only if the author knew enough to write a crude program. Radio Shack's Scripsit was one of the first word processing packages, and it was accompanied by Perfect Word. It was soon followed by Wordstar, WordPerfect, and some of the more commonly known word processors of today. In a matter of less than a decade, however, all that changed, and by the early 1990s word processing gave way to full scale desktop publishing.

Paul Brainard, founder of Aldus, is generally considered the father of desktop publishing, since he first used the term in October of 1984. He originally intended the term to describe the integration of text and graphics. Even after Brainard's first public use of the term, other terms such as personal publishing, self-publishing, electronic publishing, and computer publishing were still being used in 1985 to describe the same concept. Aldus used DTP to advertise Page-Maker software, and by the end of 1985, *Desktop Publishing* was an industry magazine. *Desktop Publishing* was sold and renamed *Publish* in 1986.

In the early 1990s, Apple's QuickTime allowed developers to integrate multimedia. The Hewlett-Packard LaserJet printer series, with up to a 600 dpi printer, debuted at a cost of $3,000. In addition, direct computer to plate printing began, which made short-run color printing cheaper and faster; Pentium processors arrived; and QMS sold its ColorScript Laser 1000 for $12,449. The mid-1990s introduced new digital presses, the first Netscape Navigator Web browser, the release of Windows 95, Adobe's PageMill, a graphical HTML editor for Web publishing, and wide-format color inkjet printers. These innovations contributed to the ease of production and subsequent growth of desktop publishing.

With all the functions of desktop publishing virtually at a publisher's fingertips, typesetting costs fell from between $110 and $150 per page to only $5 per page. DTP reduced the number of man hours required, provided greater design flexibility at or near deadlines, and decreased or eliminated darkroom and chemical use for many newspapers. In addition to higher productivity, electronic file transfer also allowed employees more flexibility. Large corporations saw other benefits, as well, such as ensuring the secrecy of sensitive documents in the pre-publication stage. DTP also facilitated the easier creation of informational graphics.

With the help of cost-effective desktop technology, catalog publishers were also able to offset increased paper costs in the mid-1990s. Ninety percent of all respondents to a 1995 *Catalog Age* Benchmarking Report were using computers to design catalog pages, and over 70 percent had upgraded their desktop publishing capabilities within the previous year, spending between $10,000 and $20,000 on

newer hardware or software. Only 11 percent offered electronic versions of their catalog at that time, but 25 percent had a separate budget for electronic media.

CURRENT CONDITIONS

The proliferation of independent desktop publishers continues. Publishers invested three times more in DTP in 1996 than in 1995 for in-house pre-press operations, management network operations, and multimedia projects. According to Jonathan Seybold, founder of Seybold Seminars on electronic publishing, digital desktop publishing has intertwined with the Internet and World Wide Web technologies. "Two revolutions are converging with the desktop revolution still incomplete even while the Internet and Web revolutions are just starting to get a foothold." Indeed, the Internet is increasingly being used for distributing magazines and publications. These online publications use software such as Tango, which makes databases available; WebCatalog, designed for web searches; and Icat, designed to provide search capabilities for catalog image templates. Sales on the Internet ranged from $40,000 to $4 million.

A relatively new form of publication are zines or E-zines, which are online magazines. Zines are easy to produce, and cost little to nothing to distribute, greatly relieving the pressure for financial success. Originating with underground publications in the early 1980s, the number of zines has skyrocketed to between 20,000 to 50,000 in the mid-1990s with only around 10—excluding major publishers—making a profit. Circulation ranged up to 50,000 subscribers.

An article in the December 1998 issue of the PMA Newsletter discusses the impact of online media on the publishing industry. New additions to Internet publishing in the late 1990s are E-books and Web-books. According to the article, there is much growth to be seen in the future in these two areas, as well as in searchable databases. The article states that while Internet publishers may compete with traditional and small publishers, the Internet also provides marketing opportunities for these same publishers.

In 1997, 200 MHz Pentium processors became commonly available for approximately $2,000. Photographic quality color printers became available for around $400, with many as low as $250, and high quality color scanners were priced at $400 to $1,000. Java, a cross-platform programming language developed by Sun Microsystems, Inc., was also beneficial to DTP.

Apple's Macintosh, an early leader in desktop publishing equipment, still dominated desktops in the late 1990s, especially with Apple's newest line of G3s and its revolutionary iMac, introduced in August of 1998. Microsoft Word and WordPerfect were the dominant word processing software. Adobe Photoshop was the top image-editing software, Adobe Illustrator the predominant package for art illustrators, and QuarkXPress the primary page layout software for designers. As publishers moved toward an all-digital production process, on-screen digital proofing became increasingly necessary.

INDUSTRY LEADERS

Many publishers have origins in DTP. For example, Para Publishing was founded by Dan Poynter in 1978 with $15,000 borrowed from his parents. Poynter had no formal background or experience in publishing. The company published books about recreational parachuting, and its first book, *Parachuting, The Skydiver's Handbook,* still sells 1,000 copies annually. Poynter is "recognized as the guru of self publishing," according to Linda Donelson in the August 1997 issue of *Writer's Digest.* He is best known for his book *The Self-Publishing Manual.*

Pfeifer-Hamilton Publishers, an imprint of Whole Person Associates, Inc., was established in 1983 by Donald and Nancy Tubesing to publish their training materials on stress management and wellness. Two of its best selling books are *The Duct Tape Book,* describing 200 outrageous ideas for duct tape and *Duct Tape Book Two—Real Stories.* Together, they have sold over 200,000 copies.

Glenbridge Publishing, Ltd. was started with $35,000 as Jim and Mary Keene's home-based company in the mid-1990s. The company distributed its thirty-eighth book in 1996. Also, Bancroft Press expanded from Bruce Bortz's family ping-pong table to a publisher of 14 books.

Publishing Arts, founded by Roger Thurber in 1988, has found a unique niche servicing desktop publishers. Its services include software support, electronic pre-press PostScript training, work flow analysis, bulletin board services, Internet installation, and Web page authoring and publishing, which alone accounted for 60 percent of its business in 1996.

Adobe Systems Inc. develops, markets, and supports software products and technologies enabling users to create information in all print and electronic media. Publicly traded on the NASDAQ, Adobe employs more than 2,600 persons, had annual sales of $894.8 million for fiscal year 1998, and is one of the leading software producers for the DTP industry. Adobe produces Adobe Acrobat, Adobe FrameMaker, Adobe PageMill, Adobe PageMaker, Adobe Illustrator and Adobe Photoshop, among many others. In March 1999, Adobe introduced Adobe InDesign, a high-end page layout program designed specifically for graphics professionals and the publishing industry. Adobe created InDesign to compete with Quark, Inc.'s QuarkXPress, and repackaged its popular page layout program PageMaker to be more attractive to mid-size businesses.

Apple Computer Inc. is a key player in desktop publishing. Apple began the personal computer revolution with the first Apple II in the 1970s, and reinvented the personal computer with the creation of the first Macintosh in the 1980s. In August of 1998, Apple reenergized its share of the computer market with the introduction of iMac, the low-cost, high performance, all-in-one system. Apple shipped 278,000 iMac's in the first six weeks, and reported sales of 519,000 iMacs in the first quarter of fiscal 1999. A company news release from March 2, 1999 announced that three leading publishing companies, Kinko's, Corbis, and PEOPLE, have selected Apple's Color-Sync technology for printing, which provides consistent desktop color management. Apple's 1999 fiscal first quarter, ending December 1998, posted a net profit of $152 million, up from $47 million in 1998's first quarter.

AMERICA AND THE WORLD

By the mid-1990s, it was reported that in-house publishing represented about 60 percent of the typesetter market in the United States. One explanation for this statistic can be found in the heavy demand for full control of "document production" within many companies. Desktop publishing certainly capitalized on this psychology in the United States, although the picture is often different in other countries.

In Japan, for example, very few companies—with the exception of newspapers and catalog publishers—have such professional tools as typesetters and drum scanners. In Japan, a printer is usually a subcontractor for its client company and utilizes the services of a designer and a trade shop to do the work.

By the early 1990s, the potential for desktop publishing in Japan greatly expanded, in part due to larger font libraries and more sophisticated composition software. In particular, QuarkXpress 3.11J stood out among composition software.

Although these developments have had enormous ramifications for the Japanese publishing industry, a general downturn in the Japanese economy has to some extent held back the progress of desktop publishing. Other reasons that desktop publishing has not caught on in Japan to the extent that it has in the United States includes: the traditional attitude of the Japanese graphic arts marketplace; the somewhat limited availability of superior-quality font designs; and the difficulties of managing two-byte characters. Hence, proprietary composition systems still controlled the Japanese market in the 1990s.

RESEARCH AND TECHNOLOGY

Xionics Document Technologies is a leading developer of embedded systems software for printing, scanning, copying, and transmitting documents to computer peripherals. They partner with original equipment manufacturers such as IBM. Embedded systems technology has allowed the continued convergence of desktop printers and copiers, creating a new category of multi-function peripherals (MFPs), which combine the functions of print, copy, scan, and fax in a single system. When embedded systems imaging equipment produces multiple original prints, it is called a "Mopier."

Computer-to-plate capability for off-set press production was emerging as an alternative to disk-to-film-plates press technology. However, electronic media will be an adjunct to, not a replacement for, printed material, and in the early twenty-first century the "paperless society" will likely still be just a concept. Innovations allowing direct-to-paper digital presses, and direct-to-plate will have an effect on the printing industry though. Also, as printing becomes more a question of pre- or post-distribution, economics will favor post-distribution printing by end users on their own equipment. Eventually, a print shop could be in every home, and the desktop publisher would be both the producer and the consumer. As the economic barriers to home generated publishing are lowered, individuals and small companies will have all the resources previously available only to larger print shops.

"*Folio's* seventh annual desktop publishing trends survey in 1997 indicated that magazine production and art departments were often eager to use new technologies. Based on 114 completed responses from production executives selected randomly in the United States, computer-to-plate (CTP) printing, digital proofing and asset-management systems appeared to be increasingly popular in the late 1990s.

More than half of the editors who participated in the survey preferred Microsoft Word to any other word-processing software, while 21.1 percent chose WordPerfect, and 10.5 percent picked QuarkXpress. Nearly half of those surveyed worked only on Macintosh; about one fifth worked on a PC; and 33.3 percent worked on a combination.

Nearly 90 percent of Art Departments used Adobe Illustrator, while 23.7 percent used Macromedia FreeHand, and 19.3 percent used Adobe Photoshop. The survey also indicated that total investment in desktop publishing has risen, particularly in consumer books. Total investments for business books averaged $437,900, while consumer magazines averaged $324,800. In the case of the latter, that represented an increase of more than 100 percent from the previous year.

FURTHER READING

"1997 American Internet User Survey." Available from http://etrg.findsvp.com/Internet/overview.htlm.

Adams, Bob. "Great Leaps." *Target Marketing,* April 1996.

"Adobe Systems Reports Record Revenue and Operating Profit for Fourth Quarter and 1998 Fiscal Year Results," 16 December 1998. Available from http://www.adobe.com/aboutadobe/pressroom/pressreleases/HTML/9812/981216.adbeq4.html.

"Apple Caps Fiscal Year With Strong Results; Company Launches Mac OS 8.5 and Reveals Over 40% of iMac Buyers are New Apple Customers," 14 October 1998. Available from http://www.apple.com/pr/library/1998/oct/14event.html.

"Apple Reports Fiscal First Quarter Profit of $152 Million, 49 Percent Unit Growth Outpaces Industry Average," 13 January 1999. Available from http://www.apple.com/pr/library/1999/jan/13earnings.html.

Beale, Stephen. "Seybold Show's Split Personality." *Macworld,* December 1996.

Bethyon, Jim. "Desktop Prepress Trends to Watch." *DTP Journal,* May 1996. Available from http://www.dtpjournal.com.

Bourrie, Sally Ruth. "Quintessentially Quark: Tim Gill." *Colorado Business Magazine,* September 1993.

Brown, Ed. "Extreme Publishing." *Fortune,* 12 May 1997.

Cozeolino, Deborah A. "Publishing Arts Recommends Bigger, Better, Faster PCs." *Computer Reseller News,* 2 September 1996.

"Desktop a Major Service for Clients." *Graphic Arts Monthly,* January 1996.

"Desktop Publishing Leads Growth in Software." *The Christian Science Monitor,* 3 April 1991.

Donelson, Linda. "Para Publishing's Dan Poynter: 'Self-Publishing is for 95 percent of the People.'" *Writer's Digest,* August 1997.

Felici, James. "Publish Premiers." *Publish,* September 1996.

Gage, Deborah. "John Warnack—Adobe Systems Inc." *Computer Reseller News,* 6 November 1995.

Harney, Kenneth R. "Senator Seeks to Broaden Tax Rules on Home-Based Business Deductions." *Washington Post,* 1 February 1997.

Karol, Michael. "Computer Use Takes Wing." *Graphic Arts Monthly,* March 1996.

———. "Desktop a Major Service for Clients." *Graphic Arts Monthly,* January 1996.

"Leading Publishers Choose Apple's ColorSync Technology: Corbis, Kinko's and PEOPLE Adopt ColorSync to Significantly Enhance Their Color Quality," 2 March 1999. Available from http://www.apple.com/pr/library/1999/mar/02colorsyncadopt.html.

Lubove, Seth. "What Might Have Been." *Forbes,* 14 August 1995.

"Macworld San Francisco 99: Apple Energizes the Publishing Industry." Available from http://www.dtpjournal.com/archives/9903mw.html.

Moskowitz, Eric. "The Rise of the 'Zine'." *The Christian Science Monitor,* 26 July 1995.

Nelson, Ted. "Things to Come." *Byte,* November 1995.

Petersen, Debbie. "Change for the Better." *American Printer,* June 1996.

Saffo, Paul. "Publishing Moves Beyond the Desktop." *Personal Computing,* February 1989.

Schwab, Robert. "Books Turned Out from Home." *Denver Post,* 17 February 1996.

"Seybold SF Covers an Industry Revolution." *Graphic Arts Monthly,* October 1996.

Smith, Daniel. "A Tale of Three Weeklies." *Editor & Publisher,* 8 April 1995.

Soberanis, Pat. "Parallel Publishing." *Publish,* 6 January 1997.

Spring, Tom. "Adobe Unveils InDesign Publishing Program: PageMaker Positioned for Lower-end Page-design Market." *PC World,* 2 March 1999.

Sreenivasan, Sreenath. "Newsletters Find Haven Online." *The New York Times,* 7 July 1997.

Sucov, Jennifer. "The Creeping Edge." *Folio: The Magazine for Magazine Management,* 1 October 1997.

———."Deconstructing the Desktop." *Folio: The Magazine for Magazine Management,* 1 March 1997.

———."Seybold Pushes Products and Process." *Folio: The Magazine for Magazine Management,* 1 November 1996.

Tessitore, John. "Desktop Publishing Wave Brings Tide of New Authors to Bookstore Shelves." *Christian Science Monitor,* 11 June 1996.

Tally, Taz, Ph.D. "Evolution of an Industry: Part One in a Series on the Graphic Arts." October 1998. Available from http://www.dtpjournal.com/archives/9810d2.html.

Trager, Louis. "Picture Perfect Software for Web Publishers Allows Users and Business to Create 'Albums' for Display on the Internet." *San Francisco Chronicle,* 11 May 1997.

Trauring, Aron. "Internet Publishing & Its Impact on Our Industry Publishers Marketing Association." Available from http://www.pma-online.org/newsletr/dec3-98.html.

Weibel, Bob. "Removable Storage for the Masses." *Publish,* June 1997.

Widman, Jack. "Looking Forward, Looking Back." *Publish,* September 1996.

Wintrob, Suzanne. "Analysts Confident Adobe Will Rebound." *Computing Canada,* 1 February 1996.

Young, Jeffrey. "Standard Bearers." *Forbes,* 27 March 1995.

—David C. Genaway, updated by David Levine
and Lisa DeShantz-Cook

DIGITAL IMAGING

Digital imaging refers to the process of recording and manipulating images with electronic cameras and computers. A digital camera is an input device that captures an image by recording it into a binary format. The binary picture is transferred from the digital camera to a computer equipped with software, which then manipulates the digital image by changing its color, size, or content. Digital images require memory storage and special ports, cables, and connectors to transfer from the digital camera to the computer. New innovations in digital imaging allow digital cameras to be plugged into the back of a desktop or laptop computer directly to transfer images. Alternately, other digital cameras use removable image storage cards. These removable image storage cards can be read by a computer without additional hardware and without the digital camera being attached in any way to the computer.

In the United States, the digital imaging market grew from 4 percent in 1995 to an estimated 18 percent in 1997. By 1998 digital camera sales jumped to 1.2 million units, more than three times the 372,000 units sold in 1996. According to a study published jointly by International Data Corporation and Future Image, the worldwide market will increase from $1.2 billion in 1997 to $5.4 billion by 2002, as technological advances enable more affordable systems to produce higher quality photos.

BACKGROUND AND DEVELOPMENT

The traditional film photography market generates more than $10 billion annually in revenues. Film photography relies on tiny crystals of light-sensitive silver compounds suspended in a coating that surrounds a transparent film. As the shutter of the camera opens, light from the brightest parts of an image are thrown onto the film and the crystals start breaking down. In developing the film, a chemical called a "developer" changes the crystals exposed into black silver, while a chemical called a "fixer" dissolves the unexposed crystals. The resulting negative shows black silver where the scene was brightest and nothing where the film was left dark (no image was recorded). However, the wet chemistry required to develop photographs has many disadvantages. It is messy and environmentally hazardous since most of the chemicals are toxic. In addition, the wet chemistry process is time-delayed—the entire developing process means that instant viewing and editing are impossible. Finally, there is always a risk of spoilage; film that is over or under developed results in poor images.

Still images like photos, slides, transparencies, and art have traditionally been converted to digital format using a process called scanning with a device called a scanner. The scanner "copies" the image and translates it to a binary format. Scanner accuracy is defined in two ways—by resolution and color information. Resolution is referred to as dpi (dots per inch) or ppi (pixels per inch). Color information is defined by the number of bits of information per color. For example, 24 bits per pixel (8 bits of each red, green, and blue) creates 1.6 million colors. The size of a pixel varies from one device to another and is, essentially, a single square unit of the same size. Digital cameras rely on the same measurements of resolution and color information.

Digital cameras do not require wet chemistry, lab processing, or scanning. Instead, digital imaging cameras create a binary image directly by recording the image on a charge-coupled device (CCD). The CCD sensor is an opto-electronic element that records light as a charge in a condenser. Developed originally by Bell Laboratories, the CCD contains an array of cells representing a picture element. Each cell converts light into an electrical charge. Pixels arranged in a straight row are called linear arrays. In 1997, CCD's accounted for about half the cost of a digital camera. Together, CCD's and storage accounted for more than three-quarters of the cost. According to Nicholas van den Berghe, vice president and general manager of the consumer division at Live Picture Inc., the combined cost of the CCD and storage should be around 15 percent of the system cost before digital cameras take off with the consumer market. Digital images created by digital cameras measure resolution in the same manner as a scanner.

CURRENT CONDITIONS

In the consumer niche of digital imaging, CAP Ventures, Inc., a market research firm, projects a 54 percent growth rate through the year 2001 for the digital camera market selling in the $500 or less range. Powerful and inexpensive personal computers combined with Internet access have created a booming market for digital cameras in recent years. Prior to the advent of the Pentium computer and the Internet, digital imaging with digital cameras was limited to a small number of computer users. According to Allen Ruster, director of the Digital Photography and Printing Services at CAP Ventures, "In the near term, the business and heavy-user home computer markets are the best opportunities for digital camera manufacturers." In a 1997 survey by the Association of Information and Image Management, 26 percent listed the Internet as the greatest market opportunity. In the previous year's survey, the Internet did not appear on the list at all.

Businesses typically use scanners to convert documents to digital format as a part of an integrated document management system. However, as increasingly larger numbers of businesses begin to do business on the Internet, digital cameras are useful, for example, in creating advertising and Web-based catalogs. According to Dr. Joseph Webb, president of Strategies for Management, "the greatest usage for digital photography is in the catalog market simply because this arena is so image-intensive." Other companies that

rely on images, like real-estate and insurance, are predicted to be the next breakthrough markets for digital cameras. Several digital imaging companies like Shepard Poorman Communications Corporation and Hollis Digital Imaging Systems predict the demise of the scanning market as digital cameras improve in image quality and price. Consumers use digital cameras to capture pictures of family and friends then manipulate these digital images for use in cards, t-shirts, and other related items. As more people begin to use the Internet and World Wide Web, consumer use of digital cameras finds a practical outlet.

In the late 1990s digital cameras were still expensive; however, prices were dropping rapidly. Competition was strong and a wide variety of digital cameras were available in a number of price ranges with varying features. Stripped-down, some low-resolution digital cameras priced to sell for as low as $130. These cameras produce a grainy picture far inferior to that of 35-mm analog film. By 1999, megapixel cameras dominated the market, with more than 1-million pixel resolution per exposure, priced upwards of $600. The average computer screen resolution is about 96 dots per inch. In contrast, an inkjet printer offers 600- to 1200 dpi, allowing near-film quality pictures to be generated on common home computers. Gains in image quality and lower prices are driving digital cameras into the mainstream, which will call for greater camera standardization and usability to drive the industry forward.

Digital imaging has suffered from a number of limitations and obstacles. A regular 35-mm camera costs about $100. In contrast, while low-end digital

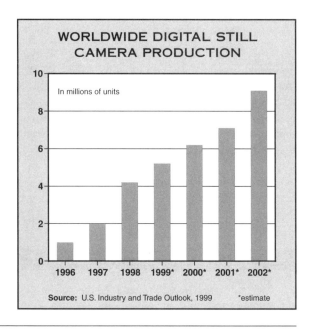

WORLDWIDE DIGITAL STILL CAMERA PRODUCTION

In millions of units

Source: U.S. Industry and Trade Outlook, 1999   *estimate

camera prices are approaching the upper-end 35mm range, added features such as flashes and interchangeable lenses can run the price up to near $2,000. Quality of digital images compared to traditional photography and printing is relatively low although expensive digital cameras can achieve high quality results. In terms of supplies, the regular 35-mm camera requires about $20 to buy film, develop it, and order prints. In contrast, the digital camera requires batteries, and photos must be printed on a special printer using special paper, or archived in a magnetic media or CD-ROM. The paper used by an inkjet printer to make a photo sells for about $15 per package of 10 sheets. Photos require 5 or 6 times the amount of ink needed to print documents or spreadsheets with ink cartridges costing up to $40.

The digital camera is only one link in the digital chain, which is why reducing the cost is not the only criteria is increasing sales and boosting the industry. Digital imaging is comprised of a network of cameras, scanners, printers, computers, software, and services. The upswing in camera sales had little to do with the new low-priced models, according to Jeff Lengyel, marketing director at Ricoh Corp. Instead, he believes that sales increased because the imaging infrastructure started to come together. Home computer prices dropped, it became easier to get on the Internet, and business on the Net boomed. Images and graphics are a big part of Net advertising and homepages. Besides dropping in price, home PCs became more powerful than ever before, and able to handle digital imaging far more easily as well as having the necessary storage space for the images. Printer quality has improved, costs for high quality printers and scanners have dropped, and companies are scrambling to put together entire systems that will work together.

The North American market for scanners will reach nearly $1.5 billion in revenue in 1999, according to InfoTrends Research Group. Storm Technology of Mountain View, California, offered the Easy Photo scanner for $299, to be used either alone or as part of an entire digital imaging system. However, flatbed scanners are of limited use in manipulating photographs. Since a glossy color photo has only 200-dpi resolution, any enlargement of such images results in poor picture quality. Alternately, the 35mm negative contains the equivalent of 3,000 dpi, therefore, professional quality pictures require a film scanner that can capture the small, densely packed frames. While these scanners have existed for years for upwards of $700, Hewlett-Packard made the technology available to consumers with the Photosmart Scanner, priced at $399 in 1999.

The late 1990s digital imaging market became increasingly competitive and dynamic as companies began to define themselves in terms of their focus on digital imaging. Kodak cites Digital Imaging as one of its core programs for aggressive growth. The company generated $400 million in digital cameras, products, and services in 1998 and anticipates that the area could add $3.5 to $4.0 billion to corporate revenues by the end of 2004. In a joint venture by America Online and "You've Got Mail," development is underway to facilitate sending photo publishing via e-mail. Kodak expects its joint marketing campaign with Intel to expose a range of consumers to digital imaging. The effort will enable consumers to have photos from their 35mm scanned directly onto CD-ROM discs, without having to buy a digital camera. As an incentive to increase consumer exposure to digital imaging, another company, IXLA Ltd. of San Francisco, California, is giving away an entry-level digital camera with the purchase of its image presentation software. The package will sell at a price of $99, including Kodak photographic inkjet paper. For the more serious

Trends **NOT JUST FOR PHOTO ALBUMS**

Birthday parties and graduations are not the only shots being captured by digital cameras. An increasing number of applications in science and medicine are being devised and marketed to take advantage of the high-resolution images offered by the technology.

An imaging system released in January 1999 by EyeDx uses a digital camera linked to a computer to screen children for eye abnormalities such as cataracts, tumors, nearsightedness, or amblyopia, also called lazy eye—the most common cause of preventable blindness in children.

Children as young as six weeks old can be screened with the system, with the camera functioning like a home camera taking photographs. Expertise in ophthalmology is not required to operate the system, so the screening can take place outside a clinical setting. Once downloaded into a computer, the software analyzes the images and generates a report with a referral recommendation.

In another application, scientists can capture high-resolution images of research results and document and analyze them with software. Eastman Kodak Company and Life Technologies, a research supply company, together offer a system with a 1.2 million pixel resolution with image analysis software that performs research calculations. The system simplifies documentation, manuscript production, and data transfer.

consumers, Epson and Kodak have reduced prices on high-end cameras and printers, further promoting the technology.

INDUSTRY LEADERS

Traditional camera manufacturers, computer software companies, and printing companies are all active in the emerging digital imaging industry. Eastman Kodak, Hewlett-Packard, Microsoft Corp., Hallmark, Epson, and Sony have all entered this emerging industry. As is the case with any dynamic market, casualties are frequent and swift. However, as of mid-1999, consumer-marketed (less than $1,200) digital cameras were available from several manufacturers including Canon Inc., Casio, Fuji, Hitachi, Kodak, Olympus, and Sharp among others.

Languishing in the digital market until the early 1990s, Kodak attributes a great deal of its success in digital imaging to the 1993 appointment of George Fisher as president. In that year Kodak lost $1.5 billion on $16.0 billion in sales. Fisher saw digital photography as a great opportunity for Kodak and proceeded with a series of divestitures to regain the necessary profitability for entering the digital imaging market, selling off most of its nonimaging businesses. Subsequent challenges followed Fisher's early successes. Price wars with Fuji Photo Film and a strong Japanese yen led to restructuring, $1.0 billion in cost cuts, and the elimination of 20,000 jobs. In 1997 the company earned only $5 million on sales of $14.7 billion, compared with 1996 net earnings of $1.3 billion on sales of $16.0 billion. A shift toward digital products and services is in the forefront of the company's growth strategy. In 1998, while sales dropped 7.8 percent to $13.4 billion, net earnings bounced back 27,700 percent to nearly $1.4 billion.

In May 1998, Kodak and the world's largest semiconductor company, Intel, announced a joint venture in digital photography and imaging, including a joint consumer marketing campaign. The agreement included plans to jointly develop products in digital imaging and update Kodak's photo finishing laboratories with Intel-based products, a broad patent cross-licensing agreement, and a collaborative consumer marketing campaign that could reach up to $150 million in spending over three years.

A wide variety of computer software companies provide software to manipulate digital images. One of the most popular is Adobe. Adobe Systems, Inc. of San Jose, California, had sales of $895 million in 1998 with 2,680 employees. Adobe provides a number of software packages including PhotoShop, its top-of-the-line package, and PhotoDeluxe, an entry-level image editor. Photoshop is one of the company's top three products that generate about 60 percent of its sales. Adobe PhotoDeluxe enjoys "bundling" or package agreements with other digital camera manufactures like Agfa, Casio, and Minolta. In total, Adobe PhotoDeluxe is packaged with more than 30 digital imaging devices. The estimated price of PhotoDeluxe was $49 in 1999.

A number of companies pursue strategies for integrating cameras and printers. For example, Epson offers a digital imaging solution by bundling together a PhotoPC digital camera ($299 in 1999) and Easy Photo software (Storm Technology). Epson America, Inc. is part of the Seiko Epson Corporation, which posted $6.1 billion in sales in 1998 and employed 44,000 people.

RESEARCH AND TECHNOLOGY

While CCDs are the dominant form of imaging technology within a digital camera, the CCD itself is expensive. A new alternative in 1997 was the CMOS. CMOS (pronounced sea-MOSS) stands for complementary metal oxide semiconductors, and is a standard computer-chip making technology in which circuits are built on thin silicon wafers. CMOS sensors require fewer batteries and are cheaper to make. The same process makes the sensors as a memory chip, while CCD sensors require a special fabrication. Additionally, CCDs require an extra chip just to read the charge value, while CMOS sensors have integrated readout chips reducing the number of parts needed in a digital camera. The cost of a CMOS sensor is anticipated at less than half of the CCD sensor.

The Advanced Photo System (APS) is a digital/print hybrid backed by Kodak, Fuji, Canon, Minolta, and Nikon. APS cameras, film, and processing equipment have the ability to "communicate" with each other and to compensate for conditions like light and film speed. APS technology allows for switching between different size photographs on the same roll of film and imprints digital information about the shot, lighting conditions, date, and other information that facilitate the developing process. The cameras have the advantage of affordability. Many models sell for between $100 and $300, and developing is available nearly anywhere offering 35mm processing. Kodak holds 60 percent of all APS camera patents.

Imagek, Inc. designed an electronic film cartridge that fits into the cavity of a 35mm camera. The cartridge stores pictures that can be downloaded to a PC/MAC and then re-used. The consumer has the advantage of being able to choose 35mm and digital format in the same camera and taking advantage of existing lenses and attachments. Imagek plans to price its Electronic Film System below $800.

The Digital Imaging Group (DIG) was launched in October 1997 with nine members—Adobe Systems Inc., Canon, Inc., Eastman Kodak Co., Fuji Photo Film Co., Ltd., Hewlett-Packard Co., IBM, Intel Corp., Live Picture Inc., and Microsoft Corp. Two months after its formation, the Digital Imaging Group more than tripled its membership, and currently has over 50 members. According to the DIG, the group is an open industry consortium whose mission is to communicate the benefits of digital imaging and digital technology as well as monitoring market response and developer recommendations. Membership gives companies the opportunity to help define the future of digital imaging technology, promote solutions, and have the opportunity to collaborate in the DIG showcase Web site and future marketing and promotional activities sponsored by the DIG. The first annual DIG Congress was held in Burlingame, California, in June 1998, where the newest and hottest tools for creating photographic-quality Web sites that download quickly and allow maximum user interaction were showcased. The DIG has launched international branches, first DIG Japan in 1998 and DIG Europe in 1999 with 11 founding members from 8 countries. The branches will help DIG extend into local markets to ultimately spread its initiatives on a global scale.

Beginning early in 1998, the DIG began the process of defining the next versions of the FlashPix and IIP specifications. FlashPix is an incredibly powerful tool for users of digital images. It uses flexible compression and color management options to offer a universal storage and exchange platform for digital imaging. By transferring to RAM, FlashPix reduces the amount of time it takes to manipulate and send a file. FlashPix accomplishes this task by using multiple-resolution versions of the image, each with half as many pixels (both vertical and horizontal) as the previous version. Each version of the image is also tiled or divided into squares measuring 64 pixels. To zoom in and out of the image, the FlashPix format allows for selection of the right resolution and tile display for each individual screen, eliminating the need to rebuild the image from scratch. FlashPix has the ability to add numerous extensions. Applications can add new storages, streams, and/or property sets that can be maintained across editing sessions of the file. Audio, for instance, can already be embedded in FlashPix images. Internet Imaging Protocol or IIP transfers a FlashPix object and transports it over a network using a request-response protocol. IIP is extremely flexible and functional as well, and can transport any FlashPix image, including tiles, transform objects, and even metadata. It eliminates the need to create and store multiple files on a server. FlashPix and IIP create a bandwidth-efficient way to allow viewers to quickly receive rich, photographic-quality images online, as well as the ability to pan and zoom into the images. It allows images to appear rapidly on screen and has the ability to print very small images in the highest resolutions that the particular hardware permits. Advocates of FlashPix/IIP believe that its capabilities present new opportunities in areas such as e-commerce and interactive communication. Over 100 products are now compatible with FlashPix/IIP.

FURTHER READING

Adobe Company Web site, 4 May 1999. Available from http://www.adobe.com.

"Adobe Ships 3 Million Copies of Award-Winning PhotoDeluxe: Easy to Use Digital Imaging Software Give Adobe Reputation of 'The Force To Be Reckoned With'." *PR Newswire*, 7 July 1997.

Avalos, George. "California Firm Sees Bright Future in Photo Software." *The Denver Post*, 12 May 1997.

Beale, Stephen. "FlashPix Format Gains Momentum." *Macworld*, December 1996.

Boyd-Merritt, Rick, and Margaret Quan. "Kodak, Intel Unroll Jointly Developed Imaging Products." *EE Times*, 29 September 1998.

"CAP Ventures Study: Users of Digital Cameras Very Satisfied." *Business Wire*, 18 July 1997.

Chakravarty, Subrata N. "How An Outsider's Vision Saved Kodak." *Forbes*, 13 January 1997.

"CMOS Goes Where CCD Has Treaded." *EE Times*, 29 April 1996.

Connor, Michael. "The Vital Lesson of Betamax." *Worldbusiness*, May/June 1996.

Day, Rebecca. "Pixel Puzzle—Building The Infrastructure for Digital Photography." *OEM Magazine*, 1 February 1997.

Deutsch, Claudia H. "There's Gold in Recycled Photographs." *International Herald Tribune*, 2 July 1997.

"Digital Cameras Monitor." *The Future Image Report*, January/February 1997. Available from http://www.digital-imaging.org.

"The Digital Imaging Group." DIG International Release, 14 April 1999. Available from http://www.digitalimaging.org/news/pr_04_14_99_1.html.

"Eastman Kodak Company." *Hoover's Online,* 3 May 1999. Available from http://www.hoovers.com.

"Eastman Kodak: Kodak Outlines Its Primary Growth Initiatives." *M2 Presswire,* 28 April 1999.

"Film Scanners." *Digital Photography Reviews,* 29 March 1999. Available from http://www.inconference.com/digicam/film1.html.

Glesi, Steve. "Kodak CEO Says Stock Is Undervalued: Photo Giant Eyes $1 Billion in Digital Revenue." *CBS Marketwatch,* 28 April 1999.

Grant, Linda. "Why Kodak Still Isn't Fixed." *Fortune,* 11 May 1998.

Holstein, William J. "Can Kodak Refocus?" *U.S. News,* 9 November 1998.

Hoye, David. "Psst! Tiny Camera No Longer A Secret." *The Arizona Republic,* 24 June 1997.

Imagek Company Web site, 3 May 1999. Available from http://www.imagek.com.

"Imaging Market Continues Steady Growth: Vendors Battle to Educate Users." *Document Imaging Report,* 16 April 1997. Available from http://www.flashpix.com.

"Innovations 1998: High-Tech Head-Turners." *Asiaweek,* 25 December 1998.

"Introduction to Imaging," 1997. Available from http://www.dpia.org/abc/abca.html.

Isaacson, Portia. "Who Will Emerge The Winner In The Business For Digital Cameras?" *Computer Reseller News,* 26 May 1997.

"IXLA Launches Major Marketing Initiative by Giving Away Digital Cameras," 14 April 1999. Available from http://www.digitalimaging.org/news/pr_04_20_99.

Jeffrey, Noel. "Getting A True Picture." *American Printer. Digital & Prepress Links Supplement,* June 1996.

"Kodak Spotlights Key Growth Engines." *Business Wire,* 27 April 1999.

"Kodak's Digital Direction." *Industry Week,* 19 May 1997.

Levy, Trudy. "Managing a Digital Image System—Choose the Ideal System to Archive and Access Your Valuable Images." *InformationWeek,* 25 November 1996.

"Megapixel Segment to Capture 95% of the Worldwide Digital Still Camera Market by 2000 According to Future Image and IDC." San Mateo, CA: Future Image, Inc., 31 August 1998. Available from http://www.futureimage.com/rel4.html.

"MGI Software Extends Market Reach in Asia-Pacific; MGI Asia Signs Building Agreements with Leading Taiwanese Scanner Manufacturers." *Business Wire,* 29 April 1999.

"NEC CSD, Epson and Sierra Imaging Announce Alliance for Windows CE Mobile Digital Imaging Solution," *Business Wire,* 15 June 1998.

Petersen, Debbie. "Digital Snap Shots." *American Printer,* March 1996.

Rossello, Rosanne. "Digital Imaging Pushes Toward the Mainstream." *The Seybold Report on Internet Publishing,* March 1997.

Ruber, Peter. "Digital Imaging Gets Real." *InfoWorld,* 1 December 1997.

Schwartz, Susana. "Digital Camera Highlights Kodak's New Image Strategy." *Insurance & Technology,* May 1995.

"Seiko Epson Corporation." *Hoover's Online,* 3 May 1999. Available from http://www.hoovers.com.

Weber, Jonathon. "Photo Technology That Lens Itself to A Better Camera." *Los Angeles Times,* 23 June 1997.

—Tona Henderson, updated by Roxanne Nelson
and Sondra E. O'Donnell

DIGITAL MAPPING

The digital mapping industry represented the convergence of several fundamental trends in high technology in the late 1990s: the increasing availability of inexpensive computer processing power to businesses of all sizes; the availability of highly accurate geographic data from imaging satellites, high-precision Global Positioning System (GPS) satellites and receivers, and refinements in older mapmaking technologies like aerial photography; and the emergence of a new science, geographic information systems (GIS), which enabled industry firms to create dynamic, highly interactive maps for visualizing, analyzing, and modeling virtually any geographic-related scenario using databases of information.

In the 1990s, the digital mapping industry emerged as a rapidly growing and widely diversified field that found ready application in industries as diverse as education, auto navigation, agriculture, banking, railroading, and telecommunications. Because of its inherent flexibility for a variety of applications, usefulness in making complex combinations of data visually understandable, and reliance on rapidly advancing technology—such as computing power and commercial uses of satellite imagery—it was poised to enjoy healthy growth in the twenty-first century.

ORGANIZATION AND STRUCTURE

Digital maps differ from traditional paper maps in that they are made up of millions of pixels—the tiny colored dots that make up graphic images on computer screens. Where traditional printed maps were painstakingly hand drawn by patient map makers after months and often years of collecting and collating data, the digitized map is often created dynamically out of layers of data and image combinations selected by the user. The digital map used by a farmer, for example, might show an area's various soil types in one view and then, with the click of a mouse, add the various types of crops being grown in the same area. The digital map for a railroad, on the other hand, might at one moment display a map showing the signals, switches, and alternate routes along the track a train is traveling and then, at the click of a mouse, call up a window showing that train's exact longitudinal and latitudinal location based on a satellite signal beamed to the train's cab. With another mouse click, the user might call up a recorded full-motion video image of the terrain and region of track the train is now passing. Unlike the traditional printed map, then, the digital map is often an interactive thing, a visual object that can be changed at the user's discretion to display the information the user wants.

When digital maps are linked to a large database of information that can be used to change the data to be viewed, they are often called "geographic information systems" or GISs. Wedded to a computerized database that permits the user to make queries or perform statistical analysis, GISs enable users to not only view data but to pose sophisticated "what-if" scenarios that can be immediately rendered in visual form.

MAPMAKING MODELS

Digital maps store data in layers of visual information that have been constructed using one of two models: the vector or the raster. The vector model uses standard geometry to plot a map's features—

such as a building or road—using the specific longitudinal and latitudinal position in space each object occupies. This method is ideal for plotting discrete objects or features on a map, but it is also expensive. The raster model, however, is cheaper and more useful for mapping continuously and/or subtly changing features such as soil type. With this model, a map is created by dividing the terrain into equally sized cells and then combining scanned or photographed images of these terrain cells together into a grid. Simply put, the vector method builds maps out of individual points while the raster method builds them out of rectangular blocks of terrain images. With the advent of high-resolution satellites that photograph the earth in precisely this rectangular, cell-by-cell way, the raster method has become the dominant method for digital mapmaking.

BUILDING A GIS

Building a GIS involves five distinct phases. First, and by far the most time consuming part of the digital mapmaking process, the printed (or analog) map is digitized. This can be done using scanners, which create photographic images of the source map and then turn them into the binary ones and zeros a computer can understand, or by using a specialized digitizing table. In this latter process, the paper map is taped to the table, the operator selects an object on the map to digitize, and then traces it with a pen-like instrument that reads or converts the object into digital information. Since a typical map has anywhere from 5,000 to 10,000 objects, digitizing is a laborious and expensive process that has traditionally been outsourced to countries in developing parts of the world.

The second stage in making a GIS is manipulating the newly digitized geographic data so it conforms to the needs of the mapmaker. For example, an analog map converted into digital data may need to have its scale (or degree of accuracy) adjusted, or the mapmaker may decide that some of the information included on the original analog map is irrelevant and can therefore be deleted.

In the third stage, a database management system (DBMS) is used to store, organize, and manage the digitized map data. The most popular DBMS is the "relational" method, which allows data to be stored in rows and columns of tables so different types of data can be compared and combined.

The fourth stage in the construction of a functioning GIS is the "query and analysis" phase: the posing of questions to the geographic database so that certain views or maps of information are displayed or

hypothetical situations explored. It is at this stage that the digital map truly becomes a GIS, offering customized maps that answer or visualize the user's questions. Two common types of analysis are "proximity analysis" and "overlay analysis." In a proximity analysis, the user might ask the GIS how many switches or signals separate a train from the next station. In an overlay analysis, however, the user might ask the GIS to integrate two different types of data—or "data layers"—such as all the road crossings, as well as all the switches that separate a train from the next station. Once the analysis is complete, the final stage of the GIS process occurs—the requested information is displayed graphically.

RELATED TECHNOLOGIES

A GIS involves several related but distinctly different technologies, all of which may be used to create the GIS. "Desktop mapping" programs are GISs that have been tailored for the desktop PC and therefore have more limited data management and customization features than GIS. Computer-aided design (CAD) systems are often used by architects, engineers, and builders to create designs and plans, but lack the data management and analytical features of GISs. Remote sensing and the Global Positioning System (GPS) are one aspect of the data gathering arm of GIS: using cameras or radar, for example, to generate digital images of the earth that can be used in a GIS. GPS is a network of orbiting satellites and earthbound receivers developed by the U.S. Department of Defense to provide users with pinpoint time and position information from anywhere on the globe. While the GPS can provide a GIS with the specific location data to create highly accurate digital map databases and in real time, it cannot provide the context ("What's over the next hill?") that a good GIS offers. Another source of data for GIS is photogrammetry—the use of aerial photographs to provide geographic images. GPS differs from photogrammetry in at least two important respects: GPS requires that the user actually be at the location whose coordinates the GPS satellites provide; photogrammetry does not provide location coordinates, but can provide remote imaging of inaccessible places.

INDUSTRY SEGMENTS

The digital mapping and GIS industry consists of four segments: services, hardware, software, and data. The services segment—which generates about one-fifth of the industry's revenues worldwide—is comprised of firms that offer GIS-related consulting, GIS system integration, analog-to-digital conversion, photogrammetry and orthophotography, and satellite imagery. Consulting firms such as UGC Consulting and PlanGraphics provide project direction for companies trying to implement GISs, as well as project feasibility studies, GIS database design, and GIS project management. System Integrators (Intergraph, for example) design and build entire GIS systems by integrating the often proprietary or standalone GIS products of software, hardware, and database vendors: they make a customer's GIS components work together. The conversion services firms convert or digitize data so it can be used within the digital GIS environment. These firms may fix errors or omissions in the primary or analog data, or assure that the conversion is clean and accurate. Because it involves the snail-paced digitization process, this segment of the GIS services industry is highly labor-intensive and therefore lucrative. Unfortunately for these firms, however, conversion generates little repeat business—data only needs conversion once. Moreover, as the world moves inexorably toward digital-only mapping, prospects for future growth in the data conversion market are slim.

The photogrammetry and orthophotography segments of the GIS services transform aerial photos into clean, sequenced map data. Photogrammetry might be considered "the science of surveying terrain from the air" and orthophotography as "the process of digitizing aerial photos." In particular, orthophotography involves smoothing out the distortions that inevitably arise from taking aerial photos of terrain so that the resulting image has a resolution of one meter (sharp enough, that is, to identify objects one meter in size or larger). Both photogrammetry and orthophotography firms must have expensive equipment and a highly skilled workforce, and they generally offer services only in the geographic regions covered by their photo archives. Nevertheless, the photogrammetry segment (which includes firms like Analytical Survey Inc. and Intera Information Technologies Corp.) is the most profitable sector of the GIS services industry.

The last segment of the GIS services industry is satellite imagery. A relatively new field, satellite imagery arose only after the conclusion of the Cold War made it possible for high-resolution spy satellites to seek commercial markets. By offering extremely fine-grained images for customers building digital maps, satellite imagery firms pose a threat to the aerial photo (photogrammetry) segment of the industry. (Also see the essay in this book entitled Satellites.)

The hardware—computers, workstations, and peripherals like printers and scanners—used in the digital mapping and GIS industries is manufactured mainly by large computer equipment firms like IBM, Hewlett-Packard, Digital Equipment, and Unisys. However, a few industry-specific firms like Intergraph and Trimble Navigation also manufacture workstations and GIS-related hardware.

The software segments of the digital mapping and GIS industries produce design or mapmaking software used to create digital maps or to manipulate and display them. The customers of this industry segment have traditionally been the industries—energy, utilities, railroads, and governments—whose mapping needs were such a vital part of their business that they had no choice but to buy the expensive, highly specialized software products that were once the sole niche of industry firms. With the rapid emergence of powerful desktop computers, however, the digital mapping software segment began to ply its wares to a wider marketplace: mainstream business and consumers. A host of software firms in the 1990s offered relatively inexpensive digital mapping products that allowed users to insert maps into their publications, multimedia presentations, animation, and Web sites. Among these firms were companies such as Autodesk, Inc., Eagle Point Software, MapInfo Corp., and Magellan Geographix. By the late 1990s, some of these firms offered digital maps via the traditional CD-ROM format and through electronic commerce sites on the World Wide Web. Similarly, high-quality maps were made available in such popular desktop graphics formats as Adobe Illustrator, Photoshop, Macromedia Freehand, and CorelDraw.

APPLICATIONS

Though the idea of integrating and displaying complex data on digital maps is several decades old, it was only with the rapid increases in computer processing power in the 1990s that business geographics (the use of digital mapping databases for business applications) reached the mainstream business world. When it did, the number and variety of applications for GIS grew by leaps and bounds. By some estimates, 85 percent of all businesses have some geographic component, and in the 1990s a tidal wave of GIS innovation arose to capitalize on the need. In agriculture, for example, GIS technology is used to find the best soils for growing crops; to plan and optimize shipping routes for transporting food and agricultural chemicals and fertilizers; to monitor and analyze crop production trends; to rate and market crop insurance policies; and to plan the application of chemicals or pesticides. In the late 1990s, more than 80 countries worldwide used GIS technology for agronomy and food planning purposes.

In banking and finance applications, GIS is used to ensure compliance with federal lending regulations; to maintain geographic distribution information on ATMs or competitors' locations; to create demographic profiles of existing and prospective customers; and to perform site analysis studies to locate branches at the best possible locations.

In police work and public safety, GIS is used to optimize the computer-aided dispatch of emergency vehicles through route planning and in-cab navigation systems; to track police and fire vehicles in real time as they respond to emergencies; and to analyze crime incidence records with map displays to learn and predict crime patterns. Firefighters also use digital maps to give them valuable information about hydrant and fire station location, hazardous materials hotspots, and building occupancy. Disaster planning agencies use GIS to create on-the-spot emergency action plans to help evacuate a region, track damaged structures for repair, or generate computer models to predict the behavior of natural disasters like floods and tornadoes.

Electric utilities use digital mapping and GIS to manage their "call-before-you-dig" telephone systems for warning construction crews of buried power lines. They also use them to determine the appropriate rates for the sale of excess energy to other utilities, to automate equipment-inventorying procedures, and to map out the "joint use" of utility poles by telecommunications firms. Similarly, oil and gas pipeline firms employ digital mapping technology to perform market analysis, manage risk, and analyze complex pipeline routes so as to take into account environmentally sensitive areas and land-use conflicts, and to make appropriate decisions regarding terrain and geology.

The federal government has historically been quick to adopt digital mapping technology and, in the late 1990s, was running approximately 250,000 GIS applications annually, from disaster planning and natural resource preservation to traffic planning projects and the planning and tracking of census statistics. Other industries that have found uses for digital mapping include petroleum (analyzing the placement of filling stations), customer-service businesses (automating call center responses), and railroads (tracking train deployment and safety).

BACKGROUND AND DEVELOPMENT

Although the science of mapmaking can be traced back to such pioneers as Ptolemy, Eratosthenes, Mercator, and Cassini, its modern development really be-

gan with the invention of the airplane at the turn of the century. To be sure, the invention of printing enabled maps to be widely disseminated for the first time, and the application of mathematical and statistical methods introduced greater accuracy, but the airplane enabled mapmakers to map previously unknown regions. Commercial aerial surveying was pioneered by industrialist Sherman Fairchild after World War I. After the end of World War II, military surveillance techniques were adapted for use in civilian mapmaking and the science of photogrammetry began to come into its own.

In the 1960s the first rough computer maps came into use, and industries such as energy, utilities, and the railroads—as well as the federal government—were employing computerized maps for such purposes as plotting pipeline routes, tracking population movements, and mapping the mineral content of geologic formations. Because computing power was still an expensive commodity, however, it took several millions of dollars just to create a customized map showing, for example, piping networks or infrastructure. Government offices and utilities could not afford to do without such mapping data, however, and still comprised three-quarters of the digital mapping industry's customer base well into the mid-1990s.

The U.S. spy satellite program of the 1950s and 1960s bore fruit for the digital mapping industry in 1972 when the National Aeronautics and Space Administration (NASA) initiated the Landsat program to survey the Earth with multispectral scanner technology, a development that marked the beginning of the systematic use of space-based remote sensing as a source of raw data for cartographers. With Landsat, mapmakers could create rapidly updateable, photo-based "thematic" maps for such specialized needs as mapping water pollution, mineral deposits, or crop health. For many years Landsat and its French counterpart (SPOT) were the only source of space-based imagery available to private mapping firms.

The birth of the desktop computer and advances in microchip manufacture and design in the late 1970s and early 1980s transformed the landscape of digital mapping. With computer processing power doubling every eight months (a phenomenon that came to be known as Moore's Law), previously impractical digital mapping applications were suddenly possible. By 1984 GIS-based vehicle navigation systems were already being used in marine and aeronautic applications, and companies like Motorola and Rockwell Automotive were hard at work on navigation systems for automobiles. In 1985 digital mapmaker Etak introduced its "Navigator" map display and vehicle positioning system, and rival Navigation Technologies demonstrated a similar routing system, "Driver-Guide," the same year. By the mid-1990s such systems were already a reality at rental car companies such as Hertz and Avis.

By 1986, Thomas Bros. Maps, the largest mapmaker in California, had sensed the change afoot in the mapping industry and began digitizing its entire map collection. With the launching of the new trade magazine *GIS World* in the late 1980s, it was clear that a new industry—digital mapping—had come into its own. For the first time in history maps were suddenly easy and inexpensive to make. By the late 1990s a typical government mapping project, such as mapping a state's population distribution, could be completed in a matter of weeks, or even days. Moreover, digital cartographers began systematizing the analytical foundations of the new GIS science by striving for standards for calculating distances and technical parameters like terrain surface slope and aspect.

In 1990 the American Automobile Association, General Motors, the Federal Highway Administration, and the Florida Department of Transportation launched a project known as TRAVTEK to develop one of the most important early demonstrations of onboard navigation and route guidance for the auto industry. The geographic data was provided by Navigation Technologies and Etak, both "street-level" digital map database providers. By 1995 Navigation Technologies had thoroughly mapped all the major metropolitan areas of the United States for the system, and Etak had completed a less detailed mapping of the rest of the country.

The collapse of the Soviet Union in the early 1990s opened a potentially major new niche for the digital mapping industry. As Russia began privatizing its military satellite system, its high-resolution earth images suddenly became available to commercial mapmakers. Not to be outdone, the U.S. government responded by permitting U.S. firms to plan high-resolution satellite systems for commercial mapping purposes. In 1995 the U.S. Navy also declassified its secret radar charts, and two American entrepreneurs began preparing a comprehensive, high-accuracy map of the ocean floor for sale to nonmilitary markets. By the late 1990s three U.S. companies had announced plans to launch and operate small commercial satellites they claimed would deliver images at resolutions of three meters or less for a few hundred dollars an image and could be used for urban planning, agricultural and environmental monitoring, making and revising maps, and even vacation planning.

A digital image of Earth. (Digital Stock.)

By the early 1990s major corporations such as McDonald's and Dunkin' Donuts were already using GIS technology to determine where to build restaurants. At the same time, Cincinnati began reducing mapping costs by sharing its GIS with local utilities. Further, the U.S. Bureau of Land Management and the U.S. Forest Service were each discussing allocating $1 billion on GIS public-land information services, and the U.S. Census Bureau was selling a rough digital city block map of the United States for $10,000. By early 1992, map users in the United States could choose from 100 different geographic databases, plotting everything from streets to soil types, and from over 200 different software packages.

The emergence of the GPS (originally developed by the U.S. government to guide missiles) as a consumer product in the late 1990s enabled industry firms to offer real-time, high-precision mapping information for customers, and GPS receivers were quickly integrated into some auto navigation systems. At this same time, the former Federal Defense Mapping Agency had been reorganized as the National Imaging and Mapping Agency, with a new mandate to promote the application of formerly military mapping capabilities for the commercial market.

PIONEERS IN THE FIELD

Among the pioneering firms in the digital mapping industry include Etak Inc., Navigation Technologies, ESRI, and GeoSystems Global. Founded in 1983 by Stanley Honey, Etak produced the world's first automated car navigation system, the Navigator, in 1985 and has licensed navigation technology to some of the biggest makers of automotive dashboard electronics. Though the sales of Navigator were limited to business customers such as restaurant guides, taxi companies, and vendors of PC mapping software, Etak—a subsidiary of Sony Corp.—was the only major company in the digital map business prior to 1985. By 1999 the company offered a GPS-based map generator to run on notebook computers with coverage across the United States, and traffic report services via cellular phones and cellular-phone connected screens.

A pioneer in the route guidance segment of the digital mapping industry was Navigation Technologies (NavTech) founded in Sunnyvale, California, in 1985. In 1988, NavTech partnered with Holland-based electronics giant Philips to develop its auto navigation system, in which it had invested more than $200 million. By the late 1990s it had accumulated detailed databases for North American and European metropolitan areas covering a population of 350 million, and less detailed coverage of sub-metropolitan areas representing another 270 million. The company supplies vehicle databases for factory or dealer installed systems on vehicles from such makers as Acura, BMW and Mercedes Benz. Aftermarket systems using NavTech databases include the Phillips Carin Navigation System and Hertz NeverLost.

ESRI (Environmental Systems Research Institute) was founded in 1969 in Redlands, California, by Jack and Laura Dangermond. In the 1970s, ESRI concentrated on developing GIS applications used in urban renewal projects. In the 1980s, ESRI became a digital mapping/GIS software company and, in 1981, released ARC/INFO, the first modern GIS integrated into a single system. ARC/INFO remained the company's flagship product and was modified to work in UNIX, Windows NT, and network computer environments. In the early 1990s ESRI unveiled ArcView GIS, a mainstream desktop mapping and GIS tool; ArcData to provide users with ready-to-use GIS data; and ArcCAD, which integrated computer-aided design (CAD) and GIS technologies. ESRI released its first consumer mapping product in 1994. In the late 1990s it positioned itself to capitalize on the "live mapping" technology made possible by the Internet and, in 1998, enjoyed sales of roughly $280 million. Ranked in 1998 as the world's forty-eighth largest provider of software by *Software Magazine,* in 1999 the company contributed software and support to federal and local livability programs and to the National Oceanic and Atmospheric Sustainable Seas Expeditions project.

GeoSystems Global of Mountville, Pennsylvania, was founded in 1967 as the cartographic services division of publisher R.R. Donnelley & Sons. In the 1970s and 1980s it expanded into customized mapping services for textbook, atlas, travel, directory, and reference publishers, and became the largest custom mapping business in the United States. In 1989 Donnelley formed a joint venture with Spatial Data Sciences and two years later acquired selected assets of Spatial Data to form GeoSystems. In 1992 GeoSystems released GeoLocate, its flagship mapping and routing software program, and in 1993 Donnelley's Cartographic Services and GeoSystems were merged as GeoSystems to form a total GIS services company. In 1996 GeoSystems entered the online publishing business with MapQuest, the first interactive mapping service on the Internet. MapQuest immediately became a World Wide Web hotspot as consumers used the service to call up "zoomable" maps of locations throughout the United States. In 1999 the company changed its name to Mapquest.com and moved its headquarters to New York City, reflecting an increased commitment to the Internet.

CURRENT CONDITIONS

As early as 1991, the U.S. GIS industry was enjoying revenues of $3.5 billion, with Pentagon spending alone accounting for one-fourth of that figure. A 1992 estimate predicted that the demand for GIS products and services by utility companies and local governments alone ensured that the GIS industry would grow 25 percent annually through 2002—with even faster growth if applications could be found to entice corporate customers and consumers. By the mid-1990s the GIS market was the one of the fastest-growing computer application markets, with an estimated value of $2.0 billion in 1995 and an 18 percent annual growth rate. In 1995 the remote-sensing arm of the digital mapping/GIS market (which included both satellite imaging and traditional aerial photography) was valued at $550 million, with potential growth to $2.7 billion by the year 2000. In 1999 the GIS software market alone was valued at $1.0 billion worldwide. Furthermore, the U.S. Department of Commerce estimated worldwide sales of GPS-related products would reach $8.0 billion in the year 2000, and by 2003 could exceed $16.0 billion

In the late 1990s growth in the digital mapping and GIS industry was expected to be fueled by applications in banking, insurance, transportation, and telecommunications, and such traditional map-using industries as environmental monitoring, utilities, and resource management. By 1999 the number of in-vehicle navigation systems shipped totaled 90,000 in North America and 900,000 in Europe. Within the industry, database formats will shift toward a universal CD-ROM format, allowing databases to be interchangeable between different manufacturers' products.

INDUSTRY LEADERS

Based in Troy, New York, MapInfo Corp. generated sales revenue of $60.6 million for the 1998 fiscal year. Its products, such as MapInfo and MapBasic, enables insurance companies and sales organizations to translate complex corporate data into easily understood maps to simplify the process of performing marketing analysis, selecting business sites, managing corporate assets and risk, and optimizing delivery routing and logistics. MapInfo sells its own digital maps to customers who can then overlay their own data on them for visual presentation and analysis, and manipulate it on any of the 400 software applications compatible with MapInfo's products. It also sells "geo-coding" products that assign latitude and longitude coordinates to corporate data containing geographic references so that data can be displayed accurately on a map. Its "MapXsite" enables Web developers and Internet service providers to create Web pages in which a company's various locations can be displayed. It was used, for example, on the Web site of the Wal-Mart discount retail chain to help consumers find the nearest Wal-Mart store. In addition, "SpatialWare" enables users to store and manage "spatial data" within traditional relational databases such as those manufactured by Oracle, Informix, and IBM.

Intergraph Corp., based in Huntsville, Alabama, is a diversified producer of hardware, software, consulting, and support services for the information technology (IT) field. Its Industry Solutions Division produces automated hardware, software, and consulting services to the process and building industries, to the infrastructure industry (including transportation, utilities, and state and local governments), and to the federal government. Its Computer Systems Division supplies high-performance graphics workstations and

PCs, three-dimensional graphics subsystems, servers, and other hardware products. Sales revenues in 1998 topped $1 billion. In 1998 sales of its GIS analysis software grew by 62 percent, and by mid-1999 Intergraph had added $30 million in new contracts to its list of major contracts worldwide.

Analytical Surveys, Inc. (ASI), produces high-accuracy digital maps that are integrated with databases in GIS applications to store, retrieve, analyze, and dis-

More On **PRISON LABOR THREATENS THE MAPPING INDUSTRY**

As the digital mapping industry emerges so does a growing threat to that industry—the use of prison inmates for mapping services. Federal and State prison industries initially contracted mainly for government service organizations, still the main market for many mapping companies. Expanded prison industries now offer geographic data conversion services to commercial markets as well.

Two of these, Texas Department of Criminal Justice, serving the Texas Department of Transportation and Texas counties, and the Unigroup at the Oregon Department of Corrections, have impacted local mapping companies. The latter group advertises to state and other governments, as well as private businesses. As a result, some Oregon mapping service providers have closed divisions or shut down entirely because of the loss of a market for their services.

On April 21, 1999 John M. Palatiello, Executive Director of the national trade association Management Association for Private Photogrammetric Surveyors (MAPPS) testified before the Subcommittee on Oversight and Investigations Committee on Education and the Workforce U.S. House of Representatives. He criticized the use of prisoners for mapping services based on the U.S. Justice Department's ruling that the current Federal law prohibiting interstate commerce does not apply to services.

Palatiello argues that mapping is part of the architect-engineer service industry, as evidenced by the states' moving toward professional licensing of mapping practitioners. Federal law requires agencies to award architect-engineer service contracts to competent and qualified firms rather than simply awarding contracts to the lowest bidder.

He criticizes the practice, asserting that using inmates for technical mapping services is questionable to public interest, since public welfare and safety is dependent on the quality of work performed. Inmates may have access to civil information such as homeowner data, property appraisal and tax assessment information. Such access could provide the opportunity for undesirable use of the private information.

play information about the characteristics of utilities networks, natural resources, transportation systems, and residential and commercial communities. ASI creates maps using aerial photography, ground surveys, and existing printed maps. It also focuses on four aspects of the GIS business: digital mapping of physical plants such as power generation facilities; photogrammetric mapping for utilities using aerial photos that have been processed to remove distortions; cadastral mapping showing property lines, property zoning, and use restrictions for local governments; and digital orthophotography for creating high-accuracy maps that look like aerial photos. In 1998 ASI had revenues of more than $88 million, up 117 percent from 1997. The company continued to grow as it signed record contracts valued at $28 million in its first quarter of 1999, only to top it in the second quarter with new contracts valued at over $35 million.

AMERICA AND THE WORLD

In the late 1990s the U.S. digital mapping industry was the world's largest, and its long history of government and private initiatives in GIS, digital mapping, and satellite sensing technologies gave it a competitive edge in the world market. Nevertheless, the United States was estimated to account for only one-quarter of the total world demand for GIS-related products and services. Although the industry did not really begin to grow until inexpensive but powerful computer processors emerged in the 1980s and 1990s, as early as 1993, worldwide revenues for computerized mapping, including software, hardware, and services, were estimated at $2.3 billion, and by the late 1990s it employed hundreds of thousands worldwide.

Despite the lead enjoyed by the U.S. digital mapping industry, however, several world regions were also at the cutting edge of GIS technologies. Japan, for example, quickly embraced auto navigation technology and, by the mid-1990s, more than a million Japanese cars had already been manufactured with navigation systems. Indeed, in 1995 alone 500,000 Japanese cars rolled off assembly lines with "in-vehicle" navigation already installed. Europe had also been a leader in the use of digital mapping to aid auto navigation, led by companies like European Geographic Technologies (EGT) and Tele Atlas. Germany was the first country in the world to complete a full mapping of its roadways for integration into in-vehicle navigation systems, and Germany's BMW was the first European car company to offer navigation technology as an option.

As early as 1974, Great Britain had played a major role in pushing digital mapping technology by launching, under the auspices of its Ordnance Survey (the national mapping agency), a complete digital database of all 70 million topographical features of the British Isles. When the mammoth project was completed in 1995, the British government began to explore the option of privatizing the Ordnance Survey—a clear reflection of the worldwide trend toward finding private, commercial uses for previously military or strictly governmental satellite technologies.

Russia also played a major role in the trend toward privatization. When the Soviet Union unraveled in the early 1990s, its previously top secret high-resolution satellite photos became available to commercial international mapmakers. In May 1995, the private Russian company in charge of managing this satellite data reached an agreement with Sweden's Satellitbild to sell two-meter-resolution satellite images to Western buyers. That same year India's IRS-1 six-meter-resolution satellite images became available for commercial use as well. These developments prompted the United States to relax its restrictions on the commercial use of high-resolution satellite images and, by the late 1990s, consortia of international companies were forming ventures to launch commercial imaging satellites for the world market. The U.S. firms Lockheed and Raytheon teamed up with the Japanese firm Mitsubishi to form Space Imaging, which promptly announced plans to launch a one-meter-resolution commercial satellite in 1997. A similar venture between the U.S. firm Ball Aerospace and Japan's Hitachi led to the formation of EarthWatch in the same period, which launched the first commercial satellite in 1997, and then declared that it had lost contact by mid-1998. EarthWatch had plans underway to launch its two high-resolution satellites in late 1999, backed by $50 million in investments.

RESEARCH AND TECHNOLOGY

Advances in digital mapping technology in the late 1990s centered around the standardization of the map objects that comprise the content of digital maps, new applications for digital mapping technology, the growth of the Internet as a platform for "live" interactive mapping, and the likelihood that high-resolution military-quality satellite images would soon become available to consumers and businesses alike. The profusion of digital mapping platforms in the 1990s and concerns over how to ensure the integrity of digital maps spurred the digital mapping industry to undertake its largest research project ever in an attempt to find objective guidelines for communicating map data. Such guidelines would include standardized or codified classification techniques for grouping map data "attributes" and logic-based systems for selecting the right graphic symbols to represent different types of map data.

The "mainstreaming" of automotive route guidance/navigation systems in the United States in the late 1990s depended on both the completion—and continual updating—of a highly reliable database for every route in the country, and a more affordable price. The Internet seemed to offer an increasingly natural environment for digital mapmakers, and the growing availability of such mapping technology on the World Wide Web was regarded as one of the key factors in the eventual emergence of a true "electronic yellow pages," in which users could not only search out addresses and phone numbers, but also detailed maps pointing out the best routes to a business. High-precision satellite images available for only a few hundred dollars came closer to reality in the late 1990s as 11 companies were given licenses for consumer GIS satellite systems, some with resolutions as sharp as 85 centimeters. A complete high-resolution mapping of the world, however, remained an unaccomplished goal by 1998 when, according to the National Imaging and Mapping Agency, still less than 10 percent of the earth had been mapped with 10-meter or better resolution.

An Electronic Chart Display and Information System was being developed for maritime navigation, which combined GPS coordinate readings with computer charts displaying water depths, coastlines, lighthouses, buoys, and other nautical objects, to tighten the "resolution" of maritime navigation accuracy beyond that offered by GPS alone. Meanwhile, the Census Bureau readied DADS (data access dissemination system), an improved data collection, analysis, and mapping system, for the year 2000 census.

FURTHER READING

"About ESRI." *ESRI Home Page,* 5 May 1999. Available from http://www.esri.com.

Analytical Surveys Inc. Home Page, 5 May 1999. Available from http://www.anlt.com.

"Analytical Surveys Reports More Than $35 Million in Contracts Signed During Fiscal Second Quarter." Indianapolis: Analytical Surveys Inc., 8 April 1999. Available from http://www.anlt.com.

"Analytical Surveys Reports Record Forth Quarter and Year-End Results." Indianapolis: Analytical Surveys Inc., 8 April 1999. Available from http://www.anlt.com.

Barkow, Tim. "Ground Truth." *Wired,* December 1995.

Biederman, Patricia Ward. "Fans Hail Map-Making Revolution." *Los Angeles Times,* 26 January 1997.

Caldwell, Douglas R. "GIS and GPS: A Marriage Made in the Heavens." *The Map Report,* 1995. Available from http://www.maptrade.org.

"The Delight of Digital Maps." *Economist,* 21 March 1992.

"EarthWatch Forges Ahead Without EarlyBird 1 Satellite." Longmont, CO: EarthWatch Inc., 7 April 1998. Available from http://www.digitalglobe.com/company/news/pr/1998/04-07_ew_forges_ahead.html.

Enge, Per, and Pretap Misra. "Scanning the Issue/Technology: Special Issue on Global Positioning System." *Proceedings of the IEEE,* January 1999. Available from http://teaser.ieee.org/pubs/trans/9902/gps.html.

"ESRI Announces Major Grants for Crime Fighting Software and Data." Redlands, CA: Environmental Systems Research Institute, Inc., 12 April 1999. Available from http://www.esri.com/news/releases/99_2qtr/law_enforce_pr.html.

"ESRI Contributes to National Sustainable Seas Expeditions." Redlands, CA: Environmental Systems Research Institute, Inc., 30 April 1999. Available from http://www.esri.com/news/releases/99_2qtr/seas.html.

"ESRI Lends Helping Hand to Federal/Local GIS Initiative." Redlands, CA: Environmental Systems Research Institute, Inc., 12 April 1999. Available from http://www.esri.com/news/releases/99_2qtr/esri_nsdi.html.

Etak Home Page, 5 May 1999. Available from http://www.etak.com.

"GeoSystems Global Corporation Adopts MapQuest.com Name and Moves Corporate Headquarters to New York." New York: Mapquest.com, Inc., 8 February 1999. Available from http//www.mapquest.com/cgi-bin/ia_find?link=ab-press_020899-1&uid=uyxduos549i6z9gx.

GeoSystems Global Home Page, 5 May 1999. Available from http://www.geosystems.com.

Ginsberg, Steve. "Digital Map Firm Finds Growth Path." *San Francisco Business Times,* 28 July 1995.

Green, Barry, and Erika Bauer. "All Over the Map." *Publish,* April 1996.

"Integraph Announces Partnership with Terrex, Terrain Experts, Inc. to Incorporate 3D GIS Visualization and Provide TerraDev™ for Geomedia(r)." Huntsville, AL: Intergraph Corporation, 5 May 1999. Available from http://www.integraph.com/press99/050599_terrex.asp.

Intergraph Home Page, 5 May 1999. Available from http://www.intergraph.com.

Jacobs, April. "All Roads Lead to the Net." *ComputerWorld,* 8 July 1996.

MapInfo Corporation Home Page, 5 May 1999. Available from http://www.mapinfo.com.

Matzer, Marla. "A Digitized Future." *Forbes,* April 24, 1995, 118-19.

Morton, Oliver. "Private Spy." *Wired,* August 1997.

"NavTech at Forefront of Market Growth for Navigation Products." Rosemont, IL: Navigation Technologies Corporation, 29 September 1998. Available from http://www.navtech.com/coinfo/releases/214.html.

"NavTech Products on the Market." *Navigation Technologies Corporation, Inc. Corporate Web site,* 5 May 1999. Available from http://www.navtech.com/market/mkt_vns_prod.html.

"NavTech Realigns Organization to Reflect Market Trends." Rosemont, IL: Navigation Technologies Corporation, 29 September 1998. Available from http://www.navtech.com/coinfo/releases/211.html.

Schott Consulting. "GIS World Stock Watch." *Schott Consulting and GIS World,* 1996. Available from http://www.schott.com.

―――. "What Is GIS?" *Schott Consulting and GIS World,* 1996. Available from http://www.schott.com.

Sena, Michael. "In-Vehicle Map Display Systems." *The Map Report,* 1995. Available from http://www.maptrade.org.

―――. "In-Vehicle Navigation." *The Map Report,* 1995. Available from http://www.maptrade.org.

―――. "A Look Back to Future Technologies." *The Map Report,* 1995. Available from http://www.maptrade.org.

Shao, Maria. "Mapping Up in Computers." *Boston Globe,* 11 December 1994.

Spicer, William. "Making Money with Digital Maps on the World Wide Web." *The Map Report,* 1995. Available from http://www.maptrade.org.

Vantuono, William. "Mapping New Roles for GIS." *Railway Age,* March 1995.

Wagner, Mitch. "Mapping Software Heads in New Direction." *ComputerWorld,* 15 July 1996.

Wilford, John Noble. "Revolutions in Mapping." *National Geographic,* February 1998.

Young, Jeffrey. "Treasure Maps." *Forbes,* 18 November 1996.

—Paul S. Bodine, updated by Sondra E. O'Donnell

DIGITAL VIDEO DISC

Digital video disc, or digital versatile disc as it is sometimes called, is well on its way to becoming the next digital home-entertainment superstar. This five-inch, CD-like disc offers twice the resolution of VHS for video purposes, never wears out, lets the user change languages at the touch of a button or watch just the ending of a favorite movie, and does not need to be rewound. The newest generation of product offers a 24-bit audio-only format that can be played in a single audio/video unit, while next-generation applications will include recordable video. Although the DVD format is far superior to that of VCRs and CDs, it cannot become the predominant video and audio medium of choice until the issue of competing technologies is resolved.

Uncertainty is therefore the main barrier limiting consumer demand for DVD. People willing to purchase the new technology encounter a problem deciding which DVD format they should buy. Early attempts to establish an industry-wide recording format fell apart when some manufacturers deviated from the initial agreed-on standards and began marketing incompatible products. Consequently, a struggle is under way that is reminiscent of the videocassette recorder wars of the 1970s between VHS and Beta formats. The DVD battle is likely to continue as companies develop and manufacture machines with new formats. In the meantime, potential buyers remain confused, with some choosing to postpone buying the new product until they can be sure they are not opting for technology that will be obsolete in the very near future.

Leading members of the electronics manufacturing and home-entertainment industries have responded by forming alliances aimed at promoting a unified format for the emerging DVD industry. These alliances have been successful in establishing a mainstream retail standard, but a few companies persist in marketing incompatible formats and in some instances distinct parallel technologies.

DVD players have nevertheless posted significant sales growth since they were first introduced in 1997. According to the DVD Video Group, manufacturers shipped 1.4 million DVD players from 1997 to 1998. Shipments for 1999 are expected to top 2 million units, making DVD the fastest-growing new packaged media format in history. Considering that a total of nearly 30 million DVD video titles have been shipped from the time the format was launched through the first quarter of 1999, the stage is set for a new industry standard to emerge—and for VHS videotapes to be stacked in the garage next to the eight-track audiotapes.

The DVD industry produces both digital home-entertainment equipment and the software (i.e., movies) that is played on it. It is the software, in fact, that propels the sales of DVD players and discs. Consequently, electronics companies need the backing of Hollywood studios to sell their hardware. Many of the industry's leaders developed and now manufacture CDs and VCRs, the leading home-entertainment formats on the market today. Some are conglomerates with operations in the both the electronics and the entertainment arenas. Time Warner's list of holdings, including Time Inc., Warner Bros., and Home Box Office, make it the world's largest entertainment and information company. Philips Electronics, the world's third-largest electronics company, owned 75 percent of music leader PolyGram until selling it to Seagram in June 1998. Sony manufactures consumer electronics and also owns Columbia Pictures.

Ever since it began, the DVD industry has been plagued with confusion over exactly who is developing which product. In April 1997, ten major electronics firms created the DVD Forum for the purpose of agreeing on a single format for future-generation DVD. The forum also promotes the industry by defining DVD format specification, issuing DVD format and logo licenses, and providing certification laboratories.

The ten original members of the DVD Forum were Sony, Philips, Toshiba, Time Warner, Hitachi, Matsushita Electric, Pioneer Electronics, Thomson SA, Mitsubishi Electric, and Victor Co. (By mid-1999 the forum had grown to include over 100 companies.) But no sooner had members reached some unity on industry standards than Sony and Philips announced they were developing products that varied from the approved format. Thus, as a concession to those firms that wish to be free to pursue whatever avenue seems promising, forum members are not obligated to develop only those products that are compatible with the DVD format.

The industry has also suffered as corporate players each strive to become the industry leader. A company can reap larger profits by inventing and owning the patent to the DVD format that ends up becoming the world's standard. As a result, many DVD products already on store shelves are incompatible with each other. For instance, first-generation DVD players, a format developed by Time Warner and Toshiba, cannot play Divx movies, a pay-for-view product introduced in 1998. While most firms stand firmly behind a single format, at least one company, Disney, has hedged its bets by releasing movie titles for both the regular DVD and Divx-enhanced DVD players.

DVD's multiple formats create distribution problems as well. When first-generation DVD products became available in 1997, they were sold through retail stores. Additionally, about 100 of Blockbuster Video's 4,000 outlets began renting DVD movies. However, Divx-enhanced equipment and software are only available at Circuit City (one of the format's pioneer backers), *the good guys!* chain of stores, and on the Divx Internet site. It is unlikely that video rental stores will jump on the Divx bandwagon in the near future since the purpose of the format is to allow consumers to buy nonreturnable movie titles. According to an ar-

ticle by Joel Brinkley in the *New York Times,* the country's video-rental retailers dislike Divx because it reduces the traffic in their stores.

BACKGROUND AND DEVELOPMENT

The story of DVD began in the early 1990s with several different groups pursuing development of the new digital format. In search of new ways to release titles from its extensive movie catalog, Time Warner paired up with electronics giant Toshiba. The race began when a competing group formed between multimedia entertainment and electronics heavy-hitters Sony and Philips. Eventually, other big-name technology and computing companies such as Matsushita, IBM, Microsoft, and Intel joined the ranks. In 1995, fearing that the industry was heading toward a winner-take-all situation in the war over competing formats, IBM called for a solution. As a result, the Time Warner-Toshiba product became the industry standard, even though it was not necessarily better. A 1996 article in *Business Week* stated that the reason the Sony-Philips partnership did not win the format war was that "they failed to court the Hollywood film industry."

The Hollywood studios, however, had mixed reactions to the new medium. Some entertainment companies, especially Paramount Pictures and Universal Studios, wanted the DVD format to have stronger antipiracy protection. Not surprisingly, Hollywood's strongest DVD advocates included Time Warner, Sony, and MCA, all companies with ties to electronics firms. Although manufacturers had hoped to market DVDs starting in 1996, those plans were delayed until the piracy issue could be resolved.

Meanwhile, Time Warner remained committed to the DVD format and was in the forefront of the movement to bring it to market. Concerns about piracy still left Hollywood uneasy, however. Finally, in July 1997 *Television Digest* reported that DVD encryption licensing issues had been resolved to the satisfaction of Universal Studios. Consequently, Universal announced they would release 10 DVD movie titles between November 1997 and February 1998. In June 1998, Disney released several titles in the new Divx format, then made a pact with Time Warner the following month for international distribution of its Buena Vista Home Movies.

Satisfied with the new encryption measures, Hollywood finally gave the go-ahead to the DVD format. In April 1997, DVD players and discs hit the stores

A digital video disc (DVD) and DVD recorder. (AP Photo/Jack Dempsey.)

in limited distribution. Retail prices for players generally ranged from $500 to $1,000, while discs cost between $20 and $30. Early releases included movies such as *Close Encounters of the Third Kind, Jumanji, Batman Returns, Driving Miss Daisy,* and *Sleepers.*

In August and September 1997, the industry was rocked by announcements from several core alliance members. First, Sony and Philips reported that they were designing a next-generation recordable DVD that deviated from industry standards. Then came word from retailer Circuit City that they would be promoting Divx (short for "digital video express"), a pay-for-view DVD that was partly incompatible with existing players and discs.

In June 1998, Divx players and discs went on sale in San Francisco, California, and Richmond, Virginia, with 30 movie titles available. A major advertising blitz heralded the new format's national launch in September 1998. By the end of the year, nearly 90,000 Divx-enhanced DVD players had been sold. But the industry's standard DVD player as developed by Time Warner and Toshiba has so far withstood the Divx challenge.

Divx is somewhat like a disposal camera in that it has limited usage. The consumer purchases a Divx movie for about $5 and then has two days from the

time he or she puts the disc into a special Divx-enhanced DVD player (which costs about $100 more than a regular DVD player) to watch the film. After that, the buyer may opt to throw the disc away, recycle it, or renew it for a longer period of time by connecting via modem with a special dial-up service. Critics of the Divx format have pointed to this need for a modem connection as one of its major drawbacks. In addition, Divx discs are not as widely available as regular DVD discs.

Meanwhile, sales of the first-generation DVD players and discs rapidly gained momentum. By the spring of 1999, two years after their debut, the DVD Video Group estimated that 1.6 million DVD players had been sold. (By comparison, in the first two years that VCRs were on the market, sales reached 200,000 units.) As cited by eUniverse, Inc., researchers predict sales of nearly 9 million players by the end of 2000, with DVD-Video sales at an estimated $1.3 billion in 2000 and $2.9 billion in 2002.

Despite such rosy predictions, the industry still faces an uphill climb. Although DVD offers better resolution and sound over rival formats, it has to contend with the more than 90 million VCRs in use as well as the more than 550 million CD players and 11 billion discs that have been sold since their introduction in the early 1980s. The DVD format must also deal with competition from upcoming technology such as Super Audio CD (SACD) and digital cable TV.

CURRENT CONDITIONS

The DVD players now popular are in the form of video players and units analogous to the CD-ROM drive on personal computers, but with far greater storage capacity. They offer superb picture resolution and give viewers several options such as widescreen or fullscreen format and alternate soundtracks that can include special commentary. Special recording techniques allow films to look even better on DVD than in theaters. When Disney released the animated feature "A Bug's Life" on DVD in 1999, the original computer data was directly channeled onto the DVD edition, producing picture quality superior to the film version. Another advantage of DVD players is that they can play ordinary CDs.

Notably lacking, however, is a unified format for DVD with rewritable capabilities. Electronics companies have proposed a variety of incompatible formats, prompting apprehension among consumers. For its part, the DVD Forum has not been entirely successful in its attempts to control the type of products that are released.

In early 1999 a group of manufacturers called the Optical Storage Technology Association (OSTA) announced plans to devise a common format in an effort to promote the development of a rewritable DVD. Competing for that new market were two main technologies, DVD-RW, backed by Sony and Philips, and DVD-RAM, backed by Hitachi and Matsushita. A third format, DVD-R, was promoted by Pioneer for the professional recording market. The OSTA group's main goal is to create a specification that allows any rewritable DVD disc to be read by any player.

Complicating the issue of rival DVD-Audio formats is Sony's Super Audio CD (SACD) player, introduced in Japan in early 1999 at a cost of about $4,100 per unit. The SACD player plays only SACD discs. Backed by Sony and Philips, it may reach U.S. markets by 2000, but it has met with resistance from music companies concerned about copyright protection. Meanwhile, the DVD-Audio format supported by Matsushita, Toshiba, Pioneer, and others will play its discs on "universal" players for DVD-Video and DVD-Audio discs. The new players will debut at a much more affordable $850 to $1,650 and have the backing of all of the major music labels except Sony Music.

Despite the format conflicts, the DVD market is growing at a strong pace. By mid-April 1999, there were more than 10 million DVD players and DVD-equipped PCs in the market. Companies independent of the major electronics suppliers have brought out their own technologies. For example, Sonic Solutions, of Marin County, California, offers DVD publishing systems for producing music, video, graphics and software for both professional applications and the consumer market. Competitive Technologies, Inc. licenses its laser diode technology to increase durability and performance in DVD drives. The company reported $133,000 in royalties for the technology during the first six months of the 1999 fiscal year and expects substantially higher revenues as the number of DVD-RAM drives approaches an expected 9 million units by 2000.

INDUSTRY LEADERS

Circuit City Stores spearheaded the development of Divx, the pay-for-view DVD that broke ranks with the existing format technology upon its debut in 1998. The actual idea for Divx came from Ziffren, Brittenham, Branca & Fischer, a leading Hollywood law firm. A research and development firm owned by Circuit City then developed the product, and Circuit City invested $100 million to become two-thirds owner of Divx. Other companies committed to the Divx format include Matsushita, Zenith, Thomson Multimedia, Disney, Universal Studios, and Dreamworks SKG. Based in Richmond, Virginia, Circuit City has over 54,000 employees and posted a net income of $142.9 million on total sales revenue of $10.8 billion for the year ending in February 1999. The company operates about 560 Circuit City Stores.

Matsushita is the world's number-one consumer electronics company. Its brand names include Panasonic, JVC, Technics, and Quasar. Matsushita is a core member of the DVD Forum, the group of top electronics firms that is setting the format standards for future-generation DVD products. Matsushita has nearly 276,000 employees and recorded sales revenues of $59.2 billion for the year ending in March 1998. For the same time period, the company reported a net income of $703 million, a growth of almost 37 percent over the previous year.

Philips, a Netherlands-based firm, is the world's third-largest electronics company. Philips has more than 233,000 employees, and 1998 sales revenues were $35.5 billion, down 5.8 percent from 1997. In June 1998, Philips sold its 75 percent stake in music

---

About... THE MANY FACES OF DVD

The most prominent feature of the DVD industry is the multitude of mostly incompatible formats encompassed by the technology. Emphasizing this point, the term "DVD" itself stands for "Digital Video Disc" by some standards and "Digital Versatile Disc" by others. Offering large storage capacity, DVD formats have the ability to replace CD-ROM, audio CD, and videotape as a new single standard, but at present the industry lacks the uniformity necessary for that to happen. The DVD format covers multiple types of media (video, audio, and computer data), falling into three broad categories: DVD-Video, DVD-Audio, and DVD-ROM.

DVD-Video (usually abbreviated to DVD) refers to the format for storage of video information. A DVD player, connected to a TV, can play movies from a DVD disc. Note that this format implicitly includes audio data as well, since movies need both video and audio data. Another related term, Divx, refers to DVD technology in a pay-per-view basis. Divx as a variation of DVD include extra data security in addition to the standard DVD copy protection. In the future, DVD-Video will evolve into "DVD-HD," an even higher capacity standard.

Even though DVD-Video has better than CD audio capabilities, DVD-Audio exists as a separate format. DVD-Audio includes additional features, such as graph-ics per track and higher quality PCM audio, and may not play in all DVD-Video players. An alternative format, the Super Audio CD (SACD) format, refers to discs with two layers: one for traditional CD audio and the other for DVD-Audio storage.

DVD-ROM, like any other technology dealing with personal computers, refers to a collection of related formats. DVD-ROM refers to any of the DVD formats that store computer data, but separate names distinguish the writable versions. The DVD-R (DVD-Recordable) format refers to a write-once disc. DVD-RW (DVD-Rewritable, previously DVD-R/W and DVD-ER) refers to an erasable format. Another erasable format, DVD-RAM only works for discs in a cartridge. Finally, the DVD+RW format is also an erasable format, but is the most compatible of the DVD-ROM formats. Data capacities of any of the DVD-ROM formats should be around 4.7G by the end of 1999.

Clearly, the many variations of DVD hinder the industry, causing confused consumers to wait for a single format that will withstand the test of time. This will probably continue until the technology ages enough for some "standards" to dominate the market. But until then, expect more variations—and more names—of DVD to emerge.

---

company PolyGram to Seagram, a Universal Studios subsidiary, for $10.4 billion. Philips offers mid-range DVD equipment that includes features such as a built-in karaoke machine and a joystick-equipped remote. The firm has paired up with Sony to develop a second-generation recordable DVD that has a different format than the one key industry leaders had previously agreed to support.

Pioneer Electronics, headquartered in Tokyo, is a world leader in audio and audiovisual products. It has more than 20,000 employees. For the year ending in March 1999, the company reported sales of $4.2 billion, a decrease of 4.8 percent over the previous year, and net income of $46.7 million, an increase of 130 percent. Its focus is on producing high-end DVD players that offer a variety of options. For example, Pioneer's model DV-700 can play DVDs, 12-inch laser discs, and CDs. Despite sluggish sales, Pioneer is committed to DVD and is developing an audio-only format.

Sony Corporation, a multimedia powerhouse, has been a major figure in the DVD industry since its inception. Early on, a DVD format developed by Time Warner and Toshiba was favored as the industry standard over one designed by Sony and Philips Electronics. For Sony, this was very much like the situa-tion the company found itself in during the 1970s, when its Betamax VCR format lost to rival VHS after a prolonged struggle. Tokyo-based Sony ended its fiscal year in March 1998 with net income of $1.7 billion, which represented an increase of 48 percent over the previous year. Sales for the company's electronics business declined 0.5 percent overall in the year ending March 1999, due in large part to sluggish economies in Asia and other parts of the world. In contrast, sales in its video category, which includes DVD-Video players, increased 11.3 percent. The company, which has 173,000 employees, reported March 1998 annual sales revenue of $51 billion. By continuing to promote formats incompatible with industry standards for future-generation audio and recordable DVD, Sony is clearly ready to do battle with its competitors.

Disney is a key player in the DVD industry because of the marketability of its movies, which include popular favorites such as *The Lion King* and *101 Dalmatians*. It has also managed to avoid committing itself to just one format by releasing titles for both regular DVD and the new Divx format, thus sidestepping one of the industry's most vexing problems. Disney has interests in Buena Vista Television, Miramax Film Corp., and Touchstone Pictures. The Burbank, California-based company has 117,000 employees and re- ported revenue of $23 billion for the year ending in September 1998. Net income was $1.85 billion, rep- resenting a 6 percent decrease over the previous year. As reported in *Television Digest,* the research firm Sanford Bernstein stated that DVD could provide in- cremental profit growth to Disney.

Time Warner Inc., one of the early proponents of DVD, realized over $50 million worth of DVD-related revenue in 1997, according to Robert Scally in *Dis- count Store News.* By July 1998, the company an- nounced that its total DVD-generated income had reached $110 million since the product first went on sale in spring 1997. The New York-based firm is the world's largest entertainment and information com- pany and has nearly 68,000 employees. Among its holdings are Warner Bros., which produces and dis- tributes movies. Time Warner helped develop DVD hoping to find a new release format for its vast cata- log of movie titles. The company's other holdings in- clude Time Inc., Home Box Office, and Book-of-the- Month Club. Figures for 1998 showed the company's net income decreased 32 percent to $168 million on $14.5 billion in revenue (which was a 10 percent in- crease in revenue over 1997). As reported by *Televi- sion Digest,* research firm Sanford Bernstein found that Time Warner'profits on DVD could range from 4 to 17 percent in the years ahead.

Toshiba, based in Tokyo, developed the indus- try's standard DVD format in a partnership with Time Warner. In addition to DVD players and discs, Toshiba introduced a computer with a DVD-ROM drive in 1997. The company's product line also in- cludes portable PCs, videocassette recorders, and elec- tronic parts such as semiconductors. For the year end- ing March 1998, Toshiba reported net income of $55.1 million, down 90 percent from the previous year, and sales revenue of $41 billion, a decrease of only 8 per- cent over the previous year. During the same time pe- riod, it employed 186,000 workers.

AMERICA AND THE WORLD

The DVD industry operates in a truly global mar- ketplace. Not only are the key players mostly inter- national conglomerates, but the product is expected to be available to consumers throughout the world. Early on, the industry divided the world into five regions, each with its own electronic code. Thus, discs pur- chased in one region cannot be viewed on players from another area. Since Hollywood releases movies in dif- ferent countries on different dates, splitting the world

into five incompatible regions allows Hollywood to maintain control over movie distribution, according to Johnnie L. Roberts in *Newsweek.* One company lo- cated in the United Kingdom has tried to thwart this system by offering DVD players over the Internet that have been modified with custom computer chips to bypass the electronic code so they can play DVD discs from any region.

Initially, there were problems synchronizing the audio hardware and software in the European market. By August 1997, however, companies had solved the problem with an alternative sound system that differed from the one used in the United States. In September 1997, *Television Digest* reported that DVD was set for an overseas launch in early 1998. In July 1998, Dis- ney signed a pact with Time Warner to allow Warner Home Video to distribute 100 DVD movies from Dis- ney's Buena Vista Home Video unit throughout Eu- rope, the Middle East, Africa, and the countries of the former Soviet Union. The pact is scheduled to remain in effect until the year 2000.

The Chinese government has been investing in its own DVD development program to foster a domestic industry. Efforts have focused on laser diode tech- nologies, MPEG-2 decoder development, and im- proved DVD manufacturing capabilities, according to an *EE Times* report. Sales growth is expected to pro- ceed slowly as Chinese consumers face the same prob- lems over competing formats that characterize the U.S. market. Still, demand for the players is expected to in- crease in China, with sales reaching 10 million play- ers annually by about 2002.

RESEARCH AND TECHNOLOGY

DVD offers high-resolution video. The five-inch disk, similar in appearance to a CD but with seven times the storage capacity, can hold up to 133 min- utes of video in standard format, wide-screen format, and letterbox format. Other features include a choice of language soundtracks and subtitles as well as the ability to view scenes from different angles. DVD also has Digital Dolby surround sound for a theater-like experience.

The DVD and DVD-ROM format allows play- back of music, video, and multimedia content. DVD- RAM, which is being developed by several competing groups, will go one step further and allow for record- ing. A forum composed of key industry electronics leaders established a standardized DVD-RAM format that had 2.6 gigabytes of storage on each side of the disc. Only a few months after that agreement was reached, however, Philips, Sony, and Hewlett-Packard began development of a DVD-RAM format that contained up to 3 gigabytes of storage on each side.

Still in the development stages is an audio-only format. To head off potential problems, representatives from the Recording Industry Association of America, the International Federation of the Phonographic Industry, and the Recording Industry Association of Japan have created an International Steering Committee (ISC) to establish an industry standard for DVD audio, according to Brett Atwood in *Billboard*. In order to set a technical standard, the ISC will listen to proposed formats developed by competing alliances. Given the history of the DVD industry, however, it is likely that whatever unified standard the ISC tries to enforce, some companies will nevertheless design and then market conflicting formats.

A standardized digital watermarking technology is being adopted by the major electronics companies that will ease the entertainment industry's concerns about uncontrolled unauthorized copying of copyrighted materials. The electronic watermarks are invisible to the user but will be recognized by consumer digital recorders or PC systems to regulate the hardware's ability to make a copy.

FURTHER READING

"About DVD." Los Angeles: DVD Video Group, 5 April 1999. Available from http://www.dvdvideogroup.com/about/press/040599.html.

Atwood, Brett. "Competing DVD-RAM Formats May Cause Consumer Confusion." *Billboard*, 6 September 1997.

"Betamax Wars All Over Again?" *Business Week*, 29 September 1997.

Brinkley, Joel. "DVD Leads Race for Movie Discs, for Now." *The New York Times*, 6 July 1998.

Brull, Steven V., and Neil Gross. "Sony's New World." *Business Week*, 27 May 1996.

"Competitive Technologies Reports Increased Royalty Growth from Laser Diode Technology Used in DVD-RAM Drives." *Business Wire*, 15 April 1999.

Daly, Steve. "Bug Screen TV." *EW Daily News*, 22 April 1999.

"Digital Video Watermarking Techniques United." Tokyo: Sony Corporation, 17 February 1999. Available from http://www.sony.com/CorporateInfo/News-E/199902/99-0217B/.

"Divx Announces Highly Successful National Launch." Richmond, VA: Circuit City, 7 January 1999. Available from http://www.192.64.204.230/help/pr010799b.html.

"DVD Video Growth Continues During First Quarter 1999." Los Angeles: DVD Video Group, 5 April 1999, Available from http://www.dvdvideogroup.com/about/press/040599.html.

Dvorak, John C. "DVD's New Spin." *PC Magazine*, 18 November 1997.

"eUniverse to Acquire Online DVD Pioneer." eUniverse, 27 April 1999. Available from http://www.euniverse.com/euniverse_corporate.asp?show=press.

"Europe DVD Launch Set for 1998." *Television Digest*, 1 September 1997.

Henricks, Mark. "Let's Get Digital." *Kiplinger's Personal Finance Magazine*, August 1997.

"Little 'Downside Risk' Seen on DVD." *Television Digest*, 1 September 1997.

Liu, Sunray. "China Government Invests in DVD Infrastructure." *EE Times*, 3 December 1998.

Newcomb, Peter. "Geekdom Gone Gaga." *Forbes*, 9 March 1998.

Palenchar, Joseph. "SACD to Battle with DVD-Audio: New Audio Format War Heats Up." *etown.com*, 23 April 1999. Available from http://www.e-town.com/news/articles/audioformats042399jpa.html.

Roberts, Johnnie L. "Home Electronics: The Disc Wars." *Newsweek*, 26 August 1996.

Scally, Robert. "DVD Shows Promise But Still Lacks Foothold in Video Market." *Discount Store News*, 26 January 1998.

"Sonic Solutions Announces DVD Authoring for Under $500: Revolutionary Sonic DVDit! Brings DVD Publishing to the Desktop." *Business Wire*, 21 April 1999.

"Sonic Solutions DVDit! Streamlines DVD Publishing With Panasonic Rewritable DVD Drive; A Single Mouse-Click Turns Corporate Productions into High-Quality DVDs." *Business Wire*, 21 April 1999.

"Study Sees Slow Growth for DVD." *Television Digest*, 4 August 1997.

"Universal on DVD Bandwagon, But Not Disney, Fox or Paramount." *Television Digest*, 14 July 1997.

Wiener, Leonard. "A CD for Movies: DVD Disks Look and Sound Great. So What's the Problem?" *U.S. News & World Report*, 21 April 1997.

Wildstrom, Stephen H. "Here Comes Movies on Disk." *Business Week*, 27 October 1997.

Yoshida, Junko, Terry Costlow, and George Leopold. "Group Hopes to Unify Recordable DVD Factions." *EE Times*, 11 January 1999.

—Katherine Wagner, updated by Sondra E. O'Donnell

DIRECT BROADCAST SATELLITE TELEVISION

INDUSTRY SNAPSHOT

Direct Broadcast Satellite (DBS) television delivers hundreds of television channels to millions of people around the world—many avid movie fans, sports junkies, and couch potatoes. Satellite owners buy slots in space and lease assigned transponder frequencies to service providers, who beam down high-powered signals in a single digital stream to individual reception dishes, some as small as a hubcap. While banned in India and China, DBS served more than 31 million homes in Europe in 1998. Two service providers dominate the U.S. market: DIRECTV, Inc., with 4.8 million subscribers; and EchoStar Communications Corp., with 1 million subscribers. Studies show that 75 percent of DIRECTV's customers have access to cable television, which costs $411 a year on average, but choose to spend $540 a year on average for DIRECTV. DBS programming includes traditional fare from the major cable networks, such as HBO, ESPN and E! Entertainment Television. DBS also offers scores of pay-per-view movies, rock concerts, and sporting events. Records peg the typical DIRECTV subscriber as male, 18-49 years old, with an annual income of at least $40,000.

While DBS claims far fewer subscribers than cable television subscribers, DBS has become the fastest growing technology for television content distribution and one of the most successful commercial applications of satellite communications. Seven million U.S. households subscribed to DBS in 1998. By 2000, industry insiders expect the number of subscribers to reach 10 million or more.

ORGANIZATION AND STRUCTURE

Direct broadcast satellites orbit 22,300 miles above the Earth. At this height, the orbital period coincides with the Earth's daily rotation about its axis. The result is that the satellite seems to hang at a constant position in the sky, allowing the reception dishes to be pointed in a fixed direction and reducing the cost and complexity of the home system.

The rights to telecommunications satellite orbital positions and transmission frequencies are assigned to individual nations by the Geneva-based International Telecommunications Union. The Federal Communications Commission (FCC), which controls U.S. slots, has reserved a portion of the broadcast spectrum and eight orbital positions for DBS. In order to allow higher-powered transmissions for interference-free reception by smaller dishes, the DBS orbital positions are spaced nine degrees apart, rather than two degrees as for conventional communications satellites. While the FCC defines and licenses DBS in terms of this higher-powered service, there is nothing to stop companies from offering direct-to-home satellite television services from conventional satellites using somewhat larger dishes. So in general, DBS has come to mean any direct-to-home television transmission from satellites, and High Power DBS refers to the FCC definition.

Originally, four of the eight DBS orbital positions were intended to serve the eastern United States, with the others serving the West. However, with current technology, three of the positions (101, 110, and 119 degrees west longitude) can transmit to the entire continental United States. Abbreviated "Full CONUS" slots, they are by far the most desirable.

Each orbital slot is assigned 32 transponder frequencies. The number of channels a DBS provider can offer depends on how many transponders the FCC has licensed it to use; generally these rights are purchased at FCC auctions. Each transponder frequency can accommodate a number of channels, depending on how compact the signal can be made using digital compression techniques. This varies with the type of programming. Sports events, with small objects moving quickly against complex backgrounds, can only be compressed three or four to a transponder. A talk show might be able to be squeezed five or six to a transponder. Since film is shot at a slower frame rate than video, it can be compressed still further. With the current mix of program types and compression technology, each orbital position provides about 200 channels from its 32 transponders.

The compression and processing of the signal happen before it ever gets to the satellite. DBS service providers maintain advanced, highly automated broadcast centers that receive programming via standard communications satellites, landlines, and videotape. From the broadcast centers, the material is transmitted to the satellite using large uplink antennas. Taped programming goes through a careful editing and quality control process before transmission, including optimization for digital compression. By contrast, live satellite programming received by the broadcast centers is generally retransmitted immediately, so the quality of the signal is dependent on that of the incoming "feed."

To receive a signal, the customer needs a small dish antenna, generally mounted on the roof. The system also includes a receiving/decoding unit, approximately the size of a VCR. This unit deciphers the signal, which is encrypted for security purposes, and decompresses it. It can only do this for one channel at a time, so watching or recording multiple programs simultaneously would require multiple decoders. The receiver is individually addressable by means of a telephone connection and a "smart card" programmed with a unique serial number. With this capability, DBS providers can activate and deactivate programming options packages, track pay-per-view services, and implement electronic countermeasures to thwart unauthorized access, or "piracy." (Also see the essay in this book entitled Digital Imaging.)

INDUSTRY REGULATION

Television broadcasting is a regulated industry, and Congress and the FCC have attempted to balance the competing interests of cable and DBS, and those industries' relationship with broadcast television. A major advantage other television services have had over DBS is the ability to provide local channels. DBS, with its limited number of satellite transponders, simply does not have the bandwidth to transmit every local station in each of the 211 television markets. Because providers recognize that lack of the local channels is the primary reason people choose not to subscribe to DBS, they are seeking to address the problem in some fashion. By making it easier to integrate local broadcast television received off the air with the DBS service, or by re-broadcasting selected network programming in the larger markets, DBS providers are hoping to attract more subscribers.

The Satellite Home Viewer Act of 1994 stipulates that DBS providers can sell local service only to customers who cannot receive acceptable broadcast television reception off the air and who have not been cable television subscribers within the past 90 days. Local network affiliates have sued to prevent DBS services from re-broadcasting their signals. This situation should be resolved by the end of the 1990s; in April, 1999 the U.S. House of Representatives voted to approve a bill that would give direct broadcast satellite service providers more equal ground on which to compete with cable carriers. "The legislation in H.R. 1554 would offer DBS providers the right to retransmit local signals back into the local markets from which they originated," according to an EchoStar press release.

While the intent of the 1994 law was to protect cable operators in addition to broadcast television, as cable continued to flourish in its monopoly markets, and prices rose several times faster than inflation, regulators began to look to DBS as a counterbalancing force. This expectation has presented problems for DBS pioneer PRIMESTAR, which is owned by a consortium of cable operators. In a bid to go from a conventional, mostly rural service to a major High Power DBS provider, PRIMESTAR sought to team with Rupert Murdoch's News Corp., which had purchased rights for 28 transponders at the Full CONUS 110-degree slot for $682.5 million in 1996. But in May 1998, the U.S. Department of Justice moved to block the deal, concerned that allowing PRIMESTAR's cable operator parents to gain control of a valuable DBS slot would be anti-competitive.

BACKGROUND AND DEVELOPMENT

Satellite dishes have been showing up in backyards for many years, as hobbyists set up receiving stations to intercept traditional analog satellite television downlinks transmitted on the "C-band" as feeds to local stations. But the 10-foot diameter antennas needed to pull in these signals, and the complications of swiveling the big dishes around to track the various satellites, limited the appeal of this technology.

In 1986, the National Rural Telecommunications Cooperative (NRTC) was formed to address a need to provide reliable and affordable services to 25 million residents of rural communities across the United States. DBS was not yet feasible because of high costs and immature compression and encryption techniques. The NRTC approached Hughes, a leader in satellite communications, about a partnership. But Hughes was working on a deal of its own with Australian media mogul Rupert Murdoch, NBC and Cablevision. Called Sky Cable, the project was to provide a 75-channel service, but the partnership collapsed.

By 1993, with some of the bugs worked out of the DBS technologies, the first DBS satellite was launched, and Hughes and NRTC had a deal—one that would attract more than 100,000 rural customers to Hughes' DIRECTV service in its first year. These customers, spread out all over the country, received a basic package of 20 channels using 18-inch fixed dish antennas, and provided much wider exposure than DIRECTV otherwise would have received in a few "rollout" test markets. Provisions in the Cable Act of 1992 assured that programming would be available to DBS.

Meanwhile, PRIMESTAR had established itself as the first direct-to-home service in 1990, operating from a conventional satellite and therefore requiring a larger (three-foot) dish antenna. After Hughes launched DIRECTV as a High Power DBS service in 1994, others followed. In 1995, an improved compression scheme, MPEG-2, increased the number of channels available to provide viewers a full complement of offerings.

Increasing convergence of telecommunications services offers new opportunities for the DBS industry. Most operators are reserving some bandwidth for expansion into data services, such as Internet access. Since DBS signals are sent as digital packets, computer data can be transmitted just as easily as video, and many times faster than over telephone lines. In 1997, Hughes Network Systems launched DirecDuo, a service combining the company's 400 kilobit per second Internet service called DirecPC with its DIRECTV offerings, using a single dish antenna.

DIRECTV scored its most successful offering in 1998. Nearly 700,000 DIRECTV customers bought a Sunday Ticket, paying $159 for the chance to watch every National Football League game of the season. The company split the profits with the NFL.

In June 1998, Unity Motion aired the first U.S. broadcast of High Definition Television (HDTV) programming via DBS. The service later expanded its programming to 24 hours a day, seven days a week, and continues to add channels.

The fastest adoption of direct-to-home digital television anywhere in the world occurred in the United Kingdom. British Sky Broadcasting (BSkyB) signed up more than 350,000 subscribers for its Sky-Digital channel line-up in the first six months following its launch date in October 1998. All totaled during the previous 10 years, the Isleworth, UK-based company signed up 3.6 million DBS subscribers and 2.6 million cable subscribers in the United Kingdom and Ireland.

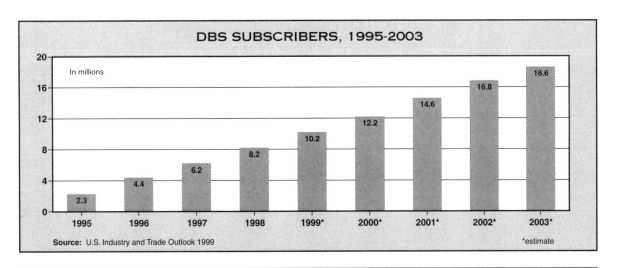

DBS SUBSCRIBERS, 1995-2003

In millions

Year	Subscribers
1995	2.3
1996	4.4
1997	6.2
1998	8.2
1999*	10.2
2000*	12.2
2001*	14.6
2002*	16.8
2003*	18.6

Source: U.S. Industry and Trade Outlook 1999

*estimate

CURRENT CONDITIONS

As of 1999, there were more than 10 million DBS subscribers in the United States, up from 8 million in 1998 and 6 million in 1997. Thousands of viewers sign on every day, and industry analysts predict more than 12 million by the year 2000. However, all the current providers are in heavy debt and operating at a loss. The operating losses are exacerbated by the providers' policy of subsidizing the cost of the customers' receiving equipment down to as low as $100 in order to attract market share. Since none of the receiving systems are compatible, if a provider goes out of business, as AlphaStar has already, customers are left with worthless equipment.

DBS firms are seeking to expand the business by serving new categories of customers. Business Vision, partnered with EchoStar, and Member Direct Television, in cooperation with DIRECTV, are providing business television to thousands of receiving sites. The programming includes tailored business news and information, training programs, industry-specific material, and proprietary packages for large firms.

In another example of DBS companies venturing into new business areas, America Online partnered with DIRECTV, Hughes Network Systems, Philips Electronics, and Network Computer to work on developing "AOL TV." DIRECTV and AOL planned to work together on a service that would combine digital satellite television programming and AOL TV's enhanced interactive TV Internet service. Hughes Network Services planned to design and build a dual purpose set-top receiver, complete with an advanced set-top box for AOL TV provided by Philips. Network Computer's contribution was to provide a complete

software platform for the new service through the company's TV Navigator software.

INDUSTRY LEADERS

Two service providers dominate the DBS industry in the United States. DIRECTV, an El Segundo, California-based subsidiary of GM Hughes Electronics, holds the top spot with 4.8 million subscribers. Littleton, Colorado-based EchoStar Communications comes in second, with about 1 million subscribers.

DIRECTV became the fifth-largest pay television provider in the United States in its first five years of operation. In May 1999, the company acquired 110,000 new customers, a 57 percent increase over May 1998 performance. And for the first five months of 1999, customer growth was up 49 percent over the same period in 1998. In an effort to expand its subscriber base that year, the DBS giant signed marketing agreements with Bell Atlantic, GTE, and SBC Communications that allowed DIRECTV to offer its satellite services to the companies' customers. To gain greater channel capacity and further seal its lead in the market, the company bought United States Satellite Broadcasting for $1.3 billion in 1998 and PRIMESTAR for $1.8 billion in early 1999. Immediately after its buying spree, DIRECTV carried all three brand name DBS services under its umbrella.

The DIRECTV service provides 175 channels from a cluster of three High Power DBS satellites. Its partner, United States Satellite Broadcasting (USSB) of Minneapolis, uses the same satellite cluster to transmit a complementary 25-channel premium movie option. About 2 million DIRECTV subscribers have al-

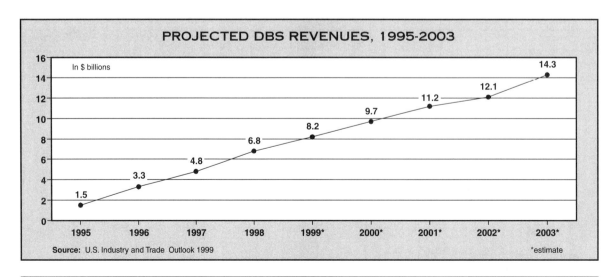

PROJECTED DBS REVENUES, 1995-2003

In $ billions

1995: 1.5
1996: 3.3
1997: 4.8
1998: 6.8
1999*: 8.2
2000*: 9.7
2001*: 11.2
2002*: 12.1
2003*: 14.3

Source: U.S. Industry and Trade Outlook 1999

*estimate

ready signed on for the optional USSB movie package. DIRECTV/USSB is the fastest-growing DBS service, adding some 50,000 subscribers each month. In addition to movies, the service's programming includes extensive professional and collegiate sports coverage, cable channels, and CD-quality audio and pay-per-view (PPV) events. DIRECTV plans to phase out PRIMESTAR service by 2002, adding 2 million mostly rural converts to the DIRECTV subscriber list. The compnay had $1.8 billion of sales in 1998, a 42 percent increase over 1997.

EchoStar Communications started its Digital Information Sky Highway (DISH) Network in March 1996. Like DIRECTV/USSB, it is a High Power DBS provider. EchoStar's market share rose from 20 percent to 24 percent from 1998 to 1999. More indicative of the company's progress was its increase in subscribers, rising from 1 million in 1998 to 2.4 million in 1999, a 96 percent increase. EchoStar transmits more than 120 channels from a Full-CONUS orbital slot, and also owns rights to East Coast and West Coast transponders from which it plans to deliver local data services, foreign language programming and other channels via an additional antenna dish. EchoStar competes by offering lower hardware prices and monthly fees. Unlike DIRECTV, EchoStar can deliver local broadcast channels in major markets. It also has the most "superstation" programming. A six to ten-channel Christian religious service from the East Coast satellite, SkyAngel, is partnered with EchoStar. Echostar had $983 million of sales in 1998, a 106 percent increase over the previous year.

AMERICA AND THE WORLD

Satellite communications is an international business, with satellites orbiting the globe and programming being transmitted from space heedless of national borders. Multinational media companies such as Rupert Murdoch's Australia-based News Corp. seek to expand into new markets. Among U.S. DBS providers, DIRECTV has been most active in pursuing joint ventures and other opportunities abroad.

Canada, Mexico, and some South American countries hold some of the orbital slots over the Western Hemisphere that could service the United States. If any of these choose to auction off transponder rights, U.S. companies can bid for them. Likewise, U.S. companies can potentially service other markets in the Americas from their own slots. Nations may attempt to control the industry by regulating the sale of de-

coders; in 1998 Argentina temporarily halted DIRECTV from competing in its market while it tried to get its own system in place.

Europe has its own active DBS market. Luxembourg-based Société Européenne des Satellites S.A. (SES) operates ASTRA, the leading satellite system, which served more than 74 million homes in Europe in 1999. More than 31 million European homes receive programming directly to a satellite dish via ASTRA. British Sky Broadcasting (BSkyB), the first service provider to offer DBS in the United Kingdom (1989), relies on an ongoing contractual agreement with SES. In 10 years, the Isleworth, UK-based company has amassed 3.6 million DBS subscribers and 2.6 million cable subscribers in the United Kingdom and Ireland, where broadcast television consists of five channels. By holding broadcast rights to the leading soccer leagues in England and Scotland, the British satellite service has also become the largest pay-TV provider.

Asia, home of 60 percent of the world's population, is a tempting target for telecommunications companies, but DBS growth there has been hampered by political and economic conditions. Japan, which can be completely covered from one orbital position and where cable television never really took off due to heavy regulation, has the most advanced satellite technology in Asia. Challenges for Japanese DBS include the Asian financial troubles of the late 1990s, a conservative business environment, and a lack of demand for Japanese-language programming outside of the domestic market. As of May 1998, SkyPerfecTV had more than 700,000 subscribers in Japan, and DIRECTV Japan had topped 100,000.

China is reluctant to allow direct broadcast to its population of 1.2 billion because of political concerns about western influences. Murdoch, whose base in Australia makes his News Corp. a natural contender in Asia and the Pacific Rim, antagonized the Chinese government by declaring that satellite television would undermine totalitarian regimes, and was subsequently constrained to low-profile participation in partnership ventures with Hong Kong and others.

Reacting to the boom in home television sets throughout that region of the world, APT Satellite Holdings Limited stepped up its efforts to secure licenses to offer DBS to homes in China and Southeast Asia. The Hong Kong-based company provides satellite service to 100 countries, mainly serving television stations, local cable operators, and master antenna systems.

In 1997, India, which also feared excessive western influences on its population of almost 1 billion, banned direct-to-home satellite television broadcast services. Amid a furor, which included a lawsuit by News Corp., it declared that the ban would only be temporary, until the government could set up a broadcast authority. A bill to establish the regulatory agency has since been introduced in India's Parliament.

In a short time Sky Network Television Limited has signed up 260,000 subscribers in New Zealand for its five pay-TV channels and analog DBS programming. The Auckland-based company is partly controlled by Independent Newspapers, which is partly owned by Murdoch's News Corp.

Another approach to the bandwidth problem might be to expand it using spot-beam broadcasts to individual markets, although satellites capable of such transmissions in the DBS frequency spectrum did not yet exist as of mid-1998. Capital Broadcasting of Raleigh, North Carolina, plans to provide local programming packages from a satellite with 61 beams by about 2001.

Technological development is also addressing the problem of "rain fade," when thunderstorms and other weather disturbances interfere with the DBS signal. Currently, satellite transmissions are focused to provide more power to wetter regions within the coverage area.

RESEARCH AND TECHNOLOGY

Advanced compression schemes allow multiple streams of programming, along with the ability to control information per transponder frequency, made DBS feasible, and research and development continues in this area. Squeezing down the signal still further would be an advantage, but providers also want to eliminate the occasional blocky digital compression artifacts that some viewers find distracting. With High Definition Television (HDTV) on the horizon, three or four times more bandwidth (or three or four times better compression) will be required to provide the same number of channels. Currently, each DBS provider uses its own format for transmitting the signal. An emerging world standard, DVB, uses MPEG-2 and also attempts to standardize other elements of the system. Still, even DVB-compliant systems from different providers are not interchangeable. (Also see the essay in this book entitled Video Displays.)

In addition to HDTV, demand for local channels drives the push for more bandwidth. Besides improving compression, other areas of technological development include higher-power transponders, which allow more information to pass through existing bandwidth because less error-correcting coding is required. Signal polarization, controlling the orientation of the electromagnetic wave transmissions, is used to isolate adjacent transponder slots and allow more of them within a fixed-frequency spectrum. Statistical multiplexing maximizes the use of existing bandwidth by assigning it upon demand, depending on the information density of a particular program being carried by a channel at a given time.

FURTHER READING

"Consumer Guide to DBS," June 1998. Available from http://www.dbsdish.com/reviews/c_report.html.

Davis, Neil W. "Asia's Communications Market Booms." *Aerospace America,* January 1995.

Gifford, James M. "The 18-Inch Business School." *Satellite Communications,* November 1996.

Hoover's Company Capsules. Austin, TX: The Reference Press, 1999. Available from http://www.hoovers.com.

"India Backtracks on TV Ban." *Wall Street Journal,* 24 July 1997.

Kiernan, Vincent. "Making Satellites More Local." *Satellite Communications,* April 1998.

La Franco, Robert. "The Unlikely Mogul." *Forbes,* November 1998.

Murphy, Beth. "Rural Americans Want Their DIRECTV." *Satellite Communications,* March 1995.

Peterson, Richard R. "Direct Broadcast Satellite: A New Generation of Television in America." 14 January 1998. Available from http://www.dbsdish.com/dbs/a0.html.

Silverstein, Sam. "U.S. Lawsuit May Trigger More Upheavals for DBS." *Space News,* 18 May 1998.

Ullman, Lawrence E. "Bent Pipes in Space." *Stereophile Guide to Home Theater,* Fall 1996.

———. "DSS: The Sky's the Limit." *Stereophile Guide to Home Theater,* Fall 1996.

Warner, Fara. "Murdoch Builds a Beachhead in China." *Wall Street Journal,* 12 December 1997.

—Sherri Chasin Calvo, updated by Denise Worhach

ELDER DAY CARE

The adult day care industry represents the broad category for establishments engaged in providing a wide variety of individual and family social, counseling, welfare, or referral services. These services were evolving rapidly at the end of the twentieth century. They might include home care by someone other than family members. Geriatric care management is a field that emerged to accommodate such services and was new to the area of general care in the 1990s. Other forms of elder day care might involve travel to a care facility on a daily or periodic basis. *Entrepeneur* magazine cited adult day care as one of the 14 hottest businesses for 1998.

ORGANIZATION AND STRUCTURE

Adult day care programs are offered in senior centers, community centers, or churches. These programs are sometimes attached to hospitals or other health care institutions. In addition, residential care facilities might provide these services should the client's care needs extend to mental and other chronic care health concerns. The 1989 *National Adult Day Center Census,* compiled by the National Council on Aging's National Adult Day Services Association (NADSA), found that the adult day care centers that responded served a high proportion of individuals with disabilities who preferred to stay in their homes rather than enter nursing homes. In 1997, NADSA compiled updated statistics based on its 1989 survey. The latter survey indicated that approximately 80 percent of the country's 4,000 adult day care facilities

were nonprofit, 10 percent were state-run, and 10 percent were for-profit institutions. Adult day care centers gave participants opportunities for social interaction and exercise along with hot meals. More than half also provided transportation to and from the home; nursing and medical services; physical, occupational, and speech therapy; counseling and social services; and personal care services such as grooming and laundry.

Inter-generational day care facilities, where both children and elders are cared for, were on the rise by the end of the 1990s in the United States. These programs often began with inter-generational programming ventures in nursing homes and continued to expand. At a time when it was not uncommon to live across the country from other family members, grandparents and grandchildren often missed out on the interaction that was taken for granted only a generation ago. Older adults and children through school age were all beneficiaries of these expanded services. One non-profit company, Bi-Folkal Productions of Madison, Wisconsin, provided programming resources to many such facilities, as well as community programs based on the inter-generational concept. As this concept continued to evolve, an increasing number of care programs across the United States reconsidered their options. The baby boomers, often caught between caring for young children and aging parents, were also referred to as the "sandwich generation," with little time and busy careers of their own. Inter-generational day care sites showed promise to alleviate the burden of the situation. On-site corporate adult day care programs, such as the one formerly housed at Stride-Rite in Cambridge, Massachusetts, were not successful in the early stages. But as the population of aging and retired workers grew, more businesses were expected to consider starting them as a benefit available to employees.

Adult day care centers were transformed as the accompanying services of speech, physical, occupational, and drug therapy became more available, attracting Medicare and private-pay patients. Another development was the expansion of outpatient care and rehabilitation to complement nursing home services. Adult day service centers focused on assisting seniors with either minimal or extensive needs. Some centers specialized in certain types of patients, namely those with early onset dementia or Alzheimer's. Typical adult day service centers provided transportation, routine health care, meals, activities, and assistance with daily activities. The demand for more intense services is expected to increase into the twenty-first century as the U.S. population ages, and as changes in technology permitted the delivery of medical services outside traditional hospitals.

According to Suz Redfearn writing for the *Washington Business Journal,* in March of 1999 the business of adult day care was "dominated by mom-and-pop operations," and statistics on regional growth were difficult to determine accurately. Adult day care centers were run as for-profit, non-profit, or state-run operations. Expenses were paid by various sources such as Medicaid, fees charged to participants, donations, grants, and private long-term care. Centers were typically run by a director, usually a nurse or social worker, with the assistance of administrative and office staff, recreation and activity personnel, case managers and social workers, therapists, nurses, and medical staff. In centers run by non-profit organizations such as community groups or churches, volunteers were crucial to providing services.

Adult day care facilities were often one component of a larger scale continuum of care for senior adults. One example is a program operated by Adventist Healthcare based in Rockville, Maryland. This operation in Takoma Park, Maryland, and also in the suburban Washington, D.C. area, grew out of a nursing home that is a sub-acute care unit. For a balance in the services, the nonprofit Adventist opened the day care center in Takoma Park in 1987. Robert Jepson, a spokesperson for Adventist, quoted in the *Washington Business Journal,* noted that, "As the senior care services industry grows, there are new levels of service that are required. This is one of those." According to Colleen Sauvage, director of Asbury Methodist Village's day program in Gaithersburg, Maryland, and noted in the same article, the business of adult day care was still a "break-even" business in the latter part of the 1990s, more than 25 years after such ventures started emerging. For many, day care was only a first step for seniors in failing health. Many assisted-living and other continuing care facilities began day care centers with a view to the future business they could provide. If a person was familiar with a long-term care center affiliated with the day care center, that long-term facility would become a reasonable choice when further care was chosen.

BACKGROUND AND DEVELOPMENT

The 1970s were flush with funding for older adults services in the United States. Federal and state monies flooded local areas as a result of the establishment of the National Institute on Aging, in May of 1972 during the administration of President Richard

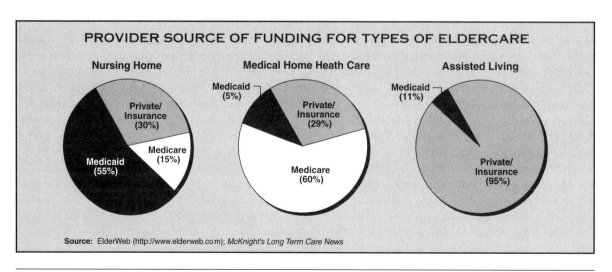

PROVIDER SOURCE OF FUNDING FOR TYPES OF ELDERCARE

Nursing Home
Private/Insurance (30%)
Medicare (15%)
Medicaid (55%)

Medical Home Heath Care
Medicaid (5%)
Private/Insurance (29%)
Medicare (60%)

Assisted Living
Medicaid (11%)
Private/Insurance (95%)

Source: ElderWeb (http://www.elderweb.com); *McKnight's Long Term Care News*

Nixon. Americans of the World War II generation were beginning to retire. People were living longer, even if they were not always without health problems. Many retired women, especially, had not worked outside the home and lived on very small retirement pensions or minimal Social Security benefits. Many of these men and women who had been born around the turn of the century came from rural backgrounds and moved to factories in the city. These citizens had limited incomes, forcing them to live at or near poverty level. A new awareness of age—both its problems and its joys—swept the country. Money was made available for senior nutrition programs and senior centers, among them adult day care. Special library outreach services grew out the needs of older adults who were homebound, hearing, or sight-impaired. Funds for large-print books and other arts-related programs for older adults were made available. Senior high-rise apartment buildings, many of them government-subsidized, went up in small towns and big cities. Local agencies on aging were set up under the auspices of state and federal programs. Church denominations started building retirement homes, along with private corporations. The dated notion of sending the aging population to "rest homes" was fading away. Better health and more leisure time were cutting through stereotypes.

Too, the demand for adult day care services developed as more women tried to balance the demands of jobs with the needs of family members. For those living near and caring for aging parents, adult day care services provided a way to be sure of elders' safety and supervision during the workday. American Association of Retired Persons statistics indicate that about 72 percent of caregivers to older people are women, more than 50 percent of whom are in the labor force,

and 41 percent of whom also care for children. Day care facilities equipped to care for individuals with certain conditions, such as Alzheimer's disease, also provided a needed respite for their caregivers. As the baby boomers moved into their older years, the demand for such services was likely to grow.

CURRENT CONDITIONS

In 1997, NADSA surveyed about 4,000 adult day care services in the United States and received about 1,600 responses. These indicated an average of about 14 participants per program, with an average ratio of one staff person to six participants. About 80 percent of the respondents were nonprofit programs, 10 percent were for-profit, and 10 percent were public or government-funded. The majority provided some type of nursing services. State licensing, certification, and accreditation standards for adult day care services vary, but most states require adherence to at least one category of such criteria. NADSA serves as a national clearinghouse for information on state-by-state licensure requirements.

The cost of attending such centers varied. One adult day care center, housed in a Baptist church in the small Arizona community of Peoria, advertised its services on the Internet in April of 1999. Basic services were offered for $6.80 an hour, and adjustments could be made on an ability-to-pay basis. As with other such centers, this one was licensed to serve people under the Department of Developmental Disabilities. Additional charges were added for: transportation, $3.50 one-way; a shampoo and shower at $12.00; toenail trim at $12.00; in-home care at $12-$13 an hour;

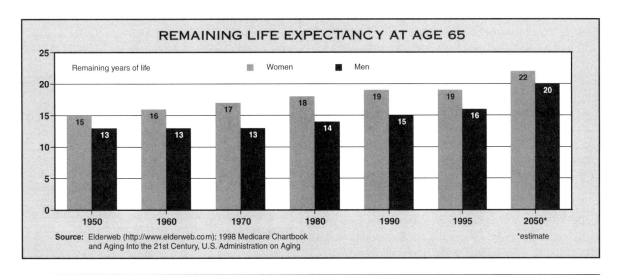

REMAINING LIFE EXPECTANCY AT AGE 65

Remaining years of life — Women — Men

	1950	1960	1970	1980	1990	1995	2050*
Women	15	16	17	18	19	19	22
Men	13	13	13	14	15	16	20

*estimate

Source: Elderweb (http://www.elderweb.com); 1998 Medicare Chartbook and Aging Into the 21st Century, U.S. Administration on Aging

overnight stay at the center was offered at a rate of $105 for a 24-hour period; and, evening care from 5:30 until 9:30 p.m. was also available from the $6.80 an hour rate.

Judith Braun, R.N., Ph.D., president and CEO of The Washington House, a continuing care retirement community, as well as past president of the National Gerontological Nursing Association, offered the following comments in a personal interview in April of 1999: "Day care is considered to be the hottest new trend in long-term care options. It provides needed socialization and some health monitoring, as well as much needed respite for the caregiver. Transportation, to and from, day care centers is one of the biggest stumbling blocks to growth. Transportation can be expensive and cause the cost of day care on a daily basis to be not much less than assisted living. Some consumers are asking, if I can pay slightly less for 24-hour care, why opt for day care?" With little if any funding from a federal level, nor much insurance coverage, yet available for day care options, growth was expected to proceed slowly for awhile. As Barbara Harry, administrator of the Asbury Methodist facility noted, "about half of the participants" families would pay for the service out of pocket. The other half would pay the $55-$65 a day through Medicaid. Most caregivers hoped that eventually the cost would be covered through insurance and Medicare. In 1999, Harry said, "That's about three to five years away."

Geriatric care managers were an important addition to the options for elder care at home. In addition to day care centers, visiting nurses and home care managers enable some people to live in their own homes longer. Programs around the country are growing. One such program in Stark County, Ohio, operates as "Family Connections" through county Family Services department. Local programs operate under the guidance of the National Geriatric Care Management Association. Newspaper reporter, Denise Sautters, writing for *The Repository,* on March 26, 1999, noted that the geriatric care manager featured in her article was, "The daughter in town," for people whose children were living elsewhere. The cost of such services was $45 an hour. Jane Pieper, the care manager, noted that with the agency as a nonprofit, they "break our service into units of times, so we are never billing for a full hour, just the time being used, so it becomes very affordable."

Another similar program featured in the March 4, 1999 issue of *The New York Times,* was located in Newport Beach, California. Sara Rimer reported that geriatric care manager Dr. Deborah Newquist filled the role of family members when they could not be available and/or lived at a distance. Rimer noted that Dr. Newquist had a doctorate in medical anthropology, received not many years ago, when the occupation of geriatric care manager did not yet exist. "The field was born in response to the nation's rapidly aging population and the health care system's complexity," said Rimer. There, where the cost of living was considerably higher than it was in Ohio, the fee might have ranged from $70 to $150 an hour. When hired at the time of a crisis, the initial fee might have been as high as $2,000 a month. Many managers were certified through the National Academy of Professional Geriatric Care Management Association, founded in Connecticut in 1994, and began administering a certification program in 1997. Rona Bartelstone, a clinical social worker in South Florida, was the founder of that program, as well as the National Association of Profession Geriatric Care Managers, based in Tucson, Arizona. The organization began in 1986 and grew to 1,200 members out of the estimated 4,000 private care managers across the United States.

Trends **EMPLOYERS AND ELDERCARE ASSISTANCE**

About 40 percent of families have to care for their aging parents, according to statistics gathered by the Associated Press from the Families and Work Institute. Oftentimes, the responsibility of having to care for aging parents on top of caring for children affects workers' ability to do their jobs. Because of the increased burden on families, businesses have begun working to broaden their investments in their employees.

In 1995, 21 of the nation's largest companies participated in a $100-million 6-year effort to improve child and elder care for their employees across the country. Some of the businesses included Business Machines Corp., AT&T Corp., Citicorp and Aetna Life and Casualty. Companies say the assistance also helps boost productivity for their workers.

According to a 1997 column by Phillip Britt, elder care programs had more than doubled in the past five years. They are now offered by 30 percent of employers, compared to 13 percent in 1991. Resource and referral services have increased to 79 percent and counseling services have reached 17 percent. Britt cited a study by the Lincolnshire, Ill.-based Hewitt Associates which surveys more than 1,000 U.S. employers to monitor employer-sponsored benefit programs.

INDUSTRY LEADERS

According to the National Adult Day Services Association, the vast majority of the 4,000 adult day care centers were still primarily private or not-for-profit institutions at the end of the 1990s. There was growth in the number of day care centers operating over the previous decade, and this was expected to continue over the next 10-15 years. In 1999, Catholic Charities was one of the largest nonprofits in the category. Asbury Methodist Village in Gaithersburg, Maryland, opened in September 1998, and it opened a day care center for older adults in March of 1999. Many church-related facilities such as these were leaders in the nonprofit sector for adult day care. The three largest for-profit companies in adult day care in the 1990s were Deerfield Senior Day Centers, based in Baltimore, Maryland and founded in 1994. Deerfield operated 13 centers in five states. Caretenders Health Corporation of Lexington, Kentucky was also a leader in the industry with 1998 annual revenues of $95.2 million and an annual growth rate of 24 percent. Caretenders provides adult day care programs in nine states. The third largest company was Active Services of Birmingham, Alabama.

In the area of geriatric care management programs, the rising star was a new company venture in 1999. Steve Barlam, a care manager in Beverly Hills, California, sold his small care management firm, staffed by himself and five other social workers, to a venture capital firm in San Francisco in 1999. The company, Bank America Ventures, sought to create an in-home care and management company with other such practices around California. Barlam stayed on as care manager and executive vice-president of the new company. Other private companies similar to this were anticipated as the need began to grow.

WORK FORCE

The nursing and personal care facilities sector grew by 22,000 workers, for a total of 1,769,000 workers. Residential care workers increased from 683,000 to 697,000 workers between 1996 and 1997. Opportunities for adult day care workers would continue to expand as the aging population demanded more such facilities and services. Census bureau data showed that average hourly earnings for nursing and personal care facilities workers was $9.53 at year-end 1997. For residential care workers, often consistent with salaries in for-profit care facilities, the hourly rate was $9.11 as of year-end 1997. Because the field of for-profit adult day care was relatively new at the end of the twentieth century, opportunities had not been fully evaluated. The professional field of gerontology, in the areas of medicine and social work was expanding as well. The number of geriatric social workers, geriatric nurses, and physicians who specialized in geriatrics continued to grow at the end of the 1990s.

Mary Brugger Murphy, director of the Washington, D.C.-based National Adult Day Services Association, said in the *Washington Business Journal,* that, "Farsighted people realize this is a logical way of delivering quality services and making money. It's telling that a program that's been grassroots is appealing to at least three large for-profit companies." In the field of adult day care, no matter what the philosophy behind it, the only direction it was taking the twenty-first century was up.

FURTHER READING

Barbour, Carol A. "Futurescape: Long-Term Care Without Walls." *Nursing Homes,* February 1998.

Braun, Judith, R.N., Ph.D. Personal interview with Jane Spear. April 1999.

Bryson, Ken. "Household and Family Characteristics: March 1995." *Current Population Reports: Population Characteristics.* Washington, DC: GPO, October 1996.

Degler, Carl N. *At Odds: Women and the Family in America from the Revolution to the Present.* New York: Oxford University Press, 1980.

Goodman, William. "Boom in Day Care Industry the Result of Many Social Changes." *Monthly Labor Review,* August 1995.

Gordon, Natalie. "Adult Day Care." *Encyclopedia of Social Work,* 19th ed. Washington, DC: National Association of Social Workers, 1995.

"Granny Care and Kiddy Care." *Forbes,* 30 December 1996.

Handbook of U.S. Labor Statistics. Lanham, MD: Bernan Press, 1997.

Martin Erickson, Lynne. "A Guide to Community." Madison, WI: Bi-Folkal Productions, Inc., 1999.

National Center for Health Statistics. *Annual Summary of Births, Marriages, Divorces, and Deaths, United States, 1994.* Available from http://www.cdc.gov/nchswww/products/pubs/pubd/mvsr/supp/44-43/mvs43_13.htm.

Neely, Esme. "Adult Day Care Industry Booms as Population Ages." *Baltimore Business Journal,* 19 January 1996.

Passell, Peter. "Day Care: Quality vs. Equality." *The New York Times,* 25 December 1996.

Phillips, Debra. "Day Care Centers." *Entrepreneur,* December 1997.

Redfearn, Suz. "Day Care for Seniors Becoming Popular Niche." *Washington Business Journal,* 26 March 1999.

Rimer, Sara. "The Growing Business of Helping Elders Cope." *The New York Times,* 4 March 1999.

Saluter, Arlene F. "Marital Status and Living Arrangements: March 1994." *Current Population Reports: Population Characteristics.* Washington, DC: GPO, 1996.

Shulte, Mark J. "Don't Stand Still, Get Financing and Go for the Growth." *Crains Small Business,* Chicago ed., July/August 1997.

U.S. Department of Labor. "Labor Protections and Welfare Reform," 22 May 1997. Available from http:/www.dol.gov/dol/asp/public/w2w/welfare.htm.

"Who's Taking Care of You?" *CIGNA Health Care Newsletter,* Summer 1997.

—Joan Giglierano, updated by Janet Whittle
and Jane E. Spear

ELECTRONIC COMMERCE

Electronic commerce has been conceived of in different ways and has been referred to by using different terms such as "Internet commerce" and "electronic business." However, the definition given by the U.S. Congress represents the most common meaning of "electronic commerce": "Electronic techniques for accomplishing business transactions, including electronic mail or messaging, World Wide Web technology, electronic bulletin boards, purchase cards, electronic funds transfers, and electronic data interchange." Therefore, in its simplest form, electronic commerce includes any business transaction handled electronically through the computer-to-computer exchange of data. Other tools that fit loosely into the "e-commerce" paradigm include electronic funds transfer, facsimile transmission, smart cards, and work flow management systems.

Nevertheless, while electronic commerce covers any form of computerized buying and selling, it is most closely associated with commerce enabled by the Internet. Indeed, the rise of "e-commerce" is inextricably linked to the explosive growth of the Internet in the mid- to late 1990s, which was in turn sustained by the convergence of telecommunications and computing technologies. Not surprisingly, most of the commercial activities on the Internet closely resemble their "real world" antecedents. Buyers browse online catalogs, request quotes, and place orders. Sellers provide online information, respond to bids, and confirm orders. Third parties provide value-added services like vendor registration and certification, specialized directories, advertising, and brokering.

Electronic commerce can be broken down into three main sectors: business to business; digital delivery of goods and services; and retail sale of tangible goods. In the late 1990s, the first category was by far the largest, with businesses using the Internet to expand their markets, lower costs, reduce inventories and cycle times, and improve customer service. The second category also represented a major growth area, with software programs, newspapers, airline tickets, and music titles all being sold and delivered electronically over the Internet. The third category, and the one that initially spurred many businesses to set up shop on the Internet, was more problematic. While certain goods—particularly computers, telecommunications equipment, books, and apparel—enjoyed enormous sales via the Internet, overall growth in this area was slow to take off.

In 1994, market researcher SIMBA Information predicted that Internet commerce would grow by an "astounding 6000 percent to become a $1 billion a year industry by the end of this decade." Considered wildly optimistic at the time, that prediction actually fell far short of the mark. By 1998, electronic commerce for all sectors totaled $51 billion. Business-to-business sales over the Internet reached $43 billion, while retail transactions for 1998 climbed to $8 billion, according to Forrester Research. By 2002, online transactions are expected to reach anywhere from $300 billion to $1.4 trillion.

In 1994, only about 3 million people used the Internet—most of them in the United States and Canada. By 1998, more than 150 million people around the world were using the Internet, and some projections estimated that as many as a billion people would be online by 2005. This expansion not only drove dramatic increases in computer, software, services, and communications investments, it made it more feasible and more profitable to do business online. Storefronts on the Internet and other commercial networks allowed consumers to browse extensive product catalogs and made it possible for them to purchase the products directly off the merchants' Web sites using credit cards or electronic cash.

Not surprisingly, many of the most prominent companies in electronic commerce were those companies already at the forefront of the emerging digital economy—computer hardware manufacturers, software publishers, telecommunications equipment makers, Internet service providers, and so on. Companies like Dell Computer and Apple Computer quickly established an online presence to sell their products. Software producers such as Adobe and Microsoft began distributing their software online. New companies like Netscape rose out of nowhere to provide the tools people needed to "surf" the Internet. Telecommunications equipment manufacturers like Cisco Systems and 3Com provided the modems, routers, and other devices needed to access the Internet. Smaller companies such as Web design firms and Internet business consultants sprouted overnight to provide the value-added services needed to keep everything running smoothly.

ELECTRONIC COMMERCE BETWEEN BUSINESSES

A considerable overlap between the different sectors in the electronic commerce industry exists, but business-to-business represents the largest and fastest growing sector, accounting for about $43 billion in sales in 1998, according to Forrester Research. Businesses use electronic networks to create, buy, distribute, sell, and service products and services. By using the Internet, businesses are able to cut the cost of purchasing, manage supplier relationships, streamline logistics and inventory, plan production, and reach new and existing customers more effectively.

Business-to-business procurement is very different from consumer buying. For example, in addition to performing authentication, online catalogs and procurement services must be able to feed order confirmations back to the customer's own ordering system. Typically, they also must be able to accept standard purchase orders rather than just credit cards or electronic cash. As a result, business-oriented online systems have developed a high degree of sophistication and have created a huge market for soft-

ware designed to give business Web sites even greater functionality.

Business use of the Internet goes beyond the simple buying and selling of goods, however. Many businesses use the Internet to lure new customers or to seek out lower-cost suppliers. For instance, Japan's national telephone company, NTT, is trying to broaden its base of suppliers by posting its requirements online—in English as well as in Japanese—and inviting bids from companies around the world. Companies like Federal Express and the United Parcel Service (UPS) have effectively utilized the Internet to cut costs, improve customer service, and increase market share by making it possible for customers to schedule, pay for, and track shipments online. Web hosting companies provide one of the purest forms of online transaction; not only do such companies sell a product that is truly "virtual" (space on the Internet), they normally accept and process orders online, bill their customers electronically, and provide service and support via electronic mail and interactive Web-based support sites.

DIGITAL DELIVERY OF GOODS AND SERVICES

Software programs, newspapers, and music CDs are ideally suited for digital distribution via the Internet. Free samples, demonstration software, or trial subscriptions are increasingly being used to attract customers. Airline tickets and securities transactions over the Internet are growing rapidly. An increasing number of banks are beginning to experiment with online banking services, and a few new banks, which exist only in cyberspace, have appeared. In the long run, according to a U.S. Department of Commerce report entitled *The Emerging Digital Economy,* "the sale and transmission of goods and services electronically is likely to be the largest and most visible driver of the new digital economy."

As of 1999, sales of software programs and subscriptions to specialized-news and information databases accounted for the bulk of this market. Software giants like Microsoft, Adobe, Intuit, Lotus, and Corel all aggressively marketed and distributed their products online either directly or via specialized software distribution sites. Long-established proprietary database services formerly accessible via direct dial or through closed networks such as CompuServe or America Online were hooked into the Internet. Additionally, most major magazines and newspapers had established an online presence, some restricting access to subscribers only, others relying on advertising to pay their way.

However, advertising on the Internet proved less profitable than many would-be online publishers had hoped. Though advertising was rife on the Internet by 1999, only the major directories and search engines were able to support themselves with advertising dollars. Advertisements usually appeared in the form of "banners" carrying the advertiser's message. Because the effectiveness of these ads was determined by how often they were "clicked" on, Internet advertising rates were based on the "click-through" percentage. Another common form of advertising is "junk e-mail"— unsolicited commercial messages sent via electronic mail. Ironically, some of the most common types of "junk e-mail" offered are to sell software enabling the user to send e-mail to millions of recipients.

Other forms of electronic delivery of goods and services include online classified ads, computer dating services, image banks, and electronic journals or "e-zines." Another major category is information brokerages or distributors such as Yahoo!, Lycos, and Infoseek. As the volume of information accessible over the Internet grows, these services have become increasingly important—and profitable.

By 1998 everything was in place to facilitate a huge growth in the market for digital delivery of music. Several online music retailers such as CDNow and Music Boulevard were well established with a large customer base. A number of different technologies were available to enable fast downloading of music data without loss of quality. Perhaps most importantly, affordable devices for recording CDs and CD-ROMs had been introduced to the market. With the right software, an Internet connection, and a recordable CD-ROM drive, a music lover could locate virtually any music online, preview it, download it, and record it on a customized CD. Though still nascent in the late 1990s, the potential upside to this market looks huge.

ELECTRONIC RETAILING

For the most part, this area is the direct electronic equivalent of traditional mail order purchasing, except that online retailers don't face the costs of printing or mailing paper, nor do they have to pay people to wait by the phones for orders. Online retailers are also able to provide many additional value added services ranging from online product demonstrations to custom product configuration. Numerous electronic shopping malls populated with virtual storefronts have sprung up on the Internet, but this particular business model has not proven extremely successful. More successful are online superstores specializing in a single product category such as computers or books. Nevertheless, traditional retailers such as Gap, Macy's, and Eddie

Trends ONLINE AUCTIONS

Online auction houses such as eBay and CityAuction offer consumers the satisfaction of garage sale prices combined with the convenience of e-commerce. Some online auction houses such as Amazon.com specialize in selling books, collectibles, or electronic items, while others such as Sotheby's Holding and Gregg Manning specialize in high-end merchandise. In 1998 the online auction market was reported at $1.4 billion, with eBay holding a reputation as one of only a very few consumer-oriented e-commerce sites that consistently turned a profit.

Online auctions typically earn money by charging sellers, who pay an entry fee as well as a percentage of the selling price. Online auctions constitute a seller's market, with sellers setting the limits. For sales of a large item such as a trailer or a car, the sellers might limit the geographic region of sale. Sellers also establish the minimum acceptable bid and the time duration of the sale. Online auction sites operate to a large extent in good faith, although most allow for feedback. Most buyers and sellers likewise are legitimate, although the environment is not immune to confidence scams. Some online auction sites offer an escrow service for new participants who are hesitant to trust the system.

Auction sites operate in a variety of ways and base rules vary from auction site to auction site. Some sites operate in "live" auction mode across the Internet. Other auction houses allow vendors to auction new products to consumers. In "person-to-person" auctions the seller establishes a time limit for accepting bids.

Bauer had considerable success with their online stores, especially during the Christmas season.

The Internet has also made it possible for manufacturers to bypass the middlemen and sell directly to customers. Retail sales from electronic commerce totaled $8 billion in 1998, yet they accounted for only about 1 percent of the overall retail market. Retailers garnered $3.5 billion in online sales during the Christmas shopping season, which represented 43 percent of their total online sales.

BACKGROUND AND DEVELOPMENT

Computer networks have existed in one form or another since the 1960s but, until recently, were generally reserved for academic and scientific exchange.

In the 1970s some companies began pioneering various techniques for transferring data in formats that could be processed on receipt, and by the early 1980s, proprietary computer networks were being put to use in the airline and banking industries.

It soon became apparent that common data formats would be needed for electronic transfers to work between different organizations, businesses, and trading communities. Standards bodies were created in the Unites States and Europe, and industry groups got together to define message requirements. During the 1980s, a number of Value Added Network services (VANs) were created to provide secure communications channels for business use. Later on, smaller VANs emerged to cater to the requirements of specific sectors, such as education. The airline industry, freight forwarding industry, and shipping industry all created networks for transmission of EDI (Electronic Data Interchange) and e-mail data.

By the end of the 1980s, EDI technology was fairly well established and posed for rapid growth. Though only 1 percent of potential users had implemented EDI, analysts expected the number of users to double every year; however, that never happened. International standards had still not attained a level that would suit all businesses. Standards, message types, and connections were complicated and confusing, making the whole process simply too much trouble for most potential users. Those who did invest in EDI did not always gain benefits though. Large retail companies could benefit by purchasing from multiple suppliers, but for the suppliers the benefits were less apparent.

During this time, rudimentary online retailing operations began to appear on bulletin board services and the large online systems such as CompuServe but, even as late as 1992, the volume of electronic commerce was so small that the term still did not exist. Though EDI fans continued to push their fading technology and online services expanded their retailing capabilities, the idea of doing business via computer still seemed a long way off.

Two things changed all this. The first was the rapidly falling price of computer hardware, which led more and more businesses to computerize. Operating systems and, particularly, the software that runs on them, grew increasingly powerful and easier to use, thereby providing a wider range of solutions to the business market and becoming more attractive to home users. The second crucial factor in the development of e-commerce was the development of the World Wide Web (WWW), a hyperlink-based system designed to make navigation of the Internet easier and provide faster access to information. The subsequent introduction of the Mosaic program (later Netscape), which provided users with a graphic interface to the WWW, was the spark that lit the Internet explosion.

While the graphic and multimedia capabilities of the Web attracted users to the Internet, the most significant factor in terms of electronic commerce was the wide range of messaging techniques, all of which were fast, reliable, and relatively secure. The Internet provided an affordable, easy-to-use, worldwide network accessible via commercially available software that not only enabled free exchange of data, but also made it possible for companies to create a visual presence for themselves in cyberspace—a virtual storefront. Though the Internet lacked the security of closed systems, its advantages far outweighed its problems, and business users rushed to get online.

In a few short years, the Internet went from being the secret playground of hobbyists and academics to a mass commercial medium. No other technology has ever been adopted as quickly. As the U.S. Department of Commerce points out, "Radio was in existence 38 years before 50 million people tuned in; television took 13 years to reach that benchmark. Sixteen years after the first PC kit came out, 50 million people were using one. Once it was opened to the general public, the Internet crossed that line in four years."

By 1994, awareness of the Internet was widespread among the business community and increasing among the general public. Enterprising virtual real estate developers began to set up Internet "shopping malls" and new start-ups launched virtual stores that existed only in cyberspace. While many of the "malls" failed to attract the level of business their developers anticipated, the more specialized shops performed extremely well. Dell Computer, for example, was soon conducting a major share of its business online. The first online bookstore, Amazon.com, did so well that traditional book chains, like Barnes & Noble, were forced to set up shop on the Internet in order to stay competitive. In addition to books and computers, CDs also seemed well suited to the Internet, and a number of online music stores appeared.

To facilitate online commerce, software developers began producing sophisticated "shopping cart" systems and secure, encrypted payment systems. Users could browse online catalogs, add items to their "cart" and, when they were finished, exit through a "check-out" where their purchases were tallied and charged to their credit card. Although the security of these systems was not always foolproof, even the earliest systems were relatively safe—certainly more secure than giving out credit card information over the telephone. Nevertheless, the public perception that hackers were lurking online waiting to steal their credit card numbers resulted in slow initial growth for electronic retailing. In fact, so many online businesses failed in 1994 and 1995, by 1996 a backlash had set in and many analysts began to regard the Internet as a passing fad.

Analysts were wrong. Growth continued slowly but steadily through 1996 and then exploded in 1997. The number of people connected to the Internet rose from 40 million in 1996 to more than 100 million by the end of 1997. Over the same period, the number of registered Internet domain names more than doubled from 627,000 to 1.5 million. In 1996 companies posted sales of $1.1 billion from electronic commerce. In addition, retailers operating exclusively on the Internet emerged, including the online bookstore Amazon.com, which recorded booming sales of $16 million in 1996 and $148 million in 1997.

CURRENT CONDITIONS

Bringing the information society to the masses was a big business in the late 1990s. Mergers and acquisitions in the Internet service provider (ISP) and telecommunications markets were commonplace as companies positioned themselves to capitalize on the growing electronic marketplace. Venture capital investing in Internet companies was up 70 percent; during the first quarter of 1998 it accounted for one-fourth of all U.S. venture funding. Consumers started to embrace online shopping, and new studies indicated that the Internet's demographics were beginning to grow more representative of the general population.

With all forms of online transactions totaling $51 billion in 1998, e-commerce appeared to be a permanent and growing method of business. In 1998 Cisco Systems was reporting sales of up to $9 million a day, and Dell Computer was selling more than $5 million worth of computer products per day. Apple Computer's online store reported sales of close to $2 million over a single 24-hour period in May 1998, and Ticketmaster Online reported revenues of $19.5 million for the first quarter of 1998. While the total amount of revenues from electronic commerce amounted to little more than a drop in the bucket, especially for retail and global sales, some analysts expect these sectors to grow rapidly in the coming years. Visa predicts that online sales will account for 10 per-

cent of U.S. retail sales by 2003, in contrast to just 1 percent in 1998, and Cisco Systems expects nearly 25 percent of all global commerce to take place over the Internet.

Furthermore, the overall picture of electronic commerce looks extremely promising. In 1998, Access Media International reported that nearly 1 million small businesses had launched Web sites, and the number was expected to triple by the end of the year. Business-to-business transactions alone were projected to climb to more than $800 billion by 2003. Online retail sales were expected to reach $103 billion, and online stock trading was expected to account for 60 percent of the discount brokerage industry by 2001, according to Forrester Research. Sales of entertainment and travel tickets bought online were predicted to top $10 billion by 2001, and online music sales were predicted to total $1.6 billion by 2002.

Despite the rapid growth in revenues, however, it was still not clear whether vendors were actually making a profit. Some analysts suggest that the cost of running an online business may make it difficult to turn a profit. In spite of its huge revenues, Amazon.com, for example, posted a loss of $27 million in 1997. Amazon.com's low profit margins have forced the company to incur losses while trying to establish loyal clientele. New software and infrastructure have simplified the task of creating Web sites friendly to e-commerce, but the costs of hardware, connections, site design, trained support staff, and marketing still make the establishment of an online store presence an expensive undertaking. According to a survey by Internet research firm, International Data Corporation (IDC), major firms were spending an average of $256,500 for Internet commerce platforms and systems. Larger web sellers were spending between $500,000 and $2 million.

For the most part, the hype about the Internet had died down by 1998 and companies were no longer coming online in search of fast profits. "Early perspectives on electronic commerce were immature," said Caroline Robertson, director of IDC's Internet Commerce research program. "Today, with more knowledge and experience, firms are hedging their bets and turning to the Internet to support—not supplant—their existing distribution strategy." Rather than counting on electronic commerce to generate a new revenue stream, companies now regarded it as a means of extending their existing distribution strategies. Web-based sales strategies were being used to decrease internal costs, streamline processes, improve customer service, and generate leads. Products and digital services marketed online included publishing and media, ticketing and reservation services, professional services, education, banking, software retailing, and electronic distribution.

At the same time, the Clinton Administration, pleased by the economic boon the Internet seemed to have brought to the United States, affirmed its commitment to unfettered commerce in cyberspace. Though the government did attempt to foist its own encryption system on the Internet—a move roundly condemned by industry and privacy advocates—it showed little interest in interfering with the Internet's "duty-free" status. President Clinton called upon all Internet users to join him "in seeking global consensus so that we may enter the new millennium ready to reap the benefits of the emerging electronic age of commerce." Vice President Gore added, "If we establish an environment in which electronic commerce can flourish, then every computer can be a window open to every business, large and small, everywhere in the world." Clinton has vowed to keep the Internet free of taxes and has been working with other countries to develop global consumer protection policies to provide consumers with the same security they are entitled to in traditional stores. Under the Internet Tax Freedom Act of 1997, taxes on electronic commerce are prohibited from October 1998 to October 2001, during which time a special committee will develop a comprehensive policy governing the taxation of Internet transactions. Nevertheless, the tax moratorium quickly met with resistance from state and local governments that felt they were losing revenues as a result.

INDUSTRY LEADERS

By all accounts, the undisputed leader in online commerce in 1998 was Cisco Systems, the world's leading manufacturer of networking equipment. Headquartered in San Jose, California, Cisco not only provides much of the equipment used to create the Internet's infrastructure, it sells a significant proportion of that equipment through the Internet. Founded in 1984 by a small group of computer scientists from Stanford University, Cisco Systems shipped its first product in 1986. Providing end-to-end networking solutions that could be used to build a unified information infrastructure or to connect to existing networks, the company grew rapidly and went public in 1990.

With its broad range of networking products and its expertise in network design and implementation, Cisco was uniquely positioned to take advantage of the rise of the Internet. From 1990 to 1998, the company's revenues soared from $69 million to more than $8.4 billion. It became a global market leader holding either the number one or the number two spot in every market segment in which it participated. Measured by market capitalization, it was the third largest company on NASDAQ (National Association of Securities Dealers Automated Quotations system) and among the top 40 in the world. By 1998, Cisco was also operating the world's largest Internet commerce site, selling more than $11 million worth of products every business day.

For all its success, Cisco is hardly a household name. The company exemplifies the business-to-business model, selling its products to corporations, government agencies, utilities, telecommunication carriers, Internet service providers, cable companies, small businesses, and educational institutions. Cisco credits its success to a flexible approach that does not try to impose any one technology on its customers, but instead provides customers with a range of options from which to choose. The company's globe-spanning operations employed more than 15,000 people in more than 200 offices in 54 countries, including about 7,400 workers in the San Francisco Bay Area.

Cisco is a leading example of what it calls a "Global Networked Business," that is, a company that "strategically uses information and communications to build a network of strong, interactive relationships with all its key constituencies." By using networked applications, the Internet, and its own internal network, Cisco claimed to be saving at least $360 million per year in operating costs, while increasing customer satisfaction and improving performance in areas such as customer support, product ordering, and delivery times. By the end of 1998, nearly half of Cisco's revenues were derived from Internet sales.

If Cisco Systems epitomized the "business-to-business" variant of e-commerce, Dell Computer was the clear leader in direct electronic retailing. Founded by Michael Dell in 1984, the company immediately differentiated itself from the competition with its unique direct-to-customer business model. By eliminating resellers, retailers, and other intermediaries between the manufacturer and the end-user, Dell was able to build powerful systems to order for its customers and to sell them for less than its competitors could sell standard, off-the-shelf computers.

By 1987, Dell had opened an overseas subsidiary in the United Kingdom, and the following year it conducted an initial public offering of company stock, selling 3.5 million shares at $8.50 each. By 1992 the company was ranked in the Fortune 500 and, by 1993, it was among the top computer-makers worldwide.

Dell was comparatively slow to move its direct marketing model online, not opening the online "Dell store" until 1996. But the elaborate, sophisticated site was well worth the wait. Customers were able to view, configure, and price systems from within Dell's entire product line; order systems online or by telephone; and track orders from manufacturing through shipping. The site also included personalized system-support and technical service items dating all the way back to the company's very first computers. Special sections for corporate and institutional customers provided approved product configurations and pricing, order and inventory tracking, reports, and contact information.

In April 1998, Dell's online sales reached $5 million per day, with more than 1.5 million customers visiting the site every week. Though most of the company's Internet sales were within the United States, Dell reported that sales from other markets had grown to 20 percent of its online total in less than one year. Overall revenues for 1998 totaled $18.2 billion, up 48 percent over the previous year, making Dell the second-largest manufacturer and marketer of computers in the United States and the third largest worldwide.

Of all the leading companies in the electronic commerce industry, Amazon.com is the purest, a true "virtual" bookstore existing only online. Founded in July 1995, the Seattle-based company set out to build an online store that would be customer friendly, easy to navigate, and offer the broadest possible selection. The store grew quickly, gathering favorable reviews in all the Internet media and selling more than $16 million worth of books in its first full year of operation.

What sets Amazon.com apart from many of its competitors—aside from the fact that it was the first—is its easy-to-use interface, broad selection, and wealth of value-added information. This type of value-added information includes both professional and customer reviews, personal notification services, and a network of "Associates" who forwarded book-buyers to the Amazon.com Web site in exchange for a percentage of the sale. In 1998 the company posted sales of $610 million exclusively from electronic commerce.

AMERICA AND THE WORLD

While the Internet continued to grow steadily in penetration and intensity in North America, it was quickly becoming a global phenomenon. Penetration levels remained by far the highest in North America— where nearly 60 million of the world's 150 million In-

ternet users resided in 1998—but international usage is growing rapidly, as is the potential for electronic commerce. In Europe, for example, Frost & Sullivan projected that total Internet commerce revenues would grow from about $1.2 billion in 1998 to $8.0 billion by 2004, while the number of Internet users was expected to increase from 16.6 to 56.0 million during that same period.

Since the United States dominates the Internet technology market, the rapid global expansion of the Internet can only do more to boost the profits of U.S. e-businesses. In 1997, U.S. exports of computer software, entertainment products (motion pictures, videos, games, sound recordings), information services (databases, online newspapers), technical information, product licenses, financial services, and professional services (businesses and technical consulting, accounting, architectural design, legal advice, and travel services) accounted for well over $40 billion. Even though the U.S. share of the e-commerce market was projected to decline from about 87 percent in 1997 to 63 percent in 2002, the huge size of the impending market guaranteed continued revenue growth for U.S. Internet companies.

FURTHER READING

"Amazon.com Announces Financial Results for Fourth Quarter and 1997 Year End." 22 January 1998. Available from http://www.amazon.com.

"Amazon.com Company Information." June 1998. Available from http://www.amazon.com.

Burstein, Daniel, and David Kline. *Road Warriors: Dreams and Nightmares Along the Information Highway.* New York: Penguin Books, 1996.

"Cisco Systems Corporate Profile." San Jose, CA: Cisco Systems, 1998. Available from http://www.cisco.com.

"Cisco Systems Fact Sheet." San Jose, CA: Cisco Systems, 1998. Available from http://www.cisco.com.

"Dell Computer 1997 Annual Report." 1998. Available from http://www.dell.com.

The Electronic Commerce Information Resource. *A Brief History of Electronic Commerce.* 1996. Available from http://www.year-x.co.uk/ec/.

Fisher, Sara, and Nola L. Sarkisian. "Holiday Mania.com: E-commerce Still a Tiny Part of Retail." *Los Angeles Business Journal,* 4 January 1999, 1.

"Industry Spotlight: Venture Capital." *The Industry Standard,* 1998. Available from http://www.idg.net.

"Industry Statistics." CommerceNet, 1998. Available from http://www.commerce.net.

"Internet Commerce Revenues in Western Europe to Reach $30 Billion by 2001." International Data Corporation, 1998. Available from http://www.idc.com.

Maladen, Carlyn. "E-Commerce Ready to Take Your Order." *Vancouver Computes!,* July 1998.

Schonfeld, Erick. "The Exchange Economy." *Fortune,* 15 February 1999, 67.

"'Twas The Season for E-Splurging." *Business Week,* 18 January 1999, 40.

U.S. Department of Commerce. *The Emerging Digital Economy.* Washington, DC: GPO, 1998. Available from http://www.ecommerce.gov.

The White House. "A Framework for Global Electronic Commerce." Washington, DC: The White House, 1997. Available from http://www.ecommerce.gov.

—Christopher C. Hunt, updated by Karl Heil

ELECTRONIC NOTEPADS

The presence of the Internet and e-mail has grown in both the work and home lives of Americans, and mobile computing makes it possible for them to stay in contact with the workplace and the world beyond. Portable computers allow individuals to carry critical business information with them in virtual offices and to access materials that are available on company networks as well as on the World Wide Web. Notebook (or laptop) computers have acquired computing power equaling, sometimes surpassing, that of standard desktop computers. As the trend toward ubiquitous computing—the notion of being connected all the time—evolves, some experts predict that notebook computers will replace desktop models altogether because of the mobility they allow.

Hand-helds and palmtops—computers weighing less than a pound—are also capable of accessing e-mail and the Internet, writing reports, and updating spreadsheets. Their size makes them attractive to consumers, students, and business people who may not need the full functionality of larger portable computers. The Microsoft Windows CE operating system, introduced in late 1996, was developed especially for the smallest computers and features software that allows automatic synchronizing of data to that on desktop PCs back in the office. The U.S. Robotics Palm-Pilot is a notable competitor to the CE-based computers.

Personal digital assistants (PDAs) have also grown more powerful and smarter since their inception. Typically, PDAs function as cellular phones, fax machines, and personal organizers. Some PDAs are beginning to use voice recognition technology to in-put information. As voice recognition capability develops and improves, this may become a standard future enhancement for such devices. (Also see the essay in this book entitled Voice Recognition Systems and Software.)

ORGANIZATION AND STRUCTURE

Once known as portables or laptops, notebook, hand-held, or palmtop computers are the lightest and smallest of their breed. Features common to notebooks include: flat-panel display screens; rechargeable battery packs; disk and/or CD-ROM drives; built-in touchpads or other pointing devices in lieu of a separate mouse; and expansion slots for Personal Computer Memory Card International Association (PCMCIA) cards, the credit-card sized devices that supply fax modem capability and extra memory. The hand-helds and palmtops use these PCMCIA slots for disk drives as well. Another common feature is a notebook's relatively high cost compared to desktop computers with similar capacities. Hand-held PDAs use a stylus or pen instead of a keyboard for input.

Screens in notebook and other portable computers are flat liquid crystal displays (LCD), which can be either passive matrix or active matrix, and may be backlit for clarity. Passive matrix displays have grids of horizontal and vertical wires, the intersections of which is a LCD element, a single pixel that either admits or excludes light. Active matrix, or thin film transistor (TFT) displays, have much better resolution but are more expensive to produce. Liquid crystal display technology was developed in the United States; however, Japan, Korea, and Taiwan produce almost all of the LCD screens. (Also see the essay in this book entitled Video Displays.)

The portable computer industry's distribution channels mirror those of the desktop PC industry, since many of the companies are the same. When customers want to buy notebook computers or any other hardware from industry leaders such as Toshiba, Compaq, IBM, or Apple, they must go through resellers who take the orders, get the products from the manufacturer, and configure, deliver, and support them. Resellers fees can add 10-20 percent to the price of a product. Because the profit margin in the notebook segment is low and the competition so fierce, manufacturers tend to keep production just below demand level. At times this can backfire, which results in shortages, fulfillment backlogs, and long waits for products when production volume is miscalculated, or when there are shortages of new or popular components such as faster chips or CD-ROM drives. Fierce competition from some of the direct sellers of mobile computers has prompted many of the industry leaders to begin selling selections of their products directly to consumers, although the majority of their sales remains in the hands of third-party resellers.

Direct-sellers, such as Dell and Gateway, fill orders they receive directly from customers. These companies then custom-configure units to their customers specifications and deliver them directly. They build machines on demand, not ahead of time, thereby eliminating the problem of storing units until they are sold and the overhead involved in maintaining inventory. This allows direct-sellers to sell at lower prices. In May 1997 one of the industry's leaders, Compaq, made the news by experimenting with direct selling, thus cutting its resellers out of some of their fees. At times, Compaq has had difficulty gauging demand for units, either coming up short of demand or having to deal with excess machines. Compaq began to institute build-to-order production, rather than build-in-advance, and began to turn inventory over faster. Custom production increased efficiency, which in turn, allowed Compaq to cut prices, improve its competitiveness, and increase market share. In a field in which the top manufacturers are evenly matched, any way to undercut the competition can make a significant difference in who comes out on top. According to Jim Schraith, vice president and general manager of Compaq's North American operations, the company's ultimate goal is to create a manufacturing and distribution system resembling that of a direct seller, while using its established network of resellers as its sales force.

BACKGROUND AND DEVELOPMENT

The Osborne I, developed in 1980 by Adam Osborne of Osborne Computer Corporation, included innovations that led the way in the evolution of truly portable computers. Weighing 17 pounds, it had a detachable keyboard, a 5-inch black-and-white display, and two floppy disk drives. It used a Zilog Z-80 microprocessor chip, an improved clone of Intel's 8080. The Osborne I not only pioneered portability, it was also credited with being the first to bundle software packages with the computer—an idea that became fundamental to selling hardware in the industry. Tens of thousands of the Osborne I portable computers were sold before it became the victim of the company's own success. In 1983, the company announced that it would build an IBM-compatible portable called the Vixen, causing buyers to stop buying the Osborne I in anticipation of the new machine. However, the announcement was premature and, without incoming orders to fund the new product's manufacture, Osborne was forced to file for bankruptcy protection. By the time the Vixen was ready to market, consumers had been wooed away by the products of a new leader, Compaq, which had been able to meet their demand.

According to author Les Freed, Compaq's opportunity to successfully take the portable computer market lead was largely due to a gaping hole in IBM's product line. In 1983 Compaq shipped the Compaq Transportable and Compaq Plus, both fully functional, IBM-compatible, portable PCs weighing just less than 30 pounds. During its first year in business, the company sold 53,000 portables and took in revenues of $111.2 million, giving Compaq the highest first-year sales in the history of American business.

In 1984 Gavilan Computer developed a truly portable machine that did not have to be plugged in. Industry commentator Tim Bajarin wrote, "The computer's clamshell design and battery-power capability made it the first serious mobile computing system." However, Gavilan could not manufacture them in sufficient quantity, and went out of business.

Apple Computer's PowerBook models, introduced to the market in 1991, set a new standard for portables. They combined long battery life with excellent display quality and a built-in pointing device. The PowerBook 170 contained an optional internal modem slot, again redefining the meaning of a mobile office computer. Apple's Duo 210, released in 1992, featured the DuoDock, an innovation that allowed the hook up to a docking station that might

A Compaq 2015 C series handheld computer. (Courtesy of Compaq.)

contain more system RAM, a larger hard drive, or more video RAM for a color monitor. The Duo could thus function fully as a desktop computer when in the DuoDock, and as an excellent portable at other times.

In 1993 another Apple innovation was the Newton MessagePad, a new type of portable known as a personal digital assistant. It was small enough to be hand-held and was offered as a personal information manager. The Newton solved the problem of keyboard size by using a stylus for input, but it promised more of this new pen-based technology than it could deliver. Apple promoted the Newton's ability to interpret handwriting, with disastrous results, because at the time its capability was relatively primitive. By 1997 when the next-generation Newton, the MessagePad 2000, reached the market, its handwriting recognition was much improved. Reviewers praised the revamped MessagePad for its robust communication and computing features. Unfortunately, early in 1998, after seven years of development and manufacturing the PDA, Apple dropped the curtain on the Newton line— the MessagePad, eMate (a Newton-based clamshell notebook for the education market), and the Newton operating system.

CURRENT CONDITIONS

In-Stat Research, a high-technology market research company, has predicted that notebook shipments and revenues will grow faster than desktops through the year 2001. In-Stat calculated a compound annual growth rate of 22.8 percent for notebook computers through the year 2001, compared to 14.2 percent for desktops.

The downside of such explosive growth was difficulty filling orders. Intense consumer demand led to long waits for delivery. For manufacturers, shortened product cycles and a rush to get notebooks to those waiting for them before their competitors did sometimes meant inadequate quality control, resulting in the release of defective products. Periodic component shortages aggravated the situation, contributing to backlogged orders and loss of market share for companies without alternative suppliers.

The industry leaders in sales of mobile computers—Toshiba, IBM, and Compaq—held onto their leadership positions in 1998, but it was a difficult year for all players in the market. Sales for the industry as a whole slipped to $35.2 billion, down slightly from

$36.2 billion in 1997, according to data from Dataquest, a unit of Gartner Group Inc. All mobile computer vendors struggled under the burden of surplus inventory during the first half of the year, which contributed to a decline in international revenue. The sales pace picked up in the latter half of 1998 with the introduction of Intel Corporation's mobile Pentium II processor and innovative thin-and-light form factors, according to Dataquest. By year's end, most vendors reported they were meeting their inventory goals.

Toshiba Corporation retained its longstanding lead in mobile computer sales, although its market share shrank during 1998. The company's notebook revenue dropped 17 percent to $6.2 billion in 1998, compared with $7.4 billion in 1997. Its share of the mobile computer market fell to 17.5 percent from 20.5 percent the previous year. IBM, number two in mobile computer sales, also experienced declines in both revenue and market share during 1998. Third-place Compaq Computer Corporation managed to increase its mobile computer revenue, despite its preoccupation with the integration of newly acquired Digital Equipment Corporation into its overall operations. One of the best showings in the mobile computer market came from fourth-place Dell Computer Corporation, which nearly doubled its market share from 5.2 percent in 1997 to 10.2 percent in 1998.

Sharp growth in international sales of handheld computers was forecast for 1999 by Dataquest. Helping to fuel this increase is the growing availability of wireless data access in handheld units, according to Scott Miller, an analyst with Dataquest. Sales in 1999 were projected at 5.7 million units valued at $1.6 billion, an increase of 47 percent over 1998 sales of 3.9 million units. Dataquest expects continued strong growth in this market with average annual sales growth of 30 percent through 2003, when sales are expected to reach 21.0 million units. "In 1998, the handheld market crossed the important billion-dollar sales threshold and is well on the way to reaching critical mass," Miller said. "Enhanced communication, including wireless access, enables a new class of applications that is ultimately the key to growing the number of handheld users."

MERGERS AND CONSOLIDATIONS

The industry saw a number of mergers and consolidations in 1997 and 1998, as cutthroat competition and price cuts affected notebook computer companies.

In early 1997 Acer Group bought Texas Instruments' notebook computer business after TI's failed attempt to gain market share at the cost of profitability.

In June 1998 shareholders in Digital Equipment Corporation, whose market share had been on a downward slide, voted to finalize Compaq's acquisition of their company.

Apple Computer Corporation, like Mark Twain, announced that reports of its demise (and/or acquisition) were greatly exaggerated. In 1998 Apple added the powerful, high-end PowerBook G3 to its mainstream notebook, the PowerBook 3400. The faster G3 also has more memory, a larger-capacity hard drive, and a higher capacity battery.

PRODUCT DEVELOPMENTS

Candescent Technologies of San Jose, California, is designing an improved screen called the ThinCRT, a 12- to 14-inch display panel that will have a wide viewing angle and will be capable of displaying television-quality motion and color along with text and graphics.

Manufacturers are also employing new technologies to extend battery life. Nickel-cadmium batteries and nickel-metal hydride batteries were the leading types until the development of lithium-ion batteries, which are more stable and hold a charge longer. Sony Corporation, a leading manufacturer of lithium-ion batteries, planned to double its production by March 1998 to meet the exploding demand. (Also see the essay in this book entitled Lithium-Ion Batteries.)

Numerous models of hand-helds, palmtops, and personal digital assistants came on the market in 1996-97. These included computers running the Microsoft Windows CE operating system. Windows CE, although less functional than Windows 95, was easy to learn for those familiar with that product. The Windows CE devices included modified versions of the popular Microsoft Word and Excel software, along with Microsoft's Internet Explorer browser. The Casio Cassiopeia was able to transmit faxes, access e-mail, and receive information via a one-way pager, in addition to being able to link and synchronize data through a docking station to a Windows 95 desktop computer. Hewlett-Packard introduced its 1000CX palmtop PC; and Philips Electronics North America Corp., the Velo 1, in early 1997. Among the strongest new competitors of these computers were several that did not run Windows CE: the Toshiba Libretto, the U.S. Robotics Pilot, and the Newton MessagePad 2000. Shipments of hand-helds, palmtops, and PDAs together were expected to total 4.8 million worldwide in 1997, an increase of about 1 million over 1996 shipments, according to Randy Giusto of International Data Corporation.

Early in 1999 Intel Corporation introduced new mobile-processor technology that the company said would allow the performance of portable computers to almost match that of desktop units. Code-named Geyserville, Intel's new technology allows a chip to operate in two modes—battery-optimized and high-performance. When a mobile computer equipped with the new technology is unplugged from an electric power source, Geyserville allows the chip to drop to a lower frequency mode, extending the life of the computer's battery. When connected to a power source, the mobile computer's processor runs at its maximum clock speed. This new technology addresses the main factor that has blocked higher clock speeds in portable computers—power consumption. "This is a revolutionary technology that will allow us to offer unprecedented levels of mobile-computing power without compromising battery life at all," according to Robert Jecmen, vice president and general manager of Intel's mobile and handheld products group. The company planned to introduce the Geyserville technology in the mobile version of its Pentium III processor, which was scheduled to reach the market at the end of 1999. The mobile Pentium III can run at 600 MHz or faster when in high-performance mode and at about 500 MHz when operating in mobile mode.

INDUSTRY LEADERS

The leading portable computer manufacturers—Toshiba, IBM, and Compaq—shuffle positions, depending on the quarter, but manage to hold onto the top three spots.

TOSHIBA AMERICA INFORMATION SYSTEMS

Toshiba America Information Systems, Inc. (TAIS), headquartered in Irvine, California, managed to hold onto its lead in the sales of mobile computers in 1998, although its market share dropped from 20.5 to 17.5 percent. Toshiba's sales also declined, totaling $6.2 billion, down 17.0 percent from $7.4 billion in 1997. According to Joseph Formichelli, executive vice president of Toshiba Computer Systems Division, the company's revenue decline could be attributed mostly to lower unit prices and not lower unit sales. He said that while 1998 saw aggressive pricing in the mobile computer market and first half inventory problems, Toshiba, by year's end, had begun to see the first measurable results of its reengineering and sup-

ply chain management and was meeting its inventory goals. TAIS is an independent operating company owned by Toshiba America, a subsidiary of Tokyo-based Toshiba Corporation.

IBM CORPORATION

Like Toshiba, IBM's Personal Systems Group (Somers, New York) experienced a strong finish in 1998, thanks in large part to its popular, new, ultra-portable ThinkPad 600 series, according to Adalio Sanchez, general manager of the company's mobile computing division. High-end ThinkPads often included 266MHz and 300MHz Pentium processors with multimedia technology and large-capacity hard drives packaged in a slimmer, lighter case. "We saw the appetite for thin-and-light grow exponentially as customers became more accustomed to the technology," Sanchez said. However, even with the strong finish, IBM's mobile PC revenue in 1998 fell 9.0 percent to $5.0 billion from $5.5 billion in 1997, and its share of the market fell from 15.1 percent to 14.2 percent. Much of the decline in mobile PC revenue, according to Sanchez, could be traced to oversupply in the first half of the year, leading to price cuts at an artificially rapid rate.

IBM's Authorized Assembler Program (AAP) provides quick shipment of custom-configured notebooks—a build-to-order program that enables resellers to deliver individualized custom solution for business customers.

COMPAQ COMPUTER CORPORATION

Much of Compaq Computer Corporation's energy was focused on the integration of Digital Equipment Corporation (DEC) into its overall operations. In the largest acquisition in the history of the computer industry, Houston-based Compaq in 1998 agreed to buy Digital Equipment (DEC) in a $9.6 billion cash and stock deal. The acquisition, which was finalized in June 1998, gave the acquiring company access to DEC's global service organization. Compaq was already the worldwide market leader in personal computer and server sales with sales of $24.6 billion in 1997.

Compaq, ranked number three in mobile computing sales for 1998, managed to register an increase in mobile computer revenue in 1998, posting sales of $4.4 billion, up 11 percent from $4.0 billion in 1997. Like both Toshiba and IBM, Compaq struggled to work off surplus inventory in the first half, forcing it to take some aggressive pricing moves. Eric Brennan, director of North American mobile product marketing for Compaq, said the company's introduction of the mobile Pentium II processor into its product line helped to stimulate sales in the second half of 1998. "By the end of the year, we had good inventory levels and met our aggressive goals," Brennan said.

Compaq's mobile computing line consists of the Armada family of productivity machines designed for business customers, and the Presario multimedia notebooks for consumers who want to stay connected to the Internet while on the road or at home.

THE SECOND TIER

The real success story in the mobile computer market in 1998 belonged to Dell Computer Corporation of Round Rock, Texas, which managed to nearly double its revenue and market share. Dell's portable PC sales totaled $3.6 billion, up 90.0 percent from $1.9 billion in 1997. The company's market share grew from 5.2 percent in 1997 to 10.2 percent in 1998. Fueling Dell's growth in the mobile market was its platform stability, attained through a commonality of components and software drivers, according to Tim Peters, worldwide general manager of Dell's Latitude line of notebook computers.

Rounding out the top five in mobile PC sales in 1998 was Fujitsu Ltd. Its revenue increased 4 percent to $2.03 billion from $1.96 billion in 1997. Steve Andler, vice president of marketing for Fujitsu, reported that the Tokyo-based company did not experience the same level of inventory problems felt by its competitors in the mobile PC market.

AMERICA AND THE WORLD

Worldwide shipments of all notebooks were projected at 16.8 million for 1998, up from 14.2 million in 1997, according to analysts at IDC (Framingham, Massachusetts-based International Data Corporation).

Canadian notebook shipments are forecast to be at 425,000 in 1998, up from 337,000 in 1997, according to Evans Research Corp. (ERC) of Toronto.

The mobile computing market in Latin America grew 64 percent in the second quarter of 1997, according to Dataquest Inc., a San Jose, California, market research company. Brazil and Mexico were numbers one and two in the region, with 288,000 and 164,000 units shipped. Several other countries in Latin America showed positive growth in portable computer shipments, including Colombia, Venezuela, Chile, and Peru.

FURTHER READING

Abraham, Michelle. "In-Stat In-sights." *Electronic News,* 17 March 1997.

Bajarin, Tim. "Back to the Luggable." *Mobile Computing and Communications,* January 1997. Available from http://www.mobilecomputing.com/articles/1997/01/9701ii.htm.

Blodgett, Mindy. "Mobile Merger Mania." *Computerworld,* 3 February 1997.

Bournellis, Cynthia. "Platform for Windows CE Added to Intellisync Family." *Electronic News,* 31 March 1997.

Carlton, Jim. "Laptop Computer Shipments Stall as Holidays Approach; Switchover to Pentium Chip Is Causing Growth Rate to Slow Markedly." *Wall Street Journal,* 23 October 1995.

Einstein, David. "Toshiba Refreshes Its Notebook Line." *San Francisco Chronicle,* 3 June 1997. Available from http://nytsyn.com/live/Prod/154_060397_112210_18879.html.

Freed, Les. *The History of Computers.* Emeryville, CA: Ziff-Davis Press, 1995.

Gambon, Jill. "NotebooksMarket in Chaos." *Information-Week,* 29 July 1996. Available from http://www.techweb.com/se/directlink.cgi?WK19960729S0025.

"GartnerGroup's Dataquest Says Worldwide Handheld Shipments to Surpass 5.7 Million Units in 1999," 27 May 1999. Available from http://gartner3.gartnerweb.com/dq/static/about/press/pr-b9924.html.

Hagendorf, Jennifer. "1999 Market Leaders: Mobile PCs—New Form Factors Give Vendors a Boost." *Computer Reseller News,* 17 May 1999, 96.

"A History of Apple Computer." Apple Computer Inc. 1997. Available from http://apple-history.pair.com.

"HP 1000CX Palmtop PC." *Electronic News,* 17 February 1997.

Kestenbaum, Jackie. "Sony Expands Lithium-Ion Battery Production." *Bloomberg Business News,* 11 December 1996. Available from http://nytsn.com/live/Tech/346_121196_22784.html.

Moore, Mark. "Entry-Level Notebook PCs Acquiring High-End Features." *PC Week,* 14 July 1997.

"New Notebook PC Design Aimed at Resisting Damage." *Wall Street Journal,* 14 October 1996.

Niccolai, James. "Top of the News: Mobile PCs Get Power Gush from Geyserville." *InfoWorld,* 1 March 1999.

"Pen Touch Sensitive Screen Featured in Casio Handheld." *Computing Canada,* 3 February 1997.

Pittelkau, Jeff. "The Newton Weighs In: Apple Newton MessagePad 2000." *MacUser,* June 1997. Available from

http://www4.zdnet.com/macuser/mu_0697/features/newton/
newton.html.

Silverman, Dwight. "Changes at Compaq Make Resellers
Nervous." *Houston Chronicle,* 20 May 1997. Available
from http://nytsyn.com/live/Tech/140_052097_102204_
31935.html.

Sinton, Peter. "Firm Is Banking on Flat-Screen Technology." *San Francisco Chronicle,* 14 July 1997. Available
from http://nytsyn.com/live/Prod/195_071497_084204_
26904.html.

Thibodeau, Patrick, and Wylie Wong. "Mobile Users Help
Laptop Sales." *Computerworld,* 23 June 1997.

"U.S. Robotics Plans Palm Pilot Upgrade." *Computerworld,*
10 February 1997.

"Worldwide Handheld Market Grew 65 Percent In 1997."
EDP Weekly, 1 June 1998. Millin Publishing, 1998.

—Joan Giglierano, updated by Judith Harper
and Don Amerman

ELECTRONIC PUBLISHING

While predicting the death of the printed page might be premature, electronic publishing, which includes formats such as CD-ROMs, the Internet, and e-books, has taken off at lightning speed. This growth has been hastened along by the mass proliferation of personal computers and the increased accessibility of the Internet. During the 1990s, content on the Internet had expanded to include Web-only e-zines and many leading print publications. By 1999 the Web was dotted with sites for literary magazines, such as *The Atlantic Monthly,* and major daily newspapers, including *The New York Times.* Even so, few of these companies have turned a profit from their e-publishing operations, and most have struggled to find reliable income sources. Regardless of profit margins, however, many publishers—whether they produce books, magazines, or newspapers—embraced electronic technology in the late 1990s for fear of being left behind by their competitors.

Traditionally, the information provided on the Internet has been free, but this no-pay policy has been a problem for online publications as they try to deliver the content that users want without charging for it. This can be a serious stumbling block, especially for specialized publications with limited appeal. Generally, online publishers gain revenue from three sources: ad banners, subscriptions, and pay-per-view. Advertising revenue can be generated in several different ways. For instance, advertisers pay a fee each time their banner is displayed on the publisher's site. Typically, these ads cost $0.005 for each exposure. In another method, publishers receive a payment—the going rate is five cents—each time one of their site-users click on an ad and are taken to the advertiser's Web site. Lastly, the publisher can receive a payment when the user buys an advertised product. This type of arrangement, which is becoming more popular, gives the publisher a percentage of the purchase price. Online sellers using these kinds of programs include Amazon.com, Barnes & Noble, and Ticketmaster.

While print publishers routinely charge for their magazines or newspapers, subscription-based publications on the Web are unusual. With only a few publishing exceptions—notably the *Wall Street Journal* and the *Economist*—Web users have shown a reluctance to pay for online content. Publishers have another option to raise revenues in the form of a pay-per-view basis, which requires readers to pay in order to download material. This method is commonly used for online fiction books and article archives. In the case of an archive, users can usually search for free but are charged a fee, running anywhere from fifty cents to several dollars, for each article they view.

Electronic media is playing an increasing role in reference and textbook publishing. In the mid-1990s, the CD-ROM format was popular for reference books. However, by 1998, its appeal had waned. Increasingly, publishers turned to the Internet as a more user-friendly format. The advantage of the Internet is that text can be easily updated, expanded, and searched. In the late 1990s publishers began offering online reference material in areas such as law and medicine. While most of these reference publishers charge a fee to access their material, Emedicine.com is a free online encyclopedia for emergency room physicians. The site was written by 400 doctors and has been privately financed. Organizers hope that the site will pay for itself through advertising by drug companies.

Trends ELECTRONIC BOOKS VS. PRINTED PAPER

E-books are a significant milestone in electronic publishing. Nevertheless this innovation, sometimes compared to the invention of the printing press, cannot be relied upon to bring the hardbound book to obsolescence. According to an article in *Economist,* the technology that promised to deliver that elusive irony called the "paperless office" not only failed to materialize, but instead succeeded in generating more paper than ever before.

Regardless, *Computerworld* maintains that e-books are "poised to become a key medium," and the potential of that medium will be some time before full realization. Benefits afforded the reader are significant. The ability to adjust the size of fonts on the screen display will be a boon to everyone who ever strained their eyes in an attempt to read unclear copy. For the visually impaired the benefits are greater still. Also, any student who lugs tens of pounds of books back and forth to school in a backpack will appreciate the ability to store the text of approximately ten full-length books into a single e-book.

E-books sell for $500 or less, a price that will fall as the technology gains acceptance and e-books prove advantageous to vendors in reducing warehouse overhead, as customers download the text of books via the Internet. Shipping costs are eliminated, as well.

Electronic textbooks seem poised for growth in the early 2000s. Sales of electronic media to schools is growing at an annual rate of 10 percent and is expected to reach over $1 billion in 2001. Online courseware is the smallest segment of the industry, but it is estimated to increase at an annual rate of 31 percent, reaching more than $40 million in 2001. Reasons for this rapid rise include the increased use of the Internet in classrooms and the acceptance of electronic publishing in the learning process.

BACKGROUND AND DEVELOPMENT

Modern publishing dates back to the 1440s and a German printer named Johann Gutenberg, who is believed to be the first European to print with hand-set type cast in molds. For the most part, printing technology remained fairly static over the next centuries, but the rise of computers in the 1970s changed that. During the 1980s almost all printing functions—such as creating artwork, setting type, and scanning photographs—became automated. There were several electronic publishing advancements in 1984. That year saw the first computer-based CD-ROM (Compact Disc-Read Only Memory); the first online magazine featuring short science fiction and fantasy stories on the BITNET network at the University of Maine; and the appearance of desktop publishing systems that integrated high-quality images and graphics with text. The 1970s and 1980s also gave birth to the Internet—a global communication system composed of thousands of interconnected networks. In 1990 Tim Berners-Lee who worked at CEKN, a European Lab for Particle Physics in Geneva, Switzerland, developed the World Wide Web. The accelerated growth of the Web in the 1990s can be attributed, in part, to its use of hypertext, the nonsequential form of writing created by Ted Nelson in 1968.

While much Internet activity has been focused on trying to make money, at least one early Internet pioneer saw the value of providing online content at no charge. Project Gutenberg, which was founded in 1971 by Michael Hart of Urbana, Illinois, continues to this day making public-domain books available for free in an electronic format. Hart's goal is to have 10,000 books online before the end of 2001. The works of authors such as Leo Tolstoy, Rudyard Kipling, and Nathaniel Hawthorne are featured on the site.

Early electronic book publishers used diskette and CD-ROM formats. In 1994 there were five or six publishers, including Chicago-based Spectrum Press, which offered books on three and a half inch and five and one-quarter inch floppy disks. Daniel Agin, who owned Spectrum, called these products "e-text" books. However, even by 1994, disks were being replaced by CD-ROMs, which had the capability of holding 300,000 pages of text and had tracks for sound and motion pictures. Because of the vast amount of space available on CD-ROMS, reference publishers, such as Grolier Interactive, adopted the technology.

In 1995 U.S. newspapers were jumping on the Internet bandwagon. In that year, 70 daily newspapers (three times as many as there had been in 1994) established an Internet presence. As reported by Steve Alexander in a June 12, 1995 article in the *Minneapolis Star Tribune,* an American Opinion Research study found that 19 percent of newspaper editors and publishers believed that the Internet would be the main competitor for advertising revenue by 2000. Early on, the *San Jose Mercury News,* owned by Knight Ridder, and the *Raleigh News and Observer* were leaders in gaining an online identity. The Mercury News made use of on-screen graphics and hyperlinks to related Internet sites to build a national readership. The site received 250,000 to 300,000 hits a day in 1995.

The phenomenal growth of e-publishing has raised questions in the areas of copyright laws and pornography. Legislators, educators, citizens' groups, and Web site owners are grappling to find solutions to these complex issues. The enormity and easy access of the Internet makes it nearly impossible to regulate, much less monitor. Recognizing this fact, the Digital Millennium Copyright Act, passed by Congress in August 1998, provided immunity to Internet service providers, such as America Online (AOL), for the copyright infringements of its customers. Even so, the vastness of the Internet has not deterred some from believing that it needs controls in the area of pornography. Many people are bothered by the fact that children can readily find pornography on the Internet. The Child Online Protection Act, which was signed into law by President Clinton in 1997, was designed to combat this problem by requiring commercial Web publishers of certain types of sexually explicit material to verify the age of Web site readers or face a penalty. However, many mainstream Web publishers were bothered by this federal law and challenged it in court. The publishers argued that the age-verification procedures would be too difficult and costly to implement, and as a result, many publishers would practice self-censorship—even if their material had not been intended to be prurient—to ensure that they did not break the law.

CURRENT CONDITIONS

After centuries of reading books on the printed page, 1998 and 1999 saw the emergence of the portable computerized book. These books, dubbed e-books, are not meant to replace traditional books—just yet. At prices ranging from $300 to $1,500, early buyers will most likely be professionals, such as doctors or engineers, who can take advantage of e-book's ability to store and update material more easily than printed text.

Several manufacturers introduced e-books in the late 1990s. Priced at $500, the Rocket eBook by Nuvomedia has the capacity to hold 4,000 pages and is the approximate size of a paperback book. The battery life of the Rocket eBook is 20 to 40 hours. Titles for the Rocket eBook are downloaded onto a computer from the Barnes & Noble Web site.

With a size of 11 inches by 8.5 inches, competitor Softbook, manufactured by Softbook Press, is larger than the Rocket eBook and, at a cost of $299, the initial price is less. However, Softbook charges a monthly subscription fee that includes access to ser-

The 3 by 4.5-inch Rocket eBook. (Courtesy of Levenger.)

vices like special publications. Softbook has the capacity to store 100,000 pages, and new titles can be downloaded directly from the Internet. The Softbook's battery life is six hours.

Another e-book maker is Everybook, which manufacturers the Dedicated Reader. With a retail price of approximately $1,500 and the capability of storing a half-million color pages, the Dedicated Reader offers two full-color screens.

On the content end, there are a growing number of publishers specializing in providing text for electronic formats. Hard Shell Word Factory is such a company. Hard Shell publishes book-length fiction and nonfiction material in various categories ranging from romance to science fiction. However, the books published by Hard Shell can only be accessed by downloading them from the publisher's Web site or on disks. Hard Shell is also offering content for e-books. Hard Shell pays its writers higher royalties than those offered by traditional publishers. Some online book publishers, however, charge writers to publish their books. This arrangement, known as vanity publishing, can cost writers $200 to $500 in upfront fees— a much lower amount than the mainstream vanity press printing where a writer can pay $5,000 to $10,000 to publish a book. Online vanity presses make the published books available on a Web site where they can be downloaded for a fee. Once a book has been published with an online vanity press, writers receive a percentage, usually 40 percent, of their book sales. Vanity press publishers include companies such as Online Originals, 1stBooks, and Xlibris.

Online periodical publishers are still trying to find out how to make their services profitable. In 1997 there were 1,700 e-zines on the Web, and most operated in the red. For one general-interest publication, the quest for profitability meant bucking the tide and doing something most other online magazines, no matter how hip and trendy, wouldn't dream of doing— going subscription only. That's just what Microsoft's online magazine, *Slate,* did in March 1998 when it asked readers to pay a $19.98 annual subscription fee. By that time, *Slate* had been around for nearly two years and had already aborted one attempt to have readers pay a fee in 1997. From its beginnings, *Slate* was intended to raise revenue through subscriptions. *Slate* first appeared on the Web in late June 1996 under the editorship of Michael Kinsley, an ex-editor of the *New Republic.* Because most of *Slate*'s editorial staff came from the print medium, the publication was short of Web-specific offerings, such as hyperlinks to other sites. However, in January 1998, *Slate* received 270,000 visits a day. A few months later, when readers were asked to fork over money for subscriptions, *Slate* received more than 17,000 orders within the first month. However, as reported by Robin Pogrebin, in a March 30, 1998, article in *The New York Times,* subscription revenue, which amounted to $340,000 at the time that article was written, fell far short of *Slate*'s annual operating costs of $5 million. In February 1999 Microsoft had a change of heart and dropped the fee. Once again, *Slate* would be free to Web users. A Microsoft spokesperson said that *Slate* would pursue advertising revenue instead of selling subscriptions.

INDUSTRY LEADERS

CNET, headquartered in San Francisco, is a leading content network in terms of audience size and revenues. The company operates a range of Web sites that offer information about computers, the Internet, and digital technologies. In addition to its Internet presence, CNET produces several nationally syndicated television shows about the Internet. The company signed a deal in February 1999 to be the exclusive provider of computer-buying guides on AOL and AOL.com. As part of the deal, CNET will pay AOL a guaranteed minimal amount of $14.5 million over the two and a half years of the agreement. Over three-fourths of CNET's sales are from its Internet operations. The company reported more than $56 million in sales revenue for 1998, an increase of 68 percent from the previous year. The company employed 580 workers in 1997.

Dow Jones & Company, Inc.'s flagship publication, the *Wall Street Journal,* appears in both print and online form. The *Wall Street Journal Interactive Edition* is one of the few Web publications that charges a fee to access its site. The Interactive Journal was launched in April 1996 and was initially available for free. By the end of 1996, however, the free access had been phased out and, by its first anniversary, Dow Jones announced that the site had a paid circulation of 100,000. Annual subscriptions are $49 and allow subscribers access to services such as business news articles, background reports on over 10,000 companies, and personal news and stock portfolios. The Interactive Journal site also features sports coverage and *SmartMoney Interactive,* a collection of personal finance and investment advice resources. Paid Interactive Journal subscribers reached more than 150,000 by November 1997. Dow Jones, which is headquartered in New York, New York, had sales revenue of $2.1 billion in 1998 and employed 8,300 people.

Knight Ridder was ahead of the times in 1993 when it launched its first Web site, Mercury Center, an offshoot of the company's newspaper franchise, *The San Jose Mercury News.* Over the next four years, the company poured $70 million dollars into online ventures without seeing any profit on its investment. In 1998 Knight Ridder's online services cost an estimated $45 million and generated $25 million in revenue, mostly from local advertising. Despite losses from Internet operations, Knight Ridder is committed to technology, and to that end, in 1998 the company moved its headquarters from Miami to San Jose to be closer to its new media division. The company operates 31 daily and 18 weekly newspapers across the United States. In 1997 the company launched the Real Cities network, which included 37 Web sites in association with its newspapers. Knight Ridder reported a 1998 revenue of $3 billion and employed 22,000 workers.

Bill Gates, the chairman and CEO of Microsoft Corporation, the world's number one software company, has said that he wants industrywide standards for electronic books. To that aim, Redmond, Washington-based Microsoft, which has a research and development budget of $3 billion a year, is working on e-book technology and is especially focusing on applications that will help foster greater acceptance of books in electronic form. In November 1998 Microsoft announced that it had created software that would vastly improve the appearance of fonts on color display screens. The new software, Cleartype, could improve the resolution of displays, such as those on many notebook computers, by nearly 300 percent. In addition to its e-book research, Microsoft produces Encarta—an electronic encyclopedia—and has created content for the Internet, including the e-magazine *Slate* and Microsoft Sidewalk, a network of local city guides. In 1998, facing increased competition in the online city guide field, Microsoft cut 25 percent of its Sidewalk staff.

Salon.com, a San Francisco-based online magazine, decided to go public in 1999. In April of that year, the publication announced an initial public offering of 2.5 million common shares, which it estimated would garner net proceeds of $27.3 million. Salon is a media company that produces a network of 10 subject-specific Web sites and a variety of online communities, which Salon expanded in 1999 with its acquisition of The Well. Like many online publications, Salon's main source of revenue comes from advertising. For the fiscal year that ended March 1998, Salon reported sales of $1.2 million, a 313 percent increase over the previous year. Also for 1998, the company reported a loss of $3.8 million and employed 74 workers. In 1999 a company spokesperson said that Salon does not anticipate showing a profit from operations in the near future.

In 1996, the Chicago-based Tribune Company, a newspaper and entertainment conglomerate, paired up with AOL to build Digital Cities, an online network providing services in cities across the United States. The Tribune Co. invested $20 million and owned 20 percent of the venture. The purpose of Digital City was to offer local content such as news, weather, and entertainment guides tailored specifically to each of its 88 U.S. markets. However, by 1998 the online city guide field had become so crowded and competitive that Digital City laid off 80 staff members. The Tribune Co. publishes four daily newspapers, including the *Chicago Tribune* and *The Orlando Sentinel.* In addition, the company owns television and radio stations and the Chicago Cubs major league baseball team. The Tribune Co. reported total revenue of nearly $3 billion in 1998—a growth of 9.6 percent over the previous year—and employed 12,700 people.

Scholastic Corporation, based in New York city, is the world's number one publisher of children's books and also produces children's television programming, videos, films, and CD-ROMS. Its Scholastic Network is an educational online service for kinder-

garten through eighth grade. Scholastic Network is the leading supplier of online courseware to the school market. Scholastic Corp. reported revenue of $1 billion for the fiscal year that ended May 1998, a 9-percent increase over 1997, and had 6,270 employees.

Competing against CNET is San Francisco-based Wired Digital, Inc. Wired Digital previously published *Wired,* the cyberspace-related magazine, which it sold to focus on Web-only operations. Wired Digital includes the Web site HotWired, which has articles on Web-related issues. Wired Digital holdings also include HotBot, an online search engine, and Webmonkey, a how-to site. In 1999 Lycos, the Internet navigation service provider, bought Wired Digital for $83 million. Total 1997 revenue reached $47 million, and the company employed 150 people in 1998.

RESEARCH AND TECHNOLOGY

One of the biggest obstacles of electronic books is that they lack the feel and appearance of printed books. To overcome this limitation, scientists at the Media Laboratory at the Massachusetts Institute of Technology (MIT) are developing electronic technology that will result in a finished product that has pages that can be turned or riffled through. Electronic ink, or e-ink, is the secret ingredient to make this possible, according to scientists at MIT. E-ink has the capability of erasing itself and redrawing new text and illustrations. Books that have e-ink will have a paperlike property but will also be able to store massive amount of data. MIT assistant professor Joseph Jacobson, who heads up the e-ink research team, says the storage capacity for these books could be as much as the entire holdings for the U.S. Library of Congress, or 17 million volumes. For this reason, the e-ink project has been dubbed "the last book." However, "the last book" is still in the development stage and won't appear on the market until 2002, at the earliest. Two business consortia of 75 companies are funding the project.

There may come a day when consumers will go to the local grocery store to do their weekly shopping and have a favorite book printed while they wait. This book-while-you-wait concept is known as on-demand printing. Companies are taking several different approaches to developing this technology. The Ingram Lightning Print project will store paperback books on a disk at a large output facility and then print the books only when needed. Similar to this idea, some companies are designing kiosks that can be put into public areas such as airports and bookstores. The kiosks will have the equipment to print out books at a customer's request. Xerox is also developing on-demand printing technology that will use its existing high-speed copiers.

FURTHER READING

Alexander, Steve. "More Newspapers Across the Country Are Launching Electronic Editions." *Minneapolis Star Tribune*, 12 June 1995.

"America Online, Inc. and CNET Announce Multi-Year, Multi-Million Dollar Content and Commerce Agreement." *Business Wire*, 8 February 1999.

Blades, John. "Books on Disk: An Idea Whose Time Has Come Unless, of Course, It's Already Come and Gone." *Chicago Tribune*, 12 July 1994.

Bronner, Ethan. "Textbooks Shifting from Printed Page to Screen." *The New York Times*, 1 December 1998.

Flynn, Laurie J. "Online City Guides Compete in Crowded Field." *The New York Times*, 14 September 1998.

Hines, Matt. "Slate Set Free." *Newsbytes*, 12 February 1999. Available from http://www.newsbytes.com.

Kaplan, Carl S. "Don't Rush to Update Copyright Laws, Professor Says." *The New York Times*, 7 August 1998.

Katz, Frances. "Salon Offering IPO, but Outlook Chancy." *The Atlanta Constitution*, 20 April 1999.

Kilsheimer, Joe. "Tribune, AOL Team up to Build Digital Cities." *The Orlando Sentinel*, 17 July 1996.

Lehmann-Haupt, Christopher. "Creating 'the Last Book' to Hold All the Others." *The New York Times*, 8 April 1998.

Lewis, Peter H. "Taking on New Forms, Electronic Books Turn a Page." *The New York Times*, 2 July 1998.

Lyman, David. "Computerized Books Have Hit the Market." *Detroit Free Press*, 10 January 1999.

Markoff, John. "Microsoft Develops Software to Improve Appearance of Screen Text." *The New York Times*, 17 November 1998.

Mendels, Pamela. "Web Publishers Testify Against Anti-Porn Law." *The New York Times*, 21 January 1999.

O'Brien, Keith. "Self-Publishers Turn to Online Vanity Presses to Get Their Works Out." *Gannet News Service*, 20 April 1999.

"The Paperless Paper." *Institutional Investor*, November 1998.

Pogrebin, Robin. "For $19.95, Slate Sees Who Its Friends Are." *The New York Times*, 30 March 1998.

"Simba Information Report Says Sales of Electronic Media to the School Market Will Grow at a Compound Annual Rate of 10 Percent from 1999-01." *Business Wire*, 19 January 1999.

"Wall Street Journal Interactive Edition Reaches Paid Circulation of 150,000 Readers." *Business Wire*, 5 November 1997.

—Katherine Wagner

EMPLOYEE LEASING

INDUSTRY SNAPSHOT

Employee leasing is one of the fastest growing emerging industries in the United States, although it is sometimes misunderstood. Many still confuse it with the temporary help industry, or assume that it involves little more than the hiring of a glorified payroll service. Rather, employee leasing (the actual leasing firms often are referred to as Professional Employer Organizations, or PEOs) involves a contractual arrangement whereby a company transfers its entire workforce and all its payroll and human resources functions to the PEO. The PEO then leases the workforce back to the client. A true full-service PEO will manage the personnel matters for part or all of a client's roster. It will provide health insurance, pay all taxes and fees, set up retirement plans, ensure compliance with OSHA (Office of Safety and Health Administration) regulations, do background checks, drug and alcohol screening, training, and counsel on health and safety issues. Such an arrangement frees the client's managers to devote themselves more fully to their core business activity, whether manufacturing a product or providing a service. A typical PEO will employ a relatively small number of its own employees while representing large numbers of workers at its client firms. For example, a PEO may have a staff of 25 to 50 workers managing the affairs of several thousand leased employees at dozens of client firms.

In the late 1990s, there were about 2,500 PEOs, which leased 3 million workers to their clients and handled approximately $18 billion in payroll. The industry grew by about 30 percent in the mid- to late 1990s and is expected to continue to grow at this rate through the early 2000s. PEO clients are typically small to medium-size companies with under 100 employees and the average client has 16 employees.

ORGANIZATION AND STRUCTURE

The National Association of Professional Employment Organizations (NAPEO) based in Alexandria, Virginia, is the primary organization serving the industry. The organization has more than 350 member companies, 15 chapters representing 45 states, and 700 offices around the country.

According to NAPEO, "the Internal Revenue Service recognizes the PEO as the employer for federal income and unemployment taxes, and case law affirms the principle that the PEO is responsible for payroll taxes." In addition, many states by statute recognize PEOs as the employer or co-employer for purposes of workers' compensation and state unemployment insurance taxes. At least 17 states have required some form of licensing, registration, or regulation for PEOs, mandating financial disclosure and reporting rules. Some deal specifically with capitalization for workers' compensation and unemployment insurance.

Employee leasing firms are as varied in size and type as the client companies they represent. One successful strategy lies in identifying and serving a particular industry niche. By targeting a particular type of client firm, a leasing company may specialize in terms of benefits offered, client size, payroll size, and risk ratios.

Different client industries require different types of expertise from PEOs. Blue-collar manufacturing firms, for example, tend to employ people with lower average salaries but higher worker's compensation claims. White-collar employees in the computer software industry enjoy higher salaries and benefits, so a PEO needs to carve out a cost savings niche by relying on its economies of scale.

Key to the growing popularity of PEOs is the relief they offer in lifting administrative burdens from the shoulders of the client's managers. The U.S. Small Business Administration (SBA) puts the average cost of regulation, tax compliance, and paperwork for smaller companies (less than 500 employees) at about $5,000 per employee versus $3,400 for bigger firms. SBA further estimates that between 7 and 25 percent of the small business owner's time is spent on employee-related paperwork.

A small business owner may be expert at his or her product or service but a neophyte when it comes to processing worker's compensation claims, providing health insurance, managing the paperwork flow, and other administrative duties. A good PEO will take over this entire realm of activity, allowing the business owner to devote him- or herself solely to the more important task of growing the business. While larger corporations have sufficient in-house expertise to handle such matters, smaller firms, especially those with 100 or fewer workers, usually lack such expertise. Few if any small manufacturers, for example, can devote a full-time manager solely to the task of monitoring and improving workplace safety. For these and other small firms, a good PEO can be extremely beneficial.

As attractive as the relief of the administrative burden can be for clients, probably the key factor for many in choosing a leased arrangement is money. Typically, a client can save an amount equal to 3 to 5 percent of gross payroll by going with a PEO. In some cases, the savings are less; in others, savings of more than 10 percent have been reported. PEOs generally charge from 3 to 6 percent of an employee's pretax salary (not including benefits), and as little as 1 percent in more competitive markets.

Small firms typically pay more for insurance and worker's compensation because their risk rating can be thrown off by a single unfortunate case. But in a leased environment, a PEO can merge a client's staff into very large pools of employees with a better overall risk rating. A single worker's compensation claim does not have the same catastrophic effect on what the company pays. The result is better coverage at a lower cost to the clients.

This type of hand-holding can take several forms. Many PEO clients are small manufacturers, such as those who provide parts to the automotive industry. These types of clients have workers who suffer from a high number of repetitive strain injuries, including cases of tendinitis, torn rotator cuff, carpal tunnel syndrome, and back injury. PEO safety managers will analyze the patterns of work and attempt to devise ergonomic solutions to avoid such problems. Often, the solution may require a job rotation program or a change in the process or equipment involved. The key is to discover the root cause of injuries, then work with management and employees to eliminate those causes.

Many PEOs save their clients money by being very aggressive about return-to-work programs. When an employee is injured, the treating physician often places restrictions on when that employee may return to work. Occasionally, such restrictions keep a worker away longer than may be necessary. PEOs have been known to work directly with physicians to help them understand exactly what is required of specific employees. In such a case, a videotape of particular workplace procedures involved may serve this purpose. PEOs may also design a temporary "bridge" job that will allow the injured employee to return to lighter duty until fully recovered. Measures like this have helped PEOs get employees back on the job sooner. This pays benefits in better morale, increased productivity, and lower worker's compensation costs.

BACKGROUND AND DEVELOPMENT

Analysts offer varied and often fanciful explanations for the historical roots of employee leasing. Some point to the mercenary soldiers employed by Britain during the American Revolution. Others trace the industry's origins to Alan Pinkerton, founder of the Pinkerton National Detective Agency in 1852, who leased security guards to the railroads to prevent theft and to recover stolen property. Since the 1940s, another pool of leased employees has been America's truck drivers. The Driver Employer Council of America reports that 30 percent of all private carriers use leased drivers, including many of the nation's largest firms.

Marianne Detwiler, senior editor of *Entrepreneurial Edge,* points out that "employee leasing was introduced in 1972 as a practice approved by the [IRS] to allow businesses to maintain a permanent staff without the personnel headaches caused by administration, paperwork, hiring and turnover."

In the 1970s, the employee leasing industry developed a negative reputation as an arrangement used only to dodge certain tax and other obligations. For example, during this period many professional partnerships—such as those owed by physicians and dentists—viewed leasing only as a way to exclude clerical and other hourly help from the retirement plans of the more highly paid managers. The Internal Revenue Service fought this arrangement in the tax courts and in 1982 the Tax Equity and Fiscal Responsibility Act (TEFRA) was enacted to ban the practice outright. TEFRA held that leased employees could be excluded from the client company's own pension plan only if the client contributed a substantial amount of money (equal to 7.5 percent of the employee's pay) to a fully vested pension plan. This could have ended the controversy, but further legislative revisions and tax court rulings muddied the situation until the Tax Reform Act of 1986 ended the pension tax-related advantages of leasing employees. The Tax Reform Act was a boon for PEOs because it forced the leasing industry to come up with a more rational reason for its existence. From that time on, the best PEOs began to promote themselves as providing more and more of the client's total personnel needs.

The leasing industry still suffers its full share of legal difficulties, however. In August 1989, embezzlement by managers sent CAP Staffing of North Carolina into bankruptcy, leaving leased employees with some $2.2 million in unpaid health claims. A few years later, Persona Management Corporation, with nearly 100 client companies representing some 8,000 workers in Rhode Island and Massachusetts, was found by the IRS to have understated clients' payroll wages in 1992 and 1993 by $60 million, and owing taxes of $13 million. These and similar incidents have created a cloud over the industry that persists to this day, despite various legal reforms and the emergence of more professional PEOs.

These incidents, even while tarnishing the reputation of the industry, have provided an unexpected impetus to its growth. Many client companies that had a bad experience with an unscrupulous PEO found that the benefits of a leased arrangement so clearly outweighed the problems that they immediately sought to sign on with another, more reputable PEO. This churning of the client base continues, with the industry in a state of flux. Numerous clients try one or more PEOs for a year or so before settling with one that meets their needs. With so many PEOs vying for attention, client companies need to exercise due diligence before signing on with one of them. Since January 1996, the Institute for the Accreditation of Professional Employer Organizations, an outgrowth of NAPEO, serves as the sole standard-setting and enforcement body for the accreditation of PEOs willing to adhere to stringent financial, ethical, and operational standards. The

process is costly, with annual accreditation fees ranging from $5,000 to $15,000. As of mid-1998, IAPEO had accredited 17 firms. In addition, NAPEO has certified nearly 200 people as Certified Professional Employer Specialists.

CURRENT CONDITIONS

Employee leasing has spread with astonishing rapidity since the mid-1980s. In 1985 there were fewer than 100 PEOs employing a total of about 10,000 workers. By the late 1990s, the industry had grown to encompass more than 2,500 leasing firms with about 3 million workers and responsibility for more than $18 billion in employee wages and benefits. A number of analysts contend that employee leasing has tapped only about 2 percent of the market's potential. They predict the industry's sales will increase by 30 percent annually for the next 10 years, according to *HRMagazine*. Furthermore, Judith G. Scott, a stock market analyst with Robert W. Baird & Co., forecasted that industry sales might reach as much as $175 billion by 2006, and the number of leased employees is slated to reach 10 million by 2000.

The growth of government regulations regarding employment, benefits, and wages has partially driven the industry, because companies, especially small ones, want to be certain that they have complied with all the pertinent regulations, but may lack the time or expertise to ensure compliance themselves. Hence, they have turned to PEOs who specialize in human resource management. In the late 1990s, PEOs generally charged between 2 and 5 percent of payroll for their expenses as well as between 9 and 20 percent of gross wages for benefits and profits, according to Carolyn Hirschman in *HR Magazine*.

The industry is enjoying growth of from 20 to 30 percent per year. Florida and Texas have the highest concentrations of PEO firms, with penetration in some regions reaching 30 to 40 percent. According to an industry report by Raymond James & Associates in St. Petersburg, Florida, seven of the largest are located in Florida, including Staff Leasing in Bradenton; the Vincam Group, Coral Gables; Paychex Business Solutions, St. Petersburg; and Payroll Transfers, Staffing Concepts International, and Automatic Data Processing, all in Tampa.

While the vast majority of the nation's 2,500 leasing firms remain privately held, *Forbes* magazine's Christopher Palmeri reported in October 1997 that 5 had gone public in the previous year. "Most trade at very rich valuations, Administaff at 42 times [1997] estimated earnings," he wrote. Some of the biggest firms, and many of the mid-sized PEOs, are pushing beyond regional boundaries in attempts to become active nationally. National Human Resource Committee, Inc. (NHRC), for example, while catering to many clients in its Metropolitan Detroit base, serves clients in more than 40 states.

Generating new business through client referrals is a popular growth strategy among PEOs. Staff Leasing's Staffleads incentive program offers new clients travel and cash bonuses of up to $1,000 for each referral. Texas-based Administaff has a client relationship with American Express (AE) under which AE refers its smaller businesses to Administaff. In Memphis, the National Bank of Commerce's small business unit has agreed to refer some of its customers to Staff Line, Inc., a Memphis-based employee leasing company.

Despite the industry's success prospects, state and federal regulations provide what many perceive to be a threat to the leasing industry. State legislation tends to be aimed at past abuses and sometimes takes a distinctly anti-leasing tack. Moreover, attempts by the Clinton Administration to broaden the availability of benefits to all workers might rob the leasing firms of their key advantage—the "one-stop shopping" approach they offer to clients in the often bewildering world of benefits. However, the threat from new state and federal regulatory change appears to be rather slight. Leasing by now is well established and provides benefits that are so obvious it is unlikely any concerted effort will now be made to ban the practice. NAPEO reports that a number of state and federal lawmakers as well as the SBA have shown support for the industry and the services it offers to businesses. In addition, officials of state and federal regulatory agencies have met with NAPEO representatives and spoken at industry events.

The IRS has undertaken a study to determine if PEOs are true employers of work-site employees. If the IRS concludes that PEOs are not true employers, PEOs' 401K plans and other benefits could lose their tax-qualified status. NAPEO has teamed with the National Association of Temporary Staffing Services (NATSS) in lobbying on behalf of legislation that would clarify staffing firm status under tax law.

Moreover, although companies transfer administrative responsibilities such as payroll, benefits, and compliance to PEOs, the companies that lease the employees from the PEOs still retain ultimate responsibility in a number of areas, according to Joanne Wojcik in *Business Insurance.* For example, if a leased

employee is injured in the workplace, the client company could be sued. In addition, if a PEO declares bankruptcy, the client company could be held responsible for wages and benefits. Hence, insurers have cautioned companies to weigh the advantages and disadvantages of employee leasing and to employ risk management strategies to minimize the potential negative consequences of leasing employees.

Another issue comes in the form of competition from national firms such as Kelly Services, the temporary help agency that in 1994 entered the leasing industry by purchasing the California-based PEO Your Staff. Given the marketing muscle of big players like Kelly, many smaller PEOs will feel the pressure. A mitigating factor might be cultural; since the vast majority of PEO clients are small firms themselves, they may prefer to do business with a smaller leasing firm that can offer more personal service, rather than with a nationwide giant.

EMPLOYEE LEASING GROWTH IN THE U.S., 1984, 2000

Number of leased employees in workforce — 10,000,000

1984: 10,000
2000*: 10,000,000

Source: *Entrepeneur,* January 1999 *estimate

INDUSTRY LEADERS

Staff Leasing, Inc., based in Bradenton, Florida, and the largest PEO in the United States, has 25 percent of its clients in the construction industry, including masons, roofers, and framers. The company has 40 sales offices in Arizona, Florida, Georgia, Minnesota, North Carolina, and Texas. It serves approximately 10,000 clients with more than 128,274 employees trained in payroll and benefits administration, risk management, unemployment services, and human resource consulting. The company caters to small- and medium-size businesses with 10-100 employees. Staff

Leasing had sales of $2.3 billion in 1998, up 28 percent from the previous year. The firm went public in June 1997.

The second largest player in the late 1990s was Administaff, Inc., based in Kingwood, Texas. Administaff operates 20 offices in 9 states and plans to add about 90 more offices in the coming years. The company focuses on small and medium companies seeking benefits and payroll management, employee records management, employer liability management, government compliance, and employee recruiting and selection. American Express owns 17 percent of the company and has a marketing agreement with it. In 1998 Administaff reported sales of $1.6 billion, up 38 percent from 1997. The company also employed 34,819 workers the same year.

Employee Solutions, Inc. is another leading company in the industry. Like many other PEOs, Employee Solutions targets small and medium companies for its employee leasing services. The company handles the administrative end of business (payroll, benefits, government regulations, etc.) and leases employees to its 1,700 clients. Employee Solutions leases about 45,000 workers in 47 states largely to clients in the transportation and service industries. The company plans to expand by acquiring Simplified Employment Services Corporation. Employee Solutions' revenues rose 3.8 percent in 1998 to $969 million.

WORK FORCE

NAPEO estimates that about 3 million Americans are co-employed in a PEO arrangement. The typical PEO client employs 14 workers with an average salary of $19,659, according to a 1997 survey. These small businesses run the gamut from accountants to zoo keepers and include every profession in between, from doctors and retailers to mechanics and funeral home directors. As a rule, those who work for such companies do not have access to the menu of benefits available to employees of larger organizations. And, as reported by Rodney Ho in the *Wall Street Journal,* a new survey by Dun & Bradstreet finds even fewer small businesses offering employee benefits. Only 39 percent of 503 small businesses polled in 1998 offered health-care benefits, a total down from 46 percent in 1996. The number offering retirement plans had dropped to 19 percent versus 28 percent in 1996.

PEO surveys indicate that employee satisfaction runs high because leased employees often enjoy a greater level of benefits than what was available to

them prior to the leasing arrangement. According to Milan Yager, NAPEO executive vice president, 97.6 percent of member companies offered a health plan in 1997, compared to 45.0 percent of small firms nationally offering health insurance. A 1997 survey showed that dental care is offered by 97.0 percent of NAPEO members, 80.0 percent offered vision coverage, nearly 90.0 percent short and long-term disability insurance, and 92.0 percent offered life insurance. More than 80.0 percent offered a 401(k) retirement savings plan.

As the leasing industry grows, the need to find experienced and capable managers becomes increasingly important. While it is possible to hire good people from related industries (for example, risk managers from the insurance profession), there will no doubt be shortages as the leasing industry expands. Given the skyrocketing growth rates of the industry, this means it is likely that some PEO firms will contract with clients but be unable to deliver the required services. This is expected to result in a shakeout and consolidation of the industry over the next decade. As stock analysts Peter Muoio and Stuart Axelrod wrote in a 1996 survey for Bankers Trust, "This shortage of management will be a key factor in keeping the industry concentrated. Although the total number of PEO companies is high, the industry shows a tremendous concentration among the largest players."

INDUSTRY INFORMATION SOURCES

NAPEO's monthly magazine, *PEO Insider,* is free to members and is available to non-members for $150 per year. NAPEO's on-line bookstore offers a number of publications, including *The Business of Employee Leasing, NAPEO PR & Marketing Guide, NAPEO Accounting Manual,* and position papers on workers' compensation, unemployment insurance, civil rights, and workplace safety, in addition to a clipping service. The NAPEO Web site at http://www.napeo.org includes an electronic phone book of service providers and a membership directory, and for members only, a state regulatory database, financial ratio survey, article library, and Web forum. The association maintains an active educational and networking program, with PEO University classes offered in 40 cities throughout the year, in addition to an annual convention and trade show in September. NAPEO can be reached by telephone at (703)836-0466, by Fax at (703)836-0976, and e-mail at info@napeo.org.

Institute for Accreditation of Professional Employment Organizations (IAPEO), the industry's primary regulatory and accreditation body, is located in Bethesda, Maryland. Telephone is (301)656-1476,

Fax (301)656-5932, and e-mail: info@iapeo.org. Information on accreditation and standards, along with the complete list of accredited PEOs, is available at the Web site: http://www.iapeo.org.

FURTHER READING

Axelrod, Stuart, and Peter Muoio. "Employee Leasing Continues to Expand." *Industry Focus/Bankers Trust Research.* New York: Bankers Trust Company, 1996.

"Benefits Tussle May Clarify Leasing." *Sarasota Herald-Tribune,* 31 January 1998.

"Boom Times for Temps." *Sarasota Herald-Tribune,* 31 January 1998.

DeGeorge, Gail. "You Do the Work, They Do the Paperwork." *Business Week,* 17 November 1997.

Detwiler, Marianne. "Employee Leasing, an Alternative Staffing Option for Small Businesses." *Entrepreneurial Edge Online,* October 1997.

"Employee Leasing Pays Off." *Corporate Detroit Magazine,* 1 March 1998.

Grantham, Russell. "National Bank of Commerce to Refer Clients to Memphis Employee-Leasing Firm." *Commercial Appeal Memphis,* 10 March 1998.

Hirschman, Carolyn. "All Aboard! The Boom in Employee Leasing May Bring Great Career Opportunities for HR Professionals." *Human Resources Magazine,* September 1997.

Ho, Rodney. "Fewer Small Businesses Are Offering Health Care and Retirement Benefits." *Wall Street Journal,* 24 June 1998.

Jones, Del. "New Boss, Same Jungle: Leasing Workers Eases Load for Small Companies." *USA Today,* 20 May 1997.

LaBar, Gregg. "Contingent Worker Safety: A Full-Time Job in a Part-Time World." *Occupational Hazards,* October 1997.

Mille, Margaret Ann. "Outsourcing Trend Drives Growth in Employee Leasing Business." *Bradenton (FL) Herald,* 3 November 1997.

Mooney. Tom. "Employee Leasing Company Owes $13 Million in Unpaid Taxes, IRS Alleges." *Providence (RI) Journal-Bulletin,* 1 December 1997.

Munter, Paul, Rene Sacases, and Larry DiMatteo. "Employee Leasing's Legal Snares." *Management Accounting (USA),* November 1997.

Palmeri, Christopher. "We Cure Small-Business Headaches." *Forbes,* 20 October 1997.

Sanchez, Mercedes, and Budd Bugatch. "Professional Employer Organizations (PEOs): Changing the Face of Business." *Alternative Staffing: Industry Report,* St. Petersburg, FL: Raymond James & Associates, Inc., 11 December 1996.

"Staff Leasing Gains Spot on Fortune List." *Sarasota Herald-Tribune,* 14 April 1998.

Sullivan, Tony L. "Employee Leasing: A Strategy to Reduce Staff Administration, Maintain Benefits, and Reduce Employee Liability Exposure." *Journal of Medical Practice Management,* August 1996.

Tippett, Karen L. "Sectors to Watch in 1997's more Sedate IPO Market." *Wall Street Journal,* 15 March 1997.

Wojcik, Joanne. "PEOs Don't Eliminate Employer's Risks." *Business Insurance,* 11 May 1998.

—John Gallagher, updated by Karl Heil

ENDOSCOPIC TECHNOLOGY

Endoscopes are medical instruments used to facilitate the viewing of areas inside the human body. In the late 1990s, the typical endoscope was a hollow tube with a tiny video camera inside, or with light-transmitting glass fibers. Images picked up via the endoscope are transmitted to a video monitor, which magnifies them and allows the doctor to examine and even operate inside the patient's body, either with no incision or with a very small one. Among doctors who routinely use endoscopes are gastroenterologists, internists, gynecologists, cardiovascular surgeons, plastic and reconstructive surgeons, orthopedic surgeons, and veterinarians.

The worldwide use of endoscopes and endoscopic surgical devices rose steadily during the 1990s as part of a large-scale trend toward the use of minimally invasive surgeries (MIS) and imaging technologies that in many cases are safer and cheaper than their traditionally invasive or "open" counterparts. The world market for MIS products was estimated at more than $4.0 billion for 1997, and the U.S. market for endoscopic technology was forecast to reach $2.8 billion by the year 1999.

ORGANIZATION AND STRUCTURE

Several multinational companies (often specializing in both medical and optical instruments) were the primary manufacturers and marketers of endoscopes in 1998. Three multinational Japanese firms produced many of the top-selling endoscopes: Olympus Optical Co., Inc., Fuji Photo Optical Co., Ltd., (also known as Fujinon), and the Pentax Corp. These companies enjoy the built-in credibility of their established lines of scientific instruments as well as their expertise in camera equipment, research that can easily be applied to endoscopic technology. Another global firm taking advantage of existing medical connections was the Bristol-Myers Squibb Co., selling endoscopes under the Linvatec brand name through its subsidiary, Zimmer Inc.

Endoscopes sometimes make their way to the U.S. market through sales representatives or subsidiaries controlled by an international manufacturer. For instance, Olympus products are shipped to U.S. and Canadian customers through a subsidiary marketing company, Cantel Industries, Inc. of Clifton, New Jersey. Other companies, such as Americo Endoscopy Services, Inc. of Miami, Florida, import and export whole lines from several endoscope manufacturers, specializing in products from such leading manufacturers as ACMI, Concept, Dyonics, Fujinon, Linvatec, Medical Dynamics, Olympus, Pentax, Solos, Storz, Stryker, and Wolf. Another firm, United Endoscopy of Ontario, California, sells and leases new and used endoscopes. The Online Medical Sales Network, owned by Medscape, Inc. of Boulder, Colorado, acts as a clearinghouse for new and used endoscopes.

HOW ENDOSCOPES ARE USED

Endoscopes have been adapted to enter many regions of the body that were previously accessible only via large incisions. As of 1998, doctors used MIS technology to perform such minute tasks as reconnecting ligaments in the knee, operating on infected sinuses, performing tubal ligation, or removing the gall bladder. Endoscopy can be performed for diagnostic or therapeutic reasons. These might include evaluating a source of pain, taking biopsies, removing foreign bodies and abnormal growths, arresting bleeding, reshaping or reconstructing tissue, and placing tubes or stents.

Endoscopes may be either rigid or flexible. Rigid endoscopes contain a solid rod lens developed by Harold Hopkins, a physicist who was largely responsible for making modern medical endoscopy a practical reality. Flexible endoscopes use a fiber-optic bundle, also developed by Hopkins, that maneuvers around curves and bends, but provides poorer resolution than the solid rod lens. The most common endoscopes are called colonoscopes, cystoscopes, fiberscopes, gastroscopes, hysteroscopes, laparoscopes, peritoneoscopes, sigmoidoscopes, and proctosigmoidoscopes.

Gastroenterologists, specialists in the digestive tract, use endoscopes routinely to locate the source of upper gastrointestinal (GI) tract bleeding, diagnose or follow up on treated ulcers, evaluate the cause of stomach pain, and find gastric obstructions. They also routinely locate and remove polyps in the lower intestinal tract by catching them with a tiny wire loop hooked to an electrosurgical cautery unit, applying current to the lasso, then tightening it enough to slice through the polyp. The area is then cauterized with a bipolar probe or a laser. Endoscopy is also used to diagnose and treat rectal pain, associated bleeding, inflammatory bowel disease, and lesions. It is widely used in a variety of gall bladder procedures.

Endoscopy has also been the most common method for detecting Helicobacter pylori, the bacterium that is believed to cause the majority of peptic ulcers. It may soon be replaced by the recently approved Pranactin test, which costs 80 percent less and requires only a breath sample that is sent to a lab for analysis. Some gastroenterologists believe that endoscopy in their field will be used less for screening purposes in the future and more for the collection of biopsy specimens and for direct intervention as simpler diagnostic methods become available. In 1998, the Journal of the American Medical Association (JAMA) published an article giving favorable review to the use of endoscopic surgery for controlling active ulcer bleeding, in conjunction with the antisecretory drug omeprazole for control of recurrent incidence.

Although endoscopy is known as the "gold standard" in diagnosing and treating some diseases, it is nonetheless an invasive technique that carries risks and requires a level of training that is not yet standardized. Although benefits to the patient can include shorter hospital stays, reduced pain, and fewer complications, these advantages can be offset by other risks. Because the manual and visual skills required for these procedures can be very different from those required for conventional surgery, the surgeon's skill and experience, as well as careful patient selection, are especially important to a successful outcome.

BACKGROUND AND DEVELOPMENT

The first endoscopes were used in the early twentieth century and resembled small telescopes with a tiny light on one end and an eyepiece, through which the doctor peered, on the other. These early instruments used fragile incandescent light bulbs at the tip that quickly overheated. Two problems challenged endoscopy's widespread use: how to safely get enough light into a body cavity and how to transmit realistic visual images. These considerations served to limit the earlier scope of application for endoscopic procedures, and kept many old-school physicians skeptical. Karl Storz is recognized as the father of cold light endoscopy, developed in the 1960s, which made incandescent bulb mounting obsolete. Storz's discovery opened the door for capturing diagnostic findings in images, and he also built the first extracorporeal electronic flash. Eventually, as the hardware developed, so did the attitudes of the collective medical community, who eventually came to accept the technology not only for diagnostic, but also for therapeutic application.

Notwithstanding, because of economic pressures, claims were made, challenging the superiority of some MIS techniques that were later disproved by long-term studies. For example, in the rush to offer laparoscopic gallbladder removals in the early 1990s, surgeons attempted the procedures after attending a weekend course, and numerous complications occurred as a consequence of inadequate training. Minimally invasive appendectomies didn't reduce length of hospital stay or complications, and many arthroscopic orthopedic procedures continued to be less successful than their open equivalents.

However, as medical schools began adding endoscopic procedure to their clinical programs, the level of skill and experience in the medical community greatly changed in the 1990s. In 1997, the American Gastroenterological Association (AGA) issued a policy statement to guide hospitals in making decisions about extending endoscopic surgery privileges to physicians. In the late 1990s, many metropolitan hospitals and clinics were well equipped with both hardware and knowledgeable professionals who were well seasoned in multiple areas of endoscopic application.

In a review of minimally invasive techniques in the journal *Endoscopy,* Dr. A. Montori expressed the viewpoint of many surgeons: "Enthusiasm for new techniques must not undermine fundamental medical and surgical principles. . .Minimally invasive surgery is in fact only a further extension of traditional surgery and not a revolution, since it simply involves replacing tactile exploration with methods requiring hand-eye coordination."

Pioneer KARL STORZ, LOOKING FROM THE INSIDE OUT

Endoscopic technology pioneer Karl Storz founded his medical instrument firm, Karl Storz GmbH & Co., in 1945. In 1960, he discovered that he could use a fiber optic light cable to send light through an endoscope into the body. (Fiber optics involves transmitting light through extremely thin fibers or rods.) Storz patented this process, called "cold light endoscopy." Next, inventors developed a remote electronic flash unit to enable endoscopes to take pictures inside body cavities. According to his company, Storz built the first extracorporeal (outside the body) electronic flash for endoscopy. In 1966, Storz teamed with Harold H. Hopkins to develop the Hopkins rod lens system, which an industry source called "the most important breakthrough in optics since the development of the conventional lens system by Max Nitze in 1879." That allowed inventors to reduce the endoscope's diameter while maintaining its photographic resolution. Years later, Storz's company improved the design with the Hopkins II optics system.

CURRENT CONDITIONS

One industry source predicts that up to 90 percent of some common procedures may be performed endoscopically by the year 2005, and another predicts that up to 70 percent of all surgeries will use MIS techniques by the year 2008; in spite of such predictions, growth has been slower than expected. Endoscopic skills are difficult to learn, and many common operations that require complex manual skills such as suturing or knot-tying cannot be performed endoscopically. Although endoscopy is widely practiced in Europe and is used in 40 different procedures in Japan, where cost containment has become an increasingly

urgent concern, only 15 percent of all surgical procedures performed in the United States are endoscopic.

Yet new technologies are making endoscopy feasible for an entirely new range of procedures. Aided by robotic instruments inside the patient that are an extension of the surgeon's hands and non-invasive imaging that can show tissue in three dimensions, surgeons can now attempt intricate procedures in previously inaccessible places and use advanced imaging systems to target tissue more accurately. Moreover, it is anticipated that robotic endoscopic surgery, using voice commands of the surgeon, may eventually help reduce the number of needed surgical assistants, especially in emergency surgeries and/or trauma center situations. In addition, streamlined approval procedures for new medical devices have made it easier for manufacturers to develop and bring new products to market in step with the pace of technological changes.

One of the most promising new applications of endoscopic technology is the treatment known as endoscopic photodynamic therapy, which technically involves the use of light-activated chemotherapeutic reactions to destroy abnormal tissue. In trial applications during the latter 1990s, it was used to halt, and in some cases cure, early gastrointestinal cancers. Despite some initial problems with systemic photosensitization (untoward patient reaction), the future of endoscopic photodynamic therapy in contrast with the more conventional thermal (heat) laser therapy remained promising.

By 1999, use of endoscopic technique in cosmetic surgery, especially for the brow and eye area of the face as well as for breast augmentation, was considered state-of-the-art technology. Again, the advantages were that endoscopic surgery offered faster healing, less surgical invasiveness, and was less harmful to surrounding tissue. For example, an endoscopic brow lift requires just a few half-inch incisions in the scalp behind the hairline, rather than larger incisions directly on the face in the brow area. After threading an endoscopic tube through one of the small incisions, the tiny instruments are inserted in another incision. Through remote viewing on a monitor, the surgeon then pulls brow muscle and tissue taut, splices them internally, and exits. Scarring is minimal, and the cost within reach of those who don't *really* need it, but would like it: from $2,500 to $4,000 in 1999.

Another growing application of endoscopic surgery is in the area of organ transplants. Endoscopic technology has advanced from simple exploratory laparoscopy followed by conventional surgery, to actual surgical intervention during laparoscopy. This greatly reduces patient risk. For example, kidney transplants previously required 12- to 18-inch surgical incisions through the abdominal muscles of the donor. With laparoscopic surgery, a small incision is made above the navel (where the kidney will be channeled out), and four small holes are also made into the skin to insert the laparoscope and surgical instruments. This drastically reduces patient pain and scarring, length of hospital stay, cost of surgery, and post-surgical complication.

Coronary artery bypasses are a $20 billion business, and many manufacturers are actively competing to develop MIS systems for this market. Patient demand for MIS heart surgery is high, and the New York University Medical Center expects to perform half of its coronary bypasses endoscopically by the year 2000. Some surgeons caution, however, that the MIS bypass procedures are more technically difficult and that several years of data will be required to judge these procedures' safety. The Blue Cross and Blue Shield Association and American Heart Association do not as yet recommend MIS coronary bypasses, but Mart Mc-Mullan, a cardiovascular surgeon, summarizes the influence of market forces: "I don't think you can underestimate it as a marketing tool. If you don't offer it, patients will go someplace else."

An increasingly common out-patient endoscopic procedure, especially during the latter 1990s, was coronary angioplasty, both non-invasive (diagnostic) and invasive (therapeutic). Threading an endoscopic catheter into a patient's main blood vessels and on into the coronary vessels, skilled specialists are able to search for plaque and other occlusions, and if any are found, can remove them all in the same procedure. This technology has drastically reduced not only the number of heart attacks in potential victims, but also the need for open heart surgery and full coronary bypass in many instances. During 1998 and 1999, new angioplastic catheterization imaging equipment was introduced that offered filmless digital imaging, producing a sharper image and also permitting viewing "in real time," even from a distant location.

INDUSTRY LEADERS

More than 100 firms manufactured endoscopic devices and components as of 1998. The industry's giant is Olympus Optical, of Tokyo, Japan, which controls 70 percent of the world endoscopic market. Olympus America, Inc. of Melville, New York, markets Olympus products in both North and South Amer-

ica. As a global high-tech manufacturer, Olympus sells scientific, medical, and industrial instruments as well as computer peripherals. It was the leading maker of flexible fiberscopes and videoscopes used for examining the upper and lower gastrointestinal tract or the bronchial tubes. Olympus also makes endoscopic peripherals, including video monitors, computer support equipment, light sources, and video processors. In the latter 1990s it began venturing into microendoscopy. Its 1998 net sales were near $2.6 billion.

A relative newcomer to the field, Endoscopic Technologies, Inc.(ESTECH) was already granted a major patent in 1999. Its RAP cannula is expected to greatly streamline endoscopic cardiac MIS, being able to perform singly what previously required several catheters and incisions to do. The RAP cannula also has the CE Mark in Europe, and FDA approval is pending. ESTECH, a privately held corporation, was founded in 1996, and already has several other products on the market, including the Window Access System, the RAP Cannula System, and the Vision System for 3-D endoscopic cardiac viewing.

Fujinon, part of Fuji Photo Optical Co., Ltd., of Omiya, Japan, makes a complete line of endoscopes including video endoscopes, panendoscopes, laporoscopes, fiberscopes, duodenoscopes, colonoscopes, and sigmoidoscopes. The company claims to make the thinnest and most flexible instruments, qualities of particular importance in pediatric procedures. Fujinon also makes a top-selling processor to carry the images gathered by its scopes.

Another firm with a strong presence is the Pentax Corp., owned by Asahi Optical Co., Ltd. of Japan. Pentax introduced the bronchial fiberscope in 1976 and had further success throughout the 1980s selling video endoscopes. Sales of Fujinon endoscopes remained strong throughout the 1990s. Their product line includes the gastroscopes, endoscopes, bronchoscopes, and duodenoscopes.

A major international subsidiary making endoscopes is Karl Storz Endoscopy-America, Inc., of Culver City, California, part of Karl Storz GmbH & Co., of Tuttlingen, Germany, still family held, with over 18 worldwide affiliates and 1,700 employees. Recent innovations include the development and refinement of: the continuous flow resectoscope with a rotating inner sheath; new pediatric endoscopes and instrumentation for urology; stroboscopes for laryngeal assessment; the ultrasonic lithotripter; a new series of high resolution microendoscopes using fiber optics to achieve external diameters ranging from 0.5-2.0 mm; and contact endoscopes with variable magnification that permitted both macroscopic diagnosis and microscopic evaluation of cell structure during a single procedure. Another big subsidiary of the Karl Storz family in 1998 and 1999 was the Karl Storz Veterinary Endoscopy of America, Inc., contributing greatly to the expanding pet care and veterinary services industry.

One U.S. industry leader is the Stryker Corporation, of Kalamazoo, Michigan, with at least a 20 percent profit growth for each consecutive year since 1977, and 10,000 employees worldwide. In 1998 worldwide sales reached $1.1 billion, according to Pam Johnson in the headquarter's financial group. The company researches, designs, and manufactures endoscopes through a California subsidiary called Stryker Endoscopy.

The largest U.S. firm specializing in endoscopes is Circon Corporation of Santa Barbara, California, which was acquired by Maxxim Medical, Inc. in early 1999. This followed Circon's solicitation in August 1998 of proposals for strategic partnerships or mergers, and the defeat of a hostile takeover attempt by U.S. Surgical in September 1998. Circon's average annual revenue of $155 million was thus married to Maxxim's $500 million of annual revenue. U.S. Surgical owned 15 percent of Circon.

Smith & Nephew Endoscopy Inc. of Andover, Massachusetts (formerly Smith & Nephew Dyonics Inc.), is a worldwide healthcare company specializing in products to facilitate arthroscopy, visualization, and minimally invasive surgery. It operates in 36 countries and employs over 12,000 people.

Other companies marketing endoscopic products in 1999 included Aspen Laboratories, Inc., Neuro Navigational Corporation, Medical Dynamics, Inc., Biometric Products, Inc., American Surgical Technologies, Inc., Imagyn Medical, Inc., Optik, and Medical Devices, Inc.

RESEARCH AND TECHNOLOGY

The field of endoscopic technology continues to be a very dynamic area of advancement. With each new equipment innovation comes a commensurate increase in breadth of application. The possibilities are seemingly endless.

In April 1999, Endoscopic Technologies, Inc. (ESTECH, a company less than three years old) received a major U.S. patent for its "Multi Channel Catheter," to be used in minimally invasive cardiac

surgery. Technically referred to in the field as a "Remote Access Perfusion (RAP)" cannula, it will singly take the place of several catheters previously needed in any cardiac surgery. For example, prior to RAP, several different catheters and multiple incisions were needed to perform the separate but simultaneous functions of delivering oxygenated blood to the body, while stopping blood flow to the heart with a balloon, and at the same time delivering drugs to the heart. RAP will allow all of this to be done, using a single easily inserted catheter, without opening up the chest. All that is needed are small "window" incisions through the ribs. These permit remote access approaches including direct aortic, femoral, sub-xiphoid, or other trans-thoracic approaches.

The RAP's impact on cardiac MISs should be far reaching. Said company president Art Bertolero, "This first patent represents our company's first step in building an important intellectual property position in the field of minimally invasive cardiac surgery. This year, there will be more than 900,000 procedures performed utilizing cardiopulmonary bypass where ES-TECH products could be utilized."

In 1998, Olympus Optical and several partners developed the first high resolution electronic endoscope less than 2.1 millimeters in diameter for observing the fine structures of the pancreas. Due to promising research in miniature video cameras and miniature flexible endoscopes, endoscopy also holds much future potential for neurosurgery. Endoscopic methods of shrinking and tightening herniated disks in the upper spine and neck were successfully demonstrated in 1998, and endoscopes are being used to relieve pressure on the brain and to assist in microsurgery by revealing structures hidden from the microscope.

One of the most important developments of the latter 1990s was the successful use of computer-enhanced robotic instruments to perform intricate microsurgical procedures. Using the ZEUS system developed by Computer Motion Inc., surgeons at the Cleveland Clinic reconstructed the small vessels of the fallopian tubes with a voice-controlled endoscope and robotically operated instruments directed by the surgeon from a console. In 1998 French surgeons used the similar Intuitive(tm) System from Intuitive Surgical Inc. to perform the first closed-chest, minimally invasive coronary artery bypass graft.

In 1998 Conceptus, a Japanese company, received approval for its STAART system for diagnosing proximal tube occlusion, a major cause of infertility. This device is a falloposcope, a microendoscope that allows surgeons to view the interior of the fallopian tubes directly, reducing the need for tubal surgery or other infertility interventions. Conceptus is also developing a non-surgical sterilization technique for tubal ligation, the most common contraceptive surgical procedure throughout the world. While the company's dedication to developing its micro-catheter and guidewire systems continued, its 1998 revenues fell, attributable to corporate restructuring and loss of distributors.

In 1995, researchers at the University of Washington (Seattle) tackled the problem of how to add the sense of touch to a physician's diagnosis. They developed an endoscopic grasping device that used a "scaleable force feedback feature," to reduce the surgeon's hand movements to a scale proper for micro-surgery and that could be programmed to limit the degree of force used. In 1998, researchers at the University of California at Berkeley further refined force feedback in a system that uses a joystick operated by the surgeon to activate robotic hands inside the patient. Commercial ventures to sell robotic manipulators on a large scale in the late 1990s included a partnership between Karl Storz-Endoscopy America Inc. and Computer Motion to market its AESOP family of voice activated and "smart" surgical devices for MIS procedures.

Imaging techniques under development for endoscopic use include a laser system that fires ultraviolet light through a bronchoscope or endoscope to induce different colors of fluorescence in healthy and diseased tissue. Another new device uses a low dose of a photosensitizing agent swallowed through an endoscope to reveal cancerous tissue in the esophagus.

As of 1999, Karl Storz was marketing its new Endovision TRICAM 3-chip video camera. The camera's most marketable feature is in providing greater detail and image magnification from a distance, so that surgeons can cauterize or suture without having to move, backup, or refocus the lenses. Storz had previously perfected an endoscopy monitoring system called "Twinvideo," a "digital picture-in-picture imaging system" capable of showing two different endoscopic images at the same time on one video monitor, allowing better coordination between surgeons performing two or more procedures on a patient at once. Physicians could combine more than two image signals by hooking up several Twinvideo systems and thus directly compare historical data from previous operations from a video recorder, CD player, or multimedia PC with the live endoscopic image.

Siemens Corporate Research continues its work on a "virtual patient" computerized system that will allow physicians to assess whether surgery is even fea-

sible in difficult areas. Using models constructed from patient data in computed tomographic images, the physician uses a mouse to navigate the anatomy under investigation and determine whether endoscopic surgery will be possible. Siemens and others also developed products that create three-dimensional images of organs viewed endoscopically.

Some observers predict that endoscopy will be influenced by two opposing developments: the further refinement of more sophisticated endoscopic methods and the evolution of better non-invasive imaging techniques to supplement or replace many existing endoscopic procedures. Reusable devices, better three-dimensional imaging, telesurgery, shared archives of endoscopic images, robotics, virtual reality, and electronic endoscopy using wavelengths of light beyond the visible spectrum to discriminate among different types of tissue are all being actively researched and developed.

FURTHER READING

"Adding Tactile Cues. (New Endoscopic Grasper Developed)." *Industry Week,* 6 November 1995.

"AGA Policy Statement," 28 April 1999. Available from http://www.wbsaunders.com/gastro/policy.

Barr, Hugh. "Gastrointestinal Tumors: Let There Be Light." *Lancet,* 17 October 1998.

Borzo, Greg. "Minimally Invasive Surgery: Can It Be Physician Friendly?" *American Medical News,* 13 April 1998.

Brooks, Michael. "Light at the End of the Gullet." *Guardian,* 15 January 1998.

"Circon Defeats U.S. Surgical Hostile Takeover Attempt," 28 April 1999. Available from http://www.circoncorp.com.

"Companies Team Up on Robotic System Instruments." *Medical Industry Today,* 26 June 1998.

"Computer Motion and the Cleveland Clinic Announce the World's First Fully Endoscopic Robotic Microsurgical Procedure." *Business Wire,* 18 June 1998.

"Conceptus's STARRT Falloposcopy System Receives US FDA Marketing Clearance for Diagnosis of Proximal Tubal Occlusion," 28 April 1999. Available from http://www.conceptus.com/press/falloprelease.html.

Erickson, Richard A. "Endoscopic Ultrasonography: A New Diagnostic Imaging Modality." *American Family Physician,* 1 May 1997.

Frieling, T., and D. Hussinger. "Endoscopy as a Research Vehicle: Potentials and Pitfalls." *Endoscopy,* March 1998.

"Galileo 1998 Annual Report," 28 April 1999. Available from http://www.galileocorp.com/company/98annual.html.

"Gastrointestinal Endoscopy." *The Merck Manual.* Rahway, NJ: Merck & Co., Inc., 1998. Available from http://www.merck.com/!!tGNk20hkItGNkp3Fn3/pubs/mmanual/html/kgkgikff.htm.

Gerzeny, Michelle, and Alan R. Cohen. "Advances in Endoscopic Neurosurgery." *AORN Journal,* May 1998.

Hamilton, Kendall, and Julie Weingarden. "Lifts, Lasers, and Liposuction: The Cosmetic Surgery Boom." *Newsweek,* 15 June 1998.

Hellwig, D., and B.L. Bauer, eds. *Minimally Invasive Techniques for Neurosurgery: Current Status and Future Perspectives.* New York: Springer, 1998.

"Helping Determine the Best Treatment: Virtual Endoscopy." *Industry Week,* 21 July 1997.

"Joint Research Team Develops Fine Electronic Endoscope for Pancreas Observation." *Nikkan Kogyo Shimbun,* 19 March 1998.

Karl Storz Homepage, 28 April 1999. Available from http://www.karlstorz.com.

Kucan, John O., M.D., and Raphael C. Lee, M.D. "Plastic Surgery." *JAMA,* 19 June 1996.

"Laser Light Unleashed Inside the Human Body May Provide Information About the Health of Tissue, Indicated by Its Fluorescence." *Medical Device and Diagnostic Industry,* October 1997.

"Maxxim Medical to Acquire Circon Corporation," 28 April 1999. Available from http://www.circoncorp.com.

Montori, A. "Minimally Invasive Surgery." *Endoscopy,* March 1998.

Okada, Shinichiro, Yoshiaki Tanaba, et al. "Single-Surgeon Thoracoscopic Surgery With a Voice-Controlled Robot." *Lancet,* 25 April 1998.

Peterson, Walter L., Deborah J. Cook, et al. "Antisecretory Therapy for Bleeding Peptic Ulcer." *JAMA,* 9 September 1998.

Satava, Richard M. *Cybersurgery: Advanced Technologies for Surgical Practice.* New York: Wiley-Liss, 1998.

Shute, Nancy. "Little Surgery, Big Plans." *U.S. News & World Report,* 28 July 1997.

"Smith & Nephew Mission Statement," 28 April 1999. Available from http://www.smithnephew.com.

Smith, Robert C., ed. "Endoscopes." *Medical and Healthcare Marketplace Guide 1997-1998.* Philadelphia: Dorland's Biomedical, 1998.

———. "Minimally Invasive Surgery Products." *Medical and Healthcare Marketplace Guide 1997-1998.* Philadelphia: Dorland's Biomedical, 1998.

"Special Section: Medical Industry Outlook 1998." *Biomedical Market Newsletter,* 31 January 1998.

Stryker Corporation Homepage, 28 April 1999. Available from http://www.endo.strykercorp.com.

Svitil, Kath A. "Robotic Surgery." *Discover,* July 1998.

"Under the Knife." *Economist,* 13 September 1997.

Werner, Curt. "For Device-Makers, Success Depends on Acquisition, R&D." *Health Industry Today,* April 1998.

Wilkins, Robert H. "Neurological Surgery (Contemporary)." *JAMA, The Journal of the American Medical Association,* 19 June 1996.

"World Renowned Neurological Spine Surgeon John C. Chiu, MD, Makes Significant Advancements in Microdecompressive Endoscopic Spine Surgery." *PR Newswire,* 15 January 1998.

—Dave Fagan, updated by Cameron McLaughlin
and Lauri R. Harding

ENVIRONMENTAL REMEDIATION

Environmental remediation removes harmful substances—ones that could harm both humans and the ecosystem—from the environment. Environmental remediation operations largely concentrate on the ground and water. Nevertheless, they also remove harmful substances like asbestos from buildings. Each year U.S. consumers, companies, and government agencies produce a substantial stream of hazardous waste, some of which winds up contaminating the air, soil, and groundwater. Some of the leading contaminants include tricholoroethylene (from dry cleaning and metal degreasing), lead (from gasoline), arsenic (from mining and manufacturing), tetrachloroethylene (from dry cleaning and metal degreasing), benzene (from gasoline and manufacturing), and Toluene (from gasoline and manufacturing), according to Patrick v. Brady *et al* in Natural Attenuation.

National, state, and local governments, as well as companies and investors, finance remediation projects. At the national level, acts such as the Carter Administration's Comprehensive Environmental Response, Compensation, and Liability Act (CERCLA) of 1980 ushered in an era of environmental protection and remediation efforts. In the subsequent years, environmental policy became a key issue in politics. Presidents Bush and Clinton adopted the environment as part of their campaign platforms, and Clinton chose Al Gore, author of the best-selling book on environmental preservation *Earth in the Balance: Ecology and the Human Spirit,* to be his running mate. Under the Bush and Clinton Administrations, more environmental laws passed, mandating that public and private land and water be cleaned, that compa-

nies abide by emission standards, that energy be conserved, and that forests be protected. With federal edicts requiring environmental remediation and protection, existing companies realized they could diversify and start offering environmental cleaning services, while entrepreneurs saw this political landscape as auspicious for launching new environmental remediation companies.

Environmental remediation constitutes a significant U.S. industry, with approximately $10.35 billion in 1997 revenues and thousands of skilled workers. Hazardous waste cleanup constituted the industry's largest segment, bringing in 75.0 percent of its revenues, while nuclear waste accounted for the remaining 25.0 percent. Federal, state, and local governments accounted for approximately 48.9 percent of the industry's revenues, while the private sector accounted for 51.1 percent. According to the EPA (Environmental Protection Agency), the average contaminated site costs $400,000 to clean up.

In its infancy, the environmental movement clashed with economic growth, bringing about a stalemate in which environmental legislation passed slowly, and companies balked at compliance, arguing they could not afford the expenditures needed to take the mandated preventative and remedial measures. However, in the 1980s and 1990s, businesses began to realize environmental and economic progress were linked together—the economy could not grow if the resources were depleted and destroyed. Therefore, well-established companies, such as Lockheed-Martin, Dow Chemical, and DuPont, jumped into the environmental fray as the industry began to take off. However, the task of toxic cleanup proved more complicated than some companies anticipated, and the industry peaked in the late 1980s, which caused companies like DuPont to abort their efforts. In the late 1990s, mergers and acquisitions became commonplace in the industry. Companies such as U.S. Filter and Earth Tech strategically acquired smaller firms to remain competitive during this period.

ORGANIZATION AND STRUCTURE

Environmental remediation services seek to remove hazardous substances that are toxic, corrosive, ignitable, explosive, infectious, or reactive, thereby making contaminated sites comply with state and EPA standards. Documentation shows that hazardous substances have deleterious effects on the environment, humans, and the ecosystem; however, some analysts argue that the extent of their impact remains unclear. Nevertheless, substances such as lead, arsenic, and metallic mercury rank among the leading hazardous substances found in the ground and in water, and all of them are known to pose serious health risks. In addition, scientific literature is rife with examples of afflictions humans suffered as a result of exposure to noxious substances in the environment. In *Ecotoxicity and Human Health,* Frederick J. De Serres and Arthur D. Bloom report on studies linking the presence of toxic substances to the propensity to develop gastrointestinal cancer, congenital malformation, stunted growth, heart disease, and strokes.

TYPES OF REMEDIATION

Environmental remediation operations rely on four general methods: thermal, chemical, biological, and physical remediation. Thermal remediation subjects hazardous materials to high temperatures to decompose them; thermal remediation subsumes a melange of incineration techniques. Traditional chemical remediation relies on the "pump and treat" technique for cleaning contaminated water. A remediation company pumps the water into a treatment tank where contaminants are removed or neutralized, then the water is pumped back into its natural basin. Newer techniques, however, allow remediation services to treat the water chemically on site, thereby obviating transportation and storage and alleviating some of the costs. Biological remediation covers techniques such as using indigenous or genetically engineered insects or microorganisms to decompose hazardous materials. Physical remediation entails collecting and containing the contaminated or toxic substances and burying them in containers. However,

this method draws criticism from environmental agencies and citizens who fear the containers could break, thereby releasing deleterious substances into the ground and water.

EPA and state-sanctioned remediation processes usually include three steps. First, the remediation contractor assesses the risks of the site and studies the soil and water contaminants. During this step, the investigator determines the site's possible hazards to the environment and to the public. Second, the remediation contractor decides which remedial method will adequately and efficiently purge the site, and considers which of the four general approaches to remediation will successfully accomplish the goal. Third, the contractor undertakes the cleanup of the site.

The EPA, along with state governments, sets contamination and pollution standards as well as criteria for establishing the risk posed by contaminated sites. The ranges reflect the different uses or locations of the contaminated areas. For residential areas, many states require that the probability of infection be 1 out of 1 million, whereas for an industrial site, states may require only 1 out of 10,000.

KEY LEGISLATION

The primary pieces of legislation governing and motivating environmental remediation include the Comprehensive Environmental Response, Compensation, and Liability Act of 1980 (CERCLA); and the Resource Conservation and Recovery Act of 1976 (RCRA). CERCLA, also known as Superfund, established a list of high priority industrial sites needing remediation. Environmental agencies and remediation firms refer to such contaminated sites as *brownfields,* or sites contaminated and no longer useable for industrial purposes and that pose risk to neighboring communities. CERCLA differs from 1970's environmental legislation because it concentrates on the cleanup and redevelopment of already contaminated sites, not on creating contemporary environmental standards. Therefore, Superfund constitutes the driving force behind environmental remediation. CERCLA entitles government agencies to several key enforcement prerogatives. They can use money from the Superfund Trust Fund to clean sites on the National Priority List, require responsible parties to finance the necessary remediation, and pursue reimbursement for Superfunded cleanups from responsible parties, according to Charles Bartsch and Elizabeth Collaton in *Brownfield.*

An influential component of CERCLA is its reliance on liability. Pollution-contributing past and present owners of a contaminated site bear the responsibility of cleaning the brownfield, and government agencies can pursue any or all of them for reimbursement of brownfield cleanup costs. With Superfund's scheme of strict liability, governments no longer need to demonstrate negligence on the part of site operators. Hence, present and past owners are responsible for any hazardous substances released on a site. Bartsch and Collaton point out that this conception of liability forces companies to implement waste and pollution reducing technologies and to clean up any hazardous materials as soon as possible to avoid the escalating costs of remediation.

RCRA amended the Solid Waste Disposal Act of 1970 that contains four key governing points: solid waste, hazardous waste, underground storage, and medical waste. This act regulates the usage, storage, and disposal of over 200 toxic substances such as heavy metals, pesticides, and herbicides. With amendments in 1984, RCRA works in conjunction with CERCLA by imposing deadlines on brownfield remediation. In contrast to CERCLA, RCRA largely governs the management of waste substances so no further brownfields and Superfund priority sites are created. Bartsch and Collaton note that the act's statutes concentrate on companies that transport, treat, dispose of, and store potentially harmful forms of waste. Under the land disposal restrictions of RCRA, the EPA establishes standards for the kinds of waste in landfills. However, CERCLA and RCRA overlap in some ways, which promotes confusion in enforcing and complying with these acts. In addition to these federal laws, each state develops legislation regarding environmental remediation and air, water, and soil cleanliness standards that work with the federal statutes.

The EPA also promotes remediation through initiatives such as the Brownfields Economic Redevelopment Initiative (BERI). Faced with a dwindling budget and congressional pressure to impose policies that do not inhibit economic growth, the EPA started a campaign to marry economic development to environmental remediation in the mid-1990s. BERI awarded loans to 10 pilot cities in an effort to foster the cleanup of hazardous sites and stimulate the economy by redeveloping the sites for business use. Cleveland, Detroit, and Bridgeport, Connecticut, were among the recipients of loans stemming from this initiative.

ENVIRONMENTAL REMEDIATION AND THE ECONOMY

As part of the growing link between the environment and economics, companies' environmental

records play a role in their ability to borrow money. When environmental laws became tougher with the enactment of bills such as CERCLA, lenders started to avoid business with companies that frequently handle toxic substances, require thorough assessment of environmental liability prior to approving loans, and circumscribe their involvement in projects by companies dealing with toxic substances. However, while bankers' policies curb the environmental degradation by companies prone to release hazardous substances, they also impede remediation since they approach such projects with caution or even refuse to finance remediation projects.

Another step the EPA has taken in its endeavor to combine environmental remediation with economic progress is to establish training programs for remediation workers and help retrain displaced workers. The EPA and the U.S. Department of Labor head an effort to bring environmental remediation courses to community colleges across the country as part of an employee training initiative. The EPA and various unions and labor groups want remediation jobs to be filled by displaced workers in the communities needing the cleanups.

Other incentive packages designed to encourage environmental remediation and urban redevelopment include Community Development Block Grants (CDBG) offered by the U.S. Department of Housing and Urban Development (HUD). Cities eligible for CDBG can use the funds for hazard assessment and cleanup if the result of the remedial efforts promotes significant housing-related needs, such as benefiting

---

Profile | **THE ENVIRONMENTAL INDUSTRY ASSOCIATION**

The Environmental Industry Association (EIA) serves the environmental remediation industry by offering information on recycling, waste generation and management, public/private partnerships for remediation and conservation projects, industry and safety standards, and international waste management policies and issues. With 2,000 environmental technology companies as members, the organization includes the National Solid Wastes Management Association (NSWMA), the Waste Equipment Technology Association (WASTEC), and the Hazardous Waste Management Association. The EIA also publishes *Waste Age, Recycling Times,* and *Infectious Wastes News.*

lower income households or eradicating slums and centers of urban blight. The Economic Development Administration (EDA) also provides grants that can help stimulate environmental remediation. The EDA's public works grants, for example, allow cities to clean up and renovate contaminated or otherwise unusable industrial sites. Finally, tax incentives, such as Industrial Development bonds, stimulate environmental remediation by offering private companies tax-exempt bonds to launch redevelopment and cleanup projects.

BACKGROUND AND DEVELOPMENT

In 1970 environmental awareness started to mount with the establishment of Earth Day on April 20 by Senator Gaylord Nelson. Nelson reports that 20 million U.S. citizens participated in the initial event, voicing outrage at the country's environmental degradation, and demanding legislation to protect and repair the environment. This demonstration of environmental concern sparked over 40 pieces of legislation requiring environmental prudence and respect, according to Nelson. These laws include policies governing the air, water, hazardous wastes, chemicals, and pesticides. In December 1970 the Environmental Protection Agency (EPA) also was established to research environmental destruction, recommend policies to combat the contamination of U.S. natural resources, and prevent environmental degradation.

Although concern for the environment manifested itself in the 1960s, bickering between the government and corporations stalled environmental remediation projects and continues to impede compliance with environmental policies. However, with legislation enacted in the 1980s requiring hazardous site cleanups and limiting the release and disposal of harmful substances, a burgeoning industry emerged with companies vying to cash in on federally mandated and subsidized environmental remediation projects. Moreover, companies' environmental records slowly became associated with their financial capabilities. In 1989, the Securities and Exchange Commission (SEC) began requesting disclosure of environmental liabilities from companies, which forced businesses to exercise more caution and discretion when disposing of hazardous substances. As the industry's success continued in the 1980s, droves of companies started offering remediation and consulting services, creating a glutted market in the early 1990s. Therefore, in the 1990s many environmental remediation operations competed for a limited number of contracts.

CURRENT CONDITIONS

In the late 1990s environmental remediation became increasingly competitive as the industry started to slow down. Government gridlock also impeded the growth of the industry during this period. The revenues for the industry's top 163 companies fell 7 percent in 1997 to $10.35 billion, including private-sector and government-funded remediation projects, according to *ENR*. Hazardous waste-related services accounted for 75 percent or $7.70 billion, while nuclear waste cleanup accounted for 25 percent or $2.56 billion. Nevertheless, the market share of these two kinds of remediation dropped in 1997. Private sector projects led the industry for the first time in 1997, accounting for an estimated 51 percent, according to *ENR*. Federal, state, and local governments together represented the remaining 49 percent of the industry's sales. Industry players expect the private sector to continue expanding as government contracts dwindle. In addition, the water remediation sector is also slated to grow and industry analysts expect the discovery of methyl tertiary butyl ether (MTBE), a gasoline oxygenate, in drinking water to boost demand for environmental remediation services in the late 1990s and early 2000s. Despite the slowdown, the amount of remediation remaining to be done is colossal. In the next three decades, analysts predict that between $373 billion and $1.6 trillion will be spent on environmental remediation, most of the funding being provided by government agencies such as the Department of Energy and the Department of Defense.

Furthermore, Judy Stringer points out in *Chemical Week* that the competitive climate of the industry forced companies to reduce their fees to compete with the plethora of companies in the business; therefore, environmental remediation companies began operating with very slim profit margins. Smaller companies also started specializing in one area of remediation in an attempt to stand out. In addition, numerous mergers and acquisitions took place in the late 1990s, as companies attempted to achieve economies of scale necessary to win contracts from major clients such as chemical manufacturers and governments. For example, Earth Technology Corporation acquired Multiservice Engineering Ltd. of Brazil, and Rust Environment & Infrastructure and Safety-Kleen Corp. merged with Laidlaw Environmental Services Inc. in 1998

Industry trends of the mid- to late 1990s include acquisitions, mergers, downsizings, and departures motivated by the environmental remediation market's saturation, according to Timothy Aeppel. For exam-

Man working in a Virginia tire recycling plant; the tires will be used as building materials. (AP/Wide World Photos/Newport News Daily Press.)

ple, DuPont Environmental Remediation Services departed from the glutted industry in 1996 due to the uncertain and somewhat ominous prospects the industry faced, and Dow Chemical's environmental remediation division merged with Radian International LLC. However, Joan Berkowitz of the environmental management firm Farkas Berkowitz & Co. predicted that the unprecedentedly low costs of environmental remediation services, coupled with the EPA's flexibility, would launch an era of heightened demand from 1996 to 1998 as companies would try to complete remediation tasks and obligations while the costs were low. In 1998 environmental remediation costs stabilized, rising by only 2.2 percent, according to *ENR*. Industry observers attribute the stabilization to the adoption of low-cost technologies and the increasing accuracy of remediation estimates.

In addition, because environmental remediation has grown less risky with the development of advanced technology, clients began seeking fixed-sum contracts instead of flexible-sum contracts as environmental remediation firms became accustomed to. Furthermore, private sector companies realized in the mid- to late 1990s that their cleanup expenditures were greater than they anticipated, which made them

more frugal, demanding lump-sum prices with no surprises.

To cope with the flooded market, many companies developed innovative practices, such as outsourcing, to stay ahead in the environmental cleanup business. Environmental operations started offering released waste testing and monitoring corporate compliance with environmental policies. In addition, they purchased sites requiring remediation, such as wastewater plants and oil wells, remediated and renovated them, then leased them back to operators. Furthermore, environmental remediation companies shifted their focus from the development of remediation plans—the sector of the industry that thrived in the 1980s—to the execution of remediation. Since environmental remediation companies have inundated the U.S. market, they have turned their attention to international contracts to stave off losses, according to Timothy Aeppel in the *Wall Street Journal*. U.S. companies have targeted Mexico, eastern European countries, and the former East Germany segment of Germany for expanding their client base.

Nonetheless, a number of factors plague the industry's progress. For example, lawyers have advised some companies to postpone environmental remediation projects until Congress finishes haggling over the Superfund reauthorization. A Republican endeavor to repeal environmental remediation and retroactive liability policies also thwarted the industry since companies did not want to comply with policies they feared might be obsolete in a few months. In 1999 Congress still continued to debate how to reform Superfund—a largely partisan dispute where Republicans fought against and Democrats fought for statutes holding companies responsible for cleaning up contaminated sites even if disposal of the toxic substances was legal at the time of disposal. Financing Superfund is another point of contention between the parties. In the past, an excise tax on oil and chemical industries funded the project, but Congress voted against renewing the tax in 1997 and continued to refuse reauthorization in 1998. EPA administrator Carol Browner admitted that the reauthorization is not likely to pass in 1999.

In the first half of 1999 the EPA added 17 new sites to its Superfund National Priority List (NPL) of sites requiring remediation, bringing the total to 1,202 at that point. Despite the legislative hurdles, Superfund has demonstrated progress in identifying and remediating contaminated sites in the 1990s. In 1997 there were 498 NPL sites where remediation had been completed, 477 sites where remediation was underway, 124 sites where remediation plans were being developed, 63 sites where the type of remediation had been selected, 180 sites where assessments had begun, and 55 sites where assessments had not begun. In contrast, in 1993 there were 155 NPL sites where remediation had been completed, 380 sites where remediation was underway, 213 sites where remediation plans were being developed, 92 sites where the type of remediation had been selected, 367 sites where assessments had begun, and 73 sites where assessments had not begun. These figures indicate that even though there were more NPL sites in 1997, the majority of the sites were either being remediated or being completed, not being assessed, or waiting for plans to be developed as in 1993.

The EPA also took steps to encourage more private investor involvement in environmental remediation in the late 1990s. The EPA removed 27,000 contaminated sites from its database of potential Superfund sites. The EPA hopes this move, coupled with its 1995 Brownfields Action Agenda, will act as a catalyst for more private sector-financed remediation. At the same time, the EPA expanded its Brownfields Pilot Program by priming the remediation pump with $200,000 for 25 sites with hazardous substances, according to Robert V. Chalfant in *New Steel.*

INDUSTRY LEADERS

Bechtel Group, Inc. ranked first with $2.2 billion in revenues from its environmental remediation services, which accounted for 20 percent of the company's overall sales in 1997. The construction giant specializes in hazardous waste and nuclear waste remediation. About 63 percent of the company's clients were in the private sector and over 60 percent of Bechtel's sales came from international customers. Besides environmental cleanup projects, Bechtel's construction division has worked on the Alaskan pipeline, the Hoover Dam, and San Francisco's rapid transit system. The Bechtel family continues to control the private company with Riley P. Bechtel as its CEO and chairman.

Safety-Kleen Corp., formerly Laidlaw Environmental Services Inc., ranked second, according to *ENR* and specializes exclusively in environmental remediation and related services. In 1998 the company reported sales of $1.18 billion and, in May of the same year, Laidlaw completed its merger with Safety-Kleen Corp and changed the company's name to Safety-Kleen in June 1998. Safety-Kleen provides hazardous and industrial waste cleanup and management services such as the collection, transportation, and processing of these substances. The company has 330 branches in the United States, Canada, and Europe. After the merger, Safety-Kleen had 11,500 workers.

International Technology Corporation (ITC) remained one of the largest environmental remediation concerns throughout the 1990s. Based in Torrance, California, International Technology provides environmental cleaning and managing services to industries and federal, state, and local governments. The company focuses on hazardous waste cleanup with services such as brownfield assessment, remediation, and restoration. Although International Technology faced many obstacles in the mid-1990s, the company posted revenues of $442.2 million in 1998, up 21 percent from 1997. Part of the company's growth was spurred by its acquisition of another environmental services firm, OHM in 1998. As a result, ITC has 60 offices throughout the country. The company also employed over 4,600 people in 1998, and Anthony J. DeLuca served as International Technology's CEO.

Morrison Knudsen Corporation, a construction company that built the Hoover dam, ranked among the leading environmental remediation firms in the late 1990s. Morrison Knudsen merged with Washington Construction Group, which specialized in environmental cleanups, in 1996. The resulting company retained the Morrison Knudsen name and Washington Construction's owner, Denis Washington, heads the company. Morrison Knudsen has four main divisions: environmental/government, engineering and construction, heavy civil construction, and mining. Many of Morrison Knudsen's contracts come from the U.S. Department of Energy and the Department of Defense. Overall, the company's sales totaled $1.8 billion in 1998 and Morrison Knudsen employed 9,000 workers.

Earth Technology Corporation USA, the result of the 1994 amalgamation of Summit Environmental Group and Earth Technology Corp. USA was another leading company specializing in environmental remediation in the mid- to late 1990s. The Long Beach, California-based Earth Tech made the strategic acquisition of HazWaste Industries in 1995 to become one of the largest and most successful environmental cleanup operations. Earth Technology offers consulting services for contaminated site investigation and remediation sites, air quality and environmental risk assessment, pollution prevention, and hazardous waste testing. Under the ownership of TYCO International Ltd., the company continued to expand in 1998 with the purchase of Rust Environment & Infrastructure Inc., strengthening its position in the industry. Furthermore, Earth Technology bought the Brazilian firm Multiservice Engineering Ltd. in 1998. After the acquisitions, Earth Technology employed about 7,000 workers in 120 U.S., European, and South American offices. Led by president and CEO Diane C. Creel, the company recorded revenues of approximately $1.0 billion in 1998.

RESEARCH AND TECHNOLOGY

Environmental remediation operations and researchers constantly seek more effective and cost-efficient technologies and methods of remediation. In the mid- to late 1990s, environmental engineers discovered they could use compact directional drilling—a horizontal drilling technique—for environmental remediation and testing for underground contamination. Unlike vertical drilling, horizontal drilling does not destroy surface objects and formations such as trees and sidewalks. Instead, it allows remediation workers to drill unimpeded by surface objects, without excavating large areas of land or disrupting nearby community activities. This method also lets workers access contaminated underground areas that cannot be reached by other means, according to *Public Works.*

Moreover, it facilitates bioremediation of leaking underground tanks and obviates bringing contaminated soil and water to the surface.

The U.S. Department of Energy (DOE), in conjunction with Texas A&M University and UOP, developed ion exchangers for removing radioactive waste to replace older inefficient ion exchangers. The new ion exchangers decrease the amount of hazardous waste generated by filtering out radioactive cesium and strontium, according to *R&D.* IONSIV can remove radioactive properties from ground water and fuel storage ponds. The DOE also created a remote assessment and monitoring tool to aid environmental remediation. The Transportable Remote Analyzer for Characterization and Environmental Remediation (TRACER) can measure a site in about a minute and reduces workers' exposure to noxious substances. Furthermore, in a joint effort with EOSystems, DOE developed an electrochemical remediation method to supercede incineration, Catalyzed Electrochemical Oxidation (CEO), which neutralizes harmful substances by encasing them in a low temperature and pressurized environment. According to *R&D,* CEO costs 25 to 50 percent less than incineration and can dispose of substances such as petroleum wastes, pesticides, and chemical weapons.

Besides the high-tech approaches to remediation, some companies have experimented with more passive, natural methods of cleaning up contaminated sites. For example, Phototech proposed to remediate the former Magic Marker site in New Jersey using an Indian mustard plant. The plant is genetically engineered so that it consumes lead while taking in water and once the plants absorb the lead the company can remove them from the site for disposal as low level toxic waste. This method alleviates the need for significant excavation and for disruption of the neighborhood. Furthermore, this method also would cost less than its high-tech counterparts—an important factor because the cost of cleanup tends to impede governments and companies from remediating sites. Similarly, ICF Kaiser International's environmental remediation division researched using cottonwood trees to absorb harmful nitrates from the ground and water around former nuclear weapon plants. Environmental remediation companies also have used short-term crops such as alfalfa and sunflowers for cleaning up sites. Likewise, researchers have experimented with using the bacterium Deinococcus radiodurans to clean up nuclear waste sites with radioactive and toxic contaminates. Researchers hope these genetically engineered bacteria will be able to degrade the toxins, yet withstand the radiation.

FURTHER READING

Aeppel, Timothy. "Environmental Cleanup Business Is Down in the Dumps." *Wall Street Journal,* 6 June 1996, 4.

Aven, Paula. "Rocky Flats may Turn to Trees for Cleanup." *Denver Business Journal,* 21 March 1997, 13A.

Bartsch, Charles, and Elizabeth Collaton. *Brownfields: Cleaning and Reusing Contaminated Properties.* Westport, CT: Praeger, 1997.

Brady, Patrick V. et al. *Natural Attenuation.* Boca Raton, FL: Lewis Publishers, 1998.

"Brownfield Sites: How Much Clean-Up? Liability?" *PR Newswire,* 15 May 1997.

"Brownfields Still Too Risky; Unless States Cut Risks, Firms Won't Build on Contaminated Land." *Industry Week,* 2 March 1998, 16.

Chalfant, Robert V. "State and Federal Initiatives on Brownfield Sites." *New Steel,* March 1997, 99.

De Serres, Frederick J., and Arthur D. Bloom. *Ecotoxicity and Human Health.* New York: Lewis Publishers, 1996.

"Directional Drilling for Environmental Remediation." *Public Works,* September 1995, 71.

Dolack, Pete. "Site Remediation." *Chemical Marketing Reporter,* 26 June 1995, SR14.

"Environment." *R & D,* September 1996, 36.

Grogan, Tim. "Estimating: The Benefits of Accuracy." *ENR,* 28 September 1998, 34.

Nelson, Gaylord. "Earth Day 25 Years Later," 20 April 1995. Available from http://www.epa.gov/docs/epajrnal/winter95/06.txt.html.

"New Jersey Firm Pursues Innovative Cleanup of Toxic Magic Marker Site." *Knight-Ridder/Tribune Business News,* 30 August 1996, 83.

Rubin, Debra K. et al. "Green Markets Lift and Shift." *ENR,* 14 July 1997, 37.

Stringer, Judy. "EPA Flexibility, Low Costs Drive Private Cleanups." *Chemical Week,* 14 August 1996, 31.

Tangley, Laura. "World's Toughest Bugs: Radiation-Resistant Bacteria May Help Scrub Contaminated Weapons-Production Facilities." *U.S. News & World Report,* 19 October 1998, 63.

"Waste Markets Start to Slide but Water Work Is an Easy Glide." *ENR,* 6 July 1998, 44.

Wright, Andrew, Debra K. Rubin, et al. "Booming Economy Keeps Green Markets Afloat." *ENR,* 6 July 1998, 37.

—Karl Heil

EXTREME SPORTS

Because most extreme sports are new, the most influential companies in the field tend to be start-up ventures founded by individuals with long histories and deep understandings of their sport and of the demographic to which they hope to cater. Bungee jump crews, skydiving trainers, and even mountain climbing companies tend to be small affairs that operate on small profit margins and quickly go under or on to other enterprises. The most consistently profitable companies in the extreme sports game are those that focus on providing equipment for the sports, and many of the leading extreme sports suppliers are cross-overs that established themselves serving more traditional sports like football, baseball, soccer, and hockey. Specialty companies catering to individual extreme sports such as snowboarding, wakeboarding, and mountain biking continue to make large gains in the market. Additionally, exposure from nationally televised events has fueled interest in the industry, which remains primarily the domain of the under-25 market. Extreme sports are among the fastest growing, in terms of participation, in the world, and companies supplying equipment and the opportunity to participate will continue to experience sales growth.

ORGANIZATION AND STRUCTURE

As an industry, extreme sports tend to vary considerably in both structure and organization. In general, the sports player has four points of contact with the industry: purchase of basic equipment, purchase of safety equipment, training, and locating a place to practice the sport. The great explosion in extreme

sports participation during the 1990s led to a proliferation of sport organizers and providers. Most new extreme sports business opportunities are in the service sector—providing equipment and opportunities for sports enthusiasts to practice and enjoy their pastimes.

Some aspects of extreme sports industries are regulated in part by government agencies. Bungee jumping from hot air balloons, for instance, requires a license from the Federal Aviation Administration (FAA). Bungee jumping from a crane requires licensing from the Occupational Safety and Health Administration (OSHA) to assure protection for the workers at the top of the crane. These sports have developed safety codes and organizations to ensure that safe practices are in place. The British Elastic Rope Sports Association and the North American Bungee Association both oversee safety standards within their industry.

ROCK CLIMBING

Rock climbing is among the most popular extreme sports. The television science program "Apple" reported that mountain and rock climbing, one of the oldest and most established of the extreme sports, experienced an annual growth rate of 50 percent in the mid-1990s.

There are two types of rock climbing practiced in the United States today. The first, and the most extreme, is called free climbing. Many rock-climbing enthusiasts prefer free climbing to all other forms of the sport. In free climbing, the climber uses only hands and feet for the actual climbing process. A rope is attached to pitons or chocks in the cliff in case of accidents. The second type of rock climbing is called direct-aid climbing; the climber attaches a rope ladder to pitons or chocks in the rock and uses the ladder to assist in the climb. Some climbers specialize in a particular type of ascent, such as vertical walls, while others specialize in different types of terrain, such as ice climbing ascending frozen waterfalls or glaciers. These types of climbs usually require additional equipment.

Of course, as rock climbing becomes more mainstream, the definition of the sport has broadened. Many weekend adventurers enjoy walking on rocks on the weekends without necessarily scaling a 90-degree granite wall. Regardless of whether climbing straight up or walking on a slight incline, rock climbers need, and seem to love, gear. The rock climbing industry has boomed in the last decade as demand for once specialty items like climbing boots, backpacks, and dehydrated food are now available at the local Wal-Mart. The Outdoor Recreation Coalition of America, a trade organization, estimates that sales for rock climbing and hiking equipment grew from just $1 billion in the early 1990s to $5 billion in 1998. Much of the industry's growth has relied on the proclivity that many consumers have for wearing hiking or climbing gear to the park or on a city stroll, even if they never intend to climb a mountain.

IN-LINE SKATING

In-line skating is one of the most popular modern sports. The Sporting Goods Manufacturers Association (SGMA) estimates that participation in the sport has grown nearly 800 percent since the mid-1980s. It has almost entirely eclipsed traditional roller-skating. The concept of in-line skates, in which the wheels are arranged in a single line like ice skate blades, dates back to the eighteenth century. Around 1750, an enthusiastic Belgian skater named Joseph Merlin devised a set of roller skates by fastening wooden spools to the bottom of his shoes. In 1823 an Englishman named Robert John Tyers created the rolito, a set of skates with five wheels per shoe in a line. The idea of the rolito traveled to the Netherlands, where skeelers became popular for a period of 20 years. In 1863, an American named J. L. Plimpton developed the first roller skate using the pattern of two wheels in front and two in back. Plimpton's pattern dominated the market in the United States for almost 120 years. Hockey players Scott and Brennan Olson developed the first modern in-line skates in 1980. The sport has since attracted more than 30 million skaters around the world and has grown into a $1-billion international industry.

In-line skaters vary from individuals interested only in skating as a hobby or an exercise, to serious aggressive skaters who compete by skating up vertical surfaces. Simple in-line skating, like traditional roller-

skating, can be performed on public streets and sidewalks. Aggressive skating, however, can require special surfaces. Rollerblade, Inc.'s Web site lists ten top aggressive skating arenas in the United States, including sites in Chicago and their home city, Minneapolis. Both kinds of skating require safety equipment, including helmets, elbow pads, and knee pads. Manufacturers of skates usually also offer safety equipment geared to the interests of the people who buy their skates. Aggressive skating enthusiasts require different forms of protection than neighborhood skaters.

Many traditional manufacturers of roller skates turned to in-line skating when the craze began in the 1980s. The in-line skates manufactured and sold today generally have four wheels, arranged in a straight line, attached to a solid plastic or leather boot. The chassis, which holds the wheels, is usually made from aluminum, glass-reinforced nylon, or a composite. The wheels themselves are polyurethane.

Most advances in the field are technical innovations to the skate itself. Rollerblade introduced two important modifications: Active Brake Technology (ABT) in 1994, and the Xtenblade in 1996. ABT allows the skater to brake simply by pointing a toe, while traditional skate brakes require the skater to press down with the heel. The Xtenblade is a children's skate that can be stretched through four sizes, allowing the skate to grow with the child.

The SGMA reports that "Not since the racquetball craze of the late '70s has the sports equipment market seen the kind of explosive growth as evidenced by inline-skating." The sport has grown faster than any other in the last decade. With total sales associated with the sport exceeding more than $1 billion annually in the mid- to late 1990s, the SGMA estimates that the market for in-line skating equipment has surpassed that of baseball, tennis, bowling, and downhill skiing. The SGMA anticipates that the in-line skating market will continue to grow at a rapid rate in the next several years.

BUNGEE JUMPING

Bungee jumping remains one of the most controversial of the extreme sports. The inspiration for it came from Pentecost Island, in the New Hebrides chain in the South Pacific. According to legend, a woman tried to escape from her abusive husband by climbing to the top of a banyan tree. When he started to climb after her, she tied vines to her ankles and jumped from the top of the tree. The vines kept her safe, but her husband fell to his death. By the time the first *National Geographic* article appeared in 1955 describing the islanders' practice of diving from the top of a tower, the practice had changed into a ritual performed by the men of the tribe, partly as a rite of manhood and partly as a fertility ceremony to ensure a good crop of yams.

On April 1, 1979, the modern sport of bungee jumping was born when members of the Oxford Dangerous Sports Club jumped from Clifton Bridge in Bristol, England. A member of the same group set a world record in 1980 by dropping from the Royal Gorge Bridge in Colorado. Although bungee jumping has a low total number of fatalities, the sport has attracted a lot of notoriety because of the inherent danger involved. For instance, an exhibition jumper named Laura Dinky Patterson died in preparation for a jump at the 1997 Super Bowl in New Orleans.

The Kockelman Brothers are among the fathers of bungee jumping in the United States. John and Peter Kockelman, engineering graduates of California Polytechnic State University in San Luis Obispo, were two brothers who formed Bungee Adventures Inc. in 1998. Bungee Adventures was North America's first commercial bungee operation, according to the company's Web site, which popularized the sport of bungee jumping by leaping from bridges over deep ravines in the Sierra Nevadas. The brothers have jumped from many diverse structures, including redwood trees, indoor coliseums, office atriums, the Golden Gate Bridge, and hot air balloons. In 1993 Bungee Adventures Inc. released the Ejection Seat, a patented human slingshot ride. The Kockelman brothers have also been active in planning safety regulations for the industry.

Bungee jumping is a largely unregulated sport though. Jump sponsors can range from unlicensed pirate jumpers to large companies. The sites of the jumps also vary widely. Jumping from public bridges is perhaps the most popular because the sites require little preparation and are plentiful. Safety concerns, however, have made bungee jumping from public bridges legal only in Oregon and Washington State. Jump sponsors can legally work from privately owned bridges, but the regulations against public bridge jumping have led to many illegal pirate jumps. Hot-air balloon jumps are also popular, but they are dependent on weather and time of day. Balloons can only fly safely in relatively still air, usually in the early morning or evening. A third option is crane jumping; however, cranes that can support the repetitive shock caused by bungee jumping are expensive and hard to find. A jump sponsor can spend between $70,000 and $150,000 for a used crane and then has to obtain permission from local agencies to set it up and use it for the business of jumping.

A snowboarder catches air on a mountain halfpipe.
(Courtesy of Burton Snowboards.)

SNOWBOARDING/WAKEBOARDING

Snowboarding is arguably the fastest growing extreme sport. Ski resorts, once hesitant to allowing snowboarders in, are now embracing them, especially during the off-season. Since the snowboard course tends to be smaller, resorts manufacture the snow (usually shaved ice) during periods of limited snowfall—much like ski resorts. During 1998, more than 60 percent of ticket sales at Southern California ski resorts came from snowboarders. Wakeboarding, performed in the wake of powerboats, is the fastest-growing water sport as the millennium approaches.

CURRENT CONDITIONS

Many small entrepreneurial companies market trips to exotic locations specifically for the purpose of pursuing extreme sports. Adrenalin Dreams Adventures, a worldwide company based in Pittsburgh, Pennsylvania, creates adventure vacation packages both in the United States and abroad. Many foreign countries have fewer regulations than the United States for governing extreme sports. In addition to two bridge bungee jumping sites in Pennsylvania, the company offers an African vacation that includes skydiving, bungee jumping, whitewater rafting, tiger fishing, and wild-animal encounters. Adrenalin Dreams Adventures, according to its promotional material, has trained and supplied sites in the United States, Columbia, Brazil, Norway, Japan, and Israel, and it supplies cord, equipment, and training to bungee jumping programs worldwide.

Most rock climbing companies tend to be small, local outfits run by climbing enthusiasts trying to make a living by introducing their sport to newcomers. Many provide training and equipment for novices and advanced instruction for more experienced climbers. A typical outing costs between $75 and $100, usually with equipment included. As with most extreme sports, there are no national companies capitalizing on rock climbing as a corporate enterprise.

The most extreme rock climbing adventure requires not only professional equipment and training, but professional guides as well. Mt. McKinley, once the most feared mountain in the world and only touched by the most skilled climbers, is now something of an extreme sports tourist attraction for the very wealthy. The *Los Angeles Times* reported that, in the late 1990s, the mountain was receiving more than 1,200 climbers a year, leaving behind an estimated several thousand pounds of trash. Professional guides for mountains like McKinley, which are highly recommended even for skilled climbers, average between $2,800 and $3,500 for a standard climb. The most challenging climbs can cost up to $10,000. One in 200 climbers who step onto Mt. McKinley never step off again.

The sale of safety equipment is accounting for a greater percentage of sales in the extreme sports market. For example, helmet sales to snowboarders increased 267 percent from the 1997 to the 1998 season. One reason for this is the increased awareness of the safety hazards associated with snowboarding. According to the U.S. Consumer Safety Products Commission, injuries among snowboarders have tripled since 1995.

The increasing popularity of extreme sports, both from a participant and spectator standpoint, is evidenced in the amount of recent television coverage devoted to such ventures. The 1998 Summer X Games, sponsored and covered by ESPN, drew 250,000 spectators and was watched internationally by 19 million viewers. Viacom Incorporated, with its MTV Sports and Music Fest, and NBC's Gravity Games are new additions to the extreme games viewer market. Some of this popularity can be attributed to the debut of snowboarding at the 1998 Nagano Winter Olympics.

INDUSTRY LEADERS

By far the biggest earners in the extreme sports arena are large sporting goods retailers. Perennially at the head of the pack is The Sports Authority, Inc., with 1998 total sales of $1.59 billion, a 9.2 percent increase over 1997. Based in Fort Lauderdale, Florida, the Sports Authority is the name in sports equipment with more than 200 40,000 square foot stores in 30 states, as well as in Canada and Japan. Second in the market after Sports Authority, Gart Sports rang in with $658 million in sales in 1998, a dramatic 188 percent increase over 1997 figures. The company doubled its number of stores to 120 in 1998 with its acquisition of Sportmart, which had stores in the West and the Midwest. Finally, Oshman's Sporting goods, with some 70 stores in the United States, had sales of $309 million in 1998, down 9.8 percent from 1997.

As for the extreme sports field more narrowly, Recreational Equipment, Inc. is among the leaders; the company posted sales of $535 million in 1997, up 10.7 percent over 1996. Figures for 1998 are unavailable. Another influential player is The North Face, Inc., which makes everything from hiking gear for frigid polar expeditions, to backpacks for use on an afternoon stroll. The California-based company posted $263 million in sales in 1998, up 26.3 percent from 1997. One of the flashier extreme sport outfits, known as much for its trendy style and chic designs as for its high quality equipment, is Lost Arrow Corporation. Lost Arrow had $170 million in sales in 1998, representing a growth of 7.3 percent over the previous year.

Smaller but still popular companies in the extreme sports industry include the fast growing Ride Sports, Inc., which did $36.5 million in sales in 1997, up more than 50 percent from the previous year. Ride made its name in snowboards, and snowboards still account for more than a third of its sales; the company is rapidly expanding into other extreme sports domains. Still widely influential is Burton Snowboards—founded by

Jack Burton, one of the founders of snowboarding itself—with estimated 1998 sales of more than $150 million. Birdhouse Projects, Incorporated, a skateboard company owned by skateboarder Troy Hawk, reported sales in excess of $10 million for 1998.

For in-line skating equipment, the leader in the field is still its founder, Rollerblade, Inc. In 1996, a survey by In-Line Retailer & Industry News named the company first among the 25 major manufacturers of in-line skating equipment, but the company does not release financial information. First Team Sports is the number two company in the in-line world, posting sales of $56.3 million in its fiscal year 1998, up 26.3 percent over the previous cycle. With hockey great Wayne Gretzky as its chief spokesperson, First Team is especially popular among young skaters. Finally, Variflex, Inc. produces more than 25 different kinds of in-line skates and is another leader in the industry. The company, which also sells skateboards and other extreme equipment, had $43.1 million in sales in 1998, down 16.6 percent over 1997.

Rock climbing and bungee jumping use similar equipment, and major manufacturers for both sports overlap. One of the most prominent manufacturers of climbing and jumping equipment in Europe is Petzl Ltd. Petzl makes and sells harnesses that are used by both private individuals and service companies. Its Crux harness is among the most popular and most copied safety devices used in sports today.

Bungee Safety Consultants, out of Portland, Oregon, offers consulting services to anyone wanting to start up a bungee jumping facility or use a bungee jump in any kind of promotional material. The group operates the highest bungee jump bridge in North America, and it helped develop the Bungee Code of Safe Practices, which is now the industry standard in all 50 states.

Bungee Adventures Inc. (BAI) is the company launched by John and Peter Kockelman in 1988. BAI organizes and performs special effects jumping as well as sport jumping. According to its Web site, BAI engineered and rigged the bungee jumping of a GMC Jimmy 650 feet in August 1992, performed the treacherous "Human Sandbag" from 200 feet, and rigged the world record setting bungee jump in Cancun, Mexico. They have also supervised over 45,000 bungee jumps safely and have launched more than 180,000 people across America and Canada with the Ejection Seat. The majority of these bungee jumps have been from cranes, with bridge jumps and hot air balloon jumps

placing second and third. Other jumps, says the Web page, have been made from hang-gliders, parachutes, and helicopters.

FURTHER READING

"1996 State of the Industry Report." *Sporting Goods Manufacturers Association,* February 1996.

Apodaca, Patrice. "Vans, Inc. to Build Skate Park at Mall in Orange." *Los Angeles Times,* 8 May 1998.

"Extreme Sports Focus Has Company on Road to Success." *Emerging Company Report,* 10 July 1998.

Forstenzer, Martin. "On and Off the Beaten Path." *The New York Times,* 16 May 1998.

Frase, Nancy. *Bungee Jumping for Fun and Profit.* Merrillville, IN: ICS Books, 1992.

Garcia, Irene. "The Height of Adventure." *Los Angeles Times,* 11 September 1997.

Johnston, Turlough, and Madeleine Hallden. *Rock Climbing Basics.* Mechanicsburg, PA: Stackpole Books, 1995.

Kroichick, Ron. "X Games Finds Snow, Beach Don't Mix." *San Francisco Chronicle,* 27 June 1998.

Luo, Michael. "As Snowboarding Popularity Soars, Injuries Multiply." *Los Angeles Times,* 23 March 1999.

Murphy, Kim. "To Some, The Height of Lunacy." *LA Times,* 1 April 1998.

Powell, Mark, and John Svensson. *In-Line Skating.* Champaign, IL: Human Kinetics, 1993.

Rappelfeld, Joel. *The Complete Blader: Basic and Advanced Techniques, Exercises, and Equipment Tips for Fitness and Recreation.* New York: St. Martins Press, 1992.

Ruibal, Sal. "Going to the Extremes Surfers Turned Alternative Tide." *USA Today,* 12 August 1998.

Skinner, Todd, and John McMullen. *Modern Rock Climbing: Free Climbing and Training Beyond the Basics.* Merrillville, IN: ICS Books, 1993.

Spiegel, Peter. "Gen-X-tremist Pitchmen." *Forbes,* 14 December 1998.

Strassman, Mike. *Basic Essentials of Rock Climbing.* Merrillville, IN: ICS Books, 1989.

Werblin, Cathy. "Complex for 'Extreme Sports' Is Proposed." *Los Angeles Times,* 12 September 1996.

"What's Hot and Why." *Inc.,* July 1998.

—Kenneth R. Shepherd, updated by Jeff Motluck

FERTILITY MEDICINE PRODUCTS AND SERVICES

The frequent decision of many couples to wait until their thirties or even later to start families has focused public attention on a relatively new industry: providing fertility products and services to those having difficulty conceiving a child. The fertility business has existed in some sense for a long time, but with medical knowledge and technical prowess expanding at an unprecedented rate, and with "miracles" being worked nearly every week, fertility has acquired a dramatic new presence in the public consciousness. So-called assisted reproductive technology (ART) has been available in the United States since 1981, and the number of births enhanced by fertility technology appears to be growing sharply. According to a Centers for Disease Control (CDC) study released in 1999 (based on births in 1996), there was a 25 percent rise in fertility-enhanced births from the previous year.

An estimated six million couples are thought to be affected by infertility. In the United States, a couple is deemed infertile if they fail to conceive after one year of unprotected intercourse (six months, if the woman is over thirty-five). Physicians in other countries advise waiting two years, meaning couples in the United States may be seeking medical help for infertility sooner, thus enlarging the pool of candidates for treatment.

Approximately 15 percent of all U.S. women of childbearing age have received an infertility service at some time, according to the CDC survey. Though the rate of infertility in America has remained remarkably constant at about 10 percent over the last 30 years,

there has been a rise in the use of infertility services occasioned by various factors. First of all, "baby boomers" have waited until later in life, when natural fertility drops off, to try to start having children. Secondly, increased use of oral contraceptives, along with the accessibility of safe and legal abortion services, have—in part—contributed to a decline in the number of babies available for adoption. Finally, the advent of high-tech treatments like *in vitro* fertilization (IVF) has made conception a real possibility for couples whom traditional methods could not help.

By 1998 the treatment of infertility had become a $2 billion a year industry. Over 100,000 patients use fertility drugs each year at a cost of more than $300 million. Non-drug costs include physicians' fees, lab costs, and hospital charges. As technological sophistication rises, costs follow suit. Typically, a cycle of high-tech fertility medicine, like *in vitro* fertilization, costs 8 to 10 times more than a low-tech method such as artificial insemination. Doctors have traditionally used low-tech methods first in their treatment regimens. But as high-tech methods become more reliable and standardized, an increasing number of fertility specialists are turning to them first. In 1996, a total of 20,659 babies were born in the United States as a result of high-tech assisted reproductive technologies.

Despite the improvements in technology, the overall failure rate for fertilization procedures is somewhere between 70 and 80 percent. Yet another downside to fertility treatment has become apparent. Now that baseline data has accumulated for more than two decades, research is beginning to show correlations between fertility drugs and certain cancers, such as breast and ovarian cancer in women.

ORGANIZATION AND STRUCTURE

The fertility industry can be divided into two broad sectors: pharmaceutical and medical. The pharmaceutical sector is dominated by two companies, Serono Laboratories and Organon Laboratories. Both firms manufacture drugs used primarily to stimulate or regulate ovulation. The drugs can be prescribed on their own, as a low-tech treatment, to assist conception. More and more, however, they are used in conjunction with a high-tech procedure like IVF in which the drugs stimulate ovulation and then eggs are collected and fertilized *in vitro* before being implanted in a woman's uterus or fallopian tubes.

Selling fertility drugs is an extremely profitable undertaking for pharmacies. A typical prescription for a woman undergoing *in vitro* fertilization includes 12 different products, including as many as 8 drugs, prenatal vitamins, and paraphernalia such as syringes and swabs. Profit margins are also higher in infertility care than for other categories of drugs pharmacists dispense. While most pharmacies make a 20 to 22 percent profit on drug sales, they earn 30 to 35 percent on infertility products, according to a 1998 article in *Drug Topics*.

The medical sector of the industry is far more complex. It includes private OB/GYN (obstetrics and gynecology) and urology practices, fertility clinics, hospitals, and laboratories. Statistics on fertility clinics are difficult to come by. One reason is the lack of agreement as to what constitutes a "fertility clinic." The American Society for Reproductive Medicine (ASRM), which for years has single-handedly assembled statistics on fertility in America, prefers the term "ART (assisted reproductive technology) practice." ART encompasses high-tech methods of fertilization such as IVF, gamete intrafallopian transfer (GIFT), and intracystoplasmic sperm injection (ICSI), all of which arose after the first test-tube babies were born in the late 1970s and early 1980s. ASRM's professional organization, the Society of Assisted Reproductive Technology (SART), had nearly 360 member practices as of 1998. That figure, according to ASRM, accounts for about 90 percent of the ART practices in the United States. The Centers for Disease Control and Prevention has released two reports on fertility clinics, giving consumers access to success rate rankings of the 300 clinics that provided data for its studies.

ART practices can be small or large, independent or affiliated with other institutions such as hospitals or universities. The larger practices have staffs of physicians, embryologists, andrologists, nurses, lab technicians, and advanced laboratory facilities where the latest techniques of micromanipulation can be performed. A small ART practice might consist of just one or two reproductive endocrinologists, a staff of a few nurses and technicians, and a small lab capable of basic fertility analyses. When it performs high-tech treatments, such a clinic generally uses a hospital lab.

Fertility treatments can be classed as low tech and high tech. Low-tech treatments might be relatively new—fertility drugs, for example, have been in use only 30 years or so—but they rely on traditional medical techniques. The most common treatments include artificial insemination, surgery, and basic drug therapies. They have varying success rates, generally lower than high-tech treatments. Success in fertility is defined as a cycle of treatment that results in the birth of a live baby.

Artificial insemination is the oldest and most common low-tech treatment. Semen, either from a woman's partner or an anonymous donor, is inserted into the vagina through a catheter; insertion is timed to occur just after ovulation to maximize the chances of fertilization. Since the 1970s, most donor sperm has been supplied by sperm banks, where it has been cryogenically preserved.

Surgery has been most often used when a woman has no fallopian tubes or when they have been blocked or damaged. Until the advent of in vitro fertilization, surgery was the only possible treatment for tubal infertility. Surgery, however, is more costly and invasive and less effective than in vitro fertilization, and during the 1990s its use declined by 50 percent.

Fertility drugs are one of the simplest low-tech methods. They can be taken orally, by injection, or subcutaneously, and they work by stimulating the ovaries to produce eggs. After approximately 36 hours, fertilization is attempted via sexual intercourse or artificial insemination. The use of fertility drugs is complicated by the powerful effects on the endocrine and reproductive systems, as well as the link to ovarian cancer. Furthermore, a large percentage of pregnancies stemming from fertility drugs result in multiple fetuses. Nationwide, about 38 percent of the live births from fertility-enhanced pregnancies in 1996 involved more than one fetus.

As a means of achieving pregnancy and birth, these low-tech methods when used on their own seem to be unpredictable. Statistics for the U.S. population as a whole are not available, but studies on small sample groups suggest that simple artificial insemination has a success rate of around six percent; when accompanied by fertility drugs, that rate can nearly triple. Fertility drugs alone have a success rate of approximately 10 percent. There are conditions when neither drugs nor artificial insemination can be used, such as when a woman has tubal problems or when a man has a low or nonexistent sperm count.

Assisted reproductive technology (ART) is at the high-tech end of the fertility treatment scale. The most common treatments are *in vitro* fertilization (IVF), gamete intrafallopian transfer (GIFT), zygote intrafallopian transfer (ZIFT), and, increasingly, intracytoplasmic sperm injection (ICSI). Freezing of sperm and embryos (known as cryopreservation) and drug therapies are often used in tandem with these techniques.

IVF is the most common high-tech assisted reproductive technology. In this procedure, eggs are removed from the prospective mother's ovaries, usually after stimulation with fertility drugs, or donor eggs are obtained. The eggs are then fertilized in a laboratory dish *(in vitro)* with sperm from the partner or a donor. Two to four of the resulting embryos are implanted in the woman's uterus. Other embryos can be cryogenically preserved for use in future IVF if the first attempt at conception is unsuccessful. IVF can be used in practically all cases of infertility, though at first it was used primarily for women with fallopian tube disorders or endometriosis, a condition in which tissue from the lining of the uterus exists and functions elsewhere in the abdomen.

In GIFT, gametes (sperm and eggs) are collected and the sperm prepared as in IVF. However, they are introduced separately into the fallopian tubes rather than the uterus and fertilization takes place *in vivo*. It was believed that a large number of eggs and high concentrations of sperm at the natural site of fertilization would increase the likelihood of conception. As IVF is refined, use of GIFT is dropping. Its slightly higher success rates do not seem to outweigh the more difficult surgical intervention that is required.

ZIFT is a hybrid of IVF and GIFT. Fertilization takes place *in vitro* as in IVF. The zygote is introduced immediately into the fallopian tube, as in GIFT, where the normal cycle of conception then runs its course. ZIFT is most often used when a male's sperm count is low or when anti-sperm antibodies are present in the woman.

NEST, or Nonsurgical Embryonic Selective Thinning and Transfer, is a new technique that helps IVF embryos live a day or so longer. This allows extra time to determine which one is the strongest and healthiest for implantation. The embryonic shell is then hatched to make it easier to attach to the uterine lining. Some experts believe this process may boost IVF success rates from about 24 percent to as high as 80 percent.

Pioneer **PATRICK STEPTOE, 1913-1988 THE "FATHER" OF TEST TUBE BABIES**

Patrick Steptoe, an English gynecologist, was one of the major innovators and developers of in vitro fertilization. Together with Cambridge University physician Robert G. Edwards, Steptoe developed the method for removing a fertile egg from a woman, fertilizing it in a test tube, then, after a brief incubation period, placing the fertilized egg into the woman's womb for the rest of the fetal development.

Born on June 9, 1913, in Oxfordshire, England, his father was a church organist, and his mother was a social worker. He studied medicine at the University of London's St. George Hospital Medical School, and became a member of the Royal College of Surgeons after being certified in 1939.

Steptoe began pursuing his interest in studying fertility problems in 1951 while working at a hospital in northeast England. During this time he developed a method for extracting human eggs from the ovaries by using a laparascope, a long thin telescope lit by a fiber optics light. At the time Steptoe had difficulty convincing other medical professionals of the benefits of laparascopy, and especially of his work with fertilization.

In 1966 Steptoe joined with Cambridge physiologist Robert G. Edwards, who had done pioneering work on fertilization of eggs outside the body. Two years later, the two were able to successfully fertilize an extracted egg. However, they had to wait another two years before an egg they fertilized in a test tube was able to reach the stage of cell growth at which it could be placed back into the womb.

Finally, in 1976, a woman who suffered from problems with her fallopian tubes agreed to attempt Steptoe's and Edward's procedure. An egg was successfully extracted from the womb, fertilized, and placed into the uterus two days later. On July 25, 1978, the first successful in vitro fertilization was realized when Joy Louise Brown was born healthy and strong.

Intracytoplasmic sperm injection (ICSI), first used successfully in Belgium in 1992, is the latest high-tech procedure to be used on a mass scale. A single sperm cell is injected directly into an egg. ICSI enables men with very low sperm counts or inactive sperm—80 percent of infertile men—to father their own children. The procedure also allows men who have had vasectomies to have genetic offspring. ICSI is seen as a useful tool for many conditions because it largely eliminates sperm as a factor in fertilization and allows physicians to concentrate on the conditions for pregnancy in a woman's body. By 1999, tens of thousands of babies had been born through ICSI.

The chance that a healthy, reproductively normal couple will conceive a child in a given month is estimated at around 20 percent. Success rates of assisted reproductive technology procedures are as good as or often better than that, ranging from about 22 to 28 percent. In 1994 6,339 IVF babies were born, 1,358 GIFT babies, and 296 ZIFT babies. Those declining numbers reflect the traditional hierarchy of treatment and an ascending scale of technology and cost.

Fertility treatment is expensive. A single attempt with artificial insemination usually costs between $300 and $500. One cycle of fertility drug treatment, which typically involves multiple drugs, can cost $2,500, and patients typically need drug treatment for two to four monthly cycles. ART procedures typically cost between $8,000 and $12,000 per treatment. Given that the *most* effective treatment results in a child barely one in four times, a high percentage of infertile couples inevitably go through more than one round of treatment. According to Kiplinger Online it is not unusual for a couple to spend at least $30,000 trying to have a child.

Only about 25 percent of traditional insurance plans and 37 percent of health maintenance organizations (HMOs) cover infertility. Even when they do, reimbursements are often limited to diagnostic costs; when they cover treatment, coverage is frequently limited to treatments that are ineffective for some patients or less cost effective than others. As of 1999 13 states mandated insurance for infertility, but coverage varies widely. Some states require a round of low-tech treatments before IVF can be attempted. Some exclude HMOs from providing coverage. Hawaii mandates nothing more than a one-time outpatient diagnostic visit. In Texas, a couple must try unsuccessfully for five years before they are considered infertile, although most physicians consider one year the defining period. Lack of insurance combined with high costs has made ongoing infertility treatments a realistic option only for the well-to-do.

But this may be changing. Infertility treatment has long been something of a gray area with insurers, but increasing demand coupled with lawsuits by those without insurance coverage seems to be leading to a more standardized approach. In June 1998, the United States Supreme Court issued a ruling stating that reproduction is "a major life activity." This cleared the way for patients denied infertility coverage by insurers to sue under Title VII of the Civil Rights Act of 1964 or under the Americans with Disabilities Act of 1990. And the number of large employers enrolled in HMOs that cover IVF is rising, reaching 22 percent in 1997 compared to 19 percent the previous year.

Patients find fertility services in a variety of ways. Many are referred by personal physicians. Some clinics advertise. Consumer groups are a valuable source of information. The most important one in the fertility area is Resolve. Besides having over 50 local offices throughout the U.S., Resolve maintains a National Helpline and compiles a referral list of over 800 fertility specialists in the United States and Canada. Another important source of information is patient support groups. Members share the names of doctors and their experiences, suggest solutions to those with problems, and help newcomers navigate the complex and often impersonal medical bureaucracy.

The Internet has become an important resource as well, enabling individuals to gain access to information about new techniques and medications that their own doctors may be unwilling to share. The number of fertility-related chat rooms is growing, and a few fertility doctors have set up Web pages to answer questions and discuss the latest medical developments. Some pharmacies sell fertility drugs online. The Web site for the InterNational Council on Infertility Information Dissemination (INCIID) also provides a wealth of material.

REGULATION AND LEGISLATION

The Food and Drug Administration (FDA) regulates the manufacture and sale of all fertility drugs in the United States. Like other pharmaceuticals, such drugs must undergo a series of stringent clinical trials and reviews before they are approved for use. According to the Pharmaceutical Research and Manufacturers of America, it takes an average of 15 years for a drug to move from the experimental stage to pharmacy shelves, a long process that contributes to high costs. Drugs are usually available in other countries years before they reach the United States but remain unavailable to American consumers. Occasionally the FDA will relax restrictions on foreign drugs. When two common American fertility drugs, Pergonal and Metrodin, were in very short supply between February 1996 and February 1997, the FDA allowed the import of substitutes from foreign suppliers.

Andrology laboratories, which work with sperm, are regulated on a federal level by the Clinical Laboratory Improvement Amendments of 1988 (CLIA-88). The law spells out strict standards of specimen control and technical supervision for labs performing "high complexity" procedures and tests, such as those connected with sperm handling. Labs are required to register with the Health Care Financial Administration and are subject to inspection by that body or an equivalent such as the College of American Pathologists (CAP). Embryology labs, where *in vitro* fertilization takes place, do not fall under CLIA-88 regulation.

The American Society for Reproductive Medicine (ASRM), together with the College of American Pathologists, has drawn up andrology and embryology lab guidelines for its member clinics. The guidelines were voluntary as of mid-1997, but efforts were underway to make them mandatory for Society of Assisted Reproductive Technology members. There are also attempts in Congress to include andrology labs under CLIA-88, a move ASRM opposes because CLIA was written for diagnostic facilities and their specific conditions. Embryology labs, the ASRM argues, engage in treatment rather than diagnosis and should be regulated accordingly.

The Fertility Clinic Success Rate and Certification Act of 1992 (FCSRCA) directed the U.S. Department of Health and Human Services, in cooperation with the Centers for Disease Control and Prevention (CDC), to develop a model program for the certification of embryology labs. Unlike CLIA-88, such programs would be voluntary and would be made available to the states to adopt at their discretion. Lack of funding has prevented the model program clause from ever being implemented.

FCSRCA also includes a provision requiring fertility clinics to report success rates for IVF, GIFT, ZIFT and other procedures to the CDC. The CDC is-

sued its second such report in 1999, based on data collected in 1996. (Previously, ASRM collected and distributed this information itself.) The 1996 data shows that nationwide IVF had a 26 percent success rate, GIFT 28.7 percent, ZIFT 30 percent, and ICSI 28 percent (where success is live birth rate per retrieval procedure). Despite the above-mentioned federal policies, the use of assisted reproductive technology by physicians and clinics is largely unregulated, and a variety of doctors dabble in fertility treatments. Since 1978 the number of clinics has increased from about 30 to over 300. Although the drug therapies are approved by the FDA, the actual practice of fertility medicine is unstructured and highly variant.

BACKGROUND AND DEVELOPMENT

The first documented case of artificial insemination in humans was in 1790. The development of infertility treatment as a discrete sector of the contemporary economy is directly linked to technological development. The most important clinical practices of the 1990s have their roots in the discoveries of the past 40 years.

The 1950s and 1960s were largely a period of research advances that only slowly made their way into practice. The first of the modern fertility-inducing substances were discovered and developed during the 1960s, when gonadotropins (hormonal substances that stimulate ovulation) were extracted from human pituitary tissue. Mass scale production was made possible when researchers learned they could also be produced from the urine of post-menopausal women. So-called menotropins are the active ingredients in the most widely used fertility drugs such as Pergonal, Humegon, and Metrodin.

Clomiphene citrate was also first introduced in the 1960s. Unlike menotropins, however, which had to be injected, it was an oral medication. Another advantage of clomiphene citrate was the considerably lower incidence of multiple births that resulted from taking it—about 8 percent as opposed to between 25 percent and 50 percent for the menotropins. During the early 1970s, A.V. Schally and R. Guillemin won the Nobel Prize for their discovery of gonadotropin releasing hormone (GnRH), a substance that enables the pituitary to secrete gonadotropins, which in turn stimulate the gonads. GnRH restored ovulation in women in whom it had apparently ceased completely.

Cryopreservation techniques date from the late 1940s, and the first successful artificial inseminations

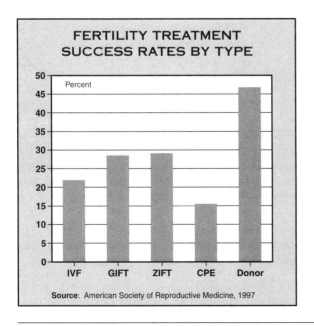

FERTILITY TREATMENT SUCCESS RATES BY TYPE

Percent

(Bar chart showing IVF, GIFT, ZIFT, CPE, Donor with y-axis from 0 to 50)

Source: American Society of Reproductive Medicine, 1997

using sperm that had been frozen were reported in 1954. An increase in oral contraception and legalized abortion decreased the number of babies available for adoption during the 1970s, helping create a demand for donor sperm. As a result, sperm banks, which could preserve sperm cryogenically, proliferated.

The major landmark in the history of fertility was achieved in England's Bourn Hall clinic on July 25, 1978, when Patrick Steptoe and Robert Edwards delivered the world's first "test-tube baby" conceived via *in vitro* fertilization. The first IVF baby in the United States was delivered in 1981 by Drs. Howard and Georgiana Jones. The 1980s were subsequently marked by breathtaking progress. Among the new developments was transvaginal ultrasound, a procedure that involved inserting a wand vaginally to collect eggs needed for IVF. It required only a local anesthetic, and no laparoscope was necessary. The first pregnancies were achieved using frozen embryos, and the first births were from donor eggs. Late in the decade, the first GIFT and ZIFT babies were born.

During the early 1990s, intracytoplasmic sperm injection (ICSI) was developed, and further refinements of the procedure continue. With this method, if there is no sperm in a man's semen, it can be surgically removed from testicular tissue and implanted using ICSI. New technologies are also being perfected that enable physicians to recognize a potent, live sperm cell among sperm that are apparently dead.

The impact of these new technologies can be seen in the growth of assisted reproductive technology (ART) since the early 1980s. In 1985, four years after the first American IVF baby, the Society of Assisted Reproductive Technology (SART) had 30 member clinics. By 1993, that number had grown to 267 clinics, and by 1999 the figure stood at more than 300. Over a decade and a half, according to ASRM, more than 30,000 IVF babies were born in the United States, and more than 50,000 babies were the result of all ART procedures.

The fertility industry has suffered occasional embarrassments. Newspapers regularly report the birth of quadruplets and quintuplets following the use of fertility drugs. During the summer of 1996 a scandal erupted when it was revealed that three doctors at the University of California at Irvine were suspected of having taken eggs and embryos from patients without their consent. As many as ten babies may have been delivered from the "undonated" eggs and embryos. The physicians were sued by 39 patients, and the incident led to the closure of the university's Center for Reproductive Health. In Virginia, another fertility doctor inseminated nearly 75 patients with his own semen and not with semen from anonymous donors as he had told them. He was sentenced to a five-year prison term for fraud.

Cloning is a result of assisted reproduction technology. In 1997 a sheep named Dolly was cloned from a single adult cell. While this was a tremendous milestone in the annals of science, it was also a development fraught with ethical and moral issues. For instance, doctors are researching the transfer of the nucleus from an older woman's egg into a younger donor egg whose nucleus has been removed. The donor egg would then be transferred to the uterus of the older patient for gestation. Using denucleated eggs is very similar to the process that led to Dolly the sheep, and this kind of ART makes the cloning of humans very possible. President Bill Clinton responded to the controversy surrounding such procedures by calling for a five-year ban on any experiments related to human cloning.

CURRENT CONDITIONS

According to the National Center for Health Statistics (NCHS), America's infertility rate has remained more or less constant for the past 30 years. In 1998 about 6 million couples experienced infertility; some 4 percent of all American women or their partners sought help for infertility or related problems in 1995. NCHS statistics, which report only on women, reflect a common bias that women are "responsible" for fertility. According to the 1999 CDC study of fertility clinic success rates, however, 25 percent of fertility problems stemmed from male disorders. Twenty-nine percent of fertility problems were due to female tubal factors, 16 percent due to endometriosis, 12 percent to ovulatory disfunction, and the remainder to other or unknown causes.

Women undergoing assisted reproductive technology usually are between the ages of 30 and 39, with 71 percent of the patients surveyed in 1996 falling into this age range. The CDC study reports that very few women under 25 use assisted reproductive technology, and very few women over 45 use it with their own eggs. Success rates for pregnancies and live births declined among women in their early thirties and declined even more sharply among women over 45. The study did not report the age of male partners of women undergoing fertility-enhancing procedures.

About 600,000 American women have turned to assisted reproductive technology (ART) at some point in their lives. Maria Bustillo, a past president of SART and a reproductive endocrinologist, estimated that between 40,000 and 50,000 cycles of ART are performed every year. Based on the current average range of ART costs, that translates to annual revenues of between $320 million and $600 million, an average of more than $1.3 million for every fertility clinic in the country. The actual figures are probably much higher because the American Society for Reproductive Medicine (ASRM) estimates that ART accounts for only approximately 5 percent of all treatment for infertility. Bustillo, on the other hand, thinks ART may in fact account for nearly one third of all fertility treatments. An article in *HealthFacts* published in February 1999 actually reports a higher figure, placing the cost of infertility treatments in the United States at $2 billion annually.

The number of ART procedures is increasing. In the past it was standard practice to begin with low-tech treatments and move on to more sophisticated technology only as a last resort. But the trend among reproductive endocrinologists (REs) is a minimal diagnosis, followed directly by ART. Whether or not this practice is justified is a matter of controversy in the profession. Cost per live delivery is the benchmark against which treatment decisions are currently made; in purely monetary terms ART averages out to nearly four times the cost of artificial insemination. For some REs, however, this does not take into account other important factors such as stress and time. ASRM is currently devising guidelines for courses of treatment.

In 1999 the *New England Journal of Medicine* published a study showing only a modest success rate for patients treated with fertility drugs, accompanied by an editorial warning of the health risks of such treatment. The risks include multiple births (there were three sets of quadruplets and four sets of triplets in the study of 932 couples), increased chance of ovarian cancer, and a drug side effect known as ovarian hyperstimulation. These risks are troubling to both health professionals and insurers. The executive director of the American Society for Reproductive Medicine called for federally mandated infertility insurance at the group's December 1998 annual meeting. Because insurance issues prod couples to achieve a pregnancy quickly, it seems to lead to acceptance of higher risk treatments. In another study released in 1998, the multiple birth rate for women under 35 undergoing embryo transfers (through various assisted reproduction procedures) in states without mandated infertility insurance was 50 percent. In the 13 states with mandated infertility insurance coverage, the rate was 37 percent.

With technological progress racing forward, certain ethical questions are becoming more urgent in the fertility industry. An area of heated controversy includes the cryogenic preservation of embryos. Professionals struggle with issues such as whether clinics and labs are obligated to maintain frozen embryos when the couple to whom they belong disappears or stops paying for their maintenance. The issue is further complicated by the absence of any legal guidelines. A clinic that chooses simply to dispose of such embryos, even after many years have passed, would almost certainly face litigation if the couple to whom the embryos belonged suddenly resurfaced. Postmenopausal motherhood presents another ethical conundrum. It is now possible, via IVF, for a woman in her fifties or even sixties to give birth to a baby. But many wonder if this is an ethically responsible choice. Questions surface about the ability of older parents to withstand the physical and emotional strains of child rearing, about the chances that the mother will survive long enough to raise the child to adulthood, and about the psychological impact of such a situation on a child.

The practice of embryo splitting generates concern that the creation of two embryos with identical genomes could produce identical twins who might be born years apart. Posthumous reproduction entertains the question of whether or not a woman should be entitled to use sperm from a dead partner if he had not given prior consent. And lastly—representing perhaps the most bizarre possibility—is the notion of whether or not society should tolerate the removal of immature eggs from aborted fetuses to be used as donor eggs. A child thus born would, in a sense, have a genetic mother who had never lived.

INDUSTRY LEADERS

Two pharmaceutical companies dominate the fertility drug industry: Serono Laboratories and Organon Laboratories. Serono Laboratories is the leader in the field with a wide range of products, primarily for reproductive medicine, but also in the areas of growth, metabolism, and immunology/oncology. Serono's parent company, the Swiss firm Ares-Serono, posted $542.6 million in fertility drug sales in 1996; 27 percent of Ares-Serono's world sales were in North America. The company predicts growth of 10 to 15 percent annually for the world fertility drug market.

Serono has an impressive list of research achievements. They launched the world's first human menotropin, Pergonal, in the 1960s; the first gonadotropin containing only follicle stimulating hormone, Metrodin, in the 1980s; and the world's first gonadotropin that could be injected subcutaneously instead of intramuscularly, Fertinex, in the late 1980s. In 1995 the company developed the world's first recombinant menotropin, Gonal-F. With this revolutionary discovery, the active ingredient in the most important fertility drugs can be synthesized. Thus, production is no longer dependent on world supplies of human menopausal urine, a fact that should ultimately bring the drug's price down. Gonal-F (follitropin alpha) is a hormone that stimulates follicle development. Gonal-F was the first drug approved by the European Union, and the FDA approved its use in 1997.

Organon Laboratories manufactures Humegon, a gonadotropin, as well as a wide range of drugs for contraception, anesthesiology, central nervous system disorders, and immunology. The company is a business unit of the Pharma health care group of Akzo Nobel, with holdings in over 50 countries.

Organon was founded in Europe in the early 1920s to develop human pharmaceuticals from the hormones present in animal organs. In addition to creating the world's first fast-acting insulin, Organon was the first to isolate and identify the male hormone testosterone in 1935 and the first to standardize the hormone progesterone in 1939. Humegon was introduced in Europe in 1963; FDA approval was not granted until 1994. Organon also received FDA approval in 1997 for its Follistim (follitropin beta), a hormone that helps stimulate the growth of follicles.

Two leading American fertility clinics are the Jones Institute for Reproductive Medicine in Norfolk, Virginia, and the Genetics and IVF Institute in Fairfax, Virginia. The Jones Institute was founded in 1981 by Drs. Howard and Georgiana Jones. They delivered America's first IVF baby at the Institute in 1981 and have delivered over 1700 more since then. The Institute offers a full range of fertility techniques. In June 1993 the Institute delivered the first baby that had been screened for Tay-Sachs disease, a fatal condition, using pre-implantation genetic testing. Jones Institute prides itself on attracting sizable research funds from private sources and the pharmaceutical industry.

The Genetics and IVF Institute (GIVF) was founded in 1984 and has achieved over 1,400 pregnancies utilizing ART procedures. In 1984, GIVF conducted its first prenatal genetic testing, and it does ongoing research on sperm separation, DNA testing, and other advanced technologies. GIVF was the first clinic to utilize non-surgical transvaginal ultrasound for the retrieval of eggs for IVF in 1985. In the early 1990s,

they became the first fertility center in the United States to offer cryopreservation of ovarian tissue.

The assisted reproduction industry is also seeing the growth of smaller, more consumer-friendly companies that focus on regional markets. For example, Matria Healthcare, Incorporated, of Marietta, Georgia, in addition to operating standard IVF clinics, also offers in-home obstetrical care and infertility treatment, including IVF services.

WORK FORCE

There are no reliable statistics on precisely how many American physicians currently treat infertility. The American Society for Reproductive Medicine (ASRM) has 8,800 members, 90 percent of whom are obstetrician-gynecologists and 7 percent of whom are urologists. Most of these members have general practices rather than fertility clinics and offer reproductive services together with other related treatments. Such practitioners provide most first-tier fertility treatment.

Various reproductive specialists work in ART practices. The most common are reproductive endocrinologists (REs), specialists who treat female infertility. An RE completes a normal medical school education, usually as an obstetrician/gynecologist, followed by a two-year fellowship in a certified RE program. A reproductive urologist diagnoses and treats male-factor infertility and completes a similar two-year, post-medical school fellowship program on reproductive medicine. According to ASRM, in June 1997 there were 650 board-certified reproductive endocrinologists and MDs enrolled in RE fellowships. Larger clinics often have a reproductive immunologist on their staff who is also an MD and whose presence—considering the growing importance of immunological factors in fertility—can be critical to treatment.

Other specialized clinic personnel include embryologists, who may be MDs or have advanced degrees in biology, biochemistry, or a related science. The embryologist is responsible for preparing embryos before and after cryopreservation. Andrologists prepare sperm for freezing and fertilization procedures; these are lab technicians with degrees in biochemistry, endocrinology, or physiology. Geneticists advise couples with potential genetic abnormalities and generally have an advanced degree in biology or genetics.

The field is beginning to see the development of a market for donated eggs. From 1989 to 1994 the number of births that resulted from the implantation of donated eggs grew from about 120 to nearly 1,300. In fact, 63-year-old Arceli Keh gave birth in 1996 to a healthy baby that grew from a donor egg. As these successes multiply, donor eggs will be in increasingly high demand. It can be a lucrative business; donors can earn up to $5,000 for donating eggs, and an egg that is suitably matched to an infertile couple may cost the couple as much as $6,000 or more.

AMERICA AND THE WORLD

In general, American reproductive science lags behind that conducted in Europe due to the stringent U.S. regulation of pharmaceuticals and the financial and societal restrictions placed on research. Drugs are usually available overseas 10 to 15 years before they can be purchased by American patients, and when they finally become available for sale in the United States, they are frequently much more expensive than in Europe or Latin America. Because of high fertility drug costs, a certain percentage of Americans prefer to buy them abroad (in Mexico, for example) despite the risks involved in smuggling them back into the country.

American fertility research also comes up short versus its European counterpart because so little of it is publicly funded. The most imposing foreign presence in the American fertility industry are the two drug companies, Serono and Organon, whose parent companies are both European.

Differences in health insurance between the United States and other countries also account for differences in reproductive technology. For example, medical insurance in Sweden pays for numerous cycles of IVF and allows doctors to transfer just one embryo as opposed to the two to four (or even more) typically transferred in the United States. This gives Swedish clinics a lower success rate of births per egg transfers. But it greatly reduces the risk of multiple births, the rate of which some observers find disturbingly high in the United States.

RESEARCH AND TECHNOLOGY

In the mid-1970s, federal funding of research on human embryos was halted in the United States when the Congress failed to fund an ethics board to review research proposals. Although the law was nullified by later legislation, it still prompted the National Institutes of Health (the major source of federal funding for medical research) to deny financial support for hu-

man embryo research. Therefore, such research must depend on private funding, some of which comes from grants established by the two drug companies, Serono and Organon. Much of the research is conducted at fertility clinics and is paid for from clinic revenues.

Research being conducted at the University of Pennsylvania School of Veterinary Medicine is showing that sperm stem cells, or spermatogonia, can be transplanted successfully from fertile mice into sterile mice. Spermatogonia are the cells that manufacture sperm. The once-sterile mice can then have healthy offspring. These sperm stem cells can also be frozen, thawed, and transplanted. The initial success in these animal trials holds promise for reversing fertility problems in men.

Some techniques are being perfected in clinical research. A handful of clinics can perform pre-implantation genetic diagnosis, which is used when a couple is at risk for X-linked recessive diseases such as cystic fibrosis or spinal muscular atrophy. In this procedure, researchers do a single-cell genetic analysis on cells taken from embryos until they find one that does not have the genetic defect. Some clinics are able to perform clinical sperm separation, distinguishing sperm by the X or Y chromosome they carry. When perfected, this treatment will enable physicians to control over 350 X-linked recessive disorders such as hemophilia, a disease that strikes primarily males. Less than 100 children have been born using this process, but it has allowed parents to avoid passing along serious genetic disorders.

An even more revolutionary advance will be the ability to remove immature eggs from a woman's ovaries (or ovary tissue itself), maturing them in the lab, and then performing IVF on them. As of late 1998 it was not possible to freeze human eggs, though it has worked on mouse eggs and embryos. The technique, if perfected, would have various applications. It would eliminate the need for fertility drugs, lowering the cost of IVF by approximately one-third, and it would eliminate the risk of side effects from the drugs. It would also enable women about to undergo cancer therapy that could conceivably destroy ovary function to bear their own children in the future or even regenerate ovaries with reimplanted tissue.

An interesting breakthrough reported in the fall of 1998 was the ability of one clinic, the Genetics & IVF Institute in Fairfax, Virginia, to ensure their patients an 85 percent chance of conceiving a girl. The clinic announced it had adapted a technique used on agricultural animals for more than a decade to select sex by relying on a sperm-sorting technique before artificial insemination. The clinic was unable to produce results for selection for boys, but it predicted that such a development was on the horizon and that many other clinics would soon offer sex selection services.

Another area of recent research concerns the safety of ICSI, the technique in which individual sperm are injected directly into eggs to fertilize them. ICSI was discovered accidentally by a Belgian doctor in 1992 and has since blossomed into a treatment that can allow 99 percent of infertile men to father children. A study published in the journal *Nature* in March 1999 warned that the injection of sperm into eggs can damage egg proteins that move chromosomes. The study involved rhesus monkeys, and it did not show any apparent genetic damage to the monkey offspring resulting from ICSI. But it indicates that there is a great deal that is still unknown about the technique.

FURTHER READING

Abma, Joyce C., et al. *Fertility, Family Planning and Women's Health: New Data from the 1995 National Survey of Family Growth,* Hyattsville, Md.: U.S. Department of Health and Human Services, May 1997.

Ackerman, Elise. "New Fangled Babies, New Fangled Risks." *U.S. News & World Report,* 22 December 1997.

American Society for Reproductive Medicine. *A Brief History of Assisted Reproduction,* January 1998.

———. *Results of Joint SART/ASRM, CDC and RESOLVE 1996 Assisted Reproductive Technologies Success Rate Report,* 1999. Available from http://www.asrm.org.

Aronson, Diane D., and Merrill Matthews. "Q: Should Health Insurers Be Forced to Pay for Infertility Treatments?" *Insight on the News,* 8 February 1999.

"Assisted Reproductive Technology in the United States and Canada: 1995 Results." *Fertility and Sterility,* March 1998.

Beary III, John F. "The Drug Development and Approval Process." *Pharmaceutical Research and Manufacturers of America,* 1996. Available from http://www.phrma.org.

Beavers, Norma. "FDA Approves Two New Fertility Drugs." *Drug Topics,* 3 November 1997.

Chandra, Anjani, and William D. Mosher. "The Demography of Infertility and the Use of Medical Care for Infertility." *Infertility and Reproductive Medicine Clinics of North America,* April 1994.

Davis, Kristin. "The Agonizing Price of Infertility." *Kiplinger Online,* 27 March 1997. Available from http://www.kiplinger.com.

"Disposition of Abandoned Embryos," *Fertility and Sterility,* May 1997.

"Embryo Splitting for Infertility Treatment." *Fertility and Sterility,* May 1997.

Golden, Frederic. "Boy? Girl? Up to You." *Time,* 21 September 1998.

Gross, Jane. "The Fight to Cover Infertility." *The New York Times,* 7 December 1998.

"Infertility: A Fertile Niche for R.Phs." *Drug Topics,* 21 September 1998.

"Infertility Treatments: Weighing the Risks and Benefits." *HealthFacts,* February 1999.

InterNational Council for Infertility Information Dissemination. "Criteria for Selecting a High-Tech Infertility Clinic," 1997. Available from http://www.inciid.org/links.html.

Kolata, Gina. "New Questions about Popular Fertilization Technique." *The New York Times,* 30 March 1999.

Larkin, Marilynn. "Male Reproductive Health: A Hotbed of Research." *Lancet,* 15 August 1998.

Levinson, Gene, et al. "Recent Advances in Reproductive Genetic Technologies." *Biotechnology,* 1995. Available from http://www.gifv.com/argt.html.

Norderberg, Tamar. "Overcoming Infertility." *FDA Consumer,* January-February 1997. Available from http://www.fda.gov.

"Oocyte Donation to Postmenopausal Women." *Fertility and Sterility,* May 1997.

Paulson, Richard. "Successful Pregnancy in a 63-Year-Old Woman." *Fertility and Sterility,* May 1997.

Phillips, Donald F. "Reproductive Medicine Experts Till an Increasingly Fertile Field." *Journal of the American Medical Association,* 9 December 1998.

"Posthumous Reproduction." *Fertility and Sterility,* May 1997.

Stabiner, Karen. "What Price Pregnancy?" *Good Housekeeping,* July 1998.

Tewari, Krishnansu. "Fertility Drugs and Malignant Germ-Cell Tumors." *Lancet,* 28 March 1998.

"The Use of Fetal Ocytes in Assisted Reproduction." *Fertility and Sterility,* May 1997.

Van Voohis, Bradley J. "Cost Effectiveness of Infertility Treatments: A Cohort Study." *Fertility and Sterility,* Vol. 67, No. 5, May 1997.

Watson, Traci. "Sister Can You Spare An Egg?" *U.S. News & World Report,* 23 June 1997.

Wright, Karen. "Human in the Age of Mechanical Reproduction." *Discover,* May 1998.

—Gerald E. Brennan, updated by Mark Crawford and Angela Woodward

FIBER OPTICS

Since the late 1950s, optical fibers have emerged as revolutionary tools in the fields of medicine and telecommunications. They are capable of transmitting light pulses containing data up to 13,000 miles without significant distortion. Optical fibers also permit the "piping" of light into otherwise inaccessible locations, which makes them useful in diagnostic procedures previously requiring invasive surgery.

According to physicists, electrical signals travel from one end of a copper wire to the other in about the same time it takes light to traverse a fiber optic cable of the same length. Both signals move only slightly slower than the speed of light. Voice transmission has traditionally been over copper wires. Originally designed for telephone service only, this system requires cumbersome switching equipment and serial amplifiers to boost the signal as it travels the distance. Copper wire is also used for television, cable TV, and computer lines, which became overloaded in the 1990s. Because of its limited capacitance, copper wire has limited bandwidth. In the old telephone system, the central office switches were so slow that even the simplest copper cables had much more bandwidth than the switches could handle. It is the processing speed of the switches, not the bandwidth of the transmission, that limits the number of telephone conversations that can travel simultaneously across telecommunication lines.

Within the telecommunications industry, fiber optics have been developed as a means of handling the data that increases exponentially every year. Amazingly, a single fiber optic strand of glass or plastic is capable of transmitting more than 10,000 times the information than conventional copper cable. Because of that, it has attracted the attention of long-distance and local telephone companies, cable television companies, and computer networks.

The fiber optics industry has been enjoying fantastic growth in the late 1990s. The leading manufacturers of fiber-optic cable have been producing at full capacity for several years. New production facilities are being built and old ones are being expanded to keep up with the growing demand. At the end of the decade, the photonics industry expected to benefit from dramatic increases in government funding for non-military research and development. Teddi C. Laurin, executive publisher of *Photonics Spectra,* called President Bill Clinton's proposed "Twenty-first Century Research Fund" the biggest dollar commitment to science in U.S. history. (Also see the essay in this book entitled Photonics.)

Technical refinements already underway promise to boost transmission capacity even higher, despite the fact that the United States is nowhere near utilizing the full bandwidth potential that fiber optics now has. The latest advances are enabling the telecommunications industry to move rapidly toward an all-optical network—one unmediated by electronic connections—which will increase carrier capacity even more. As the industry advances and as efficiency increases, costs are expected to plummet, thereby making fiber optics in the home and office a reality.

The fiber optics industry is divided into two broad segments. On the one side are the manufacturers of fiber-optic system components, such as cable, transmitters, receivers, signal amplifiers, and other specialized equipment. The other side of the industry contains the manufacturers of the actual cable. Many manufacturers have product lines that cover the spectrum, although some companies are more known for cable than components and vice versa. As a whole, the industry is split between giant companies, like Corning Incorporated or Lucent Technologies, and smaller companies, like Ciena Corporation.

The manufacturers sell their products to organizations that use fiber-optical equipment to supply a service, such as telecommunications or cable television stations; to run an information/communication network, such as that used by the U.S. government; or to other industry segments for various uses. Businesses are slowly turning to fiber optics when they install in-house computer networks, and at least one local government started wiring an entire city with fiber. For the most part, however, high-volume applications such as these are still too expensive.

Since the invention of the telegraph in the nineteenth century, most data sent along lines has consisted of electrical impulses transmitted along copper wires. Fiber optics differ in two fundamental respects—the medium of transmission is a line of glass or plastic, not copper, and pulses of light, not electricity, are the means. Lasers send pulses of light down the glass strand in an information stream that can be either analog or digital. The stream is slightly faster than an electrical current on copper, and it is unaffected by electrical disturbances that can create static in the line.

Different information streams travel down the same fiber strand separated by their wavelengths. The number of wavelengths available on a line determines how much information can be transmitted. That amount is referred to as the medium's bandwidth, and the essential difference between fiber-optic line and copper line is fiber optics' enormously higher bandwidth. A fiber strand can transmit 4,200 times more information than copper at one time—and transmit it thousands of times faster due to the higher volume of data that can be packed into the higher frequency wavelength. Copper relays, for example, can handle 24 simultaneous phone calls per second. In the late 1990s, laser and fiber optics systems were nearing a capacity of 320,000. This capacity is increasingly important as videos, sound, and other bit-heavy files get transmitted back and forth across the Internet. Copper can transmit a mere 64,000 bits per second compared to fiber optic' 10 gigabits per second, or 10 *billion* bits. Higher bandwidth means not only more information, but faster information. For example, a Web page that takes 70 seconds to load by copper will be nearly instantaneous by fiber, and an x-ray that requires two and a half hours by conventional lines takes only two seconds on fiber.

BACKGROUND AND DEVELOPMENT

Fiber optics received its first application in medicine. In the late 1950s, Dr. Narinder S. Kapany hit upon the idea of building an endoscope capable of seeing around twists and turns in a patient's body by using fiber-optic bundles. His device, which came to be called the fiberscope, consisted of two bundles of fiber: one incoherent bundle, in which there is no relationship between the order of fibers from one end of the bundle, to the other to transmit light into the body of the patient; and one coherent bundle, in which the individual fibers have the same position at both ends of the bundle, to carry a color image back to the physician. (Also see the essay in this book entitled Endoscopic Technology.)

Optical fibers were first used in the field of telecommunications in the late 1960s when it became apparent that data transmitted by laser light could be broken up and absorbed by uncontrollable elements such as fog and snow. The first optical fibers produced contained flaws that resulted in significant amounts of light loss. To boost the range of the light signal, energized atoms from rare elements were used to amplify the signal at 1.54 micrometers—the wavelength at which the fibers are able to transmit light the farthest.

Paul Henson of United Telecommunications in Kansas was perhaps the first to gamble on fiber optics in the telecommunications field. He invested $1 billion in the late 1970s; by 1982 United Telecom had one of the largest fiber-optic networks in the world, outstripping even AT&T.

The technology took off with the first deregulation of the telephone industry in 1982. Carriers competing with AT&T for long-distance business, such as MCI and Sprint, began planning their own state-of-the-art fiber-optic phone networks. By 1984 Henson was chairman of Sprint, which was announcing plans for a 100 percent fiber-optic long-distance network. The same year MCI laid its first fiber-optic line from Washington, D.C., to New York. By 1988 Sprint's entire network was fiber optic and, in 1989, the company made the first transatlantic phone call along fiber-optic line. Currently fiber-optic technology forms the backbone of the long-distance telephone industry, which has installed a total of more than 10 million miles of line.

Full implementation of The Telecommunications Act of 1996 was expected to stimulate the industry. Passed in February 1996, the law completed the deregulation of the telecommunications industry started with AT&T's break-up in the early 1980s. The law did away with the monopoly of local phone service that had been in place since 1934 and allowed anyone to compete in the market, including long-distance servers, local companies, cable television companies, and utility companies. The law also reversed the AT&T consent decree that forbade regional Bell companies from providing long-distance service or manufacturing telephone equipment. The law was intended to stimulate competition and the quick implementation of new technology. Fiber-optic companies were expected to benefit from the new situation.

Optical fibers have also been demonstrated as an ideal method of transmitting high-definition television (HDTV) signals. Because its transmissions contain twice as much information as those of conventional television, HDTV allows for much greater clarity and definition of picture; however, standard transmission technology is not capable of transmitting so much information at once. Using optical fibers, the HDTV signal can be transmitted as a digital light-pulse, providing a near-flawless image reproduction that is far superior to broadcast transmission.

CURRENT CONDITIONS

Today's telecommunication and information industries continue to be driven by the so-called "bandwidth shortage." Internet traffic is doubling regularly—a trend that will intensify as more sound and video becomes available for downloading. Voice traffic is also growing at a rate of about 20 percent annually.

The challenge is for the fiber optics industry to replace the old cumbersome copper line systems with a faster, more powerful type of electronic transmission without interrupting or slowing down a service people have come to expect. Communications companies must also weigh the cost, load, and signal differences of upgrading and revamping obsolete switching equipment from copper to optical cable versus replacing everything with a completely new fiber optics system. A hybrid approach was considered the solution by the telecommunications industry. The plan

More On **MAKING AN OPTICAL FIBER**

The manufacturing of optical fibers consists of coating the inner wall of a silica glass tube with 100 or more successive layers of thin glass. The tube is then heated to 2,000 degrees Celsius and stretched into a thin, flexible fiber. The result is called a clad fiber, which is approximately .0005 inches in diameter (by comparison, human hair typically measures .002 inches).

Optical fibers operate on the principle of what is called total internal reflection. Every medium through which light can pass possesses a certain refractive index, the amount by which a beam of light is bent as it enters the medium. As the angle at which the light strikes the medium is decreased from the perpendicular, a point is reached at which the light is bent so much at the surface that it reflects completely back into the medium from which it originated. Thus, the light will bounce back rather than escape.

In an optical fiber, total internal reflection is accomplished by a layer of material known as cladding, which has a lower refractive index than glass alone. Once light enters the fiber, it is internally reflected by the cladding. This prevents light loss by keeping the beam of light zigzagging inside the glass core.

was to use copper at one level and patch into fiber optics at another level. Later, the copper lines could be removed, and the system could be upgraded to fiber optics. Fiber optic equipment is rapidly being installed for computer network backbone infrastructure based on asynchronous transfer mode (ATM) optical switches, following the lead of the telecommunications industry. Nonetheless, not everyone sees copper as obsolete when it comes to Telecommunications. In the late 1990s fiber optics companies saw competition in the form of copper-based, asynchronous digital subscriber lines (ADSL).

Every segment of the fiber optic manufacturing industry is growing. From 1987 to 1997 fiber-optic cable was laid at a rate of about 4,000 miles a day and, by the late 1990s, more than 25 million miles of it had been installed. Nonetheless, 60 percent of that was "dead fiber," which is completely unused fiber-optic line. The remainder was used at only a small fraction of its total capacity—a reflection of fiber's enormous potential. KMI, a market research group, predicted that transmitters and receivers, which make up the bulk of fiber-optic sales, would reach $1.1 billion in sales by the year 2000; the market for erbium-doped fiber amplifiers (EDFA) was also expected to rise as networks convert to 100 percent fiber optics.

These tiny fiber optics are capable of transmitting great amounts of data through tiny light pulses. (Digital Stock.)

Thus far, fiber optics has been limited to long-distance networks. As for laying fiber optic cable, it may cost as much as $100 billion to rewire the United States and nearly a trillion dollars to rewire the world. The subscriber loop—homes and offices— remains overwhelmingly copper. The costs of moving fiber optics into the home and office are still seen as far too high—one cable operator estimated the cost at between $500 and $2,000 per home. Nonetheless, insiders predict that to-the-door fiber optics will be a reality by the year 2002.

The subscriber loop will be the next major field of conquest for the industry. That segment of the industry accounts for 90 percent of the system's total cable length. Anaheim, California, has already started converting to full fiber, investing $6 billion in a basic system and contracting SpectraNet International of San Diego to run it. The cost for the city of 300,000 people was expected to total $70 to $90 million before the project's completion in 2004. This was the first-ever attempt to link every building in a city by fiber optics.

The goal for the fiber optics industry will be to successfully merge electronic communications of all types, such as cable television and various telephone networks, into an optimal, widespread, interactive fiber-optic network. Cable may be the driving force since such a network is the key to its dream of interactive television and Internet via television and telephone. Some industry insiders believe such a union would be ideal; cable companies would possess bandwidth-rich "dumb" networks, or networks unencumbered by complex switching equipment. Phone companies, on the other hand, have extensive two-way networks—and money. The challenge will be for cable companies to change over to a two-way system. A larger challenge may be getting phone companies and cable operators to rethink their competitive relationship into a cooperative one.

INDUSTRY LEADERS

CORNING INCORPORATED

Corning Incorporated, the company that invented fiber optics, remains the world's leader in the production and sale of fiber-optic cable. The communications segment of the company, which produces fiber-optic products, accounted for almost $2 billion of the company's $3.5 billion sales in 1998. Together with Lucent, Corning provides more than 80 percent of the world's cable—nearly twice as much as its competitors. The company has been averaging some 5.2 million miles of cable annually. To meet anticipated demand, the company invested more than $1 billion in plant construction and expansion in 1999. The acquisition of Rochester Photonics Corp. (with 1998 revenue at $3 million) gave Corning access to new fiber-optic technology, such as "microlenses," which increases network performance through improved in-fiber laser focus and has transmitters and receivers that are more temperature-resistant. With headquarters in Corning, New York, the company's 45 plants employ approximately 15,400 people—reduced from 20,500 in 1997.

LUCENT TECHNOLOGIES INC.

Lucent Technologies Incorporated, of Murray Hill, New Jersey, was split off from AT&T in November 1995. It took with it about three quarters of the world-famous Bell Labs and is now one of the leading designers and manufacturers of conventional and wireless telecommunications equipment, as well as fiber optics. Employing approximately 141,600 workers, Lucent is the world's second leading producer of fiber cable, producing about 16 percent of the cable purchased for the U.S. domestic market. The company also produces a variety of other fiber-optic components, systems, and fiber/copper telecommunications systems. Sales in 1998 topped $30 billion. Despite a downturn in 1996, Lucent's fiber-optic production grew five-fold between 1991 and 1999. In 1999 the company agreed to supply its TrueWave RS fiber for Viatel Inc.'s European Network, an ambitious project to link several major European cities.

CIENA CORPORATION

Ciena Corporation of Savage, Maryland, is a relative newcomer to the fiber-optics field with a mere 841 employees. The company's primary products are dense wavelength division multiplexing systems (DWDM) for companies like MCI WorldCom, Sprint, and Teleway Japan. DWDM systems give optical fiber the ability to carry up to 40 times more data, voice, and graphic information than usual. The company is also a major supplier of erbium-doped fiber amplifiers—one of the key technologies in the change to a 100 percent optical system. Ciena employed 841 workers in April 1999. George Gilder, the fiber-optics prophet, called Ciena "the industry leader in open standard WDM." While the company's $508 million in sales in 1998 were dwarfed by those bigger corporations, sales rose by 35.9 percent over 1997.

ADC TELECOMMUNICATIONS INC.

ADC Telecommunications Incorporated of Minnetonka, Minnesota, is a leader in the design and manufacture of fiber-optic connectivity products, including transmitters, receivers, couplers, patch cords, panels, and Internet working products. The company's 8,000 employees supply customers in the public, private, and government sectors, as well as foreign nations building telecommunications infrastructures. Net sales in 1998 increased 18.5 percent to $1.38 billion. Growth was driven by two segments within the company with high concentration in fiber optics, transmission, and broadband connectivity. In addition to sales to the regional Bell companies, ADC is pushing towards acquisitions and entering the wireless and international markets. For example, the company has entered into major agreements with the People's Republic of China.

AMP INC.

Suppliers of electronic components and electrical equipment have benefited from the fiber optics boom. AMP Inc. for instance, which started in 1941 as Aero-Marine Products, grew into an international company with 45,000 employees on 5 continents. As one of the top 50 patent holding companies of the world, it supplied the aerospace, computer, automotive, utilities, and various other industries with electronic parts and

components and reached $5.7 billion in 1997 revenue. In April 1999, however, the company was acquired by Tyco International Ltd., which planned to cut costs by nearly $650 million. Plans included closing 26 administrative offices, 27 manufacturing plants, and eliminating 4,200 jobs. As a Tyco subsidiary, AMP is now the electrical and electronic components group—one of Tyco's four segments.

AMERICA AND THE WORLD

The United States has a significant lead on foreign companies in the fiber optics race. The American companies Corning and Lucent sell over 80 percent of the world's fiber cable, and companies like Ciena Corporation and ADC are at the cutting edge with EDFA and DWDM technology. Two European companies, Pirelli of Italy and Alcatel Telecom of France, are involved in development and production to the same extent as the leading American firms. Pirelli introduced the first commercial EDFA through its North American subsidiary in North Carolina. It has formed a partnership with MCI to install WDM technology on a fiber-optic line from St. Louis to Chicago. Alcatel produces EDFA and WDM as well, but its penetration into the American market has not been as pronounced.

Countries that have virtually no existing telecommunications networks are a major market—perhaps the primary market—for fiber optics. In the late 1990s, China was a major consumer of optical cable and required millions of core-kilometers of fiber optics, buying WDM systems from Lucent and Japan's NEC. In Russia, Lucent Technologies has more than $30 million invested. In 1999 Lucent joined to SviazStroy-1 (Russia's largest construction company) to form a joint venture fiber optic cable manufacturing company called Lucent Technologies SviazStroy-1 Fiber Optic Cable Company. Lucent retained a 51-percent share of the Voronezh, Russia, company. In 1999 Alcatel and Fujitsu Ltd. were preparing an 18,000-mile undersea WDM cable that would run from Australia and New Zealand to the United States, then loop back through Hawaii and Fiji to Australia.

RESEARCH AND TECHNOLOGY

Two technological breakthroughs recently transformed fiber optics—the erbium-doped fiber amplifier (EDFA) and wavelength division multiplexing

(WDM). EDFA grew out of the fundamental incompatibility of electronics and fiber optics. The optical pulses must be amplified as they travel along the fiber or else they dissipate and no longer register as signals. In the past, because they could not match fiber optics' larger bandwidth, electronic amplifiers acted as a bottleneck on the fiber-optic flow. Bell Laboratories demonstrated that a short length of fiber treated with the mineral erbium and excited with a laser acted as an optical amplifier. With the use of this type of system, electronics are no longer necessary; fiber optics' huge data capability can be exploited in full.

Wavelength division multiplexing was developed at Bell Labs in the mid-1980s. In WDM laser signals generate light pulses that can be as short as a billionth of a second in length. Each wavelength opened can be used to transmit data. The first WDMs opened transmission lines that could carry up to 2.5 gigabits per second (gbps). They were integrated into the standard fiber-optic systems. In the early 1990s researchers discovered dense wavelength division multiplexing (DWDM), which squeezes more pulses into shorter wavelengths. At the decade's end, amplifier design advances, such as Lucent's WaveStar Optical Line System 400G, expanded the operating region, thus bringing more than 40 channels operating at 10 gbps each.

Some analysts believe WDM is the foundation of all future fiber-optic technology. It enables a network to increase its bandwidth significantly without installing any new lines. One problem is that the technology is so advanced that the monitoring and diagnostic tools have not been developed to trace failures. The International Telecommunications Union has started outlining a standard for the industry, however. Insight Research Corp. projected the market for WDM components to reach $4 billion by 2002; the market analysis firm Electronicast predicted that number would rise to $10 billion by the year 2005.

The development of plastic optical fiber (POF) brought a number of advantages over glass. It is cheaper to produce and easier to work with, as well as being equal to glass in performance, flexibility, and reliability. An industry standard was established in April 1997. Landmark discoveries continue to flow from the laboratory to the marketplace. Where most were impressed by the terabit (1 trillion bit) speeds reached in 1996, Alastair Glass, head of photonics research at Bell Labs, envisions the day when one fiber-optic cable carries thousands of WDM beams with a capacity of 200 terabits per second—enough to transmit all the contents of the Library of Congress within one second.

FURTHER READING

"ADC Telecommunications, Inc." *Hoover's Online*, 1 April 1999. Available from http://www.hoovers.com.

Biancomano, Vincent J. "All Optical Net Takes Next Steps." *Electronic Engineering Times*, 23 December 1996.

———. "Communications: Optical Nets Start Seeing the Light." *Electronic Engineering Times*, 31 March 1997.

CIENA Corporation. *Hoover's Online*, 1 April 1999. Available from http://www.hoovers.com.

"Corning Acquires Rochester Photonics Corporation; Company Is a Technology Leader in Diffractive Optics and Microlens Technology." *Business Wire*, 14 February 1999.

"Corning Incorporated." *Hoover's Online*, 1 April 1999. Available from http://www.hoovers.com.

"DC Signs Multi-Phase Agreement for Distribution of Fiber-Optic Products in China." *M2 PressWIRE*, 1 October 1996.

Dobbin, Ben. "Fiber Optics Change, Speed Up World's Flow of Information." *Los Angeles Times*, 16 December 1996.

"Fiber-Optic and Optical Cable Market Demand to Mount." *China Daily News*, 21 July 1997.

Fleck, Ken. "Fiber-Optics Companies Looking at Bright Future." *Electronic Buyer News*, 23 June 1997.

Gilder, George. "Fiber Keeps Its Promise." *Forbes*, 7 April 1997.

Gruen, Adam. "Telecom Past, Present & Future: An Analysis," 1997. Available from http://www.mci.com/aboutyou/interests/technology/ ontech/hilight.shtml.

Korzeniowski, Paul. "Record Growth Spurs Demand for Dense WDM—Infrastructure Bandwidth Gears Up for Next Wave," 1997. Available from http://www.techweb.com/se/directlink.cgi/CWK19970602S0027.

Laurin, Teddi C. "Boosting R & D vs. Cutting Taxes." *Photonics Spectra*, March 1998.

"Lucent Announces Revolutionary New Fiber for Long Distance Networks." *M2 PressWIRE*, 11 Jun 1998.

Lucent Technologies Inc.*Hoover's Online*, 1 April 1999. Available from http://www.hoovers.com.

"Lucent Technologies and Russia's SviazStroy-1 Form Fiber Cable Venture." *M2 PressWIRE*, 19 Feb 1999.

"MCI Expands Fiber Optic Network." *Newsbytes News Network*, 28 January 1997.

Price, Richard. "Fiber Optics to Entwine Anaheim-Network to Link Homes, Businesses." *USA Today*, 18 July 1997.

Richtmyer, Richard."News: Reality Hits AMP—New Owner Tyco to Cut Company's Costs by $650M." *Electronic Buyer News*, 12 April 1999.

Roos, Gina. "Fiber-Optic Technology Getting Less Expensive," 1997. Available from http://www.techweb.com/se/directlink.cgi/EBN19970106S0012.

Rosen, Carol. "Lucent Technologies." *Electronic Buyer News,* 21 October 1996.

Saporta, Maria. "Lucent Emerges Among Top Employers." *Atlanta Journal and Constitution,* 1 October 1996.

Schmidt, Eric. "Communications Components: POF Extends Network Reach." *Electronic Buyer News,* 23 June 1997.

"Sprint Milestones," 1997. Available from http://www.sprint.com/sprint/overview/mileston.html.

U.S. Department of Energy. "New Energy Uses Fiber Optics to Improve Energy Efficiency in Glassmaking," February 1999. Available from http://es.epa.gov/techinfo/facts/nu-system.html.

Wirbel, Loring. "Signal Scheme Pushes Terabit Rate—Sonet Transport Catches a Wave." *Electronic Engineering Times,* 16 September 1996.

—Gerald E. Brennan, updated by Marsha Levy
and Brett Allan King

FINANCIAL PLANNING SERVICES

Financial planning is a holistic approach to personal financial management that has flourished since the mid-1980s. It is a process of analyzing a number of factors, including income, assets, present and future expenses and investments, as well as personal data such as age, health, and number of dependents, and developing a strategy to optimize personal resources and meet life goals. Financial planners use the detailed information they get from meeting with clients to make financial recommendations, including recommendations on budgeting, saving, insurance, taxes, investments, and retirement planning. Some financial planners focus on only one financial issue; others may work on many.

Financial planning services originated in the early 1960s; however, it was not until 1970 that the first fee-only planners—now a quasi standard—appeared. As an industry, financial planning came of age as America's corporations gradually replaced traditional corporate-managed pension plans with employee-managed 401(k)s and other retirement savings alternatives, forcing individuals to take on more responsibility for long-term fiscal planning. Concerns about the viability of Social Security and Medicare, coupled with growth in the number of small businesses and the self-employed, have forced many individuals who had given very little thought to retirement planning to become more knowledgeable about estate plans, insurance, home ownership, taxes, and the multitude of new financial products and investments.

The number of firms and individuals offering various forms of consumer financial advice has skyrock-eted since the late 1980s. Because there is neither a single definition of what a financial planner is, nor a consistent set of boundaries between the profession and, say, investment advising or accounting, estimates of the industry's size vary considerably. A 1997 *Barron's* report pegged the count of financial planning firms at 25,000 and entertained estimates as high as 100,000 for the total number of planners. Another calculation suggested there were as many as 250,000 professionals engaged in some form of personal financial advice. The number of those with formal accreditation is much smaller: the Certified Financial Planner (CFP) Board of Standards, one of the largest and most visible professional licensure bodies dedicated to the industry, had 33,839 members in 1999, a figure triple that of the mid-1980s.

The growth of the financial planning industry parallels the increasing accumulation of assets by Americans and greater sophistication about investments. The change in saving patterns illustrates the trend. The 61 percent of personal savings that were held in banks, savings and loans, and credit unions during the 1970s had declined to less than 38 percent by the mid-1990s. Through pension and mutual funds, households and businesses increasingly participate in huge, diversified portfolios of stocks, bonds, real estate, and even commodities. As reported in the Washington Times, pollster Peter Hart said that it took 25 years for stock ownership among Americans to double, from 10.4 percent in 1965 to 21.1 percent in 1990. It took only seven years for stock ownership to double again. By 1997 43.2 percent of Americans owned stock. Other data reveal, according to the Times article, that United States households now hold more wealth in the form of stocks than home equity.

Increasing apprehension over the competency and legitimacy of individuals practicing financial advising has accompanied the industry's growth. As a *Barron's* writer quipped, "Can't cut it as a hairstylist? Try financial planning." In the absence of universal professional or legal credentials distinguishing financial planners, several professional organizations and recent laws have sought to impose a baseline of competency and heighten public awareness of the meaning of a bewildering array of financial planning credentials.

At the same time the industry's high growth has translated into handsome salaries for many of its participants. A 1997 membership survey by the National Endowment of Financial Education indicated that the median income of planners was $90,000, up 12 percent from 1996. The International Association for Financial Planning (IAFP) estimated that the entry-level advisor may earn $20,000 per year, while experienced professionals can earn from $40,000 to more than $200,000 annually.

ORGANIZATION AND STRUCTURE

Financial planning is the process of establishing financial goals and creating a way to realize them. The process involves taking stock of all personal resources and needs, developing a plan to manage them, and systematically implementing the plan to achieve financial objectives. Financial planning is an ongoing process. A plan must be monitored and reviewed periodically so that adjustments can be made to assure that it continues to meet individual needs.

The profession involves expertise (or access to experts) in various disciplines such as estate planning, taxation, benefit plans, pension plans, insurance, investments, and real estate. Thus the consumer financial planning market has come to be fragmented across several disparate service professions in addition to those just practicing planning, and many of these services specialize in certain aspects of financial planning to the exclusion of others.

The Certified Financial Planner (CFP) Board's web site (http://www.cfp-board.org/ provides a wealth of information for those confused by the many definitions of "financial planner." According to the CFP Board, the following list of professions may provide specific financial planning services:

- Accountants
- Brokers/Dealers
- Certified Financial Planner Licensee or CFP Practitioner

- Chartered Financial Analysts (CFA)
- Chartered Financial Consultants
- Estate Planning Professionals
- Fee-based Financial Advisers
- Fee-only Financial Advisers
- Financial Adviser
- Financial Consultant
- Financial Counselor
- Financial or Securities Analyst
- Financial Planner
- Insurance Agent
- Investment Adviser
- Investment Adviser Representative
- Investment Consultant
- Money Manager
- Personal Financial Specialist
- Portfolio Manager
- Real Estate Broker
- Registered Investment Adviser
- Registered Representative
- Stockbroker.

Adding to the confusion about the variety of financial planning services, a CFP Board survey showed consumers still have many misconceptions about the role of a financial planner. The survey, conducted in February 1999 by Bruskin-Goldring Research for the CFP Board, was conducted nationally and included 1,016 adults. Among the misconceptions, 36 percent of those surveyed believed that financial planners would automatically put their assets into the best-performing stocks and mutual funds; 17 percent expected assurances from a financial planner that they would become rich; another 16 percent expected that they would be asked to pay up front for a financial planner's services.

Fees for financial advice are derived in a variety of ways, usually depending on the planner's affiliations. The methods are: fee-only, commission-only, fee-offset, combination fee-commission, and salary. It is important to note that all financial planners must disclose by whom they are paid. Aside from fee-only, the balance of these payment modes imply that financial planning is being offered in conjunction with other products or services such as investment broker-ing, banking, accounting, or underwriting. These plan-ners are often described as product-driven, as opposed to fee-only planners who are called process-driven. Also, because fee-only planners are paid by the client and do not receive commissions, they are not oblig-ated to recommend certain products or investment ve-hicles and thus are sometimes considered more im-partial than other types of planners.

Regardless of the type of planner retained, results and fees can vary widely. *Money* magazine, in a piece by Ruth Simon, reported that fee-only advisors charge a flat fee to develop a plan, typically from $500 to $6,000, depending on complexity, or an hourly fee ranging between $75 and $225. Many also charge an annual fee equal to 0.5 percent to l.5 percent of total assets to manage a portfolio. Commission-based plan-ners earn their income from commissions on mutual funds, insurance policies and other financial products they sell. A third type, the fee-based planner, uses both commissions and fees.

One way or another, the consumer will pay for the advice received. The rule of "buyer beware" still applies. Guy Halverson, writing in the *Christian Sci-ence Monitor,* described the results of a study released in 1997 by the Consumer Federation of America (CFA) and the National Association of Personal Fi-nancial Advisors (NAPFA), the trade association for fee-only planners (which has trademarked the phrase "fee only.") Of 288 Washington, D.C.-area planners and firms in a random survey, "two-thirds . . . claimed to offer fee-only services. Of those, three out of five

were earning commissions or other financial incen-tives from undisclosed third parties, such as mutual-fund companies or insurance firms." Consumer wari-ness about conflicts of interest may be part of the reason for a planner's reluctance to reveal sources of income, the study suggested. In an effort to identify those who call themselves fee-only planners but are not, the organization has developed a Fiduciary Oath which consumers can use to help them find an objec-tive, independent advisor. The 121-word oath, issued in April 1998, is available free on the group's Web site, at http://www.napfa.org, or by telephone at 888-FEE-ONLY.

In part reflecting the fragmented market, govern-ment regulation of financial planning has been uneven and complex. However, that is changing. A new law amending federal securities laws, the National Secu-rities Market Improvement Act (NSMIA), effective July 8, 1997, divided regulation between the federal government and the states. Firms with $25 million or more in managed assets remain under the jurisdiction of the U.S. Securities and Exchange Commission (SEC) while the remaining investment advisors—an estimated 16,500—revert to state regulation.

In the past some states, but not all, licensed ad-visors. Financial planners were not required to regis-ter with the SEC unless they recommended specific stocks or bonds, in which case they had to be regis-tered investment advisors. The SEC required no test, however, with the result that registration reflected lit-tle about the advisor's competency. Applicants sim-ply paid a fee and submitted a form listing their dis-

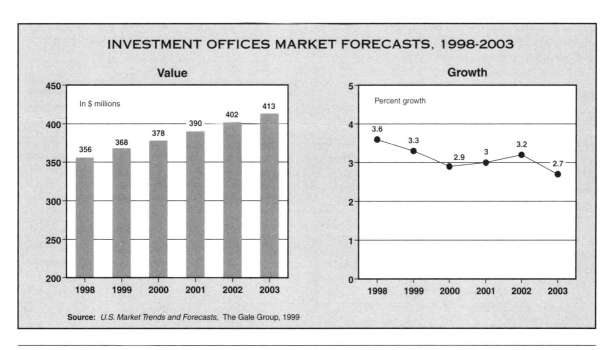

INVESTMENT OFFICES MARKET FORECASTS, 1998-2003

Value (In $ millions): 1998: 356; 1999: 368; 2000: 378; 2001: 390; 2002: 402; 2003: 413

Growth (Percent growth): 1998: 3.6; 1999: 3.3; 2000: 2.9; 2001: 3; 2002: 3.2; 2003: 2.7

Source: *U.S. Market Trends and Forecasts,* The Gale Group, 1999

ciplinary history, educational background, and investment philosophy. In 1999, while many states may not require licensure of financial planners, most state securities agencies do regulate individuals associated with investment of financial planning firms, whether or not those firms are registered with the SEC or with a state agency.

Under the new regulations, the SEC retained jurisdiction within any state that had not enacted its own regulations, but had no plans for testing or enforcing competency requirements. Many states, however, have begun to coordinate some testing requirements for new entrants to the field. As of June 1998, AICPA (The American Institute of Certified Public Accountants) reported that 15 states had a 150-hour education requirement for planners in effect, with another 29 scheduled to follow suit on a future date; in addition, 22 states prohibit commissions and contingent fees. The 1999 Media Guide to the Financial Planning Profession (CFP Board, available at http://www.cfp-board.org/index.html) states that "by the year 2000, the North American Securities Administrators Association (NASAA) plans to have an entry-level competency exam in place for all investment adviser representatives."

The states present a mixed picture. David Weidner wrote in a Wall Street Journal report that some are adapting faster than others to the new order of things: "Pennsylvania, along with [Connecticut and Washington], is considered a model in dealing with the new responsibility." Like them, the state had an active regulatory agency that worked with the SEC before the act went into effect, he said. In Ohio, one of four states that do not have separate legislation governing the practices of financial planners and advisors, a bill has been introduced to place them under minimum standards for the first time.

ASSOCIATIONS

As the industry grew, concerns about the legitimacy of financial planners arose. As a result, a number of associations emerged to promote education, expertise, professionalism and ethics in the field. These groups provide professional financial planners with information and continuing education. Many will also recommend reliable firms and individuals who are knowledgeable in financial planning. The most important of these associations include the following:

- Association for Financial Counseling and Planning Education (AFCPE) (http://www.hec.ohio-state.edu/hanna/afcpe/index.htm). Headquartered in Phoenix, Arizona, the AFCPE is a nonprofit professional organization comprised of researchers, academics, financial counselors and planners. AFCPE administers certification programs for financial counselors, including the national Accredited Financial Counselor (AFC) program; as well as certification programs for housing counselors, including Accredited Housing Counselor (AHC) and Certified Housing Counselor (CHC). It offers education and training programs at an annual conference and publishes a professional journal devoted to financial counseling and planning as well as a newsletter with a guide to resources, including Web sites, publications, and industry trends.

- Association for Investment Management and Research (AIMR) (http://www.aimr.com). AIMR has more than 36,000 members in 87 affiliated societies and chapters in 80 countries. The organization sets the highest standards in education, ethics, and advocacy for investment professionals, their employers, and their clients. Through the Institute of Chartered Financial Analysts, AIMR grants the prestigious Chartered Financial Analyst (CFA) designation.

- Certified Financial Planner Board of Standards (CFP Board) (http://www.cfp-board.org). Founded in 1985, the CFP Board exists to protect, benefit and educate the public by establishing standards in education, examination, and experience, and a code of ethics for Certified Financial Planner licensees.

- Institute of Certified Financial Planners (ICFP) (http://www.icfp.org). Founded in 1973, the Denver-based ICFP is a professional association with more than 15,000 licensees and candidate members nationwide. The ICFP seeks to establish and maintain professionalism in the field of financial planning, provide a forum for the interchange of ideas, and ensure the integrity of the profession through enforcement of a rigorous code of ethics. It sponsors continuing education programs, conducts regional conferences and advertising programs, and maintains a referral service.

- International Association for Financial Planning (IAFP) (http:www.iafp.org). The Atlanta-based IAFP, with more than 17,000 individual members and 110 chapters, brings together financial professionals from all disciplines and backgrounds to build public awareness of financial planning and to provide members with advocacy, education, and information. (In March 1999, the IAFP and ICFP announced plans to merge. The newly-named Financial Planning Association (FPA) is scheduled to be in effect by January 1, 2000.)

- National Association of Independent Public Finance Advisors (NAIPFA) (http://www.naipfa.com/). Members include firms that specialize in financial advice on bond sales and financial planning to public agencies. Headquartered in Washington, D.C., the NAIPFA seeks to build credibility and recognition of financial advisory firms and maintains high ethical and professional standards. It maintains a board of review to ensure members' compliance to standards, provides education materials to independent financial advisors and responds to legislative needs of member firms and the public agencies they serve.

- National Association of Personal Financial Advisors (NAPFA) (http://www.napfa.org/). Founded in 1983, NAPFA is headquartered in Buffalo Grove, Illinois. With more than 640 members and affiliates in 50 states, it serves as a network for fee-only planners to discuss practice management, client services, and investment selections. The association works to encourage and advance the practice of fee-only planning by developing the skills of members, increasing awareness of fee-only financial planning, and fostering interaction with other professional groups.

- Registered Financial Planners Institute (RFPI) (http://www.rfpi.com). Headquartered in Amherst, Ohio, the institute promotes professionalism in financial planning for individuals and businesses. RFPI offers classroom seminars and correspondence courses and sponsors a research program and referral service. The institute bestows the designation of Registered Financial Planner (RFP) on qualified members.

- The Society for Financial Service Professionals (SFSP), formerly the American Society of CLU & ChFC (http://www.asclu.org) Headquartered in Bryn Mawr, Pennsylvania, SFSP is a national membership organization representing 33,000 financial services professionals who have earned the CLU or ChFC designation from the American College, (http://www.amercoll.edu/default.htm), also located in Bryn Mawr. Members specialize in estate planning, investments, tax planning, wealth accumulation, and life and health insurance.

CURRENT CONDITIONS

Many well-established industries continue to vie for the financial planning market, particularly banks, investment brokerages, and insurance carriers. Firms in these industries have pursued the market through developing products or services using internal resources, through acquiring dedicated financial planning units, and through forging alliances with planning specialists. A growing number of banks are taking the plunge into financial planning, making use of training programs and services offered to large banks by Fidelity Investments, the world's largest mutual fund company. While Fidelity's training is product-neutral, it is offered in the hope that the bank will offer Fidelity Advisor funds to its clients. American Express Financial Advisors, Inc., on the other hand, focuses on smaller banks, those with $50 million to $3 billion in assets. Rather than training the bank's personnel like Fidelity, AE brings its own financial advisors into the bank to advise customers on managing their money, working up a proposal for a fee averaging $300. Other banks, like Cleveland-based KeyCorp and Chase Manhattan Corporation in New York, are developing investment business by means of in-house programs, training staff in investment planning and hiring more planners and consultants. KeyCorp will offer a "complete financial planning program" for a flat fee of $395.

These patterns suggest only some of the challenges planning-only firms may face. The growing number of Internet subscribers and the development of comprehensive financial planning software portend a vast opportunity for electronic planning-related services. Forrester Research (http://www.forrester.com), a market research firm in Boston, estimated the number of online trading accounts at 3 million in mid-1998, with that number expected to reach 10 million by 2002. In its third annual survey of online trading, Barron's found that online customers accounted for an estimated 17 percent of all retail stock trades, more than double the level of the previous year. There are more than 50 brokerage houses offering online trading, the 1997 survey found, as compared to only 12 in the first survey in 1995. With the rush of competition has come a plunge in online commissions. As reported by Barron's, Bill Burnham, an analyst for Piper Jaffray, reported that the average commission charged by the top 10 online firms was cut by more than $15.95, down from $34.65 a year earlier.

DO-IT-YOURSELF FINANCIAL PLANNING

The meteoric rise of professional interest in personal financial planning has been paralleled by an increasing number of do-it-yourself options. The number of computer software products in this field is enormous and keeps growing. Internet sites offer planning tools and a wealth of financial information.

Software programs for financial planning range in price from $40 to over $1,000; some entail more than $100 annually for maintenance of current interest and inflation rates. Quicken Financial Planner, selling for $39.95, is described by Forbes magazine as the country's leading do-it-yourself financial planning software, having "both strengths and drawbacks." Financial planning programs can calculate tax projections, net worth, cash flow, education funding, retirement savings requirements, survivor benefits, and estate taxes. Many also offer investment and cash management analysis. Most of the popular home-budgeting programs, like Quicken (Intuit), Microsoft Money, and Managing Your Money (Meca Software), contain simple retirement calculators. Likewise there are numerous retirement-specific programs, including several by leading brokerages, that offer in-depth planning tools for retirement savings.

Multitudes of Web sites on the Internet have a wide range of financial and investment information available. The free Microsoft Money Insider site (moneyinsider.msn.com/home.asp) offers information on investing, insurance, mortgages, and taxes, and has calculators for figuring retirement income and expenses. The free Money.com site (http://www.money.com) offers a similar selection. Bloomberg's Personal Finance site (http://www.bloomberg.com/personal/index.html) offers a variety of free resources, including calculators that help you save on mortgages, project your 401(k) growth, and decide whether leasing or buying a car would be your best option; market, mutual fund and stock information; and articles and interviews. In a class by itself is the free Errold F. Moody, Jr. Web site (http://www.efmoody.com). Run by a former educator with 20 years of financial planning experience and very strong opinions, the site offers up-to-date information on insurance, Medicare, Medicaid and Social Security, stocks, home-buying, retirement planning, taxes, and links to dozens of useful sites on related topics.

RESEARCH AND TECHNOLOGY

In the *Journal of Financial Planning,* author Bruce Most wrote that while technology is revolutionizing the financial planning profession, the majority of planners are behind the technological curve. Underuse may be due to lack of time to learn new software, the inability to recognize its benefits, the money

to pay for it, or in some cases, "a sort of Luddite resistance to it." Most planners aren't online, either, at least not in any meaningful way, he found.

Addressing the issue of accountability, the industry's self-governing body, the Association for Investment Management and Research (AIMR), has moved to curb abuses in an arena where advisors have presented their performance record on the honor system, with no independent verification. AIMR has introduced standards for historical performance reporting, with a recommendation for verification by an independent accountant. The subject is discussed in an article by Gerald J. Archibald, "Reporting on investment advisor performance," in CPA Journal Online at: http://www.luca.com/cpajournal.

FURTHER READING

"1999 Edition Media Guide to the Financial Planning Profession." Available from http://www.cfp-board.org/index.html.

Barrett, William P. "Bedlam." *Forbes,* 15 June 1998.

Carey, Theresa W. "Beyond Cool: Online Trading Goes Mainstream as Quality Rises and Commissions Plunge." *Barron's,* 16 March 1998.

Cross, Margaretann. "Getting Personal with Fiscal Health." *Crain's Chicago Business,* 3 February 1997.

Curtis, Carol E. "A Plan for Building Sales." *US Banker,* April 1998.

Edwards, Franklin R. *The New Finance: Regulation & Financial Stability.* Washington: The AEI Press, 1996.

Feldman, Amy. "Online Trading Begins to Reshape Brokerage Industry." *Knight-Ridder Tribune Business News,* 26 January 1998.

Foust, Dean. "For the Good Life, Hit 'Enter'." *Business Week,* 21 July 1997.

Gold, Howard R., ed. "Stretching Your Skills." *Barron's,* 28 April 1997.

Halverson, Guy. "Warning: Few Planners Are Really 'Fee Only'." *Christian Science Monitor,* 14 January 1997.

"IAFP, ICFP Boards Approve Framework of Combined Organization: The Financial Planning Association—Final Approval Awaits ICFP Member Vote," 22 March 1999. Available from http://www.iafp.org/gateway/CGI?k=GUESTLOGIN2.

McTague, Jim. "The Advice Game." *Barron's,* 4 August 1997.

Meece, Mickey. "For Financial Advisors, a Pledge on Payments (Plan to Clarify Consumer Fees)." *The New York Times,* 10 May 1998.

Most, Bruce W. "When Science Clashes with Art: The Financial Planner's Dilemma." *Journal of Financial Planning,* June 1996.

"New Survey Shows Consumers Continue to Have Misperceptions about Financial Planning Process," 19 February 1999. Available from http://www.cfp-board.org/index.html.

Ozer, Jan. "Investment Tools and Advice." *PC Magazine,* 15 May 1998.

Sestina, John E. *Fee-Only Financial Planning,* 1992.

Simon, Ruth. "The Big Bad News About Fee-Only Financial Planners: Some are Wolfing Down Commissions on the Products they Recommend." *Money,* December 1995.

"Trends in Financial and Estate Planning." *Taxes,* January 1996.

Vestner, Charlie. "E-Mazing." *Individual Investor,* July 1997.

Washington Times. "More Capital Gains, Less Urge to Tax Them." *Washington Times,* 7 July 1998.

Weidner, David. "Oversight of Financial Planners Is Mixed." *Wall Street Journal,* 15 September 1997.

Zarowin, Stanley. "The Elusive Holy Grail." *Journal of Accountancy,* October 1996.

—Kaye Brinker, updated by Shirley Gray
and Lisa DeShantz-Cook

FUTURES CONSULTING

In a rapidly changing world, decision-making in politics, business, and society is becoming more and more complex. The end of the Cold War, the fall of the Berlin Wall, and the dissolution of the USSR proved that futures much different from our normal expectations were possible. This realization induced a growing acceptance of futures consulting as a specialized profession which uses a systematic approach to explore what major changes might lie ahead and how decisions made today could influence the world of tomorrow. Futures consultants develop plausible images of the short- to long-range future for and together with their clients, and enable them to prepare for eventualities that might fundamentally affect their organization, and anticipate possible consequences of different decisions.

In 1998 the World Future Society, a nonprofit educational and scientific organization, reported that 1,134 individuals and 80 institutions from the United States participated in its professional members program, which gives a rough estimate of the number of professionals engaged in this field. With the business community going through a historic transformation driven mainly by economic globalization and the application of communication and information technologies in every area of society, a growing demand for futures consulting services in the United States and worldwide seems very likely.

ORGANIZATION AND STRUCTURE

Futures consultants address a particular aspect of a given organization—that is, the set of ideas that peo-

ple possess about the future, and how those ideas serve to impact strategic decisions affecting the organization as a whole. Highly specialized skills are used to effectively gather relevant information and to develop images of plausible futures that are communicated to clients in verbal or visual forms. Some consultants go no further than suggesting possible future images; most of them however, make recommendations about how the client could prepare for possible future events. They may also facilitate the follow-up strategic planning process; help to provide visionary solutions for company problems; train client personnel; act as catalysts between internal groups; or facilitate individuals and groups in formulating, implementing, and re-envisioning their preferred futures.

In order to analyze, envision, and facilitate change, futures consultants use methods that are fully understandable by their clients. Trend analysis and environmental scanning, whole systems analysis and global modeling, simulation and gaming, scenario building, visioning, strategic planning, and issues and change management in organizations are commonly used methods. Futures consultants acquire most of their quantitative information from published sources, research institutes, and universities. For more qualitative information, they interview individuals and experts in particular fields. Since the future cannot be predicted precisely, futures consultants use the information they gather to develop a variety of possible scenarios for their clients. It is considered an art to translate these scenarios into stories, videos, and other forms of presentation. The goal is to make the "unthinkable" seem possible, to widen the client's mindset about the future. After developing future images, futures consultants assist clients in undertaking strategic planning efforts that include determining the organization's *preferred* future or vision and the measures necessary to achieve it, often through collaborative work with groups in workshops and seminars.

While today's specialized disciplines of management consulting, such as organizational development, aim primarily to improve processes inside an existing system within a one to five year time frame, futures consulting focuses on innovation and outlooks of five to 50 years, and sometimes even more. There are many types and sizes of futures consulting businesses, ranging from individual practitioners to middle-sized firms. Some futures consultants specialize in areas such as health care or the petroleum industry, or target particular groups like multinational companies or nonprofit organizations. Older futures consulting firms are concentrated on the East Coast, mainly in and around Washington, D.C., where they have access to a great deal of information; and in California, the bellwether of the United States.

Futures consultants work for corporations, nonprofit organizations, professional societies, trade and industrial associations, educational groups, government agencies, and international organizations. They consider decision makers within the client organization their major target group and find their clients primarily through referrals and networking, one-day introductory workshops, speech-giving, and direct marketing. Collaboration and cooperation are hallmarks of the profession. Publishing is not only a form of marketing, but also a source of considerable income for some futures consultants. Membership programs and customized single or multi-client projects are the most common business models. The time-frame of typical consulting projects ranges from one month to one year and fees are levied on a project basis or charged as annual membership fees. The World Future Society serves as a forum, and their annual conferences as a market and meeting place for the field.

BACKGROUND AND DEVELOPMENT

By the beginning of the twentieth century, a few writers had laid the foundations of modern futures techniques. Ivan Bloch, a Polish banker and economist, applied statistical techniques to the first case study of contemporary warfare, and the Australian journalist George Sutherland raised trend-watching to a scientific level with the first large-scale survey of coming technological advances. The English writer H. G. Wells gained a world audience with his analysis of things to come in *Anticipations* (1902) and *A Modern Utopia* (1905).

In the United States, the need for military and commercial strategies during the two World Wars and the Great Depression supported the development of methods to foresee the future. In 1946, General Harley Arnold urged the Douglas Aircraft Company to establish a permanent center for Army-Air Force analysts and forecasters to investigate the feasibility of new means of warfare, such as jet propulsion and radar. The project grew rapidly and in 1948 became an independent nonprofit group, the RAND Corporation. Also in 1946, the Stanford Research Institute (SRI) was founded in California by a group of West Coast business leaders. SRI and RAND later became two of the most influential think-tanks in the United States and schools for many leading futurists like Theodore Gordon, Olaf Helmer, Herman Kahn, Roy Amara, and Peter Schwartz.

The planning experience of the wartime staffs carried over into the reconstruction work of the 1950s. According to Yale University sociologist Wendell Bell, after World War II, "Wartime economic controls over such things as consumer goods, raw materials, and foreign exchange gave a new respectability to the idea of planning in private enterprise-driven economies. Now, public expenditures were reviewed and policies formulated several years in advance, usually to raise the rate of economic growth." This encouraged the rise of futures studies and the development of today's most used methods. As early as in 1954, Harrison Brown of the California Institute of Technology had addressed most of the global issues of the 1980s in *The Challenge to Man's Future*. In 1958, SRI opened its Long-Range Planning Service.

AMERICAN FUTURISM GROWS

In the 1960s key publications emerged and professional institutions dedicated to futures studies were founded. In 1961 Herman Kahn founded the Hudson Institute, an independent nonprofit futures research organization. Two years later the first course in futures studies was offered by James Dator at the Virginia Polytechnic Institute. The World Future Society was formed in 1966; its newsletter, *The Futurist,* published futures oriented articles and was followed later by other new forecasting journals. Two year later, Olaf Helmer established the Institute for the Future at Wesleyan in Middletown, Connecticut, which in 1972 relocated to Menlo Park in California. From 1965 to 1966 entities such as Harvard and Yale; private corporations like IBM and Time, Inc.; foundations such as Carnegie and Ford; and the Departments of State, Health Education, and Welfare, and Housing and Urban Development were represented in the "Commission on the Year 2000" of the American Academy of Arts and Sciences. Wendell Bell pointed out in *The Knowledge Base of Future Studies* that while the Commission eventually ceased operations, it assisted in producing "a network of people interested in futures thinking that went well beyond the concerns of U.S. military researchers," and thus provided an impetus to continued futures studies.

By 1970, amidst great public interest in technological problems like aviation and aerospace, the field grew rapidly. Nonmilitary projects accounted for about a third of RAND's activities. In 1970 Arnold Brown at the American Council of Life Insurance (ACLI) who had created the first systematic trend scanning program for the insurance industry in 1969, and Ian Wilson of General Electric formed the first forum for business futurists called "Th Symposium." In 1971 Theodore Gordon founded The Futures Group in Middletown, Connecticut.

At the same time, a series of publications led to a tremendous increase in popularity of futures thinking all over the world. In 1972 the first report to the Club of Rome entitled *The Limits to Growth,* by Donella H. and Dennis L. Meadows, Jorgen Randers, and William W. Behrens was published and sold some 10 million copies worldwide. Based on J.W. Forrester's world model worked out at the Massachusetts Institute of Technology (MIT) and described in *World Dynamics* (1971), it highlighted the global nature of environmental issues and provoked the first debates about "qualitative growth" and "sustainable economies." The United Nations, together with a few multinational companies and government agencies, began funding global modeling. Other influential publications of this time included *Things to Come* by Herman Kahn and B. Bruce-Biggs; D. Bell's *The Coming of Post-Industrial Society* (1973); and Alvin Toffler's best-selling *Future Shock* (1973), which made future concern fashionable in the United States.

THE RISE OF INDEPENDENT CONSULTANTS

General expectations from futures studies in the 1970s were not met by many forecasts based on linear extrapolation that failed to account for abrupt discontinuities in development. The unforeseen OPEC oil embargo in 1973 caused growing official skepticism, and the pursuit of progressive change declined in the late 1970s with increasingly militaristic U.S. policies and a new period of growing mistrust between First and Third World nations. As a result of cuts in federal funding during the Reagan era, RAND, SRI, and the Hudson Institute began to diversify into areas besides futures research. After reaching a peak of 60,000

members in 1979, the World Future Society had lost nearly two thirds of its membership by 1985.

In 1977 Alvin Toffler, James Dator, and Clement Bezold founded the Institute for Alternative Futures, an independent nonprofit research institute in Alexandria, Virginia. That same year, Arnold Brown and Edith Weiner, also a former director of the ACLI Trend Analysis Program, founded Weiner, Edrich, Brown, Inc. based in New York City. In 1979 Joseph Coates, formerly of the U.S. Congress Office of Technology Assessment, founded J. E. Coates, Inc., a private futures consulting firm in Washington, D.C. In 1982 author John Naisbitt's bestseller *Megatrends* demonstrated the potential of the future as a business. Also indicative of its significance, abstracts of nearly 10,000 futures-related books, reports, and articles appeared in *Future Survey Annual* between 1979 and 1989.

During the 1980s leading futurists worked to improve the tools of futures research. In 1981 the Institute of Business Forecasting (IBF) was founded which started publishing the *Journal of Business Forecasting* targeting strategic planners. In the late 1980s futures consulting started its comeback as a form of independent consulting. In 1985 the World Future Society began its professional membership program with 308 individual and 150 institutional members. In 1987 the Global Business Network was founded by Peter Schwartz and four former colleagues. Responding to the growing complexity of strategic planning and decision making and based on the idea of a learning organization, it was structured as a network. The publication of Peter Schwartz's *The Art of the Long View* in 1991, which described the scenario planning method in great detail, together with other methodological publications, made futures techniques readily accessible to a broader public and contributed to an unprecedented boom of applied futures work in universities, corporations, and the government.

CURRENT CONDITIONS

Futures consulting is a small but steadily growing niche market of primarily small businesses. There were 1,134 individual and 80 institutional professional members from the United States registered with the World Future Society in 1998. This gives a rough estimate of the number of professionals engaged in this field, working as independent futures consultants, in research institutes, universities, and strategic planning departments of public and private organizations, or inhouse futures groups of multinational companies. In

1998 the number of all U.S. members of the World Future Society was approximately 18,900, about 30,000 people worldwide read their magazine *The Futurist,* and over 1,000 participants came to their annual conference in Chicago in 1998. IBF offered 5 annual conferences on business forecasting annually with up to 500 business forecasters of Fortune 500 companies.

RAND, SRI, and The Futures Group were large research and consulting organizations for which futures consulting constituted some portion of their work. In 1999 RAND employed more than 600 research professionals; U.S. government agencies still provided the largest share of support. SRI International employed over 2,700 staff worldwide and generated over $320 million in 1998, 50 percent each from government contract work and commercial clients. They diversified heavily into technology development and patenting activities as well. The Futures Group became the first futures think-tank to be acquired by a management consulting firm when it was bought by Deloitte Consulting in November 1998.

The Clinton administration emphasized the "big picture" and the long-term. In mid-1998 the presiding officers of both houses of Congress were committed futurists: U.S. Vice President Al Gore and House Speaker Newt Gingrich. In 1976, as junior members of the House of Representatives, they co-founded the Congressional Clearinghouse on the Future (CCF) to help translate futures research findings into political action. However, the client base for futures consulting clearly shifted from government to corporate and other non-governmental organizations, and new, independent futures consulting firms appeared in the marketplace.

The latest available *Futures Research Directory,* published by the World Future Society in 1995, listed 622 individuals from the United States. Of that total, 114 were based in Washington, D.C., Maryland and Virginia; 95 in New York, Pennsylvania and New Jersey; and 95 in California alone. About a quarter call themselves consultants or have a consulting firm. Almost all of which were small, from 1 to 15 employees and up to 25 associates. The existing businesses were growing rather slowly but steadily, a trend that was expected to continue into the twenty-first century. Prices for future workshops ranged between under $1,000 for one-day events to $5,500 per person for week-long scenario planning training seminars. A typical project running from one month to one year could cost $30,000 for smaller projects to as much as $250,000 or more for larger projects in mid-1999. Well- known futurists can charge $15,000 for a seminar lecture. Most of the established futures consulting firms in the United States listed a number of international clients. Salaries and fees were comparable with those charged by management consultants.

There are no specific government or business regulations directed toward futures consulting other than general labor law, the tax code, and business law, and there are no license restrictions. However, because futures consultants are privy to very sensitive information, Wendell Bell of Yale University has suggested developing a "Futurist Code of Ethics" to avoid potential abuses.

In mid-1999 futures consulting was still a small field and the market was not very competitive. However, many experts saw high growth potential. All organizations—and even individuals—are potential clients of futures consultants today. That a growing number of clients is willing to pay for this service was illustrated by two indicators. First, former non-profit research institutes, like SRI and IAF, have founded for-profit subsidiaries to serve the corporate client base. Second, top management consulting firms have strengthened their strategic planning services by training their own staff in futures consulting techniques, recruiting staff from futures consulting firms, or working with external futures consultants on an as-needed basis. Takeovers of today's leading futures think-tanks by big management consulting groups such as the acquisition of the Futures Group by Deloitte Touche in November 1998 were another possible trend.

Many experts in the field see futures consulting becoming a mainstream business within the next decade, accelerated by a transition into a global, information technology-driven economy and accompanied by fundamental organizational changes. A growing demand for futures consulting services by small and mid-sized clients in local, regional and national markets seemed very likely which could result in rising numbers of individual consultants as well as growing staffs in established mid-sized futures consulting firms. However, some experts see a possibility of diminishing demand after the turn of the Millennium.

Traditionally, futures consultants were presented with a problem description, conducted research, and produced a forecast. In the 1990s futures consulting became more communicative and participatory due to growing evidence that client involvement is key in producing effective results. Encouraging public participation in social decision-making has also come under the domain of futures consultants. Practitioners need to be able to encourage and empower people's participation in future workshops, scenario planning, and visioning sessions. Once created, future concepts have to be continuously evaluated, revised, and re-envisioned.

Some futures consultants saw the time frame for futures consulting diminishing with clients' interests shifting to short-term trends while others saw them expanding to 100 year time spans, depending on the subject studied. The role futures consultants will play in the future is as uncertain as their subject itself. Helping clients respond to anticipated changes was widely seen to become a major part of their work. James E. Alstrom suggested in *Futures Research Quarterly* that "futurists will substitute for their detached intellectualization a more deeply submerged involvement in the activities of their communities . . . supported by a mindset decreasingly dependent upon authoritative pronouncement and increasingly comfortable with constant change, incomprehensible complexity and perpetual surprise."

INDUSTRY LEADERS

The following examples were selected to show a variety of independent futures consulting firms with different business models and areas of specialization.

Coates & Jarratt, Inc., of Washington, D.C., was founded as J. E. Coates, Inc. in 1979. Among their first clients was the Environmental Protection Agency. In mid-1999 16 staff members, 6 of them futurists, worked for Coates & Jarratt, serving one of the most diversified clientele in the industry and generating around $1 million in revenue. For 40 corporate sponsors, Coates & Jarratt tracks forecasts in science, technology, and engineering around the world in dozens of fields, and notes the expected impact the forecasted changes could have on social and business environments over the next 20 to 25 years. One of Coates & Jarratt's latest multi-client projects in 1999 explored the future of packaging.

The Institute for Alternative Futures (IAF), based in Alexandria, Virginia, and founded in 1977, has directed its main focus towards the future of health care. IAF developed a seminar series for Congressional staff on long-term issues of pharmaceutical research and development in 1978 which resulted in two books on the future of pharmaceuticals. In 1999 IAF worked with a staff of 12 serving major health care providers, consumer groups and international clients such as the World Health Organization, which accounted for a quarter of IAF's client base. Starting out with small grants, IAF grew into a half-a-million dollar business

within 10 years and doubled it's revenues again after launching its for-profit subsidiary—Alternative Futures Associates—reaching up to $1.5 million in the late 1990s.

The Institute for the Future (IFTF) is a nonprofit firm based in Menlo Park, California. Founded in 1968 as a RAND spin-off, IFTF specializes in forecasting and strategic planning for information technologies, health care and the public sector. IFTF offers a variety of cost-shared membership programs in which organizations can become a member and sponsor research related to a specialized subject. Membership fees in mid-1999 ranged from $15,000 for the "Corporate Associates Program" program, to $150,000 for the "Consumer Direct" program.

The Snyder Family Enterprise located in Bethesda, Maryland, was founded in 1981 by David Pearce Snyder, a senior planning officer at the IRS who developed its strategic planning system. The small firm specialized in providing clients with a set of economic, demographic and technological assumptions about their operating environments in the form of so-called "strategic briefings"—illustrated lectures of 90 minutes to 4 hours in length, supported by 100 to 250 article reprints detailing the suggested future developments. In mid-1997 (the last available statistics) a staff of 6 supported by a network of 30 associates scanning certain print media served a mainly domestic client base of trade and industrial associations, government agencies and individual for- and non-profit organizations, generating $0.5 million in revenues.

Technology Futures Inc. (TFI) of Austin, Texas, specializes in forecasting possible technological developments and their impact on society. Founded in 1978 by John H. Vanston, a professor of nuclear engineering at the University of Texas, the firm's focus shifted from the energy sector to the telecommunications industry. Sponsored by the Telecommunications Technology Forecasting Group (TTFG), an organization financed by telecommunication companies, TFI conducted research on the development of technologies such as wireless telephoning, high-speed data transmission and local exchange networks. TFI uses mainly quantitative modeling and research tools and has a long tradition in offering training seminars in forecasting methods and practices.

Weiner, Edrich, Brown, Inc. is a small firm in New York City specializing in trend analysis. Founded in 1977, the company first developed trend analysis programs and seminars for clients and later developed their own information scanning programs for interested subscribers. In mid-1999, about 20 large corporate and seven nonprofit clients subscribed to Weiner, Edrich, Brown's trend information service derived from about 60 publications and presented monthly in a package of some 90 article abstracts.

WORK FORCE

Because of the field's holistic, multidisciplinary approach, futures consultants come from a variety of professions. While the first generation of forecasters was comprised mainly of economists, physicists, and engineers, today's marketplace prefers anthropologists, biologists, organizational psychologists, scholars of international studies, journalists, writers, and management consultants. At least as important to a future consultant as a broad education is a strong interest in the future, intense curiosity, excellent communication skills, and an open mind. Since futures consulting does not yield quick results, the work can be frustrating and stressful. A typical entry level position, such as that of research assistant, may pay $23,000 to $35,000 a year. Experienced futures consultants and researchers make about $70,000 per year. The field offers opportunities for creative entrepreneurs and those seeking to begin small businesses. Strong leadership qualities and good contacts to top management in client organizations are also essential for futures consultants.

The University of Houston Clear Lake (UHCL) in Texas was the first university in the United States to offer a Masters Degree program exclusively devoted to futures studies, which was initiated by futures author Jim Fowles and educational futurist Chris Dede in the mid-1960s. Over 70 students graduated from UHCL with an M. A. in Futures studies between 1993 and 1998, and some of them started their professional careers at major companies such as Kellogg, Coca Cola, and Enron, while others entered futures consulting firms or set up individual businesses. For people interested in a political science perspective, the Political Science Department at the University of Hawaii has offered undergraduate and graduate courses in political futures studies since 1969, and an Alternative Futures Masters Degree since 1978, directed by James Dator. Distance learning Masters and Ph.D. programs in Futures Studies for graduate students were also offered by Greenleaf University in St. Louis, Missouri. A number of professors offered courses in futures studies throughout the country, some of them after graduating from one of the programs mentioned above.

AMERICA AND THE WORLD

Most of the established futures consulting firms eventually started working internationally, whether for U.S. clients with an international market, or for clients outside the United States. Canada has been a traditional market for U.S. futurists, for consulting services as well as for publications. More recently, new markets opened up in Latin America. For example, TFI was assigned to a five year project by the Brazilian Ministry of Science and Technology to help identify new technologies of particular interest to the country in April 1999. However, many leading U.S. futures consulting firms served a mainly domestic clientele in the late 1990s.

A firm with a substantial number of foreign clients was Global Business Network (GBN), a globally oriented membership organization based in Emeryville, California. About 60 percent of GBN's more than 100 mainly multinational member companies in 1999 were based in the United States, 30 percent in Europe, and 10 percent in Asia, Africa, and Latin America. Specializing in scenario thinking and collaborative learning about the future, GBN brings strategists from those corporations together with provocative thinkers and experts in science, business, the arts, and academia from all over the world. For a $35,000 annual membership fee members subscribe to GBN's "WorldView Service" which includes meetings held in unusual international locations, a monthly book review service, reports on emerging issues and perspectives, and a Web site for online conversation among members and for access to GBN's archive. GBN also offers customized consulting for about $250,000 for an average custom-scenario-planning project. Since it was founded in 1987, GBN's revenues rose from about $1 million in 1990 to about $5 million in 1994, reaching about $11 million annually in mid-1999, generated by 45 employed staff members. GBN's worldwide network has grown to about 100 individual members and 18 associated scenario practitioners with offices in New York, Canada, Australia, England, the Netherlands, Sweden, Belgium, Italy, Singapore, Brazil, Mexico, and South Africa.

Most of the futures research conducted outside the United States has been done in academic institutions and government funded organizations. Business applications were becoming more common, but mostly conducted by in-house groups. Some independent futures consultant firms existed in Canada, Europe, and Australia. That futures consulting has remained a rather national business may also be due to cultural differences, which have to be completely understood to explore possible futures in a certain cultural context. The World Future Society remained an organization dominated by Americans with 394 foreign individuals and 43 institutions participating in its professional membership program. A truly international professional organization of practicing futurists is the World Futures Studies Federation (WFSF) with institutional and individual members from about 80 countries in 1999. It was established as a non-profit, independent, and international association in Paris in 1973. The Federation aims to stimulate cooperative futures research activities, as well as future-oriented thinking and acting, by providing a forum for the exchange and examination of information, ideas, visions, and plans for alternative, long-term futures. The WFSF organizes world conferences approximately every two years. The sixteenth world conference was planned to be held in Manila in December 1999. The organization issues a newsletter, cooperates with various other futures journals, coordinates futures research projects, and organizes introductory futures studies courses in Europe and in the Asia-Pacific region each year. Within the next few years, competition is likely to grow in global markets, and there will be increasing attempts of leading futures consulting firms to form international alliances.

RESEARCH AND TECHNOLOGY

Those techniques and methods developed by futures research pioneers in the 1940s to 1960s were widely used and have been developed further by futures consulting practitioners in the 1990s. It was also widely agreed upon that only the use of a variety of quantitative as well as qualitative methods, and a combination of analytical and visionary approaches is needed to get reasonable results. The traditional thinking pattern of forecasting—looking at the present stage of the world and speculating on how it might change—is now accompanied by "incasting"—assuming a future stage of the world and speculating "backwards" on what chain of events might have led to this situation. But whatever methods futures consultants prefer, the most fundamental impact on their work will come from the combined power of computers and software, telecommunications and the Internet.

Although reasonably priced and easy-to-use software packages for futurists were still hard to find in mid-1999, it is very likely that they will soon become available, driven by the ever growing thirst of organizations for tools that help them anticipate change

more easily and quickly. They will include tools for information scanning; trend identification; scenario creation; organizational and market assessment; strategy development; planning, creating and running dynamic systems models; and for interactive presentations. Intelligent agent technology—software programs that find, screen, and retrieve information automatically from databases and electronic mail—as well as more sophisticated expert systems that use knowledge from human experts encoded into computer systems, will make possible significant improvement in information gathering. Empowered computer performance will allow more accurate modeling and simulation of organizational and social systems based on key concepts from chaos and complexity theory. The growing supply of high-tech presentation devices and multimedia software, as well as the options offered by virtual reality, will enhance futures consulting by helping to perfect presentations of scenarios and future visions.

Telecommunications technologies and the Internet will further reduce the time needed to collect, exchange and present information. Communication technologies and software like video-conferencing, e-mail, and groupware, which allows interactive work with a group of people at different locations via computer terminals literally everywhere in the world, and the Internet as a new medium also made it possible to provide consulting services globally via the Internet. With pace of change accelerating and with appropriate tools and methods readily available, it is likely that more organizations will employ full-time futures consultants to constantly assess the latest information available, and to act upon the trends they detect.

FURTHER READING

Almstrom, James E. "The Future of Futurism." *Futures Research Quarterly,* Fall 1998.

Amara, Roy. "The Institute for the Future: Its Evolving Role." *Futurist,* June 1973.

Bell, Wendell. *Foundations of Futures Studies.* Vol. 1. New Brunswick, NJ: Transaction Publishers, 1997.

Coates, Joseph F. "An Overview of Futures Methods." In *The Knowledge Base of Future Studies,* Vol. 2, edited by Richard A. Slaughter. Victoria, Australia: DDM Media Group, 1996.

Cornish, Edward. *The Study of the Future: An Introduction to the Art and Science of Understanding and Shaping Tomorrow's World.* 2nd ed. Bethesda, MD: The World Future Society, 1998.

Fost, Dan, and Brad Edmonston. "How to Think About the Future." *American Demographics,* 1 February 1998.

The Future Research Directory: Individuals. World Future Society, Bethesda, MD: 1995.

Future Scope: The Software Toolkit for Trend Analysis, Scenario Creation & Strategy Development. The Woodlands, TX: Applied Futures International, 1998. Available from http://www.appliedfutures.com.

Garber, Joseph R. "What if. . . ?" *Forbes Magazine,* 2 November 1998.

Hill, Christian. "Consultant's Call." *Wall Street Journal,* 21 September 1998.

Kisken, Tom. "They're Looking Forward to It; Futurists Consult on Technology, Not Commodities." *Washington Times,* 5 August 1998.

Lohr, Steve. "Long Boom or Bust." *The New York Times,* 1 June 1998.

Moll, Peter. "The Thirst for Certainty: Futures Studies in Europe and the United States." In *The Knowledge Base of Future Studies,* Vol.1, edited by Richard A. Slaughter. Victoria, Australia: DDM Media Group, 1996.

"A Perfect Day." *Economist,* 22 August 1998.

Schwartz, Peter. *The Art of the Long View.* New York: Doubleday, 1996.

Sittenfeld, Curtis "Be Your Own Futurist." *Fast Company,* 1 October 1998.

Tanaka, Jennifer. "Futurism-The Trendiest Profession." *Newsweek,* 2 March 1998.

—Evelyn Hauser

Gambling Resorts and Casinos

By the late 1990s gambling had become one of the fastest growing, most lucrative, and most controversial leisure industries in the United States. About 154 million Americans gamble each year. Americans wagered $640 billion on all forms of gambling in 1997, and casino gambling accounted for about 42 percent of this total. Casinos reported winnings, or revenues, of $22 billion that same year. Gambling has also surpassed sporting events as America's most popular leisure activity based on consumer expenditures. In descending order, the country's leading gambling states are Nevada, New Jersey, Mississippi, and Louisiana. The American Gaming Association reported that gambling was responsible for an estimated 330,000 jobs nationwide, not including Native American-owned casinos. Nevertheless, with growing competition among casinos, industry revenues grew more slowly at the end of the decade than they did earlier in the decade.

Casino gambling, except in facilities managed by certain Native American tribes, is regulated at the state level. Some states, such as Nevada, have empowered gaming commissions to oversee any activity involving wagering. Other states require legislatures to approve new forms of gaming. Still, only 65 percent of Americans believe that casinos stimulate local economies, so it is often difficult to gain approval for new casinos.

Even as profits are increasing and the industry draws new players, a powerful anti-gambling lobby, the National Coalition Against Gambling, continues to block gambling proposals, defeating 30 state proposals in 1996 alone. In addition, President Clinton initiated the National Gambling Impact Study Commission to look at gambling's connection to crime and bankruptcy, and its report was scheduled to be released in mid-1999.

ORGANIZATION AND STRUCTURE

The gambling industry is divided into three main categories: pari-mutuel betting at race tracks, state lotteries, and casino gambling. Pari-mutuels suffered in the late 1990s due to competition from casinos. State lotteries are still doing well though, with lotto, daily numbers, and instant "scratch-off" tickets. Casino gambling is thriving thanks to riverboat and dockside casinos, Native American establishments, and resorts. These various forms of wagering exist in 48 states.

Casinos are the biggest money-makers and the driving force in the gambling industry. They have completely changed from their inception—moving from purely gaming houses to adult theme and fantasy parks, often with services like child care or video arcades. Casino gambling is now interlaced with 24-hour shopping malls and visual attractions like talking statues, erupting volcanoes, and mock ocean battles with pirate ships. Slot machines are proliferating in the casinos; slots appeal to gamblers because they are easily understandable and fast-paced. Originally, casinos devoted only about 30 percent of their space to slot machines, but they now devote up to 90 percent.

Casino gambling stretches well beyond Las Vegas and Atlantic City, the two U.S. cities most famous for casinos. Shortly after New Jersey approved gambling in 1976, Native American tribes, exempt from local laws as sovereign nations, realized that they too could profit. Gambling also spread to several waterfront and river states such as Iowa, Mississippi, and Illinois after state legislatures authorized the use of cruise ships and paddlewheel riverboats for gambling.

Casinos are subject to federal, state, and local regulations. Before operating a casino, gambling companies must acquire a license or reach an agreement with a state. Some states, such as Illinois, limit the number of licenses they issue, while other states do not have such limits but conduct reviews and background checks on all applicants for casino licenses. The Indian Gaming Regulatory Act of 1988 (IGRA) is the key piece of legislation governing casinos run by Native Americans. This Act led to the growth of 700 such facilities in 28 states by 1997. IGRA permits Native American tribes to engage in and regulate gambling on their lands if their lands are located in a state that allows gambling and if federal law allows for such gambling.

The industry's primary organizations are the American Gaming Association (AGA) and the National Indian Gaming Association (NIGA). Based in Washington, DC, the AGA provides the industry with statistics and information on the gambling industry around the country. Besides promoting the economic success of the industry, the AGA also promotes casino safety and responsible gambling. Providing its members with national representation, the AGA pushes for legislation to stimulate the gambling industry. The NIGA comprises 145 Native American nations and strives to protect and advance the Native American casino industry. Also based in Washington, DC, the NIGA trains tribal members to run casinos and offers seminars on improving casino business and safety.

BACKGROUND AND DEVELOPMENT

According to Dr. John Findlay, gambling in America really evolved in the 1800s during the westward migration. With little other entertainment and a belief in luck and risk taking, many American pioneers embraced all forms of gambling. Between 1800 and 1840, towns along the Mississippi River became ports for the riverboats transporting goods and people. The riverboats also became moving gambling parlors. Further west in the mining camps and small towns, public, organized systems of gambling evolved. Most of the gambling involved card games like Monte and Poker, but some wheel games existed.

As emerging cities in the Midwest, South, and West became bigger, wealthier, and more sophisticated, they sought acceptance from the East by tackling their "problems." Since the East viewed gaming as vulgar, any cities passed ordinances banning dealers and gamblers, and those caught were arrested.

While American cities started turning against gambling in the mid-1800s, a new, elegant, upscale form of gaming was evolving in Europe among the aristocratic classes—casino gambling. Casinos were different because they used large tables and machinery, such as roulette wheels. Casinos were found in elegant vacation resorts and mineral spa areas like Baden Baden and Bad Homburg, Germany, along with Nice, Cannes, and Monte Carlo on the French Riviera.

In 1863 Francois Blanc—a successful Parisian casino manager who was jailed for stock fraud—arrived in Monaco to build and run a casino there, despite wavering and resistance from his patron, Prince Charles II. Blanc brought wealth and dignity to Monaco and is considered the father of today's casinos. His management theories and rules for customer relations are used in Las Vegas casinos as faithfully as they were in the 1850s.

While casino games like Bacarrat and Roulette became popular and gained wide acceptance in Europe, a series of irregularities in U.S. lotteries and horse racing caused national scandals in the late 1800s. By 1910 almost all American forms of gambling had been outlawed.

Regulated betting on horses, overseen by strict state laws, eventually returned in the 1930s. During Prohibition, private clubs in cities offered various forms of illegal gambling—crap pits, poker, black jack, and slot machines. After World War II, Las Vegas started using its gambling resorts to attract tourists. During the 1950s, Benjamin "Bugsy" Siegel, a known gangster, saw an opportunity to elude California's strict ban on gambling and quench its citizens' thirst for gaming.

Siegel traveled to Nevada, since the state had tolerated gambling in the 1930s during the construction of the Hoover Dam, and built a luxury Caribbean-style hotel and casino called the Flamingo. Siegel contributed to Las Vegas' reputation as a rough town operated by organized crime from New York and Chicago but, with his casino, he had started something that would eventually contribute to the development of a new reputation. To attract gamblers, Las Vegas began offering inexpensive hotel rooms, food, free drinks, and famous entertainment. Soon, Las Vegas

The New York, New York casino and hotel in Las Vegas, Nevada. *(Archive Photos/R. Marsh Starks.)*

became one of the regular stops for performers like Frank Sinatra and Elvis Presley.

Howard Hughes became an investor in Las Vegas after he and his entourage moved into the Desert Inn in 1976, renting an entire floor of the hotel to stay out of range of photographers and the public. The Desert Inn management decided Hughes and his crew were a detriment to the business since they didn't gamble, so management evicted him; Hughes responded by buying the hotel. He then began buying land on the Las Vegas Strip, which prompted large East Coast Corporations like Hilton to do the same.

In 1978 casinos spread to Atlantic City; they later spread to states like Colorado, Louisiana, and South Dakota. The early 1980s saw casino resorts become more popular for guests and businesses alike, and casino growth increased dramatically by the decade's end. Casino gambling was approved in South Dakota, Iowa, Illinois, Mississippi, Missouri, and on many Native American reservations. In 1989 Iowa became the first state to allow gambling on riverboat casinos.

Also in the late 1980s, Stephen Wynn almost single-handedly changed Las Vegas by taking gambling to its next step when he built the Mirage resort. The

casino resort had a shark tank, a wild animal haven, and an artificial erupting volcano. Others soon followed suit. Old casinos such as the Sands, the Hacienda, and the New Frontier were demolished. New casinos like the Luxor—a glass version of the great pyramid with copies of Egyptian monuments and statues of Pharaohs—were built to attract tourists looking for entertainment.

Although many new casinos were introduced in various cities in the early to mid-1990s, Las Vegas and Atlantic City still claimed approximately two-thirds of 1994's gross revenues. To attract visitors, these casino resorts were becoming ever more elaborate; some even had features like malls, roller coasters, and golf courses.

CURRENT CONDITIONS

By the late 1990s, casino gambling had grown into a $22 billion industry. During this period about 154 million Americans wagered $640 billion annually on all forms of gambling. The industry's revenues increased by 5 percent between 1996 and 1997 but grew by 70 percent between 1992 and 1997. Because of fiercer competition in the industry, revenues from casino gambling grew at a single digit pace in the late 1990s, which was in contrast to the double digit growth earlier in the decade. Las Vegas controlled the largest share of the U.S. industry, accounting for 22 percent of the industry's revenues in 1997 with $4.8 billion in winnings. Atlantic City ranked second with $3.9 billion in revenues, accounting for 18 percent of the industry's overall winnings. Atlantic City's revenues grew at a faster rate than Las Vegas's in the mid- to late 1990s as the city vied with Las Vegas to be the country's leading gambling city. Mississippi ranked third with $1.9 billion in 1997, accounting for 8.6 percent of the industry's revenues, and Louisiana held fourth place with $1.2 billion in revenues, accounting for 5.4 percent. Despite the gambling industry's success in the late 1980s and early 1990s, fewer states considered gambling proposals to stimulate the economy in the late 1990s because of the country's economic prosperity, including low inflation, stable interest rates, and low unemployment.

Nevertheless, some states continued to launch new casino projects, including Michigan. In 1996, Michigan legalized non-tribal gambling and authorized the operation of three casinos in Detroit, which will be run by Detroit Entertainment L.L.C. (a partnership between Circus Circus and Atwater Casino Group L.L.C.), Greektown Casino, and MGM Grand Detroit L.L.C. According to Bear, Stearns, & Co., a Wall Street analyst firm, the three casinos should garner combined revenues of $1.2 billion a year. Temporary facilities are expect to open in late 1999, and the permanent casinos are slated to open in 2002 or 2003.

Other new casinos of the late 1990s included Las Vegas' New York-New York, a miniature version of New York City with a Coney Island-style roller coaster, a model of the Brooklyn Bridge, and a scaled down Statue of Liberty. Similar city-theme resorts based on Paris and Venice were launched during the late 1990s. The Paris-based resort has a miniature Eiffel tower, and the Bellagio, an Italian themed fantasy resort, is expected to cost about $2.5 billion, according to *Fortune*. Mirage Resorts' Bellagio also displays celebrated paintings by Picasso, Van Gogh, Monet, and Degas as part of chairman Steve Wynn's plan to make Bellagio the premiere upscale casino. In addition, older casinos such as Caesar's Palace underwent renovations during this period. These constructions and plans for new casinos should bolster the growth of the casino industry into the next century, but they also will increase competition.

The gambling industry benefited from the increase of slot machine casinos and the addition of slot machines to other casinos in the 1990s. Slot machines spurred on the industry's growth in the mid- to late 1990s, representing the majority of the revenues in U.S. casinos. In addition, because they are easy to use, slot machines appeal to novice gamblers and gamblers with small budgets, since bets are placed with coins. The high demand for slot machines goaded many casinos to change their formats to emphasize slot machines, and some even began to move away from posh

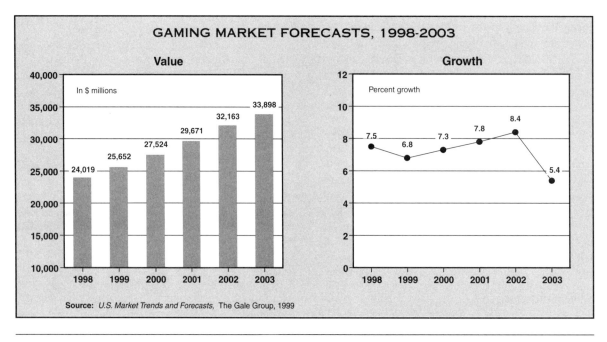

GAMING MARKET FORECASTS, 1998-2003

Value (In $ millions)

1998	1999	2000	2001	2002	2003
24,019	25,652	27,524	29,671	32,163	33,898

Growth (Percent growth)

1998	1999	2000	2001	2002	2003
7.5	6.8	7.3	7.8	8.4	5.4

Source: *U.S. Market Trends and Forecasts*, The Gale Group, 1999

theme-oriented casinos. By the late 1990s, numerous successful casinos featured only slot machines. Moreover, slot machine manufacturers began to enhance their products, making them more interactive and visually stimulating. Video gambling machines, which feature colorful, fast-paced computer generated poker games, also have proven popular for many of the same reasons. Despite the popularity of slot-machine and video gambling casinos, demand for large, themed casinos remained strong, and gambling companies continued to launch more of them during the late 1990s.

Casinos also began targeting families in the mid- to late 1990s. Casinos and resorts added family-oriented themes to their gaming houses—including carnival, ancient Egypt, and lost treasure themes—and started to provide other services to make casinos an option for family outings and vacations. These services included offering childcare for young children and alternative activities for older children. Moreover, the themes helped casino operators distinguish their gaming houses from those of other operators.

Casino owners are trying to make the experience more pleasurable for gamblers. For example, the Stratosphere features Super Tush 2000 seats. Many casinos also have designated smoke-free floors. Additionally, some casinos, including the President Casino in St. Louis, have clubs frequent players can join to earn free meals and merchandise. Casino-style gambling is also available in households via the Internet. Many such Web sites allow the user to establish an account and win or lose real money playing casino games.

Although the United States promoted the gambling industry in earlier years, in part because state governments rely on its tax revenues, the federal government grew more cautious in the latter half of the 1990s. For example, President Clinton created a nine-member national commission—the National Gambling Impact Commission—to investigate the effects of gambling on U.S. society in 1996. The commission's length is two years from its first meeting, which took place on June 20, 1997. Consequently, its report to Congress and the President is due June 20, 1999. The commission's findings could alter the gambling climate in the United States and lead to further regulation and restrictions. Furthermore, critics continued to challenge the success of the industry as an economic stimulant, arguing that most gambling cities, except Las Vegas, fail to draw visitors for extended periods. Instead, they contend that gamblers simply patronize casinos—not hotels, restaurants, and other businesses in the city—and that they do not create additional revenues for cities but rather divert revenues from other sources.

INDUSTRY LEADERS

Park Place Entertainment Corporation, with revenues of $2.5 billion, was the industry leader in 1998. It was followed by Harrah's Entertainment, Inc. with revenues of $2.0 billion; Mirage Resorts, Incorporated with $1.52 billion; Circus Circus Enterprises, Inc. with $1.47 billion; and Trump Hotels & Casino Resorts with $1.4 billion in 1998. The largest Native American casino is the Foxwoods Resort and Casino, run by the Mashantucket Pequot tribe in Connecticut, which posted sales of approximately $1 billion in 1998.

In 1998 Hilton Hotels Corporation, which formerly led the industry, split its operations in two, creating a hotel and lodging unit and a gaming unit. Hilton spun the gaming unit off as Park Place Entertainment Corporation the same year, thus catapulting the new company to the top of the industry. Park Place owns 18 casinos and 23,000 hotel rooms, including the Flamingo, Bally Entertainment Casinos, and Hilton Casinos. Park Place continued its expansion campaign initiated under Hilton's ownership by acquiring Mississippi-based Grand Casinos in 1998. Park Place's gambling operations include resorts in Las Vegas, Atlantic City, New Orleans, and Biloxi, as well as Australia and Canada.

Harrah's operates some 20 casino resorts in Nevada, New Jersey, Illinois, Indiana, Kansas, Louisiana, Missouri, Mississippi, and Arizona, as well as in Australia and New Zealand. The company focuses on establishing its brand identity and is the largest casino company in North America. Harrah's operates over 1 million square feet of gambling space. In 1999 the company announced that it would merge with Rio Hotel and Casino, thereby acquiring about 120,000 additional feet in gaming space. The company had about 25,000 workers in 1998.

Mirage Resorts mainly operates casinos in Las Vegas, but the company does have casinos and tropical theme parks in Mississippi, New Jersey, and Argentina. Some of its better known casinos are The Mirage, Treasure Island, The Golden Nugget, and Bellagio, which is one of Las Vegas's most luxurious casinos. Las Vegas-based Mirage also plans to open new casinos in Biloxi and Atlantic City in the late 1990s. The company employed about 17,100 workers in 1998.

Circus Circus owns about 10 casino resorts, including Circus Circus, the Edgewater, Excalibur, and Luxor. The company has casinos in Nevada, Mississippi, and Illinois. The company continues exploring ideas for new casinos designed to attract middle income families looking for gambling and inexpensive entertainment. The company also plans to increase its business by opening new casinos in Detroit, Las Vegas, and Atlantic City. Circus Circus employed about 20,000 workers in 1998.

Trump Hotels & Casino Resorts, Inc. ranked among the leaders in the gambling industry with Trump Plaza Hotel and Casino, Trump's Marina, Trump World's Fair, Trump Taj Mahal in Atlantic City, and Trump Indiana, a river boat casino on Lake Michigan, operating out of Gary. Together the Trump Hotels have approximately 400,000 feet of gambling space, 11,900 slot machines, and 500 table games. Owned by Donald Trump, the casinos garnered revenues of $1.4 billion in 1998. Founded in 1995, Trump Hotels & Casinos employed around 11,200 people in 1998.

During the late 1980s and continuing through the 1990s, there has been an ongoing rivalry between Stephen Wynn, the creator of Mirage Resorts, and Donald Trump. The two men compete to purchase companies that have come up for sale and even block the other's development plans in Atlantic City. While Trump has suffered financial setbacks and even near-bankruptcy with his casino investments, Wynn has established Mirage as the industry standard. Wynn's trademark is his management style. He operates his casinos with a system that rewards employees with terrific work conditions, good benefits, and vacations. In addition, Wynn believes supervisors must use persuasion rather than authority.

WORK FORCE

Casino gambling presents job opportunities for dealers, slot attendants, and pit managers, and since the industry has become intertwined with the entertainment world, there has been a huge increase in jobs in the hotel and restaurant industry. Hotel managers, bartenders, wait personnel, chauffeurs, and taxi drivers are in demand.

The melding of entertainment and gambling has been advantageous for those seeking employment in casinos. Native American gambling complexes provide an increasing number of employment opportunities. Twenty-eight states have some 700 Native American gambling facilities. The National Indian Gaming Association estimates Native American casinos employ 140,000 people. Employees at these casinos earn about $18,000 annually. According to the American Gaming Association and the National Gambling Impact Study Commission, non-Native American companies employed 330,000 workers with an average salary of $23,200 a year. About 46 percent of these employees worked in the casino portion of the operations, while the rest worked in food, lodging, and other divisions.

Trends

CASINOS: FOR BETTER OR FOR WORSE

Casinos can be the lifeblood of some communities, generating revenue struggling cities need to sustain themselves. However, long-term studies often show that cities with casinos experience economic setbacks in addition to the benefits. The benefits most often associated with casinos are increases in tourism, additional business and tax revenue, a diminishing tax burden and the creation of new jobs. However, those are frequently accompanied by crime, compulsive gambling, erosion of the work ethic, and traffic congestion.

The Casino Control Act that legalized gambling in Atlantic City, N.J., tried to counterbalance those negative effects by requiring casinos to pay revenue taxes, regulatory fees and reinvestment obligations to the state. While gambling proved profitable to the gambling industry, the revenue generated has not yet translated into meaningful urban development there, according to an article on the economics and ethics of casino gambling published in *Review of Business* in spring of 1997. The city also has not seen the funding of education and other public service programs, the article asserts. In addition, the number of retail businesses in Atlantic City has decreased by one-third, according to a citation in the article.

A study of gambling impacts by the National Opinion Research Center at the University of Chicago in 1999 determined that per capita income stays the same in communities with casinos, indicating that those communities reap more jobs, but not necessarily better jobs. And while construction, hospitality, transportation, recreation and amusement earnings rise in areas with casinos, bar, restaurant and general merchandise earnings fall, the study concluded. However, the study also determined that unemployment rates, welfare outlays and unemployment insurance in communities near casinos decline by about one-seventh and that per capita rates of bankruptcy, health indicators and violent crime rates in those areas are not significantly changed by nearness to casinos.

RESEARCH AND TECHNOLOGY

Casinos are organized in very tightly managed pyramid structures. Because such a large amount of money is in play, a massive security system has been developed using state-of-the-art camera and computer equipment. Security systems record every hand, every shuffle, and every movement of both players and dealers. Also, while attendants clear slot machines, a second security worker watches the attendant while all activity is being recorded. These systems are constantly being upgraded to keep pace with the increased number of casino patrons.

According to *American Demographics,* slot machine manufacturers are making their equipment more elaborate. For example, Casino Data Systems is working on a machine called Gold Fever, which will feature a movie that provides additional entertainment. Gambling equipment makers also launched slot machines featuring more accurate calculation software and a nudge option that allows players another chance at a jackpot. Equipment manufacturers believe that these features make slot machines more fun to play, and casino owners hope these features will encourage customers to play them longer.

The popularity of the Internet and the development of effective online security systems in the mid- to late 1990s motivated casino operators to establish online gambling sites. Although this part of the industry just began in the late 1990s, *Time* reported that it already brought in between $100-200 million in worldwide revenues. Internet gambling sites are set up so that cybergamblers can bet on sports events, participate in lotteries, and play virtual versions of casino games. The majority of the Internet gambling operations are based in the Caribbean, where there are few licensing restrictions.

Internet gambling operations, however, quickly became controversial because existing laws on gambling do not cover the specifics of the Internet in any straightforward way. U.S. federal law bans the making of bets through interstate telephone lines, but this law does not cover wagering across international boundaries, such as those that exist on the Internet where gambling operations from all over the world can set up online casinos and lotteries. Therefore, U.S. senators began introducing bills that would prohibit online gambling and punish gamblers. Major casinos have voiced mixed views. Some advocate online gambling, while others oppose it, fearing it will reduce their market shares and revenues. Most large casinos plan to wait until the controversy dies down before launching their own Internet gambling sites. Although

Congress considered several proposals to explicitly ban online gambling including the Internet Gambling Prohibition Bill (also known as the Kyl Bill), Congress has yet to approve of such a bill.

Other countries, such as Australia, support online gambling and have offered to regulate the industry. Nonetheless, with or without government support, Internet gambling is forecast to grow; the market segment was projected to reach $500 million by 2000.

FURTHER READING

Arthur Anderson LLP. *Economic Impacts of Casino Gaming in the United States.* Washington, DC: American Gaming Association, May 1997. Available from http://www.americangaming.org/media/Impact/microbg.html.

"Boomtown USA." *The Economist,* 21 December 1996.

Bourie, Steve. "American Casino Guide." *Casino Vacations,* 1996.

"A Busted Flush." *The Economist,* 25 January 1997.

Elkind, Peter. "The Number Crunchers." *Fortune,* 11 November 1996.

Findlay, John M. *People of Chance.* New York: Oxford University Press, 1986.

Goldblatt, Jennifer. "Casino Boom Fades, but Banks Find Game's Not Over." *American Banker,* 28 May 1997.

Huebsch, Kevin. "Taking a Chance on Casinos." *American Demographics,* May 1997.

Jenkins, Patricia. "Atlantic City Revenues Jump Again." *Newark Star-Ledger,* 3 October 1996.

Krantz, Michael. "Cyberspace Crapshoot." *Time,* 2 June 1997.

Labich, Kenneth, and Joe McGowan. "Steve Wynn: A $.2.5 Billion Wager." *Fortune,* 22 July 1996.

Laing, Jonathan R. "Fantasy Land: Can Ever-More-Elaborate Casinos Keep Drawing Crowds—and Money?" *Barron's,* 16 September 1996.

Mariani, Matthew. "Jobs in Legal Gambling: A New Giant in an Old Industry." *Occupational Outlook Quarterly,* Fall 1996.

Melcher, Richard A. "You Gotta Know When to Hold 'em." *Business Week,* 9 September 1996.

Mirkovich, Thomas. *Casino Gambling in the United States: A Research Guide.* Lanham, MD: Scarecrow Press, 1997.

Novak, Viveca. "They Call It Video Crack." *Time,* 1 June 1998.

O'Brien, Timothy. "Gambling: Married to the Action, for Better or Worse." *The New York Times,* 8 November 1998.

Saunders, George. "Industry Snapshot: Gambling." *Hoover's Company Information,* 1997.

Spain, William. "Crazy From the Heat." *Computerworld,* 6 October 1996.

Wagner, Jay P., and Kendall Hamilton. "Kids in Casinos? You Bet." *Newsweek,* 21 October 1996.

—Christopher Cook, updated by Karl Heil

Gaming Establishments for Adults

INDUSTRY SNAPSHOT

The concept of gaming establishments, including such high-tech diversions as laser tag, paintball, whirlyball, and interactive and virtual reality games, are generally conceived for (and usually targeted to) children and teenagers. By the 1990s, however, more adults were partaking of such pleasures, as manifested by the infusion of family amusement centers scattered throughout the United States. Arcades, restaurants, skating rinks, movie complexes, superstores, shopping centers, among several other locations, emerged as likely sources for state-of-the-art electronic playgrounds for families from many backgrounds. While many of these electronic games can be played at home by computer owners, an electronic gaming center offers sociability as well as high-tech stimulation.

The broadly defined industry of establishments anchors around electronic entertainment and grew at a phenomenal rate during the 1990s, contrary to the common perception that computer and arcade games were generally activities. By the year 2002, it was anticipated that more than 100 such centers (equivalent in size to the largest of the late 1990s) would materialize worldwide. Developers of entertainment-anchored centers could now lure adults and their families for a variety of daily and nightly purposes and shoppers might bounce between activities such as shopping, dining, movies, and video games without the necessity of locating new parking spaces.

As David Hickman, vice president of CB Commercial Real Estate Group Inc., said in a 1997 article from *Kansas City Business Journal,* "California seems to be the testing ground right now for these massive complexes. The developments are so large and so new that a lot of people in the industry are waiting for them to test it out." "Entertainment is hot," said Dan Lowe, a senior vice president with Cohen-Esrey Real Estate Services Inc., in the same article. "We're seeing it in other cities, which means Kansas City isn't far behind."

According to a February 1997 *Los Angeles Times* article, Americans spent about $8 billion annually on video games, juke boxes, and similar machines at roughly 4,500 broadly defined family entertainment places and video arcades.

ORGANIZATION AND STRUCTURE

Such innovations as paintball, laser tag, virtual reality, and video games left an indelible mark on the realm of gaming establishments in the 1990s. The first of these, paintball, was promoted as the ultimate office tension reliever and has become the sport of choice for many adults and teenagers. The game, which allows participants to play a variation of "tag" with compressed-gas paintball guns, expanded from a regional sport in the 1980s to one of international competition in the 1990s. Once in the game, players shoot small balls that splash water-soluble paint on people or objects, thus giving the game its name. Paintball operates on the "capture the flag" format, in which one team attempts to defeat the other by stealing its flag. Games last up to 30 minutes and are generally played within a five-acre area.

J.J. Brookshire of paintball equipment manufacturer Brass Eagle Inc., offered some historical perspective on paintball. He believes the evolution of the game could be traced back to the early 1970s when foresters and ranchers were exploring the most efficient means to mark livestock and trees for harvesting. In particular, according to Brookshire, BB gun maker Daisy Manufacturing Co. was approached to manufacture a gun for the aforementioned professionals. It was initially suggested that Daisy Manufacturing collaborate with pharmaceutical businesses to manufacture a soft paint "pill."

According to Brookshire in *Business First Columbus,* "No one's sure if a rancher or forester was the first to come up with the idea of shooting a friend." The first organized game of paintball, according to *Sports Illustrated,* was believed to have occurred among 12 men in June 1981 in New Hampshire. Paintball tournaments actually commenced in the late 1980s.

Paintball attracts children as young as 12 to adults of all ages. Industry insiders believed that by the late 1990s, 16- to 22-year-olds represented a disproportionately high percentage of players, with men outnumbering women by more than 9 to 1. Typically, the daily cost for playing paintball, including equipment, is about $36 according to *Paintball Store and Field Monday Report.* According to an article in *Virginian-Pilot,* about 1 million people worldwide play the game.

In an article from *World-Coos Bay,* Jack Stokes, co-owner of Hole-In-The-Wall paintball store in Coos Bay, Oregon said "It's [paintball] one of the few sports where you don't have to be a weight-lifter or a track star to play."

According to Jerry Braun, managing editor of *Paintball Sports International,* in *Business First-Columbus,* the retail realm of paintball was a $2.5-billion industry by the late 1990s. This figure included equipment sales and field fees. A serious paintball player may spend $250 on headgear and a gun, whereas a tournament competitor may spend more than $1,000 on an assault rifle alone. By 1997, worldwide revenues for the paintball industry reached roughly $275 million, according to John Henry, editor of *Paintball Store and Field Monday Report* in Newark, Delaware.

LASER TAG

Laser tag combines the two universal games of hide-and-seek and tag. Often described by its proponents as similar to paintball, but without its messiness, not to mention a tendency to become painful. Laser tag utilizes black lighting, effects lighting, booming music, and fluorescent graphics, all of which

contribute to a somewhat surreal effect. In most laser tag games, a player begins by picking a code name that is subsequently programmed into a large plastic key, activating the laser. "Tagging" is achieved when a player uses an infrared "laser" beam to deactivate opponents.

Generally, 12 to 48 players can play laser tag at any one time in an indoor space that covers anywhere from 1,500 to over 5,000 square feet. In the United States, most players spend about $6 per game, and the average game lasts 10 minutes. Since laser tag is controlled by computer software, its lasers are harmless and do not require any protective headgear. Hence, people of all ages and sizes participate in laser tag without fear of injury.

Laser Quest, one of the pioneers of the laser tag arena, opened its first center in the mid-1980s in Manchester, United Kingdom. By the mid-1990s, more than 40 Laser Quest locations existed in North America. Karin Gerner, one of the general managers of Laser Quest, said in a 1997 article from *Colorado Springs Business Journal,* "Laser Tag has a big future. It's non-violent, active participation entertainment for kids and adults. We have five centers scheduled to open this year and it's as if we can't open the doors fast enough."

Laser Storm Inc., based in Denver, is a major manufacturer and operator of laser tag systems. Although it suffered major woes in the mid-1990s, including an annual loss of $2.5 million for 1996, it also proceeded with plans for expansion. In 1997 the company signed on for 6,000 square feet in the Denver Entertainment and Fashion Pavilions, a retail and entertainment center.

Robert Cooney, president and CEO of Laser Storm, said in a 1997 interview in *Denver Business Journal* that "Our intention is to open two stores a month for the rest of the year." By the mid-1990s, Laser Storm had sold about 170 systems nationwide at an average cost of approximately $100,000. Cooney also said that in 1995, system sales contributed to roughly 95 percent of the company's revenue. In 1997, system sales accounted for only about 65 percent of Laser Storm's revenue.

"When we first opened we thought [our typical customer] was going to be teenage boys," Cooney continued in the *Denver Business Journal.* "So far, about 40 percent of Laser Storm's customers are teenagers. Another 40 percent of business is birthday parties, mostly with children 12 years old or younger. About 20 percent of those who come to a Laser Storm outlet to play are adults."

A couple enjoys the festive atmosphere of Dave and Buster's. (Courtesy of Dave and Buster's.)

By the late 1990s, Laser Storm was targeting more corporate businesses, including such companies as Lucent Technologies and Red Robin restaurants, for company outings and training sessions.

GAMEWORKS AND ITS IMPACT

One of the most high-profile companies in the American gaming industry is GameWorks, the ultimate high-tech video arcade. The company was conceived by the enormously successful film producer/director Steven Spielberg and his cofounder Skip Paul, who started the business in an attempt to merge the ideal entertainment and social experiences into one. Parent company Sega Gameworks began in 1996, as a joint entertainment venture between SEGA Enterprises, DreamWorks SKG, and Universal Studios, Inc. SEGA had the background in high-end, coin-operated video games, Universal Studios expertise was in theme park design, and Dreamworks SKG provided the creative leadership. In March 1997, GameWorks opened its first center in downtown Seattle, Washington.

One of the many games at the GameWorks center is Vertical Reality, in which adventurous guests are tied down to a seat that elevates up to 24 feet as they

attempt to shoot evil figures on the screens in front of them. Another game, Tokyo Wars, simulates a tank battle in the Japanese capital. A third game creates a virtual reality boxing tournament, while a fourth tackles sport fishing in a similar manner. In another section of GameWorks called "the cyber-living room," guests log onto computers to access the World Wide Web.

By 1999, GameWorks operated five sites and had serviced more than 9 million visitors. By summer 1999, the company anticipated opening six more sites in the United States and two additional locations in Guam and Brazil.

Another goal for GameWorks is to "cyber-link" all of its sites to each other. This means that GameWorks guests can meet and compete electronically with each other, in effect creating a self-contained worldwide network. However, this plan is an expensive proposition, as it will probably cost each GameWorks site approximately $20 million to connect with the others.

Tim O'Brien of *Amusement Business Magazine* was quoted in a 1997 *Christian Science Monitor* article, as saying "With Spielberg's name, money, and talent behind this, we will see a whole new dimension to arcades that will take to another level . . . including that of a total package for the family."

The success of GameWorks in the late 1990s had enormous impact on other competitors, particularly in terms of suburban and urban mall development. In the late 1990s, Walt Disney Co. spent millions of dollars on Club Disney, a self-described "play site" in Thousand Oaks, California.

One difference between Club Disney and Game-Works is that the former targets young families with children between the ages of 4 and 10, while the latter aims at relatively young adults during daytime and at the 20-something population at night. Disney spokesperson Andrea Borda said in *Christian Science Monitor* that "Everything here is designed for both parent and child to participate together, not watch."

Also quoted in that article, O'Brien said, "This is a change in attitude by companies going after the American entertainment dollar. Instead of giving up a day or a weekend for a theme park once or twice a year, or feeding quarters into old-style arcades every week, these both represent a new way of attracting groups of people for several hours at a time, regularly throughout a year."

During the 1990s, Odgen Corp., owner of the Great Western Forum, invested in a series of mall-based storefronts that combined live animals with motion-simulator machines. Sony Corp. was planning a gargantuan four-story entertainment center in San Francisco. Finally, Brunswick Corp., manufacturer of bowling balls and outboard motors among other products, opened Red's Rec Room at a mall in Alberta, Canada.

DAVE & BUSTER'S

Founded in 1982 in Dallas, Dave & Buster's has become one of the United States' most well-known upscale restaurants. In its success, this restaurant-arcade chain that caters to adults helped blur the distinction between dining and entertainment during the 1990s. The original Dave & Buster's restaurant concept is traceable to the late 1970s in Little Rock, Arkansas, where Buster Corley owned a restaurant beside an entertainment parlor operated by Dave Corriveau. The two men observed that many customers bounced from one establishment to another.

In the late 1990s, the company opened its fifteenth domestic location at Palisades Center Mall in Rockland County, New York. This center, a 2-million square foot retail/entertainment development, hoped to attract 20 million visitors annually.

At a typical Dave & Buster's, games represents a significant portion of revenues. As reported in *Denver Post,* in its original 12 Dave & Buster's centers, games and other entertainment accounted for 47 percent of the revenue, compared with 32 percent from food and 20 percent from beverages. This bodes well for company investors, since games typically yield a profit margin of almost 95 percent of revenues, while food and drinks yield at best a 65 percent profit margin. Dave & Buster's robust earnings and continuing popularity were recognized by an increase in its stock price, rising from $8 a share in the beginning of 1996 to $27 a share by the end of 1997.

As quoted in the same *Denver Post* article, Dave Corriveau said, "The average age of our customers is 33. We find that we attract a lot of big kids, and when they see what's here, they become even bigger kids." Dave & Buster's and similar "eat-ertainment chains", as they were termed by industry jargon, often compete with more traditional restaurants such as gourmet take-out delicatessens and new fast-food places. Given this high degree of competition, restaurant owners often contained prices, employing various forms of entertainment to jack up the volume.

The celebrity chef is one means through which "eat-ertainment chains" could achieve some distinction. For example, in central New Jersey, Nick Rentoulis operates The Town Restaurant and is a celebrity chef there. Emeril Lagasse, a New Orleans chef and TV Food Network star, fulfills a similar function. A variation of the celebrity chef attraction is the celebrity theme restaurant, such as Hard Rock Café and Planet Hollywood.

WORK FORCE

Of course, there is great variation in the composition of the labor force at the many places that qualify as electronic entertainment-anchored centers. Behind the scenes, professionals such as computer programmers are needed to create the software through which games such as laser tag and virtual reality operate. The organizations that offer gaming services and entertainment need retail workers to help customers and set up the games. Restaurant/entertainment centers need food-service staff and game operators, and many rely on teenagers, paying minimum or near-minimum wages to keep operating costs down. Employing teenagers and young adults makes sense, since these centers cater to a disproportionately young audience.

AMERICA AND THE WORLD

American entertainment centers have had enormous impact worldwide. For example, in the late 1990s, two southern California real estate developers and a few major Japanese firms were planning to build four enormous retail and entertainment centers in Japan, as reported in *Los Angeles Times*. The plan anticipates American-based malls, including such places as Wolfgang Puck restaurants and the Sports Club fitness operations. It was expected to be completed in late 1999 and to be worth more than $3 billion.

These ambitious plans for locations in Tokyo and Osaka were conceived by WPI.KOLL Asia Pacific Advisors, a partnership of two California companies, Santa Ana-based retail developer World Premier Investments and Newport Beach-based Kill Real Estate Services. The Japanese partners included Sakura and Fuji banks and Mistui Real Estate. Andrew Sun, chairman and chief executive of WPI.KOLL, said if these plans were successful, he would consider expanding the operation to other Asian regions.

FURTHER READING

"Addenda." *New York Times*, 3 November 1998.

Ball, Brian. "GameWorks comes to Play at Easton Town Center." *Business First-Columbus*, 16 January 1998.

———. "SPLAT: Paintball Purveyors Duel for Splattered Market." *Business First-Columbus*, 26 December 1997.

Burt, Wendy. "Where Stalking is Entertainment." *Colorado Springs Business Journal*, 22 August 1997.

Curcio, Frank. "Entertainment Appeals to Diners." *Courier-News (Bridgewater, NJ)*, 16 February 1997.

DeGross, Renee. "Taverns of Cavernous Proportions." *News & Observer (Raleigh, NC)*, 1 March 1998.

Friedman, Roger. "Scaring Steven Spielberg." *Premiere*, May 1999.

Fryer, Alex. "Seattle Plugs into GameWorks Virtual Arcade." *Christian Science Monitor*, 19 March 1997.

Gebolys, Debbie. "Spielberg Video Game Arcade Coming in '99." *Columbus Dispatch*, 16 January 1998.

Grover, R. "Media & Entertainment." *Business Week*, 11 January 1999.

———. "The Storyteller: How Steven Spielberg Sustains His Creative Empire." *Business Week*, 13 July 1998.

Hemmer, Andy. "'Eat-ertainment' Complex Headed Here." *Cincinnati Business Courier*, 10 March 1997.

Hertsgaard, M. "Spielberg's Other Lost World." *Mother Jones*, January/February 1999.

Iritani, Evelyn. "Southland Developers to Build Malls in Japan." *Los Angeles Times*, 21 February 1997.

Jacobs, K. "Safe New World." *New York*, 14 September 1998.

Johnson, Greg. "Whoever Get the Most Leisure Dollars Wins." *Los Angeles Times*, 23 March 1997.

Jones, Karen. "Patriot Games." *Publishers Weekly*, 13 July 1998.

Jones, Lara. "Spielberg-Backed Game Club Chain Looking for Site in Salt Lake Area." *Enterprise-Salt Lake City*, 8 December 1997.

Kirby, Kevin. "Laser Daze." *Louisville*, May 1997.

Martin, D.S. "Disney's Imagineers Go Wild with Reality-Based Park Design." *Architectural Record*, June 1998.

McLaughlin, Tim. "Dave & Buster's Looks to West Port Plaza for New Playground." *St. Louis Business Journal*, 12 May 1997.

Obermayer, Joel. "Paintball Catching on in the Triangle." *News & Observer (Raleigh, NC)*, 20 September 1997.

Peale, Cliff. "New Food, Fun Spot to Open No Time to be Bored at Dave & Buster's." *Cincinnati Post*, 29 August 1997.

Porter, Andy. "Paintball Games: Tag Takes New Attitude." *World-Coos Bay*, 21 May 1997.

Raabe, Steve. "Fine Dining? No, Fun Dining Dave & Buster's Readies Huge Food-Entertainment Complex." *Denver Post*, 5 December 1997.

"Santa Clara County Fairgrounds Plan Calls for Closer Inspection." *Business Journal Serving San Jose & Silicon Valley*, 8 June 1998.

Shors, John, II. "The Frenzied Future of Retail." *Business Record-Des Moines IA*, 2 February 1998.

Trollinger, Amy. "Retailers See Entertainment Concepts as the Next Wave." *Kansas City Business Journal*, 6 June 1997.

Vasquez, Beverly. "Laser Storm Debunks 'Fad' Concept." *Denver Business Journal*, 7 March 1997.

———. "New Restaurant Complex Offers Interactive Dining." *Denver Business Journal*, 7 November 1997.

Wood, Daniel. "Hollywood Debuts Arcades Aimed at Virtually Everyone." *Christian Science Monitor*, 14 March 1997.

—David Levine

GENETIC ENGINEERING

Genetic engineering (GE) transfers a gene from one or more cells to another cell, thereby transforming the genetic makeup of the original cell. The field of genetic engineering includes procedures such as cloning, animal transplants, gene manufacturing, and transgenic plant and animal development, all of which involve this process of cell transformation. GE research caters to or develops products for primarily two industries: medicine and agriculture.

Legislation of the mid-1990s made it possible for companies to patent not only cells and genes but also procedures for generating genes and genetic materials. Universities as well as public and private companies, especially agricultural and pharmaceutical firms, are the primary researchers and developers of genetically engineered products and procedures. However, some government agencies also either undertake or financially back genetic engineering projects. Such agencies include the U.S. Department of Agriculture, Department of Commerce, Department of Defense, Department of Energy, and Department of Health and Human Services.

While some major pharmaceutical and agricultural companies do cash in on their discoveries and developments, many other companies in this industry toil vigorously just to get by, because genetic engineering requires patience and meticulous effort in order to isolate genetic chemicals and substances such as DNA and to carry out stringent tests to check the accuracy and effects of any findings. As a result, the process also bears a high price tag and demands unflagging financing.

ORGANIZATION AND STRUCTURE

Genetic engineering research, development, and marketing are highly regulated in the United States. The U.S. Food and Drug Administration (FDA) oversees the development of genetically engineered foodstuffs. In 1999, the FDA maintained a policy of strictly monitoring and testing GE food products if they varied in nutritional value or genetic makeup. The FDA also reserves the right to require labeling of any GE food product that contains allergens that the conventional food product does not contain or any product whose nutritional content is altered via the GE process. Most of the policies pertaining to genetically engineered food products stem from the federal Food, Drug, and Cosmetic Act of 1938 (and its amendments), which stipulates the type of labeling various kinds of products must have.

Furthermore, a U.S. Department of Agriculture (USDA) branch, the Animal and Plant Health Inspection Service, monitors the research and testing of GE products such as seeds and livestock. The U.S. Environmental Protection Agency (EPA) also plays a role in regulating the industry: it establishes standards for the performance of genetically altered products in conjunction with the USDA. These two government agencies try to ensure that GE products do not pose any environmental risks such as introducing undesirable characteristics to naturally occurring plants and wildlife. These agencies have a particular concern for the possibility that a genetically modified plant might outcross with wild plants, creating new weed-like species.

In 1995, President William Clinton helped open new financial doors for the industry by amending the

U.S. code of patents with the Biotechnology Process Patent Act, extending its scope to include the development of a novel product from a specific gene in a specific cell line. A former ruling contended that a process for creating biotechnological materials could not be patented, but the 1995 policy allows the patenting of procedures that yield genes and genetic materials.

This policy has subsequently met with controversy, however, since it has led to a rush for applications for thousands of genes and gene fragments at the U.S Patent and Trademark Office. Geneticists have felt pressure to patent the general section of genetic code they are sequencing before that section is patented by someone else and the work is lost. Commissioner Bruce Lehman is quoted in an April 1999 article of *Time Magazine,* saying, "I would guess that in many cases the scientists didn't even examine the material." To prevent broad patents from resurfacing at the discovery of something useful from the genes hidden in a patent, the Patent and Trademark Office requires applications to include no more than 10 genetic sequences. The United Nations went further and called for restrictions on gene research in 1999, saying human DNA "should not give rise to financial gain."

BACKGROUND AND DEVELOPMENT

Genetic engineering of sorts has taken place for centuries: breeding of plants and animals traces back many centuries as farmers have often experimented with various cross-breeding and grafting techniques to create hybrids with more desirable features. Wheat, for example, is a hybrid of several wild grasses. Yet as a discipline of modern science it emerged around the end of the nineteenth century, becoming more pronounced and codified throughout the twentieth century. Early interest and later motivation for interest in genetics came from the work of Gregor Mendel, an Austrian botanist who studied the hereditary features in peas, pumpkins, beans, and fruit flies, according to Anthony Serafini in *The Epic History of Biology.* In 1865, Mendel established laws of genetic traits, characterizing those most likely to be transferred through breeding as dominant, while those less likely to be transferred as recessive—or the laws of heredity. His work led to theories and methods of cross-breeding.

Before genetic engineering proper could come about, scientists needed an understanding of genetics itself. Serafini argues that genetics pioneer, T. H. Morgan introduced the formal study of genetics to the twentieth century. Morgan spent most of his research

profession at the California Institute of Technology. Beginning with the work of his predecessor, William Bateson, Morgan ascertained that chromosomes were the bearers of genetic data. In 1911, Morgan and some colleagues published the first substantive article on chromosomes and genes. Morgan made other crucial discoveries including sex-linked (male and female chromosomes carry different information) and sex-limited (certain genetic characteristics are realized only in one sex, not both) genetic information. In 1926, Morgan sketched an early picture of how parents passed traits to their offspring in his book *The Theory of the Gene.*

The 1920s brought discoveries of ribonucleic and deoxyribonucleic acids, RNA and DNA, which are essential to genetic communication. RNA holds the genetic information for some viruses, while DNA carries it for most organisms. In the 1940s, scientists proved that genes carried genetic information, not proteins as some had believed. In the 1950s, researchers James Watson and Francis Crick used X-Rays to photograph DNA, leading to further understanding of the acid. As a result, they determined that DNA contained four kinds of smaller molecules hooked together in spiral chains. (This constellation of these molecules in each cell makes up the unique range of genetic information that brings about the properties in the offspring, according to Serafini.) At this point, genetic engineering began to accelerate. Max Delbruck, of Vanderbilt University, and Alfred Hershey created a hybrid virus by combining the chromosomal material from two different viruses—a creation that had powerful impact on genetic engineering research as other scientists began to attempt more arduous genetic manipulations, according to Serafini.

By 1977, a gene manufactured by researchers was used for the first time to create a human protein in bacteria. This procedure used a recombinant gene—one made from the combination of the genes from two separate organisms—to clone the protein. This feat helped to launch the industry: biotech companies and universities began to flood the field with attempts to produce marketable products. Consequently, the flurry of interest in genetic engineering provoked Congress to attempt regulating the industry by forcing researchers to concoct specimens that could not escape from their laboratories. None of the initial, and somewhat irrational, legislative proposals ever passed.

This discovery led to the development of many recombinant DNA (rDNA) projects throughout the country in the mid- to late 1970s. One of the first was in 1978, when Genentech, Inc. and The City of Hope National Medical Center created a center for developing human insulin for diabetics, using the rDNA technology. The FDA approved of the sale of GE insulin in 1982. A wave of gene and protein clonings also took place within this period, such as proteins from hepatitis B, in pursuit of a cure or treatment, and genes for human growth hormones in hope of unlocking the door to growth and development.

In the 1980s, the genetic engineering industry received the patent support it needed when the U.S. Supreme Court decided that genetically engineered products could be patented. This meant that businesses could pursue years of research and investment without the worry that another company could capitalize on their research by producing a similar product. Also in the 1980s, Kary Mullis and others at Cetus Corporation in Berkeley, California, created a technique for multiplying DNA sequences in laboratories, called polymerase chain reaction. Cetus later sold the patent to Hoffman-La Roche for $300 million, according to Genentech. In 1986, the FDA approved of the first GE crop: genetically modified tobacco, while in 1990 Calgene Inc. began testing modified cotton, which was designed to have a genetic structure resistant to herbicides. Also in 1990, GenPharm International Inc. developed the first transgenic cow. This GE creation produced human milk proteins for infant formulas, according to Genentech.

Researchers from countries around the world banded together in 1990 in an effort to develop a map of all the human genes. Known as the Human Genome Project, this grand endeavor is backed by the U.S. Government with $3 billion. Completion of the map of human genetic information entails identifying the 23 pairs of chromosomes, then sequencing all the DNA contained in the chromosomes to discover the protein each gene produces and for what purpose. The map is expected to hold the key to nearly all illnesses, from obesity to cancer. Those who launched the project expected to complete the Herculean task by the year 2005.

Profit incentives have spurred the race. In the late 1990s pharmaceutical companies and even some private laboratories were competing with the federal project, challenging conventional methods of gene sequencing. New technologies have increased sequencing speed exponentially, according to a March 1999 press release in *PR Newswire*. Those companies that manage to patent the information first will be able to profit most on its medicinal applications. Scientist J. Craig Venter, once scoffed at by peers at the National Institute of Health, provoked debate among federal scientists regarding methods of sequencing when he declared he was well on his way to completing the map by spring 2001. Leaders of the Human Genome Project announced in the fall of 1999 that they will finish the project by 2003 and have a "working draft" of the project completed by 2001.

CURRENT CONDITIONS

Life sciences, a new term to describe the industry that combines agricultural and pharmaceutical genetic engineering, has blossomed since 1996. Although life sciences is still in its infancy, there is money to be made. According to a Hoover's industry report, genetically engineered crops earned $300 million in revenue in 1996, the first year they were available. And agricultural products account for only 10 percent of sales for the GE industry. Companies are trying to seize on the potential profits and industry giants, such as DuPont Co. and Monsanto are investing aggressively. In 1998 Monsanto spent $233 million associated with the purchase of DEKLAB Genetics Corporation, Plant Breeding International Cambridge Ltd., and the international seed operations of Cargill, Inc. In keeping with an announcement of plans to rapidly build its life sciences portfolio, DuPont and Pioneer HiBred International, Inc. announced in March 1999 that Dupont will spend $7.7 billion to acquire the remaining 80 percent currently not owned by DuPont.

One of genetic engineering accomplishments that received the most media attention in the mid-1990s was the cloning of a Dorset sheep named Dolly in February 1997. Ian Wilmut and fellow researchers at the Roslin Institute in Edinburgh, Scotland, created an exact genetic replica of the "parent" sheep, using DNA from its mammary gland. However, Wilmut's announcement met a mixed reception: leaders around the world, including President Clinton, viewed this feat with skepticism and consternation. Clinton instructed a bioethics advisory commission to review dangers of cloning and banned federal funding of human cloning research. A law in England immediately went into effect outlawing researching the same procedures on human beings.

Although FDA maintains it has the authority to stop human cloning experiments in the United States, there has been no political resolve to enact a law to ban human cloning as of 1999. Predictions that a U.S. legislative ban would drive cloning projects to third world countries were fulfilled when a South Korean research team announced the first cloning of a human embryo in December 1998. The experiment will not continue to the stage of implantation in a womb until

Francis Crick and James Watson examine a DNA model. (The Library of Congress.)

local legal issues are clarified. Less controversial, a Korean government-sponsored experiment by another research team successfully cloned a cow in early 1999 using the same nuclear-transfer technology used to create the Roslin Institute's Dolly. The Korean ministry of science and technology expects to distribute embryos cloned from the 2,205-pound cow to local farms for increased meat production.

Earlier efforts in cloning calves were expected to lead to medical, rather than agricultural, advances. In January 1998, two University of Massachusetts scientists, James Robl and Steven Stice, reported that they had successfully cloned two calves, Charlie and George. According to a January 21, 1998, article in the *Chicago Tribune,* the birth of cloned calves could offer several beneficial medical treatments in the future. Genetically engineered cows could serve as neural cell donors for treatment against such nerve-damaging diseases as Parkinson's and diabetes. Additionally, cows could be genetically engineered to produce a human plasma protein that is given to people who have experienced blood loss.

Developments in genetic engineering have changed the thinking in medical research. Gene therapy, the placement of beneficial genes into patients'

cells, was, as reported in *Time Magazine's* January 1999 cover story, initially aimed to cure relatively straightforward genetic disorders. The article cites Huntington's disease and sickle cell anemia as examples of disorders caused by a single defective gene. Scientists discovered that inserting genes into cells can also be used to change cell function, broadening the range of disorders that can be treated genetically. The article describes a heart-bypass patient who is successfully treated for recurring angina with a gene that triggers blood vessel growth. In other areas, Cell Genesis, Inc. announced in a March 1999 press release that in collaboration with Children's Hospital Los Angeles and the Markey Cancer Center of the University of Kentucky they have demonstrated "efficient long term gene delivery to bone marrow cells." Since bone marrow cells further differentiate into various blood and immune cells, this therapy holds promise for treating AIDS and cancer.

Genetic engineering has also played a role in environmental remediation. Using GE technology, tree geneticists can develop trees bearing characteristics that will help them thrive even in heavily polluted regions. Transgenic trees can have greater chemical, insect, fungal, bacterial, and stress resistance than conventional trees. In addition, GE technology can produce trees with traits more amenable to industrial uses—namely, trees better suited for pulp and paper production. Furthermore, researchers hope that GE crops such as rice, corn, and soybeans will help reduce world hunger by creating crops that can also withstand predatory and destructive factors of nature.

Despite its many successes, genetic engineering and genetically engineered products still sparked much controversy into the late 1990s. Viewing it as tampering with divinely created substances, conservative religious groups opposed to genetic engineering launched political and media campaigns to impede and halt GE research, and were also known to protest at leading GE plants. In particular, the use of human embryonic stem cells—some having been created specifically for the experiment—aroused much concern. The undifferentiated cells are valuable because they can be isolated and, researchers hope, guided to form organs for transplantation. This type of controversy may become moot, however, as GE progresses. The Gene Letter cites reports that in early 1999 a team of Italian researchers at the National Neurological Institute in Milan found that a patient's own body could be the source of stem cells for organ and tissue regeneration.

Genetically-engineered products face worldwide resistance, especially agricultural products. For example, in 1996 the European Community agreed somewhat reluctantly to market corn genetically engineered in the United States by Ciba-Geigy AG. However, a trade dispute promptly engulfed the U.S. attempt to ship the genetically modified corn to the European Union. GE corn accounted for about only .5 percent of the shipment, but the European Commission stipulated that it would only accept the shipment if it was segregated from the conventional corn, and if it bore labeling that it had been genetically engineered. The United States continued to fight for the corn's 'anonymity.' While on the contrary, the backlash in Europe, fueled by 'Frankenstein' fears in Europe, was apparent in 1999 UN negotiations.

Monsanto Co. also has confronted a wave of controversy and antagonism around the globe. Much controversy has centered on the company's marketing strategies. According to an All Things Considered article featured on National Public Radio, farmers in India burned Monsanto cotton crops in retaliation to the "Terminator gene," which renders harvested seeds sterile, forcing farmers to purchase all seeds. The company also produces "Roundup" brand, a very effective herbicide, to which almost no plant is resistant—except its genetically engineered "Roundup Ready" brand line of seeds. Domestic and international protests tried forcing governments around the world to place a moratorium on Monsanto's soybeans. Likewise, Monsanto's genetically-created growth hormone bovine somatotropin or BST, designed to increase milk production, faced rejection by farmers across the globe. Further, those who have used BST must then overcome obstacles such as consumer resistance to milk from hormone-treated cows.

The industry also faces additional problems: genetic research requires persistent effort and funding even though a marketable product may not automatically result from this effort and funding. Therefore, universities often carry out initial GE and general biotechnology research projects and later sell findings to companies. Also, companies that do engage in this kind of research may only show marginal profits and may go many years without producing any product at all, let alone a wonder drug or super gene. Of the few genetically engineered products that make it through clinical study, the FDA has approved only about 10 percent for public sale. Moreover, *Standard & Poor's Industry Surveys* reported that remaining solvent was the primary goal of many companies in the industry and 90 percent of these companies employ under 200 people, with very little revenue. In addition, litigation plagues the industry. In 1996, for example, Monsanto sued two of its rivals, Ciba-Geigy

Pioneer **IAN WILMUT, 1945- A SCIENTIST IN SHEEP'S CLOTHING**

Dolly was the first successfully cloned large mammal, born to Dr. Ian Wilmut and his crew. Wilmut's experiment involved fusing a mammary gland cell from an adult ewe with an egg cell from another ewe after first removing the genetic material from the egg. By removing the nucleus from the egg cell, all genetic information was lost but the egg was still alive and healthy. Wilmut then used electricity to fuse the adult cell with the egg cell, causing the egg to pick up the genetic material from the adult cell, and begin to grow as a normal egg. The egg was then implanted into a surrogate mother.

While the experiments had been proceeding for some time, the entire process was shrouded in secrecy; only four scientists among a group of 12 researchers knew anything about Wilmut's experiments. And even after the birth of Dolly, publicity was delayed until the group could secure a patent. Once announced, the birth left in its wake a string of both admiration and outrage. The scientific community hailed the scientific breakthrough, while philosophers and religious experts warned of the dangers and implications.

and Mycogen, accusing them of using genes patented by Monsanto. Such suits take place frequently because the current patent law does not specify in great enough detail what is actually covered by the patent—whether the gene itself or the process of creating the gene.

INDUSTRY LEADERS

Founded in 1976, Genentech, Inc., a biotechnology company, develops and markets pharmaceuticals made from recombinant DNA. Some of Genentech's products include: Protropin, a hormone for children suffering from growth impediments; Nutropin, a hormone for children with renal trouble and growth insufficiency; and activase, an agent that dissolves blood clots in heart attack patients. In 1998 the company launched Herceptin, an antibody for certain breast cancer patients. That year was also a profitable first full year of sales for the non-Hodgkin's lymphoma drug Rituxan. Royalties from hepatitis B vaccines, bovine growth hormones, and Humulin (human insulin) totaled $229.5 million. The San Francisco-based company has 3,300 employees and reported a 1998 net income of $181.9 million, an increase of 41 percent from the previous year, on $1.15 billion sales revenue. Swiss drug giant Roche Holding owns about two-thirds of the company.

Amgen has also led the genetic engineering industry with its two products that exploit GE recombinant DNA technology: Epogen, the world's leading antianemia drug, and Neupogen. Epogen simulates red blood cells and is used to treat the kidney problems of renal dialysis patients, while Neupogen simulates white blood cells and is used by cancer patients undergoing chemotherapy. In 1998, Epogen and Neupogen each earned the company about $1.0 billion, a prime example of the enormous payoff potential of the industry. Based in Thousand Oaks, California, Amgen reported $2.7 billion sales revenue for 1998, up 15 percent from 1997, and a net income of $863 million. Amgen employed 5,494 workers in 1998.

St. Louis-based Monsanto Company was a pioneer in the agricultural sector of the industry. In 1996, Monsanto paid $170 million for a 40-percent ownership of DEKALB Genetics, a grain-seed producer. In 1998, the company paid approximately $2.3 billion to acquire the remaining 60-percent ownership. According to Richard A. Melcher and Amy Barrett, authors of a May 25, 1998, *Business Week* article, this increased valuation shows just how hot the GE industry is. Also in 1998, Monsanto spent $1.9 billion to purchase Delta & Pine Land, a cottonseed producer. For the year ending 1998, Monsanto reported an after-tax loss of $250 million on sales revenue of $8.6 billion. Excluding unusual expenses, such as restructuring and research and development acquisitions, after-tax income from continuing operations would have been $580 million. The company had 30,000 employees worldwide in 1998.

Monsanto is best known for its flagship chemical *Roundup,* a leading herbicide. Monsanto also has developed a variety of genetically engineered agricultural products. Roundup Ready brand soybeans, canola, and cotton are genetically resistant to Roundup brand herbicides. Seeds genetically designed to prevent insect damage include Bollgard and Ingard brands of cotton, Yieldgard and Maisgard brands of corn, and NewLeaf brand potatoes. Genes inserted in the insect-resistant seeds allow the plants to produce their own insecticides, a feature that will ensure strong market presence in coming years. Quantum brand wheat promises farmers greater yields, yield stability, pest protection, and quality. Monsanto developed YieldGard with particular concern for protecting the crop against the European corn borer.

AMERICA AND THE WORLD

Although the United States has a strong genetic engineering and general biotechnology industry, Cuba also has become quite successful in this field as well, due to Fidel Castro's multi-million dollar investment in biotechnology since the 1980s. Ironically, Cuba suffers from shortages of conventional medical supplies such as aspirin and bandages. Nonetheless, Cuba has succeeded in creating a biotechnology atmosphere that can allow it to some day compete with major industrial biotech companies and their shoals of funding sources. Spurred on by Castro, who provided the nation with free university education and directed immunologist Manuel Limonta to develop a cancer drug using genetic engineering, Cuba's research is starting to flourish. After Limonta created the drug interferon, he founded the Center for Genetic Engineering and Biotechnology, according to Linda Robinson in *U.S. News & World Report.*

Unlike the United States, European countries have remained wary of genetic engineering, and some—including Italy, Austria, and Luxembourg—have not permitted the growing of genetically altered corn. In 1997, the sale of modified corn in Europe was also a contentious issue, pitting the United States against the European Parliament. Austria, in particular, has voiced the loudest fears of GE food products: 1 million citizens signed a petition calling for a ban on genetically altered foods, according to *The Economist.* The European Union finally reached a compromise in April 1997 concerning labeling of genetically modified products. The accord requires the labeling of all 'live' GE products. Analysts contend that this action makes no sense in terms of economics and public safety because it applies to such a narrow class of products, and it will drive up consumer prices. Hence, the European Union may amend this policy in the coming years. Furthermore, European countries, as a result of their own ambivalence toward genetic engineering, own very few genetic patents, according to *Chemistry and Industry.* Even patents issued by the European Patent Office (EPO) are primarily the property of the United States and Japan, since U.S. and Japanese researchers prefer the EPO's processing procedures—which are quicker and more efficient—to those of their own countries.

RESEARCH AND TECHNOLOGY

In 1998, industry giant Monsanto Co. teamed up with Grameen Bank to bring GE cotton to Bangladesh.

Grameen Bank makes loans available to women for business startups. The purpose of the partnership, according to Judy Mann in the *Washington Post*, is to make Bangladesh less reliant on imported cotton, which it needs for its garment industry. Monsanto, the patent owner to Bollgard Cotton, is using a 10-acre farm in Bangladesh to test hybrid cotton. In the future, Monsanto will also try to remove arsenic from Bangladesh water by using water-cleaning technology.

More than anything else, the genetic engineering industry in the mid-1990s was a research campaign that yielded few marketable or FDA-approved products. Funded largely by the private sector, GE's sustenance often comes from the promise of commercial products, which serve to attract the funds of investors. As a result, GE companies must constantly research and test possible products. With robust support from pharmaceutical companies and agricultural concerns, GE researchers tend to concentrate on medical and agricultural products that will bear fruits for their financial abettors.

Gene therapy has offered some hope as a method of treating incurable brain tumor patients. Novartis Pharmaceuticals Corporation began to conduct experiments in 1997 to test the efficacy of gene therapy. Physicians relied on the mid-1990s technique of surgical removal of the tumor followed by a regimen of chemotherapy for malignant brain tumors. Researchers believe that gene therapy may one day supersede chemotherapy. According to Novartis, for example, when a herpes simplex therapy gene is injected into any affected tissue, it mingles with the DNA of the tumor cells without causing the patient to contract herpes or any other virus. This process then triggers the production of an enzyme, which, when combined with an anti-viral drug, eradicates the remaining herpes cells. Other forms of gene therapy have shown signs of success for treating lung cancer, heart conditions, cancer, and AIDS.

Cell Genesys, Inc., one company with several vaccines and gene therapy drugs undergoing Phase I/II human clinical testing, began to reap the rewards of gene technology patenting in the mid-1990's. The company has received more than $21 million for its gene activation technology for therapeutic protein production. Hoechst Marion Roussel made the most recent payment of $2 million in December 1998 when the company secured a European patent for the technology.

In 1997, an incidental experiment conducted by Johns Hopkins researchers led to speculation about and further testing of the protein myostatin, and how it controls tissue development. By removing from lab-

More On DON'T CHANGE YOUR DIET— CHANGE YOUR GENES

The first gene cloned that can suppress diet-induced obesity provides a target for the development of weight-control therapies. Human obesity, defined as more than 20% over the ideal weight, affects one-third of American adults. This amounts to 50 million people with increased risk for the development of diabetes, heart disease, high blood pressure and stroke in the United States.

Millenium Pharmaceuticals found a gene in mice that produces a protein with activity in a specific region of the hypothalamus that regulates body weight. Since human and mouse metabolisms are similar, the researchers are looking for a gene with similar roles in people.

Normally, mice fed a high-fat diet gain excess weight. A mutation in the newly cloned gene, however, allows the mice to maintain a healthy weight while fed a high-fat (42 percent fat) diet. Mice with the mutated gene also maintain a healthy weight when fed a low-fat (9 percent fat) diet with the same number of calories.

Millenium Pharmaceuticals is exploring the use of the protein product as a target to screen different compounds with the aim to develop obesity therapies. The company applies genetics, genomics, and high-throughput screening technologies to drug discovery and development.

oratory mice the genetic codes for this protein, the researchers produced rodents with more musculature than average. Researchers and analysts expected this discovery to prove beneficial for farmers, who could benefit from genetically modified beef cattle that produce leaner cuts of beef. Scientists at Moscow's Academy of Agricultural Sciences have been genetically modifying livestock in experiments for several years, according to a March 1999 *Reuters* article. The researchers have succeeded in producing pigs with an integrated growth hormone gene for faster, leaner growth, and sheep, which produce chymosine, a cheese fermenting agent.

In agriculture, researchers have focused on creating new species of plants that can resist pests and pesticides. Companies have already developed such versions of corn, soybeans, and cotton and they plan to experiment with other genetically engineered crops. In addition, some companies have sought to develop blue cotton through genetic alteration, which would save manufactures the cost of dying cotton.

FURTHER READING

"2 Cloned Calves Might Be Key to Living Drug, Organ Factories." *Chicago Tribune,* 21 January 1998.

Alison, Sebastian. "Interview-Russian Geneticist Defends Work on Pigs." *GO News,* 30 March 1999. Available from http://infoseek.go.com/.

"Amgen Announces 34% Increase in Earning Per Share and Stock Split." Thousand Oaks, CA: Amgen, Inc., 28 January 1999. Available from http://www.amgen.com/News/news99/pressRelease990128.html.

"Amgen Marketed Products and Pipeline Candidates." Thousand Oaks, CA: Amgen, Inc., 1999. Available from http://www.amgen.com/product/Pipeline.html.

Bishop, Jerry E. "Using Pigs for Transplants Shows Promise." *Wall Street Journal,* 1 May 1995.

"Cell Genesys Receives $2 Million Patent Milestone Payment from Hoechst Marion Roussel Under Gene Activation License Agreement." Foster City, CA: Cell Genesys, Inc., 16 February 1999. Available from http://www.cellgenesys.com/investor/press/.

"Cell Genesys Reports Efficient Gene Transfer to Bone Marrow Stem Cells with Lentiviral Gene Therapy Technology." Foster City, CA: Cell Genesys, Inc., 16 February 1999. Available from http://www.cellgenesys.com/investor/press/.

Charles, Dan. "Sounds Like Science: Monsanto." *All Things Considered.* National Public Radio, 16 March 1999.

"DuPont to Acquire Pioneer." Wilmington, DE: E. I. DuPont de Nemours and Company, 15 March 1999. Available from http://www.dupont.com/corp/whats-new/newsfile/990315a.html.

"Europe Lags Behind Japan and the U.S." *Chemistry and Industry,* 15 April 1996.

Flynn, Julia, and Heidi Dawley. "British Biotech's Falling Star." *Business Week (International Edition),* 6 April 1998.

"Genentech, Inc.: Corporate Backgrounder." South San Francisco: Genentech, Inc., February 1999. Available from http//:www.genentech.com/Company/backgrounder.html.

"The Genetic Crop Dust-Up." *Time Daily,* 19 February 1999. Available from http://www.cgi.pathfinder.com/time/daily/0,2960,20137,00.html.

Gillis, Justin. "Will Kids in the Next Millenium Study the Discoveries of Copernicus, Newton, Einstein and Venter?" *USA Weekend,* 29 January 1999.

Gorman, Christina. "Mighty Mouse." *Time,* 12 May 1997.

Jaroff, Leon. "Fixing the Genes." *Time,* 13 January 1999.

Johannes, Laura. "Gene-derived Obesity Drug Appears Closer." *Wall Street Journal,* 29 December 1995.

Kluger, Jeffrey. "Who Owns Our Genes?" *Time,* 13 January 1999.

"Korea Clones Cow, Seeks Mass Production-Ministry." *Reuters,* 3 April 1999.

Lemonick, Michael D., and Dick Thompson. "Racing to Map Our DNA." *Time,* 13 January 1999.

Mann, Judy. "Partnership Takes Bioscience to Bangladesh." *Washington Post,* 13 July 1998.

Melcher, Richard A., and Amy Barrett. "Grains That Taste Like Meat?" *Business Week,* 25 May 1998.

Miller, Henry. "Warning: Gene Label May Damage Your Food." *The Financial Times,* 22 April 1997.

"Monsanto Reports 1998 Fourth Quarter and Year End Results." St. Louis: Monsanto Company, 21 January 1998. Available from http://www.monsanto.com/monsanto/mediacenter/99/99jan21-quarter.html.

Novartis Pharmaceuticals Corporation. "Novartis Pharmaceuticals Corporation Study Seeks Participants for Gene Therapy to Treat Incurable Brain Tumors." *PR Newswire,* 14 May 1997.

Robinson, Linda. "The Island of Dr. Castro." *U.S. News & World Report,* 5 May 1997.

Robson, John. "Biotech Under Siege." *Wall Street Journal,* 21 November 1995.

Rudnitsky, Howard. "Another Agricultural Revolution." *Forbes,* 20 May 1996.

Russo, Eugene. "Genome Project Moves Up Deadline for 'Working Draft'." *The Scientist,* 29 March 1999.

Serafini, Anthony. *The Epic History of Biology.* New York: Plenum Publishing, 1993.

"Significant Research Findings from Michael Milkin's CaP CURE Funding: Seattle Researchers Zero in on Location of Gene for Inherited Prostate Cancer: Gene Also Linked to Brain Cancer." *PR Newswire,* 9 March 1999.

Titney, Tom. "Biotechnology." *Standard & Poor's Industry Surveys,* 1996.

"United Nations Discusses Genetics." *National Organization for Rare Disorders, Inc. Online,* January 1999. Available from http://www.rarediseases.org/odu/nol0199.html

Walsh, James. "Brave New Farm." *Time,* 13 January 1999.

Wertz, Dorothy C. "Human Embryonic Stem Cells: A Source of Organ Transplants." *The Gene Letter,* February 1999. Available from http://www.geneletter.org/0299/HumanEmbryonicStemCells.html.

———. "A New Source of Stem Cells: One's Own Body." *The Gene Letter,* February 1999. Available from http://www.geneletter.org/0299/AnewSourceofStemCells.html.

"The Year of the Triffids: Genetic Engineering." *The Economist,* 26 April 1997.

—Karl Heil, updated by Katherine Wagner
and Sondra E. O'Donnell

HEALTH SPAS

Health spas offer patrons a holistic approach to wellness that results in a relaxing, enjoyable experience in a completely stress-free environment. Modern spa facilities look to a client's total well being and offer spa-goers many options in terms of available amenities and pricing. For those desiring the full spa experience the "destination spa" will provide a personal schedule for mind, soul, and body needs. A hotel or resort with spa facilities allows guests to enjoy spa treatments, cuisine, and advice during their vacation. Businesses are also taking advantage of spas as a way to combine meetings with relaxation. A "day spa," the fastest growing segment of the industry, provides consumers with access to the spa experience at a fraction of the cost of a traditional destination spa. At-home spas and products are also a popular way to create a convenient and economic relaxing atmosphere in the privacy of the home. The newest trend in health spas and products are spas built and designed for family pets.

Spas of the late 1990s have changed dramatically from those of even 10 years prior. Men total 27 percent of the spa clientele; the boot camp style of exercise is gone; Spartan diets have been replaced with appetizing healthful meals; the image of indulgence replaced with that of total health and fitness; and spiritual rejuvenation has become an important aspect of the experience. While the number of destination spas has dropped, the number of hotel and resort spas has doubled, and the number of day spas has grown from 100 a decade ago to 3,000 in 1998.

Spas draw from techniques used by ancient peoples as well as those from the modern world. The spa experience is designed to focus on a client's total well being—physically, mentally and spiritually. Many spas actually request that patrons leave all "necessities" at home, including clothing, makeup, cellular phones, and hair dryers. The resorts provide loose, comfortable clothing and products for personal hygiene.

Destination spas focus on varying themes and specialties, allowing clients to choose a spa that suits their needs and interests. While some offer assistance in dealing with specific health concerns, such as smoking cessation or weight loss, the health benefits offered at most destination spas are relaxation, fitness, and stress reduction. Spas slow time for clients with a secure environment that is absent of demands. A rhythmic pace is set, with most spas alternating treatments and fitness classes. Schedules may not be completely filled; time is left for meditation, walks, reading, or naps. Menus are designed to nourish the body, maintain energy levels, and relax moods, without adding unnecessary calories. Destination spas offer a wide variety of rigorous fitness routines such as aerobics, boxing, cycling, walking, jogging, horseback riding, aquatics, and martial arts. These routines are balanced by relaxation techniques such as meditation, massage, hydrotherapy, journaling, and reading.

Cruise Ship spas and Hot Springs are other forms of destination spas. Combining the spa experience with a cruise ship vacation is becoming more popular every year. These sessions typically last from three days to two weeks, depending on the destination. Spas developed around natural Hot Springs are currently undergoing a resurgence in popularity. As generations of people have known, therapeutic minerals such as sulfur, iron, calcium, and magnesium found in these waters can alleviate the discomfort from arthritis, sore muscles, and chronic back pain.

Another way to obtain the spa experience is to visit a hotel or resort with spa facilities. Many luxury hotels and resorts are adding spas and outdoor recreation facilities to their properties. Surveys have found that vacationers and business travelers who patronize higher-end hotels and resorts have come to expect spa amenities and treatments. Hotel and resort owners unanimously agree that having full spa facilities gives them an edge over the competition in attracting clients. Fitness facilities with saunas, whirlpools, steam rooms, and juice bars are usually available, not to mention salons for pampering, and rooms for massage, aromatherapy, and other treatments. Group therapy and exercise are available for business people who work together.

The fastest growing segment of the spa industry is the day spa. Affluent clients leading hectic lifestyles are sharing the public's growing interest in alternative health therapies, and many beauty salons are offering these spa services in conjunction with traditional beauty services. The best of these give a taste of the spa experience without the high cost of visiting a destination spa. At a day spa clients may purchase full or half day packages, or selected services a la carte. Along with manicures, pedicures, and hair styling, the client can experience facials, yoga, various types of massages, aromatherapy, hydrotherapy, acupuncture, meditation, light and sound therapy, and other treatments offered at destination spas.

Health spas offer many differing types of treatment. Aromatherapy employs oils, herbs, and flowers for relaxation or stimulation. Aruvedic relaxation treatment combines oil and massage, dripping oil in energy centers while massaging it in. Body wraps consist of the application of herbs, seaweed, or mud, followed by a wrap as the substance penetrates the skin. Hydrotherapy may include any treatment that takes place in water or milk; since a hydrotherapy tub can cost up to $20,000, the presence of one indicates the availability of advanced treatments. Underwater music frequently accompanies these treatments. Shower hydrotherapy includes the Vichy shower with seven nozzles that hit nerve spots along the spine, and Scotch hose therapy that hits the skin in a high-pressure massage.

Reflexology is the massage of the feet; practitioners believe pressure points on the foot relate to systems throughout the body. Massage is the manipulation of the skin and underlying muscles; practitioners believe it improves circulation, rids the body of toxins, and relieves stress. Lymphatic massage manipulates the muscles to drain the lymph nodes and move waste out of the system. Reiki uses healing touch to direct universal healing energy into the body's energy centers. Swedish and sports massage get blood flowing for relaxation and get lactic acid out of the system. Acupuncturists use needles, finger pressure, or electrodes to stimulate different points on the body. These points are said to release energy flow and correspond to different body systems.

BACKGROUND AND DEVELOPMENT

Today's spas evolved from public baths, a tradition going back over 4,500 years. The Dead Sea Scrolls reveal that the site around Qumran, Jordan, was famous for its hydrotherapy and herbal medicines. Hydrotherapy was used by Hippocrates and incorporated into the healing practices of Greeks, Romans, and Egyptians. Public baths have also been found in Pakistan and in Babylonian ruins. Massage therapy has been an important aspect of Chinese and Ayurvedic healing for 3,000 years. The popularity of the public baths declined in the Middle Ages; in the seventeenth and eighteenth centuries physicians began prescribing baths and their popularity rose again. Spa popularity continued to rise with the endorsement of Vincent Priessnitz, often referred to as the father of the modern hydrotherapy movement, and wealthy Europeans in the 1800s visited spas for months, both for treatments and for socializing.

Spa-going was introduced to the United States in the 1840s by Robert Wesselhoeft and became more popular as prices began to fall and day spas began to open, allowing those with more modest means to try the spa experience. Spas benefited from the growing acceptability of alternative medicines and therapies in the 1980s. As many of those in the baby-boom generation began to age, they found traditional western medicine to have limited usefulness and to be lacking in answers. Some baby-boomers reported that doctors seemed unreceptive to treating creeping complaints—such as arthritis, back pain, and high blood pressure—in non-traditional ways. Since many people prefer not to be on long-term medication or to undergo surgery, they are turning increasingly to massage therapy, acupuncture, biofeedback, hypnosis, and reflexology. Comfortable with questioning authority and taking charge of their lives, this generation has contributed greatly to the popularity of spas.

CURRENT CONDITIONS

Modern health spa regimes have moved from extreme vigorous exercise in favor of a more balanced rejuvenation escape combining exercise, treatments, nourishment, relaxation, and pampering. Flex and strength training are emphasized, along with aerobics, water classes, yoga, and tai chi. Staff members of the same gender as the client may administer treatments in a private setting, and consideration is given to those who may feel uncomfortable shedding clothing. Various forms of massage, aromatherapy, and hydrotherapy are designed to improve circulation, relieve stress, release endorphins, and eliminate toxins.

The one topic that concerns most spa-goers is food. Gone are the days of lettuce, carrot sticks, and mineral water. In its place are wellness buffets that offer lots of fresh, bountiful, high-fiber, low-fat food and herbs. Many spas also offer classes in the preparation of wholesome and appealing foods. Several spas also publish cook books that include recipes patrons can follow to create the same helpful dishes that were offered during their stay.

While traditionally, health spas have been a feminine retreat, the current trend leans toward men as clients. Men are more educated and concerned about their own health and well-being than they were in the past and are dedicating more time to improving their health. In 1997, 27 percent of spa-goers were men, up from 9 percent in 1987, with 40 percent of the men attending with their spouses. Spas attached to fitness centers are particularly attractive to men. As introductory advertising, spas encourage businesses to reserve their facilities for meetings and offer group prices and incentive packages for men who attend these meetings. Men claim to enjoy the way spas help them unwind, recharge, and take control of their physical and spiritual well-being.

Hot trends in the industry include outside adventure activities, versa fitness, pilates, creative visualization, yoga, journal writing, warm stone massage, honey massage, Watsu water stretching, and endocrine attunement therapy. The industry's holistic approaches to health seem to be filtering into the mainstream as more doctors are trying the spa experience. Those items out of favor in today's spa are elitist attitudes, deprivation, seances, tiny meals, painful exercise, cellulite treatments, and makeup classes. *Spa Magazine* reports that 83 percent of its reader base consists of middle-aged females who have a minimum income of $75,000. Most readers of the magazine travel frequently, exercise regularly, and take nutritional supplements. Demographics further show that

their readers spend over $500 per year on personal care, health, and fitness products, and are most likely to buy personal care products at department stores.

The structure of the spa industry has changed dramatically in the past 10 years. Between 1987 and 1998 the number of destination spas and female clients declined, but the number of hotel and resort spas jumped by 50 percent. The number of male clients tripled, and the number of day spas rose from 30 to 600. Earlier spas offered very few products for sale. However, in 1998, the average spa made 40 percent of its revenue from retail product sales with the newest lines being spa products for animals. The reasons people attend spas have changed somewhat too; in 1987 reasons listed included weight management, smoking cessation, pampering, and beauty treatments. In 1997 clients said they went to spas for stress management, pampering, improved fitness, and weight management. A 1991 survey of spa clients showed that 81 percent came from large cities and surrounding suburban areas. In 1997 that figure dropped to 59 percent, with the other 41 percent coming from outlying regions. A survey of resort goers revealed that 81 percent chose a particular resort over another simply because of the availability of spa facilities.

Hotel and resort owners are expanding their services to meet the public demand. While some only carry saunas, weight rooms, steam rooms, or whirlpools and call themselves spas, many resorts are expanding to offer a large array of exercise, relaxation, and beauty services. According to an industry study, 82 percent of resort owners that felt having a spa on the premises increased perceived value of the room rate, 57 percent felt it increased their occupancy rates, and 100 percent surveyed felt having a spa gave them a marketing advantage over competitors. The survey also asked guests who did not take advantage of spa services why they did not do so. For 86 percent of these negative respondents, time was noted as a factor, while 30 percent were discouraged by the fees. Almost 65 percent of the participants said they would have used the spa facilities had these factors been eliminated.

Preferred Hotels and Resorts, a 107 member marketing consortium, reports approximately 38 percent of its members offer spa services. The group feels that this gives their members a definite advantage over hotels and resorts not offering such services. Many 4 and 5 star hotels are adding spa services, not as a destination in and of themselves, but as amenities offered by the hotel. Massage rooms, facial and body rooms, hydrotherapy rooms, meditation areas, and healthful cuisine are becoming common place in spa areas of luxury hotels. Many hotel and spa designers are invoking the art of feng shui to build the most peaceful atmosphere possible.

Although the popularity of the spa concept is steadily growing among the public, destination spas are having trouble attracting clients, simply because of the costs involved. With a typical one-week stay at a destination spa running $3000 to $4000, many people are seeking out good quality day spas to get a taste of the spa experience. Prices for services at a day spa vary greatly depending on the geographical location of the spa and the services rendered. Customers are also creating their own mini-spas at home, buying massage tables, electric massagers, hot tubs, whirlpool baths, and a whole array of spa products to relieve stress and build relationships in privacy.

Experts suggest that clients match their preferences and needs to the services of a spa when selecting a day spa. Word-of-mouth referral may be the best way to select a day spa. The spa's setting will also clue in potential clients about their seriousness—is it more of a beauty salon, filled with activity, or is the atmosphere relaxed and inviting? Other factors to consider are the variety of treatments available and skill level of the staff. Services can range from $50 for a single treatment to over $300 for a full day package.

case called Avon Centre in November 1998. This one-of-a-kind facility for Avon is located in the famed Trump Tower on Manhattan's prestigious Fifth Avenue. The Avon Centre encompasses more than 20,000 square feet on 4 floors of Trump Towers. The spa facilities include an elegant spa and salon, lecture and meeting rooms, and several beauty product demonstration arenas.

Conde Nast Traveler magazine, a leading resource for the spa industry, conducted a 1998 poll of vacationers to discover the most popular international day spas and spa resorts. The 10 most popular resorts, in order, were Canyon Ranch in the Berkshires, Lenox, Massachusetts; Canyon Ranch, Tucson, Arizona; Rancho La Puerta, Tecate, Mexico; Golden Door, Escondido, California; Cal-A-Vie, Vista, California; Skylonda Fitness Retreat, Woodside, California; Carmel Country Spa, Carmel Valley, California; Hilton Head Health Institute, Hilton Head, South Carolina; and Woodlands Spa Farmington, Pennsylvania.

The 1999 Quigley Award, awarded by *American Way* inflight airline magazine of American Airlines, for the best spa hotel treatment went to Grand Wailea Resort Hotel & Spa, Maui, Hawaii. The lauded treatment is a three-phase Ayurvedic therapy that includes a four-handed massage with heated oil.

INDUSTRY LEADERS

Contrary to popular myth, premiere destination spas in the United States are not located just in California, Florida, and Arizona. The top health spas in 1998, according to *Spa Magazine,* included Canyon Ranch Health Resort in Tucson, Arizona, where sports activities attract a clientele of 40 percent men, at a weekly cost of $2,690 to $4,354; Canyon Ranch in the Berkshires in Lenox, Massachusetts, costing $2,820 to $4,036 per week; Franklin Quest Institute of Fitness in St. George, Utah, where hiking is the favored sport, at a weekly cost of $1,067 to $1,519; and the Golden Door in Escondido, California, with custom fitness programs, costing $5,250 per week. According to the Destination Spa Group in 1998, some of the top spas in the United States are Birdwing Spa, Litchfield, Minnesota; Cal-A-Vie, Vista, California; Deerfield Manor Spa, East Stroudsburg, Pennsylvania; The Greenhouse, Arlington, Texas; and The Kerr House, Grand Rapids, Ohio.

Avon Products is the latest prominent health and beauty company to join the growing spa market. Avon opened its full-service spa and salon products show-

WORK FORCE

As with other segments of the hospitality and services industry, all types of people work for health spas. In the hotel/resort/destination end there are managers, marketers, sales people, human resource specialists, receptionists, maids, concierges, and maintenance people. Professionally, there are chefs, nutritionists, massage therapists, acupuncturists, reflexologists, fitness trainers, cosmetologists, and other treatment specialists.

In 1998 the American Massage Therapy Association claimed a membership of 35,000. The National Certification Board for Therapeutic Massage and Bodywork (NCBTMB) has certified over 33,000 professionals through its exam as of December 1998. While all do not work in the spa industry, the industry tends to hire licensed or certified therapists. The NCBTMB also accredits massage therapy schools, which require 500 or more hours of course work. Recertification requires 200 hours work experience and 50 hours of appropriate continuing education. The national exam requires proficiency in the following areas: human anatomy, physiology, and kinesiology;

clinical pathology and recognition of various conditions; massage therapy and bodywork theory, assessment, and application; and professional standards, ethics, and business practices.

Reflexologists are increasingly subject to state regulation. There are nine states and seven cities with ordinances governing reflexologists. Most require the practitioners to obtain massage therapy licenses. Some state codes call for venereal disease and AIDS testing, the purchase of an adult entertainment license, and make such businesses subject to surprise inspections by law enforcement. Several industry associations have formed to bring increased awareness, respectability, and standards to reflexology.

Cosmetologists perform a variety of functions at health spas including facials, manicures, pedicures, waxing, and other pampering treatments. Cosmetologists are regulated by state laws, most requiring graduation from a cosmetology school, passing of an exam, and continuing education. Other professionals employed by health spas may or may not be regulated under state or local laws. There are, however, a growing number of professional societies, such as the American Alliance of Aromatherapy, and the Awareness Institute Reiki Certification, attempting to self regulate with ethical and professional standards.

AMERICA AND THE WORLD

Since the 1970s millions of Americans have turned to health spas to alleviate the stress of daily life and to rejuvenate their health. A growing trend in American travel is to combine a vacation with a stop or stay at a health-restoring spa. For business travelers, spa accommodations are becoming increasingly popular alternatives to an ordinary hotel. Spa attendance need not be associated only with travel and many people are finding that frequenting day spas located near their homes is a valuable way to grab a quick rejuvenation in the course of their busy lives.

Women and men around the world are rediscovering the many advantages of spa treatments. More Asian women are taking advantage of spas that traditionally catered to male clientele. The most popular spa treatments in Asia are: Thailand, massage; Japan, bathing; Korea, exfoliation; China, herbal medicine and acupuncture; and Indonesia, herbal body treatments.

In Europe, spas were once the province of the wealthy, where they might spend months on end. Attendance at a spa was also traditionally a doctor-prescribed activity, one subsidized by government insurance. In recent years, European spas have become more Americanized, viewed as destinations in and of themselves, particularly for people in their mid-30s to mid-50s as opposed to the traditional elderly spa patrons. In the United States, Americans expect results and tend to over schedule, partaking in treatments, fitness, and classes back-to-back. European spas encourage a slower pace, one with little or no exercise, the emphasis being terrific cuisine and pampering treatments such as facials, massages, and body wraps. While some in the European industry feel their resorts should more closely resemble American resorts to attract American clients, others feel if there is no difference between the two there will be no reason to make the journey to Europe. The European perspective seems to be that clients should leave feeling relaxed, rather than "worn out."

FURTHER READING

American Alliance of Aromatherapy, 1 July 1998. Available from http://www.healthworld.com/associations/pa/Aromatherapy/aaat/index.html.

American Massage Therapy Association, 3 July 1998. Available from http://www.amtamassage.org.

"Avon Centre Opens." *Home Furnishing Network,* 15 February 1999.

"Best of the Best." *Resort Resource,* 29 June 1998. Available from http://www.resortresources.com.

CondeNast Traveler, 30 March 1999. Available from http://travel.epicurious.com/cgi-bin/travel_poll.

"From Sedona to Tucson, Great Spas." *Arizona Business Gazette,* 8 January 1999.

Health Fitness Dynamics, Inc., 2 July 1998. Available from http://www.pwr.com/HFD.htm.

Ladies Home Journal. Available from http://www.ladieshomejournal.com/Newsstand/health.htm.

Many, Christine. "MediNews," 31 March 1999.

Martin, Leslie. "Time Out." *Country Living,* 1 March 1999.

NCBTMB. 3 July 1998. Available from http://www.ncbtmb.com.

"New Patriot Inns to Feature Health Spas." *The Dallas Morning News,* 4 June 1998.

Pedulla, Tom. "Don't Sweat Over Unfamiliar Terms." *USA Today,* 28 February 1998.

Reflexology Research, 3 July 1998. Available from http://www.reflexology-research.com.

Rumbelow, Helen. "Dead Sea Scroll Writers Ran Spa." *The London Times,* 18 January 1999.

Spa Finders, 19 June 1998. Available from http://www.spafinders.com.

"Spa Industry Statistics." *Marshall Plan,* 29 June 1998. Available from http://www.themarshallplan.com.

"Spa la la la la; Los Angeles Spas." *Los Angeles Magazine,* 1 March 1999.

Spa Magazine, 29 June 1998. Available from http://www.spamagazine.com.

"The Spa Throughout History." *Dove Products,* 29 June 1998. Available from http://www.dovespa.com.

Springen, Karen. "It's a Feel-Good Millennium." *Newsweek,* 21 January 1999.

U.S. Bureau of Labor Statistics, 4 July 1998. Available from http://www.bls.gov.

Walter, Claire. "Health Spas Go Exotic." *The Denver Post,* 15 December 1998.

—Lisa Karl, updated by Susan Jensen

HOLOGRAPHY

Holography is the process of recording and reproducing a complete image of a three-dimensional object, the end product being the hologram. Holographic images are everywhere. Holograms appear on items such as driver's licenses, credit cards, compact discs, computer software packages, and greeting cards. Applications of holography can be found in the medical, geophysical, engineering, microwave, photography, printing, and tool and die making industries. Tens of millions of embossed holograms have appeared on books, software packages, and in magazines and other advertising media as major attention-getting devices or for security purposes. Among the less obvious uses of the technology are for three-dimensional "reconstruction" of parts of the body using x-ray holography; microwave holography to detect internal flaws concealed in a structure; and acoustical holography for geophysical or underwater explorations, vibration analysis, and non-destructive testing of engines and other parts.

Initially perceived by the public as a form of art or entertainment media, holography has progressed to a wide variety of serious and beneficial products in manufacturing, retailing, engineering, medicine, and industry. Holograms have proven to have greater attracting and retaining power than conventional advertising and are used in magazines, book covers, and jewelry stores for clearer display.

One of the most significant applications of holography is in the computer storage industry, where holographic storage is replacing the standard magnetic tape. According to Philip E. Ross in *Forbes* magazine, "The world wants filing cabinets small as matchboxes,

capacious as the ocean and as fast as light." With holographic capacities measured in terabytes and storage and retrieval in pages or sheets of data, holographic data storage systems just might meet this need.

Also, because of the multi-dimensional characteristics and difficulty of replication, holograms have become one of the most effective means of data security and product authentication. At the end of 1998, the holographic industry attributed 61 percent of its revenues to print security and authentication applications, according to a report by Ian M. Lancaster of Reconnaissance International in November 1998. Lancaster further reported that the use of holography for commercial packaging applications accounted for the most widespread use of the technology. According to Lancaster, the packaging industry accounted for 70 percent of embossed holographic materials worldwide.

More than 2,800 companies were involved in the production or distribution of holographic products or services in the United States in the 1990s. The industry tends to be grouped largely by function: design, origination, production, utilization, distribution, and marketing or sales of holographic products—although several companies are vertically integrated. Emerging in the 1990s are companies concerned with holographic systems, associative memories, and the application of holography to neural networks.

The industry functions like most industries, with the chain of distribution progressing from the patent or copyright holder, to the master or prototype originator, to the manufacturer or mass producer, to the retail shop, and finally, the end consumer, which may be a corporation, service, or individual.

TYPES OF HOLOGRAMS

There are two types of holograms. The first are transmission holograms, made by splitting a laser beam in two. The first beam, called the reference beam, is bounced off a mirror and strikes a photographic plate. Since it is still pristine, the waves within the reference beam are unchanged. The second beam, called the object beam, strikes the subject (an apple for example), before also striking the same side of the photographic plate. By striking the apple, the waves have been altered, which allows the plate to record the difference between the two beams, called the interference pattern. The only difference between the object and reference beams is the apple, and so the photographic plate records the shape of the apple in three dimensions. In order to view the image, a laser must be shined through the film.

The newer and more familiar type of hologram is the reflection hologram. It is created in essentially the same manner as the transmission hologram, except that the two beams strike opposite sides of the holographic plate, rather than the same side. The advantage of reflection holograms is that they can be viewed in white light, eliminating the need for another laser. The interference pattern recorded upon the photographic plate actually distorts the silver material within the film, creating the different depths within the image. Unlike stereoscopic views, the image created through holography is true 3-D. A person's eyes must re-focus to adapt to different depths, and by moving the image, one can actually see around and behind the object.

Holographic stereograph technology from researchers at the Massachusetts Institute of Technology Media Laboratory involves the convergence of stereoscopic views created from an array of true hologram images. The creation of the holographic images via reflection imagery technology facilitates viewing of the holograms under normal white light. Using stereograph technology, researchers create a spectrum of individual holograms that can be subsequently reassembled into a stereographic image composed from a sequence of true holograms. The holographic stereograph apparatus photographs a reflected image off a flat liquid crystal display screen (LCD). Holographic photography of the LCD image takes place from multiple angles, through a tiny slit, in order to create stereoscopic images for reassembly. Unlike stereoscopic views created from individual flat photographs, every image component of the holographic stereo-

graph is a separate hologram. This method of assembling smaller holograms into a larger stereograph enables the efficient generation of the holographic image from a weaker laser source, with the potential of creating inexpensive holograms—even of living objects—in a matter of minutes.

BACKGROUND AND DEVELOPMENT

A theoretical procedure for holography (from the Greek *holo,* meaning "whole," and *gram,* meaning "recording") was originally conceived by Dennis Gabor in 1948 as a means of improving the resolution of electron microscopes. Where conventional photography only captured the amplitude or brightness of reflected light, a hologram also records the interference of light waves between a single coherent light split into two beams of light waves that converge on a recording plate or film. The reference beam travels directly to the recording medium and the other beam is reflected off the object. The recorded intersection of straight unreflected light waves and the light waves reflected from an object allow a hologram to reproduce a virtual image that includes parallax (an apparent change in perspective or viewpoint that occurs with different angles of viewing).

Initially unsuccessful for its original purpose, the invention generally was dormant for several decades with the exception of attempts by Albert Baez and Hussein El-Sum at Stanford University to use x-rays to make holograms in the 1950s. Interest in holography ebbed for want of a coherent light source of consistent, unvarying wavelengths with equal crests and troughs essential to the success of the process. In the 1960s, Emmett Leith and Juris Upatnieks at the University of Michigan produced several holograms by combining Gabor's principles with Theodore Harold Maiman's laser. It was not until 1991 that physicists were able to use electron holography to reconstruct a crystal's structure, fulfilling Dennis Gabor's original goal.

Sources for holograms include light waves, x-rays, electron beams, and microwaves. Waves other than light waves have successfully used holographic principles in an increasing variety of applications. In 1994 a new holographic system for displaying 3-D images of the internal anatomy was developed. Microwaves that penetrate a variety of media have been used to detect unseen flaws in layered metal parts. X-ray technology, using the same principles, allowed three-dimensional imaging of live organisms. A new family of organic materials such as peptide oligomers

DENNIS GABOR, 1900–1979
A STUDY IN PERSISTENCE

Dennis Gabor, a pioneer in the industry, studied in Berlin, earning his degree in 1924 and his doctorate in engineering in 1927. After World War II, Gabor turned his attention to the electron microscope. His earlier attempts to develop the instrument had failed and he was determined to make a comeback in the field. His goal was to be able to "see" individual atoms. Gabor's idea was to take an electron picture. While in the initial attempts the image was distorted by problems with the lens, Gabor theorized that this could be corrected by optical means utilizing light. His theory was expressed in papers published in 1947, in which he first coined the term *hologram*. Its implications for beams of light, however, awaited only the invention of the laser.

The invention of the laser in 1960 sparked renewed interest in holography, since a constant narrow light source where all waves were in phase was now available to experimenters. The first laser hologram in 1962 ensured Gabor's reputation. In 1967, he retired from Imperial College, but continued his own research. He was able to show the application of holography to computer data processing, where it has been particularly useful in data compression. He received his highest honor in December of 1971, when he was awarded the Nobel prize in physics for his work in holography. His Nobel lecture illustrated the issues that dominated his concerns in his later years, namely the role of science and technology in society.

After Gabor was awarded the Nobel Prize, Lawrence Bartell of the University of Michigan set out to develop a holographic electron microscope. He shared his work with Gabor in 1974, and Gabor immediately began designing his own holographic electron microscope. In the summer of that year, however, Gabor suffered a stroke that left him unable to read or write. Despite this he was able to maintain contact with his colleagues. He was even able to visit the Museum of Holography in New York City when it opened in 1977. He died in a London nursing home in February of 1979.

appears promising in offering erasable holographic storage. Energy X-ray holography (MEXH), which was developed by Charles Fadley and Dietlef Bahr, relied on fluorescent atoms as detectors rather than sources to look at the structure of minute materials to make the first hologram of an atom in a solid.

Engineering applications of holography include stress analysis, checking for cracks or voids in layered or composite surfaces such as aircraft fuselages or wings, and vibration analysis. The Kirby Company, for example, studied the vibration modes of vacuum cleaner fans to streamline its product using holographic vibration analysis. Interferometry is used in the comparison of holograms taken before, after, or during non-destructive stress testing in manufacturing. Acoustic holography is applied to geophysical and underwater explorations. Microwave holography can also provide detailed surface maps. A heterodyne Mach-Zehnder interferometer was first built by students to show the feasibility of detecting sound waves in a small cell.

Other applications include a digital scale, developed by Sony Magnescale, Inc. in 1995, that is capable of measuring plus or minus 0.0086 micrometers by monitoring and measuring the phase change of a laser beam as it passes through a hologram grating. IBM introduced its 3687 holographic supermarket checkout station that could read UPC information on standard and irregularly shaped articles in 1982.

HoloScan introduced its first holographic bar code scanner in 1994.

Advertising holograms have eye-catching appeal with an exceptional rate of retention as compared with other advertising media. In a highly successful campaign, Denny's restaurant distributed hologram baseball cards as annual promotions from 1990 to 1994. McDonald's full-page hologram on the back of *National Geographic's* 100th birthday issue cost more than $1 million for space that normally sold for $200,000. The ad ran worldwide in 10.5 million copies.

In 1995 Ford Motor Company began generating full-size, full-color, photographic quality holograms of new cars directly from computer images that allowed a clinical view without the historic clay model. As early as 1973 General Motors was using holography for measuring up clay models prior to making press dies. Virtual reality will allow test drives without prototypes in the future.

Early in 1999 marketing professionals at Ford Motor Company exploited the latest holographic stereograph technology to display a full-blown prototype car called the P2000 at the Detroit Auto Show. The impressive P2000 appeared on the auto show display floor in living color, as a demonstration of future innovations planned by the auto manufacturer. In reality the P2000 was a non-existent entity, created exclusively from an array of holographic images that resulted in the visible illusion that a solid object (the car) was on display. Still more fascinating was the fact that the P2000 never existed in the engineering lab, other than as a computerized conceptualization of automotive engineers, that was displayed via LCD. Zebra Imaging of Austin, Texas, which assembled the resource-intensive P2000 display, processed an estimated three terabytes of digital data for nearly two weeks to create the final image. Zebra Imaging predicts that pending technology improvements will reduce that time-consuming process from 300 hours to a mere 5 minutes in the foreseeable future.

HOLOGRAMS AS SECURITY DEVICES

Because the production of holograms requires expensive, specialized, and technologically advanced equipment, they have generally been considered a good security device. The holograms cannot be easily replicated by color copiers, scanners, or standard printing techniques since they are governed by light diffraction as opposed to light reflection. For security purposes, Visa and MasterCard have used holograms for more than a decade. They are also used on passports in several European countries and on some government bonds and certificates in the United States.

In 1992 a series of raids in China, Taiwan, and Hong Kong turned up a counterfeit ring that was selling around 75,000 unauthorized software programs per month complete with fake holograms on the packages. A standing order for 3 million counterfeit holograms representing $150 million in losses to Microsoft was found in a shop in mainland China. In 1993 counterfeit MasterCard losses were discovered to total more than $113 million in the United States and $395 million worldwide.

To counter this security risk, Microsoft adopted a new anti-counterfeiting label, the 3M Authentication Label, which first appeared on MS-DOS 6.0 packages in 1993. This hologram label contained both an overt and covert portion. A special processing technique allowed a separate covert image to be displayed on the label when it was viewed with a special light. In 1996, the holographic seal on Microsoft's MS-DOS and Windows software helped break up a $4.7 million counterfeit operation, the largest ever in the United States. MasterCard International also introduced a new three-dimensional hologram in 1996 that was even more difficult to replicate, making counterfeit copies readily identifiable.

In 1994 Lambertus Hesselink, John Heanue, and Matthew Bashaw developed the first holographic storage system to demonstrate that holograms could store

digital data. Initially, commercialization was expected to take 3 to 5 years, but a well-funded consortium has already eliminated one year from the expected time frame. The combination of the storage of millions of data bits per page, fast retrieval rates, and rapid random access make this a highly practical storage method. Holographic Data Storage System (HDSS) calls for holographic data to be stored as pages of bits on a crystal or other optical medium.

Scientists are now examining the possibility of using holograms to display three-dimensional images, creating true 3-D television and movies. In fact, Dennis Gabor himself began such research late in his life. The fruits of these efforts can be found in the appearance of holographic goggles and even a hologram-simulation video game.

CURRENT CONDITIONS

Characterized initially by individual artistic shops and museum marketers, the holography industry has continued to be dominated by private companies. Holography has, like most new industries, experienced some volatility among its corporate players. The most active industry leaders are in the areas of advertising, engineering, medicine, mass storage media, and security. Several other companies have found specialty niches in producing holographic foil supplies or equipment.

In 1998, researchers at MIT Media Lab announced the near completion of a low-cost holographic printer that could yield high-quality holograms, as reported by Sunny Bains in *Electronic Engineering Times.* This discovery could prove to be significant in popularizing holography for a variety of applications, including marketing, graphics, and advertising. Until now, it has been difficult to reproduce quality holograms. The holography start-up firm, Zebra Imaging, reported significant inroads in 1998, toward improving the MIT printer technology for the mass market.

One of the historical challenges has been the necessity of a darkened studio with a motionless platform on which the object to be recorded is mounted in order to produce a hologram. These requirements seriously limit the type, size, and mobility of objects. Motion is achieved through a pulsating light source through a grating. Cameras revolve around the object to create transmission holograms that allow the viewer to see a 3-D object that seemingly moves as he/she moves past it. The use of digital photography and computer-generated holograms are changing the way holograms are produced. Paul Christie of Liti Holographics in Newport News, Virginia, made significant progress in eliminating the technical impediments to cheap and inexpensive laser photography during 1998. Christie created and marketed affordable holographic 8 by 10 portraiture for $400, and smaller (4 by 5 inch) images for well under $100. Christie's innovative methods not only increased product availability to the consumer, but also trimmed the price of portraits from a prohibitive level of $1,500 and higher. Christie employs advanced stereographic technology to produce 3-D images that appear to protrude from the medium, unlike primitive holographic images that appear to lay flat against a mylar backing. His technology is limited to single-color output with support for color selection.

In 1998 the holographic industry surpassed the billion-dollar milestone, although determination of an accurate total value of the industry can be difficult because by the time a holographic application becomes successful it has been absorbed by another segment, such as printing or X-ray.

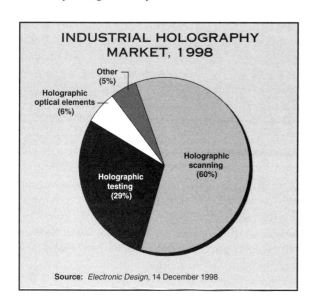

INDUSTRIAL HOLOGRAPHY MARKET, 1998

Other (5%)

Holographic optical elements (6%)

Holographic scanning (60%)

Holographic testing (29%)

Source: *Electronic Design*, 14 December 1998

INDUSTRY LEADERS

Holographic Dimensions, Inc. (HGRM), a vertically integrated manufacturer of holographic imagery, reported a 601-percent increase in first quarter sales, from $91,472 in the quarter ended March 1996, to $550,352 during the quarter ended March 1997, experiencing their first net income. The company's products are incorporated into a variety of security devices including credit cards, negotiable documents, event

tickets, and transit passes. It claims to have delivered more than 2 billion units to countries throughout the Northern Hemisphere including to major companies such as Merck Pharmaceutical and General Electric, as well as foreign governments. Its holograms are used on transit passes in eastern Europe to authenticate bank checks for Citibank. Artex Graphics acquired this privately owned manufacturer in 1994 and changed its own name to Holographic Dimensions. In June 1997, the company moved to a new 10,000 square foot facility. Holographic Dimensions also produces the online *Holography Digest: Featuring People, Companies, Technology & News of the Holographic Industry,* which is available on its Web site. In 1995 the company filed a patent for its Verigram TM Security Systems Hologram, which intended to meet the challenge of counteracting earlier mechanisms for counterfeiting holograms. In a press release dated February 25, 1999, Holographic Dimensions announced that it purchased exclusive rights to Direct Digital Holographic Printer (DDHP) technology. The new technology reputedly doubles the dot matrix image resolution from previous generations of holographic printers. Printer write speeds will increase by a minimum factor of 5 in the first iteration, and will increase by a factor of 1,000 in future iterations. The firm completed the printer prototype development phase in March 1999 and began commercial production of the printer, which will be marketed to the packaging industry.

Holographics North, Inc. produces some of the largest holograms and claims to be the only U.S. company capable of producing large format (42 by 72 inch), color, high-resolution holograms. Large-size holograms are generally used in trade shows, museums, space centers, and educational centers. The firm also creates animated stereographs, which include computer graphics, reduced or enlarged images, and onsite recordings. The maximum size of a stereograph is 40 by 50 inches.

Dimensional Media Associates (DMA) developed and demonstrated a method of projecting 3-D video images that appear to float in the air through its "augmented reality" technique. Using High-Definition Volumetric Display (HDVD), it has a prototype of a billboard advertising hologram. Currently, its foot-high versions have been shown only at trade shows but its plans call for advertising displays at point-of-purchase.

Zebra Imaging of Austin, Texas, is a start-up firm run by MIT Media Laboratory veterans Michael Klug, Mark Holzbach, and Alex Ferdman. The company, which focuses on holographic printing technology, took credit for the production of a life-size, full-color holographic stereograph display of an automobile at the Detroit Auto Show in 1999. Developers at Zebra Imaging operate in direct competition with media giants Sony and Ricoh Corporation in the race-to-market for a desktop hologram printer. Other innovative undertakings on the Zebra agenda include the perfection of monster hologram billboards.

HOLOGRAPHY IN THE MEDICAL FIELD

On June 1, 1998, Voxel issued a press release to announce that it had filed a voluntary Chapter 11 petition in response to a May 5 arbitration ruling that ordered Voxel to pay $1.9 million to General Scanning, Inc. (GSI). The two companies had entered into a contract in 1994 in which GSI was to engineer and manufacture the Voxcam imager, equipment used to produce film-based, hardcopy images of the internal structure of the body. Voxel claimed that GSI had breached its obligation under the contract. Voxel converted to Chapter 7 bankruptcy on August 8, 1998 and agreed to continue development of the Voxcam imager, pending acquisition by hologram technology giant, Holographic Dimensions, Inc.

The Voxcam is part of a system designed to interface with existing medical scanners to produce three-dimensional X-rays, and consists of a camera to convert computerized axial tomography or simply computerized tomography (CT) and magnetic resonance (MR) scans into holograms that provides an accurate interactive "road map" for physicians prior to surgery. The system converts complicated conventional CT or X-rays, which normally require a radiologist's interpretation, into a virtual model that is readily understandable by any physician. The hologram enables the physician to interact in, around, and through the image as if it were a real specimen. It allows doctors to peer inside blood vessels and assists in treating brain tumors, carotid arteries, and pelvic surgery since the viewer moves around within the image.

The potential sales of Voxcams and Voxboxes are estimated to be $800 and $200 million, respectively. Ongoing sales of Voxgram film are estimated at $450 million. There have been clinical trials of the systems since 1994. In January 1997, the U.S. Patent Office awarded patents on 13 claims to multiple exposure holograms to Voxel. Initial sales in 1996 were nearly $2.5 million, with 1997 revenues jumping to over $17.0 million. A similar Surgical Simulation Technology under research and development by Dimensional Media Associates would employ DMA's HDVD technology.

STORAGE AND SECURITY

Optitek Incorporated was founded by Lambertus Hesselink to develop his holographic storage system to search stacks of holograms in milliseconds. With this technology, mathematical operations can be performed on arrays of numbers in the memory itself without going through the processor. GTE is working with Optitek to design high-speed digital interfaces to handle transfer of data from holograms to computers.

In 1994, Tamarack Storage Devices was the leading contender in developing a way of storing 3-D holograms on film. In 1995 a consortium of research companies and academic institutions led by Tamarack received a $10.7 million award from the U.S. government. Industry participants matched funds to bring the project total to $22.5 million. On January 9, 1998, Manhattan Scientifics, Inc. purchased Tamarack and three days later Projectavision, Inc. purchased a controlling interest in Manhattan Scientifics. Projectavision relinquished control six months later, on July 30, when it sold 80 percent of its holdings to an investor group that specialized in emerging industry.

Nimbus CD International, a Technicolor Company, was one of the first companies to digitally record music on CDs. In conjunction with Applied Holographics PLC, Nimbus developed a 3-D I*d antipiracy hologram, which functions without any loss of digital information, disc capacity, or playback quality. Based in Charlottesville, Virginia, Nimbus distributes optical discs throughout North America, the United Kingdom, and Europe. In May 1998, Nimbus announced plans for a $22 million upgrade to expand its capacity to produce DVD and Divx, the newest digital disk formats. When finished, the company will be able to produce 28 million discs a year. On September 1, 1998, Nimbus merged into the Technicolor Optical Disc Division and, on March 30, 1999, Nimbus reported that the company's comprehensive total production surpassed 12 million units.

The 3M Company produces a similar version of CD security holograms as well as several security laminates, labels, and film. The DMI (Disc Manufacturing, Inc.) version can be imprinted only on non-data areas.

Control Module, Inc., which has designed and manufactured data collection and security products since 1969, offers an identification card printing and imaging system that integrates its Holonetics product with photographs and bar codes. The hologram is read and encrypted to a magnetic stripe. The optical signature is then compared to the magnetic when the card is read.

Holaxis Corporation has produced engine holograms for General Motors and Pratt Whitney Aircraft, as well as several other holographic products for other major companies.

WORK FORCE

Due to the diversity of applications, unique niche products, and the private nature of many of the companies, it is difficult to estimate the total size of the work force in the holography industry with any degree of accuracy. However, like all new and emerging industries, holography will likely create jobs that do not exist today. The growth of affiliated medical and computer fields is well documented. Trends for employment in areas associated with holography products in medicine, manufacturing, research, and advertising appear to be strong and growing. The skill level and compensation ranges from that of engineers, physicists, and optical scientists in research and development with salaries varying from $45,000 to $75,000 to machine operators at $15 to $17 per hour to minimum wage clerks in holography stores. Employment in holography is difficult to isolate. Most of the affiliated industries are growth industries, and the demand for workers at a wide variety of educational levels in these industries is likely to continue.

AMERICA AND THE WORLD

The *Holography Marketplace* lists more than 700 businesses connected with holography in more than 30 countries: 350 U.S. firms, 70 German firms, 68 in the United Kingdom, 43 in Japan, and 25 in Canada. Several U.S.-U.K. partnerships have developed to market holographic products.

Australian Holographics maintains an office in France and a research and development center in Lithuania. P.T. Pura Barutama established a hologram manufacturing plant in central Java in 1989 that employed 350 people by 1996. Ojasmit Holographics was one of five embossed hologram manufacturers in India. Holtronic Technologies, a Swiss firm, achieved a breakthrough in computer chip production with postage-stamp size silicon wafers that yield sharper images over wider areas at lower costs than conventional systems.

One of the most competitive areas is the recording materials market. One of the largest suppliers of holographic recording materials in the United States is Eastman Kodak with its red sensitive holographic emulsions, high-speed glass plates, and film. The principal competition comes from Belgium-based AGFA, and more recently Russia's SLAVICH emulsions have become available. Long sought for their high quality and resolution, SLAVICH emulsions are the only silver halide plates sensitive to multiple wavelengths used in full color imagery.

In all the world industrial market, holographic applications reached $2.8 billion in 1998. U.S. industrial consumption accounted for more than one-half ($1.7 billion) of that figure.

RESEARCH AND TECHNOLOGY

Holographic storage seems on the verge of becoming a reality. Xiao A. Shen and Ravinder Kachru reported in *Science* that data storage using holographic techniques has been developed and tested in applications such as fingerprint identification. The article states that holographic data storage is better than current technology because of its ultrahigh storage density, rapid data transfer, short data access times, and exceptional reliability. One problem preventing this type of data storage from becoming commercially viable is the slow recording rate of current holographic techniques. It will be necessary to speed this process up while not sacrificing storage density or increasing error rate.

In order to have access to vast amounts of data with lightning speed, the U.S. Department of Defense provided 50 percent of a $64 million project to commercialize a Holographic Data Storage System (HDDS) in which a gigabyte of data would fit on a pencil eraser and could be retrieved at 1 billion bits per second. Two research projects, conducted by a combination of research and corporate institutions, have been funded by the United States. The Photorefractive Information Storage Materials (PRISM) project and the Advanced Research Projects Agency (ARPA) HDSS project funded by the Department of Defense also includes IBM's Alamaden Research Center, GTE, and Rockwell International as investigators. PRISM is concerned with finding optimal media for hologram storage, and the HDSS section is investigating hardware technologies.

Holography might prove to be a valuable weather forecasting tool, as reported by the *Associated Press.* David Guerra, a Western Maryland College physics professor, is testing a telescope that has a holographic optical element as part of a research project by the National Aeronautics and Space Administration (NASA). Geary Schwemmer, a research engineer at NASA, in-

---

About... MASSACHUSETTS INSTITUTE OF TECHNOLOGY (MIT)
HOLOGRAPHY COLLECTION CAMBRIDGE, MASSACHUSETTS

Among the most distinguished schools in the field of holography is the Massachusetts Institute of Technology (MIT) in Cambridge, Massachusetts. MIT students and professors have pioneered significant research in the field. In 1993 Dr. Stephen A. Benton, Allen Professor of Media Arts and Sciences at the MIT Media laboratory, announced the MIT Museum's acquisition of a 1,500-piece holography collection from the bankrupt Museum of Holography in New York City. The pieces, which were acquired at auction, included artistic holography, historical pieces, and technical artifacts, constituting the entire collection of the former New York museum. Included in the collection were the first laser hologram, the first white-light hologram, documentation from Dennis Gabor's laboratory, and the works of many noted holographers, including Emmett Leith, Yuri Denisyuk, and Harriet Casdin-Silver.

The Spatial Imaging Group at the MIT Media Laboratory, Media Arts and Sciences Department, is a leader among holographic researchers. Also noteworthy are the artists of the MIT Center for Advanced Visual Studies. In 1994 Eastman Kodak Company of Rochester, New York donated $80,000 to the MIT Holography Program, thereby assuming the role of principal sponsor of the program.

---

vented the telescope and experiments are underway to determine if it is a cost-efficient weather prediction tool. The major importance of the holographic telescope is its ability to read atmospheric winds. It may one day replace anemometers and weather balloons that currently provide wind information.

A crystal with regularly spaced impurities that will minimize random noise and corruption of data is one storage medium under consideration by the National Aeronautics and Space Administration. Their experiments with growing crystals in space were designed to improve the quality and clarity of crystals as a storage medium. In November 1998 researchers Lambertus Hesselink, Sergei S. Orlov, Alice Liu, Annapoorna Akella, David Lande, and Ratnakar R. Neurgaonkar published supporting findings concerning the increased holographic storage capacity potential of lithium niobate and similar photorefractive materials with respect to the crystal medium.

Georgia Institute of Technology researchers have discovered a liquid crystal that, when applied as a coating on a disc, allows information to be stored as a hologram with huge capacity. John Underofler of the Massachusetts Institute of Technology is quoted in an *Industry Week* article as stating, "The entire contents of the Library of Congress could theoretically be stored in a one cubic foot crystal." In addition, retrieval will be 100 times faster than with current magnetic or optical media.

Several Advanced Technology Program projects funded by the National Institute of Standards and Technology to help corporations develop innovative products are listed in the "'98 Technology Administration Budget Highlights" of the 1998 U.S. budget. The Advanced Technology Program section noted the success of Accuwave, a 12-person fiber optic telecommunications firm that received funds to pursue research on an innovative holographic system that would allow several communications channels to simultaneously share the same optical fiber. The company is now selling three spin-off products developed with their own funds in the United States, Japan, and Europe. It is also developing a wavelength multiplexing system based on the core results of the Advanced Technology Program project funds it received from the National Institute of Standards and Technology in 1992. The projected market for multi-wave length multiplexing capable of transmitting holograms was expected to grow from $50 million in 1997 to $2 billion by the year 2000.

Pacific Northwest Laboratories developed a handheld scanner capable of producing high-quality holographic images. Potential uses include detecting radar reflective leaks in stealth aircraft, augmenting airport security, and checking cross sections of aircraft components.

There are several working research groups concerned with the development of holography, some with spin-off or affiliated corporations. The Holography Working Group headed by T. John Trout of E.I. du Pont de Nemours & Company, is involved with computer-generated holography, materials, processing, non-destructive testing, as well as optical elements, commercial applications, and standardization. The group meets at the annual International Society for Optical Engineering annual conference. The Holography and Optical Data Storage Group includes five postdoctoral and research associates as well as more than a dozen other researchers. Activities include investigation of photorefractive materials and devices, volumetric holographic data storage in a crystal, optical tomography, and computer-generated graphics.

FURTHER READING

Austin Business Journal, 23 March 1998.

Bains, Sunny. "Sony, Zebra Developing Practical Printers Based on MIT Technology—Holography Eyes Mass-Market Imprint." *Electrical Engineering News,* 9 March 1998.

Berg, Rolf H. "Peptide Oligomers for Holographic Storage." *Nature,* 10 October 1996.

Brookes, Tim. "From Credit Cards to Trade Show Displays—Holography Comes of Age." *Medical Marketing & Media,* 1 September 1990.

Carlson, F. Paul. "Holography." *Grolier Multimedia Encyclopedia.* Danbury, CT: Grolier Electronic Publishing, Inc., 1997.

"Catching Counterfeits." *Security Management,* December 1994.

"Contact DMA." Available from http://www.3dmedia.com/press.htm.

"CyberCard Signs Multiyear Distribution and Marketing Agreement." Anaheim, CA: Advanced Laser Products, Inc., 10 December 1996.

"Data Storage in Crystals." *Journal of Electronic Defense,* February 1997.

Dutton, Gail. "Holographic Storage Becomes Practical." *Inform,* July 1996.

Economist, 14 March 1998; 2 January 1999.

ENR, 17 August 1998.

"Extra Badge Security: Hot." *Security,* June 1996.

Goldberg, Ron. "How Much Is That Image in the Window?" *Popular Science,* February 1995.

Greenberg, Ian. "Exploiting the Revolution." *InfoWorld,* 18 November 1996.

Gross, Neil. "Holograms Head for the Trenches." *Business Week,* 4 December 1995.

Hamilton, Denise. "Caught by Coherent Light." *Wired,* May 1996.

Hasselink, Lambertus, Sergei S. Orlov, Alice Liu, Annapoorna Akella, David Lande, Ratnakar R. Neurgaonkar, "Photorefractive Materials for Nonvolatile Volume Holographic Data Storage." *Science,* 6 November 1998.

Hayashi, Alden M. "Six Hot Technologies for the 21st Century." *Datamation,* August 1996.

Hecht, Jeff. "Holography Finds a Home: The Museum of Holography." *New Scientist,* 9 April 1994.

Hodgson, Karyn. "Hologram Access?" *Security,* August 1996.

"Hologram Technology Goes to Work." *Machine Design,* 12 January 1995.

"Holograms on Your Hard Drive?" *Business Week,* 15 April 1996.

Kachru, Xiao, and A. Shen Ravinder. "Time-Domain Holographic Digital Memory." *Science,* 3 October 1997.

Konish, Nancy. "Holographic Market Zooms Out to Hit $2.8 Billion." *Electronic Design,* 14 December 1998.

"Lasers and Holography Becoming Tools for Weather Forecasting Westminster Work Part of NASA's New Millenium Program." *The Baltimore Sun,* 29 June 1997.

"Line Scanner Uses Holograms as Focal Lenses." *Automatic I.D.,* March 1995.

"MasterCard Creates High-Security Hologram." *America's Community Banker,* April 1996.

Montague, Jim. "Diagnosis Goes 3-D." *Hospitals & Health Networks,* 20 November 1996.

Nadis, Steve. "Two Versions of Holography Vie to Show Atoms in 3D." *Science,* 3 May 1996.

"Nimbus Introduces Theft Protection Holographic Image." *CD-ROM Professional,* November 1995.

Paperboard Packaging, January 1999.

Peterson, Richard W. "Holographic Real-Time Imaging of Standing Waves in Gases." *American Journal of Physics,* September 1996.

PR Newswire, 25 February 1999.

Richmond Times-Dispatch, 13 December 1998.

Ross, Franz, and Alan Rhody, eds. *Holography Market-Place,* Berkeley, CA: Ross Books, 1997.

Ross, Philip E. "The Hologram Remembers." *Forbes,* 26 September 1994.

Skolnick, Andrew A. "New Holographic Process Provides Noninvasive, 3-D Anatomic Views." *JAMA: The Journal of the American Medical Association,* 5 January 1994.

Stone, M. David. "Future Mass Storage." *PC Magazine,* 25 March 1997.

Testor, Seymour. "Computer Simulated Holography and Computer Generated Holograms." *American Journal of Physics,* April 1996.

Thompson, Tom. "When Silicon Hits the Limits, What's Next?" *Byte,* April 1996.

Unterseher, Fred et al. *The Holography Handbook: Making Holograms the Easy Way.* Berkeley, CA: Ross Books, 1996.

"Voxel." *Hoover's Online.* Available from http://www.hoovers.com.

Wilke, Michael. "Outdoor Ads Go to New Depth." *Advertsing Age,* 15 April 1996.

—David C. Genaway, updated by Katherine Wagner and Gloria Cooksey

HOME HEALTH CARE SERVICES

Throughout most of the 1990s, the home health care service industry thrived. All that changed in late 1997 as Medicare, mandated by the Balanced Budget Act, began implementing massive reimbursement cuts to home health care companies. The federal agency planned to decrease home care spending by $16 billion over five years. The decreased payments devastated companies and the industry was in a state of crisis. In July 1998, Milt Freudenheim reported in the *New York Times,* that most large home care companies were losing money and that shares of Apria Healthcare, an industry leader, had fallen by more than 50 percent since 1997. In July 1998, 50 home health care agencies closed their doors.

The industry endured other attacks in 1998. The *Tribune News Services* reported that Medicare administrator Nancy-Ann Min DeParle had ordered home health agencies to stop cutting care for homebound Medicare recipients. DeParle said that new federal regulations should not cause home care agencies to reduce services. Additionally, according to Matt O'Connor in the *Chicago Tribune,* home care workers have filed a lawsuit against a major home-care staffing provider asking for travel pay when commuting between home visits with clients.

Prior to the 1998 crisis, home health care seemed on a success track. In 1994 it was the fastest growing segment of health care, and the second fastest growing segment of the economy at large. Contributing to this growth were new advances in medical devices and high technology that made home care a viable alternative to institutional care. For example, respiratory patients who previously would have been hospitalized or nursing home bound were able to conduct normal working and living activities with the aid of portable oxygen systems. Home care often costs one-third less than hospital care. In addition, cancer patients, who were once confined to hospitals, could live at home and even return to work.

The focus in 1999 was to limit care to only skilled medical services and for the care necessary to cure a medical problem. Patients must show progress toward goals or their home health services may be withdrawn. An agency's goal must be getting a patient well enough in a specific number of visits to terminate care. For instance, a nurse must determine when a wound will be healed prior to treatment. Reimbursement for explaining something or teaching a patient to care for himself is only allowed once. If more is needed, according to one nurse in *American Prospect,* it must be done on the caregiver's own time or not at all.

ORGANIZATION AND STRUCTURE

Home care agencies providing health care services fall into three main categories: private or proprietary, hospitals, and public or not-for-profit. Services are differentiated by type and level of activity, such as home health aides, nursing care, and physical therapy. The home health care services industry is structured along the lines of prevention, diagnosis, infusion therapy, skilled and unskilled care, and durable medical equipment. The three largest of these segments are infusion therapy, skilled care, and durable equipment. Infusion therapy consists of intravenous products and services like antibiotics and immunoglobulins. Skilled care includes nurses, home health aides, and therapists, all under the direction of a physician. Durable medical equipment includes ventilators and respirators.

If a person is home bound and requires skilled care, Medicare pays for medically necessary home health care, including part-time or intermittent nursing care; physical, speech, and occupational therapy; medical social services; and equipment and supplies. For terminally ill patients, Medicare will pay for care provided by a Medicare certified hospice, where specialized care includes pain relief, symptom management, and supportive services in lieu of curative services.

In 1995, 18,000 home health agencies (including certified, non-certified, and hospices) were serving 7 million patients, and expenditures reached $27 billion, with Medicare accounting for slightly more than 50.0 percent of that total. Revenues for home health care services rose from $1 billion in 1980 to $30 billion in 1997. Home health care represented 8.7 percent of Medicare's budget in 1996, an increase from 2.9 percent in 1990. During that same time, the average number of home care visits per patient rose from 33 to 74.

Home health care, as defined by the Health Care Financing Administration (HCFA), is part-time or intermittent skilled care, home health aide services, durable medical equipment and supplies, and other services. To qualify for Medicare home health care, a patient's doctor must determine medical care is needed in the home; care must be intermittent; and the patient must be home bound, except for infrequent trips of short duration. Skilled nursing for wound care or injections; home health aides for personal care and physical assistance; physical, speech, and occupational therapy; and medical social services, supplies, and equipment are all included. A maximum of 28 hours per week, including a mix between all of the various providers, is allowed to qualify as part-time care.

The Joint Commission on Accreditation of Healthcare Organizations serves as the accrediting body for home care agencies. Participation is voluntary, but agencies still must meet accepted industry standards. State and local governments also serve to regulate the industry.

Nearly every segment of home health care services is hostage to public policies and funding, and there is a growing need to reconcile the aging population with the need to reduce expenditures. Some states are now imposing bans on new nursing home construction, which should channel more patients to home care.

BACKGROUND AND DEVELOPMENT

Home health care is a delivery mechanism for diagnostic, preventive, rehabilitative, and therapeutic services. Supported by technology, home care is considerably less expensive than institutionalized or hospital care. The nature of the industry is shifting as it expands. In January 1998, Medicare changed its method of payment to home health agencies. Before these changes, agencies were paid visit-by-visit without any limitations. Starting in 1998, cost-cutting procedures took effect that set limits and based payments on average costs. Critics argue that this method does not adequately cover chronically ill patient care.

Home health care appeals to insurance companies. The Medicare cuts of 1997 created a market for supplemental home health care benefits in addition to, or coordinated with, long-term care benefits. When the baby boom generation reached 50 years old they began taking care of their parents, therefore they were aware of the need for insurance to cover some of the cost. They do not want to go to nursing homes as they age. They want to stay in their own homes as long as they can and utilize home care policies. They know that Medicare will probably not cover what they will need and want. Insurance companies are moving into this niche market. Bankers Life and Casualty (BLC), along with long-term care insurance companies, pursued the home health care segment of the market. BLC enhanced its 1989 home health care policy in 1997 by offering full-time home benefits based on a "pool of money." Benefits were paid on a daily basis from $40 to $200, based on the client's option. Benefits had a weekly cap determined by the daily allowance to create what is called a "flexible deductible."

CURRENT CONDITIONS

The home health care industry felt the effects of cost saving measures by the federal government. Between 1989 and 1996, as reported by *Consumers' Research Magazine,* the number of beneficiaries receiving home health care and the number of visits per user more than doubled. In an effort to hold down costs, Medicare changed its payment system. Before October 1997, the agency reimbursed home care companies on a visit-by-visit basis with no limitations. The new system pays on an average cost basis. Because the new regulations place limitations on the number of visits, the Clinton Administration advised home care agencies not to reduce services to clients in an effort to save money. Depending on the service, payment reductions to home care agencies range from 15 to 50 percent. An indication of how crippling this has been is the news that 50 home health care agencies across Texas stopped operating in June and July 1998, as reported by Charles Ornstein in *The Dallas Morning News*. In addition, the article stated that applications for new agencies were also down.

In addition to the new Medicare fee restructuring, the HCFA has taken several steps to reduce Medicare and Medicaid fraud. According to the *Associated Press*, home health care agencies received an estimated 13 percent of the $20.0 billion of improper Medicare payments in 1997. This number, however, reflects a decrease from the estimated overpayments of $23.3 billion in 1996, according to a report by the Health and Human Services Department. In response, the HCFA has worked to cut costs, including issuing rulings establishing salary equivalency guidelines for physical, occupational, respiratory, and speech therapists providing home health services. These rulings are projected to save Medicare $1.7 billion from 1997 to 2001. The HCFA also proposed revisions to regulations that would require Medicare home health providers to conduct criminal background checks on home health aides.

Substantial discrepancies between prices paid by the Veterans Administration (VA) and the HCFA, oxygen service providers, have reduced the amount of Medicare reimbursements. The oxygen business earned $3 billion in 1996, of which Medicare paid about half. About 45 percent of the oxygen market was controlled by Apria Healthcare Group, Inc., Lincare Holdings Inc., and RoTech Medical Corporation in 1996. HCFA expects to save 40 percent on Oxygen delivery and equipment or approximately $1 billion by 2002.

HCFA is also shifting to open-ended reimbursement for home care agencies based on numbers rather than the nature of the service to a prospective payment system (PPS). The PPS plan, already initiated in some areas, sets regional limits on reimbursement rates based on the cost history of providers in a given area. The new PPS will be implemented nationwide sometime in late 2000 or more likely 2001. Meanwhile, agencies are being reimbursed on the interim payment system (IPS), which is a flat sum per patient and involves a yearly per-patient cap. One problem with the IPS is that payment is not adjusted by the severity of the illness. If the cost of care goes over the cap, the agency loses money. However, if the cost is under the cap, the agency does not get the difference. According to Biff Shea, chief executive officer at Flagship Healthcare, in *Modern Healthcare*, the IPS policy is the primary reason many home health care agencies have failed.

Shea believes that the home health care industry can survive if it streamlines its structure, institutes innovative programs, and in some cases, merges with other agencies into larger more effective units. Clinical programs must be adapted to serve the patients who have the greatest needs for their services and deal with the most prevalent diseases in the areas they serve.

Innovative programs are seeking to improve quality while maintaining costs. One program ensures early dismissal of new mothers from the hospital by sending a registered pediatric nurse to the home to check on both the mother and child's progress soon after they are discharged. Another innovative program has a specialist on phone duty 24-hours-a-day to talk with congestive heart failure patients, which sometimes solves the problem without a nurse's visit or hospital admission. Lastly, a study by researchers at Rush University in Chicago involved two groups of older patients: one group watched a series of eight two-hour videos and another group attended eight two-hour classes. The classes covered meditation and relaxation training, anxiety and depression management skills, and nutrition and exercise counseling. The patients using the videos received follow-up phone calls to check their progress. A third group received neither. Results of the study, which appeared in *JAMA, The Journal of the American Medical Association*, proved that video tapes with phone follow up worked as well as live presentations.

According to Shea, a study by the General Accounting Office concluded that "growth in the industry has been such that there were still more agencies to treat Medicare beneficiaries in August 1998 than in October 1996." Therefore, more consolidation or closure is likely. SMG Marketing Group, Chicago, agreed with this assessment in *Hospitals & Health Networks*. If HCFA requires surety bonds as a part of an agency's income, many smaller agencies will have to merge with larger firms to stay profitable. Connecticut, Louisiana, Massachusetts, New Hampshire, and Rhode Island will be particularly hard-hit as they have many small agencies.

EMERGING NICHE MARKETS

Two niche markets, behavioral and geriatric, were identified in the late 1990's and were expected to come into their own in the beginning of the next century. Behavioral or mental health home care is a short-term rehabilitation service for recently discharged psychiatric patients. "Behavioral home care during the critical four-to-six-week period following discharge helps ensure that patients take their medication, a major factor in preventing relapse," said Mary Rosedale, director of the Behavioral Home Care program at New York-based Priority Home Care in *LI Business News*. Rosedale added, "It also helps them adjust effectively to mainstream life in their communities and helps prevent rehospitalization and visits to the emergency room." As the average stay in psychiatric hospitals has been reduced from 23 to 6 days or less, the need for close follow-up care is obvious. According to The Treatment Advocacy Center in Arlington, Virginia, at least 1,000 people are murdered each year by mentally ill individuals who went off their medication.

More people are reaching the age of 100 and beyond than ever before. Most of these people do not need or want to be in nursing homes, but may need some care as they age. As reported in *Black Enterprise,* Eric Johnson and his mother Gwendolyn opened a home care agency called Geric Home Health in Cleveland that caters specifically to older Americans. Eighty percent of his staff are certified nurse assistants who help with activities such as bathing and house keeping. Geric has expanded to other cities in Ohio such as Akron and Lorian. They are also opening facilities in Detroit and Gary, Indiana. Geric's revenues have reached $12 million.

INDUSTRY LEADERS

American HomePatient, Inc. headquartered in Brentwood, Tennessee, reported sales of $403.9 million for 1998 and a net loss for the year of $39.0 million. The company's sales figure reflected acquisitions and increased revenues from home medical equipment and supplies, in addition to home health care. American HomePatient has 4,800 employees and 300 branches in 35 states. It increased its vertical integration and geographic expansion through the acquisition of a specialty retail pharmacy and four home health service firms.

Apria Healthcare Group had a net loss in 1998 of $207.9 million on $933.8 million in revenue. The Costa Mesa, California-based company has over 8,000 employees and provides home care services in 350 locations across the United States. It is the largest national home health care service provider in the United States. Services include home respiratory and infusion therapy services and the rental and sale of home medical equipment. The firm agreed to pay the government $1.7 million to settle a claim filed in 1995 charging that the company improperly paid physicians for patient referrals.

With revenue reaching nearly $19 billion dollars in 1998, Columbia/HCA Healthcare Corporation was the largest private U.S. health services provider. The Nashville, Tennessee-based company employs 260,000 people. The firm was under investigation for its business tactics in connection with a federal anti-trust suit in Texas. In June 1998, Columbia/HCA announced it was selling most of its home health care business, including all of its Texas agencies, for roughly $30 million.

Coram Healthcare Corporation (CHC) reported sales revenue of $526.5 million and a net loss of $21.7 million for 1998. The company specializes in serving chronically ill patients that suffer with asthma, diabetes, cancer, cystic fibrosis, or AIDS. CHC is based in Denver, Colorado and has 3,600 employees.

Lincare Holdings Inc., an aggressive provider of oxygen and other respiratory services in the home, is one company that has not been severely hurt by the recent Medicare cutbacks. Serving 140,000 customers in 39 states, it is one of the largest respiratory services in the nation. According to Hoover's Online, Lincare's annual revenue reached $487.4 million in 1998.

In 1998 Pediatric Services of America (PSA) reported net income of $7.0 million, an increase of 48 percent from the previous year, and sales revenue of $302.5 million. With more than 5,000 employees the Norcoss, Georgia-based company found a niche in providing home pediatric nursing and therapy to medically fragile children, along with adult respiratory therapy and other home services and equipment. PSA has 120 offices in 29 states. Since January 1997, it has acquired more than 10 health care companies, including a New Jersey nursing company, a Florida pediatric company, a North Carolina home health agency, and an Illinois pharmacy. It relies on Medicaid and Medicare for 37 percent of its revenues.

Through acquisitions and cost cutting, Olsten Corporation, the leading home health staffing company, reached $4.6 million in revenues in 1998. Olsten is the third largest temporary staffing agency and has over 1,400 offices worldwide. The company offers a full line of nursing, speech and occupational therapies, and drug infusion. Approximately 15 percent of Olsten's revenues come from Medicare. In 1998, Olsten's Health Services business had nearly 600 offices in the United States and Canada, 575,000 patient/client accounts, and nearly 700,000 employees.

WORK FORCE

According to the U.S. Bureau of Labor Statistics, in April 1997, 681,700 persons were employed in home health care services; in June 1998, the industry employed 683,000 workers. Home health aides were listed among the fastest growing occupations from 1994 to 2005. Workers are paid minimum wage and generally visit two clients a day; however, they are not paid for commuting time while traveling to homes of clients. In March 1998, Jacquelyn Peters, a caregiver for Interim Healthcare, and 48 other employees, filed a class-action lawsuit for travel pay when commuting between clients. According to the lawsuit, the workers pay falls below minimum wage.

The National Association for Health Care Recruitment, a 1,400 member organization, seeks to provide information, education, and networking for facility-based health care center recruiters and human resources professionals. Additionally, the Cooperative Home Care Associates assists home health aides in finding above minimum wage jobs.

AMERICA AND THE WORLD

With the acquisition of Sogica, France's fifth largest staffing services firm with offices in Spain, Olsten became a presence in 13 countries in 1997.

England reduced the amount it was willing to pay for nursing home residents several years ago, and Japan will not let persons into a nursing home if they have any living relatives; both policies are likely to boost home health care services. Receipts in the home health care industry in Japan began rising early on and increased 36 percent in 1994 alone.

RESEARCH AND TECHNOLOGY

Since February 1, 1997, home health agencies, along with nursing facilities, were required to submit their Medicare cost reports in an electronic format. HBO & Company's Pathways Homecare product for disease management keeps tract of clinical pathways, treatment interventions, patient-centered outcomes, and goals. It was selected by Appalachian Regional Healthcare, Inc.'s Home Services Division in 1996.

The National Association for Home Care, the largest home care trade association, was attempting to accredit information system vendors and consultants in 1996 amidst concerns that endorsement would provide an unfair advantage to such vendors.

"Nursing informatics,"—the application of information and computer science to the field of nursing—will allow a home health care nurse to remotely check on a patients' progress in their homes. According to an article by Cathy Mellett in *Michigan Today,* using Cornell University's free CUCME (See You/See Me) video conferencing software, nurses will be able to watch patients perform certain tasks and give instructions directly.

FURTHER READING

"'97 Medicare Fraud, Waste Cost $20 Billion; Losses Down from '97." *Chicago Tribune,* 24 April 1998.

"Administration Tells Home Care Agencies to Stop Cutting Service." *Tribune News Services,* 4 February 1998.

Alpert, Bill. "Heavy Breathers." *Barron's,* 2 September 1996.

"Behavioral Home Care: New Industry Finds Its Niche." *LI Business News,* 15 January 1999.

Brandstrader, J.R. "It's An Ill Wind." *Barron's,* 25 March 1996.

Brown, Ann. "Business Opportunities: No Place Like Home Care." *Black Enterprise,* August 1998.

Calico, Forrest. "Home Health Moving Toward High Touch, High Tech'." *Health Management Technology,* October 1996.

"The Care Economy." *Futurist,* March/April 1996.

"The Charm of Old Money." *Economist,* 15 March 1997.

Church, Louis. "Positioning Hospital-Based Home Care Agencies for Managed Care." *Healthcare Financial Management,* February 1996.

"Electronic Cost Reports Required for Nursing Facilities, Home Health Agencies." *Healthcare Financial Management,* March 1997.

Fogel, Lawrence A. "Reforming Home Health Care." *Healthcare Financial Management,* June 1998.

Freeman, Laura. "Home-Sweet-Home Health Care." *Monthly Labor Review,* March 1995.

Freudenheim, Milt. "Medicare Revamps System of Paying Nursing Homes." *New York Times,* 4 July 1998.

Gamble, Michael R., and Gerry D. Wilson. "Home Care Benefits Are Seriously Flawed." *National Underwriter Life & Health-Financial Services Edition,* 16 March 1998.

Gamm, Larry. "HBO & Co. Adds Home-Care Software Firm." *Modern Healthcare,* 16 September 1996.

Gardner, Jonathan. "New Home Health Rules." *Modern Healthcare,* 10 March 1997.

———. "Shifty Maneuver?" *Modern Healthcare,* 13 January 1997.

Gemignani, Janet. "Who'll Pay the Bill When Health Care Comes Home?" *Business & Health,* June 1996.

"HCFA Corrects Home Health Agency Medicare Cost Limits." *Healthcare Financial Management,* December 1996.

Heffler, Stephen K. "Health Care Indicators: Hospital, Employment, and Price Indicators for the Health Care Industry." *Health Care Financing Review,* Summer 1996.

"In Every Hundred, Ten Are Saved." *Economist,* 25 May 1996.

Kane, Rosalie A., and Carrie A. Levin. "Who's Safe? Who's Sorry? The Duty to Protect the Safety of Clients in Home- and Community-based Care." *Generations,* Fall 1998.

Kazel, Robert. "Columbia/HCA Buys Value Health." *Business Insurance,* 20 January 1997.

Koco, Linda. "Bankers L&C Still Pursuing Home Health Care Market." *National Underwriter (Life/Health/Financial Services),* 17 March 1997.

Lowes, Robert L. "House Calls: Better Pay May Bring Them Back." *Medical Economics,* 24 June 1996.

McCarthy, Joseph L. "Riding the Boom in Staffing Services." *Chief Executive,* December 1995.

"Medicare Home Health Cost Limits Increased Again." *Healthcare Financial Management,* January 1997.

Mellett, Cathy. "Virtual Nursing." *The University of Michigan: Michigan Today,* Summer 1997.

———. "Be It Ever So Jumbled." *Hospitals & Health Networks,* 5 May 1998.

Meyer, Harris. "Home (Care) Improvement." *Hospitals & Health Networks,* 20 April 1997.

Montague, Jim. "Workers' Health Is Retailer's Business." *Hospitals & Health Networks,* 20 May 1996.

Morrall, Katherine. "Possibilities, Profits, and Problems." *Hospitals & Health Networks,* 20 March 1996.

Moynihan, James J. "EDI Applications for Home Care Agencies." *Healthcare Financial Management,* May 1997.

"National Association for Health Care Recruitment." *Gale's Encyclopedia of Associations.* Farmington Hills, MI: The Gale Group, 1997.

Niedzielski, Joe. "LTC Insurers Embrace Home Care Explosion." *National Underwriter Life & Health-Financial Services Edition,* 13 October 1997.

Norlander, Dennis. "Safe Lifting on the Home Front." *Occupational Health & Safety,* September 1996.

"Nursing Home or Home Nursing?" *Forbes,* 24 March 1997.

O'Connor. "Home-Care Workers Suing for Travel Pay." *Chicago Tribune,* 13 March 1998.

Peterson, Carolyn. "Home Care Gains Acceptance for Workers' Comp Injuries." *Managed Healthcare,* November 1996.

Reschovsky, James D. "The Roles of Medicaid and Economic Factors in the Demand for Nursing Home Care." *Health Services Research,* October 1998.

Schaffer, Carol L. "Home Health Care a Viable Option." *Business Insurance,* 9 September 1996.

Schwartz, Ronald M. "Home Care Under Fire." *Nursings Homes,* September 1997.

Shea, Biff. "There's No Place Like Home: Despite the IPS, Home Health Agencies Can Survive If They Do Research and Tailor Their Services." *Modern Healthcare,* 8 March 1999.

Shriver, Kelly. "NAHC Allays Members' Concerns of Spinoff." *Modern Healthcare,* 25 March 1996.

Snow, Charlotte. "Apria to Pay $1.7 Million to Settle Kickback Charges." *Modern Healthcare,* 16 December 1996.

Stone, Deborah. "Care and Trembling." *American Prospect,* March/April 1999.

———. "Here Comes PPS." *Modern Healthcare,* 24 February 1997.

———. "Home-Care Firms Fill Chronic-Care Niche." *Modern Healthcare,* 28 October 1996.

———. "A Home-Care Link?" *Modern Healthcare,* 31 March 1997.

———. "Homing in on Home Care." *Modern Healthcare,* 27 January 1997.

———. "Post-Acute Firm Buys First American." *Modern Healthcare,* 21 October 1996.

Uretsky, Michael. "Long-term Care Insurance: It's All About Home Care." *LI Business News,* 15 January 1999.

Vanchieri, Cori. "National Disasters: Home Care's Foray into Nationwide HMO Contracting Takes a Tumble." *Hospitals & Health Networks,* 20 May 1998.

Voelker, Rebecca. "Wellness Works at Home." *JAMA, The Journal of the American Medical Association,* 24 February 1999.

Weaver, Peter. "Opportunity Knocks as America Ages." *Nation's Business,* August 1996.

Weissenstein, Eric. "GAO Traces High Income-Care Costs to Lack of Government Controls." *Modern Healthcare,* 15 April 1996.

———. "Medicare Benefit Imbroglio." *Modern Healthcare,* 10 March 1997.

———. "Squeezing Oxygen Vendors." *Modern Healthcare,* 3 March 1997.

—David C. Genaway, updated by Katherine Wagner and Dorothy L. Wood

INFANT AND PRESCHOOL PRODUCTS

Since 1980, juvenile product sales have risen from $1.7 to $4.4 billion in 1997. In fact, the baby business more than doubled from 1986 to 1997, and that did not include infant and preschool toys, an important segment of the infant and preschool market.

Cribs, car seats, strollers, bedding, and a wide variety of accessories and decorative items including baby baths, baby carriers, bath toys, bibs, books, diapers, high chairs, clothing, tethers, and even audio visual cassettes for children are among the juvenile products listed by the Juvenile Products Manufacturers Association. The organization represents about 95 percent of the juvenile products industry, and includes more than 270 companies in the United States, Canada, and Mexico.

Toy industry retail sales in the late 1990s rose at a modest but consistent 3 percent per year, for a total of $25 billion in sales in 1997. According to the Toy Manufacturers of America analyses of 1998 sales, manufacturers' shipments totaled $15.2 billion, nearly equal to 1997's shipment figure, though 1.6 percent more toys were sold, the equivalent of 3.374 billion units. Of the major product categories in 1998, the plush category increased by 19 percent and remained the strongest category, fueled by sales of Beanie Babies, Furby, Bounce-Around Tigger, and Teletubbies. Up 26.8 percent on the strength of Star Wars re-releases in 1997, 1998 sales of action figures were down 13 percent. High sales from virtual pets like Giga Pets and Tamagotchi, which were $206 million in 1997, shrunk to only $45 million in 1998. Non-powered cars such as Matchbox and Hot Wheels increased 25 percent; video game sales increased by 20

percent; building sets increased 7 percent; and doll sales decreased 3.2 percent. Approximately two-thirds of the total toy industry sales occur in the fourth quarter when many toys are bought as holiday gifts. This is beginning to level out, however, as toy manufacturers market products year round through movie and fast-food chain tie-ins.

ORGANIZATION AND STRUCTURE

Industry figures show that mass-market merchandisers became the number one class of trade for infant and toddler products. Wal-Mart, Kmart, Target, and Toys R Us are among the leading mass marketers of juvenile products. Century Products, Cosco, Gerber Products, EvenFlo Products Co., and Graco Children's Products, Inc., are among the largest juvenile products companies, with divisions including Fisher-Price, Playskool, and Tyco.

Mass-merchandisers were also a leader in the baby care category. This segment of the market includes baby soaps, ointments and bath powders, oils and lotions, bottles and nipples, and nursing accessories. These products are sold in supermarkets, drug stores, and through mass merchandisers. By 1998 the largest percentage of nursing accessories, bottles and nipples, oils and lotions, and baby bath soaps were sold through mass merchandisers, as opposed to baby powder and baby ointments, which had the heaviest sales in supermarkets.

Baby superstores are another way to sell juvenile products. In the latter part of the 1990s Toys 'R Us introduced its new Babies 'R Us, stores focusing on juvenile products, furniture, apparel, and toys.

Through these stores, Toys 'R Us was expected to become an even larger retailing force for young families. In 1998 Toys 'R Us had about 113 Babies 'R Us stores throughout the country. Baby Superstore, with outlets in 18 states, was another large infant products chain.

Juvenile products and toys are also sold through catalogs. Many parents found this easy and convenient, not to mention a time saving way to shop. There are also parent information and resource centers on the Internet as well as World Wide Web shopping directories pointing online shoppers to products for children.

In March 1999, the NPD Group reported its findings for the top toy sellers of the past year, in which 1998 saw Toys 'R Us lose its 10-year spot to Wal-Mart as the top toy retailer. Wal-Mart's toy sales held 17.4 percent of the market (up from 16.3 in 1997), with Toys 'R Us falling behind at 16.8 percent (after a 1997 market share of 18.3). Following Wal-Mart and Toys 'R Us as the top five toy retailers were Kmart, with 8.0 percent of the market, Target with 6.9 percent, and KB Toys with 4.9 percent. That same month, Toys 'R Us reported fourth-quarter had fallen 18.0 percent from the previous year.

The late 1990s saw the Internet as an emerging avenue for toy sales. Toys R Us launched an online site, and Santa Monica-based eToys opened its virtual doors in 1997. eToys claims to be the largest online store for children's products, and carries more than 10,000 items, all priced at or below prices of traditional toy retailers.

LICENSING

Toy licensing began during the twentieth century, when Richard Felton Outcault's design of the comic character "The Yellow Kid" was placed onto toys. Since then, toy licensing has become increasingly sophisticated and is reaching ever deeper into children's lives. Licensed products, such as Disney and Winnie-the-Pooh, contributed greatly to sales in such areas as baby bottles and toys. In 1997, the Toy Manufacturers Association estimated that about 40 percent of all toys sold were licensed products. Even youngsters under the age of three are affected by the onslaught of commercials and characters they encounter as part of daily television viewing, and companies continue to initiate new ways to reach these youngsters through electronic media.

Almost anywhere children go, they find products reflecting the characters they know from popular television shows and movies. Barney, the Teletubbies,

Blues Clues, Sesame Street, Winnie the Pooh, and many other Disney characters are among the most universal and there are many more. And the target age for licensees continued to grow younger. Sales of licensed products for infants alone grew by 32 percent to $42.5 billion in 1996. But not all vendors agree that licensing is the best avenue; some juvenile bedding vendors pinned products on non-licensed looks and patterns that stayed clear of major films or cartoon and comic book characters, believing that licensing is becoming a high-risk proposition.

PRODUCT SAFETY

Safety is the primary concern of parents with infants and young children. The Juvenile Products Manufacturers Association developed a Certification Program that tests products for compliance with the American Society for Testing and Materials (ASTM) standards and issues a certification seal after the product passes rigorous testing. The ASTM Certification Program covers high chairs, play yards, walkers, carriages and strollers, gates and enclosures, full-size

---

Trends   **CHILD SAFETY SEATS**

More than 60,000 children have died in traffic accidents, according to an article by the Associated Press on June 3, 1999. Furthermore, 8 out of 10 child safety seats are installed incorrectly, according to the National Safe Kids Campaign.

To curb the trend, numerous measures are being taken to protect children in the car. But with dozens of styles of safety seats and hundreds of models of cars with different-sized back seats, parents struggle to know how to install seats properly. Among the more innovative inventions are car seats that seem to have a mind of their own.

Britax, the largest baby seat manufacturer in Europe, offers several, including The Mercedes-Benz Booster Seat with Backrest. The seat boasts a built-in resonator designed to shut off the passenger front air bag systems in certain Mercedes-Benz vehicles. The system uses a small resonator built into the child seat. A low power signal from the car triggers a return signal from the resonator in the equipped seat, allowing the system to recognize the presence of the seat (and subsequently the child) and turn off the passenger front airbag.

According to government statistics compiled by the Associated Press, properly installed child safety seats reduce the risk of fatal injuries in half. Other car manufacturers, like Porsche, offer similar systems in certain vehicles.

---

cribs, and portable hook-on chairs. They continue to develop standards for additional categories including toddler beds, bath seats, bedding products, and non-standard sized cribs.

As with other juvenile products, child safety is fundamental to the development and manufacture of toys. Together with the U.S. government, the Toy Manufacturers Association leads the world in the development of toy safety standards by investing heavily in child development research, dynamic safety testing, quality assurance engineering, risk analysis, and basic anthropometric studies of children.

Toys are closely monitored and highly regulated by the federal government. The basic law covering toy safety is the Federal Hazardous Substances Act and its amendments, notably the 1969 Child Protection and Toy Safety Act of 1969. This legislation was supplemented by the Consumer Product Safety Act in 1973. These regulations were incorporated by reference in the industry's voluntary standard, ASTM F963. While toy makers are not compelled to abide by the industry's voluntary standards set forth in ASTM F963, many retailers require compliance with voluntary standards, and many manufacturers, especially the larger ones, have in-house testing laboratories that assure that all products meet or exceed government standards for safety.

BACKGROUND AND DEVELOPMENT

There is archeological evidence that simple toys were made thousands of years ago in Greece, Rome, and ancient Egypt. Later, during the Middle Ages, the colorful world of knights and fair ladies was reproduced for the pleasure of medieval children. From the end of the Middle Ages on, toy production increased rapidly, and by the middle of the eighteenth century central Europe had become the heart of the world's toy industry. Germany, particularly the city of Nuremberg, was the established toy manufacturing center of the world. In the early twentieth century, Japan, Great Britain, and the United States also began to manufacture toys on a large scale.

Toys are an important part of every child's life starting in infancy. Children learn through play, and today we know that a child's education begins long before he enters school. Babies become familiar with shapes and sounds by playing with rattles and bell toys. They learn to distinguish colors by watching mobiles. Toddlers enjoy and learn from pull toys, pegboards, puzzles, and blocks. And the preschool child uses paints, crayons, and clay to add to his enjoyment of the world.

Revolutionary educational methods, such as those of Maria Montessori and Friedrich Froebel, with their precepts of learning by doing, have taught that an interested child is a happy one. Each year, more and more toys are designed to educate as well as to amuse. For example, wooden clocks with movable hands teach children how to tell time, and alphabet blocks help them learn to spell. In addition, new methods of teaching in kindergarten influenced the pattern of toys and introduced building blocks, constructor sets, educational puzzles, and many of the toys we now take for granted. In the twentieth century, soft toys also became popular. The Teddy Bear made its debut in 1903 and remains a favorite. Advanced technology in vinyl, plastic, and foam rubber also helped to revolutionize the toy industry.

In the earliest stages of product development, many designers utilize information from sources that include parents, psychologists, educators, and other child development specialists. This background provides valuable clues to what consumers are looking for when they purchase toys and how children learn through play. Some toy manufacturers maintain in-house year-round nursery school facilities for this purpose, while others establish relationships with universities or other research facilities.

TRENDS

Toys are such an important aspect of child development that toy libraries, which function somewhat like book libraries, have sprouted both nationally and internationally. Through the USA Toy Library Association (USA-TLA), parents and professional members alike strive to create quality toys and provide play opportunities available to all children, including the disabled. In 1999 there were nearly 350 toy libraries in the United States and more than 1,000 in the United Kingdom. In an attempt to encourage participation by manufacturers, distributors, and retailers of toys, the USA-TLA offers opportunities to advertise products in publications and at conference exhibits. Ultimately, it is a win-win situation for all involved.

CURRENT CONDITIONS

INNOVATIVE NEW JUVENILE PRODUCTS

The list of new juvenile products is endless and continues to grow. Innovation and safety appear to be the driving forces. Of the more than 100 new products evaluated at the 1997 Annual International Juvenile Products Show, the industry's leading trade exhibition, safety oriented products dominated. Other important areas included products that appealed to busy lifestyles, stress convenience, or feature licensees. Among the winning products were: Glide-a-Bye Baby Bassinet by Burlington Basket Company, a bassinet with a gliding motion that keeps a baby level for sleep; Gerry Baby Products Double Take Diaper Bag; Kid Kushions's Hearth Kushion, which protects toddlers from fireplace tumbles; Car-Bar PlusA Car Seat Activity Center by The Maya Group, Inc.; Tip Resistant Furniture Safety Brackets by Mommy's Helper, Inc., which help prevent injuries caused when children climb on furniture; and White Hot Soft Bite Safety Spoon by Munchin, Inc., which turns white when baby's food is too hot. And this was just the tip of the iceberg.

By far the most radical innovation in juvenile products during the late 1990s was the very controversial extension of packaged entertainment, in the form of television shows and video games, for children under the age of two. The lovable purple dinosaur Barney got the ball rolling by appealing to youngsters from 2 to 5 years old in the mid-1990s, but by the late 1990s the British import Teletubbies was marketed to infants under the age of one. Along with television programs came computer programs, such as Jump Start Baby, which offers children as young as nine months their first formal introduction to the sun, bears, shapes, and capitalism. According to the *New York Times,* several large retail stores, including F.A.O. Schwartz and Learning Smith, began offering products for the under three set in 1998. Hasbro's talking Teletubbies plush proved so popular in 1998 that plans for 1999 included an expanded line of toys and games based on the four creatures.

The extension of marketing to babies spawned a great deal of controversy, with some arguing that it was unethical to market products to children that cannot speak the name of the item they are being encouraged to desire. The chief television critic for the Associated Press, Frazier Moore, asked in his column, "Where Does It End: A TV in the Amniotic Sac, Tuned Round-the-Clock to the In Utero Channel?" Still, marketers themselves argue that infants watch television anyway, and they are simply "filling a market niche" with appropriate material. "Would you rather have them watch *Days of Our Lives?*" Erica Lindberg Gourd, president of the Lindberg Licensing Company, asked in the *New York Times.* There were as yet no figures available for how large a market the three and under set represented, but it was certain to

draw the attention of toy and entertainment producers for the next few years.

Another important innovation in juvenile products was the proliferation of toys designed for children with disabilities. Advances in medicine, ironically, have led to a dramatic increase in the number of children with disabilities as mortality rates for premature babies and babies with severe ailments have plummeted. The American Academy of Pediatrics estimated that at least 6 million children had some form of disability, a figure that rose 20 percent from 1989-1990. According to the Toy Manufacturers of America, toys for children with disabilities represented a $2.7 billion market in 1997, and it was expected to grow faster than the toy market as a whole. The handicapped toy industry was led by familiar names like Mattel, which introduced a Barbie doll in a wheelchair in 1997, and smaller toy makers like People of Every Stripe in Portland, Oregon, which began making dolls with hearing aids and prosthetics in the early 1990s. Toy manufacturers were also offering modified versions of standard toys for use by children with disabilities.

CHILD SAFETY

Of concern to the industry during the late 1990s was a claim made by some public interest groups that PVC, or vinyl, used in toys and infant products such as tethers and pacifiers posed significant hazards to children's health. In independent tests, the U.S. Consumer Product Safety Commission (CPSC), Health Canada, and ENVIRON Corporation concluded that claims of toxic substances, namely phthalates, in vinyl used in children's toys were unfounded. The Toy Manufacturers of America stands by the safety of vinyl toys. Still, many large retailers pulled all soft rattles and tethers from their shelves, and some toy manufacturers began to phase out the use of phthalates in products for young children.

Car seat safety was also of concern in the late 1990s. A study by the National Safe Kids Campaign found evidence that 8 out of 10 child-safety car seats were used incorrectly. Infants under 20 pounds and 1 year of age were required to be placed in a rear-facing seat at a 45-degree angle to best support their necks. From 20-40 pounds, children could be seated in forward-facing car seats, and from 40-80 pounds they could use booster seats. Even when infants and toddlers were placed in the correct seats, however, the seats were often incorrectly installed—85 percent of them, according to Julie Edelson Halpert in *Newsweek.* Adding to the problems were the proliferation of car seat styles and automobiles, making it difficult for manufacturers to ensure a proper fit. In hopes of correcting some of these problems, federal laws began requiring auto manufacturers to add special bars, bolts, and tethers to make it easier for parents to secure the car seats. Auto makers and the government were also teaming up to offer roadside clinics and seat-checks to verify child safety seats were correctly installed.

INDUSTRY LEADERS

In 1998 Mattel, Inc. posted sales of $4.8 billion. Mattel's second largest core brand (after Barbie) is Fisher Price, the leader in the infant and preschool market with a history that spans more than 70 years. Mattel also includes Disney infant and preschool See N Say talking toys; Tyco Toys, which has an infant preschool line based on Sesame Street characters; and Magna Doodle and View-Master toys.

In 1998, Mattel acquired Wisconsin-based Pleasant Company, direct marketer of American Girl dolls. Mattel's software unit, Mattel Media, reached sales of $100 million in 1998. The company expected Mattel Media's extensive growth to continue, with projected sales of $1 billion in interactive products after a proposed merger with educational software leader The Learning Company was completed in 1999. Finally, Barbie's popularity in the late 1990s would culminate with the celebration of the doll's 40th birthday in 1999. According to the company, 1 billion Barbie dolls were sold in the last four decades, making Barbie the best-selling fashion doll worldwide. Barbie software continued to expand in 1999 meeting the new demands of Barbie fans. In addition, the company's Barbie Web site allows its mostly preteen customers to design a Barbie doll online. According to Mattel, about 40 percent of its sales are generated internationally, and most of its manufacturing is done in Asia, Southeast Asia, and Mexico.

Hasbro, Inc., the second largest toy company, reported 1998 net revenues of $3.3 billion, up 4 percent over 1997's posted net of $3.2 billion. Hasbro began as a family owned company in 1923. In more than 70 years it has grown from 8 family members to a company with more than 12,000 employees in facilities around the world. In 1983, Hasbro acquired certain assets of Knickerbocker Toy Company from Warner Communications. This acquisition marked the beginning of Hasbro's involvement with plush products such as Raggedy Ann and Raggedy Andy. That same year it also acquired Glenco, manufacturer of infant

bibs and sleepwear, and Tommee Tippee (producers of cups, feeding accessories, and other products). By 1985 Hasbro was the world's largest toy company, gaining access to the European market and uniting four strong divisions: Hasbro Toy, Milton Bradley, Playskool, and Playskool Baby. In 1986, Hasbro purchased certain assets of Child Guidance in addition to several games from CBS and, later in the year, the Hasbro infant line expanded with the addition of the Pur line of feeding and soothing accessories. Among its acquisitions in 1988 was the celebrated Cabbage Patch Kids line of dolls and accessories. In 1991 Hasbro acquired the Tonka Corporation, which also included Parker Brothers and Kenner Products. This addition brought new classics to an extensive collection of toys including Nerf and Baby Alive. In 1991, Hasbro grew to a $42.1 billion company with products available in more than 40 countries. In the late 1990s the entire line of infant products was part of the well-recognized Playskool division. The Playskool line offers fun and educational items ranging from baby care products to clothing and preschool toys including such classics as Mr. Potato Head, Play-Doh, and Lincoln Logs.

Hasbro credited Furby and Teletubbies for the products' contributions to its top-selling lineup for better-than-expected 1998 revenues. The company's lineup for 1999 included more Furby's, the fluffy pets that speak and react to noise and touch. The newest Furby friends included five different "international" Furby's that speak German, Italian, French, Japanese, or Spanish. Hasbro's partnership with Lucasfilm and Star Wars also took flight in 1999 with brand new action figures for the release of the new Star Wars prequel.

WORK FORCE

According to the Bureau of Labor Statistics, during the mid-1990s there were 44,300 toy industry employees in the United States, approximately 66 percent of whom were in production jobs. Toy production is labor intensive, requiring procedures such as painting, assembly, inspection, packaging, and detailing for authenticity. The costs associated with this type of production in the United States are often very high. Since the early 1950s, American manufacturers have combined domestic operations with overseas production in developing countries (where labor is inexpensive) to lower costs. It was estimated that 75 percent of toys sold in the United States were manufactured either wholly or in part overseas.

AMERICA AND THE WORLD

The United States is the largest market for toys in the world, representing about 36 percent of total toy revenue, followed by Japan and western Europe. Approximately 5,000 to 6,000 new items are introduced annually at the American International Toy Fair. The United States also led the world in toy development and in such sales support areas as marketing, advertising, and special promotions.

According to the *Toy Industry Fact Book, 1997-1998,* most toy manufacturers distributed overseas through subsidiaries, distributors, and direct sales to retailers, totaling an estimated $5.5 billion in sales each year. Of that figure $1.2 billion was exported directly. Because American toy manufacturers were preeminent in the invention and design of toys, many children worldwide desired toys and games introduced in the United States. With foreign markets so important to U.S. manufacturers, the liberalization of world trade through international trade agreements was of vital interest to those companies who sell or seek to sell overseas.

FURTHER READING

"Baby Superstore Grows in Florida." *Discount Store News,* July 1995, 6.

Canedy, Dana. "More Toys Are Reflecting Disabled Children's Needs." New York *Times: Business,* 25 December 1997.

"Cutbacks in Retailer Buying; Mattel and The Learning Company Agree to Merge." Los Angeles, CA: Mattel, 14 December 1998. Available from http://www.mattel.com/corporate/company/news_media/index.asp?section=press_releases.

"eToys Unveils Best-Selling Toys of 1998." *PRNewswire,* 10 December 1998.

Halpert, Julie Edelson. "Strapping Them In." *Newsweek,* 17 May 1999.

Hasbro, Inc. 1996 *Annual Report.* Pawtucket, RI: Hasbro, Inc., 1997.

"Hasbro Reports Record Fourth Quarter and Full Year 1998 Results Which Exceeded Expectations; Outlook for 1999 is Very Positive." Pawtucket, RI. *Business Wire,* 4 February 1999. Available from http://www.corporate-ir.net/ireye/ir_site.zhtml?ticker=has&script=410&layout=6&item_id=19618.

Juvenile Products Manufacturers Association. *Annual Report.* Moorestown, NJ: Juvenile Manufacturers Association, April 1997-March 1998.

Leonard, David, and Kathleen Kerwin. "Hey Kid Buy This." *Business Week,* 30 June 1997.

"Licensed vs. Non-licensed Items." *Home Textiles Today,* November 1996, 13.

"Mattel Commits to the Elimination of Phthalates in Teething Toys for Children Under 36 Months." *PRNewswire,* 23 September 1998.

Mattel, Inc. 1996 *Annual Report.* El Segundo, CA: Mattel, Inc., 1997.

"Mattel Reports Results For 1998 Fourth Quarter and Year in Line With Expectations." Los Angeles, CA: Mattel, 2 February 1999. Available from http://www.mattel.com/corporate/company/news_media/index.asp?section=press_releases.

Mifflin, Lawrie. "Critics Assail PBS Over Plan for Toys Aimed at Toddlers." *New York Times: Business,* 20 April 1998.

Miller, David A. "Toy Manufacturers of America State of the Industry Address." Toy Manufacturers of America, 2 February 1999. Available from http://www.tradeshowpr.com/toyfair99/releases/10.html.

Rouland, Renee Covino. "Oh, Baby!" *Discount Merchandiser,* 1996.

Slatalla, Michelle. "User's Guide; Computers and Me, And Baby Makes 3." *New York Times: Circuits,* 25 June 1998.

Supermarket Business, August 1996, 61.

Toy Industry Fact Book, 1997-1998. NY: Toy Manufacturers of America, Inc., 1998.

"Toy Manufacturers of America Release 1998 Shipments." New York, Toy Manufacturers of America, 2 February 1999. Available from http://www.toy-tma.com/NEWS/98shipments.html.

"Toys." *The New Book of Knowledge.* Danbury, CT: Grolier Inc., 1979.

U.S. Department of Commerce, Bureau of the Census. *Statistical Abstract of the United States, 1996, The National Data Book.* Washington, D.C.: GPO, 1996.

"Wal Mart Dethrones Toys 'R Us." New York: Associated Press, 29 March 1999.

—Kaye Brinker, updated by David Yosifon and Lisa DeShantz-Cook

INFOMERCIALS

INDUSTRY SNAPSHOT

The electronic retailing industry has gained more respect since its proliferation in the 1980s. The industry's best known product is the television infomercial—a 28.5 minute block of programming that resembles a television show, designed to explain and sell anything from kitchen gadgets to advice from psychic friends. By the late 1990s, infomercials evolved into a billion dollar industry segment, producing approximately 600 infomercials each year. Other industry products included television shopping channels, like QVC and the Home Shopping Network, and the "short-form," a more traditional television commercial lasting 30 seconds to two minutes with a toll-free phone number included for viewers.

In the past, electronic retailing, or direct response television (DRTV), has attracted its share of dishonest people, so the industry formed an organization to regulate itself and project a professional image. As of mid-1999, that organization was titled the Electronic Retailing Association (ERA). ERA was formerly NIMA International, and before that was known as the National Infomercial Marketing Association. ERA represents the electronic retailing industry in the United States and overseas. According to ERA statistics gathered in 1998, worldwide sales for the industry were $8.6 billion in 1996, $1.4 billion in sales was generated by U.S. infomercials, $1.4 billion from U.S. short-form, $3 billion from U.S. shopping channels, and $2.8 billion was earned by international infomercials, short-forms, and shopping channels combined. In mid-1998, ERA estimated total DRTV media buy in the United States for 1997 at $15.5 billion, and with an annual growth rate of 6.3 percent,

projected a total U.S. media buy of $23.4 billion in 2002.

But by mid-1999, the industry also experienced some growing pains, and legal problems resurfaced. ERA formed an advisory board, including a former commissioner of the Federal Trade Commission (FTC), stepping up the industry's self-regulation, and stressing that consumer protection remained its top priority. In addition, some observers feel that after years of explosive growth, infomercials have lost momentum as a selling tool. Others, however, feel the medium is in transition and ripe for a rebirth, spurred by the rapid movement of infomercials into cyberspace.

An infomercial's purpose is to show consumers how a product would satisfy a need, benefit their lives, motivate them, or solve a problem. Fitness devices are among the most successful infomercial products because they are easily demonstrated by fit, photogenic people. The more sophisticated infomercials often have a celebrity spokesperson, testimonials from satisfied customers, location shooting, a musical soundtrack, and a well-developed script. During the late 1990s, producing an infomercial cost at least $150,000, but the price could rise as high as a million dollars. Nonetheless, the potential payoff can be millions of dollars more in sales. Once an infomercial's product generates good sales, electronic retailers display the product on television channels, usually the home shopping channels. Some products may also be shown on channels related to the product, e.g., promoting fitness machines and exercise videos sports channels. The final sales venue is retail stores, where the original infomercial runs on a store's VCR, repeating and reinforcing the product's benefits to potential buyers.

ORGANIZATION AND STRUCTURE

Most electronic retailers do not invent products themselves, but instead scout trade shows and fairs—or accept submissions—for easily marketable, new inventions. For instance, the two biggest industry firms, Guthy-Renker and National Media, often buy the rights to a product from inventors and pay inventors a 10 percent (or less) royalty fee. In return, infomercial producers assume all the financial risk—and most of the payoff—for launching a product.

After finding a prospective product, the company produces an infomercial. Costs vary widely, depending on quality, but general estimates run between $100,000 and $600,000. These costs could include: $4,000 - $20,000 for the script and the same range for a director; $3,000 for props; $30,000 - $60,000 for editing; and $25,000 - $50,000 for crew and equipment. For kitchen items, a chef and a food stylist are also necessary, and live audiences add even more expense. Costs for location and a host (who may be a celebrity) are vastly divergent, and can run into the hundreds of thousands of dollars.

Industry firms usually test finished ads on focus groups before airing infomercials in specific markets. If the product generates enough response, industry firms buy more media time in diverse markets. Because response is so rapid—customers either call in or the phones are quiet—industry firms know within days if the infomercial is working or if it needs rewriting and reshooting. If the product receives positive responses, it eventually goes to home shopping channels, the Internet, and, finally, traditional retailers. If the product receives negative responses, industry firms often pull it from the air and move on to promoting other products. Due to expanding television markets, the largest firms had plenty of media time available and could launch 30 or more products per year.

Fortune 500 companies, such as Lexus, Microsoft, Apple Computer, Magnavox, Sears, AT&T, Volvo, and Fidelity Investments, added infomercials to their marketing strategy during the late 1990s, but they worked with industry firms differently than struggling entrepreneurs. Lee Frederiksen, of Frederiksen Television, Inc. in Falls Church, Virginia, described these alternative business relationships as a fee-for-service whereby a direct response marketer is hired to produce the infomercial or spot, establish both the supporting telemarketing and fulfillment structure, as well as buy media time and provide operational management. Or the marketer might provide just one or a group of these services. The advantage of this approach is maximum flexibility and control of the project while still retaining all the upside potential. The disadvantage, of course, is that the investor's capital is at risk.

The infomercial production industry reached consumers by purchasing air time on broadcast, satellite, and regional and national cable television. Infomercials are not tracked by Nielsen ratings in the manner of traditional broadcast programs, so the number of viewers is unknown. According to the Direct Marketing Association, in 1996 certain facts were documented in regards to how electronic retailers affect consumers: 74 percent of Americans reported viewing some form of direct response television, such as a home shopping show or an infomercial; and, almost 13 million people bought one or more items from a television offer.

Infomercials, and the products they sell, stand or fall on consumer reaction. Gene Silverman, president of Hawthorne Communications, advised prospective electronic retailers that at virtually every moment, an infomercial must grab the viewer's attention and convince that viewer that it is necessary to continue watching. That is because only about 1 percent of viewers will actually call the toll-free number to place an order or request information, so a company must reach a large audience to keep the response level high. Some suggested tips are: avoid telling the whole story right up front—consider how to tease an audience; use a 'grabber' that keeps an audience watching, such as "In the next half hour you will. . ." or "Stay tuned to witness an amazing. . ."; give the viewer an opportunity to think subconsciously, "I want to see this." The formula for success can be summed up in a few words: first, engage a viewer emotionally, then convince the viewer intellectually that buying the product is a smart deal.

Since electronic retailing has grown more mainstream, published a code of ethics, and more recently the "Ten Commandments of Electronic Retailing," to further improve the industry's public image. Member firms must agree to comply with all laws, from federal to local, that cover advertising and selling consumer goods. In addition, they must portray their own business operations, including revenues and profits, accurately and avoid libel or slander of competitors. Most importantly for consumers, member firms must promise: "To honor all warranties and money-back guarantees, and to establish and maintain a fair and equitable distribution system for handling customer complaints." Unlike the FTC, ERA cannot really punish violators.

BACKGROUND AND DEVELOPMENT

Infomercials began during the 1950s when television grew popular. In those days, television had little regulation, and some shows became intertwined with the sponsors. For example, some analysts believe the late 1990s corporate infomercials owe a debt to 1950s shows such as the "Bob Hope Texaco Star Theater." The show featured the Texaco logo prominently throughout, and Bob Hope interrupted the program with commercial breaks pitching Texaco's products.

In 1963, the Federal Communications Commission (FCC) set a two-minute limit on television ads, which effectively killed the infomercial. However, the two-minute limit allowed marketers to refine the short-form to pitch straightforward items like K-Tel records. In 1997, K-Tel Records was still selling records via short-form after 35 years.

When the Reagan Administration deregulated the broadcast and cable television industry in 1984, cable subscriptions expanded and infomercials reappeared. From 1984 to 1987, few federal guidelines existed, and this sometimes led to misleading ads making fraudulent claims. FTC guidelines issued in the late 1980s halted most deceitful ads by forbidding false claims and misleading presentations. In an interview with FOX News, Joel Winston, assistant director of the Federal Trade Commission's division of advertising practices, said infomercials needed policing because it was clear that some were deliberate attempts to resemble television shows for the sole purpose of fooling customers. Some viewers had never heard of 30-minute commercials and they believed they were watching standard programs. From 1987 to 1997, the FTC charged over 100 people or companies with false advertising in an infomercial. Winston commented that the FTC filed fewer charges each year because the industry had "matured" and become more mainstream.

The prestige of the Fortune 500 also has found its way into the infomercial industry: their products accounted for 10 percent of infomercials on television. In the mid-1990s, Microsoft anointed the genre by using an infomercial to help launch Windows 95, using actor Anthony Edwards from television's "ER" to explain the new operating system to consumers. High-tech and financial products lent themselves especially well to the 28-minute television format since their features were not easily summed up in a 30-second television spot. The motive was to educate consumers, fix the brand name in their minds, and point potential customers to the nearest retailer. The aim of Fortune 500 spots is to generate sales leads rather than selling products over the phone. For example, the Lexus infomercial explained its used car program and included a toll free number. Over one year, the infomercial generated 40,000 phone calls, and 2 percent of those callers eventually bought a used Lexus. Sears also ran infomercials during the mid-1990s and claimed to have doubled in-store sales on items featured in the spots.

PIONEERS

One industry pioneer is Ron Popeil, who began as a television pitchman for his father's kitchen inventions, the Chop-O-Matic and the Veg-O-Matic, during the 1950s. These products made over $1 million and drew Popeil into a career marketing his own inventions on television. Under the Ronco brand name, Popeil marketed such gadgets as the Ronco Spray Gun, the Pocket Fisherman, and Mister Microphone. His latest product in 1997 was the GLH Formula #9 Hair Spray, a tinted spray used to conceal men's bald spots. In mid-1997, Popeil claimed to have sold, at $40 each, 1 million units of GLH, which Popeil says stands for Great Looking Hair.

Other industry pioneers started during, and have survived, the unregulated days of the 1980s. For example, Tyee Productions of Portland, Oregon, a private company headed by John Ripper, produced a very successful infomercial for Soloflex in 1987. By 1997 Tyee had clients such as Philips Magnavox for their interactive compact disk systems. Another 1980s pioneer was Tim Hawthorne, of Fairfield, Iowa-based Hawthorne Communications. Hawthorne represented the infomercial's first mainstream client when the company brought Time Life Music to the air in 1986. By the late 1990s, Time Life had grown so comfortable with the genre that it sold ad time within its infomercials to other companies.

CURRENT CONDITIONS

Business continued to grow for electronic retailers into the late 1990s. From a modest start in the mid-1980s, some analysts have predicted rising sales for the industry through the early twenty-first century. According to figures from ERA, gross sales of products generated by infomercial programs rose 228 percent between 1988 and 1995—from $350 million to $1.4 billion. Some infomercials even pushed their way close to network prime time, and they are expanding rapidly into the global market and onto the Internet.

Pioneer RON POPEIL, 1935-
SALESMAN OF THE CENTURY

Ron Popeil, now considered father of the infomercial, built his career from selling his father's gadgets at a Chicago Woolworth's, local street markets and state fairs. He was still in high school and living with his grandparents but sometimes grossed as much as $500 a day on weekends by selling the gadgets he bought from his father's factory at wholesale. After a fight with his grandfather, Popeil moved out. He was only 17 years old, but he decided to make his living selling items like the Feather Touch Knife and the Kitchen Magician on the fair circuit.

Popeil soon took a partner, Mel Korey, and offered Mel 25 percent of whatever Mel sold. His first commercial arose from a suggestion by a friend who said Popeil could make a commercial for a mere $550 at a station in Florida. He decided to sell a new product, which he called the Ronco Spray Gun. The spray gun was a garden accessory that could both wash a car and fertilize a lawn. The commercials first aired in Illinois and Wisconsin and eventually spread to 100 cities. He called his first commercial a "wake-up call", realizing that he could make the same sales pitch he made on the fair circuit, but with the commercial it would reach hundreds of thousands. Soon, he decided to sell another of his father's products, the Chop-O-Matic, on television but viewers could only buy it via mail-order. Popeil convinced the stations to run the commercial for two minutes, which was longer than average. It was a grand success and the first infomercial.

Also a success was Popeil's decision to go public with the company that he now shared with Korey. The public paid $5.5 million for 22 percent. However, the more gadgets Popeil sold, the more money he borrowed. His tab had reached about $15 million in the 1980s when his bank in Chicago called his loans after another Chicago bank needed to be bailed out by the Federal government. His company declared bankruptcy. However, with the loans not guaranteed by him personally but through his assets, Popeil didn't lose his fortune. And when the bank announced an auction of the warehouse of goods it had claimed from Popeil, he offered to buy the goods for $2 million. With a new partner, Popeil liquidated some of the goods and had millions of dollars worth of products left. To recoup some of his losses, he went back to the fair circuit, hocking goods for 12-13 hours a day.

Popeil wasn't down for long when a friend suggested he go back into television marketing with a company called Fingerhut, one of America's largest mail order houses. Fingerhut had a small shopping show subsidiary where Popeil agreed to sell products. However, Fingerhut ran into financial difficulty and abandoned the subsidiary. Popeil, never one to pass up an opportunity, produced an infomercial on his own for $33,000. Selling the Ronco Electric Food Dehydrator in the nearly 30-minute long commercial, Popeil was back in business. His later success with products like spray-on hair only increased his fortune.

But the late 1990s have also produced casualties. Conducting a "State of the Industry" discussion, industry publication *Response TV* said on its Web site: "the infomercial business (has) not only lost the momentum that was propelling it through year after year of double-digit growth, it also seemed to collapse on itself like an army marching straight into the fire of enemy machine guns." The gathered industry leaders told *Response TV* that the industry was "downsizing," and that only innovative products and ads were likely to thrive in the coming years.

Legal problems have also resurfaced. In January 1998 the FTC announced a million-dollar settlement with an infomercial producer whose advertising claims were challenged. The participants of the *Response TV* gathering agreed that the industry was at a crossroads. Some said the reason for this was that the airwaves had become too crowded with similar products. One participant said infomercial producers had become arrogant, in blaming the public for recent downturns. A separate panel declared the short-form to be in better shape.

In addition to infomercials, there were at least 14 U.S.-based television shopping networks, according to ERA, including such niche-specific channels as Black Entertainment Television and FiT TV. The largest networks were Quality Value Convenience channel (QVC) Network and the Home Shopping Network (HSN). In 1997, QVC had sales of $2 billion, reached 64 million U.S. and 6 million international homes, and had 16 million active customers in four countries. On an average day, they handled 270,000 calls, with almost 84 million annually, resulting in 56 million packages shipped. QVC merchandise included: jewelry, 35 percent; home/lifestyle, 45 percent; and apparel and accessories, 20 percent. Home Shopping Network sales topped $1 billion annually, reached 70 million U.S. homes, and the network was part of a mega-merger between USA Networks and Lycos, Inc., making it part of one of the largest e-commerce entities in the world.

INDUSTRY LEADERS

Jordan Whitney, Inc. tracked the top selling infomercials each week, and published the top 100 infomercials in *The Greensheet Annual Review*. While the 1999 review (of 1998 infomercial sales) was not yet released, data for the first week of 1999 indicated the top 10 money makers as follows: Billy Blanks' hot exercise video "Tae-Bo" ranked first (and had for several months), followed by Richard Simmons' weight-loss system titled "Move, Groove & Lose." Other top sellers included Carleton Sheets real estate investment system, Express Ware infusion cooker, and Classic Country music collection. Other profitable items included the Making Money business opportunity kit, "Straight Shootin' Golf" training video, and Cellulift cellulite reducing massager.

The 1998 review, rating the 100 highest grossing industry products for 1997, listed the following: Secrets to Making Money, a home business course distributed by National Direct Corporation; Fitness Flyer, a glider-type exerciser, distributed by Guthy-Renker. Get Down the Pounds and Great North American Slim Down, both weight loss systems were also top sellers. Brown 'N' Crisp Microwave cooking bags and the Sobakawa Pillow were also popular.

The only publicly held industry firm was formerly known as National Media Corp., of Philadelphia, which changed its corporate name to e4L in February 1999. Estimated 1998 earnings at the former National Media were $330 million. Some of their infomercial products included the PowerWalk Plus treadmill, Frankie Avalon's Zero Pain topical pain reliever, the Instant Fisherman, GOO Gone, and Tony Little's Target Training System. National Media broadcasts its 3,000 half-hours of programming each week to over 370 million households in 70 countries and in 25 languages. According to the *Los Angeles Daily News*, National Media had four of the top 10 infomercials in 1998, including The Red Devil Portable Outdoor Kitchen and The Great North American Slimdown '98. The industry's largest private firm was Guthy-Renker of Palm Desert, California, with estimated 1998 sales of $500 million. Some of their infomercial products included Personal Power by Tony Robbins, which has generated $250 million in sales over the years, and the Power Rider fitness machine, which has approximately $200 million gross sales.

Another successful firm was privately held Kent & Spiegel Direct, Inc. of Culver City, California with estimated annual revenues of $200 million. The company sold 1 million Ab Flex machines—$180 million in revenues—through infomercials in the mid-1990s.

As of 1997, the company's best-selling product was the Sobakawa Pillow, a pillow filled with buckwheat husks retailing for $29.95, which is said to relieve neck strain and promote better sleep. Kent and Spiegel sold 2.3 million pillows by mid-1997.

AMERICA AND THE WORLD

Industry observers are optimistic about the global potential of infomercials. ERA held a conference in Venice, Italy in 1998, which outlined the spread of infomercials into European markets. That same year discussions with more than 50 local television stations throughout China got underway. Finally, Japan's biggest trading company purchased an almost 20 percent stake in the Asian subsidiary of Guthy-Renker.

RESEARCH AND TECHNOLOGY

Many industry firms have been researching and using the Internet as part of future expansion plans, and it is beginning to pay off. National Media offered products online through their subsidiary, Everything For Less (e4L). Guthy-Renker maintained an extensive Web site, America's Choice Mall, which pitched its own products and included links to dozens of retailers. Some industry analysts believed the Internet would not compete with television until the technology was more widespread and affordable to the average person. Nonetheless, in early 1999, the *San Francisco Chronicle* claimed that "Cyberspace is being overrun" by infomercials. In the same article, Ron Popeil declared "Our stuff is perfect for the Internet." "Steep media rates, a bevy of TV channels and the rapid emergence of electronic commerce as an economic engine have prompted the makers of infomercials to expand onto the Internet," according to the *Chronicle*. Commercial radio stations, some of which sold 28-minute media blocks to industry firms, have also become forums for infomercials.

FURTHER READING

Brennan, Judith I. "Japanese Firm Buying Stake in Guthy-Renker." *Los Angeles Times,* 19 May 1998.

Brownlee, Lisa. "Sobakawa Pillow Is Hit on Infomercials." *Wall Street Journal,* 27 May 1997.

Bunuel, Diego. "FTC, Marketers Settle Infomercial Lawsuits." *Chicago Tribune,* 14 January 1998.

"The Direct Marketing Association." New York: The Direct Marketing Association, 1999. Available from http://www.the-dma.org.

Emert, Carol. "Infomercial Breaks Early Prime Time Barrier." *San Francisco Chronicle,* 16 December 1998.

Frederiksen, Lee. "Internet or Infomercial: Which Will Turn Your Audience On?" *Marketing News,* 20 January 1997.

———. "Is DRTV Right for Me? Seven Considerations Affecting a Direct Response TV Campaign." *Target Marketing,* February 1997.

Gaw, Jonathan. "Media Firm Testing Infomercials On-line." *Los Angeles Times,* 23 November 1998.

Heusten, Frank, and Andrew Zipern. "But Wait, There's More!" 9 June 1997. Available from http://www.foxnews.com.

McLoughlin, Bill. "Infomercials Go Mainstream." *HFN The Weekly Newspaper for the Home Furnishing Network,* 28 October 1996.

Miller, Karen L. "'As Seen on TV' Now Seen All Over the Web" *The New York Times,* 2 January 1998

"Response Magazine Home." Santa Ana, CA: Response Magazine, June 1999. Available from http://www.responsetv.com.

Silverman, Gene. "Infomercials: Analyzing What Went Wrong (and How to Make it Work!)." *Direct Marketing,* July 1996.

Swartz, Jon. "Infomercials Slop Over to the Net." *San Francisco Chronicle,* 25 January 1999.

Whitelaw, Kevin. "Not Just Slicing and Dicing." *U.S. News & World Report,* 9 September 1996.

—Dave Fagan, updated by Tom Deignan

INFORMATION BROKERING

Information brokers are individuals or companies who contract to find information for a fee. Information brokers are also called independent information professionals, information consultants, and information retrieval specialists. What distinguishes these professionals, regardless of terms used to describe them, is that they work independently, rather than acting as part of the library staff or research department of a larger institution or business. Information brokers typically serve more than one client, and a good amount of time is spent on marketing in order to keep the flow of work coming from new and existing customers.

Information brokers are often self-employed small businesspeople in sole proprietorships or partnerships, though sometimes they operate as corporations. Not much capital is required to start an information brokerage, beyond knowledge of information sources and access to libraries and online resources for retrieval. Beginning information brokers generally work from home. A personal computer with a fast modem, a quality printer, Internet access, a fax machine, a two- or three-line phone system with voice-mail, business cards, and stationery are the basic tools needed to start an information brokering business. It is also helpful to have accounts with major online database vendors such as DIALOG, LEXIS-NEXIS, Dow-Jones News Retrieval, or others depending on the subject specialty of the information broker. A certain amount of information on the Internet is free, but not everything is available there, and not everything available is free; many content providers require subscriptions to access full-text articles and reports. Be-

cause timely delivery is critical to the information broker's business paying commercial database fees is often more cost-effective than using free Internet sources exclusively. The commercial vendors' sophisticated search capabilities and superior organization and indexing allow a high degree of precision in retrieval, in contrast to the relatively primitive search engines and often chaotic structure of information on the Internet.

Much attention is paid in the professional press and in various knowledge-worker newsgroups on the Internet to the question of the survival of independent information professionals now that Internet access is becoming ever more ubiquitous. Some successful information brokers believe that the advent of the Internet will actually spur demand for information brokers because the typical client has no interest in researching. Whether they lack the time or the expertise to search themselves, those willing to pay professionals to find information for them will continue to be around. The sheer volume of data that must be sifted through in order to glean what is valuable is intimidating to many present and potential customers of information brokers—as is the time investment that may be involved. The evaluation and filtering roles of trained, knowledgeable, computer-savvy information brokers thus have the potential to become even more marketable because of the efficiencies brokers bring to the Internet. Moreover, corporate downsizing and outsourcing trends of the late 1990s fueled demand for information brokers, since companies had few employees to complete time consuming research tasks. In the late 1990s, there were approximately 1,800 information brokers in 51 countries.

More On MEDICAL INFORMATION SOURCES

In a 1994 report, "Is there a doctor on-line?" *Forbes* magazine commented on the growing availability of medical information in Internet search banks and on CD-ROM for convenient home access. The article discussed the new and innovative databases hosted by a number of university hospitals. Also discussed were medical bulletin board services, the National Library of Medicine's online information service, and medical chat rooms on the Internet. Of particular interest was the fact that "Doctors are now using computers to search . . . consult . . . and keep up with the latest drugs."

Approximately three years later, in February of 1998, the *Journal of the American Medical Association, (JAMA)* published its own feedback of the increasing number of Internet-based health information resources. *JAMA* concluded that the powerful capabilities of the information resources on the Internet offered considerable promise, but were insufficient in their existing state, which lacked highly methodological systems and criteria for evaluating all resources objectively. Authors Alejandro Jadad and Anna Gagliardi concluded, "The Internet is creating new opportunities to improve decisions and communication in health care, but it can also generate many unprecedented problems. . . . If we fail to meet the current challenges, we may . . . [be] moving instead into a health care environment ruled by confusion, battles of opinion, anxiety, and unnecessary conflicts."

ORGANIZATION AND STRUCTURE

The information retrieval industry includes a host of companies providing a wide array of services. The industry's diversity results from the influence of rapidly changing technology, the ease of entry, and the number of unfilled market segments. Brokers can figure out how to fill or create a need in the market using existing technology and can profit, often with only a minor capital investment. Creativity, knowledge of market needs, and technological expertise are the most important capabilities for information brokers. Consequently, industry participants range from large online services with millions of customers to individual entrepreneurs that compile and sell information to a small base of customers. Despite this diversity, however, a few large online service providers generate the majority of industry's revenues.

TYPES OF INFORMATION

Industry observers commonly differentiate business and research brokers from consumer information brokers. Business and research information brokers largely offer numeric and bibliographic data concerning both technical and topical information. Most companies in this segment collect information and articles from primary sources and reconfigure them for electronic access. Companies may offer abstracts and text from periodicals, books, and journals, or financial and trade data, press releases, news updates, and historical company/industry information. Some companies simply obtain large, publicly available government data and repackage it into an easily accessible, understandable electronic format.

Legal and investment brokers lead the industry in terms of subscribers. Marketing, scientific, and library information services also make up another leading segment in the business and research group. The remainder of the companies in this group serves a variety of niche markets. Many of these services are designed specifically to one industry or profession, such as chemical, healthcare, civil engineering, agricultural, banking, insurance, or food service. In addition, many niche services are managed by non-profit organizations. Major players in the 1990s included U.S. firms such as CDB Infotek, Pathfinder, Advanced Research, TR Information, and LEXIS-NEXIS.

Electronic information services targeting the consumer market provide current news and financial information. In addition, though, they offer features such as electronic shopping, recreational bulletin boards and other interpersonal communication domains, weather and sports data, encyclopedias, games, travel information, home and garden advice, and thousands of other offerings. In comparison to business information services, most personal systems are inexpensive, primarily because of the number of users in the market. For instance, many consumer-oriented online services allow subscribers unlimited access for less than $20 per month. In contrast, the effective rate for many business-oriented information databases can exceed several thousand dollars per month.

AIIP

The Association of Independent Information Professionals (AIIP) reported that its membership in the late 1990s exceeded 800 information professionals in 21 countries. Its members include associate members, who earn money as information brokers at least part-time and intend at some point to make it a full-time job; and regular members, who earn a living as full-time information brokers and have been doing so for at least two years. Associate members get the benefits of interaction with peers through a private online listserve or mailing list, the opportunity to list themselves in the AIIP directory, and reduced rates at conferences and continuing education opportunities. Regular members also qualify for group discounts with online vendors like DIALOG and LEXIS-NEXIS and reduced rates for other tools of the trade such as reference books, a major benefit for their businesses.

There is no certification or licensure required to do business as an information broker, and not all information brokers join the same professional organizations. There is not a common body of knowledge or study program, so certification cannot be based on taking a specific course of study as in other professions. The diversity of activities that engage information brokers works against the idea that all practitioners receive the same training. Nor is there one major professional association to oversee the credentialing of information brokers. The AIIP probably comes the closest to being the major professional society and continues to promote itself to individuals earning any part of their incomes as information brokers. The subject specialty chosen by an information broker influences which professional associations they choose to join. Belonging to the professional organization of the subject discipline from which one draws or would like to draw, clients can be valuable both for contacts and to keep up with current topics and issues in the field. Specialized associations of librarians, such as the Medical Libraries Association and Special Libraries Association, can be similarly valuable for current awareness, continuing education, and networking. Associations frequently include chapters and divisions devoted to sub-specialties, increasing the likelihood of finding a group of peers within the larger organization.

Profile

THE AIIP—MODEST BEGINNINGS

In 1987, 26 individuals set their sights on creating a network among themselves and other information specialists, and on assisting struggling entrepreneurs. Coming together in Milwaukee, Wisconsin in 1987, this small, dedicated group formed the Association of Independent Information Professionals (AIIP). It was the first U.S. organization devoted entirely to the field of information brokering.

BACKGROUND AND DEVELOPMENT

Information brokering as a defined professional specialty dates to the 1930s in Europe. The origin was in Paris in 1935, when members of the Societe Francaise de Radiophonie organized a fee-based telephone reference service. Called S'il Vous Plait (SVP), the business was independent of any library or other institution. Though it had some true marketing talent behind it, even persuading the national postal, telephone, and telegraph agency to assign it the letters S, V, and P on the telephone dial so it could be easy to reach, the business was not financially successful until after World War II. Then, under the leadership of Maurice de Turckheim, SVP instituted a subscription fee for the privilege of accessing the service. The idea took hold and established SVP as a successful information brokering business.

In the United States, Matthew Lesko and Roger Summit independently developed information businesses in the 1950s. During the 1960s the American Society for Information Science and pioneering librarians Darlene Waterstreet, Susan Klement, Alice Sizer Warner, and Kelly Warnken put forth the innovative idea that information and librarians should not be restricted to repositories. In the mid-1970s Susan Klement drafted an outline for a course on alternative careers for librarians. The exploration of alternative careers went a step further with the publication in 1980 of Betty-Carol Sellen's *What Else You Can Do with a Library Degree*.

Other landmark publications included the *Directory of Fee-Based Information Services* (1977), first published by Kelly Warnken and produced 20 years later by Helen Burwell and Kelly Warnken's *The Information Brokers: How to Start and Operate Your Own Fee-Based Service* (1981). Sue Rugge, founder of an information-brokering service called Information on Demand, and Alfred Glossbrenner co-authored *The Information Broker's Handbook* in 1992 and updated it to include coverage of the Internet and new technology in 1995. Reva Basch interviewed 35 information professionals, many of them current or former information brokers, for her book, *Secrets of the Super Net Searchers,* published in 1996. This book gives first-hand accounts of how individuals use various tools in this field as well as their views on the future.

In a 1995 article, Alice Sizer Warner compared information brokering of the 1990s to that of the 1970s. A major, obvious difference is the extent to which computers and telecommunications broaden the scope of the brokers' access to information sources. From "heavily depending" on the print resources of local libraries, information brokers today "sometimes forget to check" print sources, so used are they to working online. She found today's information brokers much more specialized and focused. There was little guidance back in the 1970s for newcomers to the field; however, in the late 1990s, aspiring information brokers have the resources of the Association of Independent Information Professionals (AIIP) as well as the knowledge of the first generation of entrepreneurial information consultants to draw upon. Other aspects of the business have changed little. Information brokers must still be resourceful and active in finding customers. Rates of pay for services vary widely, and problems with getting customers to pay continue to plague businesses. According to Warner, the basic guidelines for starting up an information brokering service remain very similar: ". . .work hard, it takes money to make money, be able to weather a slow start, fewer big jobs are better than more little ones, keep overhead low, be well trained and experienced, treat your customers well, run your business like a business."

CURRENT CONDITIONS

The total number of information brokers stood at 1,800 worldwide in 1999, up from 334 in 1984, according to the *Burwell World Directory of Information Brokers.* Depending on the kind of search and information requested, information brokering fees vary considerably. Smaller companies usually charge about $25 for a basic search. Fees for some services of larger companies such as Lexis-Nexis, TR Information, Pathfinder, and Advanced Research start at about $100 a search, while advanced searches run several thousand dollars. Nonetheless, other companies such as CDB Infotek cut its price from $50 to $7 a search in the late 1990s to encourage more searches by its customers, who are mostly insurance companies, lawyers, and police officers.

With corporate downsizing, more companies began to rely on outsourcing in the late 1990s, which drove the information brokering industry. For example, some lawyers rely information brokers to locate facts for cases and some advertising agencies turned to information brokers for marketing research. Moreover, information brokers assist companies of all sizes that lack in-house research departments. Information brokers typically created corporate profiles, analyzed industry trends, retrieved and delivered documents, and gathered data during the late 1990s, according to the *Chicago Tribune.*

The Internet has made a significant contribution to the information brokering profession, particularly as a source for current, unpublished information. Mary Ellen Bates, principal of Bates Information Services, points out that it has also impacted delivery of search results to clients, and even finding clients. The biggest impact, though, has been in raising the awareness of people to the wide variety of information available, Bates says. She predicts that over the waning years of the twentieth century, the industry will experience a shakeout, and people who got into it because they enjoyed surfing the Internet will drop by the wayside due to a lack of subject expertise and research background. Successful information brokers will be the ones able to anticipate trends and have basic search expertise and abilities. These include excellent research skills or the ability to subcontract to those who have them, excellent people skills, the ability to market and network effectively, good time management skills, good business instincts, and the ability to do strategic planning. Bates is optimistic about the future prospects for qualified information brokers: "For every client any one of us has, there are five other people out there who don't know what information brokers are or how to find us. The market is wide open for people who have the expertise to find information. I think the bottleneck is that there just aren't that many people out there who have the full suite of skills necessary to succeed in this business."

Nevertheless, the Internet also became a point of controversy for the industry. In the mid- to late 1990s, incidents of privacy invasion started to soil the image of information brokers. Lexis-Nexis, for example, sold access to names and social security numbers to businesses and individuals through its P-Trak database accessible over the Internet. Consumers responded by demanding that the company remove their information from the database and called for some kind of regulation to prevent the sale of personal information over the Internet. Based on recommendations of the Federal Trade Commission, Congress opted for the industry's self-regulation as part of the Clinton Administration's hands-off Internet policy. Corporate information brokers including Lexis-Nexis and 13 other companies, which account for about 90 percent of the industry's business, agreed to delete personal information such as names, social security numbers, maiden names, and dates of birth from databases upon request. However, the agreement applied only to sales of this information to individuals, not to businesses, although the information brokering firms promised to sell this information only to businesses with legitimate uses for the information. Furthermore, the self-regulation agreement failed to cover the sale of information gleaned from public documents such as property deeds and divorce proceedings.

State and local governments also contributed to privacy invasion by either selling information to brokers or by hawking the information themselves. Maryland's Motor Vehicle Administration, for example, functions as an information broker by executing customized searches of the state's motorist records for a fee. In addition, the state sells a copy of its entire database for those who want it, bringing in $12.9 million in 1996. These documents provide information brokers with confidential information on people such as unlisted phone numbers, social security numbers, and physical details, according to *The Washington Post.*

Information brokers also collect and sell other kinds of information such as medical records, financial histories, and credit reports. Private information like this helps locate deadbeat parents, lost friends and relatives, and fugitives. Furthermore, it provides consumers with instant information on residential real estate values and allows them to research the qualifications of doctors and lawyers. Nonetheless, criminals can easily use it to impersonate, deceive, and stalk people, critics argue, citing a Federal Reserve Board report that suggests identity fraud is rising and that the availability of private data can make it grow even faster.

Europe, on the other hand, has taken a stricter approach, adopting the Data Protection Directive, which prohibits the transfer of commercial data to countries that have lax privacy laws such as the United States. Hence, the Clinton administration and U.S. companies continued conducting negotiations in the late 1990s with European leaders in an effort to convince them that European citizens would not experience privacy violations by U.S. business and information brokers.

INDUSTRY LEADERS

CDB Infotek, Inc. ranks among the country's largest information brokers, according to *Knight-Ridder Tribune Business News.* Based in Santa Ana, California, Infotek is among one of the few national companies hawking personal information taken from public and private records. Furthermore, the company provides access to county, state, and federal public records information such as UCC filings and related documents. Founded in 1982, Infotek boasts of 1,600 databases, containing 3.5 million public records. In 1998, ChoicePoint, Inc. acquired Infotek and Choice-

Point posted sales of $406.5 million in 1998. ChoicePoint also owns another information broker, Equifax, which specializes in credit information. However, ChoicePoint announced its plans to spin off the company in 1999.

International Research Center (IRC) was another leading information broker in the late 1990s. Based in Tempe, Arizona, IRC provides Internet-based searches on public policy, business, industry, technology, and telecommunications. Besides gathering information, IRC also evaluates it and prepares targeted reports according to client specifications. The company's principals have extensive backgrounds in the areas of computer engineering, information technology, and business and finance. The company also publishes the *Internet Resource Guide for Research and Exploration.*

TR Information Services was another industry leader and also provided personal information. The company specializes in pre-employment screening searches, asset searches, and background checks. Miami-based TR Information provides information such as social security numbers, professional licenses, fictitious names, UCC lien filings and affiliated and associated companies, and can also supply TRW consumer and business credit reports.

Several corporate owners exchanged Lexis-Nexis, while the company remained the leading information broker in the country and the world. UK/Dutch publisher Reed Elsevier became the owner of Lexis-Nexis in the late 1990s. Based in Dayton, Ohio, Lexis-Nexis targets the legal, news, and business market, providing full-text documents from law journals and selected periodicals. Founded in 1973, Lexis-Nexis now includes about 14,000 news and business sources and 5,000 legal sources. By 1999, Lexis-Nexis boasted of 1.6 million subscribers. In 1998, Lexis-Nexis booked $363.6 million in sales from its services and employed 7,100 workers. In addition, Lexis-Nexis acquired legal publisher Matthew Bender in 1998.

WORK FORCE

Those who choose information brokering as a career come to it in various ways. Some people become information brokers as the result of losing their jobs or choosing to leave them. The trend toward downsizing in the private sector has affected the information broker industry. Some corporate knowledge workers, be they librarians or other information professionals geared toward research, turn to information brokering as a way to make a living when displaced by reorganizations that eliminate jobs. Skills in information retrieval, evaluating sources, and specialized industry knowledge, along with a network of former work contacts, form a good basis for entering this line of work. Downsizing creates opportunities as well for information brokers when research and writing once done in-house are among the functions companies decide to outsource.

Knowledge workers of assorted backgrounds and experience choose information brokering as a way to increase flexibility in their schedules, such as to balance family responsibilities by working out of the home. The motivation for others is the challenge and satisfaction of self-employment. Others want to concentrate in a special area of interest in more depth than they could working for a library or other employer, so they decide to focus on finding information within that topical area (for a fee) for those not willing or able to find it themselves. There are also those who enter the field straight from library school or other professional or graduate program because they are entrepreneurial by nature. These people attended school for the professional credentials that lend authority to their businesses and to prepare themselves as thoroughly as possible to perform the work.

The 1996-97 edition of the *Occupational Outlook Handbook* forecasts that opportunities will be best for librarians working outside traditional library settings. It predicts that information brokering will be one of the growth areas for those trained in library and information science, along with positions in private corporations and consulting firms. Though positions in public, college, and corporate libraries will see relatively slow growth into the early years of the twenty-first century, entrepreneurial individuals will be able to parlay specialized skills, such as organizing and classifying information and familiarity with the universe of both print and online resources, into new careers as Webmasters, knowledge managers, researchers, and information consultants.

FURTHER READING

Arnold, Stephen E., and Erik S. Arnold. "Vectors of Change: Electronic Information from 1977 to 2007." *Online,* July-August 1997.

Basch, Reva. *Secrets of the Super Net Searchers.* Wilton, CT: Pemberton Press, 1996.

Chandrasekaran, Rajiv. "Governments Find Information Pays." *The Washington Post,* 9 March 1998.

Gullikson, Cindy T. "Information Brokers: Sailing the Sea of Change." *Searcher,* January 1997.

Levine, Marilyn. "A Brief History of Information Brokering." *Bulletin of the American Society for Information Science,* February/March 1995.

Markoff, John. "Pact to Test Controls on Data." *The New York Times,* 18 December 1997.

Rugge, Sue, and Alfred Glossbrenner. *The Information Broker's Handbook.* 2nd ed. New York: McGraw-Hill, 1995.

Sawyer, Deborah C. "Certification for Information Brokers." *Bulletin of the American Society for Information Science,* February/March 1995.

U.S. Department of Labor, Bureau of Labor Statistics. "Teachers, Librarians, and Counselors." *Occupational Outlook Handbook 1996-97.* Washington: GPO, 1996.

Warner, Alice Sizer. "Looking Back, Looking Ahead." *Bulletin of the American Society for Information Science,* February/March 1995.

Wasserman, Elizabeth. "Information Firms Agree to Limited Privacy Rules for Personal Data on Web." *San Jose Mercury News,* 22 December 1997.

Wood, Lamont. "Data Brokers Surfing for Profits Sounds Appealing but Require Special Mix of Talents." *Chicago Tribune,* 17 May 1998.

—Joan Giglierano, updated by Karl Heil

INFORMATION MANAGEMENT SYSTEMS

The field of information management systems, like so many industries based on computer technology, is characterized by consistent change. Whether the result of improvements in hardware and the underlying software, the evolution of the World Wide Web as a medium of information delivery, or fundamental shifts in thinking about the role and use of information in business and industry, information management and the systems used to implement it function in an environment that is rarely the same from one day to the next.

Information management is the means whereby information is collected, identified, and analyzed, then distributed to the points within an organization where decisions are made and customers are served. Information management systems streamline and automate the often complex processes of coordinating a company's many activities with employees, suppliers, and customers.

The field is populated at once by computer industry giants such as IBM and Microsoft, smaller but powerful companies such as PeopleSoft, Sybase, and Oracle, and as-yet-unknown startups with large doses of technological savvy and the fierce desire to reap the benefits of redefining the possibilities of what can be accomplished through technology.

Ours is an increasingly global society wherein rapid, accurate access to vast amounts of disparate information is not only demanded, but increasingly taken for granted. Employee output in the United States is 40 percent higher than it was just 10 years ago; however, businesses still feel the need to reduce costs and move with increasing efficiency in the marketplace. What fills the inevitable gaps created by the necessity to do more with less? Information; timely, accurate information. In that context, information management systems will continue to assume greater prominence while businesses, governments, and individuals become increasingly reliant upon them.

An industry study released in the spring of 1999 estimated sharp growth in the document technologies market through the year 2003. The study, a joint project of the Gartner Group and AIIM International, an information management trade group, projected that the market would grow from about $13 billion in 1998 to more than $40 billion in 2003. The study emphasized the relationship between core document technologies and such emerging technologies as electronic commerce, Web content management, and knowledge management. Among the recommendations that might be drawn from the study is the vital importance of using document technologies in all phases of an operation, whether it's corporate, government, or nonprofit in nature.

ORGANIZATION AND STRUCTURE

An information management system is built on workflow software, groupware, and reporting tools. Workflow software automates the division and assignment of work and removes unnecessary steps along the way. Examples of workflow software include project management, billing, or integrated payroll systems. Groupware incorporates a variety of software, including e-mail and World Wide Web browsers, and hardware, including fax machines and voice mail, to allow employees direct access to the information management system and each other. Reporting tools enable users to retrieve information from the information management system. Examples of reporting tools include online analytical processing tools associated with data warehouses.

With the rise of the Internet and the World Wide Web as ubiquitous and fundamental research tools, issues related to retrieving and organizing information have become increasingly important to a wider and more varied population of information consumers. Libraries, once the primary users of information management systems, no longer have exclusive claim to the need to manage vast pools of wide-ranging data. Businesses, governments, and similar institutions have developed an unrelenting need to use the tools available for controlling a steady, massive inflow and output of information.

Data warehousing and online analytical processing (OLAP) are information repositories and reporting tools that enable users to convert raw data to valuable information. Data warehousing is a variation of data migration that involves moving and transforming data from a variety of systems into a single repository. Online analytical processing software provides interactive access to multidimensional analysis of the data. There is a symbiotic relationship between the data warehouse and the OLAP tools used to mine the information since the repository structure and querying tools operate interdependently.

A data warehouse, as defined by founding father William H. Inmon, centers around a subject orientation, includes normalized data, and incorporates nonvolatile content (archival data that does not change once recorded). The subject orientation of a data warehouse may include, for example, products, customers, and inventory. The data warehouse receives information on these subjects from a variety of operational databases within the organization such as transactional (invoice databases) or records (marketing databases). The data received from these different databases is frequently coded and described in different ways and must be normalized prior to use. Disparate databases, data types, and data elements can be handled by a gateway within the information management system to integrate enterprise-wide knowledge into one useable whole. SQL (structured query language) translators accomplish the task of interpreting a variety of database types, elements, and messages from standard relational databases. Essentially, a database begins by talking to an SQL server like Oracle 7 or

IBM's DataJoiner. The SQL server provides the necessary translation using a global data dictionary and passes the information onto the next database. The internal formats of different databases vary according to the business concepts behind the database design. Thus, while the translation may be technically accurate, the SQL solution means data may require additional manipulation.

Alternately, Web-based information management systems rely on the system architecture of the client-server and a common user interface to integrate information between disparate databases. A client-server system consists of a server (a computer that contains information and serves it up at the request of a client computer) and a client (a computer that asks for information from a server). Client-server solutions can result in a lack of data cohesiveness. While operational databases are updated regularly with deletions and insertions, the data warehouse is a read-only environment in which information is loaded, then read through a series of snapshots. As the snapshots are stacked together, it becomes possible to examine data across layers of geography or time, as well as across the traditional two dimensional columns and rows of the single snapshots. The content of the data warehouse includes integrated data, detailed and summarized data, historical data, and metadata. Metadata describe the context of the information.

OLAP tools extend the architecture of the data warehouse by reading and aggregating large groups of diverse data. Richard Finkelstein, president of Performance Computing Inc., notes that the objective of OLAP is to analyze these relationships and look for patterns, trends, and exceptional conditions. The key characteristic of an OLAP is that it provides a multidimensional conceptual view of the data. Variations of OLAP include ROLAP (relational online analytic processing) and DOLAP (desktop online analytical processing). Data mining, another form of online analysis, creates a model from current information and projects this model onto another scenario where information is nonexistent. One drawback to an OLAP system is that it often requires the use of a proprietary OLAP database or warehouse without the same capacity as a standard relational database. ROLAP software allows users to make queries of a relational data warehouse.

Decentralized data and different databases abound in corporate America. Information management systems piece together information from disparate sources. Simple component information management systems link databases together based on their involvement with a part or product. For example, an inventory reorder system is a kind of information management system that tracks inventory stock and updates all databases for reorder, shipment, and payment. Because component information management systems are based on a preexisting product or need, such as the search for a part, gateways and search engines are pre-coordinated. Evolving from these product-based systems, a more complex information management system emerges to allow employees to post-coordinate their information retrieval needs. Workflow software, groupware, and reporting tools share information with each other so that, for example, employees can specify what kind of information is desired and in what format it will appear. This integration of information represents a progressive movement from piecemeal business data towards business knowledge for employee, supplier, and customer alike.

TRENDS

Many companies have already embraced Internet technology, and many more are now looking to one of the spin-offs of that technology: intranets. An intranet is an internal information system based on Internet technology such as Web services, transfer protocols, and the Hypertext Markup Language, or HTML. Although intranets use technological concepts that are prevalent on the Internet and World Wide Web, the information contained on an intranet stays securely within the company or organization managing it. Intranets are private business networks based on Internet and World Wide Web standards, but they are designed to be utilized internally. In other words, random Internet users cannot access a company's intranet; only those individuals granted specific access to an intranet can use it.

Like the Internet, intranets often require little or no training, as people who are familiar with navigating the Internet can usually become equally proficient at using intranets. Intranets can be easily maneuvered within graphics-based Web browsers, which are standard on every hardware platform in the intranet. This facilitates greater remote access without the use of wide-area-networks.

The connection between intranets and information management systems is two-fold. First, Information Management Systems are fundamental for any company trying to take advantage of intranets, since they provide the freedom to fine-tune access to data, facilitate the targeting of specific information to specific people, simplify delivery of information, and in-

corporate databases. Second, using intranets in conjunction with information management systems reduces the costs of software, hardware, and maintenance. Indeed, the two systems are so well-suited that most information management vendors are now adapting their products for intranet use, and with ever more information to manage and share, it is a trend that is sure to continue.

Emerging from the use of intranets is the trend toward the next level: extranets. Extranets are business-to-business networks operating over the Internet. When two companies allow each other access to parts of their intranets, they have created an extranet. Extranets can provide regulated and secure communications between companies, and are frequently used to aid in customer service, to facilitate transaction processing, and as an adjunct to marketing.

A number of software applications making it easier to set up and use extranets were introduced in the late 1990s. With increased ease of use and the convenience to customers and business partners of unimpeded access to a company's communications and information core, it is expected that extranet use will continue to increase dramatically until extranets become as prevalent in corporate information management systems as networks. The ease with which they let companies and customers interact will be a dominant factor in the increased use of extranets. For example, no more than 5 percent of Motorola's computer group customers used the company's extranet in January 1998. However, company executives reported that well over 50 percent were utilizing the extranet by the spring of 1999. Business-to-business use of extranets will also be crucial to their wider acceptance. For example, some companies, such as wood products maker Boise Cascade Corp., are moving their supply chains to the extranet.

Leading software manufacturer Lotus predicts that "the Internet/Intranet phenomenon will continue to reshape how people play, work, and interact in all conceivable (and maybe some inconceivable) ways. A wired world of global networks is fast replacing the world-in-a-desktop computing model." IBM's Network Computing Framework, integrated through Lotus's Domino Web Server, is an example of such an interconnected system.

BACKGROUND AND DEVELOPMENT

The first functioning document retrieval system to use electronics was demonstrated in Dresden, London, and Paris in 1931, according to Michael Buckland, Professor at the University of California, Berkeley's School of Information Management and Systems. Well before digital computers, Emmanuel Goldberg's "statistical machine" combined photocell, circuitry, and microfilm for document retrieval.

But even if Goldberg's machine provided the first hints of what an electronic information management system could do, it was not until the advent of the computer that information management began to evolve and increasingly complex systems became necessary to handle the large amounts of data generated.

The first prototype of a working business computer, the 409, was introduced in 1951. Information was fed to the 409 via a refrigerator-sized punch card unit. Punch cards—stiff cards in which holes were actually punched via machine—provided the programming and data for early computers as they "read" the sequence of holes. However, this physical means of introducing data to a computer created an environment in which an error could result in many lost hours of work. Early computer operators did not have the convenience of a backspace or delete key.

Yet information management systems evolved from the punch card machines to mainframes and spools of magnetic tape. The SQL language was introduced in the 1970s via a database system called System R. The Multics Relational Data Store (MRDS) was released in June 1976 and is believed to be the first relational database management system offered by a major computer vendor, in this case, Honeywell Information Systems, Inc.

In the 1970s, IBM mainframe computers were the prevalent systems found in business usage, whereas mini-computer platforms such as AS/400 and VAX/VMS dominated in the 1980s. The 1980s also saw the rise of the personal computer as both an individual and business tool.

It is, however, the evolution of the Internet and World Wide Web in the 1990s as a medium of information archiving and dissemination that continues to have the greatest impact upon the field of information management systems. In 1970, the average Fortune 500 company might house 8 billion characters of data in its electronic storage banks. By the year 2000, it is predicted that a similar organization will have the need to control and manage 400 trillion characters of electronic data. Current trends strongly suggest that much of this information will be manipulated by Web technology on the Internet and through corporate intranets and extranets.

CURRENT CONDITIONS

Information management systems appear in a variety of ways and for a variety of reasons. A human resource information management system (HRIMS), for example, concentrates its focus on payroll, benefits, and status information. Laboratory Information Management Systems (LIMS) are typically designed specifically for the analytical laboratory. LIMS connect the analytical instruments in the lab to one or more workstations or PCs. When data is collected by these instruments, it is forwarded by an interface to the PC where the data is stored, sorted, and organized into reports and other meaningful forms of output based on the type of information requested by the system users. Financial institutions benefit greatly from information management systems when customer account data and transaction histories are integrated. Coeur Business International offers an information management system for value-added resellers called VARoffice. VARoffice features a knowledge-base navigator to find solutions to common problems, a technical support log, and a marketing events management system. The program can be customized with Microsoft Access, VisualBasic, and an SQL server. Businesses that rely heavily on statistical analysis, such as real estate investment firms, also benefit from information management systems. Many buy-sell decisions are made according to a wide variety of market indicators. Viewing data multidimensionally across time and geography can provide invaluable information for investment decisions using an information management system. The Security Capital Group uses a multidimensional OLAP database for critical budgeting and analytical tasks.

Among their advantages, information management systems provide quick access to multiple databases holding information such as engineering parts, financial transactions, textbook titles, and customer contacts. Information management systems also encourage design reuse and reduce the time necessary to set up a new part, coordinate schedules, or change workflow processes. The Internet and the World Wide Web have spurred innovation and development of information management systems by capitalizing on the inherent network functionality of the Internet and the universality and ease of the Web browser. It is possible for all workers, suppliers, and customers to enjoy the same common interface without regard to physical location or time. Reduced hardware and software costs are prime benefits of a Web-based information management system. The formerly separate processes of document management and workflow are two applications now merging into one larger system on the World Wide Web.

Information management systems have permitted several companies and organizations to overcome costly, stifling, and sometimes dangerous business problems. The Zurich, Switzerland, police have implemented a client-server-based information system that links all police officers with a central database on suspects, crimes, and emergencies. Laptop computers allow officers to gain immediate access to central databases. This information management system speeds up the search process, allowing officers to follow up on leads immediately.

Lufthansa Air Cargo has replaced its old system, utilizing separate databases for freight depending on its point of origin, with a system that allows Lufthansa to track each piece of cargo at every stage along the delivery process. With this information, Lufthansa can develop specialized services for customers. By increasing the effectiveness of their freight operations, the company can build better relations with customers and improve profits.

Micro Stamping, Inc. cut an entire work day out of its payroll workload by putting an information management and time tracking system in place. The company chose the TC-1 Labor Management System from Datamatics Management Services as their payroll solution. The system is based on a bar-coded identity tag that employees use to gain access to the building and track job costing. It took some time for the employees to become comfortable and proficient with the system, with the greatest improvements being made once they began to equate using the cards with getting paid. The TC-1 Labor Management system is available for $4,000 for the first 200 employees.

Green Mountain Energy Resources (GMER) of South Burlington, Vermont, relies on the technological edge provided by an extranet and a data warehouse to provide the foundation of its retail marketing of electricity and electric services. GMER trades information with nearly two dozen vendors over a combination of secured Internet connections and leased lines. In addition, GMER employees can access the company's data warehouse, containing detailed customer information, through an extranet connected to the outside vendor who maintains the data warehouse. Although GMER's initial use for the data was zeroing in on customer profiles for improved marketing efforts, the company expects to use the information it collects to customize its offerings in order to appeal to a greater range of customers.

The Wave, a Web-based information management system from Century Computing Inc. located in Laurel, Maryland, uses a customized interface and integrated software and databases to expedite and improve the information-seeking process. At Williams & Wilkins, a Baltimore publishing company, using the Wave means avoiding the search process for product information. Williams & Wilkins invested almost $225,000 in the Wave, which consists of a Microsoft SQL server and PageBlazer, an application-development interface developed by The Sapphire Group Inc. of Fair Oaks, Virginia. In the future, the Wave will incorporate workflow management programs and an extranet for distributors; an extranet is a network only available to certain external companies and individuals in the same way that an intranet is only available to the employees of the company.

In 1997 PeopleSoft, Inc., one of the leading producers of powerful information management systems software, faced a problem that was best solved using information management systems and techniques. So many customers wanted the newest version of the company's premiere product, PeopleSoft 7, that they were demanding it three months ahead of schedule. In a field where even shipping software upgrades on time can be a commendable achievement, PeopleSoft's dilemma was that customers wanted its newest product early. Unfortunately, the rushed release of such a complex piece of software as PeopleSoft 7 could lead to an inferior product, undermining the success that had created the early demand in the first place. Phil Cullen, vice-president of quality for PeopleSoft, Inc., approached this dilemma by deciding to turn the company's own particular information management expertise inward. Using Web-based tools and a Lotus Notes database, along with a checklist of "universal criteria" that 50 individual departments could use to analyze the advantages and disadvantages of an early release, Cullen's team plunged into the exploration process. Within two weeks, thousands of pieces of information and minute details of input and opinion had been collected from PeopleSoft employees worldwide. Cullen's team was able to synthesize all the feedback into data that ultimately allowed PeopleSoft's upper management to make the informed decision to approve an early release. In 1998 PeopleSoft, Inc. had $1.3 billion in revenues from offices in the United States, Canada, Europe, the Pacific Rim, Central and South America, and Africa. They are headquartered in Pleasanton, California, and employ 7,032 people.

In late 1998 IntelliCorp, a leader in the information management industry, announced the formation of an industry leadership council made up of executives from companies active in information management. Council members were drawn from such prestigious companies as Andrews Inc., Deere & Company, Coca Cola Company, Fluoroware, TRW, and Nestle USA. The group held a two-day meeting in November 1998 to consider some of the more pressing challenges facing the industry as the millennium neared an end. Assessing IntelliCorp's initiative after the council's first meeting, Marie Fuggle of Nestle USA concluded that it "was an excellent forum to discuss today's pressing business process management issues, such as application integration, data integrity, and cleansing." Of data cleansing, which the council found to be one of the most costly and least anticipated expenses during implementations, Fuggle said: "I've seen double-digit man years spent to cleanse fewer than 100,000 records; there is tremendous potential to dramatically reduce these costs."

IntelliCorp, headquartered in Mountain View, California, suggested that another critical issue facing the industry is the need to stage global system rollouts in a manner that is cost-effective but still ensures continuity of corporate objectives and business processes. "Given today's requirements for daily information management between divisions and sites, corporations are looking for ways to save time and resources," according to Colin Bodell, IntelliCorp's chief operating officer. "We are developing tools and training that reduce the time and resources required to manage and control ERP systems throughout their life cycles-and make data easy for nontechnical managers to use." Elaborating on IntelliCorp's rationale for setting up

the leadership council, Ken Haas, president and CEO, said, "It's vital for us to review industry trends and the direction in which we are moving with leaders in the information management industry." He said hosting the meeting of the council helped the company to uncover "some new areas where we can add value to our customers in today's business climate."

Dramatic growth in the document technologies market was predicted by a study unveiled in April 1999 by AIIM International and the Gartner Group. The study, which was designed by AIIM, an industry trade group, and carried out by Gartner, predicted the market would reach nearly $42 billion in 2003. Emphasizing the role of the Internet in accelerating market growth, AIIM President John Mancini said the study was "an encapsulation of a vibrant market, energized by the emergence of the Web. Most organizations reported that they expect to see their spending rates more than double as they implement document technologies over the next five years. This illustrates document technologies are anchoring many of the up and coming applications such as E-commerce and knowledge management."

INDUSTRY LEADERS

Oracle, Sybase, and IBM all provide SQL gateways and OLAP software for use in an information management system. Oracle Corp., based in Redwood City, California, posted net income of $814 million on

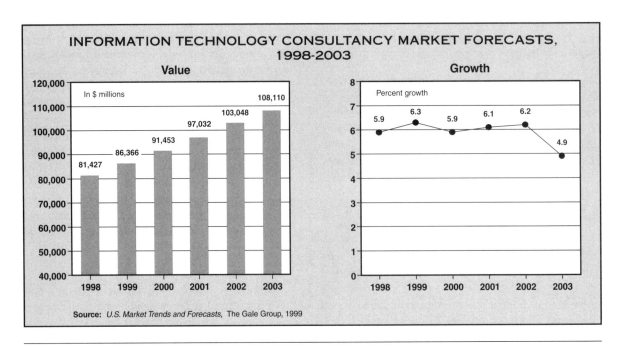

INFORMATION TECHNOLOGY CONSULTANCY MARKET FORECASTS, 1998-2003

Value

In $ millions

1998	1999	2000	2001	2002	2003
81,427	86,366	91,453	97,032	103,048	108,110

Growth

Percent growth

1998	1999	2000	2001	2002	2003
5.9	6.3	5.9	6.1	6.2	4.9

Source: *U.S. Market Trends and Forecasts*, The Gale Group, 1999

revenue of $7.1 billion in fiscal 1998, ended May 31, 1998. The company employed about 36,800 worldwide as of late 1998. Sybase Inc., headquartered in Emeryville, California, and the employer of nearly 4,200, reported a net loss of $93.1 million on sales of $867.5 million in 1998. Giant IBM, based in Armonk, New York, posted net income of $6.3 billion on sales of $81.7 billion in 1998 and employed more than 290,000 worldwide.

Other players in this market niche include Informix; Cognos, Inc.; and Arbor Software. Informix produces Metacube, while Cognos offers Powerplay and Impromptu (a reporting and querying package), and Arbor Software makes Essbase. In 1996, Arbor Software integrated Essbase with a reporting tool called Crystal Info and Crystal Reports from Seagate Software Company. Oracle revised and renamed its reporting software to incorporate OLAP functions into the Oracle relational database. Oracle's renamed product is called Discover. In April 1996, PeopleSoft Inc. began bundling Cognos PowerPlay and Impromptu OLAP tools and Arbors Essbase with its applications software.

A number of companies offer component or parts information management systems. Empart Technologies offers a product called EMPART. Other Industry leaders in the area of component information management systems are Aspect Development Inc. and Information Handling Systems. Aspect Development offers a product called Explore, while Information Handling Systems produces a component information management system called CapsXpert. Both cover more than a million parts and offer specialized search capabilities. In July 1997, Aspect introduced a new search tool called SmartMatch that allowed users to search through large databases and find parts under different naming conventions. Another company, Team Corp., offers EDA-Bridge, a Windows-based component information management system. In contrast, at least two companies offer a component information management system without a centralized database. Elixir (Incases Engineering) relies on Internet access to provide a wide variety of parts data and was priced at about $40,000 in 1997. Less expensively, OrCAD features Capture Enterprise Edition, offering parts management, parts searching, and links to online corporate databases and sold for $1,500 in 1997.

In 1998 Aspect Development Inc., based in Mountain View, California, earned more than $16 million on sales of $86.4 million and employed 659. Information Handling Systems Group Inc., the U.S. subsidiary of Netherlands-based Information Handling

Services, is based in Englewood, Colorado. The company, which is privately held, generated sales of $475 million in fiscal 1998—a 46.6 percent increase over sales in fiscal 1997. Worldwide the company employs about 3,200. In January 1997 Information Handling Systems and Team Corp. agreed to jointly develop and market an interface between CapsXpert and Explore. OrCAD Inc., based in Beaverton, Oregon, in April 1997 purchased the EDA Bridge from Team Corp., significantly expanding its leadership in the worldwide component information management systems market. OrCAD, with about 260 employees, posted net income of $3 million on revenue of $47.7 million in 1998. Sales were up more than 84 percent from the previous year, while net earnings showed an increase of 87.5 percent over 1997.

Computer Associates International Inc., characterized by chairman and CEO Charles B. Wang as the world's leading developer of client-server solutions and a world leader in mission-critical business software, offers financial and human resources management, products for Internet and Web development, and multiple-access database management systems, among many other offerings. Computer Associates, headquartered in Islandia, New York, reported net income of $1.2 billion on sales of $4.7 billion in fiscal year 1998, ended March 31, 1998. The company employed more than 11,000 worldwide. IntelliCorp, based in Mountain View, California, is one of the nation's leading providers of ERP (enterprise resource planning) life cycle management products and services. The company reported for fiscal 1998, ending June 30, 1998, a net loss of $700,000 on revenue of $24.4 million. IntelliCorp employed 138 people as of late 1998.

AMERICA AND THE WORLD

Although many of the major players in the information management systems industry have headquarters in the United States, these providers also maintain an extensive worldwide presence. Cognos, for example, has corporate headquarters in Ottawa, Canada, with U.S. sales headquarters in Burlington, Massachusetts. Cognos also has more than 32 offices worldwide in such countries as Australia, France, Germany, Hong Kong, Japan, and the United Kingdom. Lotus maintains offices in several different countries, while Arbor Software has corporate headquarters in Sunnyvale, California, and European, Middle Eastern, and African headquarters in London, England. Sybase has its world headquarters in Emeryville, California, but has other departments located in 63 countries including France, Canada, Italy, Germany, and China.

One of the industry's major software providers, SAP-AG, is headquartered in Walldorf, Germany, but also maintains several international offices.

Testimony to the growing internationalization of the information management industry came in April 1999 with the announcement of the merger of the world's leading information management trade groups. AIIM International and the International Information Management Congress (IMC) announced their merger on April 14, 1999. The combined organization will carry the name of AIIM International. In announcing the merger, AIIM President John Mancini said "this combination creates a single international resource to develop more effective and timely industry events, reports, studies, and standards."

RESEARCH AND TECHNOLOGY

In February 1998 the World Wide Web Consortium approved the extensible markup language (XML) as a standard. XML, a metalanguage that provides information about data, comes from the same common background as HTML, but is considerably more powerful and permits more efficient structure and easier exchange of data than HTML.

The advantage of XML is that it is expected to streamline electronic commerce, making it easier for companies to conduct business in the online world. XML will ease existing difficulties in sharing information on an intranet, and will allow Web searches to become more detailed and sophisticated. In addition, whereas HTML allows users to only view data, XML will allow the manipulation of data inside a browser. Microsoft included XML support in Internet Explorer 4.0, and Netscape Communications plans for Navigator 5.0 to be equipped with XML support.

A number of vendors are already producing products that use XML as a basis. For example, Sequoia Software Corp. provides an XML transaction server that lets different applications share data. Marquette Medical Systems of Milwaukee, Wisconsin, plans a Web-enabled version of its cardiovascular monitoring system that will use XML tags to consolidate and post information from various departments on a hospital intranet. (Also see the essay in this book entitled XML.)

Lotus Corp. also sees other technological trends that will continue to shape the world of information and information management. For example, e-commerce, or electronic commerce, based on the 64 percent annual growth of the Internet as a business medium and perhaps fueled by the expansion of XML, will require increased delivery of electronic catalogs and customized shopper information. Lotus predicts that improved levels of Internet Security and the merging of messaging, groupware, and the Web will allow e-commerce levels to grow to an annual volume of $300 billion within the early years of the next decade. Lotus also believes that three-dimensional data will soon be available over the Web via Virtual Reality Modeling Language (VRML).

Intranets and data warehouses will continue to proliferate, Lotus predicts, and push technology will make it easier to establish customized methods for delivering exactly what information a person wants from the vast store of material available electronically, even if a customer does not really know what might be available.

Other technologies will continue to aid the evolution of information management systems, particularly in Web-based applications. Java, Sun Microsystems's platform-independent programming language, is being used for several intranet applications (such as Novasoft's NovaWeb) and in document management systems (IntraNet's Intra.doc! 3.0). Intra.doc!, for example, permits the immediate building and posting of custom Web pages based on a customer's unique requests. The pages contain the requested information, appropriate links, and ordering information. Lotus reports that more than 1,000 IBM and Lotus programmers are working full-time on integrating Java technology. "Designed from the start for networked applications, this new programming language builds bridges where barriers used to be." Being platform-independent, Java applications can run on any computer and will not be hindered by the perpetual PC vs. Mac obstacles. The phrase to remember, Lotus says, is "Write once, use anywhere."

FURTHER READING

"15 Trends to Watch: From E-commerce to Chatting with Your Computer." Lotus. Available from http://www .lotus.com.

Adra Systems, Inc. "Intranets and Information Management Systems." Available from http://www.pdmic.com/articles/ wpintranet.html.

AIIM International, 1999, s.v. "AIIM International and IMC Combine," 5 May 1999. Available from http://www.aiim.org/ events/pressroom/aiim_imccombine.html.

AIIM International, 1999, s.v. "AIIM International/Gartner Group Worldwide Study: 'State of the Document Technologies Market, 1997-2003' Projects Will Grow to $41.6 Billion by 2003," 5 May 1999. Available from http://www.aiim.org/events/pressroom/gartner.html.

"Aspect Development Inc." *Hoover's Online,* 12 May 1999. Available from http://www.hoovers.com/capsules/51231.html.

Babcock, Charles. "Chaos Brews Beneath Client/Server Facade." *Computerworld,* 23 September 1996.

Balderston, Jim. "Push Aims to Get Smarter." *Infoworld Electric,* 26 May 1997.

Buckland, Michael. "Emmanuel Goldberg and His Statistical Machine, 1927." Available from http://www.sims.berkeley.edu/~buckland/goldberg.html.

———. "Emmanuel Goldberg, Pioneer of Information Science." Available from http://www.sims.berkeley.edu/~buckland/statistical.html.

Carrillo, Karen M. "PIM For the Enterprise Lotus Integrates Personal Information Manager with Notes and Domino." *InformationWeek,* 19 May 1997.

Castelluccio, Michael. "Data Warehouses, Marts, Metadata, OLAP/ROLAP, and Data Mining: A Glossary." *Management Accounting,* October 1996.

"Citibank Debuts Information Management System." *Operations Management,* 21 October 1996.

"Client/Server Systems Rules-Driven Searches, New User Interface Added Aspect Attacks Component-Data Management." *EE Times,* 21 April 1997.

Cole, Barb. "PeopleSoft Integrates OLAP Tool." *Network World,* 8 April 1996.

"Computer Associates International Inc." *Hoover's Online,* 12 may 1999. Available from http://www.hoovers.com/capsules/10383.html.

Dalton, Gregory. "XML Becomes A Standard; Vendors Ready Products-Language Likely to Boost E-Commerce, Ease Web Searches." *Information Week,* 16 February 1998.

Darling, Charles R. "Datamining for the Masses." *Datamation,* February 1997.

Darrow, Barbara. "Client/Server Software." *Computer Reseller News,* 3 June 1996.

"EDA Software System Manages Parts Data." *EE Times,* 16 December 1996.

"EDA Software Uses Indexed Fuzzy Matching Aspect Spins A Smart Tool to Broaden Search for Parts." *EE Times,* 14 July 1997.

"EDA-Tool Users Can Tap CapsXpert Component Database IHS, Team Forge Access Deal." *EETimes,* 20 January 1997.

"Empart Technologies Delivers World's Most Powerful Parts Information Management System: Company Announces Availability of EMPART Viewer and EMPART Publisher." *Business Wire,* 27 August 1996.

Esterson, Emily. "A Shock to the System." *Inc. Technology #1.* Available from http://www.inc.com/incmagazine/archives/15980501.html.

"The FAQs About OLAP." *Wall Street & Technology,* July 1996.

Georing, Richard. "Acquisitions Involve Pioneers of Windows-Based Tools, OrCAD, PADS Make Small But Strategic Buys." *EE Times,* 21 April 1997.

Gupta, Vivek R. "An Introduction to Data Warehousing." System Services Corp., August 1997. Available from http://system-services.com/dwintro.htm.

Henson, Row. "HRIMS for Dummies: A Practical Guide to Technology Implementation." *HR Focus,* November 1996.

Hinrichs, Randy J. *Intranets: What's the Bottom Line?* New York: Sunsoft/Prentice Hall, 1997.

Hise, Phaedra. "Human Resources: Hitting Pay Dirt." *Inc. Technology #2,* 1998. Available from http://www.inc.com/incmagazine/archives/16980891.html.

Horowitz, Alan S. "Year of the Extranet At Last?" *Information Week Online,* 5 January 1998.

Inmon, W.H. "The Data Warehouse and Data Mining." *Communications of the ACM,* November 1996.

"IntelliCorp Inc." *Hoover's Online,* 12 May 1999. Available from http://www.hoovers.com/capsules/45818.html.

"IntelliCorp Leadership Council Highlights Trends in Business Process Management." *M2 PressWIRE,* 20 November 1998.

"International Business Machines Corporation." *Hoover's Online,* 12 May 1999. Available from http://www.hoovers.com/capsules/10796.html.

"An Introduction to Lims." *LIMsource.* Available from http://www.limsource.com/intro.html.

Leon, Mark. "Query, Reporting Tools Offer Data Access, OLAP Functions." *InfoWorld,* 21 October 1996.

"Lufthansa Air Cargo." Unisys. Available from http://www.digital.com/SRC/personal/Paul_McJones/System_R/mrds.html.

Marshall, Martin. "The Connectivity Toll Gateways Let Disparate Databases Communicate But the Price Is Performance, Time, and Money." *Communications Week,* 20 November 1995.

McKinley, Tony. "1997: Predictions for the Future." *Imaging World,* 1 January 1997.

"Multics Relational Data Store (MDRS)." Available from http://www.digital.com/SRC/personal/Paul_McJones/System_R/mrds.html.

"Oracle Corporation." *Hoover's Online,* 12 May 1999. Available from http://www.hoovers.com/capsules/14337.html.

"OrCAD Adds Component Management Tool." *EE Times,* 28 October 1996.

"Parts Data for the Desktop." *EE Times,* 24 February 1997.

Patel, Jeetu, and Clark Brady. "Architecture Fit for an Intranet." *Information Week Online,* 23 March 1998.

Petzinger, Jr., Thomas. "Businesses Make a Date to Battle Year 2000 Problem," *Wall Street Journal,* date unknown. Available from http://www.fastcompany.com/online/14/humane.html.

"Research Overview." University of California-Berkeley School of Information Management and Systems. Available from http://info.berkeley.edu/research/overview.html.

Richman, Dan. "Oracle Develops OLAP." *Computerworld,* 11 March 1996.

Roberts, Paul. "Humane Technology: PeopleSoft." *Fast Company,* April/May 1998. Available from http://www.fastcompany.com/online/14/humane.html.

Ryabn, Bill. "The Computer Age Began in a Barn." *New York Times,* 29 March 1998.

Spinner, Karen. "Unlocking the Data Warehouse with OLAP." *Wall Street & Technology.* Winter 1997.

Stein, Tom. "JumboSports Inventory Problem Stores Flooded with Excess Products." *Information Week,* 14 July 1997.

"Sybase Inc." *Hoover's Online,* 12 May 1999. Available from http://www.hoovers.com/capsules/15350.html.

"System R." Available from http://www.digital.com/SRC/personal/Paul_McJones/System_R/.

Taft, Darryl K. "CBI Aims to Make A VARs Day." *Computer Reseller News,* 9 June 1997.

"Union Bank of Switzerland." Unisys. Available from http://corp2.unisys.com/infomgmt/ubs.html.

Unruh, James A. "Information: Your Most Valuable Asset." Available from http://corp2.unisys.com/infomgmt/im_primer.html.

Vadlamudi, Pardhu. "PeopleSoft Forms Partnerships to Add OLAP." *InfoWorld,* 22 April 1996.

Walsh, Jeff. "Document-Management Products Unveiled at AIIM." *InfoWorld Electric,* 12 May 1998.

Waltner, Charles. "Up-To-Data Publisher Uses Information Management System to Centralize Product Data." *Information Week,* 26 May 1997.

"Zurich Canton Police Department." Unisys. Available from http://corp2.unisys.com/infomgmt/zurich_police.html.

—Tona Henderson, updated by Don Amerman

INTERNET SERVICE PROVIDERS

By the mid-1990s, the Internet had become a common tool for communication and information dissemination and was no longer an arcane network for academia, the military, and technology organizations. By 1998, Internet service providers (ISPs) confronted not only escalating demand but also changes in the kind of services provided. As the price of computer hardware decreased and the functionality of software increased, and as more companies began to compete in the Internet service industry, customers started flocking to the Internet. By 1996 the stampede of Internet users increased even more dramatically as competition drove prices down, thus creating a quasi industry standard Internet access charge of $19.95 for unlimited monthly service. However, this method of charging customers appeared flawed to many small and large providers who reported losing money with such a pricing strategy. As of 1997, Netcom On-Line Communications Services Inc., which had matched the competitive $19.95 rate, led a campaign to begin charging higher rates and other companies followed Netcom's example. In 1998 America Online, Microsoft Network, and AT&T WorldNet, among others, implemented new price strategies that eliminated the $19.95 flat rate for unlimited use. Nonetheless, many small and medium-size ISPs continued offering flat rates at or below $19.95.

Although many companies inundated the market, the larger ISPs posted exponential revenue increases in the late 1990s: Netcom and America Online, Inc. (AOL) both more than doubled their previous years' sales. In addition, as the competition heats up, these companies have been able to increase the number of subscriptions in their services. In 1998, America On-line led ISPs with over 16 million subscribers, with CompuServe Corporation coming in second with 2.5 million. The Microsoft Network (MSN) posted about 2 million subscribers after less than two years of operation. MSN even remained ahead of telephone giant AT&T, a company some analysts predicted would dominate the market. In a complex 1998 buyout, long-distance carrier WorldCom Inc. acquired CompuServe and transferred CompuServe's consumer subscribers to AOL. Although the CompuServe consumer service remained distinct from AOL's, the move left AOL with a subscriber base of nearly 16 million. For its part, WorldCom, the fourth-largest U.S. long-distance provider, obtained all of CompuServe's corporate clientele as well as AOL's corporate-market Internet subsidiary ANS Communications. Significantly, the acquisition would catapult WorldCom to the forefront of commercial Internet access service.

The industry faces persistent changes in customer demands. While the first few major Internet service providers focused on proprietary network access and services, in the late 1990s most companies simply provided access to the World Wide Web portion of the Internet, as well as e-mail service. Those that started as proprietary services have redirected their content or gone bankrupt. ISPs also faced the challenge of providing faster Internet connections and relieving Internet congestion during this period.

The United States has about 30 million Internet users. Although the industry's revenues soared in the late 1990s with rising numbers of subscribers, many of the large ISPs, which control about 56 percent of the market, reported low profits or losses. Because of heightened competition in the industry, analysts expect the number of ISPs to drop from 6,000 in 1998 to about 1,500 in the early 2000s. In addition, ISPs are forecast to continue merging and being acquired by telephone companies as profiting through standard Internet access remained elusive in the late 1990s. ISPs posted sales of approximately $10.7 billion in 1998 and sales are forecast to more than double by 2000.

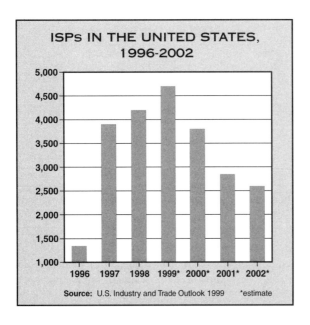

ISPs IN THE UNITED STATES, 1996-2002

Source: U.S. Industry and Trade Outlook 1999   *estimate

ORGANIZATION AND STRUCTURE

Internet service is delivered in a myriad of ways and is directed toward several distinct markets. Subscribers may access the service through a dial-up line using a conventional phone line, through a special dial-up line such as Integrated Systems Digital Network (ISDN) or similar enhanced phone-line technology, through a satellite receiver dish, through coaxial cable as used by cable television services, or through a direct connection via dedicated line such as a high-speed T1 cable. Mode of access often varies by market. In addition to the consumer market, corporations purchase Internet services as end users (e.g., for e-mail access, Web site hosting, and information retrieval) and as resellers (e.g., purchasing high-speed access and offering local service to consumers or other businesses).

Two types of providers serve the consumer market: proprietary ones, like AOL and CompuServe, and access-only ones, like Netcom and AT&T WorldNet. Besides access to the public domain of the Internet, primarily through the World Wide Web, proprietary services offer exclusive content to subscribers, such as newspapers, popular periodicals, entertainment journals, and so forth. In contrast, standard access providers deal only in Internet access.

The Telecommunications Act of 1996 provides the legislative backdrop for Internet policies of the late 1990s and the next millennium. In addition, the Federal Communications Commission (FCC) restructured phone rates in 1997, allowing schools as much as 90 percent reductions for obtaining Internet access as well as exempting Internet access providers from interstate charges for phone access. However, the FCC also mandated that businesses must pay an extra $3 above the current line fee, and Internet service providers with multiple phone lines needed to pay $9 per line beginning in July 1997. Companies expected this decision to have a negative effect on phone-line service and a positive effect on other forms of transmission including cable and wireless services.

The Internet Tax Freedom Act of 1997 (ITFA) allayed ISPs' fears that they would have to pay state and local taxes. Although some states began charging ISPs taxes in the mid-1990s, most ceased this practice when Congress started considering legislation to establish a national policy on taxing ISPs. Governing the period from October 1998 through October 2001, the ITFA exempts ISPs from state and local taxes and sanctions a commission responsible for researching the taxation of Internet commerce.

BACKGROUND AND DEVELOPMENT

THE HISTORY OF COMPUTER NETWORKS

Forbears to the Internet of the 1990s began as limited network systems for organizations to communicate either internally over short distances or externally over long distances by using computers. In the late 1970s computer networking started to grow. Organizations could afford to use this technology due to the advent of microcomputers that had the power to support several user terminals at once. With local area networks (LANs), companies or organizations could connect a cluster of microcomputers because the technology was relatively inexpensive and easy to install. LANs, however, had their disadvantages, too: they required expensive hardware to transmit large quantities of information quickly, and certain kinds of LAN systems could not work with others. Therefore, if an organization had a special LAN for its warehouse and another for its accounting department, they would not be compatible. Moreover, LAN cables could only extend about 500 meters without harming performance.

The LAN counterpart, wide area networks (WANs), existed since the late 1960s and early 1970s and used modems to send messages through regular telephone lines instead of through directly linked cables like LANs. WANs also required a host computer at each participating site that was devoted to connecting transmission lines and maintaining the operation of the system. The host computer, often called a server, functioned independently of computers using the WAN. On the other hand, WAN technology cost substantially more than LAN technology because WANs required transmission lines, modems, a special computer, and WAN software, whereas LANs simply required cabling and software. Furthermore, as with LANs, most WANs were incompatible with other WANs and with LANs.

This background created a need for a less expensive, long- and short-range, expandable networking system. A government funded agency, the U.S. Department of Defense's Advanced Research Projects Agency (ARPA), endeavored to resolve the problems with existing networking technology and developed an Internet working model later called the Internet. ARPA interconnected LANs and WANs using this model to provide the features of each computer networking system. In the mid-1970s, commercial computer companies began to develop their own closed, or proprietary, networks, which would only work with the vendor's software and hardware, although ARPA had conceived of the Internet as an open network that could allow users to communicate no matter whose software and hardware they used. Companies changed their minds, however, as computer hardware technology advances spurred new sales. The cost of computers also decreased, so companies could expect an expanding customer base, as well.

By 1982, researchers had a working version of the Internet in operation, and some major technological universities and industrial research organizations began using it. Computer science departments, in particular, led a campaign to connect all researchers in computer science via the Internet. In addition, the U.S. military also started to rely on the Internet as a standard means of communication and information transmission. At this point, the Internet became an actual tool for communication as opposed to being just an experiment. After the military began using the Internet, the number of computers connected doubled to about 500, though the amount was small relative to the number of computers connected to the Internet in the 1990s. By 1984 the number of Internet users doubled again as more government agencies, including the U.S. Department of Defense and National Aeronautics and Space Administration (NASA), started to take advantage of computer network communication.

However, researchers realized that the existing system was becoming flooded and could not hold many more connections. Consequently, the National Science Foundation (NSF) launched an effort to renovate the Internet. Although the NSF could not fund the campaign itself, it served as a clearinghouse by devising a plan and soliciting the help of International Business Machines Corporation, the long-distance carrier MCI, and MERIT, a Michigan school consortium that had developed its own computer network. By 1988, the cooperative effort of these companies and organizations laid the foundation of the Internet. Yet in 1991, this network reached its capacity, too.

The same participants plus Advanced Networks and Services (later ANS Communications, originally a nonprofit company until bought by AOL in 1995) set out to revamp the network once more, expanding it to hold substantially more connections. This renovation also took the majority of the funding away from the federal government, turning over to private industry instead. Between 1983 and 1993, the number of computers connected to the Internet increased from 562 to 1.2 million. By 1994 the number soared to 2.2 million. Around this time, the Internet became a means of communication and information transmission for private individuals because of the expanded network and the decreasing prices of personal computers (PCs).

EMERGENCE OF INTERNET ACCESS SERVICES

In the mid-1980s online services that would provide a model for ISPs began to emerge. CompuServe, an H&R Block subsidiary, had accommodated businesses with proprietary information services since 1969. Prodigy, a joint venture between Sears, Roebuck & Co. and IBM, began offering proprietary online services to the general public in 1984, and AOL (under the name Quantum Computer Services, a network for Commodore computers) went online in 1985. Netcom On-line Communications Services, Inc., one of the first true Internet services, emerged in 1988, originally providing Internet service to university students and later expanding to include residential and business clients. PSINet, Inc., founded in 1989, was one of the early Internet services to focus on business and commercial users and sold Internet access to residential providers to resell to their clients. General Electric also launched an online venture called GEnie, although the company later divested itself of the service when it failed to capture a wide following.

Technological advances in 1993—particularly the introduction of graphical Web browsers—brought mass appeal to the World Wide Web, an area of the

Internet that was previously navigable only via text-based browsers. As a result, small ISP operations cropped up all over—in major cities as well as in rural areas that the larger companies neglected. Phone companies also wanted part of the action; the regional Bell operating companies petitioned the FCC to allow them to participate. Long-distance phone carriers Sprint and MCI also vied for customers in the booming market of the mid-1990s.

As the World Wide Web started to expand, proprietary online services like AOL began to experience pressure to offer general access as other companies started offering this service. The proprietary format had become somewhat obsolete because the Web featured more diverse content, and its access was not dependent on a captive subscriber base. As a result, companies moved away from this format. IBM jettisoned its share of Prodigy and offered general Internet access instead called Internet Connection. Finally, in 1995 Microsoft introduced MSN, which at the outset provided proprietary services in addition to general access. It briefly opted to abandon the proprietary service and focus exclusively on WWW service; however, MSN later decided to stay with exclusive content offerings and to expand them to distinguish its service from that of other companies.

Before the advent of relatively low monthly fees for unlimited access, providers such as AOL and MSN charged a base monthly fee ranging from $5 to $10 per month that included 10 or 15 hours of access. After the monthly hour allocation was spent, these services charged additional fees for each subsequent hour. In 1994 these rates ranged as high as $9.80 per hour; by 1995 many were closer to $2.95 per hour; and in 1996 the flat rate of $19.95 for unlimited hours became widespread. In addition to these pricing options, many services had also offered graduated access options for higher monthly fees, such as 40 hours per month for $29.95.

CURRENT CONDITIONS

Internet service providers generated about $1.0 billion in 1993 and climbed to over $10.7 billion in 1998, according to *Forbes*. By the year 2000 ISP sales are predicted to reach $16.0 billion. There were an estimated 30 million Internet users in the United States in 1998—an increase of more than 50 percent from 1994. Analysts also predicted that the number of subscribers would jump to over 40 million by 2000. The *Wall Street Journal* reported in 1996 that about 9 million Americans logged onto the Internet daily, while

20 million used it weekly. Some estimates placed the count of ISPs at over 6,000 in 1998—up from 3,000 in 1997. While start-up ISPs continue to emerge, future consolidation of market share by mass providers such as America Online and Netcom seems imminent. *PC Week* projected that the number of operations would plummet to 1,500 by the year 2000. Despite these predictions, the number of ISPs has continued to grow and the market share of small ISPs also has increased. Small ISPs account for about 16 percent of the market according to International Data Corp., whereas large providers such as AOL and Microsoft Network account for about 56 percent

With the explosion of Internet access providers, prices have fallen drastically. In 1996, as AT&T began its foray into the market, its competitors slashed their prices in an effort to retain the customers they presently had, as well as to entice new ones. AT&T hoped to take on not only proprietary giants AOL and CompuServe but also smaller Internet service outfits by offering $19.95 flat rates and free trial hours to its long-distance phone service customers. Netcom, the largest independent access service in the late 1990s, tried to stave off AT&T's attack by reducing prices and offering fee services for free. Later, Netcom changed its mind, scrapped the flat rate, and planned to redirect its focus to business-oriented Internet service. CompuServe, after a short-lived offering of a novice-oriented service called Wow!, and PSINet announced they would also cater to the business market.

As a result of the price wars, the industry rate for unlimited access was $19.95 per month for many companies in the late 1990s. Yet this payment program had its disadvantages for both customers and providers. When AOL entered the $19.95-per-month fray in 1996 with a heavy marketing campaign, its subscriber count swelled so much that the network could not support its volume of users, triggering a threat of legal action against AOL. As a result AOL offered its subscribers additional free access time and drew back its marketing efforts. Customers suffered from congestion, busy signals, and disconnections, though they could theoretically stay online all day without incurring monstrous charges. The providers, on the other hand, though they served droves of customers, had trouble turning a profit with the flat fee. Consequently, some ISPs such as AOL, MCI, Microsoft Network, and AT&T WorldNet developed new price strategies, charging higher fees for faster connections, greater features, and heavier use. Nevertheless, smaller ISPs have relied on flat fees $19.95 or less to compete with larger companies.

<table>
<tr><td>Pioneer</td><td>TIM BURNERS-LEE
SPINNING A WEB</td></tr>
</table>

Subscription to, and usage of, the Internet is accelerating like a Formula One racer; the Internet doubles in size every ten months, and there are currently 40 million people on-line. The World Wide Web, however, is growing at an even faster rate. The Web is actually what is bringing people to the Internet, and it's the Web that is sweeping the Internet into a whole new arena of communications and entertainment. It was all the vision of one young Englishman, Tim Berners-Lee.

What Henry Ford was to the automobile industry, Tim Burners-Lee is to the Internet. He made it accessible and placed it into an arena: the World Wide Web.

The Internet and the World Wide Web are two different systems, though often mentioned in the same breath. Whereas the Internet is a systematic connection of computers and networks, the World Wide Web is what Burners-Lee calls an "abstract universe of information." Searching the Web will bring the searcher into contact with other computers; searching on the Web will bring the searcher information, documents picture, sound, animation, and possibly people.

In 1989, while working at CERN, an advanced particle physics lab in Geneva, Switzerland, Burners-Lee came up with a concept for organizing and exploring the Internet. But CERN was not interested in the Internet and shelved his proposal for a year.

When he reapplied for funding on his concept, CERN told Burners-Lee that it might be an easier way to make the telephone director available on their computer network. It got its foot through the corporate door, and was up and running in 1991.

Burners-Lee already had the technology of hypertext markup language, HTML, which is used to create Web pages. What he actually did was design a concept wherein anybody, anywhere, could build a page, then collect links with the click of a mouse, making the Web, in reality, a phenomenal, worldwide word processor. With each new page created, the Web became larger; with each link created, the Web became more inter-connected. Just one year after it was originally available, the World Wide Web was still growing exponentially.

He has admitted that if he were to do it again, he would redesign the URLs, which are the addresses for finding the Web pages. "I would have liked to have made the URLs a little cleaner. I have dots and slashes on the same thing; it's a mess."

In addition, other companies such as Concentric NetworkCorp. have paraded the $19.95 unlimited fee while factoring in other costs not covered by the so-called unlimited fee, according to the *New York Times*. On the other hand, some ISPs—FreePPP.com, Hyper Net, Inc. Internet Demographics Group, and others—went in the other direction, offering free unlimited access. These ISPs secure heavy advertising for their revenues, so if users can tolerate the ads, they can get online for free. Analysts expect ISPs to devise new means of securing revenues—such as advertising—or to limit the amount of hours subscribers can log on to the Internet in order to remain profitable, according to *PC Week*.

Given the financial struggles of the ISP industry and the deregulation of the telecommunications industry, *Business Communications Review* argues that the days of Internet access service as a stand-alone business may be numbered. Because of their lack of profitability, industry observers predict that telephone companies may purchase ISPs to run as side businesses. In addition, ISP's may enter the telephone service market, offering both telephony service, as well as Internet access, as a result of deregulation. On the other hand, ISPs may opt to face the competition by catering to specific niches in the market and offering customized service instead of just general consumer Internet access.

The late 1990s also saw the emergence of ISP wholesalers—large Internet service providers that sell access to small and medium-size providers. The wholesale relationship helps large ISPs by reducing costs associated with marketing and getting new customers, and it benefits small and medium-size ISPs by allowing them to offer more diverse services to differentiate themselves from their competitors.

The Internet faces another challenge as it has undergone many changes since its last upgrade. No longer do users expect to simply send e-mail and peruse low graphics texts; instead, they expect multimedia documents, including video and sound files. However, these require substantially more memory than text documents. Users frequently complain of slow download time, trouble connecting, and other problems associated with the growing traffic jam on the information superhighway. Hence, modification of the existing network is impending and in some cases has begun.

However, Jamie Murphy and Charlie Hofacker reported in the *New York Times* that the installation of new transmission technology, especially new lines,

---

ISPs' CHANGING ROLE

Forrester Research Inc. predicted obsolescence for the dial-up home Internet connection by the end of the millenium. It was projected that high-speed broadband connections that are "always on" would service the mass consumer market in place of the standard dial-up ISP telephone line. These plug-and-play facilities would be accessed through television cables or other direct connections, and conventional ISPs would be forced to rent time through the cable lines, leaving consumers to drop the ISP and go directly to the cable company, or to pay twice for a single service.

This impending innovation need not bring extinction to the savvy ISP. Small-to-medium sized businesses will continue to create an ongoing market for highly skilled service providers who are able to provide "worry-free" hook-ups to the right customers. Businesses with limited IS staffing, or none whatsoever, have neither the time nor the personnel to configure Internet computers for high-speed connections and are in a position to pay knowledgeable ISPs to handle the task. One ISP who follows the prescribed formula attested to a growth rate of 70 percent and higher in 1999.

does not have any economic motivation. The corporations and companies that own some of the Internet conduits have been reluctant to upgrade systems, fearing that their competitors would take advantage of technological improvements they financed. Therefore, companies have started to devise new payment models. Since Internet access fees have plummeted to around a $20 flat rate for unlimited service per month, companies are seeking to increase their revenues to make the investments in new technology worthwhile. The payment program that many companies would like to implement is a metered one where users pay for the amount of data received within a given period. With such a program, users would be charged every time they received or sent e-mail or downloaded graphically intense materials. Internet service providers feel that this plan could raise the revenues they need for technological expansions and maintenance.

In the meantime, some companies are seeking to remedy the mid-1990s Internet overcrowding by creating new online services that tailor to playing video games on the Internet to avoid the slow, clogged interface experienced on the World Wide Web. These services allow users synchronized play for two or more players. The companies also plan to charge

hourly rates for their services, according to Denise Caruso in the *New York Times.*

Many businesses turned to the Internet to boost their sales in the mid- to late 1990s; however, the results of Internet commerce—selling products and services over the Internet—remained lower than expected during this period. In 1998, Internet commerce, also known as electronic commerce, reached an estimated $51 billion, according to Forrester Research. Consumer sales through the Internet, however, totaled only $8 billion. Analysts generally agree that Internet commerce will expand significantly but disagree on how much it will grow and how long it will take to grow. For instance, Internet commerce projections for 2003 range from $200 billion to over $1.4 trillion.

INDUSTRY LEADERS

Founded in 1985, America Online (AOL) holds the greatest share of Internet customers, which numbered nearly 16 million in 1998—a third of the market by some estimates. Nonetheless, AOL faces significant obstacles in the Internet service market. AOL began offering flat rates in 1996 in an attempt to compete with Internet access providers, trying to rely on advertising and transactions for its revenue, argues Spencer Ante in the *New York Times.* However, AOL also had problems as many of its content clients started to defect. *The Atlantic Monthly, USA Weekend,* and *Newbytes,* for example, all severed their connections with AOL. These changes have left the company with somewhat of an identity crisis because its manifold content offerings distinguish its service from those of small access-only outfits, as well as from corporate operations such as AT&T and Microsoft, which has flirted more than once with proprietary content. As many journals and periodicals previously only available via AOL have set up camp on the World Wide Web, AOL had started demanding unique content from them if they plan to stay.

Stephen M. Case has led the company as CEO since 1991. In 1997 AOL posted $2.6 billion in total sales, up 54 percent from 1997, and the company employed about 8,500 people. In 1998 AOL strengthened its position in the Internet industry by reaching an agreement to buy Netscape Communications, the maker of the popular Netscape browser. When doing business over the Internet, customers seem to prefer the secure atmosphere provided by AOL, which may serve as its advantage in coming years. AOL also began seeking ways to increase revenues despite its flat-rate service fees, and the company raised its flat rate to $21.95 in 1998. In the late 1990s, the company also started selling advertising space on its sites to increase revenues.

CompuServe Interactive Services, Inc. became a subsidiary of AOL in 1998. CompuServe held second place in terms of subscribers with 2.5 million in 1998. CompuServe, like other proprietary services, found itself redefining its services and marketing strategies in an attempt to gain business clients, moving away from the residential market. With one of the strongest international subscriber bases, CompuServe offers its services in over 150 countries. In the late 1990s, CompuServe targeted mostly businesses and professionals. Though in some ways CompuServe offered more valuable proprietary content than its competitors, it lacked market focus and weathered the emergence of the Internet poorly. In 1997, after trying to spin off CompuServe, H&R Block accepted a WorldCom bid that split CompuServe's consumer and commercial sides between AOL and WorldCom, respectively.

The Microsoft Network (MSN) ranked third in terms of subscribers with about 2 million in 1998. Although a relative newcomer to Internet service, Microsoft had the distinct advantage of corporate name recognition and the ability to market the MSN start-up software with its popular Windows 95 operating system. Part of the $15 billion Microsoft empire, MSN contributed to the company's overall success and has excelled in a very competitive market quickly. However, as with other Internet service providers, MSN has tried to establish its niche. The most recent endeavor has been to build a repertoire of content selections. MSN provided between 30 and 40 unique content amenities in the late 1990s, compared to AOL's 300.

Netcom On-Line Communication Services, Inc. had about 600,000 customers in 1998, making it the largest private Internet access service. Netcom tried to stave off AT&T's attack by reducing prices and offering fee services for free in 1996. Later in the year, Netcom attempted to recast itself as a business Internet service and to create a niche service with premium rates and guaranteed access for businesses, realizing that the flat-fee recreational market was not lucrative. In 1999 MindSpring Enterprises acquired Netcom from ICG Communications, Inc. Combined, the two companies have about 1 million subscribers and revenues of $275.4 million. Netcom has subsidiaries in Canada, the United Kingdom, and Brazil as part of its growing Internet service empire.

Other industry leaders include Prodigy with about 700,000 subscribers in 1998 and Concentric Network with 225,000 subscribers. AT&T WorldNet, introduced in 1996, performed exceptionally well in its first two years of service, amassing 1.2 million subscribers by 1998. PSINet, though it began with heavy devotion to the consumer market, plans to refocus the company's service to the business market, citing lost revenues in residential customer service as the PSINet succumbed to the flat rate. PSINet had about 26,500 corporate clients in 1998 with services in 8 countries.

AMERICA AND THE WORLD

The Internet's free-form content has caused various groups to put pressure on ISPs around the world. In Germany, for example, the phone company discontinued service to a U.S. provider based on fear that German citizens could access neo-Nazi propaganda—it is legal in the United States but prohibited in Germany. France and Australia have considered taking such measures as well, according to the Human Rights Watch. Nonetheless, France, Germany, and the United Kingdom together have about 12 million subscribers, and Europe constitutes the second largest market for ISPs; however, the United States leads with 30 million subscribers. The Asia/Pacific region's market remained small in the late 1990s, accounting for only about 4 percent of the global industry's subscribers.

The Human Rights Watch also argues that since the Internet has the potential to unite thousands and thousands of people from all over the world, allowing them to engage in political discussion among other things, some countries see the Internet as a threat to their autonomy and their policies. Hence, some countries have enacted strict regulations. For example, China requires all Internet service providers to register with the government, while Saudi Arabia and Vietnam only provide government-controlled access.

Although affluent citizens of countries such as the United States, Japan, and Germany can afford personal computers and the other requisite technology for using the Internet, elsewhere in the world access is considerably less common due to cost. However, nonprofit organizations in some countries, such as the Peruvian Scientific Network in Peru, have created public computer facilities that offer Internet access for $15 a month in addition to classes on Internet navigation, according to Calvin Sims in the *New York Times*. The United Nations provided initial subsidies to the organization, which now has 22,000 members and was ranked the fourth fastest-growing network in the world behind Brazil, Mexico, and Chile, according to Sims. U.S. companies have also tried to tap into international markets. AOL Europe had 700,000 customers in 1997 and stood to inherit 850,000 more from CompuServe; AOL has also courted Japanese Internet customers. As a partner in its European venture, AOL has engaged German media conglomerate Bertelsmann AG to become what will likely be the largest pan-European service. Additionally, MSN has a pact with France Telecom.

RESEARCH AND TECHNOLOGY

Much technology existed in the late 1990s that could improve Internet service, but little had yet been implemented. Ordinary phone lines have been the culprits behind the slow transfer of information on the Internet. While integrated services digital network (ISDN) phone lines can alleviate this problem, the technology carries a high price—one neither consumers or ISPs have wanted to incur: running between $150 to $300 to install in addition to a sizable monthly service charge and per-minute fee, according to Robin Frost in *The Wall Street Journal*. ISDN is so costly because there is virtually no U.S. infrastructure to support it, unlike in Europe where it is more common. Asymmetrical digital subscriber lines (ADSL) also promise to be a solution to the lethargic tempo of Internet transmission. These phone lines can download information at a faster pace than ISDN lines although they take longer to transmit outgoing data. A related technology is digital subscriber line (DSL), another alternative to standard phone lines in the late 1990s. DSL lines have significantly greater bandwidth—carrying 256 Kilibits per second—and 24-hour connections. Other new lines included T-1, a transmission line that can transfer data at 1.5 million bits per second and is often used to connect LANs to the Internet, and T-3, a transmission line that can transfer data at 4.5 million bits per second.

Coaxial cable—used for cable television—offers yet another solution in that cables and cable modems can transmit data 100 times quicker than regular phone lines. However, again infrastructure is a problem. Cable companies would need to install new cabling capable of two-way transmissions, and only 7 percent of the cable companies can presently offer cable Internet service, according to Frost. Nevertheless, Forrester Research predicts that the number of cable connections will grow to 2.2 million in the United States. Anticipating this heighten demand, ISPs teamed up with cable companies in the late 1990s to cater to this market. For example, AT&T acquired the leading cable company Tele-Communications Inc. (TCI)—offering the Internet access service @Home and Media One, Microsoft, Time Warner—and others created the service Road Runner.

Then again, satellites may allow users to dispense with phone lines and cables altogether. Frost explains that satellites can transmit data at 400 kilobytes per second, a tenfold improvement over standard modems' 36.6 to 56 kbps speed, and thus would greatly reduce downloading time. However, sending data takes longer and satellite technology requires a sizable initial investment—about $999 for a dish and interface software, plus monthly fees beginning at $15.95 for service in 1996. In 1996, Internet access via cable generated revenues of $21 million and *Broadcasting & Cable* reported that revenues may reach $1.2 billion by 2000.

FURTHER READING

Albiniak, Paige, and Price Colman. "High-Speed Demands Fast Action." *Broadcasting & Cable,* 11 May 1998.

Comer, Douglas E. *Internet Book.* Englewood Cliffs, NJ: Prentice Hall, 1995.

Flynn, Laurie. "Netcom Bundles Services to Fend Off AT&T." *The New York Times,* 29 March 1996.

———. "Netcom's New Price Model Tailors Internet Services." *The New York Times,* 25 March 1997.

Frost, Robin. "The Internet: Is Being Online Going to Be Easier?" *Wall Street Journal,* 9 December 1996.

Human Rights Watch. "Silencing the Net: The Threat to Freedom of Expression On-line." *The New York Times,* May 1996.

"Internet Providers at War." *The Economist,* 7 November 1998.

Junnarkar, Sandeep. "New Phone Rules Will Have Mixed Effect on Net." *The New York Times,* 8 May 1997.

LaPolla, Stefanie. "Internet Outages Strain Corporate Networking." *PC Week,* 21 April 1997.

Lewis, Peter H. "An 'All You Can Eat' Price Is Clogging Internet Access." *The New York Times,* 17 December 1996.

———. "Netcom to Seek Profitable Niche: Internet Access Just for Business." *The New York Times,* 19 December 1996.

Lubove, Seth. "Mom and POPs Thrive." *Forbes,* 22 February 1999.

Murphy, Jamie, and Charlie Hofacker. "Explosive Growth Clogs The Internet's Backbone," 30 June 1996.

Rodriguez, Karen. "Internet Providers Gird for Long-Distance Service Battle." *The Business Journal,* 23 March 1998.

Schonfeld, Erick. "The Exchange Economy." *Fortune,* 15 February 1999.

Stuck, Bart, and Michael Weingarten. "Has High Tide Come for ISPs?" *Business Communications Review,* September 1997.

U.S. Department of Commerce. *U.S. Trade and Industry Outlook 1998.* Washington, DC: McGraw-Hill, Inc., 1998.

Wells, Rob. "Internet Leaders See Threat in Local Taxes." *The New York Times,* 27 February 1997.

—Karl Heil

Lasers and Laser Applications

INDUSTRY SNAPSHOT

Lasers were already a part of everyday life by the end of the twentieth century. Everything from compact disc players, to credit cards with holograms, and microchips in computers relied on the power of lasers. All of these, and numerous other products and services Americans took for granted in the 1990s, were dependent on the multi-billion dollar laser industry. Lasers were an industry that became a vital quotient among many other industries and occupations. (Also see the essays in this book entitled Digital Video Disc, Holography, and Micromachines.)

ORGANIZATION AND STRUCTURE

The term laser is an acronym for *Light Amplification by Stimulated Emission of Radiation.* A laser is a narrow, extremely focused, powerful beam of monochromatic light that is used for a variety of functions. For instance, the lasers etch information onto the surface of compact discs. Laser's qualities enable it to record far more information in less space than the old fashioned way of producing phonograph records. Lasers used in the production of CD-ROM disks condense large amounts of information, such as a set of encyclopedias or the New York metropolitan phone book, onto one disk. Another example of laser etching is in video discs, which in the 1990s promised to give videocassettes significant competition, if not replace them, as the means of providing home movie entertainment. Holograms, three-dimensional images, are also examples of laser technology at work. By the 1990s it became common practice for many credit card companies to affix holograms to their cards, thus discouraging would-be counterfeiters. Public speakers employ laser pointers when giving presentations. Laser light shows abounded in entertainment, often as an alternative to fireworks displays at public events.

Lasers have become indispensable in numerous applications. Fiber optic communications use pulses of laser light to send information on glass strands. Before the advent of fiber optics, telephone calls were relayed on thick bundles of copper wire. With the appearance of this new technology, a glass wire no thicker than a human hair can carry thousands of conversations. Lasers are also used in scanners. Any number of areas where scanners might be used are: price-code checkers at supermarkets; tags that prevents thefts of books from libraries or clothing items from stores; and inventory systems in company warehouses. Heating lasers are found to be able to drill through solid metal in an industrial setting. They remove gallstones in an operating room, or remove cataracts in outpatient surgery. They are able to precisely remove the oxidized outer layer and thus restore an art object to its original beauty. In the late 1960s and early 1970s, measuring lasers assisted scientists in calibrating the distance between the earth and moon to within two inches. They continued to provide surveyors assistance in making much smaller measurements as well. Lasers are used for guiding missiles. They aid building contractors to assure that walls, floors, and ceilings are in proper alignment. (Also see the essay in this book entitled Fiber Optics.)

In the late 1990s advances in production methods catapulted laser products into many industrial settings. Quantum cascade lasers, more compact than gas lasers, were used to sample pollutants from the air for the semiconductor and environmental industries. In addition, blue diode lasers were developed as an improvement on the infrared wavelengths, because the blue wavelength was shorter and took less space.

INDUSTRY PROFILE

The laser industry engendered several interest and advocacy groups that fostered laser use and supported technological advances. These organizations include: the Laser Institute of America, formerly the Laser Industry Association; the Laser and Electro-Optics Society; and the Institute for Electric and Electronics Engineers, or IEEE. Many significant laser manufacturers belong to the Laser and Electro-Optics Manufacturer's Association (LEOMA). LEOMA play a key role in advocating the industry in Washington and in settling disputes between companies. For example, LEOMA lobbied in Washington to maintain funding for laser research. LEOMA also had an Alternative Dispute Resolution Agreement, whereby members agreed not to initiate legal action against one another without first attempting to resolve the conflict with the help of a mediator. LEOMA reported that such mediation solved 90 percent of disputes. According to LEOMA, its 40 member companies represented 90 percent of the industry's annual North American sales.

While the federal government oversees laser research through the Technology Reinvestment Program (TRP), The National Institute of Standards and Technology, (formerly the National Bureau of Standards) has an interest in the laser industry, especially through its Advanced Development Program. The Department of Energy, the National Institute for Health, the Food and Drug Administration (FDA), and the National Aeronautics and Space Administration (NASA) are also interested in various laser applications.

BACKGROUND AND DEVELOPMENT

Laser light is produced by the process of stimulated emission, which involves bringing many atoms into an excited state. When light travels through a normal material containing more ground-state atoms than excited-state atoms, it is more likely to be absorbed than amplified. To make a laser, a special situation must occur of delivering energy that produces more excited-state atoms than ground-state atoms. This situation is called a population inversion. If light traveling through the material is more likely to collide with excited atoms than ground-state atoms, it causes stimulated emission. The material or medium then becomes an amplifier.

A laser consists of three components: an optical cavity, an energy source, and an active medium. The optical cavity, two mirrors facing one another, contains the active laser medium. One of the mirrors fully reflects light from the stimulated emission, whereas the other is only partially reflective. Light, generated and amplified by the medium, resonates back and forth between the mirrors, in a constant flux between the background and excited energy states. Some of the light transmitted by the less reflective mirror is diverted as a highly focused beam, the laser. Generally, electricity is the energy source, and the active medium can be solid-state, semiconductor, gas, or dye. One example of a solid-state laser is a ruby crystal.

PIONEERS IN THE FIELD

Albert Einstein first considered the idea of stimulated emission, a key element in laser technology, in 1917. In 1954, Charles H. Townes supplied another key element by producing population inversion in a microwave device, which he called a Microwave Amplification by Stimulated Emission of Radiation (MASER). During the 1950s, the United States and Soviet Union entered into a technology race to develop a laser, and on May 16, 1960, Theodore H. Maiman, a U.S. scientist, operated the first solid-state laser. The gas laser also made its appearance in 1960. That was the creation of Ali Javan, a Bell Laboratories engineer, working out of New Jersey. In 1962, semiconductor lasers were developed. The dye laser made its first appearance in 1966.

During the 1960s, some people within the scientific community called lasers "a solution without a problem," because they could not conceive of a practical use for them. Lasers began having commercial applications in 1961 when Theodore Maiman formed the industry's first laser company, Quantatron. Other laser companies also made their appearance, primarily producing ruby solid-state lasers.

The military took a keen interest in the use of lasers for missile guidance and other applications like the development of nuclear fusion. The federal government became a major player in laser development during the 1970s and 1980s as it tried to augment laser's existing uses. By the 1990s, laser applications were rapidly expanding in both the military and automotive fields for vehicle position sensing, crash avoidance, and profiling object surfaces from long distances. The military used laser guidance systems in smart bombs during the Persian Gulf War of 1991.

CURRENT CONDITIONS

The laser and laser applications industry in the late 1990s continued to grow quickly. The computer industry needs to etch increasingly complicated circuit patterns onto increasingly smaller microchips, requiring something more effective than the mercury light process that had sustained the microchip industry throughout the late 1980s. Cymer Inc., a company whose 1996 sales grew 350 percent from 1995, has a high-demand excimer laser, a special type of gas laser that produced ultraviolet light. In 1986 the company's founders were $250,000 in debt. With this success, they suddenly found themselves very wealthy due to the stream of clients waiting eagerly to buy their laser technology.

Design News reported that shipments of industrial laser equipment and systems for the North American market increased 40 percent in the first nine months of 1996. Cutting was the leading application for this technology, according to the report, with welding and marking rounding out the top three. While private industry grows, federal funding shrinks. *Design News* reported a 1997 study by the National Academies of Science and Engineering. This study found that funding to all areas of technological development, including laser development, had dropped. Total funding for fiscal 1997 was $43.4 billion, 5 percent less than it had been three years earlier. Included in that figure was $8.0 billion for governmental weapons research.

Weapons development continued in the late 1990s. Other laser applications continued to flourish as well. In May 1996, Laser Industries Ltd., an Israeli company, gained FDA approval for a process to remove wrinkles surgically. Other promising areas of cosmetic laser applications in 1997 were hair transplants and hair removal. Laser eye surgery continued to be one of the most widely implemented applications of laser medical technology. In March 1997, *New York* magazine referred to this process as "the most widely marketed medical procedure in history." Medical devices such as Cell Robotics' patented *Lasett,* introduced in June 1998, have replaced the stainless steel lancet used by diabetics to prick a finger in order to test their blood glucose levels. The *Milwaukee Journal Sentinel* reported in June 1997 that dentists were using a laser system to whiten teeth. The *Journal of the American Medical Association,* reported in April of 1996 on a study conducted for the treatment of warts. The outcome of that study, involving 142 patients with 703 recurrent and 25 previously untreated warts, was that pulsed dye laser therapy was highly effective and safe. The method selectively destroyed

---

More On

LASER POINTERS: TO SEE OR NOT TO SEE!

Laser pointers were developed for use as a pointing tool to guide the eye during presentations or educational instruction. However, they are proving sometimes to be more an enemy that an aide to the eye. Laser pointers contain a small diode laser that emits an intense beam of light. (A diode is an electronic device that has two electrodes or terminals.) While most laser pointers do not pose a serious risk of eye injury, some of the newer laser devices, especially green light pointers, present an increased risk of eye injury, according to Princeton University's Environmental Health and Safety Office.

If flashed directly into the eye, the laser beam can cause temporary "flashblindness," headaches, afterimages or glare, Princeton's EHS warns. Flashblindness is the temporary impairment of vision which follows the viewing of a bright light. Afterimage is the phenomenon of spots that seem to appear in the field of vision. Glare is a reduction or complete loss of visibility while being exposed to a direct or scattered beam.

Following reports of eye injuries from children's misuse of laser pointers, the Food and Drug Administration warned parents and schools of the risks. According to the FDA, the light energy of the pointers, if aimed into the eye, can be more damaging than staring directly into the sun.

Federal law now requires labeling of the product that alerts consumers to the potential hazards to the eyes. Several cities, including New York, have banned the sale of laser pointers to minors who are often perceived to misuse the devices. The devices have also caused problems at sporting events, causing teams such as the Green Bay Packers, to warn against their use. Misuse could result, as in the case of the Packers, with confiscation of the device, ejection from the stadium, a possible charge of disorderly conduct and loss of season tickets.

---

warts without damaging the surrounding skin. *Prevention* magazine in July of 1996 reported that lasers had assisted drops as a first glaucoma treatment. The report noted that, "Lasers have been used to relieve the built-up pressure in the eye that causes these vision problems—but they've only been used after eyedrops failed. A new study suggests that these beams of light may be a better first-choice treatment." The study took seven years. In all, lasers' side effects of a temporary jump in eye pressure following treatment in about a third of the patients are considered a minimal risk.

Laser printers, CDs, and other products featuring lasers continue to be fast-selling items. The fastest area of growth in the late 1990s was in sales to industry. Laser's versatility as a cutting tool, sensing device, pointer, and analyzer have found applications in many arenas. A contaminant monitor laser developed for NASA by Opotek, Inc. of Carlsbad, California, is used by the Drug Enforcement Agency to detect byproducts of illegal drug manufacturing. The same type of laser can be used for basic research in photochemistry, photobiology, diagnostics, and many chemical processes. In 1998 Opotek estimated the market for scientific lasers at about $150 million.

As with any clever mode of technology, the abuses of the laser are also rampant. In an anecdote cited by *USA Weekend* on April 24, 1999, laser pointers, the size of pencils, were discussed. The article, entitled, "Don't Point that Laser!" noted the following: "Those beams of light coming from those pen-size instruments were intended for corporate executives too polite to point with their fingers. But people of all ages know they're more fun to point at people than at presentations. Hoops fans even use them to distract players on the free-throw line. More seriously, police worry that they're the target of snipers when they see the laser light on their chests. Lasers are banned or restricted in Philadelphia; New York City; Dearborn, Michigan; Virginia Beach, Virginia; Ocean City, Maryland; Chicago Ridge, Illinois; Westchester County, New York; and in Seattle's public schools."

INDUSTRY LEADERS

The Laser and Electro-Optics Manufacturer's Association includes most of the major players in the North American laser industry. Among these are Spectra-Physics Lasers of Mountain View, California, which chiefly produces optical equipment; Bothell, Washington-based Synrad, makers of carbon dioxide lasers; Continuum Electro-Optics in Santa Clara, California, producers of solid-state lasers for various applications; Lumonics, an Ontario, Canada, company that makes lasers for product marking; and Spiricon, a Logan, Utah, producer of diagnostic lasers for use with Windows-based analysis software. Other companies that filled the *Thomas Register* in the field of laser technology are: Laser Tech of Chino, California, advertising "State-of-the-art" laser and water technology; Laser Technologies of Batavia, Illinois; Laserage of Waukegan, Illinois; and Wilmad Glass of Buena, New Jersey, advertising themselves as "Meeting laser

requirements with precision since 1951." Companies across the United States advertise services utilizing lasers for everything from ceramic cutting, to solar cell processing, to medical micromachining. In the late 1990s, many large electronics and computer companies had at least some interest in the laser industry, as did the federal government.

RESEARCH AND TECHNOLOGY

In January 1997, physicists at the Massachusetts Institute of Technology (MIT) made an astonishing announcement: the development of a single-atom laser. The MIT laser emits atoms and employs a type of matter only discovered in 1995. It was called "Bose-Einstein condensate" in honor of Satyendra Nath Bose, an Indian physicist whose work stemmed from Albert Einstein's hypotheses. This form of matter consists of a gas that is so dense and cold that atoms lose some of their individual properties and fuse into a giant superatom. These superatoms are cooled to a temperature just a few billionths of a degree above absolute zero, and at that temperature, the atoms assume some of the characteristics of light waves. The new laser, which the head of the MIT scientific team described as "a dripping faucet," emits pulses of Bose-Einstein condensate droplets. According to the July 1998 issue of *Scientific American,* light generated by this type of laser displayed properties that were explained only by quantum theory. Therefore the single-atom laser is expected to be a valuable research tool in studying atomic and subatomic properties of atoms. Scientists expected to learn more about the nature of laser light by changing the conditions that the laser is performing under and analyzing the results. These results were anticipated to solve quantum-mechanical problems and speed the development of microcavity semiconductor lasers, which could be used in the future to create optical computers. Among the practical applications for this technology was microchip etching, a field where it may represent as much of an improvement over the semiconductor laser as that was over the old mercury light process.

Medical laser developments on the horizon in the late 1990s included therapy for stroke victims, being developed at Sandia National Laboratories, as well as a new laser process promising to virtually eliminate the use of needles in biopsies. A Canadian company called Quadra Logic Technologies (QLT) developed a new type of cancer removal procedure called photodynamic therapy. The surgery uses a laser gun coupled with a light-sensitive chemical called photofrin, which acts as a catalyst in the process. The laser stimulates the photofrin, which starts a reducing reaction on the oxygen surrounding the tumor. The oxidizing reaction removes the oxygen from the cancer cells, thus suffocating them and killing the tumor. Other uses for photodynamic therapy include treatment of psoriasis, skin cancer, and ocular diseases. With laser surgery for hair loss, wrinkles, vision enhancement, and numerous other conditions already a reality, the coming years promise exciting developments in laser technology for medicine.

Industry observers in the late 1990s hoped for a breakthrough in the area of nuclear fusion as well. Nuclear fusion promised to provide cheap and abundant power without the dangers associated with nuclear fission, the conventional form of nuclear reaction. If it were to become a widely available source of energy, nuclear fusion would emerge as one of the most significant technological developments of all time.

FURTHER READING

"Almost-Painless Biopsies." *Popular Mechanics,* March 1997, 28.

Bergquist, Carl. "Using Lasers to Make Holograms." *Electronics Now,* May 1997, 20.

Blau, Melinda. "I Can See Clearly Now." *New York,* 10 March 1997, 32.

Bulkeley, William B. "Palomar Laser Hair-Removal System Cleared." *Wall Street Journal,* 11 March 1997, B-10.

"Don't Point That Laser." *USA Weekend,* 24-26 April 1999.

Eskow, Dennis. *Laser Careers.* New York: Franklin Watts, 1988.

Feld, Michael S., and Kyungwon An. "The Single-Atom Laser." *Scientific American,* July 1998.

Gleason, Suzanne Bettina. "The Laser Craze." *American Health,* March 1997.

Hecht, Jeff. *Laser Pioneers.* New York: Academic, 1992.

Knack, Maggie P. "Chronomed and Cell Robotics Sign Letter of Intent for Diabetic Laser Products." *PRNewswire,* 10 June 1998. Available from http://www.pathfinder.com/money/latest/press/PW/1998Jun10/453.html.

"Laser-Based Treatment Could Benefit Stroke Victims." *Design News,* 3 March 1997, 15.

Laser Focus World, Advances in Optics, Electro-Optics, Optoelectronics, April 1998.

"Laser Sharp." *Forbes,* 24 March 1997, 188.

Lawler, Andrew. "NIF Ignites Changes at Livermore." *Science,* 28 February 1997, 1252.

McDonald, Kim A. "Physicists at MIT Announce the Creation of an Atom Laser." *The Chronicle of Higher Education,* 7 February 1997, A-15.

McHugh, Josh. "Laser Dudes." *Forbes,* 24 February 1997, 154.

Nolan, Mary I. "A Quantum Leap In Navy AMCM Capabilities." *Sea Power,* March 1997, 15.

Normile, Dennis. "Laser Fusion With a Fast Twist." *Science,* 28 February 1997.

Opotek, Inc. *Contaminant Monitor Laser,* 1997. Available from http://www.sti.nasa.gov/tto/spinoff1997/er3.html.

Proctor, Paul. "Boost-Phase Intercept Key to ABL Deterrent." *Aviation Week & Space Technology,* 3 March 1997.

"Pulsed Dye Laser Treatment of Warts." *JAMA,* 10 April 1996.

"Vista Vision." *Prevention,* July 1996.

Wingo, Walter. "Use of Laser Systems Surges In Manufacturing Equipment." *Design News,* 3 March 1997.

—Judson Knight, updated by Marsha Levy and Jane E. Spear

LIQUID METALS

INDUSTRY SNAPSHOT

The production, use, and research of liquid metal technology spans several areas of industry, including manufacturing, aerospace, x-ray technology, and sports. *American Metals Market,* the metals information network, listed 679 vendors of various metal products on its Web site in 1999. National Aeronautics and Space Administration (NASA) space shuttle research teams have investigated the properties of liquid metals on several space shuttle flights. Space research is vital to understanding liquid metals because of what happens to them outside of earth's gravitational force. Consequently, NASA remained a key player in the industry entering the twenty-first century. Because of the many applications of liquid metals, along with the continuing research regarding possible uses, the liquid metals field is continually expanding.

ORGANIZATION AND STRUCTURE

Many professional scientific organizations oversee experimentation with the qualities of liquid metals, and look for potential uses for those qualities. Much of the research in which these scientists are engaged is conducted at universities, in the United States and around the world. These researchers periodically gather at professional conferences such as the LAM conference, which is devoted to the study of Liquid Amorphous Metals. LAM 10, the tenth in a series of such events was held at the University of Dortmund, Germany, in 1998. These events were initiated in 1966, and are held every several years since in locations throughout the world. Such meetings of the

world's leading researchers in liquid metals provide for the exchange of valuable research, as well as its professional evaluation and discernment. A list of the areas of study from which contributions are solicited, indicating some of the key topics in research, are: static and dynamic structure; electronic structure; atomic and electronic transport; magnetic properties; thermodynamics; liquid semi-conductors; molten salt-metal mixtures; expanded metals and alloys; metal-nonmetal transitions; glass transitions; qausicrystals; melting; amorphization; surfaces and interfaces; nanocrystals, intercalates, clusters; and, composite materials.

Research conducted by NASA, particularly that on the space shuttle flights, is overseen by the government agency itself. One of the key groups overseeing progress in the area of space research is "The Consortium for Materials Development in Space." Work in the industry itself, both in business research labs, falls under the jurisdiction of individual corporations that operate under standards set forth by the Office of Safety and Health Administration (OSHA).

BACKGROUND AND DEVELOPMENT

The history of human's experimentation with metals goes back at least 6,000 years, according to James Gordon Parr, author of, *Man, Metals, & Modern Magic.* However, most modern-day innovations began to emerge seriously during the Industrial Revolution of the nineteenth century. The machinery and equipment that emerged during that time allowed civilization to pursue mining in an entirely new and more efficient way. The United States exploded into the world of metal processing as a result of inventions and research that also helped build the fortunes of a few men, such as Andrew Carnegie, who innovated the manufacture of steel. Carnegie, in fact, amassed such wealth that he felt a moral obligation to give it back to the people who worked hard in steel factories and foundries, especially in western Pennsylvania.

Interest in liquid metals heightened with the advent of the "space race" in the latter 1950s and 1960s when these properties were found to render liquid metals extremely useful. Corinna Wu, in a *Science News* article "Space-Age Metals—Freed from Gravity, Materials Reveal Their Mysteries," offers this overview of NASA's role in understanding liquid metals: "Researchers would love to alloy gold with rhodium in order to produce high-temperature electrical contacts, for example. Others want to study the atom-to-atom interactions of cooling metals as they coalesce into the crystal structures that define their solid forms." But something happened when heat met gravity in these experiments. The metals were not able to alloy, or mix together, due to the currents of rising and falling material. In space, away from earth's gravity, these bothersome problems disappeared. NASA's Web pages on microgravity explain in simple fashion what the issues in this sort of experimentation are. According to the Microgravity site originating from the Marshall Space Flight Center in May 1999, "Industry spends billions of dollars each year on machine tools to manufacture products out of metal. This includes tools for cutting every kind of metal part from engine blocks to Shuttle main engine components. Cutting tool tips often break because of weak spots or defects in their composition. Based on a new concept called defect trapping, space offers a novel environment to study defect formation in molten metal materials as they solidify." The process known as "sintering," crucial to much of the work surrounding liquid metals and their practical applications, is "a bonded mass of metal particles shaped and partially fused by pressure and heating below the melting point," according to *Webster's New World Dictionary of the American Language.* NASA's authority continues to explain that, "After the return of these materials from space, researchers can evaluate the source of the defect and seek ways to eliminate them in products prepared on Earth. A widely used process for cutting-tip manufacturing is liquid sintering."

The 1990s were an exciting time period in the field of liquid metals. Lanxide Corporation of Newark, Delaware, developed one innovation, creating a pressureless proprietary process for making metal matrix composite. According to *Foundry Management & Technology,* in August 1991, "In the process, called Primex, the reinforcement, matrix and microstructural features can be varied and closely controlled, and net and near-neat shapes with complex configurations can be economically produced." The reported benefits of such a process included, "package edges designed for sealing by laser-beam or resistance welding" and "compatibility with gold, tin, or nickel electroplating."

Other developments in understanding the use of liquid metals included an engine that used "reversing flows of conductive liquid metal through magnetic fields to generate current," according to a brief article in *Popular Mechanics,* in January 1995. These developmental studies conducted at Oak Ridge National Laboratories in Oak Ridge, Tennessee, involved a generator that "harnesses electrically conductive liquid metals." The article pointed out that the technology could make it possible for an engine's ability to respond quickly to acceleration, then shrink for efficient high-speed cruise—hence, the nickname, "The Incredible Shrinking Engine." Over the decades of the latter twentieth century, development and research in liquid metals created many applications and many possibilities. According to GKN Sinter Metals company Web site, the applications for use of liquid metals are numerous. They include: porous metal flame arrestors, used where explosive or flammable gases needed to be shielded from sparks leading to ignition, also acting as "safety valves;" for flow control; and for filtration and separation of liquids, gases, and molded plastics. All of these applications from this company and hundreds of others, combined with continuing research at universities, led to useful applications in a vast number of areas affecting people's daily lives. They were: pneumatics and hydraulics; automotive; chemical; petrochemical; oil production; polymer (plastics) filtration; municipal water; waste water treatment; environmental; ammunition; aerospace; boating; food and beverage; medical and pharmaceutical; steel production; packing; and lawn and garden equipment.

The innovation that met with perhaps the most excitement was the use of liquid metal to make the heads of golf clubs. Two researchers at the California Institute of Technology (Caltech) invented the five-component metallic glass the club heads used, in 1992. The space shuttle Columbia had gone to space with similar types of glass from Caltech in a furnace created in Germany known as "TEMPUS." TEMPUS was developed as an electromagnetic levitation furnace that melted samples of metals without them touching the walls of the container or furnace. This process delivered samples that were nearly perfect. The company now in possession of the patented process is Liquidmetal Golf in Laguna Niguel, California. The five components that went into making the special metallic glass were nickel, zirconium, titanium, copper, and beryllium. The key to this process, according Jim Gorant in *Popular Mechanics,* is that after the metals are heated to a liquid and mixed, ". . . they're cooled very quickly, from about 1,500 degrees Fahrenheit to room temperature in five seconds. That's about 100 times faster than other metals are cooled, and it caused the molecules to harden randomly, rather than crystallizing into a pattern." Caltech researchers produced the original formula for the glass in 1959, working to develop materials for the space industry. It was not until 1992 that Professor William Johnson and Dr. Atakan Peker discovered the way to make it cool more slowly, enabling them to create full plates of the substance instead of the very thin strips 1959 researchers were forced to create. When announcing Liquidmetal golf clubs as one of the headlining prospects in 1998, *Golf Digest* reported that because the material was stronger and more elastic than other steel and titanium alloys, it was said to create a "hotter ball flight" as well as a "softer feel." Liquidmetal golf clubs were first produced in Japan and finally reached stores in the United States in time for the golfing season of 1998. Wu also reported in *Science News* that David Lee, head of manufacturing technology at Liquidmetal Golf, said that he and coworkers were exploring other areas where the material might be useful, especially in aerospace, marine, and for defense purposes. "Golf clubs were an easy first application for the new glass because golfers are generally affluent and willing to embrace the newest technology," Lee was quoted as saying.

CURRENT CONDITIONS

Judging by the amount of time, research, and money being invested into liquid metals research at the end of the 1990s, the industry's future looked promising. Michael Santoli reported for *Barron's* in March 1998, that LiquidMetal was a company industry executives were looking at seriously. "The gee-whiz nature of the material has enabled the company to begin selling clubs through three major manufacturers in Japan, where the golf market is particularly obsessed with technology. The prices befit the extravagant novelty that these clubs might ultimately prove to be: $5,000 for a driver with an amorphous face, eight times what the Biggest Big Bertha (particular type of club) commands here, noted Santoli." In the United States in 1998, the prices were listed more within a reasonable price range, although at the higher

end of costs. A putter went for around $400, eight-irons for $2,700, and a driver for around $500. One thing that seemed certain was that the technology searching for the "perfect" golf club remained at the forefront of the industry's mind. Again, it would likely emerge from Caltech, or some other esteemed institution, and find its way into the fortunes of business.

The true figures for the financial implications of liquid metals were difficult to determine due to the part they played in so many key industries. The budget estimates that NASA proposed to Congress in the fall of 1998 for Fiscal Year 2000 came to a total of $13.57 billion, with an increase to $13.75 billion by 2002. The allocation for life and microgravity sciences and applications alone, one of the key areas affecting liquid metals, was $263.2 million. Whatever small or large part liquid metals would play in the future, NASA projections for the next century indicated they would continue to be a significant factor in economic growth.

WORK FORCE

The market for metallurgical engineers and chemical researchers is a promising development of the ongoing experimentation and manufacturing using liquid metals. Other key positions can be found in factories and melting foundries, as laborers, skilled technicians, and business and sales managers are expected to continue.

AMERICA AND THE WORLD

According to *U.S. Industry and Trade Outlook 1998,* in 1996 domestic shipments of golf equipment totaled an estimated $2.6 billion, up 9 percent from 1995. Imports were up slightly, to reach about $581 million, and exports up 11 percent to around $766 million. Also of note was that in 1994, golf had the highest level, 30 percent, of participants who made between $50,000 and $74,000 per year. This led to a very lucrative investment for those investing in golf equipment. Due to a plentiful supply of titanium from Russia since the end of the Cold War, titanium golf clubs, too, were more affordable than when they first entered the market.

The markets for aerospace and space commerce uses for liquid metal were deemed promising as part of an industry that was increasingly internationalizing its efforts. Defense budget spending and the health of foreign economies would be factors in further exploration, research, and development for new uses of liquid metal.

FURTHER READING

Browne, Malcolm W. "Spun Liquid Mercury Metal Is Eye of a New Generation of Telescopes; Mercury Rivals the Best Glass Mirrors in Accuracy of Images." *The New York Times,* 21 November 1995.

Department of Commerce, International Trade Administration. *U.S. Industry and Trade Outlook 1998,* Washington, D.C.: U.S. Department of Commerce, 1998.

Farricker, Peter, ed. "Equipment Digest: A Matter of Substance." *Golf Digest,* 1 April 1998.

"Fiscal Year 2000 Estimates." National Aeronautics and Space Administration, 1999. Available from http://ifmp.nasa.gov/codeb/budget2000/HTML/MYB.htm.

GKN Sinter Metals Company Profile. Thomas Register, 1999. Available from http://www.sinter@thomasregister.com.

Gorant, Jim. "Liquid Gold." *Popular Mechanics,* July 1998.

"The Incredible Shrinking Engine." *Popular Mechanics,* January 1995. Available from http://www.popularmechanics.com/popmech/sci/tech/9501/TUMEVM.html.

"Metal Pouring/Filtering." *Foundry Management & Technology,* January 1997.

"Microgravity—Liquid Phase Sintering." National Aeronautics and Space Administration, 1999. Available from http://microgravity.nsfc.nasa.gov/MGImages/ABSTRACTS/MSFCMG_00153.html.

Nasch, Philippe M., Murli H. Manghani, and Richard A. Sacco. "Anomalous Behavior of Sound Velocity and Attenuation in Liquid Fe-Ni-S." *Science News,* 11 July 1997.

Peterson, Ivars. "Against the Wall." *Science News,* 6 December 1997.

"Pressureless Metal Infiltration for MMC's." *Foundry Management & Technology,* August 1991.

Santoli, Michael. "Hype or Hope?" *Barron's,* 30 March 1998.

Terrell, Peter B. "Carbon Raisers and Cast Irons." *Foundry Management & Technology,* August 1996.

Turner, Robert C., and John McKelvie. "Molten Metal Splash—the Most Visible Foundry Hazard." *Foundry Management & Technology,* July 1997.

Wu, Corinna. "Space-Age Metals: Freed from Gravity, Materials Reveal Their Mysteries." *Science News,* 24 October 1998.

—Jane E. Spear

LITHIUM-ION BATTERIES

INDUSTRY SNAPSHOT

Introduced by Sony Corp. in 1990, the lithium-ion battery (also known as the LI or Li-ion battery) has been hailed as one of the most significant developments in battery technology of the late twentieth century. LI batteries represent a rapidly growing segment of the non-lead-acid secondary battery market, which encompasses rechargeable power sources capable of running portable electronic equipment such as cellular telephones, laptop computers, and video camcorders. (Primary batteries, on the other hand, are those intended to be discarded or recycled after being used.) In contrast to their nickel cadmium predecessors, LI batteries are smaller, lighter, more powerful, and longer lasting, features that enhance the convenience and functionality of portable electronic devices.

As the popularity of such devices has grown throughout the decade, so, too, has the demand for batteries to power them. J. D. Powers and Associates, a U.S.-based consulting firm, reported domestic LI battery sales of about $1 billion in 1996 and predicted that LI battery output would quintuple by the year 2000. As the price of LI batteries drops, analysts expect that they will better compete with nickel metal hydrides, the sales of which rose to 607 million cells in 1997. Although nickel-based cells are expected to account for roughly 80 percent of U.S. rechargeable battery-cell unit shipments through 2002, LI technology will continue to make strong advances, with some analysts estimating the market at more than $4 billion by 2003. Arthur D. Little, Inc., predicts that LI batteries will capture more than 50 percent of the market for high-performance rechargeable batteries by 2003, while the share for nickel cadmium batteries will shrink to 10 percent.

ORGANIZATION AND STRUCTURE

The non-lead-acid secondary battery market in the United States is dominated by imports from Japan, mostly because Japanese manufacturers of cell phones, laptops, and other portable electronic devices were the first to respond to consumer demands for a better power source for such products. Leading the way in the development and marketing of the LI battery are firms such as Matsushita Electric Industrial (better known to consumers under the trade name Panasonic), Sanyo Electric, Sony, and Toshiba. U.S. manufacturers did not enter the market until the mid-1990s, and as a result, they lag far behind their Japanese counterparts in sales. Several of the biggest firms have even withdrawn from the market in the wake of financial losses and low consumer demand for their products.

BACKGROUND AND DEVELOPMENT

The development of the LI battery came about as a direct result of the portable electronics industry's need for a lightweight yet long-lasting power source for its products. Battery developers turned to lithium because it has the greatest energy density of any metal element and therefore can store more energy than any other kind of battery element. During the mid-1990s researchers worked with three different kinds of lithium-based batteries: lithium-metal, LI with liquid electrolyte, and LI with solid-state electrolyte. Gregory Smith reported in *Appliance Manufacturer* that of these battery technologies, LI with solid-state electrolyte received the most attention because it is safer, lighter, more flexible, and easier to work with than the others.

Batteries contain both a positive electrode and a negative electrode. In LI batteries, cobalt functions as the positive electrode, and carbon acts as the negative electrode. Electrically-charged lithium ions vacillate between these electrodes when charging and discharging. Because lithium is such a highly reactive element, early efforts to make rechargeable lithium-based batteries failed when the carbon proved unable to hold the lithium ions. The batteries would then start to smoke or even catch fire while being recharged. Finally, in 1995 researchers discovered that carbon from starches and cellulose held the most active lithium ions during charging and discharging, thereby preventing the batteries from catching fire.

LI batteries are more powerful than nickel-cadmium batteries, which for many years was the most advanced battery available. LI batteries also weigh significantly less, which is another distinct advantage over the competition. Moreover, LI batteries are an environmentally friendly alternative to rechargeable and disposable nickel-cadmium batteries. Such concerns took on added significance with the passage of the Mercury-Containing and Recharging Battery Management Act of 1996. Faced with the need to replace nickel-cadmium batteries with an equally powerful yet environmentally safer battery, manufacturers turned to LI technology. Since they last longer (and thus are disposed of less frequently) and contain no harmful substances, LI batteries seem to provide an ideal solution. However, they also carry a much higher price tag than their predecessors.

CURRENT CONDITIONS

According to an article in *PC Week,* by the late 1990s it appears that LI batteries are becoming the industry's standard power source for portable electronic devices, especially for notebook computers and communications equipment. Packing twice as much power as nickel cadmium batteries, LI batteries also retain their energy even when idle for long periods and can be used with a host of different electronic products.

For users concerned about value, however, LI batteries may not offer the best solution for powering portable electronics. They cost considerably more than nickel-cadmium batteries and nickel-metal-hydride batteries, leading to some speculation that they cannot successfully compete in the lower-end electronics market. But analysts predict that by the year 2000 the cost of an LI battery will be only about 10 percent greater per watt than nickel-cadmium and nickel-metal-hydride batteries.

In 1997, worldwide sales of LI batteries totaled an estimated $1 billion, one-fifth of total lightweight rechargeable battery sales. Demand for and production of LI batteries steadily rose throughout the 1990s. For example, in 1996 alone, Japan produced 115 million units, a 286 percent increase over 1995.

In 1998, a new form of LI battery that offers greater safety and design flexibility went into large-scale production. Thinner than traditional LI batteries, solid-polymer lithium-ion cells use a gel polymer electrolyte that eliminates all liquids and thus prevents the possibility of leaks or toxic gas emission. Because the conducting polymer is housed in an ultrathin laminated foil material, it can be bent to shape, stacked, or stamped extremely thin, allowing a range of design options not possible with standard lithium-ion cells. In addition, the solid-polymer material is fabricated in rolled sheets using less expensive oxides that permit high-volume, high-speed production. With greater energy density—115 to 150 watt-hours per kilogram compared to 70 to 110 for liquid-electrolyte batteries—solid-polymer batteries can also be recharged more than 500 times and will accept a one-hour charge. Furthermore, they more readily comply with international environmental and safety standards and so are more economical to handle and transport.

Because portable electronics are generally designed around the dimensions of their rigid components, the flexibility of solid-polymer lithium-ion batteries could make it possible for manufacturers to produce even smaller devices. The new batteries will most likely be used in high-end cellular phones, portable computers, and personal digital assistants, while lithium-ion and nickel-metal-hydride will continue to be favored in less expensive equipment. Kline & Co. estimates that global demand for lithium-polymer technology could reach $1 billion annually by 2007.

In 1998 Thomas & Betts became the first major manufacturer to mass-produce lithium-ion polymer batteries. That same year, Ultralife Batteries of Newark, New Jersey, was in full production of solid-polymer lithium-ion batteries, while Tucson, Arizona-based Moltech aimed for a midyear launch of its AA cylindrical lithium-polymer cells. Matsushita Battery began volume production of lithium polymer batteries in early 1999 and estimated that the market for solid-polymer products could be 15 million units that year. Hitachi Maxwell and Sony also unveiled plans to enter the solid-polymer lithium-ion market in 1999.

LAPTOP COMPUTERS

In 1997, computer manufacturers introduced a new line of portable computers designed for frequent business travelers: ultralight laptops weighing less than five pounds. While the absence of features such as CD-ROM and floppy disk drives helped contribute to the weight reduction, the use of LI batteries was a significant factor as well. While LI batteries offer the portable computer industry many advantages, they have also led to a rather unusual and potentially dangerous problem. Some batteries have been known to cause laptop computers to overheat and ignite, especially when they are used in the more powerful, feature-loaded computers. In particular, a few of the older Apple PowerBooks experienced battery-caused fires.

CELLULAR PHONES AND COMMUNICATIONS HANDSETS

Much of the growth in the LI market has been driven by the worldwide demand for mobile telephones. LI batteries allow cellular phone customers to use their devices for extended periods of time without having to recharge them. Manufacturers can therefore sell more phones, and battery retailers can capitalize on the popularity of LI batteries as cellular phone accessories. In 1998, for instance, 98 percent of wireless handsets in Japan used LI batteries. The demand

was considerably lower in the United States, however, with only 18 percent of sets relying on LI batteries, and even lower in Europe, where 14 percent of wireless phones were equipped with LI batteries. In 1999, Sony announced plans to begin producing LI phone packs for the growing Chinese market, which posted sales of 10 million mobile phones in 1998. Retailers expect LI batteries to be the best-selling cellular phone accessory by 2000.

INDUSTRY LEADERS

The burgeoning demand for LI batteries during the 1990s took U.S. manufacturers by surprise. Major producers lacked the technology to fabricate LI batteries and had to scramble to try to catch up to their Japanese competitors. U.S. battery makers such as Duracell and Eveready finally brought their products to the marketplace in late 1996 and early 1997.

As the international leader of alkaline battery sales, Duracell, a subsidiary of Gillette, fought to retain its dominant market position by forming an alliance with TDK Corp. of Japan. TDK had already developed the technology and procedures for creating LI batteries, so with its help Duracell intended to make a rapid entrance into the market. The battery segment of the company recorded revenues of $2.2 billion in 1996. In 1997, however, the company announced its intention to cease production of LI battery packs, although it planned to continue research and development of advanced LI battery products.

The number-two battery maker in the United States, Eveready, is a subsidiary of pet-food manufacturer Ralston Purina. More than 80 percent of its sales stem from its primary battery business. In 1996, Eveready entered the LI battery market with the construction of a new $70 million production plant. In 1999, however, citing significantly declining sales, the company declared that it was getting out of the business of making and assembling rechargeable battery packs for electronics manufacturers to include with their battery-operated devices. Instead, Eveready decided to focus on its primary battery business while continuing to market and sell rechargeable batteries to consumers under the Energizer brand name.

In 1997, NEC Electronics, a company best known for designing, manufacturing, and marketing electronic products such as microprocessors, memories, and components, announced its intention to enter the LI battery market by 1999. Its plan involved distributing batteries made by Moli Energy, a Canadian company.

Profile **PORTABLE RECHARGEABLE BATTERY ASSOCIATION**

The primary association supporting the LI battery industry is the Portable Rechargeable Battery Association (PRBA). Founded after the reclassification of nickel-cadmium batteries, which put them in the purview of the Resource Conservation and Recovery Act of 1976, the rechargeable power industry decided to create the PRBA in order to promote recycling of batteries and to focus attention on legislation affecting the industry. Based in Atlanta, Georgia, the PRBA also analyzes industry trends and performance. In addition, the United States Advanced Battery Consortium (USABC) serves the industry by conducting and encouraging research into new battery technologies and new applications of existing technologies. The Dearborn, Michigan-based US-ABC, a partnership of Chrysler, Ford, and General Motors, works on projects along with government agencies such as the U.S. Department of Energy, and the EPRI (Electronic Power Research Institute), to develop items like battery-powered autos.

In 1998, Sony, Sanyo, and Matsushita Battery together accounted for more than 80 percent of the world LI battery market. By far the most dominant manufacturer has been Sony, which introduced the first commercial LI batteries in 1990 and holds 70 percent of the market share, according to *Nikkei Weekly*. Despite some setbacks, including a plant fire in November 1995 that resulted in LI battery shortages throughout the laptop computer industry, Sony produced 48 million batteries in 1995 and expected to increase its output the following year to 72 million batteries.

In 1996, Sony announced an alliance with Sumitomo Metal Mining Company aimed at developing the technology to recycle used batteries. Together they came up with a process by which LI batteries are heated and pulverized. Iron, copper, and cobalt are then extracted from the remnants, which the companies can reuse.

Matsushita Battery and PT Matsushita Gobel Battery Industries, divisions of Matsushita Electric Industrial Co. Ltd., were also among the leaders in worldwide sales of LI batteries in 1996. Matsushita announced plans that same year to establish PT Panasonic Battery of Indonesia, a new division that would exclusively manufacture LI batteries to meet the growing worldwide demand. In 1998, Matsushita said it expected to increase its production capacity by 50 percent to 2 billion batteries per year by 2000 and open new manufacturing operations in Asia and Latin America.

Yet another major Japanese manufacturer of LI batteries anticipated a huge increase in its production capacity over 1998 figures. By late 1999, Hitachi Maxwell planned to double its monthly production to 6 million units.

Despite their success, Japanese manufacturers face stiff competition from other Asian manufacturers for their own domestic markets. South Korea's LG Chemical developed its own lithium-ion battery to compete with Sony, Sanyo, and Toshiba in 1998, and SKC created its own product for use in notebook computers. To counter these efforts, a government-sponsored initiative has led to the formation of joint ventures between Japanese and British partners that will begin production of lithium-ion cells in the United Kingdom in 1999.

RESEARCH AND TECHNOLOGY

In addition to their use in portable electronic devices, lithium-ion batteries have emerged as the pre-

ferred power supply for electric vehicles. The enactment of stricter emissions policies in states such as California, Massachusetts, and New York has prompted automakers to look into alternative fuels for the vehicles they manufacture to make sure they will comply with the new regulations. Previously, auto producers experimented with solar energy and rechargeable batteries. In October 1996, the United States Advanced Battery Consortium (USABC) signed a $106 million agreement to continue research into this technology.

While some companies have focused on nickel-metal-hydride batteries, others, such as Nissan and Mitsubishi, have tested LI batteries. Mitsubishi's vehicle was not planned as a pure electric one, but rather as a hybrid, combining battery power with a small internal combustion engine. Nissan and Sony have also jointly developed a prototype electric vehicle using LI batteries. In addition to Nissan, Toyota and Honda have announced plans to launch hybrid cars.

Supported by the U.S. Department of Energy and the USABC, Saft America, Inc. and PolyStor Corp. have also been conducting research on full-size and 50-volt LI cells for use as a high-power storage device for hybrid electric vehicles. PolyStor is also working to develop LI batteries for use in satellites.

Producers of all new battery technologies, including LI batteries, have attempted to develop standard battery sizes to limit their own production challenges as well as make it easier for hardware manufacturers and consumers to choose among the various kinds of batteries available. According to Mindy Blodgett in *Computerworld*, battery makers also plan to improve the ability of their products to communicate certain vital pieces of information. Relying on microcontrollers and special integrated circuits, these so-called "smart" batteries would let users know how much more power remained to run their equipment before a recharge was necessary. In addition, the smart batteries could efficiently allocate power to whatever function needed it the most. As James Carbone noted in *Purchasing,* such advances would help existing LI batteries last up to 20 percent longer. Smart batteries would prove especially useful for military, medical, and aerospace applications that require accurate and instant tracking of available power.

Many companies are actively investigating new applications and materials for LI technology. Nippon Telegraph & Telephone has developed a high-density LI battery with 100 hours of operation per charge for use in a prototype wristwatch phone that weighs less than 2 ounces. In 1999, Lithium Technology developed a lighter lithium-polymer battery that offered 90 watt-hours of stored energy, a fivefold increase over existing battery capacity. Several other companies are also developing a plastic lithium ion battery. Valence Technology, Inc. patented a new class of materials in 1999 that it expects will increase the energy capacity of lithium polymer batteries by 60 percent, providing a longer life between charges at lower cost. Mitsubishi has also developed a more economical process for manufacturing top-grade graphite, a key ingredient used in the LI negative electrode.

Lithium-metal, abandoned during the 1980s due to questions about its safety, became popular again in the late 1990s. Tadiran Electronic Industries in Port Washington, New York, is using it in cell phones as well as in a wireless portable modem, according to Rik Fairlie in *Computer Shopper.*

Research is also under way at Sandia National Laboratory to find better combinations of cathode materials. According to chemist Tim Boyle, scientists may be close to finding the right combinations of metals and lithium that would enable LI batteries to run long enough to replace traditional lead-acid car batteries and make long-range electric vehicles a practical possibility.

FURTHER READING

Bassak, Gil. "Makers of Rechargeables Wage Chemical Warfare to Increase Battery Capacity." *Electronic Engineering Times,* 5 January 1998.

"Battery Blues." *PC Week,* 9 February 1998.

Blodgett, Mindy. "Laptop Power Woes Drain Mobile Users." *Computerworld,* 21 October 1996.

————. "New Batteries Need Apply." *Computerworld,* 3 July 1995.

Carbone, James. "New Smart Cells Will Last Longer." *Purchasing,* 13 July 1995.

"Demand Rises But Prices Will Fall for Lithium Cells." *Purchasing,* 11 February 1999.

Dicarlo, Lisa. "Notebook Makers Feel the Heat." *PC Week,* 22 January 1996.

"Duracell Exits Rechargeable Computer Battery Business," 19 August 1997. Available from http://www.duracellnpt.com/news.d/xrchrg.html.

"Electric Vehicle Advanced Battery R&D Moves to Phase II." *EPRI Press Release,* 24 October 1996. Available from http://www.epri.com/news/releases/advbat.html.

Fairlie, Rik. "Staying Power." *Computer Shopper,* 1 May 1998.

Hara, Yoshiko. "Polymer Batteries Seek Their Niche." *Electronic Engineering Times,* 7 December 1998.

————. "Japan Revs Up Thin, Polymer Batteries." *Electronic Engineering Times,* 25 January 1999.

Hester, Edward. "Industry Corner: The U.S. Market for Primary and Secondary Batteries." *Business Economics,* 1 April 1999.

Isaka, Satoshi. "Electric Cars Enjoy New Surge of Interest." *Nikkei Weekly,* 2 December 1996.

Liotta, Bettyann. "Battery Makers Ramp Lithium-Polymer Units." *Electronic Buyers News,* 1 February 1999.

Mansfield, Simon. "LI Batteries: A Profitable Future," 5 July 1995. Available from http://www.atip.or.jp/samples/atip95.33r.html.

"Market Overview." *Battery Industry Guide,* August 1998.

Marsh, Peter. "Battery Production Overpowering." *Financial Times,* 17 April 1997.

Mooney, Elizabeth V. "Battery Business Evolves from One Acronym to Another." *RCR Radio Communications Report,* 16 November 1998.

Ondrey, Gerald. "Batteries: Full Speed Ahead." *Chemical Engineering,* February 1999.

"Ralston to Exit OEM Rechargeable Battery Business." St. Louis, MO: Ralston Purina Company, 7 June 1999. Available from http://www.ralston.com/news/news59.html.

Scholl, Jaye. "Plastic Fantastic: Will U.S. Battery Makers Cash In on a Promising Technology?" *Barron's,* 25 January 1999.

Sedgwick, David. "Limited U.S. Demand for Electric Cars." *Automotive News Europe,* 12 October 1998.

Silberg, Lurie. "Cinderella Story: Cellphone Extras." *HFN: The Weekly Newspaper for the Home Furnishing Network,* 29 July 1996.

Smith, Gregory. "Leading the Charge." *Appliance Manufacturer,* October 1996.

————. "Solid-Polymer Electrolyte Makes Lithium-Ion Safe." *Electronic Design,* 1 September 1998.

Velsmid, Debra A. "You Can Never Be Too Thin." *Computerworld,* 3 March 1997.

—Karl Heil, updated by Cameron McLaughlin

MAIL-ORDER AND CATALOG SHOPPING

Fortified by niche marketing techniques as well as by emerging computer technology, mail-order houses and catalog-based retailers experienced a renaissance in the mid-1990s. Although sales did not rise as briskly as they did in the 1980s—when the industry expanded by roughly 300 percent—they have continued to increase as a result of marketing advances based on knowledge of consumer spending patterns and demographics. Analysts forecast continued growth of approximately 7 percent into the twenty-first century. Bolstering the surge are several leading computer manufacturers who rely on catalog shopping, adding to the overall success of this industry. According to Norm Miller of the University of Cincinnati, as quoted in a Gannet News Service article, catalogs accounted for 14 percent of the retail sales market in 1998.

Mail-order and catalog shopping serves the busy lifestyles of many U.S. citizens as well as the less mobile lifestyles of the elderly. Mail-order shopping allows customers to purchase an enormous range of merchandise, including home furnishings, electronics, clothing, lawn and garden supplies, books, music, videos, and even groceries. Practically any saleable consumer item is available through a mail-order house.

ORGANIZATION AND STRUCTURE

Mail-order and catalog retailers usually do not maintain an inventory warehouse; instead, the retailers purchase products directly from manufacturers or wholesalers once orders for specific items have been received. The manufacturers or wholesalers then ship the merchandise either directly to the end-customers or to the mail-order catalog companies. This system allows retailers to avoid the overhead costs unavoidably incurred by maintaining vast on-site inventories. Many companies, such as Williams Sonoma, Inc., J. Crew, Inc., and J.C. Penney Co., Inc., also have retail stores in addition to their mail-order operations.

The mail-order and catalog shopping industry includes two primary sectors: consumer and business sales. Of these two, the consumer sector tends to garner more sales than the business sector, typically between 60 and 75 percent, leaving the business sector with about 25 to 40 percent of industry revenues. The consumer sector comprises a spate of products and services such as apparel, books, food, health care products, toys, home furnishings, and sporting goods. Key business products and services include computer hardware, data-processing products, and general office supplies.

BACKGROUND AND DEVELOPMENT

In the late 1400s, a Venetian book merchant named Aldus Manutius provided one of the first mail-order services selling Greek and Latin books via catalog, according to Ronald Vanderwey in *The Journal of Lending & Credit Risk Management.* In the United States, Benjamin Franklin used catalogs to sell scholarly literature in 1744. As people moved across the country and settled in rural areas, catalog shopping offered a convenient alternative to traveling long

Lillian Vernon, who started the catalog shopping business in 1951, appears here with some of the merchandise available through her catalogs. (AP Photo/Richard Harbus.)

distances to shop at general stores. In the mid-1800s catalogs, such as Orvis and Montgomery Ward, sprang up and started to flourish. Orvis has been marketing fishing gear since 1856. Montgomery Ward began selling general merchandise in 1872. As railway transportation improved, connecting the East Coast with the Midwest, Richard Sears and Alvah Roebuck teamed up in 1897 to offer what would become perhaps the best-known American general merchandise catalog.

Technological advances of the twentieth century propelled the industry forward. In 1913, the U.S. Postal Service began offering parcel post delivery and, in 1928, it introduced third-class bulk mail, creating an inexpensive method for sending packaged goods. The Diners Club offered the first credit card in 1950, ushering in increased demand for mail-order and catalog shopping, by providing users with a convenient and safe means of payment. Later, AT&T made mail-order shopping one step easier by introducing toll-free phone numbers, while the computer era of the 1990s has allowed mail-order houses to offer CD-ROM catalogs in lieu of print material.

CURRENT CONDITIONS

Catalog sales reached more than $85 billion in 1998, up from $81 billion in 1997, according to the Direct Marketing Association (DMA). An article in Gannet News Service quoted an industry analyst predicting that catalogs, with the help of Internet shopping, could account for 25 percent of the retail market by 2003. About 30 percent of all U.S. households may be considered heavy mail-order shoppers.

According to the DMA, circulation of catalogs went up from 13.38 billion in 1996 to 13.91 billion in 1997. The catalog portion of the industry employed over 389,000 workers in 1996 and DMA predictions point to employment reaching 447,200 by 2001. In the late 1990s, catalog sales beat out its direct-marketing competitors: television-based direct marketing and online shopping.

Catalogs originated as a way to reach consumers who lived far away from cities and were unable to shop at retail stores. Many contemporary catalog retailers operate both a mail-order business and retail operations. J.C. Penney, the largest general merchan-

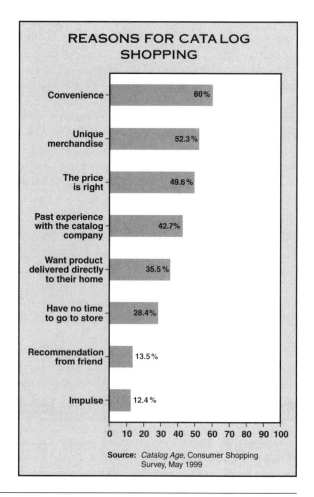

REASONS FOR CATALOG SHOPPING

Convenience	60%
Unique merchandise	52.3%
The price is right	49.6%
Past experience with the catalog company	42.7%
Want product delivered directly to their home	35.5%
Have no time to go to store	28.4%
Recommendation from friend	13.5%
Impulse	12.4%

0 10 20 30 40 50 60 70 80 90 100

Source: *Catalog Age,* Consumer Shopping Survey, May 1999

dise cataloger in the United States, also is the fourth largest retail store chain. However, one well-known mail-order retailer nearly went bankrupt when it branched out into retail store sales. John Peterman, founder of The J. Peterman Company, became famous when he was parodied on the popular television sitcom "Seinfeld." Peterman built a catalog business by selling unique clothing, such as his signature cowboy-style duster. In 1998 Peterman planned to open 70 retail stores but instead, experienced a cash shortage created by a variety of problems, including sluggish catalog sales. Peterman filed for bankruptcy in January 1999 and the company was bought at a liquidation sale in March 1999 for $10 million by retailer Paul Harris Stores Inc. Paul Harris intends to continue distributing Peterman's flagship catalog, *J. Peterman's Owner's Manual,* and keeping open at least 10 of 13 retail stores.

The DMA estimates that there are as many as 10,000 catalogs and in 1998 several hundred new catalogs entered the marketplace. One reason for the catalog proliferation is that catalogs are becoming leaning and more targeted. Like small specialty retail stores in a mall, catalogers have turned to niche marketing or segmentation. Many shoppers use catalogs to save time and, as a result, catalogs are offering fewer but more specialized items. In general, catalogs are downsizing. For instance, using the measure of the number of catalog pages distributed in a year, Spiegel Catalog Inc. reduced the number of pages it distributed from 1996 to 1997, going from 197 to 154 million. In fact, by the mid-1990s most retail catalog companies were no longer developing huge general merchandise catalogs. Instead, they used demographics and marketing research to create small specialized catalogs. Sears discontinued its "Big Book" catalog in the early 1993 and has since relied on 18 specialized catalogs—ranging from automobile parts to clothing for women size 14 and up—catering to the diverse tastes of its 24 million customers. With escalating postage and catalog production costs, general catalogs no longer offered a viable way to market mail-order products. With so many competing companies, in order to survive, mail-order houses had to make their products stand out or match the buying needs of their catalog recipients.

CHALLENGES FOR THE
MAIL ORDER INDUSTRY

Most mail-order products are discretionary or optional. Many analysts note that in the case of attenuating economic conditions, customers abandon these expenditures first. When an economic recession hit the United States in the early 1990s, mail-order sales slumped. Successful mail-order and catalog companies bear this economic fact in mind and manage their businesses accordingly. Furthermore, Betsy Dotson reports in *Government Finance Review* that six U.S. senators petitioned the Federal Trade Commission in 1996 to look into the business practices of mail-order and catalog retailers. Numerous state and local governments claim they have lost revenue from taxable products purchased by customers in their areas from mail-order companies in other states. The state of Maryland, for example, estimates a loss of $35 million a year in sales tax revenue. The senators suspect that some mail-order companies do not apprise their customers of tax obligations, according to Dot son, and called for an FTC mandate that mail-order houses must disclose their customers' tax responsibilities. On the other hand, if mail-order companies collected and tendered the taxes themselves, then they would be exempt from the mandate.

Sigmund Kiener notes in *Direct Marketing* that for mail-order companies to remain successful over the next several years, they will have to provide not only more diverse products and services but will be compelled to distinguish themselves from other companies as well. This can be done by establishing strong name recognition via umbrella brands—that is, brands that span several product or service categories—in order to build corporate identities. Kiener contends that marketing research will continue to play an important role in mail-order and catalog business, because companies will require catalogs and mail-order literature that targets its individual customers. Finally, Kiener identifies another challenge the industry must face: the need to develop a multinational customer base. When approaching international markets, however, companies must be capable of targeting a keenly defined market sector in order to succeed.

INDUSTRY LEADERS

DELL COMPUTER CORP.

Companies selling all sorts of products have experienced heightened sales through direct marketing channels such as mail-order and catalog shopping. The computer industry, for example, includes firms that rely solely on direct marketing including mail-order sales. Dell Computer Corporation has achieved enormous success using mail-order techniques, ranking number one in directly marketed sales. Headed by founder Michael Dell, the company caters to the business and government market, which accounts for about 90 percent of sales. For the year ended January 1999, Dell posted $18.2 billion in sales, a substantial increase of 48 percent over the previous year. Dell employs 16,000 workers.

FINGERHUT COMPANIES, INC.

Minnetonka, Minnesota-based Fingerhut Companies, Inc., is the second-largest catalog retailer in the United States. Fingerhut sells private-label and brand-name products and its catalogs include items such as electronics, crockery, and housewares. In 1999, Federated Department Stores purchased Fingerhut and as part of it, the catalog retailer's database of 30 million customers. Expanding its market, in August 1998, Fingerhut launched a general merchandise catalog and companion Internet site for 18- to 24-year-olds—the first such catalog of its kind. The company sent 600,000 catalogs in its first mailing of thehut.com. Fingerhut reported sales revenue for 1998 of $1.6 billion—a 5 percent gain over 1997—and net income of $75 million. The company employed nearly 10,000 people in 1998.

J.C. PENNEY COMPANY, INC.

J.C. Penney Company, Inc., located in Pano, Texas, is the leading U.S. general catalog retailer. Penney's 643-page catalog includes products such as clothing, furniture, housewares, and luggage. J.C. Penny is the fourth-largest U.S. retailer and has 1,200 department stores in North and South America. Total company revenue for the fiscal year ended January 1999 was $30.7 billion. The company employed 260,000 workers in 1998.

J.CREW GROUP INC.

J. Crew Group Inc., headquartered in New York, New York, markets casual and professional wear for men and women. The company has 100 retail and factory outlet stores across the United States and another 70 outlets in Japan. Sales revenue for fiscal year ended January 1999 were $834 million, an increase of 3 percent from the previous year. The company employed over 6,000 people in 1998.

LANDS END, INC.

Dodgeville, Wisconsin-based Lands' End, Inc., focuses on monthly catalogs featuring its casual and outdoor apparel for men and women. In addition, Lands' End provides specialty clothing for children, as well as housewares. About 60 percent of the company's sales result from catalog marketing. The firm also markets its products in Japan, the United King-

dom, and Germany. In January 1999 three of the company's outlet stores were closed and 94 jobs were cut. The reason for the restructuring, according to a company spokesperson, was that sales had risen 35 percent in 4 years while L.L. Bean staff had increased by 58.0 percent during that same time. The job cuts were for professional staff only; hourly workers in customer sales and service were not let go. The company posted sales revenue of nearly $1.4 billion for the fiscal year ended January 1999, a gain of 8.5 percent over the previous year. The company had 9,200 employees in 1998.

L.L. BEAN, INC.

Leading apparel retailer L.L. Bean, Inc., based in Freeport, Maine, issues 30 catalogs a year and operates a 24-hour, year-round retail store in Freeport. The company specializes in outdoor wear, household furnishings, and sporting goods. L.L. Bean is known for its customer service. For the fiscal year ended February 1998, the privately held company reported revenues of $1.6 billion, up nearly 3 percent from 1997. L.L. Bean employed 3,600 workers in its operations, which include 9 U.S. factory outlets and 11 retail stores in Japan.

WILLIAMS-SONOMA, INC.

Williams-Sonoma, Inc. is a leading U.S. retailer of housewares. The company, which is based in San Francisco, California, issues 5 catalogs and has

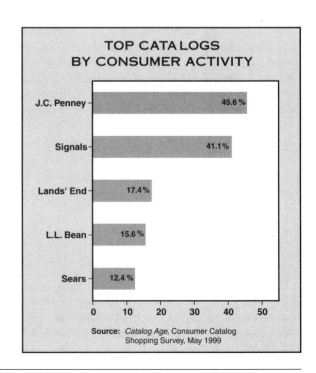

TOP CATALOGS BY CONSUMER ACTIVITY

J.C. Penney	45.6%
Signals	41.1%
Lands' End	17.4%
L.L. Bean	15.6%
Sears	12.4%

Source: *Catalog Age,* Consumer Catalog Shopping Survey, May 1999

approximately 300 stores in nearly 40 states. It sells cookware, housewares, furniture, and storage items through its namesake catalog and two other divisions: *Williams- Sonoma, Hold Everything,* and *Pottery Barn.* Two other divisions of the company are catalog-only operations and offer gardening products and bed and bath items: *Chambers,* and *Gardeners of Eden.* The company posted revenues of $1.1 billion for the year ended January 1999, an 18 percent increase over the previous year. The company employed 12,300 workers in 1998, an increase of nearly 20 percent over 1997.

AMERICA AND THE WORLD

According to *Advertising Age,* Germany purchased more catalog products than any other country. However, the U.S. mail-order industry has remained one of the strongest in the world, earning billions of dollars per year and penetrating international markets. Nonetheless, several European companies have not only done well in their respective countries, but they also have captured part of the U.S. market.

Germany's Otto Versand Gmbh & Co., controls 8.4 percent of the international mail-order market, making it the largest mail-order company in the world. The company plans to expand its catalog business into Asia, specifically targeting China, Korea, and Taiwan. The company posted sales of $13.4 billion for the fiscal year ended 1998 and employed more than 41,000 workers. Otto Versand owns brands popular in the United States such as Eddie Bauer and Spiegel, Inc. In addition to its catalog, outdoor apparel retailer Eddie Bauer has more than 500 stores throughout North America. Catalog retailer Spiegel, which is based in Downers Grove, Illinois, posted revenue of $2.9 billion in 1998 and employed 12,400 workers.

Britain's The Great Universal Stores PLC (GUS) is another one of the world's leading mail-order houses. GUS' Kay's and Marshal Ward catalogs sell more products than any others in Britain. GUS markets its wares throughout Europe and South Africa. For the fiscal year ended March 1998, the company recorded $5.6 billion in sales, a growth of 20 percent from 1997.

Mail-order shopping has increased by about 11 percent per year in Japan since it was first introduced to the country in the 1970s, according to *Nikkei Weekly.* Although 10 large Japanese companies control about 50 percent of the market there, they continue to employ somewhat antiquated marketing tech-

niques such as sending out large general catalogs. However, more efficient international companies such as Lands' End Japan KK and J. Crew have begun to flourish using niche marketing tactics as practiced in the United States.

RESEARCH AND TECHNOLOGY

Emerging database and statistical analysis technology can aid mail-order and catalog retailers in targeting consumer tastes and purchase habits. Artificial intelligence already played a decisive role in the success of some mail-order companies in the mid-1990s and promises to have an even more vital impact in the coming millennium as competition increases and technology progresses. In particular, neural networks—artificial cognitive systems that replicate the functioning of the human brain and are capable of learning—allow mail-order retailers to accurately track what products specific consumers buy, when they buy them, and how much they spend. Though they require training or "learning" time, ultimately neural networks can identify patterns in complicated sets of data, according to Sarah Schafer in *Inc.* The data provided by neural networks facilitates the development of a special catalog designed specifically for individual customers or for a group of customers with similar tastes and habits. Even though using neural networks to analyze consumer data may require some training, mail-order companies can still take advantage of this technology by enlisting the help of consulting agencies. Such technology should benefit both small companies that cannot afford a bevy of statisticians and large companies that want fast, accurate, and manageable information.

FURTHER READING

Biank Fasig, Lisa. "Sales Soar for Specialty Catalog Firms." *Gannet New Service,* 14 September 1998.

"Cashing in on Catalogs." *WWD,* 8 May 1997.

Chandler, Susan. "For 1st Time, Lands' End Turns to Layoffs; 3 Stores to Be Closed." *Chicago Tribune,* 13 January 1999.

Direct Marketing Association. "DMA Research Observatory," 1997. Available from http://www.the-dma.org/home_pages/home-obsimpac.html.

Dotson, Betsy. "Mail-order Sales: GFOA and Coalition Petition the Federal Trade Commission." *Government Finance Review,* August 1996.

"Fingerhut Launches Industry's First General Merchandise Catalog for Young Adults and Companion E-Commerce Site." *Business Wire,* 24 August 1998.

"Founder of J. Peterman Claims He Lost His Job." *The Washington Times,* 9 March 1999.

Gilgoff, Henry. "Catalogs Flooding Mail for Holidays." *Newsday,* 29 November 1998.

Horovitz, Bruce. "Catalog Craze Delivers Holiday Deals." *USA Today,* 1 December 1998.

Kiener, Sigmund. "The Future of Mail Order." *Direct Marketing,* February 1995.

Mussey, Dagmar. "Otto Expands Family-Owned Catalog Empire." *Advertising Age,* 9 September 1996.

Shafer, Sarah. "Software That Thinks." *Inc.,* 19 November 1996.

Vanderwey, Ronald. "Lending to Mail Order Companies." *The Journal of Lending & Credit Risk Management,* September 1996.

Yamamoto, Yuri. "Mail-order Companies Home in on Markets." *Nikkei Weekly,* 7 April 1997.

—Karl Heil, updated by Katherine Wagner

MANAGED HEALTH CARE SERVICES

The managed health care industry represents an attempt to fix or reduce medical costs and, for most of the 1990s, it appeared that the managed care industry was unstoppable. In 1998, however, the industry outlook had changed. Just as upstart health maintenance organizations (HMOs) had once challenged and then won control over the medical system, the pendulum once again began to shift in favor of doctors, employers, and hospitals. The result has been wide fluctuations of mergers and acquisitions. In fact, it was found in a study conducted by the Managed Care Information Center that more than 83 percent of managed care organizations (MCOs) had changed their addresses between the years 1996 and 1997. Consolidation continued to be a concern for the healthcare industry through the end of the decade.

HMOs successfully coordinated and eliminated unnecessary services, controlled use of expensive high-technology procedures, and sponsored consumer education. A MCO is a system of organized health care providers in a single or controlled structure for the co-ordination of medical services. Within this umbrella there are several types of MCOs roughly organized around the degree of flexibility, ranging from the highly regimented health maintenance organization (HMO) to the flexible point-of-service (POS) plan allowing the most freedom of choice. The preferred provider orga-nization (PPO) by definition falls in between. The greater the freedom of choice, the higher the plan's popularity as well as its cost. The term MCO is used as an operational definition of managed health care.

MCOs provide services or plans to both corpora-tions and government organizations, with Medicare being one of the largest government segments. Man-aged care was a popular option for consumers at the end of the 1990s. In 1999 the nation's 650 MCO's boasted a total membership enrollment of 160 million. MCOs provided health coverage for 86 percent of workers and their families in 1998, up from 55 per-cent only six years earlier. By 1997 one in four Amer-icans was enrolled in an HMO. There were nearly 80 million members in HMOs near decade's end. The in-surance industry expected 80 percent of the individ-ual and small group market to be purchasing true man-aged care plans by the year 2000.

The Health Care Financing Administration pro-jected that the nation's total spending for healthcare would increase from $1 trillion annually (approxi-mately $3,621 per person) in 1996 to $2.1 trillion by 2007. MCOs represented an $80 billion per year mar-ket share in the late 1990s.

While MCOs may have reduced or at least con-tained the cost of health care since their growth in the early 1990s, the industry saw shrinking profits in 1997 and 1998. According to an article in *Business Week,* several factors could have contributed to the decline of MCOs, including increased competition between insurers, employers participating in self-insurance plans, and the fact that the managed care industry was failing to cut expenses as it once did. In a survey con-ducted by the Managed Care Information Center, re-spondents ranked "increasing efficiency/profitability" as the third most important healthcare industry con-cern in 1999. The top two concerns were "complying with healthcare legislation/regulation" and "keeping customers satisfied."

In addition to fixing the costs of medical services, MCOs shifted the market from being physician-driven to MCO-driven, although not without a growing concern on the part of physicians who were pressured to accept lower fees than fee-for-service patients. Pressure on HMO earnings pushed up costs, increasing the need for further reductions. In response, some physicians formed their own physician health maintenance organizations. And many companies started to deal directly with physician and hospital providers, thus eliminating the HMOs. Sanford C. Bernstein & Co. analysts, as quoted in *Business Week,* predicted that multi-hospital chains will account for 63 percent of all hospital beds by 2001, up from 31 percent in 1991.

As competition and market penetration increased, so did mergers and acquisitions. At the end of the millennium, it was difficult to find a MCO that either had not been acquired or had acquired others.

ORGANIZATION AND STRUCTURE

Health insurance in the United States is paid for by individuals who either contract directly with indemnity (fee-for-service) insurers, by their corporate employers who pay or co-pay the premiums, or by governments who may contract either with indemnity insurers or pre-paid MCO plans. The federal government insures its employees and those eligible for Medicare (people 65 years of age and over). State governments are increasingly contracting with MCOs for workers compensation insurance; for example, state and county governments began turning to MCOs to provide insurance for those receiving public assistance.

MCOs are managerially organized as corporate staffed, contracted group practice, affiliated networks, or individual practitioners contracted through an Independent Practice Association (IPA). The driving force behind MCOs is the elimination of duplication of services. HMOs are grouped by one of the above organizational structures. Staffed HMOs employ their physicians directly on salary and services are typically provided in a single location. Group practice HMOs contract with several medical groups according to the type of service provided. A network system provides services in two or more distinct geographical units.

Traditional fee-for-service insurance plans typically allow the individual the freedom to visit any doctor or specialist and be reimbursed around 80 percent of the total costs. As a consequence, the patient could, for example, be given several separate prescriptions that combined could be redundant at best and harmful at worst. Coordination is designed to reduce this risk and lower costs. The lock-in features of HMOs

mean that patients going outside the system have no benefits and are responsible for all bills incurred with these providers. Nearly all HMOs require a gatekeeper or primary care physician who screens, evaluates, and redirects patients to participating specialists if necessary. Traditional health care has been declining since 1985 at roughly the same rate that managed care has been growing in terms of population insured.

Several MCOs use a pharmacy benefit manager and have formularies (lists of approved drugs and accepted equivalents). There are also open-ended HMOs that allow patients to go outside the defined network to obtain care from any provider in the network without first going through a primary-care physician or gate keeper but at a higher co-payment.

Doctors are paid by the contracting MCO. HMOs typically contract with a local IPA, usually for a capitation fee (per-capita average cost per member). Such a fee is variable and dependent upon demographics and local health care costs. HMOs typically pay doctors one-half to one-third the amount they would receive from fee-for-service patients and either pay on a flat rate per month per patient basis or on a per visit basis. Physicians hoping to improve revenues have started up physician friendly MCOs. Some HMOs withhold a percentage of the service fee for payout as bonuses to physicians at the end of the year if they save the HMO money by ordering fewer tests, defer visits, or cut back on procedures.

PPO plans allow members to move in and out of networks and to see specialists without a gatekeeper's approval but the member's co-payment will be higher outside the network. As high as 30 percent of PPO member patients go outside the network in the first year of membership but this number typically drops considerably by the third year.

POS plans combine the independence of traditional plans with managed care plans by allowing members to get care in or out-of-the network with or without permission with maximum benefits. Health Partners of Minneapolis pioneered POS plans in 1961 under the name Group Health Plan Corporation, but it took 25 years for POSs to become accepted. In the late 1990s, POS plans were one of the fastest growing segments of MCOs since they provided a popular mix of freedom and cost containment. They appealed to small firms because they were a less expensive option than indemnity insurance even though they cost more than HMOs. People were willing to pay for flexibility. A growing number of HMOs began offering POS plans that allowed the patient to go outside the network for service with the understanding that the co-pay may increase quite significantly.

In the late 1990s, some MCOs dropped their managed care programs for the poor and elderly. According to Peter T. Kilborn in the *New York Times,* industry leaders such as Aetna U.S. Healthcare, Kaiser Permanente, and United Healthcare ended many of their Medicaid services in states such as New York, New Jersey, Florida, Massachusetts, and Connecticut. Kilborn stated that companies claimed that cuts in government payments caused the service cutbacks. Nevertheless, the number of Medicaid beneficiaries enrolled in a managed care program of some kind continued to increase through the latter half of the decade and was expected to reach 50 percent of all Medicaid enrollees. In 1996 Medicaid paid out $16 billion in premiums for HMOs and Medicare combined.

The quality of MCO service is controlled in several ways. The National Committee for Quality Assurance (NCQA), started in 1991, serves as an accrediting body and seeks to measure the organization's ability to provide quality service by evaluating its structure and procedures based on a uniform set of criteria and statistics. The media, such as *Consumer Reports,* bases its evaluations on consumer satisfaction. Watchdog groups, such as the Coalition for Accountable Managed Care and the Center for Health Care Rights, are concerned with patients' rights as well as client satisfaction with services. Congress seeks to protect the consumer through legislation and cost containment via budget reductions, especially in the Medicare-paid programs. MCOs themselves put new doctors through a credentialing process and a recredentialing every two years, although the process is not always considered to be sufficiently thorough.

NCQA, an independent, non-government, not-for-profit organization, collects standardized data from MCOs and compiles it into the Health Plan Employer Data and Information Set (HEDIS). Fifty standards in six categories (quality improvement, physician credentials, members' rights and responsibilities, preventive health services, utilization management, and medical records) are applied in evaluating an MCO. Accreditation status based on the degree to which a set of standardized criteria for plans are met is designated as full three year, one-year, provisional, under review, or denied. Participation is voluntary for non-government MCOs but mandatory for Medicare funded contractors. Large private and public companies are increasingly requiring their health contractors to be accredited. NCQA received data from 447 MCOs in 1998.

The Utilization Review Accreditation Commission (URAC) was also cited in several MCO company reports as the preeminent accrediting body for utilization management programs. Two remaining healthcare issues are: how to maintain quality care in a cost-conscious environment, and how to extend coverage to the nation's 43.4 million uninsured persons (16.1 percent of the population).

BACKGROUND AND DEVELOPMENT

The term "health maintenance organization" was coined in the early 1970s. Although numerous bills introduced in the 1970s to institute a national universal health insurance law failed to be enacted, Congress did pass the Health Maintenance Organization Act of 1973. The Act defined the requirements for a health maintenance organization, including physician service arrangements, contracts, fiscal requirements, and safeguards to ensure solvency. Prepaid group practice plans, renamed health maintenance organizations, had already emerged in some areas of the country. The demand for managed health care was also brought about by employers seeking to curtail double digit health insurance premium hikes.

By the end of 1984 there were 16 million persons enrolled in 330 HMOs. Medicare included capitated systems in 1986. While a modest number of HMOs have been around since the 1970s and 1980s, they received a big boost when President Bill Clinton's proposed "managed competition" health care plan failed in 1993. The industry quickly responded with a more aggressive program. In 1995 the U.S. Department of Defense replaced its traditional insurance with an HMO/PPO hybrid and the government implemented its CHAMPUS (Civilian Health and Medical Program of the Uniform Services) reform initiative.

Several major changes occurred in HMOs during the 1990s: the growth of for-profit plans and the decline in nonprofit plans; the shift from vertically integrated staff and group models to vertically integrated individual practice associations and networks; increased patient cost sharing; and the shift to capitation as a means of payment to primary care physicians. There were also notable abuses, as evidenced by the U.S. General Accounting Office's claim that California Medicare risk HMOs were overpaid by $1 billion in 1995. The accusation was based on the HMO's selection of healthier Medicare beneficiaries, thus leaving more costly patients in the fee-for-service plan. Nonprofit organizations were rated more highly than for-profit plans.

Time has shown that the enactment of the Employee Retirement Income Security Act of 1974

(ERISA) has had the single greatest effect on health plans in this country. Its employee benefits statements have been broadly interpreted by the federal courts as relating to insurance mandates, medical high risk pools, and uncompensated care pools. The Health Insurance Portability and Accountability Act of 1996 increased the portability of health care coverage, limited pre-existing condition limitations, and established a program for tax-free medical savings accounts for health care purchases.

According to the American Association of Health Plans, as cited in David Azevedo's 1996 article in *Medical Economics,* more than 400 anti-managed-care bills were proposed across the states in 1996, twice as many as in 1995. Nearly every state has passed a law regarding some facet of managed health care and new bills are continually pending. An important decision by the Eastern Court of Arkansas ruled that MCOs were not required to take any willing provider who agreed to their terms and met their conditions on the basis that it was preempted by ERISA and the Federal HMO Act. Some 40 bills were introduced in Congress alone that would regulate either managed care providers or insurers, cover minimum hospitals stays for breast cancer patients, and allow patients greater freedom when choosing physicians. One bill would eliminate the "Gag clause" imposed by MCOs on physicians to prohibit them from discussing fiscal arrangements. In 1997, legislation was also being drafted that would eliminate the use of drug formularies, and a panel of legislators from nine states developed the Managed Care Consumer Protection Act to protect the rights of managed care plan enrollees.

About... THE QUALITY ASSURANCE AND PATIENT PROTECTION ACT

Managed care organizations are bringing greater scrutiny to the medical industry, and quality costs and ethics under fee-for-service were never as intensely scrutinized as in the late 1990s. In response to this scrutiny, Congress introduced the Quality Assurance and Patient Protection Act in mid-1997. Nicknamed the "Health Insurance Bill of Rights Act," this proposed legislation would guarantee the right to choose one's own doctor, the right to quality health care, the right to justice, and the right to full disclosure.

On the other hand the $77.9 billion drug industry reported a 13.7 percent sales increase in 1997. MCO members tended to receive prescriptions that were 20 percent larger than those of cash-paying customers. The majority of enrollees in HMOs or POSs were satisfied with pharmacy benefits especially when they could use national chains or local pharmacies. HMOs look at drug costs in relation to the overall cost of therapy, taking into account whether or not the prescribed drug may reduce other outlays such as hospitalization or surgery.

Dental HMOs as separate policies have increased to over 34 million according to the National Association of Dental Plans. Conventional MCOs have not been able to tap into the dental segment because dentistry has a history of demonstrated cost-cutting techniques, a gatekeeper approach to referrals, and a program of preventive care.

The merger fever in the industry in the 1990s was driven by increasing competition, regional firms acquiring plans on opposite sides of the nation to establish a national presence and increasing demand for value (quality of service for premium charged). Mergers and acquisitions resulting in mega-companies were commonplace in the late 1990s.

Among the major concerns was whether services should be MCO driven, physician driven, or end-consumer driven. Formularies, definitions of emergencies, and the general lack of provision for mental health care were some of the prevailing issues. According to one project, there was a clear correlation between formulary restriction and increased physician and emergency room visits, sicker patients, and longer hospitalizations. HMO formularies—lists of approved drugs including substitute and/or generic brand drugs—proved problematic as well. Mental health benefits were another issue of concern, particularly in regard to limitations on the number of sessions or treatment allowed by some carriers.

By the end of 1996, HMOs in the United States were recovering from higher medical costs experienced earlier in the year. POS plans, intended as a temporary hybrid to lead people to HMOs, appeared to be taking on a life of their own as a substantial number of MCOs added them to the list of options. HMO growth slowed in 1997, however.

According to the American Association of Health Plans (AAHP), which represents over 1,000 MCOs, managed care saved over $116 billion in health care costs between 1990 and 1996. In 1996, MCOs saved families with children between $375 and $500. MCOs were expected to save an additional $125 billion or more between 1997 and 2000.

The proliferation of MCOs caused increased competition between companies and fewer rate increases than analysts had predicted. Keith H. Hammonds reported in *Business Week* that insurers had low-balled prices to gain new contract bids, especially with medium-sized firms. As a result, midsize companies saw their health-benefit costs reduced by nearly 2 percent in 1997. One possible response to this trend would be for HMOs to look more like traditional insurance and for the inclusion of self-funded plans in which the employer bears some of the financial risk for employees' health care costs.

Workers compensation, a $70 billion industry, is shifting to the MCOs for coverage. Several states were using MCOs to medically manage worker's compensation claims. Every Ohio employer was required to select a worker's compensation MCO from a list of 52 certified MCOs by February of 1997. All claims were to be managed by MCOs by 1998. Evaluation of services were slated to be based on quality of care and not just the brevity of a worker's downtime. A study conducted by Bruce Sundquist, of the worker's compensation division of CAN, concluded that PPOs reduced costs for each office visit and for blood tests by 20 percent.

In mid-1997 President Clinton proposed a budget savings of $25 billion by reducing Medicare reimbursements over the next five years. This new legislation, which went into effect in October 1997, lowered the per capita Medicare payments to HMOs. Proposed cuts in MCO payments could result in the elimination of prescription drug coverage by Medicare plan providers.

CURRENT CONDITIONS

Managed care was an industry in flux at the end of the twentieth century. In 1999 Congress was reviewing several proposals to reform managed care, including legislation that would allow MCO members to request external review or sue for damages. Such legislation was driven by widely publicized horror stories of MCOs that denied care or refused to pay for necessary treatments and operations. In a 1998 case, a woman who'd had cancer successfully sued Louisville, Kentucky-based Humana Health Plan after the MCO declined to pay for a doctor recommended hysterectomy. The patient, Karen Johnson, was awarded $13 million in punitive damages.

As Congress struggled to finalize a federal "patients' bill of rights," many states moved ahead with their own initiatives. In 1997 17 states adopted comprehensive patient-protection legislation. Ten more states followed suit in 1998. States such as Missouri offered residents a wide range of protections, including the right to sue, make external appeals, see out-of-network providers, and obtain prescriptions not covered by their plan. By 1998 all states required HMOs to set up grievance procedures for patients who'd been denied treatments. Concerning external reviews, 19 states had some version by 1999. Given the widespread, bipartisan support behind the concept, many MCOs became more open to the practice. Aetna U.S. Healthcare, one of the country's major MCOs, announced in 1999 that it would begin external reviews.

At the end of the decade the "Medicare Fairness Gap" was another major issue that the managed care industry faced. The American Association of Health Plans (AAHP) urged Congress to make Medicare reform a top priority in 1999. Medicare recipients in managed care plans received more benefits at lower costs than seniors in traditional insurance plans, but the government projected that by 2004 MCOs would receive only 75 percent of the reimbursement rate of fee-for-service plans. The AAHP warned that, as a result, many MCOs might reduce benefits to Medicare patients or cease participation in the program.

A third interesting development at the millennium's end was a tentative openness on the part of the managed care industry to cover some types of experimental treatments. The AAHP suggested in 1999 that its members help pay for clinical trials of new treatments for diseases such as cancer. The UnitedHealth Group was the only MCO to announced that it would cover new, unproven cancer treatments.

Finally, cost containment was an urgent issue in 1999 when premiums were expected to increase by up to 9 percent. In the face of these increases, MCOs were urged to improve their delivery of healthcare services. Howard R. Veit, a health industry consultant, said that, "health plans that do not continually develop new and innovative ways to differentiate and appeal to consumers will simply not succeed."

INDUSTRY LEADERS

AETNA U.S. HEALTHCARE

One of the titans of the managed care industry, Aetna U.S. Healthcare, reported 1998 revenues of

$20 billion and net income of $848 million. After acquiring the NYLCare Health Plans in 1998, the MCO increased its member base by 2.1 million enrollees. That same year, Aetna acquired Prudential Healthcare for $1 billion. This move added another 6.6 million members to Aetna's rolls, making it the country's largest MCO with a total of about 18.4 million members or one in 10 Americans.

In 1999 Aetna U.S. Healthcare became the first national MCO to voluntarily submit to external review of coverage. As a result, members gained the right to appeal denials of coverage to a panel of independent physician reviewers. The decision to allow external reviews was an expansion of the company's policy of permitting internal reviews. Aetna U.S. Healthcare's president, Michael J. Cardillo, said that allowing external reviews "demonstrates our dedication to reaching out to make sure that our members get the health care they need."

CIGNA CORPORATION

CIGNA Corporation is another leading provider of health care insurance and related financial services. In the first quarter of 1999 the company reported a 20 percent increase in earnings for its healthcare division, which included CIGNA's HMO operations. The division's 1998 revenues were $21.4 billion and net income of $1.2 billion. The company's HMO had 6.7 million members in 1999.

WELL POINT HEALTH NETWORKS, INC.

WellPoint Health Networks, Inc. was one of the largest publicly traded MCOs in the United States by 1999. The company served more than 6.9 million medical members and 29.7 million specialty pharmaceutical and dental members with its HMOs, PPOs and POS plans. Wellpoint was formed in 1996 through a merger with Blue Cross Blue Shield of California. The firm initiated a public offering of 10 million shares in March 1997. The company's 1998 revenues were $6.5 billion.

COVENTRY HEALTH CARE INC.

Nashville-based Coventry Health Care Inc. had 1.4 million members in 1999 throughout the Midwest and Southeast. Of that number, almost 110 thousand were Medicaid members. After merging with Principal Health Care in 1998, Coventry recorded revenues of $2.1 billion, a 72 percent increase over 1997. The company's net earnings for 1998 were $2.9 million.

UNITEDHEALTH GROUP

In 1998 the United HealthCare Corp. changed its name to UnitedHealth Group, after a year marked by the acquisition of HealthPartners of Arizona and the decision to terminate a previously announced merger with Humana Inc. By early 1999 UnitedHealth Group had 8.6 million members, an increase of 8 percent in enrollment. The MCO division of UnitedHealth Group, UnitedHealthcare, reported first-quarter 1999 revenues of $4.4 billion. By 1999 UnitedHealthcare was providing services to members in 150 markets in the United States and Puerto Rico. The company also had an international presence, providing management services in South Africa and Hong Kong.

In 1997 United HealthCare finalized a contract with the American Association of Retired People (AARP) to provide Medigap insurance to over 5 million AARP members between the ages of 50 and 65. The availability of the program, called Medicare Select, was expanded in 1999. The plan, accessible to AARP member in 55 markets nationally, was a lower cost alternative to Medicare Supplement.

KAISER PERMANENTE

Kaiser Permanente, founded in 1945, is the largest nonprofit HMO in the United States. The Oakland, California-based company had a membership of 8.6 million voluntarily enrolled members in 1999, and a network of over 10,000 group-practice physicians. The majority of the HMO's members, 5.7 million, lived in California. The HMO also served members in 17 other states and the District of Columbia.

SAFEGUARD HEALTH ENTERPRISES

In the late 1990s Safeguard Health Enterprises, based in Anaheim, California, was a major provider of managed dental care plans catering to large- and medium-sized government agencies or private sector employees. In 1998 the company announced that it was restructuring and eliminated it general and orthodontic dental offices. Safeguard also began a transition from being a staff model dental HMO to becoming a national dental benefits company. Revenues for 1998 were $99.7 million. Safeguard had more than 1 million members in 27 states by 1999.

WORK FORCE

There were an estimated 9,933,000 persons employed in the health services industry in June 1998, according to the U.S. Department of Labor Bureau of Labor Statistics. The BLS reported that occupations in the health services field were expected to increase more that twice as fast as the entire economy. The Bureau's projections called for a 30 percent increase, or the addition of 3.1 million new health care services jobs, between 1996 and 2006.

The late 1990s were not a good time, however, to be employed in an upper-level MCO management position. In a research study conducted for The National Directory of Managed Care Organizations, and reported by the Managed Care Information Center, it was found that during 1997, more than 46 percent of MCO's senior management experienced personnel changes.

On a historical basis, employment figures and hourly wages experienced modest increases in the mid-1990s. Over 196,400 persons were employed specifically by the MCO industry leaders and over 33,000 physicians were networked or contracted with the MCOs. (MCO figures were derived solely from the reports of "industry leaders" and are incomplete since not all MCOs were included.)

FURTHER READING

Aetna 1998 Annual Report, 11 May 1999. Available from http://www.aetna.com/98annualrpt/finhigh.

"Aetna to Acquire Prudential Healthcare for $1 Billion." 10 December 1998. Available from http://www.aetna.com/news/1998.

"Aetna U.S. Healthcare to Institute First Voluntary External Review Policy for Managed Care," 12 January 1999. Available from http://www.aetna.com/news/1999.

Azedo, David. "Will the States Get Tough with HMOs?" *Medical Economics,* 26 August 1996.

Bell, Allison. "CNA Asks Whether Some MC Plans Save Money." *National Underwriter (Life/Health/Financial Services),* 28 April 1997.

"Benchmarking Guide: Consumer Satisfaction." *Hospitals & Health Networks,* 5 January 1997.

Brooks, Robette. "Reducing the Cost of Managed Care." *Inform,* April 1997.

"CBO Figures Set to Show Widening 'Medicare Fairness Gap.'" 7 April 1999. Available from http://www.aahp.org/services/communications/media/1999.

Chassin, Mark R. "Assessing Strategies for Quality Improvement." *Health Affairs,* May/June 1997.

CIGNA 1998 Annual Report, 11 May 1999. Available from http://www.cigna.com/corp/ar.

"CIGNA Reports First Quarter Results; Earnings Up 20% for Health Care Segment," 3 May 1999. Available from http://www.prnewswire.com.

Comarow, Avery. "How We Ranked the Plans." *U.S. News & World Report,* 5 October 1998.

"Congressional Bill Hits Formularies, Managed Pharmacy." *Managed Healthcare,* April 1997.

Conlan, Michael F. "Drugs at Risk." *Drug Topics,* 3 March 1997.

Cotton, Paul. "Open-ended HMOs: An Illusion of Choice?" *Journal of Business Strategy,* July/August 1996.

Coventry Health Care 1998 Annual Report, 11 May 1999. Available from http://www.coventryhealthcare.com.

"Coventry Health Care Announces First Quarter Results." 3 May 1999. Available at http://www.coventryhealthcare.com/investor/press.

Crane, Mark. "What's Holding Back Capitation?" *Medical Economics,* 27 January 1997.

DeRosa, John D. "POS Plans May be the Wave of the Future." *National Underwriter (Life/Health/Financial Services),* 28 April 1997.

Dimmitt, Barbara. "Can Point-of Service Go the Distance?" *Business & Health,* August 1996.

Findlay, Steven. "Managing the Urge to Regulate." *Business & Health,* April 1997.

Fisher, Mary Jane. "Clinton Budget to Allow PSNs for Medicare." *National Underwriter (Life/Health/Financial Services),* 3 February 1997.

———. "D'Amato Introduces Patients Rights Bill." *National Underwriter (Life/Health/Financial Services),* 28 April 1997.

Frenkel, Marcel. "Capitation, Disease Management, and Physician Liability." *Journal of Health Care Finance,* Spring 1997.

Gabel, John. "Ten Ways HMOs Changed During the 1990s." *Health Affairs,* May/June 1997.

Gardner, John. "A Push for Standards." *Modern Healthcare,* 12 May 1997.

Geisel, Jerry. "Medicare Shift to HMOs Continuing." *Business Insurance,* 24 March 1997.

Gettlin, Robert H. "Washington's Next Target: Managed Care." *Best's Review (Life/Health),* March 1997.

Gibson, William S. "Managed Care: The Cure for Health Inflation." *Compensation & Benefits Management,* Spring 1997.

Gray, Christopher. "Dental Firms Extract Market." *Modern Healthcare,* 3 March 1997.

Grimaldi, Paul L. "HEDIS 3.0 Advances Health Plan Accountability." *Healthcare Financial Management,* May 1997.

"Guaranteed Choice in Prescriptions." *Business & Health,* March 1997.

Hagland, Mark. "Dangling Modifiers." *Hospitals & Health Networks,* 5 April 1997.

"Health Care: Special Report." *Consumer Reports,* October 1996.

"Health in America Tied to Income and Education," 30 July 1998. Available from http://www.cdc.gov/nchswww/releases/98news/husrp98.

"Health Plan Efficiency Varies 'Dramatically'—Study." *Employee Benefit Plan Review,* June 1996.

"Highlights of the National Health Expenditure Projections, 1997-2007," 11 May 1999. Available from http://www.hcfa.gov/stats/NHE-Proj/hilites.

"HMO Rates Stable for Second Straight Year." *Health Care Financing Review,* Fall 1996.

"An HMO Suffers a Major Court Loss." *U.S. News & World Report,* 2 November 1998.

Hogan, William P. "Workers' Compensation Moves Further Toward Managed Care." *Managed Healthcare,* December 1996.

"Humana and United HealthCare Mutually Agree to Terminate Merger Plans," 10 August 1998. Available from http://www.unitedhealthcare.com/press.

"Independence Blue Cross and PitCairn Properties Form New Venture for Assisted Living Communities." Philadelphia, PA: Independence Blue Cross, 18 April 1997.

"Insider Spider." *Hospitals & Health Networks,* 5 April 1997.

"Kaiser Permanente Fast Facts," 11 May 1999. Available from http://www.kaiserpermanente.org/newsroom/fastfacts.

Kazel, Robert. "Foundation Health Looks to Northeast for Expansion." *Business Insurance,* 12 May 1997.

Kertesz, Louise. "Calif. Medicare HMOs Overpaid by $1 Billion—GAO." *Modern Healthcare,* 3 March 1997.

Lefton, Ray. "Aligning Incentives Using Risk Sharing Arrangements." *Healthcare Financial Management,* February 1997.

Lippman, Helen. "Another Health Explosion: It's Not Inevitable." *Business & Health,* March 1997.

Lord, Mary. "Patience for a Bill of Rights." *U.S. News & World Report.* 5 October 1998.

Managed Care Facts, 11 May 1999. Available from http://www.aahp.org/menus.

Managed Care Information Center's 1999 Healthcare Industry Trends, 10 May 1999. Available from http://managedcareinfocenter.com.

McCue, Mike. "Managed Care's Shockwave." *Managed Healthcare,* March 1997.

McNamee, Mike. "Health-Care Inflation: It's Back!" *Business Week,* 17 March 1997.

Meckler, Laura. "Fewer Americans Insured." *Associated Press,* 19 October 1998. Available from http://more.abcnews.go.com/sections/living/DailyNews/insurance981019.

Morrisey, John. "HMOs Enter the Internet Age." *Modern Healthcare,* 7 April 1997.

Moskowitz, Daniel B. "On Medicare Cuts and a Coalition." *Business & Health,* March 1997.

Nauert, Peter W. "Managed Care's 2000 Design." *National Underwriter Life/Health/Financial Services),* 28 April 1997.

Nocera, Joseph. "Two Cheers for Red Tape." *Fortune,* 26 May 1997.

Olsen, Robert E. "Employers May Want to Look at Care Options." *Business Insurance,* 27 January 1997.

Ott, Robert J. "Dental Maintenance Measures Strike the Roots of Managed Care." *Managed Healthcare,* January 1997.

"Providing Healthcare in the Age of Consumerism," 4 May 1999. Available from http://managedcareinfocenter.com.

Reynes, Roberta. "Hybrid Plans Grow in Popularity." *Nation's Business,* November 1996.

"Ruling Guts Arkansas' Any-Willing-Provider Law." *Best's Review,* March 1997.

"SafeGuard Health Enterprises, Inc. Fourth Quarter and Year End 1998 Financial Results and Agreement in Principle to Restructure Debt." *PR Newswire,* 16 April 1999. Available from http://news.stockmaster.com.

Schachner, Michael. "HMOs Are Tops in Efficiency." *Business Insurance,* 13 May 1997.

Scott, Jeanne Schulte. "Reforming Managed Care: What Are the Issues?" *Healthcare Financial Management,* March 1997.

Shapiro, Joseph P. "Seeking a Second Opinion." *U.S. News & World Report,* 8 March 1999.

Speer, Tibbett L. "The Balancing Breed." *Hospitals & Health Networks,* 5 February 1997.

Spencer, Bruce F. "1966-1975: The Decade of ERISA." *Employee Benefit Plan Review,* March 1996.

"Tomorrow's Jobs." *1998-99 Occupational Outlook Handbook,* 11 May 1999. Available from http://www.bls.gov/oco/oco2003.

"A Trial Run for HMOs." *U.S. News & World Report,* 22 February 1999.

Ullman, Ralph. "Satisfaction and Choice: A View from the Plans." *Health Affairs,* May/June 1997.

"United HealthCare Completes Acquisition of HealthPartners of Arizona," 5 October 1998. Available from http://www.unitedhealthcare.com/press.

"UnitedHealth Group Offers Medicare Select to AARP Members: Program will Expand in 1999 to Help Provide Lower Cost Alternative to Medigap," 4 February 1999. Available from http://www.unitedhealthcare.com/press/pressreleases.

"UnitedHealth Group Reports Record First Quarter Earnings of $0.72 Per Share," 6 May 1999. Available from http://www.unitedhealthcare.com/investor.q1199.

Waid, Mary Onnis. "Brief Summaries of Medicare and Medicaid," 11 May 1999. Available from http://www.hcfa.gov/stats/NHE-Proj/hilites.

Wechsler, Jill. "Giving Managed Care Payments a Tune-Up." *Managed Healthcare,* April 1997.

"WellPoint Health Networks Vision," 11 May 1999. Available from http://www.wellpoint.com/financial/vision.

Whigham-Desir, Marjorie. "What to Know About Choosing an HMO." *Black Enterprise,* February 1996.

Yovich, Tim. "Change Require Switch to HMOs." *The Vindicator,* 22 June 1997.

—David C. Genaway,
updated by Katherine Wagner and Marinell James

MASS MERCHANDISING

As reported in a *New York Times Magazine* profile, movie director Steven Spielberg was in a meeting with the consultants who design computer games for Dreamworks SKG, the entertainment company that Spielberg and two other Hollywood moguls formed in 1994. One topic on the meeting's agenda was a computer game based on the animated Dreamworks film *Small Soldiers.* "Although the film didn't do well at the box office," Stephen J. Dubner wrote, "video rentals and sales of *Small Soldiers* toys and games are so strong that Dreamworks is making a sequel, in large part to broaden the ancillary franchise."

This indicates the increasingly important role mass merchandising—such as spinoffs, tie-ins, cross-promotions, and merchandise licensing—plays in the entertainment industry. Licensed entertainment properties, such as action figures, clothing, and plush dolls, along with marketing campaigns tied to fast food chains and soft drink companies—not to mention musical soundtracks, books, and computer games—have become just as important as the original source material. Some high profile blockbuster films, including Spielberg's *Jurassic Park,* have even earned more in merchandise revenue than in ticket sales, while successful movie soundtracks often stay on the charts months after the films disappear from theaters.

In the last two decades, the licensing industry—when companies pay a fee to use the image of a sports team or an animated character, for example—has exploded. Businesses as diverse as fast food restaurants and t-shirt makers have discovered the benefits of aligning themselves with high-profile characters and images that literally sell themselves. Meanwhile, entertainment companies have discovered a vast new revenue source to help offset rising production costs. Overall, retail sales of licensed merchandise grew from $20 billion in 1982 to over $70 billion annually by the mid-1990s, according to *The Licensing Letter,* an industry newsletter.

ORGANIZATION AND STRUCTURE

Entire industries—particularly toy manufacturers—pinned their fortunes to *The Phantom Menace,* the latest installment in director George Lucas' heralded *Stars Wars* film series. Restaurant chains and others were lining up months before the film's release, forking over record fees for licensing. Some analysts predict that *The Phantom Menace* and Lucas' next two *Star Wars* installments could rake in more than $6 billion over the next decade in merchandising alone. This shouldn't be too surprising, however. It was Lucas, after all, who forever altered the licensing and promotional marketing landscape with his original *Star Wars* movie in 1977. *Star Wars* and its two successful sequels, *The Empire Strike Back* and *Return of the Jedi,* have earned an estimated $1 billion in ticket sales in the United States and more than $4.5 billion in merchandising.

The soaring revenues have come with greater expectations and some growing pains. Some critics worry that movies are being made simply to sell more licensed gadgets, rather than the other way around. Meanwhile, advertisers with a growing stake in the promotion of movies have even been known to propose script changes to maximize tie-in potential or press for earlier release dates.

Conversely, high-profile box office releases such as *Godzilla* and *Babe: Pig in the City* proved disappointing when it came to tie-ins. Even before the film was released, merchandisers were griping because the makers of *Godzilla* did not want the famed monster's image used in advertising campaigns. With licensing costs rising, such promotional ventures have become more risky. Rising costs on both sides of the licensing fence might push movie studios and restaurant chains into unprecedented alliances, enabling chains to consider films while they're still in the development stage.

Meanwhile, manufacturers who pinned hopes on a product as seemingly solid as sports merchandise—shirts, hats, and trash bins with team logos—faced losses when the major sports organizations experienced labor trouble, such as the baseball strike of 1994 and the National Basketball Association (NBA) lockout during the 1998-1999 season. Nonetheless, for both large and small businesses, mass merchandising in its various forms continues to offer important benefits to firms that spend wisely, whether it be to put the latest Disney character on a pair of socks or a *Phantom Menace* character on a pencil sharpener. So, as media companies continue to merge and expand, and books and soundtracks based on film and television become increasingly popular, marketing such spin-offs using different media is likely to become more frequent and sophisticated.

BACKGROUND AND DEVELOPMENT

Mass merchandising has been around for quite a long time, though the industry was not always as lucrative as it has been since the late 1970s. In the early twentieth century, actors and baseball players often appeared on cigarette cards, while children looking to purchase chewing gum would also get free trading cards.

Upon analysis, it was the cards, not the gum or cigarettes, that collectors came to crave. A famous Honus Wagner cigarette card from 1909—rare because the Hall of Fame player quickly demanded his image be yanked from the package because he didn't want to encourage smoking—has an estimated worth of $500,000.

Toy executive Cy Schneider asserts in his book *Children's Television* that the first licensing agreement arranged with a toy manufacturer came in 1913, when the Ideal Toy Company introduced the world to the "teddy" bear, having first sought permission from

former president Teddy Roosevelt. Companies would later use popular radio characters from the 1920s and 1930s to sell products and licensed goods. Ralston cereals, for example, offered the "Ralston Straight Shooter Manual," which told readers—presumably young boys—about the real adventures of the popular cowboy character Tom Mix. It even included the "Tom Mix Chart of Wounds," which illustrated 12 bullet wounds and nearly 50 bone fractures the cowboy purportedly suffered. The General Mills cereal company, meanwhile, organized several promotions around the Lone Ranger radio series, as did Quaker Oats with the famed detective Dick Tracy.

Ovaltine, meanwhile, targeted girls with "Little Orphan Annie's Very Own Shake-Up Mug," based on the famous character who got her start in the Sunday comics, then moved to radio, and later was found in movies and on Broadway.

PIONEERS IN THE FIELD

It was television and film that spurred real growth in this area. The first big success is familiar enough. In 1928, Walt Disney brought the character Mickey Mouse to life for the first time in a picture called "Steamboat Willie," co-starring Minnie Mouse. Within five years, Pluto, Goofy, and Donald Duck joined Mickey and Minnie in notoriety. By the mid-1930s, one million Mickey Mouse watches were sold annually, and 10 percent of Disney's revenues came from licensing its cartoon characters, according to *The Disney Touch,* by Ronald Grover. *Snow White and the Seven Dwarfs,* the first full-length animated film, released in 1937, was a huge licensing success as well.

Into the 1940s and 1950s, animated films such as *Pinocchio, Fantasia, Dumbo,* and *Bambi* all came with a line of products and cross-promotions, such as books and music. The new Disneyland theme park in California, which had fledgling television network American Broadcasting Company (ABC) as a big investor, added to Disney's already considerable ability market its own products.

With ABC backing it up, Disney was also one of the first companies to use television to sell related products. The Davy Crockett series, part of ABC's *Disneyland* series, inspired a famous national craze for coonskin caps, and the song "The Ballad of Davy Crockett" sold 10 million copies. Building on the success of *Disneyland,* the *Mickey Mouse Club* hit television airwaves in 1955. A small toy company, Mattel, also jumped on the Disney bandwagon. They advertised on the *Mickey Mouse Club* and later marketed successful tie-in products, such as "Mousegetars," a musical instrument for kids. Such early successes helped Mattel become the nation's top toy manufacturer.

Warner Brothers cartoon characters—Bugs Bunny, Porky Pig, Daffy Duck, and others—also proved to be licensing and tie-in hits for their creators. Disney hit it big again in 1964 with the mostly non-animated feature *Mary Poppins,* which produced not only inexpensive trinkets, but entire clothing lines and even shoe polish.

Nonetheless, despite Disney's success, "licensed products coming from hit movies had not been big winners" into the 1970s, Cy Schneider writes. But the release of George Lucas' *Star Wars* in 1977 changed that. Lucas' *Star Wars* trilogy, as well as the later Indiana Jones productions, generated billions in licensed product sales. In 1976 licensed toys accounted for 20 percent of all toy sales. By the mid-1980s, that figure rose to 80 percent. According to the Toy Manufacturers of America (TMA), that figure has settled at about 40 percent—although in his 1999 annual address, TMA President David A. Miller predicted an upswing "with the introduction of the new *Star Wars* series."

Before the release of the original *Star Wars,* Kenner toys signed an exclusive deal to produce toys, games, and other products based on the film for $100,000 annually, a fairly risky venture at the time. The deal made Kenner hundreds of million of dollars through the 1980s.

The effect of this on the entire toy industry should not be underestimated. By 1991, Hasbro bought Kenner; there had not been a *Star Wars* movie in nearly a decade, and merchandise sales lagged. Yet Lucas was still receiving $100,000 every year. Hasbro ended the relationship. A year later, San Francisco-based Galoob Toys was able to launch its own *Star Wars* line, and it was a success. Hasbro later returned to the *Star Wars* fold. Some industry analysts have speculated though that Galoob's successful marketing of older *Star Wars* merchandise spurred Lucas' decision to re-issue the original trilogy in theaters, thus kicking off the anticipation, and marketing frenzy, for *The Phantom Menace.*

For a large company like Hasbro, which earns over $3.5 billion annually, the *Star Wars* line represents a significant but not overwhelming portion of its revenue. Galoob, on the other hand, earns up to one-third of its $360 million annual revenue from *Star Wars* merchandise. Although licensing fees for *The*

Phantom Menace were around the once unthinkable 15 percent of wholesale revenues from the goods sold, the involvement with Lucas seemed to help Galoob's stock rebound from earlier losses. Hasbro's purchase of Galoob in 1998 may have helped as well, since it consolidated the nation's second and third biggest toy makers, not to mention each major *Star Wars* toy license holder.

CURRENT CONDITIONS

Two pioneers of mass merchandising—the Disney Company and George Lucas, the force behind the *Star Wars* industry—remain atop an increasingly competitive game. A 1995 article in *Nation's Business* put it succinctly when it said Disney "sets the gold standard," when it comes to success in the area of mass merchandising. Mickey Mouse, as Cy Schneider wrote, remains "the greatest salesman of them all."

Nearly every year in the 1990s Disney produced a lucrative animated film, from 1992's *Aladdin,* which made about $500 million worldwide at the box office alone, to *Hercules* in 1997. *The Lion King,* released in 1994, has taken in an estimated total of $1.5 billion in theaters, merchandise, and related products. Animated films are secure foundations for a wide variety of marketing possibilities and revenue sources since they appeal to the whole family and tend to include characters that can easily become cute toys or other licensed properties.

Disney has easily shown itself to be the top player in the animation game. "Aside from extensive use of the usual avenues of publicity, Disney finds promo tools through toy store displays, record albums, and merchandising and fast-food tie-ins: It's impossible to troll the mall without multiple exposures to the Disney blitz," reported *Variety* in an article entitled "High Noon For Toon Boom," which described increasing competition in the animation field.

Indeed, other entertainment companies are jumping into the animation business. "After watching [Disney] monopolize animation for six decades, rivals have boldly coughed up billions to bite into the franchise," the mid-1998 *Variety* report goes on, later adding, "Clearly, the risks are monumental. But the rewards these days can be even bigger than just ten years ago."

As profits have risen, so have costs. It takes about $100 million to start up an animation studio, and salaries for top animators are soaring, *Variety* reports.

But this hasn't stopped companies such as Dreamworks, Warner Brothers, and Fox from entering the animation game. Michael Jordan and Bugs Bunny joined forces in the highly-successful *Space Jam.* The film took in $250 million at the box office, as well as hundreds of millions more from toys, home video sales, and the soundtrack.

Disney has even lost top executives to its competitors—prominent among them Jeffrey Katzenberg, who left to form Dreamworks with Steven Spielberg and David Geffen. Despite the competition, Mickey Mouse's status as "the greatest salesman" appears safe. Home video sales, for example, are disproportionately high for animated films, and Disney rules the home video sales market. Thirteen of the top 20 all-time best sellers are Disney animated films, including *The Lion King, Snow White and the Seven Dwarfs,* and *Aladdin,* the top three. "The Disney brand name guarantees attention from retailers and consumers alike," according to *Variety,* and for the foreseeable future, Disney "would seem to have the [animation] field to itself."

The seemingly boundless revenue sources are one reason more animated programs are showing up on television. There was a time when television was, in fact, the best way to push spin-offs and licensed merchandise. As Cy Schneider wrote, "Television can do what movies cannot by virtue of its enormous reach and frequency of exposure." This has been reversed completely. As *Advertising Age* reported, these days, "most TV properties don't have the revenue potential of feature film blockbusters." Consider MTV's raunchy cartoon characters Beavis and Butthead. Paramount Pictures expanded on the cartoon's television popularity and created a blockbuster film, *Beavis and Butthead Do America,* which then led to several profitable tie-ins, from books to a successful soundtrack.

Nonetheless, there is growing potential in television for selling everything from computer games to clothes to videos, especially to and for children. From the *Mickey Mouse Club* to *Sesame Street,* television has had its long-term lucrative franchises. The Tickle Me Elmo doll, which rocked the toy industry, was a *Sesame Street* spin-off. Almost all popular television shows from the 1970s and 1980s produced tie-ins such as lunch boxes, comic books, and toys. In the late 1980s, *The Simpsons* brought television merchandising possibilities to a higher level, and the scale has only grown since then.

A leader in the field, not surprisingly, is the children's network Nickelodeon. Popular shows such as *Rugrats* and *Blue's Clues* have become spin-off

bonanzas for the network. *Rugrats* even made the transition to the big screen in 1998. Two years earlier, meanwhile, Paramount Home Video—Nickelodeon's sister company—released a home video based on *Blue's Clues,* a "detective show" for kids aged 2 to 6. The video release attracted 7,000 fans to the FAO Schwartz store in Manhattan, and 480,000 videos sold in just nine days. Two CD-Rom titles based on the show were also highly successful. *The Rugrats* show, meanwhile, spun off a CD that can be used for music and computer activities. Of course, each of these Nickelodeon-based products line the shelves of toys and children's clothing stores.

As with blockbuster films, the success of television cartoons has also raised the stakes in the industry. Many "competitors have been trying to imitate Nickelodeon's success. The Fox Family Channel, for one, will spend some $500 million to reach into this market using, among other things, the Fox Kids Network." Fox even hired a prominent executive away from Nickelodeon, Rich Cronin, to become Chief Executive Officer of the Fox Family Channel.

The competition has even led marketers to target younger and younger children. British exports the Teletubbies have spurred a "Beatlemania for 2 to 5 year-olds," according to *Advertising Age.* The Teletubbies—four, teddy-bear like, live-action figures who speak like infants and have televisions for stomachs—are designed for children as young as 18 months. Again, typical products such as video tapes, bath toys, and puzzles have proven lucrative. Tie-ins stretch all the way to TubbieCustard, a ready-to-eat, yogurt-like product based on what the Teletubbies eat on the show.

The President and CEO of Itsy Bitsy Entertainment, which licenses the Teletubbies to be broadcast in the United States, outlined the keys to a successful children's entertainment product. "For a hit, you need a property that children really like, parents approve of and that retailers will support, plus a little innovation," Ken Viselman told *Advertising Age.*

Of course, that's not as easy as it sounds. Already the increasing competition of the tie-in merchandising market has claimed casualties. For years, Equity Marketing made promotional items that were given away free by other marketers, such as Coca Cola and Exxon. Equity produced toys based on *Small Soldiers* and *The Rugrats Movie,* for example, which were given away free with the purchase of children's meals at Burger King.

Looking to expand, Equity attempted to directly sell products based on the films *Godzilla* and *Babe:*

Pig in the City, both of which failed to generate big merchandising sales and were viewed as critical and commercial failures. Equity subsequently announced it would drop out of the movie-licensing business. Equity's "misfortunes are an example of the risks smaller marketers are forced to take in hopes of riding the coattails of potential blockbusters," according to *Advertising Age.* "Such marketers as Hasbro and Mattel, for instance, do a broader array of license and non-license toymaking, which enables mem to sustain the ups and down of the film business." This also suggests that, despite worries that the quality of films will suffer in the zeal to snare tie-in deals, it appears that it still takes a good movie to sell products. As one analyst told *Advertising Age,* "If you don't succeed on the silver screen, it's very hard to have merchandise jump off the shelves."

Some feel that the advertisers and merchandisers are tinkering excessively with what, in the end, may be the most important product—the movies themselves. According to *Time,* Universal's 1996 summer movie *Flipper* was ready for theaters when studio executives approached the film's writer and director with concerns that there were only three main animal characters in the film. Toy manufacturers wanted a fourth, to round out a line of dolls. The director said it was simply too late to add another character. A compromise was forged when the studio found a turtle who appeared literally in one shot, turned it into Sam the Turtle, and then shipped him out to toy stores nationwide.

Similarly, when McDonald's expressed strong interest in the Disney film *George of the Jungle,* the studio promptly doubled the film's budget to increase the special effects and the number of animals that could be turned into toys.

As Pat Wyatt, president of licensing for Fox, acknowledged to *Time,* "Not every film is a great merchandising opportunity." Importantly, *Time* added, "not all spin-offs are aimed at junior."

Indeed, everyone eats candy and cereal, also popular tie-in products. Hershey Foods ran a theater-concession promotion with the Dreamworks film *Antz* and launched five dinosaur-themed products to go with *The Lost World: Jurassic Park.* A mass merchandising opportunity was also taken advantage of by Estee Lauder; the company produced a line of women's makeup as a tie-in with the film *Evita.*

Substantive tie-in growth for all ages has also occurred in publishing, especially with musical soundtracks. While acknowledging that "most movie tie-in books are crass rehashings of the films," *U.S. News and World Report* highlighted a trend towards higher quality tie-in volumes during the 1998 holiday season.

Meanwhile, the front page headline from a 1998 *Billboard* article announced: "Soundtracks Spark Chart Heat." As reporter Catherine Applefeld Olson wrote, "the staying power of soundtracks in [the 1990s], which kicked off with *The Bodyguard* in 1992 and has gained momentum with *Waiting to Exhale, Space Jam,* and *Titanic,* to name a few, has given record companies a new perspective on the potential of film music." Most recording companies now have departments dedicated to soundtracks, Olson explained, and "several are even outperforming the films from which they were culled." Soundtracks also serve as useful venues to debut a record company's new bands. Even television shows such as *Ally McBeal* have spawned successful albums.

The *Billboard* report continues, "With this popularity has come escalated bidding wars," as well as "increased cooperation between record labels and film studios." This is where mass merchandising seems to be headed. Cooperation, synergy, or convergence—call it what you will. Larger and larger media companies, not to mention on-line technology, have made marketing and selling tie-in merchandise increasingly sophisticated. The Web site for the hit Warner Brothers network television show *Dawson's Creek* has a complete list of songs played on the show, many available through the Warner Brothers recording arm. A media empire such as Time Warner can promote a movie and soundtrack using print media, cable television, and books since it has its own film, recording, publishing, and broadcasting arms. Feature stories and interviews on entertainment products can even pop up on a network's newscasts.

Though mass merchandising was happening as early as the 1950s with Disney and ABC, the scale and sophistication of these marketing techniques—enhanced by the Internet, which has radically altered the concept of home shopping—are sure to reshape the industry in the coming years.

WORK FORCE

Importantly, mass merchandising is not a game merely for Hollywood movers and shakers and global fast food chains. Many small and mid-size clothing manufacturers, for example, do a large portion of their business through licensing and other mass merchandising methods. "The opportunities for small companies in licensing are bigger than ever," the executive editor of *The Licensing Letter* told *Nation's Business* in 1995. Indications suggest that this industry remains "driven largely by small firms." This article highlighted several success stories in its cover story on licensed entertainment products—among them Zak Designs Inc., based in Spokane, Washington, which launched a generic children's dinnerware line in the mid-1980s. Business took off when the company obtained a license for Disney's Little Mermaid character in 1989, and revenues "increased 20-fold and employment 10-fold, to about 100 people."

There are potential pitfalls, of course, Disney for example, can bring manufacturers profits but, according to *Nation's Business,* they can be a very demanding licenser. You may also tie your product to a character suffering from overexposure, as many who invested in a license for the purple dinosaur Barney eventually discovered. Sports merchandise has also been a fickle investment given that three of the major four sports experienced labor troubles in the 1990s.

RESEARCH AND TECHNOLOGY

What's a prospective licensee to do? *Nation's Business* makes several suggestions. "Make the initial contact," to find out a licenser's requirements. This inquiry might involve hiring a consultant or attorney who specializes in the field. Be prepared to "document your qualifications," since licensers may not want to risk selling their product to an unsound firm. Knowing the market and finding a niche are important, according to *Nation's Business,* which also suggests that potential players "consider taking a risk." Being in on the ground floor of an unproven property could be lucrative.

A less costly way to play this game is to "try a knockoff." That is, if a film like *Jurassic Park* hits it big, rather than license characters from the film itself, look into products related to dinosaurs. *Nation's Business* notes that generic wildlife products did well following the release of Disney's *The Lion King.* Also be on the lookout for trends and interests that no company can own. The craze over Y2K and the new millennium, for example, proved fertile ground for manufacturers and advertisers alike.

FURTHER READING

Bart, Peter. "Give Me *Speed 2* With Lettuce, Pickles and Cheese, Please." *Gentleman's Quarterly,* March 1997.

Britt, Bill. "Teletubbies are Coming: Brit Hit Sets U.S. Invasion." *Advertising Age,* 19 January 1998.

Buss, Dale B. "Hot Names, Top Dollars." *Nation's Business,* August 1995.

Dubner, Stephen J. "Steven the Good." *New York Times Magazine,* 14 February 1999.

Friedman, Wayne. "Saying Goodbye to Hollywood." *Advertising Age,* 11 January 1999.

Grover, Ronald. "He's Big. He's Upset. He's Invisible." *Business Week,* 6 April 1998.

———. *The Disney Touch: How a Daring Management Team Revived an Entertainment Empire.* Homewood, IL: Business One Irwin, 1991.

Gunter, Mark. "The Rules According to Rupert." *Fortune,* 26 October 1998.

Hamilton, Kendall, and Devin Gordon. "Waiting For Star Wars." *Newsweek,* 1 February 1999.

Handy, Bruce. "101 Movie Tie-Ins." *Time,* 2 December 1996.

Jensen, Jeff, and Judann Pollack. "Bug Flicks Will Feast on Candy." *Advertising Age,* 29 June 1998.

Karon, Paul, and Leonard Klady. "High Noon for Toon Boom." *Variety,* 15 June 1998.

Miller, Cyndee. "TV Networks as Brands." *Marketing News,* 9 October 1995.

Morris, Kathleen. "Bated Breath in Toyland." *Business Week,* 15 February 1999.

"The Movies Go Pop." *U.S. News and World Report,* 14 December 1998.

Olson, Catherine Applefeld. "Soundtracks Spark Chart Heat." *Billboard,* 11 July 1998.

Schneider, Cy. *Children's Television: The Art, The Business and How it Works.* Chicago: NTC Business Books, 1987.

Serwer, Andrew E. "Who Gets What in the *Star Wars* Toy Deal." *Fortune,* 18 August 1997.

Snyder, Beth. "Rivals Attracted to Nickelodeon's Sweet Success." *Advertising Age,* 9 November 1998.

—Tom Deignan

MICROMACHINES

Micromachines and their parts are referred to by various names in different parts of the world. In Japan they are called micromachines. In Europe the term is MicroSystems Technology (or MST), while in the United States and the rest of Asia these machines are generally known as MicroElectroMechanical Systems—MEMS.

The micromachine industry is a direct outcome of the movement toward miniaturization that began with the development of the transistor in the 1950s, and later with the integrated circuit and the microprocessor. MEMS are expected to effect a revolution in the marketplace similar to that effected by the latter two technologies. Using batch processing of silicon chips, MEMS have the potential to create systems and components much smaller than conventional ones, with a broader range of functions at a fraction of the cost.

In 1997 the U.S. MEMS-based inertial sensor market, the largest MEMS market, reached $143 million, according to a report by the consulting firm Frost & Sullivan reported by *PR Newswire,* while the medical sensor market was $40 million. Overall, MEMS market growth currently stands at about 6 percent a year, though MEMS for the automotive and transportation sectors are growing at an annual rate of nearly 20 percent. Unlike other products of the microelectronic revolution, however, widespread commercial application has been much slower to come for micromachine research. Until 1995, one product, the pressure sensor, accounted for over 90 percent of the total U.S. market. As a result of this limited product base, together with unanswered packaging questions and long lead times for research and product devel-

opment, MEMS revenues have remained limited and growth is expected to remain slow. No micromachine company has approached the success of firms in the integrated circuit or microprocessor industries.

Companies in the automotive and medical sectors accounted for by far the largest part of MEMS sales as the twentieth century drew to a close. Established industries in the United States barely recognized the potential impact of MEMS technology on its products—micromachine producers still have to prove themselves in the market against entrenched conventional products. Characteristics that should make MEMS products profitable in the long run are size, weight, ability to solve "unsolvable" problems, and extremely low cost. As new, viable microtechnologies develop over the next 10 years, the industry is expected to expand into the profitable areas of consumer electronics, data storage, and micro-instrumentation, and to buttress its hold on the auto and medical industries.

ORGANIZATION AND STRUCTURE

About 80 U.S. companies are currently active in the MEMS area. About 20 of them are large organizations of international scope. MEMS usually comprise a very small percentage of the total production of these larger firms, though some, notably Motorola Inc. and Texas Instruments, have been working in the field since the 1970s. The remaining 60 U.S. MEMS companies are small businesses with an annual production of less than $10 million, or in most cases $5 million per year. These companies, in general, focus exclusively on MEMS and a small number of products. A significant number of small to mid-sized MEMS companies, about 30 in all, are located in the Silicon Valley. Some have been financed with venture capital, are still doing research, and have yet to bring a product to market. In the MEMS industry it is the norm for a company, big or small, to focus on a single micromachine technology to the exclusion of all others. Analog Devices produces accelerometers, Texas Instruments makes video chips, and Redwood manufactures microfluidic devices.

Despite the enormous success of the silicon integrated circuit industry, mounting a circuit on a MEMS chip has been a low priority for the industry. In 1995, only about 12 percent of the accelerometers and 8 percent of the pressure sensors sold featured on-chip integrated circuitry. Most industry observers are convinced, however, that integrated systems with on-chip electronics will play a determining role in the future of MEMS, particularly given the availability of the integrated circuit industry's existing infrastructure. Analog Devices, among others, has produced commercially successful examples of such devices.

The most common MEMS production techniques are essentially the same as those used to produce integrated circuits—material is deposited on a silicon disk. A pattern is imposed lithographically, and material around the pattern is removed, revealing the mechanism. Companies use this process to mass-produce large numbers of inexpensive micromechanisms—including micromachines with moving parts. Because the scale of MEMS production is larger than that of integrated circuits, startup companies are often able to purchase obsolete production equipment from integrated circuit manufacturers. As the MEMS industry has begun to grow, a small group of satellite industries has grown around it—businesses from other sectors devoted to the specific needs of MEMS. A small group of marketing professionals, for example, specializes in the area. More significant is the computer software industry where new CAD software and other design tools are being developed for MEMS. Microcosm and Tanner EDA are two companies that have produced such products.

Products of the micromachine industry are sold to other manufacturers for use as components in the fabrication of more complex systems. According to *Design News,* airbag accelerometers and disposable blood-pressure transducers together accounted for 30 million MEMS devices sold in 1996. The rest of the market is small enough to be virtually nonexistent. Other micro-technology applications—gas, chemical, and rate sensors, micro-relays, microdisplays, and micromachined parts—are only expected to reach full

commercialization within the next 5 to 10 years and, by the year 2000, sensors' share of the total market is expected to drop to around 50 percent.

REGULATION

Aside from the restriction of high-technology exports the President could impose for national security reasons, the only regulation of micromachines is required FDA approval for material used in medical applications. On the other hand, federal regulation of the auto industry presented opportunities for the micromachine industry. Federal fuel economy and pollution standards in the 1970s led to the development of the micromechanical manifold air pressure sensor, a critical element in the system that regulates a car's fuel to air ratio. Similarly, airbag laws created a market for the small, accurate accelerometer used in passenger safety systems.

BACKGROUND AND DEVELOPMENT

The first real impetus toward the development of the micromachine came from physicist Richard Feynman in a talk at Cal Tech in 1959. The speech, "There's Plenty of Room at the Bottom," was a feat of prescience that described the possibility of computing, mechanical production, and information storage, as well as the unique characteristics of materials and machines on the molecular level. He closed his talk with an offer: "$1,000 to the first guy who makes an operating electric motor—a rotating electric motor which can be controlled from the outside and, not counting the lead in wires, is only a 1/64 inch cube."

The first technological advance toward the micromachine was the discovery of a piezoresistive effect—a resistance charge created in silicon when it is under stress—at Bell Labs in 1954, a factor that made silicon an ideal candidate for sensors and accelerometers. Development continued apace throughout the 1960s and 1970s. Spurred mainly by funding from NASA, the first silicon pressure sensors were created. The National Science Foundation provided funding as well in the 1970s, albeit on a limited scale. Fairchild spawned a number of spin-off companies in the Silicon Valley that pursued silicon sensor technology: ICTransducers (now Foxboro/ICT) and National Semiconductor Sensor Group (now SenSym) were founded in 1972, Cognition (now Rosemount) in 1976.

A major turning point in the micromachine field was the publication in 1982 of *Silicon as a Mechani-*

A technician repairs a microelectrical component. (Digital Stock.)

cal Material by Kurt Peterson, called "the father of MEMS." The paper described the unique mechanical-structural properties of silicon. (Metals like iron, steel, and aluminum have too many structural irregularities at a microscopic level to be viable micromachine materials.) The paper was followed by the first two MEMS start-up companies in Silicon Valley: Transsensory Devices (1982) and NovaSensor(1984).

Pressure sensor designs were modified throughout the 1980s, with a great deal of impetus for these modifications coming from the automotive and medical industries. Full commercialization was finally reached around 1990. Sales of micromachine pressure sensors increased from about 3 million units a year in 1983 to over 50 million units by 1995, and continued to grow at double digit rates. There were expectations that 125 million units will be sold in first decade of the new century.

Micromachined accelerometers, used primarily as crash sensors in automotive airbag systems, are the other micromachine application brought to market on a mass scale, though nowhere near the degree of the pressure sensor. First developed between 1985 and 1990, sales have grown from about $200,000 in 1992 to $13-$15 million in 1995. A few other micromachined products have begun to enter the marketplace, including ink jet heads for printers, read/write heads for magnetic hard-drives, fuel injection nozzles for autos, and video chips for high-resolution television. The impact of these products has thus far been minimal.

CURRENT CONDITIONS

In the late 1990s, the micromachine industry ended a childhood characterized by a long period of research 'push,' and began an adolescence where a growing commercialization—it is hoped—will create market 'pull' and will draw the industry into a period of sustained growth. The lithography-based techniques of silicon batch processing developed by the integrated circuit are considered to be the key to low cost micromachining by the industry in the United States. The present infrastructure—adapting old integrated circuit (IC) production facilities to MEMS needs—is seen as advantageous for small firms wishing to enter the market. The equipment, usually obsolete by IC standards, can be purchased for a fraction of the cost of new facilities. This infrastructure is not considered optimal for generating or supporting the manufacturing energy needed to push beyond the prototype stage to the mass production stage. It is seen as a potential brake on

MEMS manufacturing technology. With MEMS limited effect on integrated circuit manufacturers, there is no need felt in those quarters to create new solutions to the problems facing the MEMS industry. With relatively low revenues, most of which are tied up in applications research and product development, the micromachine industry is at present unable to pursue those solutions on its own.

Technology is the major challenge for MEMS. Specifically, difficulties lie in finding new applications, creating a group of basic products that can be simply and easily modified to meet a broad range of customer needs, and establishing a manufacturing infrastructure to support a large market. In short, establishing the silicon-based MEMS techniques in the market will depend upon volume production, a point stressed time and again at the second Commercialization of Microsystems Conference in 1996.

The outlook for MEMS is strong, although estimates of near future growth vary. In early 1999 experts at Sandia National Laboratories, a major center of micromachine research, projected the entire MEMS industry at as much as $30 billion early in the twenty-first century. Gary Title, technology manager at 3M Corporation, projected $10-14 billion by 2001. European estimates of the world market for micromachines in the year 2002 range from $15 to $38 billion, according to *Electronic Times* magazine. Despite the variance in these estimates, the consensus of opinion favors substantial growth, though much less than the early growth of integrated circuit revenues, which reached $148 billion in 1995 and are expected to top $371 billion by the turn of the millennium.

There are a few specific areas that MEMS need to develop in order to lay a foundation for commercial success.

- The lithographic and etching methodologies of the integrated circuit industries will have to be modified to reflect micromachining's need for greater three-dimensional focus (in contrast to integrated circuitry's drive toward ever-greater degrees of miniaturization).

- MEMS need their own specialized design tools in order to continue product development. New firms are already creating computer-aided design software specifically for the micromachine industry, and a major contract was awarded in 1998 by DARPA for the development of an engineering kit to enable design engineers not expert in MEMS fabrication methods to create workable designs.

- Micromachine companies will have to develop low-cost, accurate, and implementable product testing techniques on a mass scale if potential clients are to be convinced of the reliability of MEMS products.

- One of the most serious questions to be addressed by the industry is micromachine packaging—the outer case of the micromachine that must insulate its sensitive inner workings from external factors (e.g., chemicals or electrical conductivity), without interfering with other operations of the machine.

Even when MEMS overcome these problems, manufacturers will have to compete with the "macro"-products already established in the marketplace. This means not only being smaller than the competition, but better and more versatile, with improved performance, and above all cheaper. Finally, if MEMS are to be competitive they must significantly cut the length of product development time frames. It typically takes 2 to 3 years to develop a prototype, and another 1 to 3 years to design the larger system for which the micro-component is intended.

Automobiles and medicine are expected to continue to play a large role in further development. The automotive industry is already working on a variety of sensors for suspension systems, tire pressure monitoring, even personal navigation systems. New chemical and temperature sensors are under development in the medical realm, and doctors are already postulating microinstruments able to be sent into the blood stream to perform various diagnostic and surgical functions.

By the year 2000, sensors are expected to lose their dominant market position, dropping to about 50 percent. The new driving technologies are expected to be micro-instrumentation followed at the turn of the millennium by data storage. Designers are working on integrated microsystems composed of sensors, accelerators, and regulators, as well as microactuators, which are just being perfected. Micro-applications that seemed most vital to speakers at Commercialization of Microsystems '96 include ink jet technology, high-definition video displays, optical systems, and information storage that is 100 times larger than at present, while at the same time both faster and cheaper.

INDUSTRY LEADERS

Involvement in MEMS is spread across a wide range of companies, all with varying degrees of involvement in the industry. Three large electronics companies for which involvement in commercial micromachine production is a small but growing part of their businesses are Motorola Inc., Texas Instruments, and Analog Devices Inc. In addition, there are a number of companies that began specifically as MEMS developers.

THREE DIVERSIFIED ELECTRONICS COMPANIES

Motorola has been engaged in MEMS research since the late 1970s but did not release its first product, a pressure sensor, until the mid-1980s, when it formally founded a sensor product division, called Senseon. One of the smallest Motorola divisions, Senseon's annual revenues of $25-$50 million are expected to increase to between $100 and $500 million by the year 2000. About 500 employees are working on MEMS, including about 200 engineers.

Motorola's primary MEMS products are pressure sensors for the automotive and medical markets and accelerometers for auto airbag systems. Pressure sensors outsell accelerometers about 5 to 1, but the company expects sales to be about even by 2002; chemical sensors for the industrial market are set to begin production. Research for the pressure sensor and accelerometer was conducted in-house, and technology for Motorola's new chemical sensor was licensed from a small independent company—a trend the company intends to continue in order to cut new product development time. In the future, Motorola will move toward more integrated sensor/actuator systems, and many of those will be aimed at the auto industry, an area of large potential growth and one that can spin off numerous applications into the industrial sector. The company believes sensors are likely to be the next hot commercial product and have named them as one of four key initiatives for future growth, with a commitment of future funds and manpower.

Texas Instruments (TI) has been doing MEMS work since 1977, but its first commercial application was not released until 1987—a print chip with 840 mirrors designed to print tickets and boarding passes for the airline industry. Less than 1,000 were sold, but out of that research grew TI's big micromachine application, the digital micromirror device (DMD). The DMD was designed as a video component for home television, teleconferencing, and projection theaters. The company sees it as a key technology in the high-definition television market. The DMD is TI's only current or projected MEMS product, and can be modified by adding more mirrors to increase brightness

Pioneer
DR. LARRY J. HORNBECK DMD INVENTOR

Dr. Larry J. Hornbeck, inventor of the bistable digital micromirror device (DMD) began his work in 1977 as an engineer at the Texas Instruments laboratories. For his invention he was awarded a number of respected honors, including the Rank Prize from the Royal Society of Medicine in London on March 17, 1997. Hornbeck, along with his colleague, Dr. W.E. Nelson, split the award of 30,000 English pounds.

In 1998 Hornbeck received an Emmy award from the Academy of Television Arts & Sciences for outstanding achievement in engineering for his contribution to the Digital Projection International Power Display projector, which was based on the DMD technology invented by Hornbeck and Nelson at Texas Instruments in the 1980s.

DMD is based on an array of mirrors that can be turned very rapidly. Each mirror, only 16 microns square, represents a single pixel, and serves as a viable solution to many of the problems associated with image projection.

and resolution. TI boasts that a single DMD has more moving parts than the total MEMS produced by other companies in half a year. A typical micromachine has one moving part; a DMD has half a million. To produce these TI has set up what it believes is the most advanced MEMS production facility in the world, in which 600-800 people work on developing and producing the DMD.

Texas Instrument's primary market is the video industry for home, business, and commercial markets. They are the only company producing commercial micromachines with the DMD's video applications. Competition comes from manufacturers of traditional liquid crystal displays and cathode ray tubes, primarily in Japan. These established technologies can still be manufactured and sold much cheaper than DMDs. TI currently sells about 100,000 DMDs a year, which amounts to about 20 percent of the projection display market. TI's total sales for 1998 were $8.46 billion, but micromachined products were a minuscule part.

Analog Devices, a leading manufacturer of micromachined accelerometers, is one of the mid-sized members of the MEMS world. Founded in 1965 as an electronic module company, its first MEMS product was an airbag crash sensor that was first integrated into the 1994 Saab 900. The company produces five accelerometer models currently; five others are about to go into production. Analog had about one-third of the world airbag accelerometer market in 1998, with corporate customers in all three major markets—North America, Europe, and Japan. In model-year 1998 more than 40 auto models the world over had Analog accelerometers.

Analog's sales in 1998 were estimated at $1.23 billion, of which MEMS accounted for a small but growing portion. The company announced plans to sell $320 million worth of MEMS by the year 2002, 10 percent of total revenue. MEMS revenues are expected to double annually for the foreseeable future. Three hundred Analog employees, about 25 percent of them engineers, are currently active in the MEMS division. More than 15 percent of the total staff is pursuing research and development at any given time. Together with Northeastern University in Boston, Analog is developing a low-power micromachine relay, which, if successful, will have applications that go far beyond conventional ATE relays. It should be a commercial reality sometime in the next five years. Analog is working on two major Advanced Research Projects Agency (ARPA) research contracts and pursues research actively in cooperation with the Berkeley Sensor and Actuator Center. Besides its $10-million investment in research, ADI spent more than $50 million to equip a former Polaroid facility for micromachine fabrication. In 1998 ADI announced that its fourth generation accelerometer had been designed into computer-game pads, the first MEMS application in the realm of consumer products. In 1999 it announced that it had also been designed into an earthquake sensing device, a vehicle security system, and a device to guard against back injuries.

MEMS STARTUP COMPANIES

IC Sensor, founded in 1982 as one of the first commercial micromachining start-ups in Silicon Valley, has introduced a number of technologies to the market. It put the world's first disposable blood pressure sensor into mass production in early 1984; released the first low-cost accelerometer in September 1987; produced the world's first silicon microvalve in September 1992; and developed the first accelerometer with self-testing capability in 1993.

Since 1992 the company has grown at a rate of 20 percent per year, largely as a result of sales of accelerometers to the automotive sector. They are now the largest micromachine company in the Silicon Valley. IC Sensor was purchased by EG&G Inc., a Fortune 500 Company, in 1994. EG&G IC Sensors employs over 275 workers at two manufacturing fa-

cilities, one in Milpitas, California, the other in Santa Clara, California.

EG&G IC Sensors' products are spread across the MEMS market; medical, industrial, and automotive are its leading market sectors. A special area of involvement for the company is custom silicon micromachining: applying its special MEMS expertise to meet the special requirements of particular customers. Custom microstructures have included detection cantilevers for atomic force microscopes, pressure arrays for non-invasive blood pressure monitoring, electrostatically driven micro-relays, micro-coolers for high power electronic components, and read/write coils for optical disk drives. Current product research includes motion monitoring for pacemakers and sensors for collision avoidance in aircraft.

Lucas NovaSensor produces more silicon sensors every year than any other company. Founded in 1985 by Kurt Peterson, NovaSensor's first product was a micromachined disposable blood pressure sensor monitor. In 1990 LucasVarity purchased NovaSensor. At the end of the decade more than half the company's total sales were made to the medical industry. The majority of their business is pressure sensors, but they produce proportional valves, optical switches, DNA analyzers, and microchips as well. Lucas considers itself an applications-specific manufacturer of silicon microstructures: a client presents them with a need and they customize standard products to meet it. Depending on the degree of modification, the work might take anywhere from a couple weeks to six months or more.

Lucas NovaSensor employs about 150 employees, 25 percent of whom are engineers. Half the engineers are engaged in research and development (R&D). The company produces over 1 million units a month and has annual revenues of $30 million. An early project involved development of a fuel injection nozzle for a major American automobile company who then took over its production.

Lucas NovaSensor does most of its production using wet etching or plasma etching techniques, and says they can even weld pieces of silicon together on an atomic level. Key research is now underway on deep ion reactive etching (DRIE), work begun under federal contract. The company estimates it has as much as a year's advance on other companies in this technology.

Redwood Microsystems, founded in 1988, is the world's leading producer of microvalves. At first the company intended to produce a line of micromachined valves, but soon realized the difficulty of competing with established and proven conventional products and changed focus to integrated solutions. For example, out of their very first product, a micromachined pressure regulator, they developed a "flow-stick"—a combination pressure regulator, flow regulator, pressure sensor, and shut-off valve in a 4x3x1 inch unit, about 15 percent the size and 20 percent of the cost of the part it will replace. It was first released in July 1997.

The company is the only commercial manufacturer of MEMS microfluidics. Client interest is much greater in Japan than in the United States, according to chief technical officer Mark Zdeblick, due to a long-standing interest in Japan of miniaturization for its own sake. Redwood's line of pressure and flow regulators accounts for about $2 million in revenues annually. The company has its own manufacturing facility, where about 30 people are employed. Currently Redwood is concentrating on stand-alone microfluid systems with industrial applications, in particular semiconductor-process flow-control equipment used in semiconductor manufacture. It is an area with a great deal of competition, but thus far none from MEMS companies. Driven by products like the "flow stick," Redwood is forecasting revenues of $30-$50 million by the beginning of the twenty-first century.

BEI was already a leading supplier of conventional sensors when it became involved in MEMS in the mid-1980s. Its first commercial micromachined product, an automotive gyroscope originally developed under government contract, was used in 1997 Cadillacs and Corvettes as part of an anti-skid device. Like most newer MEMS applications, its high production cost limits it to the high-end market and the company does not anticipate it filtering down to broader auto markets before the year 2000. This gyro was the first of its kind anywhere, and thus far BEI has been the only company that has been able to produce it reliably and repeatably. Over 1 million units have been sold to General Motors since the gyroscope's introduction in 1994.

The automotive industry is BEI's primary market, although it has customers in the aerospace and industrial sectors as well. In addition to the gyros, the company produces a line of micromachined mechanical sensors, position sensors, pressure sensors, and accelerometers. Micromachine output is increasing every year. Still, MEMS account for less than 50 percent of BEI's annual production, the bulk of which is still conventional sensors. BEI places a strong emphasis on research and development. About 10 percent of the 220 MEMS personnel are involved in research. One special research area is the micromechanical sensor with automotive applications; BEI

expects this sector to exhibit the most growth by the year 2000.

Breed Technologies, Inc., is a leading supplier to the automotive industry, supplying steering wheels and other plastic components as well as airbags and airbag components. Its sensor products are also used in nonautomotive applications. In 1998 it opened what it said was the world's largest facility exclusively dedicated to the manufacture of micromachined sensor devices. The 126,000 square-foot plant was built to expand the capacity of Breed's Finnish subsidiary VTI Hamlin. It was equipped to produce 10 million sensors annually, with expansion possible to 50 million. VTI Hamlin was formed 1995. Breed's sales in 1998 were $1.35 billion, an increase of 74.3 percent over 1997. It sells to 45 automobile manufacturers worldwide.

AMERICA AND THE WORLD

So far international competition in the production of micromachines is very slight, only because the market is so under-developed. U.S. companies currently account for 45 percent of world pressure sensor production and sales. Small start-up companies, which lead the drive in bringing new technologies to the marketplace, are a far smaller market force in Europe and Japan, which accounts partly for what insiders see as a slow pace of commercialization in the MEMS area. The majority of American companies in MEMS are these small start-up companies, some of whom operate with venture capital for years before releasing a commercial product. There are about 75 companies in the MEMS industry in Japan, about 35 in Germany, and a few more in other western European countries and Korea.

American companies such as EG&G IC Sensors, Analog Devices, Motorola, and Lucas NovaSensor continue to develop new products, especially new sensors, building on the success that they have achieved. New advanced accelerometers, low-pressure sensors, temperature sensors, chemical sensors, and sensors with integrated circuitry were released in 1998. Texas Instruments' digital micromirror device has the potential, according to Michael Gumport, an analyst with Lehman Brothers Inc., to exceed $1 billion in sales by the year 2000, with multi-billion-dollar sales possible in the early part of the next decade, although the development program has its critics in the company. New competition was announced in 1998 by South Korea's Daewoo Electronics in the form of a micromirror array similar to DMD except that it is controlled by analog signals rather than digital. According to Daewoo, the analog circuitry is simpler and cheaper than digital, and enables finer adjustments to the mirrors and a brighter image.

Research in the industry is very strong in Japan, and the European Commission has established a new program to promote research and development in MEMS. Japanese industry is pursuing approaches similar to those in the United States, but the 10-year, $250 million program in micromachines sponsored by the Ministry of International Trade and Industry (MITI) emphasizes miniaturizing more traditional machining methods, which has not been pursued in the United States. Nexus, the Europe-wide organization established to promote micromachines under the initiative to increase the competitiveness of European industry called Europractice, has set up what it calls a "distributed Silicon Valley." The effort spans 12 countries and involves dozens of companies and research institutions organized into a number of clusters, with members of each cluster sharing expertise and facilities, even manufacturing facilities. The hope is that this infrastructure will enable the microsystems market to fulfill its potential in Europe.

RESEARCH AND TECHNOLOGY

The university, government, and company laboratories where most of the industry's leading edge research takes place are the vital engines powering the micromachine industry. Research is critical to the development of the new technologies and products that MEMS will require to become a niche market. Funded university research is critical, because the broad interdisciplinary nature of MEMS utilizes technologies from electrical, chemical, biomedical, and mechanical engineering, as well as from chemistry, biology, physics, and materials science. Assembling the equipment and expertise required to undertake such a wide-ranging research program is beyond the means of any but the largest multinational companies. Some insiders see the "pure" research of the university lab as a potential brake on the drive toward commercial applications that are so crucial currently, and consider it essential for companies to continue their own product-oriented research.

In the middle ground are working agreements that exist between industry and academia. A model for this type of work is the Berkeley Sensor and Actuator Center (BSAC) at the University of California at Berkeley. Founded in 1987, BSAC is the foremost MEMS

center in the world. It is an Industry-University Cooperative Research Center (IUCRC) funded by the National Science Foundation (NSF), a 21-member cooperative including major companies like Motorola, Honeywell, Texas Instruments, and IBM; major government labs, like Lawrence Livermore and Sandia; and most of the major MEMS companies. Members contribute $55,000 per year to the Center and in return get access to labs, graduate students, and expertise. Some members also enter into private contracts to do targeted research at the Center, entitling them to preferential licensing rights to any technology developed.

The stated goal of IUCRCs is to give a competitive advantage to American business. Thus, membership in the Center is limited, by and large, to domestic companies. Nonetheless two foreign companies with "significant American holdings"—Daimler Chrysler and Siemens—also participate. The total BSAC staff comprises about 60 graduate students, about 8 affiliated faculty, and 6 directors. BSAC receives approximately $6 million in annual funding from NSF, the second largest IUCRC grant in the country.

An important recent development at the Center was I-MEMS—integrated MEMS—developed in conjunction with Analog Devices. I-MEMS are an array of linked microdevices, gyros, accelerometers, and other sensors built around a chip that is linked to a computer. Other current research includes work on Computer-Aided Design for MEMS, a MEMS mass spectrometer, and micro-mirrors to miniaturize scanner technology.

Important MEMS research is also being conducted at the University of Utah, the University of Wisconsin, the University of Michigan, and Case Western Reserve. Government labs active in the field include Sandia National Laboratories in Albuquerque, New Mexico, the Jet Propulsion Labs in Pasadena, California, and Lawrence Livermore Laboratories near Berkeley, California.

A measure of the industry's importance to governments throughout the world is the amount of research dollars earmarked for micromachine research. The Defense Advanced Research Projects Agency (DARPA) funded more than $131.0 million worth of research in fiscal year 1997 and 1998. DARPA is seeking $97.4 million for fiscal 2000. Funding, albeit in significantly lower amounts, is available from other federal agencies, including the National Science Foundation, Small Business Innovative Research (SBIR) program of the Technical Reinvestment Program (TRP) and cooperative research and development agreements administered by various federal agencies. Like DARPA, other agencies will be increasing their support of MEMS in the coming years.

FURTHER READING

"Aufruhr im Land Liliput." *Der Spiegel,* 1997.

Babyak, Richard J."MEMS on the Move." *Appliance Manufacturer,* February 1999.

Bak, David J., and Julie Anne Schofield. "Micromachines That Work!" *Design News,* 22 September 1997.

Biancomano, Vincent. "IC Tech Makes Silicon Sensors More Accurate and Less Costly." *Electronic Engineering Times,* 6 June 1997.

Bray, Hiawatha. "Bridging the Worlds of Real and Digital Norwood's Analog Devices Finds Success by Tailoring Microchips to Firm's Needs." *The Boston Globe,* 23 February 1999.

Bryzek, Janusz. "Starting MEMS Manufacturing Business in Silicon Valley." *Commercialization of Microsystems '96,* 6 October 1996.

"Corporate Overview." Milpitas, CA: EG&G IC Sensors, June 1997.

Drake, John. "Shirt Button Turbines." *Technology Review,* January-February 1998.

Dunn, Darrell. "TI's Next Push: Analog." *Electronic Buyers News,* 10 March 1997.

"Frost & Sullivan: MEMS-Based Inertial Sensor Suppliers Seek Out New Application Markets with High Profit Margins." *PR Newswire,* 13 October 1998.

"Frost & Sullivan: Technical Change and Profit Opportunities in Niche Markets Lure Players in MEMS-Based Medical Pressure Sensor Markets." *PR Newswire,* 13 October 1998.

Grace, Roger. "Automotive Applications of MEMS." *Commercialization of Microsystems '96,* 6 October 1996.

———. "US Market Overview." *Commercialization of Microsystems '96,* 6 October 1996.

"Inkjet Heads and Read/Write Heads for Disk Drives—Tiny Machines with a Huge Potential." *Electronic Times,* 22 June 1998.

Lee, Charles S. "Mirror, Mirror: Advanced Display Technology Reflects Brighter Images." *Far Eastern Economic Review,* 22 October 1998.

Leopold, George. "Military Invests in Microelectronic Machine Technology." *EE Times,* 21 March 1998.

Marcus, Karen. "The Challenge of Infrastructure-Supporting the Growth of MEMS into Production." *Commercialization of Microsystems '96,* 6 October 1996.

"MCC Launches Micro-Electro-Mechanical Systems Investigation." *PR Newswire,* 27 April 1998.

"Mentor Graphics, MEMSCAP, MCNC Storm the MEMS Design Market with $1.3m DARPA Funding." *M2 Presswire,* 23 September 1998.

Muller, Richard. "The Status and Promise of MEMS." *Commercialization of Microsystems '96,* 6 October 1996.

Ohr, Stephen. "Analog Devices Accelerometer Designed into PC Game—MEMS Gets Consumer Push." *Electronic Engineering Times,* 16 March 1998.

Peterson, K. "Don't Commercialize MEMS." *Commercialization of Microsystems '96,* 6 October 1996, 167-179.

Proctor, Paul. "National Laboratories Advance Microtechnology." *Aviation Week & Space Technology,* 1 December 1997.

Radford, Tim."No Small Potatoes: Small Is Not Just Beautiful But Dutiful." *The Guardian,* 23 September 1998.

Roos, Gina. "Bringing MEMS from R&D to Reality—A Handful of Companies Have Developed Microrelay Prototypes, but Full Production Is a Ways Off." *Electronic Buters News,* 26 January 1998.

"Tanner EDA and Sanida National Laboratories to Deliver New Design Kit for MEMS Technology." *Business Wire,* 1 March 1999.

"Tiny Technology: A New Lilliputian World of Micromachines: Scientists Are Creating Wasp-Size Helicopters and Building Mechanical Systems on Slivers of Silicon." *TIME International,* 2 December 1996.

VerLee, Don. "Applying MEMS to New Medical Products: a Medical Device Perspective." *Commercialization of Microsystems '96,* 6 October 1996.

—Gerald E. Brennan,
updated by Howard Distelzweig

MICROWAVE APPLICATIONS

INDUSTRY SNAPSHOT

Microwave technology applies to many industries other than the most obvious one—food preparation. Radar, medicine, chemistry, and telecommunications have increasingly relied on this form of electromagnetic energy. The entire electromagnetic range (in order of increasing frequency) includes: radiowaves, infrared radiation, visible radiation (light), ultraviolet radiation, x-rays, and cosmic radiation. In general, microwave technology includes, but is by no means limited to, some conventional mobile radios and telephones, all cellular telephones, all television broadcast channels above channel 13, satellite communications systems, radar, certain security alarms, circuits for high-speed computers, and, of course, microwave ovens.

Microwave energy has been applied to food preparation since 1950. Conventional heating combines two disadvantages—slowness and inefficiency—because it warms food gradually with heat entering from the outside. In contrast, microwaves create heat only when absorbed by the object they cook, resulting in rapid, even heating. Microwave technology works best on materials that hold some water and do not conduct electricity particularly well. Since microwaves focus energy, much less floor space is necessary in comparison to conventional heating and drying equipment.

Many other industries have reaped the benefits of microwave technology for heating and drying purposes. The chemical industry employed microwave technology in curing coatings, cross-linking polymers, and plasma polymerization. Printers and photographers have used microwave drying of film and ink curing to work more efficiently. Also, a microwave kiln

for processing of ceramic raw materials has also been successful. However, despite its success, microwave energy to heat materials is not as widespread as some of its proponents believe it should be. One reason is that radio frequency heating (RF), a related and more established technology, was more popular than microwave technology in such processes as plastics welding and wood gluing. Second, there are a great variety of microwave uses, and most use different kinds of equipment. Some companies are understandably reluctant to invest in one microwave-related product, only to realize they should have chosen another.

ORGANIZATION AND STRUCTURE

Microwave applications are found in a number of industries including telecommunications carriers, electronic device and component manufacturers, and the appliance industry. Certain firms, generally smaller companies, focus more exclusively on microwave applications, but large electronic firms, such as Matsushita, and telecommunications giants, such as Motorola and MCI WorldCom, have a great impact on the industry overall.

The wireless cable industry in the United States in 1998 had about 175 systems serving approximately 1 million customers. Although the first systems appeared in 1984, the industry never took off as expected. Most of these systems used an analog signal to provide multiple TV channels to consumers, competing with wireline cable providers, or filling gaps where conventional cable was not available. These systems primarily operated in the 2.1-2.3 gigahertz (GHz) spectrum. At the end of the 1990s, the Federal

Pioneer JAMES CLERK
MAXWELL
SHAPING THE
TWENTIETH
CENTURY

James Clerk Maxwell (1831-1879) is thought of by modern scientists as the single greatest nineteenth century scientist to have the biggest impact on twentieth century technology. Although not as famous or as well known, he is considered on a par with such notable scientists as Isaac Newton and Albert Einstein. Maxwell's work is actually the basis for which Einstein developed many of his theories, including relativity, as well as the other major innovation in twentieth century physics: quantum theory.

Maxwell focused on the observances of magnetic and electric waves of force, which he developed into his theories of electromagnetic waves, later to be known as radio waves. In 1873 Maxwell published his definitive work, *Treatise on Electricity and Magnetism* which contained these theories. During his lifetime, very few accepted his ideas, and it wasn't until about 10 years after he died that Heinrich Hertz proved Maxwell's theories correct by proving the existence of electromagnetic waves.

Lost in the notoriety of such scientists as Newton and Einstein, Maxwell's theories were actually the basis for almost all major physicists in the twentieth century, leading directly to the two main theories used in modern physics: relativity and quantum mechanics. However, it was his discovery of radio waves that runs the world as we know it. Without that one discovery, televisions, radios, cellular phones, satellites, even microwave ovens, might not exist.

Communications Commission (FCC) ruled that two-way communication could be used in this spectrum, and the new spectrum became available in the 24 GHz spectrum, which opened up new possibilities. Also, manufacturers and software developers continued to make improvements that increased the capabilities of microwave systems. The industry looked toward broadband communication of data such as Internet access as the future of the industry, and these developments attracted the attention of the broader telecommunications industry.

By 1999, microwave ovens had reached the status of a household necessity in the United States. According to a report cited in *Forecast* magazine, 93 percent of homes in the United States had a microwave. All major appliance lines included microwaves of various sizes, wattage, and features. Larger and sometimes more sophisticated models were made for commercial kitchens.

REGULATION

Like the rest of the telecommunications industry, regulation of wireless cable companies was drastically reduced by the Telecommunications Act of 1996. However, most radio frequencies, including most microwave frequencies, are licensed by the FCC, although some telecommunications companies operate on unlicensed frequencies. This gives them easier access to the frequency, but also makes interference more likely. The FCC continues to regulate the telecommunications industry to some degree in order to promote orderly development and proper competition.

Microwave ovens have been regulated by the U.S. Food and Drug Administration (FDA) since 1971. Medical devices that use microwave energy are also regulated by the FDA.

BACKGROUND AND DEVELOPMENT

The term "microwave region" is generally defined as falling in the upper section of the radiofrequency range of the electromagnetic spectrum, under that of infrared radiation. Microwave is defined differently by different groups. The FCC identifies the lower end of the range at a frequency of 890 megahertz (MHz), or 890 million cycles per second; the Institute of Electrical and Electronics Engineers (IEEE) defines microwave frequencies beginning at 1000 MHz. More general definitions extend the range from 300 MHz to 300 GHz—equivalent to 300 billion cycles per second. Regardless of the definition, the term "microwave" in general pertains to one segment of the whole electromagnetic spectrum.

German physicist Heinrich Rudolph Hertz (1857-1894) was the first person who intentionally generated electromagnetic energy at microwave frequencies in his experiments to verify the existence of electromagnetic waves. By 1920 other scientists were generating frequencies exceeding 3700 GHz; however, these relatively low energy levels could not be easily controlled. In 1931 the first microwave radio link for telephone use connected Dover, England, and Calais, France.

During World War II, major microwave innovations began in earnest. Microwave technology generated the higher frequencies necessary for the use of radar in airplanes. In 1947 the first point-to-point microwave radio relay system began, connecting Boston and New York City. By 1951 the first coast-to-coast system was in effect. By the 1960s microwave technology (specifically, two-way wireless communications) manifested itself in the citizen band (CB) radio trend. Eventually, though, because of its reputation for undependable analog transmission quality, microwave technology faced tougher times in the 1980s. Many local telephone companies also deployed high bandwidth digital services around this time.

By the 1990s, however, microwave communication technology made something of a comeback. With access to an electromagnetic spectrum formerly reserved to the military sphere, many established and start-up companies took advantage of the digital compression of video channels in the telecommunications industry. This development allowed wireless cable systems to deliver up to 200 virtual channels of video. From 1980 to the mid-1990s, the total number of licensed microwave-radio stations in the United States rose from about 22,000 to more than 100,000.

The telecommunications landscape in the 1990s appeared very different from that of any other time in history. In 1996 nearly two thirds of all long-distance telephone calls were delivered via microwave. Pager and cellular telephones represented two of the most successful examples of wireless technology. The widespread application of both products prompted many telephone companies to worry about exhausting their supply of telephone number exchanges. (Also see the essay in this book entitled Wireless Communications.)

The microwave spectrum is an enormous domain with 100 times as much frequency space for communications in the microwave range as in the whole spectrum beneath that bandwidth. A wireless cable is a broadband service that may deliver addressable, multichannel television programming, access to the Internet, data transfer services, and other interactive benefits. The wireless cable system has three main components—the transmit site, the signal path, and the receive site. These systems receive their programming from satellites that transmit a signal downward to the cable operator's receiving station. The operator then converts that signal to a microwave frequency and broadcasts it to subscribers from a transmitting tower. These signals can travel up to 50 miles.

Wireless cable customers have a rooftop antenna, a piece of equipment that receives the signal and transforms it into a cable frequency. The rooftop antenna may be installed on a single dwelling unit or on a multiple dwelling unit. These antennas generally fall into two categories—microwave antennas to capture the wireless cable signals and VHF/UHF antennas to receive the local broadcast channels. The signal is then

decoded and unscrambled for viewing. Some analog wireless cable systems use microwaves to deliver local channels.

The FCC set up rules and regulations for wireless cable operators in 1983, and the first wireless cable system emerged in 1984. For several years, the wired cable industry thwarted its program subsidiaries' attempts to sell on fair and non-discriminatory terms to new competitors. That changed in 1992 when Congress passed the Cable Competition and Consumer Protection Act, which allowed fair access to programming for cable rivals.

Until 1996, the FCC gave each wireless cable licensee the legal right to operate particular multipoint multichannel distribution service (MMDS) channels within a protected service area (PSA). Generally, a PSA's radius was 15 miles and was shielded from signal interference from other close transmissions. In 1996 the FCC overhauled this system and divided the United States into 493 basic trading areas (BTAs), each of which was auctioned to the greatest bidder. Under the new rules, each licensee operated as before, although with the implementation of BTAs, the incumbent PSAs were enlarged to cover 35 miles.

In July 1996 the FCC issued a declaratory ruling that allowed wireless cable operators to digitize their licensed channels as long as neighboring wireless cable systems suffered no interference from the analog-to-digital conversion procedure. One result of this ruling was that wireless cable could transmit up to 200 digitized channels of video, a considerable improvement over the original 33 analog channels per market.

In the United States, the wireless cable industry ballooned from about 200,000 subscribers in 1992 to 1 million by the mid-1990s. According to the Wireless Cable Association International, by 1997 roughly 5 million people in 80 countries subscribed to wireless systems. At the same time, more than 200 wireless cable systems existed in the United States. Mexico City, Mexico, particularly thrived on wireless cable with more than 600,000 subscribers in its service area.

MICROWAVE COOKING

In 1946 the Raytheon Company filed a patent applying microwaves to cook food. An oven that heated food with microwave energy was put in a restaurant in Boston, Massachusetts, for testing. The original weighed more than 750 pounds and cost more than $5,000. Given its bulkiness and expense, initial sales were not impressive.

In 1962 Dr. Roberta Oppenheimer perfected the world's first UL-approved microwave oven. While unsophisticated by the standards of the 1990s, it could prepare a 12-pound turkey in slightly less than two hours, as compared to six hours in a conventional oven. With this development making international headlines, the U.S. Government proceeded with plans to install the new ovens in homes and restaurants.

The Department of Health and Welfare eventually took responsibility for production of microwave ovens, while many scientists worried about the potential abuse of other nations latching onto microwave cooking. By the mid-1960s the Soviet Union had its own microwave ovens. By the late 1960s, many more countries were producing microwave ovens of their own.

In 1972 the North Atlantic Microwave Organization (NAMO) was founded in an attempt to prevent franchised microwave ovens produced in Communist countries from infringing upon models made in the Western World. NAMO also created standards for maximum power levels and radioactivity. By 1975 sales of microwave ovens outdistanced that of gas ranges. By the 1980s the United States and Europe were manufacturing microwave ovens in record numbers.

CURRENT CONDITIONS

TELECOMMUNICATIONS

The increasing popularity of the Internet in the late 1990s led many in the telecommunications industry to recognize the need for the capability to transmit large volumes of data without the use of landlines. With the newly granted right to use two-way digital signals, existing wireless cable companies took steps to move into this market by converting their systems to digital, an expensive proposition. Many of them found themselves in debt beyond their capability to maintain.

By the late 1990s, the FCC helped wireless cable operators branch out into high-speed digital data applications, including Internet access. At the end of the 1990s, some of the U.S. cities that offered such access included Washington, D.C.; Las Vegas, Nevada; Lakeland, Florida; Colorado Springs, Colorado; Dallas/Fort Worth, Texas; Santa Rosa, California; New York, New York; Seattle, Washington; Rochester, New York; San Jose/Silicon Valley, California; and Nashua, New Hampshire.

By 1997 a new group of products applied microwave technology to connect local area networks (LANs) at speeds of 10M bit/sec. and at distances of up to 15 miles. Companies such as Southwest Microwave, Inc. and Microwave Bypass Systems, Inc., in particular, capitalized on this relatively low-risk, low-cost trend. Unfortunately, some shortcomings in using microwave technology to connect LANs exist. These include forests, which, like high-rise buildings, can obstruct communication, poor weather, and long distances, all of which can create similar problems.

Then, in 1998 and 1999, the FCC put up for auction 986 licenses for Local Multipoint Distribution Service (LMDS) systems. These licenses for frequencies in the 28 GHz range opened up still more possibilities and attracted the interest of wireless entrepreneurs such as Craig McCaw, called "the father of cellular." Given the very large amount of transmission capability of these frequencies, the primary use of these licenses was expected to be for high-speed data transmission and Internet access.

The possibilities of broadband wireless communication in the lower frequencies used by the older wireless cable operators also attracted the interest of telecom giants. In 1999, Sprint, the third largest U.S. long-distance company, agreed to acquire People's Choice TV, American Telecasting, Wireless Holdings, Transworld Telecommunications, and Videotron USA, all wireless cable companies. At the same time, MCI WorldCom agreed to purchase CAI Wireless Systems, and Nucentrix Broadband Networks, formerly Heartland Wireless Communications, agreed to acquire Wireless One. Besides Internet access and data transmission, these assets could be developed to enable these companies to bypass the local telephone company to reach the individual home or business for regular telephone service.

MICROWAVE OVENS

Consumers were getting more value for their money when purchasing a microwave oven at the end of the 1990s. New models of microwaves had more features and more power, at nearly the same prices as earlier models. According to *Appliance* magazine's 1999 Statistical Forecast, 1998 shipments of household microwaves reached an estimated 9,329,000 units and were expected to reach 10,252,000 in 2004. Commercial microwave shipments were estimated at 185,000 units in 1998 and were projected to remain at that level through 2004.

MEDICINE

By the 1990s medicine increasingly used microwave applications. In 1996 the Prostatron became the first microwave device to treat an enlarged prostate (benign prostatic hyperplasia) in men. Manufactured by EDAP Technomed Group, this piece of machinery uses microwaves to eradicate excess prostate tissue. Restricted to medium-sized prostate glands, the procedure usually lasts an hour and can be done on an outpatient basis with local anesthetic.

In the late 1970s, Augustine Cheung, a microwave engineer, was exploring possibilities in microwave hyperthermia (heat therapy) to eventually cure cancer. Undeterred by the lack of research funds, he started Cheung Laboratories in the early 1990s to sell microwave hyperthermia systems. Even though his company experienced a $1.3 million loss on revenues of $157,618 in 1995, Cheung remains committed to his own original purpose, encouraged by studies that indicate a 90-percent response rate in applying extreme heat to destroy cancerous cells. However, the side effects caused by burning surrounding tissue often outweighed the technology's benefits. To eliminate such side effects, Cheung began applying an adaptive focusing technique called adaptive phased array (APA), developed by the Massachusetts Institute of Technology.

A third medical microwave application in the 1990s was for dissolving varicose veins. In 1996 Dynamic Associates Inc., a holding company that contains two subsidiaries—P & H Laboratories Inc. and Microwave Medical Corp.—owned the patent for a technology in which a metal wand is employed to focus microwave energy on varicose veins. The procedure disintegrates the tissue then collapses the vein. It is generally less painful than the more established practice of relying on a needle to insert a saline or acidic solution in the vein.

Microwave technology was also used in the late 1990s to treat menorrhagia, a form of abnormal uterine bleeding. A *Lancet* article describes a study in which microwave therapy was compared to laser, diathermy, and radiofrequency electromagnetic waves. With the latter three therapies, the failure rate ranged from 19 to 56 percent, and many complications ensued. By contrast, microwave therapy achieved an 83 percent success rate 6 months after treatment. In terms of safety, microwave proved superior to the other therapies, and medical staff found it easy to learn and perform.

In the mid-1990s Drs. Theodore and Wendy Guo, both employed by Potomac Research Inc., received a patent for microwave-imaging technology that could eventually replace the much more expensive CAT scans and MRI images. The National Institutes of Health and the U.S. Department of Energy have funded some of Potomac Research's efforts. Until the mid-1980s, microwaves, with relatively massive wavelengths, were considered ineffective for probing the

The Trans-Siberia line, installed by NEC and Siemens, is the world's longest digital microwave communications network. (Courtesy of NEC USA, Inc.)

human body. Since X-rays and CAT scans had shorter wavelengths, they were the preferred technology of choice. However, after the Guos helped to produce an algorithm to decipher microwaves' images, a new microwave application seemed imminent.

INDUSTRY LEADERS

In 1999 the consolidation that had been going on in the broader telecommunications industry began to grip the wireless cable segment as well. Heartland

Wireless Communications, Inc., which had been the largest operator with almost 200,000 subscribers, emerged from bankruptcy proceedings with a new name, Nucentrix Broadband Networks, and promptly entered into an agreement to acquire Wireless One, formerly the third largest operator. Nucentrix had 1998 revenues of $74.0 million, while Wireless One had revenue of $38.7 million. American Telecasting, which had been the second largest, was being purchased by Sprint, as was People's Choice TV, Videotron USA, Wireless Holdings, and Transworld Telecommunications, Inc. CAI Wireless Systems, with over 73,000 subscribers and 1998 revenue of $28.6 million, was being acquired by MCI WorldCom. Except for Nucentrix, Wireless One, and Sprint, all these companies had been experiencing negative revenue growth. Sprint had committed to spend over $1 billion in these transactions. MCI WorldCom's commitment was about $476 million.

A relative newcomer, Teligent, Inc., was founded in the early 1990s. Using broadband microwave technology, it began service in 15 cities in 1998 and planned to roll out service in all 74 of the U.S. markets in which it owned spectrum by the end of 2000. It offered local telephone service, Internet access, and other services, bypassing the local telephone companies through its wireless systems. It was certified as a competitive local-exchange carrier (CLEC) rather than a wireless cable company, but it was doing what many wireless cable companies were moving toward.

RESEARCH AND TECHNOLOGY

ENVIRONMENTAL RISKS IN TELECOMMUNICATIONS

From the mid-1970s to the mid-1990s, there were thousands of journal articles and research studies on the subject of the correlation between electromagnetic field (EMF) exposure and cancer in human beings. Although the research data was not conclusive, several studies in different countries indicate the possibility that EMF may at least contribute to some cancers in humans. The studies that explore a possible link between cancer and EMF are entirely different from other studies that focus on whether the microwave radiation can contribute to cancer. According to the Electromagnetic Energy Association (EEA), there were more than 100,000 microwave-radio stations in the United States in the mid-1990s. Harmful exposure of the public and the worker to microwave energy from these sources was extremely low. The output power of the

average transmitter employed for microwave radio is fairly comparable to that of a citizens band radio.

By the early 1980s U.S. measurements done in close proximity to microwave towers and on the rooftops of buildings near microwave antennas indicated a very positive scenario. Even in the most troubling cases, the recorded microwave levels were thousands of times below exposure limits set by the American National Standards Institute (ANSI) and the National Committee on Radiation Protection (NCRP). However, there are several epidemiological studies of people who have been exposed to above average levels of radio-frequency/microwave radiation (RF/MW) radiation in their jobs. Through their medical records and other health-related data, researchers have found some correlation between high radiation exposure and physical symptoms such as heart disease, cancer, birth abnormalities, and pregnancy miscarriage. However, to what extent these workers' problems are due to radiation exposure or to other factors (such as work or stress) was not always easy to ascertain.

With the worldwide popularity of cellular telephones in the 1990s, scientists began studying whether the radioactive effects of these devices actually posed a health threat to users. In 1994 Australian researchers concluded from their experiments that cancer-susceptible mice that had been exposed to cellular phones' radio-frequency/microwave radiation experienced two times the number of cancers as other mice. Since the Australian cellular phone industry participated in this study and had not anticipated its disturbing results, other scientists praised the validity of the study—many of them following up on its results. However, in the late 1990s, it was still not known whether the study's results and conclusion are applicable to the health of humans.

In 1995 Debbra Wright, a 42-year-old mother of three children and an employee of Bell Atlantic Mobile, sued Motorola, claiming that the cellphones she had used since the late 1980s had caused a brain tumor. The cancer, diagnosed in 1993, is close to her left ear. While at the time there were at least eight other lawsuits seeking to tie cellular phones to cancer, *Microwave News* claims Wright's was reportedly the first by a service provider employee.

While many environmental concerns about microwave energy have been completely resolved, many, if not most, of its applications have been proven reasonably safe. While microwave's most traditional purposes revolved around heating and drying, some of its most innovative uses have been in telecommunications and medicine.

MICROWAVE COOKING

At the end of the 1990s, many other applications of microwave technology were emerging. For example, a group of scientists at Boston-based Invent Resources were working on such innovations as a microwave clothes dryer that tackles metal zippers and buttons and a microwave cooking device that allows for a crispier taste.

A Cornell University study demonstrated how moisture, heating rate, and food's porosity interact during microwave cooking. By understanding these interactions, scientists hope they can improve microwave technology to produce tastier foods. Ashim Datta, a Cornell University associate professor of agricultural and biological engineering, explained, "The microwave is grossly underused. Up until now, we haven't really understood much of the physics that occur during the microwave processing of food. This research shows us the quantitative physics as to why microwave food can be soggy and sometimes unappealing and also why sometimes excessive amounts of moisture can be lost."

According to Datta, previous research on microwave technology did not calculate the interrelationship between porosity and the internal pressures that develop because of evaporation of water inside food. With the impact of internal pressure, much more moisture reaches the food's surface, while air inside a microwave oven stays at room temperature. This sometimes causes sogginess in foods. "Through understanding the true physics of microwave cooking, companies can use this information to provide better tasting and better texture of food, as well as to provide more convenience to consumers by promoting increased use of microwave cooking," said Datta.

Packaging for microwaveable meals was increasingly important in the 1990s. The most sophisticated packaging used susceptors (surface layers) to minimize the flaws of microwave cooking. These devices consisted of a plastic film metalized usually with aluminum and laminated to paper or paperboard. They often made foods crispier by improving their texture. Since producers of packaging materials continually explore methods to improve the design of susceptors, monitoring of high temperature materials is extremely important.

In 1998 Microwave Science, a Georgia software company, received a patent for a system that would allow microwave ovens to prepare food to consistent standards. This system used software and sensors in the oven, which would enable the user to input simple codes that would adjust the oven during cooking to match actual conditions of voltage, altitude, type of food, and other factors.

Manufacturers were beginning to add capabilities to microwaves that provided some of the benefits of conventional ovens, such as hot air circulation to brown foods and steamers to supply additional moisture. Another microwave oven available to consumers had true variable control. The power control on a typical microwave caused the magnetron, which generates the microwave energy, to turn on and off at appropriate intervals, but the power control on these new ovens actually varied the amount of electricity going to the magnetron, thus giving more precise control of the microwave energy.

FURTHER READING

Cahoon, Jim. "How Does Wireless Cable Work?" *Wireless Cable Association International,* 1997. Available from http://www.wirelesscabl.com.

Cheremisinoff, P.N., O.G. Farah, and R.P. Oullette. *Radio Frequency/Radiation and Plasma Processing: Industrial Applications & Advances.* Lancaster, PA: Technomic Publishing Company, Inc., 1985.

"Communities and Telecommunications Corporations: Rethinking the Rules for Zoning Variances." *American Business Law Journal,* Winter 1995.

Dagani, Ron. "Molecular Magic with Microwaves." *Chemical & Engineering News,* 10 February 1997.

"Electromagnetic Radiation and Health Risks: Cell Phones and Microwave Radiation in New Zealand." *Journal of Environmental Health,* July/August 1996.

Emmett, Arielle. "Technologist of the Year." *America's Network,* 15 January 1997.

Everything You Always Wanted to Know About Wireless Cable But Were Afraid to Ask. Washington, D.C.: Rini, Coran & Lancellotta, P.C., 1996.

"First Microwave Device to Treat Enlarged Prostate." *FDA Consumer,* July/August 1996.

Kirkpatrick, David. "Electricity, Cellular Phones, and Cancer." *Fortune,* 15 May 1995.

"Look Ma, No Wires." *Forbes,* 25 March 1996.

McVicar, Nancy. "New Studies Fuel Debate on Cellular Risks Signals May Damage Tissues." *Sun-Sentinel Fort Lauderdale,* 13 May 1997.

Philippidis, Alex. "Telecommunications Law May Expedite Cellular Antenna Approval." *Westchester County Business Journal,* 10 June 1996.

Rodger, William. "Microwave Imaging May Be Wave of the Future." *Washington Business Journal,* 21 April 1995.

Scotti, Joseph J. "Wireless Communication: The Real Competition for Local Phone Companies." *New Hampshire Business Review,* 19 July 1996.

Sharp, Nicholas C., et al. "Microwaves for Menorrhagia: A New Fast Technique for Endometrial Ablation." *The Lancet,* 14 October 1995.

Throop, John. "Cable Alternative Sees Business Upswing." *Peoria Journal Star,* 14 December 1996.

"Waiting for Wireless." *Forbes,* 13 January 1997.

Wallace, Bob. "Tide Rises for Microwave Technology." *Computerworld,* 4 September 1995.

"What Is Microwave Radio?" *Electromagnetic Energy Association,* 1996. Available from http://www.elecenergy.inter.net/eeaindex.html.

"Wireless Access Enters Real-World Trials." *Internet World,* May 1997.

"Wireless Cable Statistics." *Wireless Cable Association International,* July 1997. Available from http://www.wirelesscabl.com.

Zimm, Angela. "A Hot Opportunity: Cheung Labs Adapting Microwave Technology to Treat Cancer." *Warfield's Business Record,* 29 July 1996.

—David Levine,
updated by Howard Distelzweig

MOLECULAR DESIGN

INDUSTRY SNAPSHOT

Molecular design is the process of isolating a novel chemical compound, assessing its beneficial uses, and finding a means to synthesize it in a form optimal to the target use. Representing the research and development end of the biotechnology industry, molecular design uses computerized molecular modeling as well as specialized chemical techniques as tools to render products for profitable applications in a range of industries, including chemical manufacturing, genetic engineering, and pharmaceutical manufacturing.

While the process of creating new chemical compounds by experimentation is more than 200 hundred years old, new initiatives in molecular design have dramatically increased the speed of the entire process in the late 1990s. Researchers focused on developing new methods to aid in the discovery of novel marketable chemical and pharmaceutical agents. Major advances have been made in the tools of the trade, including protein crystallography, magnetic resonance, pharmacokinetics, and molecular biology. Combined with the recent proliferation of computer software that allows chemists to visualize and predict the behavior of new compounds, they have revolutionized the industry. Molecular design software has been used in the creation of new pesticides and drugs to treat rheumatism, arthritis, and AIDS. Molecular design has allowed many of these advances to take place through genetic research. This is an area of rapidly increasing importance in medicine and industry—in part because extraordinary advances in computing make it possible to do accurate theoretical and experimental studies of enzymes, nucleic acids, and biomolecular assemblies.

"Molecular biotechnology ought to provide unprecedented benefits to humankind," according to Bernard R. Glick and Jack J. Pasternak, authors of *Molecular Biotechnology: Principles & Applications of Recombinant DNA*. It should, they claim, offer innumerable benefits, including:

- opportunities to accurately diagnose and prevent or cure a wide range of infectious and genetic diseases

- increased crop yields through the use of genetically engineered plants

- the development of microorganisms that will produce chemicals, polymers, amino acids, enzymes, and various food additives

- enhanced genetically determined attributes of livestock and other animals

- the removal of pollutants and waste materials from the environment

Efficient and productive realization of molecular design techniques allows the biotech industry to profit from small molecule development and discovery in each of these areas. The pharmaceutical industry entirely depends upon the discovery and selective development of molecules possessing characteristics that may become profitable drugs. Also, genetic engineering continuously uncovers interesting gene activity and needs large arrays of compounds to screen against gene products for potential activity. Developers of bioremediation processes use molecular design to discover advanced synthetic treatments and accessory compounds, such as nitrification inhibitors, to optimize conditions for microorganism activity.

While college and university departments and institutes traditionally account for the majority of molecular design and research, successful business applications have attracted a tremendous amount of attention in the late 1990s and have enabled industry growth. The genetic engineering sector is responsible for much of this attention with its promise of "wonder drugs" and an "agricultural Utopia" surrounded by controversy. Major changes in molecular design technique have enabled numerous small research companies to operate with specialized core technologies and computer programs. Design companies then lease their software and technology. Alternately, they can carry out the molecular design that fuels the rest of the industry, working closely with international pharmaceutical companies such as Hoechst Marion Roussel and Bristol-Myers Squibb.

The final goal of any molecular design activity is to provide a sustainable quantity of a novel compound that offers some benefit to humans and, ultimately, financial gain for the biotech industry. A great deal of research is necessary before this ultimate goal is obtained. Yet, despite many false leads—only one drug in 10,000 makes it to market, according to Hoover's Biotech Industry Snapshot—the profits can be enormous: Amgen's Neupogen reached $1.1 billion in 1998. Genetic engineering giant Monsanto reported an EBITDA (earnings before interest expense, taxes depreciation and amortization, and excluding unusual items) of $1.1 billion for its agricultural segment, with products ranging from genetically engineered seeds to herbicides and bovine growth hormones.

BACKGROUND AND DEVELOPMENT

Humans have been using naturally occurring compounds to their benefit for thousands of years. Plants and animals provided food, medicine, and lubricating oils. New products were limited by traditional methods of screening naturally occurring substances. In contrast, the development of new substances based on knowledge of chemical properties could rarely be realized in practice. Once a novel compound with beneficial properties is isolated, it is often in a form that is unacceptable for its application say, as a drug. It is beneficial to have access to knowledge about hundreds or thousands of chemicals that display similar beneficial properties and, among those, one form just possibly will be free from any undesirable properties.

The ability to do accurate theoretical and experimental studies of enzymes, nucleic acids, and bio-molecular assemblies is inherent to "designing" a molecule, but the idea of using living things for human benefit is far from new. The use of living organisms to make cheese and bread has been practiced since 7000 B.C. Modern molecular design grew out of this larger field of molecular biotechnology. (The term "biotechnology" was coined in 1917 by Hungarian engineer Karl Ereky to describe "all lines of work by which products are produced from raw materials with the aid of living things.")

The greatest problem facing molecular biotechnicians is developing microorganisms and compounds into marketable products. Naturally occurring microorganisms rarely produce the results scientists need for commercial application. By exposing organisms to other factors, such as ultraviolet radiation, scientists induce genetic changes that might or might not produce a desired byproduct. With the recognition in 1944 that DNA (deoxyribonucleic acid, a chemical component of most living cells) held all the genetic material needed for a cell to reproduce itself, scientists began to think about creating organisms that would produce waste products that could serve as useful substances.

It was not until the late 1970s that researchers were able to apply genetic engineering techniques to molecular design. Due to the tedious nature of testing, the traditional genetic improvement regimens were time consuming and costly. In addition, the best result that this traditional approach could yield was the improvement of an existing inherited property, rather than the expansion or creation of the certain genetic capabilities. Molecular design, combined with genetic engineering, allowed these improvements to be made more efficiently.

The emergence of powerful microcomputers in the late 1970s allowed great advances in molecular biotechnology. In terms of molecular design in particular, computers proved to be important tools in the production of new chemicals. Computer databases allowed easy tracking and interpretation of huge numbers of characteristics. As microcomputing technologies improved during the 1980s, new computer programs were developed that allowed individual molecules to be displayed graphically on computer monitors. In the late 1990s, most advanced computer programs could create, edit, and print depictions of chemical molecules on the atomic level. (Also see the essay in this book entitled Molecular Modeling.)

In 1978, the genetic research company Genentech used a genetically modified *E. coli* bacterium to produce human insulin. The bacterial host cells acted as biological factories for the production of human insulin that was then purified and used by diabetics who were allergic to the commercially available porcine (pig) insulin. Genentech's product also made human insulin cheaper and more readily available to diabetics throughout the world.

Genentech was one of the most successful leaders in the molecular and genetic design industry in the 1980s. Its success inspired many imitators, only a few of which prospered. Promoters dreamed of a world in which genetically and molecularly engineered microorganisms would produce petroleum, clean up wastes, cure diseases, and repel pests. According to reports that appeared in newspapers, magazines, and television at that time, the applications of molecular design were limitless; many of those applications were being realized in the late 1990s.

The discovery and analysis of genes and their manifestations has come to be known as genomics. Coupled with other major technological advances in molecular design, the use of genomics to identify molecular targets has revolutionized the molecular design industry in the 1990s. Giant undertakings, such as the Human Genome Project, offer an abundance of information accessible on highly sophisticated computerized databases. Having identified the biological target—an enzyme, hormone, growth factor, or other protein—the researcher has a point of entry for chemical manipulation.

While computers allow the visualization of chemical interactions and large information databases, they have not entirely replaced experimentation in the lab. The final key to the technology that has made possible the massive libraries of potentially profitable biotech molecules each year is the process of combinatorial chemistry. First developed as a scheme to save time in drug research, the approach has evolved into the ability to create large numbers of organic compounds with the ability to tag them in such a way that those with optimal properties can be screened and identified. Combinatorial chemistry has reduced the time required to profile an optimum form of the compound from years to weeks.

Biological activity is dependent on the three-dimensional geometry of specific functional groups. Biomolecular research has traditionally required synthesis and screening of large numbers of molecules to produce optimal activity profiles, producing an average of one compound a week. Combinatorial chemistry allows researchers to amass libraries of large populations of molecules (100,000 in a matter of weeks) for screening compounds. Similarly, advancements of modern computers, which have become fast, small,

and affordable, allow researchers to visualize molecular structure and activity on screen rather than in a test tube. Moreover, advancements in chemical models and program interfaces allow researchers to describe the mechanisms of biomolecular activity. Finally, high throughput robotic screens identify which compounds exhibit desired activity against the target. These potential lead candidates are then sold or licensed as information to the subsequent biotech companies for further product development and marketing in the individual sectors.

Trends   THE NOSE KNOWS

Tony Czarnic has a nose for chemistry. With the ability to sniff out medicinal molecules, environmental toxins, and even the explosives in land mines, his artificial nose serves as the platform technology that will have applications in pharmaceuticals, law enforcement, and genomics.

The nose uses fiber optic bundles tipped with coded beads that will chance color when other specific molecules attach themselves. Sensors on the fiber optic bundle send unique patterns to a computer for information processing, much like receptors for our sense of smell send information to our brains for processing. This technology allows scientists keep pace with the current biotech boom in disease-related gene discovery and in gene-product screening against massive chemical libraries. In law enforcement and military situations, the technology can be used to detect explosives, illegal drugs, and chemical warfare agents.

In comparison with its namesake, the artificial nose has yet to reach the sophistication of the human nose, which can detect hundreds of different smells. But while its reactions are not quite human, scientific developer of the nose David Walt of Tufts University in Boston says the nose can detect complex mixtures including household fumes and cologne.

CURRENT CONDITIONS

Molecular design is the research "fuel" that supplies the information the pharmaceutical industry uses to formulate new drugs; the agriculture sector uses to genetically engineer crops and livestock and to make herbicides, pesticides, and fertilizers; and the biotech chemical sector needs to generate genetically engineered enzymes and technologies for bioremediation of the environment. A growing number of companies offer technologies that will produce an enormous number of potentially profitable biotech molecules. These companies offer services aimed at streamlining the process of molecular discovery and development to complement the pharmaceutical and biotech industries.

Several companies offer molecular design services tailored to suit clients' needs. For example, Pharmacopea, Inc. performs research services to develop drug discovery programs. The company generates large libraries for pharmaceutical research. These large libraries offer structure-activity data, the likelihood of rapid discovery of a suitable compound, and broad patent protection of identifiable libraries, thus slowing competitor's attempts to develop similar drugs. The company follows a strategy to manage the different aspects of molecular design with four business units. First, Pharmacopea's subsidiary, Molecular Simulations Inc. (MSI), supplies life and materials science industries with research and development software for prediction of structure and chemical interaction. Second, Pharmacopea licenses molecular libraries to outside companies for drug development. Third, the company's drug discovery program licenses candidates for drug development to pharmaceutical companies. Fourth, Pharmacopea forms collaborations to identify and optimize lead compounds for the targets provided by outside companies.

Indeed, the trend throughout the molecular design industry is collaboration. Chiron Corporation, located in Emeryville, California, has produced leads for corporate partners such as Pharmacia & Upjohn and Novartis AG. Research company Tripos specializes in software that creates virtual combinatorial libraries, and President and CEO Dr. John P. McAlister stated in 1998 that the company expects strongest future growth in software and consulting. In May 1998 researchers at Boston University and Scriptgen Pharmaceuticals announced steps toward the development of a new class of antibiotics to combat deadly drug-resistant and emerging forms of bacteria. In the realms of genetic and molecular medicine, in March 1999 Orchid Biocomputer and the University of Washington School of Medicine announced their collaboration to form The Institute for Qualitative Systems Biology.

Molecular design's highly productive technology spans beyond the limits of drug discovery applications to those of nearly any field requiring generation of small molecules. In 1994 Dr. Alejandro C. Zaffaroni, pioneer of combinatorial chemistry, founded Symyx Technologies, Inc. to apply the techniques to the chemical and electronic industries. A March 1999 press release announced Symyx's expanded collaboration worth $68 million with Bayer AG of Leverkusen, Germany, to develop catalysts for new polymer production.

Illumina, Inc. of San Diego, California, offers a new type of sensor it calls an optical nose. The fiber optics platform detects tagged sensor elements prepared according to the combinatorial chemistry technique. The sensors of the "nose" send unique chemical patterns to a computer for processing. Applications range from pharmaceutical screening to detecting environmental toxins and chemical warfare agents.

Within this industry, individual molecular design companies tend to center on a patented specialized technology that can speed the search for compounds with properties that react favorably with a desired target. Once fully established, large corporations often acquire all or part of the smaller companies and their discovery processes. Before his work on Symyx Technologies, Inc., Dr. Zaffaroni first founded Affymax Research Institute in 1988 based on combinatorial chemistry and high throughput screening technologies. The company became a subsidiary of Glaxo Wellcome Inc. in March 1995.

In an era of long-term investments, biotech companies are scrambling to maintain the funding necessary to develop products to full marketability. Molecular design's rapid library technologies combined with the unraveling of the human genetic code promises explosive growth for biotech industries, increasing productivity exponentially. More effective screening techniques minimize the time spent in pursuit of false leads in the labs, thereby allowing industry research and development efforts to focus on promising biotech compounds.

INDUSTRY LEADERS

Specialized molecular design research services are carried out in both academic and commercial environments, with many partnerships and alliances formed between the two. For example, the Molecular Design Institute (MDI) at the University of California San Francisco (UCSF) advances molecular design methods and works closely with industry. The National Institute of Health (NIH) has awarded MDI several grants covering structure-based molecular design. The institute also works to further drug discoveries.

Pharmacopea, Inc., together with its San Diego subsidiary, Molecular Simulations Inc., combines three platform technologies of combinatorial chemistry, high throughput screening, and molecular modeling software to aid the development and discovery of life and material sciences products. Revenue is generated through software sales and service, chemical compound leasing, internal drug discovery, and collaborative drug discovery. The company has collaborative agreements with agricultural and pharmaceutical companies such as Bayer Corporation, Novartis AG, and Schering-Plough Corporation. In addition to the San Diego facility, the company runs major operations in Cambridge, England, and Tokyo, Japan, to distribute software. In 1998 the company had 550 employees and reported total revenues of $92.2 million, up 14 percent from the previous year.

One of the major U.S. firms involved in the field of molecular design is Tripos, Inc., a publicly owned company founded in 1979. Based in St. Louis, Missouri, the company has a history of success in the field of molecular imaging and design software. In 1998 Tripos experienced a 15-percent decrease in its sales revenue of $25.6 million, as was anticipated with the termination of its joint venture with MDS Penlabs and investments to initiate internal chemical laboratory operations. The company expects high financial returns by combining its computer software technology with chemical synthesis. Practically every pharmaceutical company uses its patented CoMFA (comparative molecular field analysis) technology worldwide. Customers include scientific research organizations as well as biotech companies Genelabs Technologies, Inc. and Cell Pathways, Inc.

Chiron Corporation is one of the world's largest biotechnology companies. The company conducts much of its research on cancer and cardiovascular and infectious diseases in collaboration with partners from industry and academia. Swiss pharmaceutical company Novartis AG owns approximately 45 percent of its outstanding common stock. The company also markets therapeutics, blood testing, and vaccines. Headquartered in Emeryville, California, in 1998 the company had 3,247 employees, up 49.9 percent from the previous year. In 1998 the company also experienced a 36.6-percent increase in its sales revenue of $736.7 million, with a net income of $521.0 million.

RESEARCH AND TECHNOLOGY

A few companies use molecular design software strictly to develop new commercial products. A great many more colleges and universities, however, use molecular design primarily to train students in chemistry. Still, there is some overlap between the two extremes. The Department of Chemistry at the Univer-

sity of Houston, for instance, sponsors the Institute for Molecular Design (IMD), which exists to promote the exchange of information between field researchers. This information exchange helps with researching new computer tools for molecular design, attracting funds to support molecular design, and promoting computer-aided molecular design. Students as well as professional chemists utilize the programs and resources of the IMD. It is not a commercial program, however, and is therefore supported by grants from the government, private foundations, and companies in the industry.

The Molecular Design Institute (MDI) at UCSF is another example of the overlap between academia and commerce in molecular design. The Institute was established in 1993 as an academic research institute to promote the discovery, design, and delivery of pharmaceutical agents. The MDI seeks innovative partnerships between business and universities to expand their basic and applied research efforts and works closely with different agencies in the college, including the School of Medicine, the School of Pharmacy, and the biophysics program. It is also associated with the UCSF Computer Graphics Laboratory (CGL), which developed the MidasPlus program for use in molecular design. MidasPlus, an acronym for Molecular Interactive Display and Simulation, is used both for training and for commercial applications.

The USCF CGL has also introduced a number of other programs for use in molecular design. One program is AMBER, a suite of programs for performing a variety of molecular mechanics-based simulations on machines ranging from workstations to supercomputers and designed for researchers working with proteins and nucleic acids. DOCK/BUILDER/MOLSIM, is a suite of three programs also distributed by the UCSF CGL that provides a way to screen large databases of chemical compounds that have features in common with receptor targets.

Other areas of UCSF associated with the MDI have also produced software aimed to support their specific interests and needs. The UCSF Magnetic Resonance Laboratory, for instance, offers CORMA and MARDIGRAS, two programs designed to reduce error in creating molecular models. The Department of Cellular and Molecular Pharmacology, which works extensively with models of proteins, has developed four programs to help researchers working with amino acids and other protein structures. The MDI at UCSF also offers a corporate scholars program to disseminate information about molecular design and provides sabbatical positions for corporate chemists in UCSF laboratories.

CombiChem, Inc. offers its computerized Discovery Engine (trademark for its proprietary design technology) to search its virtual libraries for hypothetical compounds. With or without prior information about the target, the company generates, evolves, and optimizes potential new lead drug and agrochemical candidates for collaborative partners from the life sciences industry.

German-based CompuChem has developed a more user-friendly program called CompuChemSuite. The program allows students and educators to draw structures, make three-dimensional rotations of formulas, create color prints, label atoms for easy identification, and create animation files that allow the model to be rotated in space. This development, among others, heralds a new era in molecular design.

FURTHER READING

"About Pharmacopea: Business Model." Princeton, NJ: Pharmacopea, Inc., 1999. Available from http://www.pcop .com/business.html.

"Bayer and Symyx Expand Collaboration." Santa Clara, CA: Symyx Technologies Inc., 30 March 1999. Available from http://www.symyx.com/march1999a.html.

"Bioremediation." Birmingham, NJ: Sybron Chemicals, Inc., 1999. Available from http://www.sybronchemicals .com/biochem/bio.htm.

"Center for Molecular Design and Recognition," 1996. Available from http://dendrimers.cas.usf.edu.

"Chiron Reports 1998 Fourth-Quarter and Year-End Results." Emeryville, CA: Chiron Corporation, 9 February 1999. Available from http://www.shareholder.com/chiron/ news/19990209-6691.html.

Chithelen, Ignatius. "Etch-a-drug." *Forbes,* 12 June 1989.

"CombiChem Profile." San Diego: CombiChem, Inc., 1999. Available from http://www.combichem.com/About/.

"Combinatorial Chemistry: A Strategy for the Future." *Network Science,* July 1995. Available from http://www.netsci .org/Science/Combichem/feature02.html.

"Combinatorial Chemistry: What is Combinatorial Chemistry?" Princeton, NJ: Pharmacopea, 1999. Available from http://www.pcop.com/chemistry.html.

"Corporate Info." Emeryville, CA: Chiron Corporation, 1999. Available from http://www.chiron.com/corpInfo/ main.html.

"DuPont to Acquire Pioneer." Wilmington, DE: E.I. du Pont de Nemours and Company, 15 March 1999. Available from http://www.dupont.com/corp/whats-new/newsfile/ 990315a.html.

Glick, Bernard R., and Jack J. Pasternak. *Molecular Biotechnology: Principles & Applications of Recombinant DNA.* Washington, D.C.: American Society for Microbiology, 1994.

"Illumina: Company Profile." San Diego: Illumina, Inc., 1999. Available from http://www.illumina.com/co-profile .html.

"An Introduction to Molecular Modeling." *Network Science,* August 1995. Available from http:www.netsci.org/Science/ Compuchem/feature01.html.

"Journal of Computer-Aided Molecular Design." Leiden, The Netherlands, 1995. Available from http://www.ibc .wustl.edu/jcamd/jcamd.html.

"Monsanto Reports 1998 Fourth Quarter and Full Year Reports." St. Louis: Monsanto, 21 January 1999. Available from http://www.monsanto.com/monsanto/mediacenter/99/ 99jan21_quarter.html.

"Orchid Biocomputer Announces Collaborations with The University of Washington School of Medicine." *PR Newswire,* 10 March 1999.

"Pharmacopea, Inc. Announces 1998 Fourth Quarter and Year End Financial Results." Princeton, NJ: Pharmacopea, Inc., 4 February 1999. Available from http://www.pcop .com/pr50.html.

"Researchers Synthesize Compounds For New Class Of Antibiotics." *EurekAlert,* 12 May 1998.

"Science, Technology & Medicine: Combining Forces to Combat Disease." San Francisco: Univ. of California—San Francisco-Molecular Design Inst., 1998. Available from http://mdi.ucsf.edu/MDI_Info.html.

"Small Molecule Discovery: Oral Drugs for Major Diseases." Emeryville, CA: Chiron Corporation, 1999. Available from http://www.chiron.com/research/platforms/ smallMolecule.html.

"Tripos, Inc. Announces Fourth Quarter 1998 Financial Results." *PR Newswire,* 10 February 1999. Available from http://www.tripos.com/press/Q498.html.

Wells, William. "Combinatorial Chemistry: Making More Drugs." *Genentech Access Excellence: About Biotech.* San Francisco, 1998. Available from http://www.gene.com/ae/ AB/BA/combiChem/.

—Sondra E. O'Donnell

MOLECULAR MODELING

A powerful tool, molecular modeling utilizes computers to help predict the three-dimensional structures of molecules and elucidate their other physical and chemical properties. Its goal is to aid the rational design of compounds, including medicinal drugs, by bridging the gap between theoretical chemistry and synthetic chemistry. Theoretical chemistry employs concepts that do not always translate smoothly from the scratch pad to the bench top, and synthetic chemistry often relies on painstaking trial and error. Molecular modeling allows the display of three-dimensional models of molecules that can be rotated on screen so users can perceive atomic and molecular interactions. In the hands of highly skilled professionals, molecular modeling can provide significant insight into chemical structures and processes.

Molecular modeling complements analytical and experimental work. But just as power tools alone are not enough to build a house, computational methods alone are not enough to replace experimentation. No molecule has ever been conceived and created "from scratch" using molecular modeling alone. And all molecular modeling relies on data first obtained from experiments. Still, molecular modeling serves an essential role. Time and money limit the number of experiments scientists can run, and simulations guide their research efforts and aid their interpretations.

The chemical, pharmaceutical, and biotechnology industries use molecular modeling extensively for materials research and drug development. The chemical industry, for instance, has used molecular modeling to create better catalysts, which make chemical reactions possible even under harsh conditions, as well as to synthesize substances from new fuels to industrial lubricants. Medicinal chemists, on the other hand, have used molecular modeling to design drugs that are more potent and less toxic than their precursors.

Computational chemistry was a $2 billion industry in 1996 and experienced 25 percent annual growth through much of the 1990s. As computers get faster and scientists familiarize themselves with the software, the predictive power of molecular modeling will only grow.

More than 50 percent of molecular modeling efforts are applied in pharmacology or biotechnology. Additional applications include polymers (about 30 percent) and general materials such as metals, clays, and cements (less than 20 percent).

The major worth of molecular modeling is its predictive value. Acting as a scratch pad to test ideas and graphically display molecules, it allows scientists to predict the properties of hypothetical compounds. It also can facilitate the analysis of experimental data and suggest useful trends. For example, in 1992 Hoechst Celanese of Somerville, New Jersey began a program to bring molecular modeling to its bench chemists to get chemical insights in the shortest possible time. When chemists there used molecular modeling to develop polymers, they were able to reduce the number of chemical pairs they needed to examine from 300 to 30. Similarly, guidance from molecular modeling helps the pharmaceutical industry streamline and accelerate the discovery and development of new drugs, making these processes less expensive.

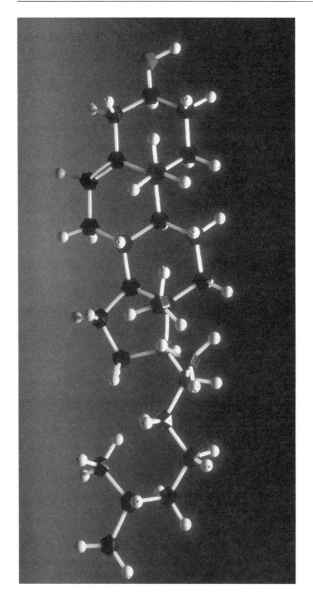

A model of a full molecule strand. *(Digital Stock.)*

Molecular modeling software treats molecules as a three-dimensional system of balls interconnected by springs. It applies mechanical constraints to the system to show the conformation (shape) that takes the least energy to maintain, to calculate the angle between two atoms bonded together in the molecule, or to reveal the location of electrostatic charges within the molecule.

Medicinal chemists may use this information to predict the biological performance of a compound, which guides the drug-discovery process. Drugs work by interacting with biological molecules in the body, such as nucleic acids (DNA and RNA), enzymes, and receptors. How well a drug interacts with its biological target depends on a concept called complementar-

ity: just as a key must properly fit a lock to open a door, a drug must bind correctly at a specific site. Complementarity, the degree of "stickiness" of the drug to the target, influences the biological activity of the drug.

Molecular modeling aids drug design by facilitating two processes: lead generation and lead optimization. Lead generation is analogous to finding the key that can fit the lock, by determining the correct chemical structure that can bind to the desired biological target. To generate lead compounds, molecular modeling takes advantage of knowledge of the three-dimensional structure of a biological target. This knowledge is obtained experimentally: the target molecule is isolated, purified, and characterized using x-ray crystallography or nuclear magnetic resonance (NMR) spectroscopy.

To find new lead compounds, scientists search three-dimensional databases of known chemical structures. These include commercial databases, such as those from Chemical Abstracts Service, of Columbus, Ohio, and Cambridge Crystallographic Data Centre, of Cambridge, United Kingdom, as well as databases available in the public domain, and in-house databases maintained by drug and chemical companies. Using technologies established by Sun Microsystems and Netscape Communications, scientists can now access chemical databases through the World Wide Web. With the Human Genome Project underway, a large database of information is becoming available on the Internet. San Diego—based Molecular Simulations Incorporated released in March 1999 its WebLab Version 1.5 with improved features that, among other enhancements, allow the biotech researcher to locate reading frames in a DNA sequence and translate them into protein sequences.

De novo drug design is an approach by which experimentally obtained knowledge of molecular properties is used to generate a lead compound. Based on the molecular properties of the region to which the drug binds, scientists can devise a chemical structure that will fit into the binding region. Molecular modeling can play an important role in creating a structure with a good fit. The chemical is then synthesized in the laboratory, tested, and optimized.

Lead optimization, the second method of designing drugs, is analogous to cutting a key to the exact shape needed to turn a lock, by fine-tuning the degree of the interaction between the drug and the biological target. To optimize lead compounds, researchers try to correlate the relationship between a chemical structure and the biological effects it produces. This area of research is called *structure-activity analysis.* It is the main focus for present day drug design, as it does not require knowledge of the biological target or its structure. First the chemist makes a series of analogs—compounds that are structurally similar to the lead compound—and tests them in the laboratory. It is necessary to use a family of analogs that range in biological activity from inactive to active. The idea is to observe how changes in molecular properties such as size, shape, electronic charge, or solubility, affect biological activity. Molecular modeling helps scientists decide what chemical modifications to make.

Optimizing the lead compound means maximizing its potency, minimizing its toxicity, and enhancing its delivery. Potency refers to how well a drug interacts with its biological target molecule. Toxicity and side effects result when drugs interact with biological molecules other than the desired target. (In the lock and key analogy, the key opens more than one lock.) Delivery deals with issues including the ability of the drug to reach its biological target in a large enough quantity to produce the desired effect. Sometimes, as when crossing the blood-brain barrier, this task is daunting. Molecular modification of the drug can affect all these properties, and modeling helps scientists decide what modifications to make.

It is important to note that molecular modeling seeks not to replace experimentation, but to improve it. Virtually every aspect of drug design still depends on data obtained through experimentation. To build a structure-activity model, compounds have to be synthesized and tested. Biochemical studies must be conducted to identify the biological target molecules. Many molecular properties that drug designers need to explore are better measured experimentally than calculated.

BACKGROUND AND DEVELOPMENT

The pharmaceutical industry was at the forefront of, and remains the driving force behind, computational chemistry. Traditional drug discovery relied on trial and error: extracts of natural substances were tested for their useful properties. In 1910, for example, Paul Ehrlich used a compound he obtained from a dye to create a drug for treating syphilis. Later, chemists made and tested large numbers of compounds and, when they identified an active compound, attempted to fine-tune it into a substance that was clinically useful. This approach has been enormously successful in finding thousands of substances that turned

out to be biologically active when tested in model systems. Since the 1970s, however, this approach has grown more expensive and less successful in yielding new medicines. The cost of synthesis and testing, especially in animal studies and human clinical trials, has risen sharply. Competition among drug companies to be the first to the market with a new product is intense, and any tool that can facilitate that process is indispensable.

In 1965 the Massachusetts Institute of Technology (MIT) introduced the first molecular modeling graphics system. By 1974 at least 19 universities and institutes had independently developed their own systems. Since then, many other organizations have developed systems, some of which are commercially available: The National Institutes of Health and the Environmental Protection Agency created the Chemical Information System; Brookhaven Laboratories introduced Crystnet; The National Institutes of Health and Bolt, Beranek, and Newman produced Prophet; Washington University in St. Louis completed MMS-X. These systems help scientists search chemical databases, display and analyze molecular structures, study chemical interactions with their biological targets, and design drugs. To aid drug-design efforts, Searle Co. of Chicago created the Moloch-2 molecular modeling system. Similarly, DuPont of Wilmington, Delaware, produced Tribble, and Rohm & Haas of Philadelphia introduced Moly. These are but a few of the many modeling systems on the market.

CURRENT CONDITIONS

Although molecular modeling is far from being able to simulate complex chemical reactions from A to Z, it is a powerful research tool. Unfortunately, several factors hinder its performance. One of the biggest challenges faced by the industry is training those without computational backgrounds to get reliable results on computers. People need extensive training to use molecular modeling properly and to familiarize themselves with strengths and weaknesses of various methods. Compounding the problem is that the computers themselves may be slow: it can take a month to perform a single calculation. In medicinal chemistry, a major limitation is the inability of modeling programs to calculate the energetics of the binding of molecules to their biological targets.

Still, molecular modeling is making headway. Computers are getting faster, cheaper, more powerful, and more accessible. Software programs are able to yield more accurate information, as well as analyze bigger molecules—some having more than 20,000 atoms. Hybrid computers emerging in the mid-1990s combined the power of supercomputers with newly developed massively parallel machines to solve big chemical problems. Greater accessibility and quickly expanding databases, such as Brookhaven National Laboratory's protein data bank, are helping researchers build upon the modeling efforts of others. Consortia formed with researchers in areas as diverse as pharmaceuticals, catalysts, and polymers has facilitated the spread of modeling knowledge. The result for chemists has been more quality time at the computer, which in turn allows for more quality time in the lab.

New technologies in the life sciences allow researchers to generate enormous libraries of molecular data through both computer programs and new laboratory methods. These molecular libraries provide starting points for experiment design in the development of compounds showing promise of usefulness and profitability in the biotech industry. For example, Pharmacopea, Inc., a leading provider of drug discovery technologies and services, has generated more than 4.5 million diverse, small molecules. CombiChem's Universal Informer Library, a virtual library, has approximately 10,000 compounds. Compounds with similar chemical properties can take on many forms, and molecular libraries must be sifted through to find the optimum form of the compound for its ultimate use as, say a drug or fertilizer. New software tools allow scientists to organize such massive amounts of data and exchange information. Novel compounds and processes can be simulated, developed, and analyzed. Researchers can interpret the properties of the molecular forms within those libraries in order to direct research efforts toward the most profitable results before they even enter the lab.

To tackle the massive undertaking of analyzing all of the chemical building blocks in terms of the rules of chemical behavior, screening vast numbers of compounds for activity with a target protein, and delivering the information in a form manageable by human scientists, many of these programs rely on high power systems. The intricate interactive graphics displayed require high-resolution systems such as Silicon Graphics® Onyx2™, Octane®, and O2™. Such powerful systems are costly and may not be available in every lab much less for every chemist. Continued advances in PC hardware coupled with low—cost and availability allow molecular modeling applications to be run under Windows NT®. Software providers for the industry have responded by directing their efforts toward producing specific programs with high visualization in a standard Windows NT® desktop environment. According to one CompuChem representative, the most important direction of the industry is the increasing availability of the Windows software at the work place for each chemist.

While great number of companies and learning institutions offer software programs and computational services designed to meet specific applications, sometimes it has been advantageous for pharmaceutical and biotechnology companies to build their own molecular modeling systems. These firms include Squib, Upjohn, DuPont, Novo, Glaxo, and Merck. For example, Merck decided to develop its own molecular modeling system to help its scientists study the geometry and reactivity of certain antibiotics. Scientists have successfully used this to design novel drug candidates, and the system has also aided the understanding of drugs' mechanisms of action.

INDUSTRY LEADERS

Molecular Simulations Incorporated (MSI) is a wholly owned subsidiary of Pharmacopea, Inc., which offers molecular design services to pharmaceutical, chemical, biotech, petroleum, and gas companies. MSI develops and distributes software to aid in all aspects of the chemical compound discovery process. The customer base is made up of Research and Development facilities of corporations from diverse industries. MSI's U.S. headquarters are located in San Diego, California. European headquarters are in Cambridge, England. In March 1999 the company purchased the remaining 50 percent of its Asian joint venture operating out of Tokyo, Japan. For 1998 MSI had 350 employees worldwide and in 1997, the last available information, reported total revenues of $56.7 million, up 19.9 percent from the previous year.

CombiChem offers services to accelerate the chemical compound discovery process for customers and collaborators in the pharmaceutical and biotech industries. The company's proprietary design technology can generate, evolve, and optimize new lead molecular candidates to be developed, manufactured, and marketed by collaborators. The company is collaborating with Novartis for crop pesticides, and Athena Neuroscience, Inc., ICOS Corporation, ImClone Systems Incorporated, Ono Pharmaceutical Co., Ltd., Roche Bioscience, Sumimoto Pharmaceuticals Co., Ltd., and Tejin Limited. The San Diego company employed 93 people in 1998 and completed its initial public offering in May 1998, raising $18.9 million. In 1998 the company had a net loss of $3.3 million on $15.1 million of sales.

Tripos, Inc. is a publicly owned company founded in 1979. Based in St. Louis, Missouri, the company has a history of success in the field of molecular imaging and design software. Tripos supplies software, sells third-party hardware, and offers research services and molecular libraries to the pharmaceutical, biotech, and other life science industries. In 1998 Tripos experienced a 15 percent decrease in its sales revenue of $25.6 million, as anticipated with the termination of its joint venture with MDS Penlabs and investments to initiate internal chemical laboratory operations. The company expects high financial returns by combining its computer software technology with chemical synthesis. Customers include scientific research organizations as well as biotech companies Genelabs Technologies, Inc. and Cell Pathways, Inc.

The Molecular Design Institute (MDI) at UCSF is another example of the overlap between academia and commerce in molecular design. The Institute was established in 1993 as an academic research institute to promote the discovery, design, and delivery of pharmaceutical agents. The MDI seeks innovative partnerships between business and universities to expand their basic and applied research efforts, and works closely with different agencies in the college, including the School of Medicine, the School of Pharmacy, and the biophysics program. It is also associated with the UCSF Computer Graphics Laboratory (CGL), which developed the MidasPlus program for use in molecular design. MidasPlus, an acronym for Molecular Interactive Display and Simulation, is used both for training and for commercial applications.

RESEARCH AND TECHNOLOGY

One of most active areas of research in which molecular modeling is being applied is medicinal chemistry. In a path of chemical reactions that ultimately ends in the development of a disease, many biological molecules are involved that can act as potential targets for drug intervention. Molecules that interact specifically with receptors or enzymes, for instance, can act as leads for creating new drugs. Molecular modeling plays an important role in this process. For example, by using molecular modeling to study a small protein in snake venom that binds to and inactivates an enzyme that helps regulate blood

Trends
A NEW AGE IN MOLECULAR MODELING

New research techniques have revolutionized the rate and reaches of molecular discovery, reshaping the chemical and biotech industries. The application of large-scale computerization to molecular research has been made possible because of the eloquence and sophistication of four main technologies in wide-spread use today:

- Genomics uncovers the secrets encoded in genes. Now an integral component of drug discovery, the technology finds target points for curing disease. Proteins control nearly every regulatory point and process in the body, and genomics identifies the protein-encoding DNA to identify sources of disease. A mutated site may incorrectly direct the over-production, under-production or miscoding of a protein product. The Human Genome Project is uncovering genetic information at an astonishing rate. (See the chapter in this book entitled Genetic Engineering.)

- High-throughput screening compares the action of thousands of potential molecular candidates against the target site once it has been identified. The robotic arms that distribute reagents into reaction wells linked to a computer for data collection have replaced the manual test-tube reaction observed and recorded individually by scientists. Next, silicon chips will replace entire laboratories, with microscopic channels serving as the site for both the reactions and data collection. Compounds that demonstrate activity against a potential target provide a source for potential lead candidates for further study and optimization.

- Combinatorial chemistry is an automated technique that produces the large libraries of compounds for high-throughput screening. Compounds may have similar active sites but exhibit different activity in practical applications. Large libraries of molecules likely contain a suitable candidate with activity limited to the desired reaction.

- Bioinformatics synchronizes the large volume of data gathered with computer software to deliver a comprehensive base of information that is making the entire molecular discovery process far more rapid and less expensive.

pressure, angiotension converting enzyme (ACE), scientists have been able to create better drugs to treat hypertension. Molecular modeling reduces the time and cost of drug discovery dramatically. Researchers at the Eli Lilly Co. screened 75,000 molecules a week for drug potential in 1997 as compared with 75,000 a year only 5 years earlier.

AIDS researchers have also used molecular modeling to study proteases—protein-cutting enzymes required for the function of the human immunodeficiency virus (HIV). When developing protease inhibitors, drug designers used computers to generate a three-dimensional structure of a related protease in order to model the smaller HIV protease. They compared the structure of the active site to that of other biologically important molecules. Medicinal chemists often compare different structures with similar biological activities to detect non-obvious likenesses. These computer simulations provided enough insight into the probable features of the enzyme's active site to be useful in designing effective inhibitors.

Correlating the three-dimensional shape of a molecule with its performance is also a useful activity in many research arenas. Scientists at Sandia National Laboratories in Albuquerque, New Mexico, developed their own molecular modeling system and used it to create synthetic substances that mimic natural enzymes' abilities to catalyze reactions. At Procter & Gamble, molecular modeling is used to develop enzymes that make detergents fast-acting. Other organizations have used it to study superconductors. Amoco uses molecular modeling to find better fuels. The use of this technology is also growing in fields as diverse as electronic, optical, and magnetic materials. Indeed, the possibilities may be endless.

FURTHER READING

Bash, Paul A., et al. "Van der Waals Surfaces in Molecular Modeling: Implementation with Real-Time Computer Graphics." *Science,* 23 December 1983.

Borman, Stu. "MEDLA Technique Calculates Electron Densities. (Molecular Electron Density Lego Assembler)." *Chemical & Engineering News,* 14 August 1995.

———. "Military Research on Cubane Explosives May Also Lead to New Pharmaceuticals." *Chemical & Engineering News,* 28 November 1994.

———. "Problems and Pitfalls of Molecular Modeling Cited." *Chemical & Engineering News,* 29 May 1995.

Bozman, Jean S. "From Supercomputers to the Desktop; Workstations Reach New Heights with Increase in Speed, Drop in Price and Off-the-Shelf Applications." *Computerworld,* 21 March 1994.

Brown, Maxine D. "Visualization Applications. (State of the Art.)" *Byte,* April 1993.

Churbuck, David. "Monster in a Box: Wavetracer Is Proving that Massively Parallel Supercomputers Need Be Neither Massive nor Expensive." *Forbes,* 22 June 1992.

"CombiChem Profile." San Diego: CombiChem, Inc., 1999. Available from http://www.combichem.com/About/.

"CombiChem Reports Financial Results for Fourth Quarter and Year Ended December 31, 1998." San Diego: CombiChem, Inc., 1999. Available from http://www.combichem.com/News/Press/990209FIN.html.

Cortino, Juli. "Apollo Delivers a Graphics Punch; DN 10000 Workstation Now Boasts High-End Graphics Capabilities." *PC Week,* 13 February 1989.

Cronin, Mary J. "Getting Drugs to Market Fast." *Fortune,* 24 November 1997.

Gund, Peter, Joseph D. Andose, Joe B. Rhodes, and Graham M. Smith. "Three-Dimensional Molecular Modeling and Drug Design." *Science,* 27 June 1980.

Krieger, James H. "Computer-Aided Molecular Design Teeming with Change." *Chemical & Engineering News,* 11 April 1994.

———. "Molecular Modeling Technology Is Dynamic and Changing." *Chemical & Engineering News,* 1 May 1995.

———. "New Software Expands Role of Molecular Modeling Technology." *Chemical & Engineering News,* 4 September 1995.

Maginnis, Ninamary Buba. "Apollo to Roll Out 3.5 MIPS Unit: Claims DN590 Turbo Bests Silicon Graphics in 3-D Workstation Market." *Computerworld,* 11 May 1987.

Moad, Jeff. "Building a Better Life. (Computer-Aided Modeling in Life Sciences Research)." *Datamation,* 15 November 1987.

"Molecular Modeling. (Molecular Modeling Software WebLab Viewer Can Be Used with World Wide Web Browser)." *Industry Week,* 16 September 1996.

"Molecular Modeling Software Debuts." *PC Week,* 6 April 1992.

"MSI at a Glance." San Diego: Molecular Systems Incorporated, 1999. Available from http://www.msi.com/about/index.html.

"Pharmacopea, Inc. Announces 1998 Fourth Quarter and Year End Financial Results." Princeton: Pharmacopea, Inc., 4 February 1999. Available from http://www.pcop.com/pr50.html.

Rotman, David. "Computers in the CPI: Designing Tomorrow's Profits." *Chemical Week,* 20 May 1992.

Seiter, Charles. "Alchemy III." *Macworld,* September 1993.

———. "MacSpartan Plus 1.1 (Molecular Modeling Program from Wavefunction)." *Macworld,* October 1996.

———. "Sculpt 2.0 (Interactive Simulations Molecular Modeling Tool)." *Macworld,* September 1997.

Siam, Khamis S., Rick D. Gdanski, Bruce E. Landrum, and David Simon. "Molecular Modeling Aids Design of Downhole Chemicals." *The Oil and Gas Journal,* 19 August 1991.

Singletary, Lynda. "Molecular Modeling Refines Genencor's Lipases." *Chemical Marketing Reporter,* 4 May 1992.

Smith, Ben. "First of the Red-hot R4000s." *Byte,* July 1992.

Studt, Tim. "Molecular Modeling Makeover." *R & D,* February 1997.

———. "Molecular Modeling Software Changes Research Techniques." *R & D,* February 1995.

———. "Promise of Rich Payoffs Drives Computer-Aided Chemistry." *R & D,* September 1993.

———. "Scientific Visualization Comes Down to Earth." *R & D,* November 1992.

"Tripos, Inc. Announces Fourth Quarter 1998 Financial Results." *PR Newswire,* 10 February 1999. Available from http://www.tripos.com/press/Q498.html.

"The Ultimate Science Story." *The Economist,* 21 August 1993.

Weber, Irene T., et al. "Molecular Modeling of the HIV-1 Protease and Its Substrate Binding Site." *Science,* 17 February 1989.

"WebLab Version 1.5 Encompasses New Versions of MSI's Web Browser-Based Software for the Life Sciences." San Diego: Molecular Simulations Incorporated, 18 March 1999. Available from http://www.msi.com/news/pressreleases/1999/pr_weblab15.html.

Wilson, Eve J. "Molecular Modeling: Computer-Assisted Innovations in Drug Design." *Alcohol Health & Research World,* Fall 1992.

Zirl, David M. "A New Tool For Chemists." *ChemNews.Com,* 1999. Available from http://www.chemnews.com/art.cfm?S=37.

—Dawn M. Levy, updated by Sondra E. O'Donnell

MORTGAGE COMPANIES

Like the broader financial markets as a whole, the industry that provides home mortgages to Americans has gone through considerable change since the 1980s. Until the mid-1980s, almost all borrowers who sought loans to finance the purchase of a home went to a traditional bank or savings and loan. Under that system, loans could take weeks to be approved; even a single credit record blemish could be disqualifying; and loan officers stressed the importance of the lender/borrower relationship typified in its most idealized form by the character of small-time banker George Bailey in the classic film "It's a Wonderful Life." Since the mid-1980s, however, everything has changed. Loans now take days or even hours, not weeks, to be approved. Once cautious lenders now bend over backwards to make loans to people with problem credit histories; and long-term relationships have all but vanished as consumers chase, and lenders compete on the basis of, the lowest possible interest rates.

These changes and others were both stimulated by, and helped fuel the growth of, private mortgage companies. Mortgage companies are firms that make mortgage loans but do not perform any other banking functions, i.e., they do not take deposits, offer checking accounts, or maintain safety deposit boxes. Initially, mortgage companies existed only to make those loans that traditional bankers didn't want to make—among them loans backed by U.S. government programs such as the Federal Housing Administration (FHA) to borrowers with less than perfect credit histories. Throughout the 1990s, however, mortgage companies soared in popularity and in importance to the mortgage lending industry as a whole. Nonetheless, most of the major mortgage companies were sub-

sidiaries of large financial institutions such as Norwest, Countrywide Home Loans, and Chase Manhattan, which had the economies of scale to compete in the industry as profit margins shrank throughout the 1990s. Smaller companies succeeded largely by tapping into niche markets such as Internet marketing and high-risk lending. The highly competitive environment of the late 1990s gave rise to numerous mergers within the industry. For example, Norwest bought its way to the top of the industry by acquiring Prudential's mortgage operations, and First Union Corp. bought The Money Store, another leading mortgage company.

In 1997, home loan "originations," or new mortgage loans, climbed 7 percent to $839 billion. Of these originations, subprime lending—lending to risky borrowers with histories of delinquency and bankruptcy—accounted for 12 percent or $100 billion. Fannie Mae, a government-mandated mortgage association, predicted that originations would rise 6.5 percent in 1998 to $878 billion, while the Mortgage Bankers Association forecasted originations to reach $1.06 trillion in 1998—which would be the industry's record high.

In the 1990s, private mortgage companies became the main source of mortgage lending in the United States. As of 1997, there were about 5,000 of these companies nationwide (out of about 12,000 total organizations making mortgage loans), and they accounted for nearly 60 percent of all originations. This was nearly double the share that mortgage companies enjoyed in 1987. In the 1990s, numerous new companies entered the industry because of low entry barriers. The second most important group by volume of mortgages was that of commercial banks, followed by the thrift industry (such as savings and loan associations), which as recently as 10 years earlier had dominated the industry. Other mortgage lenders included credit unions and life insurance companies.

The mortgage industry remained one of the country's largest in the late 1990s. Although originations were up in 1997, they still remained below the peak of over $1.02 trillion in 1993 loan originations. The record year in 1993 benefited from a wave of refinancing as mortgage rates dipped to their lowest point in years.

Many consumers may still be confused by the plethora of lending sources. Basically, however, people who shop for mortgage loans can go to one of three different types of lenders. First, there are the traditional financial institutions and their affiliates. These include most banks, thrifts, and credit unions, nearly all of which make mortgage loans. Sometimes the financial institution itself offers the loan; sometimes the loan is offered via a mortgage company owned by the institution. If a bank directs a customer to a loan office somewhere else, chances are that it will be to a mortgage company owned by the bank. Financial institutions generally underwrite their own loans, i.e., they use their own assets to fund the loan. Banks and thrifts may hold the new loan in their own portfolio until it is paid off (sometimes as long as 30 years); or they can sell the loan into the broader secondary market for mortgage loans.

Mortgage bankers and mortgage companies are more specialized. They offer the same sort of mortgage loans as financial institutions but without any other banking services. They, too, underwrite their own loans. The national mortgage companies in particular are fairly innovative about creating mortgage products with varying terms, floating interest rates, and other features to attract consumers.

According to the Mortgage Bankers Association of America (MBA), mortgage banking companies are the largest group of home mortgage lenders, followed by commercial banks and savings and loans. Mortgage banking companies operate mainly in the secondary mortgage market, using government institutions like Fannie Mae, Freddie Mac, and Ginnie Mae.

Finally, there are mortgage brokers, which are mortgage banks in that they're not financial institutions, and can be part of national companies. But there is one important distinction: mortgage brokers don't provide the money to make their loans. Instead, they play a match-making role by putting borrowers in touch with loan sources, for a fee. Especially if a borrower has had credit problems in the past, a broker can be helpful in locating more flexible lenders. A broker makes its money by collecting a fee from the lender or the borrower or both. In the best of circumstances, the lender and the broker will split the points (the fees the borrower pays), so it shouldn't cost more to borrow through a broker.

Banks and thrifts may hold or sell newly originated mortgages, but mortgage companies generally sell their new loans almost immediately, often at the end of each month. This process involves what is known as the secondary mortgage market, in which large numbers of individual loans are bundled together according to characteristics such as their term in years and their interest rate. This large bundle is then used as the basis for a security or bond that is backed by the predictable payoff schedules of the underlying mortgages. These securities are then sold on the open market, normally to pension funds and other institutional investors who consider them a reliable long-term investment. This process of "securitization" of mortgages has had two profound effects on the market. First, since the secondary market has made cash available to buy up mortgage loans, it has permitted the influx of more money into the mortgage market. This, in turn, has made more money available for loans to the consumers, and has been particularly helpful in financing loans at the lower end of the market where credit histories may be suspect. The other great effect of securitization has been the growth of mortgage companies. Since these firms lack the deep pockets of banks and thrifts, they could not possibly bear the risks involved in maintaining each of these loans in their own portfolio. By selling off the loan (and the attendant risk) to the secondary market, mortgage companies can provide a vital service to the consumer at little or no risk to themselves. This has fueled the rapid growth of private mortgage companies, which in turn has meant more choices for consumers.

The volume of mortgages sold into the secondary market varies with changes in the volume of fixed-rate lending (as opposed to variable rate loans). The higher the percentage of fixed-rate loans being made (such as in periods of low interest rates when consumers want to lock in good rates for the long term) the easier it is to secure such loans. In 1996, 56 percent of home loans were sold through the secondary market. That was down from a peak of 65 percent during 1993, when interest rates dipped to historic lows, but it represented a sizable increase over the 33 percent level of 1988, when the market was not as mature as it would later become.

As in other industries experiencing soaring growth rates, mortgage companies come in all sizes and shapes. The cost of entry into loan origination continues to be low, and many of the smallest brokers are mere mom-and-pop storefronts. But the financial sources necessary to compete and succeed as a full-service mortgage banker have increased dramatically. As a result, in terms of dollar volume the industry is increasingly dominated by the largest players, major lenders like Norwest, Chase Manhattan, Countrywide and GMAC Mortgage, which together account for tens of billions of dollars of home loan originations each year.

CURRENT CONDITIONS

The Mortgage Bankers Association estimated that home loan originations climbed 7 percent in 1997 to $839 billion and Fannie Mae predicted they would reach $878 billion in 1998, a 6.5-percent increase. Other forecasts for 1998 were even more optimistic: the Mortgage Bankers Association expected 1998 originations to surpass the 1993 record, reaching $1.06 trillion. Subprime lending constituted one of the hottest sectors of the industry, despite warnings from some industry observers such as Standard and Poor's. In 1997, subprime lending made up 12 percent, or $100 billion, of all originations. *Mortgage Banking*

forecasted the subprime market would remain strong in 1998.

Unlike the home loan upsurge of 1993 driven by refinancing, housing purchases fueled the mortgage boom of the late 1990s. The Mortgage Bankers Association expects home purchases will account for 60 percent of the mortgages in 1998 and refinancing for the remaining 40 percent. In contrast, refinancing represented about 55 percent of the mortgages in 1993.

The economic woes in Asia brought on by debt and depreciating currencies helped U.S. mortgage companies increase their refinancing loans. As a result of the Asia crisis, U.S. interest rates fell as low as 5.4 percent in mid-1998, according to *American Banker.* Many of the country's leading mortgage companies reported a significant rise in refinancing loans and applications in mid-1998.

The subprime sector continued to thrive in the late 1990s, despite criticism and warnings from a number of industry monitors. In the early days of subprime lending, mortgage companies provided loans to people with poor credit that did not exceed 60 percent of the value of their homes. However, lenders increased these loans to as much as 70 percent of the value of their homes by the late 1990s. Analysts urged mortgage companies to exercise caution in issuing loans and concentrate on profit margins instead of on the number of loans issued. Nevertheless, new companies continued to enter the market and giant financial institutions like NationsBank Corp. and First Union Corp., both based in Charlotte, North Carolina, created subsidiaries to seek out high-risk borrowers.

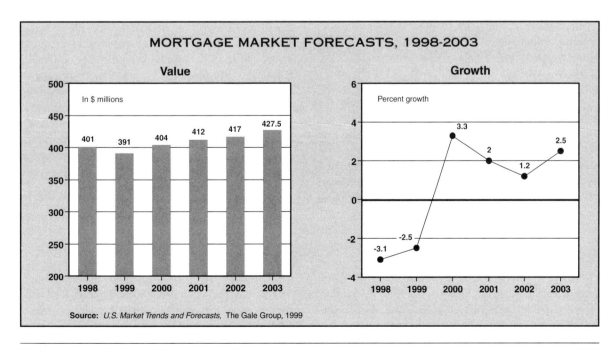

MORTGAGE MARKET FORECASTS, 1998-2003

Source: *U.S. Market Trends and Forecasts,* The Gale Group, 1999

The mortgage industry became even more competitive in the late 1990s as companies operated with very low profit margins to remain competitive. The industry's emphasis on volume fueled the competition, which also began to lead to waves of consolidation within the industry. Most of the industry's profitable companies were large mortgage brokers who could slash their profit margins and glean their profits from the plethora of loans they issued. Smaller companies, on the other hand, struggled to stay afloat or exited the business as competition started to escalate in the mid-1990s. In 1998, Beneficial Corp., Aames Financial Corp., and Cityscape all announced they were up for sale. In addition, First Union Corp., the country's sixth largest bank, announced in March of 1998 that it would acquire The Money Store, a major player in the subprime market. *Mortgage Banking* reports analysts agree that mergers will continue at least through the early 2000s.

Despite the growing trend of subprime lending, default, delinquency, and bankruptcy rates continued to rise in the late 1990s. Normally, mortgage loans have a default rate of less than 1 percent, but the high-risk market suffered a default rate of about 7 percent nationwide during this period, with even higher default rates in some markets. Even though mortgage delinquencies approached cyclic lows in the late 1990s, in part because of the country's strong economy and low unemployment rate, some analysts believe delinquency levels remained disproportionate relative to the strength of the economy. For example, in the second quarter of 1997 4.24 percent of all home loans were delinquent, according to *Mortgage Banking*. If the economy slows down, analysts expect delinquencies to shoot up rapidly. Furthermore, the country's bankruptcy level continued to reach new heights in the late 1990s, despite the nation's economic prosperity.

Technological advances continued to help the mortgage industry grow throughout the 1990s. By 1997, consumers who applied for loans for the first time in several years found that instead of dealing with a loan officer, they would more than likely confront a computer program. Computers and office automation software converted the paper-heavy and labor-intensive underwriting process into a much faster and more cost-efficient process. Freddie Mac introduced Loan Prospector, an automated underwriting service, in 1995 and by 1998 it had evaluated 2.1 million loans worth $262 billion, according to *Mortgage Banking*. About 630 mortgage companies use Loan Prospector weekly and analysts foresee greater use of such services as their functionality continues to improve.

Moreover, the greater competition in the industry gave rise to greater innovation as companies sought ways to differentiate their services from those of other companies. Two successful strategies in the late 1990s included marketing mortgages through the Internet and targeting the subprime and "no equity" market, according to *Mortgage Banking*. Online mortgage sites such as E-Loan, Mortgage.com, QuickenMortgage, and LendingTree took off in the late 1990s and were growing quickly in 1999. These sites allow home buyers to search for rates, compare rates, receive recommendations, and apply for mortgages over the Internet while saving users up to 80 percent of traditional fees. E-Loan reported receiving an average of 78 loan applications a day and receiving as many as 230 in one day in 1998; the company reported finishing 1998 with an origination volume of almost $4 billion. E-Loan claims to be able to save borrowers as much as 75 percent in fees. Web-originated loans are expected to become even more popular. An article in Web Finance (and available from http://www.fponline.com/news/news_daily/mar_mort.shtml) cites data from a Forrester Research report predicting that 1997's total of $482 million in online originated loans will rise to $40.5 billion by 2001.

Mortgage companies also explored the subprime and "no equity" niche for a new avenue of growth by offering loans for debt consolidation, paying off existing loans, and home improvement. These companies cater to borrowers who do not qualify for FHA, Fannie Mae, or Freddie Mac mortgages because of poor credit history and bankruptcy. With low profit margins in the traditional mortgage market, companies turned to the subprime and "no equity" market where profit margins—and risks—are much higher. Typically, subprime lenders charge interest rates about 6 percent higher than traditional mortgage companies. Furthermore, instead of using traditional mortgage criteria for determining credit worthiness, these mortgage companies often rely on criteria more akin to the finance industry, where the age of the previous debt is considered, not simply the amount. Mortgage companies targeting this market also use the Internet for conducting business in order to reach more people, provide greater convenience, and cut costs.

Since a healthy mortgage industry remains essential to the dream of American home ownership (and, indeed, to a healthy national economy), it seems likely that the mortgage industry will continue to develop with financial and technological innovations driving the changes. Further consolidation is likely, but smaller niche players will also have their place in a dynamic market that is so responsive to consumer demand.

INDUSTRY LEADERS

San Francisco-based Norwest Company rose to the top of the mortgage industry quickly in the late 1990s by key acquisitions in the mid- to late 1990s, including Prudential Home Mortgage Co., Directors Mortgage Loan Corp., and Wells Fargo & Co. mortgage operations. In 1998, Norwest was the country's leading originator of home mortgages and the second largest servicer of mortgage loans. Norwest began through the merger of Northwestern National Bank of Minneapolis, First National Bank and Trust Company of Fargo, N.D., and First National Bank of Mason City, Iowa in 1929, becoming the bank holding company Northwestern Bancorporation. Norwest announced in 1998 it would merge with Wells Fargo & Co.; the newly created company merged under the name of Wells Fargo & Company, with Norwest Mortgage operating as the mortgage loan division. Wells Fargo & Company provides banking, insurance, investments, mortgage and consumer finance through nearly 6,000 locations in North America and abroad. They employ 92,178 people and their 1998 net income was $1.95 billion.

Countrywide Home Loans, Inc. of Calabasas, California was another leading mortgage company and the nation's largest independent residential mortgage lender and servicer. Countrywide is the subsidiary of Countrywide Credit Industries, Inc., which has more than 7,000 employees in 550 offices in the U.S. The mortgage company has about 350 branches around the country and serves about 1.5 million customers annually. Founded in 1969, Countrywide Home Loans achieved its prominence in the industry by focusing solely on mortgages. Among Countrywide's other subsidiaries is Full Spectrum Lending, Inc. of Pasadena, California, founded in 1996. Full Spectrum Lending features options for borrowers with less-than-perfect credit, and operates out of 40 offices and their Web site (http://www.fullspectrumlending.com), which will link customers to the Countrywide Web site (http://www.countrywide.com) should they qualify for a traditional loan. The Full Spectrum Web site was launched specifically to ease the loan process for borrowers who are self-employed and have a harder time verifying their income, and those who have suffered financial hardships like job loss, debt, or divorce. Countrywide Credit Industries, Inc. closed its fiscal year on February 28, 1999 with earnings of $2.96 billion, up 53 percent from the 1998 fiscal year.

The Principal Financial Group, a diversified financial services corporation with insurance and bank-

---

About... THE MOVE TO MINIMIZE CONSUMER RISKS

Since many small and high-growth mortgage brokers are such an integral part of the mortgage industry, it is perhaps inevitable that accusations of consumer rip-offs and scandals sometimes arise. In response to these accusations, in 1996 the Federal Reserve board moved to stamp out one source of problems, ordering mortgage brokers to reveal upfront all fees that a client could expect to pay. Under the ruling, all fees levied by loan brokers and paid directly by borrowers must be included as part of a mandatory truth-in-lending statement of charges. Consumers must receive this statement within three days of applying for a mortgage. The Federal Reserve had feared that with no disclosure law on the books, some loan brokers could make their loans—particularly adjustable rate mortgages—appear more inexpensive than they really were.

---

ing divisions based in Des Moines, Iowa, ranks among the leading mortgage companies through its Principal Residential Mortgage, Inc. arm. This division was founded in 1936 and grew into one of the country's industry leaders by the late 1990s; the acquisition of ReliaStar Mortgage in mid-1998 helped the company's growth in revenues and assets. In 1998, the division serviced more than 484,000 loans totaling $41.9 billion. The company has over 250 offices throughout the world in the Americas, Europe, and Asia.

The Money Store, acquired in the late 1990s by First Union Corp., is another key player in the mortgage industry. The majority of the company's revenues come from mortgages, although the company also provides student loans and Small Business Administration-guaranteed loans. Based in Union, New Jersey, The Money Store has 200 branches around the country. The Money Store began offering mortgages in 1967 and is also the country's largest provider of home improvement loans. In 1997, the last fiscal year available, the company's sales reached $8.67 billion, up 5 percent from 1996. The Money Store's on-line loan application program, started in 1999, helped bring in $100 million in new business in its first year.

Fleet Financial Group, based in Boston, Massachusetts, is one of the largest loan servicers in the U.S., mainly in student loans and mortgages. The number one bank in New England, with 1,200 branches in the Northeast, Fleet will move to the position of 8th largest bank in the nation as Fleet Boston Corp. when its

---

acquisition of BankBoston is finalized. Fleet originates and services loans through Fleet Mortgage Group, Inc.

GMAC Mortgage Corporation, based in Horsham, Pennsylvania, is a subsidiary of General Motors Acceptance Corporation (GMAC), one of the largest financial services companies in the world. GMAC Mortgage Corporation formed in 1985, and by 1998 the company had built a portfolio of 1.1 million customers and originated more than $10 billion in residential mortgages.

The government-mandated companies, Fannie Mae and Freddie Mac, also play a significant role in the industry by ensuring that lenders have sufficient funds for low- and moderate-income, minority, and immigrant borrowers. These companies do not lend directly to home buyers, but make sure mortgage companies have enough money to lend home buyers by purchasing mortgages from lenders. Fannie Mae, the one time Federal National Mortgage Association, is the country's largest corporation in terms of assets with $415 billion. In 1998, Fannie Mae reported earnings of $3.4 billion, up from $3.05 billion in 1997. In the last 30 years, Fannie Mae has helped more than 30 million families buy homes by providing nearly $2.5 trillion in mortgage financing funds.

Congress created Freddie Mac in 1970 to ensure the availability of low-cost mortgages. Like Fannie Mae, Freddie Mac, formerly the Federal Home Loan Mortgage Corporation, serves the low- and middle-income market as well as borrowers with special needs. Because of Freddie Mac, borrowers can take advantage of long term, low down-payment, and fixed-rate mortgages. Throughout its history, the company has implemented new services and technologies to make obtaining mortgages easier. For example, Freddie Mac introduced automated underwriting, Loan Prospector, to expedite the application process in 1995. Freddie Mac announced a 1998 net income of $1.7 billion, a 22 percent increase over 1997's net income of $1.395 billion. Freddie Mac financed homes for 2.7 million families in 1998.

FURTHER READING

Binkley, Christina. "Mortgage Lenders Pursue Once-Shunned Borrowers." *Wall Street Journal,* 11 September 1996.

Brown, Steve. "Unfamiliar Waters: Those Diving Back Into Home Loans Find Altered Landscape." *Chicago Tribune,* 11 February 1996.

"Countrywide Credit Industries, Inc. Reports Record Earnings in Fourth Quarter and Increases Cash Dividend by 25 Percent." *PRNewswire,* 25 March 1999.

"E-Loan Dominates Online Mortgage Loan Industry With Total 1998 Origination Volume of Nearly $4 Billion," 13 January 1999. Available from http://www.eloan.com/s/show/press.

"Fannie Mae Reports Record 1998 Earnings of $3.418 Billion and $3.23 Per Common Share; 1998 Earnings Per Common Share Up 14.1 Percent Over 1997," 14 January 1999. Available from http://www.fanniemae.com/news/pressreleases/0137.html.

"Freddie Mac Announces Record Earnings for 1998," 19 January 1999. Available from http://www.freddiemac.com/shareholders/er/4q98.htm.

"Full Spectrum Lending Launches Web Site." *PRNewswire,* 5 January 1999.

Garrett, Joe. "Solution for Subprime Woes: Ignore Urge to Build Volume." *American Banker,* 23 December 1998.

Harney, Kenneth. "Mortgage Fees: Payment for Services Rendered or Rip Off?" *The Seattle Times,* 22 December 1996.

Hochstein, Marc. "Asia-Inspired Rate Decline Spurs New Mortgage Refinancing Wave." *American Banker,* 18 June 1998.

Hoffman, Gary. "Mortgages Sold, Resold so Fast, Firms are Losing Track." *The Detroit News,* 26 July 1996.

"Introducing the Players in the Mortgage Game." *Houston Chronicle,* 10 February 1997.

May, Michael C. "Seeking Common Access." *Mortgage Banking,* May 1998.

"Mortgage Industry Sees Opportunity In Internet Sales." *Web Finance,* 26 March 1999. Available from http://www.fponline.com/news/news_daily/mar_mort.shtml.

Prakash, Snigdha. "Experian Projects Lending Will Decline 5 percent in 1997." *American Banker,* 27 October 1997.

———. "Home Loans Expected to Top $1 Trillion of 1993 Refinance Boom." *American Banker,* 26 March 1998.

"Principal Financial Group reports 1998 Year-end Results," 24 February 1999. Available from http://www.principal.com/about/news/yearend98.htm.

"Refinance Solutions Offered Through Countrywide's Web Site." *PRNewswire,* 14 January 1999.

"Shopping for Mortgage has a Few Finer Points: With Interest Rates Low, Other Costs are Crucial." *Chicago Tribune,* 1 December 1996.

Tessler, Joelle. "Mortgage Firms Expected to Post Strong Earnings." *Wall Street Journal,* 10 January 1997.

Wise, Christy. "Three Strategies." *Mortgage Banking,* April 1998.

—John Gallagher,
updated by Karl Heil and Lisa DeShantz-Cook

Multimedia Computers

INDUSTRY SNAPSHOT

The multimedia computer industry, which barely existed in 1990, exceeded $45 billion in annual revenues by 1998. Dataquest estimates that by the year 2000 that figure will exceed $100 billion. In fact, multimedia computers have become so influential that they have literally transformed the configuration and type of most kinds of computers on the marketplace. Prior to 1995 most computers sold were traditional desktop computers, representing 74 percent of all computer sales. However, in a period of less than five years, multimedia computers have made impressive inroads into the personal computer market. According to estimates from Dataquest, as of early 1999 there were approximately 30 million multimedia computer households in the United States out of a total of 50 million households with one or more personal computers.

Because of its sudden appearance on the consumer marketplace and fast growth, it is not surprising that many have had difficulty summing up exactly what multimedia is. Multimedia is simply another name for an audiovisual (AV) personal computer with a color monitor, stereo sound, and a CD-ROM player, or other emerging technology, such as a DVD player. In fact, this information-age phenomenon is better characterized according to what it does, which is to bring together in a single computer package a variety of visual and aural media. Among these are text, graphics, video clips, animation, music, voice, and sound, and a variety of other emerging media components, including virtual reality. Any of these in any combination brought together on a computer screen are called multimedia.

In 1998 multimedia was divided into four categories: computer-based hardware (PCs, add-in boards, or CD-ROM drives); computer-based software and services (games or multimedia authoring tools); television-based hardware (set-top boxes, cable modems, or video game players); and television-based software and services (TV game cartridges or interactive TV services).

The idea of bringing together disparate media, or forms of communication, is perhaps as old as civilization itself. Whether it was the ancient Greeks combining drama, music, and dance in their plays, or eighteenth century English poet William Blake presenting his poetic works alongside artwork he created and engraved on equipment of his own design, the desire to juxtapose varieties of expression has always been present. Until the computer revolution in the last quarter of the twentieth century, however, multiple media works remained amalgamations of elements rather than cohesive wholes. With the digital technology emergent in the late 1980s and 1990s, it was possible to create seemingly endless worlds of multimedia, all of them accessible through a single box, the computer. By the late 1990s, multimedia was being used for education, training, reference, marketing, commerce, and entertainment. Multimedia has several characteristics: it is digital, integrated, diverse, and interactive. In the past, information capture and retrieval was based on the concept of analog rather than digital technology. Analog recordings of sound, for instance, are simply very good copies, whereas digital recordings—made by converting every element of sound into a series of numbers called a binary code—are virtually exact replicas. The difference might be analogous to that between an extremely good painting and a photograph. Not only does digital technology enhance the quality of pictures and sound, it brings together those elements in a way that analog technology never did. Instead of music played on an audio cassette and images captured on a videotape, two very different forms of technology, the digital world of multimedia brings together music recorded digitally on an audio compact disc with images recorded digitally on a video compact disc.

These diverse elements of sight and sound are integrated, or structured, into different packages, which are usually presented on compact discs (CDs) and sold in stores. Thus one might find, for instance, a multimedia package devoted to a musical group which would include sound recordings, video clips, sheet music, interviews with the band, and other elements. Multimedia is not for passive observation, though, like television: a part of the package is its interactivity, which means that users have choices. The disc might ask the user questions, the answers to which would result in the user being moved to new screens within the program. A multimedia presentation of Herman Melville's *Moby Dick,* for instance, might give users the opportunity to digress from the text to learn more about the nineteenth-century whaling industry.

Not just any computer can run multimedia programs. For one thing, it must have a CD-ROM (compact disc-read only memory) drive. More importantly, the large amounts of information require a computer with tremendous capacity for storing data; video and audio, in particular, take up a great deal of computer memory. Also, multimedia depends on rapid movement of images, so a computer needs a fast processor, as well as speakers and a monitor capable of delivering images of the resolution standard required for the multimedia package. These facts alone suggest that in moving to multimedia, consumers could spend literally billions of dollars on hardware and software purchases. Certainly the impetus for such expenditures materialized once the technology entered the market because it promised to add so much to everyday life. There are also the myriad supporting industries created by multimedia, such as electronic publishing, not to mention the thousands of new jobs created in areas like software development, graphic design, and content creation.

ORGANIZATION AND STRUCTURE

The multimedia industry is made up of hardware producers, large computer companies such as IBM and Intel; software producers, some of whom are giants on the order of Microsoft, while others are small, specialized entities; and a variety of other miscellaneous groups, generally tied to the software end, such as multimedia consultants.

One of the central organizations in the multimedia industry is the Interactive Multimedia Association (IMA), which provides its members with useful information relating technology, government issues, and legal affairs. Indeed, the latter two elements are every bit as important to the industry as technical knowledge is. One of the principal issues faced by multimedia developers is that of copyright law and "fair use," the doctrine that allows people to copy some material without permission under certain circumstances. Because so much of multimedia revolves around copyrighted creations, this is a key area of concern to IMA members. There are several other multimedia professional organizations, as well as several targeted publications.

Multimedia creators develop their software for different "platforms," compatible either with Apple Macintosh or IBM-compatible computers. Apple's first Macintosh, in 1984, already had extensive graphics, icons, and windows, creating an extremely user-friendly graphical user interface (GUI) that would not be widely available to users of IBM-compatible computers for several years. "Mac" also beat IBM to the punch in a number of other multimedia-related areas, including CD-ROM drives and high-speed processing technology. Microsoft Windows software, however, has given IBM-compatible computers an advantage over Apple Computer by making a similarly easy-to-use GUI available for a lower price than Mac products. Not only that, but IBM-compatible hardware is more widely used, partly because of the high number of IBM "clones" made by companies such as NEC and Compaq.

BACKGROUND AND DEVELOPMENT

The term "multimedia" has a very short history, dating back to 1990, with the advent of early packages such as MacroMind Director. In that year, the research firm Market Vision reported that some 100 potential multimedia applications existed. However, the technology and the multimedia components themselves were created in the 1970s and earlier. For example, the first known graphics software was designed in 1962 by Ivan Sutherland when he created what he called "sketchpad."

It was the growing video-game market in the 1970s that directly led to the development of the multi-

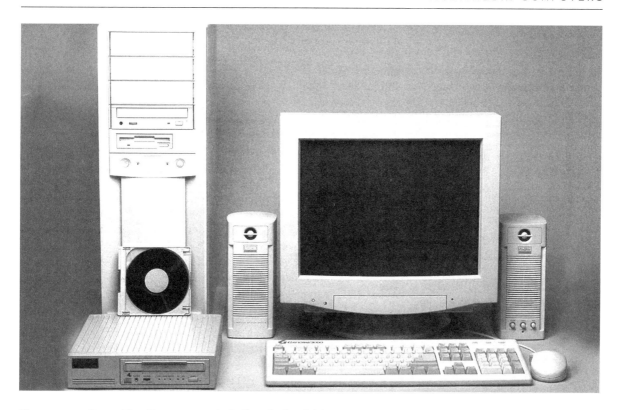

Components of a multimedia computer, including the hard drive, monitor, CD-ROM drive, keyboard, speakers, and mouse. (MediaFocus International, LLC.)

media computer. In the late 1970s companies such as Atari were worldwide leaders in this newly developed market. In fact, in 1977 Atari introduced the Atari Video Computer System. In the same year, Apple Computer's Apple II was the first mass-marketed personal computer to feature game paddles and graphics/text interface using a color display, thus making it the first computer with color graphics.

Other developments both within and outside the computer industry were critical for multimedia to grow. One of these was the introduction of the modem to the consumer marketplace. Without the availability of modems on a broad scale, the Internet and World Wide Web would never have become so popular. The Web is one of the most prolific users of multimedia and indeed has helped to increase its popularity. In 1980 this occurred on a large scale basis when Universal Data Systems introduced the first modem to connect directly into the phone line, requiring no additional power.

The most critical development to the field also occurred in 1980 when Philips and Sony created the CD-Audio standard for optical disk storage of digital audio. Several years later CD technology was adopted within the computer industry, revolutionizing personal computers.

Other pioneering efforts in multimedia continued throughout the 1980s. In 1982 Commodore produced a series of microcomputers that had custom sound, graphics, TV connectors, and text. It was also the first personal computer with an integrated sound synthesizer chip. During that same year, at the National Association of Music Manufacturers convention, a group of electronic music companies agreed to establish a set of digital transmission standards for electronic music. A year later, MIDI (Musical Instrument Digital Interface) was born.

In 1984 Philips began producing CD-ROM players for personal computers and in 1985 Atari introduced the first computer to use MIDI interface. During that same year, Nintendo introduced the Nintendo Entertainment System, which had a huge influence on the computer industry as they scrambled to develop game systems that could be used on personal computers in order to compete with the phenomenal success of Nintendo. Animation and digitized sound within personal computers were both introduced in 1986, and in 1987 Microsoft produced Microsoft Bookshelf, its first CD-ROM application.

Finally, by 1990, personal computers were being mass-manufactured with integrated CD-ROM drives. In 1991 CDTV (Commodore Dynamic Total Vision) was introduced by Commodore, featuring a CD-ROM player integrated with a computer.

Another key motivator to the multimedia market was the integration of computers into animation. This occurred in 1991 when Pixar worked with the Walt Disney Company on a full-length computer animated film, *Toy Story.*

By 1992 the first double-speed CD-ROM drives and the first stereo PC sound cards were available on the consumer marketplace. In 1993 Apple introduced Macintosh TV, which included a CD drive for both audio CDs and data CD-ROM, an internal TV and cable-TV tuner, and stereo speakers. In that same year, NEC technologies introduced the first triple-speed CD-ROM drive. By the end of 1994 multimedia computers featured on-board video, CD-quality stereo sound, and state of the art monitors.

From the beginning, entertainment and education were the driving forces behind multimedia, spawning the hybrid term *edutainment.* In 1993 consumers purchased more than 700,000 multimedia PCs and 500,000 upgrade kits, not to mention numerous multimedia packages. By 1998 the size of the multimedia market approached $42 billion. This figure would account for approximately 10 percent of worldwide information industry revenues.

CURRENT CONDITIONS

The multimedia industry continues to explode as more and more established computer giants seek to get on the bandwagon or to expand their multimedia offerings. This is because most features that once defined multimedia computers (CD-ROM drives, audio, and high-performance video) have become so omnipresent that they have influenced the development of other platforms, including notebook and network computers.

According to Dataquest, multimedia computer manufacturers face the particularly difficult challenge of keeping their leading positions. This is because they must try to address the cost-conscious consumer market while keeping up with the lightning speed of technological advances that create a short product life.

For instance, in 1998 new microprocessors and media processors began creating a multimedia evolution. Some of these new technologies include audio interconnects rapidly changing to the PCI (peripheral component interconnect) bus, DVD technology, advanced memory architecture, and the Accelerated Graphics Port (AGP) architecture. Therefore, industry leaders must stay on top of changes to computer motherboards in both the number and type of components that are being developed. If not, they will slowly fall by the wayside.

Some companies are already hitting bumps in the road. The Voyager Company, for instance, ran into trouble when it ventured into multimedia, according to *Wired* magazine. Multimedia giant Silicon Graphics, a $2.2 billion company, faced increased competition from Microsoft in the area of software, and Hewlett-Packard and Sun in the hardware division. Though there is money to be made in multimedia, clearly there are risks as well, partly because rapid changes in technology can quickly leave a company's strategies far behind.

One of the risks these companies have faced is not recognizing that one day, CD-ROM will be totally replaced by the Internet. According to the *Interactive Multimedia Sourcebook,* "Internet technology will be sophisticated enough to obviate the need for this type of CD-ROM assist. Someday, all of the multimedia content you want will reside on a server, and the Internet will be advanced enough to send it to you on demand in uninterrupted streams." They also predict that the first to reach obsolescence will be the software developers of stand-alone, educational products such as encyclopedias.

Issues of copyright and fair use still abound, leading many to attempt to set some ground rules. In February 1997 the Creative Incentive Coalition, a group of educators and multimedia professionals, attempted to establish guidelines for educators' use of copyrighted works including multimedia products. But the American Library Association and the Association of Research Libraries did not endorse their "Fair Use Guidelines For Educational Multimedia," according to *Publisher's Weekly.*

In January 1997 *Computerworld* magazine reported on "Business's Multimedia Gap," specifically the fact that sound cards and CD-ROM, the two most important elements of multimedia technology, are not widely available on the computers of corporate America. On the one hand, this seems like a negative, but for makers of multimedia hardware, it represents a market of staggering proportions. Likewise consumer interest in multimedia applications for education, entertainment, and "edutainment" are likely only to expand.

Robust growth in the multimedia market seems assured for the foreseeable future, according to a study released by Dataquest in late 1998. It pointed to the sharp growth experienced in multimedia sales between

1996 and 1997, when overall unit shipments rose a very healthy 47 percent, while revenues generated in this market climbed 52 percent. The strongest segments of the market, according to Sujata Ramnarayan, a multimedia industry analyst for Dataquest, were 3-D graphics/playback boards, voice recognition, video servers, video editing software/capture peripherals, computer-based training/authoring tools, and modeling/animation software.

Multimedia truly entered the mainstream of the consumer electronics market in 1998, Ms. Ramnarayan said, with many companies only now beginning to consider potential applications for this exciting new technology. Dataquest's study indicated that greater attention is likely to be paid to the penetration of new multimedia technologies, including DVD-ROM drives, into personal computers. Although DVD-ROM technology has a number of advantages over that offered by CD-ROM, widespread adoption of the new know-how has been slowed to some degree by a lack of software titles, cost differentials, and competing standards.

Some of the more exciting new products in the multimedia arena are expected to make their debut first in more expensive personal computers, although in time these new technologies will become more widely available at a reasonable price. Multimedia systems in the middle of the price range are adding new audio, improved video, and V.90 56Kb/s modems. Most such systems in late 1998 and early 1999 were being marketed with Pentium II (or even Pentium III) processors running at 350- or 400-MHz, hard disks with capacities of up to 9 gigabytes, PCI-based 3D video controllers with 4 megabytes of memory, PCI-based audio, and at least 64 megabytes of SDRAM. Although as recently as early 1998 DVD-ROM drives could rarely be found as standard equipment on any but the most expensive personal computers, more and more producers were including them on low- and mid-priced PCs less than a year later.

"DVD turns today's multimedia computer into a consumer electronics device," according to Martin Reynolds, an analyst at Dataquest in San Jose, California. "The problem with today's DVD solution is that it's costly." Multimedia systems equipped with DVD-ROM and the hardware-based MPEG-2 necessary to optimize its use carry added costs of up to $200, Reynolds said. He added, however, that he expected prices for DVD-equipped systems to fall quickly as the technology penetrates more and more of the PC marketplace.

The multimedia industry continues to grow, and even in the late 1990s, many industry analysts predict that a full-scale multimedia boom has yet to hit the American marketplace. Many personal computer owners in the United States, not to mention the vast overseas market, have outdated equipment that will need replacement. For the software side of the business, the future looks extremely bright, as it does also for hardware companies—provided they can stay ahead of the ever-moving technology curve.

INDUSTRY LEADERS

By 1998 the creators of Internet tools and services had become industry leaders. This is the result of many factors, including the fact that the Web is situated as the next frontier for commerce. Still, many leaders in the multimedia world produce either software or hardware. Major players in the area of animation software included Autodesk with $740 million in 1998 sales, Walt Disney Computer Software Co. Inc., and Adobe Systems Inc., which had $895 million in 1998 sales.

Corel, Aldus Corporation, and Gold Disk are all involved in the graphics software market. More specialized forms of software—for morphing, multimedia database, music clip, sound, and video—are dominated by smaller companies. Of course, smaller companies, which are more quick to respond to changes in the marketplace, are the backbone of multimedia software.

In early 1999 Corel announced a number of moves to solidify its lead as the high-volume, low-cost alternative in business productivity applications. In a particularly unique business arrangement, Corel agreed to bundle its WordPerfect Suite 8 on a line of personal computers that Gobi Inc. will rent to U.S. consumers for only $25.99 a month, after an initial setup fee of $29.99 and shipping and handling charges of $45. For $25.99 a month, Gobi provides the computer, along with unlimited Internet access, and a pledge to update all software and hardware components as necessary over a 36-month period. Corel also finalized deals with Micro Pro Inc. and Edge Corporation International to bundle its WordPerfect Suite 8 and Corel Print House Magic with PCs manufactured by those companies. In 1998 Corel had $247 million in sales.

In 1998 a new category of industry leaders also dominated by smaller companies has appeared—multimedia developers. These are the people who are designing the digital future. Most of these companies are Web site developers, including Frogdesign, which designs Web sites, and large intranet production companies like USWeb. Some firms work on corporate CD-ROMs, kiosks, presentations, and training networks. Others create CD-ROMs with the latest games and educational titles. These leaders include Brilliant Media, Cambridge Animation Systems, Cox Interactive Media, Digital Planet, and Starwave. Another category here are Hollywood's digital animation and effects houses, including one that might be considered a movie studio itself, Pixar.

Not surprisingly, however, the hardware peripherals end is much more the property of large companies. In the area of CD-ROM drives, for instance, Hitachi, NEC, Panasonic, Sony, and Toshiba are some of the competitors; a similar situation prevails in the world of flatbed and hand-held scanners, where Hewlett-Packard, Epson, Sharp, and Intel battle it out. Not all aspects of hardware peripherals are the property of such corporate behemoths, though. Turtle Beach Systems, for instance, has a niche in video boards.

Multimedia, whether in hardware or software, is a world in which mammoth corporations such as IBM, Apple, Microsoft, Silicon Graphics, and Intel can be found; but it is also big enough to include companies with just a handful of employees. Whereas tens or hundreds of millions of dollars in investment capital are required to start up a computer hardware company, a typical software title, according to Apple Computer in 1994, costs between $25,000 and $1 million to develop, not including actual manufacturing costs.

WORK FORCE

Jobs on the management, marketing, and legal side of the multimedia industry are much like their counterparts in other businesses. At the top of the enterprise are the president, CEO, and other officers. Creative directors and project managers, under the direction of a development leader or executive producer, maintain continuity on a multimedia project, coordinate the efforts to the various content personnel, and see to it that the project stays on budget. Because of the copyright issues that often arise in the industry, legal counsel is often a part of the multimedia software enterprise. Marketing personnel are key as well.

The content may be developed by content experts, specialists in a given field of information. A World War II historian who contributes to a multimedia program on great battles of the war would be an example of a content expert. Researchers are information generalists who also gather and contribute facts and data, which is compiled and turned into a narrative by editors and writers. Graphics professionals, including designers, illustrators, photographers, and scanning specialists work with the visual aspects of the multimedia project.

Moving images involve animators, both in the two-dimensional and three-dimensional forms of animation, and videographers and other video professionals. In the area of sound, there are sound designers who create the appropriate aural texture for the CD; sound researchers, whose job it is to find appropriate sounds and deal with gaining permission to use them when this is necessary; and audio engineers to handle the mixing. Information designers give order to the entire project, so that the resulting multimedia product is as user-friendly as possible; interface designers work on the interface between the images people see on their screens and the commands the computer reads; and programmers develop the scripts and codes to make it all work technically.

The greatest demand in the field is for programmers who write most of the software and who develop Web pages and Web design software. According to the U.S. Department of Labor, median earnings of computer programmers who worked full time in 1997 were about $50,490 a year. Starting salaries for graduates with a bachelor's degree in the area of computer programming averaged about $35,167 a year in private industry in 1997. One survey found that starting salaries ranged from $32,500 to $39,000 for programmers and $47,500 to $60,000 for systems programmers in large establishments, and ranged from $28,000 to $37,000 for small establishments in 1997.

The Department of Labor also reported that, in 1997, computer programmers held about 501,390 jobs and were employed in almost every industry. The largest concentration of these was in the computer and data processing services industry, which includes firms that write and sell software.

AMERICA AND THE WORLD

In the late 1990s, America still held the technological and marketing edge in the world of multimedia—the leading PC suppliers in the world in 1996 were the merged companies of Packard Bell, Zenith, and NEC Computer Systems, with Compaq Computer and IBM following close behind. However, Japanese-made hardware was an important part of multimedia from the beginning. In 1996, Sony's president, Nobuyuki Idei, said that his company planned to move into producing personal computers, in part to take advantage of the multimedia revolution. In fact, both Sony and Toshiba entered the global PC arena with new and refashioned products and marketing strategies. Similarly, Italian computer-maker Olivetti began exploring multimedia in the mid-1990s as a way to improve its outlook. Marco de Benedetti, son of Olivetti CEO Carlo de Benedetti, observed that if a typewriter manufacturer could reinvent itself as a PC company, then a PC company could become a multimedia player. Canada also has a large and growing multimedia industry. In Germany and Israel in 1997, multimedia publishing loomed on the horizon as a future growth industry.

RESEARCH AND TECHNOLOGY

New computer applications may be exciting to consumers, but their usefulness is a function of a computer's processing speed. Thus the January 1997 announcement of the Intel Pentium MMX processor was greeted with much enthusiasm. The new microchip promised to offer faster processing, clearer sound, and a higher resolution of images. The technology was initially expensive, so along with the need to develop faster processors was the need to do so more cheaply.

In 1997 Lucent Technologies was developing Asynchronous Transfer Mode networking technology, which promised to speed up the exchange of multimedia images within computer networks. *Byte* magazine in January 1997 discussed new compression algorithms, which could make possible faster-loading multimedia pages on the World Wide Web.

In January 1997 Infogear Technology Corp. demonstrated a touch-screen telephone with the capability of accessing the World Wide Web and exchanging electronic mail, and Microsoft was working on software to help bridge the gap between television and personal computing. A company called Aureal Semiconductor was developing a chip to upgrade the sound of PC speakers to that of a "surround sound" cinema.

In the final weeks of 1998 and into early 1999, the new DVD technology electrified the consumer electronics market, generating sales of more than 100,000 hardware units a week. Some industry analysts in early 1999 were predicting that sales of PCs equipped with DVD-ROM drives would top 35 million by the end of the year. The availability of DVD-ROM software is growing relatively slowly, as software companies wait until more computer owners have access to DVD-ROM drives; however, DVD-ROM drives are able to read both DVD disks and CD-ROM disks. For those who lack computer smarts, the DVD technology is also available in the form of a DVD player, which can be attached directly to a television set, much as with a VCR. However, the beauty of the DVD-ROM technology is that its users can access a world of additional information not available to those with DVD players. Thus, the owner of a personal computer with a DVD-ROM drive may not only watch the latest video release of a motion picture, but he may, if he chooses, switch from the original English-language soundtrack to one dubbed in French or Spanish. Or enjoy an interview with one of the film's stars or its director.

FURTHER READING

Apple Computer Inc. *Multimedia Demystified.* New York: Random House, 1994.

Aston, Robert, and Joyce Schwartz, eds. *Multimedia: Gateway to the Next Millennium.* Cambridge, MA: AP Professional, 1994.

Atwood, Brett. "Beatnik Makes Hi-Fi Easier on the Net." *Billboard,* 8 February 1997.

Blodgett, Mindy. "Vendors Chip in For MMX." *Computerworld,* 13 January 1997.

Bowker, R.R. *The Interactive Multimedia Sourcebook.* New Providence, New Jersey: R.R. Bowker, 1996.

Brull, Steven. "Nobuyuki Idei's Big Idea." *Business Week,* 12 February 1996.

"Corel and Gobi Break New Ground in High-Performance Technology and Software Rental." M2 PressWIRE, 30 April 1999.

"Corel Solidifies Its Leadership Position as the High-Volume, Low-Cost Alternative in Business Productivity Applications." *Business Wire,* 18 May 1999.

DeJesus, Edmund X. "Walking, Talking Web." *Byte,* January 1997.

Dillon, Patrick and David Leonard. *Multimedia Technology From A To Z.* Phoenix, Arizona: Oryx, 1995.

Feldman, Tony. *Multimedia.* London: Blueprint, 1994.

Forbes, Jim. "Inside Multimedia PCs: DVD Technology, New MPUs, AGP, Media Processors, and New Audio Strategies Spell Change." *Electronic Buyer News,* 21 July 1997.

———. "Inside Multimedia PCs: This Year's Innovations, Including DVD, Will Appear First in More Expensive PCs." *Electronic Buyer News,* 20 July 1998.

"GartnerGroup's Dataquest Says 50 Percent of U.S. Households Have a Personal Computer," 25 May 1999. Available from http://gartner3.gartnerweb.com/dq/static/press/pr-b9906 .html.

"GartnerGroup's Dataquest Says European Home PC Market Experienced Exceptional Growth in First Quarter 1999," 25 May 1999. Available from http://gartner3.gartnerweb .com/dq/static/press/pr-b9921.html.

Gordon, Jack, et al. "Virtual Reality Gets Real." *Training,* April 1996.

Kruse, Kevin. "Exploring Multimedia Internet-Based Training." *Training & Development,* March 1997.

Lawson, Stephen. "Lucent Extends ATM's Reach." *InfoWorld,* 13 January 1997.

McLester, Susan. "The Cybrid Experiment." *Technology & Learning,* March 1997.

Milone, Michael N. "Fair Use Guidelines For Educational Multimedia." *Technology & Learning,* February 1997.

Moschella, David. "Business's Multimedia Gap." *Computerworld,* 27 January 1997.

Osterland, Andrew. "Silicon Valley North, Eh?" *Financial World,* 18 March 1997.

Spahr, Wolfgang. "German Publishing Slows." *Billboard,* 15 March 1997.

Tway, Linda. *Multimedia in Action!* London: Academic, 1995.

U.S. Department of Commerce. *U.S. Industry & Trade Outlook '98.* Washington: McGraw-Hill 1998.

Veron, Marianne, and Herbert R. Lottmann. "Biblicon Valley." *Publisher's Weekly,* 3 February 1997.

Waldrep, Mark. "Status Check." *Sound & Video Contractor,* 1 February 1999.

Young, Lewis H. "Sharp Maps a New Route to Multimedia." *Electronics Business Today,* April 1996.

—Judson Knight, updated by Don Amerman

MULTIPLEX THEATER ENTERTAINMENT CENTERS

INDUSTRY SNAPSHOT

The movie theater business is thriving. In 1998, ticket sales reached a record breaking $6.95 billion and admissions rose to a 40 year high of 1.48 billion, according to Jack Valenti, chairman and chief executive officer of the Motion Picture Association of America (MPAA). The present surge in attendance traces its roots back to the 1970s and the debut of big-budget, special-effects blockbusters such as *Jaws* and *Star Wars*. They transformed and re-energized the filmmaking industry at a time when it seemed to be in danger of losing out to television.

Since then, theaters themselves have undergone tremendous changes. Old single-screen movie houses as well as those with just 3 or 4 screens have given way to multiplexes with 12 to 14 screens and megaplex theater centers containing anywhere from 16 to 30 screens. These multiplexes and megaplexes feature the latest in visual and audio technology plus motion simulation rides, virtual-reality and video games, shops, restaurants, and coffee bars.

Many observers note that various home-based entertainment options, including videocassettes, digital video discs, direct broadcast satellite, and the Internet, offer little competition in the face of such developments. In fact, as Valenti told theater owners attending the 1999 ShoWest convention in Las Vegas, the megaplexes "actually stirred increased movie theater attendance. Not only did families want to get out of the house to be entertained, they also wanted an epic viewing experience that could be found only in your theaters."

Typically, a multiplex theater has giant, curved screens, plush seating, digital stereo sound systems, and a family oriented entertainment center featuring the latest interactive games. Megaplexes have increased the comfort level of their theaters, providing stadium-style seating on highly sloped floors to ensure clear sight lines. (The seats themselves may rock or have especially high backs, and they often sport cupholders and movable armrests.) Concessions include gourmet coffee, scooped ice cream, fresh pizza, and, of course, popcorn. Newer megaplexes also add stores and full-service restaurants to the mix. The decor of these facilities is often reminiscent of the ornate, old movie palaces of the 1920s and 1930s, with Art Deco, Egyptian, Mayan, and other exotic motifs. Megaplexes thus offer patrons a chance not only to see a movie but to have dinner or a drink, play virtual-reality games, or even do a little shopping, all in an atmosphere designed to be as exciting as whatever might be playing on the screen.

ORGANIZATION AND STRUCTURE

A theater owner rents a film based on a sliding scale, thereby giving the distributor the largest percentage of gross receipts in the early weeks of a film's release and less in subsequent weeks. The exhibitor may get 10 percent of revenues during the first week, 20 percent during the second, and so on. Longer runs therefore tend to be more profitable for theaters. In general, multiplexes and megaplexes have more clout than smaller theaters in negotiating with movie studios for the best new releases because of their greater viewing potential.

About 50 percent of a theater chain's gross revenues are derived from box-office receipts, with the remainder coming from concessions. Yet concession sales actually have a much higher profit margin. In fact, theaters make about 85 percent profit on the soft drinks, popcorn, candy, and other items patrons purchase before, during, and after seeing a movie.

During the late 1990s, some prominent theater chains began to sell ownership of their facilities to a real estate investment trust (REIT). Such firms typically purchase multiplexes and megaplexes and then lease them back to the movie exhibitors. One of the biggest and most aggressive of the REITs is Entertainment Properties Trust, formed by AMC Entertainment in 1997. It acquired more than $400 million in theater and related entertainment properties in its first year of operation, including facilities run by AMC, Regal Cinemas, Loews Cineplex, and Edwards Theatres.

CURRENT CONDITIONS

While digital technology will soon allow everyone to enjoy high-resolution pictures with compact disc-quality surround sound at home, it is not expected to diminish the public's desire to go out to the movies. Analysts are optimistic with good reason; in 1998 the movie industry recorded record-breaking revenues of $6.95 billion, a 9.2 percent increase over the previous year and a 50.0 percent increase since the beginning of the decade. Admissions posted a 6.7 percent gain over 1997 figures to 1.48 billion, the largest number of moviegoers in over 40 years. Despite the widespread perception that films are aimed primarily at teenage audiences, patrons over the age of 40 formed the fastest growing market segment since 1993, up 35 percent.

One reason behind the trend toward building bigger and better facilities is that theater operators believe multiplexes and megaplexes are easier and more cost effective to operate. For example, a movie that is expected to do well can be shown on more than one screen in auditoriums that accommodate larger audiences. As its box-office receipts decline, it can be moved to a single, smaller auditorium within the same facility. With numerous movies to choose from and many theaters in which to view them, moviegoers have a greater selection of shows and show times and less chance that a movie will be sold out. The variety of choices plus the best available technology, comfort, and concessions make multiplexes and megaplexes very appealing to some people. Others, however, believe that they offer less interesting and less diverse programming because they tend to focus only on current films with the broadest popular appeal.

Another reason behind the trend toward multiplexes and megaplexes is the increased number of movie releases, especially those regarded as potential blockbusters. Film production by leading companies such as Disney has increased significantly in recent years, making theater operators fear a loss of market share if their facility cannot offer all the popular titles. The best way to prevent the hot releases from getting away, they reason, is to increase the number of screens on which they can be shown.

Stiff competition for market share has also contributed to the megaplex building boom. Theater chains interested in enlarging or just maintaining their customer base risk losing ground to rivals that are building bigger and more luxurious theaters. However, other theaters are not their only competition. Home videos and sporting events are just two of the many forms of entertainment that vie for the consumer's dollar.

Deciding where to build a center and how large to make it depends on the perceived local market and potential competition. Operators wish to maximize a multiplex's revenue per square foot and minimize its cost per square foot. Thus, some theater chains focus on markets they have identified as underserved, such as inner-city areas or medium-sized towns, where they face minimal competition in their quest to capture a new viewing audience. Others choose to go head-to-head with their rivals in well-served suburban markets.

Community resistance may also be a factor in determining where a multiplex or megaplex will be built. Finding a suitable location for such a huge entertainment center can be a highly controversial proposition in many areas. Operators must choose carefully, balancing the need to find a spot that large numbers of moviegoers will frequent with the desire to avoid antagonizing nearby residents over the added traffic, noise, and other inconveniences.

The boom in multiplexes and megaplexes is leading to the demise of one- and two-screen movie houses. Some moviegoers are attracted by the newness and glamour of the modern centers. In addition, older, smaller theaters get fewer top releases. A number of second-tier exhibitors responded to their declining market share by offering discount ticket prices on movies that had already left the multiplexes. For the most part, however, these so-called "dollar theaters" have largely fallen out of favor with consumers. This has led some owners of smaller multi-screen theaters to try a different approach—they have begun to convert their facilities into art houses that show independent productions and foreign films.

By the end of 1998, the total number of movie screens in the United States had reached nearly 34,200, up from only 31,640 the year before; the total number of theaters housing those screens stood at about 7,500. As the decade drew to a close, some industry experts feared the multiplex/megaplex building boom was helping to erode exhibitors' profits. This in turn sparked a series of mergers and sell-offs, especially among regional chains. Analysts blamed a combination of factors, including hefty construction costs and too many theaters vying for the same customers. At the same time, they acknowledged that higher film rental fees and less-than-spectacular box-office receipts of some movies that had been expected to do well also contributed to the problem.

Yet the construction of new multiplexes and megaplexes continued at a rapid pace, with some of the most notable projects getting under way in traditionally underserved urban areas such as New York and in largely African American inner-city neighborhoods across the country. Refitting older multiplexes also gained in popularity as exhibitors scrambled to keep up with innovations such as stadium seating.

Legal issues related to megaplex development also plagued some of the larger theater chains during the late 1990s. For example, a rash of mergers and sell-offs in the industry came under especially close scrutiny from the U.S. Department of Justice amid concerns that certain geographic regions were in danger of being dominated by a single theater chain. In February 1999, reporters for *Variety* noted that the Justice Department had launched an investigation of at least five major exhibitors and their relations with Hollywood studios. The probe focused specifically on booking and distribution practices that smaller theater owners claim make competing with the megaplexes nearly

impossible. Also in February 1999, *USA Today* reported that the Federal Government had filed suit against one theater chain for failing to provide seating for wheelchair users in places other than the very front row, a violation of the Americans with Disabilities Act.

Despite these concerns, major theater companies across the country are charging ahead with plans to adopt the megaplex entertainment centers format. Their goal is to transform the very concept of "going to the movies"—in short, they want to make the theater an entertainment destination in and of itself, a place where people go simply to have "fun."

At new theaters in Canada's Famous Players chain, for example, there are no ticket takers at the entrance because everyone is allowed into the large, open lobby. There they can eat and drink, play arcade games, and gather in party rooms. Movie tickets are available from automated vending machines. Famous Players is hoping that people will visit the entertainment complex and then stick around to see a movie. For those who do, the theaters boast wall-to-wall curved screens, stadium seating, and wide seats with expanded legroom.

Famous Players is only one of many theater chains aggressively pursuing entertainment dollars by offering moviegoers a unique experience. In 1995, Sony Theatres opened a state-of-the-art 12-screen complex. One of its auditoriums became the first commercial theater to show IMAX films with their special 3-D effects. (Traditionally, IMAX films have been shown exclusively in museums, science centers, and theme parks.) In other respects, too, the elaborate Sony Theatres complex is typical of the new multiplexes and megaplexes. The lobby, reached after a lengthy escalator ride past an imitation of the famous "Hollywood" sign, is a generous 8,000 square feet. The entrance to

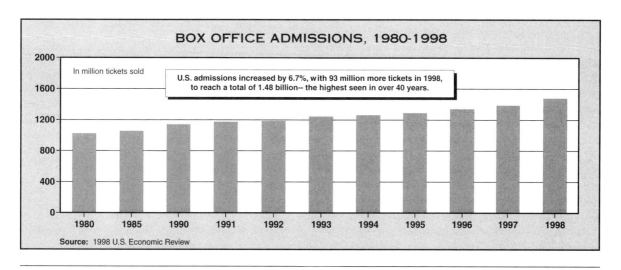

BOX OFFICE ADMISSIONS, 1980-1998

In million tickets sold

U.S. admissions increased by 6.7%, with 93 million more tickets in 1998, to reach a total of 1.48 billion-- the highest seen in over 40 years.

Source: 1998 U.S. Economic Review

each theater is decorated like the lavish movie palaces of the 1920s and 1930s.

INDUSTRY LEADERS

Among the leaders in the multiplex and megaplex theater industry at the close of the 1990s were Regal Cinemas, Loews Cineplex Entertainment, Carmike, and AMC. Somewhat smaller but also significant were Cinemark, United Artists Theatre Circuit, and GC Companies. Dominating various regional markets were a number of other chains of note, including Edwards Theatres Circuit, headquartered in California, and Clearview Cinema Group, with theaters located in suburban communities around New York City.

Based in Knoxville, Tennessee, Regal Cinemas became the country's largest theater chain in 1998 when it merged with the Act III chain. (The combined company is owned by a pair of investment firms, Kohlberg Kravis Roberts and Hicks, Muse, Tate & Furst.) It operates more than 3,300 screens at about 405 theaters in 30 states, mostly in medium-sized cities and suburban areas east of the Mississippi River. (Some of this growth occurred as a result of Regal Cinema's pre-merger acquisition of 671 screens owned by the Cobb Theater circuit.) Most of its theaters are less than 8 years old, and the company's plans call for more than 1,000 new screens to open in 1999.

In 1996, Regal Cinemas launched the first of its FunScape family-oriented entertainment complexes. These all-indoor parks feature movie theaters, shops, food courts, play areas, miniature golf courses, and high-tech video arcades with motion simulation theaters and virtual-reality games. The following year, the company signed an agreement with IMAX Corporation for 10 IMAX 3-D theaters, most of which will use the IMAX 3-D SR system.

Regal Cinemas posted 1998 sales of $707 million, a 47.6 percent increase over the previous year. About 12,000 people worked for Regal Cinemas as of 1998.

The second-largest theater chain in the United States was also created in 1998 as the result of a merger. In that year, Loews Theatres (the oldest theater circuit in North America) joined forces with Canada-based Cineplex Odeon Corporation to form Loews Cineplex Entertainment, with headquarters in New York and Toronto. It is owned primarily by Sony Pictures Entertainment (51 percent) and Universal Studios (26 percent). The company operates approxi-

mately 2,900 screens in more than 450 theater complexes located mainly in major U.S. and Canadian cities. It also has theaters in Turkey and Hungary as well as a growing presence in Spain with its joint-venture partner Yelmo Cineplex de Espana. In addition, Loews Cineplex Entertainment is a partner in Magic Johnson Theatres and Loeks-Star Theatres.

Sales for Loews Theatres in fiscal year 1998 were $413.5 million, a 10.2 percent increase over 1997. (These figures did not include Cineplex Odeon since the merger of the two companies was not completed until May 1998, three months after the fiscal year ended.) Loews nevertheless posted a net loss of $139,000 due primarily to various one-time charges. Without those charges, the company would have posted a net income of $7.6 million. More than 12,000 people worked for Loews Cineplex Entertainment as of 1998.

Carmike Cinemas is the third-largest theater chain in the United States. With headquarters in Columbus, Georgia, it operates more than 2,750 screens in about 490 theaters across 36 states. Carmike has traditionally concentrated on secondary markets (cities and towns with populations of less than 100,000), although it is beginning to make some tentative forays into larger metropolitan areas. Prior to 1998, it grew mostly by acquiring existing theaters and circuits. It then launched an effort to build new screens and expand smaller complexes as well as renovate its older theaters. Plans in 1999 called for opening 382 new screens and retrofitting 83 screens with stadium seating and digital stereo surround sound.

In partnership with Wal-Mart, Carmike also runs The Hollywood Connection, a multiplex theater entertainment center located in Columbus. The 127,200-square foot, two-story family entertainment complex features a 10 screen theater with stadium seating and Lucasfilm's THX Digital surround systems. It also contains an indoor high-tech in-line skating rink, a laser tag arena, a Ferris wheel, a 20-seat mechanical swing, a bumper car arena, a full-size carousel, an indoor 18-hole miniature golf course, a restaurant, a 7,000-square foot video game arcade, and more. Both Carmike and Wal-Mart expect this format to become increasingly popular and plan to develop and operate additional centers.

Carmike's sales for 1998 were $481.6 million, a 5 percent increase over 1997. Its net income for the year was $15 million. The number of employees in 1997, the last available figure, stood at 10,500.

Based in Kansas City, Missouri, AMC Entertainment Inc. ranks as the number-four movie exhibition company in the United States and perhaps number one in terms of innovative ideas. As of 1998, it operated about 2,700 screens in some 240 theaters located in the United States, Canada, Spain, Portugal, Hong Kong, and Japan. Additional projects are in the planning stages for elsewhere in Asia and Europe in 1999 and beyond. Since 1995, AMC has specialized in building megaplexes containing 20 or more screens. These entertainment complexes feature stadium seating with plush, high-backed seats, AMC's own High Impact Theatre System (HITS) with wall-to-wall and floor-to-ceiling screens and unique speaker configuration, and state-of-the-art computer systems to monitor everything from ticket and concession sales to the theater's temperature.

According to AMC's Web site, Stanley Durwood, the company's CEO and co-chairman and son of its founder, invented the multiple-screen theater complex idea in 1963 at a Kansas City mall. Other innovations that debuted at AMC theaters include cupholder armrests (1981), a computerized box office (1982), an ATM-style ticketing system that enables patrons to purchase tickets via credit or debit cards (1990), and a tickets-by-telephone system (1991).

In 1985, AMC took the lead among U.S. firms in overseas expansion when it constructed a multiplex in England. Ten years later the company sparked the megaplex craze by building a 24-screen theater in Dallas, an idea it then exported to Japan the following year. In 1997, AMC formed a joint venture with the Planet Hollywood restaurant chain called "Planet Movies by AMC" to develop multiplexes with the Planet Hollywood theme that combine movies, dining, and shopping in one location. Each facility offers state-of-the-art technology and innovative concession items, plus movie memorabilia. And in 1998, AMC opened a multiple-screen art-house theater (or "artplex") in Kansas City devoted exclusively to American independent films, documentaries, classic revivals, and other special shows. The artplex auditoriums are small—capacity ranges from 73 to 86 people—and feature AMC's plush new "LoveSeat" chairs for two.

In the fiscal year ending March 1998, AMC realized the highest sales in its history—$846.8 million, up 13 percent from 1997. For the same time period, however, the company showed a net loss of $24.5 million. It employed 12,700 people.

Rounding out the list of the top theater chains are Cinemark, United Artists Theatre Circuit, and GC Companies. Cinemark is based in Dallas, Texas, and operates 200 theaters and nearly 2,300 screens located

in the United States, Canada, Mexico, and 7 countries in Central and South America. Its multiplexes (usually containing 6 or more screens) can be found in medium-sized cities and the suburbs surrounding large cities. For the year ended December 1998, Cinemark posted sales of $571.2 million and net income of $11 million. That same year, the company employed 8,000 workers.

United Artists Theater Circuit, Inc. (UATC), founded by actors Charlie Chaplin, Douglas Fairbanks, Mary Pickford, and several others in 1926, has nearly 2,200 screens in 340 theaters in 26 states as well as Puerto Rico, Mexico, Argentina, Hong Kong, Singapore, and Argentina. Sales for fiscal year 1998 were $661.3 million, and the company reported a net loss of $65 million. It had 10,000 employees.

GC Companies operates about 150 theaters with over 1,100 screens under the name General Cinema Theaters. The company is headquartered in Chestnut Hill, Massachusetts, and has theaters in 24 states as well as in Mexico and Argentina, some in partnership with Hoyt Cinemas. It has also teamed up with actor Robert Redford to create a theater chain that specializes in showing independent movies; the first Sundance Cinema is scheduled to open in 2000. General Cinema posted $396.3 million in sales in 1998, down 11.4 percent from the year before. It had a net loss of $41.6 million. The company employs more than 6,000 people.

Regional powerhouses in the theater industry include Edwards Theatres Circuit, Inc. and Clearview Cinema Group, Inc. A family held firm headquartered in Newport Beach, California, Edwards has approximately 500 screens in 100 theaters, all located in California. The company's future plans call for expansion into neighboring states, with Idaho at the top of the list. Among its theaters is a $27 million megaplex in Irvine featuring an IMAX 3-D Theater with a six-and-a-half story screen and an 80-speaker digital sound system. By 2002, it is expected that a total of 13 Edwards multiplexes will contain IMAX 3-D theaters, making the company the largest single operator of such facilities. For the 1998 fiscal year, Edwards had estimated sales of $300 million, an increase of 77 percent, and employed 3,100 workers.

Clearview Cinema Group, Inc. is based in Chatham, New Jersey, and is owned by Cablevision Systems. It operates more than 280 screens in about 65 theaters in suburban New York City, including locations in Pennsylvania and Connecticut. In 1998 Clearview became a major presence in the city itself when it acquired 16 former Cineplex Odeon theaters in Manhattan. (The U.S. Department of Justice had ordered Loews Cineplex Entertainment to divest itself of the theaters as a condition of the merger between Cineplex Odeon and Loews Theatres.) The company's future expansion plans include acquiring more theaters, adding screens to its existing facilities, and building new multiplexes. Clearview posted sales of $16.8 million in 1997, the last available financial figure, a 105 percent increase over 1996, but ended the year with a net loss of $1.3 million. Its employee count checked in just short of 800.

AMERICA AND THE WORLD

In 1994, Hollywood's revenue from foreign box offices reached $2.77 billion—more than double what it was in 1986. This marked the first time that foreign theaters contributed more revenue to Hollywood than U.S. theaters did. The international marketplace continued to prove lucrative for the movie industry throughout the rest of the decade, especially in 1998. That year saw the phenomenal worldwide success of *Titanic* and 19 other films that grossed more than $100 million each, boosting overseas box-office receipts by 11 percent. As the MPAA's Jack Valenti observed at the 1999 ShoWest convention, "More people went to movies in other countries than at any time in this decade."

Many of them attended films in multiplexes and megaplexes built by the major U.S.-based theater chains, a number of which have been busy expanding into Canada, South America, Great Britain, Europe, and Asia throughout the 1990s. Steadily increasing attendance figures at these new facilities have demonstrated how popular the theater entertainment complex idea is becoming all over the world, especially in areas without an adequate number of screens or with shabby, old-fashioned, and poorly run movie houses.

But the U.S. chains face stiff competition from local exhibitors who have also jumped on the megaplex bandwagon. Canada, France, Belgium, Germany, and the Netherlands already have well-developed theater chains of their own. Great Britain has an up-and-coming player in the person of Richard Branson, owner of The Virgin Group. He won the 1995 bidding war for the MGM theater chain in Britain and has begun improving the old facilities and building new multiplexes under the Virgin Cinema name. Similar projects are under way in most major Canadian cities, in Europe's capital cities, and in mid-sized communities across the continent. A vast new market remains to be tapped in the former eastern European countries, where decent single-screen theaters are not all that common and megaplexes are unknown. Analysts predict that the most spectacular growth in multiplexes through the year 2002 will occur in Great Britain, Poland, Spain, and Germany.

Asia holds a great deal of promise as well, and U.S. theater chains have established footholds in a number of different countries. Japan, however, has tended to resist U.S. attempts to penetrate the market. Time Warner opened the first multiplex there in 1993. AMC followed suit with a megaplex in 1996; its goal is to have 600 or more screens in Japan by 2000. UCI, a joint venture between Universal Studios and Paramount, plans to have nearly two dozen theaters operating by the end of the decade. Meanwhile, they face tough competition from Japanese companies such as Shochiku, which has vowed to build even bigger and better multiplexes.

RESEARCH AND TECHNOLOGY

Multiplexes and megaplexes have flourished in part because the motion picture viewing experience has improved so much during the 1990s. Thanks to innovative new technologies, for example, theatergoers can enjoy increasingly high-quality sound systems, including Dolby Stereo and Dolby Stereo SRD, THX, Digital Theater Systems (DTS), and Sony Dynamic Digital System (SDDS). These multiple-speaker systems literally surround patrons with sound, thus enhancing the audio thrills of special-effects extravaganzas such as *Twister* and *Independence Day*.

Visual technology has been advanced by IMAX Corporation, a company that designs and distributes 3-D and giant-screen film projection equipment. (In 1997, it won the only Oscar for Scientific and Technical Achievement ever granted by the Academy of Motion Picture Arts and Sciences.) IMAX sells or leases its system to a variety of establishments, including about 160 commercial theaters, museums, and science centers around the globe; as of 1998, it also owned and operated 8 giant-screen theaters of its own. A number of chains have opted to install IMAX 3-D theaters, including Regal Cinemas, Edwards Theatres, Famous Players, and Loews Cineplex Entertainment. IMAX expects to have a presence in about 250 facilities by the end of 2000.

In addition, IMAX is poised to become a major Hollywood player with the scheduled release on January 1, 2000, of Walt Disney Co.'s *Fantasia 2000*, a

About... THX: THE SOUND AND THE FURY

THX has become the premier sound system in Hollywood, and is slowly becoming the new standard for the movie theater industry. As more theaters, intent on making the movie viewing experience as enticing as possible, are adding THX certification to their stadium-style seating and large, curving screens.

While filming *Return of the Jedi* in 1982, George Lucas noticed the problem that theater sound systems were not playing all sounds that were recorded in the studio. In order to bring the full experience of the movie to the audience, Lucas believed sound was of key importance. Lucas set about correcting this problem by developing the THX sound system.

The THX sound system is not really a set of components or equipment, but more of a performance criteria. Whereas digital sound is a new set of equipment for reading and processing the sound, THX is the way it is presented.

New movie houses trying for THX certification must design their auditoriums within certain parameters for optimal acoustics, while also following special screen speaker installation methods, rigorous audio equipment specifications, and performance standards.

All this leads up to a more naturally blended sound that uniformly reaches every seat in the auditorium, improved intelligibility of the dialogue, and decreased distortion, especially in the bass range. Speaker placement and stereo localization makes the sound appear to move across the screen or around the room. The frequency range is wider meaning the audience hears higher highs and lower lows.

THX is not a replacement for the digital sound systems currently in use in most theatres today. In fact, it can work hand in hand with any sound equipment a theater may have on hand. Digital recording is the best possible way to record the soundtrack, whereas THX is the best possible way to present the soundtrack. When the two are used in tandem, the sound George Lucas had in mind finally comes through. The digital soundtrack is like finally getting the CD player you've always wanted. THX is like having a quiet room and a great speaker system through which to play it.

---

new giant-screen version of the much-loved animated classic. IMAX will be the exclusive exhibitor of the film for the first four months of the year. According to some analysts, if *Fantasia 2000* proves to be a hit, it will give a tremendous boost to the giant-screen concept and might even pave the way for Disney to form a lucrative partnership with IMAX.

Perhaps the most exciting technological development on the horizon will put video images on par with film while granting exhibitors greater flexibility. As the 1990s draw to a close, theater owners are eagerly awaiting a digital revolution in film projection that will make the old 35mm prints obsolete. Six state-of-the-art systems made their debuts at the National Association of Theater Owners' semiannual board meeting in November 1998, and at least two of them earned positive reviews—the CineComm Digital Cinema System and the Texas Instruments Digital Light Processing Cinema System. Such a system would enable studios to transmit movies electronically to theaters, freeing them from the expense and burden of having to produce multiple prints and then ship them.

While the cost of converting the nation's 34,000-plus screens to a digital system will run about $80,000 to $100,000 per screen, it may well prove cost effective to exhibitors. Some point to the added programming flexibility as a definite bonus. Others envision being able to use their theaters to show not only movies but live onscreen events of all kinds. As an AMC executive remarked to a *Variety* reporter, "Unshackled from the limitations of 35mm prints, we'll have the ability to show anything from sporting events to a Broadway play. The true Golden Age of this business lies ahead of us."

FURTHER READING

"1998 Economic Review." *Motion Picture Association of America,* 19 April 1999. Available from http://www.mpaa .org/useconomicreview/1998.

"All-Time Box Office, Slight Dip in Production Costs Highlighted in Valenti ShoWest Address." *Motion Picture Association of America,* 12 April 1999. Available from http:// www.mpaa.org/jack/index.htm.

Allen, J. Linn. "Is Multiplex Fleet Charting a Titanic Course?" *Chicago Tribune,* 25 February 1998.

AMC Theatres, 6 April 1999. Available from http://www .amctheatres.com.

Avis, Tim. "Exhibs Tune Up for Sound Plex-plosion." *Variety,* 15 June 1998.

Banco, Anthony. "Cities: A Star is Reborn." *Business Week,* 8 July 1996.

Booth, Cathy. "Imax Gets Bigger (By Getting Smaller)." *Time,* 29 June 1998.

Carmike Cinemas, 6 April 1999. Available from http://www.carmike.com.

Chidley, Joe. "Attack of the Monster Cinemas." *Canadian Business,* 11 December 1998.

Cosh, Colby. "Welcome to Robo-theatre." *Alberta Report/Western Report,* 18 September 1995.

Crockett, Roger O. "They're Lining Up for Flicks in the 'Hood." *Business Week,* 8 June 1998.

Doll, Pancho. "At a Theater Near You." *Los Angeles Times,* 20 April 1995.

Eyles, Allen. "The Last Remaining Sites for UK Plexes." *Variety,* 15 June 1998.

Gramig, Mickey H. "More Than a Movie: Carmike Cinemas Lures Family Dollars With Games, Gimmicks." *Atlanta Journal and Constitution,* 15 June 1997.

Hindes, Andrew. "Megaplex Dominance Intact: Chain Fends Off Rivals as Company Pushes for Bigger and Smarter." *Variety,* 16 March 1998.

———. "When Prints Will No Longer Be King." *Variety,* 25 January 1999.

Iritani, Evelyn. "A Reel Challenge: U.S. Firms Make Big Push into Japan Theater Market." *Los Angeles Times,* 28 July 1996.

Johnson, Greg. "The Big Picture." *Los Angeles Times,* 5 November 1995.

Kramer, Pat. "Bold Designs Drive Expansion." *Variety,* 16 March 1998.

La Franco, Robert. "Coming Soon: A Megaplex Near You." *Forbes,* 12 August 1996.

Lehrer, Eli. "Inner-City Cinema." *Insight on the News,* 15 March 1999.

Lieberman, David. "Owners Play Key Role in Consolidation." *USA Today,* 23 March 1995.

Loews Cineplex Entertainment, 6 April 1999. Available from http://www.loewscineplex.com.

McNary, Dave. "Technology Pushes IMAX Format to Forefront with Digitally Animated Films." *Grand Rapids Press,* 14 April 1999.

Miller, Stuart. "Gotham Screen Scene's New Sheen: NYC Plays Catchup with More 'Plexes." *Variety,* 12 October 1998.

Peers, Martin. "Mega Building Punctures Profits." *Variety,* 8 June 1998.

Peers, Martin, and Andrew Hindes. "Screen Dreams Fade for Plex Tyros." *Variety,* 15 February 1999.

Regal Cinemas, 6 April 1999. Available from http://www.regalcinemas.com.

Stark, Susan. "Couple Reinvented Movie Theaters and Now Moves into Big Apple." *Gannett News Service,* 16 November 1994.

Tartaglione, Nancy. "Plex Boom Boosts Biz." *Variety,* 11 January 1999.

Tillson, Tamsen. "Canada Is Building It, But Will They Come?" *Variety,* 13 April 1998.

Wax, Alan J. "Coming to Your Neighborhood Soon! Invasion of the Mega-plexes." *Newsday Inc.,* 28 July 1997.

———. "Coming Up on Second Reel: Even Bigger Theater Plexes." *Newsday Inc.,* 23 October 1996.

White, George. "The Empire Strikes Back." *Los Angeles Times,* 1 November 1996.

—Linda Gundersen,
updated by Katherine Wagner and Deborah Gillan Straub

MUTUAL FUNDS

Mutual funds allow people to invest in stocks, bonds, and other securities without having to invest large sums of money all at once. The money from each investor, or shareholder, is pooled and the fund buys the securities. There are thousands of different funds and investors can find one to meet their specific financial goals. Mutual funds fall under one of three broad categories: stock, money market, and bond and income funds. Funds are managed by those in the securities industry, who perform the research into specific securities and add or delete securities to the funds depending on the financial goals.

The U.S. Congress and the Securities and Exchange Commission regulates mutual funds. Laws govern information that must be given to potential investors; records to be kept by investment firms; registration of funds, firms, and brokers; and recourse available to victims of fraud. There are trade organizations with standards of their own and they also work with Congress and state regulators regarding legislation. Two such organizations are the National Association of Securities Dealers (NASD) and the Investment Company Institute (ICI).

Due to a soaring stock market, Individual Retirement Accounts, and company 401(k) plans, mutual funds are more popular than ever before. From 1990 to 1997 household investments in mutual funds rose from 3 to 40 percent. The average investor is between 35 and 54 years old and has an income greater than $50,000. In 1998, mutual fund assets rose sharply to a total of $5.5 trillion, an increase of nearly 25 percent from $4.5 trillion in 1997.

Fidelity Investments led the mutual fund industry as of early 1999. Fidelity's performance in 1998 was paced by its giant Magellan Fund, with assets totaling $83 billion, Contrafund, and Blue Chip Growth, all of which outperformed the Standard & Poor's 500 Index, according to Boston-based Kanon Bloch Carre, an investment advisory firm. Other top-performing mutual fund companies in 1998 were Vanguard Group, number two to Fidelity, London-based Amvescap PLC, Capital Group Companies, and Franklin Resources Inc. Franklin Resources remained a major player in the fund business although its Franklin Templeton fund group turned in a disappointing performance in 1998.

The greatest technological advance affecting the mutual fund industry was in computers. Due to powerful hardware and sophisticated software, investment firms can manage information and crunch numbers faster and more reliably than ever before. Investors benefit from financial software and access to companies via the Internet. Like all industries relying on computers, the potential of computer crashes due to the Year 2000 Problem is a real fear. The ICI has backed the National Association of Securities Dealers' call for regular updates on investment firms' readiness.

Mutual funds pool money from several investors to invest in securities. The purpose is to allow investors to spread their risk by allowing ownership of several different types of securities. Instead of taking a sum of money to purchase 100 shares of one company, the same money could be invested into a mutual fund, which in turn owns shares of many different companies. This way an individual investor does not depend on one company's fortunes; if one company or industry is down, another company or industry in the mutual fund could be up.

There are three broad categories of mutual funds. Money market funds normally invest in securities maturing in one year or less and are known as short-term funds. Stock funds and bond and income funds invest in securities to be held for the long term. Each category is further broken down depending on investors' goals. Money market mutual funds invest in either taxable or tax-exempt securities including Treasury bills, municipal securities, certificates of deposit of banks, and commercial paper. Bond and income funds look for growth of principle and/or income from bonds, Treasury bills, mortgage securities, company debt, municipal securities, and stocks. Stock or equity funds look for a combination of growth in the price of stocks and other securities and income, or dividends, of stocks.

Mutual funds are managed professionally by those in the securities industry. They perform research on companies and securities, plus keep tabs on general market conditions. Based on their research, managers decide which securities to add or delete from a fund to achieve investors' goals. An individual investor is known as a shareholder. While a mutual fund in theory spreads risk, risk is still associated with investing, including a possible loss of the principle investment. Just as with funds invested directly in the stock market, in bonds, or other securities, money invested in mutual funds is not insured by any federal agency.

Most mutual funds list their prices with the National Association of Securities Dealers Automated Quotations System (NASDAQ) in daily newspapers. The price of a fund must be calculated every day by law. The price is the net asset value, or NAV, plus any front-end sales charges. The NAV is determined by market value of the securities owned by the fund, minus the liabilities, divided by the total number of shares owned by shareholders.

All U.S. mutual funds are regulated by the U.S. Securities and Exchange Commission, or SEC, and by federal laws. Mutual funds must provide investors with a prospectus and shareholder report free of charge. A prospectus educates a prospective investor on how to buy and sell shares; states the goals, strategies, and risks of the fund; and gives information on fees and expenses. The shareholder report contains financial statements and reviews the performance of the fund.

Four main laws also govern mutual funds. The Investment Company Act of 1940 requires twice yearly filings with the SEC, while the mutual fund administrators must keep detailed financial records. The Securities Act of 1933 states that mutual funds must offer prospectuses to investors and must register the offerings of mutual fund shares. The Securities Exchange Act of 1934 requires sellers of mutual funds, such as brokers, to register with the SEC and dictates seller and buyer relations. The Investment Advisors Act of 1940 details record keeping requirements, requires registration of investment advisors, and includes antifraud provisions.

In 1996 the U.S. Congress passed the National Securities Markets Improvement Act. This legislation calls for uniform regulation for mutual funds. While preserving states' regulatory powers, mutual funds are regulated on the federal level as far as structure, operation, and review of prospectuses and advertising. The law lowers fees paid to the SEC by the securities industry and gives the SEC exclusive oversight of mutual fund advisors.

Individual investors can buy shares in mutual funds through brokers, financial planners, bank representatives, insurance agents, or other investment professionals. Professionals can recommend funds based on clients' needs and goals, and are compensated by commissions or fees. Investors may also buy shares directly, making decisions based upon their own research.

BACKGROUND AND DEVELOPMENT

In 1868 the Foreign and Colonial Government Trust in London, England, set up the first mutual fund. It promised those of modest means the same chance at making money in securities as wealthier people. In the United States those who invested in capital markets were still the only wealthiest few until the 1920s. Until then, middle income people put their money into banks or bought stock in specific companies. The first mutual fund in the United States appeared in 1924 as the Massachusetts Investors Trust. The fund contained stocks of 45 companies and had $50,000 in assets. The stock market crash of 1929 forced Congress to act to protect investors. While risk is part of the industry, Congress passed laws to enable investors to gather as much information as possible about all types of securities, including mutual funds.

Once the country began recovering from the Depression of the 1930s, people turned to mutual funds as an alternative to investing directly in the stock market. In 1940 the first international stock fund was offered. Funds remained relatively the same, containing mostly stocks, until the 1970s when funds began adding more bonds. Money market mutual funds were also created, and tax-exempt funds offered. By the 1990s there were mutual funds for almost any investor's goals, including very specialized industry funds.

The choices facing investors have exploded since the creation of the first mutual fund. In 1940 there were less than 80 funds; in 1960, 161 funds; in 1980, 564; and in March 1999, 7,391. Assets have grown from $500 million in 1940 to almost $5.8 trillion at the end of the first quarter of 1999.

Investment professionals have added many services for investors over the years. Investors now receive information beyond the prospectus and annual report. Professionals provide tax information, retirement and general financial planning, toll-free 24-hour telephone service, newsletters, and facsimile and Internet access.

CURRENT CONDITIONS

The number of households investing in mutual funds and the amount of money they invest has increased steadily through the years. In 1990, 3.0 percent of households' financial assets were invested in mutual funds; in 1997 it was almost 40.0 percent. Out of almost 100 million households in the United States in 1997, over 37 million, or 37.4 percent of them owned shares in a mutual fund. Of the $4.5 trillion in mutual funds, 44.0 percent came from new money inflow and the other 56.0 percent came from investment performance.

Who invests in mutual funds? As of 1998, an estimated 77.3 million individuals owned mutual funds. Individuals, as opposed to banks and other institutional investors, owned 78 percent of all mutual fund assets as of the end of 1998. The average shareholder in 1998 was 44 years old, married, and employed. Median household income for the average shareholder was $55,000. As of 1998, only 17 percent of mutual fund shareholders were retired, and the heaviest concentration of shareholders fell in the 35-to-44 age bracket. In a little over half the 44.4 million U.S. households owning mutual funds, investment decisions were shared between men and women. Stock

funds are the most popular type of mutual fund with 26 percent of households owning them in 1997. For money market funds the figure was 16 percent, and for bond and income funds it was 15 percent.

The growth in assets of equity mutual funds, also known as stock funds, slowed somewhat in 1998, rising only 26 percent to $2.98 trillion, the smallest percentage increase since 1994. Net new cash flow to these funds slowed in 1998 to $159 billion from $227 billion in 1997. Funds that invested heavily in large-capitalization U.S. companies continued to capture the lion's share of the new cash inflow, compared with the flow of funds to small-cap funds. A continuing trend in 1998 was the flight of household investments from direct stock holdings into equity funds. For the fifth consecutive year, households in 1998 were net sellers of equity, with liquidations of direct stock holdings exceeding household purchases of equity mutual funds. The summer sell-off in stocks in 1998 appeared to have little effect on equity fund shareholders. August's net outflows were estimated at only 0.3 percent of total domestic equity fund assets, despite the largest declines in major market indices since the beginning of the decade. In the first quarter of 1999, the assets of stock funds jumped to a total of $3.1 trillion, an increase of about 4.4 percent from the end of 1998.

Money market mutual funds, both taxable and tax-free, ended 1998 with assets of $1.35 trillion, up a record $235 billion from 1997. This increase was more than double the previous record net inflow of $102 billion in 1997. Fueling the sharp increase in money market fund assets was the favorable interest rate climate. Inflows started 1998 substantially ahead of what they'd been in late 1997 and grew even stronger in the fall when short-term interest rates declined. The sharp drop in the stock market during the summer may have increased investors' demands for liquidity, which in turn may have given the flow into money funds a shot in the arm. By the end of the first quarter of 1999, assets in all money funds had grown to $1.44 trillion.

Bond fund assets climbed about 15 percent in 1998 to a total of $831.0 billion. Net new cash inflows totaled $74.0 billion, stimulated by falling interest rates. The net cash inflow into bond funds was the highest since 1986. The summer sell-off in stocks seemed to have little effect on the net cash inflow into bond funds. Assets in hybrid funds, those investing in a mixture of stocks and bonds, also rose 15 percent in 1998 to a total of $365.0 billion. However, the net new cash inflow into hybrid funds was down sharply to $10.5 billion in 1998 from $16.5 billion in 1997.

Outperforming both equity and bond mutual funds in 1998 were hedge funds, according to Van Hedge Fund Advisors International Inc. According to Van Hedge data, the average U.S. hedge fund showed a gain of 11.7 percent, compared with 10.0 percent for the average stock fund and 6.1 percent for the average bond fund.

Despite the sharp increase in do-it-yourself investment that has come with the emergence of the Internet, mutual fund buyers continued to make more than three-quarters of their fund purchases through professional advisers. The Investment Company Institute, the leading trade group of the mutual fund industry, reported that about 77 percent of the nearly $900 billion in new fund shares in 1998 were purchased through financial planners, banks, insurance agents, employer-sponsored 401(k) plans, brokers, and other intermediaries. ICI said most of these middlemen get paid to advise investors, and the 1998 statistics confirm that such advice is considered valuable by mutual fund buyers.

The decade-long trend of investing more assets in tax deferred securities has showed no sign of slowing. In 1985 only 21 percent of household assets invested in mutual funds were directed to tax deferred funds. In 1996 that figure rose to 56 percent. Most of this is due to the expansion of defined-contribution pension plans, IRA plans, and the explosive growth of 401(k) retirement plans.

Despite mergers among mutual fund management companies, the top five management companies' holdings decreased, as they have since 1984. In 1984 the top five companies controlled 42 percent of mutual fund assets, while in 1997 that figure was 34 percent. The trend remains the same for the top 10 management companies also—in 1984 they managed 54 percent of mutual fund assets and by 1997, 48 percent of assets.

With the stock market rising through the mid- to late-1990s, mutual funds have been an attractive investment, especially during a long bull market. However, some of the best and brightest stock fund managers are beginning to cash out. From 1996 to 1998 over 100 fund management companies sold out completely or in part. In 1997 alone, sellers made $6.3 billion. It has been pointed out that these managers are not necessarily at the end of their careers, nor have they lost their touch. One reading into the trend may be that professionals do not expect the stock market to continue its high rate of growth into the early part of the twenty-first century.

INDUSTRY LEADERS

Fidelity Investments, known officially as FMR Corporation, is the world's leader in the mutual fund industry. Fidelity serves more than 12 million customers with its more than 250 mutual funds. Based in Boston, the company in recent years has taken steps to streamline its operations and performance. Confronted by disappointing results in a raging bull market, the company, under the leadership of chairman Ned Johnson, has shed some of its nonfund assets and made major management changes. The company's former general counsel, Robert Pozen, was selected by Johnson to head Fidelity's mutual fund business. Pozen in turn set up a trio of executives to oversee the company's stock funds. Named to that team was Abigail Johnson, daughter of the chairman and heir apparent. Pozen also tried to refocus fund managers on picking the best stocks instead of concentrating on operational issues. The performance of Fidelity's funds has shown steady improvement since 1996 when its former star fund Magellan was lagging behind the S&P 500. Fidelity is a privately held company and as such is not required to report its financial performance. The most recent statistics show that its 1997 earnings topped $535 million on revenue of $5.9 billion. As of 1997, Fidelity employed 25,000 worldwide.

Vanguard Group Inc. is number two in U.S. mutual fund companies, managing almost $435 billion in assets in 1998. Based in Malvern, Pennsylvania, outside Philadelphia, Vanguard has managed to attract a high level of investment largely by word of mouth. In the process, of course, the company has cut advertising and marketing costs sharply. In another novel management twist, Vanguard outsources management on some of its funds to other companies. Privately held, Vanguard is not required to report its financial results. Its 1997 sales are estimated to have totaled about $1.6 billion. The company employed 5,000 people worldwide as of 1997.

A major force in the mutual fund business worldwide is AMVESCAP PLC, headquartered in London. Its 1998 performance placed it second in terms of average stock fund gains, according to a survey conducted by Kanon Bloch Carre, an investment advisory firm. AMVESCAP's average stock fund rose 22.6 percent in value in 1998, compared to an average increase of 26.1 percent for Fidelity funds. Although it is based in the United Kingdom, AMVESCAP generates almost 90 percent of its revenue in the United States. The company was formed in 1997 by the merger of INVESCO and AIM Management Group. AMVESCAP manages about 100 mutual funds for individuals and corporate and state institutions. With more than 4,900 employees worldwide, AMVESCAP posted net income of $156.2 million on revenue of $1.3 billion in 1998.

Although its 1998 performance was somewhat lackluster, Franklin Resources Inc. remained a major player in the mutual fund industry. Its Franklin Templeton fund group showed average stock fund gains of only 2.27 percent in 1998, putting it last among the 10 biggest equity fund managers in the United States. Its poor performance was blamed to some extent on the lagging returns of "value" stocks in 1998. Franklin Mutual Shares and Franklin Mutual Beacon, two of this group's biggest funds, reported gains of less than 3 percent in 1998. With worldwide employees numbering more than 8,500, Franklin Resources reported net earnings of $500.5 million on revenue of $2.6 billion for fiscal 1998, which ended September 30, 1998.

WORK FORCE

While a college degree is usually necessary to obtain work as a securities sales representative, more important is a person's personality and ability to sell. For someone with no sales experience, a small investment firm may be the way to break into the field. Larger firms may want to see a sales track record in the financial, real estate, or insurance fields. Early in one's career, long hours, cold calling, and rejections can be expected as a client base is built. Many people drop out of the industry due to the tough nature of sales. Those who persevere usually stay in the field until retirement because of the amount of training and education undertaken and the large amounts of money that can be made.

Education is continuous in this industry, with knowledge of economics, business, and finance an asset. Sales representatives learn how to conduct and interpret research, so that they may better advise clients. It also takes time to learn about all the products that a firm offers and to whom they should be offered. With computers a major factor in the securities industry, computer knowledge and continuing education in their use is a must.

As of 1996 about 210,500 people were securities sales representatives in the United States. These people worked in brokerage and investment firms across the country; however, the greatest concentration was in New York City and other large cities. The U.S. Bureau of Labor Statistics (BLS) stated that securities

and financial services sales representatives earned a median annual income of $38,800 in 1996, the latest figures available. It was pointed out that those in the securities field make much more than those in the financial fields. New employees go through a training period while studying for licensing exams and waiting to become a registered representative of their firm. During this period the pay is little, usually an hourly wage or small salary, but after licensing and registration, the employee will earn commissions against sales. The BLS predicts that employment in the securities industry will grow much faster than average through 2006. Factors in this prediction include strong economic growth, rising personal incomes, and more inherited wealth.

AMERICA AND THE WORLD

In the late 1990s mutual funds were present in 30 countries around the world, including Argentina, Finland, New Zealand, and Taiwan. The number of investment companies in the world totaled 22,033 in 1992 and 34,591 in 1997. In 1992 U.S. companies accounted for 17.5 percent of worldwide investment firms, and by 1997 that figure was 19.6 percent. Assets held by all investment companies rose 118.8 percent, from $3.3 trillion in 1992, to $7.2 trillion in 1997. U.S. companies held 50.3 percent of those assets in 1992 and 62.7 percent in 1997.

Asset management companies in South Korea moved in 1998 to establish relationships with foreign investment funds as a way to strengthen Korean fund operations. A Seoul-based analyst observed that "many asset management firms are trying to make inroads into the mutual fund market, but at the moment they lack in management know-how and capital capacity. So they want to set up partnership ties with their foreign counterparts." In the spring of 1999, Mirae Asset Investment Management, the first company to launch mutual funds in Korea, was involved in negotiations with a U.S. firm. Others were expected to follow Mirae's lead.

RESEARCH AND TECHNOLOGY

The technological advances that have helped the mutual funds industry have mostly been in the area of computers. Computer hardware and software development assists the industry with trading by making it quicker and more accurate. Computer technology has enabled brokers to buy or sell securities closer to the price their clients want. The proliferation of computers in the home and the development of the Internet and the World Wide Web allow investment companies to reach more potential investors than ever before. Potential investors can access a company's Web site to find information about the firm's history, past performance, future strategies, and the types of funds offered. Once an account with a company is set up, investors may be able to access it through the company's Internet site.

The greatest technological challenge for investment companies is one facing almost every industry—the Year 2000 Problem. This involves computers neither recognizing, nor interpreting correctly, the first two numbers in the year. On January 1, 2000, computers will recognize the year as 1900. Since securities dealings take place on computers, and all the investment information is stored on them, a crash of systems would be disastrous for the industry. The National Association of Securities Dealers in March 1998 proposed a temporary rule for filing reports with the NASD updates on investment firms readiness for the Year 2000. In April 1998 NASD reminded members they should have their Year 2000 plans in place.

FURTHER READING

Associated Press. "Demand Strong for Fund Advice." *Arlington Morning News,* 2 March 1999.

Atanasov, Maria. "Safer Than the Average Stock Fund." *Fortune,* 27 April 1998.

Easton, Thomas. "I've Got Mine, Jack." *Forbes,* 20 April 1998.

Fidelity Investments, June 1998. Available from http://www.fidelity.com.

Franklin Resources Inc., June 1998. Available from http://www.frk.com.

Investment Company Institute., June 1998. Available from http://www.ici.org.

"Mutual Funds Seeking Foreign Ties." *Korea Times,* 13 January 1999.

Occupational Safety and Health Administration. "SIC Major Group 62," June 1998. Available from http://www.osha.gov/cgi-bin/sic/sicser4?62.

Quinson, Tim. "Fidelity Investments Finishes First in 1998." *Washington Times,* 13 January 1999.

Reid, Brian, and Kimberlee Millar. "Mutual Fund Developments in 1998." *Investment Company Institute Perspective,* February 1999.

U.S. Bureau of Labor Statistics. "1998-99 Occupational Outlook Handbook: Securities and Financial Services Sales Representatives," June 1998. Available from http://www.bls.gov/oco/ocos122.htm.

"U.S. Hedge Funds Outpace Mutual Funds in 1998; Market Timers Score 54.4% Total Return for Year." *Business Wire,* 21 January 1999.

The Vanguard Group, Inc., June 1998. Available from http://www.vanguard.com.

—Lisa Karl, updated by Don Amerman

NEW AGE PRODUCTS AND SERVICES

The New Age products industry derives its values and sensibilities from several identifiable sources. Some are traceable to ancient human civilizations. Others were spurred on by the advent of space travel and the expanding universe of possibilities that ensued. The New Age movement that has received so much media attention in the United States since the 1980s springs from Native American practices, the philosophies of Asia and India and related religious and medical beliefs and customs, and the Utopian movements of the nineteenth century.

The driving forces of the industry have carried it into two major spheres of marketing. One encompasses products such as health and body aids, incense, crystals, books, music, herbal medicines, agricultural and organic gardening resources, and a variety of foods and beverages. The other segment provides services, including classes in yoga, meditation, biofeedback techniques, Tai Chi, and Shiatsu, as well as alternative health care such as aromatherapy and acupuncture. Even seminars and special vacation packages are among the services this burgeoning industry offers consumers.

Analysts note that the demand for New Age-related products and services has flourished in part because of the public's search for physical and mental well-being and a growing dissatisfaction with traditional Western medicine and managed health care programs. According to a random telephone survey conducted in 1998 by the Stanford (California) Center for Research and Disease Prevention, 69 percent of Americans admitted using some form of complementary and alternative medicine (CAM) during the previous year.

A study reported on in the *Journal of the American Medical Association* estimated that consumers spent at least $21.2 billion on such care in 1997, about $12.2 billion of which was out of pocket because so few health insurers reimburse patients for CAM treatments. That number is changing, however, as more and more insurance companies are rethinking their position on the benefits of nontraditional medicine.

For many years California was in the vanguard of such experimentation. Along with Arizona and New Mexico, it remains a favorite destination for those who embrace New Age philosophies. Yet alternative ideas are slowly but surely making inroads into mainstream U.S. culture. During the 1990s, traditional food, beverage, and pharmaceutical manufacturers introduced a variety of New Age-oriented products to tap into an increasingly lucrative market. Even the political arena has felt the movement's influence; the Natural Law party, which was founded on New Age principles, appeared on the ballot in 48 states in the 1996 elections.

For the most part, the New Age industry consists of numerous small businesses that furnish products and services to interested consumers. Excluded from the mix are those large, traditional firms (such as Coca-Cola Co.) that came out with New Age products only after they became popular with a substantial segment of the market. By the mid- to late 1990s, many big stores sold trendy New Age products, but at first they were available only in New Age establishments. The major exceptions were health food and grocery stores that carried New Age foodstuffs and food supplements. In the service sector, some consolidated meditation and yoga schools have emerged on the scene. One of the best known and most expensive programs teaches Transcendental Meditation (TM), a New Age philosophy that becomes a veritable way of life for many of its proponents. There is, in fact, a TM family commune in Iowa where believers can live and work together.

In 1986 the publishing sector of the New Age industry established its own trade association, the New Age Publishing and Retailing Alliance (NAPRA). It functions as a communications network for publishers and retailers of New Age books, helping them run their businesses with integrity and sell products with life-affirming intent. In 1990 NAPRA launched a journal called the *NAPRA Review* that had about 12,000 subscribers in 43 states and 16 countries by 1997. Among them are retailers, publishers, wholesalers, distributors, agents, authors, musicians, and producers of music, audio tapes, videos, and gift items.

CONFERENCES, SEMINARS, AND OTHER GATHERINGS

The rapid growth of the New Age industry can be attributed in part to the many conferences and seminars that characterize the movement. Featured speakers address topics such as the environment, dreams, nutrition, yoga, meditation, and spirituality. Among the most popular gurus on the circuit are author/physician Deepak Chopra and spiritual writer Marianne Williamson; cost of attendance at one of their programs may well run into the hundreds of dollars. The Whole Life Expo, a three-day event held twice yearly in major cities such as San Francisco and Los Angeles, brings together hundreds of vendors, speakers, and practitioners of multiple New Age disciplines. Participants learn about the latest in everything from enzyme therapy to hair regrowth products, peruse the newest books, and go to seminars conducted by well-known personalities. Some New Age events are held at the same time as celebrations marking Earth Day and the spring and fall equinoxes, while others take their inspiration from ancient religious holidays of the Druids and Native Americans and include attempts to recreate the old rituals.

BACKGROUND AND DEVELOPMENT

The sensibilities propelling the New Age industry developed from a host of different sources. Helena Petrovna Blavatsky, founder of the theosophical movement, is often credited with inspiring the New Age movement as well. When she died in May 1891, an editorial writer in the *New York Daily Tribune* declared that, "No one in the present generation, it may be said, has done more toward reopening the long-sealed treasures of Eastern thought, wisdom, and philosophy. . . . Her steps often led, indeed, where only a few initiates could follow, but the tone and tendency of all her writings were healthful, bracing, and stimulating. . . ." The Theosophical Society, which has followers around the world, espouses a doctrine that emphasizes direct and mystical contact with a divine power through meditation incorporating elements of Buddhism and Brahmanism.

The New Age movement also has some historic antecedents in the hippie and counterculture movements of the 1960s. These movements did not constitute the largest or most consistent segment of New Agers, writes Elliot Miller in his book, *A Crash Course on the New Age Movement.* He observes that New Age principles share some similarities with the 1960s movement. Yet the respect for and appreciation of nature; the movement away from materialism; the interest in non-Western thought, culture, and medicine; and the desire to create a better way of living have not been embraced by all participants in the New Age industry. Miller also argues that Asian Hinduism and Buddhism have been key influences on the New Age movement, as are the concerns about health, personal growth, and environmental conservation and protection that germinated during the 1970s.

Even those ideas had first surfaced in the United States as early as the mid- and late nineteenth century. Philosophers and writers such as Henry David Thoreau and Ralph Waldo Emerson of New England, wellness advocate Dr. John Harvey Kellogg of Battle Creek, Michigan, and the founders of the various Utopian communities across the country foreshadowed much of the later New Age movement. Around the same time, the mineral water springs in places like Hot Springs, Arkansas, and Saratoga Springs, New York, led to the construction of resort complexes that became gathering places for many of the early progressive thinkers. All of this in turn stimulated an interest in organic foods (those free of chemicals and preservatives), recycling used materials, reducing natural resource consumption, fighting pollution, and cultivating respect for the environment.

Eventually, people began seeking spiritual fulfillment and self-authenticity outside of the traditional secular and religious channels. Miller notes that the people involved in these early movements also wanted to take responsibility for themselves and the planet, concerns similar to those that later prompted the environmental and spiritual quests on which New Agers embarked.

Some practices of the New Age movement became quite common in the United States during the 1960s and 1970s; yoga and meditation, for example, had many devotees. Miller contends the movement received very little attention until the mid-1980s when actress Shirley MacLaine began promoting her New Age beliefs on television and in her books. The mass media also took note in August 1987 after the Harmonic Convergence brought together approximately 20,000 New Agers to sites considered sacred worldwide for activities that included meditation, channeling, and rituals with crystals. The event prompted innumerable articles and programs exploring the New Age movement, culminating in a *Time* magazine cover story that appeared in December 1987. The press coverage introduced a larger section of the public to the ideas, wares, services, practices, and foodstuffs associated with the New Age movement.

The confluence of these forces spawned the New Age industry. As more people started to share some of the beliefs and concerns of the original members of the New Age movement, the industry surrounding it grew. Demand for New Age-oriented products and services hit the market in full force during the late 1980s and continued to expand throughout the 1990s, especially as the millennium drew near. Consequently, many traditional businesses started offering New Age-related products, hoping to profit from the public's fascination with the not-so-new trend.

CURRENT CONDITIONS

Since private service providers and small business operations make up such a large part of the New Age industry, it is nearly impossible to come up with more than a rough estimate of sales. In 1996 revenues from New Age industry products and services combined totaled nearly $22 billion dollars. As of mid-1999, analysts pegged the global market for natural and organics products (a major component of the industry) at about $65 billion.

Health-related products in particular have boomed since the early 1980s. According to the National Center for Homeopathy, sales of homeopathic remedies in the United States hit $227 million in 1996 and are increasing by 12 percent per year. Alternative medicine as a whole earned about $11 billion per year as early as 1990, climbing to over $13 billion in 1996,

according to *Time*. As reported by the National Center for Homeopathy, a 1998 article in *Modern Healthcare* estimated the complementary and alternative medicine (CAM) marketplace at $24 billion or more with an annual growth rate pegged at close to 15 percent.

The sales of books and food products classified as New Age were estimated to amount to as much as $6 billion by the mid-1990s. New Age music sold well, too. Labels such as Windham Hill and Narada made up a significant part of the $86-million music industry in 1996, according to *Forbes*.

MARKETING NEW AGE PRODUCTS

Typically, New Age products and services were marketed in small shops in major cities and towns. The distribution network for such items was limited and, for most vendors, expansion was an option they could not afford. During the mid- to late 1990s, however, the Internet emerged as a major marketing tool for New Age vendors. Hundreds of sites offering candles, crystals, astrolites, incense, and other products have made their debut on the World Wide Web, thus enabling New Age suppliers to market their merchandise virtually everywhere without incurring significant additional expenses. Besides electronic New Age shops, the Internet hosts a number of sites advertising New Age services such as yoga, meditation instruction, and massages. Various New Age organizations also promote themselves on the Internet and provide links to related sources of information. Of course, this trend is not limited to the New Age products market. It is similar to the experience of many other industries as the Internet becomes an international shopping center.

BOOKS

Sales of New Age-oriented books dealing with religion and spirituality began to soar during the late 1980s, making that publishing category the fastest-growing one of the decade. The Book-of-the-Month Club even launched a New Age book club in 1995 called One Spirit that quickly became the most successful specialty book club in the firm's history. The genre remained on top during most of the 1990s, especially among female readers. In fact, between 60 and 70 percent of such titles are bought by women.

Quite a few U.S. bestsellers fall within the New Age genre, according to the trade magazine *Publishers Weekly,* including *The Celestine Prophecy, The Seven Laws of Spiritual Success, Simple Abundance,* and *Conversations with God.* Books linking creativity with spirituality also did well in the United States. Upon its release in 1992, for example, *The Artist's Way* had only 5,500 copies in print; by 1996, 850,000 copies had been sold.

Titles that publishers once promoted as New Age have since been reclassified as psychology, philosophy, religion, health, or fiction, thus marking the assimilation of New Age ideas into mainstream culture. Yet some authors shun the New Age label, seeing it as a liability that could lead to lower sales on account of some consumers' prejudices. For instance, *Publishers Weekly* reports that Bantam created a New Age label in 1980 but began to shy away from it by the mid-1990s because some authors did not want the New Age association. Alternative terms subsequently began to come into fashion, including "Spiritual Growth" and "Personal Growth," even if these covered only certain aspects of what was typically regarded as "New Age." Since no one has been able to come up with another name for New Age books, it remains the only inclusive label available for such literature.

As the 1990s drew to a close, the industry was undergoing some changes. Sales flattened, publishers of New Age materials consolidated, and alternative bookstores were facing a number of challenges, including increased competition from large chain operations and Internet booksellers.

BEVERAGES AND FOOD

Alternative beverages and natural foods are closely identified with the New Age movement. As with most other New Age products, they were often available at first only in smaller markets and specialty stores. By the end of the 1990s, however, they enjoyed much wider distribution and acceptance.

New Age beverage manufacturers encountered several obstacles when they tried to tap into existing distribution networks or create new ones during the mid-1990s. According to John N. Frank in *Beverage Industry,* they had trouble getting their products into stores and, if they managed to do so, the stores would often neglect New Age products in favor of traditional brands. Moreover, the well-established companies began developing their own products (such as Coca-Cola's Fruitopia) to take advantage of the growing demand for New Age products.

To address this problem, purveyors of New Age products had to choose from among several less than satisfactory options. They could, for instance, do business with small beverage distributors that served a strictly local market and thus lose out on national exposure, or they could seek out big beer distributors knowing that their products would not reach many convenience outlets and other small stores that did not sell beer. On the other hand, if they opted to go with food distributors instead, they risked bypassing the smaller stores that did not offer a large array of food items. No matter which option they chose, Frank argued, they also needed to come up with a niche marketing strategy or their products would not move quickly. Yet most New Age beverage and food operations were small and could not afford to promote their products on television or with other popular, expensive forms of advertising.

Despite these problems, New Age beverages managed to do extremely well during the 1990s. According to the trade publication *Beverage World,* so-called "alternative beverages" such as fruit juices, ready-to-drink tea and coffee, and sports drinks together reported sales of nearly $5.2 billion in 1998—about 14 percent of the market for nonalcoholic liquid refreshments. Carbonated soft drinks accounted for about 80 percent of that same market. From 1993 to 1998, the category experienced a 12-percent compound annual growth rate.

Natural and organic foods have also been a hit with consumers. According to *Supermarket News,* many traditional food stores are expanding their natural and organic food sections, and natural foods retailers such as Whole Foods Market and Wild Oats Markets have grown by leaps and bounds during the 1990s. Furthermore, organic food producers have increased the diversity of their products with some companies even manufacturing organic baby and pet food. In 1995, for example, 1,015 new products debuted—compared to only 512 in 1991. As Cyndee Miller observed in *Marketing News,* beginning in 1991 organic food sales nearly doubled. She estimated that this portion of the industry earned $3 billion in 1996 and has experienced a sales growth rate in excess of 20 percent since 1990. Sales of all types of organic products, a mere $178 million in 1980, blossomed into more than $4 billion by the mid-1990s, while sales of natural products tripled. By the end of the decade, they exceeded $12 billion.

Mainstream businesses feverishly pursued the organic and natural foods market by way of mergers and acquisitions during the 1990s. Investor Roy E. Disney bought organic frozen vegetable pioneer Cascadian Farm in 1996. H.J. Heinz Co. purchased Earth's Best, a rapidly growing organic baby food company. Such expansion moved this emerging industry "off the natural foods screen and onto the global agribusiness screen," noted Bob Scowcroft, executive director of the Organic Farming Research Foundation in Santa Cruz, California, in a *Los Angeles Times* article.

HEALTH AND HEALING SERVICES

Health and healing services such as yoga, Tai Chi, and meditation have constituted an important element of the New Age industry since its beginnings. Yoga in particular has become very popular. According to *U.S. News & World Report,* the Clinton White House made yoga classes available to staff members. Large law firms and investment banks commission yogis to teach their employees. Many physicians recommend yoga to patients afflicted with diseases like arthritis and diabetes, as well as those with cardiovascular ailments. Also, some health insurance providers have started covering expenses related to yoga and meditation. Health care facilities have even started offering yoga and meditation classes, as do some private practitioners.

Paul L. Cerrato and Aria Amara reported in *RN* that one of every three people in the United States relied on some kind of holistic or non-Western therapy in 1997. Another study conducted that same year by a different researcher put the number at about 40 percent and observed that more than half of the patients were between 30 and 50 years of age. Not surprisingly, the number of professional practitioners of non-traditional medicine in the United States rose from 200 during the 1970s to 3,000 in 1998. Even national drugstore chains like CVS, Kmart, and Walgreen's started carrying homeopathic products in the late 1990s.

Meanwhile, an increasing number of health insurance companies have started taking a serious look at the feasibility of covering alternative medical treatments in their policies. As of 1995, Washington required that all health insurance companies compensate their subscribers for all licensed and certified alternative practitioners. Analysts predict that other states will follow suit and pass similar laws.

This trend has indeed been reflected in the policies issued by several major firms. By the end of the 1990s, for instance, Mutual of Omaha was covering chiropractic care, Prudential was paying for acupuncture, and Blue Cross of Washington and Alaska was offering a plan called "AlternaPath," which covered licensed naturopathic doctors. In addition, a growing number of hospitals and HMOs are including alternative medical services in the treatments provided for their patients. The book *New Choices in Natural Healing,* a publication of *Prevention* magazine, noted that at the end of the 1990s the insurance plan that cov-

ered the widest array of alternative medicine practices was one offered by American Western Life Insurance Company of Foster City, California. It reimbursed patients for homeopathy, Ayurveda, nutritional counseling, massage, and physical therapy as part of its wellness plan. The company also offers a full-time "Wellness Line" with naturopathic doctors on call for their patients.

Much of what has come to be known as New Age or alternative medicine (increasingly referred to by the acronym CAM, for complementary and alternative medicine) is not really new, nor did it all originate in Asia. Homeopathy developed in eighteenth-century Germany. Chiropractic and naturopathy began in the United States, and people have been using herbs for healing all over the world for centuries. Practices such as homeopathy, herbalism, and midwifery were, in fact, part of mainstream medicine until the early twentieth century, when members of the medical establishment began rejecting what they viewed as "nonstandard" practices. Yet as of the end of the 1990s, reports David Plank in *Vegetarian Times,* the World Health Organization estimates that 65 to 80 percent of what is regarded as standard health care elsewhere in the world would be defined by Americans as "alternative."

Homeopathic medicines remain very popular in Europe. For years they have been sold on drugstore shelves in France and Germany and, in the United Kingdom, the government's national health insurance plan covers the cost of purchasing them. The use of herbal medicine is especially common in Germany; German physicians are far more willing than their American counterparts to recommend herbal medications to patients.

Especially popular in Germany (and increasingly so in the United States) is St. John's wort, an herb used to treat mild to moderate cases of depression. It outsells all other antidepressant drugs combined, including Prozac, in Germany. With approximately 70 percent of German psychiatrists and general practitioners routinely prescribing St. John's wort to their patients, sales soared from $23 million in 1994 to $66 million in 1996. Besides the fact that it appears to have only mild side effects compared to anti-depressant pharmaceuticals, St. John's wort is considerably cheaper, and obtaining some does not require a visit to the doctor for a prescription.

Yet some inside and outside the medical field have questioned its efficacy and safety. To address those concerns, medical school researchers at 10 centers across the United States launched a comprehen-

---

More On   AROMATIC
ESSENTIAL OILS

Aromatherapy is nothing new. It gained widespread use with Egyptian priests who produced the resin and oils in laboratories found in every Egyptian temple. They used fragrant waters during religious ceremonies for anointing rituals and they burned incense to protect against evil spirits and make prayers more effective. The smoke that swirled off incense was believed to pave pathways to the heavens, allowing prayers to reach the gods. The fumes helped worshippers enter a state of euphoria.

Today's aromatherapy is the use of pure essential oils extracted from grasses, flower petals, seeds, fruit rinds, bark, wood and other natural items. Use has become more common to cope with the stress of everyday life, such as living in a polluted city.

Some aromatic essential oils and their corresponding uses are as follows:

- Ambrette Seed oil comes from the seeds of the Hibiscus, an evergreen shrub. Its scent is said to reduce stress and nervous tension, trigger uplifting moods and lessen aches and pains, while the oil heals and moisturizes the skin.

- Chamomile oil, extracted from the flowers and leaves of the chamomile plant, is supposed to promote calm, restful sleep and good moods, as well as improve digestion and soothe the intestines. It is also thought to lessen pain, relieve menstrual discomfort, soothe inflammation, heal the skin and soothe insect bites.

- Fir needle oil, which comes from the needles of fir trees, is used to calm the spirit while the vapors open sinus and breathing passages. It, too, is used as a good mood enhancer, and at the same time is thought to encourage communication, reduce cellulite, lessen pain and remove lymphatic deposits from the body.

- Grapefruit oil, extracted from the peel of the fruit, is believed to reduce stress, cool, lift moods, improve mental clarity and awareness, sharpen the senses, increase physical strength and energy, help reduce cellulite and obesity and balance the fluids in the body.

- Manuka oil, extracted from the leaves and branches of the Manuka shrub, is used to calm, reduce stress and tension, help people to breathe easier, lift moods, improve mental clarity, loosen tight muscles and relieve aches and pains. It is also thought to be an aphrodisiac and can be used as a deodorant or a disinfectant to heal the skin.

- Peppermint oil, extracted from the whole peppermint plant, is said to cool, open sinus and breathing passages, lift moods (especially for people with slow metabolism), stimulate the brain and nerves, improve mental clarity and memory, increase physical strength and endurance, sweeten the intestines, freshen the breath, revive a person from a fainting spell or shock, increase the appetite, relieve flatulence and nausea, kill parasites, relieve pain, reduce lactation, repel insects, soothe itching skin and also act as an aphrodisiac.

---

sive study of St. John's wort in early 1999 that applies the same rigorous standards used to evaluate experimental drugs for cancer, heart disease, and other ailments. They hope to settle once and for all whether the herb works as promised, how it works, and what dangers might be associated with taking it.

The growing popularity of other New Age-oriented health regimens has prompted close scrutiny from the Western medical establishment. The results of their investigations have so far proved favorable to holistic medicine. For instance, meditation has been found to lower blood pressure, chiropractic care can eliminate certain kinds of back pain, and massage alleviates stress, anxiety, and pain, according to Cerrato and Amara in *RN*. In 1996 medical research revealed that acupuncture stimulates the excretion of analgesic and nerve-healing substances, wrote Doug Podolsky in *U.S. News & World Report*. That same year the U.S. Food and Drug Administration (FDA) decreed that acupuncture needles could be considered medical instruments.

As herbal remedies have increased in popularity, however, the FDA has begun to subject them to intense examination. Some of the claims made by dietary supplements, for instance, have been found to be false. Consequently, manufacturers have become more careful about what they claim their products can do.

INDUSTRY LEADERS

The largest retailer of natural foods in the United States is Whole Foods Market, based in Austin, Texas. (Natural foods are those deemed free of pesticides, preservatives, and artificial sweeteners and produced without being cruel to animals.) Beginning as a tiny natural foods store in 1980, it went on to pioneer the concept of selling natural foods in a supermarket-style atmosphere, and it posted sales of nearly $1.4 billion in 1998. Second quarter results for 1999 increased 10 percent over the same period in 1998, putting Whole Foods Market on track toward another profitable year in 1999.

The chain operates more than 90 stores in more than 20 states and expects to have a total of almost 120 stores by the end of 2000. Its growth can be traced in part to its aggressive expansion drive during the 1990s, which saw Whole Foods Market acquire several successful independents and smaller chains in major markets characterized by numerous well-educated and affluent consumers. In March 1999, it became the first grocery chain to launch a national online shopping service, beginning with nonperishable goods. Future plans include expanding the online service to include perishable items if customers demand it.

Wild Oats Markets, headquartered in Boulder, Colorado, is the second-largest natural foods retailer in the United States. As of mid-1999, the company operated 68 stores in 18 states and British Columbia. Sales for the 1998 fiscal year stood at almost $399 million, a 28.2 percent increase over the 1997 total. Results for the first quarter of 1999 were up 34 percent over the same period in 1998.

Wild Oats Markets has grown rapidly during the 1990s by opening new facilities and acquiring independent retailers and other natural foods chains. In 1997, for example, it entered new markets in Tennessee, Oregon, Arizona, and Illinois and opened or acquired 14 stores. In the first quarter of 1999, it announced the acquisition of 11 natural foods markets. Ten additional Wild Oats Markets are scheduled to open in 2000.

New Leaf Distributors is the largest and oldest wholesale distributor of New Age books and periodicals. Founded in 1975 and originally called Shakti Distributes, New Leaf started out by distributing the fledgling New Age Journal, as well as Dr. Ann Wigmore's books on dietary medicine, to health food stores and food co-ops in the Atlanta area. By 1976, the firm was bringing in only about $500 per week. Then a store was opened to supplement the distribution service, and in 1979 the company changed its name and sales began to rise. New Leaf posted a profit for the first time in 1983, and by 1995 sales had leaped to more than $30 million.

The Red Rose Collection is a leading distributor of New Age products such as incense, candles, crystals, and books. Using mail-order catalogs and the Internet, Red Rose also offers New Age apparel and home decorations with New Age motifs. In addition, Red Rose sells meditation and yoga paraphernalia, inspirational and instructional video and audio recordings, and an assortment of novelty gift items. According to Catalog Age, Red Rose has about 425,000 customers.

AMERICA AND THE WORLD

The New Age industry has won over many Americans, and people worldwide have embraced some of the movement's ideals and practices. According to Marketing in Europe, German demand for organic food started increasing during the 1980s, climbing 20 percent per year through the end of the decade. The market then slowed during the mid-1990s, posting gains of only about 10 to 15 percent per year. Organic food was also attracting a growing base of customers in France. A writer for Eurofood reported that the market increased by 15 percent each year beginning in the 1980s as French customers sought higher quality food and adopted healthier eating habits. The lack of an organized distribution system has hindered the industry's ability to expand even more, though.

As Yumi Kiyono noted in Nikkei Weekly, Japanese citizens have also heartily embraced the New Age movement. Spiritual books and other wares have done well, as have so-called "power stones," which facilitate meditation.

Sumit Sharma reported in the Wall Street Journal that in India—especially in Bombay—yoga, meditation, and other indigenous practices for health and stress reduction were prospering in the late 1990s. In 1996, some physicians were turning to classical yoga breathing exercises and laughing postures for their patients in the belief that they relieved stress. This spawned more than 100 laughing clubs across the country.

FURTHER READING

"The Age of New Age." Beverage Industry, March 1997.

"Americans Mingling Alternative and Traditional Medical Services." USA Today, February 1999.

Angrisani, Carol. "Chains Seen Eyeing Bite into Organic, Natural Food." Supermarket News, 12 May 1997.

Brotman, Barbara. "Finding Personal Growth in Abundance." Dallas Morning News, 14 January 1998.

Cerrato, Paul L., and Aria Amara. "Complementary Therapies: Use Research to Weigh the Alternatives." RN, February 1996.

Charles, Dan, and Bob Edwards. "Herbal Medicine." *Morning Edition.* National Public Radio, 3 October 1997.

Chillot, Rick. "Homeopathy: Help or Hype?" *Prevention,* 1 March 1998.

Condor, Bob. "Americans Increasingly Trying Alternative Medicine, Study Shows." *Knight-Ridder/Tribune News Service,* 11 November 1998.

"Financial Conference to Focus on Meteoric Growth and Global Expansion of National and Organics Products Industry." *NewsAlert,* 3 May 1999. Available from http://www.newsalert.com.

Frank, John N. "The Distribution Dilemma." *Beverage Industry,* March 1994.

Garrett, Lynn, and Bridget Kinsella. "New Age Is All the Rage." *Publishers Weekly,* 10 March 1997.

"Going Outside the Mainstream." *U.S. News & World Report,* 23 November 1998.

Grossman, Cathy Lynn. "Religious Retail Stores Have Strong Faith in Sales Soaring to Heaven." *USA Today,* 12 March 1998.

Groves, Martha. "Organic Foods: A Growth Industry." *Los Angeles Times,* 2 October 1997.

"Growing Demand for Organic Food in France." *Eurofood,* October 1995.

Gwynne, S.C. "Thriving on Health Food Whole Foods Has Grown into the Biggest Organic Supermarket Chain by Feeding on Weak Competition." *Time,* 23 February 1998.

"Health Food in Germany." *Marketing in Europe,* April 1996.

Japsen, Bruce. "Cost-Conscious Providers Take to Holistic Medicine." *Modern Healthcare,* 21 August 1995.

Kiley, Kathleen. "Have Catalog, Will Travel." *Catalog Age,* December 1996.

Kinsella, Bridget. "New Leaf Adds a New Leaf." *Publishers Weekly,* 27 January 1997.

Kiyono, Yumi. "Japanese Embrace New Age Lifestyles." *Nikkei Weekly,* 17 October 1994.

Langone, John. "Challenging the Mainstream." *Time,* Fall 1996.

Lee, Josephine, and Tom W. Ferguson. "Coin of the New Age." *Forbes,* 9 September 1996.

McCracken, Samuel. "The New Snake Oil: A Field Guide." *Commentary,* June 1999.

Miller, Cyndee. "Challenge to Fat-Free: Sales of Organic Food Nearly Doubles in Five Years." *Marketing News,* 21 October 1996.

Miller, Elliot. *A Crash Course on the New Age Movement.* Grand Rapids, MI: Baker Book House, 1989.

Monmaney, Terence, and Shari Road. "Alternative Medicine, the 18 Billion Dollar Experiment." *Los Angeles Times,* 30 August 1998. Available from http://www.latimes.org.

Nash, J. Madeline, Dan Cray, Alice Park, and Ursula Sautter. "Nature's Prozac? Despite Its Growing Popularity, St. John's Wort Has Yet to Convince Skeptics That It's Safe and Effective." *Time,* 22 September 1997.

"Nod to an Ancient Art." *U.S. News & World Report,* 13 May 1996.

"Organic Baby Food Launched." *Supermarket News,* 24 March 1997.

Plank, David. "Alternative Medicine Comes of Age." *Vegetarian Times,* April 1999.

Podolsky, Doug. "Nature's Remedies." *U.S. News & World Report,* 19 May 1997.

Sharma, Sumit. "Stressed? Inhibited? Grumpy? Join the (Laughing) Club, Indians Say." *Wall Street Journal,* 12 September 1996.

Smith, Stephen. "National Study to Examine Effectiveness of St. John's Wort." *Knight-Ridder/Tribune News Service,* 12 March 1999.

Turcsik, Richard. "High Water Mark: Premium Bottled Water Sales Keep Rising." *Supermarket News,* 24 January 1994.

Warner, Bernhard. "Whole Foods Market Joins Online Rush." *The Industry Standard,* 22 March 1999. Available from http://www.thestandard.net/articles/display/0,1449,3870,00.html.

"Whole Foods Market Announces 2Q 99 Sales and Earnings." *NewsAlert,* 6 May 1999. Available from http://www.newsalert.com.

"Wild Oats Markets, Inc. Reports First Quarter Operating Results; Acquires 11 Natural Foods Markets." *NewsAlert,* 28 April 1999. Available from http://newsalert.com.

Wind, Edgar. *Pagan Mysteries in the Renaissance.* England: Faber & Faber, 1958.

—Karl Heil,
updated by Roxanne Nelson and Jane E. Spear

NEW FOOD PRODUCTS

Ketchup and frozen dinners were considered "convenience" foods at one time. Now, an entire meal can be picked up in the grocery aisles and put on the table within minutes. In the 1990s food manufacturers responded to two major consumer motivations with their new product introductions—convenience and nutrition. Food producers launch hundreds of new products each year to capitalize on these consumer preferences. New products that appeal to both convenience and nutrition stand the best chance of surviving and creating a consumer trend. Value-added produce, such as salad kits, were among the new product offerings designed to accomplish this goal. In the latter part of the decade, more companies started to compete in this $2-billion segment of the market, trying to develop the most convenient or unique salad kit available. The emergence of "nutraceuticals" on the market also reflected the growing interest in healthy foods.

According to research conducted by The Pillsbury Co., 80 percent of U.S. meals require 30 minutes or less of preparation time, and the trend of the 5-minute meal has emerged. *Time* magazine estimated in 1997 that less than 38 percent of all meals included one item made from scratch. This market niche is known as home meal replacement. By providing ready-made or easily assembled meals without the wait and cost of dining at a restaurant, supermarkets are given the leverage to compete with restaurants for a piece of what was, in 1998, a $100-billion market. Frozen foods provide another approach to convenient and healthy food. New frozen food offerings remained strong in the 1990s, although *Frozen Food Digest* showed that marketing and stocking methods in this period hampered the success of many new food releases.

Interest in ethnic, vegetarian, and organic foods has also increased. More companies vie for this market by developing and marketing these cuisines as well as food made from organic produce. Interest in Asian, Mediterranean, and Middle Eastern food products grew in 1998 with food giants such as Quaker Oats competing against smaller manufacturers in making these offerings. Promar International, a consulting firm, estimates that 1 of every 7 food dollars in the next decade will be spent on ethnic foods. One of the leading products created to accommodate the vegetarian market was vegetable burgers. In addition, organic pot-pies, soups, sauces, and even baby food products cropped up and excelled. The natural, organic, and dietetic food segments had a combined annual growth of 20 percent in 1998, according to Hoover's, which predicted that "these foods will remain on the fringe for some time." Other industry analysts believe, however, that the growing number of organic products—more than 800 in 1998—and investment by mainstream companies demonstrates that organic products have found a permanent and significant niche.

Lynn Dornblaser, a leading food industry consultant, predicted in *American Demographics* that trends for 1999 and beyond will include a transition from low and nonfat foods to organic and all-natural selections together with an explosion of functional foods and mainstream herbal supplements. The focus will shift from fat and calorie consciousness to product enhancement and good taste as foods increasingly feature new ethnic flavors and added nutritional benefits. Supermarket products will shift from an emphasis on home meal replacement to all-in-one meal kits offering speed and convenience.

Although gourmet and specialty food items are increasingly available online, the Internet food market is not likely to revolutionize food retailing in the near future, according to Forrester Research, and it will represent less than 2 percent of consumer packaged goods revenues by 2003. Others, however, believe that online sales may provide a new frontier for global marketing and may join club stores, vending machines, and other venues as entirely new options for distributing food. Some industry analysts speculate that new products in the near future may be designed exclusively for Internet sales.

ORGANIZATION AND STRUCTURE

Food manufacturers and producers often introduce new products to meet changing or growing customer needs, to increase revenues by creating a food trend, or to accomplish both of these goals. Although many companies develop their own new products, some turn to outside operations to handle the task when they do not have the technology, expertise, or general resources to successfully produce new food products, according to Steve Berne in *Prepared Foods.* Berne also reports that companies may seek the assistance of test laboratories, market researchers, supply purveyors, and manufacturers.

Before new food products hit stores nationwide, producers usually test-market them in a limited geographical region. Companies monitor the success of the new products and determine whether they have market-staying or trend-setting power. If the products are deemed successful during the trial period, they then begin more extensive marketing. In order for new products to thrive once they are introduced, analysts note that companies must fortify them with a robust barrage of promotional strategies. Unless companies support new food products, they will never gain much attention from consumers, and if businesses let up on promoting new products prematurely, sales will start to flag and the new product will fade out of the market. Robert J. Thomas notes in *New Product Success Stories* that products succeed when they respond to the business environment and consumer demands at the time of their release and when they gain market acceptance through persistent promotion. After launching a new product, developers must track it—scrutinize the movement of the product and ascertain who buys it and why. Developers must also anticipate consumer reactions to the product and alter promotional campaigns to accommodate consumer response. *Brandweek* noted in a 1997 article that the market had been inundated "with poorly performing new products and line extensions earlier in the decade."

Among the various entities concerned with legislation related to new food products are the United States Department of Agriculture (USDA), the United States Food and Drug Administration (FDA), Center for Food Safety and Applied Nutrition, National Organic Standards Board, and an array of state, county, and municipal organizations that oversee the growing, production, and sales of foods. There are many trade organizations and groups such as The American Crop Protection Association and the Food Marketing Institute. Often, each commodity has a group concerned with lobbying and/or marketing efforts. The produce industry, for example, has its own organizations, including the International Fresh-cut Produce Association, The United Fresh Fruit and Vegetable Association, Texas Produce Association, Produce Marketing Association, Florida Fruit and Vegetable Association, Northwest Horticultural Council, and Western Growers Association protecting its interests and marketing its products nationally and regionally.

Perhaps the best example of industry oversight is found in the certification and monitoring of organic foods. As early as 1974, the USDA called for policies to govern the growing, processing, and marketing of organic foods, but no hard and fast rules resulted from these early exhortations. Yet, the USDA did provide a working definition: "organically grown food" refers to produce not treated with chemical pesticides or fertilizers, and "organically processed food" includes produce not treated with synthetic preservatives, according to William Breene in *Prepared Foods.* Farm organizations started certification programs throughout the country beginning in the 1970s and 1980s. In 1990, Congress finally passed legislation towards creating standards for certifying organic food. The Farm Act of 1990 decreed the establishment of the National Organic Standards Board, which tried to develop official standards for the organic foods industry. However, a host of certification agencies all over the country still bear the brunt of the certification task using standards they create. The USDA asked for public comment in December 1997, when it proposed new standards for organic food. As of 1999, the USDA had issued guidelines for the certification of organic meat and poultry but had not issued final regulations to establish standards for all organic products. Further complicating issues related to the standards were whether foods genetically engineered, irradiated, or grown in soil fertilized with sewage sludge could be considered organic.

CURRENT CONDITIONS

Manufacturers introduced fewer products in the late 1990s in response to consumer demand as well as a renewed focus on developing fewer products with longer staying power. Most new products are condiments, candy, and snacks. New food product introductions dropped 6 percent in 1997, according to a 1998 *American Demographics* article. In 1996 the number had dropped 20 percent—13,266 from 16,863 offerings in 1995—according to Lynn Dornblaser in *Prepared Foods.* However, the emphasis on convenient and healthy food continues. Producers introduced 2,000 reduced fat and fat-free food products in 1996—more than in any other year. With a slew of popular products such as the widening variety of home meal replacements on the market and thriving, food producers largely expanded or re-marketed existing lines and did not launch many revolutionary products in the mid- to late 1990s. A growing problem in 1997 and 1998 was dwindling shelf space in stores. Condiments, such as added interest in hot sauces and flavored mayonnaise in 1998, reflect this retrenchment.

New product introductions declined again in 1998 when 11,000 new products were introduced in the United States, an 11 percent reduction from the 13,000 introduced in 1997. Low-calorie and lowfat products began to decline in popularity in 1998, while organic and all-natural products showed significant gains. Meal kits and convenience foods continued to be dominant, while traditional "comfort" foods and indulgent desserts showed a resurgence. Sales of baking ingredients, condiments, and side dishes fell more than 10 percent in 1998, a reflection of greater reliance on meal kits and convenience foods.

Outside the United States, reduced fat products continued to expand in 1998, but a greater selection of nutritionally enhanced, or functional, foods was a dominant trend worldwide. Probiotic non-dairy foods containing beneficial organisms or substances to enhance normal function began to appear more widely in 1998. Cholesterol-reducing margarine, vitamin-fortified frozen vegetables, and even hard candy containing green tea were among the new offerings in Europe and Asia.

DINNERS, ENTREES, AND MIXES

The drive to create products that capture market share for convenience, and at least seemingly healthy food, often resulted in the release of hundreds of new dinner, entree, and mix offerings each year. In 1996 new dinner and entree releases declined by about 20 percent in contrast to 1995, when companies launched 748 new products in this category, according to Martin Friedman in *Prepared Foods.* Kim Charlet reports in *Prepared Foods* that only 597 were introduced in 1996. Charlet also writes that since 1991, sales of meal kits increased every year by over 50 percent. In 1995, this category brought in $4.2 billion, and analysts forecast sales to reach $4.8 billion in 1999. Leading this category in 1995 were frozen pizzas, with sales rising to $1.9 billion; analysts predicted sales to increase to $2.5 billion by 2000. However, most new products were merely extensions of existing lines of entrees, such as Stouffer, Lean Cuisine, Healthy Choice, and Budget Gourmet.

More companies tried to cash in on the booming frozen pizza market throughout the late 1990s. The frozen pizza category was valued at $2 billion in 1997. Kraft developed its Di Giorno Rising Crust Pizza and took it from $100 million in sales its first year to about $200 million in two years. The "rising crust" concept was popular. Tony's Pizza Service introduced its knock-off of the Di Giorno line with its Freschetta brand in 1997; sales totaled $29.2 million. Also, Kraft was successful with its Tombstone Oven Rising Pizza, a lower price pizza that rang up $35.1 million in sales in the late 1990s.

Food producers also expanded selections of prepared sandwiches. Sara Lee, Jimmy Dean, Ellio's Pockets, Chef America, ConAgra, and Owen's Country Sausages released portable convenience foods in 1995, according to Martin Friedman. Jimmy Dean also put pressure on Oscar Mayer's Lunchables by offering Tasteful Meals, which include meat, cheese, rolls, dessert, and condiments. Companies pushed this idea into prepared breakfast foods as Continental Mills launched Breakfast in a Biscuit; Swift-Eckerich brought out Breakfast Burritos; and Bob Evans introduced Breakfast Sandwiches. In addition, meat producers started tapping into the home meal replacement market. In 1997, Tyson Foods' Gourmet Selections line made its debut, offering a series of fresh refrigerated chicken dinners requiring about four minutes of microwave cooking.

Although interest in various international cuisines has remained strong, new food products in 1998 reflected an interest in more than the traditional favorites—Mexican and Italian. Interest in Asian, Mediterranean, and Middle Eastern food products increased in 1998 with food giants such as Quaker Oats and smaller manufacturers introducing new products. Ziyad Brothers Importing, for example, marketed Mediterranean foods such as tahini and hummus, while Quaker Oats expanded its Near East line with grains from that region, including bulgur and barley. Asian cuisine introductions were also evident in 1998 with such fare as sushi-at-home kits and quick fix noodle dishes. Thai cuisine also proved to be well represented with A Taste of Thai and Thai Kitchen introducing new products. Hormel introduced new Chinese, Greek, and Indian foods in 1997. Mexican foods remained popular with salsa besting ketchup as the nation's leading condiment and tortillas usurping the top spot in the baked goods category.

Smaller companies launched a host of new vegetarian burgers that showed staying power and continued to grow in popularity not only among vegetarians but also among health-conscious consumers. Gardenburger, Inc. had a 50 percent share of this market in 1998. Worthington Foods Inc. and its Morningstar Farms burger line was another market leader. Organic entree and dinner selections blossomed as well. Food producers such as Amy's Kitchen introduced a Cannelloni and Vegetables dinner plus Chicago Veggie burgers and Organic Pocketfuls Sandwiches to its line. Cedarlane Natural Foods also began offering low-fat vegetable sandwiches. Cuci's Pizza added a new selection to its pizza repertoire in 1996 with organic honey whole wheat crust pizza. In addition, A.C. Larocca Gourmet Pizzas began offering four meat-free pies featuring vegetable toppings with no artificial ingredients.

BABY FOOD

Due to the possibility of babies suffering harmful effects from farm chemical residue after consuming processed food treated with toxic chemicals, parents have grown more wary and cognizant of what they feed their children and how it is grown and processed. In addition, parents want healthy natural food for their babies, not food adulterated with unnecessary ingredients and treated with preservatives. Though Gerber Products once faced allegations of diluting its baby foods with water and starches and of adding sugar, the company announced in 1996 that it would discontinue this practice in order to maintain its strong hold on the baby food market. According to the *Wall Street Journal,* 121 of the company's 190 infant products will not include sugar or starch.

Health food companies launched products to compete with the traditional baby food producers. Growing Healthy and Earth's Best are two of the most prominent alternative producers, offering unalloyed organic foods. However, sales slumped for these new contenders and baby health food never fully caught on. Furthermore, even though the Center for Science in the Public Interest reported that Gerber diluted its products, the center failed to pique the public's interest, and Gerber retained 70 percent control of the market. Nonetheless, Earth's Best has had moderate but improving success, becoming the country's fourth leading producer of baby food. The key problem organic baby food producers face is offering competitive pricing. Yet, Gerber began to market vegetarian foods in its Veggie Recipes line in order to retain market domination.

PACKAGED PREPARED PRODUCE

A trend that started in the early 1990s and fared well by catering to both sensibilities of convenience and health consciousness was packaged salad. Its success led to the creation of numerous other new packaged produce releases. Since their introduction in 1994, salad kits continued to sell well throughout 1998 and 1999. One of the most successful food categories in the 1990s was packaged produce; new releases actually increased in 1996 instead of plummeting as they did in most other categories. Companies rolled out 552 new produce products, 115 of which consisted of fruit and 437 consisted of vegetables, according to Dana Blaesing in *Prepared Foods.* Although supermarkets traditionally offered many of these value-added products in order to promote or use up produce that neared its maximum storage limit, producers and distributors now want to participate in the market.

The leading product in the salad kits category also performed well in 1996, and, consequently, companies expanded their lines. Dole released a plethora of new salad kits given the success of the initial releases. Dole's Fresh Salad Mixes, Low Fat Complete Salads, and Salad Blends included Sunflower Ranch, American Classic, Caesar, and Spinach. These salad ensembles come with ready-to-eat greens and some also include condiments and dressing.

More companies also started catering to gourmet and organic food consumers in 1996. Fresh Express brought out its Spring Salad Mix with a blend of eight greens, and Earthbound Farm introduced its organic greens mix, The Ultimate Salad. Other companies marketing pre-packaged salads in the late 1990s included Misionero Vegetables, Capurro, and Ready Pac Produce. Some growers attempted to develop more convenient salads. J.C. Brock increased its bid to provide the most convenient salad kit with Salad 'n Seconds, a ready-to-eat salad complete with a fork. Tanimura & Antle went a bit further and expanded its Salad Time line in 1996, selling ready-to-eat salads in disposable bowls. Besides the traditional lettuce salads, companies like River Ranch Fresh Foods offer cole slaw kits containing shredded vegetables such as green and red cabbages, carrots or broccoli, and dressings, according to Lynn Dornblaser in *Prepared Foods*.

Vegetable producers churned out a larger array of packaged ready-to-use products as well. Zonie Sweets Super Sweet Corn from Arizona Tomato allows customers to enjoy sweet corn without any husking and cleaning because the corn comes ready to cook. CF Fresh debuted its Fresh Peeled Garlic, an organic product requiring no preparation. Georgia Sweets introduced its Fresh Cut Vidalia Onion Rings in 1995. Ready Pac also entered the prepared onion market, appealing to consumers' loathing of peeling and cutting onions with its No Tears Onion, which comes washed and diced. GoldMex Vegetables introduced Pepe's Green Beans in whole, cut, or sliced varieties. Companies also expanded the ready-to-eat snack vegetable market. Tanimura & Antle introduced Cool Cut Celery and Cool Cut Carrots, which come washed and cut with a container of ranch dip. Babe's Farm sought to provide convenient yet healthy prepared produce by introducing Zap-Tables, microwavable prepared baby vegetables. Babe's Farm also introduced Stirrific, a medley of unique stir fry vegetables. DeFranco & Sons also launched a microwavable corn product called Fresh Husked Corn.

In an effort to garner more fresh fruit sales, companies have begun to launch washed, sliced, and otherwise prepared fruits. For example, Fresh Express introduced Grape Escape—washed red seedless grapes removed from the stem in four ounce packages. Fresh World Farms brought out its Necta Fresh Pineapples in a few different varieties—whole cored, chunked, and sliced. Some producers also offered pre-peeled fruit. Fruit of Groveland introduced The Heart Garden Fresh Cut Fruit, providing an assortment of melons, as well as grapes and pineapple. Global Fresh and other companies began marketing Fresh Cut Apples with Dip, which includes slices of Granny Smith or Fuji apples and reduced fat caramel dip. Ready Pac Produce also introduced its ready-to-eat Fresh Melon Chunks featuring watermelon, cantaloupe, or honeydew.

DESSERTS

Food producers introduced approximately 100 new products in the dessert category in 1996. Of these new releases, gelatin accounted for 8, pudding for 27, and toppings for 65. Dornblaser attributes the influx of dessert toppings to the shoals of low-fat frozen desserts producers rolled out in 1995. However, not

all new toppings were designed for the health conscious: J.M. Smucker launched a Dove chocolate sauce and M&M/Mars added a milk chocolate/dark chocolate combination to the many chocolate toppings already on the market. On the other hand, companies such as ConAgra, Kraft, and Rich Products introduced fat-free whipped toppings—Reddi-wip fat free, Cool Whip Free, and Rich Products whipped topping in tubs and squeezable tubes, respectively. Furthermore, Bosco Products trimmed the fat from its chocolate syrup, making available a fat-free version. Hershey Foods also began offering some healthy chocolate syrups—fat-free double chocolate and chocolate mint. Hershey also marketed Special Dark syrup, a reduced fat yet semi-sweet chocolate syrup.

Morinaga Nutritional Foods introduced Mori-Nu Mates, dairy-free pudding products in lemon creme and cappuccino flavors. Instead of dairy products, these puddings use tofu. Natural Dairy Products launched the organic answer to ready-made pudding with its rice pudding. Brands such as SnackWell's and Healthy Choice continue to earn millions of dollars for their companies in part for their successful desserts. SnackWell's rolled out a fleet of reduced fat and fat-free desserts such as yogurt, ice cream, gelatins, puddings, baking mixes, candy, and cookies. Healthy Choice also offered low-fat and fat-free ice cream.

In 1998, however, the fat-free trend in dessert products began to reverse markedly. Puddings and gelatins declined in relation to 1997, but introductions of dessert toppings included an increased assortment of full-fat products. Sales of full-fat ice cream grew 10.3 percent to reach 41 percent of all ice cream sales, while sales of nonfat ice cream decreased 14.8 percent.

Two new sweeteners, Sunett and Splenda, which may have potential uses in a wide variety of dessert products, were approved for use in 1998. Reputed to taste better than aspartame—currently the most widely used artificial sweetener—they are undergoing testing and development in a wide variety of products. The most significant use of Sunett in 1998 was in Pepsi ONE, a carbonated beverage from Pepsico.

BAKED GOODS

Although there were new cookies, crackers, and other baked goods introduced in 1998, companies such as Pepperidge Farm repositioned existing products such as Goldfish crackers and Milano cookies as though they were new. Tortillas, in 1998, were the top bakery good on the market. In 1997, crackers were a

$2.7-billion food category, according to *Brandweek,* with cookies at $3.4 billion.

SNACK FOODS

When the FDA approved Procter & Gamble's Olestra fat-free substitute in 1996, an avalanche of reduced fat and fat-free chips emerged on the market. Frito-Lay offered Olean oil substitute products with one gram of fat, including Doritos and Ruffles. Procter & Gamble countered with Fat Free Pringles. Frito's Baked Lay's lead the salted snacks category in late 1997. According to the Snack Food Association, sales of "better-for-you" snacks remained stable or declined slightly in 1998, however, as consumers began to react against low-fat and low-calorie offerings and returned to traditional snacks.

NUTRACEUTICALS

A growing segment of the food industry expressed increased interest in courting the Baby Boomers, people aged 33 to 51. Nutraceuticals were thus introduced. Many of these products competed with pharmaceuticals and were food products designed to replace vitamins or other diet aids. Whether they were called "smart foods" or "functional foods," consumers spent $76 billion on these products in 1996, according to *American Demographics.* Augmented foods introduced in 1997 included Knox Nutrajoint; Uncle Ben's Calcium Plus Rice, which had calcium and vitamins added to it; and Campbell's Intelligent Cuisine, a prepared meal program introduced in January 1997 for adults with medical problems such as diabetes.

In 1998 functional foods were widely considered the fastest-growing category of new products, although federal labeling guidelines made the distinction between supplements and whole foods problematic. The Sage Group, a market research firm, states that between 2005 and 2010, the greatest market opportunities will exist for functional foods, not pill supplements, because consumers will prefer eating a few fortified foods and beverages to taking supplements that require an understanding of nutrition. Hain Pure Foods introduced a chicken broth with echinacea and zinc—both thought to boost immune function—which is the first food in the United States to contain herbal supplements. Kellogg's Ensemble line featured psyllium, which has been approved by the FDA as a cholesterol-lowering substance. General Nutrition Companies introduced a soy drink containing DHA, omega-3 fatty acids, and isoflavones—all claimed to support a variety of body functions. Omega Tech also introduced a line of DHA-enriched eggs.

INDUSTRY LEADERS

The lineup of large food conglomerates was shuffled in 1998 as a result of mergers and internal restructuring. According to Food Engineering, the largest food company in 1998 was Nestle, which had $45.38 billion in worldwide food and drink sales in 1998, followed by Philip Morris with $31.89 billion. When regulation of the tobacco industry began to heat up, the tobacco companies purchased stable food companies, according to Hoover's *Food Snapshot.* Philip Morris purchased Kraft Foods, for example, and RJR Nabisco bought Nabisco Holdings, the leading firm in cookies and crackers. Dominant food companies were involved in marketing other products as well. Unilever, the third-largest food conglomerate with $24.17 billion in 1998 sales, led the margarine, tea, and ice cream markets. Brand name foods under the Unilever umbrella included Lipton, Popsicle, and Country Crock.

The Pillsbury Co., a subsidiary of Diageo, led the food industry with 181 new products introductions in 1996, according to Steve Dwyer in *Prepared Foods.* Between 1991 and 1996, new products accounted for 13 percent of the company's sales and more than 21 percent of 1996 sales were from products less than 5-years-old. These products also bring in more than $50 million per year for Pillsbury. Moreover, 75 percent of the products introduced since 1991 have remained on the market. Since the 1970s, Pillsbury has been at the front of the convenience food movement, starting out by developing microwave dinners, baking mixes, and refrigerated bakables.

ConAgra, Inc., based in Nebraska, was the top frozen food producer in the United States in 1998, with sales of $24 billion and 80,000 employees. The company produced products for agriculture as well as prepared food items under various brand names such as Hunt's, Healthy Choice, Wesson, Rosarita, La Choy, Chun King, Peter Pan, Knott's Berry Farm, Orville Redenbacher's, Armour, Butterball, Hebrew National, and Van Camp's. Its Healthy Choice line had grown significantly with an estimated 460 line extensions as of 1998. ConAgra also formed the CAG Functional Foods Division to take advantage of projected growth in that category.

Amy's Kitchen is a leading producer and marketer of vegetarian and organic cuisine. Based in Petaluma, California, the company offers all natural organic versions of standard frozen fare such as macaroni and cheese, pot pies, and vegetarian shepherd's pie, plus an array of Mexican foods and pizza products.

AMERICA AND THE WORLD

Many U.S. food trends and products originate elsewhere in the world. In many Asian cultures, diet and health are considered integrally linked, and herbal enhancements are routinely incorporated into everyday cuisine. Unique Japanese functional products include chewing gums and soft drinks that claim anti-allergy properties, a throat candy packaged in antibacterial film bags, and health/beauty drinks that contain collagen—an ingredient used in external skin-care products.

The number of new food products launched in Europe by 2001 will increase by 15 percent, according to market research firm Datamonitor. As in the United States, desire for convenience or indulgence combine with a concern for quality and health. In the United Kingdom, a cultural preference for snacking is creating a greater market for breakfast bars and other "on-the-go" foods. In Europe, functional foods include vitamin-fortified frozen vegetables from Agro, a division of Unilever, and "smart fat" Maval yogurt that contains appetite-suppressing palm oil extract. Spanish manufacturer Union Tostadora produces lines of coffee enriched with fiber, vitamins, and ginseng. According to analyst David Jago and others, European interest in natural, organic, and artisanal food is developing in tandem with increasing ethical concerns about animal welfare and environmentally responsible food production.

FURTHER READING

Berne, Steve. "Options in Outsourcing." *Prepared Foods,* 15 April 1996.

Blaesing, Dana. "For The Third Year in a Row, with Branded Produce a Close Second." *Prepared Foods,* April 1997.

———. "Packaged Produce Products Prevail." *Prepared Foods,* 15 April 1996.

———. "Processed Meat and Poultry Offered Answers for Consumers Seeking Healthy, Alternative or Easy-to-Prepare Products." *Prepared Foods,* April 1997.

"'Certified Organic By' Labeling on Meat and Poultry Products." *Federal Register,* 12 April 1999. Available from http://frwebgate.access.gpo.gov.

Charlet, Kim. "Baby Bust." *Prepared Foods,* April 1997.

———. "Entrees." *Prepared Foods,* April 1997.

Chun, Janean, et al. "Heads Up: 1998's Hottest Trends." *Entrepreneur,* December 1997.

Dornblaser, Linda. "New Products." *Prepared Foods,* April 1997.

———. "New Products Take Steep '96 Tumble." *Prepared Foods,* February 1997.

———. "Pasta Garnishes More Meals." *Prepared Foods,* 15 April 1996.

———. "Pudding on Variety." *Prepared Foods,* April 1997.

Dwyer, Steve. "Hey, What's the Big Idea? Pillsbury Knows!" *Prepared Foods,* April 1997.

"Evolving Product Popularity Changes the Pace of Food Manufacturing." *Food Engineering,* April 1999.

"Food Marketing." *Wall Street Journal,* 4 June 1998.

Friedman, Martin. "Entrees Make Grand Entrance." *Prepared Foods,* 15 April 1996.

Hennessy, Terry. "Battle Royal: From New Immigration Laws to Labeling Requirements, a Flood of Legislative Issues Has the Produce Business in Turmoil." *Progressive Grocer,* April 1998.

"Industry Surveys: Food & Nonalcoholic Beverages." *Standard & Poor's Industry Surveys,* 27 November 1997.

"Innovations from the USA; Food Product Innovations." *Food Engineering International,* 1 April 1999.

Jago, David. "Food Products Find New Horizon; Food Trends." *Food Engineering International,* 1 April 1999.

Jago, David, and Lynn Dornblaser. "New Products: Japan; Go East, Young Man." *Prepared Foods,* April 1999. Available from http://www.prepared foods.com/1999/9904.

Kahn, Barbara E., and Leigh McAlister. "Grocery Revolution: The New Focus on the Consumer." New York: Addison-Wesley, 1997.

Martin, Kathryn. "The World's Top 100 Food & Beverage Companies." *Food Engineering,* December 1998.

McMath, Robert M. "Don't Bite Off More Than You Can Chew." *American Demographics,* March 1998.

Messenger, Bob. "Top 10 Food & Beverage Trends of 1998." *Food Processing,* January 1998.

Miller, Cyndee. "This Could Be the Year of the Roasted Garlic." *Marketing News,* 6 June 1994.

Mogelonsky, Marcia."Product Overload?"*American Demographics,*August 1998.

"New Products: North America; Health Benefits Included." *Prepared Foods,* April 1999. Available from http://www.preparedfoods.com/1999/9904.

Newton, Nell. *Food Snapshot,* 1998. Available from http://www.hoovers.com.

O'Donnell, Claudia D." Supplements Ignite Healthy Inspiration." *Prepared Foods,* November 1998.

Pawlosky, Mark. "Food: Health Food for Babies Is Slow to Grow." *Wall Street Journal,* 14 June 1995.

Perman, Stacy. "The Joy of Not Cooking." *Time,* 1 June 1998.

Stein Wellner, Alison. "Eat, Drink, and Be Healed." *American Demographics,* March 1998.

Ten Kate, Nancy. "New and Improved. " *American Demographics,* March 1998.

Thomas, Robert J. *New Product Success Stories.* New York: John Wiley & Sons, Inc., 1995.

Thompson, Stephanie. "Brandweek's Marketers of the Year: Geralyn Breig—Pepperidge Farm." *Brandweek/Superbrands '98,* 20 October 1997.

———. "Brandweek's Marketers of the Year: Mary Kay Haben—Kraft Pizza Co." *Brandweek/Superbrands '98,* 20 October 1997.

Timpe, Jennifer. "The 20-Minute Dinner Dash." *Prepared Foods,* April 1999. Available from http://www.preparedfoods .com/1999/9904.

"Trend Central." *American Demographics,* February 1999.

"USDA Tightens Organic Labeling." *Chemical Week,* 20 May 1998.

—Karl Heil, updated by Cameron McLaughlin

NOISE CONTROL
AND TECHNOLOGY

Noise pollution is endemic in modern society. Anti-noise technology, also known as active noise control, active noise cancellation, or active structural-acoustic control, is a promising approach to coping with the overload of objectionable noise. This young field utilizes speakers that silence disturbing noises by emitting an opposing noise. If the device works correctly, the new sound and the offensive one will have wavelengths that counter each other so that nothing is audible. Noise control technology holds great promise in improving sound transmission and perception in mobile telephones and other communication devices, as well as in reducing stress inducing and health threatening sounds in loud environments.

Technologies are needed to cope with various types of noise, particularly those connected with aircraft, trains, and motor vehicle traffic. Some solutions are of the more passive type, along the lines of soundproofing. Redesigning passenger compartments in cars and airplanes in order to cut down on noise for their occupants is an example of such methods, as is finding new materials effective in blocking noise within buildings and residences. Active noise cancellation technology can also be effective in such situations. An example is Barry Controls Aerospace's Active Tuned Mass Absorbers (ATMAs), which resonate at the same frequency as the engine compressors in a DC-9 airplane and have the effect of reducing cabin noise in the aircraft.

Airplanes and helicopters are among the most serious sources of noise in the United States, in urban settings and even in wilderness areas of national parks. Noise regulations adopted in the early 1990s stipulated that older planes must be modified and new aircraft must be designed with quieter engines by 1999. Lucent Technologies and Sikorsky Aircraft, in conjunction with the Naval Research Laboratory, are studying the use of smart materials to reduce helicopter rotor noise. *Flight International* reports that Bell Helicopter Textron Inc. is developing a noise-reduction plan in its Quiet Cruise system to meet new federal guidelines for aircraft that fly over national parks.

Motor vehicles of various kinds also contribute to the noise problem. Proposed solutions include highway barriers of concrete, dirt, and even waterfalls to muffle noise. The development and use of new road building materials, such as porous asphalt, is hoped to reduce the din of traffic.

Household appliances and power tools also add to environmental noise. A combination of reengineering, noise regulations, and anti-noise protection, such as headsets, are among the ways being used to tone down the clatters, whirrs, whines, and buzzing produced in residential areas. At Owens Corning, for example, acoustic engineers record the sounds of an appliance going through its operating cycles and then use different sound control systems to modify the noises. After the sounds are digitally edited, they are played to humans to get feedback on which have been most successfully quieted. Using this method—along with computer simulation—as part of the prototyping process, saves half the time needed to develop a noise control system for an appliance.

BACKGROUND AND DEVELOPMENT

Anti-noise technology is far from new. In 1936 Paul Lueg patented one of the first working active noise control systems. His process of silencing sound oscillation received patents in the United States and Germany. Another pioneer in anti-noise technology was H.F. Olson, whose 1953 article on electronic sound absorbers was published in the *Journal of the Acoustical Society of America.*

The Noise Control Act of 1972 was passed to protect Americans from noise that threatened their health and well being. It was amended by the Quiet Communities Act of 1978, Public Law 95-609, which required the administrator of the Environmental Protection Agency (EPA) to disseminate educational materials on the effects of noise on public health and the most effective means of noise control; to conduct or finance specified research projects on noise control; to administer a nationwide Quiet Communities Program designed to assist local governments in controlling noise levels; and to provide technical assistance to state and local governments in implementing noise control programs.

The Airport Noise and Capacity Act of 1990, Subtitle D of Public Law 101-508, required the establishment of a national aviation noise policy and issuance of regulations governing airport noise and access restrictions for stage two aircraft (weighing under 75,000 pounds). The Act provided for the phase out of older, noisier planes and for noise reduction to specified levels for new aircraft to go into effect in 1999, and it set civil penalties and reporting requirements for aircraft operators. It prohibited operation of certain domestic or imported civil subsonic turbojet aircraft unless such aircraft complied with stage three noise levels. Subtitle B of the same law, known as the Aviation Safety and Capacity Expansion Act of 1990, called for environmental reviews before air traffic would be rerouted during an airport expansion.

The Office of Noise Abatement and Control Establishment Act of 1996 sought to reinstate the EPA's role in noise control after funding for it was eliminated in 1982. The primary duty of the office would be to coordinate federal noise abatement activities with state and local activity and other public and private agencies. It would also be responsible for updating and developing new noise standards, providing technical assistance to local communities, and promoting research and education on the impact of noise pollution. Initially, the Office of Noise Abatement and Control would study the physiological effects of airport noise in major metropolitan areas and surrounding communities in order to propose new measures to combat the impact of aircraft noise.

The National Park Scenic Overflight Concession Act of 1997 set guidelines for air traffic over national parks in order to eliminate intrusive noise. It proposed rules for use of quiet aircraft and minimum flight altitudes within national parks, flight-free zones, and, if necessary, flight bans to prevent commercial air tours in a park to preserve, protect, or restore the natural quiet of the park. It also created a schedule for any commercial air tour operator operating within a national park to convert the operator's fleet to quiet aircraft.

Because of the January 1, 1999, deadline for implementation of restrictions on aircraft noise, much activity in the aviation field was directed toward meeting the new noise control requirements, called the Stage III rules. Older airplanes, such as DC-8s and 727s, would be grounded if they weren't retrofitted with "hush kits" to decrease noise. The Boeing Company and Raisbeck Engineering, both of Seattle, Washington, were two companies developing solutions to the problem of retrofitting older aircraft and

---

Trends **KEEP IT DOWN OVER THERE!**

Noise concerns are a large factor in the opposition of residents and citizens to airport expansions. Different kinds of noise control and airport management may help alleviate some of the problems.

For example, a June 1997 Federal Aviation Administration study showed that by changing the angle of a new runway at the New Orleans International Airport, the amount of noise experienced by nearby neighborhoods could be reduced while providing increased traffic handling capability to the airport.

According to the *Times-Picayune,* this study will be used to create national standards for runway alignment that could help with airport expansions across the United States. By laying the runway away from a neighborhood, the airplanes would not fly directly over residents. The proposed runway at the New Orleans airport would be eight degrees off parallel from the existing runway, a setup currently against FAA regulation, but the FAA feels only minor modifications need to be made to handle an airport runway system of that design.

Residents still feel it is not a real solution to the problem, since the airplanes are only a fraction off their original path. Though the airplanes may not be directly over their driveways, they can still be heard quite loudly. The best solution according to residents is not to build a runway at all.

Other ideas for reducing airport noise include holding aprons for planes waiting to take off, and installation of computer tracking systems to monitor the flight paths and noise levels of all air traffic at individual airports.

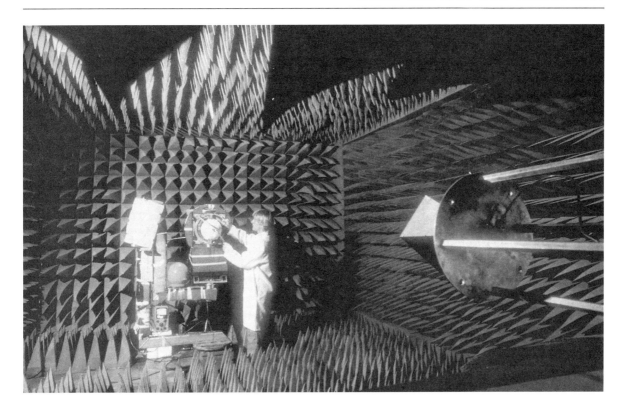

Scientist testing in an acoustic laboratory. (Digital Stock.)

redesigning new ones to bring them into compliance with the Stage III regulations. In 1996 Raisbeck recertified the Boeing 727 to meet federal requirements. In January 1997 the Federal Aviation Administration (FAA) approved the installation of Lord Corporation's NVX Active Noise and Vibration Control System in the DC-9 Series of aircraft, making it the first active noise and vibration control system to receive FAA approval on a large commercial jet.

CURRENT CONDITIONS

In the late 1990s, the noise control industry was still in its infancy, so much work was being done in the research and development area. The difficulties lay in trying to effectively block various sources of noise moving at different speeds and frequencies. Until that can be accomplished, the noise from a source such as moving traffic cannot be truly dampened. Until technology is widespread, cost is also a factor. While household appliances and products, such as dishwashers, are noisy, consumers may not be willing to pay the additional cost to control the sound.

Technology has blocked everyday noises—such as lawn mowers, leaf blowers, and weed whackers—

with the use of headphones. Noise Control Technologies produces headphones that are sold through retail outlets such as Sharper Image. Bose Corporation, based in Framingham, Massachusetts, manufacturers high-end headphones that were used on the space shuttle.

By 1999 hundreds of Boeing 727 and DC-9s had been fitted with hush kit mufflers. For the European Union (EU), however, this was not an aggressive enough step toward noise muffling. In February 1999 the European Parliament approved a ban on airplanes that use hush kits. In response, the United States threatened to ban Concorde flights into the country.

In the late 1990s there were more companies in the noise control industry than at the beginning of the decade. Firms such as Acoustical Solutions Inc.; Empire Acoustical Systems; Industrial Noise Control, Inc.; Ultimate Technologies, Inc. (UTI); Noise Cancellation Technologies, Inc.; and Andrea Electronics Corp. introduced a diverse variety of devices and materials designed to dampen noise pollution. Products ranged from acoustical windows, diffusors, and foams to UTI's telecommunications product that allows phone users to have a private conversation, even when other people are present.

INDUSTRY LEADERS

Noise Cancellation Technologies, Inc. (NCT) is a leading provider of noise and vibration reduction technology, and it is one of the most innovative companies. The firm held rights to 281 inventions as of mid-1997, including applications in active noise reduction, active vibration reduction, active mufflers, active headsets, and multimedia audio. NCT has executive offices and product development facilities in Linthicum, Maryland; sales and marketing offices in Stamford, Connecticut; product development and marketing facilities in Cambridge, England; and marketing and technical support offices in Tokyo. In 1998 NCT reported revenue of $3.3 million, a decrease of $2.4 million over the previous year.

The company uses patented active sound and signal wave management technology to reduce noise and improve sound quality. Noise Cancellation Technologies' business focuses on headsets, communications, microphones, audio systems, and fans. Product innovations include NoiseBuster and NoiseBuster Extreme! headphones, which won a Discover Award for Technological Innovation in 1994 and the Innovations '96 award, respectively. Noise Cancellation Technologies also developed Earpeace active noise control technology, used in in-flight passenger entertainment systems, and ProActive industrial hearing protection. Its ClearSpeech technology removes background noise from speech and transmits signals through telephones and radios, and it holds promise in the development of speech recognition programs. Its patented flat panel transducer technology creates a surround sound effect without the use of traditional speakers and is being produced and marketed as the automotive Top Down Surround Sound (TDSS) system with Johnson Controls, Inc. With other business partners, Noise Cancellation Technologies is working to develop markets for industrial and vehicular mufflers, technologies for quieting vehicle and aircraft cabins, and noise reduction methods for air ducts and power transformers.

Another industry leader and maker of noise cancellation headsets is Andrea Electronics, based in Long Island City, New York. Its product line is led by its best-selling NC-50 PC headset, which uses patented technology to reduce the distortion associated with many voice activated PC applications. Other devices include the Active Noise Reduction car phone and the Active Noise Cancellation near-field microphone. In 1997 Andrea introduced the QuietWare 1000 anti-noise stereo headset for the computer market. Andrea Electronics's key customers and resellers include IBM, Microsoft Corporation, Kurzweil, Dragon Systems, and NEC. In 1999 Andrea Electronics announced that it had received a patent for a head-mounted microphone. The company's products are used in pay phones and commercial, industrial, and military equipment. Andrea reported first-quarter 1999 revenues of $4.7 million.

RESEARCH AND TECHNOLOGY

Controlling the noise from jet engines is a major problem, but engineers at Georgia Tech may have found one possible solution, according to Mark Hodges in *Technology Review*. By filling a liner with ceramic beads of assorted sizes and wrapping this liner around the engine, both low- and high-frequency noises were lessened, and the ceramic beads were able to withstand the high temperatures generated by the engine. This discovery could be used to reduce the noise of commercial jet liners traveling at supersonic speeds.

Pennsylvania State University's Center for Acoustics and Vibration, NASA, and the Anti-Vibration Control Division of PCB Piezotronic announced the creation of a self-regulating vibration absorber that tracks changes in the frequency of undesirable noises and adjusts itself in response. This invention will have applications for noise control in industrial machinery, cars, and household appliances.

Professor Dimitri Papamoschou of the University of California, Irvine, created a new technology to quiet supersonic jets, such as the Concorde, which have been permitted to land at only a few airports throughout the world because of the amount of noise they produce. His invention, the Mach Wave Eliminator, reduces the exhaust noise output of these aircraft.

FURTHER READING

"The Active Assault on Cabin Noise." *Business and Commercial Aviation,* September 1995.

Andrea Electronics Corporation, 1998. Available from http://www.andreaelectronics.com/news.html.

"Andrea Electronics Corporation Announces First Quarter 1999 Results," 28 April 1999. Available from http://www.andreaelectronics.com/pr4-28-99.

"California Professor Reduces Supersonic Jet Noise." *Flight International,* 29 January 1997.

Chamberlain, Gary. "Vibration Absorber That Tunes Itself in the Works." *Design News,* 7 April 1997.

"Cincinnati Airport Gets New Aircraft Tracking System to Deal with Noise Complaints." *The Cincinnati Enquirer*, 18 July 1997.

"Company Releases New Anti-Noise Headset for Computer Use." *Newsday*, 30 June 1997.

Cox, Jeff. "Good Vibes Noise-Control Gizmos Go for Quieter World." *Denver Post*, 17 May 1998.

"FAA Says New Runway at New Orleans Airport Could be Built at an Angle to Reduce Noise Pollution; Residents Remain Unconvinced." *The Times-Picayune*, 25 June 1997.

Hodges, Mark. "The Anti-Music of the Aerospheres." *Technology Review*, January-February, 1998.

"Illinois Airport Gets New Holding Apron Designed to Reduce Noise for Nearby Residents." *The Chicago Tribune*, 17 July 1997.

Isidore, Chris. "Leaders in Air Industry Disagree about Impact of New Noise Regulations." *Journal of Commerce*, 16 February 1999.

Lavitt, Michael O. "Active Absorbers Cancel Aircraft Engine Noise." *Aviation Week & Space Technology*, 24 February 1997.

Masi, C.G. "Putting 'Quiet Shoes' on Household Appliances." *Research & Development Magazine*, November 1996.

"New Technology Quiets Supersonic Jets." *Tulsa World*, 5 January 1997.

Noise Cancellation Technologies, Inc. 1998. Available from http://www.nct-active.com.

"Noise Cancellation Technologies Reports 1998 Results," 31 March 1999. Available from http://www.nct-active.com/pr3_13_99.

"Noise Control Technology Now More Affordable." *Air Conditioning, Heating, and Refrigeration News*, February 1994.

The Noise Pollution Clearinghouse, 1998. Available from http://www.nonoise.org/.

"Quieter Helicopters Designed for National Parks." *Flight International*, 29 January 1997.

Staples, Susan L. "Human Response to Environmental Noise: Psychological Research and Public Policy." *American Psychologist*, February 1996.

Thomas, Jennifer, and Dave Hirschman. "U.S. Could Outlaw Concorde if EU Proceeds with Ban on Hush-Kitted Planes." *The Commercial Appeal (Memphis, TN)*. 18 February 1999.

"Writer Reviews New Noise-Reduction Headphones on Airplane." *The Buffalo News*, 11 April 1997.

—Joan Giglierano,
updated by Katherine Wagner and Marinell James

NUTRITIONAL SUPPLEMENTS

In May 1999, *Food Chemical News* reported that sales of nutritional supplements in the United States via the Internet rose from $12 million in 1997 to $40 million in 1998; the overall U.S. market for nutritional supplements was $13.6 billion. *Success* magazine predicted that the nutritional supplement market would reach $100 billion by the year 2005. The overall nutritional supplement market was growing at about 20 percent annually. Some of the fastest growing sectors of the industry are mineral supplements, animal feed, nutraceuticals, and phytochemicals. According to the Consumer Healthcare Products Association, approximately 70 percent of Americans were using vitamin and mineral supplements, and 25 percent were using herbal products.

The global vitamin market has been estimated at a total value of $3.3 billion—nearly half of that is the animal feed market. International leaders include vitamin manufacturers Roche, BASF, and Takeda. Sales are projected to increase about 10-15 percent annually. The retail market for botanical products was $4 billion in 1998, up from $839 million in 1991, and was growing at about 18 percent each year. Nutraceutical sales are expected to be about $12 billion by the year 2001. Private labels accounted for the highest volume of sales. Vitamins are also being placed in a variety of products, including skin moisturizers. Lancome markets a revitalizing eye treatment with vitamin E, and Avon markets facial treatment capsules with vitamin C.

The basis for the growth of nutritional supplements is because of the movement of products from health food stores to chain supermarkets and drug stores, increased advertising and more aggressive marketing, and the growing value of the herb market. Based on studies done during the late 1990s, people are more likely to treat symptoms with supplements prior to consulting a doctor, a benefit primarily due to increased information. Aging "baby-boomers" are generally well-informed and consume nutritional supplements for health maintenance/disease prevention, to reduce dependence on expensive prescription drugs, and to slow the process of aging. About 40 percent of American adults take vitamins, and 73 percent of regular users are over the age of 35. This segment is expected to grow by 23 million by the year 2007. About 30 percent of all adults take vitamin E, making it the second-most consumed vitamin after vitamin C. Furthermore, 70 percent of all doctors recommend taking nutritional supplements, and 80 percent of all doctors take some kind of vitamin supplement.

ORGANIZATION AND STRUCTURE

Nutritional supplements are produced by private manufacturers, as well as major drug and chemical companies. The *Thomas Register of American Manufacturers* lists 111 vitamin companies, 44 mineral dietary supplement producers, and 12 crude botanical drug companies. Also, there were 1,636 food product firms involved with supplements. The American Herbal Products Association (AHPA) is a national trade association that includes among its members thousands of companies that are importers, growers, manufacturers, and distributors of therapeutic herbs and herbal products. The AHPA was founded in 1983 and moved to Washington, DC in 1996 to establish a stronger relationship with the regulatory agencies.

Phytochemicals overlap the vitamin field and are defined as plant substances that are used as food fortifiers and dietary supplements. They include a wide variety of substances, including garlic, I3C, spices, soy, and herbal teas. The phytochemical market was estimated at $1.5 billion in 1996 and growing at a rate of 8-10 percent.

Nutraceuticals are compounds that have been scientifically proven to have health benefits. The market is loosely defined as foods that promote health or medical benefits, including disease prevention. The market is defined very broadly, making it hard to estimate its value and scope. Decision Resources, mentioned by Feliza Mirasol in *Chemical Market Reporter,* defines the category as "supplements that are ingested as tablets, capsules, powders, soft gels, gelcaps, or liquids, not conventional foods or products intended as the sold item in a meal or diet." Other firms, such as Find/SVP, define nutraceuticals as "processed food and beverages promoted and purchased for their medicinal properties," and *Nutrition Business Journal* defines the category as "all foods consumed for health reasons." Leading products in the market include soy isoflavones, tocotrienols, lutein, lycopene, ginkgo biloba, and St. John's Wort. Other popular nutraceuticals are creatine monohydrate, androsteniodene (andro), DHA (omega-3 fatty acid from fish), Peptidase, and calcium citrate maleate.

An article in *Chemical Market Reporter* projected growth as high as 50 percent for the U.S. nutraceuticals market. Decision Resources, a firm quoted in the same article, expected the market to reach $4.6 billion by 2003. The European market was expected to grow even faster, to $1.6 billion, showing growth of 52 percent.

Historically marketed through health food stores, direct mail, and network marketing, nutritional food supplements were also distributed through retail stores, pharmacies, discount stores, catalogs, or multilevel marketing (MLM) in the 1990s. The thousands of Kmart, Target, and Wal-Mart stores regularly selling nutritional supplements began installing displays adjacent to the pharmacies to expand herbal lines. Other chain stores such as Sam's Club and Costco installed pharmacies or nutritional supplement centers to take advantage of the booming market. With the visibility gained through chain stores, the relatively obscure herbals market caught the attention of many large over-the-counter (OTC) brand companies. Bayer Corporation, among others, is using extensive marketing efforts as well as nationally-known and trusted brand name recognition to attract nonusers to its line of herbal products.

INDUSTRY REGULATION

The Consumer Healthcare Products Association states that "Dietary supplements are considered a subset of foods under federal law and are regulated by the Food and Drug Administration (FDA) pursuant to the U.S. Food, Drug, and Cosmetic Act. The FDA has the authority to take action against any dietary supplement product found to be unsafe or making unsubstantiated or unapproved drug claims." The agency can also take action against supplements presenting significant risk of illness or injury. In addition, the Nutrition Labeling and Education Act of 1990 mandated that no health claims be allowed on food labels or advertisements unless the FDA found "significant scientific agreement" for such claims. The U.S. Pharmacopoeia (USP), a nonprofit group, was established to test supplements and assure compliance with scientific standards.

Informative point-of-purchase displays and the ability to make general claims about products were enabled by the 1994 Dietary Supplement Health and Education Act (DSHEA). The Act defines dietary supplements—vitamins, minerals, and herbs—and the limits of information about them. A supplement must contain a premeasured amount that is in the form of a soft gel, powder, tablet, capsule, or liquid. DSHEA also permits substantiated, truthful, non-misleading statements on labels and in advertising.

The limited regulatory framework established under DSHEA has been widely criticized. Companies have avoided the extensive testing requirements of over-the-counter drugs by distributing their products as supplements. The FDA's vague definitions found within the dietary supplement category have prompted numerous manufacturers to challenge the 1994 Act. The FDA treats herbs as a food, which means they do not need to be proven effective if they are safe. In 1995 the vitamin supplement industry was not heavily regulated because vitamins were considered neither a food nor a drug, and few standards regarded truth in advertising.

In late 1998, the Federal Trade Commission (FTC) issued advertising guidelines for the first time for the dietary supplement industry. The FTC also took legal action against seven manufacturers for claims made for products such as "Vaegra," a take-off on Viagra that could supposedly cure impotence, and a shark cartilage product that claimed it could cure cancer, arthritis, and circulatory problems. The Commission also targeted several weight-loss products. The FTC's advertising guidelines were posted on the FTC Web site on November 18, 1998 and also sent to industry trade associations. The guidelines essentially dictate that supplement claims be truthful, not misleading, and

Pioneer   HANS VON EULER-CHELPIN, 1873-1964
FERMENTATION AND THE START OF AN INDUSTRY

Hans Karl Simon August von Euler-Chelpin was born in Ausburg in the Bavarian region of Germany on February 15, 1873. His scientific roots ran deep—his mother was related to the Swiss mathematician Leonhard Euler.

After his early education in Munich, Wurzburg, and Ulm, he entered the Munich Academy of Painting in 1891 intending to become an artist. The problems of pigmentation led him to change his professional interest to science, and in 1893, enrolled at the University of Munich to study physics with Max Planck. His post-doctoral work in physical chemistry in 1896 and 1897 was undertaken after Euler-Chelpin received his doctorate in 1895 from the University of Berlin. Recognition came early to Euler-Chelpin—he received the Linblom Prize from Germany in 1898.

Euler-Chelpin's interests eventually shifted to organic chemistry, particularly in the area of fermentation. By 1910, he was able to present the fermentation process and enzyme chemistry into a systematic relationship with existing chemical knowledge. His book on the subject, *The Chemistry of Enzymes,* was first published in 1910 and again in several later editions.

After World War I, Euler-Chelpin began his research into the chemistry of enzymes, particularly in the role they played in the fermentation process. Apart from tracing phosphates through the fermentation sequence, he detailed the chemical makeup of cozymaze, a non-protein constituent involved in cellular respiration.

In 1929 Euler-Chelpin was awarded the Nobel prize in chemistry, which he shared with Arthur Harden "for their investigations on the fermentation of sugar and of fermentative enzymes." The presenter of the award noted that fermentation was "one of the most complicated and difficult problems of chemical research."

Also in 1929, Euler-Chelpin became the director of the Vitamin Institute and Institute of Biochemistry at the University of Stockholm, which was owned in part by the Rockefeller Foundation. Although he retired from teaching in 1941, he continued research for the remainder of his life.

Euler-Chelpin was awarded the Grand Cross for Federal Services with Star from Germany in 1959. He also received numerous honorary degrees from universities in Europe and America. He held memberships in Swedish science associations, as well as many foreign professional societies. He is the author of more than 1,100 research papers and several books. Euler-Chelpin died on November 6, 1964, in Stockholm, Sweden.

that advertisers be able to back those claims up with research. They also explain what kind of claims supplement manufacturers can and cannot make. Action taken by the FTC was in part due to the industry's rapid growth during the late 1990s, and also due to confusion on the part of supplement manufacturers after the Dietary Supplement health and Education Act of 1994 limited the FDA's authority to regulate the industry.

Maintaining compliance with regulations is important since the nutritional supplement industry is often under scrutiny. The Council For Responsible Nutrition (CRN) is a trade association representing over 80 manufacturers, distributors, and other companies in the nutritional supplements industry. It acts as a liaison between supplement manufacturers and the FTC, the FDA, and other governmental and regulatory agencies. The CRN asserts that the industry voluntarily stops the sale of unsafe products.

BACKGROUND AND DEVELOPMENT

Several companies in the food supplement industry originated from the founders' responses to physi-

cal adversity or the personal discovery of a new product, and these companies then grew phenomenally through multilevel marketing. For example, as the result of curing a stomach ulcer with capsicum, a spicy red pepper powder, Eugene Hughes and his wife began making gelatin filled red cayenne capsules and selling them to local health food stores in the mid-1960s. He added chaparral, for digestion, and golden seal, a natural antibiotic. In 1972 they founded Hughes' Development Corporation, which became Nature's Sunshine Products.

After Doug Grant recovered from a fall off a scaffold in 1989, which left him paralyzed from the waist down, he researched enzyme nutrition and developed and patented a process for the improved cellular delivery of nutrients. Although he was told he would never walk again, he fully recovered with the help of his product, won a gold medal for weightlifting, and formed Infinity2 to market an enzyme-activated nutritional system in 1993.

In the 1970s and 1980s, there was a resurgence of interest in herbal remedies in the United States. Among the early proponents of vitamins and micronutrients was Hans von Euler-Chelpin. More than 50 percent of all pharmaceuticals were made from natural sources or synthetic analogs of natural products. Beginning in the mid-1990s, an increasing number of physicians started recognizing the medicinal value of herbs and foods in curing ailments. In 1995, U.S. consumption of vitamins as food additives was 11,000 metric tons.

Nutrition drinks and energy bars also became popular in the mid-1990s. "Boost," by Mead Johnson Nutritionals debuted as an energy drink for active adults without the time to eat properly. Together, Re-Source, Ensure, and Boost represent the leading liquid nutritional supplements, a category that has grown to account for $330 million in retail sales.

Rapidly growing sectors of the nutritional supplement market have been mineral supplements, single vitamins (especially vitamins C and E), cod liver and fish oils, smaller niche products, and most recently, herbs. After a college student died from taking Ultimate Xphoria, an herbal supplement also sold under the brand name Herbal Ecstacy, the FDA warned against herbal ephedrine products that mimicked the street drug Ecstacy. Herbal ephedrine products, used for weight loss or relief of nasal and bronchial conditions, were exempted from the warning. In addition, in 1996 the FDA required all enriched foods such as pastas, breads, and cereals to contain folic acid, a trace B vitamin, in hopes of preventing some 2,500 disabling birth defects annually.

CURRENT CONDITIONS

On January 6, 1999, another resource for the nutritional supplements industry opened. The Office of Dietary Supplements (ODS), part of the National Institutes of Health (NIH), launched its new International Bibliographic Information on Dietary Supplements (IBIDS) database. The database will include published, international, scientific literature free of charge via the ODS Web site. The ODS hopes the site will assist scientists and the public in finding credible, scientific information on dietary supplements, and it was specifically mandated in the original Dietary Supplement Health and Education Act of 1994.

The late 1990's growth of herbal supplements was attributed to increased consumption by older consumers, the increasing number of pharmacies in supermarkets, increased display visibility, and health benefits substantiated by medical research. For example, because of the numerous studies that have proven sawgrass palmetto helps the prostate gland, its sales have significantly increased. The herbal market also experienced a number of shifts in market share among various herb products. Because of the numerous studies that have validated the health benefits of vitamin E, it's sales are increasing by about 5 percent per year. The sale of phytochemicals is estimated at $1.5 billion in 1998 and is projected to increase at 8 percent per year.

Without question, nutraceutical manufacturers are capitalizing on the lenient environment set forth under DSHEA and the FDA. The dietary supplement industry has grown 25 percent to 30 percent annually. Retail sales are expected to reach $12 billion by 2001.

Some popular herbs were selling so well that their natural supply was becoming endangered. Specifically, echinacea, goldenseal, American ginseng, and wild yam were becoming scarce and more expensive. What was becoming more dangerous was that some products touted to have these ingredients were adulterated, sometimes containing none of the ingredients listed on their labels. Demand for St. John's wort and kava was also exceeding its supply.

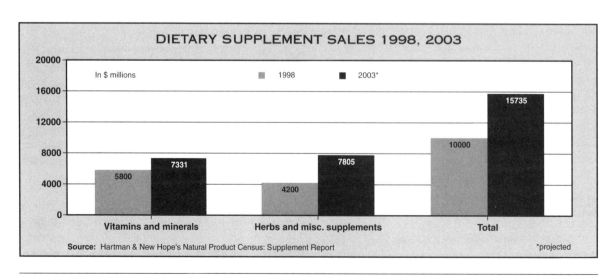

In March 1999, Switzerland-based Lonza AG and executives from Chinook Group Inc. and DuCoa LP, two U.S. companies, agreed to plead guilty to fixing vitamin prices and agreed to cooperate in an investigation by the Justice Department of a worldwide conspiracy to fix vitamin prices. Pricing information was required from Hoffmann-LaRoche, BASF, Rhone-Poulenc, and Roche Holding.

INDUSTRY LEADERS

Roche International, based in Switzerland, controls 40 percent of the international vitamin market, followed by BASF (20 percent), Rhone-Poulenc (15 percent), and Takeda (15 percent). Archer Daniels Midland Company and Henkel Nutrition and Health Group are two leading manufacturers of natural vitamin E. In response to recent scientific studies that show natural vitamin E is more effective than synthetic vitamin E, they are expanding operations to produce more natural vitamin E.

One of several domestic industry leaders is General Nutrition Corporation (GNC), with 1999 sales of $1.4 billion (18 percent growth from 1998) and almost 13,800 employees. GNC is the number one specialty retailer of nutritional supplements distributed through almost 3,900 company- and franchise-owned stores. The company planned for a total of 5,000 stores by the year 2002. Retail outlets are operated under the names GNC Live Well, Nature's Fresh, Nature Food Centres, and Amphora in the United States. GNC Live Well planned to open 1,500 outlets within Rite Aid drugstores between 1999 and 2002. In the United Kingdom, Canada, and New Zealand, stores are operated as Health and Diet Centres and General Nutrition Centres. In January 1999, GNC and GalaGen Inc. announced their collaboration on immune-enhancing dietary supplements and sports nutrition formulas.

Nature's Bounty's employment grew from 400 to 2,000 people, and sales increased from $33 million to $281 million in just 10 years through aggressive automation, acquisitions, new product development, and advanced marketing, making it one of the country's leading nutritional supplement manufacturers. In May 1999, the company announced its acquisition of Dynamics Essentials Inc., a distributor of nutritional supplements and skin care products, for $1 million. Nature's Bounty markets more than 1,000 products under the brand names Nature's Bounty, Vitamin World, Puritan's Pride, Holland & Barrett, Nutrition

Headquarters, and American Health. The company operates 77 Vitamin World factory outlet stores in the United States, opened two stores in the United Kingdom, and planned to open another 80 stores and add 150 new products in 1997. The company's net sales for the first three months of 1999 were $167.6 million, compared to $157.2 million for the same three months in 1998.

Cyanotech Corporation produces natural products from micro-algae, including Spirulina nutritional supplement, which it markets to a Hong Kong natural products company. Sales in 1998 totaled about $8.0 million. Net sales for the first three quarters of 1999 were $4.9 million, down from $5.3 million for the same period of fiscal 1998, a slide the company attributed to the costs of optimizing its NatuRose production facility.

Herbalife International markets weight-control products, health and nutritional supplements, and skin and personal care products in 36 countries. Although products are available only through a network of independent distributors who purchase products directly from the company, 1998 sales were $866 million, a 10.7 percent increase over 1997. Herbalife employs about 1,742 people, up 19.4 percent from the previous year.

Rexall Sundown sells the Sundown, Rexall, and Thompson brands of vitamins and supplements to mass-market stores, drug stores, health food stores, supermarkets, and through mail order. Total sales in 1998 reached $530.7 million, an increase of 101.5 percent from 1997. Rexall employed 1,200 people in 1998, an increase of 58.5 percent from 1997. Rexall sold about 1,300 products in 50 countries in 1999.

Natural Alternatives International is a $67.9-million independent producer of vitamins, micronutrients, and nutritional supplements, as well as innovative private label products for corporate, institutional, and commercial accounts. It was the official nutritional supplements licensee for the U.S. Olympic Committee. Natural Alternatives' 1998 sales increased 37.4 percent over 1997 and, over the same period, its number of employees increased to 128, a growth of 16.4 percent.

Other companies that are making inroads into the huge nutritional supplement field are Great Earth Vitamins and Vitamin Superstore. Based in California, Great Earth Vitamins is planning to open over 20 stores in the Washington, D.C. area by the year 2001. In addition to stocks of vitamins, Vitamin Superstores offer health books, juice bars, and

Profile METABOLIFE INTERNATIONAL

Metabolife is being called the number one herbal dietary supplement in America. The drug's founder, Michael J. Ellis, has grown wealthy selling the dietary drug that shares a key ingredient with a drug that got him arrested 10 years ago, according to an article published in *The Washington Post* on May 24, 1999.

Ellis, a former police officer, had been running a methamphetamine lab in his house, in which he and friends used ephedrine to produce the highly addictive drug. Ephedrine is a stimulant found in nature that can also be made synthetically. Ellis was arrested in a sting operation in 1989, later pleaded guilty to one count of using a telephone to further a drug deal, and received five years probation. A friend received a prison sentence of five years.

In 1992, Ellis entered into the diet supplement business with a partner to make an energy booster for weight lifters. The product contained ephedrine and caffeine. Three years later, he started Metabolife International. Now, Ellis uses ephedrine in the diet aid Metabolife 356. The fact that the ephedrine in Ellis' product comes from the ephedra plant allows the product to be marketed as an all-natural diet supplement, according to the Post's article. It thereby does not require Federal Drug Administration approval for safety or efficacy.

There have been reports of adverse reaction to products that are ephedrine-based, including 38 deaths, according to *The Washington Post*. In 1996, the FDA issued a warning that ephedrine is an amphetamine-like stimulant and can harm the nervous system and heart. A year later, the FDA proposed a rule to limit how much ephedrine a supplement could contain and length of use. Ellis opposed the rule for fear it would ruin his business. Ellis maintains the company has never been sued and he has received no complaints of adverse effects from Metabolife's users.

Metabolife and other companies formed the Dietary Supplement Safety and Science Coalition to fight the proposal, claiming FDA reports were flawed and vague, according to *The Washington Post*. Though the FDA database notes 14 cases of adverse effects and one death due to Metabolife, the organization has never provided documentation to Ellis, the article states.

---

computers downloaded with information about the health benefits of vitamins, minerals, and other micronutrients.

AMERICA AND THE WORLD

Domestic vitamin producers were meeting with competition from foreign producers, particularly those located in China; these chemical makers have undercut U.S. producers of bulk pharmaceuticals by 50 percent. For example, due to pressure from Chinese imports, vitamin C prices were falling in the mid-1990s, and they hit an all-time low in mid-1997 at $4.50 per kilo, half its value a year before. Big Western producers of vitamin C such as Hoffman-LaRoche will spend about $200 million by 2002 to upgrade facilities, improve production, and lower its cost to be more competitive. BASF and Takeda, also world leaders, are also expanding their operations in response to overseas competition; Takeda expanded its production of vitamin C by 15 percent.

Asia is an escalating market for vitamin-enriched animal feed because of increased meat consumption in Asian countries. Deregulation in Japan is making vitamins more easily available to the public. Roche and BASF are formulating joint ventures in China to manufacture vitamins and fortified animal feed. Competition from Chinese vitamin C markets is falling; only 7 of the 23 Chinese manufacturers that were in business in 1996 are still operational.

RESEARCH AND TECHNOLOGY

Research is continuing to define the health benefits of vitamins, other micronutrient supplements, and phytochemicals. A great deal of work was focused on the anticancer properties of vitamin E, vitamin C, and folic acid. A number of studies have shown these are useful in fighting Alzheimer's disease, cancer, heart disease, and birth defects. The National Institute of Health (NIH) recently recommended taking higher dosages of vitamin C. Vitamin E was proving to have an important role in cognitive function, respiratory health, immune response, and the prevention of heart disease.

According to a 1998 report in the *American Journal of Clinical Nutrition,* natural vitamin E is nearly four times more absorbable than synthetic vitamin E in pregnant women. Two new patents have been issued to Artisan Industries for a process that better processes and purifies both natural and synthetic vitamin E.

International Resource Management and Acquisitions is marketing Indole-3-Carbinol (I3C), a cancer-fighting agent that occurs in cruciferous vegetables such as broccoli. Its health benefits have been documented over eight years of medical trials.

Rexall Sundown launched several new products in 1999, including the BodySynergy™ Weight Loss System, which was based on the relationship between brain chemistry and weight loss. The research behind this product was what Rexall terms its "BodySynergy Anti-Craving Formula," a product designed to assist the brain in controlling overindulgence in food by reducing carbohydrate cravings. The company also introduced its "Osteo Basics Companion," a two-product pack featuring Osteo Essentials, a supplement containing a formula of glucosamine, Boswellia, calcium and other important nutrients to help repair and rebuild cartilage and bone." Rexall felt that this product would lead to more natural flexibility and increased freedom of movement. The second part of the two-product pack was Osteo Blend, a homeopathic product to temporarily relieve pain due to arthritis, overexertion, and muscle fatigue.

Research and development at Cyanotech was focused on its bio-engineered mosquitocide, combining a natural food for mosquito larvae, the microalgae Synechococcus, with natural toxins from the soil bacterium Bti. Cyanotech planned to reengineer the mosquitocide to increase its toxic effect and hoped to begin field trials during mid-1999.

FURTHER READING

"AHPA: Association Information." Washington, DC: American Herbal Products Association, 1999. Available from http://www.ahpa.org.

Allen, Andrea. "Regulating Nutraceuticals, Redux." *Food Processing,* September 1998.

Anderson, Duncan Maxwell. "Formula for Victory." *Success,* March 1997.

———. "Motivation Formula." *Success,* July/August 1996.

"As China Hikes Market Share." *Chemical Marketing Reporter,* 8 April 1996.

Best, Daniel. "Nutraceuticals Suit Up to Play." *Prepared Foods,* January 1996.

Chi, Judy. "Au Naturel: Capitalizing on their Names, Major OTC Firms Sally Forth into Herbals." *Drug Topics,* 17 August 1998.

"CHPA." Washington, DC: Consumer Healthcare Products Association, 1999. Available from http://ndmainfo.org/index.html.

Clark, Chapin. "Supermarkets Using Variety of Merchandising Strategies." *Capital Cities Media,* 1998.

Considine, Pippa. "A Bitter Pill for the Health Food Market." *Marketing Week,* 27 October 1995.

Croom, Edward M., Jr. "Botanicals in the Pharmacy: New Life for Old Remedies." *Drug Topics,* 6 November 1995.

"Cyanotech Reports Financial Results for First Quarter of Fiscal 1998." Kailua-Kona, HI: Cyanotech Corporation, 17 July 1997. Available from http://biz.yahoo.com/bw/97/07/17/cyan_y001_1.html.

"Diet Aid, Nutritional Drink Sales Boom." *Discount Store News,* 17 February 1997.

"Ensure an Integrated Vitamin Category." *Drug Topics,* 21 October 1996.

Fattah, Hassan. "U.S. Producers Brace for New Asian Entries." *Chemical Week,* 18 September 1996.

Freeman, Laura. "Ad Campaigns Pump Up Nutritional Foods." *Discount Store News,* 6 May 1996.

Giltenan, Ed. "Good Future in Vitamins." *Chemical Market Reporter,* 16 June 1997.

"Herbalife International Commences Operations in Thailand." Los Angeles: Herbalife International, Inc., 18 June 1997.

Kruger, Renee Covino. "Take Your Vitamins!" *Discount Store News,* February 1997.

Lee, Julian. "Drug Retailers Set to Join the Fray." *Marketing,* 19 October 1995.

Lerner, Matthew. "Nutritional Supplement Industry Gets Chemical Makers Attention." *Chemical Marketing Reporter,* 2 June 1997.

———. "Vitamins A and D Enjoy Slow but Steady Market." *Chemical Marketing Reporter,* 1 July 1996.

Levitt, Craig. "An Energized Category." *Supermarket Business,* May 1997.

Lewis, Kate Bohner. "Ulcers? Try Hot Pepper." *Forbes,* 6 November 1995.

Liebeck, Laura. "Welcoming the Wellness Generation." *Discount Store News,* 11 May 1998.

"Lonza and Others Plead Guilty to Fixing Vitamin Prices." *Chemical Market Reporter,* 8 March 1999.

Marriott, Anne. "Two Growing Chains." *Knight-Ridder/Tribune Business News,* 2 September 1997.

Mason, Marlys J. "Drugs or Dietary Supplements: FDA's Enforcement of DSHEA." *Journal of Public Policy & Marketing,* Fall 1998.

Mirasol, Feliza. "Strong Nutraceuticals Market Lures Pharma and Food Players." *Chemical Market Reporter,* 8 June 1998.

"NIH Office of Dietary Supplements Announces New Database of Scientific Literature on Dietary Supplements."

Washington, DC: National Institutes of Health, 31 December 1998.

O'Connor, James V. "Vitamins on a Healthy Road." *Chemical Marketing Reporter,* 24 June 1996.

Omelia, Johanna. "Vitamins: Skincare's Newest Rx." *Drug & Cosmetic Industry,* January 1997.

Ouellette, Jennifer. "Food Additives '95: Mainstream Neutraceuticals." *Chemical Marketing Reporter,* 29 May 1995.

Radice, Carol. "Nutritional Supplements: Adding Strength to HBC." *Progressive Grocer,* June 1997.

Rock, Andrea. "Vitamin Hype: Why We're Wasting $1 of Every $3 We Spend." *Money,* September 1995.

Smith, Elizabeth. "Neutraceutical Future Looks Bright." *Drug Topics,* 16 February 1998.

———. "Nutraceuticals Market is $86 Billion." *Drug Topics,* 15 June 1998.

Spethmann, Betsy. "Energizing the Stars." *Brandweek,* 1 July 1996.

"Supplement Sales Swing: Should Dealers Beware?" *Sporting Goods Business,* 14 September 1998.

"Sundown Vitamins Secures Exclusive License to Market Glucosamine/Chondroitin." *PR Newswire,* 31 March 1997.

Thomas, Nick. "Roche Signs Two Vitamin JV's." *Chemical Week,* 6 December 1995.

"Vitamin C Makers Seek Profits in Technology and Value Added." *Chemical Market Reporter,* 23 February 1998.

"Vitamins, Minerals, and Supplements." *Retail Business-Market Surveys,* July 1996.

—David C. Genaway,
updated by Jeff Motluck and Wendy Mason

ONLINE SHOPPING

Online shopping, or e-commerce, is big business. Consumers hoping to find a bargain or save the hassle of finding parking at the local mall, are increasingly turning to their PCs to buy products ranging from computer software, to toys, to articles from unclaimed baggage. Online sales reached $13 billion in 1998, according to the Boston Consulting Group, as stated in a *PC Magazine* article. It seems likely that the industry will continue to grow, especially with the advent of new technological advances such as personalized Internet services, which allow Web sites to cater to the individual preferences of each customer.

Online shopping represents a virtual mall, from which a wide range of goods and services can be purchased—all from the comfort of the customer's home or workplace. Items and services as diverse as books, groceries, crafting materials, mortgages, computer hardware, clothing, package shipping, stocks and bonds, mortgages, copies of newspaper articles, and Internet connections can be purchased 24 hours a day. Goods and services can come from establishments throughout the world, as long as these establishments have the software that permits them to post on an Internet site, and the software that permits them to conduct transactions online.

Although online shopping has been available since the late 1980s, this form of direct marketing did not gain in popularity until the mid-1990s. Online shopping began to penetrate the mainstream market of computer users around 1995, generating anywhere from $200 million to more than $1 billion in sales in 1996. Those figures continued to climb to an estimated $1.1 billion in 1997, double the sales posted only 2 years earlier. The Direct Marketing Association (DMA) predicts online shopping will go past the $12 billion mark by 2002.

Online shopping is still in its infancy. While many analysts agree that the online shopping industry has the potential to garner billions of dollars in sales per year—and has the potential to revolutionize the way industrial societies shop—there is considerable disagreement on when (or if) online shopping will realize this potential. In addition to consumer retailing, online shopping shows promise for business-to-business commerce. The DMA's 1999 Electronic Media Survey revealed that of its 4,500 members that have Web sites, 67 percent are targeted to other businesses.

For all its success, online shopping still only accounts for less than 1 percent of total U.S. retail sales. To increase that percentage, online shopping will need to overcome several hurdles, especially consumer mistrust of the Internet as a safe shopping arena. The key to successful online shopping involves a secure and guaranteed payment of goods and services purchased online. To try to accomplish this, consumers pay for their purchases using credit cards, and commercial sites use servers that mix up the information before transmitting it along with other security measures to prevent criminals from getting access to the consumers' credit card numbers. For the most part, there have been few reported problems with credit card use for online shopping.

Another problem many retailers face— especially brick-and-mortar retailers—is the issue of charging sales tax. Online shopping-only establishments, such as bookseller amazon.com, are not required to collect sales tax. But as established chain retail sellers, such as Tower Records, enter the Internet-selling world, the issue becomes more complicated. To gain a competitive edge, chain retailers would like to offer their customers the advantage of being able to return merchandise to one of their stores. However, in order to do that, they would have to charge sales tax on Internet purchases, a situation that is a negative in the highly competitive, low markup world of online industry.

ORGANIZATION AND STRUCTURE

Because the Web is so vast, consumers generally rely on a select number of sites that bundle retailers together. America Online (AOL), which reported total sales revenue of $2.6 billion for the fiscal year ended June 1998, has more than 400 stores on its service to create a virtual shopping mall. AOL's purchase of Netscape Communications in 1999 will further expand AOL's online services as it will acquire Netcenter, an important Internet portal. Portals, or gateways, are important to merchandisers because they are the sites where online visitors start their Internet journey. Merchandisers are eager to be listed on these frequently visited sites. One well-known portal is Yahoo!, which in December 1998, listed 27,000 stores that offered more than 2 million products. Yahoo! gets 31 million Web visitors a month, and as a consequence, companies pay to have banner ads put on the site. In 1998 Yahoo! charged four cents a day for every ad displayed on its 115 million pages. Yahoo! reported total revenue of $203 million in 1998.

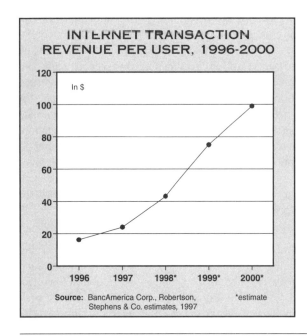

INTERNET TRANSACTION REVENUE PER USER, 1996-2000

In $

Source: BancAmerica Corp., Robertson, Stephens & Co. estimates, 1997   *estimate

Some companies on the Internet are familiar ones. Established operations such as J.C. Penney Co., Inc., Microsoft Corp., Barnes & Noble, and Citibank have active Internet sites. But alongside these household names, are upstarts such as Amazon.com and CDNow. But for both companies, the technology is the same. Online merchants offer goods and services that consumers purchase by selecting from on-screen menus or filling out on-screen forms.

While online shopping lends itself to small, inexpensive purchases, larger items are also available. Cars can be shopped for and purchased online, not only at dealership sites, but by tapping into the power of search engines or banner ads on such mega-sites as Yahoo, Infoseek, and Excite, or the growing number of online editions of Internet Yellow Pages. These sites will search for Internet locations of companies and link to sites where marketing and pricing information can be obtained, or where an actual purchase can be made. Online consumers are able to "window-shop" using their computers and make such sensitive transactions as buying stocks and bonds and finding (and applying for) home mortgages.

Like direct marketing and catalog operations, companies offering online shopping opportunities are finding that the transporting of goods, or more specifically, getting the purchased item into the hands of the consumer quickly, is a challenge. Recognizing this problem, one new Web-based company is offering shipping services for both online buyers and shippers. For a small fee, iShip.com provides carrier rates, the ability for an individual to print a certified shipping label, and a package-tracking service.

Business-to-business commerce accounts for a large chunk of online activity. Business-to-business sales represent 40 percent of online commercial transactions. And it's an area that continues to grow. Forrester Research Inc. reports business-to-business Internet commerce posted sales of $600 million in 1996 and could reach $66 billion by 2000. Stan Dolberg of Forrester Research contends analysts have been looking at the wrong sector when examining consumer online shopping growth and sales. He predicts business-to-business online shopping sales will outweigh consumer sales by 3 to 1.

Business transactions can be conducted in a way that offers advantages over personal online shopping. An Internet company can set up an "extranet" to which select business customers have access. Once an access code is entered, businesses buying supplies or services via the extranet can essentially create their own invoices, as well as keep a tally of their purchases (at the moment they type in their order on the computer screen). Some of the questions and concerns the general public has about credit card safety are wiped away by this approach.

Companies setting up Web-based businesses are faced with different challenges than their brick-and-mortar counterparts. While a company that decides to do business on the Internet will not have the same investment in a physical plant that the owner of a traditional store must make, a substantial amount of money is required for software to set up and maintain an Internet site. In addition, specialized software is needed to ensure secure online financial transactions. One company that has profited from this is IBM, which has been helping other businesses build their Web sites. In addition to providing software, hardware, and network computing services, IBM offers professional advice in areas such as site design. In 1997 IBM earned $27 billion from these electronic businesses services.

Laws and regulations for traditional retail commerce are fairly well defined while the rules for Internet commerce are still in the formation stage. Internet sales are a bust for local taxing entities because Internet firms are not required to add sales tax as a result of the three-year extension of the government's no-tax policy. Keri P. Mattox reported in an April 1999 article in *The Washington Times* that The National Association of Counties estimates that states could lose $50 billion in sales tax revenue over a five-year period. The National Association of Governors, at their 1998 meeting in Milwaukee, Wisconsin, spent time discussing this issue without arriving at a solution. In the meantime, jurisdictions with sales taxes are relying on the honesty of their taxpayers to report online (and catalog) purchases so sales taxes can be calculated. Forrester Research of Cambridge, Massachusetts, reports that governments in Europe and elsewhere are beginning to apply local laws and commercial regulations to the Web sites their citizens can access, regardless of the content's country of origin. Although it isn't clear whether a government can actually claim jurisdiction over the content of Web sites that run on servers outside their borders, Forrester suggests the smart companies won't allow themselves to be test cases.

The Clinton administration has fought to maintain an open and conducive commercial atmosphere on the Internet. In July 1997, President Bill Clinton followed the advice of his special task force on Internet commerce by calling for no new taxes or regulations. In addition to supporting self-regulation, President Clinton also promised to implement new patent, copyright, and privacy policies. However, these are regulatory issues that will be discussed and reformed for many years to come.

Besides the regulatory policies that are being implemented to assist the online shopper and the businesses online, there are publications available to help shoppers sort through all the information available concerning online shopping. In April 1997, the first magazine devoted to online shopping, *Internet Shopper,* was published by Mecklermedia. Web guide magazines offer reviews of online stores, discuss the features of each site, and recommend sites of special note or interest. The publications also offer general information such as payment methods and tips on Internet shopping.

CURRENT CONDITIONS

Many analysts wonder how much revenue online shopping has generated. While it seems certain that online shopping is a growing industry, just how fast it is growing and will continue in the future is uncertain. The nature of the industry makes it difficult to determine accurately how much revenue is being generated. While Boston Consulting Group sets 1998 Internet retail sales revenue at $13 billion, GartnerGroup puts it at $6.1 billion. The Direct Marketing Association reported electronic commerce-generated sales of $200 million in 1997. Forrester Research has put that figure at $1.1 billion. Future growth potential is even more varied. Jupiter Communications say revenue could reach $41 billion by 2002 while Forrester Research estimates the figure at $108 billion.

One problem with the Internet has been its inability to target precise demographic groups. As a consequence, Internet banner ads—which cost $17 per thousand people reached—are less than half the rate of magazines. However, when a company does get it right, it can tailor its products to a select group. Dell Computer Corp. creates customized home pages for many of its customers. The home pages offer specialized information, such as access to order and payment records. In March 1999 Dell expanded its online presence with a new shopping site, Gigabuys.com. The site offered 30,000 computer-related products services, such as product reviews. Before the expansion, Dell sold $14 million in products a day over the Web, a number which accounted for 25 percent of Dell's total business revenue.

In addition to revenue, the amount of "hits" (the number of times someone contacts a particular Internet site) is one measure of commercial activity. But unlike other areas of selling, where there is a clearer relationship between the number of catalogs sent to a consumer and the number of purchases made, no such clearcut barometer exists for the online shopping industry. Companies, such as Media Matrix Inc., Data Inc., Relevant Knowledge Inc., and Net Rating Inc. compile Internet customer information. Marshall Cohen, president of Marshall Cohen Associates (an Internet/entertainment consultant), states the problem Internet businesses currently face: no data is better than wrong data, and despite the use of "cookies" (software that records your Web habits) and online surveys, the amount of accurate data on electronic commerce is relatively small.

INDUSTRY LEADERS

A number of companies providing a wide range of goods and services are emerging as industry leaders in online shopping.

BOOKS

In the book arena, two companies continue to draw attention, as well as customers to their respective sites. It shouldn't be surprising that New York-based Barnes & Noble, Inc., the largest bookseller in the world, is one of those sites. Besides its online operation, Barnes & Noble has more than 1,000 stores. The other big name in online booksellers is Amazon.com, Inc., based in Seattle, Washington. Customers can search Amazon.com's database of 1.5 million books by title, author, subject, or keyword. One reason for the company's success has been its ability to offer discounts of up to 40 percent. It also has spent considerable amount of money on advertising; the company has not realized a profit and had a net loss of $124 million in 1998. The company, which is a Web-based concern only, also sells music and videos. In 1999 the company ventured into the auction arena. In this case, buyers are not buying products directly from Amazon.com, instead, Amazon.com customers are selling their products to other customers, with the company acting as a intermediary. Sales revenue for 1998 were $610 million, an increase of over 300 percent from 1997. The company employed over 2,000 people in 1998.

The online bookstore has rekindled retail book sales. Online book sales rose from $152 million in 1997 to $650 million in 1998, as reported in a March 1999 article in *American Demographics*. Internet shopping has made book ordering more accessible and affordable than ever. Even specialty bookstores, such as Alibris, which carries rare and out-of-print books, has taken advantage of online shopping to merchandise its product. The larger online book sites also offer their customers a chance to read current reviews of books and add their own reviews in interactive chat areas. Theories that online shopping would have a negative impact on other book sellers do not appear to have been proven as sales in traditional bookstores rose from $11.95 billion in 1997 to $12.37 billion in 1998.

BANKS

More and more banks are making their services available online. The biggest banks involved in electronic commerce include Chase, Citibank, NationsBank, First Union, First Chicago, NBD, Wells Fargo, Bank One, Norwest, and Fleet Bank. Financial institutions are still on a learning curve as to what, if any, fees they should charge, and how much the fee should be. A number of banks have begun dropping fees for online banking (and some financial institutions even "reward" online customers, still others charge more for in-person transactions). But some banks are charging anywhere from $10 to $20 per month, or a fee per transaction (including checking on an account balance). It is estimated more than one-third of the banks and savings and loans in the United States make their services available to customers via the Internet.

CLOTHIERS

As might be expected, some of the bigger retail clothiers also pop up as leaders in the online shopping industry: J.C. Penneys, Macy's, and direct-marketing leaders Lands' End, J. Crew, L.L. Bean, and Eddie Bauer. These companies are also leaders in catalog shopping. *Working Mother* magazine says these retailers have some of the easiest sites to navigate and offer customers detailed product information. In the future, nearly every well-established retailer will become an e-merchant. A December 1998 survey by consulting firm Ernst & Young showed that 76 percent of 125 traditional retailers were either already selling online or had plans to do so.

Some concern has been expressed that online shopping opportunities offered by clothiers may not reach or attract women. For some time, the number of females using the Internet has lagged behind males, but that particular gap is diminishing. The percent of females using the Internet is approaching 50 percent. What might be a more worrisome set of statistics for online sales of all kinds is not a gender issue, but an age issue. The U.S. Commerce Department survey found that between 40 and 50 percent of persons between the ages of 25 and 54 own computers, with 22 to 26 percent in that age bracket regularly going online. Only 21 percent of persons 55 and older own computers, with only 8.8 percent of that group dialing up the Internet.

Despite some optimistic predictions, not all clothiers are sold on online shopping. Ken Clark in *Footwear News* reports that companies like Nike and Rockport keep tight control over the merchandising of their products and require online retailers to obtain permission before offering the sale of their shoes online. Additionally, online shopping has an inherent limitation not faced by traditional retail stores. Customers' ability to examine merchandise before purchasing is substantially limited, even when an online shopping site has video or audio capabilities. In order for such advanced technology to work, consumers must have the same version of the software. Consumers, assuming they have the proper software, may be able to see an image of the product, but they cannot touch it or try it on.

GROCERY SHOPPING

Although on-line grocery shopping may seem difficult or impossible, this is one of the retail areas that, at least on a small scale, has shown some promise. The activities of two companies have been closely watched by analysts: Peapod, based in Chicago, and Shoplink in Boston. While specifics vary, online grocers make available to their customers general (or label-specific) products via the Internet. Usually some form of membership fee is charged. Once an order is placed, a customer is charged a delivery fee plus a percent of the entire order, and the groceries are delivered to a customer's home. Some companies give customers a choice of brand names; others just list general grocery items. Although the quality of foodstuffs can vary and the ability of shoppers to be picky about produce and other items is clearly eliminated, time-strapped individuals find this to be a viable option. In 1998 Peapod had 100,000 members who generated revenues of $69 million, an increase of 16 percent over 1997. That same year, the company employed 285 workers. Observers of the online shopping market suggest that it is one of the potential growth areas of electronic commerce.

This list of industry leaders doesn't begin to cover all of the businesses that have entered into the arena of Internet shopping. According to Jupiter Communications, online revenue by industry for 1998 were: travel, $2.0 billion; PC hardware, $1.8 billion; groceries, $270

million; gifts and flowers, $219 million; books, $216 million; PC software, $173 million; tickets, $127 million; music, $81 million; and clothing, $71 million.

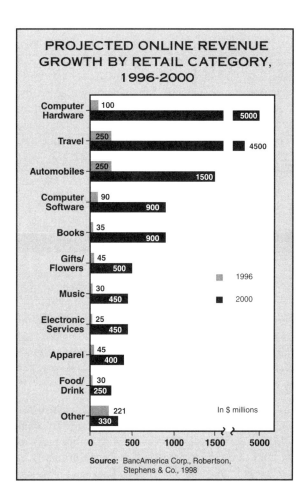

PROJECTED ONLINE REVENUE GROWTH BY RETAIL CATEGORY, 1996-2000

Source: BancAmerica Corp., Robertson, Stephens & Co., 1998

Depending on who is being quoted, online shopping either has tremendous potential or it is a medium that will not live up to its hype for some time to come. Sheri Wilson-Gray, an executive with Saks, does not believe online sales will be a cash cow for most businesses.

Saks bought an Internet "mall" site from Time Warner in 1996 for $100,000. At the time, it seemed like the right partner and the right time to try selling on the Internet. But once on Time Warner's Dreamshop site, Saks sold a $2,000 suit to one man, and some candy. The Dreamshop site is no more, and Saks has shelved plans for another foray into electronic commerce. Wilson-Gray said Saks will use its Web site to provide investors with information.

Laura Berland, executive vice president at ORB Digital Direct, an online commerce consulting firm, also offers a subdued review of online commerce. She says retailers must recognize that they are in the "covered-wagon" days of Internet enterprise and that getting into online shopping could be very expensive for companies that are particularly sensitive to bottom-line considerations.

Two stories on *The New York Times on the Web* site illustrate the wide-ranging view of online shopping as an industry. A story dated October 17, 1996, suggests that automobile sales are booming on the Web. A story a year later, dated October 16, 1997, reports that few buy automobiles on the Web, but many start their research there. Once again, the success or failure of online shopping may rest on the way sales and related activities are counted.

AMERICA AND THE WORLD

Though the United States has pioneered the Internet and has led in mainstream Internet penetration, many industrial countries around the world have undergone their own Internet revolutions. Just as the Internet allows U.S. companies to have access to customers on a worldwide basis, companies in other countries can also get access to the U.S. market just as easily.

The experience of Internet merchants in other countries has been similar to that of their U.S. counterparts. Le Shop, the first nationwide online store of its kind in Nyon, Switzerland, is aimed primarily at the Swiss market, but has sold its packaged food and personal and home care products internationally. Fromages, which sells French cheese and Sprungli, specializing in Swiss chocolate, also find themselves pleasantly surprised by the number of international customers they are now serving. As with their American counterparts, Internet businesses based in other countries find they must be concerned with logistics. For European online shoppers, the introduction of a unified currency should make shopping for products on the Internet a little easier.

One of the most ambitious and expensive Europe-based online projects is MyWorld, which gets about 5,000 visitors a day. It is owned by the giant German department store chain Karstadt and is marketing more than 150,000 items such as apparel, computers and software, and electronics. The site has posted $20,000 in sales per day and receives more than 100,000 hits per week.

Japanese companies Hitachi Ltd. and Fujitsu Ltd. have banded together and are developing a certification service for electronic commerce. They are hoping to allay Japanese fears about online shopping through their own version of security software.

RESEARCH AND TECHNOLOGY

An area where the Internet lags behind traditional stores is in the amount of time it takes to get the goods into the buyer's hands. But retailing giant Gap is looking for ways to change that. In 1998 the company, which has 1,450 stores across the United States, experimented using those stores as distribution centers to offer Web customers same-day service. Bicycle messengers in New York City were used to deliver the goods. While the bike messenger service didn't work as well as Gap had hoped, the store chain said it will try again.

The Internet offers promise in the area of personalized e-commerce sites. Features on these sites include greeting the customer by name and making buying recommendations based on the customer's states preferences. Online businesses that have incorporated personalization features on their sites have seen their revenues increase. According to Jupiter Communications, the cost to create customized sites—ranging from $50,000 to $3 million—can be recouped within a year. And Jupiter also says that nearly all of the top 25 online merchants have these features on their sites. However, merchants must obtain personal information about their customers to create these personalized sites. This fact has alarmed some government officials who are threatening regulation to limit the use of personal details, according to an October 5, 1998 article in *Business Week,* by Robert Hof. Even without federal regulations, it seems likely some consumers will not welcome this invasion into their privacy just as others will embrace the concept.

As online entrepreneurs work to develop new products and services and new ways of attracting customers to their Web sites, one major challenge faced by these companies involves the security of their sites. Surveys have shown that security is a major deterrent to online shopping for non-business consumers. Specifically, consumers are concerned about someone hacking into a site and stealing their credit card information. Customers hear stories about how hackers have broken into secure areas of the U.S. Pentagon's computers or how detailed dossiers of information can be compiled through the Internet using an individual's Social Security number and worry about the security of information they send over the Internet.

The predicament faced by Internet businesses is similar to the one faced by banks when automated teller machines (ATMs) were first introduced on the market. Bill Robbins, a spokesman for Dell Computers, said many people were initially uncomfortable making deposits at ATMs; they simply did not trust the technology. Now, ATMs are a part of many people's everyday banking. Customers are still wary of online technology. Even when they see a "lock" icon at a Web site, an indicator that a site is secure and uses encryption software, consumers will often call up the company to complete their transaction. They have a higher comfort level reading their credit card number to someone over the phone than they have typing it into a form at a Web site.

To combat this problem, some companies are developing a form of electronic currency, created when an online customer deposits money into an account. Each time the customer makes a purchase, an amount would be deducted from this electronic purse. Newspapers and others wishing to charge a small amount per item of information sought by an online customer are watching developments in this area. Credit card companies such as Visa are participating in this research.

New technology, increased access to the Internet, and a desire for convenience has pushed online shopping forward. As more efficient, user-friendly, and safe software becomes available, online shopping sales should continue to grow and revolutionize the way that shopping is done.

FURTHER READING

Belsky, Gary. "Get it Quick—and Pay Less—By Shopping on the Web." *Money Magazine,* September 1997.

Broder, John. "Making America Safe for Electronic Commerce." *The New York Times on the Web,* 21 June 1997. Available from http://www.nytimes.com.

Bryant, Adam. "Web Travel Shopping: the Surf Is Rising." *The New York Times on the Web,* 3 May 1998. Available from http://www.nytimes.com.

Calem, Robert. "Auto Sales are Booming on the Web." *The New York Times on the Web,* 17 October 1996. Available from http://www.nytimes.com.

Giussani, Bruno. "Online Holiday Sales Less Than Merry for Europe." *The New York Times on the Web,* 3 February 1998. Available from http://www.nytimes.com.

———. "To Solve Distribution Dilemma, E-Commerce Site Goes Postal." *The New York Times on the Web,* 7 April 1998. Available from http://www.nytimes.com.

Hof, Robert D. "Now It's Your Web." *Business Week,* 5 October 1998.

Holstein, William J., Susan Gregory Thomas, and Fred Vogelstein. "Click 'Til You Drop." *U.S. News & World Report,* 7 December 1998.

Judge, Paul. "From Computers to Croissants." *Business Week,* 10 February 1997.

Kaufman, Leslie. "Scrambling at the Online Mall: Can Traditional Stores Catch Up?" *The New York Times,* 23 February 1999.

Kiely, Thomas. "Electronic Commerce: Obeying the Laws of Cyberspace." *Harvard Business Review,* September-October 1997.

Krantz, Michael. "The Internet Economy: Click Till You Drop." *Time,* 20 July 1998.

Krebs, Michelle. "Few Buy Autos on the Web, But Many Start Their Research There." *The New York Times on the Web.* 16 October 1997. Available from http://www.nytimes.com.

Levy, Steve. "Bill and Al Get it Right; Their New Initiative on Electronic Commerce Could Help Turn Around a Lame Internet Policy." *Newsweek,* 7 July 1997.

Martin, Michael. "The Next Big Thing: a Bookstore?" *Fortune,* 9 December 1996.

Mattox, Keri P. "States Complain of $50 Billion Loss in Internet Tax Revenue; On-line Buying Boom Could Mean Bust for Governments." *The Washington Times,* 5 April 1999.

Mitchell, Russ. "Why AOL Really Clicks." *U.S. News & World Report,* 7 December 1998.

Mogelonsky, Marcia. "Book Biz Boon." *American Demographics,* 1 March 1999.

Reilly Cullen, Lisa. "Finally, You Could Profit by Banking Online." *Money Magazine,* September 1997.

Ross, Judith. "The Internet: Fear and Shopping in Cyberspace." *Harvard Business Review,* July-August 1997.

Steinhauer, Jennifer. "Old-line Retailers Resist Online Life." *The New York Times on the Web,* 20 April 1998. Available from http://www.nytimes.com.

Tanaka, Jennifer. "From Soup to Nuts: Shop for Groceries Without Leaving the Den." *Newsweek,* 16 March 1998.

Vizart, Frank. "A Modem, A Mouse, a Mortgage." *Business Week,* 14 April 1997.

—Karl Heil,
updated by Virginia Black and Katherine Wagner

OPHTHALMIC LASERS

Primarily due to advances in laser technology, a new market emerged in the 1990s for corrective laser surgery on the most common vision problems. These new techniques could correct nearsightedness, astigmatism, and even farsightedness. The potential market for these procedures was huge. Virtually anyone in North America between the ages of 20 and 50 years who wore glasses or contacts was eligible to have the procedure done. One analyst estimated that at least 15 million Americans were specifically eligible for a vision-correcting procedure called photorefractive keratectomy (PRK). At $2,000 to $3,000 per eye, the windfall for industry firms and their shareholders is huge. In 1998 approximately 320,000 LASIK procedures were performed, generating $1.34 billion. Some estimates claim that the number of people electing to have laser eye surgery each year will reach 675,000 people by the year 2000.

ORGANIZATION AND STRUCTURE

Two manufacturers primarily made the ophthalmic lasers used for corrective vision surgery in North America: VISX Inc. of Santa Clara, California, and Summit Technology Inc. of Waltham, Massachusetts. Summit was the first laser maker to get Food and Drug Administration (FDA) approval on the PRK surgical procedure. By 1996 the company installed 175 laser systems in the United States. The company advertised laser eye surgery directly to the public, owned vision centers that performed the procedure, and offered financing to patients for the surgery. Summit ran print ads for PRK in magazines such as *GQ, People, Redbook,* and *Glamour.* They also ran "category development" ads for the procedure on cable television, which included a toll-free number where operators referred callers to the nearest vision center using a Summit laser system. Some industry analysts criticized Summit's marketing approach, saying medical device makers should not perform procedures themselves but concentrate only on producing their instruments.

VISX and Summit dissolved their alliance under Pillar Point Partners after the Federal Trade Commission (FTC) accused them of price-fixing. While other charges against VISX stemming from a two-year investigation were dismissed in a December 1998 ruling, the FTC still challenged in 1999 the patent that has allowed the company to dominate the laser surgery market. If VISX finds the ruling unfavorable, appeals may extend the case into 2002; however, the company is confident that its many other patents will protect its ability to collect royalty fees. Meanwhile, by April 1999 VISX had filed a patent infringement suit against Nidek, Inc. and complaints against three ophthalmology centers for using the laser system central to the suit. As reported in *Ocular Surgery News,* Nidek denied any patent infringement and added that Nidek does not charge per-procedure fees.

An FDA-mandated training program is required for those performing laser eye surgery. Ophthalmologists usually perform the procedure, but some states allow optometrists to perform laser eye surgery. Some doctors have formed groups that own or control the eye surgery centers using the lasers. Other vision centers allowed doctors to use the lasers on a rental basis. Summit Technology located their vision centers in prestigious institutions such as Tufts University, Stanford, George Washington University, and the Cleveland Clinic. Start-up costs are high for laser eye surgery, with excimer lasers costing $525,000 and up to 10 percent of that amount in yearly maintenance fees. No insurance plan covers the surgery, so consumers wanting PRK pay up to $3,000 per eye.

The entire procedure takes about 30 minutes to perform, with less than a minute of that time spent under a laser whose firing pulses last less than a second. The surgery only requires local anesthetic and some drops to deaden the blinking impulse for a short time. Patients usually notice immediate vision improvement, with the final corrected vision taking a few days to develop. Industry statistics report that the vast majority of patients' vision improves to at or better than 20/40—enough to pass a drivers license exam without glasses—and that most patients achieved 20/25 or even 20/20 vision, with actual figures depending on the procedure elected. Ophthalmologists recommend that patients have the surgery done between the ages of 21 and 50, since patients older or younger than that might not get optimal results.

EYESIGHT PROBLEMS

Refraction describes the way in which light is focused by the eye. Factors affecting eyesight are the curvature of the cornea, the strength of the lens, and the length of the eye. The three problems that can result are called myopia (commonly referred to as nearsightedness), hyperopia (farsightedness), or astigmatism.

Myopia can be caused by an eyeball that is too long, or by a cornea with too much curvature, causing an image to focus just in front of the retina. Distant objects appear blurry, and can only be seen well with the aid of corrective lenses. Hyperopia is caused by an eyeball that is too short, or by a cornea that has too little curvature, causing an image to be focused behind the retina. For those who are farsighted, distant objects are more easily seen than are near objects. Astigmatism is caused by a cornea shaped like an oval or a football, rather than like a circle. Those with astigmatism have multiple focusing points and often need ocular aids to see clearly.

BACKGROUND AND DEVELOPMENT

Although lasers may be used to correct opacities and other problems resulting from diseases of the eye, they have been most aggressively marketed and developed as a means of lessening dependence on glasses and contact lenses in healthy people.

Refractive surgery began in the mid-1800s with claims that the cornea could be flattened with a spring-mounted mallet through the patient's closed eyelid, and the basic principles of incisional surgery, or keratotomy, were devised by L.J. Hans of The Netherlands in 1898. Clinical work by Japanese doctors T. Sato and K. Akiyam in the 1940s and 1950s demonstrated that transverse and radial incisions in the rear of the cornea would cause it to flatten, thus altering refraction. Visual correction was found to depend on the number, depth, and length of incisions.

In the 1960s, S. Fyodorov of the USSR performed keratotomies with multiple incisions on the anterior surface of the eye to yield greater safety and control over the degree of refractive correction. Interest in the new radial keratotomy (RK) led to a large study of the procedure in the late 1970s by the National Eye Institute. Although the technique was found to be effective, many patients experienced complications.

Ophthalmology was the first medical specialty to use lasers extensively, and clinical research on the use of excimer lasers for eye surgery began in the early 1980s. The excimer ablates rather than cuts tissue and thus is an ideal technique for precisely sculpting the corneal surface. After years of clinical trials, the FDA approved the use of lasers for moderate myopia in 1995, and industry giants Summit Technology and VISX were formed in 1985 and 1986 to introduce lasers into clinical practice in the United States.

LASIK, the newest available laser corrective procedure, evolved from a procedure introduced in the 1970s in which a thin wafer of tissue was removed from the cornea, reshaped, and reinserted into the eye. A Greek physician who used a laser to treat tissue underlying a thin flap of the cornea's surface first described in 1989 the procedure now in wide use. LASIK's dramatic results and absence of postoperative pain soon created worldwide demand, and in 1997 the FDA ruled that it was an "off-label" procedure that could be used by any licensed medical professional if it was judged to be in the best interest of the patient. In June 1998 the FDA recommended approval of LASIK using a system developed by researchers at the Emory Vision Correction Center—the first time approval has ever been granted to a physician team for a surgical system.

In late 1998 and early 1999 VISX excimer laser systems were approved to treat hyperopia and astigmatism, greatly expanding the availability of the procedure. Other companies were awaiting FDA approval or had premarket approval for systems with similar ranges of capabilities, including Sunrise Technologies and Bausch & Lomb Surgical. By some estimates, this increases the number of people potentially eligible for the procedure to 80 or 90 million—one third of the U.S. population.

RADIAL KERATOTOMY (RK)

Radial keratotomy, the original incisional technique, has been performed since the late 1970s but is no longer widely used, although improvements in surgical instruments contributed to a resurgence of interest in RK in the early 1990s. RK involves making radial cuts with a diamond-tipped knife along the cornea to weaken the sides of the eye. Ocular pressure then flattens the cornea's surface and reduces myopia. The procedure leaves scars on the cornea, however, and cuts almost 90 percent through the cornea's thickness, which tends to weaken the eye. Up to half of all RK patients experienced mild farsightedness five years after the procedure. The process also left the cornea's surface too bumpy to wear contact lenses. Despite the drawbacks, an average of 275,000 patients per year opted for RK treatment before it was largely replaced by safer and more effective methods.

PHOTOREFRACTIVE KERATECTOMY (LASER PRK)

This procedure uses short pulses from an excimer laser to sculpt only 5 to 10 percent (25 to 50 microns) of the cornea's front surface, producing a flattening effect which slightly reshapes the eye to dramatically improve vision. The entire procedure takes less than 40 seconds per eye. Excimer lasers use a specific wavelength of ultraviolet light that cannot penetrate the cornea completely or harm the eye's internal tissue.

LASER ASSISTED IN-SITU KERATOMILEUSIS (LASIK)

In 1997 the FDA approved an even more sophisticated technique which uses a two-stage process (popularly known as "flap and zap") to expose the top layer of the cornea and remove a minute amount of corneal tissue with a high degree of precision. Although LASIK is a more complex treatment and involves greater surgical skill and somewhat greater risk during the procedure itself than PRK, LASIK patients experience more rapid recovery and dramatic improvements in their vision.

PIONEERS IN THE FIELD

IBM developed the excimer laser in the early 1970s to etch microchips. An industry pioneer, Stephen L. Trokel, theorized that the laser could also be used to successfully sculpt the cornea. Working with IBM physicist R. Srinivasan, Trokel patented his idea for using excimer lasers in eye surgery in 1983. In 1985, Theo Seiler performed the first excimer laser procedure in Germany, and the first PRK was performed in the United States on a blind eye in 1987. In 1988, Marguerite performed the first PRK in the United States on a sighted person with myopia. From 1987 to 1989, several companies experimented with excimer lasers based on Seiler's work, and Trokel got the first investigational device exemption from the FDA.

Another important industry pioneer was Dr. Stephen Joffe, president and CEO of LCA-Vision. Joffe earned his medical degree in South Africa in 1967, and spent 15 years at the University of Cincinnati Medical Center. He started Laser Centers of America in 1985 as a private company, doing ophthalmic laser surgeries. He also helped found the International Nd:Yag Laser Society. (YAG referred to Yttrium Aluminum Garnet lasers, a photodisruptive laser.) LCA-Vision performed the first FDA-approved laser eye procedures in the United States, in late 1995, and did thousands of the procedures from 1990 to 1995 in Canada. Some industry analysts applauded Joffe's decision to take LCA-Vision public in 1995 by merging it into a public shell, rather than through an IPO, as did many of his competitors. This may have led to more stable stock prices for his company's shareholders, especially compared to the more volatile stocks in this industry.

Other industry pioneers include Dr. Stephen Slade and Dr. Jeffery Machat. Both are co-national medical directors of The Laser Center Inc., and both have used excimer lasers on patients since 1990. In fact, Machat reportedly performed more LASIK procedures than any other North American doctor and was the first surgeon trained to use FDA-approved excimer lasers from Technolas GmbH, VISX, and Summit. Both doctors were qualified to train and certify other surgeons in LASIK operations, and both of them lectured and trained other surgeons in the United States, Canada, Asia, Australia, South Africa, and Europe.

CURRENT CONDITIONS

The refractive surgery market has grown tremendously in the few years since ophthalmic lasers have been available, and the expanded range of procedures is bound to accelerate growth even further. Top laser vision correction facilities doubled or tripled the number of procedures performed from 1997 to 1998, and in the first four months of 1999 had surpassed the 1998-year total. As cited in the *Ocular Surgery News,* Frost and Sullivan predicts a 72 percent market growth rate for 1998-1999, since surgeons waiting for newly FDA-approved systems will be ready to invest. The high demand for refractive surgery has resulted in many ophthalmologists switching to full-time refractive surgery. Managed well, a high-volume surgeon can generate $100,000 per day. This sort of volume-geared business focus has been criticized for its heavy advertising, likened to a "feeding frenzy" on the public.

Indeed, marketing efforts have been aggressive enough to warrant intervention by federal authorities, who in 1997 seized several unapproved lasers and issued warnings about undisclosed risks and misleading advertising to 37,000 ophthalmologists and optometrists. Because patients must usually pay for laser correction themselves, many surgeons have actively pursued this patient pool with the help of large vision care ventures as a highly profitable source of income that is free of the administrative obstacles posed by managed-care plans. Other ophthalmologists, however, decline to perform the surgeries at all and consider them cosmetic procedures whose benefits may often be exaggerated.

Within the industry, the trend is definitely toward the LASIK refractive surgery over PRK procedures. In studies with patients receiving PRK in one eye and LASIK in the other, LASIK was preferred as less painful after surgery, faster visual recovery and better visual acuity. As the number of both patients receiving surgery and surgeons providing it has escalated, so has the offering of accessory instruments for cutting the flap (microkeratomes) as well as a number of spatulas, forceps, and others to maneuver it. Despite the popularity of LASIK, PRK is indicated in some situations, such as when the cornea is too thin to safely cut a flap, or if there is likelihood of physical contact with the eye, as in sports, where the flap could be lost before healing properly.

INDUSTRY LEADERS

LASER MANUFACTURERS

The two industry giants, Summit Technology Inc. and VISX, hold a monopoly on the manufacture of

ophthalmic lasers approved to perform PRK for myopia and astigmatism in the United States. In March 1998, however, federal authorities charged the two with price-fixing in a complex patent-pooling venture that had allowed them to share revenues in effectively blocking competition. The two companies were further charged with overcharging consumers by more than $40 million for the $250 royalty fee that surgeons were required to pay them per procedure. Of such royalties VISX received 56 percent, and Summit received 44 percent. Under pressure from the Federal Trade Commission, VISX paid Summit $35 million in a settlement that dissolved the joint venture. In July 1998 the FTC prohibited any further license fee agreements and required fuller disclosure to consumers by both companies.

Summit Technology, Inc. of Waltham, Massachusetts, makes the Apex Laser Workstation used for PRK surgery, and its corneal disc has been approved for the treatment of astigmatism. The company is acquiring Autonomous Technologies Corporation as a subsidiary. In November 1998 the FDA approved Autonomous' LADARVision, the only excimer system that tracks and compensates for involuntary eye movement. Summits' 1998 sales were $91.6 million, a 3.2 percent growth, with 425 employees, down 19.7 percent from 1997. Summit also owns Lens Express, the nation's most successful contact lens replacement service.

VISX, Inc. of Santa Clara, California, had 1998 annual sales of $133.8 million, up 95 percent from 1997, and 238 employees, up 45 percent. VISX manufactures its own excimer laser surgical system, complete with operating software and a system for managing patient data. With FDA approval in 1997, VISX added domestic sales to its established overseas sales of the system in 45 countries. The company offers its customers educational information about practice building and marketing on its VISX University™ Internet site. In April 1999 VISX launched an advertising campaign directed toward increasing patients' demand for procedures using VISX lasers.

Sunrise Technologies International, Inc. of Fremont, California, is a much smaller competitor, but is progressing toward its goal of becoming a leading refractive company. In 1997 the company sold its dental laser and air abrasive businesses, and over 14 months raised $31 million independent of an agent or fees. While Sunrise experienced a nearly 80 percent decline in sales for 1998, reaching only $0.6 million, its number of employees grew 56.5 percent to 36. In March 1999 the company underwent restructuring in preparation to launch its laser thermal keratoplasty

---

| Trends | LASER MANUFACTURERS BOOST OPHTHALMOLOGISTS' BUSINESS SAVVY |

Advertising and marketing seem far removed from the ophthalmologist's repertoire. But this industry relies on high-volume, out-of-pocket procedures, with the result that promotional advertising is the key to maintaining a practice and paying for continuous technological advances. Laser companies are coordinating marketing programs for ophthalmologists, offering them tools and techniques for direct mail and telephone advertising, video commercial formats and how to manage patient education seminars.

Summit Technology offers its Laser Excellence Affiliate Program to help practitioners that use Summit's lasers and their staff effectively handle inquiries with patient-education and promotional materials. The program also has developed a practitioner network and offers patients financing and a CD-ROM seminar kit, addressing patients' two main concerns—understanding the procedure and paying for it.

VISX Inc. has begun aggressively marketing its lasers on several levels. In November 1998 the company launched an online version of its marketing support program, VISX University, which aims to further practice growth. The company has also expanded its Business Development Managers program, which formulates individual practice marketing plans. The program involves a visit to the practice, analysis of area demographics and measurement of how the physician's office handles patient inquiries to determine what is needed to ultimately increase procedure volume. VISX is also embarking on a direct-to-consumer advertising campaign that will include national magazine, radio and newspaper ads. Surgeons who use VISX machines will be able to join in locally with the nationwide campaign.

(LTK) laser system. Their method uses two laser rings on the mid-periphery of the cornea to gently heat and thus shrinks—rather than cuts—the cornea. It is used to treat hyperopia, presbyopia (loss of focus due to aging), and overcorrection from prior PRK and LASIK procedures. The system is currently in use in Europe and the Americas, and in clinical trials in the United States. In January 1999 the FDA notified Sunrise that its premarket approval application for the LTK system was suitable for filing. Next, the FDA's Ophthalmic devices Panel will review the application to determine whether to recommend approval by the FDA.

OPHTHALMIC LASER SURGERY PROVIDERS

In 1997 an influential stock newsletter picked LCA-Vision of Cincinnati, Ohio, as the second-best long-term stock play after VISX in this volatile new industry. The company has active laser eye surgery centers in 18 major U.S., European, and Canadian metro localities. In 1998 the company's sales totaled $35.2 million and employed 145 workers. That year the number of procedures performed within the LCA-Vision system rose 138 percent to 23,080 from 9,715 procedures in 1997.

Laser Vision Centers, Inc., headquartered in St Louis, Missouri, operates both fixed-site and mobile excimer lasers, both independently and through joint-operating agreements. Laser Vision Centers' locations span 40 U.S. states, Canada, the United Kingdom, Ireland, Sweden, and Greece. For 1998 the company generated sales revenues of $23.5 million, a growth of 186.6 percent from 1997. The number of employees increased nearly 50 percent to 83. The March 1999 laser revenue generated at Laser Vision Centers increased 60 percent from that generated in March 1998.

The Laser Center Inc. (TLC) of Mississauga, Ontario, brought in annual revenues of $59.1 million in 1998, a one-year sales growth of 177.5 percent. Like its competitors, TLC specializes in excimer laser surgery to correct common vision problems such as myopia, hyperopia and astigmatism. The company maintains laser clinics and secondary care facilities using 7,000 affiliated local doctors. They also manage 45 refractive laser clinics, with four in Canada (in British Columbia and Ontario) and 26 in the United States. TLC invested $8 million in LaserSight in 1998 to fund development of a network of mobile excimer lasers.

In April 1999 TLC announced plans to restructure in order to focus on its core laser correction business. The corporation will use TLC Capital Corporation, a wholly owned subsidiary, for strategic investments, and negotiations are underway for the sale of Partner Provider Health, TLC's managed care division. Targets for further expanding its core business include agreements with major corporations and health management organizations (HMOs) as a source of revenue. In 1999 TLC formed agreements with Southern California Edison Co., making available discounts on services for the utility's 600,000 employees, and with the Oakland, California-based healthcare organization Kaiser Permanente, which serves 8.6 million people in 17 states and the District of Colombia.

WORK FORCE

As of 1997 only ophthalmologists could actually use ophthalmic lasers on patients. Ophthalmologists are medical doctors specifically trained in a branch of medicine dealing with the structure, functions, and diseases of the eye. After four years of medical school, Ophthalmologists spend another year as medical interns and three years as residents. In 1997 some of these doctors clashed with optometrists over who had the right to perform ophthalmic laser surgery, since so much of the process was guided by the computer instead of the human hand. In contrast to ophthalmologists, optometrists went through four years at a college of optometry, and had to pass a state exam. Optometrists prescribe glasses and contact lenses and are not licensed to write drug prescriptions or perform surgery. Some optometrists, however, began training to use ophthalmic lasers during the mid-1990s.

As of 1997 the state legislatures of Alaska, California, Colorado, New Jersey, and Virginia considered letting optometrists perform the laser procedures. Idaho already permitted some optometrists to perform laser procedures. Although ophthalmic laser surgery was something done in the caregiver's office rather than a hospital, some ophthalmologists insisted that optometrists should not be allowed to do the procedure. Other analysts claimed that as more people trusted the laser procedures, traditional optometry (selling glasses and contact lenses) could disappear unless these professionals could compete with MD's.

AMERICA AND THE WORLD

Ophthalmic lasers have been used in Europe since the 1980s. Because of international differences in the regulation of medical devices, many lasers for medical use are sold and widely used first outside the United States. Analyst Arons estimates that in 1997, 1,700 ophthalmic lasers were in operation worldwide and that up to 655,000 laser eye surgeries were performed, of which 40 to 45 percent were LASIK procedures. The number of laser corrections performed throughout the world to date may be higher than one million, and estimates of the annual world market range from $2.5 to $2.9 billion annually.

RESEARCH AND TECHNOLOGY

Many clinical studies are in progress to broaden the applications of laser techniques, but some analysts believe future innovations will not be as dramatic as those made in recent years. New techniques are being investigated for treating macular degeneration, an age-related scarring of the retina, glaucoma, and cataracts. Innovative microkeratomes, the device that creates the corneal flap, are also undergoing large-scale evaluation. Multifunction products such as Coherent's EPIC system—a three-in-one apparatus which uses a standard slit lamp to treat diabetic retinopathy, open-angle glaucoma, and cataracts—may further reduce surgeons' operating costs. In a study comparing the relative costs of PRK and high-quality contact lenses, Dr. Jonathan Javitt, an ophthalmologist at Georgetown University, found little difference between the two over a ten-year period. As more lasers are developed and approved for a wider variety of problems and procedures, he and others predict that costs to the consumer will likely decline further.

New non-laser technologies may impact the market as they emerge. The FDA has approved insertable discs and rings which slightly alter cornea's curvature to treat myopia. The procedures are considered permanent but reversible; and modifications to treat myopia are being investigated. Another technique, Radio Frequency Keratoplasty (RFK), uses radio-frequency energy to shrink the intra-stromal collagen fibers deeply within the cornea. The procedure is approved for sale in Canada and has received the CE mark in Europe, and will be marketed as less invasive than lasers to treat hyperopia, presbyopia, astigmatism and overcorrections by laser treatments.

FURTHER READING

"Autonomous and Summit Issue Joint Proxy/Prospectus Material," 30 March 1999. Available from http://www .autonomous.com/usa/pr_990329.html.

"Autonomous Technologies Reports 1998 Year End Results." *BW HealthWire,* 3 March 1999.

Bazell, Robert. "Laser Eye Surgery: It's Hot. Is It Safe?" *MSNBC,* 8 February 1999. Available from http://www .msnbc.com/news/239369.asp.

Borzo, Greg. "Eye Treatment Revolution: Providers Jumping on Laser Bandwagon (Photorefractive Keratectomy)." *American Medical News,* 13 May 1996.

Burnett, Richard. "Laser Firms Keep Eyes on the Future." *Orlando Sentinel,* 22 June 1998.

Charters, Lynda. "Laser Technology Update Presented at CLAO Meeting." *Ophthalmology Times,* 1 April 1998.

Clark, Jane Bennett. "Before You Look a Laser in the Eye." *Kiplinger's Personal Finance Magazine,* October 1997.

Drake, Cynthia. "News for You New Ways to Get Rid of Those Eyeglasses." *Investor's Business Daily,* 12 May 1998.

"FDA Advisory Panel Recommend Approval for LASIK at Emory." *Business Wire,* 5 June 1998.

"FDA Approves Autonomous Technologies' LADARVision® System; Company Announces U.S. Product Launch," 3 November 1998. Available from http://www.autonomous .com/usa/98-11-3%20FDA%20Approval%20.html.

"FDA Panel Recommends Approval with Conditions for KeraVision Intacs™, a Non-Laser Treatment for Myopia," 13 January 1999. Available at http://www.keravision.com/ si_990113.html.

Hau, Louise. "Laser Eye Surgery Winning Wider Acceptance, Observers Say." *Dow Jones Online News,* 4 May 1998. Available from http://www.nrstg1p.djnr.com.

"Huge Laser Study to Use LaserSight Keratome." *Medical Industry Today,* 25 March 1998.

"Investigator Presents Data That Got LADARVision FDA Approval." *Ocular Surgery News,* 1 March 1999. Available from http://www.slackinc.com./eye/osn/199903a/ladar.asp.

Korosko, Marian. "The Eyes Have It. Eye Care Advice." *Dance Magazine,* April 1997.

The Laser Center Inc. Company Web site. Available from http://www.lzr.com.

"Laser Performs High-Precision Corneal Surgery." *OE Reports,* November 1997. Available from http://www.spie.org/ web/oer.

"Laser Vision Centers, Inc. Announces Same U.S. Laser Revenue for March Up 60%; March Best Month Ever for U.S. Surgical Case Volume." *BW HealthWire,* 15 April 1999.

"Laser Vision Centers, Inc. Agrees to Acquire Midwest Surgical Services (MSS); Move Expands LaserVision's Services to Include Mobile Cataract Services." *BW HealthWire,* 30 November 1998.

"Laser Vision Correction Facilities Provide Technical and Financial Support." *Ocular Surgery News,* 15 April 1999. Available from http://www.slackinc.com/eye/osn/199904b/ lasvis.asp.

"LaserSite Selected for National Study." *PR Newswire,* 21 July 1997.

"LCA Vision Performed a Record 6,791 Laser Vision Correction Procedures in Fourth Quarter, Nearly Double a Year Ago." Cincinnati: LCA-Vision Inc., 7 January 1999. Available from http://www.lca-vision.com/company/ recordnumber.html.

Lipner, Maxine. "Is PRK Dead?" *EyeWorld Online,* April 1999. Available from http://www.eyeworld.org/April/cover .asp.

Mitchell, Peter. "Laser Surgery for Eye Defects—Of Proven Use or Not?" *Lancet,* 9 May 1998.

"New VISX University Internet Site Provides Resources to Create a High-Volume Practice." Santa Clara, CA: VISX, Inc., October 1998. Available from http://www.Visx.com/ eyecare/xpress/xpress_9.html.

"Ophthalmic Business: Industry Pipeline." *Ocular Surgery News,* 15 April 1999. Available from http://www.slack-inc.com/eye/osn/199904b/lasvis.asp.

Pethokoukis, James. "Eyeing the Bottom Line." *U.S. News & World Report,* 30 March 1998.

"Refractec Begins Phase III Clinical Studies of RFK." *Pr Newswire,* 20 April 1999.

"Refractive Laser Market Shows Modest Expansion." *Medical Laser Insight,* August 1997.

"Refractive Surgery Patients Prefer LASIK, Studies Report." *PR Newswire,* 9 March 1999.

Robinson, Ken. "Ophthalmic Technology Update: Lasers Go Where Scalpels Rarely Tread." *Biophotonics International,* February 1998.

Rubinfeld, Dr. Roy, Dr. Michael Lemp, Dr. Terrence O'Brien, and Dr. Paul Vinger. Interview by Diane Rehm. *The Diane Rehm Show.* National Public Radio, 20 April 1999.

Samalonis, Lisa B. "Exclusive Refractive Surgery Practices." *EyeWorld Online,* April 1999. Available from http://www.eyeworld.org/April/1319.asp.

Seppa, Nathan. "New Treatments for Macular Degeneration." *Science News,* 27 September 1997.

Smith, Robert C., ed. "Lasers." *Medical and Healthcare Marketplace Guide 1997-1998.* Philadelphia: Dorland's Biomedical, 1998.

Stone, Brad. "Zapping the Eye." *Newsweek,* 2 June 1997.

"Summit and VISX Sign Comprehensive Settlement Agreement; Pillar Point Partners Dissolved." *Business Wire,* 8 June 1998.

"Summit Tech—FTC-2: Prohibits Fee Pacts with VISX." *Dow Jones News Service,* 8 July 1998. Available from http://nrstg1p/djnr.com.

"Sunrise Technologies International, Inc. Announces Restructuring." *BW HealthWire,* 10 March 1999.

"Sunrise Technologies International, Inc. Premarket Approval Application—PMA—Accepted for Filing by U.S. Food and Drug Administration." *BW HealthWire,* 1 February 1999.

"Sunrise Technologies International, Inc. Reports Fourth Quarter and Full Year 1998 Financial Results." *Business-Wire,* 22 February 1999.

"TLC and Kaiser Permanente Form Nationwide Laser Vision Correction Services Venture." Bethesda, MD: TLC-The Laser Center Inc., 7 April 1999. Available from http://www.lzr.com/tlc.

"TLC to Form New Unit." *Reuters,* 21 April 1999.

"TLC to Take Part in Hyperopia Study." *Canadian Corporate News,* 7 July 1998.

"Trokel Testifies for VISX in FTC Patent Suit." *Ocular Surgery News,* 15 January 1999. Available from http://www.slackinc.com/eye/osn/199904b/lasvis.asp.

"VISX Files Actions Against Users of Nidek Laser System." Santa Clara, CA: VISX, Inc., March 1999. Available from http://www.Visx.com/eyecare/xpress/xpress_9.html.

"VISX Is First to Receive FDA Approval to Treat Hyperopia." Santa Clara (CA): VISX, Inc., November 1998. Available from http://www.Visx.com/eyecare/xpress/xpress_9.html.

"VISX Launches National Consumer Advertising Campaign Multimedia Campaign is Built to Increase Consumer Demand for VISX-Certified Doctors and Centers." Santa Clara, CA: VISX, Inc., March 1999. Available from http://www.Visx.com/eyecare/xpress/xpress_9.html.

"VISX Sues Ophthalmologists Over Nidek Laser Use." *Ocular Surgery News,* 15 April 1999. Available from http://www.slackinc.com/eye/osn/199904b/lasvis.asp.

Wandycz, Katarzyna. "See-Eye Ads: Laser Surgery to Cure Myopia Is a Breakthrough. So Is The Selling of It. (Photorefractive Keratectomy Surgery for Myopia)." *Forbes,* 17 June 1996.

"What Is Refractive Surgery?" *Refractive Surgery Patient Resource Center,* 22 February 1998. Available from http://eyeinfo.com/whatisrefsurg.html.

Wilson, Ellen D. "New Flap Instruments are Created as LASIK Goes Mainstream." *EyeWorld Online,* April 1998. Available from http://www.eyeworld.org/April/1312.asp

Zehr, Leonard. "Investment News." *The Globe and Mail,* 17 March 1999. Available from http://www.lzr.com/tlc/ylc_ir/investmentnews/topnews/globeandmail.html.

—Dave Fagan,
updated by Cameron McLaughlin
and Sondra E. O'Donnell

OPTICAL DATA STORAGE

INDUSTRY SNAPSHOT

During the 1990s, optical storage discs, including CD-ROMs, gained widespread acceptance and popularity. In the early 1990s, CD-ROM technology held only a niche market in academic publishing. CDs were attractive to this market because of their tremendous storage capacity—a typical optical disc can hold approximately 500,000 pages of text. One of the drawbacks to early CD-ROM technology was that it was "write only"—that is, once data was written onto a CD-ROM, it was permanent and unalterable. This prevented CDs from becoming widely accepted in other markets.

By the mid-1990s, technological advances in CD-ROM applications, such as storage capabilities for not only text, but also graphics, audio, and images, combined with rewriting capabilities, have made CD-ROMs attractive to a wide variety of markets including publishing, computing, education, and entertainment. In addition to storage capacity and versatility, CD-ROMs have gained popularity because of their durability and size, and the relative ease by which people can replicate the information stored on them. By the end of the twentieth century, optical storage may be the most popular method of information storage.

According to International Data Corp., a research firm that tracks the optical data storage industry, worldwide optical drive shipments increased dramatically from less than 1 million drives sold in the early 1990s, to 74.7 million drives sold in 1997. Heightened popularity in optical storage media has also affected the computer manufacturing market as well. Most manufacturers offer CD-ROM drives as standard or optional equipment.

The optical data storage industry includes companies that manufacture optical discs and cards and record data to them, along with those that manufacture the drives and other devices that read data stored on them. Consumer optical storage products are sold in retail computer and electronics stores, via mail-order catalogs and television shopping programs, and over the Internet, while other devices such as mass storage towers and optical memory cards are sold to government agencies and businesses.

TYPES OF OPTICAL DISCS

Optical discs are the most common kind of optical storage devices. One of the first optical discs was produced in 1978 in a joint effort by Philips Electronics N.V. and Sony Corporation This audio compact disc used CD technology to deliver digital sound and music to consumers. Philips and Sony continued to work together throughout the 1980s developing CD technology standards to store computer data. As technology advanced, new standards were adapted industry-wide. These standards evolved into the CD-ROM technology used today.

Among the types of optical discs used for data storage are compact disc read-only memory (CD-ROM), on which data is permanently written and cannot be altered; write-once, read-many (WORM), on which data can be written once before it is unalterable; and erasable (EO), on which data can be both written and erased.

Recordable CDs (CD-R) are another type of optical storage disc; they allow individuals to create their own CDs. One of the drawbacks to CD-R discs, however, is that although a user can write to different sections of the disc over several sessions, the user can write to them only once, after which time the data is permanently encoded on the CD-R.

In 1986, Philips and Sony joined forces and developed compact disc interactive (CD-I). CD-I was unique for that time, because of its ability to store text, images, sound, and graphics and through "interleaving" these types of data, present them to the user seamlessly and simultaneously. CD-I was created for the consumer market, which made it virtually incompatible with other CD-ROM drives. For this reason, CD-ROM/XA (extended architecture) was developed, thus serving as a bridge between traditional CD-ROMs and CD-Is. CD-ROM/XA allows textual data, audio, and video on the same tracks of a CD, but is compatible with both CD-ROM and CD-I drives.

Erasable, optical discs include magneto-optical (M-O), rewritable (CD-RW), and the most advanced, phase-change (PD). M-O discs can be written and erased in much the same way as a traditional magnetic disc—through the use of heat and an electromagnet. With CD-RW discs, users can both write and erase data many times, much like a traditional floppy disk. PD discs were developed as an alternative to M-O discs. PD technology is unique in that it uses multiple layers on which data can be stored. With this technology, data can be both written and erased with a single laser, thus eliminating the need for an electromagnet. Interest in this technology is fading.

Digital versatile discs or digital video discs (DVD-ROM) represent the latest technological advance in optical storage. These types of discs deliver exceptional video and audio quality. DVD-RAMs (rewritable) were put on the market in the spring of 1998.

STORAGE CAPACITY

Optical data storage is ideal for multimedia applications that include sound, images, and text because optical discs can hold much more information than the typical magnetic storage disks such as floppy disks and storing audio and video information requires a lot of memory. The typical floppy disk holds 1.4 megabytes of data. CD-ROMs appeal to users because they can hold between 600 and 700 megabytes of data. The advent of DVDs, with their tremendous storage capacity—4.7 to 17 gigabytes—may mean that DVD-ROMs will eventually replace CD-ROMs altogether. In addition, DVD drives are "backward compatible" with CD-ROMs, meaning that DVD players can play both older and various types of CDs, as well as new DVDs. For these reasons, some experts predict that DVD sales will overtake CD-ROM sales by the end of the century, thus becoming the new standard in delivering exceptional quality multimedia performance.

HOW OPTICAL DATA STORAGE WORKS

Optical data storage technology uses lasers to write data to disc and later to read it. Because lasers can encode data in smaller areas than magnetic storage technology, optical storage discs can hold much more. The laser beam of an optical disc reader, or player, strikes the disc's reflective surface and either scatters the light or reflects it back through a prism, then to a light-sensing diode that generates a small electrical voltage. This voltage, in turn, produces the binary code—a series of ones and zeros—that the computer understands and translates into meaningful information for the user.

Compact discs are 4.75 inches in diameter with a small hole in the middle and are made of a thin wafer of clear polycarbonate plastic and metal. The metal layer is usually pure aluminum that is sputtered onto the polycarbonate surface in a layer that is only a few molecules thick. The metal reflects light from a tiny infrared laser as the disc spins in the CD player. The reflections are transformed into electrical signals, and then further converted into meaningful data for use in digital equipment.

Information is stored in pits on the CD-ROM that are 1 to 3 microns long, approximately 0.5 microns wide, and 0.1 microns deep. There may be more than 3 miles of these pits wound about the center hole on the disc. The CD-ROM is coated with a layer of lacquer that protects the surface. Usually a label is silk-screened on the back.

THE MANUFACTURING PROCESS

Compact discs are made in multiple steps. First, a glass master is made using photolithographic techniques. An optically ground glass disc is coated with a layer of photoresistant material that is 0.1 microns thick. A pattern is produced on the disc using a laser; then the exposed areas on the disc are washed away, and the disc is silvered to produce the actual pits. The master disc is next coated with single molecular layers of nickel, one layer at a time, until the desired thickness is achieved. The nickel layer is then separated from the glass disc and used as a metal negative.

In the case of low production runs, the metal negative is used to make the actual discs. Most projects require several positives to be produced by plating the surface of the metal negative. Molds or stampers are then made from the positives and used in injection molding machines.

Plastic pellets are heated and injected into the molds, where they form the disc with pits in it. The plastic disc is coated with a thin aluminum layer, for reflectance, and a protective lacquer layer. The disc is then labeled and packaged for delivery. Most of these operations take place in a "clean room" since a single particle of dust larger than a pit can destroy data. Mastering alone takes about 12 hours.

The smallness of the pits and the pattern in which they are applied give optical discs their tremendous storage capacity. In contrast to magnetic disks, where data is stored in concentric sectors and tracks, data is stored on optical discs in a spiral pattern originating at the small hole in the center and reaching to the outer edges.

The primary unit of data storage on a compact disc is a sector. Each sector on a CD contains 2,352 bytes of data, and is followed by 882 bytes of error detecting and correcting information and timing control data. Thus, a CD actually requires 3,234 bytes to store 2,352 bytes of data.

The disc spins at a constant linear velocity, which means that the rotational speed of the disc may vary from about 200 revolutions per minute when the data being read is located at the outer part of the disc, to about 530 rpm when the data is located at the center.

CDs are read at a sustained rate of 150 kilobytes (K) per second, which is sufficient for good audio, but very slow for large image files, motion video, and other multimedia information. Newer drives spin at up to 24 times this rate. Still, CD access speeds and transfer rates are much slower than those from a hard disk. This is expected to change as discs are made to spin

faster and different types of lasers are used. The development of multi-spin drives in the early 1990s and ever-faster CD-ROM drive speeds have improved data access rates.

Optical storage is stable and reliable, and the discs are very durable. The surface of a CD is basically transparent. It has to allow a finely focused beam of laser light to pass through it twice, first to the metallic layer beneath the plastic where the data resides, then back to the receptors. While dirt, scratches, fingerprints, and other imperfections may interfere with data retrieval, improvements in error correction rates allow for some margin of error.

During the 1980s, U.S. companies put their research and development efforts into the magnetic hard disk rather than optical storage technology. At that time, the market for hard disks was growing because of their fast access times. The relatively slow data access time by optical drives slowed their acceptance in the market. However, Japan invested heavily in the production of optical disc devices and Japanese companies have dominated the optical storage market throughout the mid-1990s.

BACKGROUND AND DEVELOPMENT

Optical data storage technology was first used commercially in the 1960s when Philips Electronics N.V. developed laser discs known as LaserVision. Video and audio, stored together on 12-inch discs, were read from a laser light beam's reflections as the disc rotated. Variations of the reflections were translated into analog electrical impulses.

This laser disc storage technology played an important role in the development of compact disc au-

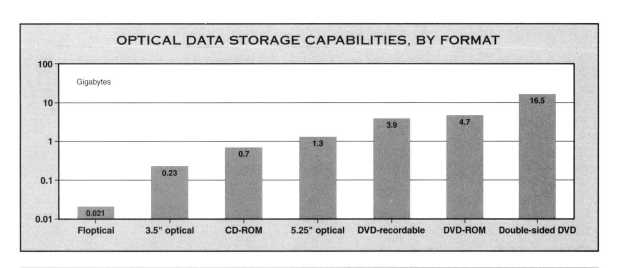

dio (CD-A) for the consumer market. The information was stored in digital, rather than analog, format. In 1980, Philips and the Sony Corporation jointly created the standard for audio compact discs (CD-A) technology known as the "Red Book." The Red Book was the first in a series of CD technology standards that are still used.

In 1984, Philips and Sony followed the Red Book with the "Yellow Book," which defined standards for the storage of large volumes of computer data on compact discs as read-only memory in addressable sectors. The Red Book defined standards only for audio. The CD-ROM discs and drives were similar to the audio CDs and drives, though with a better error correction rate and without a digital-to-analog converter. The Yellow Book provided the structure for the High Sierra Agreement published by Philips, Sony, and Microsoft in 1985. This agreement became the ISO 9660 standard governing the presentation of data on CD-ROMs that were developed and first shipped during the mid-1980s, and continued to serve as the governing standard for all CD-ROM manufacturers throughout the 1990s.

In 1989, Philips and Sony again joined to develop the software and hardware standard known as the "Green Book" for CD-I (compact disc-interactive). Although the technology failed to gain wide acceptance, the Green Book was adopted as a standard way of providing images, sound, and other multimedia functions on CD.

CURRENT CONDITIONS

At the end of the twentieth century CD-ROMs continued to be the most widely used form of optical data storage with shipments of drives topping 93 million in 1998, according to a report by International Data Corp. (IDC) in 1999. DVD-ROM shipments came close to 6 million according to the same study. IDC forecast that 19 million DVD-ROM drives would ship in 1999 and that this technology would capture 80 percent of the market by 2002. CD-RW drive sales were also expected to grow significantly in 1999. The 1998 Disk/Trend Report on optical disk drives projected that by 2001 shipments of all types of optical disc drives would top 144 million, led by DVD-ROM. Charles Van Horn, executive vice president of the International Recording Media Association, said at a DVD Production conference in August 1998, that DVD-ROM will replace CD-ROM in 105 million computers by 2002. Disk/Trend also projected a

steady rise in writable and read/write drives into the twenty-first century, with CD and DVD writable drives forecast at over 15 million in 2002, and read/write drives at almost 3.5 million.

Regarding the competition between CD and DVD, Roger Hutchinson, Ph.D., an industry expert, believes that CD-ROM and DVD-ROM technologies will co-exist for some time to come: "What I see is a ten- to fifteen-year life cycle for CD-ROM in developed countries and an even longer life cycle in developing countries—especially those with poorly-developed telephony." In addition, companies that are currently producing DVD-ROM drives—Philips, Pioneer Electronics, Toshiba, and Panasonic—have not abandoned their CD-ROM drive operations, rather they are working to improve their speeds. In 1997 a group of 10 companies agreed to a common standard for DVD-RAM, and some observers think that they will outsell writable versions of CD format drives by early 2000.

A base of nearly 100 million CD-ROM drives existed in the United States in 1997. Dataquest Inc. projected that of the total sales of CD-ROM software, 50 percent would come from games; 25 percent from reference works; 20 percent from educational CD-ROMs; and the remaining 5 percent from other products.

INDUSTRY LEADERS

Most of the leading companies in the optical data storage industry are Japanese consumer electronic giants like Matsushita, which sells its products under the brand name of Panasonic, Hitachi, Toshiba, Mitsubishi, and Pioneer. Philips Electronics of the Netherlands is also a major player in the industry. Leading U.S. companies in the industry are 3M and Hewlett-Packard. For all these diversified industrial firms, optical storage products are just a small part of their revenues. They are, however, a point of convergence of much of the research and development in the industry. For example, Hitachi, Matsushita, Philips, Mitsubishi, Pioneer, Sony, Toshiba, and JVC joined with Time-Warner and Thomson Multimedia to form the DVD Forum. Matsushita, according to Disk/Trend, was the industry leader in the sale of optical disc drives in 1996 with 18.4 percent of the worldwide market. Not content to rest on its laurels, it launched a 32X CD-ROM drive (operating at 32 times the speed of an audio CD) in May 1998. It was also one of the first, along with Hitachi, to ship DVD-RAM drives.

Toshiba, however, was the leader in DVD drives, with more different models in 1998 than any other manufacturer.

The other main segment of the optical data storage market—optical disc libraries and towers for mass storage—grew significantly in the late 1990s. Hewlett-Packard was the leader in this segment of the industry. It had 19.2 percent of the worldwide sales in 1996. In May 1998 it announced several new magneto-optical storage devices, including a new jukebox with a total capacity of 1.2 terabytes (1.2 trillion bytes). Kodak and Pioneer New Media Technologies are also important suppliers for this market.

AMERICA AND THE WORLD

In 1996, the Japanese Technology Evaluation Center (TEC) released a report comparing the optoelectronics industries in Japan and the United States. The TEC noted that annual sales of optoelectronics (optical storage discs and drives) in Japan were $40 billion, while sales in the United States were only $6 billion. This discrepancy was largely due to the fact that during the 1980s companies in the United States concentrated their efforts and interest on further developing magnetic hard disk drives instead of optical storage; the hard disk market was where a majority of sales in the United States were centered. Meanwhile, Japanese companies invested heavily in optical technology. In recent years, however, U.S. companies and universities have invested significantly in optical storage research.

According to Disk/Trend, of the 53 companies that made optical disc drives in the late 1990s, 44 were headquartered in Asia. Among the 64 manufacturers of optical disc libraries and towers, used for mass storage for mainframes and computer networks, 36 were headquartered in the United States.

Many of the major users of optical storage technology are located in the United States, and they are collaborating with Japanese manufacturers to define new formats and standards for the medium. For example, Time-Warner Inc. and Thomson Multimedia were part of the DVD Forum that produced the DVD standard, in which the U.S. movie, cable TV, video, and multimedia software industries had strong opinions and large stakes.

In late spring 1997, nine companies with major investments in high-density, rewritable optical storage (Fujitsu Inc., Hitachi Ltd., Hitachi Maxell Ltd., Ima-

tion Corp. (3M), Olympus Optical Co. Ltd., Philips Electronics N.V., Sanyo Electric Co. Ltd., Sharp Electronics Corp., and Sony Corp.) formed another group, the Advanced Storage Technical Conference (ASTC). Their goal is to develop the MO7 specification, which will use magneto-optical technology to store up to seven gigabytes of data on these single-sided removable discs.

RESEARCH AND TECHNOLOGY

HOLOGRAPHIC STORAGE

As the use of computers grows, the demand for more and more memory continues unabated. So far conventional technologies have been able to satisfy the demand, but there is evidence that there are physical laws that put a cap on what current technology can accomplish. Therefore researchers continue to search for new and possibly unconventional ways to meet the increased memory demands. Holographic 3-Dimentional methods seem to hold the greatest promise, although other approaches are also being researched and studied.

Holographic data storage has attracted a great deal of research support. A large consortium funded by the U.S. Defense Advanced Research Projects Agency (DARPA), which includes such industrial partners as IBM, Optitek, Rockwell, Kodak, and Polaroid, has been working on it, as well as Bell Labs and start-up companies like Holoplex. A significant amount of progress has been reported, though problems remain, particularly in the area of suitable materials for recording media.

A hologram is a recording of the interference pattern formed where two coherent beams of light cross. Light from a single laser is split into two beams. One of the pair picks up and carries the information, while the other, the reference beam, is reflected across the path of the first. Where they cross, an optical interference pattern forms, which is recorded on the media. In playback, a similar beam of light is shined on the recorded media along the path of the reference beam, and the holographic image is generated. If the angle at which the playback beam of light strikes the recorded media is not the same as the angle of the reference beam when the hologram was recorded, the hologram will not appear. This makes volume recording of holograms possible. If a thick recording material is used (1 mm is thick in this context), many different holograms can be recorded and played back from one location by very slight variations of angle of light.

Another aspect of holographic data storage that enables large amounts of data to be stored is that each hologram is a two-dimensional image and can contain a million bits of digital data. Because of the limitations of the material available and the need for a reasonable readout rate, the maximum number of holograms in one location is 1,000. This means that each location can hold 1 gigabit (Gbit) of data, and data can be retrieved at the rate of 1 Gbit per second. A DVD disc has a readout rate of about 10 megabits (Mbit) per second.

Several different configurations of holographic storage are being studied. Erasable write-once, read-many drives are envisioned with the capability of storing terabytes of data and reading out data at the rate of one Gbit per second. These would be suitable for applications in which data changes rarely but fast access to large volumes of data is required, such as video-on-demand and large Web-servers. Write-once 3D disks the size of DVD disks could hold more than 100 gigabytes (Gbyte), with fast access and readout rates of 500 Mbits per second could be used where data requires permanent storage but fast access, such as with medical data and satellite images. Pre-recorded 3D disks holding 100 Gbytes per disk could be used for distributing software, movies, and multimedia programs.

At the end of 1998 researchers at Bell Labs reported the development of a new holographic material that "appears to constitute a commercially viable medium with archival lifetime, shelf life, and thermal stability being the critical (non-performance) parameters." They noted that until recently other components necessary for a holographic storage system were not commercially available but that now they were, having been developed for other applications. They suggested that the nearest-term product would be a write-once-read-many times (WORM) drive. The goals for such a device would be 125 gigabytes of data on a 5.25-inch removable disk, with read rates of 30 to 50 megabytes per second.

Other researchers are working on a variation of holographic storage using a technique called spectral-hole burning. Spectral-hole burning takes place when certain materials reach a state in which they cannot absorb any more light energy. At this point the electrons of the atoms that make up the material are boosted to a higher energy level. Usually the electrons quickly lose this energy, but some materials, at very low temperatures, do not. This means that any more light at the same wavelength are not absorbed, so the material acts on the full spectrum of light like it had a hole burned in it at a certain point in the spectrum. Using the right materials, researchers have found that

they can use the phenomenon to store vast amounts of data in a very small area. Combining this with holography offers the possibility of multi-gigabyte capacities with both random-access and data-transfer rates a thousand times faster than those of magnetic hard drives, according to Tom Mossberg of Templex Technology, which is developing an optical dynamic random-access memory (ODRAM) using this method. The major obstacle is finding material that can function at higher temperatures.

Another approach to holographic storage being worked on in France proposes recording reflection gratings—a simple form of hologram—within an array of microfibers formed vertically in a disk. The interference patterns are produced along the fiber by introducing the light from each end. The wavelength of the recording light is varied, the variations containing the data. To read back the data, another light, containing every available wavelength, is introduced into one end of the fiber, and each wavelength that was recorded previously is strongly reflected. The data is decoded by analyzing the reflected spectrum. Work on this approach is in the early stages and the ideal materials and light sources have not yet been found, but patents have already been taken out on the microfiber disk and the polychromatic laser that the research has inspired.

OTHER DEVELOPMENTS

Quinta Corp., a San Jose, California, company bought by Seagate Technology Inc., the leading hard-disk drive manufacturer, has developed a system that it calls Optically Assisted Winchester (OAW) technology. It combines Winchester-type hard disk technology, like what is used in standard hard-drives, with higher capacity optical storage. The laws of physics appear to limit magnetic drives to about 40 Gbits per square inch, which Quinta says OAW will be able to surpass, at a lower price. Quinta aimed to announce its first products by the end of 1998 but was unable to.

At the other end of the capacity spectrum, but important for a growing part of the computer industry, is a new technology being developed by Ioptics Inc. called optical read-only memory (OROM). A credit-card-size OROM module can store 128 megabytes (Mbyte) per cartridge, enough for many portable applications that have low memory requirements, and much more than Drexler Technology's LaserCard. The device has no moving parts, which makes it rugged enough for portable devices, and will sell for about 2 cents per Mbyte, much less than current technologies for similar applications. Despite a $9.5-million financing package from Microsoft and others for development, by March 1999 the company had not been able to produce a product suitable for the hand-held market with its constant demand for smaller and smaller components. President of Ioptics, Lane De-Camp, said they were exploring a number of possible steps, including a larger round of funding to modify the OROM device. Sale of the technology was also being considered.

FURTHER READING

Bains, Sunny. "Holographic Films on Disk Hold Hope for Ultra-Dense Memories—Fiber Storage Reaches for Ter-abytes." *Electronic Engineering Times,* 13 April 1998.

———. "Novel Frequency Technique Supercharges Holo-graphic Recording—Spectral 'Holes' Promise Optical Stor-age to Burn." *Electronic Engineering Times,* 4 May 1998.

Bannan, Karen J. "New Devices Archive Terabytes." *PC Week Online,* 27 April 1998. Available from http://www.zdnet.com/pcweek/news/0427/27tera.htm.

"The Beginning of the End for CD-ROMs?" *Home PC,* No-vember 1996.

Broersma, Matthew. "Startup Claims Storage Advance." *ZDNN,* 18 February 1998. Available from http://www.zdnet.com/zdnn/content/0218/285977.htm.

"CD-ROM Sales by Content." *Market Share Reporter 1997.* Farmington Hills, MI: The Gale Group, 1997.

"CD-ROM Technology: History, Standards and Develop-ment." Available from http://scitsc.wlv.ac.uk/~le1812/tech/cd-tech.htm.

"Computer Storage Technology." *McGraw-Hill Encyclope-dia of Science and Technology,* 8th ed. New York: McGraw-Hill Inc., 1997.

Costlow, Terry. "Removable Storage—Ioptics Lands $9.5 Million in Financing from Microsoft, Others—Optical Rom Module Offers Low-Cost Storage in Portables." *Electronic Engineering Times,* 20 March 1998.

Curtis, Kevin, William L. Wilson, Lisa Dhar, and Adrian Hill. "Holographic Data Storage, Finally . . ." *Computer Technology Review,* Fourth Quarter 1998.

Del Prete, Crawford, Robert Amatruda, Danielle Levitas, and Wolfgang Schlichting. "Industry Outlook: All's Well That Ends Well." *Data Storage,* January 1999.

Doering, David. "Kodak's CD Library 144 CD Jukebox." *EMedia Professional,* February 1998.

Hara, Yoshiko. "Competing Rewritable-Drive Formats Aim to Usurp DVD-RAM: Upstarts Challenge DVD-ROM's Heir Apparent." *Electronic Engineering Times,* 23 March 1998.

Hara, Yoshiko, and Terry Costlow. "Japan Leaps into DVD-RAM." *Electronic Engineering Times,* 5 May 1997.

Holsinger, Erik, and Rex Farrance. "The Fastest Drives Alive." *PC World,* July 1997.

Hutchinson, Roger. "Digital Versatile Disc: The Next Gen-eration of CD-ROM," 25 January 1997. Available from http://www.ecomedia.org/sigcat/97w/dvd.html.

"IDC Study Sees Growth Ahead for DVD-ROM, Software Sales." *TWICE,* 19 January 1998.

"IDC Survey Shows Newcomer DVD to Oust Incumbent CD-ROM Technology." *Business Wire,* 31 July 1996.

Japanese Technology Evaluation Center. "Optical Storage Technology," February 1996. Available from http://itri.loyola.edu/opto/c3_s1.htm.

"Optical Disk Drive Shipments to Exceed 70 Million Units in 1997, Boosted by CD-ROM Drives, Plus Initial DVD-ROM Sales." Mountain View, CA: DISK/TREND, 1998. Available from http://www.disktrend.com/newsopt.htm.

"Optical Disk Drives and Libraries." Mountain View, CA: DISK/TREND, 1999. Available from http://www.disktrend.com/newsopt.htm.

"Optical Storage Overview." In *HP: The Optical Storage Primer.* Available from http://www.esrf.fr/computing/cs/nice/impl/optical/optical-overview.html.

"Panasonic Rides Fast Lane with 32X CD-ROM Drive." *National Underwriter Property & Casualty,* 11 May 1998.

Parker, Dana J. "DVD-RAM Finalized, High-Density Con-tenders on the Way." *EMedia Professional,* July 1997.

Psaltis, Demetri, and Geoffrey W. Burr. "Holographic Data Storage." *Computer,* February 1998.

Renstrom, Roger. "DVDs Already Start Recording Compe-tition." *Plastics News,* 24 August 1998.

SRI Consulting. "Optical Storage Technologies," 1997. Available from http://future.sri.com/TM/about_TM/aboutOST.html.

TFPL Multimedia. "Facts and Figures 1997." Available from http://www.tfpl.com/factfr.htm.

Thompson, Brad. "The PD Combo: A New Palimpsest?" *CD-ROM Professional,* March 1996.

White, Ron, and Timothy Edward Downs. "How Comput-ers Work: How a CD-ROM Drive Works." *PC/Computing,* February 1993.

—Joan Giglierano, updated by Howard Distelzweig

Optical Sensing and Infrared Sensory Devices

INDUSTRY SNAPSHOT

Scientists originally developed optical sensing devices for the aerospace and defense industry—largely for use in space probes, spy satellites, and high-tech weaponry. The technology then crossed over many industry lines, finding applications in the medical, electronics, and automotive industries, among others. The ever-popular and ever-present TV remote control, which uses an infrared sensor, shows the mass market potential of an optical sensing device that clicks with users. While the military continues to develop innovative and improved uses for optical sensing devices through government-funded research, other industries are developing their own commercial applications geared and priced for the masses. Sensors continue to pop up in a slew of consumer products—such as cars, phones, pagers, watches, cameras, and computers. As a result, even with defense budget cutbacks, insiders predict double-digit growth in overall optical sensor sales in the coming years.

Paul Saffo, a leading futurist, characterized the start of the twenty-first century as the decade of the sensor, just as the 1980s were the decade of the microprocessor. According to Saffo, sensors will eventually penetrate most aspects of life, making possible so-called "intelligent" homes and cars. But the realization of this vision depends on the development of micromachining processes, which will enable the cheap mass production of more highly efficient and compact infrared sensors.

ORGANIZATION AND STRUCTURE

Initial development of optical sensors primarily occurred in the aerospace and defense industry, largely in military and space programs. Current use and development has expanded to include a variety of industries.

Infrared sensors, the most common type of optical sensors, detect objects or conditions by identifying the heat they emit. Infrared radiation (IR) is transmitted constantly through the atmosphere and is, in varying degrees, reflected or absorbed by objects. IR energy, which is absorbed, raises the temperature of the objects. The heat humans feel from a fire, sunlight, or a radiator is infrared.

Infrared sensors have a variety of applications—military, commercial, and otherwise. The guidance systems in heat-seeking missiles, for example, depend on infrared sensors, and sensors are the key technology in night vision systems, which the military has also been instrumental in developing.

Sensors have also made a difference to ground troops. Soldiers on night guard duty at a camp during the NATO peacekeeping mission in Bosnia, for instance, often came outfitted with compact radios, night-vision goggles, infrared sniper sights, and global positioning satellite range finders.

Infrared sensors have many civilian uses as well. Weather satellites carry IR sensors to track meteorological systems. They also track pollution. Polluted water, for example, has a higher temperature gradient, which satellite sensors easily detect. Earth- and space-based telescopes integrate infrared sensors. Infrared systems are also integrated onto helicopters for finding people lost in wilderness areas; law enforcement agencies have modified versions designed to track criminals or escaped convicts. More and more, optical sensors are making their way into consumer markets. Digital cameras were made possible by optical sensors; the imaging system relies on optical sensor technology. "Smart" consumer devices, like automatic light switches—lights that turn on automatically when someone enters a room—are smart because IR sensors "know" when someone is there.

Optical sensors are produced by a variety of company types. Historically, the biggest producers have been defense contractors that manufacture sensors for specific purposes—missile guidance systems, for example. Companies like Northrop Grumman Corp. and Rockwell International Corp. continue to produce components for government projects, often in cooperation with other firms, while at the same time are expanding into broader industrial applications such as robotics. Companies that make electronics for the industrial and consumer markets also produce sensors. These firms sell their sensors to other original equipment manufacturers for use in a broad variety of industrial and consumer applications.

As the technology becomes more highly developed and less expensive, specialist companies as well as smaller start-up firms are also becoming involved in the development and manufacture of sensors. Camera companies, like Olympus Optical and Polaroid, have made important advances in sensor technology, which led to the sophisticated auto-focus devices so popular with consumers. These firms continue to be an important force in the industry as they develop digital cameras that are dependent on optical sensors. Other smaller companies, often working with proprietary technology, produce sensors for diverse, highly specialized purposes as varied as night vision, environmental monitoring, or infrared telescopy.

BACKGROUND AND DEVELOPMENT

Because infrared sensors measure heat in objects, the first ones developed were essentially thermometers that relied on a change of temperature in the measuring device itself. These early devices led to the development of bolometers, which are still used to detect infrared radiation.

The first practical infrared sensor was developed in Germany during the 1930s when research capitalized on the IR sensitivity of lead sulfide. After World War II, American researchers followed suit, abandoning the materials they had been studying and instead concentrating on lead sulfide sensors. Early IR sensors were limited to the short end of the IR spectrum. Other infrared-sensitive materials, however, soon helped extend sensitivity into the medium, and eventually into longer wavelength ranges. The introduction of semiconductor alloys, like mercury cadmium telluride, enabled infrared sensors to be fine-tuned to a specific wavelength for specific purposes.

In the early 1960s, photolithography—the repeatable imprinting of chemical or electronic patterns on silicon or other materials—made possible the first complex arrays of infrared sensors, some with focal planes of more than 1,000 elements. The refinement of such arrays would eventually make possible the focal systems for digital cameras. High-volume production of IR sensor arrays using mercury cadmium telluride took off in the 1970s and have been the dominant technology ever since. They are used in a number of applications, including missile systems and weather satellites. Eventually silicon was used and it was discovered that IR-sensitive chemicals could be "grown" on a silicon substrate and used as sensors. Other advantages of silicon included its ready availability (deriving from sand), limited frequency response, and low thermal expansion quotient.

The first generation of IR sensors is represented by the arrays developed in the 1960s; the second generation began with electronic signal readouts that could integrate output from the many elements of an infrared array. That capability was first developed in the 1970s, and reached maturity in the 1990s with large fully integrated two-dimensional arrays. Such massive arrays are common on sensor-bearing satellites, and work was underway in the late 1990s to create miniature arrays on silicon chips using MEMS (Micro-Electrical Mechanical Systems) technology. Since the 1970s, the development of the infrared sensor has directly followed upon the development of the silicon integrated circuit. (Also see chapters in this book on Astronautics, Micromachines, Satellites, and Semiconductors.)

In 1993 the Infrared Data Association (IrDA) formed to establish a low-cost universal standard to enable all infrared-based cordless data communications to work together. IrDA envisioned a walk-up, point-to-point user model, with data flying back and forth between a broad range of appliances from a variety of makers.

By 1998, IrDA reported that the IrDA standard port was rapidly becoming the most common cordless connection in the world. IrDA boasts more than 150 members—including 3Com Corp., Canon Inc., Dell Computer Corp., Hewlett-Packard Co., Motorola Inc., International Business Machines Corp., Sony Corp., and Xerox Corp. The IrDA port can be found in pagers, watches, cell phones, pay phones, printers, cameras, organizers, photo kiosks, communicators, and laptop and hand-held computers.

Two basic types of infrared sensors have been developed: one detects energy (heat), the other detects photons (light). The energy sensor detects temperature changes caused by infrared radiation. An electrical current is monitored for changes, which results in proportion to external temperature. Energy type IR sensors are relatively inexpensive and are used in various applications—from fire detection systems to automatic light switches. One technical limitation of energy sensors is that they must be insulated from the external environment to increase their sensitivity, while at the same time able to dissipate heat quickly in order to respond quickly to changes.

The most recent development in energy-type sensors involves micromachining on silicon. Manufactured using photolithography, such sensors have extremely low power requirements, yet match traditional sensors in performance. Microbolometers, devices that compare current and voltage in order to measure infrared radiation, have been developed. Micromachined IR sensors have, by and large, not moved from the laboratory into commercial production, but one foreseen application is in night vision systems for military and civilian use.

Photon-type sensors react to the interaction of light with a semiconductor. Because they react to light rather than temperature, they respond to changes much faster than energy-type sensors. Photon sensors are easily manufactured in large two-dimensional arrays, which has led to their application in advanced IR detection systems such as satellites. A major limitation to photon-type IR sensors is sensitivity to their own infrared radiation. To reduce such interference, they must be cooled to cryogenic temperatures, which requires added power and equipment. A focal point of IR sensor research is the development of sensors that don't require cooling. In 1996, after a year's work, Amber, a division of Raytheon, produced Sentinel, the world's first commercially available, microbolometer-based, uncooled, infrared imaging system. The development is eventually expected to revolutionize future production of infrared sensors.

CURRENT CONDITIONS

In the past, most of the aerospace and defense industry's sales were to the government, primarily the U.S. Department of Defense, whose sensor purchases were symbolized by heat-seeking missiles and the "smart" weapons that burst into public view during the Persian Gulf War. However, defense purchases have

since dropped significantly—defense spending has been reduced by 75 percent compared to its height during the Reagan years, according to the International Society for Optical Engineering. Consequently, aerospace and defense industry firms have been adapting applications to the civilian sector. This means finding civilian applications for technologies already developed for the military (a task made easier by the defense department, which was trying to stretch its dollars by pursuing research into military and commercial applications in cooperation with industry), as well as developing completely new sensors specifically for the civilian market.

Annual weapons procurement by the U.S. government increased by 8 percent in 1999, ending a 12-year period of decline. The Electronics Industry Association predicts that defense spending on weapons electronics will grow by $7.4 billion over the next 10 years. Total military spending in 1998 will reach $58.9 billion, and procurement of electronics for sensors for guidance and control systems will increase from $18.5 billion in 1998 to $23.8 billion in 2007. According to another forecast by Frost & Sullivan, the infrared imaging and sensors systems industry will grow by 29 percent annually through 2004. Sales of infrared FPAs alone were $283.7 million in 1996, and sales of integrated systems approached $1.0 billion. Frost & Sullivan further predicts that the most important trend affecting the infrared sensor market will be corporate consolidation among large defense contractors. Growth opportunities will be strongest in the emerging technologies used in night vision and other systems, and high-performance applications will continue to be developed as new military programs are implemented and existing technologies require large-scale upgrades.

One promising development in the late 1990s was a research consortium called ULTRA—Uncooled, Low-cost Technology Reinvestment Alliance—among Honeywell, Texas Instruments, and Inframetrics to develop uncooled focal plane array (FPA) sensors. That technology offers the potential for dramatic cost reductions over cryogenically cooled sensors, plus higher reliability, instant operation, and decreased systems costs. The sensor includes a signal conditioning circuit, analog-to-digital conversion, and signal processing functions, all arrayed on silicon chips—all the capabilities that define a "smart" IR sensor.

Work continues on standard IR technologies and materials, as well as on micromachined IR sensors. Infrared sensors are increasingly being used to monitor environmental conditions such as oil pollution, forest fires, combustible vapors, and leaks. A new generation of household smoke detectors uses an infrared sensor to detect the presence of lethal carbon monoxide. Development also continues on linear image sensors, the primary component of color scanners, and on new CMOS-based image sensors for digital still cameras, whose sales are expected to exceed $1 billion by the year 2002. A new generation of high-resolution infrared cameras is also emerging for use in machine vision systems.

The automotive industry is one of the first big customers for infrared and optical sensing devices as they become available at a competitive price. Infrared sensors are being integrated, for example, into automotive airbag systems to detect the presence of a child or small adult in a car seat, thus avoiding the inappropriate and dangerous deployment of an airbag. Other applications on the horizon include warning systems and adaptive cruise control. Unlike normal cruise control, which maintains a constant speed, adaptive cruise control would sense the presence of cars on the road ahead—by means of infrared sensors in one plan—and slow the car down to maintain a safe distance.

General Motors Corp. gave the public a peak at its new night vision system at the 1999 North American International Auto Show. The automaker—which plans to be the first to offer night vision on the 2000 Cadillac Deville—touts the feature as a way to improve driving safety by enhancing the nighttime driver's ability to detect potentially dangerous situations beyond the range of the headlamps without taking the driver's eyes off the road. GM mounted an infrared sensor on the front valence panel, with the image seemingly projected over the front edge of the car's hood, in the driver's peripheral vision. The 2000 Cadillac Evoq, a two-seat luxury roadster, sports both night vision and a rear obstacle detection system. The back-up aid uses three sensors in the back bumper—one radar and two ultrasonic—to help avert back-up collisions.

Honda Motors and other automobile companies are also testing forward-drive systems, which use optical and infrared sensors to center the vehicle, change lanes, and avoid obstacles. Lockheed Martin is testing a forward-looking infrared camera adapted from its driverless military vehicles, and forward-looking radar systems are also being developed. Some engineers predict that basic sensors could become standard automotive equipment in 3 to 5 years.

INDUSTRY LEADERS

The most important companies in the optical sensor market are defense contractors that have been involved in cutting-edge research for the government.

Recent consolidation of the aerospace and defense industry, tied to federal spending cutbacks, has left only four major players in the industry—The Boeing Company, Lockheed Martin Corp., Raytheon Company, and Northrop Grumman Corp. Citing a concern about the lack of competition for military contracts, federal regulators barred further consolidation in 1998, when they protested the proposed merger of Lockheed Martin and Northrop Grumman.

Boeing is the world's largest aerospace firm. The Seattle-based company manufactures planes, missiles, rockets, helicopters, spacefaring vehicles, and advanced communications systems. Buoyed by the acquisition of the space and defense unit of Rockwell International Corp. in 1996, Boeing also serves as the largest contractor to the National Aeronautics and Space Administration (NASA). The defense giant racked up sales of $56.1 billion in 1998.

In 1999, the U.S. Department of Defense started launching a distributed, low-Earth orbit satellite constellation that uses infrared and visible optical sensors to detect ballistic missile attacks anywhere in the world. Boeing acts as prime contractor for the first phase of the Space-Based Infrared Surveillance System (SBIRS) and subcontracts under Lockheed Martin for the second phase of the project, to be up and running by 2007. Boeing will provide all sensor payloads for the SBIRS.

Lockheed Martin, the world's second largest aerospace and defense firm, is also developing a remote sensing satellite that will provide high resolution black and white imagery, as well as multi-spectral images, to highlight chlorophyll content, chemical composition, surface water penetration, and other environmental features. The satellite's main advantage is a digital imaging sensor that can provide images with a resolution of 1 meter from 680 kilometers in altitude.

The Maryland-based company also builds warplanes and rockets and manages government projects. In 1997 sales for its electronics sector, charged with sensor development and production, hit $594 million. Total sales for Lockheed Martin reached a record $28.1 billion in 1997, but dropped down to $26.3 billion in 1998.

Raytheon and Hughes Electronics Corporation were the largest producers of infrared and electro-optical equipment at the start of 1997. Then Raytheon doubled in size when it bought the defense electronics division of Texas Instruments Inc. for $3.0 billion and the aerospace and defense division of Hughes for $9.5 billion from parent company General Motors. Also that year Raytheon supplied a major sensing system for the refurbished Hubble Space Telescope. In 1998, the company began a major joint initiative with the U.S. Army to reduce the cost of night vision sensors and broaden their commercial applications. The Massachusetts-based company expects to sell 6 million units of its uncooled infrared sensor devices over a 10-year period in military, police, automotive, and consumer markets.

The Santa Barbara Research Center (SBRC), recently acquired by Raytheon, is one of the most innovative producers of infrared sensors. SBRC specializes in integrated focal plane sensing, and for 10 years their focal plane arrays have been used in telescopes and other astronomical instruments. Basic research and development of multi-element detector arrays covers a wide range of the spectrum, from the visible to longwave infrared. In the late 1990s the company was developing multispectral sensors that could be used for emissions sensing, process control monitoring, chemical processing, and explosive detection. They have been in the forefront of the development of uncooled infrared sensor technologies.

The fourth largest aerospace firm, Northrop Grumman, became a powerhouse in defense electronics and systems integration with two acquisitions: the 1996 purchase of a defense and electronics arm from Westinghouse Electric Corp.; and the 1997 acquisition of Logicon, Inc., an information and battle-management systems maker. The electronics sensors and division of Northrop Grumman accounted for 32 percent of its sales in 1998. Total sales that year were $8.9 billion for the California-based company.

Defense applications will continue to fuel innovation as missile guidance and detection systems are upgraded and existing night vision and electronic sensor technologies are refined. Significant progress has been made in developing real-time imaging systems for satellites and high-altitude surveillance aircraft. The Global Hawk, an autonomous prototype aircraft built by Teledyne Ryan Aeronautical and Raytheon, is equipped with electro-optical and infrared sensors that can provide high-resolution images of large geographic areas in near-real time.

AMERICA AND THE WORLD

U.S. companies manufacture the majority of infrared and other optical sensors used in the United States. Foreign companies have little visibility in the U.S. market, except perhaps in the area of digital camera sensors, a market segment in which Japanese companies like Mitsubishi and Olympus Optical are very active. Innovations are being produced by small firms such as Bureau Etudes Vision Stockplus, a French company that has developed an advanced visual recognition chip that mimics the human eye and can accept infrared, video, or radar signals.

Competition for the business of the enormous Asian electronics market remains intense. The Electronic Industries Association notes that Asia "will continue as the world's premier growth market." A study released by Georgetown University estimated the market in Asia for imported U.S. defense and civil electronics was $125.8 billion in the late 1990s, and that figure does not include the People's Republic of China, home to a billion people.

The worldwide market for industrial machine vision systems totaled $4.0 billion in the late 1990s, according to the Automated Imaging Association, as demand for image capture and analysis in manufacturing processes grows in Europe, Japan, and other industrialized countries. Machine vision sales in North America were $1.5 billion in 1997 and are expected to exceed $2.0 billion by the year 2000.

RESEARCH AND TECHNOLOGY

Like most high-tech fields, research is the lifeblood of the optical sensor industry. Two key fields are MEMS (Micro-Electrical Mechanical Systems) and uncooled infrared sensors. The most important area of research affecting the optical sensor industry is the miniaturization/digitalization of sensor technology. Pressure sensors and accelerometers are already being micromachined on silicon chips, and research is underway to extend micromachining and its extremely cheap batch processing capabilities to infrared sensors.

Although commercial applications are still several years away, MEMS devices are being actively investigated in 10 projects sponsored by the Defense Advanced Research Projects Agency. Development continues on uncooled, large array, and multispectral FPA sensors as well as on a number of new technologies. Using uncooled micro-cantilevered sensors developed at Oak Ridge National Laboratory, Sarcon Microsystems is developing a line of infrared imagers, which may be inexpensive enough to be included on a wide scale in process monitoring and safety devices for cars, boats, and trains. Subminiature photoelectric optical sensors, which are more durable than fiber-optic devices and less expensive than laser sensors were being used in a variety of manufacturing operations in the late 1990s.

Bell Labs developed the world's first laser-based, semiconductor sensor. The sensor operates at room temperature and can detect minute amounts of trace gasses or pollutants (potentially parts per billion). Its power and range are unprecedented for the mid-infrared region of the spectrum. It has been called a revolutionary development for sensor applications because it opens up an new field of uncooled tunable infrared sensors.

The International Society for Optical Engineering reported on a number of projects involving uncooled sensor technology. Besides the ULTRA consortium, work is being done at Texas Instruments, Honeywell, and a number of small sensor companies, as well as in the United Kingdom, France, and Australia.

FURTHER READING

"AlliedSignal Inc." *Hoover's Online.* 11 April 1999. Available from http://www.hoovers.com.

"The Boeing Company." *Hoover's Online.* 16 April 1999. Available from http://www.hoovers.com.

Costlow, Terry. "Emerging Markets—Automotive: Safety, Comfort Drive Electronics." *Electronic Engineering Times,* 31 March 1997.

"ELECTRONICS: Honda's Automated Highway System Research." *Asia-Pacific Automotive Report,* 5 April 1998.

"Electronics Industries Association Says U.S. Defense Spending Will Rise by $7.4 Billion Over Next 10 Years." *Defense News,* 6 October 1997.

Flanagan, Dennis. "Infrared Machine Vision—A New Contender." *Sensors,* 4 April 1998.

Flanders, David. "Airborne Infrared and Ultraviolet Remote Sensing for Oil Spill Detection." *Advanced Imaging,* April 1997.

Frost & Sullivan. "Frost & Sullivan Consolidation and Price Issues Challenge the Rapidly Growing Infrared Imaging Sensors and Systems Industry." *PR Newswire,* 17 February 1998.

Hara, Yoshiko. "CMOS, CMD Parts Promise to Cut Power, Ease Integration—Sensors Jockey for Role As Successors to CCDs." *Elecronic Engineering Times,* 3 March 1997.

"History and Trends of Infrared Sensors," 9 April 1999. Available from http://www. sbrc.com/ir_history.html

"Innovative Technology Could Make Driving Safer." *Star-Tribune Newspaper of the Twin Cities Mpls-St. Paul,* 13 January 1998.

"ITT Industries Gets $35.7 Million Satellite Contract." *Newsbytes News Network,* 1 August 1997.

Johnson, R. Colin. "New Application Areas Addressed by Visual Recognition Device—Vision Chip's Circuitry Modeled on Eye and Brain." *TechWeb,* 15 September 1997. Available from http://www.techweb.com/se/directlink.cgi ?EET19970915S0046.

"Lockheed Martin: Commercial Sensing System Program Profile." *M2 PressWIRE,* 1 October 1996.

"Lockheed Martin Corporation." *Hoover's Online.* 11 April 1999. Available from http://www.hoovers.com.

"Lockheed's Vision of the Road Ahead." *Industries in Transition,* September 1997.

"MEMS Get Lift from Pentagon." *Electronic Buyers News,* 9 March 1998.

"Microcantilever-Based Devices." *NDT Update,* April 1998.

"Motorola Eyes Imaging Shift—Continues Push from CCDs to Less Costly CMOS-Based Sensors." *Electronic Buyers News,* 6 April 1998.

Shelley, Suzanne. "Proper Surveillance Can Keep a Minor Leak from Becoming a Major Event." *Chemical Engineering,* February 1998.

"STM Optimizes Optical Sensing." *Vital Publications,* 1 May 1998.

"Team to Reduce Cost of Night Vision Sensors." *Defense News,* 9 February 1998.

"Uncooled IR Detectors: Their Time Has Come," October 1996. Available from http://www.spie.org/web/oer/october/ oct96/uncoolir.html.

"U.S. Gives Go-Ahead to Merger Creating Giant Defense Company." *Tampa Tribune,* 4 October 1997.

"U.S. Global Hawk Completes First Flight." *M2 Presswire,* 3 March 1998.

—Gerald E. Brennan,
updated by Cameron McLaughlin and Denise Worhach

Outlet Centers

If ever there were a need to prove the almost insatiable appetite of American consumers for a bargain (or even the appearance of a bargain), the emergence of factory outlet malls in the late twentieth century would certainly offer ample proof of this phenomenon. By late 1998, less than 20 years after they first made their appearance on the American retail scene, outlet centers numbered more than 350. Stocking a wide range of goods, from factory irregulars to overstocked merchandise and out of season apparel, outlet stores tripled in number since the end of the 1980s when the marketing trend really caught on with American consumers. In 1989 there were about 4,500 individual outlet stores; in 1998 that number increased to more than 13,000, according to Randy Marks, president of Outlet Marketing Group of Milford, Connecticut. Marks's company tracks the nation's outlet centers and publishes *Outlet Bound, Guide to the Nation's Best Outlets.* Another measure of the phenomenal success of the outlet center concept is the comparison between the growth of all shopping centers and the growth of outlet centers in the 10 years between 1987 and 1996. While the number of all shopping centers increased about 40 percent during the period, outlet centers surged about 300 percent from 108 to 329 during the same 10-year period, according to data from the International Council of Shopping Centers.

Offering brand-name merchandise at prices sharply discounted from what it might cost in a regular retail store, outlet malls include some of the nation's most prestigious merchants such as Brooks Brothers, The Gap, Saks Fifth Avenue, Guess, Benetton, Versace, and Armani. An outlet center typically may be home to anywhere from 25 to more than 100 individual retail stores.

Though outlet stores began by offering rejected or second-quality items, as of the late 1990s, the majority of goods offered at outlet stores was of first quality.

Assessing the trend in outlet centers in the late 1990s, Marks of Outlet Marketing Group observed that the "definition of outlet has expanded to include a new category of mainstream retailers that have opened up clearance stores at outlet centers. It's the only place where designers and manufacturers decide the content of their inventory, not the store buyers who often limit the selection or create added value only at sale time."

In the late 1970s when the trend toward large outlet malls first began to take hold, there were only seven such shopping centers in the country. In little more than a decade, the fledgling retail concept mushroomed from those original seven malls in 1978 to more than 250 by 1989, with gross sales pegged in 1989 at about $18 billion. Some of the most popular factory outlets are individual stores and predate the current outlet center phenomenon. These include such locations as L.L. Bean's factory store in Freeport, Maine, and the popular VF Factory Outlet in Reading, Pennsylvania. It is, however, the rise of the large-scale outlet malls or centers that has so impressed retailing analysts in the final two decades of the twentieth century. These outlet centers range from the relatively unimpressive strip malls with only a handful of shops to the massive and elaborate outlet centers with more than a hundred top-name retailers.

ORGANIZATION AND STRUCTURE

Set up much like shopping centers and malls everywhere, the outlet centers come in a variety of shapes and sizes, ranging from the comparatively spartan strip mall to sprawling, beautifully landscaped outlet centers offering shoppers access to scores of the nation's most distinguished merchandisers and with the added attraction of bargain prices. Among major distinctions between this modern wave of outlets and the factory outlet stores of yore are the smaller scale of individual stores and the effort by today's outlet merchants to make browsing through their stores a pleasant experience. No longer must shoppers suffer the dreary, barn-like atmosphere of the old-time factory outlet. A visit to shops in one of today's upscale outlet centers is an experience comparable to a visit to the shops of regular retailers in a standard shopping center or mall.

The scale of today's outlet centers varies widely from those offering only a handful of shops (often with a common theme, such as outdoor equipment and apparel or women's clothing) to the huge shopping-center type establishments with hundreds of stores offering every conceivable type of merchandise. Although apparel accounts for by far the majority of the retailers represented in today's outlet centers, shoppers can find plenty of other products there as well. These include housewares, electronics equipment, footwear of every conceivable type, fashion accessories, perfumes and colognes, books, and even gourmet foods.

It's hardly surprising that many of the country's most popular outlet centers are located near some of the country's most visited tourist attractions. Banking correctly on the fact that Mom and Sis will eventually find a way to see that the family trip includes a shopping excursion, mall planners have gladly accommodated with major outlet centers near popular tourist destinations. In suburban Virginia, not far from the nation's capital, lies Potomac Mills, a sprawling outlet center with hundreds of merchants, large and small. Franklin Mills, outside Philadelphia, houses a similar collection of merchants. A number of outlet centers have also popped up in the Sun Belt, close to beach destinations that attract thousands of vacationers in season. One example in the latter category is Sawgrass Mills, situated 15 miles west of Fort Lauderdale. Home to close to 200 retailers, Sawgrass Mills offers more than 2 million square feet of shopping.

BACKGROUND AND DEVELOPMENT

The earliest forerunners of the modern outlet centers in the United States date back to the latter half of the nineteenth century. A number of East Coast apparel and footwear manufacturers opened up mill stores where their employees could purchase surplus goods and factory irregulars for substantial savings. Over time these mill stores were opened to the public. In the 1930s, one of the first "factory-direct" outlets was opened by Anderson-Little, a manufacturer of men's clothing. Eventually a number of Anderson-Little outlets were in operation, all of them located in relatively remote locations. In the 1940s, more companies joined the trend, using these factory outlets as a convenient way to dispose of surplus and damaged goods. Typically, the early "factory-direct" outlets were spartan, warehouse-like structures with no amenities to speak of, keeping the manufacturer's overhead low.

The modern outlet center movement was born in the 1970s. In 1974 Vanity Fair opened the first U.S. multi-tenant factory outlet center in Reading, Pennsylvania. The VF Factory Outlet was actually housed in a converted production facility. Although the first factory outlets had appeared well before then, the concept of grouping a number of outlets under a single roof or within walking distance of one another was new. Starting with fewer than 10 outlet centers in 1978, the industry exploded during the 1980s, and the number of centers soared to more than 250 by 1990. Among the forces helping to drive the surge in outlet centers during the late 1970s and through the 1980s were a reduction in the discretionary income of the average consumer, the energy crisis, increased popularity of designer fashions, and the higher value placed by consumers on quality and status. Gross sales at the nation's outlet centers was estimated at about $18 billion in 1990.

Certainly the primary force driving the expansion of outlet centers has been the unquenchable American thirst for bargains or anything that looks like a bargain. However, the rise of the real estate investment trusts, or REITs, has provided the machinery for the large-scale expansion of the outlet centers. These are large companies that are in business to develop land for commercial use. Among the REITs active in this business have been Tanger Factory Outlet Centers Inc., Prime Retail Inc., Chelsea GCA Realty Inc., the Mills Corporation, and Belz Enterprises.

The 1980s also witnessed the appearance on the scene of the mega-outlet center, of which Potomac Mills outside Washington, D.C., and Philadelphia's Franklin Mills are ideal examples. Both were developed and are operated by Mills Corporation, based in Arlington, Virginia. The company also operates the opulent Sawgrass Mills outside Fort Lauderdale, and four other mega-centers in Chicago, Dallas/Fort Worth, Phoenix, and San Bernardino County in California. Several more outlet centers on a similar scale were in the works at the end of 1990s.

PIONEERS IN THE FIELD

One of the moving forces in the emergence of the outlet center retailing concept has been Stanley Tanger, chairman and chief executive officer of Tanger Factory Outlet Centers Inc., the second largest developer of outlet malls in the country. In 1948 Tanger took over as head of the shirt manufacturing company his father had begun in 1920. Tanger/Creighton, as the company was known, went on to open a handful of successful outlet stores. Intrigued by the idea of putting together a group of such discount-price stores at a single location, in 1979 he sold off the shirt company to pursue his dream. Two years later, Tanger opened his first outlet center in North Carolina. In 1986 his son Steven joined in his venture. By the end of 1992, the company had opened 17 outlet centers but was heavily leveraged. To get out from under this mountain of debt, Tanger took the company public in 1993, using the proceeds from its initial public offering to pay off debt and further expand the company.

Another major player in the world of outlet centers has been Mills Corporation, which boasts that it has elevated its massive outlet centers to the level of major tourist attraction. With the exception of Florida, where its Sawgrass Mills outlet center ranks second to Walt Disney World, as of late 1998 the company's mega-malls were the most popular tourist draws in their respective states. The company has gone to great lengths to incorporate such features as giant video screens, huge food courts, and other attractions into its outlet centers. Speaking to CNN anchor John Defterios in November 1998, Larry Siegel, chairman and chief executive officer of Mills, said: "I think it's important to stimulate the customer as much as you can in the shopping environment. I think that people are bored of the same old shopping experience. And so what we try and do at Mills Corporation and in our projects is create something that's different and unique for the customer."

CURRENT CONDITIONS

The final decade of the twentieth century saw a less dramatic spurt in the overall number of outlet centers, but it witnessed a maturing of the retail concept to include more and more upscale brands and a growing attraction for the country's consumers, who flocked to these centers in ever greater numbers. It is estimated that about 55 million Americans shopped in an outlet center during 1998. What they found there were far more big name retailers than were present only a few years earlier. Joining some of the middle-echelon merchants in the outlet centers were such distinguished retail names as Brooks Brothers, Ann Taylor, Saks Fifth Avenue, Nordstrom, Benetton, Versace, and Armani.

The mid-1990s did witness a brief but precipitous decline in the popularity of the outlet centers. However, the expansion of the retailing concept to include some of the country's premier merchants helped to fuel a full recovery in the second half of the decade. As the outlet center phenomenon matured, industry leaders began experimenting with new gimmicks to keep business booming. In July 1998, real estate developer TRI-W broke ground in Wilmington, Delaware, for the nation's first catalog outlet center. The center, which was scheduled to open in the spring of 1999, will boast L.L. Bean and Coldwater Canyon, major catalog retailers, as tenants. Bill Wizner, president of TRI-W Corp., said of the project: "It's the first outlet center anywhere in the world that is specially dedicated to catalogs. We have been involved in the development of outlet centers for a long time, and this is the time for trying something new."

Another new concept in outlet centers premiered in the summer of 1998, when TrizecHahn Development Corporation and Gordon Group Holdings Ltd. jointly opened the Fashion Outlet of Las Vegas. Actually located about 35 miles from downtown Las Vegas, the outlet center at the California-Nevada state line brings together some of the world's top fashion retailers in a single location. With more than 400,000 square feet of shopping area, the Fashion Outlet features the fashions of such designers as Kenneth Cole, Donna Karan, Versace, Jhane Barnes, and Calvin Klein. Lee Wagman, president and chief executive officer of TrizecHahn Development, reported that response to the new outlet center has been overwhelming. "The community has eagerly embraced the opportunity to shop for their favorite designers in one place with unbelievable savings." Apparently, interest in the concept extended well beyond the immediate Las Vegas community, as Wagman added: "We've given tours to groups from as far away as Japan, Germany, and Australia, as well as hosted guests from sister cities San Diego, Los Angeles, and Phoenix."

Although outlet centers had come a long way from the warehouse-like structures of the early factory outlets, the trend toward increased amenities continued to spread during the late 1990s. Many more recent outlet centers are laid out like idealized villages, with attractive clusters of shops separated by park-like patches of greenery. In addition to making the centers more aesthetically appealing, developers have tried to add features of interest for just about everybody in the family. These amenities include kiddy rides, entertainment venues, theme restaurants, and food courts with a large variety of food vendors.

Although some observers of retail trends voiced concern in the late 1990s that the outlet center market was oversaturated with malls, most developers were moving ahead with plans to open still more retail centers. To try to gain an edge over some of its competitors, Chelsea GCA Realty Inc., a New Jersey-based real estate investment trust active in the development of outlet malls, began in 1997 to promote its brand identity as Premium Outlets. Chelsea GCA hoped this corporate-branding strategy would generate awareness among potential customers and tenants of its outlet centers. Early results indicated the strategy was paying off. Tenants at Chelsea GCA outlet malls reported average sales of $360 per square foot in 1997, against an industry average of $220 per square foot. This also represented an improved sales performance for Chelsea GCA tenants, who averaged sales of $313 per square foot in 1995 and $345 per square foot in 1996. Chelsea GCA was "focusing on new properties in larger markets," according to Tom Davis, chief operating officer. "We want to be in major markets that have international tourists. We have high-end tenants, and most of our tenants have wholesale businesses."

In late 1998 Prime Retail Inc., the largest operator of outlet centers in the world, launched a sponsorship and marketing partnership program to help buttress its branding initiative announced a few months earlier. In an attempt to firmly establish a brand identity, Prime Retail renamed all of its outlet centers "Prime Outlets." In December 1998, the company signed an exclusive marketing partnership agreement with Coca-Cola USA, under which Prime Outlets will feature only the vending machines of Coca-Cola. William H. Carpenter Jr., president and chief operating officer of Prime Retail, said that "strategic alliances with brands like Coca-Cola will create superior value for our customers, our merchants, and our shareholders. In addition to bringing added revenue, marketing partners such as Coca-Cola will tap into our growing customer base through special promotions as a way to gain exposure for the products, which in turn will provide the more than 100 million customers who shop Prime Outlets with even more value."

As outlet centers began in the 1990s to evolve into attractions in their own right, shoppers and their families seemed to be traveling farther to visit and then spending more time within the center. The average time spent in an outlet mall is four hours, according to Randy Marks, president of Outlet Marketing Group. This is far longer than the average time spent at a conventional shopping center or mall. "Willing to travel the extra distance to save as much as 75 percent on current season merchandise, this new breed of shoppers is looking for consistent value, selection, and quality, and they are finding it at the nation's factory outlet centers," Marks said.

Even with the brief mid-1990s decline in business at U.S. outlet centers, the sector showed consistent growth through all of the 1980s and into the final days of the 1990s. Nevertheless, it is unlikely to ever supplant the normal retail distribution channels that have been in place for decades, according to Andrew Groveman, president of Belz Factory Outlets and senior vice president of Belz Enterprises, based in Nashville. Belz Enterprises, involved in retailing since the 1940s, entered the outlet market in the late 1970s. The company operates a number of high-profile outlet centers in tourist destinations, including Las Vegas, Orlando, and Pigeon Forge, Tennessee, at the foot of the Great Smoky Mountains.

The real estate investment trusts that formed the real backbone of the outlet center industry in the United States for much of the late 1990s turned in a lackluster performance in terms of return on investment. In late 1998, industry insiders were predicting some improvement in the sector's prospects, based largely on the booming economy and the slowdown of outlet development. Based on indexes maintained by the National Association of Real Estate Investment Trusts (NAREIT), a trade group based in Washington, D.C., the REITs specializing in outlet malls had been outperformed by almost all other retail categories in recent years. The first indication of improved performance came in mid-1998 when outlet REITs showed a total return of 1.85 percent, better than strip mall REITs but not as strong as the 3.72 percent return reported for regional mall REITs.

INDUSTRY LEADERS

The world's largest owner and operator of outlet centers is Baltimore-based Prime Retail Inc. With 50 centers in 26 states, the company operates outlet shopping space of nearly 14 million square feet. A self-administered and self-managed real estate investment trust (REIT), Prime Retail continued to play an active role in the development, construction, leasing, marketing, and management of factory outlet stores in the late 1990s. In addition to its 50 existing centers, several other projects, including outlet malls in Puerto Rico, Maryland, and Missouri, were in the works in 1999. Prime Retail's merger with Horizon Group, finalized in June 1998, added 22 of Horizon's outlet centers into the Prime Retail portfolio. As of early 1999, the company owned almost a quarter of the outlet center space in the United States and about half of the outlet space controlled by publicly held real estate investment trusts. The company's net income in 1998 totaled $17.5 million on sales of $233.0 million. This represented a jump of nearly 200 percent in net income over 1997. The company's employment rolls at the end of 1998 totaled 1,095, an increase of nearly 100 percent over the previous year.

A solid number two in the outlet center business, Tanger Factory Outlet Centers Inc., headquartered in Greensboro, North Carolina, owns and operates 31 outlet centers in 23 states totaling 4.9 million square feet. Founded in 1981 by Stanley K. Tanger, who serves as chairman and chief executive officer, the company is a fully integrated, self-administered, and self-managed REIT. The Tanger family outlet business had its origins in a handful of successful factory outlets operated by the shirt manufacturing company Stanley inherited from his father. Convinced that this was a potentially winning strategy, in 1979 Stanley Tanger sold the shirt company so that he could devote all of his time and energy to the outlet business. The company's first outlet center was opened in North Carolina in 1981. Tanger Factory Outlet Centers posted net earnings of $11.9 million on revenue of $97.8 million in 1998. Although revenue was up 14.7 percent over 1997, net income was off 7.0 percent from the previous year. Stanley Tanger's son, Steven, serves as the company's president and chief operating officer.

Mills Corporation, based in Arlington, Virginia, is the developer and owner of some of the nation's mega-outlet centers, including Potomac Mills, outside Washington, Philadelphia's Franklin Mills, Sawgrass Mills outside Fort Lauderdale, and Arizona Mills in Phoenix. Each of these massive outlet centers hosts 200 or more stores on an average leasable area of 1.7 million square feet. Although the amenities at most of the nation's outlet centers are fairly extensive, the Mills Corp. has focused its efforts on transforming its seven regional outlet centers into tourist attractions in their own right. Most feature big-screen televisions throughout the center, an entertainment venue, and a large food court. The company, which has 1,200 employees, reported net earnings in 1998 of $23.2 million on sales of $185.4 million. Sales were up almost

9 percent from 1997, while net income totaled twice what it had the previous year.

Chelsea GCA Realty Inc. owns and manages 20 outlet centers in 12 states. A real estate investment trust, Chelsea GCA is headquartered in Roseland, New Jersey. Its outlet malls all feature high-end fashion names, including Versace, Calvin Klein, and Ralph Lauren. With about 450 employees, Chelsea GCA reported net income in 1998 of $21.4 million on sales of $139.3 million. This represented a drop of almost 25 percent in earnings from the previous year.

Konover Property Trust Inc., another real estate investment trust, operates both outlet malls and conventional shopping centers in 22 states. The company's holdings boast a total shopping area of nearly 10 million square feet. Konover Property Trust, based in Cary, North Carolina, by the year 2000 will be 60 percent controlled by the Lazard Freres investment house. Employing about 250, the company in 1998 reported a net loss of $3.0 million on sales of $69.5 million.

WORK FORCE

The outlet center industry offers a wide range of employment possibilities, from sales positions paying minimum wage to managerial positions paying six-figure salaries and higher. Unfortunately for job hunters, openings in the former category far outweigh those in the latter. More than 140,000 people work in the industry, most of them in the lower-paying sales positions in the individual outlet stores. Opportunities for higher-paying jobs exist at the store management level and also with the real estate investment trusts who own and operate most of the country's outlet centers.

Outlet operators such as Prime Retail Inc., Tanger Factory Outlet Centers, and Mills Corporation employ a number of management personnel in their headquarters operations. These companies are generally most interested in applicants with backgrounds in accounting and business administration.

AMERICA AND THE WORLD

The factory outlet center concept was pioneered in the United States, but like so many other American innovations, it has quickly made its way outside the country and put down roots not only in neighboring countries but in Europe and Asia as well. Canada has a number of outlet centers, and a few have began to appear on the Mexican retail scene. In early 1999 Prime Retail was in the process of developing an outlet center on the island of Puerto Rico.

During the latter half of the 1990s Europe saw a flurry of outlet center activity. Although many of the factory outlets found in continental Europe are of the individual, manufacturer-operated variety, similar to those found in the United States before the 1970s, there is a growing number of the outlet centers popping up. Austria, Germany, Italy, and Switzerland have attracted some of the new outlet centers.

The outlet center concept has really caught fire in the United Kingdom, where a number of such malls were opened in the late 1990s. One of the major developers of outlet centers in Great Britain is MEPC PLC, based in London. Not unlike a United States real estate investment trust, MEPC develops a broad range of real estate properties, including about 25 percent of the United Kingdom's outlet centers.

Plans were announced in the fall of 1998 for an expansion of England's Outlet Center at Cheshire Oaks that will make it the largest outlet mall in Europe. BAA McArthur Glen, the United Kingdom's leading developer and operator of designer outlet centers, announced a joint venture with BP Pension Fund, CIS (Co-operative Insurance Society), NPI, and Norwich Union for a 70,000-square foot addition to the mall. This will bring its total shopping area to 350,000 square feet, still small by U.S. standards for megamalls but bigger than any other such center in Europe. Under the agreement, the consortium of investors will get a 75 percent stake in the outlet center, the remainder of which will continue to be held by BAA McArthur Glen.

RESEARCH AND TECHNOLOGY

Recent research on the phenomenon of outlet centers has uncovered some fascinating facts and statistics about this fledgling retail trend. Among the most significant findings is the identification of this market as the fastest-growing segment of the retail industry. For the states that host them, the nation's outlet centers generate close to $500 million in sales tax revenues every year.

The majority of outlet center shoppers, according to recent market research, are typically affluent and well-educated working women who seek out bargains in brand-name merchandise. More than 40 percent of outlet shoppers estimated their annual household incomes at more than $50,000. The outlet centers of the United States received more than 500 million visits from shoppers during 1996, resulting in an average expenditure per outlet visit of $147. The appeal of the outlet centers drew shoppers from a far greater distance than conventional shopping centers, with the average distance traveled to an outlet center put at 77 miles.

Another study, commissioned by the International Council of Shopping Centers and sponsored by outlet developers and the Outlet Retail Merchants Association, produced an interesting profile of the typical outlet center shopper. The study revealed that 65 percent of outlet shoppers are married and 74 percent are female. Baby-boomers, ranging in age from 25 to 54, make up a large percentage of outlet center shoppers. The majority of outlet shoppers, just slightly more than 60 percent, report household incomes between $25,000 and $75,000, while 23 percent report incomes of less than $25,000 and 16 percent boasted incomes of more than $75,000.

FURTHER READING

Apfel, Ira. "What Is an Outlet Center? Huge Off-Price Shopping Malls Could Become the Victims of Their Own Success." *American Demographics,* 1 July 1996.

"BAA McArthur Glen Announces Institutional Consortium Joint Venture on Europe's Largest Outlet Center at Cheshire Oaks." *Business Wire,* 12 October 1998.

Bly, Laura. "Driven by Discounts: Outlet Malls Offer Day-Trippers Bargains They Can't Refuse." *USA Today,* 14 August 1998.

Booth, Cathy. "The Price Is Always Right: Outlet Malls Are Hot, But Other Retailers See Them as the Grinch That's Stealing Christmas." *Time,* 17 December 1990.

Mishra, Upendra. "SCW Development: Breaking Out of the Box." *Shopping Center World,* 1 August 1998.

"Prime Retail Launches Sponsorship & Marketing Partnership Program Designed to Build 'Prime Outlets' Brand." *PRNewswire,* 15 December 1998.

Richards, Geoffrey. "SCW Profile: Belz Outlet World Expanding." *Shopping Center World,* 1 July 1998.

Zygmont, Jeffrey. "Shoppers Plug-In to Outlets." *Christian Science Monitor,* 21 December 1998.

—Don Amerman

Oxygen Therapy

In 1664 the first experiment using compressed air in a specially-designed chamber was conducted in England, reportedly by a British physician by the name of Henshaw. The medical and scientific world could have had no idea where it would lead 300 years later. That simple, universal element, oxygen (O2), became the focus of a multi-billion dollar health care industry that captured the imagination of healers and charlatans. From the time British scientist Joseph Priestly published his own discovery of oxygen in 1774, its utilization remained primarily the domain of physicians and scientists for at least another century. Not until the 1930s, when the United States Navy began to use pure, hyperbaric oxygen therapy to treat divers suffering from decompression illness, did the use of oxygen therapy begin to be taken seriously by the medical community. The emergence of many kinds of oxygen therapies in both traditional and alternative or holistic medicine captured the attention of all generations by the 1990s. A health-conscious society looked for ways to deter the aging process, especially the post-World War II generation of the Baby Boomers. Longevity that people could not have dreamed of a century before became a commonplace expectation. Oxygen therapy as realized through alternative medicine options was driven by market demand for products that promised benefits to health and well-being.

Oxygen therapy is a segment of three major industries: health care, alternative medicine, and cos-

metics. Oxygen therapy became the general term for any method by which oxygen was introduced into the human body in order to effect some manner of healing. For traditional medicine, hyperbaric oxygen chambers became standard equipment in many hospitals. After decades of seeing oxygen therapy work for decompression sickness and resulting air embolism, physicians began to experiment with other uses. Burns, carbon monoxide poisoning, and serious flesh wounds benefited from these pressurized treatments. Other oxygen therapies for use in medicine became more advanced in such treatments as those for emphysema, asthma, and respiratory complications of newborn infants, to name a few. With the rise in the use of these therapies, the manufacture of new medical equipment surged to meet demand.

In the area of nontraditional, or what came to be known as alternative medicine, oxygen therapies became popular, even if they were not medically advised. Hyperbaric therapy crossed over to alternative medicine. In fact, even before it received widespread acceptance in the medical community, hyperbaric therapy was promoted in health spas and sports clubs for serenity, skin rejuvenation, and other miraculous cures. In addition, nutritional supplements said to purify blood, stabilize the body's metabolism, reduce stress, and remove the body of toxins were developed for oral use. Perhaps the most remarkable trend began with the opening of the first O2 bar in Toronto, Canada, during the mid-1990s. And the cosmetics industry also got into the business of selling oxygen for skin treatments.

Alternative medicine covers a broad spectrum of nontraditional practices utilizing oxygen therapy. They might include the modern technology of more widely accepted medical procedure of hyperbaric oxygen therapy adapted for non-licensed homeopathic purposes. Or, they might include other oxygen therapies such as orally ingested nutritional supplements, ozone therapy, chelation therapy, hydrogen peroxide therapy, and forms of exercise therapy. In 1992, under the auspices of the National Institutes of Health (NIH), Congress established the Office of Alternative Medicine. That same year, NIH provided $14.5 million in research to explore alternative medical options not recognized by the established medical community. No specific regulations governing such practices or medicines were established, however. In 1994, the Dietary Supplement Health and Education Act offered even more freedom to alternative medical providers by determining not to regulate this area through FDA standards.

INDUSTRY REGULATION

The health care system in the United States is a highly regulated industry. The U.S. Food and Drug Administration (FDA) sets national standards and guidelines for any medical treatment. Any oxygen therapy for use in an approved medical setting is subject to regulations regarding the licensing of qualified personnel, the safety and effectiveness of the equipment used, and the authorization of any medicine that might be used in administering treatment.

The American Medical Association (AMA) also offers its discretion in approving medical practices. In addition, professional societies for physicians, researchers, and other medical personnel set standards for conduct in the practice of utilizing the technology. Health Maintenance Organizations (HMO'S) and major insurance companies, too, provide monitoring when determining appropriate oxygen therapies. Continued medical research into various therapies expands the market for these products and services annually. Finally, the licensing of cosmetologists under state testing programs also offers additional regulation of industry practices.

BACKGROUND AND DEVELOPMENT

According to Lawrence Martin, M.D., Chief of the Division of Pulmonary and Critical Care Medicine at Mt. Sinai Medical Center in Cleveland, Ohio, ". . . although oxygen's life-supporting role was understood early on, it took about 150 years [since Priestley's discovery of it as a separate gas] for the gas to be used in a proper fashion for patients." He goes on to state

that, "For the first 150 years after discovery, therapeutic use of oxygen was sporadic, erratic, controversial, comical, beset by quackery, and only occasionally helpful." The first time that oxygen was reported to have been used as a therapy was by a doctor named Caillens in France in 1783. Details of this case were unknown. In 1874 in Geneva, Switzerland, however, Jurine published his results of the daily oxygen inhalation treatments of young woman in failing health due to tuberculosis, or a condition causing similar deterioration. Throughout the entire nineteenth century, research and experimentation continued. Nothing proved to be significant until 1917, when physicians Haldane and Barcroft began to administer oxygen therapeutically, primarily to relieve respiratory illnesses.

In 1928 the progress of oxygen treatment in the form of hyperbaric oxygen therapy suffered a severe blow. Wealthy industrialist H. H. Timken of Canton, Ohio, known for his worldwide production of roller bearings, entered into a million dollar venture with Dr. O. J. Cunningham of Kansas City, Missouri. The *Journal of the American Medical Association (JAMA)*, in its 5 May 1928 issue reported that, ". . . during the past two weeks the newspapers have recorded that Mr. Timken, of roller-bearing fame, was financing the construction of a 'million dollar sanitarium' for the treatment of diabetes 'by a new and deeply guarded method' in Cleveland, Ohio. . . . reports stress the fact that the chief feature of the 'sanitarium' is a huge steel tank sixty-four feet in diameter and five stories high. The new tank is in the form of a huge steel ball instead of a cylinder." It was Cunningham's theory that diabetes, pernicious anemia, and cancer were due to an anaerobic form of pathogenic bacteria.

However much he made these claims, Cunningham offered no proof of his theories. After a few years of use without success, the property fell into further disrepute, changing owners several times throughout the 1930s. In 1941 the huge steel ball was dismantled for use as scrap metal for the World War II war effort. While advances continued in the use of bedside oxygen tanks and tents for varying degrees of life support, hyperbaric therapy would not begin recovering from the Cunningham folly until 1939. At this point the U.S. Navy began to treat deep-sea divers suffering from decompression sickness, also known colloquially as "the Bends," with this specialized therapy. Different from the Cunningham experiment and others that simply used compressed air, these chamber treatments involved only compressed pure oxygen. During World War II studies in high-altitude sickness were also conducted, using hyperbaric and other oxygen therapy technology. Acceptance of hyperbaric oxygen therapy was slow to emerge. Studies continued into the 1960s and 1970s with claims that it could treat anything from hair loss to senility. These claims were never fully supported. Other studies indicated that the therapy showed some measure of success in the treatment of burn patients, wounds, and serious infections, such as gas gangrene.

The use of the hyperbaric oxygen chamber as a crossover between the worlds of traditional and alternative medicine became a widespread phenomenon in the 1980s. Famous rock star Michael Jackson reportedly slept in a hyperbaric chamber, a practice he continued long after treatment for facial burns he suffered in an accident while filming a television commercial. Canada's *MacLean's,* magazine, reported on 29 September 1997 that professional athletes used hyperbaric oxygen therapy on a routine basis. Vancouver Canucks hockey team trainer Dave Schima was quoted as saying, "We have great results with charley horses and deep bruises . . . use it on a daily basis." The *American Journal of Sports Medicine* also reported, it was noted in that same article, that their studies suggested hyperbaric therapy in this area seemed to have no more than a placebo effect. Dr. Albert Bove, who co-authored the study, also added that, ". . . if it works for the players, it may not need to be medically proven."

Forbes magazine also reported in December of 1996, on a another variation of this treatment. "Popping up in gyms nationwide," reporter Katrina Burger reported, "is something called the Hypoxic Room, a $32,000 8-by-8-by-7 foot plastic chamber in which the oxygen level is just 15 percent—a level you'd find at 9,000 feet above sea level." The claim by Nicholas Cohotin, vice president at Hypoxico, Inc. where the machine was made, was that his machine "will give you a 30-minute workout in just 15 minutes." He also made the claim that the machine could be effective simply by sitting inside of it. New York pulmonary specialist Dr. Robert Kutnick is quoted as well. He says that, "You may feel you've exercised ten minutes, but you're still only exercising five minutes." Whether or not such a machine worked was left up for question by Burger. Another example was the Hyperbaric Oxygen Clinic in Santa Monica, which offered sessions in their chambers to those recovering from plastic surgery, adding further to the miracle claims of the treatments.

The origins of use of oxygen therapy in the world of alternative medicine is more difficult to pinpoint. It too grew out of authentic medical research. The "wellness movement" that began in the nineteenth century throughout Europe and America gave birth to much of what eventually became known as the "New Age Movement" that emerged during the 1960s social revolution. European spas for health treatments were a centuries-old tradition. The ancient health and beauty treatments of China and the Far East, Egypt, and along the Mediterranean for everything from mud baths to breathing in mountain air were well-established, revered traditions long before anyone ever set sail for the new world of the Americas. The movement of the 1950s and 1960s toward eastern religions gave an opening to reconsider the western traditions by which many Americans were raised, particularly after World War II. The prevalence of tuberculosis sanitariums even into the 1940s, often placed in rural or mountain settings for the purer air, prompted the experimentation into the uses of oxygen.

Dietary herbal supplements were offered for better circulation—and that involved getting oxygen to flow more freely throughout the body. Into twentieth century America people amassed vast fortunes from tonics and treatments that offered no verifiable medical validity. Some treatments were harmless. Others were not. Even as late as the 1980s the FDA reported a death and injury from the ingestion of hydrogen peroxide. Industrial strength hydrogen peroxide was illegally promoted to treat Acquired Immunodeficiency Syndrome (AIDS), some cancers, and at least 60 other conditions. The product was sold as "35 percent Food Grade Hydrogen Peroxide," that was diluted for use in "Hyper-oxygenation therapy." The formula proved to be fatal to one child in Texas in 1989, and was particularly toxic to several other children due to its highly-corrosive qualities.

Despite warnings of the harmful aspects of such nontraditional practices, the industry managed to grow into an $18-billion dollar market by 1996, as reported by the *Nutrition Business Journal* and referenced in a series of articles in the *Los Angeles Times* by staff writers Terence Monmaney and Shari Roan. In that article they reported that even insurance companies began to look at various alternative treatments as viable and offered some reimbursement for certain procedures. A significant 35 percent of Californians polled in 1998, they reported, had admitted to the use of high-dosage vitamins, once only a bastion of the alternative lifestyle. The market for homeopathic remedies in California alone totaled $3.65 billion dollars, up 100 percent from 1994 to 1998. California was long considered the forerunner in such experimentation.

Two interesting commercial venues opened for oxygen therapy by the 1990s. One was that of the oxygen bars opening first in Toronto, Canada, then gaining serious popularity in Hollywood and New York. When *Science World* magazine first reported on the opening in Toronto in December of 1996, customers could stop in for 20 minutes of pure oxygen, pumped in through the plastic plugs in their noses, for a mere $16. In January of 1999, *Parade* magazine reported on the latest celebrity craze. Actor Woody Harrelson and his wife, along with holistic physician Dr. Richard DeAndrea, opened an organic food restaurant on Sunset Boulevard in Hollywood. A 20-minute serving of oxygen there was available for $13. Other well-known television and film stars carried oxygen tanks with them to their sets.

Another area where oxygen therapy began to climb into prominence was in the cosmetics industry. In his article for *Vogue,* in May, 1997, columnist Charles Gandee investigated the treatment. His focus was an exclusive spa in the SoHo section of New York City, named "Bliss," which catered to the rich and famous. For the less rich and famous, one might wait three weeks for a $120 oxygen facial. Explaining the fascination with oxygen facials Gandee quotes Bliss owner, Marcia Kilgore, "There are those who believe the reason your skin ages is that there isn't enough oxygen available for the cells to perform their regular functions." Some physicians disputed this claim, according to Gandee. "They're playing on the perception of the consumer that somehow oxygen, which is certainly an essential component of life, when applied directly to the skin will provide a benefit. And I would say that I'm not aware of any scientific literature that shows any benefit at all from this sort of treatment," says John Bailey, M.D., the director of the Division of Cosmetics and Colors at the FDA. Kilgore herself remained convinced of the benefits, referring to a device known as a pulse oxymeter, that she claims measures the levels of oxygen in skin. Some plastic surgeons agree with her treatment, and popularity seemed to indicate that the trend was not going to decline.

PIONEERS IN THE FIELD

The earliest pioneers in the discovery of oxygen's therapeutic benefits would list Haldane and Barcroft, certainly, in the area of traditional medical treatments. The U.S. Navy itself was unparalleled in its use and investigation of hyperbaric oxygen therapy, and that paved the way for other medical doctors and researchers to further its use. Authors of the book *Hyperbaric Oxygen Therapy,* Richard A. Neubauer, M.D. and Morton Walker, D.P.M. were devoted to the ongoing study of the benefits of that form of oxygen therapy. In his forward to the book, well-known scientist Dr. Edward Teller, Director of the Lawrence Liver-

more Laboratory in California, offered enthusiastic support for hyperbaric oxygen therapy, and for the physicians' efforts in promoting its use. He notes that, "For the past three decades, hyperbaric oxygen has been applied worldwide. Unfortunately, its use has been much more restricted in the United States than in other countries . . . Many lives, limbs, and minds could be saved by introducing HBOT(Hyperbaric Oxygen Therapy) into all hospitals and using the treatment after every major surgical operation . . ."

One of the best-recognized authorities on oxygen therapy as an alternative medicine is Ed McCable. Known as "Mr. Oxygen" because of his book, *O2xygen Therapies—A New Way of Approaching Disease,* he traveled the world promoting various forms of oxygen therapy. His activities were curtailed on 7 April 1998 when he was arrested by the United States Justice Department on counts of tax fraud.

The rise of support for this industry was often held directly accountable to two factors. One represented the general distrust the population holds for government and its regulations. Another was the progress that medicine made throughout the twentieth century, and that progress made people imagine that all diseases were curable. Whatever the method, it was worth the try.

CURRENT CONDITIONS

According to the *U.S. Industry and Trade Outlook '98,* health care would continue to dominate the marketplace into the next century as it had for the previous decade. The major challenge that faced oxygen therapy in traditional medicine was research and development. Private companies, such as Sechrist, a leader in the field of hyperbaric therapy equipment and other respiratory products, would provide much of the funding for further experimentation. One such product involved was long-term patient-triggered synchronized assisted ventilation in infants. A case study during the early 1990s by a team led by Nadarasa Visveshwara, M.D. of Valley Children's Hospital of Fresno, California, proved the procedure to be safe and effective in very low birth weight infants with uncomplicated respiratory failure. Such innovative research would continue to affect the increased usage of various forms of oxygen therapy.

The challenges of hyperbaric oxygen therapy extend further, according to Neubauer and Walker. The field of HBOT was relatively young by medical standards even at the close of the twentieth century. Only since the 1960s had valid research and results been followed. Consequently, many doctors graduate from medical school knowing little about this therapy. They would come to accept HBOT for certain conditions, such as the wounds, burns, air emboli, carbon monoxide poisoning, and chronic bone infections. The medical profession, as a whole, however, would not yet accept its use for many other conditions that hyperbaric doctors already recognized. These treatments included coma related to head injuries, bruising of the spinal chord, stroke, and multiple sclerosis. For instance, HBOT is widely used in Great Britain for the treatment of multiple sclerosis. Other conditions that Neubauer and Walker noted were treatable with hyperbaric oxygen therapy included cranial nerve syndromes, peripheral neuropathy, various orthopedic conditions, gangrene, frostbite, diabetic retinopathy, cirrhosis, and Crohn's disease, to name a few. It was estimated that there were under 400 hyperbaric chambers in use in the United States by 1998, and that about 100,000 patients are treated with HBOT each year. With increased exposure of the benefits of this ther-

---

More On **OXYGEN THERAPY AND HEALING**

The date was June 9, 1980. Two police officers were patrolling the northwest area of the San Fernando Valley in California when they saw a man running in circles. The officers took quick action when they realized the man was on fire—his upper body and head blazing with blue flames. They hurried from their patrol car, wrestled the man to the ground and rolled him in the grass until the fire was extinguished.

The man on fire was Richard Pryor. He had accidentally set himself ablaze. The officers' next impulse was to take Pryor to Sherman Oaks Community Hospital, where the doctor determined third-degree burns covered his face, ears, chest, arms and abdomen. His chances of survival were less than 50 percent, and if he lived, scarring would be horrible. However, Pryor was fortunate to go on acting for years to come, largely thanks to hyperbaric oxygen therapy, used by Dr. Richard Grossman in his treatment, according to "Hyperbaric Oxygen Therapy" by Richard A. Neubauer, MD, and Morton Walker, DPM.

During that summer, Pryor entered the oxygen chamber at least once daily for an hour at a time. Later the chamber facilitated the healing process of unburned portions of Pryor's skin from which his doctor had taken skin for grafts. The procedure uses pure oxygen at higher-than-atmospheric pressure to help overcome diseases associated with a lack of oxygen in the tissues. Pryor continued to use oxygen therapy after his burns and grafts had healed.

apy, and increased research findings, the future of HBOT did hold promise.

The state of alternative medicine and its promotion of the many forms of oxygen therapy was ever-expanding. The *New England Journal of Medicine* conducted a national survey that was published in January of 1993. The results of the survey revealed that people visited nontraditional practitioners for some therapy far more often than they visited all U.S. primary-care physicians. In 1990, there were an estimated 425 million visits to alternative medical practices. $10.3 billion, or 75 percent of the total outlay of expense, was paid out of pocket. $12.8 billion was paid out of pocket for all traditional hospital care in the United States. Oxygen therapies in alternative medicine included specially designed deep breathing exercises, often followed with the assistance of a personal trainer, hydrogen peroxide therapy, oxidative therapy, oxone therapy, ionization, and the ingestion of oral stabilized oxygen products. Many of the oxygen compounds for ingestion, in the form of dietary supplements continued to flood the market.

The Internet was inundated with sales of oxygen therapy products. Established businesses and new business start-ups appeared on the Internet and offered consumers thousands of products involving oxygen therapy. Among them were Crossroads, "The Oxystore," and Bio-Karmic Technologies, all California companies. Crossroads offered the "world's largest collection of products, tools, books, audio, and video tapes relating to oxygen and detoxification." The health value of many of these products, considered questionable, came with warnings even by the businesses themselves. The disclaimer included on the Crossroads Web site stated that, "The products described are intended solely for informational and research purposes only, and are not intended to diagnose, treat, cure or prevent any disease. Persons with any health related problem should consult a health care provider for guidance." This company indicated that a list of physicians "knowledgeable in oxygen/ozone or holistic oriented therapies," was available upon request. What was not mentioned usually was that some of these therapies, such as hydrogen peroxide therapy, were even considered dangerous. Yet these disclaimers did not slow consumer purchases.

Another impact felt by this market was the unprecedented growth of health spas. The number began to grow so rapidly into the 1990s that it was nearly impossible to calculate. These spas included holistic health centers that could offer one-day, one-week, or extended stays for treatments. Americans patronized many of the clinics that had opened in Mexico offering cancer treatments not approved in the United States. Even department stores began to cash in on the business of in-store therapeutic facials. As the world welcomed high-technological advances, an American public began to turn to health products that were born often of ancient health practices.

INDUSTRY LEADERS

The business of oxygen therapy is part of a diverse number of professions, occupation, and industries. It includes medical professionals and trained technicians, cosmetologists, alternative health practitioners, medical equipment manufacturers, health spa owners, hospitals, and business owners who sell related products. Still, the key manufacturers of hyperbaric oxygen chambers are important to note. They include: Environmental Tectonics Corporation of Southhampton, Pennsylvania; Mediscus Group of Trevosie, Pennsylvania; Reneau, Inc. of Stafford, Texas; Reimers, located in Northern Virginia; and Sechrist Industries, Inc. in Orange County, California. The fact that they remained predominantly small, privately held companies, with average earnings around $10 million dollars annually at the end of the 1990s was indicative of the industry's youth.

Research and development of hyperbaric treatments is the focus of several laboratories around the United States. They are: Ocean Hyperbaric Center in Florida, also operating the American College of Hyperbaric Medicine from that facility; Baptist Medical Center in Jacksonville, Florida; Lifeforce, in Baltimore, Maryland; Texas A & M University Hyperbaric Laboratory at College Station, Texas; and the Undersea Hyperbaric Medical Society, Inc. of Kensington, Maryland.

Other standard oxygen equipment, such as monitors, analyzer, and transmitters, were products of a multitude of medical equipment companies and companies that dealt simply with oxygen-related products. The Alpha Omega Instruments Corporation of Rhode Island is a rising company in this area of the industry.

WORK FORCE

At the end of the 1990s, health care was the dominant employer in most cities. A labor force of 7.8 million in 1990 grew to 9.3 million by 1995. Due to an aging population of the post-World War II generation, health care showed no ceiling for its growth potential.

The need for medical and support staff in hospitals, medical offices, and clinics for oxygen therapy were projected to keep growing, as well.

As in many other aspects of the alternative medicine market, true projections were difficult due to the nature of the business. Every worker from chiropractors to herbal supplement specialists to health bookstore staff to production factories reaped the benefits of this multi-billion dollar business. Because those who seek out alternative care tend to be affluent, well-educated members of the population with the resources to experiment, the economic implication was growth in exponential increments. This was true of the work force in the cosmetics industry, too, as oxygen therapy facials and similar body therapies became a more-rooted piece of the profits.

AMERICA AND THE WORLD

While America lagged behind the rest of the world in the use of hyperbaric therapy and alternative medicine, it was catching up near the end of the twentieth century. American wealth, education, and growing travel options helped to create more options in seeking health and beauty care. While many Americans continued to seek treatments at spas in Europe and Mexico, the growth of similar facilities in the United States had begun to offer them such opportunities closer to home.

America continued to be the world leader in traditional health care, both in medical services and equipment manufacturing. Economic indicators were that the predominance of the United States was not likely to shift. Estimates of 1995 revenues were held at $841 million in exported medical services alone. The greatest portion of this income resulted from visits by foreign citizens to clinics in the United States for treatment. As the possibilities for hyperbaric oxygen therapy grew from increased research, America was considered likely to dominate the field, particularly in the manufacturing of equipment.

FURTHER READING

"Brain Injury Improves with Hyperbaric Oxygen." *Reuters Health Information,* 27 May 1998.

Burger, Katrina. "Lots of Pain; No Gain." *Forbes,* 2 December 1996.

FDA Backgrounder. "Milestones in U.S. Food and Drug Law History," April 1999. Available from http://www.fda.gov.

Gandee, Charles. "Air Apparent." *Vogue,* May 1997.

Goldstein, Debra. "Oxygen Bar." *Science World,* 6 December 1996.

Health Monitor. "Athletes on Air." *Maclean's,* 29 September 1997.

"High-Pressure Chambers Could Help Prevent Paralysis." Reuters Health Information, 10 May 1998.

"Hyperbaric Technologies." Thousand Oaks, CA: Hyperbaric Chamber Systems & Management, 1999. Available from http://www.hyperbaric.com.

Lewis, Carol. "Every Breath You Take." *FDA Consumer,* March-April 1999. Available from http://www.fda.gov.

Martin, Lawrence, M.D. "Oxygen Therapy: The First 150 Years." Cleveland, OH: Mt. Sinai Medical Center, January 1999. Available from http://www.mtsinai.org.

Monmaney, Terence, and Shari Road. "Alternative Medicine, the 18 Billion Dollar Experiment." *Los Angeles Times,* 30 August 1998. Available from http://www.latimes.org.

Neubauer, Richard, M.D., and Morton Walker, D.P.M. *Hyperbaric Oxygen Therapy.* Garden City, NY: Avery Publishing, 1998.

Oxygen & Ozone Therapies, 1999. Available from http://www.oxytherapy.com.

Oxygen Therapy Page, 1999. Available from http://www.iconz.co.nz/cliffs/oxy/index.html.

OxyRegeneration. "Frequently Asked Questions About OxyRegeneration Plus and Stabilized Oxygen," 1999. Available from http://www.ideaconcepts.com/oxyfaq.html.

Scott, Walter. "Personality Parade Questions." *Parade,* 3 January 1999.

U.S. Industry & Trade Outlook '98. Washington, DC: GPO, 1998.

—Jane Spear

PARALLEL PROCESSING COMPUTERS

Parallel processing computers are of two basic types: vector computers, in which a single processor can perform more than one operation at a time, and multiprocessors, which use many processors in alliance to break difficult problems into pieces that are solved by different processors simultaneously. Multiprocessing computers come in a number of different configurations, and were the fastest and most powerful computers at the end of the twentieth century.

The technology behind parallel processing computers has been around since the 1960s, a decade before the first microprocessor was announced by the Intel Corporation. Since then, many companies—from IBM to Cray Research—have improved on the technology that interconnects the processors and allows multiple smaller processors to perform more quickly than one large one. Parallel hardware architectures were usually reserved for supercomputers. Up until the late 1980s, physicists needing number-crunching computers to simulate nuclear explosions and aerodynamic engineers modeling fluid dynamics could turn nowhere but to expensive supercomputers. Their calculations could bog down even the fastest lone processor.

With the advent of relational databases in the mid-1980s, businesses as well as researchers and scientists could collect very large amounts of data and store them in a systematic way. Retrieval of this information fell into the domain of the parallel processor and was gradually finding a market in many standard business applications from analysis of the stock market to modeling earthquake-safe architecture. By the late 1990s large-scale parallel processing had reached 5 continents, the exceptions being Africa and Antarc-

tica. At the end of 1998, of the world's 100 most powerful computers, 45 were being used for research, 24 for academic purposes, 14 in industry, 9 for government classified operations, and 8 for further development by computer manufacturers worldwide. Of the research installations that specified the kind of research done, weather was the most common, with energy research specified next most frequently. Uses in the industrial installations were spread among a number of applications including electronics, databases, and finance.

The structure of the parallel and supercomputing market is driven, in large part, by hardware advances. While it is the architecture of microprocessors that defines parallel processing, it is the leaps-and-bounds advances in their speed and miniaturization that make supercomputers much more compact than the room-size computers of the 1960s and 1970s. The power of the supercomputers of the early 1960s were on many desktops at the end of the 1990s.

On the hardware side, parallel processing computers fell into several categories: supercomputers, often called "heavy iron;" clusters of small computers linked together to act as a single computer; and mid-range computers. The supercomputer segment of the industry was dominated by a small number of U. S. and Japanese companies such as Silicon Graphics Inc. (SGI), International Business Machines (IBM), and NEC Corporation. A larger number of companies, again, almost all American and Japanese, produced mid-range computers used especially for

---

Pioneer **SEYMOUR CRAY, 1925-**
THE HENRY FORD OF THE COMPUTER INDUSTRY

Seymour Cray was born on September 28, 1925, in Chippewa Falls, Wisconsin. The eldest of two children, Cray revealed his talent for engineering while still a young boy, tinkering with radios in the basement and building an automatic telegraph machine by the time he was ten years old. Cray's early aptitude for electronics was also evident when he wired his laboratory to his bedroom, and included an electric alarm that sounded whenever anyone tried to enter his inner sanctum. While attending Chippewa Falls High School, Cray sometimes taught the physics class in his teacher's absence. During his senior year, he received the Bausch & Lomb Science Award for meritorious achievement.

While serving in the U.S. Army during the final years of World War II, Cray used his natural gifts in electronics as a radio operator and decipherer of enemy codes. After the war, he enrolled in the University of Wisconsin, but later transferred to the University of Minnesota, where he received his bachelor's degree in electrical engineering in 1950 and a master's degree in applied mathematics the next year.

Cray began his corporate electronics career with Engineering Research Associates (ERA). When he joined the company, it was among a small group of firms on the cutting edge of the commercial computer industry. One of his first assignments with ERA was to build computer pulse transformers for Navy use. Cray credited his success in such endeavors to a top-of-the-line circular slide rule that enabled him to make a multitude of calculations needed to build transformers. In a speech before his colleagues at the supercomputer conference, Cray recalled feeling "quite smug" about his accomplishment until he encountered a more experienced engineer working at the firm who did not use complicated slide rules, but preferred to rely on intuition. Intrigued, Cray put away his slide rule and decided that he would do likewise.

Cray's seminal work in computer design features the semiconductor as a component to store and process information. His dense packing of hundreds of thousands of semiconductor chips reduced the distance between signals and thus ushered in the dawn of the supercomputer. Seeking to process vast amounts of mathematical data needed to simulate physical phenomena, Cray built what many consider to be the first supercomputer, the CDC 6600. To fields such as engineering, meteorology, biology and medicine, the supercomputer represented a technological revolution akin to replacing a wagon with a sports car in terms of accelerating research.

A maverick in both his scientific and business pursuits, Cray eventually started his own company devoted entirely to the development of supercomputers. A devoted fan of *Star Trek,* a 1960s television show about space travel, Cray often included aesthetically pleasing touches in his computers, such as transparent blue glass that revealed their inner workings.

---

heavy graphics and database applications. The cluster computers were a development arising from researchers in need of processing power but without the funds for a supercomputer. It used off-the-shelf PCs and Fast Ethernet connections to generate formidable computing power.

On the software side, most software used by supercomputers was developed by the computer manufacturer specifically for their machines. Generally, the investment in a supercomputer was for a particular purpose and the software and hardware were chosen together to accomplish that purpose. On the other hand, off-the-shelf software was available for a variety of mid-range computer applications such as graphics, mathematical simulations, and database applications.

BACKGROUND AND DEVELOPMENT

The first parallel computer architecture appeared in 1959 with the delivery of the IBM 7030, affectionately known as "Stretch." With a performance measurement of approximately one megaflop, or 1 million instructions executed per second, the 7030 was the most formidable computing machine of its time. It was comparable in speed to the average desktop personal computer of 1992. It was delivered to Los Alamos National Laboratory to model nuclear explosions, but only eight were ever manufactured. Other government labs, such as Lawrence Livermore and the National Aeronautics and Space Administration (NASA) competed for high-speed computing machines to perform complex aeronautical and fluid dynamics calculations. The birth of the first single processor CPU, the Intel 4004, was another 12 years away.

Control Data Corporation (CDC), founded in the late 1950s, developed the CDC 6600 in 1964 and the CDC 7600 in 1969, both exceeding a megaflop. Other giants of the early parallel processing supercomputing field included Burroughs, Sperry-Rand, and Texas Instruments. CDC was the starting place of a man who was later referred to as the father of the supercomputing industry—Seymour Cray, who left the company in 1972 to found Cray Research. Cray Research dominated the supercomputer scene of the 1980s with

---

its freon-cooled Cray-1, Cray-2, and X-MP models. Soon new competitors arose to capture some of Cray's dominant market share. Convex, Sequent, and Alliant developed competing systems, but for those who could afford the million-dollar price tags (mainly government laboratories and engineering departments at major research universities), a Cray computer was the first choice.

The late 1980s saw the production of the first non-American parallel processing supercomputers for the general market. Companies like Hitachi, NEC, Meiko, and Fujitsu began marketing computers to compete with Cray and CDC. The breakup of the former Soviet Union and the end of the Cold War caused a marked decline for supercomputers during much of the 1990s. University research that depended on heavy number-crunching, such as oceanography and meteorology modeling, plus the growth of commercial applications such as power generation and transmission, securities and stock market data modeling, high-definition television, and even virtual reality, kept the market alive. These and other high-bandwidth applications relied on parallel rather than serial processing of data.

By the mid-1990s, led by the parallel and multi-processing hardware of Intel and its P6, or PentiumPro chip, computer manufacturers like IBM, Sun Microsystems, and Silicon Graphics began to develop architectures to take advantage of greater throughput. Database giants Oracle Corp. and Sybase Inc. also used parallel architectures to quickly manipulate and retrieve records in relational databases. Their products represented the first forays of parallel processing and supercomputing into software products for standard to high-end business applications. This meant that parallel processing was nearing the desktop of the average personal computer.

Microsoft Corporation, champion of the personal computer market, also entered the small end of the parallel computing market. Several personal computer lines used parallel processing in server applications. Sun Microsystems developed the SPARCCenter computer lines in 1993, using 8 to 20 parallel CPUs. Silicon Graphics (SGI), a vendor known for high-performance graphics rendering, purchased Cray Research in 1996 and developed its own parallel processing computer.

CURRENT CONDITIONS

SUPERCOMPUTERS

At the end of the 1990s several manufacturers each claimed to have the world's fastest computer. In

1996 Intel's parallel processing computer known as ASCI Option Red broke the teraflop barrier (1 trillion operations per second). This computer used a parallel arrangement of 7,264 PentiumPro chips to create nuclear simulations at Sandia National Laboratory. It was developed as part of the U.S. Department of Energy's (DOE) Accelerated Strategic Computing Initiative (ASCI) for modeling of the effects of aging on nuclear warheads. In 1998 NEC Corporation began to ship its SX-5 Series supercomputers. The standard system used 16 CPUs each running at 8 billion operations per second (GFLOPS). Up to 32 CPUs could be linked together, which NEC said would produce the fastest vector processing computer in the world. In 1999, however, Fujitsu announced that it would begin to ship a new vector computer with peak performance of 9.6 GFLOPS, outpacing the SX-5.

In the meantime, in 1998 IBM announced that it would build a computer called Pacific Blue for the U.S. Department of Energy, which would run at sustained speeds of 3.88 TFLOPS. It was to be built for the Lawrence Livermore National Laboratory using 5,800 processors. In 1999, however, the most powerful computer actually in use was Mountain Blue, built by SGI for Los Alamos National Laboratory and running at 3.08 TFLOPS. Like Pacific Blue and Sandia's ASCI Red, Mountain Blue was developed as part of the DOE's ASCI program. The DOE also planned a 30 TFLOPS machine by 2001 and a 100 TFLOPS computer by 2004.

CLUSTER COMPUTERS

Also in 1998 a team at Los Alamos announced their "supercomputer," which was actually a cluster of 68 PCs that could operate as a single computer at the rate of 47 GFLOPS. What was most noteworthy about it was the cost—approxiamately $313,000, roughly 10 percent of the cost of a conventional supercomputer. This computer, called Avalon, was a "Beowulf-class" computer, a development in parallel processing that began in 1994 among NASA scientists. Thomas Sterling and Don Becker, working at the Center of Excellence in Space Data and Information Sciences (CESDIS), a NASA contractor, put together 16 desktop computers using Ethernet connections and called it Beowulf. It was an instant success, and a movement began, first among government researchers but soon moving toward commercialization.

Beowulf clusters used off-the-shelf hardware and publicly available software, most significantly the Linux operating system, a version of Unix that is available free, but required considerable knowledge of computer networking to put together. In May 1999

Profile   MAN VS. MACHINE?

At the tender age of 22, Gary Kasparov won the title of World Champion in 1985 from world renowned Anatoly Karpov. Born in Baku and currently living in Moscow, Kasparov is the youngest person ever to attain this title. His early teacher and mentor was Mikhail Botvinnik, World Champion for more than a decade beginning in 1948 and the engineer who pioneered Russian computer chess.

Founded long before Kasparov was born, the Association for Computing Machinery(ACM)—the first and foremost international scientific and educational organization dedicated to advancing the art, science, engineering and application of information technology—had continuously brought the leading computer-chess systems and their developers together to compete and exchange ideas. It was only fitting, then, that ACM would sponsor the matches between Kasparov, and DEEP BLUE, a super computer developed at the IBM T. J. Watson Research Center in Yorktown Heights, New York, by Feng-Hsiung Hsu, Murray Campbell and Joe Hoane, under the supervision of Chun-Jen Tan.

In 1994, an early version of DEEP BLUE won the 1994 ACM International Computer Chess Championship at Cape May, New Jersey. Still, until DEEP BLUE, the world's leading chess players had an edge on the best computer-chess systems, although there were periodic computer wins against grandmasters. Even Kasparov, who had, before DEEP BLUE, never lost a match to a computer opponent, had lost individual rapid-chess games. However, experts agreed that early games were not an appropriate test of the relative abilities of either Kasparov or the computers.

The first true test came in 1996, when Kasparov was pitted against DEEP BLUE, which at the time was capable of calculating 100 million board positions per second. Kasparov was defeated. A year later, Kasparov agreed to a rematch with a new and improved DEEP BLUE, which had 256 chess co-processors, and was much more powerful than its predecessor. Kasparov's loss at the 1997 match marked the first time a World Champion Grandmaster had ever been beaten by a computer in a refereed match. Many saw the loss as heralding a new age in computing technology and artificial intelligence, but some, such as leading author, physicist, and psychologist David Stork, agreed that "few . . . feel deeply threatened by a computer beating a world chess champion any more than . . . [by] a motorcycle beating an Olympic sprinter."

The true impact of the match remains to be seen, but IBM hopes that it will be able to use the chess-specific processing to learn more about other computationally intensive problems in molecular dynamics.

EBIZ Enterprises demonstrated a fully configured Beowulf Clustered Super Computer, a 16 node cluster that was priced at under $15,000. This machine ran a standard test problem in 12 seconds, compared to the three seconds required by the Cray T3-E, which cost $5.5 million. According to the company, this made supercomputer power available to many people and organizations without the funds for a conventional supercomputer or the knowledge to build their own cluster.

CHIPS

At the other end of the computing scale, individual chips were also being developed incorporating parallel processing instruction within the chip. Making the most news at the end of the 1990s was the Merced IA-64 chip being jointly developed by Intel and Hewlett-Packard. A 64-bit processor, as opposed to 32-bit like the Pentium, it was designed with Explicitly Parallel Instructions Computing (EPIC). This parallel processing within the chip would make it at least twice as fast as previous Intel chips, according to the designers. It would also incorporate previous generation instruction sets for backward compatibility.

Merced was not the first 64-bit processor, though. Digital Equipment Corporation introduced its 64-bit Alpha processor for its servers and workstations in 1993, but it did not make the impact on the industry expected of the Intel chip when it will be put into production sometime in the year 2000. In the meantime, Elbrus International, a Russian computer company, announced in May 1999 the design of a processor that it claimed would operate faster than Merced. It also used internal parallel processing. Elbrus had taken out 70 patents on its design and was looking for a Western firm to help manufacture the chip.

Another innovation on the horizon of parallel processing was optical computing. Researchers struggling with scaling problems in parallel architectures were working with light rather than electrical signals to compute. Ten processors fully electrically connected require 100 wires, and the problem is squared as the number of processors increase. Using the speed of light and fiber optic technology rather than the speed of an electrical pulse through wire has a theoretical potential of 2 terabits per second. The implementation, however, is expensive and daunting. Positioning systems for light pulses must be micro-accurate. Light

---

beams through fiber optic wires also suffer attenuation, or weakening of a signal over longer distances; lasers solve the problem, but with huge costs. Honeywell, Lucent Technologies, and Motorola, among others, have already invested research dollars into developing marketable optical computing solutions.

INDUSTRY LEADERS

Relatively few companies solely market parallel computers and, to some large companies, parallel offerings represent a small portion of their revenues. In addition, the way companies report their income makes it difficult to determine the contribution of parallel processing to the bottom line.

In 1995 the industry began consolidating with the merger of several key players, including Cray Research with Silicon Graphics, and Convex Computer with Hewlett-Packard. Several other mergers are expected into the year 2000 as configuration of all high tech industries continued to shift in response to technological and market changes.

Minneapolis-based Cray Research, the dominant leader in the 1980s, saw its supercomputer and parallel computer market share decrease in the 1990s. Its T3D and T3E lines represent parallel computing solutions. Silicon Graphics, which bought Cray Research in 1996, led the 1998 list of the top 500 supercomputer sites, with seven of the top 10 and 46 of the top 50. It had a total of 183 installations in the entire list. In 1998 and 1999 the company established relationships with both Microsoft and Intel and added Linux to its set of operating systems, positioning itself to take advantage of developments in the low end as well as the highest end of the computer market. SGI reported 1998 sales of $3.1 billion, an increase of 15.3 percent over 1997.

Armonk, New York, based IBM was still the world's largest computer company at the end of the twentieth century. Practically synonymous with large computers for years, IBM built a market share of almost 80 percent in the 1960s and 1970s. It introduced the first computer to eliminate vacuum tubes in 1960 and the first laser printer for computers in 1975, among many other innovations. It introduced the PC in 1981, but failed to capitalize on the growth of the low-end of the computer market and went into a steady decline. In 1994 it posted its first profit in four years, and in 1997, Deep Blue, an enormous parallel processing IBM computer, defeated the world chess champion, Garry Kasparov, in a six game match. IBM was com-

missioned in 1998 by DOE to build Pacific Blue, a 3.88 TFLOP computer for the Lawrence Livermore National Laboratory. IBM reported 1998 sales of about $81.7 billion, a growth of 4.0 percent from 1997. Forty-three percent of that, or $35.4 billion was from hardware sales.

Hewlett-Packard, of Palo Alto, California, the world's second largest computer company, acquired Convex Computer in 1996 to offer the Exemplar line of parallel processing computers. The Convex division experienced "very good early acceptance of its technical servers." Hewlett-Packard reported 1998 sales of slightly over $47.06 billion, an increase of 9.7 percent over 1997. In 1999 it split off its testing, measurement, and medical electronics division into a separate corporation.

Intel, well-known for its dominance of the processor market, has been selling parallel computers since about 1985. It built the 1.3 TFLOPS ASCI Red for the Sandia National Laboratory, but its Paragon line of parallel computers is the standard business offering. It also planned to begin shipping its Merced 64-bit parallel processing microchip in mid-2000, which was expected to eventually bring parallel processing to the ordinary desktop computer user a few years later.

Meiko, a Japanese company not well-known in the United States, made a massive parallel computer, the CS-2. Other Japanese companies making inroads in the American supercomputing market include Fujitsu, Hitachi, and NEC. However, these companies have stronger offerings in vector-based supercomputers, and lack significant massively parallel computing solutions.

Tandem, NCR, and Compaq are new players entering the symmetric multiprocessing (SMP) market. They offer relatively small servers designed for mainframe and UNIX network replacement.

WORK FORCE

Employees in the supercomputing and parallel processing computer industry mainly come from engineering or computer science backgrounds. Due to the theoretical work involved, a small percentage may come from mathematics or other hard science fields. Nonetheless, the growing multidisciplinary perspective used by many university research centers affects the work in parallel processing as well. According to the Caltech Concurrent Computation Project, which researched parallel computing from 1983 through 1990, a wide range of disciplines were recruited to tackle different aspects of the technology. It was also noted that the traditional interdisciplinary field for the project, computational science, is not well understood or implemented either nationally or within the university structure.

According to the *Occupational Outlook Handbook* published by the U.S. Bureau of Labor Statistics, computer scientists, computer engineers, and systems analysts held approximately 933,000 jobs in the late-1990s, including 58,000 who were self-employed, and these were expected to be the three fastest growing occupations through 2006. Median earnings of this group were about $46,3000.

AMERICA AND THE WORLD

The United States has dominated the supercomputer and parallel processing computer market since its inception. Although research in the former Soviet Union was concurrent with similar U.S. research in the 1970s and 1980s, fewer marketable products resulted. Japanese companies increased their share in the 1980s and more convincingly in the 1990s. Parallel processing computer product offerings in other nations are nearly nonexistent.

Starting in 1988 the University of Mannheim in Germany maintained a list of the "Top 500" supercomputer sites worldwide. Machines were ranked in terms of speed and power. The listing affords an excellent set of benchmarks concerning the international community with respect to sophisticated parallel processing technology. In the November 1998 list, U.S. companies built 443 of the 500. The remaining 57 were from the Japanese companies NEC, Fujitsu, and Hitachi. All of the top ten were U.S.-built, and only three of the top twenty were Japanese.

RESEARCH AND TECHNOLOGY

There is much relevant research on parallel processing computers. While a significant amount of research considered hardware architecture, a growing body of research looked into the complexity of writing software for parallel hardware architectures. Scalability of parallel architectures varied, and some architectures handled certain mathematical problems (algorithms) better than others. Input/Output (I/O) throughput is also a research area in supercomputing.

Research was being done on three basic parallel architecture types at the end of the 1990s: Symmetric

MultiProcessing (SMP), Massively Parallel Processing (MPP), and clustering technology. SMP uses a number of CPUs but they share one memory. This approach is good for large databases, for example, which are continually updated. Because the memory is shared, it is easier to update. MPP, on the other hand, utilizes many processors which each has its own memory and copy of the operating system. This approach works well for massive problems that can be broken into pieces that can be worked on simultaneously. Clustering architectures are similar to MPP except that they are in fact many separate machines liked together in a high-speed network.

Described by one programmer as "fiendishly difficult" and something that "should be considered illegal at most sites," parallel software programming was still in the early stages of development at the end of the 1990s. Software testing is often difficult to execute due to the lack of repeatability and dependence on the relative timing of one processor versus another. Writing software for parallel systems often involves mathematical proofs rather than brute testing, something beyond the scope of many programmers. Also, different types of parallel architectures support different types of software—what works on one may not work on another. Significant research has begun on a standard communications protocol in parallel processing computers. A standard for a *message-passing interface,* the parallel computing version of an operating system, is being developed by international forums and computer groups.

Open MP, an applications programming interface (API) standard announced in December of 1997, was intended to ease some consternation on the part of applications programmers developing code for parallel processing systems. APIs afford portability between hardware platforms by shielding the programmer from the idiosyncrasies of the proprietary machine codes. Open MP, developed in tandem by SGI and software developers Kluck & Associates, received endorsement from Digital Equipment, IBM, Intel, and others. Representatives from Dow Chemical and DuPont also voiced optimism regarding the potential of the new standard.

While supercomputers tended to be evaluated based on their CPU throughput, input/output requirements were a major consideration as well. Mapping the human genome, for example, requires just as much I/O throughput as CPU brute force due to the massive amount of data needed for input. Meteorological modeling can have billions of datapoints. Such *grand-challenge applications* push the frontiers of parallel processing research and development.

Research centers involved in the parallel processing and computing industry include the Center for Research on Parallel Computing (CRPC), a consortium of universities led by Rice University in Houston, Texas. The CRPC is a National Science Foundation Science and Technology Center. Other research centers include the Institute for Parallel Computation at the University of Virginia, the Center for Applied Parallel Processing at the University of Colorado at Boulder, and the Parallel Architecture Research Laboratory at New Mexico State University.

Supercomputing centers which offer supercomputing expertise and facilities are numerous across the country. Many work closely with national laboratories such as Fermilab in Illinois and Lawrence Livermore in California. Notable supercomputer centers include the Pittsburgh Supercomputer Center, the Minnesota Supercomputer Center in Minneapolis, and the Maui High Performance Computing Center in Hawaii.

FURTHER READING

Adams, Charlotte. "SMP Clusters Offer Low-cost Alternative to Supercomputers." *Federal Computer Week*, 19 October 1998.

Babcock, Charles. "A New View of the Parallel Universe." 18 December 1995. Available from http://www.computerworld.com/home/print9497.nsf/all/SLsuperD3EE.

———. "Software Lags Hardware's Fourfold Leap." 17 June 1996. Available from http://www.computerworld.com/home/print9497.nsf/all/SLfourIA26A.

Bains, Sunny. "'Fully' Connected." *OEM Magazine*, 1 February 1997.

Brown, Chappell. "FPGA Blends Parallel Architectures." *EE Times*, 22 April 1996.

"EBIZ's thelinuxstore.com Unveils the Element-L Beowulf Super Computer Cluster." *Business Wire*, 20 May 1999.

Foley, John, and Martin J. Garvey. "Parallel Lines Unveiled." *Information Week*, 9 September 1996.

"Fujitsu to Roll Out 9.6 GFLOPS Vector Supercomputer." *Japan Industrial Journal*, 21 April 1999.

Halfhill, Tom R. "Inside IA-64." *Byte*, June 1998.

Hara, Yoshiko. "Multimedia Chips." *EE Times*, 5 May 1997.

Hunt, Laura. "Massicely Parallel Processing." *Computerworld*, 15 February 1999.

"Interconnect Contract Kicks Off Quest—U.S. Starts Path to 30 TFLOPS Computer." *Electronic Engineering Times*, 5 January 1998.

Mason, Scott. "SMP Provides a Mirror into Your Server." *Network Computing*, 1 May 1997.

McGrath, Steve. "Supercomputing Gets a New Hero." *Communications News*, August 1998.

Nash, Kim S. "Behind the Merced Mystique." *Computerworld*, 6 July 1998. Available from http://www.computerworld.com/home/features.nsf/all/980706rc.

"NEC Claims 'World's Fastest' Supercomputer." *Computergram International*, 8 June 1998.

"Open MP API Created for Cross-Platform Parallel Apps." *Computergram International*, 29 October 1997.

Pickering, Carol. "Blue Mountain." *Forbes ASAP*, 22 February 1999.

"The Power of Multiprocessing." *VAR Business*, 15 November 1996.

Robertson, Jack. "Intel Goes to 1 Trillion Ops." *Electronic Buyers' News*, 23 December 1996.

"Russia: A New Super-fast Microchip Designed by Elbrus International."*Moskovskie Novosti*, 23 March 1999.

Santo, Brian. "Team More Than Doubles the Speed of Chess-Playing Computer." *EE Times*, 24 March 1997.

Sharp, Oliver. "The Grand Challenges." *Byte*, February 1995.

"Speedier at Los Alamos." *Aviation Week & Space Technology*, 12 October 1998.

———. "NT Courts the Parallel World." 19 May 1997. Available from http://www.computerworld.com/search/AT-html/9705/970519SL20ntdb.html.

Thompson, Tom. "The World's Fastest Computers." *Byte*, January 1996.

U.S. Department of Labor. Bureau of Labor Statistics. *Occupational Outlook Handbook.*Washington, DC: GPO, 1998.

Watterson, Karen. "Parallel Tracks." *Datamation*, May 1997

Wilck, Jennifer. "Chemical Makers Welcome Open MP Interface." *Chemical Market Reporter*, 1 December 1997.

Young, Peter. "Programming for Parallel Processors Too Often Is a Problematic Procedure." 8 May 1995. Available from http://www.computerworld.com/home/print9497.nsf/all/SL16para.

—Christopher Kasic,
updated by Gloria Cooksey and Howard Distelzweig

PASSENGER RESTRAINT SYSTEMS

INDUSTRY SNAPSHOT

Prior to 1970, passenger safety in automobiles mainly depended on operator skill, which put a premium on measures like drivers education. There were obvious limits to that approach, however, as a certain number of accidents were inevitable. At that time the transportation industry began to debate the feasibility of different ways to help passengers survive crashes. Gradually, technological improvements were introduced. Seat belts became mandatory, and later the simple lap belt gave way to a more complicated shoulder-and-lap belt system.

By 1990 public interest in safety had mounted to a pitch that saw major improvements in passenger restraint systems. New government regulations spurred the development of devices like driver's side air bags in autos, followed by passenger side air bags, and later by the development of side-impact air bags and child safety seats.

Experience with the first generation of these systems generated debate as to whether safety devices themselves sometimes caused injuries or deaths. This concern initiated the development of de-powered bags and other products. As the safety industry edged toward the year 2000, the trend was toward development of a fully integrated system in which a smart seat could adjust the speed of deployment of air bags and other safety features depending upon the height or weight of the person in the seat. While much of the debate and development of passenger restraint systems involved the automobile industry, similar debates were taking place in other transportation industries. For example, in 1997 the federal government began reviewing recommendations that would require child safety seats in airplanes.

BACKGROUND AND DEVELOPMENT

Despite years of debate throughout the 1980s, it wasn't until 1993 that the federal government mandated that automobile manufacturers begin installing air bags in all vehicles. Prior to that, air bags were installed in some European models and in a few domestic cars as well. Air bags work as a supplement to lap-and-shoulder belts in the event of an accident that propels the driver or passenger toward the steering wheel, dashboard, or windshield. Deployed by electronic sensors at the moment of a crash, air bags inflate in a fraction of a second and cushion the forward hurtling passenger.

Air bags seized the public's imagination and soon carmakers, after years of avoiding any mention of safety issues for fear of scaring consumers, began to sell safety in their advertisements. Fewer than 1 percent of American-made cars contained an air bag in the mid-1980s; by 1997, however, virtually all new vehicles sold in the United States had at least one, and 60 percent also had a passenger side air bag. As of September 1, 1998, government regulations required all passenger cars, vans, and light trucks to contain dual front air bags. Several states, including New York, Ohio, Arizona, Indiana, and Texas, ruled that consumers can sue car manufacturers for failing to equip cars with air bags, even if the cars were produced before laws were passed requiring them to be installed. Pennsylvania, Mississippi, and Idaho, however, have since ruled that car manufacturers cannot be sued in such cases.

Government and industry figures indicated that air bags were saving lives. Crashes resulted in roughly 1.4 million air bag deployments through 1996, including 1.2 million on the driver's side and 200,000 on the passenger side. Since 1986 an estimated 2,000 lives have been saved by air bags. Significantly, some 520 of those lives were saved in 1996 alone, indicating that as air bags became universal, their benefits grew.

Intense debate continued, however. First, safety experts maintained that side-impact air bags were needed to save even more lives. Secondly, the occurrence of several deaths apparently due to air bags deploying so fast that they killed occupants, led to questions about whether air bags needed to be de-powered or even disengaged at the owner's request.

It was clear that while an air bag mounted on the steering wheel or dashboard saved lives in head-on collisions, it did little for side-impact crashes. Indeed, the sensors telling an airbag to inflate were mounted on the front of the car and would not be activated in the event of a side crash. The idea of a side-impact bag also ignited consumers' imaginations, and soon all the major car companies and their suppliers were rushing to develop systems. A variety of side-impact systems were proposed, but by 1998 only expensive luxury vehicles had them as standard features, and few people were requesting them as added options. Some side-impact bags inflate near the driver's or passenger's knees; others pop out from near the head rest or from a door panel. Volvo was among the first car manufacturers to actually offer such a system.

The second key question in the air bag debate involves whether air bags should be de-powered or even switched off at the consumer's request. This question arose out of reports that air bags were deploying at minor low-speed bump crashes, and striking occupants with such force as to injure or kill them. A review by the Centers for Disease Control (CDC), looked at 32 such deaths that had occurred between 1993 and 1996. The CDC reported that while only 1 death occurred in 1993 when fewer than 1.0 percent of all vehicles had dual air bags, there were 18 such deaths during the first 11 months of 1996 when the percentage of dual air bags had risen to 11.4 percent. Young children and small or elderly women seemed to be at particular risk. Young children who were improperly restrained—or not restrained at all—in the front passenger seat were sometimes struck by the inflating airbag. Small or elderly women sometimes sat so close to the steering wheel that the bag struck them while in the act of inflating, instead of merely cushioning them as they fell forward. The CDC reported that of the 32 deaths, 21 had occurred among children who were not properly restrained. Nine were children who had been in rear-facing child safety seats in the front seat.

As media reports of such incidents mounted, the safety industry rushed to placate fears. Air bags, they pointed out, had saved far more lives than they had cost. There is confusion and there is concern about air bags. Unfortunately, most of the concerns are misplaced, Brian O'Neill, president of the Insurance Institute for Highway Safety, told the *Washington Post.* The simple act of buckling up eliminates the risk of serious injury from an airbag for almost all adults, and putting children in the back seat eliminates the risk entirely for children. The benefits of air bags, particularly if one follows those instructions, greatly outweigh any risks.

Two solutions have been offered to eliminate the potential problems air bags can cause. One is to "de-power" airbags so that they inflate 25 to 35 percent slower (first generation air bags deploy at a rate of 200 miles per hour). The answer to the question lies in determining the type of accident the industry hopes to guard against. Air bags were originally designed to save lives in high-speed head-on collisions, during which occupants are thrown forward at such speeds that a bag needs to inflate almost instantaneously to do any good. But a bag can inflate at a slightly slower rate—with less potential for injury—if the accident is a slower fender-bender type. Either option involves engineering compromises and trade-offs.

There was also discussion of a cut-off switch, which would allow an operator to disengage the passenger-side airbag. Safety regulators, however, feared that consumers would switch off air bags due to unfounded worries about their defects and, thus, compromise their own safety. In 1997 the Big Three automakers said they were installing cut-off switches on the passenger side of some, but not all, two-seaters and pickups, where babies or small children may be at risk in deployment. A few manufacturers, such as Subaru and Volvo, have refused to produce cut-off switches, insisting that their cars are safest with the air bags fully operational.

In late 1997 the government's National Highway Traffic Safety Administration (NHTSA) began allowing Americans who met certain narrow height or age requirements to have a cut-off switch installed in their cars. The process is cumbersome, however, requiring a formal application and approval procedure with the NHTSA itself. By the middle of 1998 the federal government had issued 30,000 cut-offs for approvals, but consumers soon found that government permission was not enough: many auto dealers refused to install cut-off switches, afraid they'd be held liable should an injury occur as a result. According to the NHTSA, of the estimated 25,000 auto dealerships nationwide, only 400 were willing to install cut-off switches in 1998. The Automotive Service Association advised its members not to install the devices, out of safety and liability concerns.

By spring 1998, Ford Motor Co. announced that all of its cars, as well as the Ford Windstar minivan, would be outfitted with side air bags over the following two years. Side air bags were initially offered as an option on the Mercury Cougar coupe, then became standard on the Lincoln sedans and other Ford luxury models. The company promised that by 2000, side bags would be added to all other models.

While the air bag debate continued to be the loudest in the passenger restraint field in the late 1990s, renewed attention was also returning to earlier mechanisms such as head restraints and seat belts. Starting in 1969, the federal government had required head restraints—a primary defense against whiplash injuries—to be installed in all automobiles. However, two studies by the Insurance Institute for Highway Safety found that, by the late 1990s, head restraints had morphed into more comfort oriented "head rests," thus losing much of their protective function. In 1998 the NHTSA was considering new regulations that would raise the height of head restraints, and require them to lock in position so as to stay in place during an accident.

Car manufacturers in the late 1990s were also revisiting the idea of head restraint systems. In 1998 Saab became the first car maker to offer "active" head restraints, which actually cradle a passengers head in the event of an accident. Unlike air bags, the system—developed in part by General Motors and expected to become more widely available in GM cars—does not require professional repair or resetting after a crash.

With all the technological advances, however, simply "buckling up" remained the primary and most effective passenger restraint system in any vehicle. The NTHSA estimated that using seat belts can reduce the risk of death in an accident by 45 percent for front-seat occupants. Unfortunately, less than three-quarters of passengers reported wearing seat belts, even though every state but New Hampshire required it by law.

Child safety seats also provoked intense public debate in the mid- to late 1990s. This debate grew out of concerns that improperly restrained children, such as a baby placed in a rear-facing child safety seat in the front seat, were at greater risk from inflating air bags, as well as from a crash itself. The CDC report noted that children were more likely to move around or lean forward in the front passenger seat, and that

Deployment of passenger air bag with crash dummy.
(Courtesy of TRW.)

adult-sized shoulder belts may not fit properly. Also, because children are shorter than adults, they may be more likely to have their heads or necks struck by inflating air bags. Smart bags would likely reduce this danger, but in the meantime, the NHTSA and other safety groups endorsed the recommendation that all children ride restrained in the back seat in appropriate safety seats or wear safety belts.

These safety concerns were a boon to manufacturers of child safety seats. Laws in all 50 states and the District of Columbia required that young children ride in safety seats. However, as consumers who rushed to buy the equipment soon learned, child safety seats could be confusing and easily misused. The *Wall Street Journal* reported that nearly 80 percent of child safety seats in cars and vans were used improperly, resulting in an estimated 600 deaths annually for children under the age of five. Further adding to the confusion was the multiplicity of models—dozens of child safety seats were on the market in 1999.

To correct such problems, in 1997 the NHTSA proposed rules backing a General Motors Corp. design that would change the ways child safety seats are attached to vehicles. The new design requires vehicle makers to install fixtures that anchor child safety seats, through a series of straps and buckles, to the automobile. A drawback of the system is that it would raise the price of child safety seats, from approximately $55 to more than $100, which could discourage some consumers from buying them.

Some vehicle manufacturers responded to safety concerns by building child safety seats directly into the rear passenger seat of their vehicles. This, too, led to confusion. The *New York Times* reported that in July 1997 the Chrysler Corp. was forced to send instructional videos to some 135,000 customers after receiving complaints that child seats built into its minivans malfunctioned. Complaints focused on whether restraints could retract and trap, or even choke, young children in their seats. No injuries or deaths were reported, but some parents were reported to have cut the belts away to free their children. Chrysler maintained there was no defect in the seat, and hoped that the videos would help resolve the problem. In 1998 General Motors produced a video called "Precious Cargo—Protecting the Children Who Ride With You" and offered it free to anyone at 4,000 Blockbuster Video stores around the country. The video showed parents how to correctly install various child safety restraint systems.

The NHTSA reports that child safety seats, when properly installed, reduce the risk of death in automobile accidents by 69 percent for children, and 47 percent for toddlers. In 1996 alone, the agency asserts, an estimated 365 lives were saved by child safety restraint systems. More than half of all the children who died in car accidents in 1996 were completely unrestrained.

In addition to the proliferation of child safety seat regulations, a number of states in the late 1990s began requiring children to ride in the back seat. Children in Florida and Minnesota must ride in the back seat until they are 16; in Tennessee they cannot ride in the front until they are 13. As often happens in the safety industry, cautionary steps taken by these states will likely domino throughout the country in the coming years.

Child safety seats also figured in a long-running debate in the airline industry. For decades, airlines permitted children under the age of 2 to ride for free, if held in their parent's lap during flights. The National Transportation Safety Board had long recommended that aircraft restraint systems for toddlers be made mandatory. The Commission on Airline Safety and Security agreed with the recommendation and forwarded it to the Federal Aviation Administration (FAA). In the late 1990s the FAA was reviewing the proposal, but

expressed doubts about making such a requirement, saying that the benefits gained from child safety seats might not outweigh the cost to airlines and passengers.

CURRENT CONDITIONS

One of the hottest trends in the industry in the late 1990s was toward "smart" air bags that would use seat sensors to determine the height and weight of the occupant and use that information to determine the rate of bag inflation. RufNorth America developed the SiSonic sensor, a silicon-chip sensor for use in smart air bag systems. Given the financial stakes in designing a hot-selling system, automakers were keeping most of their research to themselves. But *Ward's Automotive Reports* noted in July 1997 that development was obviously a high priority. The journal quoted a Nissan spokesman as saying, "It's certainly where the industry is headed."

The rush to develop "smart systems," however, was dealt something of a blow early in 1998 when the NHTSA began investigating "sensitive" air bag systems on approximately 800,000 General Motors cars and 400,000 Chrysler cars. While the investigation was ongoing in mid-1998, early results indicated that the systems sensors were susceptible to water corrosion.

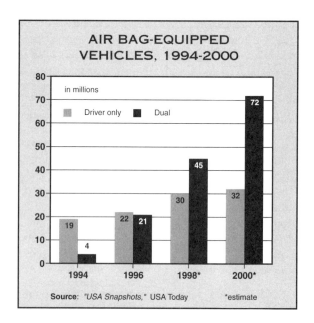

By 1999 the buzzword in the passenger restraint industry was still "smart." The NHSTA asked NASA's Jet Propulsion Lab to assess advanced air bag technologies. Such technologies were meant to reduce the rate of injury to infants, children, and out-of-position adults at the moment of air bag inflation. The NHSTA also published guidelines for a gradual phase-in of advanced air bag systems in all passenger cars and light trucks. The first-stage goal was for 25 percent of vehicles to meet new advanced air bag standards by model year 2003, with 100 percent compliance by 2006. The Alliance of Automobile Manufacturers, an organization that represents the auto industry on safety and environmental issues, met it 1999 with the NHSTA to discuss advanced technology air bags.

TRW Inc., one of the world's largest suppliers of restraint systems, predicted there would be 28.5 million side-impact bags in use by the year 2000, and 60.0 million by 2005. A brisk overseas market will contribute to this boom, as will the development of integrated smart systems that link seat, bag, and belt in one complete package.

The government set standards for head air bags in late 1998. The first cars to incorporate the sausage-shaped bags were imports from BMW, Mercedes-Benz, and Volvo. The head air bags deploy from the roof above the front doors of the vehicles and provide an added measure of protection in car rollovers or accidents with secondary impacts, such as a collision with a pole or tree.

In its continued efforts to improve restraint systems, the industry also focused on "smart seating." For example, in 1998 Volvo was developing a new type of car seat that would reduce whiplash-related injuries sustained during a rear-end collision. The seat back and head rest moved with the passenger to reduce forward rebound and spread the forces of impact more evenly.

INDUSTRY LEADERS

MORTON INTERNATIONAL

In response to public concern for safety, many companies have rushed to develop systems or products. One industry leader is Morton International, which produces the chemicals and inflating technology used to deploy air bags. In 1996 Morton and Autoliv AB of Sweden combined their air bag businesses, creating the largest automobile occupant restraint firm in the world. Morton's 1998 sales were $2.53 billion.

Although the Chicago-based Morton is best known as the salt processor with the umbrella girl on its labels, the company first found itself in the air bag business because it manufactures sodium-azide, long used to inflate air bags. Given concerns about the safety of sodium-azide (based upon its volatility, re-

cycling, and cost disadvantages), Morton announced in the late 1990s production of a non-azide inflator for driver-side air bags for an Asian carmaker.

Although sodium-azide will probably be used for some time, other makers of non-azide and stored-gas inflators such as Denver-based OEA and Allied Signal, which makes inflators in a joint venture with Sequa, known as Baico, began nibbling away at the market share of the bigger competitors.

BREED TECHNOLOGIES

Breed Technologies manufactures seat belts, air bag systems, air bag inflators, and electronic crash sensors. Through a joint venture in the late 1990s with Siemens AG, Breed was working on "intelligent" restraint systems that would "provide optimum protection for all occupants in every crash scenario," according to company literature. The company reported net sales of $1.3 billion in 1998.

TRW INC.

Companies providing an entire smart package are likely to have an advantage in future markets. In the late 1990s the industry leader appeared to be TRW Inc., a Cleveland-based firm with 1998 sales of $11.8 billion. TRW claimed a 36 percent share of the air bag market in the United States, and was doing even better in overseas markets. The first vehicle to feature TRW's complete occupant restraint system was the 1998 Mercedes-Benz M-Class. The company was able to draw on the technical expertise of its aerospace and defense lines to keep its air bag technology on the cutting edge. TRW also enjoyed a healthy cash flow, which was expected to help as the company worked toward a totally integrated passenger safety system. The 1998 purchase of technologically sophisticated Magna International, which specializes in air bag and steering wheel operations, helped to solidify and extend TRW's position in the field.

In 1999 TRW signed 12 production contracts with 6 different automakers worldwide to develop advanced, integrated safety systems. These systems will feature enhanced pretensioners, energy management systems, buckle switches, dual-stage inflators, an inflatable "tubular torso restraint," and head and knee air bags.

Another major development was the Distributed Systems Interface (DSI) that TRW created with Motorola and introduced in 1999. The DSI allowed automakers to add new safety features without redesigning a vehicles entire restraint system.

OTHER INDUSTRY LEADERS

Clearly, with seats becoming platforms for safety systems, companies that produce seats are themselves candidates for industry leadership. These include the Southfield, Michigan-based Lear Seating, which boasted 1998 sales of $9.1 billion, and Milwaukee, Wisconsin-based Johnson Controls, which had 1998 sales of $12.6 billion. Both companies reported brisk sales of safety related equipment in the late-1990s. In 1999 Lear introduced the TransG seat system, which included safety features such as cushion restraints, inflatable air collar restraints, side bolster air bags, and four-point, all-belts-to-seats restraints.

With an explosive 54 percent growth to sales of more than $1.6 billion in 1997, and 1998 sales totaling 1.8 billion, Collins & Aikman of Charlotte, North Carolina, is also quickly becoming a major player in the domestic car safety seat arena. Overseas competitors include Sweden's Autoliv, Germany's Temic, and Japan's Takata.

FURTHER READING

"Agency Checks On a Problem With Air Bags." *The New York Times,* 24 February 1998.

"Alliance Adds 10th Automaker with Fiat Membership." *PR Newswire,* 12 May 1999. Available from http://biz.yahoo.com/prnews/990512.

"Automakers Reach Consensus on Air Bag Improvements." *CNN Interactive,* 15 November 1996. Available from http://www.cnn.com/US/9611/15/air.bags.

Bowers, Faye. "Child Safety vs. Higher Cost of Travel: Hard Choices." *Christian Science Monitor,* 21 March 1997.

"Breed Reports FY 98 Fourth Quarter Earnings and Fiscal Year 1998 Earnings Results," 28 September 1998. Available from http://www.breedtech.com/news.

Brown, Warren. "Car Dealers Refusing to Switch Off Air Bags." *Washington Post,* 1 June 1998.

———. "How To Buy A Safe Car." *Washington Post,* 22 February 1998.

Chartrand, Sabra. "Patents." *The New York Times,* 22 September 1997.

Federal Motor Vehicle Safety Standards; Occupant Crash Protection. Washington, D.C.: Department of Transportation, National Highway Traffic Safety Administration, 1998. Available from http://www.nhtsa.dot.gov/airbag/proposed/advbag.

"Ford to Offer Side Air Bags on All Models." *CNN Interactive,* 8 April 1998. Available from http://www.cnn.com/US/9804/08/ford.side.airbags.

"From Swivel Seats to 4-Point Belts, Lear's TransG Seat System Offers Maturing Baby Boomers Comfort, Confidence," 1 March 1999. Available from http://www.lear.com/news.

"General Motors Offers Free Child Passenger Safety Video at Blockbuster Video." *General Motors,* 3 April 1998.

"Government Sets Standards for Head Air Bags." *CNN Interactive,* 30 July 1998. Available from http://www.cnn.com/US/9807/30/new.air.bags.

Harler, Curt. "The Great Air Bag Cut-Off Debate." *AutoInc. Magazine,* March 1998.

Huelke, Donald F. "An Overview of Air Bag Deployments and Related Injuries." *Society of Automotive Engineers,* 1995.

"Inflatable Seat Belts Could Prove the Safest System." *Car Today,* April 1997.

Jensen, Cheryl. "Safety Devices That Can Save Your Neck." *New York Times,* 29 May 1998.

Johnson Controls Inc. Company Description, April 1999. Available from http://www.johnsoncontrols.com.

"Lear 1998 Sales Top $9 Billion," 3 February 1999. Available from http://www.lear.com/e/e2.

Libertiny, George Z. "Air Bag Effectiveness—Trading Major Injuries for Minor Ones," 1995.

MacDonald, Sue. "You Need to Be a Savvy Consumer When Selecting a Car Seat." *Gannett News Service,* 29 May 1997.

Meredith, Robyn. "Chrysler Sends Out Videos After Child-Seat Complaints." *The New York Times,* 26 July 1997.

Morton Financial Overview, 13 May 1999. Available from http://www.morton.com/finc/overfinc.

Morton Milestones, 13 May 1999. Available from http://www.morton.com/comp/mile/prflmile.

NHTSA Safety Fact Sheet: Advanced Air Bags, 13 May 1999. Available from http://www.nhtsa.dot.gov/airbag/abpress/adv.

Nomani, Asra Q. "Autos: Regulators Plan Safety Rules for Child Seats." *Wall Street Journal,* 13 February 1997.

"Operation ABC '98: Mobilizing America to Buckle Up Children." *National Safety Council,* 18 May 1998.

Perez-Pena, Richard. "Albany Court Allows Suits Over the Lack of Air Bags." *The New York Times,* 17 June 1998.

Russell, Christine. "Keeping Them Safe: With the Controversy Over Air Bags, How Can Parents Protect Their Children?" *Washington Post,* 17 December 1996.

"Sensor for Smart Air Bags and Parking Assistance." *Automotive Engineering International Online,* December 1998. Available from http://www.sae.org/automag/topprod/1298p11.

"A Series of New Contract for Occupant Safety Systems Enhances TRW's Leadership in Advanced, Integrated Systems." *BusinessWire*, 1 March 1999. Available from http://www.businesswire.com.

"Some Importers Delay De-Powered Air Bags." *Ward's Automotive Reports*, 7 July 1997.

"TRW and Motorola Develop Innovative In-Vehicle Network Architecture, the Industry's First Open Standard for Advanced Safety Systems." *BusinessWire*, 2 March 1999. Available from http://www.businesswire.com.

TRW Annual Report 1998, 13 May 1999. Available from http://trw.com/98annual/fin_highlights.

Ward, Sandra. "Goin' Like 60: Airbag Boom Speeds Ahead." *Barron's*, 24 June 1996.

"Whiplash Studies Lead to New Car Seat." *Automotive Engineering International Online*, December 1998. Available from http://www.sae.org/automag/toptech/1298t09.

———. "Money Bags: Who Will Be the Winners in the New Airbag Boom?" *Barron's*, 22 January 1996.

—John Gallagher,
updated by David Yosifon and Marinell James

PET PRODUCTS AND SERVICES

As of the late 1990s, Americans owned about 120 million cats and dogs, slightly more cats than dogs. This figure, staggering as it is, does not include the hundreds of thousands of other pets, including tropical fish, birds, reptiles, and amphibians that Americans have taken to their hearts. And pet owners, most of who consider their pets part of the family, are generous with these animal family members, lavishing close to $27 billion annually in the late 1990s. This figure does not include the cost of veterinary services, which in 1998 totaled more than $11 billion. Spending on pet food rocketed in the late 1990s, making this one of the fastest growing segments of the entire food industry. Total spending on pets rose sharply in the

1990s, with the latest figures available in 1999 showing that spending went up over 30 percent between 1994 and 1996. Services for dogs increased markedly, with new markets opening up in services traditionally reserved for children, such as day care, Halloween costumes, and birthday parties.

Analysts estimate that American spending on basic pet-related goods (not including veterinary services) will jump to $28.5 billion by the year 2001. Large chain pet supply stores are to be found in shopping centers, large and small, across the country. Additionally, the major discount retailers, including Wal-Mart and Kmart, boast expansive pet supply sections, as do a number of the country's larger department stores.

A vast industry has grown up to meet the needs of America's pet owners and their animal charges. On one side, the industry is dominated by a handful of large corporations dealing in most of the traditional (and not so traditional) products that are needed to keep a pet healthy, well-fed, comfortable, and entertained. On the other side is a vast network of loosely organized suppliers of more exotic products and services. Most of the companies in this latter group are relatively small, and most handle a limited number of products, unlike the supermarket-scale offerings of the large pet retail companies.

The range of products available for pets in the United States is mind-boggling, particularly for those who have no pets themselves. Among the products and services marketed for pets are such basics as pet foods, leashes, bird cages, aquariums, pet toys, and veterinary care. However, in recent years, more and more unusual products and services aimed at pets and pet owners have come to market. Some of the more un-

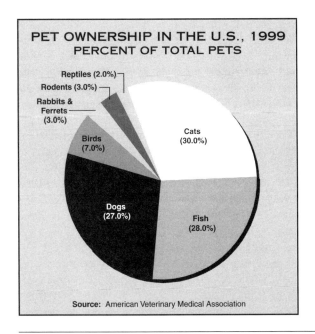

PET OWNERSHIP IN THE U.S., 1999
PERCENT OF TOTAL PETS

Reptiles (2.0%)
Rodents (3.0%)
Rabbits & Ferrets (3.0%)
Birds (7.0%)
Cats (30.0%)
Dogs (27.0%)
Fish (28.0%)

Source: American Veterinary Medical Association

usual pet products include health insurance, elaborate housing for dogs and cats, furniture to fill up such housing, and even audio tapes to encourage your bird to talk. Among the services are a broad range of training programs, grooming, pet sitting, and walking.

ORGANIZATION AND STRUCTURE

Among the large corporations dedicated to serving the needs of American pet owners and their pets are three corporations based in the southwestern United States. PETsMART Inc. and Petco Animal Supplies Inc., based in Phoenix and San Diego, respectively, are the top two retailers of pet supplies. Veterinary Centers of America (VCA), based in Santa Monica, California, operates a vast network of full-service animal hospitals providing health care for American pets. VCA operates nearly 160 animal hospitals in 26 states as well as a network of veterinary labs. Those laboratory services are used by more than 13,000 animal hospitals in 49 states for the testing of pet blood, urine, and tissue. Competing with the large pet retailers for the consumer's pet supply dollars are the giant discount retailers, such as Kmart and Wal-Mart, most of which aggressively market pet foods and some other basic pet supplies.

The other side of the pet supply industry is made up of a number of smaller companies, each of which generally markets a narrow range of pet products or services. In many cases, these companies may sell only a single pet product or device, or a family of closely related such products. Included in this group, of course, and an exception to the rule of limited product offerings are independent pet stores, which generally offer a full range of pet products. These non-chain pet stores are found in downtown shopping centers as well as in the smaller regional malls throughout the country. In some cases, pet products or services are marketed by a single division of a larger enterprise, as is the case with some of the pet benefits packages, which represent only a tiny segment of the business of a full-service insurer or benefits packager.

BACKGROUND AND DEVELOPMENT

Although American companies have been meeting the needs of American pet owners for decades, the major forces in the pet supply industry at the close of the twentieth century were all of relatively recent vintage. Small independent retailers had been the norm

until the build-up of nationwide chains and megastores in the 1980s and 1990s.

PETsMART Inc., headquartered in Phoenix, is the country's number one retailer of pet supplies. It traces its origins to the vision of a California-based pet supply wholesaler who decided in the 1980s that he could make a lot more money if he opened his own retail outlets. The wholesaler decided to open his first retail store in Las Vegas and hired Jim and Janice Dougherty to operate it. Called the Pet Food Supermarket, the Las Vegas outlet did a booming business, leading soon to the opening of four more stores in the Phoenix area. The Doughertys, managing the fledgling chain of Pet Food Supermarkets, met Ford Smith, a graduate of Harvard Business School, and the trio decided to introduce the superstore format into the pet business. Using Toys "R" Us as their model, they opened two PetFood Warehouses in Arizona in 1987. The following year another seven stores were opened in Arizona, Colorado, and Texas. PetFood Warehouse was redubbed PETsMART in 1989. At about this time, Jim Dougherty left the company for health reasons, followed a short time later by his wife. PETsMART brought in Sam Parker, who had previously worked for Jewel Supermarkets, as chief executive officer. Parker redesigned the company's strategy as well as the layout of its stores. In the early 1990s the chain added a new range of services at its outlets, including grooming, veterinary services, and obedience classes. It also broadened its product range to include birds and fish. The company went public in 1993. In the late 1990s it operated more than 500 stores in the United States, Canada, and the United Kingdom.

Petco Animal Supplies, the number two U.S. retailer of pet supplies, operates more than 460 stores in 37 states and the District of Columbia. Its retail superstores, each averaging 15,000 square feet in area, sell about 10,000 products, ranging from collars and leashes to dog houses, grooming supplies, and pet foods. Petco evolved from a San Diego area veterinary supply store called Upco, which opened in 1965. When it decided to market a full range of pet supplies in the late 1970s, the company changed its name to Petco. By 1988, the company had grown to about 40 stores and was purchased jointly by the Spectrum Group and the Thomas H. Lee Co. Shortly after the takeover, Petco acquired two pet supply chains, more than tripling its number of stores. By early 1990, however, the company found itself in financial hot water, its advertising costs having mushroomed to promote its schedule of periodic sales. Under a new management team, headed by Toys "R" Us veteran Brian Devine, the company launched a new policy of everyday-low-prices for its premium pet foods, which increased traffic and stimulated sales of other products as well. The company stabilized financially and in 1994, with nearly 200 stores, went public.

One of the largest networks of full-service animal hospitals in the United States is operated by Veterinary Centers of America. Founded in 1986, VCA's goal from the start was to become a leader in the field of veterinary services. In its second year, VCA acquired the West Los Angeles Veterinary Medical Group. It has continued to grow through the acquisition of leading veterinary hospitals across the country. To finance its expansion, the company successfully completed its initial public offering of stock in October 1991. Although the IPO was launched on the American Stock Exchange, the company's stock is traded on the NASDAQ. The company joined with Heinz Pet Products in early 1993 to introduce a premium line of pet food called Vet's Choice. In 1996, VCA merged with Pets Rx and the Pet Practice. That same year the company set up the largest veterinary diagnostic laboratory in the United States. Nine veterinary diagnostic laboratories across the country were consolidated to form Antech Diagnostics. VCA's laboratory services are available to veterinarians across the country, who also are encouraged to consult with VCA's staff of more than 50 board-certified veterinary specialists.

CURRENT CONDITIONS

The array of pet products and services available to pet owners in the United States and abroad continues to grow. Among the products that debuted at the annual Pet Products Trade Show in Atlanta in the summer of 1998 were a number of interesting items likely to turn up soon on the shelves of pet stores across the country. These included Wordy Birdy, from Wordy Birdy Products, a $30 tape recorder that will play continuously (or until the tape wears out) a bird owner's recorded message of the phrase or phrases he would like his pet to learn. Another product sure to gladden the hearts of cat owners everywhere is CatFinder, offered by Pet Friendly for $40. This product is a radio-remote device that attaches to the collar of a cat so that its owner can track it down in a pinch. Pet-Ag introduced its $7 Emergency Feeding Kit that contains everything one might need to feed an orphaned raccoon, kitten, porcupine, or other small mammal. A company called Petcraft offered a $35 Serenity Pet Casket, lined with blue satin and large enough to hold a departed pet of up to 15 pounds.

With the growing market in pet foods, specialized segments such as pet bakeries and herbal supplements for dogs and cats have emerged in the late 1990s. A gourmet dog food manufacturer, Canine Caviar Inc. of Anaheim, California, went into business in 1996 and two years later had franchises all over California expected to bring in $3 million in 1999. Several chains of canine bakeries operate in California and in the West, with business expected nationally and internationally. With the late 1990s obsession with alternative medicine comes homeopathic and herbal veterinary medicine. While the number of non-traditional veterinarians is not known, the practice seems to be growing, according to a 1999 article in the *Arizona Republic*. High-tech medicine such as organ transplants, laser surgery, chemotherapy, and insertion of pacemakers is increasingly being used on animals as well.

A small but growing number of American companies have begun offering pet-related benefits to their employees. American Management Systems, an information consulting firm based in Virginia, pays the kennel bill for its employees who must board their animals when they are sent out of town on business. Many companies offer to pay a portion of its employees' veterinary bills. Though only .1 percent of all pets in the United States were covered by insurance as of 1998, this seems to be a growing market, as evidenced by increasing business at several firms that specialize in veterinary insurance.

For the pet superstores such as PETsMART and Petco, a significant percentage of their revenue is derived from the sale of pet foods. The competition for the pet food dollar tightened considerably after 1994, when Wal-Mart introduced a premium brand of pet food at a price notably lower than the major brands of pet food. Many of the other major discounters followed Wal-Mart's lead. From mid-1997 to mid-1998, sales of pet food at the major discount chains rose more than 16 percent. Regular supermarkets, which until the 1990s had been the primary source for U.S. pet food purchases, took note of the competition from the discounters and began introducing their own brands of pet food and sharply discounting some of the name brands they carried.

Perhaps the most surprising phenomenon in the pet supply market has been the resilience of the small, independent pet shops. Although many were predicted to fold under the pressure of competition from the pet superstores, most of these independent pet shops have demonstrated amazing staying power. The superstores generally don't deal in the sale of dogs and cats, although some of them participate actively in pet adoption programs. The small neighborhood pet shops al-

---

PRACTICAL PET PRODUCTS?

A Chinese Pug named Frodo was the first canine ever to be neutered and implanted with a solid silicone testicular implant. Frodo's transformation shows the extent to which pet products and care have grown into an unusual industry. The procedure took place in Castro Valley, California where Dr. Cynthia Edelman performed a three-minute procedure on the 16-month-old pug. Implants, made of solid silicone, have the texture and feel of a gummie bear, according to Gregg A. Miller, inventor and president of the Missouri based CTI Corporation.

Neuticles, as they are called, are 100 percent safe and will never flake, leak or cause any adverse reaction, Miller said in a press release for his company. Five sizes of the false testicles are available for canines. They are sold to veterinarians for $89 to $129 per pair for the silicone models, and $25 to $32 a pair for the polypropylene version. Neuticles are also available for horses and bulls.

Pets can also be pampered with the invention of gourmet pet food, which includes pasta for dogs. Thompson's Pet Pasta Products, Inc., owned by Coldwater, Kansas native Richard Thompson, specializes in making dog food out of pasta that resembles meatballs and ziti.

Thompson knows about pasta, having built up the American Italian Pasta Company, 74 percent of which he and investors sold in 1991 for $50 million, according to a 1998 article in *Food Processing*. When traveling in Italy, he conceived of the idea to cook pasta for pets when he saw the native Italian people cooking pasta for their dogs.

Though the company lost $13 million in 1996, according to *Forbes*, Thompson's Pet Pasta Products had grown to $20 million in 1998. Some of the products include: Beef-flavored and Bacon Liver-flavored Woof-a-Roni, which are chewy pasta bones; Labonies, which are crunchy bones flavored with real lamb; and Petzels, chewy beef-flavored twists.

And Avid Canada, a microchip company, has invented PETtrac, a worldwide computerized tracking system for companion animals. To activate the system, a chip is injected in the animal, the microchip number is entered into the patient's records and is recorded on a patient identification sheet which is forwarded to the company. Each participating animal is registered in the PETtrac database, using the clinic as a tracking site. The company has numerous back-up systems to guarantee the constancy of its tracking abilities.

---

most all sell cats and dogs, in addition to fish, birds, and other small pets. Many pet owners, it turned out, felt more comfortable dealing with the pet stores from which they had originally acquired their pets, guaranteeing these smaller retailers a decent level of repeat business.

Veterinary Centers of America by the late 1990s had become the largest provider of pet care in the United States. In addition to its network of freestanding veterinary hospitals and its chain of clinical laboratories, VCA in late 1998 owned an interest in Vet's Choice, a joint venture with Heinz Pet Products, and an interest in Veterinary Pet Insurance Inc., the nation's biggest pet health insurance company.

Pet insurance, available not only in the United States but in Canada and the United Kingdom as well, is a relatively new business and one that is expected to show growth as both the scope and the cost of veterinary care climbs sharply. In Canada, pet insurance has been available since 1989, although as of 1998, less than 1 percent of that country's 7 million cats and dogs had been insured by their owners. According to Valerie Goddard, operations manager of Pet Plan Insurance, based in Mississauga, Ontario, many pet owners are unaware that such a product is available. Or, she said, many owners who are aware of the availability of pet coverage "just don't feel it's going to happen to them," meaning a medical crisis for their

pet(s). Pet Plan, according to Goddard, covers all treatment costs provided the animal was insured before the accident or illness. Covering only cats and dogs, Pet Plan charges up to $42.25 a month for coverage.

INDUSTRY LEADERS

Although supermarkets and the large discount chains compete in segments of the pet supply market, particularly pet foods and the most basic pet maintenance products such as collars, leashes, and flea sprays, the industry itself is divided between two large superstore chains and hundreds of independent neighborhood pet shops. These are PETsMART and Petco.

The industry leader is PETsMART, headquartered in Phoenix, Arizona. After going public in 1993, it began to expand rapidly through acquisition, adding 40 stores in 1993, 50 more in 1994, and acquiring a Midwest chain of pet superstores, Westheimer Companies. PETsMART has operated in Europe since 1996. As of 1998, PETsMART operated 468 stores, including its Canadian and European outposts. Its 1999 sales topped $2 billion.

Number two in the pet supply market is Petco Animal Supplies Inc., headquartered in San Diego. With

---

more than 450 stores in 37 states and the District of Columbia, Petco derives a little more than 40 percent of its total revenue from the sale of premium pet foods. The company's selection of products numbers about 10,000, including pet toys, grooming supplies, collars, leashes, aquariums, pet bedding, and pet enclosures. Like its larger rival, Petco does not sell cats and dogs, although it does offer fish, birds, and reptiles. It also follows PETsMART's lead in sponsoring pet adoption programs. For fiscal 1999, ended January 31, 1999, Petco reported a net loss of $2.4 million on revenue of $839.6 million. The company's revenue was up 12 percent from the previous year.

Analysts predicted in the mid-1990s that between them PETsMART and Petco, following the superstore blueprint established by Toys "R" Us in the toy industry, would quickly dominate the pet industry, where neighborhood pet shops made up the bulk of the competition. Unfortunately for the pet superstores, the competition from both the neighborhood stores and the pet departments of the large discount chains has proved more formidable than originally anticipated. Analysts have revised their market predictions, suggesting now that it will be some time before the two superstore chains dominate the pet supply market.

In the area of health care for pets, Veterinary Centers of America Inc. ranks number one in the United States with more than 150 animal hospitals in 26 states. In addition to its full-service veterinary hospitals, VCA operates the country's largest network of veterinary laboratories. Its 15 diagnostic labs provide services to more than 13,000 animal hospitals in 49 states. The labs provide a full range of diagnostic services, including testing of blood, urine, and tissue. VCA's animal hospitals account for more than 70 percent of the company's revenue. The hospitals' services range from basic services such as vaccinations, neutering, and routine exams to specialized surgeries for most household pets. Headquartered in Santa Monica, California, VCA owns a 50 percent interest in the Vet's Choice premium pet food brand, a joint venture with Heinz Pet Products. The company also owns a share in Veterinary Pet Insurance Inc. The company posted net income in 1998 of $16.3 million, an increase of 45.5 percent over the previous year. Revenue in 1998 totaled $281.0 million, up 17.4 percent from 1997.

WORK FORCE

Employment in the pet supply and veterinary services industries is difficult to quantify, because many of the independent retailers and animal hospitals involved in the business are private and thus not required

to report such information. Employment opportunities in the pet supply business range from entry-level sales jobs and main-office clerical positions through top-level management positions with the leading superstore chains. Within the veterinary care segment of the pet industry, jobs range from support personnel through veterinary surgeons and specialists.

As of 1998, PETsMART Inc. employed 18,800, an increase of more than 21 percent from its employee rolls of 1997. The number-two pet superstore chain, Petco, employed 9,400, up by almost 65 percent from the previous year. Veterinary Centers of America Inc. reported a total payroll of just over 3,000 employees, up almost 40 percent from 1997.

AMERICA AND THE WORLD

The pet industry is alive and well outside the United States, particularly in Canada and the United Kingdom. Britons, in particular, have been noted for their obsession with their pets. Of the two big pet superstore chains, only PETsMART operates outside the United States. The company, as of 1998, had 84 retail outlets in the United Kingdom and 12 in Canada. PETsMART in 1996 acquired Pet City Holdings PLC, which operates more than 50 stores throughout the United Kingdom.

Pet insurance, a concept that has begun to catch on in the United States, is also making headway in Canada and the United Kingdom. So far, however, less than 1 percent of Canadian pet owners have opted to insure their pets. In the United Kingdom, with a total of more than 50 million pets, about 15 percent of pets have been insured by their owners, according to 1998 data from Euromonitor.

Pet Healthcare Services, a U.K. pet insurance specialist, in early 1999 launched an online information service for pet owners. The Web site offers a wide range of information about caring for one's pets and provides an e-mail notification service to remind pet owners when vaccinations or flea control treatments are due for their pets. The market for pet products and services is booming in the United Kingdom and was estimated in 1998 at about $3.2 billion annually. The market for pet food reportedly grew by about 20 percent between 1994 and 1998.

RESEARCH AND TECHNOLOGY

The pet industry, like almost every segment of the economy, is turning to high technology to develop products for pets and pet owners. One product certain to appeal to any pet owner who has ever been traumatized by the loss (temporary or permanent) of a pet that strayed away is offered by a Canadian firm. The PetNet microchip, barely larger than a grain of rice, is implanted under the skin of a pet for identification purposes. Pets that have been "chipped" are registered with PetNet, a registry of all pets that have been implanted with such a microchip. Anitech Enterprises Inc. of Markham, Ontario, which developed the PetNet microchip, said the technology makes it much easier to locate lost pets, sparing both pet owners and pets a lot of grief.

FURTHER READING

Bidwell, Carol. "Furry Friends, Big Bucks: Pets Generate Billion-Dollar Industry; Doting Owners Eager to Make Animals' Lives the Cat's Meow." *Arizona Republic,* 2 March 1999.

"The Bionic Dog (Anitech Enterprises' PetNet Microchip Pet Identification Product)." *Computing Canada,* 11 April 1996.

Earnest, Leslie. "Dogs Collar the Market in Pet Pampering: Animals: From Bakeries to Veterinarians, Businesses Increasingly Are Catering to Pets, Especially Canines." *Los Angeles Times,* 12 November 1998.

Harrison, Bette. "New Gadgets May Be Useful to Your Faithful Pampered Pet." *Atlanta Journal and Constitution,* 26 June 1998.

Hunter, George. "Owners Increasingly Pampering Pets." *Gannett News Service,* 22 March 1999.

Kellner, Tomas. "Fido's Insurance." *Forbes,* 30 November 1998.

"Kolorfusion Inc. and Pet Friendly Inc. Enter Licensing Agreement." *Business Wire,* 26 January 1999.

"Natural Critter Care (Growing Popularity of Natural Care, Which Includes Non-processed Whole Foods and Organic Products)." *Earth Action Network Inc.,* 1998.

Phillips, Vicki. "If You Can't Shop with the Big Dogs, Stay Out of the Mall." *Shopping Center World,* 1 June 1998.

Polsky, Carol. "Beyond the Goldfish Bowl: Today's Elaborate Home Aquariums Include Everything from Shark Tanks to Mini-Coral Reefs." *Newsday,* 19 November 1998.

"Sun Alliance: Pet Healthcare Services Launches 'Cyberpet' Service for UK Pet Owners." *PressWire,* 9 March 1999.

"Veterinary Centers of America Inc. Reports Second-Quarter and Six-Month Financial Results; Company Reports 33% Increase in EPS on Record Earnings and Revenues." *Business Wire,* 23 July 1998.

White, George. "Like Cats and Dogs; Pet Supply Superstores Have Got a Fight on Their Hands." *Los Angeles Times,* 24 July 1998.

—Don Amerman

PHOTONICS

The photonics industry champions an evolving technology whereby light and other radiant energy forms, measured in photons, are generated and harnessed. The science of photonics replaces the electron, now dominant in electronics, with the photon. Photons are uncharged particles of light, and scientists see in them an opportunity to move bits of data at speeds higher than anything previously known in the world of electronics. Photonics uses light (both its linear and non-linear properties) for information processing and communication; light is emitted, transmitted, deflected, amplified and detected by sophisticated optical and electro-optical instruments and components, lasers, fiber optics, and sophisticated hardware and systems. Photonics research in the late-1990s was geared toward communications, computer processing, and the generation of energy. Researchers experimented with optical memory, storage devices, computer buses, optical network interfaces, and photon-based processors, all of which could drastically speed up communication and computing processes. Despite initial doubts in the scientific community, the growing consensus is that, just as electronics transformed the twentieth century, photonics may spark a technological revolution in the twenty-first.

BACKGROUND AND DEVELOPMENT

In the twentieth century, electronic technology revolutionized areas as varied as medicine, manufacturing, and defense, and sparked new industries such as computer science and telecommunications. By harnessing the electron, scientists are able to store, process, and transmit information through wires. Electrons are interacting, charged particles whose power—electricity—is manifested in electronic products such as the computer. The electronic integrated circuit (chip), which often contains millions of rapid information-processing transistors, is the foundation for all electronic products—everything from computers to missiles to VCRs. While the advances wrought by electronics have been nothing short of revolutionary, electrons do have their shortcomings. Given the charged nature of electrons, the transmission of data runs the risk of "cross talk," noise sparked by their unwanted interaction. To be effective, electrons must pass through wires and, while a chip might hold millions of transistors, it can only accommodate hundreds of wires to transport the information they contain. In essence, there is more information being produced than there is capacity to transport it, so information traffic "clogs up." In order to overcome such "bottlenecks" in electronic processing, scientists are integrating photonics and opto-electronics (a hybrid technology combining electronics and photonics) into electronic products.

Photonics (often called optics) uses light instead of electricity to process and store information. Photons are neutral particles and, as such, carry no electronic charge; they are thus not affected by electromagnetic interference. Where electrons require barriers such as wires to keep them from interacting with one another, the photons in streams of light can cross paths with no adverse consequences. Though they are often passed through fiber optic cable, photons can be beamed in all directions, thus providing a great number of parallel, interconnected data channels. Data transmission is "clean," with information travelling unhindered on independent channels of light. Given the neutral nature of photons, non-optical techniques are required for putting data onto these beams of light, and so-called "photonic circuits" still depend on electronic technology. Photonics also means more bandwidth, with photonic processes measured in trillion hertz (terahertz), as opposed to the fewer than 10 billion hertz (gigahertz) reserved for electronics. Given this high bandwidth and capacity for interactivity and parallel information processing, photonics researchers envision devices that are cheaper, faster, and lighter than anything ever delivered by electronics.

Researchers first explored photonics in the early 1950s, but experiments using light from the sun and from mercury arc lamps proved unsuccessful. Laser and the transistor were born a scant decade apart, yet it was the transistor that would triumph from the 1960s on. Early laser experiments for optical computing led many scientists to conclude that high heat dissipation and inadequate materials made photonics an improbable endeavor; but advancements in laser technology (in particular the use of room-temperature laser) encouraged more vigorous research into optics. With the advent of semiconductor lasers and optical fiber in the early 1970s, photonics research gathered momentum, particularly in the communications industry, where industry leaders saw the implications for high-speed data transmission. That need for speed, accompanied by the growing view that electronic computers left little room for evolution, sparked a renewed photonics industry that began to flourish only in the mid- to late 1990s.

In 1999, the Holy Grail of many photonics researchers remained the perfected "photonic crystal." Much as semiconductor chips can manipulate electricity, this artificial structure can transmit light, bend it, and make it turn corners with a minimal loss of light. Scientists have already been able to bend light in the laboratory, but photonic chips are still on the workbench. Despite the revolutionary applications of photonics in telecommunications, current communication systems require electronic circuits at either end; light signals must pass through these circuits to be converted to electrical signals—a process that slows down the communication process. The development of all-photonic circuits was expected to bring tremendous increases in speed and efficiency, bring that much closer vice president Al Gore's vision of a high-bandwidth national information infrastructure.

CURRENT CONDITIONS

Photonics is already a consumer reality. Anyone who makes long-distance telephone calls, listens to compact discs, or is charged through supermarket laser price scanners is experiencing the results of photonics technology. But this is just the tip of the iceberg. Researchers are discovering new and varied ways of applying photonics in fields as vast as home entertainment, telecommunications, optical computing, defense, and microscopy.

Photonics today is a multi-billion dollar industry, though accurate measurements depend largely on which photonic industry subgroups are taken into account. According to the Photonics Development Center, the bulk market for optical communications is growing at 40 percent annually; by some estimates this would make it a $15 billion industry by 2004. Nonetheless, the top companies dedicated to photonics technology in 1999 showed net sales far in excess of the estimated $2.8 billion industry calculation for that year. What was clear was that photonics would become an increasingly important industry, as research continues to usurp the traditional role of electronics.

OPTICAL STORAGE

The more photonics research translates into affordable consumer products, the more individuals and institutions can expect to see revolutions in the way they store their information. Optical storage technology has grown considerably since the early 1980s. Among the most ubiquitous optics products available today is the compact disc. With the growing presence of personal computers, consumers in the late 1990s were using CD-ROM (compact disc read-only memory) on a regular basis and increasingly were receiving computer software on CD-ROM, capable of holding hundreds of megabytes of data. WORM (write once, read many) disc technology post-dated the CD-ROM and has a storage capacity measured in billions of bytes (gigabytes). In the late 1990s, many institutions began replacing paper and microfilm storage with optical storage. Digital video disk (DVD) technology also materialized commercially, along with stand-alone DVD players and DVD computer peripherals. In late 1998, Fujitsu Computer Products of America unveiled the world's first 1.3 GB 3.5" Magneto-Optical Drive. Magneto-optical media is resistant to moisture, shock, dust, and other dangers and can be rewritten more than 10 million times, making it an appealing long-term storage option. In mid-1999, Memorex began shipping its multifunctional CD-RW drive, which made CDs as simple to use and create as magnetic floppy disks. Another area of research involves holographic storage, whereby information is stored as light onto crystal fibers. Some predict that erasable optical memory will eventually replace magnetic disks as the storage medium of choice. (Also see the essay in this book entitled Optical Data Storage.)

TELEVISION

Electro-optic technology may also transform television, with the traditional boxy television set being replaced by the flat panel display; this technology is also applied to computer monitors. The billion dollar flat panel display industry exists thanks to beam-steering applications, a key component derived from photonics research. Electro-optics may also mean greater consumer choice and freedom from the restrictions of local cable TV providers: with photonics technology, electrical TV signals turn into optical signals capable of travelling through fiber optics over long distances. (Also see the essay in this book entitled Video Displays.)

TELECOMMUNICATIONS

A major force behind the development of photonic technology is the growing use of optical fiber by the telecommunications industry. The fiber is small, light, durable, resistant to corrosion, and difficult to tap. In addition, its broad bandwidth makes it the media of choice among long-distance carriers. Fiber optic telephone systems are another photonics application already familiar to most consumers. If the industry's plans to deliver high-definition television with two-way communication pan out, many buildings and homes may see their traditional copper wire replaced by fiber cable—an expensive proposition that will require tearing out old network lines. Among the crucial advances in photonics has been the development of the optical fiber amplifier and error correction; with this technology, electrical impulses are sent to a local phone office where a switch modulates a laser to convert those impulses into optical form. Wave Division Multiplexing (WDM) is another technology helping to augment the capacity of optical fibers; with this technique, multiple laser pulses of different hues are sent simultaneously down a singular tiny fiber, increasing a fiber's capacity dozens of times.

Digital transmission is nothing new. The first form of transmission was Morse code, used for decades as a form of sending simple messages over long distances. Fiber applications didn't materialize until 1983, when New York and Washington, D.C. were united by a transmission trunk using glass fibers and transferring data at 45 million bits per second. Early 1996 brought phone company installation of 2.5 gigabyte fiber-optic equipment; that same year, MCI quadrupled its Internet backbone capacity and data could move at 40 billion bits per second. The transmission of data at trillions of bits per second is no longer an impossibility, due largely to advances in photonics.

Despite the advantages of fiber lines, changing from electrons to photons was not cost-effective for many phone companies. Until the advent of optical amplifiers, 16-signal fiber lines required a $1.2 million investment every 19 to 25 miles. Optical amplifiers are just as expensive, but only two are needed every 350 miles or so. According to *Forbes*, phone companies were expected to spend nearly $10 billion on this technology between 1997 and 2001. As for laying fiber optic cable, it may cost as much as $100 billion to rewire the United States, and nearly a trillion dollars to rewire the world. But as companies raced to meet increasing demands for fiber in the late 1990s, the increased supply brought down prices. Despite competition in the form of copper-based, asynchronous digital subscriber lines (ADSL), fiber-optics continued to advance the telecommunications industry, thanks largely to photonic innovations.

In mid-1999, Lucent's Bell Laboratories was working to take WDM a step further by multiplexing a virtually limitless number of channels on a single fiber. Where 40 to 80 channels is the state-of-the-art for WDM technology, Lucent's "chirped-pulse" WDM technique promised the ability to multiplex 300 channels, all within an 80-nm segment of the spectrum. That same year, Lucent unveiled a single-laser, time division multiplexing system that would quadruple information transmission to 40 Gbps—enough to send 500,000 phone calls per second over a single fiber optic cable. MCI WorldCom was expected to test the system by year's end. At a time when companies were pushing toward a record of 1,000 fibers per 1-inch cable, this means radically faster and cheaper data transmission, which the industry needs to keep up with a growing number of consumers and their demands for high bandwidth capable of sending data, voice, and video on demand. (Also see the essays in this book entitled Telephony and Voice Mail Systems.)

PHOTONIC COMPUTERS

One major goal of photonics research is optical computing. *PC Magazine* suggested that by 2005 "a mainstream computer may run at a clock speed of 10 gigahertz, pack a gigabyte of memory and 100 gigabytes of storage, weigh four ounces, run for weeks at a time on battery power, and display a crisp resolution of 10,000 by 10,000 pixels." Inspired by the possibilities of light, researchers dream of the day where computers consist of several processors communicating and connecting with one another in massive parallel interconnections based on photonics. In addition to computer-to-computer fiber-optic links, photonics research is evolving to provide solutions at increasingly minute levels: links between circuit boards inside computers, chip-to-chip connections on individual circuit boards, and optical connections within the chips themselves. The ultimate success of all-optical computing will likely rest in the successful development of all-optical processors. In 1999, there were already patents on the world's smallest laser, photonic light-emitting, and micro-resonator devices; jointly, these three devices are the basis of a light-based "photonic" logic circuit expected to revolutionize computers. Photonic devices are similar to current semiconductor integrated circuits, so thanks to microcavity technology and the devices' planar structure, they can be built into current semiconductor wafers, integrating more high-speed features on a single chip than electronics ever could. With the use of lenses, lasers, and holograms, some organizations are currently developing optical computers. The ultimate success of all-optical computing, however, will likely rest in the successful development of all-optical processors. (Also see the essays in this book entitled Holography, Lasers and Laser Applications, and Parallel Processing Computers.)

MILITARY

In addition to providing commercial products based on photonics technology, researchers are combining light beams and electrical pulses in various military-related applications. Given the durability of cable, and light's immunity to electromagnetic interference (EMI), weapons systems-based photons rather than electrons may be more reliable in battle conditions. Fiber optic cable may provide the solution to the military's need for secure, jam-resistant communications and, in the in the late 1990s, low speed optical communications were already used in shipboard applications at terabyte speeds. A proposed high speed optical digital computer network will have effects on avionics, satellites, and ground platforms. The fiber-optic, high speed Synchronous Optical Network (SONET) has been adapted for military data and voice transmission. The Air Force and AT&T worked toward perfecting a ruggedized optical connector (ROC) for potential use in helicopters and tactical fighters. The military has also shown an interest in photonic memory as a means of creating databases of interactive battlefield visualization systems; the current synthetic aperture radar (SAR) technology requires equipment so large that the electronics and their power supply must be carried in separate trucks. With photonic technology—particularly dense, system-on-

a-chip photonics and free-space optical components— such battlefield tools could conceivably fit in one's hand. Companies like VLSI Photonics currently work toward achieving such computing density. Photonics technology may also allow the military to improve on its radar technology by helping to detect electromagnetic radiation, in order to track and avoid jamming signals.

MICROSCOPY

With the aid of photonics technology, scientists are better prepared to view the world at the microscopic level. At Hamamatsu Photonics, Dr. Hiroyasu Itoh developed the framing streak camera in 1992. With a shutter speed of 50 billionths of a second and capabilities for taking pictures at less than a millionth of a second, this photonic camera allowed him to capture clear, detailed photos of the process by which the pores of different types of cells open and close. Physicists at Cornell University have successfully applied photon physics to monitor the cellular presence of serotonin, a primary brain chemical. This new microscopy has revolutionized biochemistry, allowing biologists to track molecular movement deep inside living cells, without destroying or damaging the cell. Whereas previous microscopy precluded the study of certain molecules, this new method gives visibility to previously unobservable molecules by employing the additive energies of multiple photons to spark fluorescence in them. Multiphoton instruments were previously the sole creations of researchers, but Bio-Rad Laboratories received license from Cornell to commercialize the instrument. In 1999, physicists learned to determine the position of fluorescent molecules in a solid matrix with a resolution finer than a light wavelength; by probing with an ultra-precise frequency laser, they could study how chemically identical, adjacent fluorescent molecules react to light.

INDUSTRY LEADERS

There are literally thousands of companies using photonics, though not all are engaged exclusively in the field. Lucent Technologies, Bell Communications Research (Bellcore), Pirelli, and Corning are some of the major players in the photonics industry. Despite the presence of giant corporations dedicating part of their research and development costs to photonics, it is important to note that there are a myriad of smaller companies providing important technological innovations as well.

Lucent Technologies, with 141,600 employees and 1998 sales of more than $30 billion, is a telecommunications powerhouse. Locally, the U.S. company is the top producer of software and telecommunications equipment, providing everything from wireless networks and switching and transmission equipment to telephones and business communication systems. Globally, Lucent is a leading developer of telecommunications power systems and digital signal processors. The company sells primarily to telecommunications network operators like AT&T, which accounted for 15 percent of sales in 1998. Its products are chiefly the result of technology provided by Bell Labs. Lucent's fiber-optic production grew five-fold between 1991 and 1999, the year the company agreed to supply its TrueWave RS fiber for Viatel Inc.'s European Network, an ambitious project to link several major European cities.

Telcordia Technologies, formerly Bell Communications Research (Bellcore), was created after the breakup of AT&T in 1984 as a research institution for the so-called "baby Bells." The company changed its name to Telcordia in 1999, the year after it became a subsidiary of the defense contractor Science Applications International Corp. Telcordia provides software to 80 percent of U.S. telecommunications networks and is a key provider of telecommunications software globally. Annual sales exceed $1 billion. The company dedicates one-tenth of its efforts to research, with its 5,270 employees engaged mainly in consulting and software programming.

Pirelli is perhaps best known for producing high-performance tires, but 51 percent of the Italian company's $5.8 billion (unofficial) in sales in 1998 came from the company's Cables and Systems sector, which produces optical fiber, power, and telecom cables. Most of Pirelli's 36,211 employees work at plants outside Italy. Pirelli's cable unit, with 20,000 employees at 65 plants in 21 countries, produced notable breakthroughs in 1998, particularly in the area of cable fiber-count. In response to the 288-fiber-count cable (288 fibers in a 1-inch cable), the company soon launched 432-count cable. That was followed by 720-fiber RILT (Ribbon In Loose Tube) cable and RILT 864 cable; this brought more and faster data transfer per fiber-optic cable.

Despite its reputation for consumer glass products, Corning Incorporated is a leading world producer of fiber-optic cable, having sold all but 8 percent of its glassware and cookware operations. In 1998 alone, the company's 15,400 employees (down from 20,500 in 1997) at 45 plants worldwide produced nearly $3.48 billion in revenue; more than half of that came from the company's Communications unit, which produces cable and photonic components, lenses, and liquid crystal display glass. Through its Specialty Materials unit, the company manufactures laboratory equipment and emission control substrates. In 1999, Corning invested more than $1 billion in plant construction and expansion. The acquisition of Rochester Photonics Corp. (a company with 1998 revenue at $3 million) brought access to new fiber-optic technology, namely "microlenses," which increase network performance through improved in-fiber laser focus, and transmitters and receivers that are more temperature resistant.

With 841 employees, CIENA is a telecom equipment maker that provides wavelength division multiplexing (DWDM) systems for giants like MCI WorldCom, Sprint, and Teleway Japan; its DWDM systems give optical fiber the ability to carry up to 40 times more data than usual. While the company's $508 million in sales in 1998 were dwarfed by those bigger corporations, sales rose by 35.9 percent over 1997.

Pioneer DR. DAVID PAYNE

Though photonics is largely the business of research teams at universities and giant corporations, there are individuals who stand out for their contribution to the field. In 1997, *Forbes* called Dr. David Payne "perhaps the leading scientist behind two key inventions in photonics over the past decade and a half."

A physicist at Britain's University of Southampton, Payne was a key force behind two important inventions: the optical fiber amplifier and error correction. The former facilitates the magnification of a light pulse's reach, amplifying light without having to convert it to electrical pulses and back again and tripling data transmission speeds yearly. The latter is an enhancement to the amplifier that corrects distortions that may occur when light pulses are stretched to their limit in distance and speed. Both of these technologies can be implemented in fiber already buried underground.

AMERICA AND THE WORLD

The United States is one of the world's largest consumers of photonics technology and has been researching photonics for nearly half a century. The Rome Laboratory in Rome, New York, became one of the Air Force's four "Superlabs" in 1990 and enjoyed a budget of nearly $293 million. Its photonics center is one of the world's leading facilities, yet it has drawn fire for alleged corporate biases in sharing photonics capabilities with private industry. Despite a 1989 joint agreement with the State of New York to engender cooperative photonics research between the public and private sectors, critics accused the laboratory of favoring large corporations over small- and medium-sized regional business; most of the lab's contracts went to large corporations like General Electric, General Dynamics, Northrup, ITT, Westinghouse, AT&T, and Bell Laboratories. In Texas, the STARTech technology business development center announced the creation of the Photonics Development Center, meant to be a key global center for the optical communications market. The $3 billion in funding came from the University of Texas at Dallas, industry giants like MCI WorldCom, Nortel Networks, Alcatel, ADC Telecommunications, and Fujitsu Network Communications, and a group of venture capital firms.

RESEARCH AND TECHNOLOGY

Despite nearly a half-century of related research, the photonics industry was basically in its infancy at the end of the twentieth century. While many photonic products were already on the market, much research remained to make photonics a more viable commercial option in the future. Researchers were investigating in many different areas, with many different techniques. Photonic crystals, photonic switches, photonic processors, and quantum information technology were just a few of the technologies brewing in laboratories worldwide.

PHOTONIC CRYSTALS

Photons' appeal is also their handicap. Despite the greater freedom of movement that photons enjoy, they are not as easy to channel as electrons. Microelectronics researchers have been able to control electrons with the help of semiconductors: by using an electric field, scientists can control the movement of electrons across a semiconductor's "band gap." This technology has provided the base for minute solid state transistors and for the advancement of electronics in general. Photonics research, on the other hand, has lacked a similar light "semiconductor" and spent most of the 1990s looking for a way to isolate and manipulate certain wavelengths of light.

One of the major barriers to developing photonics crystals was size; an effective crystal would have to be several times smaller than the ones used in inte-

grated circuits. Researchers at Bell Communications Research used a drilling technique to design a crystal that filtered out certain wavelengths of microwave radiation. Others built photonic crystals from colloids (fine solid particles suspended in liquid). In 1997, electrical engineers and physicists at the Massachusetts Institute of Technology (MIT) used X-ray lithography to build the first photonic crystal to function at an optical wavelength. By drilling strategically spaced, microscopic holes in a silicon strip, they were able to trap light of the infrared wavelength—just what the telecommunications industry uses in fiber optics. With this new technology, light can be bent and controlled much in the way electrons are in integrated circuits.

PHOTONIC SWITCHING

With rapid-fire growth in the telecommunications sector and a boom in fiber-optic communication networks, the 1990s saw a rapidly growing need for photonic switching devices. Photonic switching systems make for cheaper and more reliable transfer of information. Switching can occur when light flows through the tunnel-like active optical waveguide, and an electrical current or beam of light alters the index of refraction. Another technique bringing ultra-fast photonic switches consists of shaping a pulse of light that can be read by a mask; if the pulse has not been grated to the correct shape, it will not pass through. With millions of dollars for research and development, researchers were studying the use of optical switches in nonlinear optical switches, semiconductors, polymeric film, and micromachined movable mirrors. Despite advances, there were still many barriers to photonic switch development. Photons are less easily manipulated than are electrons, and photonic switches have generally been longer than electronic switches. Likewise, the speed and voltage requirements of different switching components are not uniform throughout the device. When it comes to using fiber over long distance, light must be converted to electricity and back again, thus slowing down the process.

Nonetheless, Lucent predicted that all-optical devices allowing cross-connected signals would be on the market before 2000. The ElectroniCast Corp.'s *Photonic Switch and Matrix Technology and Market Global Forecast* foresaw major growth in world sales of photonic switches and switch matrices used in fiber-optic networks. Sales are predicted to reach $3.2 billion in 2006.

In the late 1990s, North America accounted for most of the world's fiber-optic photonic switch consumption. With the reconfiguration of fiber networks, the sale of photonic switches was expected to drastically bite into the market dominance by conventional switches. Likewise, photonic switch and switch matrix production was expected to soar to a value of $2.29 billion in 2006. Telecommunications equipment was predicted to command at least a 40 percent share of optical switch sales by 2001. With demand for high-speed opto-electronic integrated circuits expected to grow, greater sales of photonic switches won't be far behind. Given the ubiquity of the technology, individual consumers would receive a double advantage: drastically reduced communications charges and radically improve data throughput speeds.

QUANTUM INFORMATION TECHNOLOGY

In 1998, applied physicists at Stanford University reached a long-sought goal: they developed a "single-photon turnstile device," the first device capable of creating a beam of light composed of a steady stream of photons. By overcoming the noise caused by microscopic variations in ordinary light, the device paved the way for scientists to advance in nascent, cutting-edge fields like quantum information technology. This new research area brings new computation and encryption techniques with major implications for the future of mainstream computers and telecommunications devices. Quantum computers, for example, could solve problems millions of times quicker than the most powerful supercomputer of today. A research team from IBM Corporation, the Massachusetts Institute of Technology, the University of California-Berkeley, and the University of Oxford has reportedly built the world's first computer modeled on the principles of quantum mechanics.

Photonics advocates dream of the day when information processing is entirely optical, whereby light is used to define the transmission of a signal beam. The final result, once again, is greater speed; with all-optical processors, computers, telecommunications equipment, and other devices will be able to operate without having to translate between electrons and photons. The main barrier to all-optical signal processing continues to be the properties of the materials it requires. Increasingly, laboratories are recognizing the strengths and weaknesses of both photonics and electronics, and are working toward a hybrid technology called opto-electronics, whereby electricity is used to manipulate the transmission of light through a material. Some laboratories, such as Bellcore, have already made progress in the development of photonic integrated circuits (these chips are also known as "opto-electronic integrated circuits" or "optical integrated circuits"). In 1999, Nanovation Technologies, Inc.

patented its functional, fully integrated optical circuit based on photons. The company claimed that a photonic chip would be up to 1,000 times smaller than semiconductor circuits based on electrons, and could multiply chip speed and data capacity by up to 1,000.

While photonics is on the rise, it won't necessarily mean the demise of electronics: future technology will likely have both electronics and photonics technologies working in harmony, with photons picking up the slack in those areas where electronic technology is sluggish.

FURTHER READING

Amato, Ivan. "Designing Crystals That Say No to Photons." *Science,* 20 March 1992.

Banks, Howard. "The Law of the Photon." *Forbes,* 6 October 1997.

Bellcore Becomes Telcordia. *Newsbytes News Network,* 9 March 1999.

Brown, Chappell. "Technology: As Cost Drops and Capacity Rises, Researchers Up the Ante in Data Links—Optical Interconnects Getting Supercharged." *Electronic Engineering Times,* 25 May 1998, 39.

———. "Technology: Darpa Program Seeks Next-Generation Chip-Level Interconnect—Optics Tackles VLSI Data Bottleneck." *Electronic Engineering Times,* 1 June 1998, 41.

"CIENA Corporation." *Hoover's Online,* 1 April 1999. Available from http://www.hoovers.com.

"Corning Acquires Rochester Photonics Corporation; Company Is a Technology Leader in Diffractive Optics and Microlens Technology." *Business Wire,* 14 February 1999.

"Corning Incorporated." *Hoover's Online,* 1 April 1999. Available from http://www.hoovers.com.

Dalton, Larry R. "Polymeric Electro-Optic Modulators." *Chemistry and Industry,* 7 July 1997.

Fast Facts About Telcordia. Available from http://www.bellcore.com/newsroom/fastfacts/index.html.

"First Device That Produces Light—One Photon At a Time." *Business Wire,* 11 February 1999.

"First Patents Issued For "Revolutionary" Photonic Devices." *Newsbytes News Network,* 11 January 1999.

"Fujitsu Computer Products of America Introduces the World's First 1.3 GB 3.5 Magneto-Optical Drive." *Business Wire,* 22 November 1998.

Galatowitsch, Sheila. "Defense 2010; Ten Technologies That Will Change the Way We Build Systems, Fight Wars and Envision Defense." *Defense Electronics,* December 1992.

Griffiths, Andrew. "Money-Go-Round: Race Starts for a New Generation of Microchips Below the Salt." *The Daily Telegraph,* 10 April 1999.

"The Light Stuff: Hamamatsu Photonics." *The Economist,* 21 November 1992.

"Lucent Commercializes 40-Gb/s Systems." April 1999. Available from http://www.laurin.com/Content/Apr99/lateLucent.html.

"Lucent Technologies Inc." *Hoover's Online,* 1 April 1999. Available from http://www.hoovers.com.

MacLean, Lisa M. "Photonics: A Complicated Future Ahead?" *Telecommunications,* March 1994.

"Memorex Releases New CD Collection." *M2 PressWire,* 11 May 1999.

Muscoplat, Rick. "What Fiber Glut?" *America's Network,* 15 September 1998.

Pennisi, Elizabeth. "Photons Add Up to Better Microscopy." *Science,* 24 January 1997.

Peterson, Ivars. "Drilling Holes to Keep Photons in the Dark." *Science News,* 2 November 1991.

———. "Drilling into the Infrared." *Science News,* 28 March 1992.

Photonics Development Center FAQ. Available from http://www.photonics-center.com/faq.htm.

Photonics Spectra Home Page. Available from http://www.photonicsspectra.com.

Pirelli and AT&T Labs Announce Multi-Wavelength 40gbps Breakthrough On Single Mode Fiber. Available from http://www.pirelli.com/cgi-bin/news/shownews .pl?id=201.

"Pirelli S.p.A." *Hoover's Online,* 1 April 1999. Available from http://www.hoovers.com.

Pirelli S.p.A. Press Release. Available from http://www.pirelli.com/cgi-bin/news/shownews.pl?id=189.

Regalado, Antonio. "Intellectual Capital." *Technology Review,* 1 January 1999.

Schiff, Debra. "Switch Hitting in Photonics." *Electronic Design,* 15 December 1997.

"STARTech Creates Photonics Development Center; Participating VCs Manage $3 Billion in Funds; Leaders Position Telecom Corridor to be Global Center of Network Evolution." *Business Wire,* 25 October 1998.

"Success Reported In Revolutionary Photon Chip Tests." *Newsbytes News Network,* 17 December 1998.

Taubes, Gary. "Photonic Crystal Made to Work at an Optical Wavelength." *Science,* 5 December 1997.

"Telcordia Technologies." *Hoover's Online,* 1 May 1999. Available from http://www.hoovers.com.

Thyfault, Mary E. "Networking: Photonics Lets Users Get Most From Fiber—Technology Speeds Deployment, Cuts Carriers' Costs." *InformationWeek,* 30 November 1998.

Van den Berg, Rob. "MICROSCOPY: Molecular Imaging Beats Limits of Light." *Science,* 31 July 1998.

Watson, Andrew. "PHOTONICS: Optical Circuits Turn a Corner." *Science,* 9 October 1998.

Welter, Therese R. "Electronics Takes a Bride." *Industry Week,* 7 May 1990.

Wirbel, Loring. "Technology: Photonic Circuits Easing Into Silicon Optical Benches." *Electronic Engineering Times,* 8 March 1999.

Wu, Corinne. "Light Gets the Bends in a Photonic Crystal." *Science News,* 16 November 1996.

Young, Ruth C., and Joe E. Francisc. "Secrecy as a Factor in the Spread of New Technology: Photonics in the Rome Labs." *Focus,* Spring 1994.

—Brett Allan King

PHOTOVOLTAIC SYSTEMS

Photovoltaic (PV) systems, which convert sunlight to energy, have existed for approximately 160 years. The term "photo" stems from the Greek *phos,* which means "light." "Volt" is named for Alessandro Volta (1745-1827), a pioneer in the study of electricity. "Photovoltaics," then, could literally mean light-electricity. A French physicist first noted the photovoltaic (PV) effect in 1839, when he built a device that could measure the intensity of light by observing the strength of an electric current between two metal plates. During the following 110 years, scientists experimented with different materials in an attempt to find a practical use for PV systems. It was not until the latter 20th century that solar energy became practical and economical enough to warrant its broad-scale marketing as one of the primary energy sources of the future. In the 1990s alone, the price of solar energy dropped 50 percent as technology continued to advance.

Solar energy has enormous potential. The sheer abundance of solar energy gives an indication that it could be the foundation for a worldwide energy system. The industry has its share of concerns, however. Although efforts are being made to reduce costs, solar energy systems are still rather expensive. Nonetheless, by building upgraded, innovative photovoltaic systems and equipment, manufacturers are providing jobs and reducing the rate of consumption of fossil fuels. Extensive use of solar energy technology will have a beneficial impact on air pollution and global climate change. PV technology can also help generate ethanol and methanol, which can become additional fuel sources themselves.

Equally important, there are few power generation technologies as environmentally friendly as PV systems. During operation, PV generates no noise, hazardous waste, or pollution. These systems are used in a wide variety of applications, including wireless and cellular communications, recreational vehicles and boats, off-grid homes, and crop irrigation systems. In developing countries, PV systems are used for water purification, water pumping, and vaccine refrigeration.

In the 1990s PV applications went from being "niche" suppliers of electricity to bringing technology to the threshold of big business. In 1998 alone the worldwide PV solar cell market reached $2 billion, and was growing at the rate of 24 percent per year.

The statistics regarding sunlight illustrate why the photovoltaic industry is growing so rapidly. The amount of sunlight that strikes Earth each year, combined with the winds that flow from it, is nearly equivalent to 1,000 trillion barrels of oil. Scientists estimate that harnessing just one-quarter of the solar energy that falls on the world's paved areas could meet all current global energy needs comfortably. They also predict that by the year 2025, solar energy could provide 60 percent of the electricity and 40 percent of the fuel needed.

Solar power has long been recognized as a potentially inexhaustible, inexpensive source of energy. Within solar power, there are active and passive systems that include solar thermal and solar heating, cool-

THE FORCE BEHIND THE PV PHENOMENON

Photovoltaic (PV) systems cannot operate without the sun—the basis of the solar system and the source of heat, light, and energy for the Earth. About 93 million miles from the Earth, the sun is 864,00 miles in diameter and has a mass about 330,000 times that of the Earth. Scientists predict that the sun will live approximately 10,000 million years (it is presently about 4.5 billion years old). It is predicted that the sun will remain stable and continue to burn hydrogen for about the same amount of time. At the end of its life, the sun will dilate and its surface temperature of 5,800 degrees Kelvin will be cut in half. The sun will then become about 50 times larger and about 300 times brighter, becoming what scientists call a "red giant."

Nuclear fusion at the core of the sun is responsible for changing hydrogen into helium. The helium travels to the surface of the sun and appears in the form of light. About one-third of the light is diffused by clouds or particles in the air when it enters the Earth's atmosphere. Once this energy hits an object on the Earth, it is absorbed and then redistributed through the object via conduction, convection, or radiation—all processes of transferring heat molecularly. Modern solar energy is a means of capturing this energy and redistributing it to heat and cool buildings, to operate engines and pumps, to heat water and swimming pools, and to power appliances.

ing, and lighting; and photovoltaic, or solar electric, systems. Although both systems gather and contain energy, they distribute it in different ways. PV cells consist primarily of silicon, the second most abundant element in the earth. When silicon is combined with other materials, it exhibits electrical properties in the presence of sunlight, generating direct current (DC) electricity. Electrons are charged by the light and move through the silicon. This is known as the photovoltaic effect.

The first experimenter to successfully convert sunlight into electricity was French physicist Edmond Becquerel (1820-1891). Scientists later discovered that the metal selenium was particularly sensitive to sunlight, and during the 1880s, Charles Fritts constructed the first selenium solar cell. His device, however, was inefficient, converting less than 1 percent of the received light into usable electricity.

The Fritts selenium solar cell was mostly forgotten until the 1950s, when the drive to produce an efficient solar cell was renewed. It was known that the

key to the photovoltaic cell lay in creating a semiconductor that would release electrons when exposed to radiation within the visible spectrum. During this time, researchers at the Bell Telephone Laboratories were developing similar semiconductors to be used in communication systems. By accident, Bell scientists Calvin Fuller and Daryl Chapin found the perfect semiconductor: a hybridized crystal called a "doped" cell made of phosphorous and boron. The first solar cells using these new crystals debuted in 1954 and yielded a conversion efficiency of nearly 6 percent. Later improvements in the design increased the efficiency to almost 15 percent.

In 1957 Bell Telephone used a silicon solar cell to power a telephone repeater station in Georgia. The process was considered a success, although it was still too inefficient to penetrate the general marketplace. The first real application of silicon solar cells came in 1958, when a solar array was used to provide electricity for the radio transmitter of Vanguard 1, the second American satellite to orbit the Earth. Solar cells have been used on almost every satellite launched since.

Today there are about 100,000 people utilizing solar power and living "off the grid," or independent of utility companies. The cost for installing photovoltaic systems in an average home falls in the range of $6,000 to $10,000. Most systems in this range are capable of producing about 800 to 900 watts of power, enough to operate most of the basic electrical needs without the cost of monthly utility bills. By contrast, the startup costs of powering new homes can be as high as $15,000.

Under current market conditions a photovoltaic system will pay for itself in about 15 years. In the 1990s electric companies were charging about 10.5 cents per kilowatt-hour used for power. By contrast, PV systems cost approximately 20 cents per kilowatt-hour to operate—an amount that is predicted to decrease to less than 10 cents per kilowatt-hour by the turn of the century.

In addition to home systems, there are several large facilities across the United States that provide solar energy to others. A new solar plant being built in the Nevada desert by Enron and Amoco Corporation will be able to produce 100 megawatts of power—enough to supply a city of 100,000 people. Hopes are to sell energy for about 5.5 cents per kilowatt-hour.

The Solar Energy Industries Association reported that the potential U.S. market for photovoltaics is approximately 9,000 megawatts, translating into a

$27 billion market. Expected to require more than 1,200 megawatts of PV power by the year 2000, the fastest growing markets for the systems include the military, telecommunications, rural electrification, and utility sectors.

Solar power generates about $350 million per year, and experts predict this amount to increase to $1 billion per year by the year 2000. The Solar Energy Industries Association reported that worldwide sales of photovoltaic products increased by 14 percent from 1995, reaching more than 90 megawatts in 1996. Companies in the United States held a 43 percent share of this $1 billion global market. The American industry may be experiencing an even larger surge in growth though. In June 1997 President Bill Clinton announced before a United Nations meeting on global warming that the United States plans to put a million more solar panels on American roofs by 2010, with the goal of reducing greenhouse gases. The program offers a 15 percent tax credit, with a $1,000 cap for solar thermal panels and a $2,000 cap for photovoltaic panels. About half of all states already have sales and property tax waivers or tax credits to promote solar energy.

The plan has already gained some momentum. A year after Clinton's speech inaugurating the Million Solar Roofs Initiative, the Department of Energy awarded $5 million in TEAM-UP grants. TEAM-UP, which stands for Building Technology Experience to Accelerate Markets in Utility Photovoltaics, is a program designed to assist in developing commercial markets for a wide range of solar photovoltaic technologies. TEAM-UP, managed since 1994 by the Utility PhotoVoltaic Group, is in partnership with the utility industry and the U.S. Department of Energy. It provides cost sharing for selected PV business ventures in the United States, and because funding is provided by the U.S. government, TEAM-UP support is restricted to U.S. firms. The Utility PhotoVoltaic Group is a nonprofit association of 90 electric utilities and electric service organizations in the United States, Canada, Europe, Australia, and the Caribbean, cooperating to accelerate the commercial use of solar electricity. The DOE's $5 million grant was awarded to 14 solar electric businesses in the Utility PhotoVoltaic Group, and also helped attain an additional $27 million in private funding, to be used to support 1,000 systems in 12 states and Puerto Rico. "TEAM-UP helps bring photovoltaics to the mainstream market," said Dan Reicher, Assistant Secretary for Energy Efficiency and Renewable Energy at the Soltech conference in Orlando, Florida, and as quoted in *Regulatory Intelligence*. "TEAM-UP stimulates the market by reducing risk, cutting costs, and drawing more cus-

Close-up image of a solar collector. (Digital Stock.)

tomers to the market earlier." The Million Solar Roofs Initiative has already received 500,000 commitments. According to the Solar Energy Industries Association, the proposal for the million roofs will help deliver reliable PV generated electricity to American consumers at a competitive price, lead to the construction of new plants in over 20 states, create 70,000 jobs in the PV industry, and increase the U.S. industry share from 40 percent to 60 percent.

Cities such as Santa Monica, California, began programs to reduce energy use by fossil fuels, and replace it with something more environmentally sound. Santa Monica, which has dubbed itself the "Sustainable City," formulated a policy in 1993 which will strive for a 16 percent reduction in citywide energy use by 2000. In a project funded by the California Energy Commission, the U.S. Department of Energy, and Edison Technology Solutions, the Pacific Park on the Santa Monica Pier will be home to the world's first solar-powered Ferris wheel by August of 1998. It will cost about $365,000 to convert the Ferris wheel to operate on a 50-kilowatt photovoltaic system, and is expected to save the park $7,000 a year in energy costs. "High-visibility sites are being selected in order to enhance public awareness and education of the benefits of renewable solar energy," says Vikram Budhraja, president of Edison Technology Solutions, as quoted in the *Los Angeles Times*. Another highly visible site touting the benefits of PV was the White House Christmas tree. Christmas 1997 saw the first solar powered tree lit at the White House, an event symbolic of President Clinton's commitment to a cleaner environment and to expanding the use of solar energy.

CURRENT CONDITIONS

Wind energy had been the world's fastest growing electricity source until 1997, when it was surpassed for the first time by the growth rate of PV installations. Global PV capacity was approximately 750 MW by the end of 1998. Moreover, technological advances reduced the cost of PV-generated electricity to that which was comparable with peak-load electricity from traditional U.S. utilities. At the same time, experts calculated that PV fields covering 250,000 km (less than 10 percent of Nevada, for comparison) would be sufficient to cover the electricity demand for the entire United States.

U.S. manufacturing of PV modules covered approximately 20 percent of the world market in 1997, equaling shipments of $175 million, up substantially from 1996's $131 million. Shipments of solar thermal collectors increased to 8.1 million square feet, up from 7.6 million square feet in 1996. Exports constituted about 5 percent of total shipments, mostly to Canada, Taiwan, Sweden, Germany, and Korea.

In October 1998, the National Design Museum in New York held an exhibit displaying more than 20 solar-powered consumer products, including sundials, coolers, fountains, call boxes, light sources, cooking devices, lanterns, cars, medical equipment, laptop computers, and lawn mowers. Use of these and other solar products is far less widespread in the United States than in Europe and Asia.

INDUSTRY LEADERS

PV research and manufacturing continues to attract big investors. In August 1998, the multinational British Petroleum Company (BP) announced its intentions to merge with Amoco. At the time of the announcement, BP already owned about 10 percent of global PV production capacity. Amoco, in turn, is co-owner of Enron Corp., which has major stakes in Solarex Corporation. BP publicly announced its intentions to help reduce global warming and carbon dioxide pollution by raising investments in solar energy from $100 million per year to $1 billion within a decade.

The world's largest manufacturer of solar modules is Siemens Solar, the photovoltaic division of the Siemens Company, the German global electronics giant. The company has produced about one-fifth of the total installed base of PV power worldwide. As of mid-1997, Siemens had produced a little more than 100 megawatts of PV modules.

Solarex, a business unit of Amoco-Enron Solar, is the largest U.S.-owned manufacturer of photovoltaic products. Founded in 1973, the company, based in Frederick, Maryland, has participated in some groundbreaking projects, such as supplying about 40,000 square feet of the PV modules that made up the roof array located at the 1996 Olympics swimming facility in Atlanta, Georgia. The modules provided almost 350 kilowatts of electric power, which saved 25 to 30 percent of the building's total electric bill, or about $33,000 per year. The company also has a 4-megawatt project coming on line in Hawaii in 1998 and a project for upwards of 50 megawatts to be installed in India over the next several years. Employing over 600 people, Solarex markets its products in more than 55 countries worldwide. The National Renewable Energy Lab in Golden, Colorado, which is part of the U.S. Department of Energy, contracted with Solarex in August, 1997, to conduct further research on thin film photovoltaics. Amoco's proposed merger with the British Petroleum Company will greatly enhance the research and production capability of Solarex, making it the largest PV company in the world, with annual sales of approximately $150 million—a 20 percent share of the global market.

Canon, Inc., the Japanese camera and office equipment multinational, announced its teaming with Energy Conversion Devices, Inc. of Troy, Michigan, to form a joint venture called United Solar Systems Corporation (USSC), specializing in thin-film technology. In 1998 USSC had a production capability of 5MW, but plans to expand to 25MW rapidly.

Smaller companies like ARDI (Advanced Research and Development Incorporated) in Athol, Massachusetts, are also making their mark in the industry. The company has developed the see-through solar window and received development contracts from the U.S. Department of Energy and the Air Force for the window batteries. The company holds 120 patents, mostly in light, optics, and electric power. The solar windows, which can produce enough electricity to power an entire house, are projected to be sold in stores within the next 10 years.

Boston-based Spire Corporation, with 115 employees and $14 million in sales at the close of fiscal 1998, opened an office in Denver, a move that reflects the rising demand for photovoltaic modules. Spire provides products and services to photovoltaics, optoelectronics, and biomedical markets worldwide. Their equipment is used by the PV industry world wide, in 142 facilities in 38 countries, for manufacturing solar modules.

In a corollary development, a small Arizona company called Fire, Wind and Rain announced in March 1999 that it had developed a new battery charger which would deliver 25 percent more power from solar panels than competing models. Dubbed the "Power Advantage 30," the patent-pending charger seeks out the maximum power point of solar panels, then readjusts for changes in sunlight, temperature, and battery voltage. The company realized a 25-percent increase in growth in 1998.

AMERICA AND THE WORLD

In the summer of 1998 the Second World Conference and Exhibition on Photovoltaic Solar Energy Conversion was held in Vienna, Austria, attracting 2000 global delegates who presented over 1100 papers. There were also more than 450 exhibitors at the event. Many of the same attendees returned in October to visit "Nieuwland," a solar-powered project community in the Netherlands near Amsterdam. All sloped roofs in the community face south at an angle of 20 degrees, and the direct current collected from the solar modules is converted to alternating current suitable for the powering of household appliances and the power grid. Ultimately, the community will have 5000 houses, an apartment building, a sports complex, schools, and a daycare center, all powered by solar energy.

Japan is the leading country for *installations* of PV panels, but the cost is about four times as high in U.S. dollars than traditional sourcing from utility companies. However, Japan has a well-planned subsidy program for residential solar roofs, about half the cost. In early 1999 Japan co-sponsored a 2-day seminar on "Photovoltaic Technology in India and Japan," held in New Delhi, which covered 26 presentations and served as a nucleus for the exchange of information and technology. Japan and India remain second and third largest producers of PV cells, behind the United States. Their production output during 1997-1998 was 8.2MW and 11MW respectively.

A joint collaboration between USSC and KVANT, Russia's leading PV technology enterprise,

resulted in a development and testing program for Russian space missions. USSC's solar cells were assembled into modules by KVANT, then incorporated into all Soviet/Russian space vehicles during a five-hour space session in November 1998. Another interested participant in this project was Sovlux, a Russian-American joint venture owned by KVANT, Michigan's ECD, and the Russian Ministry of Atomic Energy. USSC is the world leader in amorphous silicon alloy PV production, holding all records for high efficiency cells and modules.

The European Union, like the United States, has also implemented a subsidy program for solar homes, amounting to about $50 million annually as of 1998. Australia continues to be on the forefront of alternative and renewable energy applications as well. This is partly due to the geographic remoteness of areas in Australia where conventional electricity is not practicable. The 1999-2000 Olympic games in Sydney will showcase the country's technology, with many of the Games' village homes being outfitted with PV cells. A joint venture between the University of South Wales and Pacific Power, known as Pacific Solar, has been developing technology to set up the first manufacturing facility for PV products, with products on the market by 2002.

India, the United States, and Germany are the biggest markets for PV systems. The Indonesian, Pacific region, and Central and South American markets are also growing. The Pacific region purchased 25 percent of all PV modules sold in the mid-1990s, and European countries bought 25 percent. North American countries, primarily Canada and the United States, accounted for 18 percent of sales. The remaining 36 percent were scattered throughout the world. More developing countries' predilections for PV systems have caused the solar power market to grow an average of 15 percent per year between 1973 and the present.

Much of the research being done on PV systems is concentrated in the United States, although some American companies are involved in joint ventures with foreign manufacturers. For example, Energy Conversion Devices of Troy, Michigan, produces a metal roofing solar battery system that can replace a roof on an ordinary house. United Solar, a subsidiary of Energy Conversion Devices, makes the batteries in conjunction with Canon of Japan.

German-owned Siemens has teamed up with the Department of Energy's National Renewable Energy Lab in Golden, Colorado to research the film. In April 1998 Siemens Solar Industries and the Northwest Energy Efficiency Alliance, a consortium of Northwest electric utilities, state and local governments, public interest groups and the private sector, signed an agreement to work together in cutting energy use and production time in the manufacture of silicon crystals for photovoltaic cells and computer chips. Foreign companies have also begun acquiring many U.S. high technology solar manufacturing companies. Siemens purchased ARCO Solar, which is now known as Siemens Solar; British Petroleum bought Advanced Photovoltaic Systems, making it a subsidiary of BP Solar; and Solec International, a U.S firm, is now controlled by Sanyo and Sumitomo, two large Japanese corporations.

Ironically, 70 percent of the solar cells and solar-power systems manufactured in the United States are exported to Third World countries. Exports increased almost 40 percent in the mid-1990s. The export rate is expected to increase considerably, since about one-third of the world population lives without electricity. Although many of these countries initiated aggressive electrification programs, costs are too high to build large power plants or extend the electrical grid to thousands of the remote villages without power. Consequently, household solar power systems may be an economically and environmentally sound alternative in these areas.

India is becoming a major world producer of PV modules, and the Indian government intends to install solar-powered telephones in every one of the country's 500,000 villages. By the year 2000, Mexico plans on electrifying 60,000 villages via solar power. In Zaire, Hospital Bulape treats 50,000 patients every year and depends exclusively on solar power for everything from x-ray machinery to air conditioning systems. In Morocco, solar panels are sold in open markets next to carpets and produce.

Even in countries with immediate and easy access to electricity, solar power and the use of PV systems are growing. There is a large-scale national program in place in Japan in which the Japanese government subsidizes homeowners for nearly half of the cost of a rooftop PV array. Between 1994 and 1996, 12 megawatts were installed, and an additional 12 to 15 megawatts were installed in 1997 alone. In fact, the Japanese government has increased its national budget for photovoltaics about 15 percent per year since 1992. In Tokyo there are nearly 1.5 million buildings with solar water heating, more than in the entire United States. The Japanese Ministry of Trade and Industry's goal is to install solar cells on more than 70,000 homes by the year 2000.

In Germany, the world's largest and most technically advanced rooftop photovoltaic plant was in-

stalled by Siemens Solar on the hall rooftops of the New Munich Trade Fair Center. With a peak output of one megawatt, it will feed around one million kilowatt hours of solar power into the grid of the Trade Fair Center. In 1997 Germany's Ministry of Research and Technology announced it would provide financial support for two large solar manufacturing plants, and in Berlin, Germany, the city's construction industry made a commitment to install solar collectors in 75 percent of all new buildings.

RESEARCH AND TECHNOLOGY

The United States, in the past 20 years, has spent approximately $1.4 billion in research and development of solar power and photovoltaic systems. In 1996 alone, the U.S. research and development budget totaled $62.5 million, compared to Japan's $130 million and Germany's $55 million. In April 1999 the DOE announced an additional $5 million in awards to 18 universities around the country, specifically earmarked for PV research. Designated areas of research focused on reducing cost of PV systems, increasing electricity output, and developing longer lives for PV cells.

In February 1999 the DOE's National Renewable Energy Laboratory (NREL) set a world record for thin-film solar cell efficiency, now increased to 18.8 percent for the copper indium gallium diselenide (CIS) cell. Because CIS thin-film technology has impressive outdoor reliability and stable conversion efficiencies, the new record is important to terrestrial and space applications.

Modern PV systems are being equipped with control inverters that can change normal solar energy into AC current for use in households. Significantly, researchers are producing solar batteries that are in the 34 percent efficiency mark. That compares to earlier cells that were about 4 percent efficient. State-of-the-art, direct motorized tracking devices that aim the PV cells directly at the sun at all times during the day are helping to improve systems by collecting more heat. Additionally, solar power and the PV industry are making inroads on traditional power generating industries. Oil-fired power plants, for example, operate at only 35 percent efficiency.

One of the goals of PV system researchers is to improve the storage system currently in use. Another is to reduce the number of components in a system. The primary pieces of equipment in any solar system are the photovoltaic panels, which absorb and contain sunlight so that it begins conversion into useful power.

Although they are made primarily of silicon, other materials have begun to be used, such as gallium-arsenide, which is used in the Russian space station Mir.

The number of panels needed in a given situation depends on the amount of energy required. For an average house, the number is determined by the kilowatts per hour actually used. Each panel generates about 50 watts of DC electricity for each hour of sunlight, and batteries are needed for the storage of the energy so it can be used when needed. A power center must also be part of the system to regulate the flow of electricity going into the batteries so they are not overcharged and to control the energy leaving the batteries. Inverters, which convert solar power into electricity, must also be obtained for a PV system. A generator is needed as a separate power source to serve as a backup if anything goes wrong and to replenish the system after a cloudy day.

Storage has long posed problems for solar energy researchers. Batteries are currently the top cost-effective method of storing power. They receive power from the inverters and store it until it is drawn upon. The number of batteries needed depends on the amount of power needed. The batteries provide adequate storage and require only modest attention. However, they must be replaced about every 10 years at a cost of approximately $1,000 each. Researchers are seeking other, more inexpensive storage sources, such as thermal mass walls made of concrete, brick, adobe, or drywall; and super-insulated stress-skin panels to line walls. These panels are composed of a combination of oriented stranboard (which is similar to plywood) and chlorofluorocarbon-free styrofoam.

Prabir Dutta, professor of chemistry at Ohio State University, found a way to trap light energy and then store it chemically. Using a molecular cage, he found a way to mimic photosynthesis. The charged light enters the cage and is then trapped in a zeolite cage, which prevents the charged molecule from returning to its donor molecule.

NASA is also looking at ways to increase the amount of energy to be stored. The agency is experimenting with the use of a Solar Power Satellite (SPS), which can deliver enormous amounts of energy to the Earth. This can be accomplished by building huge photovoltaic structures (estimated to be as large as Manhattan) that are designed to deliver 5 to 10 gigawatts of electrical power. Just one of these monoliths would be sufficient to power Connecticut. The inventor of SPS, Dr. Peter Glaser, notes that they will be expensive to build but cheap to operate and environmentally safe.

According to the U.S. Department of Energy, as researchers discover more efficient storage materials, the availability of appropriate storage could enhance the contribution of renewable energy by about 18 quadrillion British Thermal Units (BTUs) per year by the year 2030 in the United States alone. Another goal of PV researchers is to find a suitable substitute for silicon as a semiconductor of sunlight. Today, single-crystal silicon provides the framework for the PV industry. In 1995 alone, the material accounted for 61 percent of all PV shipped. Polycrystalline and semi-crystalline silicon accounted for another 26 percent. Two products that show tremendous potential are amorphous silicon, which requires only 1/50 to 1/100 the silicon used in other technologies, and cadmium telluride (CdTe).

FURTHER READING

"Alliance and Siemens Solar Industries Agree to Share Cost of Demonstrating New, More-Efficient Silicon Crystal Production Process." *Business Wire,* 7 April 1998.

American Solar Energy Society. "Factbase on Solar Energy," 1997. Available from http://www.sni.net/solar/new .htm.

Barron, Kelly. "I'm Greener Than You." *Forbes FYI,* 9 March 1998.

Brooks, Nancy Rivera. "California News and Insight on Business in the Golden State; Solar Revolution; Sun Will Power Santa Monica Ferris Wheel." *Los Angeles Times,* 18 June 1998.

The Canadian Renewable Energy Guide. Ottawa, ON: Solar Energy Society of Canada, 1996.

"Fun in the Sun: Solar-powered Products Light the Next Millennium." *The Earth Times,* 9 August 1998. Available from http://www.elibrary.com.

Graebner, Lynn. "Innovative Solar Plant Fires Up the Mojave." *Business Journal Serving Greater Sacramento,* 10 June 1996.

Hasek, Glenn. "Solar Shines Brighter." *Industry Week,* 20 April 1998.

"Indian Government." *M2 Presswire,* 1 February 1999.

"Industry Group 99, Energy Department Awards Contracts to Universities for Photovoltaic Research," 2 April 1999. Available from http://www.elibrary.com.

"Introduction to PV Technical," 1997. Available from http://mnrc.ucc.ie/rems/pv/pvtech01.htm.

Kraul, Chris. "A Fresh Jolt; Falling Prices for Photovoltaic Cells Give New Life to Solar Industry." *Los Angeles Times,* 28 May 1997.

Miller, Molly. "The Future is Bright." *Mother Earth News,* 12 October 1997.

Quinn, Randy. "Sunlight Brightens Our Energy Future." *World & I,* 1 March 1997.

Robicheaux, Gina. "Silent Night, Solar Night." *Capitol Report,* 9 December 1997.

Robinson, Gail. "Process Ups Solar-Cell Efficiency." *Electronic Engineering Times,* 23 September 1996.

Santangelo, Mike. "Rethinking Solar Power in the 90s." *Newsday,* 28 January 1997. Available from http://www .ttcorp.com/upvg/index.htm.

Solar Power: Global Market Growing 24% a Year. *National Journal's Daily Energy Briefing,* 8 April 1999. Available from http://www.elibrary.com.

"Solar Thermal and Photovoltaic Collector Manufacturing Activities," 1 June 1999. Available from http://www.eia .doe.gov.

"Spire Corp. Establishes Denver Office; To Be Headed by Expert on Renewable Energy Policy." *Business Wire,* 11 September 1997.

"Spire Helps Launch Solar Fabrik's German Factory for Production of Photovoltaic Modules." *Business Wire,* 11 October 1997.

Sweet, William, ed."Power & Energy." *IEEE Spectrum,* January 1999.

"To Go Green, Get Ready to Spend Green." *The Christian Science Monitor.* 31 March 1999. Available from http:// www.elibrary.com.

"United Solar Photovoltaic Modules Successfully Installed on MIR Space Station." *PR Newswire,* 3 December 1998.

U.S. Department of Energy. "World-Record Solar Cell a Step Closer to Cheap Solar Energy," 25 February 1999. Available from http://www.nrel.gov.

U.S. Department of Energy National Center for Photovoltaics, 1997. Available from http://www.eren.gov/pv/ aboutpv.html.

—Arthur G. Sharp,
updated by Roxanne Nelson
and Lauri R. Harding

PHYSICAL FITNESS PRODUCTS

Helping people get fit is big business. During the 1990s, physical fitness products of every type—from exercise videos to treadmills—began appearing with increasing frequency, not just in commercial gyms, but in people's homes. The typical American's penchant for comfort, convenience, and privacy focused new attention on this segment of the broader sporting goods industry. According to the Sporting Goods Manufacturers Association (SGMA), sales of sporting goods, including equipment, apparel, and athletic footwear, reached $45.6 billion in 1998 for growth of only 1 percent, the smallest rate of growth in the industry in the preceding 10 years. However, exercise equipment sales accounted for $17.5 billion in 1998—up 1.7 percent from 1997. The Association states that 50 million households own exercise equipment, and fitness equipment sales have grown every year since 1987.

The SGMA also found that consumer interest in achieving and maintaining fitness not only helped increase equipment sales to clubs, but also enabled manufacturers to promote equipment sales to corporate offices, colleges, training facilities, resorts, and apartment buildings, creating miniature gyms and making fitness more convenient. The American Council on Exercise (ACE), a nonprofit health and fitness organization, also concluded that working out at work became popular as people tried to fit exercise into busy schedules. ACE found that state-of-the-art facilities were showing up in major corporations in the United States, including Gap, Oracle, Clif Bar, and 3Com.

Buoyed by the Surgeon General's pronouncement that "physical activity is the key to good health for all Americans," individuals of all ages, but particularly the elderly, were investing both time and dollars in their own physical fitness. The amount of media attention devoted to and general information available on health issues such as weight, body image, diet, sports, and exercise compound the probability that wholesalers' and retailers' promotional messages will sink into the collective consciousness of modern consumers.

Manufacturers of exercise products have tried to meet the needs and desires of potential customers by developing products that are not only efficient and simple to use, but also enjoyable and reasonably affordable. While reaching peak fitness levels and enhancing personal appearance are still enormous motivators for certain age groups to engage in fitness activity, a growing group of adult men and women are exercising to improve overall health and energy. Industry analysts predicted that ever greater numbers are taking up some form of regular exercise.

From the period of 1987 through 1997, statistics compiled by the SGMA indicate that the top exercise participation trends included, among others, such areas as: step aerobics; use of free weights and resistance machines; indoor and outdoor fitness walking; use of treadmills, stair-climbers, and Nordic ski machines; and in-line skating. The two strongest sports categories in the United States in 1997 were those of "extreme sports" and fitness equipment. The SGMA also noted that wholesale exercise equipment sales grew by 9.8 percent in 1997, with treadmills accounting for $1.6 billion. (Also see the essay in this book entitled Extreme Sports.)

ORGANIZATION AND STRUCTURE

Fitness items are typically sold by the actual manufacturers, either directly to retailers, where price mark-up occurs before sale, or via distributors, who in turn sell to retailers. Often, high-end manufacturers give a retailer exclusive rights to sell their product in a certain region. Fitness products reach customers through a variety of outlets, the most notable being large sporting goods stores. New and innovative marketing methods include infomercials and by mail-order, which have become excellent ways to sell exercise videos and some exercise machines. The Internet also became a fresh marketing avenue for the promotion and sale of such products.

During the later 1990s, producers of fitness products witnessed significant changes within the industry. In 1996, mergers, acquisitions, and initial public offerings (IPOs) occurred with relative frequency. The largest notable acquisition in the area of sporting goods was that of Spalding Sports Worldwide, by Kohlberg, Kravis, Roberts & Company. Estimated at over $1 billion, the deal was touted as the largest ever seen by the industry. Notable IPOs included those of companies Ridgeview Inc. and The North Face Inc. Mergers continued in 1998, with Icon acquiring trademark rights to NordicTrack; Cybex acquiring Tectrix; Precor obtaining Pacific Fitness; and Schwinn buying Hebb Industries as well as GT Bikes. Analysts expected such continued activity industry-wide for the next few years. Deeply concerned with maintaining and increasing market share, the SGMA reported that manufacturers and smaller retailers were aware of the need to sell to, and compete with, huge retailers such as Sports Authority, MC Sports, Big 5, and Gart Sports, who recently merged with SportMart. Retailing behemoth Sears was the leading seller of exercise equipment in the late 1990s.

Trends **PRODUCT LIABILITY REFORM**

In the late 1990s the Product Liability Reform Bill, designed to address the degree of product liability, generated from millions of dollars worth of frivolous lawsuits, was of great interest to the physical fitness industry. The bill eliminates joint liability between retailers and manufacturers of physical fitness equipment, thus making retailers responsible for their own negligence, and also reduces the dollar amount of awards given to claimants when misuse of drugs was proven to be a factor in the injury.

BACKGROUND AND DEVELOPMENT

In the late 1980s, the home-exercise segment of the wholesale fitness market stood at $750 million and was growing fast. Factors contributing to the emergence of the home-exercise phenomenon included convenience, proximity, the scarcity of available free time, as well as the added comfort and security of privacy—an issue of particular concern to those lacking confidence in either physical appearance or athletic ability. In 1988, *Forbes* magazine noted the comment of one expert who explained the reasoning behind people's preference for home-versus-health-club: "When you couple a new behavior with a new environment, like a health spa, it represents a double threat to people, so they prefer to stay home." By the early 1990s, this concept became a mantra in the ads of at least one exercise equipment manufacturer. The Trotter Company beckoned the market with its theme, "For those who consider exercise a matter of privacy."

In the late 1980s, membership in health clubs began to level off after a period of sustained growth, and the major creators of exercise equipment realized the need to reorganize. Companies such as Nautilus Sports/Medical Industries and Universal Gym Equipment found themselves joined by such competitors as Precor, Inc. in the race to grab sales. Precor succeeded in creating its own niche by catering to consumers willing to pay for high quality equipment that would stand up to years of use. Whereas in the early 1980s a treadmill, for example, could be purchased for as little as $200; by the decade's end, a sturdier and better designed product could be bought for about $1000, a price not considered unreasonable.

Interestingly, Nautilus, designated the "grandfather" of the exercise equipment companies by industry insiders, chose not to push its products aggressively into the home exercise market at that time. The firm, founded in 1970 by Arthur Jones, continued to focus on and provide its products primarily to health clubs.

Adding to the convenience of home exercise equipment was the introduction of the exercise videotape. A $5.8-billion market by 1993, this segment of the industry faced significant challenges in initial distribution of its products in the early 1980s. Kathy Smith, a veteran in the field of exercise tapes, discussed her first commercially available video titled "Ultimate Workout" in *Billboard* magazine: "We didn't have distribution anywhere. I couldn't find it in the stores. It was very tough getting shelf space, getting distribution, and getting the word out without a big advertising machine behind you."

Fitness branches out to multimedia with books and interactive videos. (Courtesy of GMP Fitness.)

Contibuting to the difficulty of distribution was the lack of seriousness with which the industry viewed the coming aerobics boom. Smith noted in the article her belief that aerobics would be much more than a passing fad and that the industry would eventually realize this. A prophetic statement, since by 1992 Smith's combined 12 exercise videos sold more than 5 million copies. Names of other exercise gurus, particularly women, became common in American households by the 1990s. Models and actors, as well as professional trainers, cast their hats into the exercise-video ring by the late 1990s, sometimes with mixed results. Among the most successful entrepreneurs in this genre was Jane Fonda, who by 1989 alone made over 11 such tapes. While most exercise videos were initially geared toward aerobics and aerobic dancing, by the early 1990s, stress management, stretching, body sculpting, and toning were highlighted topics as well.

In 1999 hundreds of videotapes were available, though not necessarily on the shelves of large sporting goods stores. Discount retailers such as Target carry some of the more popular ones, but the mail-order industry has the edge on exercise video sales. One such retailer, Collage Video, offers more than 400 videos through their catalog. In business since 1987, Collage features what they consider to be the best exercise videos. Their mix of offerings from step aerobics, floor aerobics, toning, and strength training are being joined by videos featuring the latest trends in exercising, including yoga, Pilates, kickboxing, ethnic dance, sports-specific training such as golf, cycling, and running, and even mini-trampolining. Popular multi-video producer The Firm, whose lofty goals promise "visible results in 10 workouts," offers its unique brand of aerobics and strength training through catalogs, like Collage, and also through its Web site. New phenomena Tae Bo™, the kickboxing craze trademarked by Hollywood's Billy Blanks, offers videos via its Web site and through infomercials, which began airing in late 1998.

Another phenomenon affecting the industry as a whole is the increasing interest of elderly Americans in exercise, health, and general fitness. According to the Fitness Products Council, research indicates that the percentage of people 55 years of age and older who engaged in some form of frequent exercise skyrocketed by 73 percent between 1987 and 1995. The SGMA found that in 1998 fitness club enrollments grew by 125 percent for people aged 55 and up. Medical research reports and studies discussed in the media gave credence to the idea that debilitation is not an inevitable consequence of old age. The *Harvard Health Letter* noted that, "Losing muscle and bone is

The G BALL helps maintain physical health and promote overall well-being. (Courtesy of GMP Fitness.)

no more inevitable than developing a spare tire." Regarding strength training, the newsletter also declared that the practice could be "the closest thing there is to the fountain of youth." By the late 1990s, the perception of anyone being "too old to exercise" had almost evaporated.

CURRENT CONDITIONS

Fitness product sales are booming. Wholesale revenues for fitness products were $2.7 billion for 1997, up from $2.1 billion for 1996. According to the Fitness Products Council, "sales of exercise equipment in 1996 rose at twice the rate of all sporting goods, footwear, and apparel combined." The two most significant markets to watch include older Americans, exercising mainly to sustain health and vitality, and younger people, interested in exercise primarily as a means to improve physical attractiveness and body image.

Although total industry sales at the end of the 1990s were beginning to show slightly less growth, the exercise equipment market continued to rise as more people exercised, at home, at the gym, or at an alternative facility, such as in the workplace. By 2001,

the fitness equipment retail market is expected to reach $4.9 billion. That figure represents a 6.6 increase each year from 1996 to 2001, slower growth than the 11.4 percent annual increase realized from 1990-1994.

Product trends in the late 1990s included sales of such items as: abdominal exercisers (also known as "ab trainers"); low impact aerobic exercisers, or "elliptical cross-trainers;" weight resistance machines; recumbent bikes in which the user semi-reclines; treadmills; and various original videos. Specifically noted in 1997 was the air walker, a flat-folding machine touted as providing "a complete workout" while inflicting no pounding impact on the body. Costing between $149 and $199, air walkers, produced by various manufacturers, were in such demand early in the year that some retailers couldn't keep them on their shelves. Dozens of "body-part-specific" trainers and equipment were hawked via late-night television and on infomercials in 1998 and continuing in 1999. Now a staple in clubs, elliptical trainers remained popular after their introduction in 1997. While treadmills continue to reign as the best selling equipment for home use, a resurgence in sales of exercise bikes began, in part due to the popularity of new group cardio classes, such as the group cycling class Spinning. Heart rate monitors and body fat measuring devices became popular and continued to sell in 1998 and into 1999 in conjunction with larger equipment. In 1998 sales of heart rate monitors were $67.5 million, double 1993's $33.0 million, according to David Tappan, director of marketing at CardioSport, one of the largest monitor manufacturers.

The American Council on Exercise (ACE), a non-profit health and fitness organization, says that products to watch for in 1999 include elliptical trainers, whose sales were still growing; interactive cardio machines and Web-connected interactive fitness machines; and more offerings in gym classes, day spas, and alternative exercises videos such as Tai Chi and yoga. Innovation is the driving force behind creating new and better ways to get and keep Americans exercising, and the exercise equipment industry is proving that it is more than happy to keep up with the pace.

According to statistics compiled by American Sports Data, Inc. (ASD), the great proportion of Americans report that they believe in the value of exercise, but less than 20 percent actually engage in such activity with any regularity. The fitness products industry had this target group in its sights and was currently seeking innovative ways to motivate members of this inactive segment. An ASD survey found that while one quarter of the population is completely sedentary, 28 percent are active fewer than 50 days per year. On a positive note, 55 percent of the survey respondents said they were "more interested in exercise now than two or three years ago."

INDUSTRY LEADERS

Utah-based ICON Health & Fitness, Inc. is the world's largest manufacturer and marketer of fitness equipment. The company produces elliptical motion trainers, cross-country ski machines, treadmills, stationary bikes, strength trainers, and other equipment under the brand names that include Weider, Reebok, ProForm, Weslo, IMAGE, JumpKing, Healthrider, and NordicTrack. ICON's total sales were $750 million for fiscal year 1998 and the company employed 4,800 people.

ICON's channels of distribution include direct sales (via the Internet and 800-numbers), Workout Warehouse (the company's catalogue), department stores (Sears), mass merchandisers (Wal-Mart and Kmart), sporting goods stores (Sport Authority and Gart Sport Mart), specialty fitness retailers (Busy Body), and catalog showrooms (Service Merchandise).

Precor Inc., a subsidiary of Chicago-based Premark International, Inc., manufactures treadmills, elliptical fitness crosstrainers, and stairclimbers. According to a company press release, Bothell-based Precor has had a five-year steady growth pattern for both commercial and international sales. For the fiscal year ended 1997, Precor contributed over $100 million in revenue to boost Premark's total sales volume to $2.4 billion.

In December 1997, Precor filed a patent infringement lawsuit against NordicTrack and Keys Fitness Products Inc. The suit claimed that the companies had infringed on a patent for Precor's EFX Elliptical Fitness Cross Trainer, first introduced in March 1997. The lawsuit was settled against Keys Fitness on 1 April 1998, with Keys agreeing to no longer sell its E-Trainer. Other lawsuits are pending.

In late 1998 Precor announced it had acquired Pacific Fitness Corporation, manufacturer of high-end cardiovascular and flexibility equipment, with a move planned for both operations in July 1999. "The centralization of the facilities will enable Precor to ensure the standard of excellence in all areas of total fitness: cardiovascular, flexibility and strength," Precor president Bill Potts said in a company news release.

AMERICA AND THE WORLD

In 1996, Nordic Track added international distributors and contracted with dealers in the Philippines, Singapore, Indonesia, Malaysia, Brunei, and Scandinavia. Additionally, the Minnesota-based company has operations in Canada, the United Kingdom, and Germany. According to a company press release, the company's total worldwide sales reached $504 million in 1995. NordicTrack also signed a deal with Sears in October 1997, making its products available in the giant retailer's Canadian stores. Bothell, Washington-based Precor Inc. is a subsidiary of Premark International Inc., which markets products to over 100 countries.

FURTHER READING

Barrie, Michael. "Exercise as Theater." *Nation's Business,* June 1995.

Beardi, Cara. "Staying Fit G&G Fitness Sees Big Growth in Exercise Equipment." *Buffalo News,* 23 June 1998.

Braham, James. "Making Exercise More Fun (or at Least Tolerable)." *Machine Design,* 10 October 1996.

Collage Video Complete Guide to Exercise Videos. Minneapolis, MN: Collage Video, 1999. Available from http://www.collagevideo.com/.

Fitzpatrick, Eileen. "Flabby Fitness Vid Market Needs New Retail Regimen." *Billboard,* 5 August 1995.

Goldstein, Seth. "Fitness Vids Are Shaping Up As Big Force in Market." *Billboard,* 25 December 1993.

"Good Year Ahead." *Fitness Products Council,* March/April 1997.

Grieves, Robert T. "Muscle Madness." *Forbes,* 30 May 1988.

Halverson, Richard. "Keeping in Step with Fitness." *Discount Store News,* 17 February 1997.

"Health & Fitness Video: More Than Just Aerobics." *Billboard,* 16 November 1991.

"A Hopeful Future." *Fitness Products Council Letter,* May/June 1997. Available from http://www.sportlink.com/fitness/newsletters/may-jun97/index.html.

Kaydo, Chad. "Battle of the Bulge-Busters." *Sales & Marketing Management,* October 1996.

Levine, Joshua. "Fancy Coatracks." *Forbes,* 15 February 1993.

Light, Larry. "Caution: Dueling Sweat Machines." *Business Week,* 30 January 1995.

Lustigmann, Alyssa. "Fitness Quest Gets Grip on Excel Venture." *Sporting Goods Business,* June 1995.

McCartney, Jim. "NordicTrack Sees Sales at Sears as Chance to Rebound." *Saint Paul Pioneer Press,* 1 October 1997.

Minkoff, Jerry. "Exercising Options." *Discount Merchandiser,* February 1994.

Paula, Greg. "Exercise Equipment Puts on Magnetoheological Brakes." *Mechanical Engineering,* May 1997.

Riddle, John D. "1999 State of the Industry Report." North Palm Beach, FL: Sporting Goods Manufacturers Association (SGMA), 1999. Available from http://www.sportlink.com/research/1999_research/99soti/99soti_index.html.

"Sports Hit Parade Lists Top Favorites." North Palm Beach, FL: Sporting Goods Manufacturers Association, 15 April 1997. Available from http://www.sportlink.com/industry/media/m97-1.html.

Touby, Laurel. "Fitness Investigates: Heart-Rate Monitors." *Fitness,* March 1999.

"What's Driving Sporting Goods?" North Palm Beach, FL. Sporting Goods Manufacturers Association (SGMA), 26 February 1999. Available from http://www.sportlink.com/press_room/1999_releases/m99-008.html.

—Alice Janes,
updated by Katherine Wagner and Lisa DeShantz-Cook

POLYMERS

Polymers are synthetic or natural compounds formed by chemically linking simple molecular units called monomers. The term "polymer" traditionally has been understood to mean a plastics material. Today "polymer" suggests a much larger focus, encompassing the cutting edge of high-tech materials science with much of the emerging technology still in a research or developmental phase.

Synthetic plastics make up the bulk of resin production and historically have been the primary focus of technical development. Plastics are created when materials such as petroleum, coal, and natural gas are broken down into components—such as ethylene, methane, acetylene, butadiene, propylene, benzene, naphthalene, toluene, and xylene—then react with other materials and agents to form polymers.

Plastics materials are divided into two main groups: thermoplastics and thermosets. Thermoplastics soften when heated and harden when cooled, enabling them to be repeatedly reheated and remolded. In general, chemical changes do not take place in thermoplastics during processing. Thermoset resins can be heated and molded only once because they undergo chemical change during processing that renders them insoluble and infusible. Composite plastics, which are known for their high strength and light weight, are most often thermoset resins that have been reinforced with glass, boron, graphite, or polyamid fibers.

Plastics are used in the following industries: transportation (motor vehicles and parts, railroad equipment, ships and boats, aircraft, military vehicles, and recreational equipment); packaging (containers, rigid and flexible packaging); building and construction (pipe, conduit and fittings, structural material, doors, windows, skylights, other fixtures); electrical/electronic (home and industrial appliances, electronic components); furniture and furnishings (rigid and flexible types); and consumer and institutional products (health care and medical products, toys and sporting goods, disposable food serviceware, hobby and graphic arts supplies, clothing, and miscellaneous products).

The U.S. plastics industry evolved rapidly during the second half of the twentieth century and contributed significantly to the economy. In 1998 polymer production rose 3.2 percent to 91.7 billion pounds. According to *U. S. Industry and Trade Outlook '99*, shipments of plastic products totaled an estimated $47.3 billion in 1998 and were forecast to reach $49.2 billion by 1999. Plastics constituted the country's fourth largest manufacturing industry and accounted for about 20 percent of the general chemical industry's revenues. Including jobs from captive plastic product operations—for example, from plastic automotive parts being molded in automobile plants—the industry had a work force of 1.3 million employees in 1996. Furthermore, when upstream supplier industries are factored in, the industry's sales amounted to $366.4 billion, and the polymer industry accounted for 2.3 million jobs, or nearly 2 percent of the U.S. work force.

The United States is the world's major net exporter of plastics with an excess of exports over imports of $7.7 billion in 1998. Mexico and Canada absorb about one-third of U.S. exports, followed by the Netherlands, Belgium, Japan, China, and Taiwan. However, the Asian economic problems of the late 1990s impeded trade as Asian companies cut back on purchases and were less willing to purchase U.S. polymer products because of the strength of the U.S. dollar relative to their devalued currencies. Some Asian countries were also increasing their own production of polymer resins and products.

ORGANIZATION AND STRUCTURE

The plastics industry has three main components: resin suppliers, machinery builders, and processors.

RESINS

Petrochemicals, which are processed into many materials other than plastics, account for only 6 percent of total gas and oil production. A portion of petrochemical feedstocks are processed into various resins. The feedstock is reacted into monomer, then polymerized into raw plastics material. For example, vinyl chloride monomer becomes polyvinyl chloride (PVC).

Raw thermoplastic polymer takes many forms, including powders, granules, and pellets. Additives can be used to modify such performance characteristics as fire resistance or greater strength. Additives include lubricants, antioxidants, antistats, blowing or foaming agents, colorants, flame retardants, heat stabilizers, organic peroxides, plasticizers, and ultraviolet stabilizers.

Thermoplastics are divided into commodity and engineering resin types, although some resins—depending on how they are processed—may fall into either group. Engineering plastics have high heat resistance, high impact strength, and other superior physical properties; however, they also cost about twice as much per pound as the commodity plastics. Engineering resins include acetyl, nylon, acrylonitrile

butadiene styrene (ABS), and polycarbonate (PC). They are used for automotive engine parts, appliance parts, business machine and computer housings, mechanical gears, and other applications.

Commodity plastics, which includes ABS, polyethylene (PE), polypropylene (PP), polystyrene (PS), polyethylene terephthalate (PET), and PVC, are used for flooring, plastic bottles, packaging, and other low-impact applications.

In 1994 plastics materials and resins totaled $37.7 billion in shipments and created jobs for 692,000 workers. Average hourly earnings were $19.37. In 1996 sales of injection molding resins rose 6 percent; however, a slowing economy resulted in an estimated 4-percent drop in sales for 1997.

MACHINERY

Plastics are molded into desired shapes using one of more than 15 processes. Injection molding equipment, which was developed in the 1920s, is the most commonly used. Other processes include blow molding, extrusion, compression molding, thermoforming, rotational molding, casting, pultrusion, filament winding, stamping, and calendering. Equipment has become increasingly complex and increasingly automated. Computer automation has taken plastics molding from what was once considered something of an intuitive "black art" to a highly controlled, scientific process. Entire plants are now automated—from inventory and scheduling to processing and shipping. In the early 1980s computer-aided design/computer-aided manufacturing (CAD/CAM) was developed. CAD/CAM allows mold makers to create drawings on a computer screen and make alterations in the design quickly, as needed, rather than painstakingly creating and recreating pen-and-ink drawings on paper. Soft-

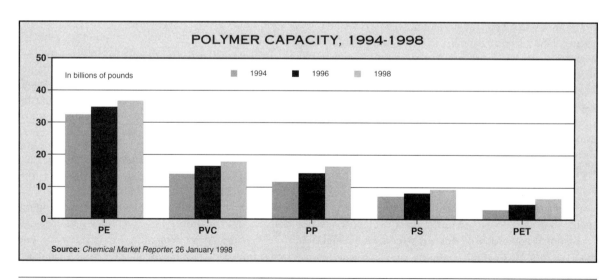

Pioneer GUILIO NATTA, 1903-1979
MOLDING AN INDUSTRY

Guilio Natta was born on February 26, 1903, in Imperia, Italy. Having read his first chemistry book at age 12, he quickly became fascinated by the topic. At age 16, Natta graduated from high school, and in 1921 entered the Milan Polytechnic Institute, earning his doctorate in chemical engineering in 1924, at the early age of 21.

Following graduation, Natta remained at the Polytechnic Institute as an instructor. He was promoted to assistant professor of general chemistry in 1925, and to full professor in 1927. In 1938 he became director of the Institute's Chemical Research Center where he remained for the rest his career.

Natta was always concerned with the practical results of scientific research and believed that science should serve chiefly to meet the needs of business and industry. One of his early practical breakthroughs was the discovery of an effective catalyst for the synthetic production of the important chemical methanol.

In the early 1930s Natta became interested in the chemistry of polymers, or large molecules. In the late 1930s he used his expertise to contribute to Italy's self-sufficiency efforts, especially in the development of new methods to produce synthetic rubber. Following the conclusion of World War II, Natta continued his research in polymer chemistry, subsidized by the Montecatini Company.

On March 11, 1954, Natta and his Montecatini research group synthesized linear polypropylene, a high polymer with even more desirable chemical properties than polyethylene, which had been synthesized by Natta's close friend Karl Ziegler. Natta's plastic, the first of its kind, proved capable of being molded into objects stronger and more heat resistant than polyethylene. It could be spun into clear fiber stronger and lighter than nylon, spread into clear film, or molded into pipes as sturdy as metal ones. Natta and his colleagues soon discovered other high polymer plastics, including polystyrene.

Natta did not inform Ziegler of his discovery, and Ziegler was greatly disturbed by Natta's failure to live up to an earlier agreement between the two to share their research. The two scientists appeared together at the 1963 ceremony in Stockholm at which they jointly accepted the Nobel prize in chemistry.

In 1959 Natta contracted Parkinson's disease and was already seriously crippled by it at the time of the Nobel prize award ceremony. He retired from active work in the early 1970s and died at Bergamo, Italy, on May 2, 1979, from complications following surgery for a broken femur bone.

In the course of his career, Natta authored or co-authored over 500 scientific papers and received nearly 500 patents. He was the recipient of numerous gold medals and at least five honorary degrees for his scientific contributions.

---

ware has taken much of the guesswork out of mold design. Further, designs can be tested on-screen, thereby saving time and model-making costs.

PROCESSING

Processing combines materials and machinery to create finished consumer goods. In 1990 an estimated 35,000 plastics processors (all categories combined) operated in the United States, running from two or three machines to several hundred. The three types of processors are custom, captive, and proprietary. Custom processors create components for other manufacturers to use in their end products; for example, a custom processor might make engine parts for the automotive industry or refrigerator door liners for the appliance industry. Most custom processors work very closely with the product manufacturer and may be involved in decisions about materials and mold design. A subgroup of custom processors, called contract molders, have little involvement with their customers beyond molding the actual product; the manufacturer simply buys time on their machinery.

Captive processors are manufacturers that acquire equipment to mold specific parts for their own products.

Manufacturers generally install plastics processing equipment only when they require a large enough volume of parts to make such an investment economical. In such a case, a manufacturer might still use outside vendors to fill a portion of its needs, thus keeping in touch with the market and providing a backup operation. Proprietary processors, on the other hand, make the products they will sell under their own company name.

BACKGROUND AND DEVELOPMENT

Development of the first commercial plastic in the United States is generally attributed to John Wesley Hyatt, who developed cellulose nitrate (celluloid) in 1868 as a substitute for ivory in billiard balls. In 1907 Leo H. Baekeland developed phenol formaldehyde molding compounds, and in 1909 he successfully produced a phenolic plastic called Bakelite. Over the next four decades 18 more polymers were developed, along with the necessary equipment to process them. High polymers, as they are currently known and used, were developed in Italy in the early 1950s in the labs of Guilio Natta and his associates.

The United States, Germany, and England were leaders in developing plastics and finding applications for them. Companies that were pioneers in the industry included E.I. du Pont de Nemours (DuPont), Westinghouse, the Foster Grant Company, Farbenfabriken Bayer, General Electric Company, Eastman Kodak, and Dow Chemical Company.

George Eastman (later of Eastman Kodak) developed transparent film for cameras in 1889. In 1908 the United States pioneered cold molded plastics for electrical insulation. A year later Hugh Moore founded the Dixie Cup Company to produce disposable plastic cups in response to laws prohibiting shared drinking cups on trains to help curb the spread of tuberculosis.

The Formica Products Company was started in 1913 to produce reinforced plastic insulators. Laminated products began to replace moisture-absorbing vulcanized rubber in electrical applications during the electrical revolution happening in industry at that time. Westinghouse, the Formica Products Company, and the Bakelite Company worked side-by-side and often head-to-head in this industry. The very profitable Formica Products Company became a subsidiary of the American Cyanamid Company in 1956.

In the 1930s General Electric formed a separate engineering and marketing department for plastics, DuPont began injection molding plastics, the Rohm & Haas Company introduced Plexiglas acrylic coating, and Dow Chemical USA began producing styrene.

The industry did not begin to realize its potential, however, until the end of World War II when the U.S. government released the formula for low-density polyethylene (LDPE) to the civilian market. Polyethylene (PE), first produced in England in the 1930s, was soon discovered to have outstanding dielectric (nonconductive) properties that made it useful as insulation material for radar. After the war, industrial investigators around the world began to experiment with the new plastic and soon discovered that PE could be used in diverse applications such as pipe, film, and squeeze bottles. It rapidly became the most widely used plastic and today accounts for 40 percent (by weight) of all plastics used. In the next 50 years, the plastics industry grew from a sales volume of 2.8 billion pounds in 1945 to 79.2 billion pounds in 1995.

CURRENT CONDITIONS

The polymer industry is the second largest sector of the broad chemicals industry behind pharmaceuticals, accounting for about 20 percent of revenues. In 1998 stagnant plastic prices and rising raw material prices offset the U.S. polymer industry's increased productivity and the world's greater demand for related products. In addition, the strength of the dollar versus a number of Asian currencies slowed the growth of the industry's revenues during this period. Production of polymers rose 3.2 percent in 1998, reaching 91.7 billion pounds. The leading resin types included phenolic with 3.9 billion pounds, urea with 2.6 billion pounds, and polyester with 1.7 billion pounds. The top thermoplastics were polyvinyl chloride (PVC), with 14.5 billion pounds; polypropylene (PP), with 13.8 billion pounds; high-density polyethylene (HDPE), with 12.9 billion pounds; and low-density polyethylene (LDPE), with 7.6 billion pounds. In the late 1990s, plastics production ranked as the country's fourth largest manufacturing industry. The United States was also the world's largest consumer of plastics.

The current popularity of plastics, particularly as a substitute material for wood and metal, led to the estimated 4.4 percent growth in industry shipments in 1998—valued at around $47.3 billion. Analysts predicted just over 3-percent growth in 1999. This slowing of the growth trend was expected to end after 1999, with shipments predicted to grow 4 percent annually through 2003.

With a $7.7 billion polymer trade surplus in 1998, the United States depends heavily on exports for the industry's growth. In 1997 exports accounted for 25 percent of shipments. However, Asia, the key export market of the 1980s and 1990s, approached saturation in the late 1990s as Asian producers increased their production capacities nearly to the point of meeting their domestic needs. China, the largest importer of polymers, reduced its imports from the United States by 12 percent from 1990 to 1994. However, China is predicted to remain a net importer through the early 2000s.

Furthermore, the Asian economic crisis of the late 1990s stifled demand for polymer imports. *Chemical & Engineering News* reported that many analysts believe polymer sales to the Asian countries affected by bad debt and currency depreciation will drop by 15 to 30 percent and continue to hamper overseas sales until the early 2000s. The Asian economic woes also caused prices to fall worldwide because Asian producers began exporting greater quantities of polymers, selling their products for substantially less than producers with stable currencies such as those in the United States and the European Union. Consequently, U.S. and European manufacturers had to lower their prices to remain competitive.

Growth segments in the industry included construction, including plastic lumber, millwork, and composite beams; health care, including pharmaceuticals and diagnostic materials; electronics; and household goods. A study by the Freedonia Group, an industrial research firm, forecast growth of more than 3 percent annually through 2001. Polyvinyl chloride was expected to remain the dominant resin type. An example of innovative plastics use in construction is the laminated glulam wood beam, pioneered by Daniel Tingley, director of the Wood Science and Technology Institute, Ltd. The beams are comprised of layers of wood products bonded together with high-strength, fiber-reinforced plastic to create large beams used in bridge construction and other engineered structures. Automotive use of plastics continues to grow, but at a slower pace; however, the average light vehicle is predicted to add 10 percent more plastics in 1997.

Plastic packaging, though a mature segment of the plastics industry, was still strong, accounting for 21.8 billion pounds, or about 26 percent of the domestic sales and captive use in 1997. A study by Frost and Sullivan, another industry research group, expected revenue from this market to reach $44 billion by 2003, a volume of about 26.6 billion pounds.

Competition was expected to increase from some Asian and Middle East countries, with the result that producers in the United States and Europe began to emphasize the production of specialized and higher value products, such as engineering thermoplastics (ETP) and high-temperature plastics. Mark Witman, director of plastics technology for Bayer Corporation, said in a presentation at the Engineering Thermoplastics 1999 conference that the global market for ETPs should reach 2.2 billion pounds. A study by Kline and Company, a New Jersey consulting company, predicted that the market for high temperature polymers would grow at a rate of 10.2 percent annually, reaching $8 billion by 2007 from $3.1 billion in 1997, driven in part by continued growth in computers and other electronic devices.

Biodegradable polymers were a very small part of the industry at the end of the 1990s, but they were predicted to experience explosive growth. According to Greg Bohlmann of SRI Consulting, this market would increase 35 percent per year by 2001, to 70,000 metric tons per year. North America was the largest market, but Bohlmann expected that demand would grow more quickly in Europe because of a European Union directive urging the use of biodegradable packaging. Some big producers such as BASF, Eastman Chemical, and Bayer have entered the market with technologies for biodegradable thermoplastics such as polycaprolactone and polyester-based products. Dow Chemical formed a joint venture with Cargill to produce lactic acid polymers, which have the added environmental attraction of being produced from renewable resources such as sugar.

RECYCLING

Although plastics make up only about 1 percent of solid waste by weight, their general bulk makes plastic waste products highly visible. Also, most plastics are not naturally biodegradable. Clean thermoplastic trim and reject waste that is the byproduct of the molding cycle has long been recycled. Postconsumer waste and thermoset waste are more difficult to recycle. Thermoset waste must be ground up and used as filler. In the 1970s, so-called advanced recycling technologies were developed to reclaim industrial wastes and x-ray films. The 1970s and 1980s, however, saw an increase in plastics being used for packaging, thus creating a greater volume of plastics in the waste stream. In 1980 no PET soft drink bottles were recycled, but consumer concern drove the industry to initiate recycling and, by 1992, 40.6 percent of PET bottles were being recycled. In 1997 nearly 1.4 billion pounds of plastic bottles were recycled, the highest amount ever. However, because the use of plastic grew strongly that year, the rate of recycling showed a decline. The recycling of all kinds of plastic bottles grew, with pigmented HDPE bottles, such as those used for laundry detergents, showing the greatest increase—14.9 percent.

When plastics are recycled, the post-consumer products must first be sorted by resin type, then shredded or granulated into uniform pellets. The plastics material is then cleaned of contaminants and food residue. It is dried, heated, filtered to remove any remaining contaminants, forced though an extruder at 475 degrees Fahrenheit to form pellets, then marketed. The process is expensive, and recycled plastic generally cannot be reused in food-contact applications. Recycled plastic also may have decreased performance characteristics. Those considerations result in a limited market for the recycled resin.

Companies such as Eastman Chemical, Hoechst Celanese, Shell Chemical, and DuPont have used methanolysis and glycolysis technologies to recycle PET soft drink and other food-contact bottles back into monomers that can be purified and reused for food packaging. Amoco uses hydrolysis to recycle PET; DuPont and BASF recycle polyamides back into raw materials; and Batelle, Inc. recycles commingled post-consumer plastic waste into petroleum products.

One recycling process, thermal decomposition, uses 1,000 degree heat in an oxygen-free environment to convert plastics back to liquid petroleum. The liquid product can be refined and reused as new plastic, synthetic fiber, high-quality lubricants, and gasoline. The process also produces small amounts of solid carbon and gas, both of which can be used.

An industry-funded project to recycle plastics from computers went into limited commercial service in 1998. The engineering plastics used in computers are inherently valuable, but the effort of recycling makes them expensive, especially in comparison with the somewhat depressed resin prices common at the end of the 1990s. One difficulty is that so many different types of plastics are used in computers.

INDUSTRY LEADERS

The polymer industry at the end of the twentieth century was dominated by the large diversified chemical companies. The three largest were European-based conglomerates. A German-based company, BASF AG, reported $14.8 billion in polymer sales in 1998. Europe constituted the company's biggest market, followed by North America, Asia, and South America. BASF and its 97 subsidiaries manufactured plastics, colorants and finishing products, chemicals, health care products, and oil and gas products. The company had manufacturing plants in about 40 countries and marketed its products to 170 countries.

Another German-based company, Bayer AG, had $17.2 billion in revenues from polymers in 1998. The company's polymer segment accounted for 32 percent of 1998 sales. Bayer had six companies that produce polymers, including Bayer Faser GmbH (fibers) and Wolff Walsrode AG. In the late 1990s, Bayer continued to globalize and expand its production capacity to remain on top of the industry. Bayer and its 350 subsidiaries around the world produced not only polymers but also a whole array of chemical products, including pharmaceuticals, agricultural chemicals, automotive products, and electrical products.

DuPont, the largest U.S. chemical company, had $6.9 billion in 1998 polymer sales, roughly the same as 1997 sales. DuPont's polymer division serves the chemical, construction, packaging, automotive, electrical, textile, and transportation industries with its plastic products. In 1999, Wilmington, Delaware-based DuPont underwent a significant reorganization, streamlining operations from eight major segments to three. The company was also in the process of spin-

ning off Conoco, its oil and gas subsidiary, and was planning to move its polyester business onto joint ventures with foreign companies. In 1998, the company employed 101,000 workers.

GE Plastics, a subsidiary of General Electric, reported $6.7 billion in polymer sales in 1997, a 2.9 percent increase over 1996. The company also had about 14,000 workers in 1997. In an effort to increase its global presence, GE Plastics began a joint venture with Bayer AG in 1998 to develop more resistant automotive coatings. General Electric Company was the nation's fifth largest corporation with nearly $100 billion in 1998 sales, producing aircraft parts, appliances, industrial equipment, and materials such as polymers. General Electric also owns GE Capital Corp., a leading financial services company, and the broadcasting behemoth NBC. GE Plastics accounted for about 7 percent of the parent company's total sales.

Midland, Michigan-based Dow Chemical posted 1998 revenues of $5.1 billion from its "Performance Plastics" segment plus $3.8 billion from its "Plastics" segment, accounting for about 28 percent and 20 percent respectively of the company's overall sales. These figures represent a decline of about 5.6 percent from 1997. Dow Chemical, the country's second largest chemical manufacturer, restructured itself in the late 1990s, selling off its non-core businesses to concentrate on chemical production and agricultural genetic engineering to produce materials for polymers. Dow Chemical operated 114 production plants in 33 countries and employed 39,000 workers in 1998.

WORK FORCE

The number of employees in plastics manufacturing and wholesale trade in the mid-1990s, not including upstream production, was estimated at 1.3 million workers in 19,463 establishments, according to the Society of the Plastics Industry. Employment in the plastics industry has grown consistently since the 1980s, while other manufacturing industries watched their workforce decrease by 4.3 percent. California employed the most workers in the industry, accounting for 9.4 percent of the industry's employees. Ohio was second in employees, with 8.6 percent, followed by Michigan, Illinois, Texas, Pennsylvania, Indiana, and New York. Texas is an important state in terms of resins and plastics materials as most of the country's feedstocks and petrochemicals are produced there. The largest share of miscellaneous plastics products are produced in California and Ohio, and Michigan is the largest producer of molds for plastics. California and Ohio produce the most plastics machinery. California is also the largest in captive production of plastics products. In the 1990s, Arkansas was the fastest growing state in terms of employment, expanding by 125 percent between 1991 and 1996.

AMERICA AND THE WORLD

In 1998 the United States continued its long-standing plastics trade surplus, totaling about $7.7 billion. Plastics molds and machinery, however, had a deficit. Although plastics imports from Mexico rose from $216 million in 1991 to $398 million in 1996, exports to Mexico tripled in that time—from $617 million in 1991 to $1.781 billion in 1996.

In the mid- to late 1990s, the United States led the world in plastics consumption, accounting for nearly 25 percent of world consumption of the five major thermoplastics: HDPE, LDPE, PP, PS, and PVC. The European Union ranked second with 26.7 percent; Japan third with 8.7 percent; China fourth with 6.9 percent; South Korea fifth with 3.9 percent; and Taiwan sixth with 3 percent.

A plastics machinery boom that began in 1993 cooled off in 1996 as consumption slipped 2.3 percent from a record $3.44 billion set in 1995. The downward trend was predicted to continue through 1997, then rise again to reach $3.72 billion in 1999.

RESEARCH AND TECHNOLOGY

MATERIALS TECHNOLOGY

Plastics have had a bad reputation environmentally, not only because most forms do not biodegrade, but also because manufacturing polymer resin creates large amounts of hazardous waste in the form of organic solvents and contaminated water. The U.S. Environmental Protection Agency reported that 567 million pounds of toxic waste were generated from plastics production in 1992, and about one-quarter of that was released directly into the nation's land, air, and water.

In 1994 Joseph DiSimone, a chemical engineer and associate professor at the University of North Carolina at Chapel Hill, announced that he had pioneered a more environmentally friendly way to create polymers. Rather than mixing monomers, an initiator compound, and large amounts of water or organic solvent

together to form polymers, then draining off the water or solvent, DiSimone used supercritical carbon dioxide as a substitute bonding medium for the water or solvent. A supercritical gas is one that is under such high pressure its density is more like that of a liquid. Adding surfactants to the mix helped the polymer chains to form in the supercritical gas, which can be harmlessly vented off when polymerization is complete. The process also holds promise for creating modified polymers with greatly enhanced physical properties. A drawback is that the equipment needed to create supercritical carbon dioxide is expensive; however, the process eliminates the need for petroleum-based solvents and saves the high cost of cleanup. Research continues on this method for largely eliminating toxic waste from the manufacturing process.

The U.S. market for water-soluble polymers continues to increase as paint, coatings, adhesives, and cosmetics manufacturers are forced to replace volatile oxygen compounds (VOCs) with environmentally friendlier formulations. Water-soluble polymers include starch-based (86 percent), natural hydrocolloids (4 percent), polyvinyl alcohol and other synthetic polymers (3 percent each), and cellulose ethers (2 percent). State legislation banning phosphates in detergents has resulted in demand for water-soluble polymers, which also are used in water-treatment, food processing, and pharmaceutical applications. A study by Frost and Sullivan predicted that the market would grow to $20 billion by 2003, driven largely by increased use by the water and waste water industries.

Natural oils such as soybean, corn, and linseed can be used as monomers. Epoxidized soybean oil has been used for several years as a plasticizer for PVC, and it has the advantages of being biodegradable and a renewable resource. Ongoing research in this area is being conducted by Dr. Alec Scranton of Michigan State University.

Polymer composites are lightweight, high-strength, corrosion-resistant materials that came to the forefront in applications for the aerospace industry. With the end of the Cold War, the composites industry took a precipitous downturn because, although composites' outstanding properties make them a natural for transportation, construction, marine, medical device, and sporting goods applications, their cost can be prohibitive. As the cost of wood products rise, however, composites have become more attractive, and the industry is slowly regaining momentum. Shipments of composite materials reached 3.22 billion pounds in 1996, up 1.6 percent over 1995, and growth was expected to continue at 1.6 percent through the end of the decade.

APPLICATIONS

High-tech applications for new generations of polymers continue to proliferate. Researchers recently discovered that conjugated (alternating single and double bonds between the atoms of a molecule) polymers can be used as the active layer in electroluminescent devices such as light-emitting diodes (LEDs) and flat panel displays. Conjugated polymers, particularly polyphenylene vinylene (PPV), have shown electroluminescense and photoluminescence across the full spectrum. Researchers Arthur J. Epstein of Oregon State University and Alan G. MacDiarmid of the University of Pennsylvania are researching a new class of compounds—semiconducting, highly conducting, and superconducting organic and inorganic polymers. One group of organic polymers acts like synthetic metals in that they exhibit the magnetic and electronic properties of metal but have the mechanical properties of organic polymers.

As technology transfer continues between U.S. government laboratories and industry, the National Aeronautics and Space Administration (NASA) has offered its research on thin-film and coating technologies. In aviation, high-tech "smart molecule" polymers are being developed for applications such as permanent de-icing of aircraft.

In the medical arena, polymers are used in transdermal systems for drug delivery including hormone replacement, pain control, and heart stabilization. Penederm Inc. has developed a polymeric system designed to deposit and hold drugs and skin-care agents at targeted levels on and in the upper layers of skin. Polymers also are used in orthotic and prosthetic devices.

In other innovative uses, in the late 1990s the U.S. Army developed a method for encapsulating vaccines in biodegradable polymers; the slow-release capsules promote the formation of antigens in the intestines before the vaccines can be broken down by digestive juices. LifeSciences Corporation has introduced an artificial polymeric skin for use in treating patients who have life-threatening burns. The artificial skin allows new skin to develop beneath it, then it gradually biodegrades. The company has submitted the product for FDA approval and has begun manufacturing the skin for export to countries where its sale has been approved.

FURTHER READING

American Plastics Council. "The Evolution of Plastics Recycling Technology." Washington: Society of the Plastics Industry, 1994.

"Bayer Director of Plastics Technology Mark Witman Expects the Global Market for Engineering Thermoplastics Will Reach 22 Billion Lb." *Chemical Market Reporter,* 22 March 1999.

"Breaking into the Big Time." *Chemical Week,* 10 June 1998.

"Despite Tighter Regulations and Market Pressures, the U.S. Plastic Packaging Market Promises Healthy Growth Fueled by Emerging Technologies and Growing Applications." *PR Newswire,* 2 February 1998.

DiSimone, J.M., et al. "Dispersion Polymerizations in Supercritical Carbon Dioxide." *Science,* 15 July 1994.

Facts & Figures of the U.S. Plastics Industry, 1996 Edition. Washington: Society of the Plastics Industry, 1996.

Fourth Annual Plastics Industry Outlook: 1997-1999. Livingston: The CIT Group, June 1997.

Fox, Karen Celia. "Cleaner Manufacture of Plastics—With a Bit of Bubbly." *Science,* 15 July 1994.

Freedonia Group, Inc. "Plastic Processing Machinery to 2001," June 1997. Available from http://www.freedonia group.com.

———. "Plastics in Construction to 2001," September 1997. Available from http://www.freedoniagroup.com.

Lindsay, Karen. "ICE '97 Wrap-Up." *Composites Design & Application Magazine,* New York: Composites Institute, March/April 1997.

McElligott, Suzanne. "China Still Dominates Plastics Markets; But Pricing Is under Pressure." *Chemical Week,* 18 June 1997.

McHugh, Josh. "Annual Report on American Industry: Chemicals." *Forbes,* January 1997.

"New Applications and Environmental Trends Are Driving Growth in Water Soluble Polymer Markets." *PR Newswire,* 12 December 1998.

Plastics Recycling Update. Portland, OR: Resource Recycling, Inc., June 1997.

Probe Economics, Inc. *Contribution of Plastics to the U.S. Economy: An Economic Impact Study of the Plastics Industry.* Washington: Society of the Plastics Industry, 1996.

Riordan, Teresa. "Rethinking Plastics from the Ground Up." *The New York Times,* 11 September 1994.

Rosato, Dominick V. *Rosato's Plastics Encyclopedia and Dictionary.* New York: Hanser Publishers, 1993.

Rubin, Irvin I., ed. *Handbook of Plastic Materials and Technology.* New York: John Wiley & Sons, Inc., 1990.

Storck, William J. "North America: U.S. Chemical Industry to See Modest Growth next Year as Economy Cools." *Chemical & Engineering News,* 15 December 1997.

Toloken, Steve. "Industry Hopes Recycling Project Computes." *Plastics News,* 25 May 1998.

U.S. Department of Commerce. International Trade Administration. *U.S. Industry & Trade Outlook '99.* Washington: McGraw-Hill, 1999.

Wolfe, Joanne. "Good News for Plastics and Designers." *Plastics Design Forum,* November/December 1994.

"Worldwide Sales of High-Temperature Polymers May Reach $8 Billion in 2007 vs. $3.1 Billion in 1997." *Plastic News,* 28 September 1998.

—Joanne Wolfe,
updated by Karl Heil and Howard Distelzweig

PREMIUM BOTTLED BEVERAGES

INDUSTRY SNAPSHOT

The premium bottled beverage market (also known as the "New Age" or "alternative" segment of the industry) consists of single-serve fruit juice and juice drinks, ready-to-drink tea, sports drinks, and pre-packaged iced coffee. It does not, however, include alcoholic beverages, which are regarded as a separate category. Nor does it typically include bottled water, despite the fact that a number of beverage manufacturers include bottled water in their product lines.

While carbonated soft drinks are by far the most popular form of nonalcoholic bottled beverages with about 80 percent of the market, juices, teas, and especially sports drinks have been making significant inroads. In 1998, according to the trade publication *Beverage World,* single-serve fruit beverages, ready-to-drink tea and coffee, and sports beverages posted combined sales of nearly $5.2 billion. Such alternative beverages had a 12 percent compounded annual growth rate from 1993 to 1998 and claimed about 14 percent of the market for nonalcoholic liquid beverages.

ORGANIZATION AND STRUCTURE

Producers of premium bottled beverages include companies of all sizes, from industry giants Coca-Cola and Pepsi to specialty firms such as Snapple Beverages and even small regional manufacturers. Distribution varies according to a company's array of products and how each is manufactured. Coca-Cola and Pepsi dominate the distribution system in the United States by virtue of their size and market share.

Beverages are formulated and packaged using either a hot-fill or cold-fill processing method that is determined in part by the nature of the product in question. Hot fill, in which bottles are filled with hot liquid and immediately sealed, is the accepted method of bottling iced teas, for example.

During the late 1990s, in response to the public's growing concern about *E. coli* and other food-borne diseases, manufacturers began paying extra attention to the bottling process in an effort to prevent contamination. Juice bottlers in particular have boosted quality control measures and turned to pasteurization (which kills potentially harmful bacteria) for added safety.

FRUIT JUICES AND JUICE DRINKS

Fruit juices and juice drinks (that is, beverages containing less than 100 percent fruit juice) are the second most popular type of beverage in the United States after carbonated soft drinks. They are typically available in single-serving portions that consumers might purchase in food service establishments and convenience stores or from vending machines. Although juice consumption declined during the 1980s, it began to climb once again during the 1990s. Health-conscious consumers, clever marketing, expanded distribution, and a wider variety of flavors are credited with reversing the downward trend and boosting sales.

In creating new flavors they hope will capture the public's fancy, juice makers experimented with juice blends as well as with single-fruit juice drinks. For example, aronia berry juice cocktail first appeared on store shelves in 1998. The aronia berry is among those substances being touted as a so-called "functional food" with antioxidant properties. The drink has been

In 1996 David Marcheschi (left) and Chris Connor, founders of Water Joe, produced water that contained caffeine.
(AP Photo/Charles Bennett.)

marketed as having all the benefits of cranberries but with a milder taste.

READY-TO-DRINK TEA

Although ready-to-drink tea had already been on the market for several years when brands such as Snapple and AriZona arrived on the scene, it had not yet caught on with consumers in a very big way. But Snapple and AriZona changed all that with single-serve, ready-to-drink beverages that actually tasted like brewed tea.

Snapple hit the national market in 1988. It enjoyed several good years during the early 1990s before sales fizzled in the middle of the decade, dropping nine percent in 1995 and eight percent in 1996. Under new ownership since 1997, Snapple has begun to recover market share, posting a 14 percent increase in case sales during the first quarter of 1999 over the same period in 1998.

AriZona Iced Tea was launched by Ferolito, Vultaggio & Sons in 1992 to compete with Snapple. Its unique packaging and competitive pricing helped draw consumers to the brand. In 1996, AriZona reported $2 billion in annual sales and claimed a market share of more than 17 percent.

Lipton and Nestea, the traditional distributors of bottled iced tea, responded to their new competitors by forging alliances with Pepsi and Coca-Cola, the undisputed leaders in the soft drink industry. "With the distribution and marketing might of Pepsi and Coke behind them, Lipton Original and Nestea may overwhelm Snapple," *Forbes* magazine predicted in 1996. Snapple executives stated that they hoped to take advantage of their rivals' entry into this market segment, but by 1997, Lipton and Nestea were the top-selling ready-to-drink teas.

That same year, Quaker Oats sold Snapple to Triarc Companies, a New York-based holding company. As Nikhil Deogun observed in the *Wall Street Journal,* "Although Triarc got Snapple for a fire-sale price of $300 million (Quaker Oats took a big loss, selling Snapple for $1.4 billion less than it had paid), the acquisition still was a gamble."

Although increased competition reduced ready-to-drink tea prices in late 1996, the industry expected steady growth through the remainder of the century. Yet the trendiness of the product poses unique dangers that can impact the bottom line. "The 'premium' beverage business is as distinct from the soda-pop business as Tommy Hilfiger is from Levi's," noted Deogun. A Triarc executive concurred, stating,

"We're not in the soft-drink business; we're in the fashion business."

SPORTS DRINKS

Sports drinks claimed a three percent share of the beverage market in 1998. Gatorade, owned by Quaker Oats, was the leading sports drink in the United States at the close of the decade. Despite increased competition in the form of new sports drinks from Pepsi and Coca-Cola and other beverages, it still claimed nearly 80 percent of the U.S. sports drink market in 1998 and was responsible for 37 percent of the $4.6 billion in sales and profits its parent company posted that same year. According to a *Wall Street Journal* article published in February 1999, Quaker Oats officials were greeted with some skepticism when they projected a continued average annual growth rate of 15 percent for Gatorade. (It was a prediction some analysts believed was too optimistic.) Yet as the article went on to note, Quaker Oats had plans "for increasing availability of the product at 100,000 'high sweat' sites and a new bolder-flavored line called Fierce."

As a reporter for *Brandweek* observed, "Under twin challenges from Coke's POWERaDE and Pepsi's All Sport, Gatorade has experimented more with offbeat flavors and packages, including the sports bottles, to broaden consumption occasions of the $1.1 billion brand. [The new] flavors are the first from Gatorade to eschew actual fruit names; they're described simply as light-tasting fruit-flavor blends." The Gatorade Frost line posted sales of $100 million in its first six months on the market and had $148 million in sales and about a nine percent market share in its first year.

Gatorade's chief competitors, Coca-Cola's POWERaDE and Pepsi's All Sport, together account for most of the remaining 20 percent of the sports drink market, with POWERaDE claiming 11 percent (up 22.4 percent in sales in 1998) compared to 7 percent for All Sport. Prospect Ridge Beverage Co. entered the sports drink category in late 1998 with a product called Starter Fluid. The name was licensed from the Starter sportswear firm and endorsed by basketball star Scottie Pippen. However, previous attempts to market similar licensed sports drinks, including Everlast, Nautilus and Spaulding, have failed.

Sports drinks face another challenge in their efforts to snag a bigger share of the beverage market—criticism from health professionals. While doctors and others in the medical field agree that encouraging athletes to drink more fluids is a laudable goal, they harbor more than a few doubts about the true nutritional benefits of sports drinks. In fact, the high sugar content of products like Gatorade translates into more calories, and its very acidic nature (coupled with the high sugar content) helps promote tooth decay.

More On **SPORTS DRINKS**

Physical fitness fanatics gulp down over one billion dollars worth of sports beverages every year. Gatorade, with 80 percent of the market, is among the 50 leading brand name sellers in supermarkets. So what is the big attraction? According to David Whitford in *Fortune,* the sports beverage, "Looks like something Sam would serve with green eggs and ham." Where did it come from? Dr. Michael Cade of the University of Florida invented the beverage in the early 1960s to rehydrate the Florida Gators, the school football team. Cade's first recipes failed to pass the taste test and some players went so far as to heave the stuff after drinking it. It was Mrs. Mary Cade, the doctor's wife, who came up with an idea to introduce lemon juice in the formula. The lemon juice did the trick, and made the difference between drinkable and indigestible. Dr. Cade made the stuff in his lab until 1967 when he sold the rights to Stokely-Van Camp.

Are sports drinks particularly beneficial? Nutrition experts claim that a quart of water can be just as beneficial except during an ultra-strenuous workout that lasts for 90 minutes or longer.

CURRENT CONDITIONS

Total United States beverage consumption in 1997 set a record at $178.9 billion worth of drinks sold and consumed. According to a 1998 *Beverage World* market overview, the upward trend was expected to continue. Predictions are that the figure will reach $200 billion by 2010 as consumers seek out alternatives to soft drinks and tap water.

In 1997, companies began responding to increased consumer interest in maintaining good health and proper nutrition by creating a new group of products called "functional foods" or "nutraceuticals." These included drinks augmented with herbs such as ginseng or other substances touted as having antioxidant properties. According to *Forbes,* an estimated $30 million worth of herb-enhanced beverages were purchased in 1997. This broader category of drinks included not only the vast number of green tea drinks on the market, but also products such as V-8 Splash Tropical Blend drink, which contains 100 percent of the Recommended Dietary Allowance for vitamins A and C.

Iced-coffee drinks emerged as a growing segment of the beverage industry in 1997 with nearly 41.2 gallons consumed per person. Kraft/General Foods had a difficult time finding a niche for their Cappio brand coffee beverage in 1996, but PepsiCo-Starbucks and Nestle saw their sales rise in 1997 and again in 1998. For PepsiCo's product, the increase in consumption appeared to stem from the use of the popular Starbucks name as well as the fact that it was marketed as a coffee-flavored milkshake. Frappucino (another PepsiCo product) enjoyed a 64.1 percent share of the market in 1997, and Nescafe Blended Iced Coffees took a distant second place with a share approaching 11 percent.

Entering the pre-packaged beverage market in 1998 were various dairy-based "smoothie" drinks such as Triarc's WhipperSnapple and Hansen's Natural line. They joined an array of yogurt-based drinks, the sales of which had increased 91.3 percent to

$15.9 million in 1996. Tracking milk or other dairy drinks is done only on a limited basis by the beverage industry, however, since they are technically regarded as food items. To help make sure this category remains part of the milk industry rather than the beverage industry, the International Dairy Foods Association announced plans in 1997 to begin brokering the production and marketing of new products between dairies. The association also hoped to spur development and production of fruit and coffee drinks targeted at children and young people.

INDUSTRY LEADERS

Quaker Oats Co. leads the premium bottled beverage industry as a result of Gatorade's success among sports drinks. Gatorade was the creation of Dr. Michael Cade, a researcher at the University of Florida who invented the greenish-yellow liquid to serve as a hydrating replacement for body fluids lost in athletic

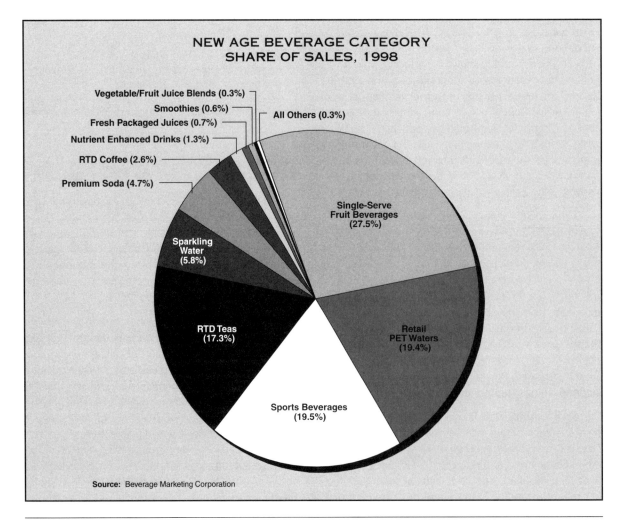

NEW AGE BEVERAGE CATEGORY
SHARE OF SALES, 1998

Vegetable/Fruit Juice Blends (0.3%)
Smoothies (0.6%)
Fresh Packaged Juices (0.7%)
Nutrient Enhanced Drinks (1.3%)
RTD Coffee (2.6%)
Premium Soda (4.7%)
All Others (0.3%)
Single-Serve Fruit Beverages (27.5%)
Sparkling Water (5.8%)
RTD Teas (17.3%)
Retail PET Waters (19.4%)
Sports Beverages (19.5%)

Source: Beverage Marketing Corporation

competition and during hot weather. Players for the Florida Gators football team who drank the concoction had fewer problems with dehydration and showed increased efficiency and greater endurance. In fact, on January 1, 1967, after the Gators beat Georgia Tech in the Orange Bowl by a score of 27 to 12, Georgia Tech Head Coach Bobby Dodd told *Sports Illustrated* magazine that his team lost because "we didn't have Gatorade. That made the difference."

Since then, Gatorade has often appeared on the sidelines at sporting events ranging from little league baseball games to professional tennis matches. It has also served as the official drink of sports organizations such as Major League Baseball, the National Football League, the National Basketball Association, the National Hockey League, and NASCAR.

Dr. Cade sold the rights to Gatorade to Stokely-Van Camp in 1967. Quaker Oats bought Stokely in 1983 when Gatorade sales checked in at about $120 million. Under its new owner, Gatorade enjoyed wider distribution and an expanded product line of new flavors. By 1998, the popular sports drink was posting sales of $1.5 billion. "Gatorade defines the category," declared Jesse Meyers, publisher of *Beverage Digest.* "There is not a beverage category in any country in the world that is so dominated by one producer."

Coca-Cola produced about 6.5 billion gallons of beverages in 1997 compared to PepsiCo's 4.5 billion gallons, most of it in the form of carbonated soft drinks. These companies dominate the alternative beverage field with an assortment of familiar brands, including Coca-Cola's Minute Maid and Fruitopia fruit juices, Nestea iced tea, and POWERaDE sports drink. Meanwhile, PepsiCo distributes Tropicana and Ocean Spray fruit juices, Lipton iced tea (the market leader in its category with a 42 percent share in 1998), and All Sport sports drink. The Tropicana line alone, which includes brand names such as Tropicana Pure Premium, Season's Best, and Dole (known mostly for its pineapple products), posted an estimated $1.9 billion in sales in 1997. The following year, Tropicana's owner, Seagram Co. Ltd., sold the company to PepsiCo for $3.3 billion. Fruit juices are an especially popular alternative beverage, claiming about seven percent of the nonalcoholic liquid refreshment market.

Ocean Spray Cranberries, Inc., is a grower cooperative founded in 1930. It has been credited with reinventing the cranberry by coming up with new products and marketing strategies. Among the group's most successful endeavors are the "Crave the Wave" juice blends, estimated to account for about 80 percent of sales. In addition, its Mauna Lai blend of

guava-based juices "established the category of tropical fruit drinks," according to *Industry Week.* The Wellfleet Farms premium 100 percent juice line, which debuted in mid-1998, was the most successful product launch in the company's history; about 400,000 cases were shipped in its first six weeks on the market. Ocean Spray operates in 46 countries, including the United Kingdom, Australia, and Switzerland. It had total sales of $1.48 billion in 1998, a 3 percent increase over the 1997 figure.

Nantucket Nectars was founded by Tom First and Tom Scott, who met while attending Brown University. The pair started in business as provisioners in Nantucket Harbor and then opened a deli, where they began tinkering with concocting drinks. Their products include juice nectars, a "Super Nectars" line of functional drinks and herb-infused teas. Located in Cambridge, Massachusetts, Nantucket Nectars employed approximately 100 people in 1997 and posted sales in the late 1990s of $45 million. In December 1997 it formed a partnership with rival Ocean Spray. Under the terms of the agreement, Ocean Spray acquired a major stake in Nantucket Nectars, which was expected to continue operating as a free-standing company while taking advantage of the bigger firm's purchasing power and production expertise.

The primary product line for South Beach Beverage, a Norwalk, Connecticut-based company, is SoBe herbally enhanced beverages, which debuted in 1995. They are the market leaders in their category, which has seen sales jump from almost zero in 1996 to about $30 million in 1997. Company executives claim SoBe drinks differ from the competition in that they are sediment-free, 10 percent juice, and "drinkable." They include fruit blends, teas, "faux cocktails," and a fruit-vegetable juice blend called Orange Elixir. The company has been credited with giving herbal drinks greater market visibility.

Among producers of ready-to-drink teas, Lipton (owned by PepsiCo) enjoys by far the largest market share. Yet two other brands, Snapple and AriZona, have attracted attention with quirky advertising, innovative packaging, and trendy flavors.

Snapple Beverage Corp. was established in 1986 in Brooklyn, New York. Founders Lenny Marsh, Hymie Golden, and Arnie Greenberg regarded their product as an alternative to sweet soft drinks. The national success it achieved during the early 1990s can be traced in part to a humorous series of television advertisements featuring Wendy, the "Snapple Lady." She was a bona fide marketing department employee of the company who read and answered customers' letters to Snapple on the air. Sales soared, reaching over $700 million by 1994, the year Quaker Oats bought the firm for $1.7 billion.

Beverage World named Snapple "The Beverage of the Decade" in 1997. Not long after receiving that honor, however, Quaker Oats sold Snapple to Triarc Companies in response to several years of declining sales that analysts blamed on distribution difficulties and a lack of promotion. A holding company with interests in several different industries, Triarc had already been credited with resurrecting the Mistic brand of teas and juices. Since acquiring Snapple, Triarc has worked to turn the brand around, posting a 14-percent increase in case sales in the first quarter of 1999. It also introduced a number of new products in 1999, including WhipperSnapple smoothies, Snapple Farms juices, a line of herbal enhanced fruit drinks and teas called Elements, Mistic brand Italian Ice Smoothies, and Sun Valley Squeeze fruit-flavored drinks.

Ferolito, Vultaggio & Sons, purveyors of the AriZona Iced Tea brand, started in business as beer distributors in Brooklyn, New York, during the 1970s. Their fleet eventually grew from one Volkswagen bus to twenty-five trucks. In 1986, they decided to try *making* beer rather than just delivering it. They experimented first with brewing malt liquors, then branched out to iced teas in 1992. Within two years, the AriZona brand was posting $300 million in sales.

The company's innovations in packaging, including larger-than-average portions and trendy "good-for-you" formulations featuring green teas and ginseng, helped build the AriZona brand. In 1997, however, *Brandweek* noted that Ferolito, Vultaggio & Sons had "seen its growth stall from explosive levels earlier in the decade." The firm was criticized for lacking advertising and consumer promotional plans. Furthermore, a variety of distribution problems led to numerous sales problems for the company's line of iced teas and juice drinks. But it rebounded in 1998 and launched distinctive new products such as AriZona Asia Plum Green Tea, Blue Luna Iced Coffee, and AriZona Total Sport Extreme Thirst Quencher. As of 1999, the AriZona brand of ready-to-drink teas accounted for $500 million in sales, ranking just behind Lipton and Snapple.

WORK FORCE

Increased regulations and more sophisticated equipment in bottling plants have created a need for better trained and more highly skilled employees in the beverage industry. Specialized courses of study such as the Beverage Technician certification program at Florida International University assure employers that their workers are properly educated.

Management-level employees are expected to have degrees in the sciences or engineering, with follow-up training and education from trade-specific groups such as the International Society of Beverage Technologists. For areas such as quality control, employment requirements might require candidates to possess a degree in microbiology, biology, chemistry, or field science. Additional experience in statistical process control, blending, flavors, and sanitation is considered a plus.

AMERICA AND THE WORLD

U.S. companies dominate the worldwide beverage industry. Among the exceptions are two firms based in Mexico, PanAmerican Beverage and Pepsi-Gemex. PanAmerican Beverage, a Coca-Cola-affiliated distributor with 19 percent of the Latin American market, ranked ninth internationally in 1997 with about $2.5 billion in sales. Pepsi-Gemex, a Pepsi-allied bottler with 50 percent of the Mexican market and $498 million in sales in 1997, ranked fortieth.

During the mid-1990s, there was concern among manufacturers that Europe was lagging far behind the United States in its demand for sports drinks. According to Tara Parker-Pope in the *Wall Street Journal,* Germany led Europe in its consumption of sports drinks at mid-decade, and Italy was the second-largest market. Gatorade, which was not even introduced in Italy until the late 1980s, claimed 80 percent of its market by 1995. But the popular product fizzled in France due to distribution problems and stiff competition from a Coca-Cola product called Aquarius that was manufactured especially for European consumers. Gatorade finally gave up on the French market in 1993. In Belgium, however, it was the top seller in 1995 with a share of 36.8 percent, up from 27.3 percent the previous year. In Spain, on the other hand, Aquarius enjoyed a full 49 percent of the market. It did not do as well in Germany, where the country's own labels and small-brand drink offerings outsold Aquarius, causing a drop in market share from 27.6 percent to 21.2 percent from 1993 to 1994.

Due to the fact that beverage preferences vary widely from country to country, there are numerous locally based producers of bottled drinks. By and large, Americans tend to drink less fruit juice than

Western Europeans, partly because of the popularity of soft drinks. In the Asian market, carbonated drinks are popular, but consumers also favor canned coffees and teas as well as mineral water. In Japan, for example, Georgia brand iced coffee, a Coca-Cola product, is a top-selling item.

RESEARCH AND TECHNOLOGY

Formulation and flavoring are subjects of ongoing concern for beverage companies. With growing consumer demand for vitamins, minerals, and other health-related products, the challenge for flavoring companies trying to keep up with this trend is to provide beverage companies with nutritionally sound yet tasty products. "A lot of healthy products have unpleasant tastes, and flavors combined with nutraceuticals overcome this problem," observed Hans-Peter Voss, vice-president of Wild Flavors, in a 1998 *Beverage World* article.

Flavor chemists are blending herbs and vitamins with exotic flavors from nature. In 1996, kiwi-strawberry was especially popular; in subsequent years, it was cranberry and mango. The new flavors for 1998 included unusual tropical fruits such as starfruit and persimmon as well as various vegetable mixtures, namely those chosen for their antioxidant benefits, including orange-carrot, orange-tomato, and apple-green bell pepper. The late 1990s also saw drinks with additives such as potassium, ginseng, and echinacea gain in popularity.

Dairy products are also beginning to enter the prepackaged beverage market in a big way, most often via iced coffee drinks and smoothies. Producers faced several challenges in formulating these beverages, however. For instance, Triarc's WhipperSnapple uses real dairy products instead of gum substitutes, yet it is marketed without calling attention to its dairy content. Juice companies such as Hansen's and Odwalla also manufacture competing smoothie-type products.

FURTHER READING

"The Artal Group." *Economic Review*, January 1998.

"The Beverage World Top 50." *Beverage World*, July 1998.

Blamey, Pamela. "Mooove Over Soda: Could the Next Trend in Beverages Come from Milk-Based Drinks?" *Supermarket News*, 27 January 1997.

Bolt, Kevin. "Premium Soft Drinks." *Beverage World*, March 1995.

Brewster, Elizabeth. "The Great Carrot Cover-Up." *Food Processing*, May 1997.

"Clearly, Colorfully Canadian." *Beverage World*, 15 June 1998.

"Country Pure Foods to Acquire the Quaker Oats Company's Ardmore Farms Business." *PR Newswire*, 16 July 1998.

Cuneo, Alice Z., and Louise Kramer. "Aquafina Takes the Middle vs. Upscale Water Brands: Pepsi-Cola's Midprice Entry Readies First TV Effort." *Advertising Age*, 22 June 1998.

Danyliw, Norie Quintos. "Tooth Trouble." *U.S. News & World Report*, 30 June 1997.

Deogun, Nikhil. "Soft-Drink Marketers at Triarc Deftly Give Snapple Back Its Buzz." *Wall Street Journal*, 14 December 1998.

Dwyer, Steve. "Innovative to a 'Tea'." *Prepared Foods*, 3 June 1999. Available from http://www.preparedfoods.com/1999/9904/9904ferolito.htm.

"Fruit Beverages Scope." *Beverage World*, July 1998.

"Industry Surveys: Foods & Nonalcoholic Beverages." *Standard & Poor's*, 27 November 1997.

Khermouch, Gerry. "Still Winging It." *Brandweek*, 27 October 1997.

———. "Tom Scott, Tom First: Founders, Nantucket Nectars." *Brandweek*, 3 November 1997.

———. "Triarc's Smooth Move." *Brandweek*, 22 June 1998.

Lee, Diane. "Industry Snapshot: Beverages." *Hoover's Online*, 3 June 1999. Available from http://www.hoovers.com/features/industry/beverage.html.

Lefton, Terry. "Beverage Player Greenhorns in on Gatorade Turf with Starter, Pippen." *Brandweek*, 27 July 1998.

"Liquid Stats." *BeverageWorld.com*, 3 June 1999. Available from http://www.beverageworld.com/bevinfo.html.

"Lizard Wizards Try to Put Drinks in Your Gizzard." *Beverage Industry*, February 1996.

McCormack, Scott. "Zen in a Bottle." *Forbes*, 18 May 1998

McMurray, Scott. "Drumming Up New Business: Quaker Marches Double Time to Put Snap Back in Its Snapple Drink Line." *U.S. News & World Report*, 22 April 1996.

Meushaw, Tony. "Quality Time." *Beverage World*, 15 February 1998.

"Ocean Spray and Nantucket Nectars 'Juice Guys' Team Up," 9 December 1997. Available from http://www.oceanspray.com/press/press.asp?ID=121.

Parker-Pope, Tara. "Europe's Sports-Drink Industry Thirsts for Demand Enjoyed by U.S. Market." *Wall Street Journal*, 17 February 1995.

Phillips, Bob. "Coffee Run." *Beverage World*, April 1998.

"Portola Packaging Receives NSF Certification for Cap Snap Water Bottling Equipment." *Beverage World,* April 1998.

"Portola Packaging's Push-Pull 'Sports Caps' Provide Product Shelf Impact and Tamper Evidence." *Beverage World,* April 1998.

Prince, Greg W. "What It Takes." *Beverage World,* April 1998.

Prince, Greg W., and Eric Sfiligoj. "The Beverage Market Index for 1993; Five Out of Six Drink Categories Experienced Growth in 1992, Making for a $159 Billion Retail Business." *Beverage World,* May 1993.

———. "Reality Drinks." *Beverage World,* September 1994.

"Quaker Oats Expects Rising Gatorade Sales to Surpass Food Sales." *Wall Street Journal,* 18 February 1999.

Rasmusson, Erika. "Snapping Back into Action." *Sales & Marketing Management,* October 1997.

Reidy, Chris. "Ocean Spray Seeks to Keep Its Distribution by Pepsi Exclusive." Knight-Ridder/Tribune Business News, 10 August 1998.

Roth, Daniel. "Just Call Us Cockroaches." *Forbes,* August 26, 1996.

Russo, Laurie. "As Good as It Gets." *Beverage World,* April 1998.

"Seagram Sells Tropicana Products to PepsiCo for $8.8 Billion Cash." *Nation's Restaurant News,* 3 August 1998.

Sfiligoj, Eric. "Annual Beverage Market Index." *Beverage World,* May 1998.

"Snapple's New Look: Lemon." *U.S. News & World Report,* 31 March 1997.

"Stirring the Porridge." *Economist,* 5 November 1994.

Theodore, Sarah. "Gatorade Growth Taps 'Active Thirst.'" *Beverage Industry,* April 1998.

"They Want You to See Clearly Now." *Beverage World,* 15 May 1997.

"The Top 10 Soft Drink Review." *Beverage World,* 15 March 1998.

"Triarc Reports First Quarter 1999 Results." *NewsAlert,* 18 May 1999. Available from http://www.newsalert.com.

Turcsik, Richard. "Aronia Berry Juice Making a Big Splash." *Supermarket News,* 6 July 1998.

Whitford, David. "The Gatorade Mystique." *Fortune,* 23 November 1998.

"World Survey of Soft Drinks Industry." *Economic Review,* March 1992.

—Linda Dailey Paulson, updated by Jane E. Spear

PREMIUM NON-ALCOHOLIC BEVERAGES

INDUSTRY SNAPSHOT

Throughout the 1990s, many breweries and wineries cultivated a whole new set of customers. Those Americans who never, or seldom drank alcohol, or might not drink alcohol due to an expected driving situation represented a market to which the industry had not targeted previously. The anticipation that premium non-alcoholic beverages could create a competition for breweries and wineries with soft-drink makers and bottled water distributors for a market share made the venture appealing. Throughout the 1990s, manufacturers produced and marketed non-alcoholic beverages that tasted like the quality beer or wine they wanted to imitate. They were able to maintain a niche market, that represented about 1 percent of U.S. beer and wine sales.

The legal definition for non-alcoholic beer and wine indicated a beverage containing less than 0.5 percent alcohol by volume. A glass of orange juice, due to natural fermentation, has 0.2 to 0.5 percent alcohol. By comparison, most light beers have 1.9 percent to 4 percent alcohol by volume. Regular beers contain 4 percent alcohol on average. Imported beers might contain up to 7 percent. Typical wines range from 10 percent to 14 percent alcohol by volume.

Brewers created non-alcoholic beer by utilizing two different processes. One involved removing alcohol from standard beer after brewing using heat or vacuum distillation. The other stopped fermentation before the alcohol content went over 0.5 percent. Some critics warned that the trace amount of alcohol in non-alcoholic beer or wine could trigger a recovering alcoholic into a relapse. Yet according to a drug prevention source, a 150 pound man would have to consume 30, 12-ounce non-alcoholic beers in one hour to get a blood-alcohol concentration of 0.10 percent.

ORGANIZATION AND STRUCTURE

Most non-alcoholic beer sold in the United States comes from the four biggest American brewers: Anheuser-Busch Companies Inc., with O'Doul's; Miller Brewing Company, with Sharp's; Adolph Coors Company, with Coors Cutter; and The Stroh Brewery Company with Stroh's. The import market is small. This market includes non-alcoholic brews from the following well-known beer exporters: Canada's Excel; England's Bass Barbican NA, and Kaliber NA; Germany's Clausthaler NA, and Haake-Beck NA; Holland's Buckler NA; the Philippines' San Miguel NA; and, Switzerland's Moussy NA. The smaller non-alcoholic wine market appears to have only two notable firms. One is Ariel Vineyards of Napa, California, which specializes in de-alcoholized wine exclusively. The other is Sutter Home Winery, Inc. of St. Helena, California, the nation's fourth largest vintner. Sutter primarily makes regular wines but also offers a non-alcoholic line under the label of Sutter Home Fre.

Manufacturers initially sell non-alcoholic beer and wine through beer and wine wholesalers and distributors. From that point, liquor stores, convenience stores, health food outlets, and supermarkets sell these products to consumers. Some retailers display the non-alcoholic products adjacent to their regular beer and wine. Others place them with soft drinks or fruit juices.

Some critics charged that brewers created non-alcoholic products to acclimate children to the taste of beer, as well as to create brand loyalty. One critic went further to say that marketing non-alcoholic beers was similar to marketing candy cigarettes. This represented a poor model for children to follow. Others criticized non-alcoholic brews as a ploy to allow beer makers to advertise their brand names in situations where beer advertising was banned. The beverage industry countered by saying it was creating another option for those abstaining under certain circumstances, and for health-conscious beer drinkers. Because non-alcoholic brews closely resemble alcoholic beer, some retail chains and individual stores restrict sales to people over 21, although no law requires it. One circumstance that occurred at a major manufacturing plant in Ohio, for instance, in the mid-1990s created a flap among union workers and management. The company charged that a worker was violating a policy of no alcohol in the workplace when he was caught drinking a non-alcoholic beer on a work break. The worker had no idea that the product did contain some alcohol, even if it was a minuscule amount. The union and the company settled the dispute, and the worker was able to retain employment. Such complications gave cause to many critics concerns. Other critics accused brewers of profiteering since they priced their products as high as their alcoholic lines, even though the non-alcoholic products carried no excise taxes.

NON-ALCOHOLIC HOME BREWING

Though the non-alcoholic beer industry continued to grow in the 1990s, the large breweries dominated the market. While specialty breweries had grown much faster than the beer industry overall in the 1990s, these smaller companies did not make significant amounts of non-alcoholic beers. So many drinkers who preferred the taste of special recipe micro-brewed beer turned to creating their own at home. Available kits allowed the home brewer to have stout, porter, or flavored beer, without the alcohol.

With no fancy equipment and only one or two extra steps, the latest masterpiece from the home brewer could be made a non-alcoholic product. Home brewers who rendered their beer non-alcoholic began to share their recipes over the World Wide Web, and to develop a small but faithful following as well. The beer-making process follows the normal procedure right up to the fermentation stage, the point at which the beer gained its alcoholic content. At this stage, the home brewer has several options. The cheapest method is merely dilution with water. A brew that is diluted 50:50 with water cuts the alcohol content to approximately roughly in half to only 1.5 percent. The chief complaint for this process is that the beer tastes too watery.

The most popular form of removing the alcohol from the beer seems to be cooking it. By placing the beer into a large pot and allowing the liquid brew to reach a temperature of 180 degrees, the alcohol is cooked away. The longer it is left in the oven, the more alcohol is cooked out. The true alcohol level, depending on how long it is cooked, usually goes down to less than 1 percent. This is slightly above the legal .5 percent limit for what is considered non-alcoholic.

The drawback to this method is that the beer tastes as if it has been cooked. Home brewers agree that, once bottled and given a few weeks to age, the cooked taste does evaporate. The issue that emerges with this process is that once cooked, the yeast used to carbonate the beer is also cooked away. The yeast is added again during the cooling stage to carbonate the flat beer naturally. When finished, the brewer has a totally unique product.

BACKGROUND AND DEVELOPMENT

The popularity of non-alcoholic beer and wine rose in America in the 1980s. But it was not the first time Americans drank such products. During Prohibition, enacted by law of the U.S. Congress from 1920 until it was lifted in 1933, many major American breweries survived by making malt syrups and near-beers, which qualified as non-alcoholic. When Prohibition ended, U.S. brewers roared back into production. Near-beer almost disappeared from the market. During the late 1980s and early 1990s, near-beer appeared again, repackaged as an upscale refresher for adults. Some industry analysts wondered what came first: consumer desire for a non-alcoholic beer; or, brewers buying ad space to tell consumers they desired the product. Some analysts speculated non-alcoholic beer was a logical step after light beer, with its lighter taste and lowered alcohol content. It gained popularity. Miller Brewing Co. was the first major U.S. brewer to offer a non-alcoholic brand when it launched Sharp's in 1989. Anheuser-Busch followed in 1990 with O'Doul's non-alcoholic beer. Other competitors followed the trend throughout the early1990s.

Beginning in 1994, brewers advertised heavily. This created a recognizable image for their non-alcoholic labels. That year, marketers targeted health-conscious consumers. Before this, they targeted beer lovers who abstained in certain situations. By going after health-conscious consumers, non-alcoholic beer marketers competed for an audience that normally consumed other beverages between activities, such as iced teas, bottled water, fruit juices, or sports drinks. For instance, Anheuser-Busch introduced its "Cool Down with O'Doul's" campaign in 1994. Miller's ran ads featuring cold, sweaty bottles of Sharp's, edited with footage of people playing softball, basketball, and football. The German non-alcoholic beer Haake Beck ran an aggressive campaign in Colorado that same year, partnered with a Denver fitness center. The campaign featured cholesterol screenings, 10K runs, bike races, and Haake Beck samplings. The ads featured fit, attractive, young people to back up what was termed, "The Haake Beck Body" promotion. Market research later showed the campaign raised sales of Haake Beck 600 percent.

CURRENT CONDITIONS

Non-alcoholic beer sales were predicted to rise 2 to 3 percent in 1997, according to Matthew Hein, director of statistical and information services for the Beer Institute, a brewing trade group. Domestic sales were predicted to rise 0.5 to 1.5 percent, and soft drinks were predicted to increase by 3.5 percent. Hein also reported that beer's share of total beverage consumption fell in 1995 against competition from bottled water and soft drinks. According to an article by Tara Parker-Pope, based in London, for *The Wall Street Journal,* in July of 1995, "Despite heavy promotion and a slew of new brands, the market for no-alcohol and low-alcohol beers has lost its kick. In nearly every European market, consumption has fallen dramatically in the past two years, forcing several brewers to discontinue brands, drop advertising campaigns and scale back production." Industry analysts disagreed if non-alcoholic beverages would grow appreciably past the current level of 1 percent of the U.S. beer market. According to another industry commentator, non-alcoholic beer sales peaked in 1990 and failed to grow between 1991 and 1997. According to the Consumer Price Index for 1997, non-alcoholic beverages posted the second highest hike in prices, after pork, 3.7 percent. This trend possibly had more to do with the introduction of more blended juices and teas than increases in the prices of non-alcoholic beers and wines.

In a *Milwaukee Journal Sentinel* article, an Anheuser-Busch and Miller distributor reported non-alcoholic beer sales of about 1 percent total, while a Stroh's distributor reported 2 percent of sales coming from non-alcoholic brews, with one-half of those represented by Old Milwaukee NA. Fara Warner reported in *The Wall Street Journal,* in May of 1995 that sales of nonalcoholic brews slumped about 13 percent in

1994, to two million barrels. Marketers were trying to "woo drinkers back to the slumping category with new advertising campaigns, reformulation and giveaways of the brews at events like bass-fishing tournaments." According to industry sources, Anheuser-Busch spent the most on advertising of any brewer to promote its non-alcoholic label. Anheuser-Busch spent $10.3 million in 1994 for O'Doul's promotions, but only $3.1 million promoting it in 1995. As of late 1996, O'-Doul's appeared to be the top-selling non-alcoholic brew. Sharp's was the next best seller.

The most varied products were in the non-alcoholic wine category, since there were as many potential varieties of non-alcoholic wine as regular varieties. For instance, Sutter Home Vineyards produced the following types of non-alcoholic wines: White Zinfandel, Chardonnay, Spumante, and Sparkling Brut. For the winter of 1996 and 1997, Sutter Home introduced a complete point-of-purchase display system for retailers of "Sutter Home Fre Alcohol Free Entertaining Center." Sutter Home also offered mail-in or instant coupons to entice potential new customers. The company reported a 28 percent growth for the category in 1995 and claimed to have 50 percent of the non-alcoholic wine market in 1996.

INDUSTRY LEADERS

In 1998, Anheuser-Busch of St. Louis, Missouri was the world's largest brewery and had the best-selling non-alcoholic beer, O'Doul's. The company had 1998 annual sales of $11.2 billion and 23,344 employees. Anheuser-Busch's best-known alcoholic beers included: Budweiser, Bud Light, Busch, and Michelob. The second best-selling non-alcoholic beer in 1998 was Sharp's from Miller. Miller, of Milwaukee, Wisconsin, was owned by Philip Morris Company. In 1998 annual Miller beer sales were $4.1 billion. Philip Morris also owned 20 percent of Molson Breweries of Canada, and 100 percent of Molson's U.S. brewing operations. The Molson Companies Limited of Toronto, Ontario, was Canada's leading brewer with 1998 sales of $1.09 billion and 4,560 employees. Molson produced the non-alcoholic beer Excel through its Molson Breweries division, a joint venture shared with Miller and Australia's Foster's beer.

The third-largest U.S. brewer was Adolph Coors of Golden, Colorado, with 1998 annual sales of $1.9 billion and 5,800 employees. Coors' non-alcoholic brew was Coors Cutter. The fourth-largest U.S. brewer was Stroh Brewery of Detroit, Michigan, which was acquired in 1999 by Miller. The company made

Stroh's NA and also acquired Kingsbury Non-Alcoholic beer after buying out G. Heileman Brewing Co. of La Crosse, Wisconsin. Miller's acquisition of Stroh's and other such large-scale purchases of the smaller breweries were expected to affect sales of all products into the next century. Pabst of Milwaukee, Wisconsin, also bought by Miller in 1999, made non-alcoholic versions of Pabst and Hamm's beer. A much smaller U.S. brewery, Saranac-Matt Brewing Co. of Utica, New York, made the first non-alcoholic, dark microbrew, Black Forest NA. Additionally, one major foreign brewery, Guinness PLC of London, England, participated in the industry. Guinness had 1998 annual sales of $5.37 billion and 13,494 employees. Though best known for its Guinness stout and Harp lager, the company also produced the non-alcoholic beer, Kaliber.

One wine industry leader in the late 1990s was Ariel Vineyards, which calls itself "the world's largest producer of award-winning premium non-alcoholic wine." Ariel makes its wines from premium varietal grapes from Sonoma, Paso Robles, Napa Valley, and Monterey. The company caused a shock in 1986 when it won a medal against wines with alcohol in a blind taste test. Ariel continued to win medals for its wines throughout the 1980s and 1990s, although the wines mainly competed in non-alcoholic wine categories. Ariel's closest competitor, Sutter Home, did not introduce non-alcoholic wines until 1992. By 1999, Ariel had an array of de-alcoholized wines on the market, including Blanc, a blend of Chenin Blanc, Riesling, Muscat Canelli, Gewurztraminer, and Johannesburg Riesling; Rouge, a blend of barrel aged Zinfandel and Pinot Noir; Chardonnay; Cabernet Sauvignon; White Zinfandel; and Johannesburg Riesling. Ariel markets products in the United States, Canada, in several European countries including Finland and Iceland, in Japan, Australia and New Zealand, and in the Caribbean.

In addition, Ariel Vineyards received an important celebrity endorsement during the 1990s,which may have given them credibility with West Coast consumers, from television chef Graham Kerr, the former host of the "Galloping Gourmet," television series of the 1970s. He cooked with, and drank Ariel's de-alcoholized wines on his syndicated cooking show in the 1990s. A traffic accident he and his family suffered in the later 1970s, along with increasing health concerns due to heart trouble caused Kerr to re-think his approach to cooking and eating. As a "born-again Christian" Kerr and his wife became advocates of heart healthy cooking, as well as the decision against consumption of alcohol. Also, the influential *Univer-sity of California at Berkley Wellness Letter* praised non-alcoholic wines, specifically Ariel's, as a safe source of antioxidant compounds, which may reduce the chance of heart disease. The *Wellness Letter* also praised the nutritional benefits of non-alcoholic wine because "removing the alcohol eliminates many" empty calories. Non-alcoholic wines were reported to have less than one-third the calories of regular wine, about 20 to 30 in five ounces, versus the usual 100.

AMERICA AND THE WORLD

Throughout the 1990s, the United States was the only nation with a major share of the premium non-alcoholic beverage market, according to an industry market analysis firm. Some analysts also believed the foreign market for American non-alcoholic brews could grow. Statistics showed U.S. exports grew 20 percent between 1994 and 1995 for non-alcoholic beer to $8.7 million, an 800 percent increase from the $1.1 million exported in 1991. This was likely due to foreign fascination with U.S. brand names, stricter drunk driving laws, or growing acceptance of non-alcoholic beers in Muslim countries, where full-strength beer was usually forbidden for religious reasons.

The Wall Street Journal reported in December of 1995 that sales of nonalcoholic beers in Saudi Arabia, for instance, grew at a double-digit rate from 1992 to 1995. The 250,000 barrels consumed there was only a fraction of the estimated 187 million barrels reportedly consumed in the United States. But at that time when beer sales in Europe and America were not growing, such a significant increase in sales as those in the Middle East were considered impressive. The difficulty in Muslim countries was in advertising. In her article Tara Parker-Pope said that, "To avoid any association with beer, the nonalcoholic brands are called malt beverages. With no ads for malt-beverages products allowed, nonalcoholic beer can only be marketed through special promotions, contests and flashy store displays..." Understanding the audience in these countries was a specific problem. "Getting to know your audience is even harder if your product appeals to women, brewers say," reported Parker-Pope. "Sales of Bass' Barbican with Lemon malt beverage are booming in Saudi Arabia, and company officials suspect it's women who like it best," said Huw Williams, sales director for Bass Beers Worldwide. "But in a country where the women are covered head-to-toe, and they can't drive, and they can't speak to you on the street, we can't be sure," he added, according to Parker-Pope.

In the mid-1990s, Iran had at least one known brewery. This plant produced two million bottles of non-alcoholic beer per year for export to other Muslim nations. The revolutionary government seized the brewery in 1979, after the Shah's overthrow. Throughout the 1990s it was run as a government-backed foundation. In Pakistan, the Murree Brewery Co. made regular and non-alcoholic beer, despite a government ban on alcohol. The brewery was forbidden to advertise or run more than two eight-hour shifts in a day. However, enough Pakistanis consumed beer for the brewery to make profits of 23.1 million rupees, or $770,000, in 1993. Some analysts believed American breweries would have a definite advantage against such small competitors if Muslim markets would open to them further.

Spain also entered the non-alcoholic beverages market with Whissin, an abbreviation of "whiskey sin [without] alcohol." Espadafor, a family-owned firm in Granada, Spain, spent more than two years researching and developing this whiskey substitute. A new spirit of health consciousness and awareness of dangers of mixing drinking and driving drove sales of non-alcoholic beers and wines in Spain upward, as well. Espadafor was working on developing rum without alcohol, into the late 1990s, according to Jane Walker in the *Irish Times.*

RESEARCH AND TECHNOLOGY

Industry firms used competing technologies to remove alcohol, or keep it from forming in their premium beverages. Some analysts cite Ariel Vineyards' de-alcoholization process as a superior technology because it made Ariel products taste as if it contained alcohol, with a superior rating. While competitors removed alcohol from wine using a heated evaporation process, Ariel used a patented cold ultra-filtration/reverse osmosis process. According to company literature, Ariel pumped the wine into a processing tank and it flowed along a double membrane to extract water and alcohol. What was left over was a thick wine concentrate that was returned to the storage tank and recycled several times. After this, upon adding water,

they reconstitute it into a virtually alcohol-free beverage that tastes like a regular wine without the bite of alcohol.

To make Whissin, Espadafor blended sugar, barley, maize, and wheat, heated and pasteurized this blend using a method that prevented the sugars from fermenting into alcohol. Then the company added "secret aromas" to give Whissin the flavor of whiskey.

FURTHER READING

"Beer Sales Likely To Grow 0.5 Percent To 1.5 Percent This Year." *Kane's Beverage Week,* 23 September 1996.

Causey, James E. "Stagnant Sales May Mean End of Non-Alcoholic Beer Trend." *Knight-Ridder/Tribune Business News,* 23 December 1996.

"Iran To Export Non-Alcoholic Beer To Islamic Countries." *Food & Drink Daily,* 4 October 1994.

MacLeod, Helen R. "Non-Alcoholic Beer a Potent Export Brew." *Journal of Commerce and Commercial,* 14 May 1996.

"Pakistan's Murree Beer Plant Battles Prejudice." *Food & Drink Daily,* 18 July 1994.

Parker-Pope, Tara. "Brewers Dismayed as Drinkers Decide that Suds Are a Dud without Alcohol." *Wall Street Journal,* 6 July 1995.

———. "Non-Alcoholic Beer Hits the Spot in Mideast." *Wall Street Journal,* 6 December 1995.

"The Price Was Right." *Progressive Grocer,* 1 April 1998.

Scarpa, James. "Marketing Exercise. Non-Alcoholic Beverages." *Restaurant Business Magazine,* 20 January 1994.

"U.S. Is Biggest Low/Non Alcohol Beer Market." *Beverage Industry,* 22 November 1996.

Walker, Jane. "Substitute Takes the Punch out of Whiskey." *Irish Times,* 7 February 1998.

Warner, Fara. "Ads Try to Lift Ailing Non-Alcoholic Beers." *Wall Street Journal,* 11 May 1995.

"Wellness Made Easy." *University of California at Berkley Wellness Letter,* January 1997.

—Dave Fagan,
updated by Laura Lawrie and Jane E. Spear

PRINTERS AND
PRINTER ACCESSORIES

With the explosion of the home and office computer markets in the 1980s and 1990s, consumer demand soared above its previous level. Since more people started relying on computers, the need for computer peripherals and components, such as printers and printer cartridges, also increased. As printers became more prominent, their prices went down. Lee Gomes reports in *The Wall Street Journal* that printers costing around $500 in 1995 sold for about $200 in 1996. By 1998 low-end color inkjet printers were sold at a street prices under $100. However, ink and toner cartridges provide printer manufacturers with a continuous source of revenue, giving manufacturers an incentive to sell their products at lower prices.

While manufacturers produce a number of different types of computer printers, the inkjet and laser printers dominated the market in the mid-to-late 1990s. A few years after its introduction, the inkjet printer quickly became the industry's best-selling printer technology—especially for home use—because of its price, functionality, and features.

A rapid expansion in business computer networks and the rapid rise of Internet technology in the late 1990s inspired interest in shared printer technology. Printers multiplied rapidly throughout offices as new print server hardware eliminated the need for PC-controlled printing devices. Other new technology inspired software systems that promised to enable remote printing across the Internet.

According to the U.S. Census Bureau, operations manufacturing peripherals such as printers, fax machines, and scanners garnered $16.5 billion in revenues in 1995, a $2-billion increase over 1994 sales

and more than $3 billion over 1992 sales. The Bureau also reports that 787 operations produced peripherals including printers in 1994. These operations employed 55,601 workers and about 50 percent of them maintained a staff of 1 to 10 people.

ORGANIZATION AND STRUCTURE

The computer printer industry includes three key technologies: the dot-matrix, inkjet, and laser printers. However, with superior quality offered by the inkjet and laser printers and with their falling prices, consumer demand for dot-matrix printers plummeted in the early 1990s, leaving the model nearly defunct.

A host of factors, such as print quality, speed, and printer capability, affect the cost of a printer. Measured horizontally and vertically, the number of dots per inch (dpi) determines the print quality or resolution. The industry standard in the mid-1990s was 300 by 300 dpi. However, some printers have more advanced capabilities allowing them to print 400, 600, even over 1000 dpi. Printers capable of producing higher dpi ratios are better suited for printing graphics and images. Rated by pages per minute (ppm), inkjet printers can churn out 1 to 3 text pages per minute, whereas laser printers can print 4 to 8 text pages per minute. For graphics and images, inkjets take substantially longer and laser printers require some extra time. Most printers in the mid-to-late 1990s could print on paper, labels, and envelopes.

Dot-matrix printers originally led the computer printer market, but in the 1990s they verged on extinction and were hard to find. The once industry-standard dot-matrix printer lost its appeal in the 1990s because its technology failed to advance as the technologies of competing printers forged ahead by providing users with increased capabilities and enhanced print jobs. Dot-matrix technology employs some basic typewriter principles: the print head strikes a ribbon making contact with the paper to print characters. Of the computer printers, the dot-matrix is the cheapest and easiest to care for; however, the speed and print quality of dot-matrix printers lags far behind competing printer technologies spurring on its demise. Moreover, dot-matrix printers generate a lot of noise while printing, in contrast to the other two kinds. Replacement ribbons ran about $10 to $40 in 1999.

Phillip Robinson explains in the *San Diego Union-Tribune* that monochrome laser printers function in a similar way as copying machines, relying on the same technology. A set of rollers advance the paper through the printer and the printer dispenses toner to printed areas of the paper and uses heat to permanently bond it to the paper. This system creates a fast, reliable, and flexible printer with high quality resolution. Furthermore, laser printers can hold more sheets of paper than competing models and print on both sides of the paper. However, they require a new toner cartridge about every 2,000 to 5,000 sheets of paper. Toner cost from $10 to $400, depending on the printer, in 1998.

Inkjet printers, on the other hand, work by funneling ink through small nozzles in the printer head where it makes contact with the paper, according to Jon Pepper in *Nation's Business*. The inkjet printer gradually evolved with its adoption of smaller and smaller nozzles since its inception, allowing it to produce enhanced quality print jobs. Technological advances also made the mid-1990s inkjet printer a viable alternative to the laser printer, not only for home use, but also for office use. In the mid-1990s, the industry-standard inkjet printer included color and monochrome capabilities and contained two ink cartridges. The color cartridges include three base colors—red, yellow, and blue—to help produce photorealistic print jobs. These printers have a separate black cartridge for text documents; however, some economy models do not contain a separate black cartridge and produce a lackluster black by mixing the colored ink. Inkjet printers need new ink cartridges about every 500 to 1,000 sheets of paper. The cost of cartridges ranged from $10 and $200 in 1999. In addition, most inkjet printers require special coated paper to produce optimal outputs, which ran between $5 and $20 per ream in the late 1990s. Inkjets also work best with special overhead transparency film, which cost between $15 and $30. Lasers, however, still seemed to

have the advantage, as the cost per page was lower for lasers than for inkjet printers in the late 1990s.

Besides these standard technologies, a number of specialty printers exist. These specialty models largely serve the image-arts sector. Jon Pepper argues that wax thermal transfer printers produce high quality overhead projection transparencies, but they have limited capabilities for general and business-related printing needs. Pepper also notes that a related printer, the dye sublimation printer, creates some of the most compelling graphic images by injecting the ink in variously sized dots and allowing the colors to bleed together to yield more realistic images. Therefore, these printers offer a superb option for anyone needing to print photographs, advertisements, and otherwise graphically intense documents. A new line of inkjet printers, phase-change inkjet printers, also hit the market in the 1990s, providing a faster inkjet solution for color printing. Averaging about four pages per minute, the phase-change printer works by melting ink sticks and spraying the molten form on to the paper where it becomes solid again.

The North American Graphic Arts Suppliers Association (NAGASA) serves the industry by linking manufacturers, retailers, and users of computer printers designed for the graphics-arts market. The NAGASA's members include printer industry behemoth Hewlett-Packard. The association strives to enhance its member's distribution channels, reducing their costs, and improving their business. The NAGASA also provides a non-commercial forum for discussing matters relevant to the graphics-arts and printing-related industries and encourages research to help advance printer technology.

CURRENT CONDITIONS

With about a 30 to 40 percent household-market penetration of computers, the sales of computer printers also sprang up in the mid-1990s. Despite stagnating computer sales, the printer industry experienced brisk sales in the mid-1990s, constituting one of the hottest products in the computer industry. Given the increased affordability and demand for color printers, most manufacturers started offering only color-capable inkjet printers in 1996. Since printer manufacturers started selling printers at greatly reduced costs with low profit margins, they began to rely more on the sales of inkjet and toner cartridges to bolster their revenues. Printer makers mark up these after accessories by as much as 70 percent, according to

Lee Gomes in *The Wall Street Journal.* Some industry observers expect worldwide sales of printer accessories to climb to $18 billion by the year 2001.

According to John Roberts and Al Senia in *Computer Reseller News,* in a survey by CRN Inside Spending, companies were likely to spend less on printers in 1998 compared with 1997. This was due to a sharp drop in prices expected in 1998. Color inkjets were very popular with small (57 percent of those surveyed, up from 37 percent in 1997) and mid-sized companies (85 percent, up from 70 percent in 1997). Monochrome inkjets saw a decrease in use in 1998 in large corporations, 61 percent in 1998 as opposed to 73 percent in 1997, and in mid-sized companies (66 percent, down from 68 percent in 1997). In small companies, however, the use of black-and-white inkjets was unchanged, at 46 percent.

Fortified by low prices, printer manufacturers actively began targeting home users, especially families and children in the mid-1990s. Hewlett-Packard, for example, marketed its DeskJet 682C to children by bundling the CD-ROM-based "Mickey and Friends Print Studio" project kit, which includes 200 Disney images such as those of Mickey Mouse, Donald Duck, and Pluto for creating customized calendars, posters, banners, name tags, and diary pages, according to Stephen Manes in *The New York Times.* Other companies offer similar packages: Canon's printers include software from Hallmark for creating cards as well as software from Crayola for arts-and-crafts projects.

INKJET PRINTERS

In 1999, inkjet printers typically cost between $90 and $500, while laser printers cost between $350 and $1,000, though higher-end versions of both models carried a much higher price tag. The average inkjet printer cost less than $200 in 1999, a more than 50-percent drop in price since 1993 (the time when they debuted), fueling the heightened demand for them.

Despite a few perennial problems and stigmas associated with inkjet printers—especially lower-end ones—such as having smudgeable text and producing inferior documents, lower prices and enhanced features have made inkjet printers popular for general home and business printing needs. Joe Ward reports in *USA Today* that Lyra Research projected that inkjet sales would increase from 24 million (79 percent of all computer sales) in 1997 to over 46 million (84 percent) in 2001. Conversely, sales of personal laser printers were expected to decrease from 4.6 million (16 percent of all computer sales) in 1997 to 3.4 million (6 percent) in 2001. Multifunction printers, such

as Hewlett-Packard's mopier, were expected to overtake sales of personal laser printers from 1997 to 2001, increasing from 5 percent to 10 percent of all computer sales.

The inkjet printers of 1999 allowed greater dpi ratios—some even generated over 1,400 dots per inch, which made them strong competitors in the printer market. These new lines of inkjet printers provide quality and speed comparable to laser printers, especially to lower-end laser printers. Furthermore, inkjet manufacturers developed special color ink cartridges to let users produce graphic print jobs with outstanding quality, as well as ink that allows users to print on ordinary copy paper.

OFFICE PRINTER MODELS AND TECHNOLOGY

Because of the high cost of printers—especially laser printers—many companies and organizations cannot afford to supply each computer user with a printer. Yet according to *Managing Office Technology,* printers account for as much as 60 percent of the traffic on the network. Therefore, software developers, as well as businesses and organizations, began to explore printer networking options in the 1980s and especially in the 1990s. With a central controlling system, a company or organization can link a number of computers to only 3 or 4 printers. Manufacturers, including Hewlett-Packard, developed laser printers that can be directly connected to local area network (LAN) ports to function as a LAN print station, according to Erik Delfino in *Online.* Prior to this technology, companies had to attach LAN printers to a special computer connected to the LAN, whereas with these new printers, companies can dispense with the special computer and attach the printers directly to the LAN. Moreover, companies have developed radio transmitters that allow mobile computer users to print documents via radio transmission. With transmitter kits, businesses, schools, hospitals, etc. can connect all computer users to a print station. These transmitter kits ran about $239 in the mid-1990s. Also new to the market, in response to rising need for printer access, peer-to-peer printing services became a common enhancement to the new print server technology. Peer-to-peer printing services conserve precious network resources by allowing users to bypass network servers altogether and transmit print jobs directly to the print servers.

Through advancements in networking technology during the 1990s, the local area networks evolved into wide area networks (WANs) that spanned buildings and even geographical locations. Through enterprise networking technology multiple distinct WANs could function as one giant network. Internet technology inspired the business-centric intranet environment, replete with private Web server technology, and many businesses maintain Internet connections in addition to private networks. Printer technology advanced in step with every network advance, and before the end of the decade Internet-based printer technology emerged. The Internet Engineering Task Force (IETF) quickly established a Printer Working Group (PWG), assigned to the task of defining an Internet Printing Protocol (IPP) for Web-based printer communication and security. Even pending the approval of formal protocol standards, print-server manufacturers and software developers moved in to capitalize on the new market. In the absence of a protocol Osicom Technologies and Castelle rushed to incorporate Web-based printing into their products by means of common e-mail protocols. Hewlett-Packard in collaboration with Microsoft developed a proprietary Internet Printing Protocol and then came forward late in 1998 with the HP JetDirect 500X Internet print server, priced at under $500 for Token Ring. Unlike fax technology, Web-based printing supports the transmission of finished, full color documents to remote printers, outside the limitations of the corporate intranet.

In the 1990s, printer manufacturers also introduced multi-capability computer peripherals. Canon Computer Systems refers to its models as "convertibles," according to Melissa J. Perenson in *PC Magazine*. Multi-capability peripherals usually include printer, copier, scanner, and fax faculties. Instead of purchasing all the individual components—which could run

thousands of dollars—computer users, in particular those with limited budgets, could invest in convertible peripherals, which cost only about $600 in 1997. Yet lower priced multi-task peripherals just contain inkjet printers, so users seeking higher-end functionality still may have to purchase separate components.

Another permutation of the multifunction peripheral is the mopier, a document server with fax, laser printer, and copier capabilities. Coined by Hewlett-Packard, "mopier" refers to multiple print original printers that allow network users to print multiple copies of a document. In the mid-1990s, the mopier challenged the photocopier industry. Designed for durability and heavy printing loads, the mopier can replace the need for a printer in a network printer environment where all documents requiring copying are computer generated. *Purchasing* reports that some analysts predict that the industry may sell as many as 200,000 mopiers by the year 2000.

Xerox Corporation, sensing that it needed to become a "player" in the printer/copier market, launched several new products in mid-1998, including network laser printers, color inkjet printers, replacement cartridges for Hewlett-Packard's laser printers, and digital copiers. In response to blurred distinction between printer/fax/copier functions, Xerox developed multifunction copiers in direct competition to multifunction printers such as the mopier. Xerox further teamed with Lotus Development Corporation and announced in 1998 a breakthrough software technology that supports remote Internet-based multi-function printer capabilities by means of the standard office copy machine. The prototype system was designed to accept document input through the office copy machine and transmit the image through the World Wide Web server for output in the Lotus Notes e-mail format. Xerox further indicated that the system could provide OCR functions to convert documents transmitted from the copy machine into live text for further word processing on the receiving end. Observers expressed reservation over the new Xerox copier technologies, pending further testing. By early 1999 Xerox announced the release of five new multi-function Work-Centre devices targeted to the small office/home office (SOHO) market.

INKJET CARTRIDGES

With the escalating demand for inkjet printers, the consumption of inkjet cartridges soared because users usually must replace the cartridges with every ream of paper they go through. Consequently, users dispose of millions of inkjet cartridges per year, fueling concern from environmentalists. Ink cartridge makers tend to

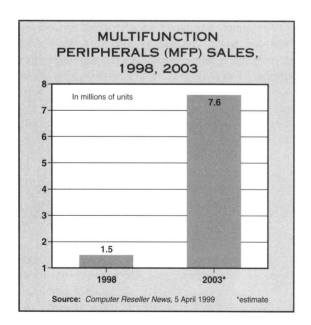

MULTIFUNCTION
PERIPHERALS (MFP) SALES,
1998, 2003

In millions of units

7.6

1.5

1998   2003*

Source: *Computer Reseller News,* 5 April 1999   *estimate

design their products so they cannot be refilled; however, some operations recycle the cartridges by refilling them. Companies such as Hard Copy of Longmont, Colorado, can successfully refill most inkjet cartridges and then sell them for about half the price of new ones. In addition, companies offer pick and delivery amenities, making their services more affordable and convenient than the traditional retail ink cartridge services. Cartridges make up a key aftermarket source of revenue for printer makers, which helps them keep the prices of the actual hardware low. Leading industry presence Hewlett-Packard Co. alone earned $3.4 billion from sales of inkjet and laser toner cartridges, according to Lee Gomes in *The Wall Street Journal.*

INDUSTRY LEADERS

Hewlett-Packard Co. (HP) led the printer industry in 1998 with its popular laser and inkjet printers. Deriving 80 percent of its revenues from computer system and computer peripheral sales, HP constitutes a computer industry powerhouse. Lewis E. Platt headed the company as CEO and HP posted sales of $47.1 billion in 1998. Employing 124,600 workers in 1998, the company provided the electronics market with leading products since the 1930s, when HP manufactured oscillators. The company designs its printers to meet the needs of a diverse range of users—from home computing to workgroup use—and its core printer lines include the LaserJet 6, the LaserJet 5, the Color LaserJet, the DeskJet 300, the DeskJet 400, the DeskJet 600, the DeskJet 1000, and the DeskJet 6000 series. Moreover, HP has been at the forefront of many of the industry's technological advances.

Epson America Inc., a division of Seiko Epson Corp., was the world's second leading printer producer in the mid-1990s. The Japanese company provides a host of state-of-the-art laser, inkjet, and dot matrix printers including the Stylus Color 800, Stylus Color 1520, Stylus Color 3000, Stylus Photo, EPL-N1200, EPL-N2000, LQ-870, and LQ-670. In 1998, Reijiro Hattori served as the company's chairman and Epson employed 31,000 workers around the world. With the stiff demand for computer printers in the 1990s, the company's sales climbed dramatically from 1992, cresting at $6.1 billion in 1998. Over 50 percent of the company's sales derive from printers and other computer components, which Epson has manufactured since 1982.

An International Business Machines Corp. (IBM) spinoff, Lexmark increased its hold on the computer

Trends | **NO DARKROOM NO COMPUTER**

Photography enthusiasts who are eager to try one of the new digital cameras, but who dislike the notion of working with a computer, have an alternate option. Early in 1999 Sony introduced the FVP-1 Mavica Photo Printer. The Mavica, a new concept in printing, creates 3-7/8 by 5-1/2-inch photographic images from 3.5-inch floppy disk. The process is as simple as it sounds—pop a floppy disk into a compatible camera; take one or more pictures. Pop out the floppy disk; place it into the printer and print the image. The Mavica hardware includes a self-contained floppy disk drive. An s-video outlet on the printer supports optional direct connection to a television or video camera via cable. The printer cannot and will not connect to a desktop computer.

The printer employs dye sublimation transfer technology to create images of 1.41 million pixels, an excellent level of detail, depending on the resolution at which the picture was taken. An easy-to-install ink ribbon cartridge fuels the printing mechanism. For brave-hearts who would save, edit, or otherwise enhance the images before or after printing, a Windows-based software bundle comes with the printer hardware. Sony's FVP-1 Mavica Photo Printer sells for a street price of well under $500. It weighs seven pounds and prints a photo in less than three minutes. Mavica is designed for compatibility with the Mavica FD81 camera.

printer market in the 1990s, becoming one of the key players in the industry. Deriving three quarters of its sales from computer printers and related wares, Lexmark excels in offering quality printers at competitive prices. Since Lexmark manufactures all of its printer components, the company can sell its products at a lower price than other printer markers. Lexmark produces all of the standard technologies: laser, inkjet, and dot-matrix printers. Besides its printers, Lexmark manufactures toner cartridges, inkjet cartridges, coated paper, and connection cables. In 1998, Marvin L. Mann led the company as CEO and in 1998 Lexmark garnered $3.0 billion in sales, up 2.1 percent from 1997. In addition, the company employed 8,800 workers.

Canon Inc. provides a wide range of laser and inkjet printers. Based in Japan, Canon trails only Hewlett-Packard in laser color printers sales. In 1997, Fujio Mitarai was the company's CEO and the company brought in $24.4 billion in revenues, climbing nearly 15 percent from 1997. The company also employed 78,767 workers. Canon's core printers include the BJC-240 series, an affordable line of color inkjet printers; the BJC-620 series, a higher-end color inkjet printer; Multipass C2500, a convertible printer with fax, copier, scanner, and printer capabilities; and the LBP-465, a mid-range laser printer featuring 600 dpi resolution. Canon's products also emphasize new technology. Its inkjet printers, for example, rely on Bubble Jet technology, which allows them to print on cotton, silk, as well as leather. Moreover, Canon promotes printer cartridge recycling.

Other important computer printer manufacturers that produce inkjet, laser, dot-matrix, and specialty printers include Digital Equipment Corp. with sales of $13 billion; Texas Instruments Inc., which posted revenues of $8.5 billion; Brother International Corp.; Panasonic, a division of Matsushita, a leading Japanese electronics manufacturer; and Okidata Inc., a U.S.-based subsidiary of Oki Electric Industry Co., Ltd. of Japan. The Xerox Corporation's digital copiers and other printing products accounted for 36 percent of its $19.4 billion in revenue in 1998, and the company expected to increase their market share by the turn of the century.

RESEARCH AND TECHNOLOGY

In 1996, Oberg Industries Inc. began using a new stamping technique for producing complex metal components of computer printers, according to Richard J. Babyak in *Appliance Manufacturer.* Oberg expects the new stamping process to drastically cut costs of production and improve the overall design of the components. This process costs less because creating parts through stamping is cheaper than creating them through metal injection molding or pulverized metal fabrication—the competing methods. Printer manufacturers have used these parts as base yokes and armature in laser and dot-matrix printers.

Furthermore, Hewlett-Packard led a campaign in 1997 to make computer peripheral connections to local area networks (LANs), wide area networks (WANs), and to the Internet entirely seamless and independent of hardware and operating systems. HP's JetSend allows users to transmit text and images to peripherals without needing to know the configurations of the hardware—whether it has a Windows 95, Windows NT, or a Mac O/S operating system. This technology promises to help integrate the Internet and mobile communications technology with computer peripherals. JetSend lets a user send data via the Internet to a remote printer (or any remote peripheral), according to Scott Berinato in *PC Week.*

Lexmark was among the companies in 1998 to develop new technologies intending to produce higher quality inkjet prints. Photorealistic output was a top priority, and new print heads and inks were launched. Epson built in new utilities to help with cleaning and aligning print heads, as well as nozzles. Network color laser printers also were improved, and prices continued to fall as quality rose.

FURTHER READING

Babyak, Richard J. "Cutting the Cost of Complexity." *Appliance Manufacturer,* June 1996.

Berinato, Scott. "HP to Launch 'Appliance Bid'." *PC Week,* 21 July 1997.

"Consolidation Continues, Despite Strong Sales." *Purchasing,* 11 July 1996.

"Could New Mopiers Hasten the Demise of the Copier?" *Purchasing,* 22 May 1997.

Delfino, Erik. "A Printer Primer." *Online,* May-June 1995.

Dominianni, Cheryl. "Printers: Low Prices and Superior Color Bring Photo-Quality Printing to the Desktop." *Windows Magazine,* 15 June 1998.

Flynn, Laurie. "Market for Home Color Printers Is Booming." *The New York Times,* 20 May 1996.

Fusaro, Roberta. "Users Doubt Copier/E-mail Combo," *Computerworld,* 21 September 1998.

Gomes, Lee. "Computer-Printer Price Drop Isn't Starving Makers." *Wall Street Journal,* 16 August 1996.

Manes, Stephen. "Banner Days for Inkjet Printers." *The New York Times,* 30 April 1996.

Mangis, Carol, "Internet Printing," *PC,* November 1998.

Matzer, Marla. "Showing a Softer Side of Hardware." *Brandweek,* 7 October 1996.

Narisetti, Raju. "Pounded By Printers, Xerox Go Digital." *Wall Street Journal,* 12 May 1998.

Pepper, Jon. "All That's Fit to Print." *Nation's Business,* December 1995.

Perenson, Melissa J. "Convertible Printers." *PC Magazine,* 25 June 1996.

Peterson, Marilyn, "Network Printing Takes Off," *Managing Office Technology,* July-August 1988.

Roberts, John, and Al Senia. "Company Product Spending." *Computer Reseller News,* 29 June 1998.

Robinson, Phillip. "Laser Printers Still Beating Inkjet? Battleground is Cost Per Page, 'Duty Cycle.'" *San Diego Union-Tribune,* 12 May 1998.

Ward, Joe. "With So Many Printers, Which Do You Buy?" *USA Today,* 11 March 1998.

"What Is a Mopier?" *Purchasing,* 17 April 1997.

"Xerox Cuts Deeper Swath Through HP's Printer Heartland With New Products, Supplies, Partners." *M2 Presswire,* 16 June 1998.

—Karl Heil,
updated by Laura Lawrie and Gloria Cooksey

PROFESSIONAL EXECUTIVE RECRUITING

INDUSTRY SNAPSHOT

Executive research specialists, sometimes known as headhunters, seek and place management personnel domestically and internationally in a wide variety of positions and industries. Companies retain the services of an executive recruiter to access a global network of candidates far beyond the scope of an in-house human resources department and to locate the *right* candidate in a fast and efficient manner.

Executive search firms are non-licensed organizations that primarily place senior executives who earn a minimum of $50,000 per year. Top-level firms may restrict themselves to jobs paying $100,000 and above per year. Realistically, the differences between firms are disappearing as the industry sorts itself out and companies diversify.

When industry and business are operating at high levels, executive search services are in great demand. As downturns occur, businesses hire fewer managers, which cuts into the industry's employment levels and profits. Consequently, executive search firms are expanding their specialties to include areas such as outplacement, consulting, finance, benchmarking, employee testing, and temporary services. These additional services, combined with the expansion of the global market, provide an expanding opportunity for executive research firms.

ORGANIZATION AND STRUCTURE

The process of executive recruiting is multifaceted. A detailed job description, in writing, must be prepared by the search firm and client company at the onset. The recruiter then conducts an extensive search, contacts prospective candidates, and performs reference checks. Client interviews are arranged with the top two or three prospects from the pool of candidates. The most-promising candidate is selected.

The industry is divided into generalists and specialists. Some firms, such as Phyllis Solomon Executive Search Inc., based in Englewood Cliffs, New Jersey, concentrate on specific industries and clearly defined levels of management. Solomon focuses on middle- to upper-management personnel in the health care field. Smaller firms such as Solomon also tend to seek relatively localized niches within the industry. Larger companies like Korn/Ferry tend to be more diverse and serve a wider array of clients in widespread geographical areas. They, too, constantly seek new clients in diverse businesses to serve. For example, A. T. Kearney Executive Search, which has been in business for more than 50 years, announced in 1997 that it was establishing an office in Santa Monica, California, to service the entertainment industry. It is vital to the success of executive search firms that they constantly establish niches and respond rapidly to changes in the business world.

Executive recruiting is becoming increasingly specialized. Contemporary recruiters use state-of-the-art technology to ensure the personnel recruited suitably fit the intended positions. They use tools such as computer software and paper-based tests to analyze items such as executives' skills and personality traits, then compare them to the requirements of the positions to be filled. Recruiters cannot trust luck, subjectivity, or hunches to select candidates. Clients can pay executive recruiting firms as much as one-third of a candidate's first year's salary as compensation, which means neither side can afford mistakes in matching the right candidate to a specific job. Recruiters can earn as much as $750,000, and repeat business, for the most high-profile job searches.

Firms generally work on one of two fee bases: contingent or retained. Contingency means that the client pays no money until a person is placed. Firms that work on a contingency basis usually recruit junior or mid-level executives, and only are paid if the search is successful for the client. Under the retained structure, the client typically pays one-third of the fee up-front, another third halfway through the search, and the final third upon placement of a candidate. This fee can be as much as 33 percent of the position's annual compensation. The fee structure varies with the client's needs and the candidate's availability. In some cases, clients need people immediately—and temporarily. In others, they can afford long lead times to replace outgoing personnel or assume newly created positions.

Often recruitment firms are called upon to place executives on a temporary basis. Many businesses today operate in a project mode in which they assign specialists to teams designed to complete a specific task. Once the task is completed, project members are reassigned or let go. Clients may need executives to fill in for short periods of time for key personnel. At other times, individuals may want to work only for a set period. These new practices have opened doors for recruitment firms to place executives on a temporary basis, which impacts how they work. Placing temporary staff members generally means shorter time frames in identifying, testing, and placing executives. Clients seeking temporary personnel typically need them immediately. Consequently, recruiters sometimes must identify promising candidates quickly.

BACKGROUND AND DEVELOPMENT

The emergence of the U.S. executive recruitment industry can be traced back to the 1940s as businesses, growing after World War II, had a dearth of acceptable in-house candidates for promotions. For the most part, in the industry's first decades, the different types of recruiters were interchangeable. There was no sharp division of labor between personnel recruiters and executive search specialists.

In the early 1990s, a high-profile executive search helped reshape the industry. In early 1992, IBM launched a major search for a new chief executive.

The corporation hired two top recruiters, Gerry Roche and Tom Neff, both of whom were acknowledged leaders in the field. (Both men have been included consistently in the top 250 executive recruiters in the United States.) This was an unusual move because Roche and Neff worked for different companies, Heidrick & Struggles and SpencerStuart, respectively. IBM also sidestepped a practice common in the executive recruiting industry known as "client blocks," in which major executive search firms do not approach individuals placed in jobs by competitors. Moreover, IBM was not shy about letting the world know how its search for a CEO was going. In fact, in a break with tradition, the corporation made public the names of executives who were ostensibly among the finalists for the position. The resulting publicity worked to the benefit of the executive search industry. For the first time, business experts and members of the public came face-to-face with an industry that had toiled in relative obscurity for most of its existence.

The notoriety helped fuel growth in the executive recruitment industry as executives from companies of all sizes became acquainted with the notion of professional recruiting firms. At the same time other changes in business practices spurred greater demand for these services. The global market proved to have an impact on American businesses, and recruiters found themselves involved in worldwide searches for executives to fill slots in multinational corporations. There was also a revolution in the American workplace. Corporations began downsizing thousands of people to become "leaner and meaner." Those laid off included many high-ranking executives. Executive recruiters picked up some of the slack by matching laid-off professionals with new positions.

Ironically, the executive search industry experienced its own downsizing. Between 1992 and 1995, almost one-fifth of the country's retainer-type executive firms went out of business. Many of those remaining had to cut back staffing. In effect, they eliminated less productive recruiters.

CURRENT CONDITIONS

Many firms have opened offices in places heretofore ignored by executive recruiters. The majority of the top executive search firms in the United States are based in New York. Large numbers are based in Chicago, California, and Texas. However, areas such as Miami, Florida, are now home to large firms, which are establishing offices there to take advantage of emerging markets. Since hundreds of multinational corporations are running Latin American offices from Miami, many key executives for those firms are being recruited from that area. Among the executive search firms that opened new offices in Miami in the 1990s are Korn/Ferry International and Heidrick & Struggles.

Industry experts estimate that one office needs to sustain between $1 and $3 million in business per year. Income is based to a great extent on location, however. For instance, fees for executive recruiters' services may vary greatly between major geographic locations such as New York and Miami. Money is only part of the entire operation. Executive recruiters also need access to candidates with diverse backgrounds and skills. Because U.S. companies increasingly form joint ventures with companies in other parts of the world, there is a need for executives who not only speak foreign languages, but understand foreign cultures as well. The search for executives who can do both is best conducted by specialists in the field.

An example of a growing company is Raymond Karsan Associates, based in Wayne, Pennsylvania. The worldwide firm has 450 employees in 24 offices. In 1998, for the fourth consecutive year, Raymond Karsan Associates was named one of the fastest-growing privately held companies by *Inc.* magazine. "Our company's growth has been fueled by corporate America's realization that human talent is their most important asset," says CEO Rudy Karsan. "We are proud to be included in this prestigious *Inc.* 500 ranking which salutes our sales growth of approximately $3.6 million to $36 million during the past five years."

One of the industry's strengths is that some of its segments are recession-proof. For instance, Phyllis Solomon specializes in recruiting for the health care field in advertising, medical education, public relations, and middle- to upper-management positions in the pharmaceutical industry. She chose her niche in part because medicine is a fairly stable area of employment. Her firm provides an excellent example of how niche-driven the executive search industry is.

The areas of specialization are increasing. A. Kearney Executive Search, for example, recently opened an office in Santa Monica, California, to service the worldwide media and entertainment industry. The service is fairly new to the company, which has been in business for 50 years. It employs 3,600 employees overall, 2,300 of whom are consultants. Kearney is a prime example of an aggressive firm that fills in niches in the business environment and hires the

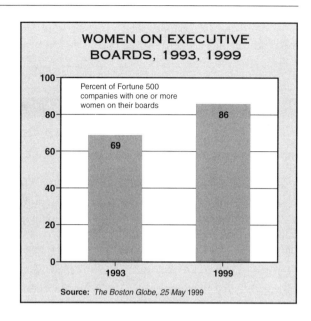

WOMEN ON EXECUTIVE BOARDS, 1993, 1999

Percent of Fortune 500 companies with one or more women on their boards

1993: 69
1999: 86

Source: *The Boston Globe, 25 May* 1999

most qualified people to service them. The fact that so many niches still exist is an advantage for the executive search industry.

According to the Association of Executive Search Consultants (AESC), searches were up 3 percent during the third quarter of 1998 with 3,070 searches booked by member companies, compared to the same quarter in 1997. Executive demand is up 14 percent at service businesses and 9 percent at communications companies. The AESC represents 160 member firms worldwide with a total of more than 700 offices and 3,000 consultants.

An important issue arising in the late 1990s is that of recruiter ethics. In July 1997, John R. Walter resigned as president of the AT&T Corporation, after just seven months in that position. Although many laid sole responsibility at the feet of AT&T's board, there were some experts who voiced concern with the entire executive search system. As Judith Dobrzynski reported in the *New York Times,* the recruiters involved may not have heeded signs that the search was flawed, although many recruiters feel that the only way to ensure this happens in the future is to fundamentally change the way recruiters are paid.

Kennedy Information, the publishers of *Executive Recruiter News,* an independent newsletter of the executive recruiting profession, says that clients must have a clear understanding of the search firm's replacement policy *before* booking a search. Search firms working on a contingency basis will usually guarantee a candidate for 60 days, while a search firm working on retainer will guarantee the candidate for a year or more. Should an executive leave before the duration of the time period, the firm should replace the candidate at a reduced or free rate.

INDUSTRY LEADERS

For more than 20 years, Korn/Ferry International has been ranked number-one in the executive recruiting industry. According to the March 1999 issue of *Executive Recruiter News,* revenue figures for the worldwide firm totaled $339.08 million in 1998, followed by number-two ranked Heidrick & Struggles' $324.8 million. Heidrick & Struggles, however, edged out Korn/Ferry in U.S. sales for 1998 with revenues of $178 million, compared to $177 million.

Korn/Ferry International has been in the executive search industry since 1969. The company operates as one firm worldwide with more than 71 offices in 41 countries. Korn/Ferry recruits executive personnel for Fortune 500 companies in areas such as marketing, management, and finance. By the late 1990s, the company had successfully completed over 70,000 searches.

Heidrick & Struggles, on the other hand, has been in the executive recruiting business since 1953. They operate 55 offices around the world. Organized into practice groups that specialize in areas such as information management, mining, and aerospace, the search firm recruits chief executives, boards of directors, and senior-level managers for Fortune 500 companies, not-for-profit organizations, and start-up ventures. In 1998, Heidrick & Struggles acquired rival Fenwick Partners.

WORK FORCE

The executive search industry does not employ large numbers of people, and the majority of the companies in the industry do not require a wide variety of specialists. Many are sole proprietorships or small businesses. For example, the Curtiss Group, based in Boca Raton, Florida, employs 12 people and brings in about $1.5 million per year. Companies like Curtiss employ recruiters, data processing and testing specialists, experts, and support personnel such as administrative assistants. Another example is the Compass Group, based in Birmingham, Michigan, which employs only 22 people. The company, named one of the "50 Leading Retained Executive Search Firms" by *Executive Recruiter News,* earns between $2 and $5 million per year. Most of its employees are retired

executives from Ford Motor Company. Only five of them are full-time employees.

Even industry leaders Korn/Ferry (1998 total worldwide employees: 1,432) and Heidrick & Struggles (1998 total worldwide employees: 1,412) do not have the large workforces one might expect from companies generating sales in excess of $300 million a year.

The majority of the recruiters are well-educated people with advanced degrees. One of the most common degrees among successful executive recruiters is the MBA, because it helps recruiters understand the world of business and management. One of the hallmarks of successful executive recruiters is in-depth knowledge of the fields in which they specialize. Another is time in the industry. The average age of the top 250 executive recruiters is 55. They each average nearly 23 years in the business. Women and minorities make up a small but growing share of the industry's personnel. There are 28 women in the current top 250 recruiters, but only a handful of minorities.

AMERICA AND THE WORLD

Many of the top executive search firms in the United States have established offices in numerous foreign countries. For example, A. T. Kearney Executive Search currently has a multinational network of recruiting professionals with expertise in all principal industry and functional sectors. In fact, Kearney operates more than 60 offices in 30 countries. The Curtiss Group, based in Boca Raton, Florida, operates offices in Holland, Brazil, and Tokyo, in addition to its Florida sites in Boca Raton, Fort Lauderdale, Miami, Jacksonville, and Tampa Bay. Other large firms, e.g., Korn/Ferry International, Heidrick & Struggles, and Spencer Stuart, operate offices throughout the world. This trend will continue as the global market expands and multinational corporations continue to form. As they do, American executive search firms are likely to have a deep impact on international searches.

RESEARCH AND TECHNOLOGY

Computers have revolutionized the world of executive recruiting. Firms compile and reference large databases containing the names of people who can fill particular jobs with particular companies. Many executive search firms operate proprietary computerized information systems and employ in-house specialists to implement, maintain, and enhance them. For example, Compass Group maintains a computerized database of more than 21,000 profiles and resumes of top candidates.

In recent years, executive search specialists began using software to help clients identify personality traits, simulate a day at the office, present models on how to conduct interviews properly, and a host of other tasks designed to facilitate the placement and hiring process. Software packages can range from $600 to $3,000 or more. State-of-the-art software and hardware have enhanced recruiters' abilities to place the right people in the right positions.

The Internet poses both challenge and opportunity for the industry. In June 1998, Korn/Ferry International and *The Wall Street Journal* announced the launch of "Futurestep," an Internet service set up to recruit mid-level executives. Potential candidates log on to the system, answer informational questions, and respond to an assessment profile in lieu of submitting a resume. The information is then screened electronically and candidates who match current client requirements are called for a videoconference interview and must undergo a standard reference check.

Although some on-line recruiters are thought to be resume wholesalers, because they solicit resumes via Web sites, many executive recruiters are expected to forge alliances with Internet content developers by the turn of the century.

FURTHER READING

"AESC Online—Association of Executive Search Consultants." New York: Association of Executive Search Consultants, 1999. Available from http://www.aesc.org.

Bennett, Julie. "Answering the Call: Not All Recruiters are Created Equal, So Ask Questions." *Chicago Tribune,* 1 February 1998.

Burgess, Scott. "Boca Raton, Fla., Executive Search Firm Prides Itself on Luring Client." *Boca Raton News,* 11 March 1997.

Bushnell, Davis. "Suitors Line Up for Executives Recruiters: Roll Out the Limos in Headhunting for a Big Payoff." *Boston Globe,* 1 March 1998.

Directory of Executive Recruiters. Fitzwilliam, NH: Kennedy Publications, 1997.

Dobrzynski, Judith H. "An Ethical Role for Recruiters." *The New York Times,* 29 July 1997.

Drake, Samantha. "HR Firm is After One-Stop Shopping." *Philadelphia Business Journal,* 11 April 1997.

"Executive Recruiter News" Fitzwilliam, NH: Kennedy Information LLC, 1999. Available at http://www.kennedy-info.com.

Fitzwilliam, N.H. "Heidrick & Struggles Top U.S. Executive Search Ratings." *Business Wire,* March 16, 1999. Available from http://www.djinteractive.com.

Goodman, Cindy Krischer. "Giant Search Firms Make Miami Their Latin American Hub." *The Miami Herald,* 9 June 1997.

"Heidrick & Struggles" Chicago, IL: Heidrick & Struggles, 1999. Available from http://www.heidrick.com.

Hoover's Company Profiles. Austin, TX: The Reference Press, 1999. Available from http://www.hoovers.com.

Korn/Ferry International Home Page. Los Angeles, CA: Korn/Ferry, 1999. Available from http://www.kornferry.com.

Kunde, Diana. "Execs Finding Short-Term Opportunities." *The Dallas Morning News,* 26 January 1997.

Lee, Chris. "The Hunt for Skilled Workers." *Training,* 1 December 1997.

Logue, Charles H. *Outplace Yourself: Secrets of an Executive Outplacement Counselor.* Holbrook, MA: Bob Adams, Inc., 1993.

"Raymond Karsan Associates." Princeton, NJ: Raymond Karsan Associates, 1999. Available from http://www.raymondkarsan.com.

Richtel, Matt. "A New Executive-Recruiting Service on the Web." *The New York Times,* 8 June 1998.

Schellhardt, Timothy D. "Downsizing Thinned Ranks; 'Up-and-Coming' Go Fast." *Wall Street Journal,* 26 June 1997.

Sibbald, John. *The New Career Makers.* New York: HarperCollins, 1995.

Sileo, Olia. "Matchmaker, Matchmaker." *The New Jersey Record,* 9 April 1997.

—Arthur G. Sharp, updated by Laura Lawrie and Lori Lewis-Chapman

PUSH TECHNOLOGY

Push technology is a means of delivering information to networked users without the time-intensive research users are often required to do to get the information they desire. "Push" products, such as news delivery services, filter information based on consumer preferences and send it directly to subscriber hard drives whenever they are hooked up to the administering network. It enables volumes of information to be delivered without the necessity of spending countless hours on the Internet. For end-users, push technology makes it possible to "subscribe" to certain Web sites and information services that periodically send messages and information to users without constant solicitation. In many cases, subscribers determine how much and how often information is sent along.

As Web surfing became more popular in the early 1990s, companies found that it was more difficult to attract visitors to Web sites and keep them coming back. According to Amy Cortese in *Business Week,* Web sites need repeat visits in order to sell advertising, which, although still not a major source of income, "remains the most promising way to make money."

The Web needed to become a more profitable business medium, and push technology seemed to fit the bill. The broadcast technology supporting television and radio has been updated to exploit the Internet, and computer users ("viewers" or "listeners") can "tune in" to favorite sites ("channels") to get the information they want and need.

Push technology has seen many ups and downs since PointCast pioneered it in the mid-1990s. Many vendors have come and gone, but it seems as if push technology, in one form or another, is here to stay.

Pull technology, or actively searching out and "pulling" information from a Web site, remains the most commonly used technique for retrieving information from the Internet, and search engines such as Infoseek, Yahoo, HotBot, and Excite help users locate the desired site. The process can be extremely time-consuming and tedious, and users often become frustrated when unable to find exactly what they want.

According to Peter Weinstein in *Technology and Learning,* push technology can best be explained in terms of "who initiates and manages the transfer of content." Most people use push technology every day, if they use the Internet at all, when they send and receive e-mail. E-mail uses a very simple form of push technology. In other words, when you write an e-mail message, you then "push" it out over the Internet to the intended recipient.

PointCast, Inc., based in California, was the first company to see potential in delivering actual Web page content to individuals instead of the other way around. The roots of this new technology can be traced back to 1992, when Christopher and Gregg Hassett developed a product called *Journalist,* designed to deliver a customized electronic newspaper to CompuServe and Prodigy customers. Although *Journalist* flopped, the Hassett brothers went on to develop a new way of delivering customized news, soon to become PointCast.

PointCast began sending news and advertising directly to computers in 1996. Shortly thereafter, several other Silicon Valley firms, including Marimba and BackWeb, entered the market, each offering technologies to distribute and update software. Marimba was able to deliver Web content to all types of systems, mainly because its application, Castanet, was written in Java.

In order to receive pushed information, users download and install proprietary software. A push server can then send select information through broadcast "channels." The server manages distribution and maintenance of all available channels, although individual clients receive only those channels they have specified. Using the push software, users can configure it so that they can receive what they need, when they need it.

A "netcast" or "webcast" is a simple form of push technology. A server broadcasts the program over the Internet and individual computer users can tune in to the channel, just like tuning in to a television or radio program. The next step up from a netcast or webcast is the "news and information service," which is delivered to computer users in the form of an interactive screen saver. PointCast uses this technology.

In 1998, Marimba developed Castanet. This suite of software tools not only distributed interactive multimedia content, but could also distribute software applications and updates. This technology was particularly useful in many fields, but especially in the education market.

CURRENT CONDITIONS

There are several key advantages to using push technology. Because push can automatically download information to a hard drive, the information can then be retrieved offline, yielding the potential for greatly reduced Internet traffic jams. Another key advantage is that software or content updates can occur automatically and do not require any intervention from the end-user; this is particularly useful for organizations or companies that have extensive computer systems. But although push technology offered several important benefits, it quickly fell out of favor not long after its arrival in 1997, as end-users were barraged with junk e-mail, advertising, and the like. Push was regarded by many as a "bandwidth hog" or "bandwidth bandit," and in fact, many organizations refused to use the technology, or stopped using it because the information overload caused so many systems to crash. Hewlett-Packard Co., without actually banning employees from using PointCast, actively discouraged them from downloading it.

One of the more serious potential problems results from the use of push technology's ability to automatically update and distribute software throughout an entire organization. This ability is both an asset and a potential liability; if the updated software contains viruses, this can have devastating implications for an organization. PointCast addressed this problem in 1997 with a program called "I-Server." I-Server enabled companies to have PointCast content sent once, to the company server. Management could then decide whether or not to rebroadcast content to employees, customers, or both.

By the end of 1997, many critics believed that push technology failed to meet its promises or expectations. Although push companies promised an increase in advertising revenue on the Web due to the potential for direct advertising, this did not fully materialize. And although push was touted as "the next step in the evolution of the Internet," according to Amanda Lang in the *Financial Post Weekly,* most end-users and companies preferred to stick with pull technology. To many, it still seemed smarter to go looking for what you needed, when you needed it. In this way you retained control over what, and how much, was downloaded to your computer. Fear of viruses being directly downloaded and the invasion of privacy that could occur through automatic downloads were other strikes against push technology.

Critics of push technology cite several reasons for uneasiness with the technology. First of all, many say that pure push does not really exist. Basically, all push technology begins with pull technology, in that the end-user must first contact the server to initiate delivery of information. With netcasts, users must actively choose to tune in and must keep to the schedule determined by the provider of the netcast. According to Glyn Moody in *Computer Weekly,* as "clients draw down content on a scheduled basis," most of the technologies described as push really are pull.

Many critics and users alike are worried that once responsibility for delivery of content is relinquished to someone else, privacy could be compromised, thereby increasing the likelihood of more viruses, data corruption, and pirated information. Many organizations are understandably wary of allowing outsiders into proprietary computer systems.

In addition, contrary to expectations, push technology actually added to bandwidth overload in the late 1990s. Rather than relieving ever-increasing Web traffic jams, the additional traffic created by end-users trying to sign up for automatic content delivery further increased the already limited Internet bandwidth.

Many argue that push technology is not needed at all, rather much more efficient pull technology that enables easier access to information on the Internet.

More On PUSHING TO THE MASSES

One push application with a potential for commercial viability and universal appeal would be pushed news broadcasts. Pushed newswires could be purchased via subscription, for direct and automatic download on a regular basis, directly onto the hard disks of subscribers' computers. This application parallels the delivery of a daily newspaper onto the subscriber's front porch on a daily basis. An emerging push broker such as Marimba Castanet would be likely to host such online services. A push broker might contract with a universally accessible cable television channel—PBS for example—as the communications medium, in which case a subscriber would not need a telephone modem and Internet connection to receive the download.

In order to receive pushed news a subscriber would equip a home PC with appropriate client (receiver) software. State-of-the-art Web browser software in general provides sufficient client services to receive the pushed data, but push service brokers in most instances would require that users install proprietary client software. Some would provide specially configured versions of one of the more popular Web browsers such as the Microsoft Internet Explorer or the Netscape Navigator. If a broker used a television channel as the communications medium, then the hardware requirement for subscribers would involve a PC equipped with television tuner and antenna.

The data sources available to subscribers would be determined by contracts concluded by the push broker. For example, if a push broker contracted with ESPN for sports news, then that news would be one of the options available to the service subscribers. If the broker contracted only with small Web content providers, only those respective services would be available to the subscribers. The types and sources of data content for push downloads are as boundless as the Internet itself. Among the endless possibilities are news and sports channels, software update channels; channels to download recipes; channels with lesson plans for teachers; stock market channels; weather channels, even cartoon channels. Individual subscribers would be free to pick and choose which data feeds to accept. Downloaded data would be stored permanently on the hard disk of the subscribing computer. The subscriber would access the data at his or her convenience. Unwanted or obsolete data could be erased from the hard disk like any other data file.

Many systems professionals believe that a new technology standard is needed, such as Microsoft's "channel definition format" or "CDF". CDF is written in extended markup language, "XML," and has been offered by Microsoft as a possible new industry standard. Both Microsoft and Netscape have incorporated CDF into their browsers, Internet Explorer and Netscape Netcaster, reportedly providing smoother and more enjoyable Web access.

Because so much of the early pushed information—junk e-mail, advertising, etc.—tarnished the perception of push technology and the companies that developed the technology, early push pioneers such as Marimba and PointCast developed new terminology. Terms such as "remote administration management," or "smart agent" are now used to avoid unfavorable associations with earlier failed products.

There are still many possibilities for push technology. Many companies have found that the best use for present-day push technology is within their own organizations over the company Intranet. By developing their own channels, companies can direct the information sent to employees and can monitor Intranet volume as well as content.

Push technology, mainly that of PointCast, Back-Web, and Marimba's Castanet, is being used more and more by U.S. federal government networks, according to Richard W. Walker in *Government Computer News*. The Treasury Department, the Agriculture Department, and several smaller agencies such as the Office of the Assistant Secretary of the Army for Research, Development, and Acquisitions, the National Institutes of Health's AIDS research plant, and the National Institutes of Health's Warren Grant Magnuson Clinical Center, have all been implementing information delivery systems since early in 1998. The Defense Department entered into an agreement with Network Associates, Inc. to deliver updates of McAfee antivirus software to its 2 million users using BackWeb's technology. Due to concerns about security, however, the Air Force banned commercial push software until the issues were addressed satisfactorily.

INDUSTRY LEADERS

Sunnyvale, California-based PointCast pioneered the push technology category. The company was founded in 1992 by Chris Hassett. Years later, when Hassett left in 1997, David Dorman took over as president. When the push category fell quickly out of favor, Dorman began repositioning the company as a "smart-agent-based news-and-information service for corporate customers." Dorman resigned in early 1999 after accepting an offer to lead a $10-billion joint venture designed to combine the international networks and traffic of both AT&T and British Telecom. Although a new CEO and executive vice president, Phil Koen, succeeded Dorman, Dorman remained Point-Cast's chairman. In April 1999, *Internet News* reported that former CEO Chris Hassett was attempting to buy back the company.

The PointCast Network gathers up-to-the-minute local, regional, and international news as well as industry-specific information, and delivers it to computer desktops. PointCast's Intranet Broadcast Solution suite of products gathers and coordinates information flow from a variety of Intranet sources. These sources may be corporate alert bulletins, news from key business partners, industry intelligence, information on suppliers, and so forth. The Intranet Broadcast Solution is also designed to reduce traffic congestion by more efficient caching technologies. In late 1998, PointCast announced its plans to market in Europe with the sale of two new releases of its Point-Cast Network in the United Kingdom and Germany, two of Europe's fastest-growing Internet markets. To deliver content, PointCast would work with its European media partners *The Economist, Reuters, Deutsche Presse-Agentur,* and others. The Canadian edition of PointCast Network was launched in 1996 and a Japanese edition was launched in late 1997. By 1998, PointCast had more than 1.2 million viewers of its network worldwide. A series of failed buyout negotiations with such heavyweights as Rupert Murdoch's News Corporation, NBC, Microsoft, and others plagued the company in the late 1990s. Despite such setbacks, in February of 1999 *ClNet News.Com* reported that PointCast intended to move forward with plans for a possible joint venture with BellSouth and other phone giants to offer high-speed Internet access over telephone wires. To begin building brand awareness for the possible venture, the company was in preliminary discussions with advertising agencies.

BackWeb Technologies, Inc. is another industry leader based in San Jose, California and Ramat-Gan, Israel. BackWeb also has offices in Chicago, New York, Canada, the United Kingdom, and several other countries. A 35-year-old former Israeli army paratrooper named Eli Barkat led BackWeb as CEO. Back-Web formed partnerships with many of the world's leading corporations including Microsoft, Hewlett-Packard, Sun Microsystems, and others. BackWeb provides business customers with Internet communications systems and applications for managing critical business operations such as customer service, competitive analysis, and sales.

Among BackWeb's key products are an Internet communications software system called BackWeb Foundation, and a customer relations/sales package called BackWeb Sales Accelerator. BackWeb Foundation gathers important data in any format and delivers it to desktops throughout an organization. Sensitive to the bandwidth complaints that helped to drive original push technologies out of favor, BackWeb developed its Polite Communications technology. The Polite Communications system is capable of adjusting the rate of data transmission to complement the available bandwidth, thus, reducing bandwidth congestion. Added components to BackWeb Foundation further increase data transmission efficiency by compressing data and allowing users to both interrupt and resume data transmission.

BackWeb Sales Accelerator delivers key information such as new promotions, pricing, product announcements, and so on to organizations' sales forces. Additional system modules scan the Internet for market updates and industry news while other modules enhance organizations' internal messaging capabilities and provide access to industry-specific subscription services. Both products are designed to fit seamlessly into customers' existing management systems. BackWeb has licensed its software to more than 200 corporations including Rite Aid, Compaq, and Cisco Systems. It has estimated annual sales of $20 million.

Marimba, Inc., founded by four members of Sun Microsystem's original Java team, is also based in California, in Mountain View. Kim Polese, one of Marimba's founders, is CEO. Marimba originally focused on content delivery, but by the late 1990s had turned its attention to developing applications enabling corporations to distribute and update software remotely via the Internet, corporate Intranets, and extranets. Marimba's suite of Castanet products use client-server technology to update and maintain off-the-shelf or custom applications. Castanet includes powerful security features such as authentication and encryption, among others. Organizations can add new modules to the Castanet system as needs expand. In April of 1999, Marimba filed to sell nearly 3.6 million stock shares in an initial public offering (IPO). Sale of the shares was expected to give the company an implied market value of nearly $387 million based on more than 20 million shares that would be outstanding following the IPO at about $17 per share. Marimba markets products worldwide.

Diffusion, Inc., is also based in Mountain View, California. Dr. Richard Schwartz founded Diffusion in 1995 and James Gagnard is president and CEO. Diffusion specializes in the Customer Relationship Management (CRM) market and has found a niche for itself in the financial services industry. Products like Diffusion's Customer Relationship Management (CRM) 3.0 software can automatically coordinate and manage key functions such as informing customers when account balances drop too low or when a fund transfer has taken place.

In addition, both Microsoft and Netscape include push tools in their browsers, Internet Explorer and Netscape Communicator, respectively. These tools automatically download Web pages, create channels, and display Web content on the user's desktop, and can be implemented without traditional Web browsers. Microsoft's Managed Webcasting is more closely integrated with its Internet Explorer browser, and is more easily configured than Netscape Netcaster. Netcaster is a television-based "Channel Finder" and is considered by some reviewers, including Jeff Bertolucci, to be superior to Managed Webcasting at delivering popular news channels such as ABC-News.com and CNNfn. Netcaster is not integrated with Netscape's browser, however.

Even America Online, Inc. (AOL) entered the push world with a program that can fetch AOL content, Web pages, and e-mail, according to preferences specified by AOL users.

AMERICA AND THE WORLD

Many American companies have yet to make a big impact in the international market, particularly Europe, mostly due to slow and unreliable telephone lines, which sometimes ceased to function when receiving heavy volumes of information all at once. Because of this, one of the most successful companies is a Canadian company, Lanacom, Inc. Led by CEO Tony Davis, Lanacom's Headliner (launched in December 1996) "reads" Internet news sites, and then delivers that information to registered users. The content is delivered to the desktop via a ticket-tape bar that runs on the top or bottom, or vertically along the side of the screen. Information can also be delivered in the form of a screen saver or can be downloaded directly to the user's hard drive. Of the leaders in the American market, BackWeb has had the most success getting established in Europe.

RESEARCH AND TECHNOLOGY

Tibco, a subsidiary of Reuters, is an international leader in application management products that offer real-time event-activated information transfer throughout organizations. Tibco's technology is called "publish and subscribe," and its product is TIB/Rendezvous. In the summer of 1998, a PointCast corporate press release announced that an engineering team had successfully integrated TIB/Rendezvous into PointCast's Central Broadcast Facility, thereby enhancing the timeliness and efficiency of information from the PointCast Network. Information is directed to PointCast's Central Broadcast Facility via satellite, leased lines, and the Internet. Formatted information can now be multicast by a single update, and can be transmitted throughout all servers simultaneously and in nearly real time. TIB/Rendezvous uses significantly less bandwidth because it can simultaneously send single messages to millions of servers and end-users rather than performing the same function millions of times for millions of servers and end-users.

Most analysts predict that push technology will continue to evolve through the turn of the century. As the technology evolves, society will no doubt continue to wrestle with the social, behavioral, and privacy issues raised by a technology that can now enter our lives with little intervention on our part.

FURTHER READING

Afzali, Cyrus. "PointCast Founder Preparing to Take Control of Push Pioneer." *InternetNew.com,* 3 April 1999. Available from http://www.internetnews.com.

Bertolucci, Jeff. "Browsers Get Pushy." *PC Computing,* 1 October 1997, 149.

Borland, John, and Kawamoto, Dawn. "Marimba Ups IPO Offering Price." *Bloomberg News Special Report to CNET New.com,* 28 April 1999. Available from http://www.news .com.

———. "PointCast Pushes Ahead with Net Venture." *C\NET News.com,* 25 February 1999. Available from http://www.news.com/News/Item.

Caruso, Denise. "My Life as a Mailbox/Garbage Can, or How I Came to Hate Push Technology." *New York Times,* 24 March 1997, 5.

Chandrasekaran, Rajiv. "The Big Push? New Technology Could Change Way Web Is Used." *Washington Post,* 11 May 1997, HO1.

Cortese, Amy. "A Way Out of the Web Maze." *Business Week,* 24 February 1997.

"Diffusion Home Page." Mountain View, CA: Diffusion, Inc., 1999. Available from http://www.diffusion.com.

Duvall, Mel. "Push Pioneer Turns to CRM Market." *Interactive Week Online,*20 January 1999. Available from http://www.zdnet.com/intweek/stories/news.

Eads, Stefani. "Can BackWeb Soar Where PointCast Stumbled?" *Business Week Online,* 30 April 1999. Available from http://www.businessweek.com.

Foremski, Tom. "Push Technologies." *Financial Times,* 12 March 1997, 6.

Gold, Howard R., and Kathy Yakal. "PointCast, Others Send News and Data Direct to the Desktop." *Baron's,* 12 May 1997, 58.

Lang, Amanda. "Push Came to Shove." *Financial Post Weekly,* 21 February 1998, IT3.

"Marimba-Managing the Internet." Mountain View, CA: Marimba, Inc., 1999. Available from http://www.marimba.com.

Moody, Glyn. "Pushing Technology Off the Net." *Computer Weekly,* 14 May 1998, 66.

Niccolai, James. "PointCast Pushes into U.K., Germany." *The Industry Standard,* 30 November 1998. Available from http://www.thestandard.com.

Strom, David. "The Best of Push." *Web Review,* 18 April 1997. Available from http://webreview.com/97/04/18/feature/index.html.

———. "PointCast Names Koen CEP." *CNNfn,* 4 March 1999. Available from http://www.fn.com.

———. *Push Publishing Technologies,* 13 May 1998. Available from http://www.strom.com/imc/t4a.html.

Walker, Richard W. "Charms of Push Technology Are Pulling Users In." *Government Computer News,* 23 March 1998, 78.

Weinstein, Peter. "Pushing and Pulling on the Web." *Technology and Learning,* 1 January 1998, 24.

"Welcome to BackWeb." San Jose, CA: Backweb Technologies, Inc., 1999. Available from http://www.backweb.com.

"Welcome to Pointcast." Sunnyvale, CA: PointCast, Inc., 1999. Available from http://www.pointcast.com.

"Who's Pushing in Europe." *Wall Street Journal Europe,* 2 June 1997, 30.

Wilder, Clinton, and Justin Hibbard. "Pushing Outside the Enterprise: Companies Begin to Tap Push Technology's Potential as a Sales and Marketing Tool." *Information Week,* 4 August 1997, 20.

Wong, Wylie. "VARs Push Technology to Corporations: Developers' Solutions Target Specific Niches and Applications." *Computer Reseller News,* 9 February 1998, 99.

—Amy Pennington-Boyce

RAW JUICE BARS

INDUSTRY SNAPSHOT

Driven by healthy eating habits and the demand for convenient food, raw juice bars began springing up in the United States in the 1990s. Although health food stores offered such concoctions as low-fat fresh fruit and vegetable mixtures and "smoothies" (shakes with fruit and added nutrients) since the 1980s, they did not begin to penetrate the mainstream market until the following decade. Achieving initial success and popularity on the West Coast—primarily in California—they soon began to spread across the country. However, only large cities and university towns with residents of diverse tastes tended to sustain stand-alone juice bars, that is, operations functioning mainly as juice bars. In other areas, stores, restaurants, health clubs, gyms, and coffee houses integrated juice-bar amenities into other food services.

The juice bar explosion helped manufacturers of blenders and juicers thrive during the 1990s, selling commercial models to establishments offering juice bars, as well as consumer models to people interested in replicating favorite raw juice elixirs at home. Juice bars not only cater to people seeking healthy refreshments, they also compete with fast food, delicatessen, and supermarket home meal replacements by offering a convenient alternative. With ample fruit, yogurt, and supplemental nutrients, juice bar offerings serve as breakfast, lunch, or snack fare. Juice bar beverages also allow customers to get recommended fruit intake by just consuming one drink, instead of several pieces of fruit. Besides containing vitamins from fruits and vegetables, juice bar products may also include other essential ingredients, such as calcium and protein, when low-fat dairy products or fortified soy products are part of the mixture.

Supermarkets and fast-food chains began test marketing juice bars and offering smoothies in the late 1990s. In 1997 *Restaurants & Institutions* reported that there were about 800 juice bars in the United States with total revenues of $340 million. Of those 800 establishments, California accounted for 34 percent, or 275, while the remaining 66 percent were spread throughout the country, primarily in large cities and college towns. *Entrepreneur* cites juices and smoothies for creating revenues in excess of $500 million for 1998. With plenty of room between the East and West Coasts, as well as overseas, industry analysts predict the expansion juice bars would help the industry see profits of $1 billion by 2000.

ORGANIZATION AND STRUCTURE

The juice bar industry's key companies include those that concentrate on selling fresh blended juices and smoothies. These juice bars, however, may also offer products such as low-fat muffins, snacks, sandwiches, soups, and bottled water. In addition, operations such as cafes, restaurants, and supermarkets provide juice bar services to augment the primary selection of products. Many gyms, fitness centers, and health clubs offer customers juices and smoothies, often mixed with extra protein from sources such as eggs, soy, or whey. Also, some operations focus on being "beverage bistros," selling nearly equal amounts of gourmet coffees, sodas, and juice bar offerings.

Primary concoctions sold by juice bars include a spate of mixed fruit and vegetable juices such as apple, orange, banana, guava, papaya, carrot, cucumber, and beet juices, as well as smoothies. Smoothies are shakes made of fresh fruit juice, ice, and either frozen yogurt, sherbet, or soy milk, and are often fortified by wheat grass, ginseng, protein powder, vitamin C, spirulina, bee pollen, and/or wheat germ. Juice bars frequently market these nutritional supplements as enhancers of the immune system and energy boosters, based on research on the effects of homeopathic substances. Some juice bars use only fresh fruit juice, while others use a combination of prepared and fresh juice. Using only fresh juice creates a number of difficulties for juice bars, in that the price of fresh fruits— especially exotic produce—fluctuates throughout the year; fresh fruit is highly perishable, and employees may have a hard time extracting juice from fruits without the appropriate consistency. Consequently, smaller operations, experimental juice bars, and sideline juice bars often opt for canned and bottled juices to avoid these problems.

In *Restaurants and Institutions*, Beth Lorenzini recommends that juice bar operators display plenty of fresh fruit at all times, even if they use prepared juices, and that they should install three compartment sinks in the juice-preparation area to promote frequent cleansing of equipment and utensils. Moreover, Lorenzini urges entrepreneurs to invest in top-quality blending and extracting accouterments. She argues that heavy-duty blenders capable of emulsifying at 32,000 revolutions per minute (rpm)—not the standard 16,000 rpm blenders—work best for juice bars. Though these blenders bear a high price of $800 to $1,200, they can endure frequent, high-output use, and produce the best emulsions. Since juice bars often must run blenders and extractors from open to close, juice bar owners should consider having a spare blender and maintaining a stock of spare parts as well. Lorenzini also contends that in many regions of the United States operators should couple a juice bar with other offerings such as bakery, vegetarian, and health-food products.

BACKGROUND AND DEVELOPMENT

The food bar phenomenon of recent business history began in the 1970s with the salad bar. Restaurants sprouted up that centered on the salad bar concept, and supermarkets began offering salad bars in addition to regular items, according to Bob Ingram in *Supermarket Business.* With demand for convenient and healthy food, salad bars caught on quickly by providing products to meet both of these needs.

Shortly after the introduction of the salad bar, restaurants and stores began adding other services such as pizza bars, coffee bars, olive bars, fruit bars, and sandwich bars. Furthermore, establishments started focusing exclusively on one or more of these products, as witnessed by the influx of cafes and coffee houses in the 1990s. Nonetheless, with the exception of the salad bar, many of these concepts did not offer particularly healthy fare, thereby alienating a significant segment of the potential customer base.

In addition to these forebears, the juice bar industry has antecedents in the soda, ice cream, and frozen yogurt parlor and coffee house crazes of earlier years. Many juice bar operators in the 1990s strategically placed units near high schools and universities, as well as near businesses and stores, hoping to attract a crowd interested in healthy beverages and a pleasant atmosphere for socializing. Like its predecessors, the juice bar provides what sociologists have termed "third places" in contrast to the primary and secondary places of home and work. Third places offer environments where people can meet for casual conversation, according to Gerry Khermouch in *Brandweek.* Khermouch also reported that scholars attribute the popularity of such places to the suburbanization of the United States, and to the emerging numbers of people who work out of the home. Because of these factors, cafes, juice bars, and other such places provide venues for renewed social connection. To function as third places, juice bars must emphasize atmosphere and location in addition to convenient and healthy products. That is, they must be within walking distance of target customers and provide a relaxed, gregarious environment.

In the 1980s, health food stores began to flourish, offering not only organic and low-fat foods, but also a particular style of deli service. Many of these health food stores, particularly those on the West Coast, pioneered the juice bar, bringing in blenders and juice extractors and mixing up assorted fruits and vegetables along with nutritional supplements. As these kinds of beverages grew more popular, California entrepreneurs realized that demand was strong enough to start launching stand-alone juice bars in the late 1980s and early 1990s.

CURRENT CONDITIONS

In the late 1990s, juice bars represented one of the hottest trends in the food service industry. Demonstrating steady growth throughout the 1990s, the number of stand-alone juice bars increased from 150 in 1990 to about 800 in 1997, with California alone boasting 275 of these establishments, according to James Scarpa in *Restaurant Business*. In 1997, the industry garnered approximately $340 million in sales and some analysts predict that the industry's revenues will reach $1 billion by 2000, according to *ID: The Voice of Foodservice Distribution*. James Scarpa also reported in *Restaurant Business* that a juice bar spanning 1,100 square feet can gross up to $1.5 million in just one year with an initial investment of $150,000. And Minneapolis-based investment firm Piper Jaffray reported in *Entrepreneur* in 1998 the restaurant industry growth at 3 percent, with the smoothie segment growing at an annual rate of more than 30 percent. For the most part, juice bars simply require a comfortable cafe-style atmosphere, refrigerator, blenders and juice extractors, and fresh fruit and vegetables. Produce and serving supplies make up the bulk of overhead owners must incur, so owning and operating a juice bar is quite affordable, comparatively speaking. Moreover, employees need very little training, which contributes to juice bars' ease of operation.

Juice bar owners characterize clients as maturing baby boomers and "generation Xers" who are often concerned with consuming healthy foods. Besides the success of small chains and independent juice bars, corporate food service operations announced their forays into the juice bar industry in the mid-1990s. TCBY Enterprises Inc. and International Dairy Queen Inc. planned to open specialty shops offering freshly made fruit juice and smoothies.

Unlike other beverage trends and beverage bars, juice bars can market healthy products as guilt-free, yet enjoyable, while coffee houses must choose not to rave about the salubrious qualities of java, nor can bars and pubs promote the physical benefits of alcoholic beverages. However, some juice bars try to tempt more customers by adding sugar, honey, and higher-fat dairy products to their juices and smoothies, intending their products to suffice as meals, not simply as beverages. In the attempt to spread themselves across the country, the juice bar industry targets shopping centers and strip malls, just as coffee houses and frozen yogurt parlors do. In addition, juice bar owners seek to operate in conjunction with stores and even automotive service stations, setting up juice bars on the sites of these other establishments. To compete with fast-food chains, juice bars open early, providing the breakfast crowd with a fast, healthful alternative to traditional breakfast fare.

Some industry analysts expect juice bars to become the next major U.S. restaurant trend by the year 2000, supplanting cafes, according to Rita Rousseau in *Restaurants and Institutions*. Juice bars that origi-

More On FRESH JUICE

Juice bars may be enjoying a sweet success but regulations by the Food and Drug Administration (FDA) could sour the industry. After a batch of fresh apple juice contaminated with E. coli bacteria led to the death of one child and the illness of 66 people in three western states and Canada in 1996, a nationwide debate erupted over the safety of fresh juice.

The FDA took subsequent steps to prevent future contamination, including suggesting warning labels for juices that were not pasteurized. According to the FDA, unpasteurized juice can contain bacteria that makes people ill. Those at high risk include children, older adults, and people who have weakened immune systems. The various microorganisms that can cause foodborne illnesses have been found in apple juice, apple cider, orange juice, and frozen coconut milk, according to the FDA.

A 1997 assignment by the FDA to inspect unpasteurized cider operations generated eye-opening data. While the agency found no detection of pathogens in a finished product to be sold to the public, it found that one firm's apples tested positive for Salmonella. The assignment also uncovered fecal coliforms and E. coli in the wash water used at several of the companies.

Though industries have contended that good manufacturing practices and increased inspections should be enough to ward off contaminants, the FDA said more needs to be done. Labeling also addresses the need for a warning until juice processors implement measures to control pathogens, the FDA noted on July 8, 1998. The FDA suggested the voluntary labeling program to curb the outbreak of foodborne illnesses. However the risk of contamination is low, as more than 98 percent of fruit and vegetable juices are pasteurized.

nally burgeoned in California are prepared to expand throughout the nation, including the Midwest and Southeast. For example, Carole Clancy reports in the *Tampa Bay Business Journal* that one juice bar alone, Planet Smoothie, plans to operate about 30 juice bars in the Tampa Bay area by the end of the 1990s.

Entrepreneur listed Juice Bars as one of the "12 hottest businesses for 1999." Research uncovered revenues in excess of $500 million for 1999, due in part to expansion from the West to the East Coast. Juice Gallery, a publishing, media, and research company based in Chino Hills, California, also has high hopes for the future of the juice and smoothie industry. Dan Titus, director of Juice Gallery, predicts more diversity among menu options toward the close of the

A sampling of Jamba Juice smoothies, blended-to-order.
(Courtesy of Juice Club, Inc.)

century, as well as improvements to existing equipment and new equipment designs as the industry continues to grow.

Responding to juice bar popularity, full-service restaurants, grocery stores, and fitness centers have opted for juice bars in order to cash in on the demand for various juice concoctions and smoothies. Equipment manufacturers also made it easier to set up juice bars by developing blenders and juicers for kiosks and carts for use in airports, campuses, convenience stores, and health clubs, according to *Restaurants and Institutions.*

James Scarpa reported in *Restaurant Business* that adding juice bar capabilities to a restaurant can significantly boost sales. As consumer dietary trends shift away from alcoholic beverages as a lunch time potable, restaurants can increase revenues by pushing fruit juice concoctions and smoothies, which bring in considerably more money than their soda and ice tea soft drink counterparts. Restaurants can, according to Scarpa, successfully sell juice bar elixirs by presenting them as upscale drinks served in attractive glasses replete with garnishes.

While franchises accounted for most of the growth in the juice bar industry in the late 1990s, juice

bar consultancies have also cropped up to help those entrepreneurs choosing to go it alone. Juice Gallery owner Dan Titus offers a comprehensive package as a franchise alternative that takes prospective juice bar owners through all the steps to opening and running a successful business. Chris Cuvelier, owner of Juice & Smoothie Bar Consulting helps clients in the United States as well as overseas avoid some of the common industry mistakes. These consultants draw from their own experiences as juice bar start-ups, including successes and things they could have done better, to lead others to successful ownership.

INDUSTRY LEADERS

Juice Club, Inc., with its Jamba Juice bistros, was one of the more successful juice bars in the 1990s. Founded in 1990 by Kirk Perron, the San Francisco-based juice bar company had 76 stores in 1998, all of which were located in California, according to *Inc.* However, CEO Perron intends to expand his operations to 1,000 units by the turn of the century with the help of equity partnerships. According to Michael Adams in *Restaurant Business,* Juice Club, Inc. expects to garner $100 million in revenue by the late 1990s. (While Adams reported that a single Juice Club unit alone could achieve up to $1.5 million in sales, estimated 1997 revenues for the company totaled approximately $4 million, according to *Ward's Business Directory.*) Perron created Juice Club to offer consumers an alternative to both fatty fast foods and to insipid health foods, and his Jamba Juice shops emphasize quality and healthy eating by using fresh fruits and vegetables for beverages. Perron plans to convert all his juice bars to the hipper Jamba Juice concept, which provides sandwiches and soups in addition to juice concoctions. "Jamba" is a west African word meaning celebration, according to Perron, who wants his Jamba Juice units to offer customers a festive atmosphere as well as exciting, healthy drinks.

Smoothie King, based in New Orleans, has expanded its franchises across the United States. In 1998, Smoothie King operated 165 outlets in 10 states and had sold the rights for 229 franchises in various locations throughout the country. The company plans to continue expanding with 12 new franchises under way in the Austin, Texas, area—all of which are scheduled to be complete by the year 2000. Each unit costs about $150,000 to set up, but operators expect to glean $500,000 in annual sales. Smoothie King was founded in 1973 by Stephen and Cynthia Kuhnau and began franchising in 1989. Stephen Kuhnau develops all of the company's emulsions and studies nutritional trends and findings to provide up-to-date products for his health conscious customers. In addition to smoothies, Smoothie King offers health products, such as vitamins and minerals, and competes with general health food stores. *Entrepreneur* magazine acknowledged the success of Smoothie King in 1995, ranking the juice bar operation the number one specialty beverage franchiser in its annual "Franchise 500" list. In 1996, the company reported sales of $21 million. In 1998 Smoothie King announced plans to expand overseas and reports international interest from countries such as Canada, Mexico, Korea, and South America.

Atlanta-based Planet Smoothie vied with Smoothie King in the race to bring juice bars to the East Coast. Founded in 1995, Planet Smoothie planned to expand from 85 stores to more than 300 stores by the end of 1999, including expansion overseas with 5 stores in London and another 12 stores slated to open in the United Kingdom during the year. Most of the new stores are expected to be located in shopping centers. Planet Smoothie relies on franchising to expand its presence. Under its policies, the corporation subsidizes the opening of new Planet Smoothie outlets and unit operators share profits with the Planet Smoothie corporation. In 1997, it cost about $70,000 to start a new Planet Smoothie unit and, with corporate subsidies, franchise owners only had to pay part of that figure, according to Carole Clancy in *Tampa Bay Business Journal.*

Juice World is a promising juice bar chain with bold ambitions. In 1996, the company operated only 3 outlets with 9 more in development, but planned to have 150 franchised outlets by 1999. Founded by accountants Michael and Carol-Dana Fullam as a business for their daughter, Juice World blossomed quickly. In 1996 the Fullams ran juice bars only in California, but intended to disperse the chain throughout the country, with destinations such as Chicago and the East Coast. Juice World's northern California locations allow the company to have unlimited access to the organic fruits and vegetables it uses for its concoctions. Based in Arroyo Grande, California, Juice World hopes to garner $120 million in revenues by 2000, according to Joan Holleran in *Beverage Industry.*

Other leading smoothie and juice bar operations include: Edina, Minnesota-based Orange Julius's Just Juice concept; an International Dairy Queen venture, which had 410 stores open in 1998 and signed contracts for 15 more franchises to begin operating throughout the country; San Diego-based Fresh Blend Smoothie and Juice Bar, which began in 1994 and operates 11 juice bars in California, Arizona, and Nevada, reporting 45 percent sales increases since opening; and Scottsdale, Arizona-based Sun City Squeeze, which ran 105 mall and health club juice bars in the mid-1990s with intentions to open about 200 more by the year 2000.

AMERICA AND THE WORLD

Overseas expansion is on the minds of many of the companies growing in the United States. Analysts agree that there is room for everyone both here and in the international market. After offering their Orchard Blend Smoothie in TCBY stores, TCBY launched their subsidiary, Juice Works, in 1998, and plans to open franchises internationally after further development of the concept in the United States. Ice cream giant Baskin-Robbins offered up its BR Smoothie in 100 locations outside the United States in 1998, including Australia, Europe, and Guam, and hopes to move into Canada in the future.

FURTHER READING

Adams, Michael. "Smoothie Operator." *Restaurant Business,* 10 October 1996, 80.

Castagna, Nicole G. "Smoothing Out the Juice Bar: Extract Profits from Growing Interest in Produce-based Beverages." *Restaurants & Institutions,* 15 September 1997, 110.

Clancy, Carole. "Smoothie Bars: Serving Up the Next Food Fad?" *Tampa Bay Business Journal,* 30 May 1997, 1.

Holleran, Joan. "Squeezing Fresh, Healthy Profits." *Beverage Industry,* April 1996, 25.

"Juice Gallery Offers 1999 Predictions for the Juice and Smoothie Industry." *Business Wire,* 15 December 1998. Available from http://www.thejuicereview.com/juice_smoothie/juice_gallery_predictions%20_1999.htm.

Khermouch, Gerry. "Third Places." *Brandweek,* 13 March 1995, 36.

Krummert, Bob. "A Growth Bonanza for Smooth Beverages." *ID: The Voice of Foodservice Distribution,* June 1998, 66.

Lorenzini, Beth. "Turn Up the Juice." *Restaurants & Institutions,* 1 February 1995, 113.

Phillips, Debra, et al. "Entrepreneur Magazine's 12 Hottest Businesses for 1999: Juice Bars." *Entrepreneur Magazine,* 1999. Available from http://www.entrepreneurmag.com/entmag/hotbiz99/juice.html.

"Planet Smoothie Blends Nutritious Quick Fix." *Shopping Center World,* December 1998.

Plotkin, Hal. "Seeking Quality, Juicer Squeezes Out Franchisees." *Inc.,* July 1997, 25.

Rohland, Pamela, et al. "SmartPicks Top Businesses for 1999: Juice Bars." *Entrepreneur Magazine,* 1999. Available from http://www.entrepreneurmag.com/startup/topbiz99/juice.html.

Rousseau, Rita. "Squeezing Profits from Juice." *Restaurants and Institutions,* 15 October 1995, 142.

Scarpa, James. "Be Fruitful." *Restaurant Business,* 15 January 1997, 93.

"Squeeze to Please." *Restaurant Business,* 1 July 1996, 147.

Teague, Elaine W. "Juice Bar Franchises Pour Into the Global Marketplace." *Entrepreneur International Magazine,* March 1998. Available from http://www.entrepreneurmag.com/page.hts?N=5900.

———. "Virgin Versions: Smoothie Operators Sweet Talk Customers into Alcohol-Free Concoctions of Fresh Fruit Juices." *Restaurant Business,* 20 November 1996, 103.

—Karl Heil, updated by Lisa DeShantz-Cook

RETAIL AUTO LEASING

Retail auto leasing is emerging as one of the hottest segment in the auto industry. Before 1970 only large corporations had access to leasing opportunities. General Motors Acceptance Corporation (GMAC) developed a new simplified retail lease service plan in 1970 and by 1982 introduced its Direct Leasing Plan, which offered the advantages of affordable leasing to individuals. Approximately 3.0 percent of total retail sales by all companies were leases in 1982. By 1992 the percentage had risen to 20.4 percent and by 1999 to 33.0 percent. The Ford Motor Company led the way in the leasing market. In 1993, leases accounted for 66.0 percent of Ford's total retail market and was responsible for the Taurus being the best selling car in America. According to *The Detroit News,* a record 11.1 million individual leases expired in 1999 driving a huge number of customers into dealer showrooms to look for a new vehicle.

ORGANIZATION AND STRUCTURE

Ford, General Motors, and DiamlerChrysler introduced retail leasing in the late 1960's. Before that only large corporations who could afford to lease large fleets of vehicles had that opportunity. The automakers controlled retail leasing through their system of dealerships and captive financing arms—private subsidiaries of the auto companies, General Motors Acceptance Corporation (GMAC) and Ford Motor Credit Company (FMCC), for example. They set up leasing desks at designated dealerships and one salesman was designated as the lease specialist. The dealership was and still is the pass through agent, and does not usually own the vehicle at any point in the transaction—the automaker owns the vehicle until it is sold to the leasing company. In the early days of leasing, the captive finance arms such as General Motors Acceptance Corporation (GMAC) or Ford Motor Credit Company (FMCC) had to supply the lease. Banks and credit unions later took over some of the lease contracts.

At first glance one might think that the major automakers have the lease market to themselves. That is not the case though captive finance companies hold 66 percent of the leasing market while banks have 29 percent, and independent finance companies and credit unions have the remaining market. Major auto companies still use their vast network of dealerships to sell retail leases. In the late 1990s, however, leasing was so popular that almost every salesman in every dealership was equipped to sell a lease. The purchaser can go with the captive financing company; or, if he can find a better deal with an independent finance company, he can have the automaker transfer the ownership of the vehicle to that company. The customer can also go to one of the many independent leasing companies that have entered the market in recent years and they may supply the type of vehicle the person desires.

NICHE MARKETS

Newer companies are beginning to develop niche markets. For instance, *Success* pointed out that PMH Caramanning, a full service marketing company located in Farmington Hills, Michigan, has targeted companies that lease or purchase less than 30 vehicles with their new unit, Business Vehicle Services (BVS) in cooperation with General Motors. According to PMH president Peter McAteer, "These businesses don't usually qualify for corporate rates. They have to buy retail. But we train individuals at a participating auto dealerships to act as fleet managers for each company they deal with."

Auto-buying services have expanded into the lease market as well. One can hire a lease-hunting professional to find the best lease for a fee of between $300 and $500. Car Bargains, AutoAdvisor, and CarSource are three such businesses mentioned in *Money* that will track down the desired vehicle and close the deal. Professional lease hunters usually do better than amateurs. Internet lessors are working the World Wide Web and an astute hunter can now find a good deal anywhere in the world. Two sites to find information on are Edmund's Web site (www.edmunds.com) and Microsoft's CarPoint (www.carpoint.msn.com). Both offer prices, reviews, and an up-to-date listing of rebates. A shopper can click on IntelliChoice (www .intelichoice.com) to check manufacturers' leases and Carwizerd (www.carwizerd.com) to check the latest residual factors. Lastly, a new market niche is developing, the used-car lease fueled by high returns of expensive vehicles and the advent of the auto "superstore." (Also see the essay in this book entitled Used Car Superstores.)

TYPES OF LEASES

Leasing companies use two types of leases. Most leases are closed-end where the lessee is not responsible for any end-of-lease payment. The other type of lease is open-end. The lessee or consumer takes the risk regarding the market value at the end of the lease. If the vehicle is worth more than the residual value or amount for which the vehicle can be purchased, the lessee must pay the difference if he chooses to purchase it. If the vehicle is worth less, the lessee may negotiate a rebate. In both types of leases the vehicle may be returned or purchased. The closed-end lease with a manufacturer subsidy or a subvented lease is the most popular of the two leases.

GOVERNMENT REGULATIONS IMPACT LEASING INDUSTRY

The federal Consumer Leasing Act of 1976 (CLA) was enacted for consumer use as an alternative to installment sales, reported *Business Lawyer*. As leasing became more prevalent in the early 1970s, the federal government realized that the consumer was confused as to what he was actually buying, a situation that was used by a few unscrupulous leasing companies. CLA requires that a leasing company must make certain disclosures in writing. The lessor or owner of the vehicle may be the automaker's captive finance arm or a

bank or finance company to which the automaker sells the lease and the vehicle. The name of the lessor can be found on the back of the contract. The lessor must give a brief description of the leased property. He must disclose the total amount of the initial payment required, including the acquisition fee or what the dealer pays the leasing company, usually $200-$500, to handle the lease for the vehicle. Marking up these fees increases profits. It may also include the adjusted capitalized cost, which is the capitalized cost minus the capitalized cost reduction. This can also be negotiated. The cap or capitalized cost is the purchase price and includes fees, taxes, warranty charges, insurance, and interest costs, and must be included in this disclosure. The capitalized cost reduction is also called the down payment on the lease and can be negotiated.

The lessor must disclose penalties for late payments or delinquencies. This includes early termination liability or the amount the lessee must pay to terminate the lease early. It can range from 30 to 100 percent of the remaining amount of the lease. The lessor must explain the warranty and who is responsible for the upkeep of the vehicle. Excess wear and tear is the amount the lessee pays for damage to the car at the end of the lease. It is not negotiable. The lessee should probably have it fixed himself. The lessee needs to know if the leasing company has a flexibility on moving clause. Some local and regional leasing companies do not allow the lessee to take the car when moving to another state. Some states also require the lease taxes to be paid again even if they have been paid to another state.

At the end of the lease the lessee has certain rights under CLA. The customer may have the option to purchase the vehicle. This is called the purchase option. At the end of the lease, the vehicle can be purchased for a "fixed" dollar amount or "fair market value." The "fixed" dollar amount is determined at the beginning of the lease, while the "fair market value" is determined at the end of the lease. The fixed purchase option is usually the better way to go. Both options can be negotiated if the lessor is willing to talk. The lessee must be given the residual value at the beginning of the lease. The purchase fee, usually $250, must also be disclosed. The purchase fee or the amount paid for the right to buy the vehicle can be negotiated.

If the lessee does not purchase the vehicle, he must pay the disposal or disposition fee, which covers the cost of moving, cleaning, and disposing of the car. This is charged by the leasing company and is waived if the vehicle is purchased; however, it can be negotiated. Penalties for default or early termination must be reasonable.

Regulation M, revised federal rules that went into effect in October 1997, requires a standardized leasing form and simple language that tells the lessee exactly what the terms are. These terms include monthly depreciation, monthly rent charge, and the monthly payment. Monthly depreciation is the adjusted capital cost minus the residual value, divided by the number of months of the lease. The monthly rent charge also called the money factor is extremely important. It is the lease rate, or the cost of interest, on money borrowed. It is found by subtracting the monthly depreciation from the monthly payment. The monthly payment is the average monthly depreciation and average monthly rent charge, as well as federal, state, and local sales taxes.

State governments began to realize that some abuses existed in the leasing industry. At least 10 states have studied the leasing industry and enacted or amended consumer protection statues covering automobile leasing. *Business Lawyer* reported that state government appears to be focusing on three issues: the punitive nature of default charges; gap insurance; and wear and tear damage. Illinois, Maryland, New Hampshire, New York, and Wisconsin have statutes, which restrict the charge for early termination to a reasonable amount. States are beginning to require lessors to disclose whether they are providing gap insurance or informing the lessee that he must provide his own. Gap Insurance protects the lessee from paying the difference between the lease payoff and the vehicle's insured value if it is stolen or totaled. The dealer cost is about $200 and this insurance is vital to the lessee.

Federal law authorizes lessors to determine the standards for abnormal damage to the vehicle. State law in Connecticut, Illinois, Maryland, New Hampshire, New Jersey, New York, and Wisconsin is stepping in to help determine what is "normal" and what is "excessive" wear and tear. With the popularity of leasing, more states are expected to develop comprehensive state consumer leasing statutes. This trend was apparent at the National Conference of Commissioners on Uniform State Laws where a committee to draft a Uniform Consumer Leases Act (UCLA) was formed. More protection for both the lessee and the lessor is expected shortly.

Another aspect that state governments are looking into is the mileage allowance. The lessee is allowed to drive a certain number of miles a year, usually between 10,000 and 15,000 miles. If the total mileage of the lease is exceeded, the lessee must pay a fee, usually 12 to 15 cents per mile. If more miles are needed, that can be negotiated at the beginning of the lease. Some Lessors will give cash or credit for vehicles re-turned that used less than the allowed mileage. If a lessee exceeds his mileage allowance, the price he pays can be extremely painful to his wallet.

CURRENT CONDITIONS

Conditions for both leasing companies and lessees are expected to be good well into 2000. The prices of 1999 models of most major companies are holding the line or even being reduced a percent or two. Ford is reducing overall prices, GM is holding the line, and DiamlerChrysler has an increase of only 0.1 percent. Foreign carmakers are dropping prices even more. According to William Wilson, an economist for Comerica Bank in Detroit, "Automakers have no choice. They're forced to lower prices to promote sales." In spite of falling car prices and lower interest rates, the cost of financing a new luxury vehicle is more than some house payments. The monthly payment for a $29,000 car with 10.0 percent down and an 8.5 percent three-year loan is about $824.00, the same as a 30-year mortgage payment on a $160,000 house. That is why 1999 was considered the year of the lease.

The "baby boomers" are in their prime buying years now and many of them want the high-end luxury vehicles. According to *Consumer Trends,* the most likely buyers of new lease vehicles are between the ages of 35 and 54. As long as government regulations and the tax environment are favorable, boomers will continue to lease. Either they can't afford to finance a car like a $43,000 Yukon Denali at $850 a month or they want to keep that $43,000 working for them in other financial markets. At the end of 2 or 3 years they still have the option of buying the vehicle or leasing another brand new vehicle. The boomers are money savvy and are likely to take the deal that will net them the most money in the long term.

Regulation M has changed the leasing market. Michael Kranitz, head of LeaseSource, an online guide to automotive leasing in *Crain's Cleveland Business* said that "the new rules should take some of the fear out of leasing." The lessor must disclose the terms of a lease in clear simple terms. Most lessors include free gap insurance, which covers that difference between the lease payoff and an insurance settlement if the car is totaled or stolen. A financed vehicle does not have this protection. Most lessors today do not create unfair wear and tear charges. They want the lessee to stay with them. A vehicle owner would also be responsible for the same repairs before selling the vehicle. Also, if the lessee expects to drive more than

15,000 miles a year, conditions of most leases, he can negotiate a higher mileage at a slightly higher cost.

The Internal Revenue Service rules favor leasing luxury cars for business use, according to Andrew Blackman, a certified public accountant with Shapiro & Lobel, in New York City, in *Kiplinger' Personal Finance Magazine*. Tax breaks are higher and business write-offs for a leased car are easier. A business owner who buys a vehicle is only allowed to deduct part of the cost while the lessor can deduct the full cost of the lease.

NEW TREND

The latest idea in the lease business is the used-car lease. With the huge number of 2- and 3-year leases returned in 1999, the market for used-car leases heated up. "A used-car lease lets people step up to a nicer car than they could otherwise afford," said analyst Art Spinella of CNW Marketing/Research in *Money*. According to GE Capital Auto Financial Services, a leasing firm, only 2 percent of used-car shoppers purchase a lease. Sandra Derickson, GE Capital Auto Financial Services' president, predicted in *Money*, "We think used-car leasing will be one of the fastest-growing parts of the industry." One in ten luxury cars such as Mercedes-Benz and BMW are used-car leases. With all the expensive Explorer and Expedition sport utilities vehicles (SUV) coming back from new car leases, Ford is offering used-car leases to people who would still like a SUV but still could not afford the residual price. A vehicle that is 2- or 3-years old has already taken its major depreciation and its value will decline much more slowly in the next three to four years. For example, a new Ford Explorer XLT will lose 42 percent of its value in the first two years, and only 45 percent more in the next four years, according to Automotive Lease Guide, a research firm, in *Money*. A used-vehicle coming off a two year lease in good condition with low mileage can be a reasonable deal for both the customer and the used-car lessor as well.

PITFALLS IN THE LEASING BUSINESS

When lease companies offer high residuals and low monthly payments, they can get stuck with a glut of returned lease vehicles. If the used-car market is hot, they can get rid of them there. If the residual of the used vehicle is higher than the street value, the lessor will have to take the loss. In 1998, approximately 80 percent of the cars leased for two years were returned to the leasing company. Lenders are losing an average of $1,400 a vehicle, according to Lee & Mason of Maryland Inc., a Boston company that sells residual-value insurance, in *Automotive News*. The leasing business can be tricky according to Dick Schliesmann, executive vice president of Wells Fargo Bank in Walnut Creek, California, and chairman of the Consumers Bankers Association in *Automotive News*. The lessor needs to know the street value of the vehicle at the end of the lease. The buyer also needs to know the value of various currencies on the world money market. Said Schliesmann, "In leasing, you have to know not only the value of a car, but what the value of the yen or the deutsche mark is going to be." For instance, if the Japanese Yen goes from 85 per dollar to 120 per dollar as it did in 1996-1997, then a new Honda or Camry will be worth less than an old vehicle coming off a lease. Why should a customer purchase an old car when he can have a new one for less? Therefore, banks and credit unions are discontinuing short term leasing where the vehicle returns are high and leaving it to the captive finance companies.

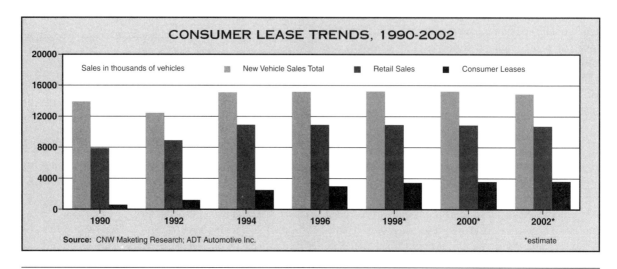

CONSUMER LEASE TRENDS, 1990-2002

Sales in thousands of vehicles ▪ New Vehicle Sales Total ▪ Retail Sales ▪ Consumer Leases

Source: CNW Maketing Research; ADT Automotive Inc.

*estimate

INDUSTRY LEADERS

Ward's Business Directory of U.S. Private and Public Companies lists Ford Motor Credit Company (FMCC), General Motors Acceptance Corporation (GMAC), and Nissan Motor Acceptance Corporation (NMAC)—financial arms of the major automakers—as the major captive lessors. Both GMAC and FMCC have been in existence since the beginning of the auto industry, and they jumped into retail leasing in the late 1960s. *Automotive News* wrote in August 1998 that GE Capital Auto Financial Service, a major supporter of DiamlerChrysler leases and a major player in the lease business, did not renew its deal with Diamler-Chrysler because of potential loses. DiamlerChrysler Financial Corporation took over leasing responsibilities for DiamlerChrysler. The top independent auto lessors include Wheels Inc., Automotive Rentals Inc., Executive Car Leasing Co., Leasing Associates Inc., Always Rent A Car Co., Langhome Leasing and Messenger Service, Franklin Equity Leasing Company, Selex Systems Inc., A-Drive Corp., Jake Sweeney Auto Leasing Inc., PHD Penske Leasing, and American Honda Finance Corp.

AMERICA AND THE WORLD

According to Daniel Howes in *The Detroit News,* the company that wins the race to be a world company will be the one that learns to use emerging technology to manage changing markets, customer preferences, and a diverse work force. Jacques Nasser, Ford Motor Company's president and chief executive has issued a challenge to Ford to become a "world-class consumer products company." He wants to create a worldwide company that would offer a variety of services including sales, rental, leasing, and financing. General Motors chairman John F. Smith Jr. agreed. "The global auto companies of the future . . . are going to be more focused on the total life cycle of the vehicle and how their company participates in that there's no end to it." He also said, "As I look out, I don't see it being just a hardware game. I'm talking about info-tainment coming into the vehicle controlled by the manufacturer in such a way that we bill for the service." Apparently, Smith would lease "info-tainment" whether the customer bought or leased the vehicle.

According to *Consumer Trends,* European vehicles tend to be more popular with American lessors. In 1997, American consumers leased for example, 66 percent of Mercedes' and 62 percent of BMW's.

A total of 55 percent of cars leased were European while 31 percent were American.

DOWNSIDE TO THE WORLD MARKET

Nissan Motor Acceptance Company (NMAC), the finance arm of Nissan, Japan's number two automaker, held third place in the number of leases outstanding in the United States in 1999. Bob Thomas, president of Nissan Motor Corporation, U.S.A., prophetically said in 1992, "Two years down the road you're going to be looking at those vehicles again. They will probably compete with your new vehicles. You've got half of your asset still remaining. You haven't depreciated it out. This is the risk side of it." Because it overestimated the value of its residuals, Nissan lost $2 billion in 1998 on returned leased vehicles. The economic crisis in Asia in the late 1990s made matters worse. Honda Motor Company and Toyota also had serious losses, but not as deep as Nissan's. A lease company entering the world market must not only know the expected residual value in the home country, but must also keep a close eye on world economies as well.

NEW TECHNOLOGY

Not to be outdone by Ford and General Motors, DiamlerChrysler Financial Corporation moved to electronic training in the leasing business. Use of an Intranet to train its leasing staff is expected to eliminate the need for thick manuals. LearnLinc I-Net is an electronic classroom tool made by Interactive Learning International Corp., of Troy, New York. More accurate leasing at a lower training cost and at a speedier pace are impressive results of the new technology. According to Don McCloud, manager of training and personnel development at DiamlerChrysler, in *The Detroit News,* "Leasing has become as increasingly large part of our business over the last six or seven years. And with state and federal leasing rules changing all the time, we can now be confident that the right information is getting to the right people" at each of DiamlerChrysler's offices worldwide. Ford is looking closely at this new technology and expects to implement a version by 2000.

FURTHER READING

"The ABC's of Leasing." *House Beautiful,* December 1997.

"Auto Leasing." *Consumer Trends,* International Credit Association, 1998.

Bivins, Larry. "Auto Lease Campaign Spells Out Agreements." *The Detroit News,* 10 December 1997.

"Buying or Leasing a Car." *Consumer Reports,* April 1998.

Connelly, Mary, and Charles M. Thomas. "New Lease on Life." *Automotive News,* 23 August 1993.

Coulombe, Charles A. "Little Fleet: a New Approach to Leasing Lets Small Business Zoom into High Gear. (PMH Caramanning's Business Vehicle Services Auto Leasing Service)." *Success,* October 1997.

Edgerton, Jerry. "Leasing in the Lap of Luxury: (at a price you can afford)." *Money,* October 1998.

———. "Secondhand News: Automakers Are Increasingly Pushing Used-car Leases. Here's When One Makes Sense." *Money,* 1 April 1999.

Gelb, Joseph W., and Peter N. Cubita. "An Overview of State Automobile Leasing Legislation. (1997 Annual Survey of Consumer Financial Services Law)." *Business Lawyer,* May 1997.

GMAC: A Long Tradition of Leadership. GMAC Corporation, 1999.

Gruber, Gerald H. "Recovering Hidden Values in Retail Lease Portfolios." *Journal of Retail Banking,* Fall 1992.

Harris, Sheryl. "Car Lease Math Goes Public New Rules Should Take the Surprise Out of Popular Transaction." *Detroit Free Press,* 9 March 1998.

Hearn, Albert D. *Auto Lease Guide,* 1999. Available from http://www.leaseguide.com.

Henry, Ed. "Don't Buy a New Car—Lease It." *Kiplinger's Personal Finance Magazine,* December 1998.

———. "Tax Breaks Favor Leasing: IRS Rules Deliver Fat Write-offs for Business Cars." *Kiplinger's Personal Finance Magazine,* May 1997.

Henry, Jim. "Residual Losses Force GE to Quit Diamler-Chrysler Leasing." *Automotive News,* 24 August 1998.

———. "Value Subtracted: Average Residual Losses Are Up to $1,400 a Leased Vehicle." *Automotive News,* 23 March 1998.

Howes, Daniel. "Strategy: To Win, Companies Must Change Quickly Management Speed Will Determine Worldwide Success." *The Detroit News,* 21 December 1998.

Keel, Keith. "Auto Retailing: Changing Trends in Jobs and Business." *Monthly Labor Review,* October 1998.

Miller, Stephen E. "Economics of Automobile Leasing: The Call Option Value." *Journal of Consumer Affairs,* Summer 1995.

Phillips, David. "Car Sales on Record Pace." *The Detroit News,* 8 April 1999.

Sakurai, Joji. "Nissan Struggles in Sea of Debt: Automaker Misread Consumer Trends to Fall on Hard Times." *The Detroit News,* 16 February 1999.

Smith, Rebecca. "New Rule: Car Dealers Must Provide Clear Information on Auto Leasing." *San Jose Mercury News.* Distributed by Knight-Ridder/Tribune Information Services, 18 September 1996.

"Summary of Consumer Credit Laws." *Credit and Financial Issues: Responsive Business Approaches to Consumer Needs.* Washington D.C.: U.S. Department of Commerce, May 1995.

Suttell, Scott. "Fed Steps in to Clear Up Confusion in Auto Leasing." *Crain's Cleveland Business,* 27 October 1997.

Wilkinson, Stephanie. "Intranet Training Tool Gets a Road Test." *PC Week,* 2 February 1998.

Ward's Business Directory of U.S. Private and Public Companies. Detroit: Gale, 1999.

—Dorothy L. Wood

RISK MANAGEMENT SERVICES

Risk managers help protect their own organization or their clients from the effects of risk. Some industry analysts defined risk as "the possibility that a future event may cause harm," adding, "risk includes potential opportunity as well as harm." Without some risks, companies could not grow, since some risks lead to large gains. Without risk management services to analyze potential risks, companies could make costly mistakes and lose business.

The contemporary risk manager's job usually involves predicting and controlling or preventing losses within the organization and determining the proper amount of insurance to cover actual losses. The goal of any risk management service is to protect an organization from harm and position it for gain.

Risk management is essentially a sequence of decisions. Anything that could interfere with the company's progress must be identified. Risk managers examine methods for dealing with these potential problems, and choose the best method. This method must then be implemented and monitored. In the late 1990s the major issues facing risk managers included the rise in natural disasters around the world, the implementation of stricter environmental policies, the proposal and adoption of new health care policies, the Year 2000 problem, and the increase in large corporate mergers and acquisitions.

ORGANIZATION AND STRUCTURE

The risk manager is an insurance broker who advises clients on insurance and risk; an independent consultant on risk, who works for a fee; or a salaried employee who manages risk for the employer. The profession's largest trade group, The Risk and Insurance Management Society, Inc. (RIMS), classified risk management service providers as anyone who protects an organization's financial and physical assets; bought insurance/risk transfer products for an organization; manages an employee benefit program; administers a self-funded property/casualty and/or employee benefits insurance program; or buys risk control services from independent suppliers.

Risk managers and risk management services first identify what the organization potentially may lose. In a disaster like a chemical spill or fire, the company can lose physical property, such as buildings, vehicles, and equipment. They can also lose income after a disaster, since they are unable to do business while things are rebuilt or replaced. Companies can also lose personnel to a disaster. Employees would not necessarily need to die or be severely injured for the company to suffer losses. Any time employees miss work and draw benefits, the employer pays for it. Another potential risk is liability. If the company produces something that accidentally harms its customers, the company could be liable for damages.

Risk control is intended to stop losses before they occur. One risk control technique is exposure avoidance, which means abandoning or not participating in an activity that could bring a loss, such as deciding to stop manufacturing children's pajamas with asbestos fibers. Other techniques for risk control are loss prevention, which means reducing the chance of a certain loss, or loss reduction, which means anything to lessen the severity of a loss, such as disaster planning. Another technique is the segregation of loss exposure—

keeping valuable assets in a variety of locations. Examples of segregation are splitting up the company's inventory in different warehouses or sending its delivery trucks along different routes so if an accident occurs in one location, the company will not lose everything. Another form of risk control is contractual transfer that shifts some legal and financial loss to another party. This is done by leasing or subcontracting risky activities, such as toxic chemical transport, to another firm that then shares the liability for a mishap.

Risk financing means paying for the losses that *did* occur, and this is done by either transfer or retention. Companies transfer losses by sharing responsibility for risks with other parties, such as contractors, or by taking out insurance policies with commercial insurance providers. Insurance generally covers property risks, liability risks, and transportation risks. Transfers completed without commercial insurance carriers often involved paying into a mutual insurance arrangement or "pool" maintained by other organizations sharing similar risks. In contrast, companies retain losses by paying for their own losses themselves by establishing a special funds or by taking out loans.

Risk managers buy commercial insurance several ways, but the standard way is through an agency or broker. According to one industry source, there were 70,000 agency/brokerage firms in the early 1980s, but by 1996, this number had fallen to 44,000 and could fall to 35,800 by the year 2006, due to mergers and acquisitions or an inability to compete. Risk managers can buy insurance from exclusive agents, like State Farm and Allstate, and direct response sales, like USAA and GEICO.

The simplest form of retention is current expensing of losses, which means paying for the loss like any other current expense. Another method involves using an unfunded loss reserve, like noting the loss as a potential liability to be paid later. Another financing method is a "funded loss reserve," which means drawing from a company fund set aside for that reason. The company might also borrow the money to pay for the loss. The most complex retention method involves the use of a "captive insurer," a private insurance carrier owned by the company and used to insure itself and its international subsidiaries. Many U.S. Fortune 1000 companies own captive insurance companies, and set them up offshore in locations such as Bermuda.

BACKGROUND AND DEVELOPMENT

In 1995, Fortune 1000 companies spent $18.2 billion on traditional risk financing—45.2 percent of risk

financing costs, while alternative financing expenditures reached $22.1 billion. This led some analysts to believe more corporations preferred to retain risk to save on traditional insurance. According to one survey, the preferred way to fund alternative financing was through some form of self-insurance, which was chosen by 92 percent of risk managers.

Many risk managers believed the cost of risk fell during the mid 1990s, with 60 percent of managers reporting a decrease in 1996, compared to 43 percent in 1995. Better "loss control" and higher risk retention helped lower costs. Other industry statistics confirmed the cost of risk dropped in 1995, to $6.49 per $1,000 of revenue, a 22 percent decline over three years.

As risk managers analyzed potential new problems, the insurance industry responded with even more products. As more companies did business on the Internet, some mistakenly assumed their existing general liability policies covered losses accrued from electronic transactions. In 1997, American International Group Inc. (AIG) introduced a policy called InsureSite to "respond to a company's third-party liability for loss of money or electronic funds resulting from the theft of credit card data due to business conducted on its World Wide Web site." As the information superhighway expanded, more risk managers also had to plan for telecommuters—62 percent thought their companies would allow more telecommuters in the next five years. And as more of the workforce sat at computers, 55 percent of risk managers reported higher repetitive motion claims, although 73 percent said their companies had programs to reduce the problem.

During the 1990s, insurance carriers marketed products covering all calamities. Several carriers offered kidnapping and extortion policies, especially designed to cover a company's top executives and their families when traveling or living abroad; some of these policies pay $25 to $50 million for hostage negotiations. Aon Corporation offers insurance against hostile takeovers for smaller companies, and the policy covered up to $5 million in legal expenses to thwart an unwanted buyer. American International Group Inc. (AIG) also offered political risk insurance for companies doing business abroad in case their overseas locations were nationalized or confiscated by an unexpected new government.

CURRENT CONDITIONS

According to the Risk and Insurance Management Society (RIMS), the industry's new growth will come from operations management, including safety and loss prevention, environmental risks, and ethics; not from finance, as some analysts contend. In addition, RIMS expects more small and mid-sized companies to add risk managers to their staffs or to include risk management as part of the responsibility of these companies' chief financial officers or treasurers. Because of the trend towards risk management services among companies of all sizes, more insurance brokers are charging fees for their services, instead of receiving commissions for selling insurance products.

According to the "1997 U.S. Risk Management Survey," the issues of Superfund legislation, product liability, tort reform, Occupational Safety and Health Administration (OSHA) policy, and Medicare strongly affected their work. According to the survey, 75 percent of risk managers call civil justice and tort reform "a significant factor in their everyday lives." Only 17 percent believed the Private Securities Litigation Reform Act of 1995, which encourages courts to punish lawyers who pursued frivolous lawsuits, has helped protect their companies.

Almost 90 percent of risk managers believe the Kennedy-Kasselbaum Health Care Reform law will not help their companies, although the law provides access to group health care plans for small businesses. Risk managers also must consider the revamped Family and Medical Leave Act, which allows employees for companies with at least 50 workers up to 12 weeks of unpaid leave for family or medical emergencies. However, about 43 percent of risk managers think this Act will have a negative effect on their companies, including reduced productivity and stress on workers covering for missing colleagues.

In the late 1990s, risk managers faced not only the escalation of natural disasters, but also the increased stringency of environmental regulations. *Risk Management* reports that the 1990s brought on five times as many natural disasters as the 1960s and that insurance companies pay 15 times what they paid in the 1960s. In 1996, for example, there were a record 600 catastrophes worldwide, which caused 12,000 deaths and $9 billion in losses from insurance. Experts frequently attribute the rise of natural disasters to global warming, which they believe will lead to greater windstorms, floods, droughts, and crop damage in the future.

During the late 1990s, corporate risk managers also started to focus more on ensuring their companies' compliance with federal environmental regulations. By addressing environmental issues such as pollution, waste management, and environmental liability, risk managers have the potential to aid companies in in-

creasing their profitability and competitiveness, according to *Risk Management.* The United States promised to reduce its greenhouse gas emissions to 7 percent below the levels of 1990 by 2010 and Congress considered a bill in 1999 that would provide incentives for businesses to cut gas emissions prior to the deadline. Risk managers also must assist in the compliance with the Environmental Protection Agency's stricter standards for ozone and particulate matter. Gridlock continued to hamper the cleanup of contaminated sites in the late 1990s. In 1999, Congress continued to debate the Superfund program, which promotes the remediation of contaminated sites. The debate over Superfund has stalled in funding, but *Risk Management* predicts that Congress may pass a bill that provides tax credits for the cleanup of contaminated sites.

Congress also proposed new legislation that would affect how the Resource Conservation and Recovery Act of 1976 treats the cleanup of solid and hazardous waste. *Risk Management* expects incremental reforms such as the revision of emission limits for hazardous air pollutants from incinerators. Risk managers also will have to address the "Clean Water Action Plan" introduced by Vice President Al Gore. This plan includes strategies for reducing polluted runoff and stopping wetlands reduction in an effort to gain 100,000 acres of wetlands by 2005.

Furthermore, risk managers had to countenance the Year 2000 problem during the late 1990s. Because older computer systems relied on a two-digit year designation, they were not designed to handle the date change from 1999 to 2000. Systems that are not Year 2000 compliant could crash or malfunction when the date change occurs. Consequently, the Year 2000 Problem could affect risk managers' service vendors who are not prepared for the problems. In addition, risk managers have had to develop management strategies and insurance products created to mitigate the force of the problem. Nonetheless, some risk managers are concerned that the new computer systems with the four-digit year designation will not be able to compare data from before the date change.

With mega mergers and acquisitions taking placing in almost all major industries, risk managers started becoming part of merger and acquisition teams in the late 1990s, according to the Risk and Insurance Management Society. Both buyers and sellers began to rely on risk managers to develop solutions to problems and obstacles that cropped up during the merger and acquisition process. For example, risk managers on the buying end must examine a target company's insurance policies, expenditures, loss experience, and other agreements and policies that could affect man-

About... **ECONOMY, COMPANY, AND COMMUNITY: THREE LEVELS OF RISK MANAGEMENT**

Risk management has benefits on three levels: economy, company, and community. An economy's risk is the wasted resources, both natural and man-made, destroyed by or used to fight accidental losses. For example, resources are wasted by fires when buildings are destroyed. An effective risk management program for an economy minimizes the resources consumed and improves the allocation of resources.

Certain companies or organizations also face risks for potential and actual losses. An effective company risk management program will enable the organization to distinguish between good risks and unnecessary ones. This allows the company to become more prosperous—without interfering with normal activities—while reducing the cost of risk.

A community's risk combines a company's and an economy's risks. Successful risk management on this level focuses on effects of actual or potential losses on a particular community.

While carrying out the duty of protecting the economy, companies, and the community, risk management services must work together to examine the interests of all levels, since all three have similar risks and similar resources allocated to establishing and maintaining risk management programs.

aging the company's risks and figure out ways to overcome any hurdles found in managing the prospective company's risks. Because of the brisk merger activity, risk managers can arrange insurance coverage so that it removes harmful liabilities from the balance sheets of companies to be acquired, according to *Business Insurance*.

In the late 1990s, companies began to voice concerns about new kinds of risk and insurers have sought ways to accommodate the new needs of businesses. These insurance innovations largely were policies that protect companies from poor financial performance by guaranteeing specific levels of earnings. One of the first of such policies was Honeywell Inc.'s, which covers its profits from overseas sales. Hence, if the dollar's value increases and thereby lowers the value of its overseas profits, the company files a claim. Other kinds of policies protect companies from losses if they result from circumstances beyond a company's control. These new policies provide risk managers with new tools for dealing with risk and preventing losses.

INDUSTRY LEADERS

One of the leading insurance brokerages offering risk management consulting is J & H Marsh & McLennan, Inc., a subsidiary of Marsh & McLennan Companies, which garnered sales of $7.2 billion and had 36,000 employees in 1998. They offer consultation on medical and legal cost containment, claims management, loss control, and employee benefits. The company formed through the merger of Johnson & Higgins, Marsh & McLennan, and CECAR of France, becoming the world's largest insurance broker.

The second highest grossing insurance firm is Aon Corp. with 1998 annual sales of $6.4 billion and 44,000 employees. Aon acquired brokerage Alexander & Alexander Services, another risk management consultant, in 1996, and the combined firm provides risk management through a subsidiary, Aon Risk Services, Inc. Aon Corp. has two major lines of service: a brokerage and consulting line and an underwriting line.

Some major insurance carriers also provide risk management support along with their policies. The largest of these is American International Group, Inc. (AIG), with 1998 sales of $30.7 billion and 40,000 employees. The company offers service through a division called AIG Risk Management, Inc. and wrote $3 billion in special risk premiums in 1996. The Chubb Corp., with 1998 sales of $6.3 billion and 11,000 employees, offers risk management through its Chubb Services Corp. and has special policies for energy, financial, and high-tech firms. Another carrier providing risk management is Reliance National, a subsidiary of Reliance Group Holdings, Inc. with 1998 sales of $3.36 billion and 6,640 employees.

Several firms only offer risk management consulting services to other companies. Some examples include: Shelter Island Risk Management Services; Mutual Risk Management Ltd.; E.W. Blanch Holdings, Inc., which services insurance companies; and Betterley Risk Consultants, long-time publishers of a newsletter named *Betterley's Risk Management*.

WORK FORCE

The Risk and Insurance Management Society, Inc. reported that 7,800 of their individual members handled some or all risk management tasks for their employers or clients in the late 1990s. According to a survey of risk managers reported by Logic Associates, companies with sales of $200 million or less employ a full-time risk management staff of two. Annual salaries for risk managers at smaller companies was around $65,000. Companies with sales of $2 to $4 billion typically have risk management departments with professional workers who report to the chief financial officer. Companies with $4 to $7 billion in annual sales usually have risk management departments with four professional workers. Companies with over $7 billion in annual sales have risk management staff of five or more. Risk managers' salaries at sizeable companies can be as high as $300,000 per year plus bonuses.

AMERICA AND THE WORLD

U.S. risk managers often base a company's captive insurance office in another state or country because of the tax advantage. The top U.S. states for captive insurance companies are Colorado, Illinois, Vermont, and Hawaii. Common off-shore captive domiciles include Panama, Barbados, and Grand Cayman. The world leader for captive insurance companies is Bermuda with over 1,300 firms. In 1997 at least 350 of these belonged to U.S. Fortune 500 companies. Bermuda's liberal corporate tax laws also attracts many global specialty insurance and reinsurance firms.

As for competing in the world market, one industry analyst had the following advice for risk management providers: "For globalization to be truly successful, risk managers will have to deal with the cultural and legal differences among countries without varying the services and economic protection their companies provide. Indeed, global thinking networking of worldwide risk management partners will be the factors that set the top risk managers apart from their peers."

RESEARCH AND TECHNOLOGY

Computer-aided analysis and tracking is an important tool for risk managers. Many risk managers believe computer technology makes their jobs easier. In a 1997 survey of risk managers, 77 percent of risk managers had Internet access at work, 67 percent had e-mail links to their insurance consultant or broker. In addition, 67 percent said online access to claims information was the Internet's most important feature. In another survey covering technology, approximately 60 percent of risk managers believe they will eventu-

ally be able to process claims reviews electronically and conduct videoconferences with insurers. Furthermore, *Risk Management* reports that most risk managers use the Internet for information gathering, researching products, services, and regulations, among other things. Around 33 percent of risk managers using the Internet use it to exchange information and about 13 percent use it to review claims.

FURTHER READING

"American International Group Web site." Available from http://www.aig.com.

Aon Corporation, Alexander & Alexander Services Inc., and Radford Associates. "1997 U.S., Risk Management Survey." Available from http://www.aon.com.

Bradford, Michael. "Internet Usage on the Rise for Risk Managers." *Business Insurance,* 30 April 1997.

"The Chubb Corporation Web site." Available from http://www.chubb.com.

Feldman, Paul. "Risk Managers' 'Global' Concerns." *Risk Management,* June 1998, 64.

Head, George L., and Stephen Horn. "Overview of the Risk Management Process: Chapter 1." Available from http://www.bus.orst.edu/faculty/nielson/rm/chapter1.htm.

Katz, David M. "Cost Managers About to Become Asset Managers." *National Underwriter Property & Casualty/Risk & Benefits Management Edition,* 2 December 1996.

———. "New RIMS President Delillo Sees RM Future in Operations, Not Finance." *National Underwriter Property & Casualty-Risk & Benefits Management,* 27 April 1998, 3.

———. "RMs Earning More, Headhunter Observes." *National Underwriter Property & Casualty-Risk & Benefits Management,* 26 May 1997.

———. "RMs to Ask Vendors: 'Ready for 2000?'" *National Underwriter Property & Casualty-Risk & Benefits Management,* 19 May 1997.

Kloman, Felix. "Of Mice and M & M." *Risk Management Reports,* June 1997.

Kroll, Karen M. "Covering Non-traditional Risks." *Industry Week,* 1 February 1999, 63.

Mills, Evan. "The Coming Storm: Global Warming and Risk Management." *Risk Management,* May 1998, 20.

Risk and Insurance Management Society, Inc. (RIMS) Web Site. Available from http://www.rims.org.

Roberts, Sally. "1998 RIMS Report: Risk Managers Increasingly Involved in M & A." *Business Insurance,* 11 May 1998, 38.

———. "Interet Brings Wide Web of Exposures." *Business Insurance,* 30 April 1997.

"The Structure of the Bermuda Insurance Industry." Available from http://www.bermuda-inc.com/cgi-win/bermuda-inc.exe/bim.

Telegro, Dean Jeffery. "A Growing Role: Environmental Risk Management in 1998." *Risk Management,* March 1998, 19.

Wojcik, Joanne. "Gaining a Higher Profile: Risk Management Increasingly Important in M&A Activity." *Business Insurance,* 5 October 1998, 2.

—Dave Fagan, updated by Karl Heil

Robotics and Industrial Automation

Robots, including programmable and multifunctional devices (often with a wide range of motion), are used to perform diverse tasks in industry, particularly in manufacturing. The commercial use of robots spread as factories automated. Robots appeal to industry in two situations: first, when they can perform a task faster and more accurately than humans (in some cases, tasks impossible or unsafe for humans), and secondly, when they are more cost effective.

The industrial automation industry is only 25 years old, yet it has grown immeasurably in that quarter of a century. In the 1980s there were no more than 1,500 robots existing worldwide. According to statistics from the Robotic Industries Association (RIA), the United States had about 88,000 industrial robots in place in 1998. The world total was 711,500, according to a report from the United Nations Economic Commission and the International Federation of Robotics, reported in the Financial Times. The world leader by far is Japan, where almost 60 percent of the world's robots are in use. In 1997 Japan used 277 robots for every 10,000 workers in manufacturing, followed by Germany with 90. Sweden and Italy each had just over 60 per 10,000 workers. Estimates suggest over 350,000 people are employed worldwide in the robotics field. These numbers attest to the growth of the industrial automation and robotics industries, which will likely accelerate well into the twenty-first century.

Robots serve numerous U.S. industry sectors, including aerospace, automotive, food and beverage, pharmaceuticals, semiconductors, and textiles. Among the functions they perform are: arc and spot welding, assembling, coating and painting, dispensing, hazardous materials handling, inspection, loading, and packing.

ORGANIZATION AND STRUCTURE

The robotics and industrial automation industry is made up of companies that produce robots and other industrial automation machines (accessories such as "grippers", or "hands"); those that supply the software that controls them; and others, called system integrators, that bring the pieces together for a specific application for a specific customer. The 1998 Robotics Industry Directory, published by the RIA, listed more than 125 suppliers of robots and related automation products. The association itself included more than 175 manufacturers, distributors, system integrators, accessory suppliers, research groups, and consultant firms. The customers of this industry are primarily manufacturing companies, with the automotive industry being the largest segment. Each year, however, more and more manufacturers in other industries such as food processing, electronics, and consumer goods invest in robotics and other automation systems. Computer chip manufacturers are becoming an increasingly important part of the market. Other fields, such as medicine, are also taking advantage of the special advantages of robots.

A small number of very large corporations, most headquartered outside the United States, manufacture most of the world's robots and industrial automation systems. However, the larger number of mid-size and small companies, focusing on the needs of a specific industry or application, have expanded the frontiers of robotics. Typically, the automation supplier and the customer work closely together to develop a system to meet the specific requirements of the application and site.

BACKGROUND AND DEVELOPMENT

In the 1890s, Nikola Tesla built the first radio-controlled vehicles in response to his vision of smart mechanisms that could emulate human movements. These were known as "automatons" until 1921, when a Czechoslovakian novelist and playwright, Karel Capek, featured robots in his play, *R.U.R.,* short for "Rossum's Universal Robots." The term "robot" comes from the Czechoslovakian word *robota,* which translates loosely into "serf," or compulsory labor. The word caught people's fancy, but robots did not exist in any great number outside the human imagination. It was not until the 1940s that true robots became reality. They were closely tied to the invention of computers.

Serious robot research began in the late 1950s when George Devol and Joe Engelberger developed the first industrial modern robots, known as Unimates. Devol earned the first patents for parts transfer machines. Engelberger formed Unimation, the first company to market robots, and consequently he has been called the father of robotics.

In the late 1960s, researchers at the Stanford Research Institute produced the first robot prototype, an experimental robot called Shakey. This machine processed information via a small computer and was capable of arranging blocks into stacks through the use of a television camera, which it used as a visual sensor. By itself, Shakey was not especially useful. It did, however, encourage other researchers to pursue useful functions for robots.

General Motors Corporation (GM) teamed up with the Massachusetts Institute of Technology (MIT) in the mid-1970s to develop robots. Using GM funds, MIT researcher Victor Scheinman refined a motor-driven arm he had invented. His work led to the production of a programmable universal manipulator for assembly (PUMA), which marked the beginning of the so-called robot age. Because success in developing industrial robots did not come easily, there were failures galore in the early stages of experimentation.

In the early 1980s robotics was expected to be the "next industrial revolution." Zymark Corporation produced the first robots manufactured specifically for use in a laboratory in 1982. A few years later, Perkin-Elmer Corp. introduced the MasterLab, and Fisher

Scientific Co. offered the MAXX 5, but neither was successful and both projects were dropped. In 1985 U.S.-based companies reported orders for a record 6,200 robots. Large corporations like General Electric (GE), IBM, and Westinghouse got into the robotics business, along with many smaller companies.

In the mid-1980s, however, the boom turned to bust when the huge market that had been predicted failed to materialize. The big name companies shut down robot operations, and many smaller companies merged or went out of business. The automobile industry accounted for more than 70 percent of robot orders, and cutbacks in capital investment there had devastating consequences. New orders for robots fell to just 3,700 in 1987.

Between 1987 and 1992 robot manufacturers improved the reliability and performance of their products, which would help to establish themselves in industries other than automotive. In 1991 Zymark introduced the XP robot, which featured programmable speeds and operated three times faster than other units in existence. That same year Hewlett-Packard Co. developed its Optimized Robot for Chemical Analysis (ORCA), which used a special methods development language to operate. These machines revolutionized the laboratory robot industry and set the stage for important advances in the field. Robots were also developed for assembly, material handling, and many other applications.

In the late 1990s robots were becoming more commonplace in the laboratory and other sites, especially manufacturing plants. Contemporary robots are much more advanced than their ancestors with the changes in recent years.

Thus far there have been three generations of robots, each of which show an increasing ability to accomplish more difficult tasks. Though some boast complex features, many amount to little more than electronic arms. In some cases each ensuing generation of robots is simply a more state-of-the-art arm. For instance, there are robotic arms today equipped with tools to assist surgeons in performing delicate operations—a far cry from the primitive first generation of robots.

The first generation of robots comprised industrial robots (such as information and painting robots and robots for education and automation in injection mold and welding lines). Some were used in semiconductor and disk assembly, wafer inspection, and wafer disk carriers. Next came the second generation, which gave birth to cleaning robots, security robots, and intelligent and assembly robots. As technology advanced, a third generation appeared. This group included more advanced service robots. This time, they did more than clean: they were personal robots. There were also medical/welfare robots used for rehabilitation and support for the elderly. In addition, this generation introduced cellular, navigation, biped, multi-arm and finger, and harvesting robots. Some featured artificial intelligence. There were also space robots, micro-robots for bionics, robots to work in hazardous environments, and maintenance robots.

Robots are dependent to a great extent on developments in computers. Like computers, their intelligence control systems are based on microprocessors. These systems provide continuous two-way communication between the robot's microprocessor and the arms. Whether the robots are classified as " playback" or "sequence" types, they rely on their microprocessors for directions.

Playback robots are capable of memorizing and repeating movements programmed by human operators. Sequence robots are less expensive than playback since manufacturers build their programs directly into the machines. Often, these robots move from point to point or from one assembly station to another. In either case, they work at a lower cost than humans, which accounts for their growing popularity. Comparisons between humans and robots on a typical production line suggest that robots far outperform humans at less cost overall. Moreover, they can function in places that pose hazards to humans. These advantages account for the surge in the number of industrial robots currently in place and the increasing number predicted to be installed in the near future.

Robots are classified as either industrial or non-industrial. Industrial robots are used primarily on assembly lines. Robots with grippers perform tasks such as loading and unloading presses and other machines. A second type can use its grippers to manipulate tools and spray paint, weld, grind, drill, or rivet. Non-industrial robots perform an entirely different range of services. For example, police departments use robots to detect bombs. This practice reduces the dangers that human officers might face in locating and defusing explosives. A Japanese university has developed a robot that simulates a human jawbone. The robot emulates human chewing motions, which the researchers hope will help them develop new dental treatments. A California-based manufacturer has invented a robot that performs hip replacements in dogs. Other companies have created robots that can patrol buildings as security guards; lift briefcases, open doors, and pour drinks for wheelchair-bound people; and clean washrooms. Of course, NASA used robots to traverse the moon and Mars.

CURRENT CONDITIONS

After the severe slump in the mid- to late 1980s, the robotics industry made an impressive comeback. By the mid-1990s, the industry enjoyed a series of record-breaking sales years, with annual revenue increases of as much as 25 percent. Although both the automotive and non-automotive segments performed well, actual unit shipments still fluctuated slightly between positive and negative growth in these years. Nevertheless, from 1992 to 1997 the industry posted gains in new orders of 131 percent.

There were 88,000 robots installed in U.S. factories in 1998, according to the Robotic Industries Association (RIA). Over 12,000 new units valued at nearly $1.1 billion were shipped in 1997; this was the first year annual shipments surpassed the $1.0 billion mark. An inevitable slowdown in this growth occurred in 1998, but industry experts remained optimistic about the future. Donald Vincent, executive vice president of the RIA, noted with satisfaction that material handling had supplanted spot welding as the leading application for new robotics equipment. Other robust application markets included arc welding, assembly, coating, and materials removal.

INDUSTRY LEADERS

The largest manufacturers of robots and industrial automation machines were multi-national corporations such as FANUC Ltd. and Yaskawa Electric Corporation, both of Japan, Thyssen AG of Germany, and Elsag Bailey Process Automation N.V. of the Netherlands. FANUC, Yaskawa, and Thyssen have U.S. subsidiaries. Rockwell International is the largest U.S.-based manufacturer of automation products, but not robots per se. Adept is the most important U.S. company manufacturing robots.

FANUC Robotics North America, Inc. is the Rochester Hills, Michigan-based subsidiary of FANUC Ltd. of Japan. Originally called GMFANUC Robotics Corp., the firm was founded in 1982 as a joint venture between General Motors and FANUC Ltd. It became a wholly owned subsidiary of FANUC Ltd. in 1992. While created in part to supply the auto industry, FANUC has diversified to serve most U.S. industries requiring robotics technology. In 1998 it expanded operations in Ohio, Mexico, and Brazil and had 28,000 robots installed worldwide. Its 1998 sales were approximately $370 million, an increase of 37 percent over 1996, and it employed a labor force of

1,200. Its parent, FANUC Ltd., posted 1998 sales of $1.73 billion, an increase of 16 percent over 1997.

Giddings & Lewis, Inc., with headquarters in Wisconsin, is a subsidiary of Thyssen AG. It manufactures industrial automation equipment in Canada, Germany, and the United Kingdom, as well as in the United States. The company primarily serves customers in heavy industries such as automotive, defense, and aerospace. It had 1996 sales of $763 million dollars (the last year that information was made public), and employs about 3,100 people.

Rockwell International Corp., once a defense industry giant, is the largest U.S.-based industrial automation company. Between 1984 and 1998 it made more than 50 acquisitions and divested itself 30 operations, getting out of the airframe and automotive components business altogether. It even sold off its semiconductor business in order to further concentrate on industrial automation. Rockwell reported 1998 sales of $6.75 billion, an increase of 13 percent over 1997.

Motoman, Inc., a subsidiary of Yaskawa Electric Manufacturing Co. of Japan, was founded in 1989, and by 1998 had more than 9,000 robot installations. It is the third-largest robot maker in North America. Between 1992 and 1997 it experienced compounded sales growth of over 35 percent. It employs over 450 people and is headquartered in West Carrollton, Ohio.

Adept Technology has installed over 10,000 systems worldwide designed to handle, assemble, and package many kinds of products. Its products simulate the movement of the human shoulder, elbow, and wrist. It also sells PC-based software to run its robots. Adept's 1998 sales were $98.4 million, an increase of 18.8 percent over 1997. The electronics industry accounted for 40 percent of its sales, compared to 16 percent to the automotive industry.

PRI Automation is the leading U.S. supplier of automation systems for computer chip manufacturers, with 90 percent of the market. Its hardware and software automate the movement of silicon wafers between different steps of the manufacturing process, reducing the risk of error and contamination. Intel Corp. accounts for 22 percent of its sales. Other major customers include Samsung and Motorola. Between 1992 and 1997 PRI experienced annual growth of at least 32.0 percent. Growth from 1996 to 1997 was 53.1 percent, to $169.5 million. Sales growth for 1998 was only 5.1 percent, to $178.2 million, because of the slow-down in microchips. Another major supplier to the chip industry is Brooks Automation, Inc. Its equipment uses vacuum technology to move, align, and hold the silicon wafers in the manufacturing process. The

company supplies about 90 percent of the vacuum robots used in the semiconductor industry. Brooks' 1998 sales were $99.9 million, an increase of 15.6 percent over 1997.

Other important U.S. robotics companies include Cognex Corp., the world's leading manufacturer of hardware and software systems that function as robot eyes with more than 70,000 vision systems shipped; Gerber Scientific, Inc., which makes automated manufacturing systems for the apparel, optical, signmaking, and printing industries; Integrated Surgical Systems, Inc., with 1998 sales of $6.1 million; and Computer Motion, Inc., with 1998 sales of $10.6 million. Integrated Surgical Systems, Inc. and Computer Motion, Inc. both manufacture robotic systems for use in surgery.

WORK FORCE

Automation and robotics have a mixed effect on employment. Proponents argue that the increasing use of robots will add jobs. After all, there must be humans to design, build, and repair them. Opponents suggest otherwise. They say that more robots performing tasks heretofore carried out by humans will eliminate jobs. Early evidence does side with the proponents. The industry has generated more jobs in manufacturing, sales, and computer maintenance than it has eliminated. Although there are no hard figures at this point to substantiate either claim, it must be remembered that the robotics industry is in its infancy. Also, since it is allied closely with the computer industry, there may be a spillover effect between the two.

The industrial automation and robotics industry is also linked with other industries in a symbiotic manner. For example, there is a close relationship with the computer-aided design and computer-aided manufacturing (CAD/CAM), bionics, and laser industries. Jobs and career paths abound in all these industries. There is a growing need for robotics specialists in almost every industry, including electronics, shipbuilding, construction, automobile manufacturing, aerospace, computers, and medical technology. Job titles include robot programmer, robotics engineer, robotics repair person, robotics designer, mechanical engineer, robot sales representative, robotics assembly supervisor, and robotics software writer to name a few. Yet, with new jobs come increased demands for new skills. This is where the escalating use of industrial robots has an impact on the labor force.

Workers need new skills to cope with the new robots. There has been a reduction in the number of semi-skilled workers as the result of industrial automation. The labor force needed in an automated plant requires skilled workers such as maintenance engineers, electricians, toolmakers, and computer programmers. Without such people, industry and robots cannot function. Thus, the increase in industrial automation and robots has created a demand for more training, without which neither industry nor robots can survive.

AMERICA AND THE WORLD

American researchers are in the forefront of the development and use of robots. Ironically, the United States ranks only twentieth in per capita consumption of numerically controlled machine tools, one of the leading types of industrial automation. Japan leads the world in robot technology. The majority of the industrial robots in use today are found in Japan. In fact, at least one Japanese factory uses an assembly line of robots to make still more robots. Japan's lead in robot use is expected to narrow, however, according to a report by the UN Economic Commission and the International Federation of Robotics, which forecast growth in Japan of only 5 percent between 1997 and 2001, but 50 percent growth in the United States.

The United States still occupying a significant place in the development of robots is somewhat surprising. In the early 1980s, the American robot industry grew quickly due in part to large investments by the automotive industry. However, the promising start to the fledgling industry faltered when the integration of robots into production lines lagged and the economic viability of industrial automation and robots faded. As a result, there was a noticeable shakeout in the robot industry. Most of the American manufacturers went out of business, consolidated with others, or were sold to Japanese and European competitors. For a while, only one U.S. company, Adept, continued to produce industrial robot arms.

RESEARCH AND TECHNOLOGY

Researchers work constantly to upgrade the quality and efficiency of robots. They concentrate primarily on true robots for industrial use. A true robot operates independently and automatically from a self-contained program built into it. There is also a class of robots called telecherics, which are human-operated machines. These machines can possess many of a true robot's features, but they are always under human di-

rection by cable or radio links. They serve such purposes as handling radioactive or explosive materials and sample specimens on the ocean floor. In all cases, though, operators behind the scenes must manipulate them. They are not as numerous as true robots.

True robots are generally stationary industrial robots located in factories. Early models handled assignments such as welding or painting that posed hazards to humans. These robots tend to be cumbersome. Researchers have developed a new generation of light-duty and inspection robots that address different problems. Modern true robots carry out monotonous, repetitive tasks with a high degree of precision. Some share work with human workers. Ironically, contemporary robots look nothing like the "creatures" portrayed in early movies, literature, and plays. Researchers have developed a new breed of robots with manipulators (the arm that defines the machines' capabilities); controllers (the components that store information, instructions, and programs used to direct the manipulators' movements); and power supplies that drive the manipulators, which are smaller and more efficient than their forerunners. They have also improved on robots' degrees of freedom, geometrical configurations, and envelopes.

DEGREES OF FREEDOM

A robot's applications and flexibility are determined by its number of degrees of freedom (the number of movements it can perform). Many industrial-type robots are limited sequence by nature; that is, they are restricted to a low number of movements. The degrees of freedom are related closely to the robot's geometrical configuration.

GEOMETRICAL CONFIGURATION

Industrial robots feature four principal geometrical configurations: articulated, revolute, or jointed-arm; spherical (also called polar coordinate); rectangular (or Cartesian); and cylindrical. They can also be vertically jointed, horizontally mounted, and/or gantry or overhead mounted.

ENVELOPE

A robot's envelope is the three-dimensional contour formed by the motion of the end effector (a device used to produce a desired change in an object in response to input, such as a gripper) or wrist moved completely through the outer limits of motion.

As computers become more powerful, researchers make more changes to robots' degrees of freedom, geometrical configurations, and envelopes. That, in turn, means robots will become more flexible and capable of more advanced functions. In only one-quarter of a century, researchers have made remarkable strides in robotics technology. Thus, the development of and need for advanced robots will continue to grow—as will the industrial automation industry.

THE FUTURE

At the end of the twentieth-century the robotics industry was cautiously optimistic about the future. The automotive industry continued to be the dominant market, but electronics, aerospace, food and beverage, and appliance manufacturing showed signs of strong growth as markets for robots, according to a study for the Robotic Industries Association by Ducker Research Company. Major technological factors on the horizon that boded well for the industry were the development of PC-based control systems, stimulated by the simultaneous development of low-cost PC-based vision systems. Vision systems, along with improved sensor technology, increase the possibilities for robot applications in currently labor-intensive processes. A survey of robotics professionals in *Robotics World* magazine reported that the shift away from proprietary control systems toward an open architecture would also be an important part of the future. Agreed upon interface standards pose a significant hurdle in the path to this future.

FURTHER READING

"1998 Industry Survey: Cautious Optimism the Industry Watchword." *Robotics World,* 1998/1999.

"Cognex Corporation Reports Record Revenue and Earnings for the Fourth Quarter and Full Year of 1997." Natick, MA: Cognex Corporation, 1998. Available from http://www.cognex.com/press/release/finance/q4.html.

"Leading Technology-based Companies." *Crains Detroit Business,* 16 March 1998.

"Leading the Charge to a Productive 21st Century." *Robotics World,* Fall 1998.

Murray, R. M., et al. *A Mathematical Introduction to Robotic Manipulation.* CRC Press, 1994.

"New Robotics Market Study Sees Substantial Growth Opportunities for Industry." Ann Arbor, MI: Robotics Industries Association, 1998. Available from http:// www.robotics.org/htdocs/whatshot/market_study.html.

"Robot Orders Rebound in Third Quarter." Ann Arbor, MI: Robotics Industries Association, 1999. Available from http:// www.robotics.org/htdocs/about/3rdquarter.html.

"Robotics." Menlo Park, CA: SRI Consulting, 1998. Available from http://future.sri.com/TM/aboutROBO.html.

"Robotics Industry Has Best Year Ever in 1997." Ann Arbor, MI: Robotics Industries Association, 1998. Available from http://www.robotics.org/htdocs/whatshot/fourthquarter.html.

"The Robotics Market: Assessment and Forecast." *Robotics World,* 1998/1999.

"Rockwell Automation and Cognex Corporation to Enter into Global Relationship." *Business Wire,* 7 July 1998.

"World Trade: More and More Robots Populate World's Factories." *Financial Times,* 14 October 1998.

Zheng, Y. F., ed. *Recent Trends in Mobile Robots.* Singapore: World Scientific, 1993.

—Arthur G. Sharp, updated by Howard Distelzweig

SATELLITES

The demand for satellites and the launching systems that set them into orbit is booming. According to *Hoover's Online,* the satellite industry is expected to increase 20 percent a year in the foreseeable future. Governments, companies, and organizations have deployed satellites to accomplish all sorts of tasks such as enabling accurate meteorological forecasts, obtaining strategic and military intelligence, exploring the galaxy, facilitating telecommunications, transmitting television signals, providing high-speed Internet access, positioning and navigational information, and enhancing map making.

The United States has been the dominant participant in the communications satellite market since its beginning and now manufactures 70 percent of the world's satellites. But a growing contingent of other countries such as France, Russia, Japan, and the United Kingdom also make influential contributions and are capable of heavy competition with the United States.

Launch systems, used to propel the satellites into space as well as for other launching purposes, are big business. U.S. launch vehicles and related equipment brought in $3.4 billion in 1998 and that number is expected to increase to $3.7 billion in 1999. To make space launches more efficient, companies have been developing reusable launch pads that should result in cost savings for getting spacecraft into orbit. Furthermore, U.S. satellite manufactures reported sales of $8.3 billion in 1997, representing over 60 percent of the satellite revenues worldwide.

In order for large-scale satellite communications networks to succeed, companies offering these services must find ways to reduce the cost of satellite-based communications so they are viable in the consumer market. Satellite manufacturers have already taken initial steps in this direction, creating small satellites that cost less than $20 million, in contrast to the $100 million they once did.

ORGANIZATION AND STRUCTURE

Satellites serve as active repeaters of transmitted signals and, therefore, as an alternative method of sending information both short and long distances. Instead of wire, short-wave radio, cables, or fiber optics, communications satellites can send signals without interference across long distances and geographic boundaries. In addition, satellites are economical because their cost of operation does not depend on distance. Satellites, moreover, can relay signals from one terrestrial transmitter to a number of receivers within the coverage vicinity; they can also transmit broadband signals and hence can send large quantities of data. Furthermore, satellites can cover a wide area. With enough satellites in the proper configuration, they could cover any point on the globe. In practice, however, the International Telecommunications Union (ITU) and the U.S. Federal Communications Commission (FCC)—regulatory bodies that oversee the development and operation of telecommunications technology—often restrict the coverage of satellites to a much more limited area.

Communications satellites function by taking the signal from an Earth-based transmitter antenna and relaying it to a receiver antenna elsewhere on Earth. That is, satellites contain equipment that receives signals, amplifies them, and sends them to Earth receiver sta-

Four radio telescopic satellite dishes scan the sky. (Digital Stock.)

tions. Hence, these features make satellites ideal for the one-to-many point transmissions of radio, television, data, and video.

Satellites can transmit and receive broadband microwave signals at a variety of different frequencies, which are allocated for specific uses. The Ku-band (extending from 10.7-18.0 gigahertz) and the Ka-band (18-31 gigahertz) frequencies were expected to replace C-band (3.70-7.25) frequencies for Earth stations with immobile antennas or Fixed Satellite Services (FSS) in the mid-1990s. Steven Adamson et al. in *Advanced Satellite Communications: Potential Markets* also predicts that Ku-band transponders, or receivers, would outnumber their predecessors, the C-band transponders, by the late 1990s. However, they note that companies, organizations, and individuals have a significant investment in C-band technology, especially in Earth station C-band equipment. About 90 percent of U.S. television stations employ C-band satellite technology. Moreover, the typical backyard satellite dish receives C-band frequencies and there are an estimated 3 million U.S. households with such receivers. In order to placate both sides, companies have developed and launched satellites with both C-band and Ku-band capabilities. Also, according to Steven Adamson et al., Ku-band satellite use is likely to grow further because of the competitive cost of us-

ing very small aperture terminals (VSATs) with powerful Ku-band transmissions. VSATs convert wideband satellite signals to narrower bands for low data rate services such as paging and faxing. Paging services began focusing more attention on VSAT technology in the mid-1990s to enhance two-way paging and to move away from terrestrial paging channels. Companies such as PageMart Wireless invested millions of dollars in VSAT satellites because they believe it will make two-way paging more reliable and easier to manage. Mobile Satellite Services (MSS) such as ships, cars, trucks, and airplanes use L-band (1.5-1.6 gigahertz) frequencies, and Broadcast Satellite Services providing direct satellite broadcasts use S-band frequencies (2.0-2.7 gigahertz). The government reserves Q-band (44 gigahertz) frequencies for its use.

Space satellites are propelled into orbit by spacecraft or rocket boosters. Satellite services rely on different kinds of orbits depending on the kinds of tasks they perform and on the size of the satellites. The most frequently used orbits include: low Earth orbits (LEOs), medium Earth orbits (MEOs), and geostationary orbits (GEOs). Early satellites orbited at low Earth altitudes of 400 to 1,000 feet. However, many satellite projects under way in the mid- to late 1990s also called for low Earth orbiting satellites. MEOs cover altitudes of about 6,000 miles from the Earth and work best for larger satellites. Many of the communications satellites in the mid-1990s, however, used geostationary orbits, where they orbit at an altitude of 22,300 miles. From this point, the satellites' rotation mirrors the Earth's, causing the satellites to maintain a constant position relative to the Earth. However, this orbit can only hold about 150 satellites and was almost full in 1997, according to William J. Cook in *U.S. News & World Report.*

The FCC and the ITU regulate satellite-related communications industries. The FCC focuses on issues concerning U.S. domestic use of satellites, while the ITU handles aspects of communications satellites with international ramifications. The FCC opened up the skies for U.S. satellites by rescinding the regulatory distinction between domestic and international satellites in a policy called Domestic International Satellite Consolidation (DISCO) in 1996. This policy allows satellite service providers access to international markets. However, the move did not make the U.S. market more accessible to international satellite companies. On the other hand, the ITU allocates the use of various frequencies to different user groups and controls satellites in GEO. The ITU makes its decisions concerning satellites use and radio frequencies at its World Administrative Radio Conferences.

In 1997, 70 countries signed an accord to open up their telecommunications markets at the World Trade Organization (WTO), paving the way for global satellite communications services. About 50 percent of the countries in the accord lacked efficient modern telephone systems, according to William J. Cook in *U.S. News & World Report.*

BACKGROUND AND DEVELOPMENT

Russia launched the first successful satellite, the sputnik, on October 4, 1957, taking the lead in space exploration. This event inspired the United States to redouble its efforts to catch up with and surpass Russia as the Cold War continued to brew. Less than a year later, on February 1, 1958, the United States launched its first satellite, becoming the second nation in space. On November 3, 1960, the National Aeronautics and Space Administration (NASA) launched its first satellite, Explorer 8, beginning the first of many NASA space expeditions.

Satellites first entered the commercial arena in the 1960s, originally providing alternative channels of data transmission for international telephone and tele-graph services. That is, satellites competed with undersea cables for use by telephone and telegraph services. In the 1970s, companies started to deploy satellites within the United States for commercial purposes. These satellites not only transferred telephone signals for businesses, they also relayed network data. Companies relied on satellites for point-to-point and point-to-multipoint transmissions, between, say, an office and a production plant.

In addition, television networks began implementing satellites to send and receive transcontinental relays of broadcast signals in the 1970s. Satellites ultimately had a revolutionary effect on television broadcasting; with satellites, networks could cull the best resources from all the stations in the network. Stations could transmit or receive signals from other network stations via satellites. Later, television stations acquired portable Earth stations, allowing them to travel from event to event, to broadcast live from events, and to rove around town looking for events to broadcast.

CURRENT CONDITIONS

In the mid- to late 1990s the communications satellite industry experienced strong growth as some lucrative markets developed and the prospect of a satellite-dominated communications industry came about. Throughout the late 1990s, investors pumped dollars into satellite companies. According to Jeff Cole in the *Wall Street Journal,* telecommunications companies allocated about $42 billion altogether for new satellite-based systems in 1997. Not only did companies plan to expand the cellular phone and television uses of satellites, they also aimed to provide Internet access service and direct-to-home television, in order to seize some of the cable industry's share of the television market. According to the Satellite Industry Association and Furton Corp., U.S. satellite manufactures gleaned $8.3 billion from satellite sales in 1997, accounting for 61 percent of the world's $13.5 billion in satellite revenues. Worldwide revenues are forecast to reach between $30.0-40.0 billion by 2008.

Participants in the industry branched off in two directions: one building small low-cost, low-orbit satellites, and the other building large high-cost, high-orbit satellites. But no matter which form of satellite companies plan to work with, they intend to put in orbit an infrastructure of satellites that will allow phone, Internet, paging, television, and any other kind of data transmission from just about any point on the planet, superseding the telephone and cable lines that extend across vast expanses of industrialized countries. The number of commercial satellite launches continued to climb. The International Launch Service (ILS)—a joint venture led by Lockheed Martin Corporation—reported having 49 launches scheduled through the end of 1999, in contrast to 1995 when only 20 satellites were launched by all services. The ILS's backlog of space launches has an estimated value of $3 billion. Moreover, the Teal Group predicted that in the next decade, 1,800 more will be propelled into space. Lower satellite manufacturing costs spur these endeavors on: whereas it once cost about $100 million apiece to make a satellite, Motorola could churn them out for a fraction of that cost, at $20 million each, by the late 1990s.

TELECOMMUNICATIONS

Steven Adamson et al. predict that increasing demand for cellular phones, fax machines, and voice message services will fuel the deployment of more low Earth orbit (LEO) satellites. They suggest that the number of mobile communications users could reach 100 million throughout the world by 2000. An example of this growth is the expansion of services of Iridium World Communications Ltd., an international point-to-point telecommunications network using 66 satellites in low orbit. In May 1997, Iridium launched 5 satellites using a McDonnell Douglas Delta 2 booster, placing the first batch of its 66 satellite constellation into orbit. The Iridium network is designed to link the telecommunications satellites with mobile phones, solar powered phone booths, fax machines, and pagers. Iridium began service in late 1998. Supported by Hughes Electronics, Spaceway also wants to compete in the telecommunications market by using 8 geostationary satellites to provide standard telephone, fax, data, video conferencing, and even Internet services. This network is expected to be in operation beginning in 2002 for North America.

BROADCAST SATELLITES

Broadcast satellites send audio, video, and data signals directly to subscribers. Steven Adamson et al. contend that in order for broadcast satellites to compete with alternative communication media, broadcasters must glean their profits from charges to users or advertisers and they must pull in revenues from their offerings on a limited number of channels. Video direct-broadcast satellites, however, carry high prices and consumers only use such services on special occasions, if at all. However, video direct-broadcast satellites can compete among consumers concerned with convenience, according to Adamson et al. They

also state that geographic location may favor video direct-broadcast satellite services where alternatives are remote.

The U.S. direct-to-home television service grew quickly in the mid- to late 1990s, nabbing over $2.75 billion from the cable industry according to *Television Digest.* Each year about 1 million people switch to direct-to-home service and several hundred thousand reduce their cable subscriptions to the basic offering plan. *Television Digest* reported that in 1995, 2.2 million people opted for direct-to-home television, 4.4 million people did in 1997, and 9.6 million people did in 1998. Direct-to-home television is flaunted as having better sound and image quality, plus a greater selection of channels.

INTERNET SERVICE PROVIDERS

Satellites have also become a medium of Internet access, as researchers have sought faster ways of transmitting and downloading data. This segment of the industry could have a potential market of over $20 billion in 2005, according to Merrill Lynch. Traditional telephone lines cannot send large amounts of data quickly. Even upgraded to maximum capacity, about 56 bits per second in the late 1990s, telephone lines cannot compete with satellites, which can allow voice modems as well as send information at about 28 megabytes per second. Satellites could lower monthly hookups for phone companies from the current rate of over $1,000 to between $50 to $100. Software magnate Bill Gates and cellular phone pioneer Craig McCaw began a project to supply Internet service via satellites in 1997, called Teledesic. The Teledesic project calls for the construction, launching, and operation of as many as 288 satellites with over a $9 billion price tag. Motorola Inc. is building the satellites for the network. With Motorola's expertise in building satellites for similar networks, such as Iridium, and with the expectation of robust demand, Teledesic is slated to begin service in 2003. In addition, several other such projects were either underway or being planned, including Lockheed Martin's Astrolink and Loral Space's and Alcatel's Cyberstar/Skybridge.

Some companies already offer wireless Internet access service. Metricom, for example, has had moderate success with its service even though it only has standard bandwidth of 33.6 kilobytes per second. Internet service providers (ISPs) use low-altitude satellites, which will reduce transmission time and require less energy than higher altitude satellites. Satellite ISPs, however, must promote their services better in order to capture a greater share of the market. According to Matt Richtel in the *New York Times,* only about 90,000 people subscribed to satellite Internet access services in 1998. Dunn also attributed the lack of success of satellite ISPs in part to the cost and technical configuration involved with setup. Dunn calculated the costs to be about $800 for the satellite accouterments, $40 per month for satellite access service, plus about another $20 per month for an Internet access provider. However, satellites deliver data at a much greater rate than any other modem on the market—1000 times faster than plain old telephone lines—and they also appeal to people in other countries in remote areas inaccessible by cable. Hughes Network Systems is the leading satellite ISP with its DirecPC service.

GLOBAL POSITIONING SYSTEMS

Global Positioning Systems (GPS) operate based on satellites and identify exact locations of users. The military first developed GPS, which runs on 24 U.S. Department of Defense satellites, for strategic and navigational purposes. Since then businesses have begun integrating the technology into a variety of products: cellular phones, dispatch hardware, and computers. The price of GPS equipment has also dropped spurring on accelerated demand for it. For example, the laptop PC card SkyMap by Etak listed at $299 in 1998 and is expected to fall even lower in the following years. Depending on the model, a GPS monitor can locate its whereabouts within 10 to 300 hundred feet of its actual position.

GPS has also experienced increased commercial popularity. The U.S. Department of Commerce predicts that this sector of the satellite industry alone might bring in as much as $8.0 billion by 2000 and $16.0 billion by 2003 in worldwide sales. The biggest use of GPS has been for car navigation, which accounted for about $334 million in revenues in 1997. Automotive use is slated to continue to being the leading application of GPS, and sales are forecast to reach $1.6 billion by 2001. Nevertheless, GPS is also used for aviation, marine, military, tracking, and surveying purposes. For example, shipping and transit services have implemented GPS to increase the efficiency of their services. With GPS in place, dispatchers always know where their vehicles are and assist them with directions, with finding alternate routes, and in emergencies.

Concern over millenium complications surrounded the timing mechanisms for GPS satellites in June 1999. Failures in the synchronicity of the satellites threatened to degrade data transmission and disrupt network connections, interfering with the information transfer necessary for everything from weapons navigation to fishing detectors. The problem was expected to be resolved before the August 21 deadline, the date the timing systems 20-year clock switched back to zero.

OTHER APPLICATIONS

Defense projects have also goaded the satellite industry on by using satellites for such varied purposes as tracking the weather and spying. Additionally, in 1998, NASA began efforts to award a $600 million a year contract to a team of companies that will control or monitor more than 100 existing and planned NASA spacecraft, as reported by Peter Behr in *The Washington Post*. Two teams, one headed by Lockheed Martin and the other by Boeing Co., hope to change the way NASA scientists gather information from research spacecraft. According to Behr, the two teams envision a day when information gathered from space probes or satellites will be relayed to scientists on the Internet.

In 1998, the U.S. Naval Academy began teaching midshipmen to navigate using satellites, instead of relying on a sextant and stars. An article in *Newsweek* states that the Navy made this change because it believes that its high-tech systems are more reliable than traditional methods.

A small, albeit costly, segment of satellite production goes to space exploration projects. Recent missions, such as that by the Galileo, have photographed areas of celestial bodies that astronomers and other scientists wish to study but which are impracticable for human space missions. For example, in 1997 the Galileo took pictures of Europa, one of the Jupiter's moons, in order for scientists to study whether life exists on the planet.

In 1997, Space Imaging, Inc. designed a satellite with photographic equipment that can accurately capture the landscape of the Earth in great enough detail to spawn a new epoch of cartography, according to Richard Rapaport in *Forbes*. The company also intends to create a digital library of the images collected by the satellite, so cartographers can consult it to see if the images they need already exist. If additional photographs are needed, Space Imaging will establish stations in North America, Europe, and Asia that can instruct the satellite to photograph specific areas. Space Imaging predicts that this technology will spark a $7 billion industry by 2000.

CHALLENGES TO THE INDUSTRY

The industry suffered a glitch in May 1998, when Galaxy IV, a communications satellite, experienced technical problems and rendered 45 million pagers useless for several days. According to Adam Rogers in *Newsweek,* no one saw the possibility of problems in having nearly 90 percent of all pagers using Galaxy IV. The article states that industry officials claim the failure rate of satellites is only 1 percent. In addition to the pager problems, when the five-year-old satellite had its computer and back-up computer failed, several broadcasting and data networks also went down.

While satellite capabilities and demand have increased and strengthened in the 1990s, the satellite industry must also recognize a number of obstacles in its course of orbit. With all the space operations in the last few decades, the upper atmosphere is becoming inundated with cosmic debris. Thousands of rocket parts, shot satellites, and a host of other miscellaneous spacecraft components orbit around the galaxy, creating a perilous environment for new spacecraft. According to *The Economist,* 500 active satellites circulated throughout space, while some 2,000 inoperable ones, 1,400 used rocket boosters, and over 1,000 other pieces of debris polluted outer space in 1997.

INDUSTRY LEADERS

Hughes Electronics is the leading satellite manufacturer, producing about a third of all GEO satellites. The company owns more than 80 percent of PanAmSat, a 17-satellite network that is expected to launch six more satellites by the year 2000. This unit of General Motors offers satellite services such as DirecTV and DirecPC, its direct-broadcast and Internet access services, respectively. Hughes Electronic also has received government contracts, including ones for work on the Galileo and the Milstar program. As part of the company's competitive strategy, Hughes Electronics increases the power and efficiency of its satellites every 2 or 3 years, allowing the company to provide any frequencies customers want. In 1998, the company posted revenues of $5.9 billion and employed 15,000 people.

Lockheed Martin provides the Defense Department with space and satellite technology and plays a role in the commercial satellite market. For high-speed Internet access, the company is developing Astrolink, a nine-satellite system that will cost $2 billion. Lockheed Martin has designed spacecraft for Motorola's satellite network, equipment for the Hubble Space Telescope, satellites for weather monitoring, satellites for Global Positioning Systems, technology for Iridium, and A2100 communications satellites. The company also announced it would acquire the COMSTAT, a satellite access provider, to offer satellite communications services. In 1998, the company recorded sales

of $26.2 billion, a net income of $1.0 billion, and 165,000 employees.

Loral Space & Communications Ltd., a high-technology company headquartered in New York and specializing in satellite manufacturing and satellite services, is the third largest satellite producer. The company posted sales of $1.3 billion in 1998. Loral owns a 42-percent share of Globalstar, a consortium developing a LEO satellite system for wireless communication, as well as a 51 percent interest in Space Systems/Loral, the company's dominant satellite manufacturer. The company also owns the communications service providers CyberStar, Skynet, and Orion Network Systems.

In 1998, Motorola was awarded a multi-billion dollar contract to build Teledesic's 288-bird system. Teledesic hopes to provide satellite Internet access to millions of users across the world with a network of some 800 satellites offering broadband and digital data transmission capabilities. Motorola also owns a 20-percent share in the 66-bird Iridium system, which boasts that users can make phone calls from anywhere in the world with a cellular phone. In 1998, Motorola booked $29.3 billion in revenues, had a net income of $962 million, and employed 133,000 people.

AMERICA AND THE WORLD

As the price of fiber-optic cable dropped, its demand increased, taking a sizable chunk of the international telephone service business away from satellites. For example, in the late 1980s Intelsat handled about 50 percent of international phone calls, but in 1997 it only handled about 20 percent. As a result, companies such as Intelsat that once thrived on international phone service, have turned to the direct-to-home television market in Asia, which according to *The Economist,* constituted one of the most rapidly expanding markets in the mid-1990s. In 1997, this market had worldwide revenue of $13.5 billion and Eric Le Proux de la Riviere of Communications & Space Euroconsult predicted that it will climb as high as $30.0-40.0 billion by 2008. Southern Asia is predicted to account for the greatest share of growth with 400 percent, followed by Latin America with 230 percent, Middle East and Africa with 220 percent, and Asia Pacific with 70 percent, according to de la Riviere. Revenues in North America are expected to grow by 50 percent during this period.

France, Russia, and the United Kingdom, among other European countries, and Japan have played instrumental roles in the progress of the satellite industry. Companies from these countries have contracts extending into the next millennium to collaborate on some of the largest satellite projects on the drawing boards. France teamed up with Motorola for Iridium and Russian contractors are working on the Teledesic project. Boeing is collaborating with Ukranian, Russian, and Norwegian companies to create a mobile launch system, the Odyssey. In addition, these countries have thriving satellite industries of their own. Russia, for example, developed the Proton spacecraft, which can carry up to seven satellites in just one mission. Also, France's Arianespace is the world leader for satellite launches, accounting for 60 percent of the market. According to Burton I. Edelson et al. in *Satellite Communications Systems and Technology,* the European and Japanese satellite industries have technological advantages over the U.S. industry in part because the governments in European and Japanese countries have traditionally provided more support to satellite development.

RESEARCH AND TECHNOLOGY

In addition to the satellites, the launches that send them off into space are increasingly important. According to Eric Schonfield in *Fortune,* currently planned satellites exceed the available number of launch pads. Companies, including Lockheed Martin, are developing reusable systems that should reduce the cost of a launch—currently running from $10 million to $149 million—by one-tenth. In the late 1990s, NASA sponsored the production of the X-33 and X-34 programs, which promote the creation of reusable launch vehicles. The prototypes of Lockheed Martin's X-33 and Orbital Sciences' X-34 are forecasted to be completed by the end of 2000.

Satellite producers and operators constantly look for ways to reduce costs while maintaining the technological advantages of satellites in order to make their products financially accessible to mass markets. Sea Venture, a bevy of international companies led by Boeing Commercial Space, has been developing a mobile offshore launching platform, the Odyssey, for satellites. Tim Furniss reports in *Flight International* that the Odyssey would provide the advantages of launching satellites at the equator, where the Earth's rotation is the fastest and the path to geostationary-transfer orbit, a stage of orbit prior to the final route to geostationary orbit, is the shortest. Therefore, launching satellites from equatorial points takes less energy than from other points.

FURTHER READING

"Activate the Money Star: Satellite Operators." *The Economist,* 3 May 1997, 56.

Adamson, Steven, David Roberts, et al. *Advanced Satellite Communications: Potential Markets.* Park Ridge, NJ: Noyes Data Corporation, 1995.

Agres, Ted. "Companies Vie for a Slice of High-Stakes Space-Launch Pie." *R & D,* January 1997.

Behr, Peter. "Firms Vie to Operate NASA's Spacecraft." *The Washington Post,* 26 June 1998.

Cole, Jeff. "New Satellite Era Looms Just over the Horizon." *Wall Street Journal,* 18 March 1997, B1.

Cook, William J. "1997: A New Space Odyssey." *U.S. News & World Report,* 3 March 1997, 44.

"Direct-to-Home Satellites." *Television Digest,* 7 April 1997.

Dunn, Ashley. "Satellite Fantasies: 'Scuse Me While I Kiss the Sky." *New York Times,* 12 June 1996.

Edelson, Burton I., et al. *Satellite Communications Systems and Technology: Europe, Japan, and Russia.* Park Ridge, NJ: Noyes Data Corporation, 1995.

Elstrom, Peter. "The Internet Space Race." *Business Week,* 1 June 1998.

Furniss, Tim. "Launch Odyssey: The First Geostationary Satellite Launch from an Offshore Platform Is Scheduled to Take Place in 1998." *Flight International,* 19 March 1997, 32.

Gordon, Gary D., and Walter L. Morgan. *Principles of Communications Satellites.* New York: John Wiley & Sons, Inc., 1993.

Leopold, George. "Will August Rollover of Critical Devices Disrupt Satellites?—Lawmakers Probe GPS Timer." *Electronic Engineering Times,* 17 May 1999.

McGraw-Hill Companies and U.S. Department of Commerce. *U.S. Industry and Trade Outlook.* New York: McGraw-Hill, 1999.

Rapaport, Richard. "Satellite Mapping." *Forbes,* 24 February 1997, 107.

Richtel, Matt. "Start Ups Pin Hopes on an Internet Route Through the Sky." *New York Times,* 30 November 1998.

Rogers, Adam. "A Satellite Glitch Reveals a High-Tech Bottleneck." *Newsweek,* 1 June 1998.

"Satellite Growth Predicted." *Television Digest,* 7 September 1998.

Schonfeld, Eric. "Blasting Off the Cheap Way." *Fortune,* 2 February 1998.

"To Boldly Dump: In Space, Nobody Ever Tidies Up." *The Economist,* 29 March 1997, 87.

Wayner, Peter. "Sky-High Dreams for the Internet." *New York Times,* 22 May 1997.

—Karl Heil, updated by Katherine Wagner

SECURITY PRODUCTS AND SERVICES

The security industry comprises a wide array of corporations that furnish personnel and products designed to protect public and private property and individuals from a variety of problems such as theft, arson, and personal attacks. Services include security guards, private investigators, and consultants. Products range from armored cars to X-ray scanning devices to bank vaults. In addition to securing tangible things like people and objects, it became increasingly important during the 1990s to develop technologies capable of securing intangibles, such as intellectual property and software-stored information or data. Throughout the world it is an especially important industry in view of real and assumed threats to national security, petroleum pipelines, nuclear power plants, and the global economy, among others.

ORGANIZATION AND STRUCTURE

The security industry contains several distinct fields: civil and military service, public safety, private home and business security, data and information security, personal and consulting services, and a variety of guard services. The guard segment includes personnel like bodyguards, border patrol officers, customs officials, private detectives, and park rangers. The industry contains many categories of services and products that are related by one common goal—the protection of individuals, groups, and property.

Numerous relatively small firms dominate the product manufacturing segment of the industry. Large firms such as Borg-Warner, through its Burns sub-

sidiary, Pinkerton's, Inc., and Wackenhut dominate the guard segment of the industry, which provides executive protection, special events and strike coverage security, and patrol services, among others. Well known companies, such as ADT and Brinks, lead the home and industrial security systems industry. To demonstrate the volatility of the industry, though, the acquisition of ADT by Tyco International indicated the ongoing competition for position in this rapidly growing field. Overall, the industry reported revenues of about $39.3 billion and employed approximately 2 million workers in the mid- to late 1990s. During this period security equipment accounted for roughly $2.0 billion and is expected to reach $4.3 billion in 2001, according to Frost and Sullivan. The American Society for Industrial Security predicts that the industry's revenues will grow 8 percent through 2000 and by 7 percent through 2004. The home security market was expected to produce $14.0 billion in 1999.

BACKGROUND AND DEVELOPMENT

The concept of a "police department" is relatively new. King Louis XIV of France maintained a small group of 40 inspectors in the sixteenth century. Their primary job was to report on individuals' movements—not necessarily provide security for them. Beginning in 1633, the city of London hired watchmen to guard its streets at night. That practice carried over to the United States well into the nineteenth century. In 1829, Sir Robert Peel founded the first true police force in England by reorganizing the London metropolitan police force. The officers became known as "bobbies," in honor of Sir Robert.

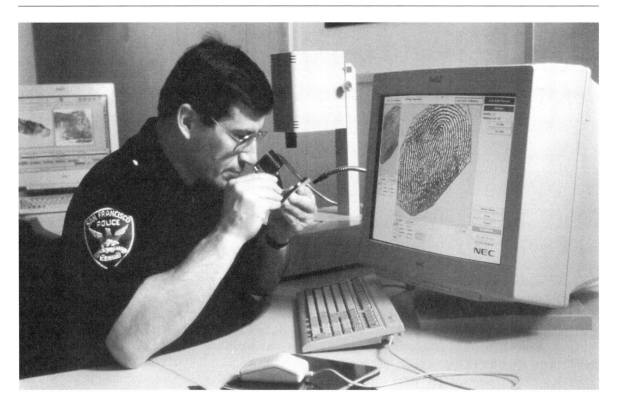

A police officer uses the Automated Fingerprint Identification System by NEC to compare millions of fingerprints in an instant. The system works faster and more accurately than a human assistant could. (Courtesy of NEC USA, Inc.)

The first organized U.S. police department came into existence in New York City in 1845. Boston became the next city to establish its own police force. Gradually, other cities formed police departments. Private security, however, was still relatively unknown—until Allan Pinkerton came along. Pinkerton is generally considered the father of private security. In 1850, he organized Pinkerton's National Detective Agency in Chicago. Eleven years later he recovered a large sum of money stolen from the Adams Express Company and uncovered a plot to assassinate President Lincoln. Those coups enhanced his reputation and accelerated the development of the private security industry, which was helped by the industrial revolution.

As industry grew in the late nineteenth century in the United States, owners looked for ways to protect their property. This was especially true in the western sections of the United States as ranchers and manufacturers expanded throughout the territories. Not surprisingly, companies like Pinkerton assumed much of the responsibility for protection of private goods and property. They took over the security for banks, department stores, museums, and other private buildings. That led to a spin-off industry of security system design (such as safes and vaults). Then, as home owners began to see the value of personal property security, companies

like ADT formed to provide it. Concomitantly, there was an outgrowth of the industry to provide security for government and privately owned facilities like nuclear power facilities and oil pipelines. These demands created a need for better-trained protection personnel and more sophisticated security systems.

Starting in the late 1980s, technology made it possible for people to get away from traditional ways of buying products and banking. For example, people no longer needed to do their banking or shopping in person. They could do either of these by utilizing automated teller machines (ATMs) or using computers, which added to the need for and development of security systems. Naturally, if people chose to do their banking at 2 a.m. through out-of-the-way ATMs, they ran a risk of becoming victims of criminals. That risk called for heightened security measures to be provided by banks. In addition, there grew a need for security systems for computerized transactions made by businesses, banks, financial institutions, and private citizens. The increasing use of computers to conduct business of all kinds had a dramatic impact on the security industry. Companies of all types emerged to fill the need. As a result, the commercial security services industry grew rapidly. That growth shows no signs of slowing down. In fact, the security industry is one of the fastest growing—and most diverse—fields of employment in existence today.

The security industry expanded rapidly in the wake of highly publicized incidents such as the bombing of New York's World Trade Center in February 1993 and the bombing of the Oklahoma's Alfred Murrah Federal Building in April 1995. As a result of these incidents, the security firm Wackenhut, among others, grew by 20 percent and the government called for legislation mandating more stringent security measures. Furthermore, because of employee outrage at the stream of corporate downsizings in the 1980s and 1990s, more industries turned to security firms to protect their executives from employee retaliation. Between 1980 and 1996 the number of security companies rose from 70,000 to 160,000 and the number of security employees grew from 975,000 to 2 million. Between 1992 and 1996, the industry's revenues grew from $29.1 billion to $39.3 billion, according to the American Society for Industrial Security (ASIS).

CURRENT CONDITIONS

The security equipment sector of the industry is forecast to grow 13 percent annually, reaching $4.25 billion in 2001, according to Frost and Sullivan. *Security Management* reports that three trends of the mid- to late 1990s will fuel this sector's expansion: increasing public concern about crime, federal and state budget cuts in public safety spending, and advances in security equipment. This sector produces three kinds of equipment: perimeter security, interior security, and access control devices. Interior security and access control equipment together account for about 97 percent of the sector's revenues, according to *Security Management.*

In April 1999 SecureRite.com, a division of Clark Security Products, which is the nation's largest distributor of security products, announced an alliance with over 500 independent locksmiths from across the country to offer on-line marketing of a wide array of home security products. Orders taken on-line will be completed by the nearest affiliated locksmiths. The company hopes to attract more than 2,000 additional locksmiths as affiliate members by the year 2000. In 1999 Clark Security Products was a $100 million company with 12 warehouses nationwide.

Sales of perimeter security equipment, which includes video motion detectors (VMDs), microwave sensors, and barrier sensors, totaled $19.7 million in the mid-1990s and are predicted to hit $39.1 million

by 2001. VMDs are expected to spur most of the growth in the perimeter equipment market. In the mid-1990s, VMDs ran about $9,500, but prices continued to fall due to heightened competition in the industry. The access control portion of the industry remained the largest in the 1990s and *Security Management* predicts that it will continue to represent about 50 percent of the sector's sales through 2001, when access control equipment sales are slated to reach $2 billion. Falling access control prices, which cost about $921 in the mid-1990s, should spark the growth of these security products. Finally, the interior security equipment segment of the industry had sales of $675 million in the mid-1990s and is expected to have sales of $1.86 billion by 2001. Glass break sensors and closed-circuit television (CCTV) are forecast to lead the growth in interior security equipment.

A growing area of increased interest (and need) is in software security processors for banking, the Internet, and enterprise security application. These products use encryption technology embedded in hardware to help safeguard sensitive data that may be electronically communicated, for example, as in direct-deposit banking or credit card purchases over the Internet. A leader in this area is Compaq's Atalla Security Products, which offers a full line of Network Security Processors (NSPs) designed to move money through ATMs, EFTs etc. securely. Theft of computer hardware is also of rising concern. Philadelphia Security Product's Flexguard Security System offers cable lock kits and pin lock kits to prevent desktop and laptop model computers from being stolen while connected to systems hardware.

As to information security technologies and practices, at the Internet Security Conference held in San Jose, California, in April 1999, CyberSafe Corporation announced the release of a Centrax 2.2 upgrade to its newly acquired intrusion detection product suite. It is the only product to integrate host and network based intrusion detection, vulnerability assessment, and policy management under a single user-friendly interface. Host-based intrusion detection is directed at responding to internal compromises of a system (which account for 80 percent of unauthorized access), while network-based intrusion detection monitors external attack on the system's security integrity. CyberSafe Corporation was founded in 1991 and is privately held. Its products are designed to secure electronic business, such as its award-winning Trust-Broker (TM) Security Suite, or Defensor (R) and Centrax (TM) systems.

Also in 1999, JAWS Technologies Inc. announced an alliance with Offsite Data Services Ltd.

to offer companies both on-line and off-site backup and recovery software to ensure that client companies have uninterrupted and secure access to their information data. Strategic Research President Michael Peterson predicted to *Byte Magazine* in 1999 that "annual US revenues for this type of on-line backup service will grow from a current $10 million to 200 million over the next three years."

In the credit card area in 1999, transaction card suppliers began an industry-wide transition in their magnetic stripe credit cards, to higher "oersted" card products. (Oersteds measure electrical energy needed to encode a transaction card.)

INDUSTRY LEADERS

Many companies in the security industry concentrate on specific niches. For example, Executive Protection Associates, Inc. (EPAI), based in Reno, Nevada, offers a broad range of security services including electronic debugging, background investigations, and anti-stalking operations.

In the field of personal security services, enterprises that dominated the market in 1998 and 1999 included such notables as Flatfoot Investigation and Protection Agency (whose visibility was enhanced when it supplied bodyguard services during the 1996 Summer Olympics Games) and the Anvil Group, which provides executive protection against terrorism, extortion, and kidnapping. Anvil also provides investigative services for alleged celebrity stalking. Other established protection service companies are Bodyguard Elite, Corporate Protection Professionals, Inc., International Protection Services, and the National Bodyguard Network.

EPAI comprises several companies whose missions are to supply specific security-related products. County Communications, based in Silicon Valley, California, is a full-service radio communications engineering company specializing in communications scrambling systems and debugging for protective service and high-risk security applications. It is also a leading designer and manufacturer of surveillance equipment. Another of its companies, also based in Silicon Valley, is Layton and Associates, which provides licensed security and event staffing. Their personnel include Police Officer Standard Training (POST) trained security officers and event staff familiar with all aspects of security management and event security. A third arm is Executive Protection Associates, which is headquartered in Germany. The company provides

full service security throughout Europe. EPAI is but one of many corporations in the security field that offers diverse security on a worldwide basis.

One of the leading producers of security equipment is SafePak Corporation, based in Portland, Oregon. SafePak develops and sells specialized deposit collection and ATM equipment to the banking industry, which is one of the biggest users of security services. The company developed a deposit retrieval system for night depositories and ATMs, which is considered the standard for the industry. SafePak's system dramatically reduces transportation and personnel costs involved in customer deposit collection and increases security for the deposits themselves. Moreover, it reduces dangers to bank customers, to the security personnel who are responsible for their safety, and the protection of banks' property and assets.

SafePak also produces other state-of-the-art equipment designed to protect banks' property. Much of it is in response to the trend away from direct-deposit banking, which resulted in an increase in the number of customers who do their banking transactions around the clock via automatic teller machines. But as technology made it possible for people to bank 24-hours-a-day, it also increased the chances that they might become victims of enterprising criminals who also plied their trade around the clock. Thus grew the need for new security devices and guards to protect property and physical well being.

Other SafePak products include special locks for cash cassettes on ATM machines, and time-delay lock boxes for ATM keys. The company is always developing new products in response to increasing security needs—and to keep a step ahead of its competition, which is also cashing in on the escalating need for state-of-the-art technology systems.

Wackenhut Corporation, founded by CEO and chairman George Wackenhut, ranked among the industry's largest security firms in the latter 1990s. By 1999, it had received two new lucrative accounts: first, as primary security provider for IBM at its world headquarters and 37 other locations in 14 states; and second, to provide fire and emergency services for Ciba Specialty Chemicals, commencing in May 1999 at Ciba's Alabama facility. Based in Palm Beach Gardens, Florida, Wackenhut serves the commercial, industrial, and governmental security markets. Wackenhut also provides special security services such as airport security, executive security, and investigation. The company operates in 48 states and has a presence in 50 countries. Besides security services, Wackenhut's subsidiary Wackenhut Corrections also runs approximately 40 prisons throughout the country. Wackenhut's revenues rose 56 percent in 1998 to $1.8 billion, with a net income of $9.3 million, up 40 percent before adjustments. Key new contracts that began in 1998 included providing services to AT&T, the Kennedy Space Center, and Bank of America. The company employed 56,000 people in 1997 but, by 1998, internal growth resulted in a 45-percent increase of leased employees, from approximately 16,500 up to 25,000 in the same year.

The best known company in the security business is Pinkerton's, Inc., which lists approximately half of the Fortune 500 companies as its clients. Ironically, although its name draws instant recognition, it is not the largest in the security industry—that honor goes to Borg-Warner. The company's chief focus is on integrated security systems (i.e., combining high-tech electronic access control and monitoring tools). However, it offers a variety of services, such as searches for missing persons; patent and trademark infringement investigations; security system consulting; design engineering; project management; security system sales, installation, and service; and guards. (Pinkerton's guard service generates 96 percent of the company's revenues.) The company operates about 220 offices located in Asia, Canada, Europe, Mexico, and the United States.

When Pinkerton bought northern California-based Omega Corporation and Cincinnati-based J. L. Torbec Company in 1995, the company began expanding domestically and internationally. In 1996, acquisitions included Beltran's Security and Investigation Services; Colt Protective Services; Distribution Associates South; Security Services; and two Canadian security firms, Protection Canadlarme and VCS Securite, Inc. The trend continued in January 1997 when Pinkerton's acquired Security GmbH of Germany. Six months later, it acquired Steel S.A., a leading uniformed officer security provider based in Santiago, Chile. The latter purchase was in keeping with Pinkerton's strategic expansion of its Latin American operations. Steel, established in 1991, was Chile's second largest private security firm with 1996 revenues of approximately $10.6 million. It employed 2,000 security officers throughout Chile.

Pinkerton's is a growing company, which attests to the expanding security industry. The company has grown about 15 percent per year from 1986 to 1997. Revenues increased from $244 million in 1986 to over $1 billion in 1997. There has been a concomitant growth in employment; the company employed 38,000 people in 1990. By 1998, Pinkerton's had 47,000 employees worldwide.

Sensormatic Electronics Corporation, based in Boca Raton, Florida, is another industry leader worth noting. The company is the world leader in electronic security. It is a fully integrated supplier of electronic security systems to retail, commercial, and industrial markets and manufactures integrated source tagging, i.e., anti-theft labels, which are used by more than 1,000 companies worldwide. The companies apply the labels during the packaging or manufacturing processes. Soft and hard goods retailers employ the company's electronic article surveillance (EAS), closed circuit-television (CCT), and exception monitoring systems to cut down on shoplifting and internal theft. Sensormatic contracted with British Petroleum, Saks Fifth Avenue, and Chevron Oil to provide security products for their facilities. Sensormatic's success is indicative of the growing need for security-related products and services worldwide. In 1998, the company posted sales of $986 million and employed 5,800 workers.

WORK FORCE

There are approximately 2 million people employed in the security services and equipment industry, including 750,000 security guards (also called security technicians, patrollers, or bouncers), 132,000 production workers, 90,000 private investigators, and 16,500 armored car guards. There are also about 6,200 consultants and engineers in the field who design and implement security plans to protect personal property and goods. They generally work closely with company officials to develop comprehensive security programs to fit individual clients' needs. They also generate policies and procedures on the effective destruction of critical documents and the protection of data processing and other machinery. Once their systems are implemented, they remain responsible for overseeing their effectiveness and amending the plans as needed.

As one indication of the seriousness of the security industry in meeting society's needs, educational requirements for consultants have become quite rigid. In the late 1990s, many companies preferred to hire security consultants with at least a college degree. Ideally, consultants should have a well-rounded education including courses in business management, communications, computers, sociology, and statistics. They should (but are not required to) have experience in police work, government, or other fields of crime prevention as well. The security industry needs a large variety of trained and experienced employees to develop and implement products and services required to combat sophisticated terrorists and criminals.

Estimates predict that the security field will continue to grow well into the twenty-first century, creating numerous jobs for security guards, security managers, and other related personnel. In the late 1990s, the security service sector was the seventh fastest growing service industry in the country, according to the American Society for Industrial Security. Private security workers will be used increasingly to supplement or replace police officers in such activities as courtroom security, crowd control at airports, and at special events such as the Olympics. Meanwhile, others in the field will be employed by firms developing and selling security systems.

AMERICA AND THE WORLD

The world market for security services is projected to expand by 8 percent annually through 2000, according to the American Society for Industrial Security. ASIS predicts that worldwide revenues from the industry will reach $61.8 billion in 2000 and continue growing, reaching $87.9 billion in 2005. The United States has the largest security market, followed by Europe and Asia ($5.4 billion). Developing economies are forecast to drive the growth of the industry during this period.

Some notable international companies offering personal protection services, crowd control, security escorting, etc. in 1999 included David R. Marks International, European Security Operatives, the International Bodyguard Association (Italian), International Protective Services, South Africa's John Soulglides, and Australia's Titan Security.

A relative newcomer to the international counter surveillance market is Electronic Security Products, Inc. (ESP, Inc.), which caters exclusively to the intelligence community, law enforcement agencies, and private sector security-oriented enterprises. Of particular note about ESP is its design market for covert surveillance devices, not far from what one would imagine in James Bond thrillers. For example, ESP designs and markets video glasses, which appear as ordinary eyeglasses but in fact contain a complete video and recording device. Whatever the wearer sees and hears will be fully recorded. So also is the capability of ESP's writing pens and jewelry broaches, each containing video/audio recording devices. ESP will custom-design devices to "turn almost any object into a stealth surveillance camera." The company is based in New York City.

RESEARCH AND TECHNOLOGY

Research and technology are fueling the growth of the security industry. In every field of the industry, researchers are producing innovative, technologically advanced products that are revolutionizing the industry. Ademco Security Group, a division of the Pittway Corporation, is one of the largest manufacturers on Long Island, New York, developing and implementing technologies that enhance security procedures and lower product costs. It markets over 1500 security products, and worldwide helps protect 15 million businesses, offices, homes, government agencies, factories, etc. One form of its security technology is in its surface mount devices that replaced its batch processing system, in which circuit boards go through a series of steps in batches of hundreds or thousands. In the late 1990s, the company began using flexible manufacturing, whereby machines can complete a board of one design within two minutes and then make another of a completely different design.

Ademco is also active in wireless applications. Ten years ago, the company developed a wireless alarm system called AlarmNet. By reducing reliance on phone lines to send messages to monitoring companies, this product had immense implications in the home security area of the industry. If there is a problem with the phone systems, the warning systems are useless. So, Ademco developed AlarmNet, which employs a cellular-like wireless radio frequency signal that sends multiple signals in case of trouble. Products and systems like surface mount devices and AlarmNet enhance the provision of security and assure growth for the entire industry. Pittway's 1998 annual report, released in April 1999, showed record sales and operating earnings. King Harris, company president, attributed sales growth to new products such as Ademco's Lynx self contained wireless system. Pittway also reported a 26 percent increase in first quarter sales for 1999.

Sensormatic Electronics Corporation is also aggressively pushing research and technology. For example, the company is integrating its UltraoMax technology, which involves acousto-magnetic principles, with other label products. One result will be the incorporation of UltraoMax right into bottle labels, which will reduce labeling costs and packaging steps for manufacturers and cut down on theft at the point of sales. Sensormatic's earnings were up 20 percent in the first three quarters of fiscal year 1999, due in part to sales increases of UltraoMax systems to the Wal-Mart chain. In 1999, UltraoMax was the fastest growing technology in the electronic article surveillance (EAS) industry, accounting for $400 million in sales for the period of March 1998 to March 1999.

SafePak Corporation continually develops and markets products that improve security for bank tellers, armored car drivers, business managers, and other people involved in the transfer of funds. The company manufactures and sells specialized deposit collection equipment and ATM security equipment to the banking industry. Among the products it has developed are night deposit and ATM deposit retrieval systems, a cash bar system to lock in existing cash cassettes in ATMs, and optical deposit counters for night deposit safes. These eliminate the need for two bank employees to attend a night deposit safe, while also allowing armored guards to retrieve deposits in bulk from the safes without the presence of the bank employees. Similar security-related products are being developed constantly by firms in all niches of the industry.

FURTHER READING

American Society for Industrial Security. "The US Security Market." Available at http://www.asisonline.org/stat11.htm.

Atalla Security Products, 25 April 1999. Available from http://www.tandem.com.

Bowman, Erik J. "Security Tools up for the Future." *Security Management,* January 1996, 30.

Brintliff, Russell L. *Crimeproofing Your Business: 301 Low-Cost, No-Cost Ways to Protect Your Office, Store, or Business.* New York: McGraw-Hill, 1994.

"CFC International, Inc. Reports 1999 First Quarter Results." *PR Newswire,* 22 April 1999.

"Clairvest Group Inc. Acquires Second Largest Electronic Security Operations in Australasia." *Business Wire,* 17 March 1997.

CyberSafe Corporation, 24 April 1999. Available from http://www.cybcrsafc.com.

Electronic Security Products, Inc. 25 April 1999. Available from http://www.esp.com.

Encyclopedia of Careers and Vocational Guidance, Vol. 4. Chicago: J. G. Ferguson Publishing Company, 1997.

Flexguard Security System, 25 April 1999. Available from http://www.flexguard.com.

Fried, Edward R. *Oil Security: Retrospect and Prospect.* Washington: Brookings Institution, 1993.

"JAWS Technologies Signs Sales & Marketing Alliance With Offsite Data Services, Ltd." *Business Wire,* 22 April 1999.

Lowry, Tom. "Fire Alarm Maker Tyco Rescues ADT." *USA Today,* 18 March 1997.

Martin, William Flynn. *Maintaining Energy Security in a Global Context.* New York: The Trilateral Commission, 1966.

"Pinkerton Continues Expansion in Latin America; Makes 50 Percent Joint-Venture Equity Investment in Chile's Steel S.A." *Business Wire,* 1 June 1997.

Pittway Corporation, 28 April 1999. Available from http://www.pittway.com.

Pradnya, Joshi. "Ademco Finds Island Good Fit." *Newsday,* 31 March 1997.

"Profits of Doom: After Oklahoma." *The Economist,* 13 May 1995, A27.

Raffaele, Elizabeth. "At Local Companies, Protecting Executives Is a Big Concern—and a Big Business for Security Experts." *Pittsburgh Business Times,* 17 March 1997, 1.

"SecureRite.com Launches New Model for E-Commerce Transactions." *Business Wire,* 21 April 1999.

"Sensormatic and Wallace Announce Production and Distribution Agreement." *Business Wire,* 11 February 1997.

"Sensormatic Third Quarter Earnings Increase 20% Over Prior Year." Company Press Release, 28 April 1999. Available from http://biz.yahoo.com.

The Wackenhut Corporation Press Release Page, 28 April 1999. Available from http://www.wackenhut.com.

"Welcome to the New World of Private Security." *The Economist,* 19 April 1997, 21.

—Arthur G. Sharp,
updated by Karl Heil and Lauri R. Harding

SEMICONDUCTORS

Among the largest modern industries throughout the world are those involved in the development, manufacture, and sale of semiconductors. Any device that is described with the terms "solid-state," "integrated circuit," or "microchip," uses semiconductors. These miniaturized circuits have expanded into almost every major piece of new equipment used by humans over the past 20 years. Cellular phones and communications, fuel-efficient automobiles, televisions, microwave ovens, photocells, and microcomputers all rely on semiconductors in order to operate. Since the first large-scale emergence of semiconductors in the late 1950s, production in the United States alone has become a multi-billion dollar industry. Government agencies debate the importance of semiconductor production in national policy. It is difficult to imagine the modern world without the influence of semiconductors. (Also see chapters in this book entitled Advanced Ceramics; Photovoltaic Systems; and Wireless Communications.)

Although semiconductor production and sales are regarded as well established rather than emerging industries *per se,* analysts agree that there is still considerable growth to come. Microcomputers, the largest industry to use semiconductors, generate about 50 percent of all income for the semiconductor industry. New technologies improve the performance of microprocessors—only one segment of the larger semiconductor industry—every 18 months on the average. In addition, manufacturers of computers and other users of semiconductors have increased their use of high-performance chips in their machines. Upper-end computer vendors regularly increase the power of desktop computer consoles. Off-the-shelf equipment standards grew from 4 megabytes of random access memory (RAM) in 1995, to 64 megabytes by the end of 1998. More remarkable still is an endless proliferation of miniaturized "embedded" systems—full-blown computer systems that are integrated into the control functions of common appliances and devices. Embedded processors are at once very small yet very powerful, replete with operating systems and software applications. They achieve seamless levels of design integration with the appliance or device as a whole, such that the presence of the processor may be ignored at the very least and frequently is undetectable.

In 1997, manufacturer shipments of semiconductors and related products reached $68.72 billion. Early in 1999 the Semiconductor Industry Association (SIA) reported global semiconductor industry's sales were up 3.3 percent from the same time in 1998, despite economic turbulence in Asia. SIA forecasts projects accelerated global industry growth at 17-19 percent annually through 2001, when worldwide sales could reach $222.3 billion.

The semiconductor industry is divided according to the type of semiconductor produced. Each type has a separate function. All semiconductors, however, are broadly similar. They are all made from materials that conduct electricity; *conductors* (such as copper, iron, and aluminum) and *insulators* (such as rubber, glass, and wood). Semiconductors are important because they can change the way an electric current behaves, or even change one form of energy (such as light) into another form (such as electricity). Transistors, perhaps the most important form of semiconductors, are particularly important because they can control the flow of a very large electric current by means of a very small electric current at another point on their surface. They can act like switches in conducting electric current. For example, some transistors conduct electricity well only over a certain voltage—the amount of effort needed to move electricity in a current from one place to another. When the threshold voltage is reached, the transistor stops resisting the current and becomes a conductor of the current. This ability of transistors to act as both resistors and conductors of electricity allows them to serve as switches. Different settings of different switches allow information to be stored and communicated. This basic property of semiconductor material allowed scientists to develop the microprocessors and microcomputers that have so influenced the modern industrial world.

All semiconductor chips are manufactured using basically similar processes. They are generally made from a silicon matrix, composed of melted sand embedded with small crystals. Although other raw materials have been used to make semiconductors, including some plastics and ceramics, sand is most common; it is plentiful, inexpensive, and it works well. To make a semiconductor, a manufacturer melts sand into a column. Usually these columns are between six and eight inches in diameter, although recently they have expanded to 12 inches. The columns are cut into a series of thin wafers. Each wafer is then implanted or printed with a series of small circuits, which vary according to the function of the chip. The wafer is then cut into chips, which are sold to computer manufacturers, makers of electronic equipment, and hobbyists.

It is the imprinted circuits that make semiconductors function. They can be placed on the silicon matrix in a variety of ways. During the melting process, the manufacturer introduces impurities in the form of crystals of phosphorus, aluminum, boron, or gallium (called *dopants*), which change the semiconductor's ability to conduct electricity. This is commonly done by treating the wafer with chemicals. The first chemical makes it react like a piece of photographic paper. Next, a template called a photomask is placed over the wafer. The wafer is then treated with light-sensitive chemicals that cause tiny metal lines, some no thicker than 1/25 of a micron—finer than the finest human hair—to be deposited on its surface. Another way to imprint a circuit on a wafer is to flood the wafer with other dopants. The wafer is then heated to induce the dopant's atoms to line up in the desired pattern. Still another way is to shoot atoms of the

dopant directly into the surface of the wafer. All these processes can be repeated on several different levels, so that a single microchip may contain several layers of semiconductors within its surface.

Manufacturers divide semiconductors into two large categories: analog and digital. Analog semiconductors pass electricity in continuous waves of fluctuating voltage. They can amplify or regulate voltages, coordinate signals between different systems, or convert data from analog or linear signals into digital signals and back again. Analog integrated circuits (ICs) are used in amplifiers, electronic musical instruments, and electronic analog computers. Digital semiconductors process information as a series of extremely high-speed pulses, using the ability of transistors to function as on/off switches. Each pulse that passes through the circuit switches a transistor "on" or "off." Thus digital circuitry requires only two voltage levels ("on" voltage and "off" voltage) to communicate exact information quickly and accurately. High-speed microprocessors, such as Intel Corporation's Pentium processors, are capable of passing hundreds of millions of pulses per second that can then be translated into other types of information, through binary (two-digit) communication languages. Digital semiconductors are subdivided into three functional types: memory chips, logic chips, and microprocessors.

MEMORY CHIPS

Memory chips are made specifically to store information. Memory chips may be read-only memory (ROM) or random access memory (RAM). Some semiconductors (volatile memory chips) lose the information they store when their power is interrupted, while others (nonvolatile memory chips) can retain data through a loss of power. In addition, there are several different classes of memory semiconductors. Dynamic random access memory (DRAM) chips are most common in personal computers. They store information quickly and easily, and allow it to be accessed rapidly. The counterpart to the DRAM chip is the static random access memory (SRAM) semiconductor. SRAM performs the same functions as DRAM, but much faster. Unlike DRAM, SRAM does not require a constant electric current to operate—it can retain information with less current and operate much faster than DRAM. However, SRAM is more complicated to manufacture and thus costs more than DRAM, so its use in computer systems is less common. Continually expanded processor power and function necessitates a corresponding upgrade in RAM modules. Extended data output random access memory (EDORAM) modules may be required for faster machines that process greater quantities of digitized data simultaneously.

The flash memory chip is a nonvolatile semiconductor that can be erased and reprogrammed electrically. One example of a computer chip that uses flash memory is the binary input/output system (BIOS), a ROM chip that checks the hardware for system memory and the presence of installed devices such as disk drives. The BIOS directs the computer through the process of initial program load (IPL) of the operating system. Flash memory chips are found in communications equipment as well as in computing devices.

MICROPROCESSORS

Microprocessors are a specific type of chip used primarily in computers, but they are also important to the telecommunications, electronics, and automobile industries. They are sometimes called central processing units because they control and coordinate the processing of data from all other points of the computer. They consist of a series of specialized integrated circuits contained in a single chip. Microprocessors are what make computers such powerful tools. Microprocessors can pack thousands or even millions of transistors into a very small area—in some cases, less than the size of a human fingernail. The best-known of these microprocessors are the series manufactured by Intel Corporation, including the popular Pentium series.

LOGIC DEVICES

A third category of semiconductors is logic devices. They control the ways in which information is transmitted and interpreted within a single electronic system. While most other types of semiconductors can be used in different types of equipment without major changes, logic devices usually have to be designed to fit into a particular system. There are three main categories of logic devices: complex programmable logic devices (CPLDs), field programmable logic devices (FPGAs), and application-specific integrated circuits (ASICs). The two programmable logic devices are fairly standard across the industry. Their value lies in the fact that manufacturers can modify them to suit their particular needs by using electrical codes. The ASICs have to be designed and constructed for a particular function, and thus tend to be more expensive.

The manufacture and sale of semiconductors is so important to the U.S. economy that Congress holds hearings on the industry to discuss its impact on national policy. Worldwide semiconductor sales are brisk, according to the *Global Sales Report* of World Semiconductor Trade Statistics (WSTS), with eastern Asian and Pacific Rim countries providing the bulk of sales from U.S. and Japanese manufacturers. According to the Semiconductor Industry Association worldwide sales of semiconductors reached $10.88 billion for February 1999. This was a sight increase in sales from the worldwide sales of $10.54 billion in February 1998.

ENCRYPTION DEVICES

Early in 1999 industry leader, Intel Corporation, acknowledged plans to develop a new ASIC called an encryption chip, for a variety of applications including on-line banking and commerce transactions. Encryption technology originally emerged in the late 1990s as virtual private networks (VPNs) proliferated among business and industry. In order to achieve security over these networks, companies turned first to software packages but soon looked to hardware solutions for greater privacy. As a hardware component, the encryption chip would significantly expand the complexity of the array used to encrypt the data, far beyond the original U.S. Data Encryption Standard (DES) that permits a maximum of 56 computer digits. In addition to the expanded array, the dedicated encryption chip would support multiple passes of the data through the chip before the process would be complete for transmission. Encryption chip technology would be useful in a variety of security applications, including the protection of copyrighted electronic materials, such as videotaped releases, from unauthorized duplication.

BACKGROUND AND DEVELOPMENT

Semiconductors occur regularly in the natural environment. In 1874, Ferdinand Braun used crystals of galena, an ore of lead, to make a simple semiconductor device to regulate electric current. Any atom that has more than three and less than six electrons in its outermost energy level can be a semiconductor. Inert gasses such as helium and neon and rock-like materials like mica have eight electrons in their outermost energy level and are very good insulators. Metals such as gold, silver, and copper are excellent conductors because they have only one electron in their outermost energy levels. The best semiconductors, such as silicon and germanium, have between three and six electrons. Even then, however, they have to be put through a manufacturing process in order to become commercially useful.

In the days before widespread development of semiconductors, scientists worked and experimented

---

SIDNEY BENZER
PHYSICIST AND BIOLOGIST

American physicist Seymour Benzer was born in Brooklyn, New York in 1921. Benzer, the son of Polish immigrants, was a scientific prodigy. He first attended Brooklyn College on a Regents' Scholarship at the age of 15. A biologist by choice, Benzer elected to study physics because he knowledge of biology was too advanced for the undergraduate curriculum at the college. He continued his physics curriculum into postgraduate work and later, as a graduate student at Purdue University in Illinois during World War II, he performed research into radar technology for the U.S. government. It was there that he identified the germanium crystal that led to the development of the first transistor, the key component of solid-state electronics. Benzer eventually joined the physics faculty at Purdue University, although in 1953 he rekindled his interest in biology. He moved to Pasadena in 1965 and went to work at the California Institute of Technology

(Caltech), where he experimented with mutant fruit flies, called *drosophila melanogaster.* Through his work at Caltech, Benzer earned a reputation as one of the pioneers in the field of molecular biology. He was recognized as the first scientist to develop a "map" of a human gene.

Ironically Benzer's eccentricities in pursuit of his science sometimes overshadowed his discoveries. One of his least understood habits of this semiconductor pioneer was his preoccupation with eating samples of unusual organic matter, not the least of which were his own drosophila experiments. Additionally he ate crocodile tails, cow udder, a variety of animal brains, fish lips, caterpillars and more.

In 1983 Benzer was awarded the National Medal of Science. His biography, *Time, Love, Memory,* was published in 1999.

---

with other devices that could perform the same functions. Thomas Edison observed the principle behind the electron tube—the idea that an electric current would flow in only one direction through the device—as early as 1883. The electron tube was first developed in 1905 by Sir J. Ambrose Fleming, who used it to detect high frequency radio waves. It works on the principle of heating or "cooking" electrons off a heated metal plate in order to affect current flow. Because this heating had to take place in a vacuum to prevent the plate from melting or oxidizing, these tubes were also called vacuum tubes. Electron tubes were common in early radio receivers and were common to nearly all telecommunications devices until the late 1950s and early 1960s. They are still seen in some microwave ovens, x-ray machines, and radarequipment.

Although the electron tube was indispensable in the development of the radio industry, it had its own problems. Electron tubes were bulky, inefficient, and fragile. In 1948, three scientists working at Bell Laboratories developed the first practical solid-state equivalent of the electron tube. Walter H. Brattain, John Bardeen, and William Shockley created the first transistors with the idea of replacing the tubes with something less fragile. The transistors were virtually unbreakable, gave off almost no heat, and were very small—in some cases no larger than the tip of a man's finger. In 1952 one of the original developers, William Shockley, further refined the transistor, making it less fragile and more reliable.

In 1958, Jack Kilby created the first integrated circuit (IC), a complex electronic device that incorporated one or more semiconductors. Kilby's IC combined transistors with other electronic devices, such as resistors and capacitors, to create a solid-state electronic device. It represented a great advance over existing electronic devices because it was less fragile and more compact. The miniaturization potential of the IC made possible the development of the microcomputer in the 1960s.

The history of the modern personal computer (PC) took another great leap forward in 1971 when Intel Corporation created the first microprocessor. The microprocessor made possible the coordination of great numbers of ICs into a single system. Only four years later, IBM introduced its first PC, and in 1976, Apple Computer Inc. introduced the first model in its popular Apple line. The PC had left the laboratory for the office, the classroom, and the home. Even more astounding were the strides made as embedded systems permeated the manufacturing environment. Embedded systems are complete one-chip computers that perform a comprehensive spectrum of maintenance functions for the electronic operation of a device or appliance. By the mid-1990s embedded systems were standard features on automobiles, security devices, household appliances, elevators, computer testing systems, and office machinery. The variety of potential applications for these systems will not be realized for years to come.

CURRENT CONDITIONS

According to the Semiconductor Industry Association (SIA) the computer industry accounts for roughly half of semiconductors sold in the mid- to late 1990s. Worldwide semiconductor sales totaled near $137 billion in 1997, but fell in most areas during 1998. SIA analysts blamed the economic crisis in parts of Asia for the drop in sales. Beginning in late 1997, Asia started to suffer from bad debt and devalued currencies, a condition that drastically reduced sales to the region. For example, the devaluation of the Yen relative to the U.S. dollar accounted for a $1.7 billion drop in Japan's semiconductor market in 1998. Although the Asia/Pacific region was forecast to be the hottest growing market in 1998 with expansion of 24 percent predicted, analysts re-evaluated the region's potential in mid-1998 and projected only 3.2 percent growth that year, a figure that proved not too low.

Nonetheless, the SIA believes the worldwide semiconductor industry will rebound in 1999 partially because of the tremendous growth of Internet usage. From 1999 through 2001, the industry organization forecasts robust growth of 17 percent or more as the industry recovers from slow growth in 1997 and declining sales in 1998. By 2001, the industry should bring in $222.3 billion, according to these predictions. In 1998, the United States continued to have the largest semiconductor market, accounting for 32.7 percent of the world's sales and by 2001 the U.S. market is slated to reach 33.1 percent, according to the SIA.

Oversupply in the global DRAM market resulted in diminished sales since 1996; although SIA reports indicate that the world inventory stabilized late in 1998. During the interim, sales fell by approximately 21 percent in 1997. Once DRAM regains a production pace in keeping with demand, semiconductor analysts predict that DRAM sales will rise rapidly— by 26 percent in 1999, and by 35 percent in 2000 and 2001.

The U.S. market for very low-end personal computers costing under $1,000 was blamed in part for stagnant microprocessor revenues in 1998. Nonetheless, sales surpassed 1996 levels by a significant margin. The U.S. represents about 42 percent of the world's microprocessor sales, which will most likely experience renewed growth by 1999 and should remain strong through 2001 at which time sales could soar to $41.6 billion, according to SIA reports.

INDUSTRY LEADERS

INTEL CORPORATION

Maker of the first microprocessor, Intel is the leader in sales of semiconductors industry-wide. In 1971 Intel's founders created the 4004 series microprocessor, which had 2,300 transistors and a processing speed of 60,000 instructions per second. Intel's modern Pentium series processors regularly contain more than 5 million transistors and access them at a processing speed of 400 million instructions per sec-

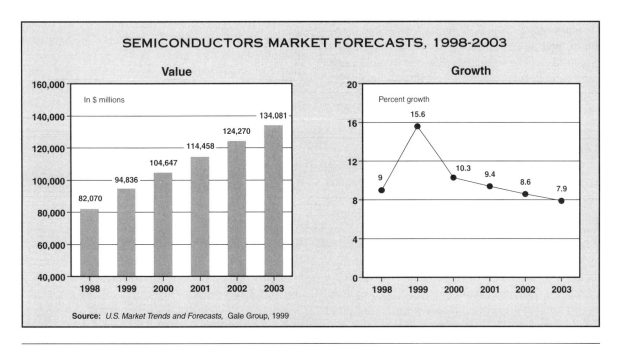

SEMICONDUCTORS MARKET FORECASTS, 1998-2003

Value

In $ millions

1998	82,070
1999	94,836
2000	104,647
2001	114,458
2002	124,270
2003	134,081

Growth

Percent growth

1998	9
1999	15.6
2000	10.3
2001	9.4
2002	8.6
2003	7.9

Source: *U.S. Market Trends and Forecasts,* Gale Group, 1999

ond or better. The worldwide leader in sales of semiconductors, the company reported $26.3 billion in total revenues in 1998, with sales growth of 4.8 percent. Intel has become a household word in the United States because of the popularity of its Pentium microprocessors and its commercials advertising "Intel Inside." Between 1987 and 1997, sales increased from $1.9 billion to $25.07 billion, an average annual increase of about $2.3 billion.

Intel dominates the industry in the sale of microprocessors, with about 90 percent of all sales worldwide. Its major rivals are Advanced Micro Devices (AMD) and Cyrix, both of which produce microprocessors that rival Intel's Pentium series in performance. AMD K6 series microprocessors retail at about 25 percent less than the equivalent Intel product, the Pentium II. The Cyrix equivalent of the Pentium II, the 6x86MX, sells at between 50 and 60 percent of the Intel product. However, neither Cyrix nor AMD has Intel's manufacturing capacity or its name recognition. Another rival of Intel in the microprocessor market is Centaur Technology, which introduced a Pentium-equivalent chip, the MMX-compatible IDT-C6, at a retail price of only $150. Market researchers predict that these manufacturers will see their greatest sales in lower-end PCs that cost $1,500 or less.

MOTOROLA, INC.

The second-largest American producer of semiconductors is Motorola Inc. In 1997 Motorola ranked fifth in size among the world's semiconductor producers, with worldwide sales of about $6.2 billion or 21 percent of the company's overall sales, by 1998 Motorola moved into third position with estimated revenues of $6.9 billion, behind the American corporation Intel and Japan's NEC. Much of the material produced by Motorola goes into cellular telephones and other telecommunications equipment. Its production is broader than Intel's, with sales peaking in memory chips, logic chips, and analog semiconductors.

TEXAS INSTRUMENTS INC.

Texas Instruments (TI), which had for years been a major manufacturer and distributor of computer equipment, has begun to specialize in the production of semiconductors. In April of 1999 Gartner Group's Dataquest market research group reported that Texas Instruments Incorporated (TI) was the leader in analog semiconductors with a 10.8 percent market share in 1998, in a marketplace that totaled $21.1 billion worldwide. The report estimated that 80 percent of the top 10 computer manufacturers were shipping products featuring the TI 1394 analog chip family. TI covers 68 percent of the digital cellular phone market according to the study. TI makes and sells an assortment of both digital and analog semiconductors, but its greatest strength lies in the creation of digital signal processing semiconductors (DSPs). TI used these devices in electronic toys in the 1970s, but they are beginning to emerge as important components of high-speed modems and telephone technology.

AMERICA AND THE WORLD

The chief competitors of the American semiconductor industry are Japanese. NEC Corp., Toshiba Corp., and Hitachi. These companies all ranked among the top 10 semiconductor producers worldwide. NEC was ranked second only to Intel in semiconductor production with overall sales of $39.9 billion in 1997. Toshiba ranked fourth in 1998, and Hitachi ranked seventh. Other top 10 semiconductor manufacturers are scattered across the world. Samsung in South Korea was one of the top companies in terms of worldwide sales, with revenues of $5.8 billion in 1997. Philips in the Netherlands is number eight, with revenues of $4.23 billion.

Worldwide semiconductor sales were forecast to fall to $134.6 billion in 1998, but should begin an ascent in 1999 and reach $222.3 billion by 2001. The United States has the largest semiconductor market in the world, accounting for an estimated 32.7 percent of the industry's global sales in 1998. The Asia/Pacific market (Singapore, Korea, China, Taiwan, and India) ranked second, accounting for 23 percent, followed by Europe accounting for 22.7 percent, and Japan accounting for 21.6 percent, according to the Semiconductor Industry Association. Industry analysts predict that the Asia/Pacific region will experience more growth in semiconductor sales than any other region in the early 2000s as the region recovers from its economic crises of the late 1990s.

RESEARCH AND TECHNOLOGY

Researchers continue to experiment with semiconductors in order to reduce price and increase performance. One simple way to reduce the cost of chips is to increase the size of the wafers they are made from. The industry standard until recently had been to use wafers cut from silicon columns that were only four inches in diameter. By 1997, wafer size had increased to between six and eight inches in diameter.

Soon, industry analysts predict, manufacturers will move to a 12-inch or 300-millimeter size wafer. The increased wafer size will allow semiconductor makers to effectively double their chip capacity. However, the *Standard & Poor's Industry Survey* report on semiconductors suggests that chip manufacturers are somewhat slow in adopting the new size because they are wary of the expenses involved. However, the same source predicts that the new 300-millimeter wafers will come into common use by the year 2000.

Currently, semiconductor manufacturers are experimenting with using new technology to bring their merchandise directly to consumers. They plan to place the entire series of circuits that make up the modern microcomputer on a single chip. This "system on a chip" technology could revolutionize computer manufacturing and electronic retailing. The creation of single chips that function like entire computer systems would allow the building of smaller, more powerful electronic devices and would speed the creation of new products. The first step in the development of "systems on a chip" is the integration of the function of memory chips and logic chips in a single semiconductor. LSI Logic Corp., a company that specializes in the production of logic chips, already manufactures limited quantities of combined memory-logic chips. They have also begun development of specialized system chips for digital cameras and televisions. In June of 1997, LSI Logic and another manufacturer of these two types of devices—Micron Technology Inc.— announced plans to combine their research efforts in order to develop single-chip systems.

Another technology that emerged in the late 1990s as commercially important is the digital signal processor (DSP). A DSP's only function is to change an analog signal into a digital one. However, it is capable of handling these signals at speeds up to 10 times faster than the average microprocessor. DSPs have recently come down in price, and new technology allows them to be easily programmed. Although sales of DSPs amount to only a small portion of the semiconductor market, experts suggest that demand could grow by as much as 40 percent over the next ten years. Some of the new applications in which DSPs could become important include voice-activated computers, videoconferencing, and downloading of digital television programs, movies, and games through consumer's television sets. Texas Instruments controls about 45 percent of the DSP manufacturing industry. The U.S. firm, Lucent Technologies Inc., ranked 14 among the world's largest semiconductor manufacturers. Currently Lucent Technologies has an additional 29 percent of the DSP market, and the rest of the DSP industry is divided between several other firms, including Motorola Inc. On June 2, 1998 Motorola and Lucent Technologies announced that they would form a strategic alliance, called Star*Core, to develop "next generation" DSP technology.

Key to producing more powerful semiconductors is increasing the number of transistors that can fit on a single chip. The number of transistors on a single chip controls the chip's power. In 1971, when Intel produced its first microprocessor, its transistors measured 10 microns in size—much smaller than the original transistors first produced in 1948. In 1996, however, manufacturers regularly produced semiconductors containing transistors that measured a quarter of a micron or less in size.

Although semiconductor technology has advanced tremendously in the past 30 years, scientists are already predicting that there may be limits on how far semiconductor technology can progress. Dr. Gordon Moore, one of the founders of Intel, has suggested that, even though the power of semiconductors doubles about every 18 months, the progression may not last long. Dr. Moore foresees a limit to semiconductor power that may be reached in the next 10 years. In particular, he hints that it may not be possible for linewidths—the size of individual transistors on a single microchip—to be reduced to less than 1/10 of a micron. That would limit how many transistors could be packed into a chip. Researchers are trying to bypass this limit by placing semiconductors deeper inside a chip instead of in a small layer close to the surface, but this technology is not yet commercially viable. In April of 1999 Lawrence Berkeley National Laboratory announced that researcher Othon Monteiro developed a method of applying copper inlay to the semiconductor wafer instead of the common aluminum alloys in general use. The copper reportedly supported accelerated speeds with better insulation, greater stability, and potentially smaller circuit runs.

FURTHER READING

"1996 Annual Survey of Manufactures." Washington, DC: U.S. Department of Commerce, Bureau of the Census. Available from http://www.census.gov.

"1997 Current Industrial Reports." Washington, DC: U.S. Department of Commerce, Bureau of the Census, August 1998. Available from http://www.census.gov.

Agres, Ted. "Roadmap Points to Crucial Semiconductor Needs." *R & D,* February 1998.

Arlington Morning News, 19 January 1999.

Capital Investment in Semiconductors: The Lifeblood of the U.S. Semiconductor Industry. Arlington, VA: National Advisory Committee on Semiconductors, 1990.

Dick, Andrew Ronald. *Industrial Policy and Semiconductors: Missing the Target.* Washington, DC: AEI Press, 1995.

Electric Power Research Institute, Inc. *Signature.* Summer 1998.

Goldstein, Andrew, and William Aspray, eds. *Facets: New Perspectives on the History of Semiconductors.* New Brunswick, NJ: IEEE Center, 1997.

Globalisation of Industrial Activities: Four Case Studies, Auto Parts, Chemicals, Construction, and Semiconductors. Washington, DC: Organization for Economic Development Publications and Information Center, 1992.

Howell, Thomas R., Brent L. Bartlett, and Warren Davis. *Creating Advantage: Semiconductors and Government Industrial Policy in the 1990s.* San Jose, CA: Semiconductor Industry Association/Dewey Ballantine, 1992.

Lawton, Thomas C. *Technology and the New Diplomacy: The Creation and Control of EC Industrial Policy for Semiconductors.* Brookfield, VT: Avebury, 1997.

"Semiconductor Equipment." *Standard & Poor's Industry Surveys,* 1 May 1997.

Semiconductor Industry Association. "Global Semiconductor Sales to Decline 1.8 percent in 1998," 3 April 1999. Available from http://www.semichips.org/news/pr060398 .htm.

Semiconductor Industry Association. "Semiconductor Sales Worldwide Total $10.88 Billion In February Industry Is Up In Sales 3.3 Percent from Last Year," 5 April 1999. Available from http://www.semichips.org/stats/shares.htm.

Semiconductor Industry Association. "World Market Sales and Shares for 1991-1996." Available from http://www .semichips.org/stats/shares.htm.

"Semiconductors." *Standard & Poor's Industry Surveys,* 31 July 1997.

Semiconductors and the Electronics Industry: Hearing before the Subcommittee on Science, Technology, and Space of the Committee on Commerce, Science, and Transportation, United States Senate, One Hundred First Congress, Second Session. Washington, DC: GPO, 17 May 1990.

Willett, Hugh G. "Embedded Is Where It's At," *Electronic News,* 15 February 1999.

Yu, Peter Y., and Manuel Cardona. *Fundamentals of Semiconductors: Physics and Materials Properties.* Berlin and New York: Springer, 1996.

—Kenneth R. Shepherd,
updated by Karl Heil and Gloria Cooksey

SMART CARDS

A smart card is a device that contains a microprocessor chip capable of storing large amounts of memory. Smart cards are different from magnetic stripe cards in that the latter hold only a fraction of the amount of information—such as account holder's name and account number—as the former. Smart cards come in two varieties: "intelligent" cards, which can perform complex functions and have both a read and a write capacity; and memory cards, which store and gradually deduct value as it is used. A simple cash card or the telephone cards popular in Europe and east Asia are specific examples of memory cards. Examples of intelligent cards are medical records cards that contain patients' vital statistics, prescription and allergy information, and medical histories. Some of these cards may also include a digital version of one's photo identification.

Smart cards are the same size as credit cards and are used for financial transactions, for security purposes, for long-distance phone accounts, to maintain medical and other records, and for a variety of related purposes. Eventually, there will be smart cards with multiple applications, which were already in development in the late 1990s. Students at certain universities, for instance, could use a single card to gain access to certain areas of campus restricted to outsiders, to access library records and grade information, and to record the status of their financial accounts, not only with the tuition office but even at the student cafeteria.

One industry analyst has calculated that adapting to a smart card society would carry a cumulative price tag of $10 billion, which has kept smart cards from catching on in the United States. But by the late 1990s,

with such groundbreaking events as the introduction of "Visa Cash" at the 1996 Olympics, the United States was steadily increasing its use of smart cards. In fact, according to *U.S. News & World Report,* the number of smart cards being used in North America reached 16 million by the late 1990s. Although use of smart cards in the United States remains well behind use in Europe, industry observers expect U.S. use to increase. Nevertheless, analysts' forecasts vary widely. For example, the Smart Card Forum predicts the number of smart cards in the United States to reach 2.5 billion by the year 2001; Forrester Research puts the number at 600 million and Schlumberger Electronic Transactions, one of the industry's leading smart card producers, expects the number to be 273 million. Some analysts expect U.S. use of smart cards to increase substantially around 2000 because the patents on smart card technology will expire around this time, allowing companies to adopt the technology at a far lower cost. Worldwide, smart card sales reached $1.8 billion in 1998 and are forecast to jump to $5.0 billion by 2003, according to Frost & Sullivan.

Not surprisingly, people are wary of this technological development, which only came into being in the mid-1970s. To some, smart cards seem to represent a monolithic gateway for another person to invade one's privacy; to others, they bring to mind the type of surveillance detailed in George Orwell's *1984.* In a mid-1990's survey of World Wide Web users, censorship and privacy were found to be the two most important concerns, and nearly 40 percent of respondents claimed that they reported false information when registering at a Web site. Such fears are understandable and expected in the face of a technological innovation that can potentially change everyday life as fundamentally as can smart cards.

Most experts believe that smart cards, however, will offer individuals more privacy—not less—because the encryption, or coding, on them makes it nearly impossible for another person to use. Industry analysts discuss the day when smart cards will be pervasive, and in the late 1990s, the day was rapidly approaching for Americans. In the 18-month period from January 1996 to mid-1997, the industry experienced near-exponential growth in the United States, a growth that was forecast to continue. In addition, by the mid-1990s some form of smart phone card was in use in 50 countries worldwide.

ORGANIZATION AND STRUCTURE

Smart cards initially had three discrete functions—electronic purses, replacements for magnetic-stripe technology, and value-transfer cards—although some smart cards of the late 1990s supported multiple applications, including applications well beyond these three. The electronic-purse function refers to systems designed to replace cash and coin with electronic credit. As a replacement for magnetic stripe technology, smart cards were designed to replace credit and debit cards and provide superior security. Finally, as value-transfer cards, smart cards were designed to serve phone cards, copy cards, and so forth where users transfer cash value to the computer-chip cards.

There are also a variety of marketing applications for smart cards, including "loyalty programs," in which the cardholder accrues points toward a gift from the card-issuing institution. An example of this would be frequent-flyer miles earned toward a free plane ticket. Sometimes smart cards themselves become the commodity, as with card collecting—a booming side industry. Banks and other card-issuing institutions ultimately benefit from such unused cards. A $5 card issued by NYNEX during the 1992 Democratic National Convention in New York City, for example, was valued at $2,500 five years later.

Two principal industry-related organizations are the Smart Card Forum (SCF) and the Smart Card Industrial Association (SCIA). The former, established in 1993 by Citicorp, Bellcore, and the U.S. Treasury Financial Management Services Division, included some 230 corporations and government agencies in Europe and the Americas in 1997. SCF promotes public policy initiatives in support of smart cards and works to develop both cooperation and competition among members of the industry. SCIA was formed in 1989 and includes manufacturers, integrators, re-

sellers, users, issuers, consultants, and nonprofit and educational institutions involved in some aspect of the smart card industry. It sponsors CardTech/SecurTech, a conference for members of the advanced card and security technology industries; keeps members and the public informed about developments within the industry; publishes a newsletter, *Smart Link;* and educates the public about the developing smart card industry. SCIA also provides links to principal financial card-issuing associations—Europay, MasterCard, and Visa—at its online Web site. In an effort to become the premier trade association for the smart card industry, the SCIA "relaunched" itself in early 1997 and has increased its efforts to educate businesses and the public about the industry's potential.

BACKGROUND AND DEVELOPMENT

A key element in the development of the smart card was the microchip, which was invented by Texas Instruments engineer Jack Kilby and Fairchild Semiconductor engineer Robert N. Noyce in 1959. Until that time, there was a direct relationship between a computer's size and its power. When, in 1971, Intel Corporation scientist Ted Hoff created a tiny silicon chip capable of holding as much memory as ENIAC, an early computer that weighed 18 tons, it was clear that the information industry was about to undergo monumental changes. Three years later, in 1974, Frenchman Roland Moreno conceived the idea of marrying chip technology with a credit card-sized device, and the smart card was born. When, in 1980, Arlen R. Lessin, an American, learned about the smart card, which was then virtually unknown in North America, he said: "I knew the moment I saw the card demonstrated that it would revolutionize the way we conduct both our business and personal lives." Lessin obtained the rights from Moreno to market the card in the United States, and he founded the first U.S. company in the industry, SmartCard International, Inc.

Smart card technology spawned a demand for computer chips capable of fitting inside a card and undergoing the same wear and tear as magnetic stripe cards. In Europe, this technology was developing in the late 1970s and early 1980s as U.S. banks were just beginning to adopt the magnetic swipe card and as automated teller machines (ATMs) proliferated.

The reason for the lag in smart card use in the United States had its roots, ironically, in the high quality of U.S. telecommunications services. Running checks on credit cards via the phone lines was easy for U.S. merchants; hence, they felt little need for a card that would make it possible to instantly verify the customer's account information. In France, however, where phone services were not nearly as advanced as in the United States, smart cards were an appealing alternative. By the mid-1990s, Roland Moreno's home country alone had some 20 million banking smart cards and millions more phone cards in use.

Smart card use in the United States was minimal until the nation's two leading credit card companies, Visa and MasterCard, began to see them as a way to curtail credit-card fraud. In the mid-1990s, such fraud in the United States accounted for some $500 million a year in losses and $1.7 billion annually worldwide.

In 1995, three large financial institutions helped foster a major development that paved the way for wide use of smart cards. Europay, MasterCard, and Visa, all credit-card licensing institutions, developed a set of technical standards—called the "EMV" specifications after their combined initials. These standards ensure that cards will be compatible with one another, preventing the proliferation of competing systems that could create costly failures analogous to Sony's Betamax brand of video-cassette playback technology.

CURRENT CONDITIONS

In the mid- to late 1990s, there were approximately 140 smart card projects at some stage of implementation in the United States, and the numbers were rapidly growing. During this period, there were some 420 million smart cards in the world, and it was predicted that by 2000 there would be 3.8 billion. Of these 3.8 billion, only 600 million are forecast to be sold in the United States; however, that would be a substantial increase from just 16 million sold in the late 1990s. U.S. smart card growth was projected to be highest (182 percent annually) in gaming cards, which were expected to increase to 500 million by the year 2000; followed by identity cards, projected at 400 million; and transportation cards, estimated to number 200 million by the year 2000. According to Frost & Sullivan, smart card sales worldwide totaled $1.8 billion in 1998 and are slated to rocket to $3.7 billion by 2001 and $5.0 billion by 2003.

Because of excitement over smart cards in the early 1990s, numerous companies flooded the market with smart card technology as the number of competitors rose by 250 percent between 1992 and 1997, according to *Electronic Business.* Production equipment for smart cards jumped from $2 million to $1.36

billion during this period as companies prepared for a smart card revolution. Despite the number of companies selling smart cards and smart card equipment, consumer demand remained limited, and some analysts predict that fewer than 2 billion cards will be in circulation by 2000.

The lackluster demand for smart cards is attributable to the lack of smart card infrastructure in the United States. By the late 1990s, the United States lagged behind most other industrialized countries in adopting smart card technology. The United States accounted for only 3 percent of smart card sales in the mid- to late 1990s, while Europe accounted for 70 percent and Asia and Latin America the remainder. France, the country that pioneered the smart card, led with smart card readers in numerous locations throughout the country. France also unveiled its electronic purse system in 1998 during the World Cup tournament there in an effort to completely replace cash and coins. France also issued medical smart cards to all families to facilitate the country's national health care system. Analysts link the lack of demand in the United States to a variety of factors, including the reluctance of U.S. companies to pay patent royalties on smart card technology and the pervasiveness of magnetic-stripe technology, according to *PC Magazine.* Because the 17-year patents on smart cards were issued in the early 1980s, they are set to expire around 2000, at which time analysts expect U.S. companies to begin a more aggressive foray into smart card technology. U.S. bankers, among others, also contend that implementing smart card technology would cost too much because of the ubiquity of magnetic-stripe technology, which is used in ATMs and credit-card readers around the country.

The Clinton Administration took steps to increase the country's use of the new technology in the late 1990s. By late 1999, the government expects all federal employees to carry smart cards serving a variety of purposes: identification, access, and banking. The government also plans to pay social service benefits electronically and pay government vendors electronically by late 1999. In addition, government officials identified $640 billion of services and programs that could be converted to the smart card system, including student loans, Medicare, and Medicaid. Ultimately, the switch to smart cards is predicted to reduce federal paperwork and expenses.

As a consequence, the Smart Card Forum issued a highly optimistic prediction that 2.5 billion smart cards will be in use in the United States by 2000. Other estimates remained more conservative. Schlumberger predicted that the North American market would reach

273 million cards by 2001 and 543 million by 2005. In terms of market share, Dataquest expects the Americas to account for 20 percent of the smart cards sold in the world by 2001, and it expects the United States to be one of the leaders in smart card development, along with Germany, Japan, and France. In addition, Europe is predicted to account for 40 percent of the world smart card market in 2001, and Asia is expected to account for 25 percent.

Despite its slow start, some analysts predict that the American market for smart cards will grow rapidly. According to Catherine Allen and Jeffrey Kutler, writing in *Smart Cards: Seizing Strategic Business Opportunities,* this growth could be attributed to the following factors: adaptation of universal standards (EMV specifications), declining costs of implementation, accumulating market experience with smart cards, the need to remain technologically competitive, the increasing development of wide-area networks such as the Internet, and the inability of magnetic-stripe technology to stay abreast of developments in digital information storage and retrieval.

One of the country's first widespread launches of the smart card took place in New York City. In late 1997, Chase Manhattan and Citibank issued 50,000 smart cards to consumers. New York City, consequently, became the country's crucial testing ground for smart cards. These banks installed smart card readers in 500 stores on New York's Upper West Side. Although Visa launched a smart card experiment during the 1996 Olympics, the card failed because of too few readers in the area. However, Chase Manhattan and Citibank hope New York's dense population and the strategic placement of the readers will help to avoid these problems. Merchants also welcomed the cards because they reduce the labor needed to process transactions since smart cards do not require customer signatures or phone-in verification.

In addition, major drug store chains around the country adopted new point-of-sale technology that was compatible with smart cards during the late 1990s. Rite Aide, for example, began introducing smart card readers in its 3,900 stores in 1998. With the imminent use of smart cards for Medicare and Medicaid benefits, drug stores made this move to be able to process sales from their Medicare and Medicaid customers. Many major supermarket chains also have deployed smart card compatible technology.

In the late 1990s, the cost of a smart card ranged from 80 cents for one containing 1 kilobyte of memory, to $15 for one that could hold 8 kilobytes. A point of sale (POS) terminal upgrade (needed in smart card transactions) cost a bank about $500 per unit.

INDUSTRY LEADERS

Although many of the companies and institutions that use smart card applications are well-known, such as Visa and MasterCard, those involved in smart card technology are far from household names: Schlumberger Ltd. and Gemplus, for example.

Schlumberger Ltd., headquartered in New York, is an international company with annual sales of more than $11.8 billion in 1998, up 11 percent from 1997, and with offices in approximately 100 countries. Under its electronic transactions division, Schlumberger developed a smart card reader for Apple Newton notebook computers in France. Despite its production of smart card technology, Schlumberger is primarily an oil services company.

Headquartered in France, Gemplus Card International was the world leader in smart cards and magnetic stripe cards in the mid- to late 1990s. Created in 1988, the company employed approximately 2,900 people in the mid-1990s and supplied products to more than 80 countries worldwide. With total production capacity of 900 million plastic smart cards in 1998, Gemplus brought in total sales of approximately $648 million that year.

In the mid- to late 1990s, Gemplus controlled 28 percent of the industry; Schlumberger, 24 percent; CP8 Oberthur, 14 percent; Soliac, 14 percent; Giesecke & Devrient, 10 percent; and all others (including IBM, Philips Communication Systems, and Toshiba America), 10 percent.

Chip manufacturers are major component suppliers to the smart card industry. Among chip manufacturers, the leader was Motorola, with 20 percent of the industry, followed by Texas Instruments and SGS-Thomson, with 15 percent each, and Siemens and Hitachi, with 10 percent each. The remaining 30 percent of the chip market was held by all other companies involved, including Oki Semiconductor and Philips Semiconductor.

AMERICA AND THE WORLD

In the mid- to late 1990s, smart cards were one technological area in which the United States did not lead the world, although SCIA predicted that it would within a decade. During the 1990s, France was at the forefront in smart card development, with the rest of Europe and the Pacific Rim close behind. In the mid- to late 1990s, Denmark had a stored-value cash system called Danmont, and Germany's national health insurance program issued users smart cards. Japan, Singapore, and many of the emerging eastern European nations were increasingly basing their monetary systems on smart cards.

In the late 1990s, only about 3 percent of the world smart card market was in North America, compared to 70 percent in western Europe, 11 percent in South America, 10 percent in Asia, and 6 percent in the rest of the world. By the year 2000, it is projected that North America's share will rise to 12 percent, with western Europe still in the lead with 40 percent, followed by Asia with 30 percent, South America with 10 percent, and the rest of the world comprising 6 percent of the market.

RESEARCH AND TECHNOLOGY

In the 1970s, Intel founder Gordon Moore postulated that computer chip capacity and performance would double every 18 months, while prices would decrease at a similar rate. This concept, called "Moore's Law," applied mostly to microprocessor chip development. In the mid-1990s, because the smart card industry was such a new one, the cards' capacity was not growing at the rate predicted—yet. But already in 1996, the industry was looking to rapidly grow as chip memory increased from 8 to 64 kilobytes and even 256 kilobytes. As memory expands, so does the likelihood that one day smart cards will constitute tiny personal computers and even multimedia systems with voice and video capacities.

With the increase in memory capacity, the trend is toward multiple application smart cards—that is, cards that can perform diverse functions. Other developments that were in progress in 1997 included smart card systems that would allow secure access for users on the Internet or other networks. Hewlett-Packard, in conjunction with Informix and Gemplus, was an innovator in this technology, which it marketed as the ImagineCard. Overall, the Internet was expected to greatly expand the range of smart card applications, and *America's Community Banker* reported in March 1997 that it would soon be possible for some bank customers to download cash online. In 1997, France launched a nationwide program that would ultimately replace cash with smart cards.

In the mid-1990s, the Smart Card Forum predicted that around the end of the decade there would be extensive building of infrastructures to support smart card systems, as well as a growth in their ap-

plications. The Forum forecast that the late 1990s would see the implementation of a mass issuance of cards and an emergence of better biometric identification systems—identification based on characteristics such as the size and shape of one's hand and one's fingerprints. The Forum also predicted that by the end of the decade, multi-function cards will make their appearance, along with widely used identification cards and the "electronic wallet," or multi-function financial smart cards. However, U.S. implementation of smart cards remained slow by 1999, and analysts revised their predictions, indicating that these smart card innovations would not be deployed until the early 2000s.

Smart card hardware and peripherals were other areas achieving significant growth in the 1990s. The high-tech smart cards of the mid-1990s require high-performance and yet user-friendly readers and other devices. Created mostly in Europe, such devices as modems with integrated smart card readers allow for secure electronic commerce, home banking, and public online transactions. Such readers are currently priced in the $75 to $200 range, but prices are expected to drop. Such large corporations as Microsoft and Sun Microsystems have developed server software to support readers and handle smart card transactions and to facilitate electronic commerce. Microsoft's Windows-based cards cost issuers about $3, whereas Sun's Java-based cards run about $20.

In 1997 four large players in the smart card industry teamed up to form the JavaCard Forum. Founded by Gemplus and Schlumberger and joined by Bull CP8 and De La Rue Card Systems, the JavaCard Forum's premise is to utilize the power of the Java platform to run multiple applications and its built-in security to greatly advance standard smart cards. The Forum has targeted the banking, telecommunications, and information technology markets for the development of Java Cards.

FURTHER READING

Allen, Catherine A., and William J. Barr, eds. *Smart Cards: Seizing Strategic Business Opportunities.* Chicago: Irwin Professional Publishing, 1997.

Castelluccio, Michael. "Wearable Computers." *Management Accounting,* April 1997, 60.

Church, George. "Leave Your Cash at Home." *Time,* 13 October 1997, 64.

Coulton, Antoinette. "Examining Why Acceptance Lags in the U.S." *American Banker,* 29 April 1998, 5A.

Dvorak, John C. "Inside Track." *PC Magazine,* 6 April 1999, 89.

Egan, Jack. "The End of Cash and Carry." *U.S. News & World Report,* 27 October 1997, 61.

Filippo, John San. "ATMs: The Next Generation." *Credit Union Executive,* March/April 1997, 20.

Fraone, Gina. "Smart-Card Vendors in for a Squeeze." *Electronic Business,* December 1998, 32.

Frook, John Evan. "Internet 'Smart Cards' on the Way." *Interactive Age,* 1 November 1996.

Kaplan, Jack M. *Smart Cards: The Global Information Passport.* Boston: International Thomson Computer, 1996.

Kingson-Bloom, Jennifer. "Drugstores Update Card Systems." *American Banker,* 12 October 1998, 1.

Mitchell, Richard. "The Smart Card's Chief Advocate." *Credit Card Management,* April 1997, 26.

"More Smart Cards: Access from the Inside Out." *Security,* April 1997, 24.

Mulqueen, John T. "V-One Secures New Clients." *Communications Week,* 4 November 1996, 87.

O'Sullivan, Orla. "From France, A Glimpse of Things to Come." *ABA Banking Journal,* March 1997, 57.

Roberts, Bill. "Internet Gives Smart Cards Whole New Life." *Computing Canada,* 3 March 1997, 14.

"Smart Card Factoids." Smart Card Forum, 1998. Available from http://www.smartcrd.com.

"Smart Card Resource Center." Amerkore International, 1997. Available from http://www.smart-card.com.

Tetzeli, Rick. "And Now for Motorola's Next Trick." *Fortune,* 28 April 1997, 122.

Trager, James. *The People's Chronology.* New York: Henry Holt and Company, 1994.

—Judson Knight, updated by Karl Heil

Smoking Cessation Products and Services

Not until the final decades of the twentieth century did smokers finally get an arsenal of potent weapons to use in the fight to "kick the habit." Before that, people who chose to stop smoking had little choice but to grit their teeth and go cold turkey. It is true that there were some earlier over-the-counter products that claimed to minimize the pain of quitting, but recent studies by both public and private researchers have shown that about the only thing these products reduced was the consumer's bankroll.

Counseling services also were available for most of the second half of the twentieth century, with most of the earliest ones relying heavily on hypnotherapy. Such services, many of them now affiliated with national and regional counseling services, continue to be available. In the 1960s, in the wake of the first urgent warning about the dangers of smoking, a number of stop-smoking programs, built around the concept of group therapy, started appearing. Such therapy, which typically worked with a group of smokers over a period of several weeks, claimed to be more successful than individual efforts in helping smokers quit.

Although health alarms about the use of tobacco products first sounded in the 1960s, it was not really until the last two decades of the century that smoking began to face strong social disapproval. Smokers who could ignore or withstand the increasingly vocal disapproval of nonsmokers often were persuaded to quit smoking by the health warnings issued by such organizations as the American Heart Association and the National Cancer Institute.

Almost all of the more effective smoking cessation products appearing in the final quarter of the twentieth century fall into the pharmaceuticals category. Originally, all pharmaceuticals were introduced as prescription only products, but some of the first to appear have since been approved for over-the-counter sale. The earliest available products provided users with an alternate source of nicotine after smoking had been stopped. Such nicotine-substitute therapies were delivered first in a chewing gum and later in transdermal (through the skin) patches. In the last half of the 1990s, two further means of delivering nicotine were introduced: a nicotine nasal spray and a nicotine inhaler.

Perhaps the most potent of the smoking cessation products was the last to be marketed commercially. Available by prescription only, Zyban is a oral medication that alters brain chemistry to relieve cravings. For smokers worried about an increase in weight, Zyban has the added appeal of helping to control appetite in the wake of smoking cessation.

The smoking cessation business is actually divided into two segments, the largest of which is a branch of the pharmaceutical industry. The second, and smaller, segment consists of counseling services, hypnotherapists, and self-help smoking cessation programs, such as SMOKENDERS.

The pharmaceuticals segment of the smoking cessation industry is made up mostly of large, diversified pharmaceutical companies, some of them international in scope. The smoking cessation products of these companies, in most cases, represent only a small percentage of their overall production and business. For example, SmithKline Beecham PLC, the marketer of Nicorette chewing gum and NicoDerm CQ transdermal patches, mainly produces health and beauty aids.

Within the pharmaceutical-based smoking cessation aids, there is a division between those marketed over the counter, such as Nicorette chewing gum and some of the transdermal nicotine patches, and other, more potent products, such as Zyban, nicotine nasal spray, and the nicotine inhaler. The latter category of products is available only by prescription in the United States in the late 1990s.

The services segment of the smoking cessation industry is often made up of groups formed by hospital and medical staff, volunteer organizations, addition counselors, and psychologists. Often these groups offer personalized quitting advice. Behavioral or supportive therapy can be done in groups, by telephone contacts, through written materials, and even individual counseling.

Many smoking cessation services have incorporated the use of the newer pharmaceutical tools into their programs. For example, in the late 1990s, SMOKENDERS, which got its start as a program built around the concept of group therapy, was marketing a smoking cessation kit, which included pharmaceuticals, that individuals could follow on their own.

BACKGROUND AND DEVELOPMENT

For as long as there have been smokers, there have been those among them who made a conscious decision to try to quit smoking. For centuries the only option open to these smokers was to suffer through the often-painful symptoms of nicotine withdrawal. Not until the twentieth century did any products appear that claimed to be effective in reducing nicotine cravings. Although there was undoubtedly some placebo effect from early over-the-counter products, the Food and Drug Administration (FDA) announced in June 1993 that all such products were ineffective and would be withdrawn from the market after existing supplies ran out. Most of these products were sold as chewing gum or oral medication and carried such brand names as Cigarrest, Bantron, Tabmint, and Nikoban. In announcing the FDA decision, then-Commissioner David A. Kessler, himself a physician, said, "Smoking is one of the nation's leading public health risks, and we favor any safe and effective method for helping people kick the habit. However, to reduce smoking-related illnesses and deaths, smoking deterrents have to work."

More than a decade before the FDA's withdrawal of some of these over-the-counter smoking deterrents from the market, the first nicotine-replacement product in the form of a chewing gum had made its debut. Called Nicorette and introduced originally by Marion Merrell Dow Inc., each piece of gum contained four milligrams of nicotine. Chewing an average of six to nine pieces daily, a smoker could gradually cut down on the number of cigarettes smoked without suffering sharp withdrawal pains. Still on the market, Nicorette claims a one-year quit rate of 10 to 15 percent. A month's supply of Nicorette costs about $120.

During the 1980s, pharmaceutical companies introduced a new nicotine-replacement delivery system with the transdermal patch. The patches, in varying strengths depending on the magnitude of the smoker's habit, are applied directly to the skin and worn for 12 or more hours daily. Once the smoker has given up smoking and has gradually reduced the patch-delivered nicotine to its lowest level, he or she can stop using the patch and, ideally, stay off cigarettes. Like Nicorette, the various nicotine-replacement patches claimed a one-year quit rate of 10 to 15 percent. A month's supply of the transdermal patches ranged in price between $100 and $110.

The emergence of the fledgling smoking cessation industry was set against the backdrop of an increasingly health-conscious American landscape. Another potent factor helping to convince smokers to quit was the growing social unacceptability of smoking. This trend found its way into legislation that banned smoking in a wide range of public places. Additionally, smoking in the workplace was also becoming rare with many places of business banning smoking altogether on their premises or limiting it to a few locations. The pressure on smokers to quit grew steadily stronger.

PIONEERS IN THE FIELD

The breakthrough in drug therapies aimed at smoking cessation came in 1984 with Marion Merrell Dow's introduction of nicotine polacrilex gum— Nicorette. A number of over-the-counter products designed to help smokers quit remained on the market after the arrival of Nicorette. However, subsequent studies showed that apart from a possible placebo effect, these products were without any practical value. In 1992, another medium for nicotine replacement therapy was introduced—the transdermal patch. A number of companies, including Marion Merrell Dow Inc. and Parke-Davis, introduced the patches under such brand names as Nicoderm, ProStep, Habitrol, and

Nicotrol. The patches, available in a variety of strengths, were at first available only by prescription, as was Nicorette. Nicorette and Nicoderm, introduced by Marion Merrell Dow, were subsequently acquired by international pharmaceuticals giant SmithKline Beecham PLC, based in the United Kingdom.

Among the pioneers in the non-drug programs aimed at stopping smoking, perhaps the best known and one of the earliest successes was SMOKENDERS. Founded by the wife of a dentist in Phillipsburg, New Jersey, the program attracted a wide following and was built around the concept of group therapy techniques. Smokers interested in quitting would join the program and pay a fee to SMOKENDERS. Weekly sessions over six or seven weeks could eventually lead smokers to stop smoking. In its original form, the program did not use any pharmaceuticals; more recently, those enrolled in SMOKENDERS have the option of including pharmaceuticals. SMOKENDERS continues to attract a number of enrollees and now includes a program that can be followed by an individual outside of the group setting.

CURRENT CONDITIONS

The late 1990s brought a number of important changes to the smoking cessation industry. Notable among these was the federal government's 1996 decision to allow over-the-counter sales of Nicorette nicotine-replacement chewing gum and Nicoderm and Nicotrol transdermal patches. Previously, smokers interested in quitting could obtain these drug therapies only with a doctor's prescription. ProStep and Habitrol transdermal patches remained available only by prescription.

Exciting new possibilities started emerging in early 1996 when the FDA approved Nicotrol-brand nicotine nasal spray for sale by prescription only. The nasal spray contains nicotine that is absorbed through the user's nasal lining into the bloodstream. Like other nicotine-replacement therapies, this product is intended for use over relatively short durations—no more than six months. As with all nicotine-replacement products, the user could become addicted to the nicotine in the new medium. For these cessation products to be most effective, users must gradually reduce their intake of nicotine until they have completely weaned themselves off the substance.

A little more than a year after the introduction of Nicotrol nasal spray, the FDA approved a Nicotrol nicotine inhaler, also available by prescription only.

Users puff on a plastic mouthpiece containing a nicotine cartridge to receive approximately four milligrams of nicotine, about one-third of the nicotine in a regular cigarette. Like the chewing gum, transdermal patches, and the nasal spray, the one-year quit rate for the inhaler was estimated at 10 to 15 percent.

The biggest leap forward in smoking cessation technology came in June 1997 when Glaxo Wellcome introduced Zyban into the prescription market. A tablet taken twice daily, Zyban offered a novel alternative to the gum, patch, and inhalant delivery systems and, more importantly, showed a far higher degree of effectiveness than any of the predecessor drug therapies. The drug, also marketed as an antidepres-

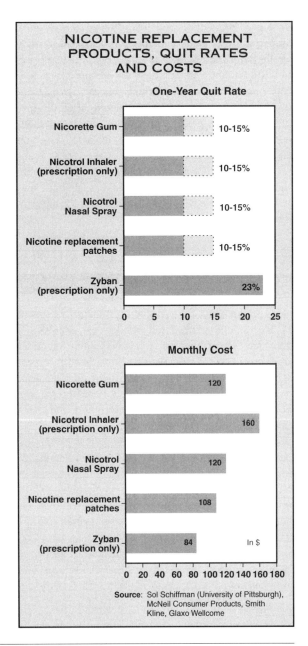

NICOTINE REPLACEMENT PRODUCTS, QUIT RATES AND COSTS

One-Year Quit Rate

Product	Quit Rate
Nicorette Gum	10-15%
Nicotrol Inhaler (prescription only)	10-15%
Nicotrol Nasal Spray	10-15%
Nicotine replacement patches	10-15%
Zyban (prescription only)	23%

0   5   10   15   20   25

Monthly Cost

Product	Cost
Nicorette Gum	120
Nicotrol Inhaler (prescription only)	160
Nicotrol Nasal Spray	120
Nicotine replacement patches	108
Zyban (prescription only)	84

In $

0 20 40 60 80 100 120 140 160 180

Source: Sol Schiffman (University of Pittsburgh), McNeil Consumer Products, Smith Kline, Glaxo Wellcome

sant called Wellbutrin SR, raises dopamine levels in the brain, thus reducing the smoker's craving. Early studies point to a one-year quit rate of 23 percent, about twice that achieved with previous drug therapies. The cost of a month's supply of Zyban is estimated at $84 to $100, which is less than any of the rival treatments.

According to Information Resources, "In 1998, sales of over-the-counter nicotine-replacement products exceeded $568 million, nearly double total sales of 1996. . . . Prescriptions are soaring too. Sales for the 12 months that ended September 1998 totaled $184.4 million, up 154 percent from the previous year."

Even with successful products, quitting smoking is no easy feat. A national poll conducted by the Hazelden Foundation in 1998 showed that it took former smokers an average of 18.6 years before they finally quit. The poll also revealed that most smokers had tried to quit an average of 10.8 times before they finally succeeded. Current smokers revealed to Hazelden pollsters that they had already tried quitting an average of 3.4 times. In announcing the poll results, Elliott Driscoll, manager of smoking cessation services for Hazelden New York, said, "These numbers reflect the serious nature of nicotine addiction. Nicotine is a powerful drug, just like alcohol and heroin, and those who want to quit often relapse in spite of their good intentions."

INDUSTRY LEADERS

The dominant force in the drug therapy segment of the smoking cessation market is SmithKline Beecham PLC, whose over-the-counter nicotine-replacement products account for more than 90 percent of that market. Based in England, SmithKline Beecham is one of the largest pharmaceutical companies in the world with a broad range of prescription and over-the-counter drugs and health products. Among these products are Geritol vitamins and Aquafresh toothpaste and such prescription drugs as the antidepressant Seroxat/ Paxil. In addition to its two main U.S. smoking cessation products (Nicorette and NicoDerm CQ), which together control more than 90 percent of the over-the-counter market, the company markets different smoking cessation patches in Europe and Australia. SmithKline Beecham posted net income of just over $1 billion in 1998 on sales of about $13.4 billion. The company employs more than 58,000 people worldwide.

Glaxo Wellcome Inc., the U.S. subsidiary of U.K. pharmaceuticals giant Glaxo Wellcome PLC, is head-

quartered in Research Triangle Park, North Carolina. The company markets the prescription drug Zyban, the only oral pharmaceutical that reduces the craving for nicotine. The medication, also marketed as the antidepressant Wellbutrin SR, has the highest one-year quit rate of any drug-based smoking cessation product. The U.S. subsidiary employs approximately 8,500 people, while Glaxo Wellcome PLC has a worldwide work force of about 53,000. The parent company, along with Merck and Novartis, is one of the world's three largest manufacturers of prescription drugs. In addition to Zyban, the company manufactures Zantac, used to combat heartburn; Zovirax, a herpes treatment; Ventolin and Serevent, anti-asthmatic medications; and Combivir and Epivir, used in the treatment of HIV and AIDS. The company earned $3.05 billion in 1998 on sales of $13.25 billion.

The McNeil Consumer Products division of Johnson & Johnson markets three products in the arsenal of smoking cessation drug therapies. These are the Nicotrol transdermal patch, available over the counter, and the Nicotrol nasal spray and Nicotrol inhaler, both of which may be purchased only with a prescription. Johnson & Johnson, headquartered in New Brunswick, New Jersey, is the world's largest manufacturer of health care products, as well as the most diversified. In addition to a wide range of consumer products like Tylenol, Motrin, Band-Aid bandages, and Reach toothbrushes, the company produces and markets a wide range of medical equipment and pharmaceuticals through a number of its subsidiary operations. Important pharmaceuticals in the Johnson & Johnson product line include the antihistamine Hismanal, Ortho-Novum oral contraceptives, and Ergamisol, a cancer drug therapy. The company employs more than 90,000 people worldwide. Johnson & Johnson posted net income in 1998 of about $3.1 billion on sales of about $23.7 billion.

Novartis AG, based in Basle, Switzerland, is the distributor of the Habitrol transdermal nicotine-replacement patch. Formed in 1996 by the $27 billion merger of Ciba-Geigy and Sandoz, Novartis' business focuses on three key areas: agribusiness, health care, and nutrition. The company's nutrition division produces Gerber baby foods and related products, while its agribusiness segment markets pesticides, herbicides, and fungicides to help protect farmers' crops. The health care division produces about 60 percent of the company's total revenues, and its products include both prescription drugs and over-the-counter products. Employing about 87,000 worldwide, Novartis posted net income of $3.6 billion on revenue of $21.3 billion in 1997.

WORK FORCE

The international pharmaceutical industry, which manufactures and markets most smoking cessation products, employs hundreds of thousands of people around the world. The jobs available in the industry range from clerical to management positions in the pharmaceutical companies' offices. For those with an interest in chemical and medical research, this industry offers a broad range of opportunities, for it is through these companies' ongoing research that new products are brought to market.

Employment levels in the non-drug smoking cessation services field are relatively low. Most of these operations involve individual counselors or small teams, the majority of whom are trained professionals. There is a fairly limited number of support jobs available in these operations.

AMERICA AND THE WORLD

Although U.S. smokers may have felt more pressure to quit than smokers elsewhere in the world, there is a swelling tide of international opposition to the smoking habit. As in the United States, the pressure springs not only from health concerns but also from the fact that the smoking habit is becoming increasingly socially unacceptable. Many smoking cessation products are marketed internationally. In some countries, products not available in the United States are being sold. Some of the major players in the smoking cessation market abroad are the same companies active in the field in the United States.

SmithKline Beecham Consumer HealthCare in November 1998 launched the NiQuitin CQ brand of nicotine-replacement transdermal patches in the United Kingdom, Belgium, and Sweden. The company's move into Europe was one of a number of moves to try to spread its U.S. smoking cessation success to other countries. Two months earlier Smith-Kline Beecham had announced its acquisition of the Nicabate transdermal patch, the number one smoking cessation product in Australia and New Zealand. In May the company received approval to enter the vast Chinese market with a transdermal nicotine-replacement patch that was licensed internationally (except in Canada and South Korea) by Alza Corporation. In very early 1998, SmithKline Beecham unveiled plans to expand the range of dosage formats with the licensing of an oral nicotine product from TheraTech Inc. SmithKline Beecham is investing close to $20

million in the United Kingdom to try to capture a majority of the U.K. smoking cessation market with the NiQuitin patch. The United Kingdom has about one-fourth as many smokers as the United States. Unlike some of the other nicotine-replacement patches marketed worldwide, NiQuitin CQ offers a personalized behavioral support plan to be followed in conjunction with use of the patch. In launching NiQuitin in the United Kingdom, John Clarke, chairman of Smith-Kline Beecham Consumer HealthCare Europe, said, "Two hundred forty people a day are dying from their habit, and smoking is predicted to become the number one preventable cause of death and disease in the world by the year 2005. We believe we can make a real difference in improving public health. Europe represents a tremendous opportunity for the future."

In early 1999, Glaxo Wellcome, which markets Zyban, applied for permission to market the smoking deterrent drug in Europe. Available by prescription in the United States since 1997, Zyban is the only drug of its kind, an oral medication that reduces a smoker's craving for nicotine. Early tests have shown it to be the most effective of the smoking cessation drug therapies. In announcing its plans to introduce Zyban in

<table>
<tr><td>About...</td><td>THE GREAT AMERICAN SMOKEOUT</td></tr>
</table>

In 1971, Arthur P. Mulvaney of Randolph, Mass. came up with an idea that could improve Americans' health while supporting youth and education at the same time. His idea came to be called the "Great American Smokeout." The genius behind Mulvaney's proposal was a plea to people to give up smoking for a day and donate the money they would ordinarily spend on a pack of cigarettes to a high school scholarship fund.

Within five years, the Smokeout spread across the country when the American Cancer Society organized the first Great American Smokeout. In 1998, 6 percent of America's 48 million smokers tried to give up smoking for that day, according to the American Cancer Society. The day of the Smokeout is now more popular than even New Year's Day—infamous for the commencement of new resolutions—as a time when Americans try to quit smoking.

The event takes place annually on the third Thursday of November. Now, the Smokeout has evolved again to include teenagers, whose smoking habits are on the rise. Between 1991 to 1995, the number of teenagers who smoke rose from one-quarter to one-third of the teenage population, according to The Centers for Disease Control.

Europe, Glaxo Wellcome officials projected the international market in smoking cessation products to be more than $800 million in 1999.

In early 1999 doctors at three Ontario hospitals experimented with a program of counseling aimed at helping patients suffering from smoking-related ailments. Aimed specifically at patients in three hospitals in Cambridge and Kitchener, Ontario, the program directs primary care physicians to give their patients a "one-minute unequivocal message to stop smoking," according to Patricia Smith, a professor of health studies and gerontology at the University of Waterloo. "Since smokers are more likely to be hospitalized than nonsmokers, we are taking the program to where we know the smokers are."

RESEARCH AND TECHNOLOGY

A national poll conducted by the Hazelden Foundation in the second half of 1998 looked at the various methods used by smokers to try to quit. A number of current smokers said they had tried to quit by gradually reducing the number of cigarettes smoked until they gave them up altogether. Other smokers tried a similar technique by switching to cigarette brands with progressively lower nicotine levels until they had weaned themselves off cigarettes completely. Others reported they had tried to kick the habit by stopping smoking abruptly, the so-called cold turkey approach. Other smokers sought out the comfort and support of group, while others buddied up with one other individual or turned to a formal support group, such as Nicotine Anonymous. The poll also revealed that most smokers were none too proud of their habit. Almost 20 percent of smokers reported that they had tried to hide the fact of their smoking from family members, employers, or coworkers. Among other findings in the Hazelden poll: Only 80 percent of current smokers see smoking as a health hazard, compared with nearly 93 percent of former smokers.

A market research study in the United Kingdom revealed that smokers there spent more than $160,000 daily in 1998 trying to quit. Britons' expenditures for smoking cessation products jumped sharply in 1998, climbing about 15 percent to more than $61 million. Euromonitor, a market research company, reported that advertising by producers of nicotine-replacement drug therapies, coupled with the government-funded antismoking campaign, was beginning to rival the tobacco companies' advertising expenditures of more than $160 million in 1998. The Euromonitor study revealed that smokers trying to quit spent most of their money on nicotine gum, which accounted for more than half of total sales of nicotine-replacement products. U.K. sales of patches appeared to have dropped slightly in 1998, according to Euromonitor. The report predicted that the 13 million U.K. smokers will continue to spend more on smoking cessation therapies, particularly as both social and medical condemnation of the habit grows. The study indicated that about two-thirds of British smokers would like to quit. Euromonitor predicted that U.K. smokers will spend about $95 million a year on nicotine-replacement drugs in 2002 if present trends continue.

In April 1999, researchers from Nabi in Boca Raton, Florida, along with cooperating scientists from the University of Houston-Clear Lake and the University of Minnesota, presented results from pre-clinical studies of a vaccine to help prevent and treat nicotine addiction. The Nabi-academic research team reported that Nabi-NicVAX, an experimental conjugate vaccine, had been shown in animal studies to generate elevated levels of high-affinity antibodies to nicotine. Researchers said that purified antibodies generated in laboratory animals in response to vaccination with Nabi-NicVAX were able to significantly reduce brain nicotine concentrations in rats. In an assessment of Nabi's research into the vaccine, Dr. Robert Naso said, "We are excited about the results obtained thus far with Nabi-NicVAX in these animal models. The antibodies generated in response to vaccination with Nabi-NicVAX appear to be preventing nicotine from reaching receptors in the brains of the treated animals. We expect that blocking uptake of nicotine by the brain will greatly reduce the addictive effects of nicotine. If similar effects can be achieved in humans, we may be able to use the vaccine to prevent nicotine addiction or to help tobacco users kick their nicotine habits."

Commenting on the promising vaccine research by Nabi and its collaborators, Dr. Alan I. Leshner, director of the National Institute on Drug Abuse, National Institutes of Health, said, "Research has shown that a combination of pharmacological and behavioral treatments can more than double the odds of success for individuals who try to quit smoking. Just as with other drugs, however, ultimately our best treatment is prevention. If the promise of the basic research on this vaccine extends to effectiveness in humans, it may not only help individuals trying to quit but may also prevent nicotine addiction in at-risk individuals."

FURTHER READING

Clark, Andrew. "Glaxo Brings Anti-Smoking Drug to EU." *Daily Telegraph,* 3 March 1999.

"FDA Announces That No Over-the-Counter Smoking Deterrent Works." *Food and Drug Administration Online,* 1999. Available from http://www.fda.gov/bbs/topics/NEWS/NEW00408.html.

"Glaxo Wellcome Inc." *Hoover's Online,* 1999. Available from http://www.hoovers.com/capsules/43846.html.

Irwin, Aisling. "Smokers Pay a Fortune to Kick the Habit." *Daily Telegraph,* 10 April 1999.

"Johnson & Johnson." *Hoover's Online,* 1999. Available from http://www.hoovers.com/capsules/10824.html.

"Nabi-NicVAX Data Presented at the Society for Research on Nicotine and Tobacco Meeting." *PRNewswire,* 19 April 1999.

"National Survey Shows It Takes Smokers an Average of 11 Attempts Before They Quit for Good." *Business Wire,* 11 November 1998.

Nordenberg, Tamar. "It's Quitting Time." *FDA Consumer,* 1 November 1997.

"Novartis AG." *Hoover's Online,* 1999. Available from http://www.hoovers.com/capsules/52941.html.

"Novopharm Ltd. to Obtain Exclusive Chewing-Gum Technology for Canada and United States from Premedent Technology." *Business Wire,* 25 November 1997.

"Questions and Answers about Finding Smoking Cessation Services." *National Cancer Institute Online,* 1999. Available from http://cancernet.nci.nih.gov/clinp...ng_Smoking_Cessation_Services.html.

"Quit-Smoking Products Could Thrive After Settlement." *Reuters,* 15 June 1997.

Rock, Andrea. "Quitting Time for Smokers: New Products and Programs Can Quadruple Your Chances of Success." *Money,* 1 January 1999.

"Scott-Levin: Zyban Smokes Competition." *Business Wire,* 20 October 1997.

"SmithKline Beecham PLC." *Hoover's Online,* 1999. Available from http://www.hoovers.com/capsules/41844.html.

"SmithKline Consumer HealthCare Launches NiQuitin CQ in Europe." *PressWire,* 27 November 1998.

"Star Tobacco & Pharmaceuticals Inc. a New Innovative Competitor in the Emerging Tobacco Cessation Product Market." *Business Wire,* 14 October 1997.

"Treatment Works . . . When You Choose to Stop Smoking." *APA Online,* 1999. Available from http://www.psych.org/public_info/nicotine.html.

—Don Amerman

SOFTWARE CONSULTING

Software consultants evaluate how, and which, new systems can replace old ones, or how old systems can be modified to cope with new organizational realities. Modern business and government grow more complex by the day, and it is necessary that their computer systems be modified to keep pace with the rapid changes in software. The technical expertise needed to make these modifications makes organizations less able to carry out such tasks themselves. With increased attention to the bottom line, a full-time trainer on staff to make these periodic changes is an extra expense that companies do not need. Enter the software consultants who are up-to-date on the software changes needed by the business or government agency and are hired as contractors who complete the job and move on. Software consultants are also brought in to modify a company's computer software so that it performs tasks more efficiently, write new applications specific to the client company's needs, develop new applications for a specific department, or to integrate the operations of various departments.

The demand for software consultants is expected to grow at a rapid rate into the early years of the twenty-first century. Among the factors fueling this growth will be the need for specific expertise driven by rapid changes in most industries, and a growing willingness by most companies to hire outside consultants. Certainly the international trend toward maximization of profits by strategic downsizing will play a major role in the growing use of consultants. Information technology (IT) consulting, on which U.S. companies spent about $12 billion in 1997, is expected to more than double by the year 2000, according to the International Data Corporation (IDC) of Framing-

ham, Massachusetts. A huge chunk of this IT consulting is in the area of software applications, although some involves hardware and structural problems.

The sharp growth in the demand for software consultants during the late 1990s was driven in part by two specific areas of corporate concern, one generally short term in nature and the other of a more enduring nature. Worries about Year 2000 problems in essential software applications fueled a big jump in the use of consultants. While much of this business needed to be completed before the arrival of the year 2000, there were those who predicted that Y2K business would keep consultants busy well past the January 1, 2000, deadline (see chapter on Year 2000 Compliance Products and Services). Another major endeavor for U.S. corporations has been in the development of enterprise resource planning, and a number of outside consultants have been kept busy in meeting those needs.

ORGANIZATION AND STRUCTURE

Software consulting encompasses many types of computer work and its boundaries with other industries are often vague. The field ranges from large multinational management consultant firms with billion dollar budgets to one-person shops that bring in $100,000 or less per year. What they all have in common is a client who contracts them as outside service providers to work on a computer problem on a project basis. A project may be a day or two in length to a year or longer. Some contracts are renewed indefinitely until a consultant becomes, in many respects, indistinguishable from a normal full-time employee.

One side of the industry is comprised of large firms—the so-called Big Six accounting firms and big software producing companies. These firms are distinguished from the thousands of smaller software consulting companies by the fact that although software consulting is a growing sector of the larger firms' services, it is not normally their primary service. Arthur Andersen, for example, offers software consulting, but its major business is accounting; Oracle Corporation's software consulting is an adjunct to its software manufacturing. The clientele of such large companies are almost always organizations of equivalent size with comparable financial resources, that is, other large firms and government agencies. Large companies, like Computer Science Corp., whose primary service is outsourcing, are also adding consulting to their portfolio of computer services, though government contracts, middle to long term, are their main source of consulting revenue.

In the United States the lion's share of software consulting is performed by small companies, partnerships, or individuals. Companies often begin as one-or-two person operations and grow as their reputation builds. They are offered more work than they are able to handle alone and then expand to take on extra employees. These smaller operations generally have from 1 to 10 employees and tend to specialize in a few particular types of projects. They can be in a particular business sector, or involving specific applications, computer languages, and operating systems that are within their expertise.

Staying current or even ahead of technology is a critical ongoing process for software consultants. Consultants' fees relate directly to the demand for the skills mastered, and it is the new and uncommon abilities that are in greatest demand. Familiarity with SAP software, a popular but relatively new set of business applications in the United States, brings significantly higher fees than a familiarity with UNIX, a system that is important, but with which a great deal of consultants are conversant. Consultants frequently accept work outside their skill set at a fraction of the rates normally paid in order to get experience in a new application. According to the Software Contractors' Guild, the software consulting industry encompasses numerous abilities: 171 different applications, 55 computer languages, and 24 operating systems, in all more than 500 skill classifications.

Consultants find clients in different ways. Some advertise or have Web pages, however word of mouth plays an important role. A sizable number of consultants get new clients only through referrals. Once consultants or companies have completed an impressive job, they can rely on new client referrals because there are so few consultants in relation to the amount of work at any given time. One group of independent consultants, known as software contractors, does not organize their own jobs; they rely instead on computer placement agencies, similar to temporary employment agencies to find work for them. Contractors provide a resume to an agency that describes in depth their skill set, conduct an interview, and indicate their availability. When work is available, usually within a few days, the agency notifies the contractor. Clients pay the contractor's fee, which has been specified or negotiated in advance, plus an additional 30 to 60 percent to the agency. *Contract Professional* magazine estimates that software consultants who find work through placement agencies comprise, by far, the largest share of the software consulting industry.

Agencies encompass a large sector of the software consulting industry and are located throughout the country. Many large temporary employment agencies provide placement service for software contractors. The nationwide chain, Kelly Services, for instance, has Kelly Technical Services. There are also larger and smaller independent agencies.

The Software Contractors' Guild acts as a job clearinghouse for contractors, consulting companies, agencies, and clients. For a $12 annual membership, contractors can post resumes online, noting their skill-set items and relocation options. According to observers, listing with the Guild brings more work offers than most members can single-handedly manage, and the organization has steady turnover. Contractors frequently have their own Web pages to advertise their special skills.

Although both are self-employed and work with software for clients, a few rough distinctions can be drawn between software contractors and software consultants. Contractors, in general, work through agencies, at least while they are getting started in the business; they tend to work exclusively on-site at the client's place of business; their projects range from a day to indefinite renewal; the projects they work on tend to be more clearly defined, and of more limited scope; and they tend to spend more time "writing code," that is, creating computer programs. Contractors, who number in the tens of thousands, comprise the majority of the software consultant industry. Consultants tend to work on a project between 3 to 9 months. Often, they are required to take an active role in client's problem definition and needs analysis. The first weeks or even months of a project at a mid- to large-sized company, usually involve a series of meetings and interviews with different members of staff.

Only afterwards can the technical problems be approached.

The technical work performed by software consultants varies. Sometimes older software is modified to run in a different system or in an ensemble of different applications. Occasionally a program is written from scratch, though that usually means patching together routines a consultant keeps in his or her "tool kit."

The decision to outsource an IT function was viewed increasingly in the late 1990s, not just as a quick fix, but as an integral part of a company's long-term business strategy. According to Frank Casale, executive director of the Outsourcing Institute of Jericho, New York, "an organization needs to analyze its core competency. Anything from that point on could be a candidate for outsourcing." Among the reason for increased outsourcing are to be able to react quickly to market shifts, to have access to highly skilled personnel, and—most importantly—to cut costs. Companies considering the outsourcing of an IT function are cautioned to carefully determine the cost of that function. "Estimating cost is more complicated that people think," Casale says.

For corporations that outsource IT functions, the benefits may be either obvious or difficult to quantify. Some of the benefits, such as improved performance, the ability for the company's full-time staff to concentrate on its core competency, and a reduction of operating costs, can readily be seen and measured. However, some of the more subtle benefits of outsourcing may take time to become apparent. "If four years ago you had told someone you could use outsourcing to increase morale, you would have been laughed at," Casale says. Today, however, most top IT executives realize that outsourcing one or more functions can reduce the pressure on an overtaxed staff, creating a more hospitable working environment for full-time employees in the IT department. "Then it becomes a tool to create a good work environment," says Casale. "It's tough enough to keep these people as it is. It becomes a perk."

REGULATION

Section 1706 of the Internal Revenue Code is the most troublesome regulation for software consultants because they fall into three tax classes: 1099 workers, W-2 workers, and those who have incorporated. The latter two are legally uncomplicated, however, the former falls into the IRS's gray zone. W-2 workers are paid by the placement agency for which they work. The agency collects the fees from the client and cuts the contractor a paycheck with income tax already de-

ducted. The advantage of not having to keep track of taxes is offset by the numerous tax breaks not available to W-2 employees. Self-employed consultants who have not incorporated are considered 1099 workers. Although they are ostensibly independent, by working on-site and using the client's equipment, they may be considered for tax purposes regular employees of the client, i.e. as workers who should be in the W-2 class. As such, 1099 contractors risk being audited and forced to repay deductions made as self-employed workers. Their client's are also at risk of litigation for unpaid benefits or failure to withhold income taxes.

Thus, it is an independent consultant's advantage to incorporate, even if he or she works completely on their own. Incorporation as a business sidesteps these problematic income tax questions. The Software Contractors' Guild expressly advises clients looking for contractors to hire only those who have incorporated, or who are W-2 employees of a contract placement agency.

There are certain contractual restrictions on software consultants. Because of the sensitive client information to which they have access, consultants are usually required to sign confidentiality agreements. Their placement agency contract requires them to wait a year after the conclusion of such a contract before accepting independent work with the same client. Professional ethics require that when a contractor is offered the same job by different agencies, the first offer is accepted.

BACKGROUND AND DEVELOPMENT

The rise of software consulting as a profession parallels the expansion of computers throughout the business world. Not long after this expansion began, computer manufacturers began to realize that they had to provide many more services to the companies installing their computers than was possible for them. The in-house programming and computer department soon realized they were incapable of maintaining the cutting edge skills necessary to adapt to the swiftly evolving computer industry.

Led by pioneers like Jerry Weinberg and Ed Yourdan, the first software consulting firms opened in the 1960s. They arose in response to software packages that were difficult to use, and to software vendors that offered inadequate support for complex projects. Software consulting began mediating between inflexible software and the increasingly helpless software user.

Pioneer   ED YOURDAN
SOFTWARE CONSULTING

Ed Yourdan is, in his own words, "a daredevil parachutist, alligator trainer, sword swallower, Himalayan mountain climber, raconteur, advisor to Hollywood stars of ill repute, bon vivant, connoisseur of McDonald's hamburgers, author of numerous books, and, from time to time, walks on water and leaps over tall buildings in a single bound." The energetic and interesting Yourdan is also one of the pioneers of software consulting.

In 1964, during his undergraduate study, he was hired by Digital Equipment Corporation to write programming for two of their mainframe computers. During his career he worked on over 25 different mainframes, developing his deep understanding of programming.

It was during the 1970s that he developed one of the most popular methods of software analysis and design. Working with Peter Coad, Chairman of the consulting firm Object International, Inc., they came up with the Coad/Yourdan methodology. Called simplistic by others, their method focused on the importance of traceability and the reduction of complexity. In order to achieve reduction of complexity the concept of "sub-

jects" was developed. "Subjects" was a mechanism for logically grouping objects identified by similarities and differences. The analysis model developed with his methods were represented in five layers on one diagram; the layers included subject, structure, attribute, service, and class and object.

The diagramming techniques were to be easy to use, with a lot of importance placed on the attribute layer, emphasizing a division between data and process. Research focused on analysis but Coad and Yourdan also support the design phase. The design methods were developed as an extension to the original analysis methods.

Yourdan Founded his own consulting firm, Yourdan, Inc., in 1974. During the 12 years that he ran the firm, it grew into a staff of 150 with offices throughout North America and Europe. The company was sold in 1986, and is now a subsidiary of IBM.

He has written over 200 technical articles, and 24 computer books, including a computer crime novel which he admitted was, at best, mediocre. He is currently working as a freelance consultant, focusing on the year 2000 computer glitch.

CURRENT CONDITIONS

Robust growth in the software consulting business was expected to continue well into the new millennium. Total IT consulting revenues, not all of which involved software, hit $8.50 billion in 1995 and were expected to hit $18.50 billion by the year 2000, according to data from IDC. Total projected IT consulting revenues for 2000 were broken down as follows by IDC: $1.27 billion for business process reengineering; $1.10 billion for change management; $480 million for business strategy; $2.20 billion for process improvement; $4.20 billion for IT strategy; $5.00 billion for IT design; $1.60 billion for operational assessment; $850 million for needs assessment; $739 million for benchmarking; $499 million for capacity planning; and $573 million for maintenance planning.

Two of the hot-button projects for which consultants were in demand in the late 1990s included ERP and Y2K. Consultants specializing in ERP systems were hard at work in the final years of the millennium developing the next generation of decision-support systems, known in the business as strategic enterprise management (SEM) applications. On the Y2K front, the late 1990s saw a frantic race to bring millions of software applications and hardware systems into com-

pliance before the arrival of the new millennium. It is estimated that $2.3 billion will be spent by 2000 just bringing federal computers up to date. Worldwide, the estimated cost is expected to eventually total between $200 and $500 billion.

The other defining trend in the American software consulting industry is the severe shortage of qualified workers. According to the Information Technology Association of America, in the late 1990s, there were around 190,000 job vacancies in the computer field. Computer staffing companies and software companies are feeling the shortage. As a result, it is a seller's market and salaries are lucrative. The Year 2000 Problem has drawn many of the best people away from other work, creating even more need, which has thus far been filled by computer workers from overseas.

As of mid-1997, consultants who were experienced in SAP, a client/server software package that enables companies to integrate many of their commercial, manufacturing and financial functions in one system, earned the highest rates. A good SAP programmer can demand—and get—$200 an hour from clients. According to the magazine *Contract Professional,* demand for consultants who can work in Windows NT, Java, and PeopleSoft is growing. Businesses are also looking for consultants with experience in local area networks (LANs) to construct company intranets.

INDUSTRY LEADERS

The bulk of software consulting in small to large companies is done by tens of thousands of small companies throughout the nation. Each company—some as small as a single worker—has its own area of expertise, such as a particular application, a certain industry sector, and 1 or 2 computer languages. There are large companies active in the industry, but in general they did not become that way by doing software consulting, nor is it currently an area of special expertise. The Big Six accounting firms—Arthur Andersen, Coopers & Lybrand, Deloitte & Touche, Ernst & Young, KPMG Peat Marwick Thorne, and Price Waterhouse—include software consulting as part of a broad package, which includes management, financial, and other types of consulting. Anecdotal evidence points to an increase in software consulting revenues, but exact figures are not available.

Arthur Andersen & Co. is the world's largest accounting firm and part of Andersen Worldwide. Andersen Consulting is currently the world's largest management and technology consulting firm, with multinational clients from a wide range of industries. They consult on anything and everything that has to do with cutting-edge technology and training, and they work directly with major computer and software suppliers. The late 1990s witnessed an energetic effort by Andersen Consulting to break away from Arthur Andersen. The struggle for independence continued well into 1999 and remained unresolved. Based in Chicago, Andersen Consulting had a workforce of 62,000 people in 1998. The company posted total revenue in 1998 of $8.3 billion, up 25 percent from the previous year. Big software developers (e.g., Microsoft Corporation, Oracle Corporation, Sybase, Inc.) increasingly generate revenue—estimated between 25 and 50 percent—from consulting as well.

In 1999, Computer Sciences Corp. (CSC) was the largest computer service provider. With more than 600 offices in more than 100 locations worldwide—primarily in Europe, the Pacific Rim, and the United States—California-based CSC is also among the world's leaders in information technology (IT) consulting, systems integration, and outsourcing to global industries and government agencies. In fact, almost 30 percent of CSC's sales were government contracts. For fiscal 1999, which ended March 31, 1999, CSC posted net income of $341 million on revenue of $7.7 billion. This represented a jump of 31 percent in net earnings and a 16-percent increase in revenue. CSC's 1998 workforce of 45,000 showed an increase of nearly 7 percent over the previous year.

Although competition is keen, a number of other large companies competing against each other proved that the industry is growing, with clientele enough to spare. The smaller companies also experienced growth at the century's close. Florida-based Computer Management Sciences, a provider of information technology consulting and custom software development services across a network of 15 American sites, had net sales of $76 million at the end of their fiscal year for 1997. This is an increase of 54 percent over the previous year, and they also experienced a 38-percent increase in their 736 person workforce. In 1999 they were acquired by software company Computer Associates International for $415 million.

CIBER—whose name is an acronym for "consultants in business, engineering, and research"—is a leading provider of information technology consulting services, with more than 70 percent of their sales coming from the CIBER Information Services Division. This division provides information technology consulting and temporary and outsourced computer staffing services. The company has more than 50 offices in the United States and Canada, and at their fiscal year end in June 1998, they reported net sales of $550.4 million, an increase of 110 percent from the same period of the previous year.

A similar situation exists with staffing agencies; in all, there are approximately 1,400 nationwide. Leaders in the field consist of traditional employment agencies with a nationwide network of offices and clients, who over the years expanded from clerical services into technical services. Manpower Inc. is the world's largest temporary employment company, with more than 3,200 owned and franchised offices in 50 countries. More than 2 million workers around the world have been placed in jobs through Manpower. The company also provides permanent employment opportunities, as well as employee testing and training. With almost $9 billion in worldwide sales, they were the industry leader in 1998 sales. Switzerland based Adecco SA, the world's largest employment agency, operates more than 3,000 offices in 48 countries and supplies both temporary and permanent personnel to some 200,000 clients. They were formed with the merger of Switzerland's Adia and France's Ecco, and they specialize in placing white-collar workers and professionals, including those in information technology. They had a 1998 net revenue of $140.9 million. Olsten Corp. is the third largest temporary staffing agency in the world, operating more than 1,400 offices in the United States and 13 other countries. They, too, have branched into information technology, with overall net sales of $4.6 billion at the

More On SOFTWARE CONSULTANTS: USE WITH CAUTION

A shocking reality of outsourcing excess sank into the minds of corporate executives in 1997 following a revelation from AT&T that during the previous year the telecommunications conglomerate came very close to topping the one billion dollar mark in expenditures for consultants. That fact led one major business journal to dub the telecommunications conglomerate, "king of the consultant junkies." Much more serious than name-calling were the concerns that surfaced over the notion that mega-sized corporations were not in complete control of their own agendas with regard to strategic policy-making; perhaps of equal concern was the fact that AT&T was by no means the biggest spender in the outsourcing arena of the late 1990s.

The *Journal of Accountancy* voiced valid concern in 1998 when it cautioned companies to beware the vagaries of the outsourcing information technology tasks—including software maintenance and development—to outside contractors. Despite the cautionary commentary, the *Journal* went on to enumerate the potential benefits of the modern consultant-laced business culture. Short-term benefits included lower short-term cost, more effective divestiture of capital, and greater expertise and resource availability in the outsourced area. Long-term benefits were described as better resource utilization through greater ability to focus on the corporate discipline.

end of the 1998 fiscal year. Finally, the fourth largest employment agency worldwide, Kelly Services, Inc. provides about 750,000 employees to 215,000 clients. Kelly was once primarily an agency providing clerical help but has now expanded to other industries including technical and professional workers. In 1998 they had total sales of $4.1 billion.

WORK FORCE

Precise statistics regarding the number of active software consultants are scarce. The Software Contractor's Guild, a group of software contractors/consultants who post their resumes on a shared Web site in order to attract wider access to the clients, has more than 500 names registered, but this is the merest tip of the iceberg. The U.S. Bureau of Labor Statistics reports there are around 500,000 information technology/information systems consultants, which includes hardware as well as software consultants. Insiders at

some of the placement firms estimate the number at around 2.2 million; *Contract Professional's* unofficial estimate is around 1.5 million.

Independent software consultants usually have a college degree, and often an advanced degree as well, in computer science, engineering, or business. Independent consultants generally require about two years experience working in a company before they generate work on their own. Some software consultants have professional engineering licenses issued by the states, but clients do not generally expect such licensing. A few consultants also have systems certification issued by software companies like Novell, Inc. or Microsoft, but such certification is regarded by most consultants as window display and extraneous to their true qualifications.

One of the main challenges for consultants and contractors is keeping up-to-date with the rapid changes in the computer world. To this end, many read the latest computer periodicals and maintain personal reference libraries of the latest computer manuals. A great deal of information is available from the Internet, and free of charge. All of the major computer magazines have Web sites and all of the businesses associated with computers and software maintain an online presence where they publish press releases and other updates. Occasionally they will attend a formal course; but being self-employed, they have to pay for such courses themselves and earn no income while attending. Instead, many seek out work that will bring them into practical contact with technologies and systems of interest.

It is not unusual for a qualified, reputable software consultant to earn $100,000 or more per year. Even contractors who work primarily through agents do not find it difficult to earn a six-figure income. Average income for newcomers to the industry—consultants or contractors who have put their time in with a firm and struck out on their own—is around $55,000 per year. In addition, because consultants tend to work on short-term projects, usually no longer than nine months, they have more flexibility to schedule vacations. On the other hand, as self-employed persons, consultants have to take responsibility for their own taxes, health insurance, and retirement plans.

AMERICA AND THE WORLD

Being a profession where so much work is distributed by referral and personal reference, consulting depends on establishing face-to-face, individual relationships with clients. For that reason, domestic workers do most software consulting in the United States. What foreign competition does exist—for example, the growing numbers of computer specialists from the former Soviet Union—is as yet unorganized and poses little threat to Americans, if only because of the serious shortage of qualified personnel that currently exists in the United States.

However, the Internet has made it possible for international consultants to work on U.S. client software. The consultants come from India, Indonesia, or eastern European countries. The Software Contractors' Guild has a French chapter, and is working on creating an India chapter. These consultants find clients that transmit the work electronically, which is becoming easier to do. It is then distributed to a crew of workers who finish the job much more quickly—and for a much lower price—than domestic manpower. Software workers in India do extremely high-quality work, and they will work for $15 an hour instead of the $75 or $80 an American would charge. Consultants in India list on the Software Consultant Guild's Web site, as well as with placement services. The Internet is used to organize the jobs as well. Companies seeking consultants, as well as employment agencies, are now using the Internet with more frequency. A company can advertise jobs on its own Web site, or they can list open positions with one of the many huge job banks that have sprung up on-line.

FURTHER READING

"1996 Top Staffing Revenues—U.S.-Based IT Companies." *Contract Professional*, July/August 1997, 11. Available from http://www.ciber.com.

Adecco SA Home Page. Available from http://www.adecco.com.

"Andersen Consulting." *Hoover's Online*, 29 May 1999. Available from http://www.hoovers.com.

Andersen Consulting Home Page. Available from http://www.ac.com.

Caruso, David. "Command Performance." *Intelligent Enterprise*, 5 January 1999.

"Computer Sciences Corporation." *Hoover's Online*, 29 May 1999. Available from http://www.hoovers.com.

"Computer Services." *Moody's Industrial Review*, 4 April 1997.

"Computers: Commercial Services." *Standard & Poor's Industry Surveys*, 6 March 1997. Available from http://www.csc.com.

Gow, Kathleen. "PeopleSoft Consultants Thrive in Sellers' Market." *Contract Professional*, May/June 1997, 12-14. Available from http://www.iscg.com.

Greenberg, Ilan. "Consultants See Action." *InfoWorld*, 27 April 1998.

Isaacs, Nora. "Call in the Outsiders." *InfoWorld*, 17 May 1999.

Kelly Services, Inc. Home Page. Available from http://www.kellyservices.com.

Kenneally, Christopher. "How Long will the Good Times Last?" *Contract Professional*, July/August 1997, 22-28. Available from http://www.manpower.com.

Mayer, John H. "NT Experts in Driver's Seat." *Contract Professional*, March/April 1997, 30-31.

"The Millennium Bug." *Contract Professional*, May/June 1997, 8.

Murdock, Michelle. "Who Ya Gonna Call?" *InfoWorld*, 10 March 1997.

National Association of Computer Consultant Businesses (NACCB). Available from http://www.naccb.org.

Newman, Judy. "Y2K Problem Brings Profits-Finding Solutions Lucrative Work for Consultants." *Wisconsin State Journal*, 29 November 1998, 1E.

Olsten Corp. Home Page. Available from http://www.olsten.com.

Oracle Corp. Home Page. Available from http://www.oracle.com/.

Sybase Corp. Home Page. Available from http://www.sybase.com.

Weil, Nancy. "Oracle Setting Up Consulting Centers, Ships Enterprise Bundle." *InfoWorld*, 29 April 1998.

—Gerald E. Brennan, updated by Don Amerman

SPECIALTY COFFEE

Coffee is the world's second most-traded commodity, after oil. The premium variety is arabica coffee, which forms the basis of the U.S. specialty or gourmet coffee industry and has powered the nation's coffeehouse revival. According to the industry's trade group, the Specialty Coffee Association of America (SCAA), there were around 7,200 gourmet coffee outlets in the United States in the late 1990s with more than 70,000 employees. That number stands in stark contrast to the 250 cafes in 1979. The specialty coffee industry also generated over $1.5 billion in sales in the late 1990s, representing about 35 percent of all U.S. coffee sales during this period. According to the SCAA, the industry grew quickly during the 1990s— about 25 percent per year. The SCAA believed the gourmet category rejuvenated coffee sales as a whole, reversing a decline from the 1960s that did not perk up again until the early 1990s.

As coffee prices rose during the 1990s, some analysts predicted that the specialty coffee business could only prosper. Since an ordinary cup of coffee was already considered expensive, specialty roasters and retailers believed consumers would spend slightly more for gourmet coffee. The array of products was never wider; retailers added more flavors to whole beans and variations to the basics of espresso and steamed milk. The more clever retailers added coffee shakes and iced tea concoctions such as chai to their menus, to outdo competitors who offered mere iced lattes. Since most specialty retailers also retailed whole beans, their stores added home espresso machines, coffee grinders, and other brewing paraphernalia for add-on sales.

Many industry firms did all they could to increase market share: they ran catalog sales departments, added retail locations, and competed for new wholesale clients, such as restaurant chains and supermarkets. Several industry firms started sites on the World Wide Web during the 1990s to sell coffee beans over the Internet. Some roasters even created private label blends for their institutional customers. Starbucks Corp.'s Nordstrom Blend, for example, was created for the upscale department store chain. Courting corporate accounts became increasingly important because the top place for drinking coffee was the workplace in the late 1990s.

After growing in any of roughly 20 countries, coffee beans passed through many middlemen and brokers before coming to industry firms in the United States. Usually, the beans arrived green or unroasted, whereupon industry firms bought and roasted them in small batches. From there the beans reached consumers through several channels, including: supermarkets, gourmet delis, fancy food stores, houseware/gift stores, mail order, mass merchandisers, the Internet, specialty coffee stores, and coffee cafes. In non-proprietary retail stores, such as supermarkets, specialty coffee came prepackaged or in bulk, depending on the individual retailer's store format. An estimated 29 percent of specialty coffee sales in 1996 were in supermarkets.

Industry firms often sold their beans through a combination of supermarkets, their own bean stores and/or cafes, mail-order, and the Internet. There were

3,250 cafes, 2,125 coffee bars and kiosks, and 1,800 coffee carts selling coffee in the United States in the late 1990s, according to the SCAA. Furthermore, the SCAA predicted that the number of specialty coffee retail outlets would hit 10,000 by 1999, including 4,500 cafes, 3,000 coffee bars and kiosks, and 2,500 carts. The difference between a bean store and a cafe is that the former emphasizes selling beans (and assorted brewing gadgets) so consumers can make gourmet coffee at home, while a cafe prepares single drinks for customers to consume on the premises or to take out. Many industry firms such as Starbucks sell whole beans as well as individual drinks at their stores, and serve coffee drinks to consumers in two forms: the filtered, drip coffee familiar to most Americans, and European-style espresso, a more concentrated form of the brew, which is harder for consumers to make at home. Shots of espresso are "pulled" from espresso machines by cafe workers called "baristas," a coffee bartender of sorts. Most espresso beverages have one or more shots combined with steamed or foamed milk to make such drinks as cappuccinos, caffe mochas, or cafe au laits.

The Specialty Coffee Association of America is a non-profit trade organization with more than 2,500-member companies including roasters, retailers, exporters, and coffee brokers in the late 1990s. The group states its purpose as being to "serve the specialty coffee industry through the development and dissemination of information that fosters coffee excellence within the trade." It is concerned with developing coffee quality standards, but also organizes trade shows and collects educational information for its members.

According to an early 1990s study used by the SCAA, about 22 percent of Americans bought specialty coffee. The study noted above-average consumption in the Pacific, Middle Atlantic, and New England states. The study found gourmet coffee drinkers tended to be slightly more affluent than average and lived or worked in big cities. Gourmet coffee consumption also rose with the drinkers' educational level. Those who finished college bought 49 percent more gourmet coffee on average and those with some post-graduate education bought 71 percent more. They also found that households with kids and two working parents bought 28 percent more gourmet coffee. The SCAA described their typical customer as "an educated urban resident with the disposable income to spend on fine coffee."

BACKGROUND AND DEVELOPMENT

Until the 1960s, nearly all Americans bought their coffee at the supermarket. During the late 1960s, some entrepreneurs opened shops carrying hard-to-find gourmet food items, such as specialty coffees, aimed at affluent consumers. Some of these businesses even roasted their own coffee, to control the degree of roast and keep the coffee fresh. By 1969 the United States had about 50 specialty coffee stores. During the early 1970s, 100 gift/houseware stores and 1,200 specialty food stores carried gourmet coffee. In 1975 a killing frost in Brazil devastated the coffee crop, which raised coffee prices by 500 percent. Large roasters tried to calm consumer sticker shock by selling coffee in 13-ounce cans instead of the usual 16-ounce. Since consumers got less for their coffee dollar, some of them switched to the more flavorful gourmet blends following a quality versus quantity consumer trend.

Throughout the 1970s the industry experimented with roasting beans darker to make a smokier, more distinct coffee than the lighter supermarket roasts. Thus, many consumers came to associate dark roasted coffee with gourmet coffee and many specialty coffee companies developed proprietary house blends during the 1970s. Decaffeinated coffees became a popular seller during the 1980s, with 17 percent of the population drinking it by 1988. The demand for flavored coffees emerged in the mid-1980s, causing producers to add flavors such as cocoa, vanilla, or hazelnut in liquid or powder form to coffee beans. This required little capital investment and allowed specialty shops to sell flavored coffees at a higher price. Industry firms tried many different flavors, and several became big hits, particularly by attracting new, younger coffee drinkers to the customer base.

Some coffee purists scoffed at flavored coffees, despite their apparent popularity. Starbucks, for example, refused to flavor its beans, but sold flavored syrup to add after brewing. Syrups provided retailers with more sales options than simply flavoring coffees. These could be used in Italian sodas, granitas, and other drink concoctions popular with the 18-to-35-year-old cafe patron. These drinks could also be sold at a premium. Standard flavors included vanilla, hazelnut, and raspberry; but companies such as Boyd Coffee expanded their lines to include creme brulee and wild huckleberry flavored syrups, and Stasero added praline, marshmallow, and a combination of passion fruit, orange, and guava. Marketing syrup-flavored drinks proved to fuel creativity from employee and customer alike. Signature drinks offered by some retailers included "Lemon Meringue Pie Italian Soda," "Nutty Buddy"—a mocha spiked with three nut-flavored syrups—and "Starburst"—white chocolate and lemon syrups mixed in sparkling water.

Another trend included consumer requests for organic coffees. However, the industry in the 1990s could not tell if consumers would pay more for the harder-to-find organics. Certainly more emphasis was placed by retailers on the beans' growing environment. One growing environmental and economic concern within the industry was the plight of wintering songbirds. The shade trees sheltering coffee bushes of Central and South America have long been home to migratory birds. Ornithological surveys have found 150 or more bird species living in traditional coffee plantations. Strong demand for coffee and advice from the U.S. government caused growers to convert their land to so-called "sun plantations." U.S. Agency for International Development (AID) spent $81 million in efforts to get growers to change planting methods to increase volume. (Economic studies completed since dispute those assumptions.) The process of changing these once-fertile habitats from shade tree to sun plantation, started in 1978, has caused a decline in the migratory bird species population in these traditional locations.

Increased attention to the plight of the birds meant coffee drinkers began asking for shade-grown beans in an attempt to change the trend. Companies including Thanksgiving Coffee marketed specially labeled coffees to educate coffee lovers about the issue. According to a 1997 *Knight-Ridder/Tribune News Service* article, most specialty coffee is actually shade grown. The Specialty Coffee Association of America says most mass-market coffees are grown on sun plantations, where volume and price are a bigger factor.

Growth of the roaster/retailer segment shows how the industry evolved during the 1970s and 1980s. In 1979 there were about 50 coffee roaster/retailers in the United States; by 1989, there were 400. Growth of specialty coffee retail stores (no roasting on premises) was also dramatic: there were 250 of these stores in 1979 and 1,000 by 1989.

CURRENT CONDITIONS

The specialty coffee industry reaped sales of approximately $1.5 billion in the mid- to late 1990s, but the Specialty Coffee Association of America predicts that the industry's revenues will double by the end of the decade, reaching $3.0 billion. About 49 percent of the U.S. population drinks coffee and the average consumer drinks 3.3 cups of coffee a day—the highest level since 1962 when 64 percent of the population consumed coffee.

With strong demand for specialty coffee, more competitors entered the business during the late 1990s, with varied success. General Foods captured some market share from the smaller players with its line of Gevalia Coffees, sold only by mail-order. Procter & Gamble, maker of Folgers, entered the specialty coffee fray in 1995 with its purchase of Millstone, which it distributes to about 7,000 stores. In addition, another mass-market coffee producer, Chock full o' Nuts Corp., bought an industry firm called Quikava in 1994. Based in Boston, Quikava is a chain of drive through espresso shops that offers franchising. Quikava kept expanding and Chock full o' Nuts set a precedent for other established retailers to enter the market. In 1998 there were 20 Quikava outlets and development of these franchises continued.

Retailer J.C. Penney Company of Plano, Texas, announced in early 1997 they would open JC Java gourmet coffee bars inside J.C. Penney stores. Working with the Coffee Group, a consulting firm in Costa Mesa, California, Penney planned to put 60 JC Java's in their west coast stores from 1997 to 1998. The Coffee Group hoped to franchise the stores and get them into three-quarters of the 1,200 total J.C. Penney stores. The consultants also started coffee bars called Caffe Tazza inside Gottshalks department stores.

Some industry analysts wondered if the market could bear another mass-market gourmet coffee chain or whether some competitors might fail. One industry trend of the late 1990s was the consolidation of specialty coffee companies (or the rumors of such consolidation), as smaller competitors scrambled to compete with the industry giant, Starbucks Corp. For instance, in 1997 Java City of Sacramento, California (with 1995 annual sales of $32 million, and 40 retail units) merged with wholesaler Caravali Coffees of Seattle, Washington. The new company expected to gross $50 million in the late 1990s, and was held by Cucina Holdings, Inc. Caravali began in 1983 as the wholesale division of Starbucks, and sold separately to private investors when Starbucks changed hands in 1987. Caravali ran only seven retail stores, but had a big wholesale network covering North America, the Pacific Rim, and Europe. This was Java City's second merger, having already combined in 1993 with a 68-unit bakery chain, La Petite Boulangerie, a move that allowed Java City to scale back on stores and raise revenues.

Some analysts said the industry trend toward consolidation indicated that the specialty coffee industry was maturing, and that mergers and acquisitions brought needed capital. Ted Lingle, head of the Specialty Coffee Association of America, said in a published story, "We see growth peaking in this industry around the year 2010, and between now and then you'll see a slow but steady increase in the number of mergers. After that, I don't think you'll see merger mania tapering off until after the year 2020."

"The definition of specialty coffee is changing," wrote Donald N. Schoenholt in a 1998 *Tea & Coffee Trade Journal* article. "The lines between specialty and commercial products are beginning to blur. The big companies' threat to the existence of regional brands increases. This is so even as specialty coffee's appeal continues to grow across the land. Our ranks have swelled, been thinned, and filled again with specialty coffee businesses that are in significant ways different kinds of businesses than those of the movement's founders. Many are extensions of much bigger companies whose primary products and services often have more to do with tobacco and soap than they do with any kind of coffee. None of this is bad by itself. But things have changed. . . . Today, 'specialty coffee' most often means a beverage of flavored coffee in a 12 oz. container to go. Enough said. Things change."

Schoenholt wrote that aggressive business tactics by big companies served to "alienate some companies from their specialty coffee community roots." The roots of the industry, he wrote, was in a strong and viable independent group of businesses with the sole mission "to never let the blight of coffee sameness again creep over the land."

Because of the widespread devastation caused by Hurricane Mitch in 1998, some specialty coffee prices were forecast to rise in 1999. Hurricane Mitch ripped through Central America in the fall of 1998, destroying the coffee crop and infrastructure of the region's producers such as Guatemala, Nicaragua, Honduras, and Costa Rica. While the hurricane was not expected to affect the overall supply of coffee, it was predicted to limit the availability of some specialty coffees. In particular, the hurricane damaged at least 10 percent Nicaragua's organic crop and sent the price of Guatemala Antigua coffee soaring to about $13 a pound.

INDUSTRY LEADERS

It goes without saying that the highest-grossing industry firm in the late 1990s was Starbucks Corporation based in Seattle, Washington. The company posted 1998 sales of $1.3 million, up 35 percent, and had more than 2,000 retail locations spread throughout the world. Starbucks also distributes its specialty coffee to about 3,500 supermarkets. The company began in 1971 with one store in Seattle. Three entrepreneurs—Gordon Bowker, Jerry Baldwin, and Zev Siegl—founded the original business. They named it

after a character who loved coffee from Herman Melville's classic novel *Moby Dick*, and they developed the now-familiar mermaid logo. Starbucks originally sold bulk tea and specialty coffee beans by the pound. They did not add a coffee bar to sell drinks until 1984. The coffee bar idea came from Howard Schultz, who was the company's marketing director. Schultz quit the company in 1985 to start a chain of espresso cafes like those he'd seen in Milan, Italy. He called his cafes Il Giornale, and they served Starbucks coffee. In 1987, Schultz raised money from private investors and bought Starbucks from its founders for $3.8 million. The venture paid off for Schultz, whose personal fortune was $100 million in 1997, 75 percent of which came from Starbucks stock.

During the late 1980s, Starbucks built a larger roasting plant, started a mail-order catalogue, and opened stores in British Columbia, Oregon, and the Chicago area. By 1992, the company grew to 165 stores and offered stock on the NASDAQ (National Association of Securities Dealers Automated Quotations System) exchange. Their specialty sales division landed prized institutional accounts throughout the 1990s including: Nordstrom's coffee bars, United Airlines, Barnes and Noble, ITT/Sheraton Hotels, Westin Hotels, and Star Markets. Starbucks also offered some of their catalogue items on the Internet through America Online. In 1994, they had 425 U.S. stores and bought a smaller competitor, The Coffee Connection, Inc. In 1995, the company also bought a minority stake in Noah's New York Bagels, Inc., a coffee and bagel chain based in Golden, Colorado.

Starbucks began joint ventures from 1995 to 1997 to get its coffee into other products, including: Double Black Stout, a dark beer with a shot of espresso, developed with Redhook Ale Brewery; Frappucino, a bottled iced coffee beverage, developed with Pepsi-Cola Co.; and a line of Starbucks coffee-flavored ice creams marketed with Dreyer's Grand Ice Cream, Inc., and sold in supermarkets. One of the company's few failures was a carbonated coffee beverage called Mazagran. Joint ventures extended to non-food items as well, including the sale of music CDs in Starbucks stores, a concept developed with Capitol Records's Blue Note Jazz label.

Starbucks opened almost one new store per day in the late 1990s, including five on a single day in Toronto. During this period, Starbucks expanded to the Pacific Rim, opening stores in Hawaii, Japan, and Singapore. The expansion effort helped the company realize its goal of having 2,000 stores by the year 2,000. Part of the company's expansion campaign also included the acquisition of Seattle Coffee Company.

About... THE COFFEE-CHAIN NAME GAME

For two specialty coffee chains, inspiration lies behind the name. Starbucks, which started out as a single shop in Seattle, derives its name from the coffee-loving first mate in Herman Melville's adventure tale, *Moby Dick*. In 1982, Howard Schultz joined Starbucks as director of retail operations and marketing. Schultz, after visiting Italy and seeing the popularity of espresso bars there, convinced the company's original founders to try out a similar coffee-bar style in downtown Seattle. It was widely popular and prompted Schultz to found a new company, Il Giornale, in 1985.

When Schultz acquired the assets of Starbucks in 1987, he was faced with a decision: keep the Starbucks name or keep Il Giornale. Il Giornale, the name of the largest newspaper in Italy, had been inspired by the daily routine the name suggests of getting a pastry, a paper and a morning cup of coffee. However, after the acquisition, Schultz had to weigh the pros and cons of both names. The decision was hashed out in two meetings—one with major investors and the other with employees. Despite his attachment to the name he created, Schultz agreed with one consultant who said the Italian name was obscure, hard to spell and hard to pronounce. Starbucks also had more widespread recognition, largely due to mail orders, while Il Giornale was still new. In addition, Starbucks represented something purely American. The decision was clear: the Starbucks name stayed.

The founders of Caribou Coffee also derived their name from an inspiration. In fact, the idea for the business developed from an inspirational trip to a mountain range. That experience later yielded the name. Founders Kim and John Puckett were inspired to start their chain of specialty coffee shops after a long climb to the top of the Sable Mountains in Alaska. After reaching the summit, they looked across the Denali mountain range and watched a herd of wild caribou in the valley below. At that moment, they felt very small but lucky to see such beauty. That's when they realized they wanted to do something special with their lives and later hit on the idea of creating a place where people could enjoy good coffee and conversations in a place that would feel as good as the view from atop the mountain range. The name Caribou Coffee was born.

Seattle Coffee Company operates 68 cafes primarily in the United Kingdom, under the names Seattle's Best Coffee and Torrefazione Italia brands as well as a roasting and packaging facility. Furthermore, Seattle Coffee products can be found in about 1,600 grocery stores nationwide. Starbucks bought the company in order to penetrate the European market. Despite critics calling them the "golden arches" of the specialty coffee industry, the company's cash registers kept ringing. Starbucks claims to serve about 4 million customers per week.

Second Cup Ltd., a Toronto-based firm, moved to the much coveted number two spot behind Starbucks in 1998 with 607 locations worldwide. The company is the parent to U.S.-based Gloria Jean's, a mall-based retailer that predominantly sells flavored whole-bean coffees. The company announced in late 1997 that it was combining operations with Coffee People, Inc., a Portland, Oregon, chain with 45 locations. Second Cup also provides coffee for use on Air Canada and VIA Rail Canada.

The West Coast competitor, publicly held Diedrich Coffee of Irvine, California, ranked third with 1998 sales of $150 million, about 1,500 employees, and 363 retail locations. Diedrich acquired another leading specialty coffee company, Coffee People, Inc., in 1999, propelling the company towards the top of the industry. Diedrich has stores and carts located in 38 states, including Texas, Colorado, and California, plus wholesale and mail-order divisions, and roasts its own coffees from regional plants. The company also planned to open cafes in bank branches owned by Home Savings of America. Diedrich was founded in 1912, owns Central American plantations, and is credited with designing and manufacturing "one of the world's most popular batch roasting machines."

Caribou Coffee, started in 1992 with a mere $200,000, was the fourth largest coffee retail chain in 1998. The privately owned company had 120 locations in Minnesota, Michigan, Ohio, Illinois, Georgia, and North Carolina in 1998 and also provides coffee to Delta Airlines. Planned expansion was to take Caribou Coffee throughout the Southeast and Midwestern United States. Another major player in the industry was Green Mountain Coffee, Inc. of Waterbury, Vermont, which posted 1998 sales of $55.8 million and had 410 employees. The firm sells gourmet coffee to 750,000 catalogue patrons and has 4,000 institutional customers. Green Mountain also runs about 12 cafes in the Northeast.

One of Starbucks' original founders, Jerry Baldwin, went on to run privately held Peet's Coffee and Tea in the San Francisco Bay area (34 retail cafes in 1997). Another Starbucks founder, Gordon Bowker, sat on the board of Peet's and Redhook Ale Brewery. In 1992 Starbucks expanded into northern California, thus competing with its own creators.

The independent cafe and retailer had long been an integral part of the growth of specialty coffee, however, they continued to face challenges from Starbucks in the late 1990s. Independent retailers feeling stomped on by giant Starbucks did not merely leave those business owners in their cups. In Boulder, Colorado, for example, in 1998, 10 local, independent cafes banded together to promote their stores. This effort included distributing coupons and to-go cups printed with a message promoting independent cafes—a message Solo Cup Co. refused to print because it provided cups for Starbucks.

AMERICA AND THE WORLD

Gourmet coffee comes from about 20 different countries. Free trade between the United States and producer countries is vital to the industry, since the domestic crop is so small. The only gourmet coffee grown on U.S. soil comes from the Kona area on the island of Hawaii. But Kona's crop was impractical for two reasons: price and authenticity. The coffee costs more than similar-tasting Latin American coffees, because American coffee pickers did not work for Third World wages. Since the beans are so expensive, scams occasionally surfaced. Case in point, in 1996 a Berkeley, California wholesaler got caught diluting Kona beans with cheaper Latin American beans, after having fooled consumers, and some in the industry, for years.

Other specialty beans came from the Arab states and East Africa, including: Yemen, Ethiopia, Kenya, Tanzania, and Zimbabwe. The final group of coffees came from the Malay Archipelago, including such areas as Sumatra, Sulawesi, Java, and New Guinea. The most prominent coffee-growing region was Latin America. Brazil grew one-third of the world's coffee, but only a small portion of that was gourmet quality. The second-largest coffee-producing country was Colombia, which produced the most consistent coffee according to some analysts. Mexico, Ecuador, Peru, and Venezuela produced coffees most often used by specialty purveyors for blends, although better varieties from these countries were sometimes sold unblended. Some analysts believed Costa Rica grew the region's finest coffee, particularly the estate coffee, La Minita, from Tarrazu.

Conditions in Guatemala perhaps best represented the challenges facing industry firms doing business in the so-called Third World nations. The region produced a distinctive, sought-after coffee, but had a history of poverty, political turmoil, and human rights abuses. During 1994 and 1995, some human rights organizations picketed Starbucks, saying the company ignored the desperate conditions of Guatemalan coffee workers. Some analysts believe the company was singled out for attack because of its prominence and because the company was known for taking a stand on social issues. Starbucks countered that they did not own or control any of Guatemala's 33,000 coffee farms. The company also stated that they bought less than one-half of 1 percent of the world's coffee crop and lacked the leverage to solve entrenched social problems. However, in 1995 Starbucks wrote a "framework for a code of conduct," outlining what they expected from their suppliers: "We are dedicated to working with others to raise standards of health, education, workplace safety, and economic well-being in all communities where we do business."

Since 1997, Starbucks has collaborated in Guatemala with Appropriate Technology International (ATI), on a program to improve efficiency and lessen environmental impact on some of Guatemala's small coffee farms. In 1996, Starbucks gave CARE (an international relief and development organization) a $250,000 donation, making it the charity's largest North American donor. Starbucks also merchandised "CARE packages" of coffees from countries where the charity operated (e.g. Kenya), donating some of the profit from those bean sales to CARE.

Despite the challenges presented with obtaining raw product abroad, there existed various international opportunities for specialty coffee purveyors outside the United States, particularly in the United Kingdom and Asia. Locations with the best opportunity for success included Singapore, Hong Kong, and Jakarta. Franchises in the United Kingdom included Seattle Coffee Co., Coffee Republic, Aroma and Costa Coffee with Nestle announcing plans in April 1998 to open several Nescafe CoffeeHouse franchises and Starbucks prepared to enter the market as well.

The primary challenge facing specialty coffee companies in the late 1990s continued to be how to expand while making their companies more competitive against the dominant Starbucks. The Specialty Coffee Association of America stated the greatest opportunities for retailers were between 1979 and 1983, but says ample room remains in the market. Orders were up 95.4 percent in 1998 in coffeehouses alone. "Specialty coffee is not a novelty anymore," says Michael Bregman, Second Cup Ltd., chairman and chief executive officer. "Most markets are fairly well served today, although there's lots of opportunity for growth. So, to go into a new market from scratch and expect them [consumers] to embrace a brand new entrant into what's becoming a fairly competitive landscape requires a lot of capital, a lot of patience, and entails a lot of risk. We think that will continue to be the pattern."

According to a report from the International Coffee Organization, global coffee consumption may rise 12 percent from 1996 to the year 2000, with U.S. coffee drinkers accounting for 5 percent of that. In volume, this would be 14.19 billion pounds of coffee per year. Sue Gillerlain, in an 1998 market analysis appearing in *Specialty Coffee Retailer,* stated that although the industry was "facing adulthood and along with it domestic consolidation" there remained "opportunity for the small independent retailer to take customer service, community and product quality all the way to the bank."

FURTHER READING

Andrews, Margaret C. *Avenues For Growth: A 20-Year Review of the US Specialty Market.* The Specialty Coffee Association of America, 1992.

Barron, Kelly. "J.C. Penney Hopes Its Coffee Bars Will Cater to Average Consumers." *Knight-Ridder/Tribune Business News,* 21 January 1997.

"Coffee's Rising." *Beverage World,* October 1996.

"The Cup Runneth: Retail and Specialty Products Are Helping Grow the Coffee and Tea Market." *Beverage Industry,* April 1997.

Dewar, Heather. "Decline in Shade Trees for Coffee Bushes May Be Lined to Decrease in Migratory Songbirds." *Knight-Ridder/Tribune News Service,* 29 January 1997.

Diedrich Coffee Company Web site. Available from http://www.diedrich.com.

Gillerlain, Sue. "State of the Industry Report 1998." *Specialty Coffee Retailer,* June 1998.

Gugino, Sam. "A Man Who Knows His Beans: If It Were Up to John Martinez, Everyone Would Be Drinking Estate Coffee." *Cigar Aficionado,* August 1997.

Kramer, Louise. "Starbucks, P&G, Seattle Coffee in Grocery Scuffle." *Advertising Age,* 16 February 1998.

Kugiya, Hugo. "Seattle's Coffee King: Starbucks Boss Howard Schultz." *The Seattle Times,* 15 December 1996.

"A Look at the Latest in Retail Trends." *Tea & Coffee Trade Journal,* September 1997.

McDonald, Barbara. "Specialty Coffee Prices May Heat Up in Hurricane's Wake." *Supermarket News,* 18 January 1999.

Riell, Howard. "Harnessing Java's Jolt." *Supermarket Business,* March 1997.

Robert, Nancy. "Summertime Syrup Drinks." *Specialty Coffee Retailer,* June 1998.

Schoenholt, Donald N. "The Times They are a Changing." *Tea & Coffee Trade Journal,* April 1998.

Schulaka, Carly. "Boulder, Colo., Independent Coffee Shops Team Up to Battle Corporate Chains." *Knight-Ridder/Tribune Business News,* 15 June 1998.

"Second Cup Opens in Jerusalem, Israel." *Nation's Restaurant News,* 20 January 1997.

Specialty Coffee Association of America. Available from http://www.scaa.org.

Thanksgiving Coffee Company Web site. Available from http://www.thanksgivingcoffee.com.

Williams, Norman . "California Merger A Sign that Specialty Coffee Industry Is Maturing." *Knight-Ridder/Tribune Business News,* 28 March 1997.

———"Sacramento, Calif., Chain to Join with Wholesale Giant." *Knight-Ridder/Tribune Business News,* 27 March 1997.

—Dave Fagan,
updated by Linda Dailey Paulson and Karl Heil

SPECIALTY TOURISM

Specialty tourism, or special interest travel, is a growing segment of the leisure travel industry. Special interest travel is the portion of the industry geared to those seeking destinations and activities not usually included in traditional vacation itineraries. Rather than placing high priority on relaxation, comforts, entertainment, or standard tourist activities, specialty travelers seek active interaction with destination environments. They shun the label "tourists," feeling the term implies travel on more regimented itineraries, in large groups, or to highly publicized and commercialized locations. Special interest travelers prefer to be classified according to the specific travel experiences they pursue. In general, however, special interest travelers actively seek destinations, sites, or experiences that have not been developed for tourist activity.

The concept of "specialty travel" is better defined by its more specific interest categories such as adventure, nature, culture, sport, spiritual, vocational, and study tourism. An exhaustive list like the one in the *Specialty Travel Index* includes more than 300 activities. Activities on special interest tours vary from abseiling to yoga, and some target members of specific affinity groups such as women, students, families, singles, gays/lesbians, farmers, veterans, Christians, golfers, divers, or bird watchers. Activities preferred by the general population—like skiing, power boating, motor travel, flying, luxury cruises, gambling, or resort travel—are generally not considered part of the specialty travel industry.

In general, the specialty travel industry has benefited from some emerging social, technological, and economic trends. Most importantly, travel has become easier, faster, and more important to our lifestyle. The cost of air and surface travel has been going down. There are more roads, air routes, airplanes, and surface vehicles to transport travelers to destinations previously very difficult to reach. Information for travelers is more abundant and more available. There are more businesses offering specialty services. The expanding network of local providers of lodging, guides, transport, equipment, and otherwise facilitating exploration of areas without a formal tourist infrastructure is growing rapidly. A prosperous economy has afforded more people the high incomes and security to expend discretionary income for the exotic experiences that specialty travel provides. And finally, specialty travel responds to the public's increased interest in healthy, active, educational activities. Many segments of the specialty travel industry complement interests in fitness, life-long learning, physical achievement, and a healthy lifestyle—trends that are often identified with the aging Baby Boomer generations. The World Tourism Organization (WTO) predicted that cultural tourism would be one of the hottest travel trends for the twenty-first century.

ORGANIZATION AND STRUCTURE

There is no single organization or publication that speaks for the specialty travel industry, though several private entities attempt to provide unifying promotional services based on common needs for insurance, working with political or environmental policies, or for commercial promotion. Some operators are members of such traditional travel associations as The American Society of Travel Agents. The Adventure

Travel Society of Boulder, Colorado, a private organization, has attempted to provide a forum for discussing adventure travel trends and problems. Each year they hold a World Congress for adventure travel at a different venue around the world. The organization, however, has no position on travel policy, nor does it include any democratic participation of members in establishing guidelines or directions. Generally, organizers of specialty travel may work with airlines or other transportation companies and derive a portion of their earnings from ticket commissions. In the 1990s, however, airlines dramatically reduced commissions to agents and some operators left the matter of reaching remote trip destinations in the hands of the traveler.

The lack of a unifying body for this segment of the travel industry also leads to marketing confusion. Often, adventure travel land operators sell services through conventional travel agents, adventure agents, or directly to the consumer. This sometimes creates a dysfunctional marketing problem as diligent consumers may collect information from three or more different sources describing the price and features of a single adventure experience with varying criteria. Most specialty travel companies have Internet sites, which further complicate the problem of identifying and distinguishing services as unique. No conventions or common agreements have emerged to establish order in the marketing channels. Generally, consumers pay a fixed retail price, which may include commission for booking agents and re-marketers at 10-35 percent, depending on booking volume and marketing commitment.

The retail costs of specialty travel vary greatly with destination, group size, duration, and types of service included. According to the Travelon Web site, which holds a database of several thousand trips, the cost of a guided, full-service, 8- to 12-day trip in Asia, Africa, or Latin America ranged from $900 to $2,500. Exploration cruising in the Amazon, Galapagos, or Antarctica generally cost between $200 and $400 per person per day. Himalayan trekking, African overland camping safaris, and other large group participation trips appealing to budget-minded travelers are usually priced under $100 per day, but may tally more than $200 per day. Cost was often a function of government fees. In Bhutan, for example, all local service providers were required by the Bhutan Tourism Ministry to charge overseas operators standard rates averaging more than $200 per person per day. The greater part of most African safaris was the cost of fees for park entry, camping, and vehicle entry. Cost of tips to guides on all trips is usually additional. Consumers of specialty travel tend to enjoy above average wealth, but trips must still be priced competitively. Specialty travel groups from different companies often meet at campsites, favored hotels, trail heads, key locations, or remote airports and participants compare notes on price, quality, leadership, and experience. Every company understands the paramount importance of customer loyalty derived from having the best trip at the best price.

Though lacking any formal, collective organization, specialty tourism is categorized according to certain functional characteristics or business-types. Tourism promotion offices are often associated with national, state, or regional government agencies and they usually promote all types of tourism. Inbound or receptive operators help groups of visitors or individual tourists and coordinate various portions of the overall itinerary, including lodging, transfers, activity reservations, guides, and meals. These inbound operators rely on local specialized service providers. These may be trekking, rafting, or diving operators, lodge owners, ski resorts, tour bus owners, or the owners and managers of any number of services. Most agents and operators who organize and conduct these trips are not members of organizations such as the American Society of Travel Agents or United States Tour Operators Association, who serve to set standards and track development of the broader leisure tourism industry.

Specialty travel also relies on outbound operators, particularly in the case of foreign travel. Outbound operators design itineraries, print brochures, select inbound operators, specify services, negotiate prices, and promote services offered by their businesses as unique products for a national or international market. Often travelers who purchase vacation packages from outbound operators are not aware of this distinction. Outbound operators may rely on travel agents or independent trip organizers to fill trips. Each of the agents employed to reach the public may also specialize in some aspect of specialty travel, or more generally in leisure travel. Many travel agents have developed an interest or expertise in locating and evaluating special interest trips and the industry as a whole. Operators may try to fill trips through direct booking of clients and with the help of their own public relations agents. Increasingly, this purely promotional end of the specialty travel industry has proliferated to include the Internet, e-mail, video, magazines, database marketing, travel shows, and product or service cross-marketing schemes to reach prospective specialty travelers. All of these participate in the specialty travel industry, but none define it individually. Operators of specialty travel trips distin-

A women's whitewater rafting group. (Courtesy of Mariah Wilderness Expeditions.)

guish events less by the common standards than by the uniqueness of itineraries, leaders, style, qualifications, and value of services.

One of the best ways to assess the size and diversity of the industry is to attend one of the many adventure travel shows scheduled annually in large cities, including Chicago, Atlanta, Madison, Cincinnati, San Francisco, Baltimore, and New York. These shows bring participants, providers, tourist bureaus, guides, media publicists, adventure travel site operators, airlines, hotel and lodge owners, and others with interest in adventure travel together. One can also gain a good sense for the diversity of this segment of the industry from the travel advertising sections of magazines such as *Outside, Sierra, Backpacker, Escape* or *Men's Journal.*

ADVENTURE TOURISM

Adventure tourism is a broad term covering several smaller segments of specialty travel, all related to active pursuit of extreme sports, remote destinations, and unusual experiences. Increasing numbers of people are pursuing active, physically, and intellectually challenging recreational experiences both close to home and in the most remote regions of the earth. In response to the demand for special travel information

and services, thousands of small businesses around the world have emerged in the past 50 years.

Included are the more narrowly defined categories of adventure travel such as ecotourism, exploration cruising, trekking, mountaineering, rafting, kayaking, nature tourism, cultural tourism, SCUBA diving, dog sledding, and a panoply of other recreational outdoor sports. Many organized tours include a combination of these and other activities. All of these activities require a greater amount of exertion, higher degree of risk, and greater emphasis on the natural and cultural encounters of participants than conventional travel. Conversely, adventure tourism avoids or minimizes emphasis on luxury accommodations, night life, dining, relaxation, shopping, museums, or entertainment. However, more and more conventional tour and cruise operators are expanding or redefining itineraries to include more active adventure activities as they detect market demand for authentic natural, cultural, and physical exploration on more spontaneous itineraries.

ECOTOURISM

Another large segment of the specialty travel industry is ecotourism. While not completely distinct from adventure tourism, ecotourism focuses on the experience of nature and culture while also paying attention to the economic and environmental impacts of travel itself. The adventure component of ecotourism may be more intellectual than physical. Some ecotourism operators seek the highest accommodation standards possible and avoid placing clients in circumstances demanding excessive physical exertion or use of primitive accommodations. Others presume clients are fit and flexible and that they anticipate the physical and intellectual challenges that accompany reaching pristine locations and/or cultures.

Ecotourism operators share a concern for enfranchising local communities in the economic process and benefits of tourism. Companies like JOURNEYS International and International Expeditions also have non-profit organizations or service divisions that help train local people in tourism related fields and support schools, clinics, or local community projects. They view this as a way to help create a political and social environment for environmental preservation. Ecotourism is a process of learning, training, and improving the travel experience for participants and local hosts. It is also a way to move toward goals of sustainable activity and generate local community benefits without harming the local cultures or environments.

The recognized authority on ecotourism is The Ecotourism Society. This organization has memberships in various classes ranging from travelers to operators to researchers, all concerned with improving the standards and effects of ecotourism. They publish many pamphlets and brochures of interest to anyone trying to get started in the ecotourism business.

NATURE TOURISM

People more frequently formulate vacations around the primary objective of seeing and enjoying nature. Similar to ecotourism, nature tourism seeks nature for its own sake with less focus on human culture and less explicit concern for conservation or preservation. Bird watching, SCUBA diving, botany exploration, African wildlife safaris, sport fishing, whale watching, and other trips seek out nature and provide interpretation and education. Such trips may or may not support active conservation of the places they visit.

SPIRITUAL TOURISM

Increasing numbers of people join similarly educated or religiously oriented travelers to further spiritual understanding. Organized pilgrimages to holy places in the Middle East have taken place for decades, but in recent years more tours have promoted New Age spiritual orientations to visit ancient sites not usually associated with modern organized religion,

such as the Mayan ruins of Central America or Stonehenge in Britain. Other trips adopt an agenda of self-realization similar to the vision quest of some Native American religions, without its doctrinal components. Many Americans explore Buddhism or other Eastern beliefs by joining tours to important religious sites in Asia from the monasteries of Tibet and Nepal, to the ashrams of Hindu India to Islamic monuments of Pakistan or central Asia, to sacred sites of Native Americans in the United States.

SPORT TOURISM

Many people seek active vacations focusing on specific fitness activities. Bike trips, kayaking, golf, horseback riding, trekking, climbing, orienteering (competitive compass navigation), and even marathons increasingly draw people from all around the world to organized tours or events that may take place in exotic locations. Rafting, ballooning, sailing, and walking trips may require less physical exertion, but still demand a level of physical involvement, knowledge, and disciplined focus beyond the requirements of conventional leisure vacations. These types of vacations are typically organized by an individual or a company with knowledge of the sport and access to the specialized equipment required to perform the activity. They market expertise, access to optimal environments, the quality of their equipment and guides, and their ability to effectively coordinate necessary travel arrangements. The Discovery Channel's promotion of Eco-challenges, in which teams from around the world compete to navigate a difficult course over difficult and varied terrain, has popularized a variety of sport tourism skills.

AFFINITY GROUP TRAVEL

Demographic factors offer another way to focus specialty travel events. Participants may be all members of an organization, occupation, ethnic group, or marital status. Operators organize trips for singles, families, grand parents and grand children, gays/lesbians, farmers, doctors, wine and food lovers, educators, students, or seniors. This kind of trip provides an experience tailored to specific common expectations and preferences of the group. Sometimes groups have an occupational focus that defines the primary goals of the trip. Health professionals, for example, may choose to take a trip like the Himalayan Health Expedition, on which they have a full program of contact with local clinics, local healers, and shaman. A local doctor stimulates continuous dialogue with local people about health issues. Some operators offer an extensive variety of trips specifically geared to physicians.

Groups of people embarking on specialized trips appreciate knowing fellow participants will have the same personal and lifestyle views. Gay and lesbian tours are quite common, often with adventure or ecotourist themes. Participants feel more comfort in knowing personal qualities such as sexual orientation or marital status will not create problems or confusion for other participants on the trip, allowing more focus on the actual themes of the experience.

BACKGROUND AND DEVELOPMENT

The industry known as "specialty travel" was largely developed due to the increasing accessibility of once unknown, unattainable, or presumed hostile environments. Demystifying the dangers of wilderness, natural terrain, foreign travel, and wildlife created a psychological acceptance of the citizen as explorer and the traveler as student. Popular books, magazines, and movies about remote and wild places or attractive exotic locations also helped establish widespread desire to experience these places. Television programming on cable channels such as the Discovery Channel, the Travel Channel, the Learning Channel, and Animal Planet constantly remind viewers of the world they can explore. Additionally, specially designed clothing, luggage, medicines, and the spread of the English language have all facilitated adventure travel. Vastly expanded international air service has made it easier and quicker to reach exotic locations. And Peace Corps volunteers and other returned international workers bring back information on remote places and services for travelers. Increasingly, local residents of attractive adventure destinations were acquiring specialized activity knowledge, a hospitality infrastructure, and familiarity with international languages to allow them to act as guides and hosts for foreign visitors.

Prior to the 1970s, when the first special interest travel companies developed, travel excursions to remote areas were truly an adventure, undertaken without the benefit of guide books, organized services, or knowledgeable local interpretation. Simply reaching foreign lands was an all-consuming activity and contacting area diseases was expected. In the 1970s and 1980s, pioneering companies like Mountain Travel, Earthwatch, JOURNEYS, and American Wilderness Experience established consistent activity and information-based itineraries that took the logistic hassles out of exotic travel and made it safer and healthier. Still, many people viewed specialty travel as more demanding or more uncertain than it really was and early growth was slow. Gradually, popular perception came

to match reality, and this has spurred growth for all types of specialty travel.

In the 1990s, political and nonprofit environmental and wildlife preservation organizations began an almost religious support of ecotourism. Previously, conservation organizations viewed tourism as a destructive force in natural habitats. Research, however, demonstrated the economic rationale for some tourist activity helping natural and cultural preservation. Organizations such as the World Wildlife Fund, Conservation International, Sierra Club, and Nature Conservancy sponsor trips for members. They derive significant funding from adventure advertising in publications, and these groups actively support and facilitate development of accommodations in and adjacent to natural preserves where they conduct research.

This alliance between adventure travelers, local residents, and environmentalists serves as significant rationale in development planning for new facilities. The Sierra Club has always offered many trips that easily qualify as "adventure travel" or "ecotravel." More recently, organizations such as the World Wildlife Fund, Nature Conservancy, and Conservation International have offered more comfortable, less-physically demanding ecotravel. Some of these organizations are investing in large, luxurious expensive lodges adjacent to the natural areas they seek to preserve. The traveler who desires pristine nature and culture experiences (and will pay well for it) provides tangible, measurable, and direct measure of nature preservation benefits. This has become more convincing to policy makers than hypothetical and elusive rationales of preserving genetic diversity, protecting natural capital, balancing global gas emissions, or even reducing flooding from disturbed watersheds. Increasingly, adventure travel companies are closely aligned with efforts to preserve natural and cultural environments.

The growth of specialty travel as a broad industry in the last 20 years also reflects globalization of the underlying activities. In a world economy people are more interested in seeing the rest of the world, not just their own community, in the context of their own experience and interests. The concept of "world records," "wonders of the world," and "world class experience" have drawn people to take up hobbies and past times that extend that sense of personal interest worldwide. Specialty travel providers must understand not only tourism concepts, but also the underlying interests of the travelers.

Another important element in the development of an expanding specialty travel industry over the past two decades has included equipment innovation. It is now possible to travel lighter, more comfortably, and more safely to previously hostile or inaccessible places. Safer climbing equipment, SCUBA gear, rafts, and other gear have taken much of the previous risk out of more adventurous travel. Lighter, stronger fabrics, better medicines, improved maps, field guides, and custom luggage have all become added incentives to prospective travelers seeking to turn fantasies into actual exploration.

PIONEERS IN THE FIELD

The merger of two of the oldest adventure travel companies formed Mountain Travel-Sobek (MTS) in 1991. MTS offers relatively high-priced group travel to all continents and is often considered a pioneer in both designing itineraries and promotional techniques. They currently offer more than 100 trips around the world. The company has changed ownership several times since its founding in 1967 and it is currently based in California.

JOURNEYS International, founded in 1978 by a former Peace Corps Volunteer and his wife, specializes in active natural and cultural explorations to more than 60 worldwide destinations. Many of JOURNEYS trips support local conservation and cultural preservation projects. Local experts in each destination lead the group's programs. JOURNEYS is particularly known for Himalayan trekking, active African safaris, and small group adventure cruises.

American Wilderness Experience (AWE) is one of the oldest U.S. adventure travel companies. AWE describes its mission as promoting adventure travel, with dedication to program quality, customer service, and a commitment to support wilderness preservation, recycling, and ecologically sensitive tours. All AWE programs take place in North America.

CURRENT CONDITIONS

Economic prosperity in the United States, retirement security, the financial success of baby boomers, and the information revolution have all served to expand the specialty tourism industry in the late 1990s. The Internet and the World Wide Web have made information about travel more accessible to anyone with a computer. They have also enabled travelers to contact local operators in remote places directly, resulting in slightly less use of U.S.-based travel organizers and agents. According to *Travel Weekly,* since the

mid-1990s airline ticket revenues have declined drastically as airlines reduce commissions and complete their own sales. While some adventure travel promoters suggest that this is a reason to expect travel agents will sell more adventure travel (a high-price product with at least a 10 percent commission to agents), fewer and fewer consumers are using travel agents to make their arrangements.

Yet, ironically, the same forces that expanded the industry have constrained the growth of new and established companies. The full employment economy has reduced the frequency and duration of American vacations, especially among the educated and high-income demographic groups. This has limited the growth of international trips and more lengthy expeditionary travel. The average length of American vacations was decreasing. As baby boomers aged, they were more able to afford the relatively high price of organized adventure travel. However, the debilitating effects of aging have constrained participation in more active and physically demanding activities such as trekking, skiing, mountaineering, and SCUBA diving.

Other difficulties have also arisen. Highly publicized stories of criminal or terrorist actions against tourists in Egypt, Uganda, Turkey, and Colombia have created a generalized fear of foreign trips in travelers who might otherwise leave the country. The risk of AIDS, cholera, virulent TB, and malaria in developing countries may seem like imposing obstacles to would be travelers. There is a trend toward higher visa fees, higher tourism taxes, and increased park visitor fees in many foreign destinations. This was pushing the cost of international travel above the rate of inflation, or the rate that travel prices increase in North America.

These trends of shorter vacations and perceived instability favor U.S.-based operators of domestic adventure experiences such as cycling, rafting, whale watching, canoeing, and skiing. Participation in these activities within the United States insulates customers from political risk and provides a complete adventure experience in a relatively short time period. Similarly, Canada, Europe, Australia, and New Zealand tend to be viewed as safe, stable, healthy destinations, and these will probably witness a higher rate by Americans visiting for specialty travel tours than less-developed areas of the world.

The Internet posed a dilemma for specialty tourism operators. If they create a Web site accessible to the public, they very visibly compete with other agents selling the same trip. This is particularly true if the site accepts direct bookings through the Web site or if they publish a toll-free telephone number for reservations. No tourism operators feel confident that a Web site will substitute for the traditional color brochure or catalog, yet virtually every operator feels a need for a credible Web presence. As a largely information-based industry, many operators feel Internet promotion will be increasingly important in the next decade and will provide an essential, if not fully defined promotional tool.

NEW BUSINESS START-UPS

Because reputation and references are so important for acquiring customers, new operators expect 4 to 6 lean years while getting started. Many who lack substantial start-up capital must keep a part time job as the business becomes established. Still, many newly established adventure travel companies do not survive into a second or third year. Due to the relatively high risk involved with travel to less-developed countries, insurance to cover professional liability and accidents is very expensive, especially for new operators without a proven safety record. This, combined with the well-known litigious character of the American consumer, has ended the existence of many start-up specialty travel businesses.

Another frequent cause of business failure is related to limited business opportunity. Specialty operators, for example, often have problems if they can only offer certain tours during certain seasons, and if the market they serve is too narrowly focused. Often, the specialty travel market is dispersed and hard to reach through traditional marketing avenues. Many excellent, well-planned, and fairly priced trips do not depart because the promoters failed to recruit enough participants in time to meet deposit or air reservation deadlines. When a specialty trip is sold to a broader market to achieve minimum enrollments, trip organizers and operators are often faced with participants with varied expectations and purposes. Still, according to the World Tourism Organization, as cited by the Ecotourism Society, 595 million travelers in 1997 spent an estimated $425 billion, and this expenditure was expected to grow by about 6.7 percent per year over the next two decades. The *Green Travel Newsletter* quotes the International Travel and Adventure Exposition organizers as estimating that Adventure travel is a $200-billion dollar industry, of which only 37 percent of tours are booked through travel agents.

INDUSTRY LEADERS

There are no dominant companies in the specialty travel field, though within different categories there are recognized leading firms. One of the first specialty travel companies, Earthwatch is unique as a nonprofit organization that actually sponsors scientific research on which travelers participate as paying expedition members. Earthwatch works with scientists who make support arrangements for volunteer assistants, and as a non-profit organization, some of the trips costs' are tax deductible.

International Expeditions, based in Helena, Alabama, specializes in quality guided nature explorations with particular focus on tropical rainforests and the African savannahs. They emphasize strong academic leadership and invest in training for many local guides in travel destinations. Another company, Wilderness Travels, was founded by former staff members of Mountain Travel in the late 1970s and offers quality group nature and cultural trips throughout the world. They have strong programs in the Galapagos, Peru, Turkey, and the Himalayas. Generally catering to the higher income market, these trips offer the best available standards of accommodation and dining in remote locations.

Backroads offers more than 150 different active vacations—bicycling, walking, hiking and multisport—in more than 85 destinations around the world. Abercrombie and Kent (A&K) of Oakbrook, Illinois, is an up-scale market, traditional travel company that bridges the conventional leisure travel market and specialty travel fields. Well known for cruises, safaris, and escorted trips to exotic locations, A&K is one of the most successful operators marketing its programs worldwide, primarily through travel agents. A&K has 27 offices worldwide and their tours travel to 100 countries across the globe.

Victor Emanuel Nature Tours (VENT) specializes in birding tours. One of the oldest birding companies, VENT offers trips featuring expert birders and uses the best available accommodations for its relatively high-priced programs. They are also designing a program for birding cruises. In 1998-99 they offered nearly 140 tours.

WORK FORCE

The Adventure Travel Society estimated in 1996 that there were more than 80,000 adventure tour operators worldwide. The Specialty Travel Index listed 600, most of whom were operators based in North America. This list just included the larger companies selling to the U.S. travel industry. The typical specialty travel operator was a small business employing the owner and 2 to 5 other people, none of whom were certified travel agents. There were no formal academic credentials required, though some guides required local licenses.

One of best aspects of working in the specialty tourism industry is the nature of the clientele. The prospect and committed traveler is usually healthy, well educated, and enjoy a high level of income. While this clientele has high expectations of responsiveness, communication, efficiency, and accuracy, they tend to be pleasant to talk with, reliable in paying expenses, and honest. Employees of specialty travel firms need to match these clients' standards for communication skills and integrity.

Most employees and owners of specialty travel companies do not spend time leading trips. While a single owner-operator-guide may be a basic model for operation, most people find that the challenge of running a profitable specialty travel business has more to do with understanding business, advertising, computers, communication, personnel management, and legal compliance than navigating difficult terrain. Most growing companies promoting international specialty travel require a competent staff of writers, sales people, reservation agents, bookkeepers, and computer technicians to remain profitable. Many companies contract with guides as freelancers for individual trips or for a season of trips. Professional credentials, licenses, or training may be required.

While leading or guiding trips may be the most fun and hold the most glamour, guide pay and benefits are usually quite low, and the work can be physically and psychologically exhausting. Guide burnout is common, and extended guiding can be hard on a marriage. Also, the work is often seasonal. Still, more people are seeking guide positions than are available for many types of trips. Most companies hiring guides require demonstrated leadership and communication skills, authoritative knowledge of the skills or contents of the activity, and some previous experience in the field. International specialty travel operators often hire local guides in destination countries, and company employees accompanying groups during international travel is relatively uncommon.

Specialty travel, especially adventure travel, is often a risky business. Owners of adventure companies are constantly concerned about safety, liability, and accurate record keeping. Errors in bookings, planning, reservations, or judgment can have extreme financial, legal, or medical consequences. At the same time, travel is traditionally a low-paying industry. According to the 1998-99 Occupational Outlook Handbook

quoting, *Travel Weekly,* "1996 median annual earnings of travel agents on straight salary with less than 1 year experience were $16,400; from 1 to 3 years, $20,400; from 3 to 5 years, $22,300." The article notes the problem this creates in competing for good people who can earn more in other industries.

In order to promote and sell the services a specialty tourist business offers, staff must have first-hand knowledge of the tours' activities and destinations. Being a specialized business, it requires more first-hand knowledge than generalized tour operators need. High quality, detailed written materials, reading lists, check lists, and pre-departure booklets must be constantly rewritten and revised to emphasize the capacity of the operator to provide a safe and satisfying trip.

Owners hiring staff into public or client contact positions must be cautious in educating the staff to represent the company's policies and products accurately. Satisfaction with the personal treatment a company affords the traveler is a major factor in the participant taking future trips or recommending the company to friends.

AMERICA AND THE WORLD

Adventure tourism growth is an international phenomenon, especially in Europe, where longer vacations are required. In general, adventure vacationers from Europe take trips more than three weeks in duration, while American and Canadian citizens generally take trips of two weeks or less. The challenge of permits, visas, acquiring local transport, and foreign languages and culture often compound the adventure for travelers outside of the United States and provide further incentive for the traveler to seek the help of a specialized operator to assist with these requirements. Responsible adventure travel operators provide extensive safety, medical, cultural, environmental, and ecological information to foreign-bound travelers to minimize problems, as many areas attractive to adventure travelers have no established local tourism industry. Accommodations, meals, standards of sanitation, legal and security services, and transportation fall far short of what would be reasonable minimum expectations in the United States.

Many international specialty travel operators pay special attention to the Travel Advisories and Warnings issued by the United States Department of State in planning or canceling trips to troubled areas. In addition, the advice and standards established by the Center for Disease Control in Atlanta often form a basis for the health and immunization suggestions given by operators to clients traveling overseas. Both of these organizations have Web sites and e-mail lists to which operators may subscribe for current information.

For Americans traveling overseas the most popular adventure destinations include the Himalayas for trekking, east and southern Africa for safaris, southern Europe for bicycling and sailing trips, Costa Rica and Belize for tropical nature tours, Peru for hiking and pre-Columbian culture experience, and Galapagos Islands of Ecuador and Antarctica for exploration cruises. Europe, perennially popular with conventional group tourists, also has a thriving specialty travel industry focusing on walking, bicycling, traditional cultural experiences, and dining and natural environment exploration.

Outer space is the new frontier for future adventure travel. Several companies suggest they are prepared to book commercial spacecraft as soon as it becomes possible. More terrestrial limits for future specialty trips include circumpolar exploration cruises and icebreaker expeditions to the North Pole. In Asia, companies are offering hiking trips to remote parts of Tibet and Yunnan, China, climbing in Kyrgystan, dinosaur digs in Mongolia and sea kayaking in the Far East. In Africa, adventurous travelers now travel in Mozambique, Ethiopia, Mali, Burkina Faso, Chad, and Cote d'Ivoire. Kilimanjaro climbs are extremely popular; however, Niger, Sudan, Somalia, the Congo, Rwanda, Algeria, and Libya are still beyond the interest of even the most adventurous traveler.

In Latin America, emerging destinations include Panama, where visitors combine tours of the Canal with rain forest exploration. In Bolivia, the native cultures of the Andes, Amazon rain forest, and Inca ruins are attracting increasing numbers of visitors. The unique ecosystems and reverse seasons of Argentina and Chile and the spectacular scenery of Patagonia hold increasing interest for North American visitors.

Significantly, however, most specialty travel trips Americans take are within North America. Canadian and U.S. National parks and forest wilderness trips are very popular. Departures of hiking, bicycling, horse-packing, canoeing, birding, diving, and rafting trips within North America are far more numerous and varied in cost, duration, and amenities than those that leave the continent. Marketing support from local,

state, and regional tourism boards eager to attract tourist to their areas can provide critical financial and even management assistance to companies seeking to bring specialty tourist to their own back yards.

FURTHER READING

"Adventure Travel Society." Englewood, CO: The Adventure Travel Society, 1999. Available from http://www.adventuretravel.com.

"Ecotourism Guidelines for Nature Tour Operators." North Bennington, VT: The Ecotourism Society, 1993. Available from http://www.ecotoourism.org/textfiles/stats.txt.

"Ecotourism Statistical Fact Sheet." North Bennington, VT: The Ecotourism Society. Available from http://www.ecotoourism.org/textfiles/stats.txt.

"Explorers Index." *EXPLORE Magazine,* 1999. Available from http://www.hillside-visual.com/explore/explorers/weblinks.html.

Green Travel Newsletter. Auburn, MA: Green Travel Network, 1999. Available from http://www.greentravel.com.

Jacobs, Judy. "Evolution of Operators." *Travel Counselor Special Report,* February 1999.

Karwacki, Judy. "Indigenous Ecotourism: Overcoming Challenges." *The Ecotourism Society Newsletter,* January-March 1999.

Lindberg, Kreg, et al. *Ecotourism: A Guide for Planners and Managers,* Vols. I & II. The Ecotourism Society, 1993.

McLaren, Deborah. *Rethinking Tourism and Ecotravel.* Kumarian Press, 1998.

Occupational Outlook Handbook 1998-99. Washington, DC: U.S. Bureau of Labor Statistics, 1998. Available from http://stats.bls.gov/ocohome.htm

"Queen of the Mountain: Operators are Developing More Women-only Itineraries." *Travel Weekly,* 10 October 1996.

"Specialty Travel Index." San Anselmo, CA: Specialty Travel Index ONLINE, 1999. Available from http://www.specialtytravel.com.

Specialty Travel Online. San Anselmo, CA: Specialty Travel Index ONLINE, 1999. Available at: http://spectrav.com/.

The World Tourism Organization. "World Vision 2020." *U.S. Department of State Travel Advisories,* 1997. Available from http://travel.state.gov.

—Will Weber

SPY AND SURVEILLANCE EQUIPMENT

INDUSTRY SNAPSHOT

Due to an increasingly affluent and litigious society, and an ever more competitive business climate, the demand for spy and surveillance equipment has never been greater. Many companies that manufacture surveillance products experienced double-digit growth in sales revenue from 1997 to 1998. Most retail sellers are independently owned stores with names such as Counter Spy Shop, Spy Mart, or Spy Shop International. Purveyors of spy equipment benefit from society's paranoia—they sell both the surveillance equipment and counter surveillance equipment. Widespread use of the Internet has lead to more spy shops—legitimate and otherwise—establishing Web sites to push their wares.

There are many reasons why people feel the need to outfit themselves with spy and surveillance equipment and there are plenty of gadgets to meet their needs. For businesses, these gadgets could save proprietary information. According to an April 2, 1999, article in *Time* magazine by Daniel Eisenberg, it is estimated that there was $25 billion in intellectual property thefts from U.S. corporations in 1997. To stem that tide, businesses are becoming more diligent in ferreting out dishonest employees. This process may be as simple as having a ceiling-mounted video camera or it may be as sophisticated as tiny video cameras secreted in walls, clocks, or lamps. Closed-circuit television sets are used to monitor areas such as retail stores and libraries. Retail establishments also use electronic tags, which trigger an alarm if someone tries to take the merchandise out of the store without having the tag deactivated or removed.

Everyday people turn to spy equipment both for protection and to gather or confirm information. Tiny cameras hidden in plants or trees can survey the doorway of a home, while motion detectors can detect intruders on property. Concerned parents are hiding cameras in pictures and even stuffed animals to watch over their children's care givers. Tracking devices allow non-custodial parents to keep track of their children's whereabouts; voice changers allow women to sound like men on the telephone or answering machine; and heat sensors let people figure out if that noise they heard in the middle of the night was a burglar.

ORGANIZATION AND STRUCTURE

With the popularity of spy equipment and the rush to meet the demand, many surveillance devices are very affordable. Once the province of law enforcement, employers, and the media, the average person may now have access to the latest spy equipment and all types of people are taking advantage of its easy availability. Sellers say their customers want to obtain information or confirm a suspicion. Reasons range from cheating spouses, monitoring of empty homes and apartment hallways, monitoring of nannies and babysitters, to the recording of conversations with employers to back up age- or sex-discrimination claims. Night vision binoculars can be very helpful to farmers trying to catch poachers, and those who fear bomb threats can check their mail with a portable bomb detector kit.

REGULATION OF SPY AND SURVEILLANCE EQUIPMENT

In September 1998, the Federal Communications Commission (FCC) ruled that the telecommunications

BEHIND THE
SCENES
OF THE NFL

By the end of the century the National Football League (NFL), like an untold number of businesses, customarily used video cameras as a security device, and few gave the practice a second thought. Early in 1999 the *New York Times,* and the *Washington Post* reported that video camera surveillance in NFL locker rooms was on the rise. In January of 1999 an estimated 25 percent of NFL franchises, including the New York Jets, reportedly had installed and were using video cameras in the players' locker rooms. Owners and agents justified the practice, at least in the case of the Jets, as an attempt to crack down on locker room thefts, in particular during practice sessions.

The Players' association acknowledged that it, too, was aware of the practice and that the franchises were operating within their rights to tape the players even in the locker rooms. One franchise owner, Art Modell, upheld the players' right to privacy and condemned the practice of video-taping the locker room. Modell asserted that he would never tolerate the practice.

---

industry had another 20 months in which to comply with a 1994 federal law that would allow law enforcement agencies to conduct increased surveillance activities on digital telephones. Companies affected by this decision include AT&T Wireless Services, Lucent Technologies, and Ericsson. Originally, telecommunication manufacturers had an October 1998 deadline to add new features to network switching equipment that law enforcement officials use. These enhancements will provide increased capabilities, such as being able to monitor more phone calls at one time and to handle call forwarding and conference calling features. The FCC deferred making a decision on network enhancements that might interfere with an individual's right to privacy, such as providing information about the location of cellular callers. In the late 1990s, technology could only locate the cellular network transmitter that was closest to the cellular user. However, companies were working to pinpoint the caller's location within 20 feet. This technology will be used in the 911 emergency system, but it is still undecided if it will be included in law enforcement surveillance networks.

It is illegal in the United States to manufacture, sell, or plant listening devices in order to eavesdrop on other people's conversations. It is also against federal law to import or advertise the devices that make eavesdropping possible. This law falls under the Om-

nibus Crime and Safe Streets Act of 1968. Any device that has no other purpose but "the surreptitious interception of wire, oral, or electronic communications" is illegal. As spy equipment sales increase, the Federal government has been cracking down on spy stores. In 1995, for example, U.S. Customs officials shut down 40 spy stores in 20 cities, charging them with the sale of illegal listening devices. The law is different, however, where it concerns the taping of one's own conversation, in person or over a telephone. That situation falls under state law and most state laws indicate that consent only has to be obtained from one person to record a conversation. Fourteen states indicate permission for recording must be obtained from all parties taking part in the conversation. Video taping is a different matter. Under federal law, it is generally allowed without the tapees knowing, as long as there is no accompanying audio recording. Exceptions to video recording include, for example, the setting up of video cameras in a company bathroom.

The contradictions within the federal and state laws are many. For example, someone can tape your conversation as long as they are with you, but not tape your conversation from a remote location. Someone can audio record on his or her own property without telling the other person, but cannot do that on the other person's property. In terms of criminalization, video recording is generally ignored, the consensus being it is alright as long as there is no audio.

The U.S. Congress passed a law in the fall of 1996 with stiff prison terms and fines for those convicted of corporate espionage. Unfortunately, this has not slowed the sale of counter surveillance equipment within the business community. Even with unequivocal federal laws concerning listening devices, it is an estimated multi-billion dollar industry in the United States. Millions of dollars worth of such devices are sold to U.S. citizens each day, purchased illegally from U.S. spy shops, through mail order, or via the Internet from foreign countries.

BACKGROUND AND DEVELOPMENT

Spy and surveillance equipment, especially the more sophisticated materials, used to be reserved for law enforcement. For years federal authorities turned a blind eye to those selling illegal bugging equipment, but ads began appearing in magazines from suppliers around 1980. As orders poured in and entrepreneurs set up shop, federal authorities began closer scrutiny of the shops. The reason was because law enforcement was seeing too many of the devices in the hands of criminals. According to the government, many offerings at spy shops are illegal and are for purposes such as corporate espionage, drug dealing, kidnapping, and other criminal activities.

CURRENT CONDITIONS

Today spying is not just for professionals, it's for everyone, including executives, spouses, lovers, and neighbors—not to mention criminals. Industry estimates show that sales grew from $10 billion in 1985 to $40 billion in the late 1990's.

Federal authorities are still cracking down on the sale of illegal listening devices. In March of 1997 the then largest chain of spy shops, The Spy Factory, was shut down after owner Ronald Kimball, formerly a Drug Enforcement Administration agent, plead guilty to importing and selling illegal bugging equipment. The transmitters sold by the company were stronger than the Federal Communications Commission allowed and they used frequencies reserved only for the U.S. government and military.

It is becoming easier to record other people without their knowledge, yet harder to detect when it is being done. All of this contributes to a more suspicious and careful society and helps to drive the trend in counter surveillance equipment, according to the National Association of Investigative Specialists (NAIS). Among other reasons given for the trend are the high divorce rate, greater disposable income, and increasing numbers of people starting home-based businesses. Since many such home start-up firms are in the information field, their owners are concerned about the need to protect their proprietary data.

With the cold war over, unemployed surveillance specialists are being recruited by major corporations to spy on competitors. From 1997 to 1998, the FBI almost tripled its investigations into corporate espionage. A survey of 38 federal law enforcement agencies reveals the most common ways in which corporations are spied upon: hidden cameras, 83 percent; audio bugging, 71 percent; still photography, 68 percent; and night vision systems, 63 percent. Intercepting various communications is popular too: through computers, 17 percent; electronic mail, 17 percent; cellular phones, 14 percent; and satellite transmissions, 11 percent.

The U.S. State Department estimates over $888 million worth of eavesdropping devices are sold in the United States each year, with an estimated $8.2 trillion in losses to targeted U.S. corporations. The Department says there are almost 3000 sellers of spy

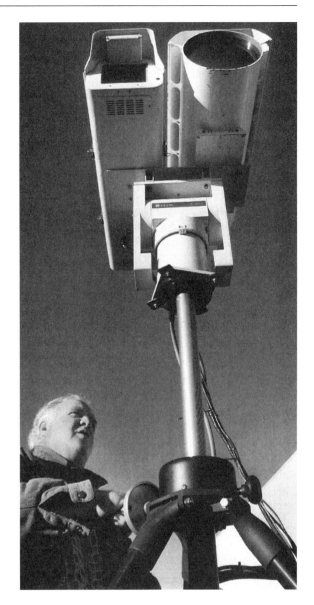

A U.S. Border patrolman demonstrates a surveillance camera during the Immigration and Naturalization Service's annual conference. (AP Photo/Eric Draper.)

equipment who offer over 712,000 illegal bugging devices, with equipment priced from $15 to $2,895. The sellers make huge profits; the State Department estimates an annual figure of $812,000 per company. These numbers do not include the legal sale of eavesdropping devices to law enforcement. Many who sell spy equipment protest that they themselves do not sell listening devices outlawed by federal law, yet almost all acknowledge that the contraband equipment can easily be bought elsewhere.

There are three basic categories of equipment available through spy shops—do it yourself audio and video surveillance, counter surveillance, and personal or corporate protection. For surveillance, there are large cameras for deterrence and small ones that can be hidden just about anywhere—in a briefcase, a tree or houseplant, a pair of glasses, a radio, or even attached to a fiber-optic cable that can be easily slipped under a door. Supersensitive microphones have made for higher quality audio recording. A recorder the size of a credit card or cigarette pack can be slipped into a pocket and a transmitter can be hidden in a pen, the back of a tie, or in a hat.

To catch those who may be "wired" or to find that hidden camera, spy shops offer counter surveillance equipment. A bug detector that looks like a pager will vibrate when it detects hidden microphones. There are products that will disable a listening device while still allowing the phone itself to work. If you feel like someone is watching you, the industry abounds with private investigators who will "sweep" your home or office, looking for equipment.

For personal protection there are motion detectors, heat sensors, bomb detectors, bulletproof clothing, umbrellas, cars, and an electrified briefcase to protect laptop computers. Tracking devices to keep track of items or people can be easily hidden, just as cameras and bugging devices. Communications gadgets include voice changers and voice scramblers. Semen testing kits are available as well to detect the substance's presence on clothing.

The cost for spy equipment varies widely; one store said its anti-tapping systems run from $300 to $60,000 and its bug detectors vary from $500 to $40,000. Tracking devices can cost up to $20,000. A top-of-the-line video camera and system may cost $4,500, but one for individual use can be had for $400. A car with armor, ramming bumpers, bulletproof glass, blinding lights, and smoke, tear-gas, and oil slick generators can easily run over $100,000. An electrified briefcase goes for $895, voice changers for $300, semen testing kits for $60, and sunglasses equipped with small mirrors so you can see who is following you cost $10.

INDUSTRY LEADERS

Spy shop owners are generally secretive and cautious. There is no industry organization per se, but most shops are related to private detectives and investigators. Some of the more well-known spy shops are Quark International in New York, The Spy Shop in Chicago, and Spy Supplies International in Gwin-

nett, Georgia. Those with more than one location include the Counter Spy Shop, U-Spy, and Spy Outlet.

The equipment for sale in spy shops comes from various sources. Military- and law enforcement-grade equipment may be adapted for civilian use. Some items are consumer electronics products retrofitted or rewired for surveillance work, either by the manufacturer or the owner of the spy shop. Leading manufacturers include Checkpoint Systems, Inc., Sensormatic Electronics Corp., Sentry Technology Corp., Ultrak, Inc., and Vicon Industries, Inc.

Thorofare, New Jersey-based Checkpoint Systems, Inc., manufactures closed-circuit television systems and electronic tags, which are put on store merchandise to detect shoplifting. Checkpoint has a 33 percent share of the U.S. retail surveillance market. For the year ended December 1998, the company had sales of $362 million and over 3,600 employees. Checkpoint has 350,000 surveillance system in place around the world and its clients include American Stores Company, Canadian Tire, Toys "R" Us, and Pep Boys.

Sensormatic Electronic Corporation, based in Boca Raton, Florida, holds more than 50 percent of the anti-shoplifting surveillance market. The company makes closed-circuit television and video systems, electronic tags, and labels. The company reported sales of $987 million for the year ended June 1998. This represented a decrease of nearly 4 percent from the previous year. For 1998 Sensormatic had a net loss of $37 million and 5,800 employees. The client list for Sensormatic includes Kmart, Hill's Department Store, Hudson's Bay Company, and The Home Depot.

Sentry Technology Corporation of Hauppauge, New York, manufacturers retail surveillance products and its clients include Lowe's Home Centers and Target Department Stores. Sales for 1998 were $28 million, a 15 percent increase from the previous year. The company employed over 200 employees in 1998, an increase of 19 percent from 1997.

Ultrak, Inc. of Lewisville, Texas, is a leader in the surveillance equipment field. The company designs, manufactures, and services many types of video surveillance systems and sells items under license from Mitsubishi, Panasonic, and Sony. Using a variety of proprietary brand names, Ultrak markets products such as cameras, digital recorders, and audio equipment. A publicly held company, Ultrak reported sales of $195 million in 1998, up 3.4 percent from 1997. The company had net sales of $3.6 million and employed 710 employees in 1998. In March 1999 the company sold its 10 percent ownership of Securion 24

Co., which was the sole distributor of Ultrak products in Japan. This move will allow Ultrak to expand and add additional distributors in Japan. Ultrak was named one of America's 100 fastest growing companies by *Fortune* magazine in 1997.

Vicon Industries, Inc. manufactures 600 surveillance and security products, such as video recorders and cameras, monitors, and motion detector devices. Vicon's clients include Bank One Stadium in Phoenix, Arizona; the MGM Grand Hotel and Casino in Las Vegas, Nevada; and the U.S. Postal Service. For the year ended September 1998, Vicon had 217 employees and reported sales of $63 million, an increase of 23 percent over the previous year.

WORK FORCE

The *Occupational Outlook Handbook,* published by the U.S. Bureau of Labor Statistics (BLS), notes that private detectives and investigators spend much of their time on surveillance. Licensing is required by most state and local laws, yet there is no formal training required. Most people in the field, however, tend to be on their second career, frequently having retired from the military or from law enforcement. There were approximately 58,000 people working as private detectives and investigators in 1996, with about 17 percent of these self-employed. Forty-two percent worked in retail stores, with another 36 percent employed by detective agencies. The BLS predicts the field will grow as fast as the average through 2006. Income varies widely, with security and loss prevention directors and vice presidents of security earning an average of $67,700 in 1996, investigators earning an average of $37,800, and detectives in retail stores earning an average of $19,100. Private investigators fees range from $50 to $150 per hour.

The National Association of Investigative Specialists surveyed its members and predicted the following specialties would be hot for 1998: insurance claims investigation, process servers, background checks, missing persons location, surveillance, executive protection, countermeasures, fraud investigation, criminal investigation, and accident investigation. Domestic investigations, namely divorce cases, used to be the number one specialty and the biggest income provider to many private investigators; they are now listed as number 13 on the NAIS list. The specialty of information broker was among the top five until recently; in 1998 it was listed at number 20. Child abuse investigations were not thought of as a specialty until recently; they are now listed at number 18 and the NAIS

predicts the trend will continue. The NAIS also notes that fraud investigations of all types are on the rise.

AMERICA AND THE WORLD

While use of eavesdropping devices outside of law enforcement is illegal in the United States, such usage may be legal in many other countries. Overseas companies need merely place advertisements in magazines or set up shop on the Internet to conduct business where federal law enforcement has no significant jurisdiction. The equipment coming into the United States is imported mainly from France, Germany, Lebanon, Italy, Canada, Israel, England, Japan, Taiwan, and South Africa. The U.S. State Department estimates $496 million worth of illegal surveillance equipment is imported into the United States each year.

Ultrak, an industry leader in the design and manufacture of surveillance and security equipment, announced in May 1998 that it was forming Ultrak Europe to manage much of the company's overseas business. In 1996 and 1997 Ultrak purchased four companies in France, Germany, the United Kingdom, and Italy. Those companies, along with one in South Africa, comprise Ultrak's foreign holdings. Ultrak sold off its Japanese affiliate in 1999. Headquartered near Dallas, Texas, Ultrak offers a comprehensive line of systems and products for the surveillance and security products markets. The firm is traded on the NASDAQ under the symbol ULTK.

RESEARCH AND TECHNOLOGY

While technological advances in many areas of the industry are impressive, perhaps the most significant advances are evident in video surveillance. Cameras can now photograph through an opening as small as 0.0625 inches, allowing them to be hidden just about anywhere, including inside telephones, ceiling speakers, desk lamps, even stuck behind a tie or under a hat. The Sony EVO is billed as the world's smallest videotape recorder, able to fit in the small of the back or in a fanny pack.

The newest in video surveillance comes from Loronix Information Systems, Inc. in Durango, Colorado. The company developed a closed circuit television (CCTV) that records digitally, allowing for better picture quality, along with the ability to fax, print, or send images over the Internet with complete security. The system eliminates the need for videotapes and VCRs and was designed to allow use on companies' existing surveillance systems.

FURTHER READING

"40 Stores Selling Spy Equipment Are Raided." *Star Tribune,* 6 April 1995.

The American Society for Industrial Security Home Page, 7 July 1998. Available from http://www.asisonline.org.

Barrett, Greg. "Gumshoes, Government and You: Is Everyone a Spy?" *Gannett News Service,* 24 March 1998.

———. "James Bond Wannabes Beware." *Gannett News Service,* 24 March 1998.

Casimiro, Steve. "The Spying Game Moves Into the U.S. Workplace." *Fortune,* 30 March 1998.

"Checkpoint Becomes Pep Boys' Exclusive Provider of Loss Prevention Systems." *NewsAlert,* 5 March 1999. Available from http://www.newsalert.com.

The Counter Spy Shop Home Page, 6 July 1998. Available from http://counterspyshop.com.

De Yampert, Kathy. "You Spy? Store Lets You Do the Snooping." *Gannett News Service,* 25 July 1995.

Eisenberg, Daniel. "Eyeing the Competition." *Time,* 22 March 1999.

"Federal Authorities Shut Down the Spy Factory." *Reuters News Service,* 10 March 1997.

Goldstein, Marilyn. "516 Spies Who Came in From Burbs." *Newsday,* 7 April 1995.

The Granite Island Group Home Page, 22 June 1998. Available from http://tscm.com.

Malanowski, Jamie. "Silicon Bond Looking to become a Superspy?" *Time,* 1 June 1997.

Markoff, John. "A Call for Digital Surveillance Is Delayed." *The New York Times,* 14 September 1998.

The National Association of Investigative Specialists Home Page, 19 June 1998. Available from http://pimall.com/nais .html.

The National Security Institute Home Page, 22 June 1998. Available from http://www.nsi.org.

Nurse, Doug. "Scoping Out the Spy Shop: Eyes and Ears— Gwinnett Store Carries Gadgets for Private Citizens' Undercover Research." *The Atlanta Journal and Constitution,* 23 November 1997.

"Sensormatic Receives Five-Year Commitment from Hudson's Bay Company to Install Anti-Theft Techonolgies in All Its Stores." *NewsAlert,* 27 January 1999. Available from http://www.newsalert.com.

"Ultrak Announces the Formation of Ultrak Europe." *Business Wire,* 11 May 1998. Available from http://www .businesswire.com.

"Ultrak Announces Sale of Japanese Affiliate; Company Sells Ownership Interest in Securion 24 Co., Ltd." *NewsAlert,* 10 March 1999. Available from http://www.newsalert .com.

"Ultrak, Inc." *Hoover's Online,* 2 July 1998. Available from http://www.hoovers.com.

"Ultrak Introduces 5-Inch Miniature Surveillance Domes." *Business Wire,* 15 June 1998. Available from http://www .businesswire.com.

U.S. Bureau of Labor Statistics Home Page, 12 April 1999. Available from http://www.bls.gov.

—Lisa Karl, updated by Katherine Wagner

SUPERDRUGS

Infectious diseases such as bacterial pneumonia, meningitis, and tuberculosis were considered conquered during the 1970s. Once among the leading causes of death throughout the world, it seemed that antibiotics—penicillin, erythromycin, and tetracycline—were on the way to eradicating these killer diseases. Due to over-prescription and careless use of antibiotics over the years, however, resistant strains of the old diseases evolved and are proving difficult, if not impossible, to treat with the older drugs. Death rates from diseases long in abeyance are on the rise at alarming rates. Drug-resistant bacteria—superbugs—have precipitated the dawn of the post-antibiotic era, and the search for new "superdrugs" is underway. Major pharmaceutical companies have enough faith in the quest to invest millions of dollars in small start-up companies using cutting-edge technologies like genetic engineering to develop tomorrow's antibiotics, which will eliminate the resistant strains of superbugs.

The International Congress of Infectious Diseases reported that resistant infections can triple the cost of hospital care, and the Institute of Medicine, a part of the National Academy of Sciences, estimated that the cost of treating resistant infections in the United States may be more than $30 billion per year. Antibiotics themselves account for 10 percent of all pharmaceutical sales, and the world market was estimated at $22 billion annually. Thus far, few new superdrugs have been approved to combat the resistant strains, but the research goes on—both as a search for weapons to use against diseases and to keep the antibiotics market share high among pharmaceutical sales.

ORGANIZATION AND STRUCTURE

The "superdrug industry," while part of the long-established pharmaceutical industry, is actually emerging as an industry in its own right. Although tremendous demand exists for these products, superdrug companies engage almost exclusively in research. The industry has brought virtually no products to market, and most of the smaller companies have not yet turned a profit, existing on venture capital, government grants, and research and development.

The industry can be divided into two broad sectors. One is comprised of traditional pharmaceutical companies, large multinationals who, for the most part, have been manufacturing antibiotics since the 1950s. The result of years of pharmaceutical research and the basis of future research efforts are libraries consisting of hundreds of thousands of chemical compounds. Most of these compounds have been developed and tested over the years but have not been used in commercial pharmaceuticals or prototypes. They may be chemical variants of commercial pharmaceutical ingredients. They may be compounds that have exhibited interesting or useful characteristics that companies were unable to exploit in medicines. Compounds may be derived from animal or botanical sources, or, increasingly, may be designed on a molecular level to possess particular pharmaceutical properties. New technologies in drug design have increased tremendously the pace at which compounds are being added to these chemical storehouses of knowledge. (Also see chapter in this book on Molecular Design.)

Traditionally, when a new drug is sought to cure a disease, the compounds in these vast chemical libraries are tested on the pathological organism or condition on a mass-production scale until one compound exhibits a promising or desired result. It is then refined into a medication fit for human use. When bacteria emerge that are resistant to a particular antibiotic, the traditional response is to find another agent that will defuse the resistance and "piggyback" it onto the antibiotic, enabling it to function again. It has been determined in the medical world that bacteria will eventually develop resistance to such combinations. Consequently, drug research is moving away from simple modification toward techniques like gene technology and automated drug screening to develop novel agents that bacteria have never encountered.

With the failure of pharmaceutical science to deal with viral illnesses (like HIV), and with the rapidly increasing number of resistant bacteria, smaller, high-tech start-up companies appeared in the 1980s and 1990s. Such companies sought to approach the problem of resistance from a different angle. Rather than "piggybacking" new drugs onto old drugs to break bacterial defenses, these companies began to use techniques like genetic engineering to determine weak points in a pathogen's DNA. The techniques are usually based on the companies' own proprietary technologies, which they developed themselves or licensed from a university.

The most important start-up companies in the superdrug industry produce no pharmaceutical products themselves. Some license proprietary technology to traditional pharmaceutical companies for use in research programs. For example, Genome Therapeutics developed a database of genetic information on the most important drug-resistant bacteria, and then licensed particular sequences of its staphylococcus aureus database to Schering-Plough for its superdrug research.

Smaller companies frequently form research partnerships with pharmaceutical firms. The small firms bring unique technology to the partnership, and the larger companies bring their chemical library and company infrastructure. Pharmaceutical products resulting from such research are licensed exclusively to the larger partner, with the smaller receiving a licensing fee and royalty payments. The smaller firms reap the benefit of the partner's enormous research, product development, marketing, and distribution resources. The larger partner usually also contracts to make equity investments in the smaller firm and milestone payments as predetermined stages in the development process are passed. Among the collaborations:

- Cubist Pharmaceutical has collaborations with Bristol-Myers Squibb Co., Merck & Co., Neurogen Corp., Helios, Novartis Pharma AG, and ArQule. Cubist will use its proprietary technology for drug lead selection and whole-cell screening.

- Genome contracted with Astra Hassle AB for over $22.5 million to develop therapeutic, diagnostic, and vaccine products for use against gastrointestinal and other diseases caused by the *Helicobacter pylori* bacterium. The company also has a $45-million collaboration with Schering-Plough Corp. targeting anti-infectives for drug-resistant *Staphylococcus aureus* and other strains.

- Microcide has an agreement with Pfizer for genetic research with the aim to produce novel classes of broad spectrum antibiotics. Collaborations have produced milestone payments and are potentially worth $32 million to Microcide for each product developed. In 1999 the agreement was expanded to include the investigation of compounds for animal health markets.

REGULATION

Superdrugs, like all pharmaceuticals, are subject to approval by the U.S. Food and Drug Administration (FDA) before they can be sold in the United States. They must be proven safe and effective for human use. To that end, they are required to undergo pre-clinical tests followed by three clinical trials on healthy and ill human subjects. The entire approval process can last as long as 15 years; however, the FDA has sought to reduce the length of time for the final approval process. A user fee program, which was refined under the Food and Drug Modernization Act of 1997, allows the FDA to hire more reviewers to speed up approvals. In 1998, 30 drugs received approval in an average of 11.7 months, compared with a 30-month average per drug before user fees. The law also requires the FDA to aim to review "priority" drugs within six months, and to facilitate patient access to experimental drugs.

To facilitate patient access the FDA has two fast-track programs that might apply to certain classes of superdrugs. "Expedited development and review" applies to drugs designed for patients with diseases that are considered life threatening, or that cause major, irreversible consequences. Among these are diseases or infections for which there are no satisfactory therapies, like drug-resistant tuberculosis and pneumonia. The FDA expedites the review of experimental therapies that qualify for this program. The "accelerated approval program" is intended for new drugs that provide meaningful therapeutic benefits to patients that

Pioneer ALEXANDER FLEMING, 1881-1955
FATHER OF PENICILLIN

Alexander Fleming was born in a farmhouse in Lochfield, Ayrshire, Scotland, on August 6, 1881, and educated in modest circumstances. While pursuing an M.B. and B.S. at London University after his successful completion of medical school in 1906, Fleming concurrently accepted a job at St. Mary's Medical School as a junior laboratory assistant. In 1908 he earned his degrees with honors, and immediately passed the surgeons' exams. However, Fleming chose to stay in laboratory research, focusing mainly on the prevention and treatment of bacterial infection. He was at the forefront of his area of expertise and, despite the imperfections of the first antibacterial agents, remained dedicated to the belief that a safe and effective antibacterial substance could be found. Fleming was particularly motivated to find an effective yet safe substance after witnessing the horrible suffering caused by bacterial infections during World War I.

In 1928, Fleming serendipitously discovered his second and most famous antibacterial substance: penicillin. Ironically, one of the main factors that led to the discovery of penicillin was Fleming's own untidy habits. Instead of the normal practice of promptly discarding bacterial culture plates, Fleming held on to his plates far beyond their usefulness. On one particular plate he noticed that a strange mold contaminant had inhibited the growth of the disease-causing bacteria that had been cultured on the plate. Fleming isolated the mold for further investigation, and named the bacteria-killing component of the mold "penicillin."

Fleming, however, was unable to effectively communicate the potential importance of his discovery. His colleagues had little interest, and Fleming could not clearly express that penicillin, unlike former bacteriolytic agents, could actually inhibit disease-producing bacteria. He subsequently made only a few unenthusiastic references to penicillin in later papers and lectures and used it mainly as a laboratory convenience for keeping his vaccine cultures free of certain bacteria. It is unclear if Fleming actually realized the therapeutic powers of penicillin. His writings are vague on this point.

After news of penicillin spread, Fleming began receiving most of the recognition and fame for its discovery. He was knighted in 1944 and in 1945 shared the Nobel Prize in medicine. He died in 1955.

existing treatments lack. This program is generally limited to drugs for patients who are unresponsive or intolerant to other available therapies. The FDA may place certain restrictions on the early approval. For example, use may be limited to certain clinics or to specially trained physicians, or contingent on the accompanying provision of other medical procedures.

BACKGROUND AND DEVELOPMENT

In 1928, Alexander Fleming accidentally discovered the lethal effects that penicillin has on bacteria. The fungus killed colonies of bacteria. Although Fleming established that penicillin killed *Pneumococcus* and *Streptococcus* bacteria, it was not until 1941 that Howard W. Florey and Ernst B. Chain purified penicillin and demonstrated its antibiotic properties at Oxford University.

Work on penicillin continued throughout the 1940s and by the 1950s, and penicillin was recognized as a miracle drug. It was soon joined by other antibiotics, including the cephalosporins, tetracycline, streptomycin, erythromycin, and sulfa drugs.

In the 1970s most doctors believed that infectious diseases would soon be wiped out. This optimism

proved premature, however, and by the 1990s, the medical community recognized that many illnesses believed to have been conquered were reappearing. Since 1985, with the appearance of drug-resistant strains, tuberculosis rates have begun rising dramatically in the United States, the country that once had the world's lowest incidence of the disease. As Judith Braffman-Miller wrote, "In 1941, 10,000 units of penicillin administered four times daily for four days cured patients of pneumococcal pneumonia. Today a patient can receive 24,000,000 units of penicillin a day and still die of pneumococcal meningitis." It is estimated that in 1998 more than 1 million Americans contracted an antibiotic-resistant infection, and 60,000 died from it.

Ironically, the success of antibiotics over the last 40 years has contributed directly to the rise of resistant strains. The longer bacteria are exposed to a drug, the faster that resistant strains are able to become dominant. In the 1940s, when penicillin was being developed, researchers noted that whenever the drug killed a batch of germs, some survived and displayed resistance to its properties. Those bacteria would then multiply and pass the genes of resistance on to future generations. In bacteria such reproduction occurred with breathtaking speed, and new generations appeared every 15 minutes or so. Furthermore, bacteria were observed as being able to exchange genetic material via little packets of DNA called plasmids. Drug-resistant bacteria were in this way able to pass resistance on to as-yet nonresistant strains, which would then reproduce.

Doctors and patients both contribute to the problem. For example, doctors often prescribe antibiotics when they are not indicated as treatment for the common cold, an illness caused by any number of viruses that are not responsive to antibiotics. Patients, on the other hand, often stop taking antibiotics as soon as they start feeling better instead of continuing the full regimen prescribed by a physician. In such cases, resistant bacteria are thus given an opportunity to survive, multiply, and become dominant. In 1996, the Centers for Disease Control and Prevention launched a public service campaign against the overuse and misuse of antibiotics.

Pharmaceutical companies responded by fighting the problem one-on-one: if a bacterium develops an enzyme to digest an antibiotic, researchers combine two drugs, the original antibiotic and another to short-circuit the enzyme. The strategy is defensive and reactive in that scientists wait for resistance to develop and then act to modify an old solution to the new development. But bacteria are able to develop resistance more quickly than scientists can react. This is particularly true in regard to patients with compromised immune systems.

The drug of last resort during the late 1990s, the one that doctors turn to when infections are resistant to all others, is vancomycin. More than 95 percent of hospital-acquired *S. aureus* infections are resistant to penicillin or ampicillin. Vancomycin is the only effective drug for these cases. But even this is not an ideal antibiotic. Known to produce severe side effects and inefficient at penetrating the brain, vancomycin is ineffective against penicillin-resistant meningitis bacteria. Additionally, in 1989 hospitals began reporting rapid increases in vancomycin resistance in enterococci (VRE), also common in hospitals. Hospitals began to see how increased VRE can lead to cross-resistance in *S. aureus*. Strains of *S. aureus* with intermediate resistance to vancomycin were reported in Japan in 1996 and in two different states in the United States in 1997. For the time being, there is no drug to follow up treatment with vancomycin. Public health officials fear that we could be rapidly approaching a window of vulnerability in which the existing antibiotics are no longer effective and new ones have not yet been developed to take their place.

In early 1997, the FDA approved a new antibiotic, sparfloxacin, manufactured as Zagam by Rhone-Poulenc Rorer. Studies later that year showed its efficacy in treating lower respiratory tract infections caused by *S. pneumoniae* and other bacteria. Other new drugs are on the horizon but most are awaiting FDA approval. The payoffs of large investments of time and money in research may be near; however, several companies have antibiotics from novel classes in Phase II and Phase III clinical trials.

CURRENT CONDITIONS

In early 1999, IntraBiotics, Inc. had in-licensed four novel classes of antibiotic technologies. The company had three products in Phase II trials including ramoplanin ointment, designed to prevent hospital-acquired *S. aureus* infections. The company licensed rights to develop and market the drug in the United States and Canada from Bioresearch Italia. Cubist Pharmaceuticals formally initiated both Phase I and Phase II clinical trials for daptomycin, which targets vancomycin-resistant enterococci, methicillin-resistant *S. aureus,* and the intermediately resistant *S. aureus* strains. Pharmacia and Upjohn's Zyvox, another first in a new class, entered Phase III trials, after very promising Phase II results against numerous enterococci, *S. aureus S. epidermis* isolates, including vancomycin-resistant strains.

Other researchers are looking into vaccines, which may be a better defense against bacterial disease than antibiotics, since they utilize the body's natural defenses. Wyeth-Lederle Vaccines and Pediatrics developed a vaccine shown to protect infants from infection by pneumococcus bacteria, the leading cause of ear infections and deadly meningitis. Merck & Co. are developing a pneumococcal vaccine for children to supplement the adult vaccine. In addition, some companies are developing medications to deal with drug-resistant fungi, which presents a potential problem for individuals with compromised immune systems.

Paradoxically, future success in this industry will entail scaling back sales and controlling the distribution of antibiotics. Physicians and public health officials agree that bacteria will find a way to adapt to new drugs. The Center for Disease Control (CDC) is recommending that doctors prescribe antibiotics only when clearly necessary and has issued more stringent guidelines for the use of all antibiotics. It has also been suggested that antibiotics be rotated—that is, that certain antibiotics should be taken out of circulation for a time to limit bacterial exposure to them; but research in Great Britain in 1998 found a common bacterium strain resistant to streptomycin, an older drug to which it had never been exposed and that had not been used for decades.

New evidence emerged in 1998 that growth promoters—minute concentrations of antibiotics—in the food supply may be encouraging resistance. Henrik Wegener, a Danish researcher, sequenced the gene responsible for vancomycin resistance and found resistance-related mutations among animals but not among people, suggesting that some resistant bacteria may be passed to humans from animals. He also found that a growth promoter now used in poultry is chemically similar to Synercid in the United States and launched as the next powerful line of defense for vancomycin-resistant infections. Studies have already shown that animals are resistant to Synercid; and the next powerful antibiotic in line for human use after Synercid, Ziracin, is almost identical to a growth promoter widely used in poultry.

In 1999, two strains of the most common hospital bacteria, staphylococcus and enterococcus, were resistant to nearly all antibiotics, including tetracycline, streptomycin, and sulfa drugs as well as common disinfectants like formaldehyde, chlorine, and iodine. A danger now looming is that vancomycin-resistant enterococcus will pass its resistance on to S. aureus, a common source of hospital infection. Vancomycin remains one of the few drugs to which methicillin-resistant bacteria responds. That susceptibility too may be weakening; in at least four cases S. aureus failed to respond to vancomycin. In 1998, British health authorities found a strain of Pseudomonos aeruginosa, which causes serious secondary infections in cystic fibrosis and leukemia sufferers, that was virtually resistant to all antibiotics. In cases of vancomycin-resistant enterococci—up to 30 percent in some hospitals—the death rate is well over 50 percent.

A recent survey of major American and Japanese pharmaceutical companies showed that 50 percent had cut back or completely ended antibiotic research programs in the belief that the market was saturated. Nonetheless, the number of medicines and vaccines in development rose from 79 in 1994 to 125 in 1996. The most promising are believed to be the drug families that include Pharmacia & Upjohn's linezolid, Rhone-Poulenc Rorer's Synercid (quinopristin/dalfopristin), and Pfizer's Trovan (trovafloxacin). Shering-Plough is resuming development of another promising class, the everninomicins, after having abandoned efforts 20 years ago because there was no market for it.

In 1998, the FDA granted limited approval for Synercid, one of a group called streptogramins that is also the first new antibiotic type to have been approved

in a decade. In clinical trials with patients who had severe infections associated with gram-positive bacteria, 88 percent responded to Synercid, while only 50 percent responded to vancomycin. One new investigational drug is linezolid, which is active against a broad range of bacteria that includes S. pneumoniae, the leading cause of illness and death from severe infection in the United States, and two other common causes of hospital-acquired infections. Linezolid is one of the oxazolidinones, which act by inhibiting protein synthesis. In one case, the linzolid supplied by Pharmacia and Upjohn under the accelerated approval program is attributed to saving the life of a patient who contracted a vancomycin-resistant bloodstream infection.

Approved through the accelerated global development program in late 1997 was Pfizer's Trovan® (trovafloxin), which is regarded as a potential superdrug. It was approved for the largest number of uses ever included in an initial drug approval in the United States. It is also the first oral antibiotic ever approved for oral use in surgery. Trovafloxin is a once-daily drug that is expected to be most effective in dealing with penicillin-resistant pneumococcus. It works by interfering with bacterial reproduction. Other drugs approved in 1998 were cefdinir, a broad-spectrum cephalosporin; grepafloxacin, a fluoroquinolone intended to treat lung infections; and rifapentine, the first new anti-tuberculosis medication in 25 years.

The long-term strategy of a large segment of the pharmaceutical industry is being determined by drug resistance. The search for superdrugs has presented a new set of challenges. Among them is the need to develop novel agents, i.e., drugs that bacteria have never been confronted with and to which they have little resistance. Only one new chemical class of anti-infective drugs was approved by the FDA between 1976 and 1996. Additionally, the industry has to continue to develop innovative research methods if it expects to find effective new agents quickly. If it is to go on the offensive against resistant bacteria and prevent resistant strains from reaching epidemic levels, pharmaceutical firms must also learn to predict how bacterial resistance develops against new antibiotics. Finally, a breed of instant tests is needed that will enable doctors to distinguish bacterial infections from viral infections.

INDUSTRY LEADERS

Cubist Pharmaceuticals, founded in 1992, has identified as drug targets 20 enzymes that bacteria use to bind amino acids into protein. In 1998 the company changed its corporate strategy from drug discovery and development to a fully biopharmaceutical corporation by restructuring and adding a marketing team. Cubist plans to launch its new antibiotic Daptomycin in North America and will enter marketing agreements for its launch in Europe and Japan. In addition to its focused efforts on Daptomycin, the company has a proprietary technology to identify therapeutic targets and create high-throughput screening assays for promising drug leads available for licensing.

Cubist has collaborative agreements with Bristol-Myers Squibb, Merck & Company, and Pfizer to develop anti-infective drugs in its target-based Synthetase Program. Cubist has agreed to screen various genetic targets it has sequenced against compounds in the libraries of its partners. Partnerships with ArQuele, Neurogen, and Helios use Cubists technology to screen the partners' diverse sets of potential drug compounds. In early 1999 Cubist signed a research and licensing agreement with Novartis Pharma AG for use of Cubist's proprietary technology for the discovery and validation of novel antibacterial targets, potentially worth $33 million for Cubist.

Genome Therapeutics, founded in the mid-1980s, is one of the pioneers in the superdrug industry. Genome's corporate focus is researching the genetic basis of disease. It conducts human gene discovery programs to identify the genes responsible for asthma and osteoporosis. The company's superdrug research centers on its pathogen program. The two most important technologies are whole genome pathogen sequencing, which involves decoding and representing the genetic structure of a pathogen, and bioinformatics, which is the application of computers, software, and databases to the analysis of genomic research in order to compare sequences and identify a gene's function. The ultimate goal of such genomic sequencing is to select particular genes as targets of drug action.

On August 1, 1995, Genome entered into a partnership with Astra Hassle AB to develop therapeutic, diagnostic, and vaccine products effective against gastrointestinal illnesses caused by *H. pylori* bacteria. In exchange for exclusive use of Genome's *H. pylori* database, Astra agreed to pay the company between $11 and $22 million, depending on which goals were met. In 1998, Genome extended its agreement to grant Schering-Plough exclusive access to its *S. aureus* genome sequence. Schering-Plough paid Genome $3 million up front, and depending on research results could pay another $10.3 million. Genome could also earn up to $43.5 million in research and milestone payments, along with royalties on any Schering products that come out of the research.

IntraBiotics was founded in Sunnyvale, California in 1994 to produce a range of novel antimicrobials based on naturally occurring substances called host defense peptides. The peptides are normally produced by an animal or human's immune system to protect the host from infection. This research has led IntraBiotics to develop a class of antimicrobial drugs called Protegrins that kill bacteria and fungi before attaching to their lipid membranes, a mechanism unique to this product. Its product Protegrin IB-367 aerosol entered Phase I trials to demonstrate efficacy in treating respiratory infections, including those caused by drug-resistant bacteria and fungi. Applications of the drug-resistant bacterial are being evaluated. The company also had three other products in Phase II trials and two in lead optimization, based on four in-licensed novel classes of antibiotic technologies in 1999. The company completed a private placement raising $23 million in 1999 with international groups of private investors.

RESEARCH AND TECHNOLOGY

Researchers in the field of superdrugs generally have a background in biology, genetics, molecular biology, or biochemistry. Because of the importance of genetics to superdrug development, individuals with expertise in bioinformatics—the use of computers to analyze, track, and correlate the enormous amount of data generated by genome analysis—have become particularly valued. Knowledge of combinatorial chemistry and assay development—the practical chemistry of pharmaceuticals—is also very useful. Advanced training in molecular biology, molecular genetics, or biochemistry is often required.

Federal funding for antimicrobial resistance research rose from $7.8 million in 1992 to an estimated $13.8 million in 1998—a 75 percent increase. The Pharmaceutical Research and Manufacturing Association estimates that 15 percent of the pharmaceutical industry's outlay for research and development—an expected record $24 billion in 1999—is devoted to new anti-infectives. Accordingly, research spending in 1999 for this category (includes antifungal, antiviral, and antibiotic drugs) is projected to reach $3.4 billion. The search for superdrugs has called forth a number of new pharmaceutical research methods. The most revolutionary of these is related to the deciphering of the genome of drug-resistant bacteria and the search for individual target genes. One such technology is "genetic sequencing"—identifying genes in DNA fragments. Fragments from different individual organisms are compared to establish the function of par-

---

> *More On* WEAPONS DERIVED
> FROM NATURE
>
> A drug derived from a protein found in the host's defense arsenal may be the next weapon against Superbugs; and it has the advantage of several points of attack. XOMA Corporation's genetically engineered Nuprex is derived from bactericidal/permeability-increasing protein (BPI), found in human white blood cells.
>
> The drug targets serious infections and complications of trauma and surgery. These infections include antibiotic resistant infections as well as the deadly infection meningococcemia, primarily affecting children and caused by the same organism that can cause meningitis. Inflammatory response to the poisonous endotoxins from the cell walls of some bacteria can rapidly worsen from flu-like symptoms to organ failure and death. Survivors may suffer neurological damage and loss of limbs.
>
> Phase III clinical trials are underway for the drug, which utilizes BPI's properties to kill bacteria and heighten the efficacy of antibiotics. It's action works to make bacterial cell walls more permeable, killing bacteria and facilitating antibiotics' mechanisms. It also blocks inflammatory response by binding to endotoxins and neutralizing them.
>
> Once available, the drug may be a defense against such severe infections as perforated colon or appendicitis, as well as serious lung infections often affecting cystic fibrosis patients. The company has also developed a topical formulation of BPI to treat eye infections such as corneal ulcers.

ticular genes. Once a particular gene has been connected with a particular function, perhaps for a bacterial resistance mechanism or for the reproduction or survival of the organism, the search can begin for drugs to attack, disable, or block the gene's expression.

Other simpler and relatively cheaper strategies cut down the expense and time to develop new drugs. New approaches cripple or inactivate bacteria instead of killing them so that resistance is less likely to develop. Nobel laureate Sidney Altman and his team at Yale University are looking to restore the sensitivity of bacteria to existing drugs. Their experiments use synthetic genes that target the bacterium's own genetic material and prevent it from expressing resistance, in effect forcing it to inactivate the substances that make antibiotics fail. These "search-and-destroy" gene sequences resemble an enzyme found in all cells and so have the potential to be used in any kind of genetic material. This technology has been licensed for commercial development by Innovir Laboratories of New York City.

Some efforts to revive the potency of older drugs involve defeating the chemical mechanisms by which bacteria expel or break them down. Antidotes to penicillinase, the bacterial enzyme which renders penicillin and its cousins ineffective, already exist, and researchers at Tufts University are developing a compound to block the cellular mechanism with which bacteria pump tetracycline and similar drugs out before they have a chance to work.

Others are looking beyond the exploration of how bugs develop drug resistance to the larger issue of who gets infected, who is at risk, and how the host's metabolism and physiology contributes to the spread of disease. One new model stresses the importance of understanding the host's role in the development of infection and proposes combining antitoxins and other boosters of immune function at strategic times with traditional antibiotic therapy. A French team working with Eli Lilly has used imaging technologies to identify bacterial concentrations at various stages of disease and determine the key points at which specific therapies may work most effectively in concert with specific events in an individual's response to infection.

One of the most promising lines of research to have emerged in 1998 was the discovery of a key protein that tells bacteria when to release the toxins that destroy vital tissues and organs. Dr. Naomi Balaban of the University of California at Davis and collaborators at Panorama Research and the University of Maryland found that removing a critical signal protein, RAP, prevented the secretion of bacterial toxins and that immunizing animals with the toxin-activating protein protects them from infection. Because this treatment does not kill bacteria but merely prevents them from secreting toxins, resistance is unlikely to develop.

Another strategy may be an old therapy that predates the widespread use of antibiotics—phage treatment with viruses that invade and finally kill their bacterial hosts. Efforts are also under way to develop new antibiotics from other microbial sources, as opposed to micro-modification of existing chemical compounds. For example, University of Wisconsin researchers discovered an antibiotic-producing microbe in the alfalfa plant that protects the plant's roots from bacterial disease. They are investigating whether it can be used against human diseases. Other researchers are looking into biological sources of antibiotics, including bees, algae, plants, and insects.

FURTHER READING

"1999 Survey: New Medicines in Development for Children." Washington, DC: Pharmaceutical Researchers and Manufacturers of America, 1999. Available from http://www.phrma.org/charts/nda-c98.html.

"Bacteria Remain Antibiotic Resistant." *ReutersHealth,* 13 March 1998.

Beavers, Norma. "Doomsday Bugs." *Drug Topics,* 4 May 1998.

Boyce, Nell. "Evidence Links 'Superbug' Bacteria to Livestock Feed." *Milwaukee Journal Sentinel,* 6 April 1998.

Braffman-Miller, Judith. "Beware the Rise of Antibiotic-Resistant Bacteria." *USA Today Magazine,* 1 March 1997.

Brickner, Steven J. "Multidrug-Resistant Bacterial Infections: Driving the Search for New Antibiotics." *Chemistry & Industry News,* 17 February 1996.

Chin, Jason. "Resistance is Useless." *New Scientist,* 12 October 1996.

"Continued Search for Anti-Infectives." *Applied Genetics News,* 1 April 1998.

"Counterattack on Germs." New York: Pfizer, Inc., 1998. Available from http://www.pfizer.com/science/counter attack.html.

"Cubist Pharmaceuticals 10-K405." *EDGAR Archives.* Securities and Exchange Commission, 31 March 1997. Available from http://www.sec.gov/Archives/edgar/data/912183/00009-12057-97-010962.txt.

"Cubist Pharmaceuticals, Inc.: 1998 Annual Report." Cambridge, MA: Cubist Pharmaceuticals, Inc., 1999. Available from http://www.cubist.com.

"FDA Advisory Panel Recommends Approval of Synercid(r) for Treatment of Severe to Life-Threatening Infections; Synercid Represents First New Class of Antibiotics in U.S. in More Than Ten Years." *PR Newswire,* 19 February 1998.

"Genome Therapeutics Corp. 10-K." *EDGAR Archives.* Securities and Exchange Commission, 27 November 1996. Available from http://www.sec.gov/Archives/edgar/data/356830/0000950135-96-005167.txt.

Gianturco, Michael. "Superbugs, Superdrugs." *Forbes,* 3 March 1997. Available from http://www.forbes.com/forbes/97/0310.

"IntraBiotics Begins Phase I Clinical Trial of Protegrin IB-367 Aerosol for the Treatment of Respiratory Infections." Mountain View, CA: IntraBiotics, Inc., 20 January 1999. Available from http://www.intrabiotics.com.

"IntraBiotics Begins Phase II Clinical Trial of Ramoplanin Ointment for the Elimination of *Staphylococcus aureus* from the Nose." Mountain View, CA: IntraBiotics, Inc., 13 January 1999. Available from http://www.intrabiotics.com.

"IntraBiotics, Inc.: Corporate Profile." Mountain View, CA: IntraBiotics, Inc., 15 December 1998. Available from http://www.intrabiotics.com.

"IntraBiotics Raises $23 Million in Private Placement, Names Additional Board Member." Mountain View, CA: IntraBiotics, Inc., 1 February 1999. Available from http://www.intrabiotics.com.

"Infectious Diseases: The Battle Against Antibiotic Resistance: Sequential Pathogenesis and Biological Response Modifiers." Available from http://www.lilly.ca/RESEARCH/r_infec6.html.

"Infectious Disease: Britons Find 'Superbug' That Defies Most Potent Medicines." *Chicage Tribune,* 28 April 1998.

"Killer Bugs: Round Two: Daniel Green on How a Generation of Antibiotics Could Save the World." *Financial Times,* 25 April 1998.

Knudson, Mary. "The Hunt Is On for New Ways to Overcome Bacterial Resistance." *Technology Review,* 11 January 1998.

Leff, David N. "Nobelist Finds Synthetic Gene Reverses Bacterial Resistance." *BioWorld Today,* 5 August 1997.

Levy, Stuart B. "The Challenge of Antibiotic Resistance." *Scientific American,* March 1998.

Maugh, Thomas H. "Scientists Find New Way to Foil Staph Bacteria." *Los Angeles Times,* 17 April 1998.

"Microcide Expands Existing Antibiotics Collaboration with Pfizer to Include the Discovery of Animal Health Products." *PR Newswire,* 13 January 1999.

"Microcide Pharmaceuticals, Inc.: Corporate Profile." Mountain View, CA: Microcide, Inc., 1998. Available from http://www.microcide.com/corp.html.

National Institute of Allergy and Infectious Diseases, National Institutes of Health. "Fact Sheet: Antimicrobial Resistance." Bethesda, MD: U.S. Department of Health and Human Services, March 1998. Available from http://www.niaid.nih.gov/factsheets/antimicro.htm.

Nemecek, Sasha. "Beating Bacteria." *Scientific American,* February 1997.

"New Drug Approvals in 1997." Washington, DC: Pharmaceutical Researchers and Manufacturers of America, 1998. Available from http://www.phrma.org/pdf/charts/nda97.pdf.

"New Drug Approvals in 1998." Washington, DC: Pharmaceutical Researchers and Manufacturers of America, 1999. Available from http://www.phrma.org/charts/nda-c98.html.

"New Drug Shown Effective Against Vancomycin-Resistant Bacteria." *EurekAlert,* 9 March 1999. Available from http://www.eurekalert.org/releases/nwu-nds030999.html.

"New Studies Compare Antibiotic ZAGAM to Biaxin; Quinolone ZAGAM Offers Rapid Bactericidal Activity." Collegeville, PA: Rhone-Poulenc Rorer, Inc., 30 December 1998. Available from http://www.rp-rorer.com.

Nichols, Mark. "Outbreak: Doctors Are Struggling to Control Drug-Resistant Bacteria." *Maclean's,* 9 September 1996.

Nuttall, Nick. "Superbug Defies Antibiotics." *Times,* 23 April 1998.

Pfeiffer, Naomi. "FDA Decision Soon on New Resistance-Fighting Antibiotic." *Drug Topics,* 21 October 1996.

"Pharmaceutical and Biotech Firms Are Taking on Drug-Resistant Microbes." *The Scientist,* 10 June 1996. Available from http://ds.internic.net/pub/the-scientist/the-scientist-960610.

"Pharmaceutical Industry." *S&P's Industry Surveys,* April 1998.

"Rising Costs of Antibiotic Resistant Infections Place Burden on Health Care System; Experts Discuss Strategies for Better Resistance." *PR Newswire,* 18 May 1998.

Rubin, Robert J., et al. "The Economic Impact of *Staphylococcus aureus* Infection in New York City Hospitals." *Emerging Infectious Diseases,* January-March 1999. Available from http://www.cdc.gov/ncidod/eid/vol5no1/rubin.html.

Smith, Robert C., ed. "Anti-Infectives." *Medical and Healthcare Marketplace Guide 1997-1998.* Philadelphia: Dorland's Biomedical, 1998.

Tanouye, Elyse. "Merck Discovers New Way to Attack Bacteria." *Wall Street Journal,* 8 November 1996.

"Vaccine Protects Newborns from Infection." *USA Today Health,* 2 February 1999.

"Zyvox™ (Linezolid), The First of a New Class of Antibiotics." Bridgewater, NJ: Pharmacia and Upjohn, Inc., 23 March 1999. Available from http://www.pnu.com/press_display.asp?174.

—Gerald E. Brennan,
updated by Cameron McLaughlin
and Sondra E. O'Donnell

Systems Integration

In its purest form, systems integration involves fitting together the ideal combination of personnel, technology, networks, services, and databases to solve a business problem or pursue a business opportunity. One of the fastest growing service areas within the information systems industry, systems integration has been driven by fast-paced change in both business and technological environments during the 1980s and the 1990s. Drawing from traditional systems development approaches, systems integration nevertheless differs from this traditional systems model in a number of ways. The general assumption of most traditional systems development is that most—if not all—of the scope of the problem being attacked is within "design control" of the project. Traditional development assumes that the various parts of a system can be engineered to fit together and concentrates more on the development of applications and databases, giving little concern to interfacing those applications and databases. Systems integrators attack these development problems from the opposite direction, concentrating on building interfaces to make all system components work together.

As many companies turned to prepackaged computer software in the 1980s and 1990s, they realized that these products, while admirably functional for the price, did not perform company-specific tasks as efficiently as possible. Because companies and organizations may rely on separate applications for tasks such as word processing, spreadsheets, and data mining, they must constantly switch programs when working on tasks requiring more than one application. Consequently, systems integrators dramatically increased their presence in the marketplace in the mid-1990s.

Systems integrators take multiple applications such as word processors and Internet browsers, as well as operating systems, and unify or integrate their capabilities to meet the needs of individual clients.

Among the companies specializing in systems integration are Electronic Data Systems Corporation, Andersen Consulting, American Management Systems Inc., Perot Systems Corporation, and TRW Inc., which in 1997 paid $1 billion to acquire BDM International. Additionally, many leading computer hardware vendors such as Hewlett-Packard, Unisys, AT&T, International Business Machine Corp. (IBM), and Digital Equipment Corp. (DEC) provide systems integration services. To meet the need for very specific systems integration tasks, there are hundreds of specialty companies and start-ups that offer such services. Systems integrators generally do not restrict services to products they developed, but instead integrate any company's applications and hardware into a coherent system designed around the goals and specifications of their clients.

In the latter half of the 1990s, systems integration (SI) constituted one of the three most popular professional computer services in the United States. The U.S. government was the largest consumer of systems integration services, and thus the government's demand for systems integration affected the industry as a whole. In the mid- to late 1990s, as Congress attempted to reduce spending and the deficit, the systems integration industry felt the adverse effects of government spending reductions and caps, although analysts expect the corporate market to compensate for the industry's loss of government clients.

A growing segment of the systems integration business is Web systems integration, which employs open standards and Internet technologies as the glue to hold pre-built components together. According to an analysis of this burgeoning field by the University of Colorado Business School, "some of the key success factors in Web systems integration include selecting the right architecture, dealing with packaged application components, working with software vendors, and assessing legacy applications." The success of such Web integration projects can sometimes depend on careful project management and a grasp of organization politics.

ORGANIZATION AND STRUCTURE

The systems integration (SI) process usually contains five steps: planning, design, development, implementation, and operation. SI brings about interaction between the hardware platform, software applications, and the operating system, and creates a base for all subsequent system-related uses and modifications, according to Debi Nelson in *National Underwriter Life & Health-Financial Services Edition.*

Since systems integration is like a permutation or avatar of custom computer programming, Alan R. Earls explains in *Computerworld,* the initial stage of the integration process is one of the most crucial: clients must clearly specify exactly what capabilities they would like their systems to have and what the goals and requirements are. Systems integrators must also proceed carefully at this stage, ensuring that they fully comprehend client needs in order to deliver the expected service.

Furthermore, systems integrators and clients must take pains to draft thorough contracts that specify the tasks to be performed, as well as the deadlines for those tasks. Earls urges companies to conduct a rigorous selection process to make sure they choose systems integrators with skills and fees amenable to their needs. The screening process should involve lawyers, technicians, and contract specialists so that all aspects of the SI contractor are examined prior to selecting a SI firm and signing a contract with the integrator.

Earls noted that companies should consider the location of the systems integrators as well. If both parties cannot solve a problem via the phone, then an on-site visit is warranted, which could cause significant delays if the systems integrator has to travel a long distance. In fact, on-site service and special attention make up some of the most important features systems integrators can offer, according to a *Computerworld* survey, which small, nearby SI firms may excel at providing.

Depending on client needs and project specifications, systems integrators may use prepackaged software exclusively. They may also need to design custom applications or outsource this task to a custom software developer. In addition, many systems integrators cater to specific markets, such as information system and manufacturing system markets, and they specialize in certain kinds of technology and computer system-related skills. Therefore, companies and organizations seeking SI services select firms based on the firms' focal markets and aptitudes. SI firms usually have a team of systems integrators work on contracts, so a given firm may have specialists in various aspects of system integration and employ specialists in various computer environments such as Windows and Unix.

BACKGROUND AND DEVELOPMENT

With the proliferation of computers into homes and businesses during the 1980s and 1990s, the demand for diverse computer applications increased. In the beginning of the computer boom, custom software constituted the most prevalent kind of applications for businesses. Companies would contract software developers to create applications to suit individual needs. Computer programmers would design everything from workplace automation software to customer information databases. However, custom development had two significant drawbacks: cost and lack of standardization. Other than financial powerhouses, most companies could not afford custom software development except in financially prosperous times. Furthermore, without industry standards, custom software clients could have trouble upgrading software and ensuring that all divisions had the same operating systems and compatible software, which sometimes hindered interaction between various branches of a company.

By decree of the U.S. Justice Department in 1969, IBM had to start selling its software separately from its computer hardware, ending IBM's stronghold on the prepackaged software industry and opening the doors for vigorous competition. Consequently, a plethora of software developers sprouted in the wake of the Justice Department's decision. Prepackaged software offered an economical solution to the needs not only of small and medium businesses with tight budgets, but also to home computer users who used computers largely for uniform tasks such as word processing. Since software development required little capital investment, programmers could tinker away at novel and improved applications with very little financial risk. As a result, the prepackaged software industry blossomed in the 1980s and bore substantial fruit in the 1990s, producing high quality products at much lower costs than custom-made counterparts. Therefore, the custom software industry began to slow down as the prepackaged software industry soared ahead. Nonetheless, because of their unique tasks, many businesses and organizations still required custom applications to increase the efficiency and functionality of company software. This need continued to feed the custom software industry. However, another option emerged as well: systems integration. The systems integrators began to adapt prepackaged operating systems and applications to fulfill the requirements of the businesses and organizations.

CURRENT CONDITIONS

Systems integration recorded $43.9 billion in revenues in 1998, according to *Standard and Poor's Industry Survey*. The industry's biggest spenders were manufacturing, banking, and government. U.S. government clients included the U.S. Department of Defense, the National Aeronautics and Space Administration, the Environmental Protection Agency, the Federal Aviation Administration, and the National Oceanic and Atmospheric Administration.

Despite government cutbacks and downsizing in areas of the government such as the Department of Defense, there is still a need for systems integration in the civil sector. Although SI firms lost some government contracts as the number of federal employees decreased with government spending reductions, the demand for systems integrators stood poised to increase as government agencies continued to outsource more projects. Moreover, business demand for systems integration grew considerably in the mid-1990s and analysts expect the demand to expand significantly, thereby offsetting any losses of government contracts. Businesses require systems integrators to make operating systems function in harmony with other applications in a way unique to the individual businesses. Unlike custom software design, however, systems integration allows companies to take advantage of the low-priced general capabilities of prepackaged software, and have them modified to meet company specifications and requirements without the financial and time constraints of entirely customized software suites. *Standard and Poor's Industry Survey* predicted a 15-20 percent increase in the commercial sector through 1998. Therefore, many SI firms that used to court government clients planned to launch forays into the commercial market.

About... **SYSTEMS INTEGRATION INDUSTRY ORGANIZATIONS**

Two organizations serve the systems integration industry: the Independent Computer Consultants Association (ICCA) and the National Association of Computer Consultant Businesses (NACCB). Founded in 1976, the ICCA reported having over 1,500 members and 24 chapters in 1999. The St. Louis-based association consists of entrepreneurs who are technical specialists in all aspects of computer hardware and software including systems integration. Before becoming a member, computer consultants must pledge to uphold the organization's code of ethics. In addition, the non-profit ICCA keeps members apprised of legislative activity that could affect small businesses and entrepreneurs, and it offers certification examinations. On the other hand, the NACCB lobbies for policies that will strengthen computer consultants' opportunities. The Washington-based association also uses the Internet to let computer consultants post their resumes to attract clients and requires its members to adhere to a code of ethics. The 300 businesses around the country that make up the NACCB work with contract computer consultants, including those who provide systems integration services. The member businesses are those that need temporary technical computer support.

The commercial market's use of system integration grew extremely quickly in the late 1990s. Individuals looked to system integrators for assistance in consolidating hardware and software components purchased from different vendors. Because of the high turnover rate in the information technology sector, and the lack of in-house technical expertise, system integrators were also essential in developing unique, customized front-office applications for Fortune 500 organizations.

INDUSTRY LEADERS

Of the companies specializing in systems integration, Electronic Data Systems Corporation (EDS) is by far the largest, reporting sales of nearly $17 billion in 1998. The company posted net earnings of $743.4 million in 1998, an increase of 1.8 percent over its net income in 1997. Founded by Ross Perot, who now heads rival Perot Systems, and later acquired by General Motors (GM), the company employs 120,000 people worldwide. Although it was spun off by GM in 1996, EDS business with GM still generates nearly a quarter of its annual sales. Headquartered in Plano, Texas, EDS has an alliance with MCI WorldCom, under which the two swap assets, employees, and services. Although systems integration represents a substantial segment of the company's total business, EDS handles a wide variety of systems consulting assignments.

Another major company specializing in systems integration is Andersen Consulting, a subsidiary of Andersen Worldwide. Based in Chicago, Andersen Consulting employs more than 62,000 worldwide. Its alliance with parent firm Andersen Worldwide, a major international accounting company, has been filled with discord in recent years, and an effort is under way to break away from its parent. Andersen Consulting works closely with major computer and software suppliers. Its 1998 sales totaled $8.3 billion, up about 25 percent from the previous year.

Based in Fairfax, Virginia, American Management Systems Inc. designs and integrates technological solutions for a wide variety of businesses worldwide. Although its largest individual customer is the U.S. government, the company's biggest market is the telecommunications industry, whose companies account for about 30 percent of AMS sales. With 8,100 employees, AMS posted net income of $51.8 million on revenue of $1.1 billion in 1998. Net income was up more than 66 percent from 1997 levels, while sales showed an increase of more than 21 percent from the previous year.

Ross Perot's newest venture, Perot Systems Corporation, bears its founder's name. Based in Dallas, Perot Systems provides technological consulting and services, including both systems management and integration. Among its leading customers are Swiss bank UBS; East Midlands Electricity, a British utility; National Car Rental; and Tenet Healthcare. The company shed its private status in early 1999. More than 90 percent of its employees are shareholders. In 1998, the company reported net income of $40.5 million on revenue of $993.6 million. Perot Systems employs about 6,000 people worldwide.

TRW Inc., a widely diversified corporation based in Cleveland, Ohio, entered the systems integration business with its 1997 purchase of BDM International, an information technology company that sells computer systems to both government and private sector customers. TRW as a whole employs nearly 80,000 people worldwide. The company posted net earnings of $477 million on revenue of $11.9 billion in 1998.

A *Computerworld* customer poll ranked Unisys Corp. as one of the highest in terms of technical aptitude and customer service. Unisys offers systems integration services to both its corporate and government clients. Unisys' forte is building information architecture systems to allow clients to efficiently manage, store, and analyze data. When constructing a system, the company considers not only the data but also the customers, industry trends, business strategies, and competition in order to make the information system optimally functional. Furthermore, Unisys provides services in countries throughout the world. The company also has strategic alliances with Microsoft Corp., Hewlett-Packard Co., Sun Microsystems, PeopleSoft, Oracle, and Tandem. In 1998, Unisys posted net income of $813.7 million on revenue of $7.1 billion. Net earnings were off less than 1 percent from the previous year, while revenue was up nearly 26 percent from 1997. Unisys earned revenues of $378.0 million for its systems integration services out of $2.0 billion in total for its information services division. Overall, the company brought in $6.3 billion. Unisys also employed 36,802 employees, and Lawrence J. Ellison was the company's chairman and CEO in 1998.

Hewlett-Packard Company (HP) also received a significant amount of praise in the *Computerworld* survey. Besides being a major provider of computer systems, servers, and peripherals, HP also leads in the system integration service. In 1999, Lewis E. Platt served as HP's CEO. The company posted net income of $2.9 billion on revenue of $47.1 billion in 1998. HP also maintained a staff of nearly 125,000 employees in 1998. After decades of work in electronics—starting in the 1930s by developing oscillators and then later by producing calculators, computers, and printers—HP began to offer computer-related services, including systems integration, in the 1990s and quickly became a leader in the field.

With products such as the popular Internet search engine Alta Vista, Compaq Computer Corporation is another key computer and Internet software and component producer that provides systems integration services as well. The company bought Digital Equipment Corporation in 1998. That same year, Compaq posted a net loss of $2.7 billion on sales of $31.2 billion. Led in early 1999 by Benjamin M. Rosen, chairman and acting CEO, Compaq employed more than 70,000 people worldwide.

Align Solutions Corp. specializes in systems integration and led the industry in innovation in the mid-1990s. With executives from companies such as Perot Systems Corp. and Andersen Consulting, the fledgling company competes with larger well-established operations because of its leaders' experience and vision. Align Solutions employs people versed in advertising, writing, graphic design, and public relations in addition to its computer programmers. This meld of expertise allows the company to provide unique systems integration solutions. Julia King reports in *Computerworld* that Align can woo a broader base of clients because of its staff's diversity, by combining technical and creative skills. In 1997, Richard Scruggs served as the company's president and CEO.

AMERICA AND THE WORLD

As the world economy becomes increasingly dependent on computer technology, the demand for systems integration services has witnessed rapid growth on the international scene. To meet that demand, systems integrators around the world were busy in the closing days of the 1990s striking alliances to provide such services in both the industrialized countries and the Third World as well.

In June 1998 Digital Equipment Corporation, now a part of Compaq Computer Corporation, agreed to establish a new joint venture company with Beijing Founder Electronics Corporation, the leading systems integrator in China. The new company, which will be called Beijing Founder Di Cheng Information Technology Company Ltd., will become China's largest provider of network and systems integration services. China's booming information technology market is projected to experience a 35-percent compound annual growth by the year 2000. The Chinese market for systems integration was estimated at $71.2 million in 1996 and was predicted to hit $237.0 million by 2000.

In early 1999, Siemens Computer Systems announced the formation of a strategic partnership with BSG, one of the leading systems integrators in the United Kingdom. Under the agreement, Siemens will combine its comprehensive portfolio of information and communications services with BSG's expertise in developing innovative information technology applications.

Industry analyst IDC reported in late 1998 that Asian systems integration markets were continuing to grow at a steady rate despite the region's economic troubles. According to IDC's report, the growth potential for systems integrators is the greatest in China, India, and Taiwan, which are expected to see a compound annual growth rate between 26 and 49 percent in the 5 years from 1997 to 2002. In China and India, the Internet and government initiatives were expected to fuel much of the growth in local systems integration markets, as reported by IDC.

RESEARCH AND TECHNOLOGY

Integrating the Internet into other applications constitutes a major area of research within this industry. Besides systems integration firms, prepackaged software developers such as Microsoft Corp. also strive to combine the potential of the Internet with standard office applications. Presently, most systems have largely segregated desktop and Internet capabilities that require different programs to manipulate them. The desktop component includes files and applications, whereas the Internet component includes an expanse of hypertext and multimedia files accessible with an Internet browser. Difficulties such as the switch from Hypertext Markup Language (HTML) files for the Internet to non-HTML files for the desktop impede this integration, according to Ashley Dunn in the *New York Times*. However, the successful integration of these capabilities could lead to the reduction of applications that a business, organization, or individual requires. Moreover, adding Internet structure to desktop files could result in a reduction of the plethora of windows through which one must ferret in order to access a file in a Windows 95 or a Mac Operating System environment.

The Internet also has stimulated research into the development of integrated systems for Internet service providers (ISPs). As demand for Internet access escalated in the mid-1990s, a spate of telephone companies rushed to begin offering such service. SI firms such as Technology Applications Inc. worked on developing systems to allow ISPs the efficiency of integrated Internet servers for network interface, online security, communications access, networking management, implementation, Web development, administration, and maintenance, according to Dan O'Shea in *Telephony*.

FURTHER READING

Alexander, Steve. "More than Just Hardware." *Computerworld*, 26 February 1996.

———. "Top-Down." *Computerworld*, 26 February 1996.

"Carleton Pure-Advantage Program Targets Systems Integrators as Business Partners." *Business Wire*, 5 August 1998.

"Digital and Beijing Founder Electronics Combine to Create China's Largest Systems Integrator." *M2 PressWIRE,* 3 June 1998.

Dunn, Ashley. "Internet Explorer 4.0 and the Unified Field Theory." *The New York Times,* 16 April 1997.

Earls, Alan R. "Who to Choose?" *Computerworld,* 26 February 1996. Available from http//:www.computerworld .com/search/AT-html9602/960226SYSINTSLsysint2.html.

Hoover's Online. Austin, TX: The Reference Press, 1999. Available from http://www.hoovers.com.

"Information Services." Blue Bell, PA: Unisys, 1997. Available from http://www.unisys.com/annual/at_a_glance.html.

King, Julia. "Goliaths Losing Ground in Systems Integrator Market." *Computerworld,* 26 February 1996.

———. "IS Firm Looks Beyond Tech Skills." *Computerworld,* 21 April 1997.

Mullich, Joe. "Trends: Will the Real Network Integrator Please Stand Up." *InternetWeek,* 13 July 1998.

Nelson, Debi. "Identifying 'Hidden Costs' When Buying Software." *National Underwriter Life & Health-Financial Services Edition,* 3 March 1997.

O'Shea, Dan. "IPAC a Hot Launch Pad for Internet Business." *Telephony,* 29 January 1996.

"Siemens Computer Systems Announced Partnership with Leading System Integrator, BSG." *M2 PressWIRE,* 1 March 1999.

Uimonen, Terho. "IDC Bullish on Asia Systems Integration Arena." *ComputerWorld Today,* 22 October 1998.

"Welcome to Hewlett-Packard." Palo Alto, CA: Hewlett-Packard, 1996. Available from http://www.hp.com/.

Wood, Peter C. "Computers: Commercial Services Industry Survey." *Standard and Poor's Industry Surveys,* 6 March 1997.

—Karl Heil,
updated by Don Amerman

TELEMEDICINE

Telemedicine refers to a broad spectrum of tele-communication tools, information systems, and imaging technologies that can be used to supplement the practice of conventional medicine and facilitate the exchange of information needed for diagnosis and treatment. In a statement to Congress in 1998, Col. Jeffrey Roller, Deputy for Telemedicine and Advanced Technologies for the U.S. Army, defined it as "the convergence of technological advances in a number of fields including medicine, telecommunications, computer engineering, informatics, artificial intelligence, robotics, material science, and perceptual psychology."

Often broadly defined as the transfer of electronic medical data from one location to another, telemedicine encompasses a range of emerging technologies that may enable a healthcare revolution in the 21st century. After a decade of often inconsistent progress, there was little consensus in 1998 about telemedicine's cost-effectiveness, but experts generally agreed that it was approaching a level of professional acceptance and commercial viability that would permanently and radically transform the practice of medicine throughout the world.

Applications range in complexity from the relatively simple transfer of digitized images or data via phone lines or the Internet to consultations and videoconferencing, to the monitoring of patients at home, or the direction of surgery or diagnostic procedures from a distance. Most applications have evolved from government-funded pilot programs, and a substantial proportion of telemedicine's advances were initially developed to meet the needs of military medicine and to improve health care in remote areas.

Telemedicine typically involves interactive, *real-time* transactions (such as videoconferencing) that may require dedicated networks or even satellite links or *store-and-forward* systems that allow data, images, or patient information to be transmitted from a personal computer and inspected at the receiver's and sender's convenience. Transmission media include phone lines, coaxial or integrated services digital network (ISDN) lines, satellites, and other peripherals. Although complex dedicated networks provide the infrastructure for many institutional applications, telemedicine is rapidly evolving to encompass software and products for affordable desktop systems that can integrate voice, video, and data.

ORGANIZATION AND STRUCTURE

Still in its infancy, telemedicine is available primarily to large institutions such as medical centers and prisons. According to a Business Communications Co. report, in 1997 medical centers accounted for $462.5 million of the industry's $642.6 million in sales; the remaining sales were divided among military, correctional, educational, and residential markets. In 1998, more than 700 companies supplied products and services for remote consultations, home health, teleradiology, telepathology, patient monitoring, distance education, and research.

The most popular application of telemedicine is the transmission of images in radiology, pathology, and dermatology, which do not require the patient's real-time involvement and can circumvent numerous legal problems created by cooperative diagnosis and treatment across state lines. The transmission of still images is also a well-established practice that Medicare and some other third parties will reimburse. Telemedicine in prisons, where the cost of patient transportation is exorbitant, has been highly successful. Interactive conferences for remote consults and distance education for practicing physicians and medical students are also becoming more widespread. In 1998, most managed care organizations were still examining the cost savings of telemedicine for home health care and many other applications.

HOME HEALTH

According to government estimates, home health spending reached $18.2 billion in 1998. Telemedical applications can range from phone-based call centers to integrated home telemonitoring systems that track the progress of chronically ill or recovering patients. In numerous pilot projects, at-home monitoring has been shown to reduce doctor and emergency visits and enable fewer home health nurses to see more patients more frequently in a shorter amount of time. TeVital, a leading supplier of home-based monitoring equipment, estimates that per-cost home health visits can be reduced by one-third to one-half through the use of sensing and video systems. Although home health telemedicine promises enormous potential savings, only a handful of mostly university-based programs existed in the United States in 1999.

At least one special pilot program may promote more wide-spread use. American TeleCare, Inc.'s $1.5 million project launched in February 1999 installed systems in 100 patients' homes to link them with staff at Veteran's Hospital in Tampa, Florida. Connected via ordinary phone lines, the systems transmitted heart and lung sounds and vital signs in real time between patient and hospital care staff. The initiative was expected to demonstrate improvements in accessibility of care and lower care costs, with fewer emergency room visits and inpatient days. Initial physician, patient and nurse responses were very positive.

RURAL HEALTH

According to the Health Resource and Services Administration, telemedicine was used to deliver patient care, primarily radiology, in approximately one-third of all rural hospitals in the United States in 1996, and 40 percent of those programs had existed for one year or less. The most common applications were for diagnostic consults, data transmissions, and chronic disease management. Many rural hospitals are limited by the high cost of telecommunication technology, but federal attempts to offset those fees with a subsidy program were partly dismantled in

1998 by service providers' attempts to levy additional taxes. In January 1999, physicians in underserved rural areas became eligible for Medicare reimbursement for telemedicine services, with payment shared among practitioners. Although Federal Medicaid law does not recognize telemedicine as a distinct service, services administered via telemedicine applications may be reimbursed at the State's option, according to a Department of Health and Human Services' Health Care Financing Administration Web Page. At least 14 states reimburse for services provided via telemedicine applications for reasons including improved access to specialists and reduction of transportation costs.

BACKGROUND AND DEVELOPMENT

Although interest in telemedicine has been revived by the technological advances in the late 1990s, the use of communications technology to improve information-sharing and connect patients with doctors located elsewhere is not new. One of the first applications in the United States was a closed-circuit television system devised for a Nebraska state psychiatric institute in the 1950s. The National Aeronautics and Space Administration (NASA) began using telemetric devices to monitor the condition of astronauts in space in the 1960s and later to deliver health care to the Papago Indians of Arizona in the 1970s. Other early projects included a telemedicine station at Boston's Logan Airport to deliver emergency care to travelers, and an experimental network that used satellite-based video to provide health care in isolated regions of Alaska.

International prototypes of low-cost telemedicine to link rural populations with health care providers included the Memorial University of Newfoundland's satellite-based audio and teleconferencing network that connected institutions throughout the province and was later linked to Kenya and five Caribbean nations. Using a government satellite, an Australian pilot project was begun in 1984 to provide health care to a remote group of islanders. In 1989, NASA established a satellite consultation network that used voice, video, and fax to aid earthquake victims in Soviet Armenia and was later extended to help burn victims after a railroad accident in Russia.

The U.S. government has actively supported a broad variety of mostly university-based demonstration projects for several decades, but many of its activities have never been systematically evaluated.

Thirty-five organizations in nine government agencies spent more than $646 million on telemedicine projects between 1994 and 1996, but in 1997 the General Accounting Office found the projects to be poorly coordinated, and a Department of Commerce report questioned their cost-effectiveness.

After the National Information Infrastructure (NII) identified telemedicine as a key focus of information technology, joint agency ventures were reorganized to fulfill the requirements of the Telecommunications Reform Act of 1996 (TRA), which mandated better reporting and evaluation of all federal telemedicine initiatives. Medicare was mandated to begin paying for some telemedicine consultations in 1999. Telecommunications carriers were required to provide service to rural health care providers at rates comparable to those of urban areas in that state, with the support subsidy programs.

Yet the distribution of funds, capped annually at $400 million, has been slow. An Office for the Advancement of Telehealth update states that as of February 1999 105 applications were waiting Federal Communications Commission (FCC) approval, and over 200 additional applications were near completion for FCC submission. The FCC subsequently assigned the Universal Service Administrative Company (USAC) to audit applications and administer the program. USAC recommendations outlined in a March 1999 report are intended to simplify the process and allow growth in health networks.

In 1996 the National Library of Medicine and the Health Care Financing Administration, which administers Medicare, began a new series of demonstration projects to evaluate the use and cost-effectiveness of telemedicine in a wide variety of clinical settings. The NLM announced two additional projects in September 1997, and in 1998 awarded 24 contracts to various organizations to develop novel medical projects demonstrating Internet applications. These projects, including free Medline access on the Internet, with links to U.S. and international journals, continued to receive funding from the Fiscal Year 1999 Presidential Budget of $171.3 million for the NLM.

Additional funding to rural areas has been made available since 1993 through the U.S. Department of Agriculture (USDA). The 1999 Distance Learning and Telemedicine Loan and Grant Program had $150 million available for loans and $12.5 million for grants. As of March 1999 the program had funded 252 projects totaling $68 million, improving health care in more than 725 hospitals and rural health care clinics.

This doctor uses a teleconferencing system, which allows him to consult with a co-worker remotely. (Courtesy of NEC USA, Inc.)

CURRENT CONDITIONS

Many visionary projections about the future of telemedicine have not been realized, and early grant-funded projects suffered from lack of focus. In addition, market projections are difficult because products and services are often part of larger investments in telecommunications technologies and healthcare delivery systems. Nevertheless, the Association of Telemedicine Service Providers (ATSP) reported in 1999 survey results indicating a 90 percent growth in 141 U.S. telemedicine programs' activity levels from 1996 to 1997, with future growth suggested by first quarter 1998 statistics. The C. Everett Koop Institute estimates that as insurers recognize the savings provided by electronic links to patients and as technologies improve, telemedicine will become a $20 billion market consisting of software and hardware, biomedical equipment, and a standardized telecommunications infrastructure.

Other market studies concur. Business Communications Company, for example, estimated the value of the U.S. market for telemedicine at $650 million in 1998, and predicted it would reach $3 billion by the year 2002. Overall growth is expected to be 35 percent annually from 1998 to 2002, with a 42 percent increase in public sector investments and 89 percent growth in sites. Prison telemedicine sites are expected to grow by 280 percent, and military investment is expected to double by 2005. The market for overall healthcare-related information, however, is projected to grow by only 3 percent per year.

In keeping with these predictions, the ATSP survey found that telemedicine programs for prison populations accounted for twenty percent of the reported activity. Remote care services were most commonly used for specialist consultation and second opinions; however, increasingly, telemedicine is being used for chronic illness management, emergency care, follow-up care, interpretation of diagnostic exams and home health care.

According to Feedback Research Services, the U.S. market for telepathology, teleradiology, and videoconferencing systems is approximately $100 million. Telemedicine-related videoconferencing systems in Europe, North America, and the Pacific Rim accounted for $250 million in revenues, and worldwide sales of products and services approached $520 million in 1997. Annual worldwide growth is estimated at 15 percent, and Europe and the Pacific Rim may account for telemedicine expenditures of $1.4 billion by the year 2001.

Frost & Sullivan estimated sales of picture archiving and communications systems (PACS) and teleradiology systems in the United States—which accounts for 81 percent of the market—and Europe at $368.8 million in 1998. A growth rate of 28 percent would yield a total annual market of $1.6 billion by the year 2004.

A 1998 Healthcare Information and Systems Society survey of senior healthcare executives also supported these projections: more than one-third of the organizations surveyed used telemedicine, 10 percent planned on using it within the next 21 months, and 28 percent were investigating its use in the future. In addition, 93 percent of telemedicine program managers surveyed by *Telemedicine and Telehealth Networks* planned to expand by 2003.

OBSTACLES

Although the cost of typical applications is quickly falling, telemedicine is not a common feature of the average medical practice. The most significant obstacles to its widespread use are licensure constraints, malpractice concerns, lack of reimbursement, technical compatibility problems, and physician resistance.

Technology. Many interactive applications require high-bandwidth carriers and are dependent on switched public network—expensive media not yet balanced by the overall cost savings of many telemedicine applications. Although networking solutions for expensive real-time teleconferencing and high-level data exchange will continue to be critical, lack of integration and standards have discouraged many institutions from investing heavily in transitional or obsolescent technology.

Liability. Electronically administered medical care that transcends a single jurisdiction poses significant new licensing, credentialing, and malpractice problems. Except for military physicians, who are licensed in one state but may practice anywhere, physicians who wish to practice telemedicine across state lines must be licensed wherever they provide care. Although reciprocal licensing schemes have been proposed by the Federation of State Medical Boards, they have thus far been rejected by the American Medical Association and other influential physicians' groups. Malpractice claims have also already been made for misdiagnoses by consulting physicians based on inadequate image transmission. Several states have devised limited special-purpose licenses, but reciprocity among states is not expected until the year 2000 or later.

Reimbursement. Until physicians are reimbursed for providing electronic and remote services, telemedicine is likely to remain limited. Feedback Research Services reports that U.S. telemedicine programs were reimbursed at most $4.2 million in 1997, and expects 1999 services to collect less than $10.0 million. At least 14 states now have policies for reimbursing Medicaid for limited telemedicine services, but they often lack specific guidelines. Yet, because of the vagueness inherent in Federal Medicaid law, States have the flexibility to reimburse the costs unique to telemedicine applications, such as technical support or line-charges. As service caps become more universal and evidence of telemedicine's cost-effectiveness accumulates, managed care organizations may begin reimbursing telemedicine more widely, or even requiring its use when direct patient-physician interaction is not essential. Columbia/HCA was criticized in 1998 for requiring some patients to be examined remotely instead of face-to-face—a cost-cutting move that was criticized by physicians and patient advocates as further removing patients from their doctors.

Physician Resistance. In addition to malpractice concerns, logistical and political barriers also exist among individual practitioners who perceive increasingly centralized and cooperative medical care as a threat to their livelihood. Many physicians also express resistance to expensive technologies that cannot be easily integrated into an existing medical practice. Because patient records still exist substantially in paper form, data from electronic transactions must often be manually added to a medical record, adding another level of administrative labor. Rural physicians, among others, express reservations about giving up existing referral structures in favor of monopolistic networks mandated by large health care centers, and urban specialists accustomed to authority over their local resources express misgivings about relinquishing control over the quality of information available to them from distant sources. Many physicians cite inconvenience in existing telemedical consultation procedures and inconclusive evidence that telemedicine is in fact a better way to practice medicine.

Some observers believe that telemedicine will become one facet of a larger movement toward integrated health information systems that can streamline medical record-keeping and administration, which now account for up to 40 percent of the cost of medical care in the United States. Large-scale coordination of administrative and clinical data may dictate the use of multimedia electronic patient records and a level of information sharing and networking compatibility that raises serious questions about the security and confidentiality of patient data.

INDUSTRY LEADERS

Service providers and device manufacturers are quickly stepping in as telemedicine moves from a grant-funded series of pilot projects to a mature industry incorporated into mainstream health care. Telecommunications providers such as BellSouth and AT&T are participating in pilot projects to provide networks capable of integrating voice, video, data, and advanced imaging.

Ethernet LANS and ATM networks are also being considered as backbones for multiservice networks, but experts believe significant compatibility and reliability problems still remain. Cisco Systems, a network provider, has expressed intentions to capture half of the health care network market and faces aggressive competition from 3Com and Bay Networks.

American Telecare is prominent in the home health care market. Its Personal Telemedicine System works with a personal computer over phone lines to send and receive physiologic data. Images can be

---

Trends

HYPERLINKED HEALTH RECORDS

The days of costly and inefficient information systems and medical mishaps due to confused paperwork are numbered. Soon Information such as allergies to medications, doctors' names and health plan status will be instantly available to authorized viewers. Updating clinical data and administrative information will be immediate, and there will be no more written prescriptions for pharmacists to decipher or for patients to lose.

Healtheon has taken on the task of making accessible a comprehensible database of health information. The Santa Clara, California company uses its software to link doctors, patients, laboratories, hospitals, HMOs, insurance companies and employers over the Internet.

Although other companies have long sold information-management software to hospitals and doctors' practices, Healtheon is the first to base its software and systems entirely on the Internet.

The company's founder, Jim Clark, cofounder of Netscape, targeted the market because it is the largest single market in the world. Worth $1 trillion, the industry wastes as much as $270 billion on inefficient information systems.

---

stored and filed with patient information and notes. TeVital also produces devices for home health care that allow two-way video interaction between the patient and provider with an ordinary phone line and incorporate a range of sensors for measuring vital signs.

PictureTel, another videoconferencing provider, offers high-end graphics and group conferencing and participates in several Department of Defense pilot projects. Intel owns 10 percent of the Andover, Massachusetts company, which produces videoconferencing units with a range of technology requirements, including ISDN, T1/E1 or ATM backbones. Applications include everything from operating room and emergency care to consultations via local Internet connections.

Vtel, the dominant video systems provider, produces videoconferencing and multimedia systems designed specifically for medical use that allow bedside input from endoscopes and other devices. The company claims to have 1500 systems installed worldwide. The Austin, Texas company is second behind PictureTel, with customers such as Microsoft and the Drew Medical Center. Telemedicine products and accessories, including receivers, digital cameras, software kits and viewing stations are highly adaptable from ISDN to ATM configurations, and Windows, Sun or Macintosh platforms. Product Distributors include Ameritech and Sprint long-distance carriers.

MedVision, Inc., a software company, produces a utility for viewing MRI, x-ray, and other image and text data on any standard PC. The independent private company located in Minneapolis, Minnesota develops software for medical practice management. Customer base includes the U.S. Department of Defense, the University of Arizona, Canada's TechKnowledge, and the U.K.'s United Medical Enterprises.

AMERICA AND THE WORLD

Developing nations have actively promoted telemedicine as a way of obtaining specialty care for their citizens in outlying areas, and international telemedicine consultations in turn circumvent some of the legal problems of providing interstate care domestically. International patients are linked through many consortia in Canada, Europe, and the United States, including WorldCare Limited, a partnership between Duke University Medical Center, Massachusetts General Hospital, Johns Hopkins School of Medicine, and the Cleveland Clinic Foundation. In Malaysia, telemedicine is a cornerstone of the government's ambitious Multimedia Super Corridor, although investment was scaled back in 1998 in response to the region's economic difficulties. India participates in several consulting networks for obtaining second opinions and transmitting pathology and other data. In 1998 the first African telemedicine network was established in Mozambique.

World Care Technologies, Inc., a Cambridge, Massachusetts company provides telemedicine and medical management services accessible through the Internet. In 1999 the company formed a strategic alliance with Data General Corporation, a leading information systems provider, and MarkCare Medical Systems, Inc. a medical imaging systems distributor. The alliance combines telemedicine and Personal Archiving and Communication Systems (PACS) to interconnect health care providers. Initial installation sites included hospitals and clinics in Spain, Portugal, and Romania.

Canada has a long history of providing networked medical services to its remote provinces. The European Union has long advocated the use of information technology to reduce inequalities in European health care, and the European Commission has launched feasibility studies for its planned Global Emergency

Telemedicine System. Australia has been particularly aggressive in establishing telemedicine sites and, as a result, telemedical revenue grew from $36 million in 1997 to an estimated $54 million in 1998, and is expected to reach $4 billion by the 2005. In Great Britain, archaic record-keeping systems, bureaucratic opposition, and concern that short-term commercial interests would prevail over long-term goals have led to a few telemedicine trials but no large-scale applications.

RESEARCH AND TECHNOLOGY

Military medicine is an ideal laboratory for telemedicine technologies because of its freedom from reimbursement and licensure issues, and because its very purpose is to provide timely specialty care to remote locations. Portable medical communications systems and sensors for on-site assessment of key vital signs are being developed for possible future use on isolated job sites or in health care settings. New electronic formats for medical information are also being developed, along with a personal information carrier intended to bridge the gap between treatment and access to a complete medical record. The importance of teleradiology was affirmed in 1998 during the U.S. mission to Bosnia-Herzegovina, where all radiological exams were conducted from neighboring countries. Numerous projects in teledentistry, teledermatology, telepsychiatry, and telepathology are in progress, including experimental uses of artificial intelligence to aid medical decision-making under battlefield conditions and high-resolution diagnostic imaging provided by forward medical units to distant treatment centers.

Telemedicine is also being used outside clinical settings. Virgin Airlines and Princess Cruise Line both offer telemedicine services to travelers. A Florida homeless shelter has used telemedicine, especially to treat common ailments in homeless children. As the cost of technology falls and private companies gain a better understanding of the unique needs of health care information systems, experts believe such commercial applications for routine health monitoring or emergency care will likely become more commonplace.

FURTHER READING

"American TeleCare, Inc.," 16 April 1999. Available from http://www.americantelecare.com.

"American TeleCare, Inc. Launches TeleHomeCare Project at Veterans' Hospital in Tampa, Florida." Eden Prairie,

MN: American TeleCare, Inc., 16 April 1999. Available from http://www.americantelecare.com/PR.txt.

"Army TMED Projects." Available from http://www.ttad .org/pages/projects/armyproj.html.

"ATSP '98 Telemedicine Report Chronicles Industry Growth, Diversification." *BW Healthwire,* 7 April 1999.

Bergeron, Bryan P. "Telepresence and the Practice of Medicine." *Post Graduate Medicine,* April 1998.

Bowermaster, David. "Costs of a High-Tech Cure." Available from http://www.msnbc.com/news/168627.asp.

Burns, Patrick. "Changing Times and the Business Case for 'Telestuff'." *Health Management Technology,* July 1997.

"Case Study: MedVision." Redmond, WA: Microsoft Corporation, 17 April 1999. Available from http://www.micro soft.com/NTServer/nts/exec/casestudy/MedVision.asp.

"Complete Product Line." Available from http://www.vtel .com.

"CorpTech Company Capsule for MedVision, Inc.," 16 April 1999. Available at http://www.corptech.com/Research Areas/CompanyCapsule.cfm.

"Data General, MarkCare Join Forces with WorldCare, Firms to Offer Integrated PACS/Telemedicine Systems." *PACS and Networking News,* February 1999.

"Data General, MarkCare Medical Systems and WorldCare Technologies Announce a Strategic Alliance to Provide Integrated Clinical Information Management Solutions to the Healthcare Industry." Westboro, MA: Data General Corporation, 17 April 1999. Available from http://www.dg.com/ news/html/01_12_99.html.

Davis, Stephania H. "What's Holding Up the Telemedicine Explosion?" *Telephony,* 1 June 1998.

Dudman, Jane. "Health and Efficiency (Telemedicine in the United Kingdom)." *Computer Weekly,* 31 July 1997.

Evans, Jim. "Telemedicine: A Picture Is Worth . . ." *Health Management Technology,* January 1998.

"Fact Sheet: Telemedicine Related Programs." Available from http://www.nlm.nih.gov/pubs/factsheets/telemedicine .html.

"Federal Telemedicine." Available from http://www.cbloch .com/about.html.

"HCFA Model for Telehealth Out of Step with Current Practice." *Medical Outcomes and Guidelines Alert,* 18 June 1998.

Hoovers Online, 16 April 1999. Available from http://www .hoovers.com.

"The Internet and the Future of Telehealth." Available from http://www.iftf.org/telehealth.html.

Janah, Monua. "Health Care by Cisco." *Informationweek,* 23 February 1998.

"Killer Apps: The Telemedicine Breakthrough." *America's Network,* 15 January 1998.

Kim, Howard. "No Telemedicine 'Rush'," *American Medical News,* 4 May 1998.

Laino, Charlene. "Virtual Medicine, Real Benefits?" Available from http://www.msnbc.com/news/168944.html.

Larkin, Marilynn. "Telemedicine Finds Its Place in the Real World." *Lancet,* 30 August 1997.

"Latest Analysis Suggests a $4.2 Million Reimbursement Level for 1997 Telemedicine Services." *BW Healthwire,* 25 March 1999.

Lindberg, Donald A. B. "Fiscal Year 1999 President's Budget Request for the National Library of Medicine." Statement to the House Appropriations Sub-Committee on Labor, HHS and Education, 18 March 1998. Available from http://www.nlm.nih.gov/pubs/staffpubs/od/budget99.html.

Linkous, Jonathan D. "Telemedicine Information & Resources: Predicting the Market for Telemedicine." Available from http://www.atmeda.org/resources/marketreports.html.

Magenau, Jeff L. "Digital Diagnosis: Liability Concerns and State Licensing Issues Are Inhibiting the Progress of Telemedicine." *Communications and the Law,* December 1997.

Martin, Sean. "New Budget Law Could Boost Telemedicine's Future." *American Medical News,* 15 September 1997.

"Medicaid and Telemedicine." Health Care Financing Administration, U.S. Department of Health and Human Services, 31 March 1999. Available from http://www.hefa.gov/ medicaid/telelist.html.

Meredith, Helen. "Exporting Skills Good Medicine for Health Care." *Australian Financial Review,* 17 July 1998.

Nairn, Geoffrey. "Internet Set for Key Role in Healthcare." *Financial Times,* 1 April 1998.

"New Rules: Medicare to Pay for Interactive Consults Only." *Modern Healthcare,* 29 June 1998.

"NLM National Telemedicine Initiative." Bethesda, MD: National Library of Medicine, 5 April 1999. Available from http://www.nlm.nih.gov/research/telemedinit.html.

"Obstacles to Telemedicine's Growth." *Medical Economics,* 24 November 1997.

"PictureTel: Industries and Applications," 16 April 1999. Available from http://www.pictureTel.com.

"The Present Offers a Small Glimpse of Telemedicine's Future." *BBI Newsletter,* 1 May 1998.

Robinson, Kevin. "Telemedicine: Technology Arrives, But Barriers Remain." *Biophotonics International,* July/August 1998.

Rosenberg, Robert. "Telemedicine: An Expensive Prescription?" *Business Communications Review,* May 1997.

"Rural Providers Take $300 Million Hit As FCC Bows to Political Pressure." *Modern Healthcare,* 29 June 1998.

Sani, Rozana. "Ministry Cuts Back on Telemedicine." *New Straits Times,* 25 May 1998.

Sherter, Alain L. "Using Telemedicine to Bring Care to Homeless." *Health Data Management,* March 1998.

Smith, Robert C., ed. "Telemedicine." *Medical and Healthcare Marketplace Guide 1997-1998.* Philadelphia: Dorland's Biomedical, 1998.

Snyder, Karyn. "Telemedicine: The New Frontier." *Drug Topics,* 4 August 1997.

Sorelle, Ruth. "Vision for the Future: Health Care Options Grow With Rural Telemedicine." *Houston Chronicle,* 7 July 1998.

———. "Vision for the Future: Medicine On-Screen." *Houston Chronicle,* 5 July 1998.

———. "Vision for the Future: Telemedicine May Be Just What the Doc Ordered in Space." *Houston Chronicle,* 6 July 1998.

———. "Vision for the Future: Telemedicine a Virtual Reality of the Future." *Houston Chronicle,* 8 July 1998.

"A Telemedicine Primer: Understanding the Issues." Available from http://www.atsp.org/telemedprimer.html.

"Testimony Before the House Committee on . . . , Subcommittee on Health and Environment." Available from http://www.ttad.org/pages/congress/testimony050598.html.

"Universal Fund Program: Options for the Future." Rockville, MD: Office for the Advancement of Telehealth, February 1999. Available from http://telehealth.hrsa.gov/univtxt.htm.

"Universal Service Administrative Company Report to the FCC: Evaluation of Rural Health Care Program." Washington, D.C.: Federal Communications Commission, 29 March 1999. Available from http://www.fcc.gov.

"USDA Streamlines Loans and Grants Program." Washington, DC: United States Department of Agriculture Press Release, 25 March 1999. Available from http://telehealth.hrsa.gov/rusgrant.html.

"Vtel: The Company." Available from http://www.vtel.com.

"What Is Telemedicine/History of Telemedicine." Available from http://208.129.211.51/WhatIsTelemedicine.html.

"World Care Technologies Company Profile," 17 April 1999. Available from http://www.worldcaretech.com.

—Cameron McLaughlin, updated by Sondra E. O'Donnell

TELEPHONE SERVICES AND ACCESSORIES

In a society as dependent upon high-speed telecommunications as this one is, it should come as no surprise that telephone users have grown increasingly enamored of the wide variety of add-on products designed to make phone service even more useful. These products range from the relatively simple Call Forwarding feature, which sends incoming calls to another number, or voice mail, to the more sophisticated Caller ID box, which lets the user know who is calling.

For the most part, the vast array of telephone accessories and services were developed by research and development teams at some of the country's better known telecommunications companies. An explosion of mergers and acquisitions during the late 1990s made this a corporate landscape subject to sharp changes from day to day. For the most part, telephone users avail themselves of these services through local service providers, although the product or technology may have been developed originally by another telecommunications company. Among the more popular telephone services and accessories are call block, call forwarding, caller ID, call waiting, call waiting ID, repeat dial, return call, signal ring, 900-call block, the cordless digital spread spectrum telephone, and conference calling.

The upsurge in U.S. telecommunications industry megamergers was traced by many to the Telecommunications Act of 1996. Intended to deregulate the industry and stimulate competition, the statute instead appeared to set off a massive wave of corporate mergers. In 1996 alone the total value of mergers in the telecommunications industry was estimated at close to $80 billion. Of the original seven Baby Bells, five remained: Bell Atlantic, SBC Communications (which absorbed Baby Bell sibling Pacific Telesis), BellSouth, Ameritech, and US West.

ORGANIZATION AND STRUCTURE

In the United States, the face of the telecommunications industry was forever altered in 1984 when the Justice Department's antitrust ruling broke the giant American Telephone & Telegraph (AT&T) into seven regional companies, one of which was Bell Atlantic. It should be noted, however, that Bell Atlantic's acquisition in the late 1990s of Baby Bell sibling NYNEX for $25.7 billion doubled its size and made it the number two U.S. telecommunications service company after its former parent. Its scheduled merger with GTE promised to double the company's size again.

Mergers and acquisitions continued to change the structure of the U.S. telecommunications industry throughout the second half of the 1990s. As of early 1999, the principal basic telephone service providers in the United States were SBC Communications, BellSouth, Ameritech, US West, MCI WorldCom, Sprint, Bell Atlantic, and GTE, the last two of which had announced but not finalized plans to merge. In addition, there are numerous small independent telephone companies located throughout the United States. These and other companies such as AT&T, Lucent Technologies, and Northern Telecom also develop and market some of the highly successful new add-on services and devices.

Almost all of these companies, independents included, offer customers a broad range of add-on services and accessories, including caller ID, call block, and call forwarding. In addition to these services, American consumers have a number of other products to choose from, such as the PowerDialer from Technology Arts of Massachusetts. PowerDialer was designed to automatically redial busy numbers as quickly as the local telephone company could process the calls, as fast as 25 times in a minute. The product, which retailed for $249 in the late 1990s, is marketed directly by Technology Arts and is not available through local telephone companies.

The future promises an even broader range of services for telephone consumers with the spread of fiber-optic wiring, which will allow faster and better data transmission over telephone lines. A number of major telephone service providers also acquired an interest in television cable companies in preparation for the day when they would begin to offer television connections over telephone lines—and that day is not far off.

BACKGROUND AND DEVELOPMENT

Upheaval in the U.S. telecommunications industry in the mid-1980s, resulting from the Justice Department's antitrust ruling, left telephone companies in a brand new competitive arena. Home and business telephone users, who had previously rented equipment from the local telephone company, now purchase their own equipment and pay local providers for hooking up to their networks. Although most telephone companies offer a range of telephones for sale, consumers usually find they can get a better deal at the local discount chain or an electronics store.

Most telephone companies soon realized there was a virtual gold mine in marketing add-on products. Suddenly, services that previously had been available only to sophisticated business users were being sold to home service consumers. These included call forwarding ability and the ability to dial back the number of the last caller (even if the phone was not answered). Some such services were even offered on a per-use basis. For example, a telephone customer unable to get to a ringing phone in time could punch the star key and two numbers, typically "69," to activate this service, for which he or she would then be charged 75 cents or $1. Those who chose to have access to this service at all times paid a monthly fee for unlimited use.

Among the most popular services marketed by local telephone service providers are call block, which allows telephone customers to block all calls from certain telephone numbers, and call forwarding, which routes all calls to another telephone number or to voice mail when the phone is busy or not answered. Also particularly popular is caller ID, the use of which requires a small box with a window to display a telephone number. This feature allows customers to determine the number (and sometimes the name of the caller) from which a call is coming.

The technology for cordless telephony has improved significantly since such equipment was first marketed. Reception on early cordless telephones left a great deal to be desired, and many purchasers of such early equipment soon abandoned it and returned to corded phones. In the late 1990s, digital spread spectrum technology vastly improved the reception and transmission quality of cordless telephones.

CURRENT CONDITIONS

The U.S. and international telecommunications industry in the late 1990s was marketing a mind-boggling array of telephone accessories and services. Available from local telephone service providers, and in some cases from independent retailers, these accessories ran the gamut from caller ID boxes to a range of telephone instruments, both corded and cordless.

The telephone selections available to consumers alone was staggering in its variety. Only 20 years ago, choices would have been relatively limited. One could buy a console, wall, or princess telephone in black, white, or pink. With Ma Bell's control on telephones loosened by deregulation, a typical discount store routinely stocks a selection of about 50 cordless phones, 30 phones with cords, and at least a dozen cellular phones. That does not include the telephone/answering machine combinations, of which one might find at least half a dozen. Better yet, the increased competition in this marketplace has sent prices plummeting. In late 1998 or early 1999, a 25-channel cordless telephone could be found at most discount retailers for only $100, about half what it would have cost only a year earlier.

In 1997, for the first time, cordless telephones outsold corded phones by 28.2 to 27.8 million. Jim Barry, a spokesman for the Consumer Electronics Manufacturers Association, predicted that the gap between cordless and corded phone sales was likely to grow larger over time. "What you're getting with a cordless phone is convenience," Barry said. "And the technology of cordless telephones is getting better." Cordless telephones also proved to be a very popular gift idea. Ameritech, one of the Baby Bells, reported that about 45 percent of all its cordless telephones are sold in November, just in time for Christmas gift giving.

There are a number of reasons for the sharp increase in popularity of the cordless telephone, not the least of which is significantly improved reception. The first cordless phones on the market allowed a user to walk from one room of the house to another without dragging a telephone cord along with them, but they were subject to considerable interference, had a limited range, and lacked security. The first cordless phones transmitted sound from the handset to the telephone's base using an analog signal. Neighboring cordless phone users often found snippets of other conversations breaking into their own. Even transmissions from household baby monitors sometimes interfered with cordless phone calls. Modern cordless models broadcast over frequencies that are less crowded, offering much clearer signals. Even better, some new cordless phones use digital signals, reducing the chances that conversations would be intercepted. Sounds are converted into computer code, and then transmitted between the base and the handset.

In addition to increased dependability, cordless telephones today are available in a number of different models. Early cordless phones, operating on frequencies between 43 and 49 MHz, were highly susceptible to interference from computers, fluorescent lights, and other such devices. Transmissions at such low frequencies generally were not able to penetrate walls or other such obstructions. Most of these early cordless phones, few of which are still available in stores, operated over 10 channels. If interference was encountered on one channel, the phone would switch automatically to the next.

Improved reception is available on 25-channel analog cordless phones, which manage to avoid interference by using more channels. Some of the 25-channel phones come with built-in Caller ID. If longer range and still clearer reception is required, 900-MHz analog phones are a good choice, according to CEMA's Jim Barry. He said that some such telephones operate dependably at three-quarters of a mile from the base. He pointed out, however, that since the signal is uncoded, the user runs the risk of having his or her conversations intercepted. That danger can be avoided if you opt for a 900-MHz digital phone, which convert sounds into code for transmission from the handset to the base. To ensure even better reception, some 900-MHz phones use digital spread spectrum technology. If interference is encountered on one channel, the phone searches for a clear channel as far

away as possible from the one that is blocked. This technology increases the clarity of reception and range. Finally, the ultimate cordless phone as of the late 1990s was the 2.4-GHz model, available only from Panasonic. These phones have twice the range of the 900-MHz models and offer increased clarity.

Although the performance of cordless telephones sharply improved, for many users the tried and true corded telephone was first choice because of its dependability and security. Other attractive features of corded phones are the lower price and the knowledge that they will still function in a power outage, something that cannot be said of cordless phones. The phone line itself supplies all the power needed to operate a corded telephone. For the style-conscious, corded phones are often the logical choice since they offer the widest variation in style and are available in novelty shapes and most colors. For those who must use the telephone while typing or using their hands, a headset phone may make sense.

Of the add-on telephone services and accessories, the three most popular features are call waiting, caller ID, and voice mail, in that order. Jeff Small, a marketing official with Ameritech's consumer division, said that the call waiting feature is compatible with any telephone. When a user with this service is on the telephone and someone else calls, an audible signal can be heard on the line. The user may click the receiver button or push "flash" to answer the new call. No special equipment is needed for this service, although customers must pay a monthly fee to the local service provider.

Unlike call waiting, caller ID service requires special equipment, specifically a LCD screen to display information about incoming calls. Some newer models of phones, both corded and cordless, have a caller ID screen built in, or consumers who decide to opt for this service can purchase a small caller ID box with such a screen. Customers pay a monthly fee for caller ID service and also a rental fee if they use a caller ID box supplied by the telephone company. Voice mail systems are covered in a separate essay elsewhere in this book.

Increasingly popular in the late 1990s were two-line phones that allowed customers to use a line hooked up to a computer modem as a second voice line when the computer was not in use. Other telephone accessories or features available on the market included storage for telephone numbers called frequently, speakers for hands-free telephone use, and an answering machine for those who prefer that to voice mail.

INDUSTRY LEADERS

A leading player in the market for telephone services and accessories is Bell Atlantic, the largest of the surviving Baby Bells. Bell Atlantic's acquisition of Baby Bell sibling NYNEX doubled the company's size. Further expansion is on the horizon in the form of a planned merger with GTE Corporation. Based in New York City, Bell Atlantic is the second largest telecommunications services company after AT&T, although in many sectors it is a bigger player than its former parent. Bell Atlantic provides local telephone service to some 40 million homes and businesses in a 13-state area stretching from Maine to Virginia and includes the District of Columbia. In 1998, Bell Atlantic posted net income of nearly $3.0 billion on revenue of $31.6 billion. Net earnings showed an impressive increase of nearly 21.0 percent over 1997, while revenue was up by 4.5 percent.

Lucent Technologies, former equipment manufacturing arm of AT&T, is today the largest U.S. manufacturer of telecommunications hardware and software. Based in Murray Hill, New Jersey, the company's products range from integrated circuits to sophisticated business communications systems. Lucent is also home to Bell Laboratories, AT&T's former research and development division. In fiscal 1998, ending on September 30, 1998, Lucent reported net income of $970.0 million on revenue of $30.1 billion. The company's net earnings were up almost 80.0 percent over 1997, while revenue climbed 14.4 percent.

Based in San Antonio, SBC Communications is second only to Bell Atlantic as a provider of local telephone service. With almost 37 million local-access lines in the states of Arkansas, California, Connecticut, Kansas, Missouri, Nevada, Oklahoma, and Texas, the company is the umbrella organization for such familiar subsidiaries as Southern New England Telecommunications, Southwestern Bell, and Pacific Bell. SBC is also active on the international front, holding interests in telecommunications companies in 10 countries outside the United States. The company reported a jump of almost 173.0 percent in net income in 1998 to $4.0 billion. These earnings were drawn from total revenue of $28.8 billion, up 15.8 percent from 1997. SBC announced plans to purchase Ameritech, a Baby Bell sibling based in Chicago.

Serving about 21 million local telephone customers in more than 25 states, GTE Corporation announced plans to merge with Bell Atlantic. The resulting company will serve 63 million local telephone customers in 38 states. GTE's largest local telephone operations in 1998 were in Florida, California, and

Texas. GTE posted net income of $2.2 billion in 1998 on revenue of $25.5 billion. While revenue was up 9.5 percent, the company's earnings were down 22.3 percent from the previous year.

In the late 1990s, AT&T, parent of the Baby Bells, was busily exploring ways to get back into the local telephone business that it lost when the company was broken up in 1984. In an effort to advance this strategy, AT&T acquired TeleCommuncations Inc. The purchase gave AT&T access to about 18 million homes through cable hookups. The company hoped to upgrade one-way cable lines into two-way connections, allowing AT&T to offer telephone, cable television, and high-speed Internet access over these connections. The company reported net income in 1998 of $6.4 billion, up nearly 38.0 percent from the previous year. AT&T's 1998 revenue totaled $53.2 billion, an increase of 3.7 percent over 1997.

Headquartered in Atlanta, BellSouth Corporation is a major provider of local telephone service in nine southeastern states. It is looking to Latin America for new business opportunities to offset some of the losses expected in local U.S. markets due to increased competition under deregulation. BellSouth posted 1998 net income of $3.5 billion on revenue of $23.1 billion. Net earnings showed an increase of 8.2 percent over 1997, while revenue rose 12.5 percent over the previous year.

MCI WorldCom Inc., based in Jackson, Mississippi, is a major player in the long-distance telephone market as well as a marketer of some telephone services and accessories. Formed by the 1998 merger of MCI Communications and WorldCom, the company has operations in more than 60 countries. In 1998, it reported a net loss of $2.7 billion on revenue of $17.7 billion. Revenue showed an increase of 140.5 percent over the previous year.

Based in Chicago, Ameritech is one of the surviving Baby Bells created by AT&T's 1984 breakup. SBC Communications announced plans to acquire Ameritech. As of 1999, the company served more than 12 million local telephone customers in Illinois, Indiana, Michigan, Ohio, and Wisconsin. Ameritech has also made inroads into the cable television market in a number of Midwest cities. The company has international interests in telecommunications companies in Belgium, Denmark, Hungary, and Norway. It reported net income of $3.6 billion in 1998 on revenue of $17.2 billion. Earnings were up 57.1 percent from 1997, while revenue was just over 7.0 percent higher than in the previous year.

Headquartered in Brampton, Ontario, Northern Telecom Limited is a major manufacturer of telephone equipment. Its products range from elaborate business communications systems to personal telephone equipment. About 60 percent of the company's revenue is generated by sales in the United States. In 1998, Northern Telecom reported a net loss of $537 million on revenue of $17.6 billion. The 1998 revenue represented a jump of 13.8 percent from the level reported the previous year.

Sprint Corporation, like most players in the U.S. telecommunications market, has irons in a number of fires. Already the number three long-distance provider in the United States, the company also provides local phone service, ranking second after GTE Corporation in the world of non-Baby Bell telephone service. The company's local service division boasted more than 7 million customers in 19 states as of early 1999. Its net income in 1997 totaled $952.5 million on revenue of $14.9 billion. Although revenue in 1997 was about 6 percent higher than in 1996, net earnings showed a decline of almost 20 percent.

Based in Englewood, Colorado, US West Inc. is the smallest of the Baby Bells, providing local telephone service over about 16 million lines. The company moved aggressively to establish itself as a provider of cable television service. It was also trying to discard the reputation for poor service that earned it the nickname "US Worst." In 1998 US West posted net income of $1.5 billion on revenue of $12.4 billion. Earnings were 28.1 percent higher than in 1997, while revenue was up about 20.0 percent from the previous year.

WORK FORCE

It is virtually impossible to isolate the segments of the telecommunications industry responsible for some of the specialized services and accessories covered here. The industry as a whole is a major employer in the United States as well as in most other Western countries with a sophisticated communications infrastructure. The world's growing dependence on communications technology is likely to ensure that this sector remains a major employer for the foreseeable future. It is possible, however, that some of the rationalizations in the industry brought by mergers and acquisitions may from time to time bring job reductions at some of the companies that are major players in this field.

According to employment records from the late 1990s, major employers in the telecommunications industry included Bell Atlantic Corporation, with a pay-roll of more than 140,000; SBC Communications Inc., which employed close to 130,000; GTE Corporation, 120,000; and AT&T Corporation, about 108,000. BellSouth Corporation employed more than 88,000 as of 1998, while MCI WorldCom Inc. reported a payroll of 77,000 that same year. As of 1997, Chicago-based Ameritech Corporation employed close to 75,000, and Sprint Corporation employed nearly 65,000, according to 1998 data. US West Inc., based in Englewood, Colorado, had a payroll of nearly 55,000 as of 1998. Canadian-based Northern Telecom employed 73,000, according to 1997 statistics.

Employment opportunities within the telecommunications industry run the gamut from entry-level clerical positions, to researchers and engineers, to high-paying management positions at the head of some of the industry's major players. For young people interested in participating in the technological revolution that continues to sweep this country and the world, the telecommunications industry is at the heart of this revolution, sponsoring much of the research that has moved technological know-how forward during the late twentieth century.

AMERICA AND THE WORLD

The love affair with useful telephone services and accessories is not limited to the United States alone. Virtually all of the technology that has made possible most of these tools has either been exported to or developed independently in most of the countries of the industrialized world. And the advances are not limited to the industrialized world alone. Telephone customers in some of the developing countries are also getting an opportunity to avail themselves of these telephone products.

RESEARCH AND TECHNOLOGY

Just when it seems technological advancement has reached its limits, a company steps forward to announce a new ground-breaking product or a forward-looking variation to an existing product. Built on the popular caller ID technology, a new product called privacy manager was introduced in parts of Chicago and Detroit in the fall of 1998 by Ameritech. Caller ID was designed to help users screen out unwanted calls, particularly calls from telemarketers and other sales personnel. However, cagey telemarketing firms managed to dodge this barrier by using legal means to block both their identities and telephone numbers. Privacy manager uses caller ID technology to identify incoming calls from phone numbers that are either "unknown" or "unavailable." Such calls are intercepted by a recorded message that asks the caller to identify himself or herself. If the party placing the call chooses to disclose his or her identity, the call rings through to the privacy manager customer, who then hears a brief recording identifying the caller. The customer then has three options: accept the call, decline the call without explanation, or decline the call and have privacy manager ask that the caller not call again. In introducing the product, Diane Primo, Ameritech's president of product management, said: "The message is loud and clear. Our customers simply want control over telemarketing."

One of the technologies that futurists have talked about endlessly for the last several decades has been the so-called picture phone, which allows both parties to a conversation to see each other. Although such telephones are available, thus far the technology is still rather shaky, the pictures not so clear, and the cost prohibitive for most telephone customers. This is one long-promised technological innovation that is almost certain to materialize in the early years of the twenty-first century. Another innovation offered by a number of electronics companies is the screen phone, which allows users to display caller ID information, surf the Web, or check e-mail. Sort of a marriage between a telephone and a computer, Cidco's iPhone was designed to appeal to customers who want to be able to check e-mail without booting up the PC. The iPhone retails for about $500.

A number of telecommunications companies are expected to aggressively pursue the cable television market in the next few years. Already the technology exists to offer cable television over existing telephone lines. Ongoing work to install fiber optic telephone lines throughout the country will certainly step up action on this front in the near-term future. US West, which already offers 120 digital channels of television entertainment and information over telephone lines in the Phoenix area, is moving to offer the same sort of service in metropolitan Denver.

FURTHER READING

Cantwell, Rebecca. "US WEST, TCI Going Head-to-Head for Cable Customers." *Denver Rocky Mountain News,* 7 October 1998, 1B.

Cummings, James. "Hold the Phone! Options Are Ringing Off the Hook." *Atlanta Journal and Constitution,* 3 December 1998, BE14.

Davidson, Paul. "Who's Next on Frenzied Telecom Merger Front?" *USA Today,* 12 May 1998, 3B.

Day, Rebecca. "Phone Home: Phones of the Future That Do It All. Now . . . . " *Popular Mechanics,* 1 May 1998, 92.

"Dialtone: PowerDialer—High-Tech Gadget Helps You Break Those AOL Busies." *Work-Group Computing Report,* 24 February 1997.

Gelmis, Joseph. "A Roundup of Hot Games, Gadgets & Gizmos from the Consumer Electronics Show." *Newsday,* 21 July 1994, B29.

Hoover's Online, 26 April 1999. Available from http://www.hoovers.com.

"Huaxu, Motorola Form Smart Card Joint Venture; Agreement Promises Bright Future for Smart Card Industry in China." *Business Wire,* 22 January 1998.

Irvine, Martha. "Phone Company Offers Service to Filter Out Sales Calls." *AP Online,* 23 September 1998.

Mason, Charles. "Cox Says Early Foray's Bearing Fruit." *America's Network,* 1 June 1998, 58.

Mathoda, Ranjit. "All Hell Breaks Loose in the Telephone Industry." *B.C. Intell. Prop. & Tech. F.,* 1998.

Meyers, Anne. "Family Tech: Smart Ways to Make Home Life Easier: Technology Keeps Ringing in New Customer Phone Services." *Atlanta Journal and Constitution,* 14 February 1999, H3.

"Motorola Israel Develops Cellular Voice-Dial System." *Xinhua News Agency,* 29 January 1997.

"NCTI Introduces Clearspeech-Phone Filter at Winter CES-Digitally Cancels Noise for Telephones." *Business Wire,* 7 January 1999.

Phillips, Sharon. "Ameritech EVP & CFO—Interview." *Wall Street Corporate Reporter,* 5 August 1998.

"US Robotics Announces Major Move into ADSL." *Newsbytes News Network,* 3 March 1997.

—Don Amerman

Telephony

Telephony covers the transmission of any sort of data over wired or wireless networks and encompasses the many changes within the trillion-dollar telecommunications industry. The computers and electronics industries figure prominently in telecommunications devices, such as satellites, switches and phones, as well as the computer-telephone integration (CTI) technology used in faxes, voice mail, call centers, voice recognition, video-conferencing and interactive voice response systems. Mergers, technology and regulations constantly reshape the broad-ranging telephony industry.

Telephony data flies back and forth across industry lines in more ways than one. Long distance telephone service revenues hit $92.7 billion in 1997, with hefty increases projected. Insiders predict Internet telephony will reach $20 billion annually by 2000. One research organization estimates that 35 percent of all phone calls will be made using Internet-based public phone networks by 2002, potentially creating a $60 billion market. The satellite telephony industry alone may exceed $35 billion annually by 2005. Through convergence, the new-generation telephony company may eventually offer local, paging, long-distance, cellular, and Internet phone services all priced right and specially packaged. For the consumer, these convergent technologies may one day mean one number, one phone, and one bill.

ORGANIZATION AND STRUCTURE

The industry consists of three main businesses: provision of services to consumers, corporations and individuals; installing infrastructure from production of hardware to deployment of software; and managing or providing business services for these business activities within the industry and to consumers such as Yellow Pages publishing and custom database maintenance.

Voice is encoded and decoded through the telephone itself into electrical signals. These are transmitted over a network of copper or fiber optic cable, radio or satellite transceivers, and switches between one or more other telephones or networks. The majority of telephone services are designed for speech transmission, but with the advent of computerization and digitization, networks transmit other data as well. These include facsimile documents, audio and video, and big packets of secure data. Consumers want plain old telephone service (POTS), cellular telephone service, and Internet connections; corporations need sophisticated telephony networks for broadband transmission of voice, data and even video.

"There are 600 million phones in the world, which is why telecommunications is a trillion-dollar business," stated Andrew J. Kesler in *Forbes* in 1998. "These analog lines aren't going away, but you can augment them with digital technology. . .There's a lot of room for new business now that telco competition is allowed. Anyone can lease a pair of wires from a regional Bell for $22 per month and use them to offer 155 megabits per second for $45,000 per month."

GOVERNMENTAL AGENCIES

The telecommunications industry is regulated by the Federal Communications Commission (FCC). This independent agency, created in 1934, regulates interstate and international communications that originate in the United States and are transmitted via radio, TV, wire, cable and satellite. As new technologies developed, for example, this agency has undertaken the task of allocation of the electromagnetic spectrum for transmission of television and wireless communications signals. The FCC traditionally has attempted to maintain a balance between the stronger market players while ensuring markets remain open to competition.

At the state level, public utilities commissions add another layer of regulation. These bodies, which do the bidding of state lawmakers, originally granted local franchises to local-service providers and regulated utilities, namely gas and power companies. The National Association of Regulatory Utility Commissioners is an umbrella group designed to be sure there are uniform regulations for public utilities. Other levels of government responsible for various regulations, primarily for oversight of such things as franchise granting and infrastructure construction, exist at the county and municipal levels.

STANDARDS BODIES AND TRADE ASSOCIATIONS

The predominant standards body for the telephony industry is the United Nations's International Telecommunication Union, based in Geneva. This body assists governments and the private sector alike by providing a forum for determining technical methods by which data is sent. A good example is the ratification of the V.90 standard for 56K modems. The American National Standards Institute approves and publishes United States telecommunications standards. An array of other bodies, such as the IEEE, promulgate standards as well. The United States Telephone Association, Telecommunications Industry Association, Multimedia Telecommunications Association and National Exchange Carrier Association are among the various industry trade organizations formed to protect the interests of member companies within the industry.

IMPACT OF REGULATION

Regulation of the U.S. telecommunications market has primarily been shaped in the courts by antitrust actions brought against AT&T. In a 1949 case, the United States Department of Justice claimed that the Bell Operating Companies practiced illegal exclusion by purchasing goods from Western Electric, which was a part of the Bell System. The case, settled in 1956, resulted in AT&T holding on to Western Electric with the condition that they not enter the computer market. The second major antitrust suit, *United States*

v. AT&T, was initiated in 1974. The allegations included that AT&T monopolized the long distance market and again asserted its relationship with Western Electric was illegal. The government sought divestiture of AT&T-owned manufacturing and long distance businesses. The company broke up in 1982 after years of legal wrangling and formed seven regional Bell operating companies (RBOCs). The Baby Bells remained regulated monopolies, each with an exclusive franchise in its region. AT&T later spun off NCR and Lucent Technologies.

THE TELECOMMUNICATIONS REFORM ACT OF 1996

Although the break-up of AT&T was the watershed legal event causing telephony to evolve and thrive, perhaps the most notable factor pushing its convergence with the computer industry was the Telecommunications Reform Act of 1996. Congress, through this legislation, removed barriers to competition throughout the telecommunications industry and effectively paved the way for the industry to seek cross-industry alliances such as with computing. Telecommunications reform was spearheaded by the guidance of Reed Hundt, chairman of the FCC, who shepherded the Act through Congress during his tenure. (He stepped down November 1997.)

At the bill signing, President Bill Clinton called the Act, "truly revolutionary legislation that will bring the future to our doorstep." He said "the information revolution is changing the way we work, the way we live, the way we relate to each other. Already the revolution is so profound that it is changing the dominant economic model of the age. And already, thanks to the scientific and entrepreneurial genius of American workers in this country, it has created vast, vast opportunities for us to grow and learn and enrich ourselves in body and in spirit."

"But this revolution has been held back by outdated laws designed for a time when there was one phone company, three TV networks, no such thing as a personal computer." Clinton said the Act would help "our laws catch up with our future. We will help to create an open marketplace where competition and innovation can move as quick as light. An industry that is already one-sixth of our entire economy will thrive. It will create opportunity, many more high-wage jobs, and better lives for all Americans."

Despite these promises, industry leaders chafed at regulatory challenges. Richard D. McCormick, chairman and chief operating officer, US West Inc., was among them. In a 1996 address he told the USTA that "where Congress may have paved the way, the Federal Communications Commission has blasted some unbelievable potholes. The FCC's proposed rules on interconnection, unbundling and resale are not competition—they're confiscation."

As *Fortune* magazine noted, the legislation is resulting in corporate mergers and legal battles rather than better and more competitive consumer communications services. Rather than creating new networks from the ground up, companies are buying and selling customers to gain revenue, buying companies to gain market position.

The resultant effect of the Telecommunications Reform Act of 1996 on telephony and other related communications businesses may take years to surface or to comprehend their impacts. As Walt Sapronov stated in *Business Communications Review,* "One area almost certain to see turmoil soon is the dual, overlapping roles of the FCC and state regulators." As an example, "Essentially, Congress has usurped the long-held prerogative of state public service commissions to determine whether, how and which competitors may provide local telecommunications service."

Confusing issues further are taxes levied on telecommunications services. These include federal, state and local charges for programs such as Universal Access, 911 service and subsidizing school and hospital telephone service. Universal Access is a federal program designed to give rural residents and people in low-income brackets basic telephone service. What constitutes "basic" has been widely debated. The state of California, for example, in 1998 included a 0.41 percent charge to consumers be used to discount school, library and hospital bills. On one bill for one phone line in San Francisco, as many as 11 agencies may tax phone use.

New entrants to the telephony market are perceived by telecommunications companies to have an unfair competitive advantage. Primarily, the grousing has been directed at Internet service providers who are unregulated and are not subject to the numerous taxes telcos are. The FCC had not yet, in 1998, regulated IP telephony. Regulatory constrictions on ISPs were being made on a select basis, solely on the complaints of telephone companies.

With technologies merging and established, older ways of doing business seemingly antiquating by the day, the idea has been posited that telephony should be unfettered from all regulation. "The fact is, the FCC is becoming irrelevant," wrote Michael Surkan in *PC Week.* "The blueprint for telecom deregulation has become a laughing stock as courts overturn FCC pro-

nouncements. The public is also taking a dim view of the massive sales of the radio spectrum as many purchasers default, and personal communication service rollouts are mired in delays and high costs."

"In a world where long-distance-call prices keep dropping, the old mantra of regulation for the purpose of ensuring affordable universal phone service sounds increasingly hollow. We would be better off subsidizing needy phone users directly than condoning a convoluted regulatory scheme that breeds inefficiency and political warfare."

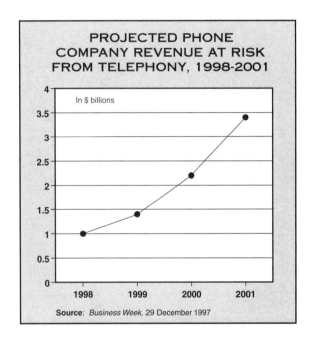

PROJECTED PHONE COMPANY REVENUE AT RISK FROM TELEPHONY, 1998-2001

Source: *Business Week,* 29 December 1997

BACKGROUND AND DEVELOPMENT

The history of telephony is entwined with the development and advances in electronics, telephone and computer for communication. "The telephone utterly revolutionized human communication," stated Isaac Asimov. Hyperbole? Hardly. It was telegraph and telephone that propelled the desire for increasingly faster and more instant means of communications. Alexander Graham Bell is credited with inventing the telephone, initially to send voice via telegraph. Bell patented the device in 1876. Thomas Edison was the first to improve upon the invention.

Switching technologies have driven telephony development and deployment throughout the United States as it progressed from mechanical to analog to digital switching. The network and telephony devices are useless unless switching works properly to connect calls, whether for voice or data. In the early days, an opera-

NetSpeak product manager Ross Schindler demonstrates the WebPhone, which allows users to speak to and see others via the Internet. (AP Photo/Paul Sajuma.)

tor manually plugged and removed circuits from a switchboard to initiate and terminate calls. The first technology leap was initiated in 1889 by Alom B. Strowger, an irate undertaker whose business was being diverted to a competitor by a less-than ethical operator. The Strowger system eliminated the need for a human to connect calls by utilizing mechanical devices to make a connection. This technology was standard throughout the United States for a period of about 50 years.

Beginning in about the 1940s, a series of analog switches were developed to replace huge and cum-bersome devices. The new devices included cross-bar switches, the electronic switching system and stored program control switches. Electronic switching systems were the first marriage of telephony and silicon. Computer technology was used within these systems to make operations efficient and thus reduce costs.

Regulation of the U.S. telecommunications market was shaped by antitrust actions brought against AT&T 1949, 1956 and 1974. The company finally broke up in 1982 after years of legal wrangling, forming seven regional Bell operating companies (RBOCs) in 1984.

The 1970s, along with litigation against industry monolith AT&T, brought digital switching to the fore. These were faster, smaller and more cost efficient devices. A digital switch could accommodate between 1000 and 10,000 subscribers on a network. These devices eventually automated and centralized maintenance. The late 1970s and 1980s were the age of fiber; the 1990s belonged to wireless, specifically digital wireless.

Contrary to laudatory visions about the promise of digital technologies, George Gilder, writing in *The Economist* in 1993, predicted the future was not as bright for older, entrenched technologies like the telephone. "Contemplating their revenues of tens of billions of dollars, their laboratories full of new technology, their millions of mostly satisfied shareholders and customers, their multiplying masses of trade publications and cover-stories in national magazines, telephone and television executives all too often seem unaware that their basic technologies are dead," he wrote. "In order to see the future of telecommunications, it is necessary to lug the dead body out of the way first."

The telephone network was formed on twisted pair copper wires, but in the 1990s various means became available to transmit large bundles of data economically without wires. Peter Huber stated in a 1993 *Forbes* article that the "massive repositioning of wire and radio" had truly begun in the 1980s. "When the Bell breakup was approved in 1982, MCI was feverishly building a microwave network. Government lawyers concluded that the long distance, radio-based market was competitive, while the local, landline network remained a monopoly. AT&T was carved up accordingly," he wrote, "but even as the ink was drying on the divestiture decree, the microwave towers were being dynamited to the ground. The long distance network was being taken over by fiber optic glass."

At that time other emergent technologies included cellular systems and low-power cellular or "personal communications services" networks. Huber estimated, at that time, the cost to companies for these various technologies was vastly different and the economics of scale constantly widening. In 1993, the cost associated with creating infrastructure for cellular networks was estimated as $1,000 per subscriber, while traditional copper wired landlines cost about $1,500, with the costs increasing. Transmission equipment developed in the 1990s called Synchronous Option Network, or SONET, were fiber-optic transport systems that increasingly provided the backbone for ATM and broadband switching systems over which both voice and data can be carried. A

steady, industry-wide transition toward an all-optical network was progressing in the late 1990s; however, at that time the technology was not deemed cost-effective to make these types of networks commercially available. According to *Telephony,* companies such as international carriers with large investments in fiber-optics were poised to be the first to employ these networks. Throughout this era, the industry became increasingly reliant upon computers for all aspects of telephony operations.

CURRENT CONDITIONS

Major driving forces in U.S. telecommunications, according to a 1998 analysis in *Business Economics,* are multi-fold. Dramatic reductions in the costs of transmission, information processing and switching—which were brought about by lowered costs of equipment such as integrated circuits and computers—as well as technology improvements, meant corporations could offer services affordably. Value on these networks has shifted from the infrastructure to content and system interface, resulting in a panoply of services. Despite this good news about corporate cost-of-operations price drops, in mid-1998, consumers were still waiting for that trickle down to reach them.

Mergers and increased competitiveness caused companies to vie for customers in every sector, down to the heavy-use home user. The new generation telephony company wants to provide local, long-distance, cellular, paging, and Internet services and specially packaged services to consumers. The latter is seen as a lucrative area for these companies. BT, GTE and WorldCom are among the companies whose 1997-era strategy was to wrest control of the local market to sell those services. This also created some seemingly odd bedfellows. Cable-modem possibilities to connect to the elusive "final mile" meant matches were attempted with companies such as TCI, Cox and Comcast to bring telephony services to consumers. With about 65 percent of homes in the United States connected to cable service in 1998, according to Standard & Poor's, it would make sense for these companies to bring telephony to the home market, however; cable is, for the most part, omni-directional. There were many technology obstacles to overcome, but the possibilities were still being explored. And companies in other market niches, such as utilities, attempted to get a piece of telephony for their investors by investing in hybrid companies.

INDUSTRY LEADERS

Deregulation made the telephony market less of a free market and more a free-for-all with merger mania making musical chairs of service market segments between 1996 and well through 1998, with the ultimate economic and regulatory results remaining to be seen. In 1997, the long distance market alone was valued at $82 billion annually. The triumvirate of AT&T, MCI, and Sprint had a 95-plus percentage market share in 1997, but another 20 companies were expected to enter the market, each taking about a 2 percent bit. Baby Bells and name brands supposedly have a better market position; however, GTE estimated competition would eventually take 30 percent of its local customer base. Consumers wanted a wide range of services at low costs.

LONG DISTANCE PROVIDERS

AT&T Corp. remained the United States' leading long-distance telephone carrier in the 1990s. The company, which had 90 million customers and 128,000 employees in 1998, posted more than $53 billion in sales that same year. With the advent of deregulation, increasing competition and restructuring placed AT&T's focus on communications services included services such as wireless phone service, Internet access, and international telephone services. The company also had been seeking a deal to cement its market position in the cable-phone segment.

WorldCom was founded in 1983 as discount long-distance carrier LDDS. The company grew through a series of acquisitions with some 40 competitors. Approval on a $37 billion merger with MCI was pending regulatory approval in 1998. WorldCom reported well over $17 billion in revenue in 1998.

Sprint, in addition to providing long-distance service, took the challenge of providing retail products to consumers in 1997, according to *Brandweek*. The company, which owns one of the largest fiber-optic networks, created neighborhood telephone stores with Radio Shack.

There is truly no stagnation in this vibrant and ever-changing industry. Throughout 1998, existing companies continued to spin off and merge as well as consolidate services and refine their business focus to maximize profitability. Entrenched telecommunications companies appeared to be at a competitive disadvantage within the telephony market. Those companies that burst onto the scene in the wake of regulatory reforms appear to have done so successfully for their willingness to explore new revenue opportunities related to those pursuits traditionally associated with the telecommunications business model.

Qwest Communications International Inc., once an obscure telecommunication provider, became the fourth-largest long-distance service provider in the United States in 1998. Primarily operating in the western United States, the company was constructing an 18,400-mile fiber optic network for more than 130 cities, which will later be extended into Mexico. The company was once a part of Southern Pacific Rail Corp. and leveraged its ties to that business to install its network along railroad rights-of-way. Qwest installs networks for companies such as Frontier, WorldCom, and GTE alongside its own network and sells network capacity to various parties. With the 1998 purchase of LCI International, which was twice its size, Qwest became a contender in the long-distance service market with more than 2 million customers and $2.3 billion in revenue.

Other operating long distance companies in 1998 included Frontier Corp. and Telco Communications Group. Labyrinthine regulation regarding the market conditions under which Baby Bells were allowed to enter the long-distance service market effectively barred them from this market.

LOCAL SERVICE PROVIDERS

Bell Atlantic Corporation was among the local service providing companies that emerged from the AT&T break up. This Baby Bell purchased NYNEX—another Baby Bell—in 1997 to give it sales of $30.19 billion that year; 1998 sales topped $31.5 billion. The company provided local telephone service in 13 northeastern states and Washington, D.C. In addition to its array of domestic local service and related telephony services—such as consumer marketing, directory management, and wireless and calling-card services—Bell Atlantic also was invested in telecommunications in 21 countries in 1998 including Indonesia, Mexico, New Thailand, and the United Kingdom.

SBC Communications boasted of providing local telephone service in seven of 10 top metropolitan areas in 1997 and cellular telephone services in 78 markets. Its sales were $28.78 billion in 1998. Under its corporate umbrella were well-known industry brands including Cellular One, Pacific Bell, and Southwestern Bell. Its other services included Internet access, paging, and directory publishing. The company had investments in nations such as Chile and France.

GTE served some 23 million local telephone customers in 28 states in 1998. It posted sales of more than $25 billion that same year. Various GTE subsidiaries also provided cellular, Internet hosting and airline telecommunications services as well as served as a contractor for the United States Department of Defense and various national security agencies. Its operations extended to Canada and South America.

Many local carriers went global following deregulation and the freeing of international markets. U.S. West Communications Group was among those companies that operated Telewest Communications, a United Kingdom cable telephony. It also had invested in cable in the Netherlands, Belgium and the Czech Republic. Other prospering Baby Bells include BellSouth and Ameritech.

Non-RBOC local carriers proliferated in 1997. Many traditionally long-distance service providers attempted to break into this potentially lucrative market through mergers and acquisition. Emergent local service providers, which are highly regionalized by the business's nature, include RCN in Princeton, New Jersey, Northwest Iowa Telephone Co. and McLeod USA, both Iowa companies; USN Communications in Chicago; and Winstar Communications and Teleport, both based in New York City. *Telephony,* in a 1997 article, stated local competition, in addition to the Telecommunications Act of 1996 and eager community leaders, helped make telephony in rural areas often more sophisticated than in urban settings. Abingdon, Virginia, for example, in 1996 installed fiber throughout its downtown area and installed public terminals for community information access; and Iowa had the largest state-owned fiber optic network in the United States in 1997. Other competitive local-exchange carriers (CLECs) in 1998 included ICG Communications, Intermedia Communications and NEXTLINK Communications.

Wireless communications companies increased their profile in the wake of technology advances and deregulation. Major companies invested in this niche for providing cellular telephony services include Air-Touch Communications, Nextel Communications, United States Cellular, and Western Wireless. There were also several cellular companies operated by the Baby Bells, GTE, and long-distance companies in the $29.7 billion cellular telephone market in 1998 including Bell Atlantic/NYNEX Mobile. PCS, digital wireless technology, is a highly competitive wireless arena with, in 1998, an estimated four PCS providers per market. In addition to consortia formed by large companies previously named, other companies engaging in this business include Omnipoint,

NextWave Telecom, General Wireless and Chase Telecommunications.

Telephony products cut a wide market swath. These include consumer products such as calling cards and actual handsets to sophisticated frame relay and network switching products, or software and servers for high-end corporate users or service providers. Among the companies making telephony hardware and software available in the 1996 to 1998 period were high-profile companies such as AT&T, Siemens Rolm Communications Inc., Lucent Technologies Corp., Northern Telecom, Pacific Bell, and Internet telephony players IDT and VocalTec Communications. Also active in this area were Mitel, NTT, Teleport Communications Group, NetFrame Systems Inc., Rhetorex Inc., PairGain Technologies, Cubix Corp., and Madge Networks Inc.

AMERICA AND THE WORLD

Traditionally, telephone services in nations other than the United States have been state-run. Many state monopolies have been privatized. Changing this industry internationally was the creation of a 1997 World Trade Organization agreement in which representatives from about 70 nations said they would open their national markets to international competition. Nations ratifying this represented 90 percent of world telecommunications revenues. From this, investment between international companies and joint ventures between companies have created a crazy quilt of alliances and services for Internet service provision, infrastructure construction and similar activities. These include Concert, which couples BT and MCI Communications with assistance from Telefonica de Espana; Global One, formed by Sprint, Deutsche Telekom and France Telecom; and two AT&T ventures: WorldPartners, which is AT&T plus 30 other companies in North America, Europe, and Asia; and Unisource, which was formed with Switzerland, Sweden, Spain and other phone companies.

British Telecommunications PLC was once the United Kingdom's government-run telephone company. The company offers a wide range of service, including international service—despite the fact that in 1998, an estimated 97 percent of its revenues were from U.K. operations. The company posted $26.145 billion in 1998 sales. BT had made a bid for MCI, which was eventually purchased by World Com. It did have a 20 percent stake in the United States service provider which was worth $7 billion.

Deutsche Telekom AG, Europe's largest telecommunications provider, had 1997 sales of $37.5 billion. The company continued expansion in 1998, investing in Asia, Europe, and the United States, the latter of which is through Global One, a joint venture with Sprint and France Telecom.

Standard & Poor's estimates the Latin American markets, namely Argentina, Bolivia, Chile, Mexico, Peru and Venezuela, will benefit the most from privatization. Despite this atmosphere for free market telephony, Brazil, Ireland, Greece and Spain have not opened their markets. The latter three nations were expected to do so sometime in 2003.

RESEARCH AND TECHNOLOGY

Technology advances have outpaced expectations. The changes have been amazingly rapid, from digital switching to fiber-optics and beyond. Computers play an increasingly important role in telephony through development and deployment of technologies such as voice over networks. The past 20 years in this industry were amazing, but it is predicted these next years will herald more developments in telephony than were brought about in the previous 50-year span.

Computing, photonics, satellites and other technologies have become increasingly sophisticated, thus altering the foundation on which communications transmissions are made. Some telephony companies remain content to attempt to maximize their copper-wired infrastructure as long as possible without sacrificing service quality. Significant capital investments, after all, have been made. Additional investments would be absorbed through service rate hikes.

The telephone network was designed based on conjecture that each call was three minutes in duration with no more than nine minutes worth of calls made during peak use hours. In 1996, the problem became the emergent modem use which meant tied up lines for upwards of 15 minutes. Because Internet service providers and subscriber-based online services have arranged for users to incur no charges for local calls, a web surfer can stay on indefinitely with no cost to her and there is no revenue for those local providers. That same year, local phone providers began lobbying government agencies for the right to charge Internet users for local access. The problem is further compounded by technology. According to *The Economist,* telephone companies have $30 billion invested in the older circuit-switching infrastructure alone, however, packet switching technology is a digital,

more efficient technology which would solve network traffic problems. Examples of the latter technologies include Asymmetric Digital Subscriber Line (ADSL) and Integrated Services Digital Network (ISDN). But as that newspaper pointed out, companies "seem to be thinking more about recovering the investments they have already made than promoting alternatives." Bolder companies are experimenting with photonics and creating SONET pathways. New networking technologies mean construction of new networks and thinking about evolutionary business and technology changes in layer after layer of telephony companies.

For equipment manufacturers, changes in the dynamics of the telephony market coupled with technological advances have made executives shift focus. Nortel, as an example, had more than 110 million digital switching lines internationally in 1998 in addition to SONET and microwave transmission products. Prior to deregulation Tellabs Inc., for example, primarily made digital cross-connects for switching telephone traffic over large networks based on circuit switching. In the late 1990s, this was being replaced by packet switching, an industry segment dominated by companies such as Cisco Systems. Digital technologies are needed to enable voice traffic to be carried with data via IP networks. As Bruce Upbin pointed out in a May 1998 *Forbes* article, "telephone technology is changing so fast that a hot product today could be obsolete in just a few years."

That's why companies such as Tellabs are investing in new technologies. It bought into photonics in 1997 with a $6 million purchase of the IBM wavelength-division multiplexing technology. This technology allows light waves to be split to create more network bandwidth. In 1998, Lucent's Bell Laboratories was working with optical switching and Advance Intelligent Networking technology, wherein service "intelligence" placed in databases rather than switches was being deployed. Links with cable operators to provide wireless services were being explored by telephony companies.

Voice and data transmission networks are moving in the coming decade from traditional networks to specialized high-bandwidth networks such as Internet Protocol or IP networks. In fact, John A. Roth of Northern Telecom stated in a March 1998 presentation that telecommunications is making a "historical move from dialtone to Webtone." By Webtone, he means new generation telephony networks designed to carry data and voice traffic by using IP networking. The creation of these types of networks would eliminate outdated copper line transmission and enable businesses and individuals to simply mix and match an array of services from traditional telephone conversations to conducting teleconferences.

"In 1996, the volume of data traffic on carrier backbone networks exceeded the volume of voice traffic," said Roth. "This historic event signaled the fundamental transformation of networks dominated by voice to networks dominated by data. Data networks are the foundation of the world of Webtone." Nortel anticipates Internet users to number 250 million internationally by the year 2000, with 300 million on the World Wide Web by 2003. The forecasts for 2020 put United States Internet use at 80 percent of the total population. Indeed the early adapters seem to be large corporations most able to invest capital in these types of cutting-edge systems. Boeing and Ford Motor Company were among those companies that deployed IP networks for their international, internal communication needs. Small business and consumer adoption of these technologies traditionally lags behind early adopters, with wide-spread use occurring as prices fall. Nortel claimed in 1998 the move was toward a "massive and sophisticated" public network.

FURTHER READING

"$4.4 Billion Bid for LCI Makes Qwest a Big Deal." *The Sacramento Bee,* 10 March 1998.

Asimov, Isaac. *Asimov's Chronology of Science & Discovery,* Edition 1. 1994. HarperCollins Publishers, 1994.

Berinato, Scott, and Stephanie LaPolla. "A Brewing Culture Clash." *PC Week,* 8 September 1997.

Carter, Wayne. "United They Stand: Industry Groups Are Making Progress in Developing an All-Optical Network. " *Telephony,* 15 September 1997.

Economides, Nicholas. "U.S. Telecommunications Today." *Business Economics,* April 1998.

The Evolution of the PBX: White Paper. Research Triangle Park, NC: Northern Telecom, ND.

Gilder, George. "The Death of Telephony: Why the Telephone and TV Will Not Be the Stars of a Communications Revolution." *The Economist,* 11 September 1993.

Hammel, Steve. "Nickel-and-Dimed: Thanks for Paying Your Phone Bill. You Kept the Tax Man Happy." *U.S News & World Report,* 18 May 1998.

Hanley, Michael. "Small Towns, Big Plans." *Telephony,* 2 June 1997.

Hofacker, Richard Q., Jr. "Telephone." *Collier's Encyclopedia,* Edition 1997.

Huber, Peter. "Telephony Unbottled." *Forbes,* 18 January 1993.

Kesler, Andrew J. "Digital Picks Up the Pace." *Forbes,* 1 June 1998.

Kim, Steve. "The 'E-telecom' Experience: A Streamlined View of the Network Promises a New Day for Carriers and Customers By Replacing Multiple-and Often Disparate-Databases." *Telephony,* 20 April 1998.

McCombs, Harold. "Mixed Signals: How the Telecommunications Act Affects You." *American City & County,* August 1997.

McCormick, Richard. "Tenets of Telephony." *America's Network,* 15 November 1996.

"The Real Target Is Your Dial Tone." *Fortune,* 24 November 1997.

"Remarks on Signing the Telecommunications Act of 1996." *Weekly Compilation of Presidential Documents,* 12 February 1996.

Rendleman, John and Scott Berinato. "IT, Telecom Cultures Clash." *PC Week,* 25 May 1998.

Roth, John A. *The Webtone Opportunity.* Research Triangle Park, NC: Northern Telecom, March 1998.

Sapronov, Walt. "Pondering Long-term State Preemption." *Business Communications Review,* September 1996.

Schroeder, Erica. "Telephony Services Will Be the Talk of Las Vegas." *PC Week,* 1 April 1996.

Shipside, Steve. "Wired Workers." *The Guardian,* 21 May 1998.

Smith, Kelly. "Promises That Didn't Ring True." *Money,* April 1998.

Standard & Poor's Industry Surveys—Telecommunications: Wireless. Standard & Poor's, 25 December 1997.

Standard & Poor's Industry Surveys—Telecommunications: Wireline. Standard & Poor's, 19 March 1998.

Stockford, Paul. "The Promise of Computer-Telephony." *Electronic News,* 31 March 1997.

Surkan, Michael. "The Case for Treating Telcos Like ISPs." *PC Week,* 27 April 1998.

Taninecz, George. "Act, React: the Telecommunications Act of 1996 Is Slowly Shaping the Corporate-Communications Markets of Tomorrow." *Industry Week,* 6 January, 1997.

Telephony 101: An Introduction to the Public Network. Research Triangle Park, NC: Northern Telecom, 1994.

Timmer, Joel. *Telecommunications Services Snapshot.* Available from http://www.hoovers.com.

Trends in Computing and Telephony: White Paper. Research Triangle Park, NC: Northern Telecom, ND.

Upbin, Bruce. "Survival Technique: Paranoia." *Forbes,* 18 May 1998.

"The War of the Wires." *The Economist,* 11 May 1996.

Warner, Bernhard. "Brandweek's Marketers of the Year: Tom Weigman, Sprint." *Brandweek.* Available from http://www.brandweek.com.

"What Is Telephony?" *Dallas Business Journal,* 5 January 1996.

Yovoich, B.G. "Convergence Creates New Executive Breed." *Business Marketing,* January 1995.

—Linda Dailey Paulson,
updated by Denise Worhach

TIME CAPSULES

Who among us could withstand the excitement of finding and opening a sealed time capsule buried for many years, which has been storing various objects considered representative of some forgotten era of history? For that matter, who among us would not be interested in contributing to the official contents of a sacrosanctly-sealed time capsule to be opened 100 or 1000 years from now? Apparently, the world cannot get enough to satiate its interest and fascination with the past—from the surge in the antiques market, to the movie *Somewhere in Time,* to the near-frenzied captivation with the sunken ship *Titanic.* In the year 2001, more than 30 countries around the world will collaboratively launch KEO, a satellite time capsule programmed to reenter earth's atmosphere in 50,000 years. Millennium mania has clearly contributed to the capitalization of the market, and experts have stated that by 2000, more than 10,000 sealed time capsules will be in existence around the world. The trouble is, will posterity be able to find them?

ORGANIZATION AND STRUCTURE

Although globally represented, the industry is loosely organized and structured, united more by common interest than anything else. This is not to imply that the conglomerate membership is comprised of laymen. In 1990 the International Time Capsule Society (ITCS) was established to promote the careful study of time capsules and to document their existence in a continuing registry database. Its membership includes some impressively-credentialed scholars and experts in the field. The ITCS's first conference received press coverage from *The New York Times,* the *International Herald Tribune,* the *London Daily Mail,,* the Associated Press, CNN, ABC, and National Public Radio.

Headquartered at Oglethorpe University in Atlanta, Georgia, the ITCS chose that location as most appropriate because Oglethorpe is the site of the famed "Crypt of Civilization," the swimming pool-sized time capsule buried there. The Crypt is recognized in the *Guinness Book of World Records* (1990) as "the first successful attempt to bury a record of this culture for any future inhabitants or visitors to the planet Earth."

ITCS has articulated its fourfold mission "to maintain a registry of all known time capsules; to establish a clearing house for information about time capsules; to encourage study of the history, variety, and motivation behind time capsule projects; and to educate the general public and the academic community concerning the value of time capsules." The Society holds annual conferences at Oglethorpe, and ITCS members from around the world attend these meetings to pool their knowledge and discuss time capsule projects.

While some companies do turn a tidy profit from manufacturing time capsules, and others by sponsoring their theme or burial, the money-making end of the industry is on the retrieval, showcasing and, in some instances, selling of the contents of a retrieved time capsule.

BACKGROUND AND DEVELOPMENT

Time capsules existed long before given their dubbed name. King Esarhaddon of Babylon, Assyria, and Egypt buried cuneiform inscriptions, small statues, and other treasures of the time into temple foundations. Although primarily intended for the *afterlife,* future lives and peoples became additional beneficiaries of this buried legacy. This practice of burying treasure and communications into the hollowed cornerstones of buildings has continued into present times. However, it was not until 1938 that the term "time capsule" was used to refer to a sealed container that held special objects and communications intended for posterity. The Westinghouse Electric Corporation is credited with adopting that term for its 1938 seven-foot long torpedo-shaped container created for the 1938-1939 New York World's Fair in Flushing Meadows. At the exact moment of the autumnal equinox at noon on September 23, 1938, it was buried 50 feet into the ground at this site. Westinghouse followed up with another time capsule buried for the 1964-1965 New York World's Fair.

The 1938 capsule contained, in part: an alarm clock, a can opener, eyeglasses, a fountain pen, an electric lamp, a miniature camera, a nail file, a safety pin, a slide rule, a toothbrush, a watch, a Mickey Mouse cup, a Sears Roebuck catalogue, cigarettes, a baseball, a deck of cards, a dollar bill, seeds, and the Holy Bible. By comparison, the 1964 capsule contained, in part, a plastic heart valve, a transistor radio, contact lenses, a ball-point pen, a rechargeable flashlight, a Polaroid camera, birth control pills, freeze-dried food, a computer memory unit, filtered cigarettes, tranquilizers, antibiotics, credit cards, a bikini, a Beatles record, and a fifty-star American flag.

Westinghouse's 1938 time capsule was made of hardened alloys, mostly copper, which Westinghouse called Cupaloy; the 1965 capsule was stainless steel. Both were lined with a layer of Pyrex glass and filled with nitrogen to prevent decomposition of the contents. Westinghouse also had printed details about the location of the capsule in "The Book of Record," which was printed on archival paper and distributed to libraries around the world. Both time capsules are to be opened in the year 6939 (5000 years from the 1939 capsule). Their novelty and futuristic appeal captured the public's attention, and in Montreal, Canada, a time capsule was buried to honor Expo 67 (to be opened in 2067). Expo 70 in Osaka, Japan, also commemoratively buried a capsule to be opened 5000 years later, in 6970.

Prior to the Crypt of Civilization and KEO, most time capsules were more modestly created and stored. Since time capsules (as we now think of them) were not widely publicized until the 1930s, many were directed to be opened 100 years after they were buried

(a technologically *long time* back in 1938), making the twenty-first century a potentially busy time for capsule enthusiasts. Unfortunately, more capsules have been lost than found. For example, as of early 1999, no one had yet found the famous time capsule containing the signatures of 22 million Americans, intended to be buried ceremoniously at a Valley Forge centennial celebration in 1976 by President Gerald Ford. After it had toured the nation, the capsule was stolen from a van at the burial site. It has until the year 2076 to be found and opened on time. Additionally, the 1983 cast of television's "M*A*S*H" buried a time capsule containing series props, scripts, and costumes in a secret spot of the Twentieth Century Fox parking lot but, unfortunately, a massive Marriott Hotel was later built on the site. In 1953 residents of Washington buried (somewhere on the grounds in Olympia) a two-ton time capsule to celebrate Washington's territorial centennial. The state legislature subsequently failed to approve funds to mark the burial site. A similar incident occurred in the town of Lyndon, Vermont. An iron box containing items from the town's centennial celebration in 1891 was mentioned in the newspaper at that time, intended to be opened in 100 years, or 1991. However, in 1991 residents searched everywhere without success. No city has yet beaten the record of Corona, California, though, which has misplaced 17 time capsules since 1950. The ITCS faithfully tracks any known data on the whereabouts of these and other missing capsules and actively solicits information from anyone possessing knowledge.

In 1960 the Union of American Hebrew Congregations (the central body of Reformed Judaism) sponsored a well-publicized time capsule to be opened at the millennium. Many world figures were asked to contribute their thoughts and opinions to the contents of the capsule. Lyndon Johnson, then Senator, foresaw the end of racial segregation. Israeli Prime Minister David Ben-Gurion saw the future of the Soviet Union as transformed into a "free and democratic" country and that peace would come for the Arabs and Israelis. Eleanor Roosevelt thought there would someday be a Jewish president. In any event, because the Union was moving offices in Manhattan in 1999, it tried to retrieve the capsule. Alas, it wasn't found even though newspaper clippings indicated that it was installed in the building's "walnut-paneled boardroom."

Andy Warhol created no less than 610 time capsules in his lifetime—in the form of cardboard boxes filled with then-current memorabilia. He often kept a box at his desk, calling it a "time capsule in progress." Warhol died in 1987; 10 years later, in 1997, *Harper's Magazine* published a partial inventory of Warhol's

Time Capsule 416, which was filled between 1981 and 1984. The contents included an exhibition announcement of Linda McCartney's photographs, along with a color photograph of Paul McCartney and Willem de Kooning posing with a de Kooning painting; a complimentary ticket to "Marilyn Monroe's 51st Birthday Party (a posthumous celebration); another party invitation to Senator Christopher Dodd's fortieth birthday party; an envelope from Universal Pictures containing a press release announcement for Joe Don Baker starring in *Fletch;* a fan letter from Miss Chrissie Suleski of Bloomfield, New Jersey, asking Warhol to help her meet members of the rock band, Duran Duran; 5 canceled U.S. postage stamps; shoelaces printed with Wonder Woman, Batman, Robin, Green Lantern, and Captain America; an autograph request from teacher Peter James Therrien; and two complimentary admission tickets to the "Women of the 80s" party at The Cat Club. Contents from these and other Warhol time capsules are stored at the Andy Warhol Museum in Pittsburgh.

PIONEERS IN THE FIELD

Until KEO came along in the latter 1990s, the most impressive capsule effort was the creation and ceremonious dedication of the "Crypt of Civilization." In 1936 Dr. Thornwell Jacobs, then-president of Oglethorpe University, approached *Scientific American* magazine editors about publishing an article soliciting the cooperation of "industrialists and philanthropists" to help to make his brainchild a reality. Jacobs wanted his generation to "seize the opportunity to preserve for the future a complete record of how we live, and to give to the generations of thousands of years hence a carefully thought out record of what we have accomplished up to the year 1936." So taken were the editors, they heartily endorsed the project in the magazine and set themselves up as a clearinghouse for suggestions, advising potential volunteers, assistants, and interested parties to communicate directly with them.

The generated response was enormous. Jacobs noted in his April 1937 diary, "We have been in *Time,* . . . 'Reader's Digest,' Walter Winchell's radio column . . . and in newspapers from London to Australia." Following an NBC broadcast and an article in *The New York Times* about the intended project, famed photographer and inventor Thomas Kimmwood Peters (1884-1973) expressed his interest in official involvement. Jacobs appointed him as archivist of the crypt, and together they created and refined their manifest

More On TIME CAPSULES

Times Capsule, Inc. is a creator of Times Capsules. Their products, they say, employ technology to preserve books, documents, metals, plastics and almost any type of archival materials for the life of the times capsule itself. The company asserts the Times Capsule is a container, custom built to a customer's specifications, with a controlled environment to protect and preserve materials for centuries. A patented Vapor Phase Deacidification process is used to chemically treat the contents with a mild organic alkaline substance which neutralizes the acidity of paper and renders its life expectancy 25 to 40 times greater than untreated paper, according to the company. Times Capsule, Inc. even offers a 500-year guarantee against fire and flood damage should such natural disasters occur where the capsule is stored.

Some of the items Times Capsule, Inc. suggests can be stored in a times capsule are:

- Photographs
- Signature scrolls
- Essays
- Telephone books
- Credit cards
- Current newspapers and magazines
- Flags
- Clothing
- State-of-the-art electronic equipment
- Seeds
- Forecasts of what life will be like from educators, legislators, students, theologians and businesspeople.

ideas into reality. It was decided that the crypt was to be sealed for 6177 years, or until the year 8113 A.D. The date was calculated by using the starting date of the first recorded calendar, 4241 B.C. Exactly 6177 years had passed between then and 1936. Therefore, Jacobs that envisioned the history recorded and left for posterity in the crypt would represent the mid-point of human recorded time.

The crypt itself was somewhat of a scientific oddity in that it was not a "capsule" *per se,* but rather an epic-scale room-sized chamber actually built underground. The chamber lay on granite bedrock in the foundation of Phoebe Hearst Memorial Hall on Oglethorpe's campus, chosen because Jacob anticipated the solidly-structured building would stand for at least "two to five thousand years." The chamber itself had a two-foot thick stone floor and a seven-foot thick stone roof. The only visible sign of the crypt was its stainless steel door, complete with commemorative plaque. After consulting the Bureau of Standards in Washington for technical advice on the preservation of stored items, Jacobs directed the building of several stainless steel receptacles lined with glass and filled with nitrogen to prevent oxidation once sealed. David Sarnoff, president of Radio Corporation of America, dedicated the door at a Paramount News-filmed public ceremony on May 28, 1938.

Jacobs had envisioned the contents of the crypt to be similar to those found in a museum—including not only accumulated formal knowledge but also samples of "pop" culture and curious items reflective of various cultures. First came the massive amount of documents and written artifacts, constituting more than 800 works on the arts and sciences. The microfilming, undertaken by student assistants, took over 2 years to complete and ended up taking 640,000 pages of microfilm. The cellulose acetate base film that was used had a life expectancy of six centuries, according to the Bureau of Standards. However, as a backup, a duplicate copy of specific writings was made on paper-thin metal film. Some of the items included the Bible, the Koran, the *Iliad,* and Dante's *Inferno.* Added to this was producer David O. Selznick's original copy of the "Gone With the Wind" script and hundreds of newsreels.

Voice recordings and motion pictures were also added to the crypt's contents, along with electric machines, microreaders, and film projectors. In the event that electricity was not around at the time of the crypt's opening, a generator operated by a windmill was included, as was a hand-magnifier to allow visual review of the microfilms with the naked eye. Of interest in the crypt's contents was the inclusion of voice recordings of Hitler, Stalin, Roosevelt, Mussolini, and Chamberlain. For balance and comprehensive treatment the voices of Popeye the Sailor and a champion hog caller were also included. Several everyday items were included to reflect contemporary culture: a Donald Duck doll, a set of Lincoln Logs, a quart of Budweiser beer, and several pictographs. The very first item encountered upon entry to the crypt is a machine to teach the English language in order to help decipher the crypt's contents.

The crypt was sealed ceremoniously on May 25, 1940, amid world news of an impending world war. One of the last items to be placed in the crypt was a steel plate from the *Atlanta Journal,* which reflected the world's news. Dr. Jacobs directed his speech toward the prospective discoverers of the crypt, telling them, "The world is engaged in burying our civilization forever, and here in this crypt we leave it to you." The massive steel door was then closed and welded shut.

CURRENT CONDITIONS

By far, the most ambitious and universal effort to date is the scheduled launch of Planet Earth's KEO satellite, scheduled for the year 2001. The brainchild of French artist Jean-Marc Philippe, KEO's concept was given form by a team of France's leading scientists and engineers who mostly worked voluntarily to get this non-profit project off the ground. The name KEO was derived from research into the most common phonemes (k, e, and o) in the world's most widely spoken languages. After seeking world support and publicity, the global outpouring was extensive. Engineers, scientists, scholars, businesses, students, and the general public all shared in ideas and plans. KEO actively solicits persons who wish to record messages to be included in the time capsule; the information is to be stored on glass-tempered CD-ROMs, complete with instructions in universal symbolic images that will hopefully be decipherable by the world's descendants. KEO's main risk is the possibility of collision with space debris or a micrometeorite, and its less-than-57-degrees angle of orbit was chosen for that reason. However, if space pollution continues at its present rate, KEO will most likely succumb to space.

For the persistent enthusiasts and the optimists, though, all is not for naught. There are some 50-year gems waiting to be opened, including one to be opened in 2045 in Sandusky, Ohio. Its contents purport to capture "the triumphs and tragedies of life in America during 1995." Included in its contents are Pop-Tarts, a "Buns of Steel" video, a purple Wonder Bra, crayons, and a Twinkie. Not far from Sandusky is the town of Euclid, Ohio, where a seven-foot torpedo-shaped time capsule is scheduled to be opened in 2043. This capsule intends to reflect life in Euclid, including the assembly-line routine, the town's Polka Hall of Fame, and a history of town organizations. Some capsules are more esoteric in content, such as the one buried by the National Car Rental company. It contains fifty years of car-rental memorabilia, mostly in the company's trademark green color. Its opening is scheduled for 2022.

INDUSTRY LEADERS

Building on Dr. Jacobs' vision, The ITCS remains the recognized historian and tracker of the world's time capsules, albeit that information on their respective existences is by voluntary disclosure to the Society. Among its founding members are some notables. Knute "Skip" Berger, executive director of the Washington Centennial Time Capsule project, is also author of "Time Capsules in America" in *The People's Almanac #2* (1978). Paul Hudson, registrar at Oglethorpe University, has written and lectured extensively on the Crypt of Civilization. He also is a history lecturer at the University. Another distinguished founding member of the ITCS is Dr. Brian Durrans, an anthropologist as well as deputy keeper in the ethnography department of the British Museum. Founding member William Jarvis is also head of acquisitions/serials at Washington State University and author of "Time Capsules" for the *Encyclopedia of Library and Information Science* (1988).

None of this is to imply that one must be rich and famous; part of an official federal, state, or municipal team; or participating in an event to create a time capsule. Millennium madness has brought everybody into the act. Gillian Barr, of the company BarrTek, which sells custom-engraved aluminum time capsules, commented in a 1997 *Newsweek* article that sales had tripled in the previous year. The Rhodes College Class of 1998 buried their college memories at their alma mater in Memphis. *Parents* magazine followed the 1998 story of a Palm Bay, Florida, family who opened up their one-year time capsule "buried" in the closet the previous year. It was intended to remind the family members what they were like a year prior, including what their hopes, dreams, and values were at that time. Although the contents may have been insignificant to outsiders—crayon drawings from the four-year-old, a Beanie Baby, and a business card of a parent's new entrepreneurship—the items had great significance to the respective members who could reflect on their gauged growth. Touted as a great family activity, "The Family Treasure Kit" that they used was available for purchase by the general public.

Other time capsule products were readily marketed in local stores and were also available on the Internet. For example, a company known as Treasure Baskets To Go offered time capsules for capturing special events such as weddings, births, or graduations. Intended more for personal entertainment than official posterity, the packaged kits did not warrantee any minimum life expectancy for the time capsule itself.

AMERICA AND THE WORLD

Through the continued efforts of ITCS to organize and track time capsule projects on a global level, the sharing of data and the commonality of interest have both greatly contributed to the industry's enhanced appeal. As the 1990s neared completion, enthusiasts around the world felt the need to preserve as much as they could about the twentieth century for posterity. In 1996 ITCS became part of the "Team-Tidskapsler" project in Copenhagen, which represented the largest time capsule burial in continental Europe to date. Another major undertaking was the BESTCapsule 2001 project, coordinated by the Kinki University in Osaka, Japan. The latter's focus was on the environment, and the contents of its proposed time capsule will be of more academic than popular interest as it will be retaining various soil and water samples, as well as preserved biological specimens. All in all, "time in a bottle" was the thing to have at the close of the century. As of 1999, ITCS's Paul Hudson indicated that time capsule inquiries were up to a dozen a day.

FURTHER READING

Beyer, Lisa. "Where, O Where, Did They Put the Future?" *Time,* 27 July 1998.

Butler, Declan. "Space Time Capsule Could Send a Message to the Future." *Nature,* 8 January 1998.

"Creating a Family Time Capsule." *Parents,* February 1998.

Hamilton, Kendall, and Steve Rhodes. "Our Gifts to the Future: Books, Beer and a Wonderbra." *Newsweek,* 7 April 1997.

Hudson, Paul. "The 'Archaelogical Duty' of Thornwell Jacobs: The Oglethorpe Atlanta Crypt of Civilization Time Capsule." *Georgia Historical Quarterly,* Spring 1991.

Jacobs, Dr. Thornwell. "Today - Tomorrow." *Scientific American,* November 1936.

"Lost In Time." *Harper's Magazine,* April 1995.

Olshan, Jeremy. "A Brief History of Time Capsules." *Queens Tribune,* 1998.

"Seniors Put Their Past Six Feet Under." *Chronicle of Higher Education,* June 1998.

"Warhol's Later Work." *Harper's Magazine,* October 1997.

—Lauri R. Harding

USED CAR SUPERSTORES

INDUSTRY SNAPSHOT

The 1990s introduced a new trend in purchasing a used car. Gone were the stereotypes, haggling, pressure, and distrust. Emerging was a new buying experience called the used car superstore. This noteworthy trend tapped into what prospective car buyers wanted most—clearly marked pricing, huge inventories containing a variety of makes and models, a no-pressure sales environment, and warranties. In 1996 the new industry had only 10 units across the country. By the close of 1998 that number climbed to 66 and was growing according to the "1999 Used Car Market Report" published by vehicle redistribution company ADT Automotive.

ORGANIZATION AND STRUCTURE

Used car chains such as CarMax and AutoNation have expanded on the "superstore" idea pioneered by such giants as Office Depot and Home Depot. As in these superstores, there are a wide variety of products offered at a low price. Unlike their traditional counterparts in used car retailing, these new automotive superstores offer buyers the opportunity to shop more conveniently. Prospective buyers at a used car superstore shop in a showroom, using a computerized touch-screen kiosk to view vehicles. They are able to create their own financial profile on the computer, which helps determine how much of a down payment and what kind of monthly payments they can afford. From this profile, they receive data from the computer showing their possible choices within their price and preference range. The computer gives consumers printouts on their choices, with details such as mileage and options. Computers also allow superstores to track inventory, allowing each location to stock cars that are popular to a particular area, which, in turn, helps save money by reducing the length of time cars sit on the lot.

Used car superstores get their cars from various sources including trade-ins from customers, lease turn-ins, and wholesalers. Many people who lease cars turn them in at the end of the lease; these are considered good cars for resale as they are usually only a few years old and have been well taken care of. While many new car franchisers get the first pick of returned lease vehicles financed by their maker (for example, leased Fords financed by Ford Motor Credit), about two-thirds of leases are financed by non-automobile maker companies. With the popularity of car leasing, this gives a steady supply to the used car industry.

While leasing provides a steady stream of used cars to superstores, most of the cars on non-franchised used car lots come from wholesalers. Wholesalers hold auctions periodically, but only professional car buyers take part. Manheim Auctions, with 63 locations in the United States, is the largest auctioneer of used cars in the industry. Manheim gets its cars from lease turn-ins, rental fleets, repossessions, and overstocked dealers.

In addition, unlike traditional showrooms, the used car superstore offers buyers the opportunity to choose between competing brands: Ford or Chevrolet, Toyota or Honda. This was a major innovation, and in this regard it is interesting that electronics superstore Circuit City, through its company CarMax, has been a leader in this emerging industry. "Imagine what it would cost to buy a TV," CarMax head Austin Ligon said, "if Circuit City had to have 15 different stores to sell 15 brands of televisions."

Other advantages abound. Used car superstores place an emphasis on convenience. They feature extended hours—in some markets until 10 p.m.—and full amenities including cafes, childcare centers, and community rooms.

Trends USED CAR SUPERSTORES: BUYING IN STYLE

The modern used car buying environment is enhanced by a number of physical comforts, not the least of which is the opportunity to conduct the selection process in a temperature-controlled showroom rather than on an outdoor lot. Many superstores now have hosts or hostesses, whose job it is to make customers feel as "at home" as possible. Waiting areas are furnished with comfortable seating, and often customers can sip coffee from an in-store coffee bar while "shopping" on the computer. At some superstores, customers with children are even able to place their youngsters in an onsite day-care center. Apparently, used car dealers in the 1990s have adopted the philosophy not only of the soft sell, but of the comfortable sell, as well.

BACKGROUND AND DEVELOPMENT

For as long as there have been cars, there have been used car sales. The used car industry has grown dramatically since the post-World War II boom in automobile sales led to an increasing number of used cars sold. From the growth of that industry, a stereotype emerged. Just as there is a stereotypical "traveling salesman," so there has been a stereotypical used car salesman: pushy, aggressive, male, wearing a loud coat, he was sure to browbeat a hapless old lady or a frightened pair of newlyweds into making a purchase they could not afford or did not want.

True or not, this stereotype seemed accurate to many Americans in the latter part of the twentieth century. Used car buyers might have generally had positive experiences, but those who had negative ones were more likely to remember and talk about those experiences. Coupled with the stereotype was the idea that purchasing a used car was somehow sleazy or shady. As new car prices climbed ever higher, consumers began revising their opinion of used cars, and new players in the market have forced a change in the way we view used car sales people. By the late 1990s, new car departments of dealerships averaged 58 per-

cent of total dealership sales, used car departments accounted for 29 percent—more than four times the figures from a decade ago—and service and parts contributed 12 percent.

A number of factors contributed to the increase in used car sales. One was the economic slowdown of the late 1980s and early 1990s, a worldwide phenomenon. Another was the high number of available two- or three-year-old cars, a by-product of the explosion in automobile leasing that began in the early 1990s. A third factor, one that had also contributed to the increase in leases, was the high cost of new cars. As the shift toward increased used car sales began, a change in the used car industry was inevitable.

In the 1980s, something new had developed in retailing, and it didn't come from inside the auto sales industry: the concept of the "superstore" and its cousin, the warehouse buying club. Usually massive stores with high ceilings and broad aisles, superstores and warehouse clubs offered low prices and a wide variety of choices. Instead of going to a cramped local hardware store that offered only a few brand options, for instance, a "do-it-yourselfer" could shop at a hardware superstore and pay lower prices and have more choices. The idea caught on not only in hardware, but also in office supplies, electronic equipment, groceries—and automobiles. The used car superstore concept offered more benefits than traditional used car dealers such as money-back guarantees, better warranties, and after-sale service.

The auto superstore took elements from the other types of superstores and combined them with revolutionary changes in the method of selling cars. By eliminating a regular commission system, salesmen did not have the incentive to push buyers toward the most expensive car; since commissions were based on unit volume rather than price, the salesperson was more likely to encourage the buyer toward a purchase that would create the greatest customer satisfaction. Customers were indeed more satisfied. A mid-1990s study showed that CarMax had a 98 percent customer-satisfaction rate, whereas the National Association of Auto Dealers (NADA) reported an average satisfaction rate of only 85 percent for traditional dealers.

Among the leading issues faced by used car superstores in their battle against traditional dealerships in the 1990s were the franchise laws of many states. Many state governments look favorably upon automobile dealers, who provide the state treasuries with enormous sales tax money and flood the local economy by purchasing large amounts of advertising. Hence, many states have laws that make it extremely difficult for a new superstore to enter the market.

CURRENT CONDITIONS

U.S. automakers have viewed the emergence of the used car superstore industry with ambivalence. On the one hand, they appreciate the improved reputation of auto showrooms offered by the superstores. Hence, Chrysler, in January 1996, made the unorthodox move of giving auto superstore CarMax a franchise in Duluth, Georgia. On the other hand, the traditional dealership system, with its large numbers of relatively small companies, offered Detroit far more control than the emerging used car megastores. As for the traditional dealers, few are able to pretend any longer that the superstore concept is not taking hold in the auto sales business. Many are frightened, and some are trying to compete.

There is plenty of reason for alarm among traditional dealers, which are generally family-owned businesses. Whereas a typical dealership cost about $4 million in the mid-1990s, the price tag for a superstore could easily be five times that much. In addition, the number of traditional car dealerships has been consistently declining. In 1951, there were 47,500 dealerships in America, but by 1997 that figure had dropped by more than 50 percent, totaling 22,600, and analysts predict that the number would go down to 15,000 within the next few years. Predictably, dealerships that are growing are those who sell 400 or more cars per year. For the rest, overhead costs are rising, and profit margins are declining.

Dealers, frightened of the encroachment by upstarts such as the used car superstores, fought back with competition and through the legal system. On February 7, 1996, a group of dealers put together Driver's Mart, a chain of superstores that was projected to grow to 100 units by 2001. By April of 1998, AutoNation acquired Driver's Mart. "Our partnership with the Driver's Mart retailers accelerates our rollout of the AutoNation USA stores in many key middle market cities," said Steven R. Berrard, president and co-CEO of AutoNation, Inc. "The acquisition of Driver's Mart establishes relationships with many of the country's leading automotive retailers. This reflects our shared belief in the used car megastore concept."

Traditional dealers would be wise to learn from some of the advantages of the superstores, especially the increased customer satisfaction. Despite the seeming trend toward the consumer-oriented dealership, marketing research reports car dealerships rate at the bottom in customer service. In the late 1990s the nation's Better Business Bureaus received more complaints about automobile dealers than about any other industry.

Traditional dealers can, however, take heart from market research showing that superstore prices outpace those of the used car market in general. In late 1997 the average new car cost $22,000, the average used car cost $12,000, and the average sale at AutoNation was $13,000-$13,500. Similarly, old-fashioned dealers can draw comfort from a 1997 *Auto Marketing* survey, which showed that many customers were still happy with traditional dealerships. As the survey concluded, "Used car superstores have some retooling to do before they will be able to sell to the general public." The survey added that the appearance of the dealership has much more to do with consumers' responses than traditional dealers might guess; one expert estimated that 40 percent of the customer's impression hinged on this factor, an area in which the new superstores excel.

The entire car sales industry in 1998 was a $651 billion market. In the mid-1990s, the used car superstore industry was lead by only a few chains, and one leading analyst predicted that neither of the two leaders, CarMax and AutoNation, would have more than an eight-percent share of the used car market in 2001. However, while in the mid-1990s used cars accounted for almost 50 percent of all car sales and the share looked like it would grow, by early 1998 the tide was turning. New car manufacturers reacted by holding the line on prices and offering sales incentives to consumers. CarMax president Austin Ligon said in a 1999 *Chicago Tribune* article: "There is still an enormous opportunity in used cars. The environment is challenged now, but it won't last forever. This is a cyclical business."

Meanwhile, wholesale prices of used cars remained the same, while well-informed consumers demanded better prices. In January 1997 profit margins for used cars were at 11.1 percent; by January 1998 they had fallen to 10.8 percent. As a result, stock prices of all used car superstores had fallen, some drastically. While some analysts remained skeptical as to whether the superstore concept would work, others felt it simply needed fine-tuning. One thing the superstores were learning is that while customers rate their experiences at the megastores as positive, they were not willing to pay the price for the service. Already thought of as an expensive place to buy a used car, superstores are working hard to change that image.

INDUSTRY LEADERS

CarMax Group, owned by electronics superstore giant Circuit City, was a pioneer in the industry. In

1993, CarMax opened its first store in Richmond, Virginia, and many predicted that the concept would not take hold. In 1995, however, it did some $288 million in sales in just four months. Late in 1995, the company acquired a Chrysler dealership outside of Atlanta, thus breaking one of the traditional auto sales industry's unwritten rules: that a publicly owned company would never own an auto sales franchise. CarMax posted $1.47 billion in sales in fiscal year 1999, way up from 1997 revenues of $510 million. However, CarMax continued to operate at a loss. Net income plunged from a loss of $9 million in 1997 to a loss of $34 million in 1998, but there are signs of recovery. In 1999 CarMax reported a loss of $23.5 million. In early 1999, CarMax had 30 locations including two freestanding new car dealerships.

After reaching the $1 billion mark in sales in 1998, but still operating at a loss, CarMax is focusing on building smaller satellite stores with inventories up to 200 in existing markets and adding new car franchises to become profitable. "If we had to do it over again, we'd probably build smaller stores. You don't need an inventory of 1,000 cars when 400 cars would still give consumers a tremendous selection," CarMax president Ligon said in a 1999 *Chicago Tribune* interview. "We're still confident in the used car concept and still sell twice as many cars per store as anyone else does."

In an effort to build a national automotive retail brand—automotive sales, service, and rental—in 1999 Republic Industries, parent of AutoNation USA, changed its corporate name to AutoNation, Inc. The company, led by former Blockbuster Entertainment group head H. Wayne Huizenga, has more than 380 new car franchises in 20 states and 45 AutoNation USA used vehicle superstores. AutoNation decided to reorganize and relocate the used car superstores next to the company's new car dealerships, in effect, merging the two. In January 1998, Republic reportedly took a $150 million write-off to cover the costs. This setup allowed the company to encourage dealers to accept trade-ins and move returned leases from the new dealers to the superstores. Superstores would then have a selection of better cars. AutoNation's 1998 revenues were $17.5 billion ranking them 83 on the 1999 Fortune 500 list of America's largest companies.

AutoNation also made other changes, particularly in the way of staffing and salary. Previously, the company employed retailers from the Blockbuster chain; however, they soon learned that running a car operation was not the same as running a video operation. To combat these problems, they brought in experienced automobile industry people, lowered inventory from 700-1,000 cars to 500, and began to pay their employees on commission rather than salary and bonuses. While some industry experts criticized AutoNation for this move—worrying that a commission-based sales staff might increase customer apprehension by pressuring them to buy more expensive vehicles—the company structured the commissions on volume and customer satisfaction. Thus, an employee receives the same commission regardless of what car they sell; they receive an additional commission or bonus based on how satisfied the customer was with their purchasing experience.

WORK FORCE

Like the traditional automotive sales industry, jobs at used car superstores are divided between management, administration, service, and sales. While sales are the key element in both types of businesses, salespeople at used car superstores are taught to listen to customers and to help them find the car that best suits their needs, rather than to use other tactics to make sales. Salespeople in this emerging industry are generally on salary, or receive a commission tied to unit volume and customer satisfaction, rather than to the dollar amount of a given car sold.

The increased focus on the customer is evident in the service area as well. For example, at AutoNation, all members of the staff, including service technicians, are taught how to handle customers—in line with the company's guiding principle of making "customers for life." This is a particular challenge in the area of service, since buyers do not tend to be as loyal to a dealership for service as they do for sales. Some used car superstores, such as AutoNation, have their own onsite service units with National Institute for Automotive Service Excellence-certified technicians.

FURTHER READING

"AutoNation, Inc." *Hoover's Company Profiles,* April 1999. Available at http://www.hoovers.com.

Brickman, Joanne. "Used Car Superstores: A Revolution in Used Car Buying." *Woman Motorist Used Car Buying Guide.* Available at http://www.womanmotorist.com.

Cedergreen, Christopher W. "Automotive Superstore." *Ward's Auto World,* February 1997.

"Circuit City Stores, Inc.—CarMaxGroup." *Hoover's Company Profiles,* April 1999. Available at http://www.hoovers.com.

DeGeorge, Gail. "Republic Learns Cars Ain't Videos." *Business Week,* 9 February 1998.

Edgerton, Jerry. "Stay Off His Lot! The New Way to Buy an Old Car." *Money,* 1 June 1998.

Eldridge, Earle. "Circuit City Fine-Tuning Its Used Car Chain Idea." *USA Today,* 24 February 1999.

———. "Used car Superstores Make Shopping Fun—But Their Prices Can Be Beat." *Money,* September 1996.

Ellis, John W., IV. "Used car Buyers Generally Happy with Purchase." *Auto Marketing,* 7 April 1997.

Gelsi, Steve. "The New Deal." *Brandweek,* 30 September 1996.

Harris, Nicole. "Superstores: Buying Used—without Feeling Used." *Business Week,* 19 February 1996.

Harte, Susan. "Used Cars: Improved Quality, Choices Appeal to More Drivers." *The Atlanta Journal and Constitution,* 15 September 1997.

Hartnett, Michael. "Superstores Reshape Used Car Business." *Stores,* June 1996.

Light, Harry. "Ford Buys Used car Concept." *Business Week,* 19 December 1996.

Mateja, Jim. "Used car Superstore Branches Out from Big Foothold." *Chicago Tribune,* 5 March 1999.

McLean, Bethany. "Companies to Watch: Tarrant Apparel Group, First South Africa, CarMax." *Fortune,* 17 March 1997.

Naughton, Keith, et al. "Revolution in the Showroom." *Business Week,* 19 February 1996.

Ratliff, Duke. "Car Superstores: Pedal to the Metal." *Discount Merchandiser,* March 1996.

Sawyers, Arlena. "For Many Used car Sellers, It's Service with a Smile." *Auto Marketing,* 7 April 1997.

Seraflin, Raymond. "Car Dealers Go High-Tech vs. Superstores." *Advertising Age,* 26 February 1996.

———. "Spielvogel Auto Group Joins Mounting Used car Derby." *Advertising Age,* 15 January 1996.

"Three Trends Are Reshaping Auto Finance." *ABA Banking Journal,* February 1997.

Vlasic, Bill. "Trend: Used car Dealers." *Business Week,* 13 January 1997.

Wernie, Bradford. "Huizenga Developing Primer in Selling and Renting Cars." *Auto Marketing,* 7 April 1997.

Yung, Katherine. "Advances in Computer Technology Forcing Improvements in Auto Dealer Industry." *Gannett News Service,* 30 March 1998.

———. "Circuit City Releases Fiscal Year 1999 Results." *PR Newswire,* 6 April 1999. Available at http://www.prnewswire.com.

———. "NADA Data 1998." The National Automobile Dealers Association, 1998.

———. "New Name an Important Step Forward." *Company News On-Call,* 6 April 1999. Available at http://www.prnewswire.com.

———. "Republic Acquires Driver's Mart." *Company News On-Call,* 22 April 1998. Available at http://www.prnewswire.com.

———. "Slow-Growth CarMax Opts for Marathon Race." *Auto Marketing,* 7 April 1997.

———. "Used car Chain CarMax Cuts Back Growth Plan, Delays Entry in L.A." *Dow Jones Business News,* 23 February 1999. Available at http://www.djinteractive.com.

———. "Used Car Market Report." ADT Automotive, 1999.

—Judson Knight,
updated by Lisa Karl and Lori Lewis-Chapman

USED COMPUTER EQUIPMENT RESELLING

The vast and growing enterprise in used computer equipment reselling is less sharply defined than many other emerging industries. In fact, in the late 1990s, members of the industry were even in dispute over the very meaning of the word "used" as it applied to computer equipment. Nor was there a single organization, or group of organizations, to advance the cause of the used computer business; the ones that do serve computer dealers tend to make little distinction between those who sell new and those who sell used equipment.

Many industries are dependent on others; but used equipment sales exist purely as the result of new equipment production, particularly through upgrading existing equipment. A common theme throughout the used computer equipment business—at least among sellers who deal with the general public—is that people expect the resale value of computers to diminish only slightly with the passage of time, whereas it is not uncommon for a $2,000 system to be virtually worthless after 5 years.

The technology of computers is changing quickly, and that is the basis for the growing industry in computer equipment reselling. Computer power doubles about every 18 months and many manufacturers hype the latest and greatest model, creating a healthy supply for the used equipment market. Dealers are able to buy and sell equipment that is slightly out of date, but still quite viable; by reselling it, they extend the lives of computers, save customers money, and tap into a vast and growing source of profit. Consumers who are starting up a business and do not have a lot of capital; who have never owned a computer before and are intimidated by the technology and prices of new computers; and who want a second computer for the home, are the primary market for used-computer equipment.

In a 1998 study of the used computer market, International Data Corporation (IDC), a market research company, observed that the used market had been a very minor player in the computer industry for a number of years. However, according to IDC, "recently it has become a concern for new PC vendors." As buyers become aware that they can purchase a full-function computer with few compromises for such a low price, sales of new entry-level computers may well be affected. IDC predicted that "used PC vendors will continue to represent both a valuable resource and a form of competition for new PC vendors." Even more intense competition between used computers and new entry-level models is foreseen by IDC if "compelling new software applications that would drive users to upgrade to new high-end hardware do not appear." IDC's figures for 1997 show that used computer systems accounted for nearly 15 percent of computer shipments. It predicted the shipment of used systems would increase exponentially, growing at a 14 percent compound annual rate to a total of 9.9 million units by the year 2002, up from 5.5 million in 1997.

Sellers of used computer equipment are generally either retail stores or dealers. Although there are a few chains in the industry, notably Computer Renaissance, most retailers of used computers are small business owners. The *Wall Street Journal* offered an example of how one such store, Compuplan, does business.

When a woman in Cedar Hill, Texas, wanted a computer to perform routine household operations such as keeping her finances, she went to Compuplan and purchased a used IBM 486 computer for $699. Her computer originally belonged to American Airlines, who used it for the airline's reservations system. Thus it did not have a great deal of consumer-oriented amenities, such as software. So Compuplan, which bought the unit from American for $250, invested another $300 in upgrading it. It then added $150 to the price (27 percent of the original investment) and sold the computer to the customer.

Retailers sell equipment of greatest interest to the consumer market: software, PCs, peripherals (printers, etc.), and the occasional network card or memory chip for the do-it-yourself computer enthusiast. Dealers, on the other hand, sell all those things and more—including large systems for networking an entire company—but they do so in larger quantities. Typically, if a consumer were to call a dealer and ask to buy or sell just one PC, the dealer would refer them to a retailer. Hence the difference between retailers and dealers is to some extent in what they sell, but more significantly in how they sell it. Dealers generally operate in an ordinary office, with a large storage and testing area in back, and do little of their business face-to-face; rather, they are highly dependent on telephone communications. Generally they buy from, and sell to, other businesses, including other dealers. They make their money primarily because of the information they possess: they know that on one side, Company X needs a certain item and is willing to pay $1,000 for it, and that on the other, Dealer Y has the item priced at $750. The dealer in the middle, because he is able to link up the two companies, makes the $250 profit.

One of the leading trade organizations for used computer sellers is the Computer Dealers and Lessors Association (CDLA). Founded in 1981, the CDLA brought together the Computer Lessors Association, which has existed since 1967, and the Computer Dealers Association, formed in 1972. As its name implies, the CDLA's constituency includes businesses that lease computer equipment; in fact, according to figures provided by the organization, leasing accounts for more than twice as much revenue annually as used equipment sales. Besides sellers and lessors, the CDLA includes maintenance companies, refurbishment/reconfiguration firms, transportation companies, financial institutions, original equipment manufacturer (OEM) finance companies, software distributors, and industry consultants. Among its principal services to the industry, and to the public, is the CDLA's Code of Ethics, which its more than 300 members have signed. Since 1974, a standing committee has arbitrated hundreds of cases regarding ethics violations.

More On **USED COMPUTER INDUSTRY ASSOCIATIONS**

Several organizations from different areas of the computer industry are of great interest to the used computer business. Among the most important are:

- The Computer Leasing and Remarketing Association
- The Business Products Industry Association
- The Business Technology Association
- The Computing Technology Industry Association
- The Information Technology Association of America

All these groups represent some configuration of business people including storefront resellers, wholesale dealers, value-added resellers (VARs), and lessors.

More central to the life of the used computer business than industry associations, however, are arenas and forums where dealers can exchange information about available equipment. Retailers, and to a certain extent wholesale dealers, watch for news of liquidations and auctions, including those run by local governments or federal institutions. Salespeople and equipment brokers often interact with each other over the telephone in a complex network of interactions that spans the globe. A dealer in the Midwest, for instance, may learn that an end-user (buyer) in San Francisco needs 300 personal computers. So she calls her contact in Denmark, who then gets in touch with a supplier in Australia. The Australian supplier puts in a call to a dealer in Los Angeles, who has the equipment and sends it. And thus the 300 PCs may travel around the world, back up the chain, in order simply to travel from Los Angeles to San Francisco. Outsiders might ask why the L.A. dealer was not put directly in touch with the San Francisco end-user, but to equipment dealers, the answer is obvious: without the profit that accrues to a dealer as middleman, he is unable to continue to exist as a business and the next time someone comes looking for equipment, they may be unable to locate it because there is no one to track it down.

Although voice interaction over the telephone remains a key element in arranging the movement of goods within the used computer industry, brokers also rely on weekly publications announcing equipment for sale, and are dependent on information-age technology to keep up-to-date on equipment offerings. A company with a large quantity of token rings to sell, for instance, might set up a fax broadcast to dealers and end-users all over the United States or the world. The Internet is an emerging means of exchange as well. Numerous companies have their own Web sites, and there are sites as well for entities such as Daley Marketing Corporation (DMC), which sells primarily to dealers. Founded in 1980 as an IBM computer broker/lessor, DMC is in the business of providing timely, accurate, and detailed industry information through regular publication of its *DMC Computer Price List, DMC Broker and End-User Market Value Report,* and other items.

The market for used computer equipment is composed of three distinct segments: refurbished, used, and liquidated equipment. Refurbished equipment runs the gamut as far as quality is concerned, but all refurbished systems are previously owned computers that have been reconditioned. Many refurbished computer systems are sold with warranties. Used equipment, on the other hand, may or may not be reconditioned. Finally, liquidated computers generally represent last year's models that were never sold. According to Christine Arrington, an analyst for International Data Corporation, the used computer market "has been evolving from a dumping ground for unwanted and under-powered systems to an acceptable source of low-cost hardware to fit a variety of budget and power ranges." She predicted increasing competition between the new and used computer markets but said they probably will remain highly interdependent.

Late in the 1990s, cost-conscious school systems around the United States increasingly began to turn to refurbished personal computers to meet their needs in the classroom. The appearance on the used market of more and more used Pentium-based PCs has helped fuel this demand. Refurbished PCs are attractive to the folks running U.S. public schools for a number of reasons, not the least of which is the savings that can be realized. Many school systems operating under tight budgets are forced to cut corners on such basic supplies as paper and pencils, so an opportunity to save money on high-end purchases like computers and peripheral equipment is appealing. By going the used-computer route, school boards can double or triple the number of computers they can put into the classroom. Of the growing school market, Brian Kushner, chief executive officer of ReCompute, an Austin, Texas-based company that markets refurbished PCs, said: "To get three to four times the computational resource for the same dollar—that's an enormous leverage.

Schools don't need—and often don't want—powerful systems targeted at multimedia, engineering, and software compilation applications."

BACKGROUND AND DEVELOPMENT

In 1993 an article on used computers in the Stockholm-based periodical *Tomorrow* approached the subject from a characteristically "green" northern European angle: concern over the environmental impact of non-recyclable computer equipment. According to the article, the German Ministry of the Environment reported that western Germany alone generated some 800,000 metric tons of "electronic waste." This included batteries, cables, and other small items, but the bulk of it was in larger information and office systems. The situation pointed out the fact that computer equipment became obsolete at a quick rate, such that many companies considered it easier to dump such equipment into a landfill than to set about reselling it. The infrastructure for such reselling, in the form of a healthy computer resale industry, was clearly only then developing—or at least, people's awareness of it was still in its early stages.

There was a time when IBM literally dumped old PCs, PC/XTs, and PC/AT models offshore to create an artificial reef, but that day is long gone. In 1997 *Computerworld* magazine reported that the industry giant had begun selling refurbished equipment on the World Wide Web. In fact, it was a 1956 U.S. Justice Department consent decree, restraining IBM's actions in the used equipment market and other areas, which laid the groundwork for the existence of the used computer industry. Of course, it would be many years before computers themselves became widely available to ordinary consumers, but the explosion in PC use during the 1980s paved the way for the growth of used-computer sales.

Yet there was a period of lag, just as the used-car business only came into its own approximately a decade after the advent of widespread sales of Fords and other models. For most of the 1980s and early 1990s, used equipment computer sales were primarily among dealers; only later did the industry see the appearance of numerous storefront retail operations. A study by the Gartner Group for the Computer Leasing and Remarketing Association at the end of 1993 found that volume had not grown for three years starting in 1991, a fact analysts attributed to caution on the part of consumers, as well as to the economic recession. In 1993, however, the volume of used-computer leasing and sales was $19.4 billion, and by 1994 the figure had grown to $21.4 billion. Of that, approximately 30 percent, or $6.42 billion, was in used computer sales.

Aside from the growth in the economy and the differing methodology used to obtain the observations (for example, the first was a survey, the second a straight dollar accounting), the change can be attributed to rapid developments in computer technology during the middle and latter part of the 1990s. In quick succession, IBM upgraded the processing speed of its personal computers such that whereas a 286 was acceptable in 1990, by 1997 the technology had gone through three generations, to a 386, then a 486, and finally a Pentium processor. At the same time, the speed of Pentiums had also accelerated. Other changes were afoot as well: for instance, widespread access to the Internet dictated a need for faster and faster modems, and old 9,600- and 14,400-baud models were being cast off in favor of 28,800 or 56,000 models. The business world saw a revolution in local area networks (LANs), which required their own extensive range of equipment in order to be established. In upgrading their computers and systems, individuals and businesses had to go somewhere to sell off the old and, in many cases, to purchase the new or almost-new.

By 1995 IBM was back in court challenging the 39-year-old Justice Department decree, but it faced strong opposition. One opponent, the very same judge who had presided over the original case—now 84 years old and still sitting on the bench—was removed from the case by a federal appeals court on the grounds that he could not be impartial. Another foe, Computer Leasing & Remarketing Association attorney Kevin Arguit, would not be so easily moved, though. According to the terms of the disputed decree, IBM was prevented from immediately reselling returned equipment; instead, it had to wait 60 days and then offer it first to used-equipment vendors at certain prices. These prices, which the company's representatives said were unreasonably high, further delayed sales of IBM's equipment. If the decree was lifted, Arguit responded, IBM would dominate the market. The dispute raged on.

CURRENT CONDITIONS

The used computer equipment business in the mid-1990s remained the province of entrepreneurs and independent businesspeople. Diamond Data in suburban Atlanta is not an atypical operation. Composed of fewer than a dozen employees, including sales, technical, administrative, and shipping personnel, it deals almost exclusively in IBM equipment, which it trades

with end-users and dealers around the world. Among the company's priorities are staying ahead of the technology curve and looking for the "hottest" equipment; maintaining competitive pricing; keeping abreast of information flow, both in terms of advertising its wares among other dealers and staying aware of equipment being offered for sale; and keeping a tight watch over inventory. The latter, according to company president Mark Moore, is a key to successful operations: "it doesn't matter what equipment you have," he said, "if you can't keep track of it by part number and lay your hands on it quickly when you need it, it doesn't do you any good."

The number of households in which people own computers has risen from 28.5 percent in 1992 to 39.5 percent in 1996. Between 1995 and 1996, 48 million used computers were sold in the United States; in 1996, that represented 18 percent of all computer purchases. In 1996, 23 percent of used computer buyers were also first-time owners; in 1997, that number had risen to 28 percent. With the price of new computers dropping—some cost under $1,000—the price of used equipment is dropping as well. Another factor contributing to lower prices is the introduction of new, more powerful computers about every year and a half. The top-of-the-line new computers range from $2,000 to $4,000 and lose about 60-75 percent of their value in just three months. According to a Delaware location of Computer Renaissance, the average price of a used computer was less than $500 in early 1998, down from an average price of $900 in early 1997.

Prospective buyers need to beware when buying used computer equipment. Just as in used cars, the reputation of the dealer is critical. Customers need to make sure the equipment has little wear and tear and, more importantly, will accomplish the tasks they need. Most people looking to buy used computers want a machine that has basic word processing software, accounting features, and database management capabilities. If someone is looking to run the latest software, especially on PCs, a used computer may be of little use. In the first half of 1997, 35 percent of used computers sold ran on a 386 or slower processor, 46 percent did not have a CD-ROM drive, and 69 percent did not have a modem. Customers can ask about the history of the machine—most come from business lease returns, trade-ins, or customer returns. Warranty information is important too; most offer a 90-day warranty, and the quality of the service department of the store should be top-notch.

One of the phenomena observed in the used computer market late in the 1990s was the growing entry of Pentium-powered PCs. As new computer buyers snatch up the latest Pentium II and Pentium III models, their Pentium I-based equipment is hitting the used market. This has caused a number of computer resellers to question the wisdom of even stocking older computer systems such as 386- and 486-powered models. PCs powered by the now-ancient 286 chip are already extinct. Another trend seen in the used market has mirrored what has been happening in the new computer market: Prices are moving downward across the board, driven to a large extent by an oversupply of powerful refurbished systems, many of which feature warranties. As of late 1998 full-featured Pentium models were selling for about $600.

INDUSTRY LEADERS

The largest sellers of used computer equipment are associated with vast corporate entities: in addition to IBM's resale wing, AT&T Systems Leasing Corp. and GE Capital are important players. At another tier are high-volume dealers such as USA Computer in Long Island or Daktech in Fargo, North Dakota.

Two of the major players in the used computer market are Computer Renaissance (CR) and ReCompute International. Formed in 1988, Computer Renaissance is a chain of more than 200 used computer stores across the United States and Canada. The company's revenue in 1998 was estimated at $160 million, up nearly 50 percent from $108 million in 1997. Headquartered in Minneapolis, Minnesota, Computer Renaissance now ranks thirty-sixth in sales among the top U.S. computer retailers. Most of CR's retail outlets show more computers than the superstores, displaying an average of 30 systems per store. Shoppers are encouraged to tinker with the equipment before making a decision to purchase. All stores take trade-ins.

ReCompute International, based in Austin, Texas, refurbishes personal computers purchased from large companies that are upgrading their equipment, and from PC manufacturers that are liquidating unsold units to make room for new models. Brian Kushner, ReCompute's CEO, says, "We're the undertakers of the PC industry." For many computer users, individual as well as corporate, the older technology in some of the used computers marketed by ReCompute and others in the industry is more than sufficient for their needs. "The vast majority of buyers out there are paying for way more computer than they need," according to Dale Yates, a systems administrator for McLane Company, based in Temple, Texas. Yates and others responsible for corporate computer buying decisions are finding that there's no need to supply someone whose responsibilities are largely confined to word processing, for example, with a computer designed to perform far more sophisticated functions.

Other companies in this industry include Second Source, with six stores in Delaware and Pennsylvania; Computer Exchange, which matches buyers and sellers for a 10 percent commission; and Boston Computer Exchange, a phone-based buying and selling dealership that reported $32 million in sales in 1996. The Internet has several used-computer selling sites, running from manufacturers that sell refurbished models to auctions.

WORK FORCE

Generally, a used-computer operation, whether a wholesale dealer or a retail store, must employ at least one class of worker: salespeople. Salespeople, whether they work behind a counter or over the phone, may receive a salary, but usually commissions are used as an incentive for high performance. Because they generate the company's profit, salespeople are usually the most highly paid, and can often earn in the high five-digit figures, or even over $100,000 a year.

Also important are technical personnel, whose job is to evaluate equipment for problems, and they fix those problems as they arise. Tech workers may earn $20 an hour or more. In addition, used computer businesses, depending on their size, may employ shipping and receiving personnel, inventory workers, and administrative assistants.

AMERICA AND THE WORLD

The used computer business continues to grow internationally, where buyers in emerging countries are thrilled to purchase slightly used American equipment at a discount. Trading goes on between America and the economic powerhouses of Western Europe and the Pacific Rim, but a future area of growth is likely to be "second-tier countries," such as developing nations in Eastern Europe, the Middle East and Central Asia, East Asia (including China), and parts of Latin America and Africa.

One international market that was booming in the waning days of the twentieth century was Brazil, where the supply of used computers in early 1999 was estimated at about 6.8 million. Many of these systems had been acquired from larger companies at cut-rate prices, according to Loja dos Micros, a Sao Paulo-based seller of used systems. Another player in the Brazilian market is Celty Informatica, also based in Sao Paulo. Both companies predict that as the devaluation of the Brazilian currency increases the prices of new computers, the demand for used equipment will grow even stronger.

FURTHER READING

Albert, Sam. "Beware: Black-Market Chips Are Hot." *Computerworld,* 12 August 1996, 37.

"Brazil: Growing Market for Used Computers." *South American Business Information,* 26 January 1999.

Computer Dealer & Lessors Association Home Page. Available from http://www.cdla.org.

"Computer Industry Failing to Recycle Outdated Models." *Japan Times Weekly International Edition,* 27 May-2 June 1996, 14.

"Computers a Stupid Investment? (ReCompute Sells Used Equipment)." *Electronic News,* 20 July 1998, 40.

Dallabrida, Dale. "Savings Can Be Big On Used Computers." *Gannett News Service,* 18 February 1998.

Dennis, Raoul. "Second Time Around." *Black Enterprise,* August 1996, 26.

Di Simine, Mario. "Satisfaction Guaranteed." *Success,* May 1996, 8.

Doan, Amy. "Born-Again PCs." *Forbes,* 5 April 1999.

Eisenberg, Anne. "Used-PC Bargains Add Appeal to Life in the Slow Lane." *New York Times,* 4 March 1999.

Flynn, Laurie J. "Just Drive a Used PC Off the Lot and Save." *New York Times,* 23 February 1997, F-10.

Flynn, Mary Kathleen. "Oldie-But-Goodie Computers." *U.S. News & World Report,* 8 January 1996, 63.

The Grow Biz International Home Page, 14 July 1998. Available from http://www.growbiz.com.

Harrington, Mark. "Top Ten Retail Innovators: No. 4-Computer Renaissance." *Computer Retail Week,* 16 November 1998, 36.

Hays, Laurie, and Bart Ziegler. "U.S. Favors Relaxing Decree Restricting IBM; Justice Department Stance On 1956 Limitations Is Victory For Company." *Wall Street Journal,* 20 July 1995, A-3.

Johnston, Marsha W. "Taking the Byte Out of Electronic Waste." *Tomorrow,* April/June 1993, 10.

Karl, Lisa Musolf. "Used, Not Obsolete." *Baltimore Business Journal,* 26 January 1998.

Levy, Melissa. "Hand-Me-Downs Are Becoming Big Business." *Star Tribune,* 5 August 1997.

"Low Risk In Buying Used." *Purchasing,* 16 June 1994, 44.

Mackenzie, Ian. "Lower Pentium PCs Set to Invade Used Computer Market." *Computer Dealer News,* 22 June 1998, 30.

Manes, Stephen. "Is There An Afterlife For PCs?" *Informationweek,* 17 June 1996, 164.

Mardesich, Jodi. "Those Who Feel Abused Over Used Computers, Sue." *Computer Reseller News,* 10 June 1996, 99.

Mehling, Herman. "The PC Pipeline." *Computer Reseller News,* 27 March 1995, S-23.

Munk, Nina. "Going Once, Going Twice, Sold!" *Forbes,* 21 October 1996.

Panagos, John, and Lee Shein. "New Systems Raise Demand For Used AS/400s." *3X/400 Systems Management,* October 1994, 92.

Rigdon, Joan E. "FTC Inquires of PC Rivals On Used Parts." *Wall Street Journal,* 17 July 1995, A-3.

"Secondhand Blues." *Computerworld,* 31 March 1997, 45.

"Secondhand Computers Hold Appeal." *Minneapolis Star Tribune,* 8 March 1999, 9E.

Stuckert, William. "A New Lease On Technology." *American City & County,* December 1994, 10.

Taylor, Kieran. "Recycled Rewards." *Data Communications,* June 1996, 68.

"Technology Yard Sale." *Association Management,* October 1996, 123.

Templin, Neal. "Computers: Corporate Castoffs Fuel Market For Used PCs." *Wall Street Journal,* 10 June 1996, B-1.

———. "Computers: Midnight at the Oasis of Microprocessors." *Wall Street Journal,* 29 November 1995, B-1.

"Used Computer, Leasing Business Flat, Poll Says." *3X/400 Systems Management,* January 1994, 22.

Vijayan, Jaikumar. "Suits Over Used PCs End." *Computerworld,* 4 March 1996, 32.

Wagner, Mitch. "Got Old, Washed-Up PCs? HP Offers Cold Hard Cash." *Computerworld,* 23 October 1995, 50.

Wasserman, Todd. "News: Refurb Chains Rethink Inventories—Retailers Alter Their New-to-Used Product Ratios to Help Sustain Margins." *Computer Retail Week,* 28 September 1998, 8.

Whelan, Carolyn. "Refurbished Systems Shift to Schools." *Electronic News,* 20 July 1998, 6.

"Where Will You Buy PCs in the New Millennium?" *Purchasing,* 19 October 1995, 79.

—Judson Knight,
updated by Lisa Karl and Don Amerman

VIDEO DISPLAYS

Advanced video displays provide enhanced image resolution and definition using both new and existing display technologies. The advanced video display industry is primarily based on two technologies—advanced cathode ray tube (CRT) displays and flat-panel displays (FPDs)—that emerged in research laboratories in the 1980s and in the commercial market in the 1990s.

With a Federal Communications Commission (FCC) mandate in April of 1997 requiring the replacement of analog displays, manufacturers began creating products to meet the demand for new display units. These advanced video displays took the form of high-definition television (HDTV) receivers, which provide superior resolution, color, and detail compared to conventional receivers and offer a quasi-three-dimensional picture. HDTV relies heavily on a digital version of previous CRT TV and computer monitor video-display technology. HDTV producers and television broadcasters planned to launch the industry commercially in 1998; the first digital shows were expected by fall of 1998.

The advanced video display industry also includes a set of new technologies used mostly in laptop computers. Portable computer equipment requires lightweight yet powerful and functional technology; hence, computer makers turned to flat-panel video displays in the 1990s to avoid large, clunky monitors for laptops. Flat-panel screens are simply thin displays capable of capturing high-resolution images. According to the U.S. Display Consortium, the flat-panel display market in 1998 had some $11 billion in revenues and was expected to reach $20 billion by 2000. Stanford

Resources Inc. estimated the liquid crystal display (LCD) market would reach 2.27 billion units valued at $21.8 billion by 2004. *Publish* estimated in 1998 that the market for flat-panel displays would grow by 16 percent annually through 2003 with the CRT market expanding 5 percent.

As companies began to develop HDTV sets in 1997, they not only worked with the standard CRT technology but started experimenting with flat-panel technology as well, because as the size of a CRT display increases, its thickness and weight balloons as well. The alternatives to CRT-based displays, however, remained inferior in terms of image quality and impractical in terms of cost in the mid-1990s.

ORGANIZATION AND STRUCTURE

HDTV

In contrast to conventional analog TV with its 525 horizontal lines, HDTV offers 1,080 horizontal lines, providing much clearer images and detail. A standard television receives analog TV signals as radio signals undergoing constant changes and creating a nearly square picture. An HDTV, on the other hand, receives signals digitally as binary electronic signals, which the receiver then translates into a stream of images—rectangular, as in movie theaters—virtually free from broadcast distortion. HDTV provides a 16/9-inch width-to-height ratio compared to the 4/3-inch ratio of conventional TV. Moreover, HDTV also delivers digital sound, comparable in quality to an audio compact disc.

HDTV hardware employs state-of-the-art computer technology to make it efficient and highly functional. Digital TV transmitters use computer technology to

---

Trends   MICRODISPLAYS ON THE HORIZON

Bigger, flatter screen displays settled onto contemporary desktops, as researchers' heads turned toward further development and refinement of the tiniest, micro liquid crystal displays. Analysts expect the miniaturized screen displays to enter the market full force soon after the turn of the second millenium forecasters predicted a $400 million market for the displays by 2004.

Two Japanese manufacturers, Sony and Seiko-Epson, took the lead in the micro display arena,. In 1998 the two companies comprised the bulk of the $350 million micro display market. A string of ten or more competitors followed in lethargic pursuit, hesitant over what some perceived as a limited applications arena for the technology. In 1999 the micro display marketplace confined itself to camera and camcorder displays, but ongoing innovations that contributed to reduce the cost of the manufacturing technology during the 1990s stand to define the viability of the industry at any point in the future. Anticipated applications abound for the tiny viewers, most prominently on cellular telephones and in other communications equipment. Yet, many developers see the phones and photographic viewfinders as a limited market niche—not to mention the end of the trail for micro displays. Others maintain that those applications in reality foreshadow a diverse assortment of many more lucrative uses for micro screens, applications that loom in the offing.

The current state of the technology is based in standard CMOS transistor concepts. This fact, combined with ongoing improvements in sub-micron manufacturing procedures, stand to topple the cost barriers that prevent the LCD displays from permanently replacing the older polysilicon displays on game readouts, pagers, and other small electronic items.

compress the signals for broadcast, allowing them to send two programs in one broadcast channel. Analog technology can deliver only one program per channel. Reciprocal technology must be present on the receiving end to interpret the digital signal.

In 1997 different industry factions continued to vie over which kind of scanning transmission technology HDTV systems should use. Computer makers backed progressive-scan systems—technology compatible with computer monitors. The TV industry on the other hand, sought to implement interlaced scan systems—technology incompatible with computer monitors. This scan system would have enormous ramifications for consumers in that for about $100, computer users could upgrade their computers to re-

ceive HDTV signals, while HDTV sets cost $2,000 or more. However, the computer-friendly progressive-scan technology cannot deliver the high-resolution of interlaced-scan technology. Progressive scanning would provide 525-line resolution for general programs and 720-line resolution for 35-millimeter films; interlaced scanning would deliver 1,080-line resolution. Nonetheless, David Moschella reported in *Computerworld* that computer industry companies contend that in time progressive-scan systems could surpass interlaced scan and provide superior pictures as the technology advances. In 1997 some major broadcast networks planned to offer programs using interlaced scanning, much to the chagrin of the computer industry.

HDTV LEGISLATION AND POLICIES

The Telecommunications Reform Act of 1996 officially launched the foray into digital television in the mid- to late-1990s. With exhortation from House Speaker, Newt Gingrich, and Senate Majority Leader, Trent Lott, part of the FCC's HDTV policy included handing out broadcasting licenses for free instead of auctioning them off as the agency usually does. Thomas W. Hazlett argued in the *Wall Street Journal* that the decision to give away HDTV air space will require tax payers to foot an $11 billion bill and it will cause the government to lose as much as $70 billion in revenues.

As a trade-off for gratis air space, the FCC wanted to impose a standard that would govern all digital television broadcasts. In 1996, the agency began to review proposed standards for digital television which included 18 HDTV formats, including formats for wide-screen pictures and sports broadcasts, according to Albert R. Karr in the *Wall Street Journal.* The FCC faced robust debate between a computer-industry alliance—headed by Microsoft Corp., Intel, and Compaq Computer Corp.—and a cadre of TV broadcasters. The dispute centered on the integration of computer and TV technology that would enable computers to function as TVs and TVs to function as computers. The computer alliance fought for a standard that would allow computers and TVs access to the same signals, whereas the TV broadcasters, dubbed the Great Alliance, insisted on a format that would exclude existing computer technology from functioning as displays. The computer alliance urged the FCC to either adopt a standard amenable to both computers and HDTVs or not to impose a standard at all. Finally, in 1997 the FCC backed down on its plan to impose a standard and decided to let the market determine the format. Also see the chapter entitled Digital Interactive Television.

Though the FCC expected stations to start broadcasting HDTV signals starting in 1998 and offer complete digital programming by 2006, the agency also required that stations and networks provide analog signals via their traditional channels. Therefore, viewers with conventional TVs need not worry about losing access to TV programs until 2006, when they will have to purchase an adapter or an HDTV set. In addition, these policies do not govern cable and satellite TV services, which may begin offering HDTV to compete with free television services.

Prior to the Telecommunications Act, the FCC began actively encouraging research into digital television by participating in its development. In 1987, the FCC decided to help the TV industry create a new standard of television or advanced TV (ATV). Later on, the new technology became known as high-definition television.

The National Association of Broadcasters (NAB) provided a forum for the exchange of ideas related to the HDTV advanced video displays. Serving all sectors of the broadcast industry, the NAB offers amenities such as reports on legislation and technology that affect broadcasters and information on public and government relations. The NAB played an instrumental role in representing the concerns of the TV broadcasters and networks while government agencies developed HDTV policies. Each year the NAB holds a convention to highlight new technology and discuss current issues. In 1997 the convention centered on HDTV and the FCC policies that had begun to unfold.

FLAT-PANEL DISPLAYS

Liquid crystal displays (LCDs) make up the most common form of flat-panel display. LCDs work by having a layer of material that can regulate light and turn each picture element or pixel in an image on and off, according to Alfred Poor in *PC Magazine*. LCD video displays comprise two primary kinds of laptop computer monitor technologies and constitute one of the costliest components of portable computers. One of the more expensive technologies used in higher-end products are thin-film transistor (TFT) screens, which provide the best image quality in terms of color saturation, response time, brightness, and color depth, according to Steve Preston in *EDN*. Lower-end laptops rely on super-twisted nematic (STN) screens, which cannot deliver the quality TFT screens can. In particular, the pixels in STN screens take longer to turn on and off, thereby creating slower response times. Though manufacturers cut the original response time of earlier STN displays in half, they still lag with response times of 150 milliseconds, compared to TFTs'

35 milliseconds. Moreover, STN screens offer color depths of only 16 to 18 bits per pixel, whereas TFT screens can support twice as many bits per pixel. STN technology can also cause the display to shimmer and wave because of the way it creates a 256,000-color palette from eight primary colors.

Manufacturers integrated flat-panel displays into an array of products such as watches, wide-screen wall TVs, and military, nautical, and aviation devices. Flat-panel technologies such as LCD displays make ideal components for these devices not only because of their size and weight, but also because they require substantially less power than CRT displays. However, the United States, though it pioneered much of the flat-panel technology and conducted seminal research on flat-panel displays, remained on the periphery of flat-panel production. U.S. firms either lack the capacity or the capital to successfully produce flat-panel displays, according to the Office of Technology Assessment in *Flat Panel Displays in Perspective*. Therefore, the Clinton administration established the National Flat Panel Display Initiative (NFPDI) to help the United States stake out a larger share of the market. Led by the U.S. Department of Defense, the NFPDI began in 1994 to foster new research into developing flat-panel displays in the United States, especially for defense purposes.

The Video Electronics Standards Association (VESA) provides oversight to this segment of the advanced video display industry. VESA creates standards that allow the industry to develop technology systematically and uniformly without chaos. The standards VESA develops enable manufacturers of computers to measure and represent video display qualities in a common format.

BACKGROUND AND DEVELOPMENT

Video-display technology used in desktop computers and TVs uses the same engineering to present images. Manufacturers employed this long-standing technology, the cathode ray tube (CRT), ever since the first TVs were made. CRTs function by projecting a beam of electrons from one end of the tubes to the other where the electrons cause a layer of chemical phosphors to glow, revealing different colors.

CRT-based television technology remained stagnant for several decades. The analog TV technology of the mid-1990s paralleled that of the 1940s and 1950s. Early televisions of the late 1920s relied on 90-line resolution with monochrome pictures that flickered across the screen. However, the technology improved almost on a yearly basis at first. Between 1931 and 1939, resolution expanded from 120 lines to 441 lines. RCA released a 441-line video display in 1939 that sold for $600, or about half the cost of a new car, according to the *New York Times*.

The National Television Standards Committee (NTSC) established the TV broadcast format in 1941 that governed the industry until the FCC's 1996 decree that TV broadcasters convert to digital TV transmission by 2006. The NTSC's standard mandated that TV stations broadcast 525-line programs in the United States. With few alterations, this defacto standard remained for more than five decades, even though technology existed for higher-resolution broadcasting.

The modifications to the NTSC standard largely included making amendments for color broadcasting. Initially, the FCC adopted an ineffectual color-wheel method for color broadcasting in 1950. CBS developed the color-wheel technique, but it could only produce basic and inaccurate colors. The color wheel worked by creating the illusion of full color with a color wheel spinning inside the TV set, according to Joel Brinkley in the *New York Times*. In 1951, RCA introduced a different color system, which many companies and analysts extolled. Brinkley stated that RCA's electronic method created full-color images by shining three separate color images onto the screen. Consequently, the FCC repealed its original decision and made the RCA system the new standard.

In the 1970s and 1980s, companies such as Zenith Electronics Corp. and a number of Japanese companies led by the Japanese Broadcasting Corporation (NHK) started to research new television formats using digital technology. These digital TV (DTV) projects led to the development of both digital standard-definition and digital high-definition television. The goals of this research were to create televisions with better resolution and to imbue TV pictures with a near three-dimensional quality and increased speed of image scanning. Japan premiered its HDTV capabilities at the 1984 Los Angeles Olympics and began a 1,125-line resolution direct-broadcast service in 1989 called MUSE. Later, through combined effort, NHK and Sony Corp. produced the regularly used HDTV system Hi-Vision, which promoted further development of HDTV technology.

However, developers could not integrate CRT displays into smaller electronic devices such as laptop computers, watches, calculators, and portable monitoring displays, because CRT displays require ample space for tubes. Moreover, the larger screens became,

the more unwieldy they became with CRT technology because the size of the tubes increases with the size of the screen. The Office of Technology Assessment reported that large U.S. electronics corporations developed alternative or advanced video displays by the end of the 1970s working with LCD, plasma, and electroluminescent technologies. This research produced simple screens capable of presenting text and numbers as used in calculators and watches. However, U.S. researches halted much of their research at this point, leaving the technology in an embryonic state, while Japanese companies continued to experiment with LCDs and developed active-matrix LCD displays for portable TVs in the 1980s. With this foundation in place, Japanese video-display manufacturers such as Sharp Corp. and NEC Corp. enhanced and refined existing flat-panel display technology in the 1990s and conducted research on new flat-panel and advanced video-display technology.

CURRENT CONDITIONS

HDTV

In 1997, the HDTV industry was just starting. Television broadcasters such as the Home Box Office (HBO) and Discovery prepared digital shows to usher in the digital age of television in 1998. TV hardware manufacturers readied themselves to ship HDTVs to retail outlets. Analysts predicted that the new sets would cost initially between $2,000 and $7,000 depending on the screen size. Significant price drops were anticipated as demand would increase. By an FCC order, analog TV broadcasting would cease in 2006, stranding some 230 million conventional TVs in obsolescence and stimulating demand for their successors or for adapters. With the mandatory equipment upgrade, U.S. TV viewers might be compelled to spend an estimated $150 billion to obtain HDTV sets by 2006, according to Brinkley.

Depending on the outcome of the conflict between the computer industry and the TV broadcasters, users may have the option of using their computers as HDTVs or their HDTVs as Internet browsers. The TV set, however, dominates the market: in contrast to the 35 percent figure for computers, about 99 percent of all U.S. households have a TV. While TV manufacturers prepared to roll out HDTVs, the computer industry, led by Compaq Computer Corp. and Gateway 2000 Inc., readied the launch of computer home theaters with full computer and TV capabilities. Gateway introduced such a product in 1996, but it has received tepid market response. The TV industry attempted to merge Internet browsing and TV capabilities with its WebTV, but it too has failed to attract consumer interest.

Many broadcasters plan to offer digital television long before the FCC deadline. Judy Bloomfield reported in *HFN* that network and VHS stations in 30 leading U.S. markets expressed intent to introduce digital television by early 1999. Thus an estimated 43 percent of U.S. viewers would receive digital TV before the next millennium.

As a result of the FCC mandate, semiconductor manufacturers plan to glean heavy business from the demand for mixed-signal semiconductors to control the new transmission and reception equipment. Robert Ristelhueber reported in *Electronic Business Today* that TV users will have to replace or upgrade over 200 million television sets by 2006. Therefore, Dataquest predicted that the digital TV semiconductor market will grow to $718 million by 2002.

The joint venture between the industry giants Microsoft and NBC, MSNBC, took its first step towards the new digital TV age and era of HDTV in 1997, when the cable broadcaster moved to a predominately digital studio. The move to the new studio prepared MSNBC for HDTV broadcasting as well as for Internet broadcasting. For its regular network, NBC announced it would provide HDTV prime time programs and conventional broadcasting at other times. In addition, CBS planned to offer both progressive- and interlaced-scan HDTV, while ABC was still considering relying on progressive scan HDTV in mid-1997.

FLAT-PANEL VIDEO DISPLAYS

The Office of Technology Assessment (OTA) reported in *Flat Panel Displays in Perspective* that world revenues from this collection of advanced video displays totaled approximately $11.5 billion in the mid-1990s and predicted that sales would rise to as much as $40 billion in the next millennium. At this time, U.S. producers accounted for only about 3 percent of global sales. The U.S. Department of Defense, however, initiated Clinton administration-backed plans to bring the U.S. producer share up to 15 percent by 2000 through funding and incentives for companies committed to producing FPDs in the United States.

Flat panels used for portable computers accounted for the bulk of the worldwide sales. Consumer electronics applications of FPDs made up the next-largest group of products, followed by commercial, business, industrial, and transportation applications. Military use amounted to less than 1 percent of worldwide flat-panel sales. Of the various flat-panel technologies, liquid crystal displays (LCDs) accounted for 87 percent of all

FPDs sold. The OTA expected LCD technology to retain this market share into the twenty-first century.

Since mass commercial production began around 1990, Japanese companies have led the FPDs industry. Nonetheless, other Asian countries including Korea and Taiwan are also key players in the global flat-panel industry. In contrast to the United States, Japan invested billions of dollars in its flat-panel industry, according to the OTA, which allowed the Japanese industry to prosper quickly as demand for FPDs in laptop computers burgeoned. As the decade progressed, this investment pushed the Japanese market to the forefront in both flat-panel production and sales.

The Video Electronics Standards Association (VESA) reached an accord for a new flat-panel standard in 1997. With the standard in place, manufacturers would no longer confront difficulties stemming from incompatible connection types, pin counts, and pin placement in laptop computers, according to *Computerworld.*

Electronic News predicted in early 1998 that a combination of conditions could result in a shortage of LCD panels beginning in late 1998. Instead, oversupply damaged the market. Prices dropped from a mid-1990s high of $995 to $350. By 1998, some manufacturers were reportedly selling panels in quantity for $250 or less in order to unload them. Most of the fabrication facilities were mandated to operate at 20 to 50 percent capacity beginning in 1998 and companies such as Hyundai delayed making major capital investments in fabrication facilities. During the course of 1998 the retail value of LCD displays fell nearly 50 percent—from $1,670 for a 14-inch display at the end of 1997, to under $1,000 by the end of 1998.

Stanford Resources Inc. subsequently found in mid-1998 that stagnant demand in the portable computer market and large installed TFT-LCD capacity caused prices to drop—the first such drop in market value since the technology was developed. Demand could not offset the price decreases. Passive LCD module manufacturers were about the only part of this segment that fared well. *Electronics News* predicted capacity would remain tight through 2000, with the resultant effect a more stable market for TFT-LCD products as well as TFT equipment and materials producers. Growth in the industry's capital spending was projected to begin in late 1998 and continue into early 1999.

COMPUTER MONITORS

As shipments and prices declined during 1998, consumers realized new payoffs in every aspect and dimension of computer display technology. New CRT and FPD displays came to market that were not only cheaper, but bigger, clearer, thinner, and more durable. Vendors introduced new 19- and 21-inch big-screen monitors, many in the slim packaging afforded by refined FPD technology. *PC Magazine* evaluated CTX International's 21-inch EX1200 and praised the high-clarity and maximum resolution of 1,600 x 1,200 that could be had for less than $1,000. EIZO Nanao Technologies' FlexScan T960, a similar device, received equal approval. Raytheon meanwhile introduced a new 21-inch rear-projection monitor with 1,280 x 1,024 resolution. The device was less than 13 inches deep, weighed only 32 pounds, could withstand 9 g's of force, and was touted for its clarity.

INDUSTRY LEADERS

CRT HDTV LEADERS

Leading producers of HDTV technology include Zenith Electronics Corp., Sony Corp., and Panasonic. Zenith Electronics devoted millions of dollars to HDTV research in the 1980s and helped to pioneer much of the HDTV technology. Zenith's research allowed the company to develop an HDTV transmission system that the FCC adopted in 1996. Zenith's work on HDTV also won the company an Emmy award for primetime engineering. In addition to its HDTV endeavors, Zenith is one of the leading manufacturers of televisions and VCRs in the United States, despite financial losses throughout the 1990s. Zenith employed 6,800 workers and posted sales of $985 million in 1998. LG Group owned 55 percent of the company and, according to Hoover's, was to assume control of the company in 1998 under Chapter 11 bankruptcy protection.

Sony Corp., an international electronics leader, stepped up its efforts to be a key producer of HDTV hardware. In 1997 Sony launched a video display capable of handling both traditional 525-line analog as well as 1,125-line digital broadcasts. In 1998 the company employed 177,000 workers worldwide and together with its subsidiaries posted sales of over $51 billion.

Matsushita Electric Corp., a subsidiary of Panasonic Broadcast & Digital Systems Company, also played a crucial role in the development of HDTV technology. Some of the first TV networks and stations to begin switching to digital hardware selected Panasonic's equipment for their stations. In 1998 Matsushita posted sales of $59 billion worldwide.

FLAT-PANEL DISPLAY LEADERS

Despite a disappointing 26 percent decline in 1998 due to the Asian economic crisis, the FPD market rebounded early in 1999. Analysts attributed the improvement to an increased demand for thin-film transistor technology that was necessary to accommodate a rise in the sale of laptop computers. The swell in demand led to price increases of 25 percent and higher from major suppliers. During the first quarter of 1999 the United States shipped 136,000 units according to Stanford Resources, as reported in *Electronic News.* That number was projected to grow to 299,999 in the fourth quarter.

Most of the leading flat-panel display companies were based in Japan, including Sharp Corp. Sharp was one of the first Japanese companies to follow up on initial U.S. research on FPDs in the 1970s. When U.S. companies such as Westinghouse and RCA halted their flat-panel experimentation, Sharp began exploring the technology. The company held 37 percent of the market in 1998 and made displays for products such as airplane instrumentation, calculators and computer screens. Moreover, Sharp continued to research building larger LCD displays through 1998. Sharp had a staff of 47,981 employees and posted $13.5 billion in revenues in 1998.

Toshiba Corp. was the world's second-largest of FPDs producer in the 1990s. It also led the world market in portable personal computer manufacturing. Collaborating with International Business Machines Corp. (IBM), Toshiba manufactured advanced video displays for the computer and the consumer electronics industries. Toshiba also produced a diverse selection of electronics and energy products. Toshiba employed 186,000 in 1998, when it reported $41 billion in total sales.

NEC Corp. ranked third in FPD production in the 1990s. Besides its video displays, NEC is a leading computer producer in Japan and the world's second-largest manufacturer of semiconductors. The company also owned 50 percent of U.S. computer company Packard Bell. NEC employed 152,450 people and posted total revenues of $36.9 billion in 1998.

In addition to the industry giants, there are quite a few prosperous companies in this industry segment, many of which are involved with the U.S. Display Consortium. The U.S. Display Consortium or USDC, created in 1993 as a government-industry response to the Flat Panel Display Initiative, has as its mission to ensure that this segment of the high definition display industry remains "on the leading edge." The group has been instrumental in creating and growing industry manufacturing infrastructures, and has funded more than 35 projects related to materials and components manufacturing since 1993. Those projects have been awarded to companies across the United States, including Vermont and Texas. In June 1998, the USDC was awarded an additional $10 million by the Defense Advanced Research Projects Agency (DARPA) for continuing research for the U.S. FPD industry. Among its more than 100 members, the USDC counts FPD manufacturers, developers, users, and equipment manufacturers and suppliers. These include companies such as Candescent Technologies Corporation, Compaq Computer, Planar-Standish, Texas Instruments, Three-Five Systems, and Universal Display Corporation.

Candescent Technologies attracted significant attention during the mid-1990s when it embarked on intensive research to perfect field emission display (FED) technology for flat display graphics applications. Candescent, once known as Silicon Video, is not alone in the quest for a high-voltage FED phosphor to mimic the function of CRT operation at the pixel level, although many in the industry look to Candescent to accomplish the painstaking project. Indeed, Japanese manufacturer Sony purchased an option for the production rights to the Candescent technology should the effort succeed. Candescent persists in the development effort where dozens of other organizations have failed, not the least of which was Motorola. The technology, if perfected, will facilitate FPD technology in the graphics display arena where active matrix liquid crystal display (AMLCD) technology fails because of limitations in viewing angles, clarity, and power consumption. Despite ongoing technical advancements in Asia Candescent continues as one of a dwindling number of U.S.-based industries involved in that field, although PixTech Incorporated announced its intention in the first quarter of 1999 to undertake a similar research project.

Three-Five Systems, Inc., is a Tempe, Arizona-based manufacturer of LCDs and LEDs for a wide range of devices from pagers to military controls. About 90 percent of its annual sales are attributable to business from original equipment manufacturers in the United States and Europe. Its largest customer has been Motorola. The company posted sales of $95 million in 1998, a growth rate of more than 12 percent over the previous fiscal year, and had about 460 employees.

Planar Systems, Inc., with $129 million in 1998 sales, was North America's largest independent maker of industrial displays. Their electroluminescent displays, CRTs, and active- and passive-matrix LCDs were made for customers such as AlliedSignal and Siemens for products including industrial controls, aircraft instrumentation and point-of-sale systems. The company purchased Standish Industries, a maker of lower-end liquid crystal displays, but in 1999 Planar

announced discontinuance of its FPD products because they were too expensive to manufacture in consideration of the limited demand. The Planar Systems rollback left PixTech Incorporated in a bind as intermediary supplier of the Planar products. PixTech rebounded and agreed to purchase Micron Technology Incorporated, and announced an intention to begin research and development work toward perfecting FED technology for larger, brighter, slimmer screens.

RESEARCH AND TECHNOLOGY

The existing commercial CRT technology of the 1990s posed problems for developing large-screen TVs and monitors: weight and depth substantially increase with the size of the screen. Hence, larger desktop computer monitors are difficult to make so that they can actually fit on a desk. Sensitive to this problem, manufacturers started to examine placing electron guns at the side of the screen, reducing the tube depth and thereby making CRT video displays smaller and lighter, according to Alfred Poor in *PC Magazine*. TFT-LCD displays slowly began emerging on the market. NEC Electronics Inc., in late May 1998, introduced flat-panel color monitors designed for desktop computing. These TFT-LCD monitors, 18.1- and 15.4-inch displays, were estimated to cost between $2,100 and $4,000. *Publish* estimated that "flat-panel displays will still cost three times as much as comparable CRTs in 2001."

NEC and Sharp developed laboratory prototypes of LCD-based computer monitors that provided computer users with larger screens without increasing the weight and depth of the monitors. The cost of producing large-screen LCD displays was much greater than producing smaller ones—those under 20 inches diagonally. Consequently, Poor believes that LCD monitors will not compete in the large-screen market until their prices drop. In addition, researchers continue to hone CRT displays for HDTV sets. HDTV specifications call for resolutions of 1,920 lines by 1,080 pixels.

While some companies expanded their LCD technologies, many U.S. and Japanese companies turned to competing flat-panel technologies in an effort to carve their niche in that market. Backed by Advanced Research Projects Agency (ARPA), U.S. producers experimented with electroluminescent and plasma displays, which they hope will ultimately provide better resolution and more competitive prices than the standard LCD technology. Research on large flat-panel displays focused on color plasma technology, which producers believe will appeal to the market of 40- to 60-inch corporate and public wall-hanging displays. IBM prototyped its high-end Roentgen monitor late in 1998, with a 2,560 x 2,048 flat-panel display resolution. Companies also plan to integrate plasma flat-panel technology into emerging HDTV sets, but plasma HDTVs bore a hefty price of about $15,000 in 1997, making them financially accessible only to the corporate market. Furthermore, plasma displays could provide only a contrast ratio of 120:1, while CRT displays could deliver a ratio of 300:1, giving CRT technology an advantage in terms of image quality. Nonetheless, with adequate sales and expanded production, the prices of large-screen plasma displays could drop by 30 percent, according to Alfred Poor in *PC Magazine.*

The United States Display Consortium announced in May 1998 that it would begin exploring new markets for flat-panel displays, particularly field emission displays, projection display systems, and organic light emitting diodes. The consortium estimated the projection display market alone would exceed more than $7 billion by 1999. Markets for that technology include corporate presentations, education and training, and entertainment, as well as miniature liquid crystal displays. In a 1998 press release, the consortium stated that several areas that could benefit from these sorts of products but have not yet been exploited, include areas such as home appliances, transportation, and medical instrumentation.

FURTHER READING

Ascierto, Jerry. "Candescent Delays Plant, Replaces CEO." *Electronic News,* March 1999.

Bloomfield, Judy. "HDTV Getting a Push." *HFN: The Weekly Newspaper for the Home Furnishing Network,* 24 March 1997.

Brinkley, Joel. "TV Goes Digital: Warts and Wrinkles Can't Hide." *The New York Times,* 3 March 1997.

————. "Who Will Build Your Next Television? 2 Industries Fight for $150 Billion Prize." *The New York Times,* 28 March 1997.

Brodesser, Claude, Michael Freeman, and Richard Katz. "The Resolution Will Not Be Televised." *Mediaweek,* 14 April 1997.

Brown, Peter. "LCD Shortage Looms." *Electronic News,* 30 March 1998.

Dailey Paulson, Linda. "Liquid Crystal Displays Decline in Market Value." *Newsbytes News Network,* 29 June 1998.

Dorsch, Jeff. "Only One Fab to Add Capacity in '98." *Electronic News,* 30 March 1998.

————. "1999 Promises A Better Year in FPD Equipment, Materials." *Electronic News,* 1 February 1999.

"Flat-Panel Standard." *Computerworld,* 19 May 1997.

"The Good, the Bad, and the Flat." *Publish,* March 1998.

Hazlett, Thomas W. "Industrial Policy for Couch Potatoes." *Wall Street Journal,* 7 August 1996.

Karr, Albert R. "FCC Is Expected to Move Forward on HDTV Proposal." *Wall Street Journal,* 9 May 1996.

Krantz, Michael. "A Tube for Tomorrow." *Time,* 14 April 1997.

Moschella, David. "Wintel Has Right HDTV Idea." *Computerworld,* 19 May 1997.

"NEC Expands Flat-Panel Offerings." *PC Week,* 1 June 1998.

Office of Technology Assessment. *Flat Panel Displays in Perspective.* Washington: GPO, 1995.

Poor, Alfred. "Future Display Technology." *PC Magazine,* 25 March 1997.

Preston, Steve. "Designing Graphics Systems for Notebook Computers." *EDN,* 16 April 1997.

Ristelhueber, Robert. "Chip Makers Eye HDTV Bonanza." *Electronic Business Today,* July 1997.

"Television Timeline." *The New York Times,* 2 December 1996.

—Karl Heil,
updated by Linda Dailey Paulson and Gloria Cooksey

VIDEO RENTAL AND RESELLING

As the price of video cassette recorders (VCRs) plummeted and the cost of cinema admission rose, the demand for video rentals and sales increased in the late 1980s through the late 1990s. In 1998, movie admission for new releases was approximately $7.75 for general admission, whereas video rental fees were about $3 at major video rental outlets and even less at in-store video departments. Nevertheless, video rentals and sales slowed around the middle of the decade as the industry's revenues declined in 1995 and grew slightly in the following two years.

When the industry began, video renters, including video stores and chain grocery stores' video rental departments, were reaping modest profits simply by shelving the leading new releases and some perennial favorites. However, in the late 1990s, the market grew more competitive with a glut of shops striving to gain market shares. Consequently, those companies unable to change with the times exited the video rental scene. The most significant types of companies to quit the business were retail and grocery chains that did not want to invest additional effort and money into fortifying and promoting their video rental services. Besides the escalating internal competition, the industry also faces multifaceted external competition from cable movie channels, which offer an abundance of newly released movies. Furthermore, new satellite services providing direct-to-home movies were also striving to convert video rental customers to its convenient, albeit more pricey, method of watching movies at home.

Nonetheless, the industry has clearly rebounded from 1995 and has continued to expand, despite the greater internal and external competition. The in-store sector of the industry witnessed modest revenue increases in 1998 with sales of about $2.48 billion, while the rest of the industry posted approximately $14.9 billion in revenues. Analysts also predict that demand for rental videos will continue to be strong until at least the year 2002.

ORGANIZATION AND STRUCTURE

Operations providing video rental and sales are largely divided into two groups: exclusive video rental shops or video specialty shops (VSS), such as Blockbuster Video and Hollywood Video, and video rental departments of supermarkets and general retailers, such as Kroger and Wal-Mart. However, given the increasingly competitive market, some supermarkets and general retailers turned to video rental chains to run their video rental services.

First run movies usually come to video about 6 months after their initial release, whereas they come to pay-per-view service after another 1 to 3 month window and to cable movie channels after an additional 3 to 5 month window. Video rental operations usually pay between $50 and $80 for each first-run video cassette for rental use and between $10 and $15 for sell-through use. However, movie studios began considering alternative pricing methods to replace the flat price approach with pressure from video specialty stores such as Blockbuster. The alternatives include a revenue sharing program where consumer demand would dictate the price of the cassette, which would allow VSSs to purchase more copies of each movie. Such a system would help VSSs make more copies of a movie available to their customers. VSSs objected to the flat price because it forces them to pay the same amount for both blockbusters and flops.

In addition to offering videos, video rental shops may also provide video games and CD-ROMs for rent. Larger VSSs often carry rental videos in laser disk format, which provides a crisper image and sharper sound, and VCRs. Many national VSS chains diversified in this manner, and in-store services have followed this pattern in order to compete. Besides their rental items, VSSs often sell a host of concessions such as candy, microwave popcorn, and soda, as well as new and used video cassettes. Most in-store video outlets also sell new and used video cassettes.

Video specialty shops and in-store shops may cater to specific crowds. VSSs may court the adult crowd by providing an X-rated section, although many larger companies have averted potential problems by removing adult sections or not even introducing them. Small and independent video shops often concentrate on, or exclusively offer, art and foreign films. Furthermore, a number of in-store shops only rent and sell G, PG, and PG-13 movies, targeting the family crowd and not wanting to offend the sensibilities of shoppers who might object to R-rated fare.

A host of video cassette purveyors or distributors serve video rental operations, and many operations have several distributors. Distributors include Wax-Works Video Works, The Movie Exchange, and Ingram Entertainment Inc. WaxWorks provides videos to rental operations and promotes video rental. Its clients include Kroger, Jitney Jungle, and Harps Food Stores. The Movie Exchange was another large distributor in the mid- to late 1990s with over 200 rental accounts and over 1,000 sell-through accounts. Ingram Entertainment Inc. has over 3,000 accounts, most of which are in-store video departments. Distributors have several problems though. For example, Kroger Co. announced in 1997 that it would pare its distributors down to just one and began taking bids to see which distributor would win its contract. Even more devastating for distributors was Blockbuster Entertainment Corp.'s 1996 decision to buy directly from movie studios. Such moves have begun to alter the overall structure of the video distribution market as other companies have sought to imitate them.

The primary association serving the video rental industry is the Video Software Dealer Association (VSDA). With headquarters in Encino, California, the VSDA promotes home video rental through conventions, newsletters, education, and industry reports. The VSDA also provides members with screening videos and retailing handbooks to help them market new re-

leases and remain competitive. Established in 1981, the VSDA had 3,500 small independent and large multi-branch company members by 1997. The VSDA's accomplishments include lobbying for and helping bring about the adoption of state and federal anti-piracy laws, as well as the maintenance of competitive pay-per-view windows.

BACKGROUND AND DEVELOPMENT

The VCR appeared in 1975, planting the seeds of the video rental industry. New entertainment services also emerged around this time, including cable television. The VCR complemented cable because it allowed users to tape television movies and shows. Shortly after the introduction of the VCR, movie studios released video cassettes of classic movies to add to their revenues. The advent of the VCR/video cassette combination presented consumers with more entertainment options. No longer did they need to rely on the movie theaters' or premium cable channels' schedules to see movies; instead, they could see them whenever they wanted by purchasing sell-through videos, giving consumers a great convenience. However, sell-through videos carried a financial burden since few consumers could afford to pay $10 to $25 every time they wanted to see a movie.

Therefore, video rental shops emerged to serve the market that wanted the convenience of home video without the expense of sell-through video cassettes. Video rental caught on quickly because, after an initial $150 to $500 investment for a VCR, people could rent a cassette for a lower price than they could go to the theater. Video rental especially filled the family entertainment niche where consumers needed tickets for the entire family costing $20 to $30 *vis-a-vis* a $3 expenditure to rent a video. By 1985, the industry posted revenues of $3.5 billion and by 1990, it posted revenues of $9.8 billion, according to the VSDA.

CURRENT CONDITIONS

The VSDA reports that approximately 27,000 video rental outlets were operating in the late 1990s, down from 31,000 in 1990, which the VSDA attributes to consolidation and the rise of the video megashops. The average video store of the late 1990s consisted of 3,000 square feet of store space occupied by 5,400 video titles. Superstores, in contrast, consisted of 4,800 square feet of store space and over

11,000 titles. Overall, the industry rebounded from its first year of declining sales in 1995 as sales rose slightly the following two years, reaching $16.6 billion in 1997. In 1998 industry revenues rose an estimated 5 percent, climbing to $17.4 billion with the help of *Titanic,* the video that generated the most revenues in rentals and sell-throughs. In addition, video rental revenues account for about 57 percent of the total revenues for a movie, well outweighing theater earnings. Moreover, despite some cries of alarm from industry analysts, Paul Kagan Associates Inc. contends that video rentals and sales will continue to grow, reaching $19.1 billion by the year 2000.

Video rental operations have achieved success due to the 87 percent VCR penetration—87 percent of all U.S. households have a VCR. In addition, about 65 million U.S. consumers patronize a video store once per week, and video stores received about 33 billion visits annually in the late 1990s, making video watching the most popular leisure activity in the United States, according to the VSDA. In addition to soaring video rentals, the industry has experienced increasing success with video sales. U.S. consumers also purchased approximately 600 million sell-through videos a year during this period, according to Paul Kagan Associates.

Nonetheless, other modes of entertainment continued to compete with the video rental industry in the late 1990s. Alternative forms of in-home entertainment such as digital television, pay-per-view, direct-broadcast satellite remained a challenging force for video rental stores during this period. These alternatives provide a number of distinct advantages over video rental, namely, higher resolution for digital television and some greater conveniences such as not having to return videos for pay-per-view and direct broadcast movies. However, these forms of in-home entertainment also cost significantly more, lack features such as being able to pause and rewind movies, and have a far more limited selection than video stores.

VIDEO SPECIALTY SHOPS

Dominating the industry in both video rentals and controlling a growing share of video sales, VSSs looked strong in the late 1990s after a successful rebound from 1995's receding revenues. In 1998 video stores brought in about $15 billion in sales, according to *Supermarket News.* VSSs also began implementing some money saving policies to redefine the purchasing of video cassettes during this period. Blockbuster Video announced in late 1996 that it would eliminate the middlemen and buy directly from movie studios, and Dan Alaimo of *Supermarket News* expects this

move to initiate a trend as VSSs attempt to reduce costs. In addition, Blockbuster reached agreements with movie studios to receive discounts for purchasing large quantities of movie videos and negotiated deals to eliminate the flat pricing system of movie studios.

In the late 1990s, VSSs earned approximately 80 percent of their revenues from video rentals, 10 percent from video sales, and about 10 percent from game rentals and miscellaneous sales. The VSDA reports that the average VSS had sales of $300,000 during this period, and that VSSs accounted for 85 percent of all video rentals, while in-store operations accounted for the remaining 15 percent. However, in-store operations dominated the video sell-through market, holding a 55 percent share of the market.

An increasing number of VSSs had become publicly traded companies in the mid- to late 1990s. Whereas in the early part of the decade there was only 1, by 1996 there were 10, although 50 percent of the VSSs were small stores with 1 or 2 outlets. Nonetheless, *Business Week* ranked 2 VSSs—Movie Gallery and Movies—among its top 25 "Hot Growth Companies" due to their strong sales, growth, and returns on investment.

IN-STORE VIDEO RENTAL OPERATIONS

In store video outlets continued to hold their market share throughout the late 1990s, accounting for about 15 percent of the industry's revenues. In 1998, this sector of the industry posted sales of an estimated $2.48 billion, up 6 percent from 1997. In-store operations have also made new buying agreements with video purveyors. A growing trend in the late 1990s, shared-fee transactions, allowed video rental departments to purchase video cassettes for $10 each and then split the rental profits with the purveyors—often about 50 percent for each party. Supermarkets have also attempted to compete with video specialty shops by launching guaranteed availability campaigns like VSSs have tried. Video shops promised to have copies of new release blockbuster movies such as *Titanic* in stock, or their customers were entitled to watch them free of charge. Shared-fee agreements make such promotions possible because video stores can order substantially more cassettes with such a program since they cost a fraction of the full $50 to $80 price.

Furthermore, in-store operations have borrowed another trick from VSSs—showing videos in the store. Having monitors in the store allows video departments to promote new releases, older titles, and even B movies. Pat Natschke Lenius reports in *Supermarket News* that in-store outlets with monitors have had marked success, but supermarkets must also remain cautious and sensitive to the diverse tastes of their customers. Therefore, they tend to only show G and PG movies and shun movies with extensive violence or profanity. Some in-store video shops have also gleaned profits from renting videos purchased at low sell-through prices and then selling them as used movies. Video departments could easily recoup their investments and earn profits using this system. In addition, many in-store operations established permanent and diversified sell-through sections that include video games as well.

Besides convenience, the key weapon wielded by in-store video operations has been pricing. In contrast to the standard new release price of $3 and $2 for other titles at Blockbuster and other large chains, supermarkets charge an average of $2.33 for new releases and $1.25 for other titles. For video games, in-store operations charge an average of $1.98. Such pricing strategies give in-store departments strong leverage with consumers interested in value, as well as those interested in convenience.

Though many supermarkets and general merchandise stores run their own video rental shops, an increasing number rely on outside companies. With competition billowing and national chains expanding, in-store operations found it difficult to keep up without the expertise of professional video rental companies. Dan Alaimo reports in *Supermarket News* that about 38 percent of retail stores with in-store video rental outlets favored having outside companies run them. Special video rental operations also emerged that cater to retailers. BlowOut Entertainment Inc., for example, largely depended on Wal-Mart and Kmart in 1997, with 160 outlets in Wal-Mart stores and 28 in Super Kmart centers. However, BlowOut planned to branch out on its own in part because Blockbuster Video began to court Wal-Mart.

Store-run in-store video rental operations accommodating new trends in the video rental industry prospered in 1996 and 1997, while those reluctant to change found it difficult to compete, forcing four major supermarkets—Dominick's Finer Foods; Kash n' Karry; Meijer; and Stop and Shop Supermarkets—to close their movie shops. Part of the strategy of successful in-store operations included increasing new release inventories, expanding overall inventories, and implementing new promotional plans, according to Alaimo. In the late 1990s, supermarket video departments kept inventories composed of 37 percent new releases and 63 percent other titles. Alaimo projects new releases gradually will constitute a greater share of the in-store inventory and expects new release to account for 40 percent of the inventories by the end of the decade. Some stores experimented with even larger volumes of new releases in order to test the market and carve a new niche. Moreover, supermarket video departments found it beneficial to expand their overall supply in order to stay in the video rental race.

Alaimo also writes in *Supermarket News* that in order for in-store video departments to remain competitive in the next millennium they need to unflaggingly increase their inventories and enhance their methods of inventory management. Furthermore, they

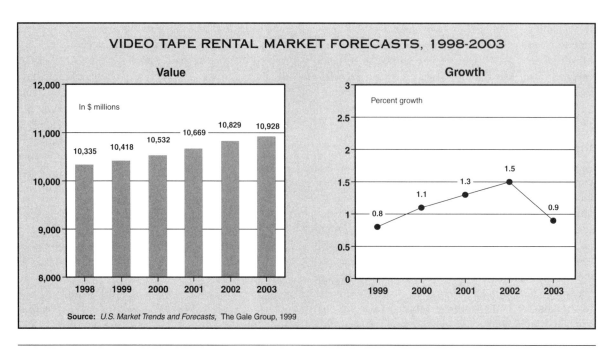

Source: *U.S. Market Trends and Forecasts,* The Gale Group, 1999

must supply on-going marketing support for their inventories and take advantage of category-management technology. To improve efficiency and control, analysts recommend implementing computerized inventory management tools, so they can keep track of orders and rentals and see what sells and what does not. In-store operations must also pay close attention to the sensibilities of their clients and stock their departments accordingly in order to avoid costly overhead that does not move.

INDUSTRY LEADERS

Blockbuster Entertainment Group, a subsidiary of Viacom Inc. since 1994, led the video rental industry in the 1990s. According to *Video Business,* Blockbuster controlled about 27 percent of the market in the mid- to late 1990s. In 1998 the company earned $3.9 billion, including revenues from its other concerns—music retail and theme park operation. Blockbuster has over 4,000 stores dispersed through all 50 states and another 2,000 stores in 26 other countries. Altogether, the company employs about 80,000 workers. Blockbuster, however, has faced problems of slumping growth and leadership. In 1996, Viacom hired William R. Fields, a former Wal-Mart executive, to revitalize the company, but he quit after one year. The resignation of Fields surprised the industry because he had prodigious ambitions for the company; he envisioned Blockbuster as selling a variety of additional wares including CDs, computer software, and movie merchandise. Moreover, some of Viacom's key shareholders have requested that Viacom spin off Blockbuster, fearing a restructuring of the video rental industry. Heeding their advice, Viacom chairman Sumner Redstone announced the parent company would sell about 20 percent of Blockbuster in 1999.

In 1997, Blockbuster formed an alliance with Sony Electronics in order to keep up with advancing video technology. Under the alliance, Blockbuster displays and demonstrates Sony's Digital Versatile Disc or Digital Video Disc (DVD) players, and Sony offers video rental coupons with purchases of its DVD players. DVD is an emerging audio and video laser format that can hold substantially more data than its predecessor the CD, CD-ROM, and laser disc. Viacom dispensed with "Video" as part of Blockbuster's name, to emphasize the company's multimedia entertainment offerings. In addition, Blockbuster moved into the in-store sector of the industry by opening departments in Wal-Mart stores, and Blockbuster plans

to expand its presence in Mexico using the Wal-Mart-based stores as its vehicle.

Based in Wilsonville, Oregon, Hollywood Entertainment Corp. grew quickly in the mid-1990s to become the second largest national video rental chain. With a series of acquisitions and expansions, Hollywood Video has marched across the country to keep pressure on Blockbuster and to secure its hold as the number two video chain. In 1999, Hollywood Entertainment operated over 1,200 Hollywood Video superstores in 42 states—a dramatic increase over its 25 stores in 1994. Hollywood Video successfully competed with small VSSs, as well as in-store departments, for selection. Part of Hollywood Video's strategy includes providing an upbeat atmosphere complete with neon lights and many television monitors playing movies. Headed by founder Mark J. Wattles, Hollywood Entertainment posted sales of $763.9 million in 1998. Moreover, each Hollywood Video outlet brings in an average of $900,000 per year—three times the national average—according to Scott McMurray in *U.S News & World Report.*

Other key video rental stores include Movie Gallery and Video Update. Movie Gallery was the country's third largest video store chain in the late 1990s with about 860 stores in the United States, plus another 100 franchised stores. Targeting small suburban towns, Movie Gallery brought in $267 million in 1998. Video Update, ranked fourth with 780 outlets around the country and in Canada. In 1998 Video Update's revenues rose to $156.2 million. Video Update also owns the Moovies chain, which has about 240 stores in 15 states primarily on the East Coast.

Of the in-store video operations, Kroger Co. has had some of the greatest successes and has been on the vanguard, experimenting with new approaches to marketing videos. In the mid-1990s, Kroger brought in television monitors to boost movie rentals and sought to cut its video department costs by dealing with only one movie distributor. Kroger also tested various marketing techniques in certain areas to see if they might lead to a more successful way of stocking in-store video departments, including expanding its offerings and concentrating on new releases. Although small compared to large chains, Kroger devotes between 600 and 700 square feet to its video departments, which the chain packs with popular titles. In addition, Kroger began stocking audio books, sell-through videos, and video games. Kroger marketing strategists rely on the area demographics of each store and base inventory decisions for individual stores on this information, according to *Supermarket News.*

AMERICA AND THE WORLD

The United States leads the world in video rentals and sales. With the majority of the movies domestically produced and almost 90 percent VCR penetration, the home video industry thrives in the United States. However, Australia, Canada, and Japan also have strong VCR bases, which make their home video markets strong and key target areas of U.S. video specialty shop chains and video cassette distributors.

U.S. movie studios did well abroad in the mid-1990s in terms of video rentals and sell-throughs. In 1996, they posted revenues of over $3.4 billion from video rental and sales abroad, according to Don Groves in *Variety*. International customers showed heightened interest in video rentals and purchases after activity ebbed in 1995. In addition, VCR penetration increased throughout the world, and video piracy has decreased. Peter Dean reports in *Billboard*, for example, that VCR penetration hit 64 percent in the European Union, while video piracy dropped by as much as 28 percent in the United Kingdom.

RESEARCH AND TECHNOLOGY

With a 1995 dip in sales and the emergence of competitive alternatives to video rentals and sales, companies were seeking ways of maintaining and increasing their customer base. Supermarkets have provided promotions giving customers movie rental discounts with the purchase of home meal replacements, such as deli prepared entrees. Kroger has experimented with leasing space to the fast food chain Popeye's Chicken and Biscuits, and linking these restaurants to its video departments with each of them issuing coupons for the other. Furthermore, Blockbuster Entertainment launched a promotional campaign with Planters nuts and Hollywood Entertainment teamed up with Domino's Pizza to offer free movies with pizza purchases. With such promotional campaigns underway, in-store video shops await the outcome of the sales strategy. VSSs may forge alliances with restaurants if these strategies prove auspicious.

Moreover, as new forms of in-home entertainment become available, such as digital and satellite television and pay-per-view packages, video rental operations must turn to new technology to hold onto customers who might begin flirting with alternative forms of entertainment. Video rental stores, therefore, embraced a new format of laser disk recording and playback in the mid-1990s, the Digital Versatile Disc

(DVD). DVDs can store between 4.5 and 17.0 gigabytes of data, which translates to 135 to 540 minutes of playing time. Besides offering more disk space and better audio and video qualities, DVDs also have interactive capabilities, which allow users to witness multiple angle shots of a single scene, read sets of multiple subtitles, and move to favorite parts of movies by pressing a button. DVD players sold for approximately $500 in the late 1990s. Video outlets, however, do not plan a full-scale introduction of these disks. By 1996, DVD hardware had reached only about 8 percent of the U.S. population; however, analysts predict it will grow to about 32 percent by 2007, according to Bob Geistman in *Supermarket News*. Moreover, recording capabilities for DVD hardware are years away.

In order to track industry performance and consumer habits, the VSDA introduced VidTrac in January of 1996. The point-of-sale service collects data from a large sample of video rental operations throughout the country. More than 4,500 stores participate in VidTrac, including 9 of the most successful rental chains. The VSDA plans to tabulate and circulate the data each week, offering rich and accurate statistics and projections for the video rental community.

FURTHER READING

Alaimo, Dan. "Harris Teeter Looks to Heat Up Video with HMR Tie-in." *Supermarket News,* 9 June 1997.

———. "Keeping Pace in the Race: The Competition in Home Video Is Tough, But Supermarkets Are Still Doing Well." *Supermarket News,* 13 April 1998.

———. "Kroger Lifting Curtain on More Video Rental 'Stores'." *Supermarket News,* 20 November 1995.

———. "Rental Bloom: Seeding the Department with New Releases." *Supermarket News,* 14 April 1997.

———. "Rental Properties: Supplies Say Chains in Video Rental for the Long Haul Need to Apply More Sophisticated Approaches to Inventory." *Supermarket News,* 20 January 1997.

Dean, Peter. "The U.K. and Europe." *Billboard,* 11 January 1997.

Geistman, Bob. "Time to Take Stock of New Technologies." *Supermarket News,* 22 April 1996.

Groves, Don. "O'seas Video Takeout Makes Comeback Bid." *Variety,* 3 March 1997.

Lenius, Pat Natschke. *Supermarket News,* 3 February 1997.

McClellan, Stephen. "Viacom Hit by Lackluster Blockbuster." *Broadcasting and Cable,* 28 April 1997.

McMurray, Scott. "Time to Hit the Fast-Forward Button." *U.S. News & World Report,* 26 August 1996.

Sweeting, Paul. "Vid Into Period of Adjustment." *Variety,* 8 June 1998.

Video Software Dealer Association. "A White Paper on the Future of the Home Video Industry," 1997. Available from http://206.71.226.123/whitepaper/WHITPAPR.HTM.

—Karl Heil

VIRTUAL COMMUNITIES

INDUSTRY SNAPSHOT

Virtual communities are at the interface of two powerful forces in the Internet: community and commerce. The Internet had its origins as a community of scientists in the 1970s, and when the public-at-large was given access to the system, which enabled individuals scattered across the globe to communicate cheaply and easily using tools like e-mail, USENET, and bulletin boards, it was only natural that people with similar interests would seek each other out and set up communities in cyberspace. Private companies played a large role in the Internet's privatization. The next logical step was an attempt to commercialize the large e-communities of people with similar interests.

Virtual communities are a true emerging industry and, as such, accurate statistics are difficult to come by. That the Internet comprises an enormous community, a kind of transnational community, is undeniable however. In the United States alone, some 80 million adults used the Internet March 1999, more than twice the number in 1997. One third of households on the Internet spent 10 or more hours a week online, and nearly 80 percent of all Internet households spent 45 minutes online per visit. In early 1999, there were nearly 30,000 distinct USENET groups, each with a narrow topic of discussion. Many virtual communities that function through Web sites are as focused as USENET groups, others have mass memberships, representative of a broad segment of the Internet population. That mass community in turn subdivides into countless sub-communities, some vast, some minuscule. It remains to be seen whether virtual communities are mass phenomena or niche phenomena. If groups tightly focused on specific topics or specific

demographic groups are the hardier breed, then efforts undertaken by some successful and well-focused groups to expand to a mass audience may be ultimately flawed.

ORGANIZATION AND STRUCTURE

A community is defined by *Merriam Webster's Collegiate Dictionary* as "a group of people with a common characteristic living together within a larger society." A virtual community is also made up of individuals united by some common need or interest, but the group "lives together" only in the cyberspace created by computers and the Internet. Thus, while most traditional communities are united by geographic factors—they live in a particular city or neighborhood with particular characteristics and problems—the common factors uniting virtual communities are much more multifarious. A hobby, a business, a research interest, or personal exigency can form the basis of an online community. Modern telecommunications and the Internet make it possible for a butterfly aficionado in Ohio to communicate with a lepidopterist in Africa as cheaply and easily as one's next-door neighbor. Like any community, members of a virtual community must be able to interact with one another, but unlike "real" communities, members of virtual communities may never meet face-to-face.

The difference between a Web site and a virtual community can be subtle. But the characteristic all communities share is that members are able to interact with one another—members communicate information or opinions and others can respond. Interaction takes many forms: bulletin boards or newsgroups where members can post messages and respond to messages others have posted; listservs, which distribute each member's e-mail to all other members and can be responded to by all members; chat rooms, where members converse in real-time by means of their keyboards; or, graphical environments where members create a brand new visual appearance and interact with the simulacra of other members.

Some virtual communities are operated for-profit. e-Steel (http://www.esteel.com), for example, is a community that engages in buying and selling steel. Others are non-profit. The InterNational Council for Infertility Information Dissemination, a not-for-profit organization devoted to collecting information to help infertile couples, set up its site (http://www.inciid.org) so such couples could network, share their experiences, and provide support. Some virtual communities are consumer oriented. These, in turn, can be further subdivided into geographic communities, demographic communities, and topical communities, each characterized by a different type of common feature. A geographic community takes a certain place as the common ground, for example, the Total New York Web site, which includes news of events in the city along with personal ads and chatrooms for people living in or planning to visit New York City. Demographic communities are based on personal characteristics such as race, age, or gender. ThirdAge, a virtual community for people over 55, is a demographic community. Topical communities are based on specific interests other than geographical location or demographics. Among the tens of thousands topical communities are sites for investors, guitarists, or lovers of the works of Herman Melville. Finally there are mass communities, like TalkCity and AOL, that include some or all of the specific communities mentioned above.

In contrast to consumer communities are business-to-business communities. Some carry out the functions of business or professional associations, commodity and stock exchanges, or support groups. One type—the vertical industry community—serves a particular industry, for example the automobile industry, and enables the workers to network efficiently and solve common industry-related problems. e-Steel provides an online exchange where members can buy and sell steel. John Hagel III and Arthur G. Armstrong, in their book net.gain, call vertical industry communities "one of the more widespread forms of early business community." Members of functional communities share a particular profession, for example, marketing people or accountants. Geographical communities provide forums similar to Chambers of Com-

merce or Rotary Clubs, where businesspeople in a particular city or region can air problems and network. Business category communities serve distinct groups within the larger business community, such as small businesspeople or franchise owners.

The designations "consumer-oriented" and "business-to-business," betray the commercial basis of most virtual communities. Even non-profit groups have to raise operating funds. Virtual communities rely on a variety of sources for operating revenues. Some obtain money from a single type, others use various sources simultaneously. One source of revenue are fees charged to users. These include monthly subscription fees, hourly usage fees, and service fees. These fees consist of charging members to download information or software or for automatic notification of the availability of products at a particular price. Start-up communities with a small membership or whose demographic profile or management are yet unproven rely on such revenue sources, when they are starting out, at least. Member fees are also a way for communities who so desire to keep advertising off their Web pages. Communities whose members pay a membership fee are most resistant to permitting advertising on their community sites.

Advertising, in particular banner advertising, is sought with varying degrees of success by many communities. Virtual communities and their individual forums and chat rooms are attractive to advertisers because they provide access to individuals with a specific demographic profile. Forums on parenting will be attractive to manufacturers of safety seats for babies and toys; travel chat for seniors will be attractive to cruise companies and drug manufacturers. Communities must reach a certain critical mass—a certain number of members who visit the community regularly for a specific period of time—before advertisers will consider them viable however. In general, the cost of advertising is based on the number of "hits" the Web site receives, that is how often a page is visited by members or the public. As of spring 1999, however, there were no universally accepted procedures for calculating the real significance of a Web site's hits.

Some virtual communities use sponsorship as source of revenue, a form similar to advertising in some respects. A sponsor underwrites a community or one of its areas that is directly related to one of its products or services. For example, a pharmaceutical company might sponsor the health forum at a senior citizens' community. A link to the company's Web site would be included in the sponsored forum and clicking it would connect members with a page containing information on the company's drugs and their uses, with the company's customer service, etc. The sponsor's link functions not only as an advertisement, but as an information resource for forum and community members. Like advertising, sponsorship fees are usually based on a Web site's traffic. Unlike advertising, which is often short-term and variable, the very existence of a forum, chat area, or even community can depend on a particular sponsor.

Requirements for membership vary in different communities. Some are open to anyone who clicks on the community's site. Others require members to register first, either for the entire site or for particular areas. Registration can be limited to giving a name, valid e-mail address, and selecting a password; it can include a broad range of personal data including address, telephone and fax number, date of birth, gender, occupation, hobbies and interests, and other demographic information. Some sites that require registration, however, also have special guest areas. Some sites require that members download and install special software in order to interact in specialized site environments. Some sites or areas of sites are limited to particular demographic groups: to women, to people over 18 years of age, or to children, for example.

The form of interaction varies from community to community as well. Most are text based as members communicate through typed messages that are sent as e-mail in discussion groups or appear instantaneously in chat. Interaction in some communities, in particular the vast network of special-interest newsgroups known as USENET, are completely uncensored. Participants can and often do say anything they want. Freedom of expression and information is counterbalanced by frequent "flames"—posts in which one participant insults others in crude, abusive language. To prevent "flame wars" from taking over, some communities draw up explicit guidelines for member interaction. Communities also use discussion moderators who monitor the content of postings before they go online and try to control the tenor of community discussions so they do not become too unfriendly. Under-moderating is considered more effective than over-moderating. Moderators can also be responsible for introducing new members, settling arguments, making sure discussions stay more or less focused, and passing on community news. Chat hosts are similar to discussion moderators, but they work in real-time discussions online rather than a bulletin board-style posting of e-mail.

In addition to the virtual communities themselves, there are companies that provide goods and services related to communities. Internet service providers can give a community prominence by placing it on their main screen. Some, like AOL with its member profiles, public and private chat areas, and member services, constitute highly successful virtual communities in their own right. Search engines have been developed to help Internet users navigate the increasingly complex world of online communities. Other companies manufacture software needed to manage member interaction, advanced graphic interfaces, or other specialized needs of virtual communities. Furthermore, virtual communities increasingly crossover into other media, like television tie-ins, or even into real-world communities, when online groups organize real-life get-togethers.

BACKGROUND AND DEVELOPMENT

The history of virtual communities is the history of the Internet itself. Originally commissioned by the Department of Defense, the first network—named ARPANET after the Advanced Research Projects Agency, which provided the funding—was set up in 1969. It was comprised of four "nodes:" UCLA, Stanford Research Institute, University of California at Santa Barbara, and the University of Utah. By 1971 the network had expanded to 15 nodes. More importantly, e-mail was invented that year, making possible personal correspondence over the network. In its early years, the Internet community was comprised primarily of natural scientists and Defense Department people. Access to the network was progressively expanded, from ARPA researchers, to military and government-funded researchers, and then to the academic community as a whole. By the early 1990s the U.S. government had made a major financial commitment to developing the so-called Information Superhighway. The growth of the Internet took off around 1989. Host computers grew from around 28,000 to 100,000 between 1987 and 1989. In 1990 they reached 300,000, in 1992 1.0 million, in 1994 3.0 million, in 1996 12.8 million, and in 1997 19.5 million.

One of the first significant communities within the Internet was USENET. USENET is a system of newsgroups, each devoted to a specific topic, in which participants post their opinions in the form of public e-mails and respond to the posts of others. The system was born in 1979 when graduate students at Duke and the University of North Carolina developed software that enabled messages to be sent and posted outside the ARPANET. To participate, one needed only the software to post and read messages, which its developers distributed for free, and access to a USENET server. By the beginning of 1980, two articles a day were being distributed by three newsgroups, by the end of the year there were 15 groups. By 1988 the number of groups had exploded to 11,000, and in 1998 it had reached nearly 30,000 with millions of messages posted daily.

CompuServe, one of the first private services that enabled networking by computer was founded in 1979. CompuServe provided e-mail service, electronic bulletin boards, and chats. The service caught on quickly and, by 1985, had approximately 100,000 subscribers, all of whom had to dial up CompuServe computers to participate because the Internet was still limited to universities and the government. One of the legendary virtual communities, The WELL—the Whole Earth 'Lectronic Link—was founded in February 1985 by Stuart Brand, the founder of the Whole Earth Catalog, and Larry Brilliant of Networking Technologies International. The WELL was far more than a subscription e-mail service like CompuServe. For $8 a month and $2 an hour WELL members became part of a highly literate, fanatically committed community of users. They shared their thoughts and lives with each other, and became far more devoted to their virtual friends than many people are to their real ones (once even organizing medical evacuation from India for a community member who was near death). The WELL called its discussion groups "conferences"; each conference was run by a "host" who moderated the discussion.

By the end of 1987, The WELL had passed the break-even point, though continual equipment upgrades ate up most profits. In 1989, when the Loma Prieta earthquake rocked the San Francisco Bay Area, The WELL was for a short time one of the few ways the Bay Area had to communicate with the outside world. In November 1990 it had 5000 registered members; by August 1994, after the Internet had been opened to the public, the number had doubled. Primarily a space for conversation at first, The WELL provided members with access to the Internet for the first time in January 1992. The explosion of the Internet in the mid-1990s and the concomitant increase in the number of Internet Service Providers caused WELL membership to taper off to about 7,000 by the mid-1990s. In April 1999 The WELL was purchased by online magazine Salon, an event that raised the fear among old-line WELLbies that the community might soon be invaded by advertising and online shopping.

In the mid-1990s virtual communities began appearing at an explosive rate. America Online, with 1 million subscribers, expanded its service into the World Wide Web; Geocities was founded promising a virtual community of millions based on free Web pages. Toward the end of 1997 investors discovered virtual communities: Yahoo purchased Geocities for $3.5 billion. NBC and Hearst Communications invested $34 million in one of the largest virtual communities, TalkCity. By 1999, there were so many online communities that specialized search engines were being developed to help the public find groups that matched their interests. One of the most interesting developments of the latter half of the 1990s was the rise of virtual communities, like the Palace, that were based on graphics rather than text.

CURRENT CONDITIONS

There are few reliable figures available as of spring 1999 on the number of virtual communities. For one thing, they are only beginning to emerge as an industry in its own right and have yet to be precisely tracked. For another, there is no widely accepted agreement on precisely what constitutes a virtual community: Is it a group of individuals who know each other and communicate regularly online? a collection of chat rooms and bulletin boards where anyone in the world can post messages as often or as little as they like? a community of Web page owners who never communicate? One indication of how large the population of virtual communities in the Internet might be are the approximately 30,000 USENET groups in existence in 1998.

Every year the members of virtual communities better reflect the demographics of the United States at large. The spread of personal computers into more and more homes is partly responsible. According to *The State of the Net,* by 1997 there were nearly three times as many personal computers in use in the United States. as in 1990. The explosive increase in the use of the Internet has also contributed to the breadth of virtual community membership. About 80.0 million adult Americans, 38 percent of Americans over the age of 16, were online as of March 1999, according to Intelliquest Research. That was up from just over 36.0 million in 1997 as reported in *The State of the Net.* Intelliquest Research also reported that another 18.8 million adults planned to be online by the year 2000. Even more crucial for Web site operators and advertisers, in 1997 nearly one third of Internet households spent 10 or more hours a week online, and nearly 80 percent spent 45 minutes or more online per visit, according to *The State of the Net.*

The virtual communities themselves are as diverse as the people who join. The membership of The Palace, a graphics-based community, is 60 percent males between 17 and 31 years of age. iVillage is populated primarily by women between 25 and 49. SeniorNet members are men and women from 55 to 102 years old. There are thousands of others of varying degrees of interest, including sites for mothers (The CyberMom Dot Com—http://www.thecybermom .com/), for veterans (Veterans News and Information Service—http://www.vnis.com/), for kids (Children's Express—http://www.ce.org), for new college graduates (College Grad Job Hunter (http://www.college grad.com/), for African Americans (http://www .blacktalk.com/), Christian singles, (http://www .creativeye.com/singles/), for experts in different fields (http://expertise.cos.com/), for New Agers (http://www.newage.com/Newcyber/), for gourmets (Epicurious Food), pet owners (http://petnet.detnews .com/), for arts and craft types (http://www.craftnet village.com/), for investors (http://www.stock-talk .com/stocks/list.shtml), for history buffs (http://www .thehistorynet.com/), for car owners (http://cartalk .cars.com/), for horse owners and breeders (http:// www.horsenet.com/overfence/index.html), and even for individuals interested in outer space (http://www .outerorbit.com/).

Businesspeople are another target group of virtual communities. Growth in this sector is spurred by the pervasiveness of computers in business as well as the rise in e-commerce, which Forrester Research predicts will increase from $41 billion in January 1999 to $327 billion in 2002—a conservative estimate by most accounts. Professional associations represent one common, traditional type of business community that has successfully transplanted itself to the Internet. Industry.net, the Web's largest community of engineers, has moved beyond the traditional model. It offers its members the opportunity to network; hold discussions and do business with each other; and to access information in its vast databanks of technical reference materials, manufacturers catalogs, trade organizations, etc., all online. The group has annual revenues of approximately $80 million. The Cambridge Information Network provides an online forum where chief information officers can gather and discuss their experiences and common problems. In early 1999 the group had about 1,400 members throughout the world who could also use features like on-call experts and an article database. The large consulting companies are also finding ways to effectively expand their business through online business communities. "Online Consulting," at Ernst & Young's ERNIE Web site, offers managers at small and mid-sized companies access to consulting expertise they would not be able to afford otherwise. For $18,000 annually, members can access ERNIE's databank of information and submit questions that are then forwarded to the best-qualified consultant, and answered within two workdays.

Some of the larger communities have experienced rapid growth in the latter half of the 1990s. Before April 1998 a total of 4.0 million people visited Talk-City; in March 1999 the site claimed it had 5.0 million one-time users and 1.5 million regular members. TalkCity homepages grew from 300,000 in June 1998 to 1.3 million in March 1999. Between February and November 1998 the membership of iVillage increased by 170,000 to 740,000. Women.com went from a start-up membership of 1,300 members in the mid-1990s to 4.0 million visitors a month at the beginning of 1999. Growth is not always the result of conventional publicity such as advertising. At the end of 1996 The Palace was still selling the software required to access its site and it had about 50,000 members and 300 individual Palace sites. Once it started giving the software away in August 1998, word of mouth brought in new members at a rate of 1,000 to 2,000 a day, The Palace did no advertising. By March 1999 its approximately 1,000 Palace sites had received 6.0 million visitors.

Growth in members—particularly in the groups that do not charge a membership fee—does not immediately translate into profitability. Those communities rely on sources of revenue like advertising. Advertisers appreciate the ability to easily reach concentrated groups from a particular demographic range, but are often unsure how to evaluate the effectiveness of an ad at a Web site. An ongoing question is how to measure the audience of a Web site. It is not as straightforward as determining the circulation of a magazine or even the audience of a television program. The most common means of measuring a Web site's traffic has been to count the number of "hits," or how many times it is accessed in a particular period. Counting hits only, however, is unsatisfactory because a visit of 20 seconds or less is the equivalent of a visit that lasts 2 hours. Another model had advertisers pay a rate based on the number of times visitors actually clicked on their ads looking for further information about a product.

In 1997, the authors of the book net.gain predicted that within the following few years advertisers would be willing to pay only for actual sales generated by a Web site. Such cooperative ventures have been on the increase, in particular with smaller Web sites and advertisers. But only one year after net.gain appeared, Hosting Web Communities reported that there was little evidence that a widespread move toward the "commission" model had taken place. Acceptance of Web-based advertising on a mass scale, and not simply in the blue-chip sites that have accounted for 80 percent of ad revenues, will depend on the development of clear, acceptable standards for measuring and evaluating traffic at Web sites. Filtering software that enables Net surfers to remove all ads from their screen is just another factor that will complicate advertisers acceptance of the Web as a medium.

Like much e-commerce on the Web, by spring 1999 few virtual community sites to date have broken even—not to mention making a profit. Nonetheless, there has been no lack of investors and strategic partners who believe in the commercial potential of virtual communities. iVillage, for example, lost $11.3 million from July 1995 to December 1996, $21.3, and $32.4 million in the first nine months of 1999. The community signed contracts with AOL in July 1997, Charles Schwab & Co in December 1997, with Intel in June 1998, with AT&T in October 1998, and with NBC in November 1998. In September 1998 the Hearst Company and NBC invested $34.0 million in TalkCity. In January 1999 Yahoo announced the acquisition of Geocities for $3.5 billion in stock.

A number of different types of companies are growing up around the virtual communities. Software developers produce software needed to make specialized interaction possible in a virtual setting—for example, the purely graphical interaction of The Palace—or to streamline more traditional forms of interaction. The German-based blaxxun is a leading producer of Virtual Reality Modeling Language (VRML) software needed to create 3-D environments. Tribal Voice, founded by John McAfee, produces networking software that enables groups to communicate online by voice messaging as well as traditional chat and bulletin boards.

Specialized search engines have been developed to help cope with the growing number and offerings of virtual communities. Agents Inc.'s engine, www .firefly.com, searches for communities as well as individual members with specific interests. Talkway (www.talkway.com) is itself a community whose registered members can search the 50 or so thousand different USENET forums for groups with similar interests. Anyone can do keyword searches in USENET using Dejanews (www.dejanews.com).

INDUSTRY LEADERS

The Internet is a community of communities. In some respects, every site on the Web, insofar as it attracts a group of individuals with a specific interest,

could be said to comprise a virtual community. Some have set themselves up with the express purpose of fostering community, among all people or a subgroup. The largest virtual communities are usually not the most representative as "communities." The leader, Geocities, boasts hundreds of thousands of members thanks to its free homepages, but the degree to which a real "community" of users exists is questionable. The following communities are some of the most representative and successful of the commercial virtual communities.

TALK CITY

Talk City is one of the largest, best known and fastest growing of all virtual communities. Founded in 1996, it grew out of an earlier community run by Apple Computer, eWorld. When Apple announced it was closing the service, eWorld's Peter Friedman and Jenna Woodhull decided to set up a new home for the displaced community and in summer 1996 Talk City was the result, a community for everyone.

Talk City's specialty is moderated thematic communities in the general areas including Family, Entertainment, College, Teens, Auto, Business, Computing, Shopping, People, and Spirituality. In addition, there are special areas on games, news, art, and music. Conversation in each area is run by trained moderators, the "Conference City Crew." One can register as a member of Talk City with one's name, e-mail address, and a password, or visit as a guest. General membership is free, but certain services must be paid for (placing a personal ad, for example). Talk City's 2.4 million regular members spend an average of 26 minutes per visit online, and visit four or more times a month, more than members of other online communities, according to Media Matrix.

Talk City's revenue comes from three sources. Advertising accounted for about 65 percent in 1998. Corporate Services, primarily setting up virtual communities for private companies, brought in about 40 percent of revenues at the end of 1998. Member transactions, such as fees for additional memory, accounted for about 10 percent of revenue. New Talk City products in the future could include online meetings, seminars, or presentations. The company generated $1.5 million in sales in 1998 and employed 82 people.

IVILLAGE

iVillage, a virtual community for women, was founded in June 1995 by Candice Carpenter and Nancy Evans and went online in January 1996. Carpenter used her experience with other sites, including ParentSoup and Parent's Place—two communities for parents—and AboutWork in setting up iVillage. The idea behind the new site was to provide a network for women to turn to find help for their everyday problems. In 1997 a strategic alliance with AOL was finalized in which iVillage was placed in three AOL channels and was given special AOL keywords. The community was off and running.

iVillage consists of 12 channels on topics including Family, Health, Work, Money, Food, Relationships, Shopping, Travel, and Astrology. Each channel provides members with access to expert advice, chat areas, discussion groups, book lists, and book discussions. The site provides links to about 50 different experts each week, some of which have regular electronic office hours. iVillage has more than 1,500 ongoing discussion groups and holds about 800 chats a week. Discussions range from breast cancer to problem teens, and are moderated by approximately 1,100 so-called community leaders. Membership in the community is free and registration is required. iVillage had some 740,000 members in November 1998. Eighty-four percent of iVillage's members are women, mostly between the ages of 25 and 49, but areas like the parenting area are also well-visited by men. At the beginning of 1999, iVillage called itself the largest virtual community for women.

iVillage obtained some $65 million in risk capital from approximately 25 companies. AOL, Lycos, and Excite made deals to use iVillage content on their women's channels. NBC agreed to invest in the site and to provide advertising for it during prime-time. Most of iVillage's ongoing revenues come from sponsoring, from companies like Nissan and Polaroid, and advertising. Future growth is expected to come from online shopping. iVillage owns the company iBaby, an online shop that sells about 20,000 baby products. It also has agreements with Amazon.com, N2K Inc, and 1-800-FLOWERS, Inc. iVillage totaled $15 million in 1998 sales and employed 200 people.

SWOON

SWOON is a virtual community for people interested in personal relationships, friendship, romance, and sex. Its members, overwhelmingly young, female, and single, come to the site to meet and chat with members of the opposite sex and for information on finding or improving a relationship. The site includes a number of special features. "Newsflash" presents daily news on the subject of relationships. Members can look for partners in the online "Personals." Daily horoscopes predict one's romantic future and describe one's perfect mate. "Jane Err" takes questions and offers advice about all sorts of relationship questions.

Members can share their experiences at "Success@ SWOON Forum." SWOON's online environment is entirely interactive and includes many chat areas and discussion groups.

SWOON was developed by Conde Net, the online subsidiary of Conde Nast, publisher of such magazines as *GQ, Glamour, Details,* and *Mademoiselle.* A portion of SWOON's site content comes from CondeNast publication's. SWOON revenues come from banner advertising and from online shopping arrangements. Sixty-five percent of SWOON members have shopped at least once online. Membership in SWOON is free. Members are only required to register if they want to place a personal ad; ads are restricted to people over 18 years of age. Some SWOON members have begun holding get-togethers offline.

THE PALACE

The Palace is one of the most unique virtual communities on the Web. Unlike many others whose communication and information exchange are text based, encounters at The Palace take place in an graphical environment where members change their appearance at will, exchange cartoon gifts, and "say" very little. In the words of its co-founder Mark Jeffrey, it is a "vision theater," more like a party than a discussion. People come to The Palace to play not to discuss.

Encounters at The Palace take place in areas called palaces, which are designed by The Palace by participating companies or by members. The Palace provides the software packages needed to create one's own palace or to access others free of charge at its Web site. Members create their individual graphic appearance—their avatar—which represents them in whatever palaces they visit. They can also design objects that can be used as gifts or weapons in encounters with other avatars. Verbal communication—when it takes place—occurs in comic-style speech balloons. More typical, however, is a spontaneous playacting using ones imagination and graphic resources. There is a rich variety of palaces to visit, each governed by the rules its creator has set down. Some are highly regulated, others have no rules and are definitely not for beginners.

The Palace had approximately 600,000 users in March 1999, mostly between 17 and 31. About 60 percent of them were male. Many members visit The Palace every day and tend to remain longer than visitors to most other virtual communities. That owes perhaps to the degree of individual creativity that comes into play and the richness of its thousands of individual palaces, which range from television themes like

"South Park," to kids palaces, to adult palaces like "Sin City."

Originally The Palace software had to be purchased and members who wanted access to the entire site had to pay. Since August 1998, software has been distributed free of charge. As of spring 1999, one can use the entire site without charge. The software needed to construct a palace site of one's own is distributed to anyone who wants it. Revenues come from advertising, which can be fed automatically into some or all palaces. The Palace, Inc., the parent company of the community, also develops graphical virtual environments for other companies, who then bring their servers into The Palace network. The Palace, Inc. and its clients often establish partnership relationships and share subsequent advertising revenues, for example.

WORK FORCE

Little data exists on the workforce in virtual communities. Certainly a whole range of business people, from venture capitalists to marketing and advertising specialists, computer experts, from software developers to network developers, and online content providers, such as writers and artists, are necessary for the successful startup and operation of a virtual community. Of all the jobs connected with the field, the most characteristic and unique is the online moderator. Moderators are responsible for keeping chats on topics and making sure everyone gets his or her say. Discussion group moderators make sure participants adhere to guidelines, do not "flame"—use abusive or insulting language—other members, and resolve disagreements. A number of communities require their moderators to undergo special training and AOL has set up a school for volunteer chat moderators.

AMERICA AND THE WORLD

Virtual communities are more successful and highly developed in the United States than in other countries. This is due to a variety of factors. The Internet began taking off as a mass medium there a good 2 to 3 years before other nations. The United States has been and remains at the cutting edge of computer technology. Another factor for American dominance may be the linguistic foundation of communities: people communicate with one another primarily by language, and thanks to American popular culture exports such as television and popular movies, English had become the de facto world language. In this connection it is interesting that, FortuneCity, the third largest virtual community after Geocities and Xoom, is owned by a British company, FortuneCity Ltd. Internet use is growing rapidly in Europe. Between 1996 and 2000, use is expected to grow by more than 300 percent in Germany, and 600 percent in Great Britain and the Netherlands. Surfers in those nations will eventually discover existing communities and found their own. As Internet use spreads, it is to be expected that other nations, in particular from Europe and Asia, will also play a role in the development of virtual communities. blaxxun, for example, a leading producer of VRML software is a German firm.

RESEARCH AND TECHNOLOGY

One of the most critical technological challenges facing virtual communities is the development of effective means of measuring Web site traffic. Such tools would involve some sort of qualitative analysis of a "hit" that would distinguish an accidental hit by a person looking for something else on the Web from a legitimate visit. As measured in early 1999, page views can indicate a visit of 15 seconds or a half hour. Only when advertisers know what they are buying into will they buy Web ads confidently. And only when advertisers buy confidently will advertising revenues filter down to mid-sized and smaller sites.

The tools that make virtual communities possible are becoming more sophisticated every day. PowWow software was developed by Tribal Voice to improve virtual communications in corporations, in particular multinationals. It incorporates not only traditional chat and discussion groups, but also Internet-based voice communication capabilities. That enables multiple users to speak with each other simultaneously without long distance charges. Inevitably such software will filter down into general circulation where it will enrich interaction in regular online communities.

The graphics capabilities of virtual community sites will inevitably expand as VRML (virtual reality modeling language) makes full animation possible and as wider bandwidth becomes available to the average Internet user through higher speed modems, ISDN lines, and the like. Animation and other sophisticated graphical interfaces will spread out of "pure" graphic sites such as The Palace and into the more traditional communities and business sites.

FURTHER READING

Amlot, Robin. "Stockbroking on the Internet: Navigating a Web of Financial Knowledge." *Independent,* 7 April 1999.

"Big Five Accounting Firms Establish Positions In Online Information Market." *Electronic Information Report,* 26 June 1998.

"Blaxxun Interactive." *Hoover's Company Capsules,* 1 April 1999.

Claymon, Deborah. "Web Magazine Salon Buys Online Community the Well." *Knight-Ridder/Tribune Business News,* 8 April 1999.

Clemente, Peter. *The State of the Net.* New York: McGraw-Hill, 1998.

"Community Fever," 30 September 1998. Available from http://www.iconocast.com/icono-archive/ICONO.093098.html.

Davy, JoAnn. "Online at the Office: Virtual Communities Go to Work." *Managing Office Technology,* July-August 1998.

Dyson, Esther. *Release 2.0.* New York: Broadway, 1997.

Figallo, Cliff. *Hosting Web Communities.* New York: John Wiley & Sons, 1998.

Flinn, John, and Laura Rich. "Nancy Evans & Candice Carpenter: iVillage Is Building Virtual Communities for Grown-ups to Call Home on the Internet." *ADWEEK,* Eastern Edition, 23 September 1996.

Hagel III, John, and Arthur G. Armstrong. *net.gain.* Boston: Harvard Business School Press, 1997.

Hammel, Sara. "Online Feminine Mystique." *U.S. News & World Report,* 1 March 1999.

Ioannou, Lori. "Going Public With iVillage. How the Gloria Steinem of the Internet Built the Largest Online Women's Network and Became a Darling of Wall Street." *Your Company,* 1 Febraury 1999.

Ludlow, Peter. *High Noon on the Electronic Frontier.* Cambridge, MA: The MIT Press, 1966.

Maclachlan, Malcolm. "Electric Communities Plugs New Net Creation: 3-D World." *Business Journal,* 16 September 1996.

Moran, Susan. "Rise of Seniors On Net Creates An Opportunity." *Web Week,* 23 September 1996.

Olofson, Cathy. "Tribal Voice Has A Virtual Powwow." *Fast Company,* 1 December 1998.

Rheingold, Howard. *The Virtual Community.* Reading, MA: Addison Wesley Publishing Co., 1993.

Violino, Bob. "IT Management: Where CIOs Meet Online—High-Level IT Executives Take to Members-Only Web Sites to Discuss Technology and Business Issues." *Information-Week,* 27 April 1998.

Weise, Elizabeth. "Forget the Net, Usenet Is the Way to Go." *USA Today,* 16 June 1998.

—Evelyn Hauser

VIRTUAL REALITY

People know of virtual reality chiefly through science fiction or even games. Indeed, virtual reality, or VR as it is commonly referred to in the industry, may seem like something out of science fiction, but it is real and, by the latter part of the 1990s, it was on the verge of becoming a part of everyday life. Virtual reality is, as its name suggests, a simulated version of reality wherein users feel they are "really" walking on a beach, flying a fighter jet, performing heart bypass surgery, or whatever else the VR software is programmed to do.

Jaron Lanier, founder of VPL Research, was the first to coin the term "virtual reality." Other related terms include "artificial reality," coined by Myron Krueger in the 1970s; William Gibson's "cyberspace," first coined in 1984; and such terms as "virtual worlds" and "virtual environments," which first were used in the 1990s. The term "virtual reality" is today used in a wide variety of ways, often leading to some confusion. As originally coined by Lanier, the term was meant to describe total immersion in a three-dimensional computer-generated world.

While VR has caught on as a pop culture gimmick, VR has not yet developed into a big business. The industry is characterized by languishing technology and small, undercapitalized companies. Slow growth rather than explosion was the rule of the day in the mid-1990s. However, by the late 1990s, virtual reality had started generating business largely thanks to the settlement of patent disputes that had gone unresolved from 1993 to 1997. The market for virtual reality, which totaled just under $500 million in 1997, was estimated to have grown to nearly $1 billion the following year, an increase of almost 100 percent.

Although its entertainment potential is fairly obvious and was the first area to be exploited by the fledgling VR industry, virtual reality has some more practical educational applications that were being explored seriously as the millennium neared its end. VR is expected (by its proponents) to reshape the relationship between information technology and people, offering a variety of new and novel ways to communicate information and visualize processes. Virtual reality allows the creation of a three-dimensional virtual environment that can be rooted in reality or abstract. Among the former could be such real systems as buildings, landscapes, human anatomy, crime scenes, automobile accidents, and spacecraft. Representations of abstract systems might include magnetic fields, mathematical systems, molecular models, and population densities.

Computers have changed greatly since their inception. Early computers, in fact, lacked many of the elements users in the 1990s took for granted, such as memory and monitors. In the 1950s, computer scientists connected a typing board to a computer and the notion of a monitor emerged soon afterwards, followed in the early 1960s by a movable pointer, which was quickly nicknamed a "mouse" because of the tail-like wire attached to it. Later came the idea of a graphical user interface, or GUI, which allowed users to talk to or "interface" with the computer; an example of a GUI is an icon that users click to access a particular function. The icon is the side of the interface that the user sees, whereas the computer responds to a set of commands activated when the user clicks on the icon.

The basic concept underlying VR has been around for decades, although it only began to take its present shape in recent years. Simulators such as those used to train truck drivers and airline pilots were obvious forerunners of current virtual reality technology. It took the emergence of the computer and its ability to generate complex images and simulate interactive environments to truly energize the VR concept and spark the birth of a new industry.

Many people helped lay the groundwork for VR. In 1950 Douglas Engelbart envisioned a world of small computers that people would use for communication—an utterly foreign concept at a time when computers were mammoth structures that might fill up an entire house and yet be capable of little more than simple addition and subtraction. In 1960 J.C.R. Licklider predicted that the human mind and the computer would work in close harmony in his essay "Man-Computer Symbiosis." This, too, seemed doubtful in an age when programmers could only communicate with the computer through punched-hole tape.

History ALDOUS HUXLEY: THE FATHER OF VIRTUAL REALITY?

While the immediate roots of virtual reality go back only to the early 1980s, some of the fundamental technologies actually came into being along with the computer in the 1940s. Some, however, might see an even earlier root as far back as the 1930s, when Aldous Huxley's futuristic novel *Brave New World* depicted cinema-goers of the future accessing a full sensory experience through a contraption called a "feelie."

By the 1960s the notions that would later come to fruition as virtual reality were rapidly taking shape. In 1962 Morton Heilig built the Sensorama cubicle, which gave the user the illusion of driving a motorcycle. In 1965 Ivan Sutherland, "the father of computer graphics," had already imagined computer users being immersed in a separate reality created by graphics. In addition, Myron Krueger, a significant VR pioneer who in 1970 became the first to use the term "artificial reality," built the first of his many "responsive environments" in 1969. Called GLOWFLOW, it involved a platform surrounded by a screen. Viewers stood on the platform, and as they walked around, the shifting of their bodies' weight caused various pictures to appear on the screen.

From these early days the development of virtual reality was the product of a bizarre amalgam of players: computer scientists, many of whom worked in university research labs; unconventional visionaries; and military and civilian personnel from the Department of Defense and the National Aeronautics and Space Administration (NASA). The government was an important contributor to VR research. After the Soviets launched the first space satellite, Sputnik, in 1957, the U.S. government reacted by launching vast new programs in military and flight engineering and science. Out of this came the Advanced Research Projects Agency (ARPA), which developed the beginnings of the Internet—then called the ARPANET—and invested in what would become virtual reality.

Futhermore, the military provided funding for J.C.R. Licklider, helping him to explore his ideas of "man-computer symbiosis." With its vast budget, the Defense Department facilitated the first use of a virtual reality system in the 1970s. NASA, on the other hand, had less money to spend, but its scientists were also interested in the possibilities for VR use in flight training and other aspects of space flight. Because of its limited budget, NASA was a key element in helping to develop relatively less expensive VR technology. NASA also explored the idea of telepresence, which would make it possible for someone to "do" something in one place while sitting in another. Following this concept, in July 1997 NASA programmers on earth were able to operate a vehicle that rolled over the surface of Mars and collected soil and rock samples.

PIONEERS IN THE FIELD

Jaron Lanier was a leader in the early development and commercialization of virtual reality technology and products. Lanier is called the pioneer of virtual reality and is recognized for coining the term. Virtual reality was the name he gave to the goggles, gloves, and software that allow people to interact with each other in worlds generated by 3-D graphics. Lanier also developed software that made VR commercially viable.

Born in 1961, Lanier grew up in New Mexico, dropped out of high school, and set out to be a musician rather than a computer genius. Lanier was already developing the technology that would alter the future of humankind by the time he was in his twenties. Working with Atari in the early 1980s, he earned enough royalties from his "Moondust" video game to quit and start his own company. Legend has it that when *Scientific American* called to discuss a new programming language he had developed, the 22-year-old Lanier was embarrassed to tell them his company had no name, so he made up the name VPL Research Inc. on the spot.

Lanier founded VPL Research in 1984 and headed the company until 1992. During that time, the company made many of the early advances that would later enable interactive, networked 3-D games like "Doom" and "Quake." "VPL's groundbreaking efforts and research have become an important influence on many virtual reality and 3-D graphics products that succeeded the company," according to Sun Microsystems, the company that later acquired VPL.

When Lanier left VPL in 1992 because of differences with Thompson-CFS, the French technology conglomerate that helped finance him, he gave up his patents. During the next four years, Greenleaf Medical financed VPL Systems. Greenleaf fought a four-year battle in bankruptcy court to keep Thompson from gaining exclusive control of the VPL patents. In February 1998, Sun Microsystems announced it had acquired VPL for an estimated $4 million. The deal settled debts and released approximately 35 patent applications, 12 of them already granted. The acquisition is looked on favorably by Wall Street and many in the VR industry.

Jaron Lanier has continued his involvement in the VR field as lead scientist for the National Tele-Immersion Initiative, a coalition of research universities working to create the next generation of virtual reality applications on the Internet.

CURRENT CONDITIONS

In 1997 the virtual reality marketplace was valued at $480 million, according to a March 1998 *New York Times* article. By the end of 1998, that figure was close to $1 billion due to significant growth in the industry. One of the factors that contributed to its relatively slow growth during the mid-1990s was the legal battle involving VPL Research Inc. The legal battle involved custody of the patent rights to much of the technology that defines virtual reality. Since there was such uncertainty in the industry over the patents, interest in starting new companies waned during the four-year court battle (1993 to 1997).

That situation changed in 1998. By acquiring VOL, Sun Microsystems now has the rights to the patent portfolio and technical assets of the company, which extend to networked 3-D graphics, human-

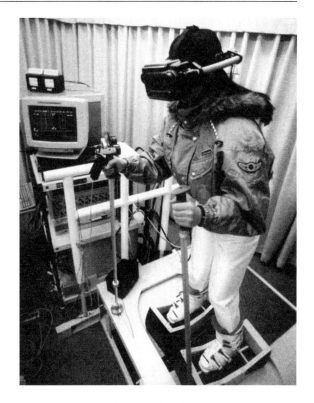

A woman using a virtual reality skiing system. (The *Bettman Archive/Newsphotos, Inc.*)

based body input, and 3-D window systems. The acquisition provided stability in the volatile industry as a whole. According to Stuart Davidson, a partner in Labrador Ventures, a California high-tech venture capital firm, "this will help virtual reality get out of the cottage-industry stage. At the very least, by establishing hardware and software standards for the technology, Sun Microsystems should end costly duplication of effort among companies developing virtual reality."

In the late 1990s, virtual reality applications were taking hold in wide-ranging segments of American life. Among the areas touched by VR were entertainment, design and engineering, medicine, education and training, sales, and the military.

Entertainment was an early area of VR application, and it remains significant in the late 1990s. For instance, a restaurant chain offers patrons the opportunity to experience virtual reality-based games. The Evans and Sutherland Computer Corporation developed a system in late 1996 that inserts the viewer into a virtual setting on live television. In 1997, research at Carnegie-Mellon University involved a VR application that would make it possible for someone watching a sport on television to view the action from anywhere on the field of play. In June 1998, Disney opened DisneyQuest, a new family entertainment experience at Downtown Disney in Orlando. DisneyQuest features futuristic games and rides that use motion-based simulators and virtual reality environments. Disney partnered with Silicon Graphics, a leader in the VR field, for this project. DisneyQuest's "Explore Zone" is the entertainment world that features VR. Finally, a controversial area of VR entertainment in the late 1990s was virtual sex or "cyber sex."

In the area of design and engineering, software for three-dimensional modeling assists designers in creating prototypes. Thus, a designer or engineer can analyze a product through VR without having to build an expensive model. One of the many cost advantages offered by virtual reality is its ability to speed up the design and testing process—a valuable asset in an era of shorter product development cycles and rapidly changing generations of products. VR gives architects the ability to design and "build" whole structures and allows their prospective clients to "walk through" them. Many software companies also offer programs for the general public that allow users to create residential floor plans the way professionals create them. Industrial engineers also create virtual factories with employees, robots, machines, and products to explore better ways to make the factories function.

Medical advances in VR technology include the National Institutes of Health's development of "virtual bronchoscopy," a virtual and noninvasive imaging of the bronchial tree within the human respiratory system. Other advances make it increasingly possible to study human anatomy, without actually cutting open a cadaver, and to improve surgical techniques through virtual operations. Coined "Cybersurgery," VR is a crucial tool in neurosurgery where a 3-D picture of the brain helps surgeons pinpoint the location of a brain tumor with extreme accuracy.

Educational and training applications of VR technology are widespread, ranging from knowledge of purely theoretical or historical interest to highly practical applications. "Rome Reborn," an ambitious project being developed at UCLA in the late 1990s, would walk users through versions of Rome from 850 B.C. to 450 A.D. Virtual reality could also be used to help people from a wide variety of occupations—doctors, factory workers, fighter pilots—improve their work by simulating their activities.

Examples of VR applications in sales and marketing include uses in real estate like Home Debut, which provides virtual tours of homes for sale. *Forbes*

looked at VR technology enlisted by the marketing firm Coopers & Lybrand in an effort to predict the buying habits of 50,000 music consumers. Also, the journal *I/S Analyzer Case Studies* predicted that an increasing number of businesses would use VR technology because VR authoring software was now compatible with most programming platforms, and the cost of head-mounted displays (HMDs) and other equipment was dropping.

The military was one of VR's first advocates. In the late 1990s, virtual reality was being used more frequently to simulate combat, and experiments were exploring ways it could be used in actual combat. Called Simnet, VR was used to train soldiers on real-to-life tank and helicopter training simulations for the U.S. Army. One promising area is that of telepresence, which allows remote command functions to orchestrate activities in a distant location.

Still very much in its infancy, VR technology in the late 1990s was being used extensively in the engineering, pharmaceutical, and entertainment fields. As noted, its value as a teaching tool in medicine, particularly surgery, has been recognized, and expansion of its use in this area can be expected. Almost any field in which it is helpful to construct a model and manipulate in real time can benefit from virtual reality technology. The images in VR simulations will become increasingly more realistic as computers grow ever more powerful. ScienceNet speculates that within 50 years, virtual environments that are essentially indistinguishable from real life will be readily created by computers.

INDUSTRY LEADERS

Silicon Graphics Inc. is one of the significant players in the VR field. Silicon Graphics computers are the dominant platform for virtual reality in the late 1990s. The company is a leading supplier of visual computing and high performance systems. Its products include a broad range of computers, from desktop workstations to servers and high-end supercomputers. With corporate offices in Mountain View, California, and offices in 60 sites throughout the world, Silicon Graphics manufactures and markets its systems to the communications, energy, entertainment, government, manufacturing, and science industries.

Silicon Graphics is providing VR technology to the new DisneyQuest entertainment complex in Orlando. Its Onyx2 Infinite Reality Systems are providing the computer graphics and high performance for the virtual reality experience. This same visual super-computer is currently used by the National Center for Supercomputing Applications (NCSA), a unit of the University of Illinois. This supercomputer allows researchers to process high-resolution visualizations of their applications as they run them.

In June 1998, the company announced the release of its Cosmo Page FX for Windows 95 and Windows NT. Cosmo Page FX is a web authoring tool that enables 2D graphics and Web designers to add depth, motion, and interactivity to images and type for use in online advertising and Web site design. The advantage of this new tool is that users do not need to be technically savvy in 3-D, programming, or Web development to use it.

The June 1998 edition of *PC Magazine* named Silicon Graphics' Cosmo Worlds 2.0 the editor's choice of interactive Web content development tools. Recently made available for Windows applications, Cosmos Worlds 2.0 creates real-time interactive 3-D worlds for the Web. The magazine noted its fluid handling of 3-D objects and programming support for animations and interactions. At a list price of $999, the software is still out of reach for many PC users. The company also makes about a dozen other 3-D software products.

In fiscal 1998, which ended June 30, 1998, Silicon Graphics posted a net loss of $459.6 million on sales of $3.1 billion. The company's sales were down more than 15 percent from their levels in fiscal 1997. Led by Richard E. Belluzzo, chairman and chief executive officer, Silicon Graphics employed more than 10,000 people worldwide in 1998.

A chief competitor of Silicon Graphics is Sun Microsystems, Inc. Although not a high-profile player in the virtual reality field, the company's 1998 acquisition of VPL Research will change that. The company was expected to establish hardware and software standards for the industry with this acquisition.

Sun has been a leading manufacturer of graphics workstations used for mechanical computer aided design (MCAD). Founded in 1982, Sun is a leading provider of hardware, software, and services for the Internet. With more than $8 billion in annual revenues, Sun can be found in more than 150 countries around the world.

In the area of virtual reality, Sun has developed the JAVA 3-D View Model (a virtual reality viewing model), virtual holographic workstations, and virtual portals (three-screen immersive projections displays). Sun Microsystems' Java 3-D API is an application-programming interface used for writing 3-D graphics applications or Web-based 3-D applets. It provides an abstract, interactive imaging model for behavior and control of 3-D objects. The specification for this language is actually a result of collaboration between Sun Microsystems, Silicon Graphics, Intel Corporation, and Apple Computer. Java 3-D is designed for use in virtual reality systems, 3-D games, CAD applications, MCAD systems, and the design of Web pages and 3-D logos.

Headquartered in Palo Alto, California, Sun employed more than 22,000 people worldwide in 1998. The company, led by Scott G. McNealy, chairman and chief executive officer, reported net earnings of $762.9 million for fiscal 1998, ended June 30, 1998. This represented little change from its net income in fiscal 1997. Fiscal 1998 sales, totaling $9.8 billion, were up nearly 14 percent over the previous year.

Autodesk is the fourth largest PC software company worldwide. Its software products are focused on design solutions and visualization. Its Autocad, Autodesk, and Picture This software is used by architects, designers, engineers, animators, scientists, film makers, and educators to more easily conceptualize their ideas. Based in San Rafael, California, Autodesk posted net earnings of $90.6 million on sales of $740.2 million in fiscal 1999, ended January 31, 1999. Earnings showed an increase of nearly 500 percent over fiscal 1999, while sales were up a more modest 19.9 percent. As of spring 1999, Autodesk was led by Carol A. Bartz, chairman and chief executive officer. Other significant players include Polhemus Inc. and Virtual Reality Inc.

Government and university entities also play a role in VR, the most prominent of the former being the Department of Defense and NASA. Among the latter are the University of Illinois, home of the National Center for Supercomputing Applications (NCSA); the University of Washington; and the University of North Carolina at Chapel Hill.

WORK FORCE

Until virtual reality becomes widely used, jobs in this area will remain limited to design and production roles, though even these positions are limited. For example, in its heyday, VPL employed only about 35 individuals. However, the advantage for those interested in entering the field is the fact that its territory is largely unmapped, and VR in the late 1990s is still to some extent a world open to visionaries.

AMERICA AND THE WORLD

Industry analysts in the 1990s expressed concern that America would fall behind other countries. This theme is familiar to those who observed the auto industry or various fields of electronics—Americans may have made the original innovations, but the Japanese were often more successful in developing and marketing the products. By the late 1990s, it appeared that Japan might well take the forefront in VR technology as well. Advantages enjoyed by the Japanese include the fact that Japanese industry in general—and high-tech industry in particular—operate according to national objectives, thus offering a modified form of the central planning espoused by command economies while enjoying the advantages of a free economy. The number of Japanese patent applications in the 1990s was double the number of those in the United States. Germany, France, and the United Kingdom also promise to be major players in the world of VR.

In the fall of 1998, Hong Kong Polytechnic University announced the installation of a $1.7-million virtual reality laboratory. The facility will substantially enhance the university's health education capabilities. Susie Lum, senior executive manager for nursing, said the facility "lowers risks associated with training on human patients and establishes standards and optimization of specific procedures."

To help prepare policemen in Australia's New South Wales to deal more effectively with such complex emergencies as hostage situations and major disasters, a VR training device called Minerva was introduced in early 1999. The video-based equipment simulates real-life crises and helps trainees to make split-second decisions. New South Wales Police Minister Paul Whelan, in introducing the VR trainer, likened its technology to simulators used in training race car drivers and airline pilots.

RESEARCH AND TECHNOLOGY

In the late 1990's, VR technology seemed to be advancing only in the research labs and not in the marketplace. "While there's plenty of creative ferment and experimentation in the VR scene, there isn't a boatload of money being spent," according to a 1997 *Forbes Digital Tool* magazine article. The only area where technology is progressing is in high-end industrial applications such as the creation of prototypes of commercial jets and cars.

Much of the discussion about VR technology focuses on Virtual Reality Modeling Language (VRML) 2.0. VRML is a standard language for describing interactive 3-D objects and worlds on the Internet. Like HTML, the modeling language typically used on the World Wide Web, VRML is a Web-authoring software, but it also gives users the ability to create sophisticated three-dimensional environments. It adds interaction, graphics, and extra dimensions to online communication.

A VRML Consortium was formed as the official mouthpiece for VRML evolution to provide a forum for creating and promoting standards for VRML and 3-D content on the Web. The consortium approved VRML 97 as the ISO standard in December 1997. In 1998, the nonprofit group was comprised of 65 organizations and, in March of that year, began work on formalizing its organizational structure by forming an executive committee and task groups to work on marketing and specification issues. Although many of the larger technology companies including Apple Computer, Cosmo Software (a Silicon Graphics company), Microsoft, Oracle, and Sony had joined the consortium, other major players, including Sun Microsystems, have not yet announced their support of VRML.

Central to the development of new VR technology is the controversy surrounding immersion technology versus wearable display gear. The primary piece of equipment for the VR experience is the head-mounted display, or HMD—a helmet hooked up to the computer that includes tiny monitors (television screens) to cover each eye. The screens each show slightly different views that, when viewed simultaneously, produce the illusion of looking at three-dimensional objects. Also inside the HMD is a tracking device that follows the user's head movements and changes the on-screen images accordingly, in order to maintain the sensation that one is operating within a fully spatial, rather than two-dimensional, realm. The HMD also includes speakers to further enhance the experience. Virtual reality users often avail themselves of tactile devices, most commonly a sensor glove, which is connected to the computer like the HMD. The glove senses movements of the user's hand and helps him or her to "move" within the virtual world seen through the screens on the headset. The headgear and the glove create an illusion of depth and the ability to manipulate objects. With prolonged use, these devices have proven to be awkward and uncomfortable. Head-mounted viewers such as Nintendo's Virtual Boy were expensive and ultimately unsuccessful. However, the most realistic computer-generated 3-D world is currently displayed using these wearable displays.

A new wave of lightweight, head-mounted displays called PDs (personal displays) were expected to debut in 1998 from Retinal Displays. These PDs are seen as an improvement to the older, uncomfortable, and often awkward head-mounted displays. PDs are used with new visual personal computers that feature hardware-accelerated 3-D graphics.

Many scientists have come to embrace the idea of immersing a user in a 3-D environment on a computer screen without the use of wearable displays. Researchers are currently experimenting with these immersion VR environments. NCSA's computer animated virtual environment, or CAVE, at the University of Illinois at Chicago, is one such example. These environments completely surround the user, in effect transporting him or her to a different world through VR. The Laboratory for Integrated Medical Interface Technology at the University of Washington is another immersive environment. Other new immersive interface technologies are the Vision Dome from Alternate Realities Corporation, Immersadesk from Pyramid Systems, and the Immersive Workbench from Fakespace.

The first virtual reality experiment to be conducted in outer space took place aboard the space shuttle in April 1998. The Neurolab experiment tested visual orientation in a weightless environment. Four mission specialists spent about an hour and a half in headgear showing a computer-generated simulation of their laboratory.

Researchers in the late 1990s were looking at ways to improve the limitations of 3-D computer imaging on a two-dimensional display. Viewing 3-D scenes is still somewhat disorienting and has an unnatural feel. Objects in 3-D scenes are very difficult to grasp without jiggling them with a control device. Also, seeing virtual objects from different points of view currently requires the use of several screens.

Volumetric imaging is one development being researched in the late 1990s by Parvis Soltan at the Naval Command, Control, and Ocean Surveillance Center in San Diego. Soltan's research uses volumetric imaging devices, which place points of light in all three dimensions using a panel that is twisted into a helix. The image is projected onto the helix, which is spinning very fast to make it virtually invisible, and it can be viewed from the top as well as the sides. Soltan's device looks crude and is very loud, but the images it creates are surprisingly good. Two private companies have already started marketing the technology.

Another technology in development in the late 1990s is the solid-state crystal ball. Elizabeth Down-

ing is researching a whole new way to create 3-D images—by creating these images inside a solid piece of glass. The technology involves intersecting lasers in a fluoride-glass cube which contains elements that fluoresce when struck by these lasers. The energy created by the two intersecting beams release visible photons, thus creating the image. Applications for the crystal ball technology include medicine, air traffic control, design engineering and, eventually, 3-D television.

Virtual reality is being used in a hospital-based project in Atlanta to help rid veterans of the Vietnam War of some of the lingering psychological effects of that experience. Where traditional psychological therapy has largely failed to ease the post-traumatic stress that has plagued these veterans for decades, virtual reality seems to be having a positive effect. This was but one of more than a hundred VR applications outlined at an international conference, called Medicine Meets Virtual Reality, held in San Francisco in early 1999. Medicine has embraced both full virtual reality, and partial or augmented reality, in which the real and virtual worlds are blended together. Some of the problems that medicine has been addressing with VR technology include agoraphobia, anorexia, and impotence. Boston's Artificial Reality Corporation has created a virtual environment for the training of physicians that allows trainees to experience both the smell and the feel of the patient and the operating room. Of this simulation, Peter Larson of ARC said, "When they go into the virtual world, they carry a backpack that contains a reservoir of smells. The computer follows their eye movements and when they look at something, the computer gives them the smell to go with it."

FURTHER READING

"Add-Ons Enhance CAD Simulations." *R&D*, February 1997.

"AlterVue Systems Releases First Practical Virtual Reality Application for Widespread Business Use." *Business Wire*, 12 May 1998.

Balderston, Jim. "SGI Signs VRML Deal With Netscape." *InfoWorld*, 3 February 1997.

Brown, Ed. "The Virtual Career of a Virtual Reality Pioneer." *Fortune*, 2 March 1998.

"Cosmo Software Ships Cosmo PageFX, A New Web Authoring Tool for Designers." *Silicon Graphics Web Site*, 1998. Available from http://www.sgi.com/newsroom/press_releases/1998/june/pagefx.html.

Coy, Peter. "This Is Joe Blow-Dry, Live From Mars." *Business Week,* 18 November 1996.

CyberEdge Information Services Inc. "Virtual Reality Market Measured," 1999. Available from http://www.cyberedge.com/home/www/3a1.html.

Ditlea, Steve. "False Starts Aside, Virtual Reality Finds New Roles." *The New York Times,* 23 March 1998.

Dobson, Roger. "Science: Virtual Sanity." *Independent on Sunday,* 17 January 1999.

Dunn, Ashley. "Virtual Reality Through a Crystal Ball." *The New York Times,* 19 March 1997.

Dvorak, Paul. "Engineering Puts Virtual Reality to Work." *Machine Design,* 20 February 1997.

"Extending Beyond VRML 2.0." *InfoWorld,* 25 November 1996.

Gage, Deborah. "Virtual Reality: Net to Take On New Dimensions." *Computer Reseller News,* 24 February 1997.

Hayward, Tom. *Adventures In Virtual Reality.* Carmel, IN: Que, 1993.

"HK Polytechnic University Establishes $1.7m VR Lab." *Newsbytes News Network,* 30 November 1998.

"Honey I Shrunk the Monitor." *Forbes Digital Tool,* 9 June 1997.

"Hotel Room of the Future." *Futurist,* March/April 1997.

"How Businesses Are Cutting Costs Through Virtual Reality: 30 Seconds." *I/S Analyzer Case Studies,* March 1997.

"It's Called Shopping For Homes From Home." *Marketing News,* 14 April 1997.

Koselka, Rita. "Playing the Game of Life." *Forbes,* 7 April 1997.

Krumenaker, Larry. "Virtual Assembly." *Technology Review,* February/March 1997.

Larijani, L. Casey. *The Virtual Reality Primer.* New York: McGraw-Hill, 1994.

Larner, Monica. "For the Appian Way, Hit Command-A." *Business Week,* 14 April 1997.

"NSW: Virtual Reality to Give Police Edge in Crisis Management." *AAP General News,* 12 February 1999.

Radosevich, Lynda. "Virtual Reality Tools Come of Age." *InfoWorld,* 9 December 1996.

Rheingold, Howard. *Virtual Reality.* New York: Touchstone, 1991.

Swerdlow, Joel L. "Information Revolution." *National Geographic,* October 1995.

Teresko, John, John Sheridan, and Tim Stevens. "Winning Technologies." *Industry Week,* 3 December 1997.

"Times Books to Publish *The Visionary Position.*" *M2 PressWIRE,* 16 March 1999.

Ulfeder, Steve. "The One That Got Away." *Computerworld,* 20 January 1997.

Valendorpe, Linda. "Breathe Easier With New Bronchoscopy." *R&D,* February 1997.

"Virtual Reality Market Study Continues; First Longitudinal Study Will Document Billion Dollar Market." *Business Wire,* 9 September 1998.

Von Schweber, Linda and Eric. "Teams of Workers Will Visually Explore Virtual Prototypes Together and Interactively Conduct Simulations Through VR Techniques." *PC Magazine,* 9 June 1998.

—Judson Knight, updated by Don Amerman

VOICE MAIL SYSTEMS

The imperatives of economic competition in the 1980s and 1990s and the attendant claims and pressures on personal time spawned by the information age created a demand for faster, cheaper, and more efficient messaging technologies. By the early 1980s, improvements in computer technology made improved messaging technologies available for business systems. Chief among these messaging systems is voice mail.

By 1997, there were in excess of 50 million voice mailboxes worldwide. The messaging industry—for both voice mail and fax transmissions—is experiencing 20 percent annual growth. Market research estimated the total worldwide messaging market at more than $5 billion in 1998, and the market is expected to exceed $10 billion by the year 2000. With such a massive market available, there has been a concerted effort among vendors to develop a unified single-station method for receiving and processing messages. Indications are that these unified messaging services are destined to thrive on the Internet due to the high level of integration intrinsic to that environment and to the exceptional versatility of Web browser software. Across the Internet, where all systems converge, ongoing advances to improve the quality of voice transmission across IP networks will contribute to the realization of universal messaging.

BACKGROUND AND DEVELOPMENT

Voice mail was pioneered by small firms in the late 1970s, but the essential precondition making its development possible was the introduction of touch-tone phone service in the mid-1960s. The familiar touch-tones were actually computer codes that for the first time enabled phones and computers to communicate with each other.

Seizing the opportunity provided by this new information transfer capacity, small firms developed the basic store-and-forward technology, which digitizes spoken phone messages and stores them on hard disk in designated mailboxes, from which they can be converted on demand back into voice. These messages can then also be rerouted to other users, deleted, or saved for future access.

In the late 1970s a few small firms such as Comintern, of Burlington, Massachusetts, and Sudbury Systems, of Sudbury, Massachusetts, made the first store-and-forward voice mail systems commercially available to specialized users. Comintern had been active in answering services and beepers; Sudbury sold specialized systems for hospitals.

ECS Telecommunications of Dallas, renamed VMX Inc. in 1982 for its main product line, the Voice Message Exchange, offered one of the earliest corporation-wide voice mail store-and-forward systems for business clients. VMX founder Gordon Matthews invented basic voice messaging technology to avoid the huge volume of memos, letters, and phone slips and the frustrating phone-tag scenarios that encumbered the many corporations and organizations then served only by answering machine technology.

In 1981 IBM and Wang introduced voice mail products, which lent credibility to the nascent industry. In 1982 Rolm Corporation made its PhoneMail system available, the first such product able to be fully integrated into a Private Automatic Branch Exchange (PABX). Also in 1982, Sperry Univac introduced the first system to be integrated into an automated office package.

From that point developments in voice mail technology involved decreased size and costs, increased reliability, greater ease of use, broader compatibility with PBX (Private Bank Exchange) systems from many vendors, and more flexibility—early systems required that both parties using the system be subscribers to it, while later systems required only one subscriber. From the mid-1980s, sales of voice mail systems logged steady increases. In 1984 alone, for example, sales nearly tripled from $40 million to over $100 million. Yet the market remained barely tapped. From 1987 to 1991, sales increased at an average annual growth rate of 42 percent.

In the late 1990s, voice mail systems were based on proprietary software, which often made unmediated communication between systems extremely difficult or impossible. Therefore, by 1998 the overriding developmental direction of the voice mail industry was concentrated in the race to develop affordable integrated systems to unify the disparate messaging technologies. Graham MacArthur, director of the London-based Data Connection Ltd., compared this situation to that of e-mail in the late 1980s—when third-party software developers created a profitable niche by developing gateways between non-compatible systems.

Until late 1997, voice mail systems were connected by AMIS (audio messaging interface standard) protocols. AMIS links were originally analog-based: one system basically dialed another system—a process that presented its own compatibility complexities—and forwarded the message in audio form as many times as required. This added further problems to the process because of the inherent degradation of sound quality during the forwarding process. AMIS was adapted to a digital format, but the problems in dialing up non-compatible systems remained.

CURRENT CONDITIONS

Due to the shortcomings inherent in current voice messaging technology, a group of nine telecommunications vendors combined to push for the adoption of a new standard for voice mail interoperability known as voice profile for Internet mail (VPIM). The group is a powerful one, composed of industry leaders such as Centigram Communications, CTI Information Systems, IRdg, Lucent Technologies, Northern Tele-

com (Nortel), Octel Communications, ReadyCom, Siemens Business Communications, Unisys, and Applied Voice Technology. According to In-Stat, a market research firm, the original 9 companies together held more than 70 percent of the North American voice mail systems market, amounting to more than 31 million voice mailboxes. In the late 1990s, more than 40 companies made contributions to the development of the VPIM standard. *Data Communications* reported approval of the standard by IETF in 1999. VPIM as approved complied with the multipurpose Internet mail extensions (MIME) standard for Internet messaging to provide uniform methods of transmitting e-mail, fax, and voice via e-mail gateways. A free software package called Sendware was among the first implementations of the new standard.

By 1997 market revenues totaled $2.3 billion even in the wake of a slowed growth pattern of 10 percent. Some industry realignment occurred and some new companies moved into the list of the top 10 industry leaders. These included Active Voice and Comverse Technology, which took over fourth and fifth place, respectively, each with under 6 percent of the market. Market researchers projected continued major growth in both subscriber and transaction volumes, and estimated that the total messaging market would double by the year 2000. Telecommunications companies anticipated an imminent retooling of the market in the direction of inter-operability solutions such as VPIM. Most underwent preparations to develop open systems to meet the expected demands of that market. In 1998 traditional players in the voice messaging market, such as Lucent Technologies Inc., Northern Telecom Ltd., and other computer telephony vendors produced gateways to support VPIM.

FRUSTRATIONS AND OPPORTUNITIES

Voice mailboxes have become so widespread in the United States that the problems and inconveniences affecting users have become a common cultural experience and, at times, a fertile source for humorists. Voice mail shares with e-mail and fax the potential for message overload, with attendant demands on time required for replaying and appropriate follow-up or deletion. This particular problem is not specifically attributable to any of the messaging technologies; it is a result of the sheer volume of messaging done in society. It is, however, amplified by the increasing use of commercial broadcast and network messaging, which makes it possible to send one message to numerous recipients at a very low cost. Horror stories of this type of intrusive marketing abound. *Business Week* cites one company in Col-

---

More On   SORTING THE (VOICE) MAIL:
OPERATOR ERROR

      Voice mail systems at one time served only the largest vendors and corporations. The purpose of voice mail, it seemed, was to impact customer satisfaction by eliminating all voice-to-voice contact with designated representatives. The systems gained increasing visibility during the 1990s, and replaced telephone voice message recorders in the smallest businesses and in many homes. Increased prevalence of voice mail spurred debate over its value. Opponents of voice mail challenged the expedience of automation against the diminishing human contact in an automated society.

      The benefits of voice mail were irrefutable, but the applied technology left large factions of the populace simmering in frustration when caught in an automated voice mail loop that allowed no exit to speak to a live operator. Voice mail is a microprocessor-based automated environment. As such it functions effectively contingent

upon proper implementation. As with a vast majority of computer problems, difficulties experienced with voice mail systems are frequently caused by operator error. A malfunctioning or improperly programmed voice mail system may be an extreme annoyance to callers. It is likewise irresponsible to leave voice mail systems running wantonly—Messages must be monitored, and timely response should be the norm. Callers who leave messages both appreciate and expect a response.

      Purists who eschew automation altogether must in turn recall the days of live telephone operators and consider the stereotypical Ernestine, the "ring-dingy" telephone operator characterized by comedienne Lily Tomlin. Ernestine, based on one comedy writer's recollection of a pre-automation telephone operator, could frustrate on a par with the most annoying and unresponsive of voice mail systems.

---

orado, for example, that dialed each room in a hospital with a voice commercial for a liquor store.

The nature of voice mail as a system and as a way of communicating and doing business has given rise to other specific problems and annoyances. Impenetrable, labyrinthine automated customer response systems too often present seemingly endless options, transfers, and dead ends; they appear to frustrated users as designed to guarantee the impossibility of reaching live, comprehending, human assistance. The canned phrases of voice mail systems such as "Your call is important to us" and "No one is available to take your call right now" have become part of the vernacular, often delivered in bitter ironic frustration.

Critics of the social effects of voice mail usage cite the increased isolation of individuals, which the technology supports. In an article on problems associated with voice mail, Bernard Beck, a Northwestern University sociologist, contends that, "A few years ago there were stories about cocooning—how everybody was staying home. Now, in the workplace, there may be a similar thing—a kind of strange individualization. The less we have to deal with people, the better. We don't know that other people will do what we expect them to do." Critics who decry the intrusion of work into private and family time regularly cite the invasive role of voice mail, as well as that of the other messaging formats, in breaking down the separation of home and office.

In addition, an interesting array of useful voice messaging technologies and services have come to the

fore since 1997. Wildfire Communications, Inc., for example, designed a personal assistant technology that would enable a user to set up voice mail and enter caller contact data using voice commands. In 1997 Intel and Microsoft, along with a venture capital firm, made a $12 million investment in Wildfire. The voice-activated Wildfire interface offered users voice messaging, call routing, and voice dialing. The company has several versions of the technology available for a broad range of customers, from network carriers to individuals. Following the success of Wildfire in North America, in 1999 a British telephone firm, Orange PLC, adapted the hands-free system to meet the needs of telephone customers in the United Kingdom.

In mid-1998, Motorola announced its Portable Answering Machine—a pager that allows users to hear voice mail simply by holding the pager to the ear. The service, marketed by Conxus under the brand names Pocketalk and PageNet, uses an oversized pager that holds four minutes of messages, and was available in nine metropolitan areas, with seven more areas scheduled to offer the service in 1999.

The use of voice mail in educational settings has also become increasingly more common since the early 1990s. Suzanne Prescott, professor of education at Illinois' Governor's State University, developed a pilot software program that allows students doing homework to dial a local number, punch in a security code, and choose to answer assigned questions, leave questions about homework, or hear detailed assignment descriptions for the next day's class. Students

---

can also receive communications from other students in private voice mailboxes and play educational games by punching in answers on their phones. In addition, parents can listen to messages from teachers. The system is easily adaptable. At Bright Elementary School on Chicago's South Side, for example, the system is constructed to meet the specific bilingual needs of that district. Prescott explains: "The system is geared to hone the English-speaking skills of the Spanish-speaking students. Because it's a voice system, the teachers can listen for pronunciation, coherency, etc." Other such systems allow schools to broadcast messages to all parents and eliminate lost or forgotten messages, to alert substitute teachers when regular teachers call in sick, and to alert parents in truancy situations.

According to educators, children seem to prefer the interactive nature of phone systems to the isolation of workbook assignments. Furthermore, the ease of accessibility of a simple telephone obviates the exclusionary need for expensive computer equipment—a significant consideration in lower-income areas. Educators and voiceware experts predict that in an era of widespread financial constraint, the low overall cost of such systems will spur their continued use and development, and make them attractive supplements to traditional teaching.

The ease of voice mail extends even to those unable to afford a phone. Seattle's Worker Centre initiated Community Voice Mail (CVM), a service that provides homeless persons with individual voice mailboxes and access codes. Designed to overcome the enormous disadvantages the homeless face in communicating with potential employers and landlords, CVM empowered the homeless to receive messages in pursuit of employment and housing. A subsequent $100,000 grant to CVM from the Harvard Innovation Program and the Ford Foundation financed the Community Technology Institute, which assisted other communities nationwide in developing similar voice mail programs.

For business travelers away from home, Sony's Voice File Recorder combines the convenience of voice mail with the low cost and efficiency of e-mail. Users record and store up to 495 messages into the hand-held ICD-80 recorder, ready for downloading at the nearest kiosk or Internet hook-up. The Voice File Recorder converts the messages into WAV files for attachment to any e-mail transmission. Recipients receive the e-mail and listen to the voice mail attachment on any computer equipped with a sound card and speakers. Maxon America's Responder offers the same ease of use, without the intermediary of Internet e-mail service. The Responder functions as a bi-directional voice mail system that receives messages from any phone via cellular transmission, and stores the transmission for later recall at the user's convenience. A user response system records the user's reply and transmits the message directly back to the original caller. Even more convenient is the touch-tone phone-based iTalk server from TellSoft Technologies Incorporated. The iTalk system runs on RealAudio from RealNetworks. Callers relay voice mail over the telephone to the iTalk server, and the recipient can then access the voice mail through an Internet address on the World Wide Web.

Potentially the most annoying voice mail system of all might be a new offering from Spanlink Communications Incorporated and Nuance Communications Incorporated. The two firms joined forces to market a touch-tone voice-response answering system. The package runs under Lucent Technologies Incorporated phone system, Intuity Conversant. This product differs from common systems that request callers to communicate via the touch-tone phone pad. Instead, Spanlink's call center package and Nuance's speech recognition software provide automated response to callers' voice queries and requests. The caller speaks into the telephone and a computer answers back.

INDUSTRY LEADERS

The drive to develop advanced inter-operability and to get systems into the market expeditiously received a major boost as a result of a recent merger of two important telecommunications leaders. In July 1997 Lucent Technologies purchased Octel Communications for approximately $1.8 billion, uniting 2 major firms with complementary strengths in the messaging field. The new entity is known as Lucent Technologies Octel Messaging Division. Octel, the world's market share leader in voice processing technology, sells voice mail systems in more than 70 countries and holds a multiplicity of patents in voice mail, automated attendant, and integrated messaging. Lucent Technologies estimated that more than 80 million Octel voice mailboxes were being used in 90 countries worldwide in 1998—more than half for residential voice mail and about a third for wireless voice mail. One product developed in this area is its INTUITY Integrated Messaging for Lotus Notes and Lucent Unified Messenger for Microsoft Exchange, which can be used for voice, fax, and e-mail message management via telephone or PC. Octel voice mail products are used by a variety of businesses, telephone companies, cellular services, government agencies, and educational institutions. The company also provided voice mail outsourcing in 1997 to corporations such as Ameritech, Citicorp, EDS, Ford Motor Company, and J.P. Morgan. Lucent also has a long track record of developing advanced messaging products and is particularly strong in providing outsourcing and professional services, which will be crucial in the dissemination of next-generation messaging products. Lucent Technologies Inc. posted sales of $30.1 billion in 1998. The Octel Messaging Division alone employed more than 3,000 people worldwide.

Northern Telecom Limited, better known as Nortel, is the Canadian-based manufacturer of numerous telecommunications products, including voice messaging technology. In 1998 U.S. customers accounted for approximately 60 percent of the company's $17.5 billion in sales. Nortel's array of telecom products include switching, enterprise, wireless, and other network systems.

In 1998 Comverse Technology, Inc. ranked among the top five firms in the voice mail industry in terms of market share. Based in Woodbury, New York, the company's TRILOGUE and Access NP product lines supply voice and fax messaging, personal assistant, and information services to its customers in the telecommunications services segment. TRILOGUE is designed for use by network operators and is able to accommodate 1 million mailboxes and 45,000 hours of voice storage. The company had 1998 sales of $696.1 million.

Another notable company in the industry is Brooktrout Technology, Inc., which primarily develops hardware and software applications to be used in all sorts of electronic messaging, such as voice processing systems for voice mail. The company had 1998 sales of $100.9 million, a third of which was generated by sales of their Merlin Mail voice messaging and auto attendant system. Ironically, Brooktrout's top customer is messaging competitor Lucent Technologies.

RESEARCH AND TECHNOLOGY

The convergence of voice mail and e-mail achieves increased visibility as technology firms race to perfect and release products for efficient voice transmission across the Internet. The basic capability is available and the quality continues to improve as innovations in cellular phone technology contribute to the state of voice compression products. Two prominent hardware developers, Cisco and Motorola, each foresee richer products for Internet voice mail transmission. Both companies intend to invest $1 billion by the year 2005 toward the development and manufacture of e-mail, voice mail, Web pages, and other Internet-based telecommunication for mobile access. Software leader Microsoft Corporation, in partnership with British Telecom, will develop software product lines for similar purposes. A new Microsoft platform code-named Chimera is nearing reality under the terms of Wireless Knowledge LLC, a joint venture between Microsoft and QualComm.

At mid-year in 1998, Hammer Technologies Incorporated released an IP test system to monitor voice quality across the Internet and across private intranets. The system alerts designated personnel whenever voice degradation reaches a pre-defined limit. The package includes simple network management protocol (SNMP) diagnostics tools. Systems such as this that improve the quality of voice transmission across digital bandwidths may serve to accelerate the growing use of Internet-based voice messaging services.

FURTHER READING

1997 Lucent Technologies Annual Report, 3 May 1999. Available from http://www.lucent.com.

"Acquisition: Lucent Technologies to Purchase Octel Communications for $1.8 Billion." *Cambridge Telecom Report,* 21 July 1997.

Biagi, Susan. "Hammer Introduces Test System for IP." *Telephony,* 20 July 1998.

Bounellis, Cynthia. "Microsoft, Intel Invest in Wildfire." *Electronic News,* 27 October 1997.

Bruno, Lee. "Calling All Messages." *Data Communications,* 7 April 1999.

"Digital Watch/Infotech: Managing Information Overload. All Your Messages in One Place." *Fortune,* 12 May 1997.

"Educational Voice Mail Moving to the Head of the Digital Classroom." *Chicago Tribune: Education Today,* 23 April 1995.

Edwards, Morris. "The Move to High-Speed Wireless." *Communications News,* April 1999.

"A Familiar Voice Is At Hand." *Chicago Tribune: Womanews,* 22 September 1996.

"A Few Words on the Latest Way to Communicate: V-Mail." *PC Week,* 9 June 1997.

Flanagan, Patrick. "Lucent Acquires Octel to Round Out Its Product Line." *Telecommunications,* October 1997.

"Future Phones." *Working Woman,* May 1983.

"Internet Gets A Voice" *Telephony,* 10 August 1998.

"Interoperability: Vendors Set for EMA Show—Push for Voice Mail Standard." *Computer Reseller News,* 17 March 1997.

"Is Voice Mail a Secure Line?" *Chicago Tribune Business,* 8 March 1995.

Kosiur, David. "Building A Better Messenger; VPIM Dials Up MIME in Its Quest to Bring Universal In-box to Desktops." *PC Week,* 30 March 1998.

"Look, Ma! No Hands!" *Communications News,* March 1999.

"Lucent Technologies: Lucent Technologies to Purchase Octel Communications for $1.8 Billion." *PressWire,* 18 July 1997.

Lucent Technologies Octel Messaging Division Profile, July 1998. Available from http://www.lucent.com/octel.

Mollenauer, Jim. "Zen Again: The Art of Voice Compression." *Telecommunications,* February 1999.

Nelson, Scott Bernard. "Gadgets for the Frequently Mobile." *Kiplinger's Personal Finance,* April 1999.

"'Not Home' Please Hold." *The Economist,* 18 December 1993.

"A Pager That Talks: Motorola's Voice-Mail Pager Is A Boon to Road Warriors Tired of Trying to Decipher Alphanumeric Messages." *Fortune,* 11 May 1998.

"PC-Based Voice Mail Systems: Replacing the Receptionist." *PC Magazine,* 17 January 1989.

"Phone Follies: Is Anyone Out There?" *Chicago Tribune Sunday Magazine,* 15 October 1995.

"A Plan to Link Voicemail Systems Via the Net." *The New York Times Cybertimes,* 20 April 1997.

Popular Electronics, May 1999.

"Software Funnels Voice, Fax, E-Mail to One Mailbox." *Computerworld,* 24 February 1997.

"Still an Infant Technology: Voice Mail." *Modern Office Technology,* June 1985.

"Unified Messaging Means No Escape." *Computerworld,* 2 June 1997.

"Vandals Give Frontera Grill a High-Tech Fright. Hackers Take Over a Phone System." *Chicago Tribune,* 18 February 1996.

"Voice Mail Delivers the Message." *Office Administration and Automation,* March 1993.

"Voice Mail Interoperability Debate." *Computer Reseller News,* 16 March 1997.

"Voice Storage and Retrieval: An Overview." *Telecommunications,* September 1988.

"VPIM Lets Mail Systems Talk to Each Other." *PC Week,* 17 March 1997.

"White Paper: Lotus: The Right Call: A New Era of Messaging." *Computer Reseller News,* 14 July 1997.

"Your New Computer: The Telephone." *Business Week,* 3 June 1991.

—Peter A. di Lorenzi,
updated by Linda Dailey Paulson and Gloria Cooksey

VOICE RECOGNITION SYSTEMS AND SOFTWARE

Voice recognition (VR) systems and software are used in a wide range of applications, from automating commercial phone systems to enhancing personal productivity. The technology may appeal to anyone who needs a hands-free approach to writing or who would like to accomplish a computing task with the least amount of effort. However, the development of VR software has encountered many formidable obstacles, most of which have plagued the industry since its inception. Nonetheless, VR technology has advanced and become mainstream to the extent that businesses and health care professions of all sorts have turned to voice recognition solutions for everything from providing telephone support to writing medical reports.

Indeed, voice recognition is becoming a standard software option. Major software developers provide simple VR technology in many of their applications, including the Microsoft and Apple operating systems. This VR technology allows users to issue basic commands via a microphone, such as turning on the computer and opening and closing applications and files. The increasing popularity of VR software and devices in the late 1990s pushed the industry's revenues between $500 million, according to some estimates, and above $1 billion, according to others. Furthermore, analysts predict that the industry's sales will grow to $8 billion by the year 2000.

The leading voice recognition products of the late 1990s united 2 components that were only found separately in the previous 5 to 10 years: large vocabularies and continuous recognition. Top-of-the-line speech-to-text software, for example, wielded 60,000

word vocabularies and could process continuous speech. Also, technological advances have made VR software and devices more functional and user-friendly in that many are programmable and versatile, not requiring training or speaker dependence. Moreover, most contemporary VR products can perform their tasks with over 90 percent accuracy.

According to a 1999 report in the *Journal of Information Science,* technology breakthroughs in VR waned with the approach of the year 2000. The industry nonetheless generated interest on a variety of fronts, including the discovery of new potential for improved VR technology associated with Intel Corporation's Pentium III processor. Other innovations included the implementation of a VR-based medical transcription service across the Internet, and rudimentary VR-based airline ticketing systems. On the International front, AT&T Labs announced its intention to prototype a VR-based Chinese-to-English translator, and activities by U.S.-based Microsoft Corporation furthered the notion that a comprehensive voice-activated version of the flagship Windows-based operating system could materialize early in the twenty-first century.

Judith Markowitz in *Using Speech Recognition* traced the development of speech recognition devices back to Alexander Graham Bell in the 1870s, though the result of his research was the telephone. Several decades later, a Hungarian scientist, Tihamer Nemes, sought a patent for a speech transcription apparatus that relied on the sound tracks of movies. Nemes

```
┌─────────────────────────────────────────────────┐
│  More On    SPEECH                               │
│             RECOGNITION:                          │
│             ENABLING THE                          │
│             DISABLED                              │
│                                                   │
│           One particularly beneficial appli-     │
│   cation of computer speech recognition is in     │
│   the education of the disabled, as well as       │
│   people unable to operate keyboards. A speech    │
│   recognition system can help hearing-impaired    │
│   students to speak by providing them with        │
│   visual feedback when they attempt to form       │
│   words. Conversely, the systems can receive      │
│   verbal instructions from physically disabled    │
│   pupils unable to enter information on a          │
│   keyboard.                                        │
│           Speech recognition has also been used   │
│   in factories to control machinery, enter data,  │
│   inspect parts, and take inventory, thereby      │
│   opening up a wealth of employment oppor-        │
│   tunities previously closed to those with        │
│   disabilities.                                    │
└─────────────────────────────────────────────────┘
```

wanted the device to recognize and transcribe speech sequences. However, the patent office rejected the proposal. VR technology did not advance as quickly as Bell and Nemes had hoped. About 90 years after the initial endeavor to create a speech transcriber, AT&T Bell Laboratories finally developed a device that could recognize speech, in particular, digits when uttered by a human voice. Matching a vocal stimulus with prerecorded patterns, the device required a lot of tuning before it could recognize someone's speech, yet it was said to have almost 99 percent accuracy once successfully tuned.

Research in the mid-1960s taught developers a lesson: voice recognition technology depended on perceiving subtle and complex verbal input—abilities researchers could not reasonably hope to imbue their devices with, according to Markowitz. Consequently, researchers limited their focus to a series of lesser goals that one day might lead to a more comprehensive and powerful voice recognition system. They devoted their study to developing devices that could recognize a single person's voice, known as speaker-dependent technology. The devices used verbal stimuli punctuated by small pauses to allow the machine to process the input, and had small vocabularies of about 50 words. Speaker-dependent technology requires a training period—the speaker records sample pronunciations so that the device can create an archive of speech patterns and note a speaker's idiosyncratic inflections and cadences. Speakers must pause after each word with discrete devices. Hence, continuous speech is not possible with such tech-

nology and using a discrete-word device demands patience.

The rudiments of continuous speech recognition did not come until the 1970s. This technology only became functional in the 1980s and remained under refinement in the 1990s. Threshold Technologies, Inc. created the first commercial VR product in the early 1970s, according to Markowitz. Threshold's VIP 100 had a small vocabulary and used a discrete-word, speaker-dependent format, but Markowitz reported that it proved moderately successful nonetheless.

Goaded by these successes, the Advanced Research Projects Agency (ARPA) started to experiment with voice recognition technology. ARPA pushed for large vocabulary, continuous speech-processing devices and helped launch the industry's collaboration with artificial intelligence research, according to Markowitz. ARPA also took a comprehensive approach to voice recognition technology, exploring the influence of word meaning, word structure, sentence structure, and contextual and social factors. By 1976, ARPA created systems that had vocabularies over 1,000 words, could process some continuous speech, could recognize the speech of several language users, had an artificial syntax, and recognized better that 90 percent of their input, according to Markowitz. ARPA contracted Carnegie Mellon University (CMU), Bolt Beranek and Newman (BBN), and Massachusetts Institute of Technology (MIT) to build these systems.

Markowitz reported that CMU developed one of the most successful early VR systems, Harpy, which could recognize over 1,000 words with an error rate of about 5 percent. CMU also implemented hidden Markov modeling (HMM) technology in its DRAGON device, which generated or predicted letter sequences based on language immersion, according to Markowitz. HMM became a staple part of most of the following major VR applications. By 1985, 1,000-word systems were still considered large, especially for commercial products, though Speech Systems, Inc. developed a product with an extremely large vocabulary for its time in 1986, the PE100. The PE100 could recognize as many as 20,000 words in continuous speech, and the system was not speaker-dependent. In the late 1980s, Dragon Systems raised the ante by creating a 30,000 word device, though it required discrete speech. Continuous speech VR technology became much more viable in the 1980s and so did technology that could tolerate some background noise. The 1980s also brought the advent of portable VR devices, according to Markowitz. The machines of the early 1980s sold for as much as several thousand dollars and only had small vocabularies, whereas those of the late

1980s sold for a few hundred dollars replete with vocabularies over 1,000 words.

As PC prices fell in the mid-1990s, companies began to develop computer-based VR applications. In 1994, Philips Dictation Systems led the foray with software containing a large vocabulary that could process continuous speech. VR also began to expand its commercial potential at this point: companies integrated VR technology in VCR remote controls, air traffic control devices, and general computer software.

CURRENT CONDITIONS

Judith Markowitz reasons in *Using Speech Recognition* that VR technology has a multitude of obstacles to overcome on the road to human-like voice recognition—the same ones that always impeded VR technology, only now the focus is on refining the technology. These hindrances include: more than 20,000 frequencies to recognize in human speech, homophones, integrating contextual information, marking boundaries within continuous speech, variability among speakers, and noise or other interference. Nonetheless, voice recognition software and devices have begun to grow in the 1990s as the technology has become more reliable and the cost of computer hardware has decreased. VR technology accounted for a modest but expanding portion of the overall software industry's estimated $60 billion in sales in 1997 and for a small percentage of the hardware industry's $106 billion in 1997. *Speech Technology* estimated that the industry's revenues reached about $500 million in 1997 and TMA Associates predicted that the market for voice-recognition systems and software would climb to $8 billion by 2001. Other forecasts say VR technology will bring computers to about 60 percent of all U.S. households, up from about 35 percent in the late 1990s. The release of the Pentium III processor by Intel Corporation in March of 1999 was a further boon to VR applications, according to Metagroup senior analyst, Ashim Pal, who was quoted by Lindsay Clark in *Computer*. Pal predicted among the most significant benefits of Pentium III would be the potential for improved efficiency in VR applications, especially for large document processing. VR software vendors, including Lernout & Hauspie, Dragon Systems, and IBM Corporation, reportedly tailored proprietary software programs to optimize the benefits of the new chip.

Large software developers including Microsoft and Novell have already integrated VR technology into their everyday products. Other software makers plan to add voice recognition interfaces to their applications. The purchase by Microsoft Corporation of an 8 percent interest in VR development firm Lernout & Hauspie late in 1998 gave credence to speculation that the Windows operating system vendor might incorporate full-blown VR into an operating system before the year 2005. IBM obtained a license to use Eloquent Technology, Inc.'s Eloquence in its VoiceType VR software, according to Scott Berinato in *PC Week*. PureSpeech introduced a VR-based e-mail program, Juggler, in 1997 that provides text-to-speech functionality and stores up to 10 speakers' voices. Also, NEC plans to offer Kurzweil's VoicePad voice-based word processor and plans to sell it with its high-end office line computers, according to Berinato. VR industry leader, Dragon Systems, announced early in 1998 that it would begin packaging VR technology for ActiveX programmers and developers.

Some of the more recent developments in VR technology have led to software applications such as Dragon Systems' NaturallySpeaking, that can process continuous speech without sacrificing a rich vocabulary (60,000 thousand words). Although NaturallySpeaking does make occasional blunders, it marked an advance in VR design because, unlike previous applications that either required discreet speech or intermittent recognition of continuous speech, NaturallySpeaking can do both to some extent. This software also allows users to program it using macros for abbreviations and it can perform tasks such as cutting and pasting through verbal commands. After the introduction of NaturallySpeaking, Dragon's competitors, IBM and Lernout & Hauspie, launched similar products: ViaVoice and VoiceXpress, respectively.

Not only has standard dictation software benefited from the advances in VR technologies, businesses have turned to voice recognition applications to perform many tasks including providing automated telephone service, selling and trading stocks and bonds, and providing general information. Banks, brokerages, credit corporations, telephone services, online databases, and other businesses chose VR technology because it could deliver an estimated 97 percent accuracy rate and save thousands of dollars, according to Ripley Hotch in *Communication News*. In addition to identifying 97 percent of the speech it encounters, VR software products made fewer mistakes in general than did their human counterparts, about 30 percent fewer on average. Hotch also expects corporate deployment of voice recognition software to increase, as companies realize cost savings associated with fewer receptionists and telephone representatives due to VR technology. Furthermore, Judith Markowitz reported in

Using Speech Recognition that many companies boast of significant returns on investment: Verbex Voice Systems devoted $1.8 million to VR automation and the technology saved Verbex enough money in nine months to cover the investment.

In the late 1990s, more businesses turned to voice recognition systems to handle customer telephone calls, among other things. For example, stock broker-age firm Charles Schwab & Co. uses a VR system by Nuance Communications to handle 45,000 calls a day for stock quotes, and voice-automated stock trading became a reality on the Internet at a site called E*Trade. UPS also implemented a VR system by Nu-ance for its 125,000 daily callers, which tells them where their packages will be delivered or where they were left. UPS said that the VR system costs only $1.75 a call, whereas employing a customer assistant would cost $4 a call.

However, lower-end VR software is plagued by inefficiency, according to a *Business Week* study. Products from Kurzweil, IBM, and Dragon Systems all needed extensive acclimation—several hours worth—as well as supplementary correction even for a short dictation, as reported in the study. These products, on the other hand, highlight the advances in the industry: whereas this technology was once state-of-the-art and cost thousands of dollars, it now represents economy-grade technology costing under $100.

Advances in the 1990s have also made VR technology a possible ingredient in security software. Key-ware Technologies' Voice Guardian, introduced in 1997, can recognize users' voices with 99 percent ac-curacy, according to Scott Berinato in *PC Week*. The VR software records and stores voice prints of network users, then verifies network user voices when anyone attempts network access. In 1997, Voice Guardian cost $50 per client. Moreover, Berinato says that Dell Computer Corp. plans to offer Voice Guardian with its servers. Keyware also announced it will produce a Web-based version as well.

INTERNET "SPEAK"

The untapped potential of the Internet attracts VR systems developers for a variety of innovative pur-poses. New VR-based special access applications for the disabled, introduced in 1998, includes several speech-activated Web browsers and a talking Web browser from IBM Corporation. Conversational Com-puting Corporation, known as Conversa, launched Converse Web, an inexpensive (under $70) voice-activated Web browser that allows any user with a multimedia computer to traverse the expanse of the Internet via verbal commands, without using a mouse or keyboard. Motorola took the concept one step fur-ther with its innovative Voice Markup Language (VoxML), a voice-activated language for voice-based browsers and Web pages. Motorola indicated its in-tent to submit VoxML to the World Wide Web Con-sortium for use as a standardized language. VoxML holds the potential for Web-based telephone conver-sations, whereby users would converse with the In-ternet over standard telephone lines.

MEDICAL TRANSCRIPTION

Early in 1999 voice recognition vendor Applied Voice Recognition Incorporated (AVRI) reinvented it-self as e-DOCS and announced its intention to spe-cialize in voice recognition for medical transcription applications. In the process AVRI acquired at least six medical transcription companies between April 1998 and the same month in 1999. AVRI indicated that the acquisitions provided services for as many as 5,000 physicians. The new focus put AVRI in competition with MedQuist Incorporated, which employs human transcription personnel. AVRI further indicated an in-tent to retain its original name, while doing business as e-DOCS.net and trading on the NASDAQ exchange under the new symbol, e-DOCS.

The new e-DOCS transcription service runs on AVRI's Voice Commander 99 software, provides ser-vices to physicians via the Internet, and offers 24-hour online turnaround for transcribed documents. Physi-cians may earn discounts as high as 20 percent for those who realize the highest accuracy rate of 95-100 percent. The discount incentives are an effort to en-courage optimization of the technology, which neces-sitates that dictators speak very clearly. AVRI offers contracts to physicians that include handheld dictation equipment along with the basic computer and printer. The Voice Commander software, conceived in 1994, was patented in 1997. AVRI underwent comprehen-sive reorganization in 1999 and forecast $20 million in revenues all together for that year.

INDUSTRY LEADERS

A key innovator in this industry and developer of highly acclaimed VR applications has been Dragon Systems, Inc. Founded in 1982, Dragon focused pre-dominantly on speech-related technology. In 1984, Dragon's VR technology became the first to be inte-grated in a portable computer. ARPA also commis-sioned Dragon to develop speaker-independent, con-tinuous speech recognition applications in the mid-1980s. In 1990, medical application developers used Dragon's technology for a speech recognition information management system. Dragon also produced DragonDictate, the first commercially available 30,000-word vocabulary PC application. In 1991 and 1992, IBM and Microsoft licensed Dragon System's VR technology, which became part of IBM's VoiceType and Microsoft's Windows 95. By 1994, Dragon had increased DragonDictate's vocabulary to 60,000 words, the industry's largest at that time.

In 1997, Dragon introduced its meritorious NaturallySpeaking, combining a large vocabulary with continuous speech recognition capabilities as the world's first general purpose large vocabulary continuous speech recognition application. The same year the company marketed itself under the "The Natural Speech Company" umbrella. Cofounder James K. Baker served as the company's chairman and CEO and Janet Baker was the president in 1998. James Baker worked on the Dragon project while a graduate student at CMU. The company received two PC World, World Class Awards in 1998 for Naturally-Speaking: one for best voice recognition and one for most promising software newcomer. Naturally-Speaking also outsold its major competitors—IBM's ViaVoice and Lernout & Hauspie's VoiceXpress—in units and revenues.

Kurzweil Applied Intelligence, Inc. has also produced numerous voice recognition products. Kurzweil specializes in voice-centric technology for business and medical use. Founded in 1982, the company is based in Waltham, Massachusetts. Kurzweil's latest line of products include speaker-independent technology coupled with a large vocabulary, which does not require training, designed for computers. Kurzweil offers various grades of its Voice product line such as VoicePad, VoicePlus, and VoicePro. These applications have vocabularies ranging from 17,000 to 60,000 words, all with over 90 percent accuracy, according to Kurzweil. In addition, Kurzweil develops VR applications for medical fields such as radiology, cardiology, orthopedics, pathology, and primary care. Computer makers such as NEC bundle Kurzweil's VoicePad with business-grade computers.

In 1997, Kurzweil announced it would merge with a Belgian company, Lernout & Hauspie Speech Products N.V., which develops speech recognition technology as well, and take on the Lernout & Hauspie Speech Products label. The resulting company reported sales of $211.6 million in 1998 and had 1,100 workers. Microsoft subsequently purchased a minority share of Lernout & Hauspie in 1998 in order to expedite the company's development of VR Web browsers and other related technologies. The two companies will cooperate and share their technology and Lernout & Hauspie will supply VR technology for Microsoft's Windows operating system.

Voice Control Systems, Inc. (VCS) develops speaker-independent continuous and discrete VR technology as well. Some of VCS's core products include Ready Receptionist, WordBuilder, and VoiceDialer. Dialogic also uses VCS's technology in its Antreas Software, VR/160p, VRSoft, and VR/40 applications. In addition, VCS develops speech recognition hardware such as DVM2 and DVM4. VCS's products focus on empowering users to access and operate computers and other electronic devices via their voices. In 1998 the company posted $14.2 million in sales and Ronald H. Larkin headed the company as CEO. VCS also acquired Voice Processing Corporation in 1996, expanding its VR technology production capabilities.

Fonix Corporation attempted to redefine VR technology by developing new approaches to voice recognition. Fonix was dissatisfied with the direction voice recognition software was heading and sought alternative technology and models to replace some of the industry standards of the mid-1990s. Incorporated in 1985, Fonix strives to develop speaker independent, real-time, natural language software that can house large vocabularies and recognize speech with greater than 97 percent accuracy. Salt Lake City-based Fonix conducts research and creates VR technologies, which it then licenses to other companies. In 1998 the company employed 94 workers.

International Business Machines Corporation (IBM) continued to have a strong presence in the industry in the late 1990s. IBM's core voice recognition product during this period was ViaVoice, in its executive, office, and home versions. ViaVoice, a continuous speech program, features a 64,000-word base vocabulary, a 260,000-word backup dictionary, voice correction, and recognition of a wide range of voice frequencies. In 1997, ViaVoice ranked among the best selling speech recognition applications. IBM also makes Simply Speaking and Simply Speaking Gold, VR word processing applications. In 1998, IBM garnered $81.6 billion in sales.

The AT&T spinoff, Lucent Technologies, carrying on the vision of Alexander Graham Bell, extensively develops voice recognition technology. Specific to VR technology, Lucent creates security systems, voice processing technology, and telephones. One of its key products is Conversant, an automated speech recognition application with a 2,000 word vocabulary that allows clients 24-hour access to their accounts.

Profile JANUS AND JANUS II, CARNEGIE MELLON UNIVERSITY

Assorted research programs involving speech recognition technology are underway at the Interactive Systems Laboratories (ISL) of Carnegie Mellon University in Pittsburgh, and Universitat Karlsruhe in Germany. JANUS and JANUS II speech-to-speech translation research systems, are promising prototypes with which researchers have established speaker-independent continuous speech-to-speech language translation. With the original JANUS interface and later, under JANUS II, the scientists demonstrated automated articulation of spontaneous—and even poorly spoken—language recognition. Specific language translators under development in the JANUS and JANUS II programs include English, German, Spanish, Korean, and Japanese. Because it is intrinsically processor-based, JANUS ultimately affords the added capabilities to access automated databases. This characteristic makes the system appropriate for reservation booking systems for hotels, common carriers, and elsewhere.

Under the direction of Alex Waibel, Debbie Clement, and Silke Dannenmaier of ISL, JANUS is supported in part by the JANUS consortium of corporate sponsors from the United States, Japan, Korea, and France. Consortium members receive a software license and a copy of the source code. Other projects at ISL include a voice operated driving information system (VODIS), and GlobalPhone, a project for multi-lingual speech recognition for phone-based data collection.

Lucent also develops speech recognition technology for faxes and computer networking, and has developed Speech Application Platform, a programming platform for creating speech-based applications. Based in Murray Hill, New Jersey, Lucent employed 141,600 people in 1998 and posted over $30.1 billion in sales.

RESEARCH AND TECHNOLOGY

VR STANDARDS

In addition to battling traditional obstacles such as creating large vocabularies and implementing contextual information, The Speech Recognition Application Programming Interface Committee—which includes IBM, Dragon, Kurzweil, and Philips Dictation Systems—also wants to develop a programming interface in order to standardize VR software. This programming interface will enable independent software developers to integrate VR technology into their applications. The committee plans to distribute this interface without royalties, according to B.G. Yovovich in *Business Marketing.*

Even though the VR technology of the mid-1990s appears advanced relative to previous technology where users had to pause after each word or train the software, it still requires substantial refinement. One of the preeminent voice recognition applications of 1997, NaturallySpeaking still made a few errors at a demonstration, tripping over common expressions such as "chiefs of staff," which it transcribed as "cheese of staff," according to *PC Magazine.* Moreover, analysts contend that technology that cannot deliver at least 95 percent accuracy is unacceptable to most users.

Fonix Corporation argues that the technology of the mid-1990s can advance voice recognition applications and devices no further. The statistical modeling procedures such as hidden Markov modeling may require replacement, according to Dr. Victor Zue, a researcher at MIT. Consequently, researchers have looked to artificial intelligence for answers, in particular, to neural networks that simulate the performance of the human brain and are capable of learning from exposure to language. VR researchers hope that neural nets can supplement or replace reliance on statistical models of speech-sound frequency. This technology should reduce the effects of age, pitch, volume, and dialect in speech recognition.

NEW APPLICATIONS

In the late 1990s, researchers applied voice recognition technology to the automobile in an effort to transform the car into a mobile office, replete with e-mail and Internet access that could be activated and operated via voice commands. VR-based applications as designed for cars would control computers, radios, cell phones, televisions, and other gadgets. Such voice recognition technology would additionally control a car's entertainment system. Delphi Automotive Systems' Network Vehicle and Microsoft's Auto PC along with systems from IBM and Clarion Corp. were scheduled for production before the year 2000.

Representatives of major airlines announced in 1998 that research into VR-based ticketing systems holds the promise of expediting passenger services. American Airlines and United Airlines, purportedly leaders in the implementation of such systems, indicated that systems were already in use but remained "schedule-driven," and required significant human intervention.

In 1998 *Telephony* reported a project by AT&T Labs to develop a prototype VR-based Chinese language translator. The development effort, in conjunction with the Chinese Academy of Sciences and ATR Interpreting Telecommunications Research of Japan, is based on an AT&T project that successfully translated English into Spanish. The success of the five-year China project holds promise for on-the-spot Chinese-to-English translations for tourists and business travelers in the orient. The technology could ease the performance of simple but crucial functions such as hailing a cab and ordering food.

FURTHER READING

"About Kurzweil AI." *Kurzweil Applied Intelligence, Inc. Home Page,* 15 April 1997. Available from http://www.kurzweil.com/company/.

Baldwin, Gary. *American Medical News,* 15 February 1999, 28.

Berinato, Scott. "Biometrics Tools Guard Network." *PC Week,* 14 April 1997, 6.

———. "Software Gets Voice Interface." *PC Week,* 21 October 1996, 27.

Brennan, Mike. "'Wired' Cars Are Coming." *Denver Post,* 28 February 1998, C1.

Cawkell, Tony. "Tracking Fast Moving Technology: The Progress of Speech Recognition." *Journal of Information Science,* January 1999, 79.

"Cheese of Staff." *PC Magazine,* 10 June 1997, 10.

Clark, Lindsay. "Businesses to Get Voice Boost with Pentium III." *Computer,* 11 March 1999, 39.

Computer Telephony Integration Makes Voice Processing More Affordable. Frost & Sullivan, 1997. Available from http://207.88.20.210/ns-search/.

"Corporate Milestones." *Dragon Systems, Inc. Home Page,* April 1997. Available from http://www.dragonsys.com/general/milestones.html.

Darwin, Jennifer. "Public Company Finds New Voice in Medical Transcription Business." *Houston Business Journal,* 26 February 1999, 6.

"Dragon Systems: Dragon NaturallySpeaking Selected for Two 1998 PC World World Class Awards." *Presswire,* 18 June 1998.

Flint, Perry. "Bigger Than the Internet? (Speech-Recognition Technology May Aid Airlines in Ticket Distribution)." *Air Transport World,* September 1998.

Foremski, Tom. "Speak Up to Access All Areas." *Computer,* 5 November 1998, 50.

Hickman, Angela. "The Web Finds Its Voice." *PC Magazine,* 1 December 1998, 29.

Hotch, Ripley. "Open the Pod Door, HAL." *Communications News,* March 1997, 54.

Markowitz, Judith. *Using Speech Recognition.* Upper Saddle River, NJ: Prentice Hall PTR, 1996.

Marshall, Jonathan. "When Computers Listen to You: Voice Recognition Systems Becoming More Sophisticated." *The San Francisco Chronicle,* 12 May 1998, C1.

Sechler, Bob. "Small-Stock Focus: Applied Voice Recognition Transforms itself to Catch Web Wave, But Technology Isn't Perfect." *Wall Street Journal,* 5 April 1999.

Shmelling, Sarah, "In Other Words . . . ." *Telephony,* 16 November 1998.

"Technology Overview." *Fonix Corporation Home Page,* 1997. Available from http://www.fonix.com/fonixtechnologies.html.

"Voice-Activated Software Progresses." *The Plain Dealer,* 8 December 1997, 6C.

Wallace, David G. "It Rights It Wrong." *Business Week,* 21 April 1997, 23.

"Web Talking." *PC,* 15 September 1998, 12.

Yovovich, B. G. "Technology Has Found New Voice." *Business Marketing,* July 1995, 3.

—Karl Heil, updated by Gloria Cooksey

WATER AND AIR FILTRATION AND PURIFICATION SYSTEMS

INDUSTRY SNAPSHOT

Concerns about environmental quality helped the residential water and air purification industries flourish during the late 1990s. To varying degrees, both industries exhibited characteristics of a new or suddenly vibrant market. They are both highly fragmented and comprised of a large number of small companies manufacturing and distributing across various product lines. As the century neared its close, however, each industry presented signs of a shaking out, with a few large companies developing a brand consciousness in the consumer market.

Both industries are growing at great rates. In the late 1990s, the water quality products industry was valued at $25 billion worldwide, including all forms of treatment, filtration, and purification. The U.S. home water purification market was valued at over $1 billion and continued to expand. According to a trade group, the market for residential drinking water treatment nearly doubled from 1990 to 1995. Sales of portable units targeted for use outside the home were estimated to be about $15 million, but growth in that niche was shrinking. By 2000, the U.S. water filter market was expected to reach $2.32 billion. The air quality products industry was also on an upward trend. Sales of air purifiers, including the fast-selling portable air cleaners, grew by more than 10 percent a year in the mid- to late 1990s.

In the late 1990s, both industries faced similar challenges. Each segment of the industry sold products that could be used either at a particular location in a home or throughout the whole house. Encouraging consumers to move from inexpensive entry-level purchases to whole-house purification systems was the

next challenge for these industries. Furthermore, each segment began introducing more sophisticated filtration devices in the late 1990s, each capable of removing more harmful substances than its predecessor. Through various educational marketing techniques, the industry hoped to make consumers aware of the benefits and advantages of these new products. Additionally, consumer awareness of both air and water quality issues, especially in the home, continues to rise, due in large part to new regulations requiring the disclosure of such information and the consumer's ability to have his or her own home tested for air and water purity.

ORGANIZATION AND STRUCTURE

Both the water and air purification industries are comprised of companies that produce finished units, component manufacturers, and assemblers of finished units. Products are sold to industrial and commercial users as well as to residential homeowners. Although the largest industry leaders maintain their own networks of dealers and distributors, the large majority of firms sell products directly to retail outlets for resale.

WATER QUALITY PRODUCTS INDUSTRY

Products sold by water industry participants include softeners, reverse osmosis units, ultraviolet units, distillation units, ozonators, carbon and noncarbon filters, filtration carafes, faucet-mounted models, countertop models, and personal filtration units. Components manufactured for those products include mineral tanks, valves, controllers, membranes, faucets, and filters. Retail operations in the industry generally have a high percentage of revenues—sometimes as high as 70 percent—derived from recurring sales of consumables such as servicing equipment, replacement parts, and filters.

Retailers and manufacturers in the water treatment industry are represented by the Water Quality Association (WQA). The WQA is a not-for-profit international trade organization founded in 1950. The agency counted 2,200 members, all corporate manufacturers and retailers. As reported by the survey, the purchaser of water quality products and components is usually a dealership or original equipment manufacturer. As in many industries, assemblers and component manufacturers who make finished units sell more units to dealerships than to original equipment manufacturers.

The water quality products industry is not regulated by a government agency. Typically, however, units are labeled for retail sale with indications of how fine a filtration or purification system has been installed. The National Sanitation Foundation International "Standard 42" indicates a filter equipped for handling aesthetic problems such as taste, smell, and appearance, while "Standard 53" indicates a filter equipped for handling basic health problems such as lead and organic compounds. Such filters normally indicate the specific contaminants they can handle. The most resistant filters—labeled as being certified "absolute one micron"—are those that can filter parasites.

The Environmental Protection Agency (EPA) did not regulate the manufacture or distribution of water-filter units in the late 1990s. However, EPA policies and guidelines, as well as statutes such as the Safe Drinking Water Act of 1974 have had a great impact on the industry. The Act contained water quality guidelines that many communities in the country failed to meet; the 1996 reauthorization of the Act made certain provisions more rigorous. Thus, while communities fail to meet federal water standards and the public grows more skeptical of the water it drinks, the water quality products industry benefits.

The Safe Drinking Water Act Amendment of 1996 was signed into law in August 1996. Congress overwhelmingly approved the bill, which authorized billions of dollars to improve deteriorating water systems. The funds represent a sharp increase in spending for water systems, both municipal and rural. The law also included a "right to know" provision that requires water authorities to disclose what chemicals and bacteria are in drinking water and requires public notice of any dangerous contaminants within 24-hours

of discovery. The bill also imposes a duty on the EPA to develop and apply more rigorous standards to fight cryptosporidium and other common drinking water contaminants posing significant health risks. Beginning in 1999, water utility companies were required to report what elements were found in their water. This information would allow consumers to make better choices when purchasing home water filtration products, and the responsibility placed on the EPA reflects a shift in federal policy away from identifying new pollutants toward controlling the most dangerous ones. The impact of the Act is difficult to predict; however, its passage reflects a growing discontent among Americans about the quality of water. That discontent makes itself felt in the booming sales figures for companies in the industry.

AIR QUALITY PRODUCTS INDUSTRY

The air quality products industry manufactures and markets air filters and purifiers for both whole-house applications and portable use. Within those two applications, there are three general types of air cleaners on the market: mechanical filters, electronic air cleaners, and ion generators.

Mechanical filters, which may be installed in whole-house or portable devices, are of two major types. The first type, known as flat or panel filters, normally consists of a dense medium, such as coarse glass fibers, animal hair, or synthetic fibers, which are then coated with a viscous substance such as oil to act as an adhesive for particulate material. Flat filters may also be made of "electret" media, which is comprised of a charged plastic film or fiber to which particles in the air are attracted. Although flat filters may collect large particles well, they remove only a small percentage of respirable-size particles.

The second type of mechanical filter is the pleated or extended surface filter. Due to its greater surface area, this type of filter generally attains greater efficiency for capture of respirable-size particles than do flat filters. This allows an increase in packing density without a significant drop in air flow rate.

In electronic air cleaners, an electrical field traps charged particles. Electronic air cleaners are usually electrostatic precipitators or charged-media filters. In electrostatic precipitators, particles are collected on a series of flat plates. In charged-media filter devices, the particles are collected on fibers in a filter. In most electrostatic precipitators, and some charged-media filters, the particles are ionized, or charged, before the collection process, resulting in a higher collection efficiency.

Like electronic air cleaners, ion generators use static charges to remove particles from indoor air. They act by charging the particles in a room, so they are attracted to walls, floors, or any surface. In some cases, these devices, which come in portable units only, contain a collector to attract the charged particles back to the unit. Both electronic air cleaners and ion generators can produce ozone. Some systems on the market are hybrid devices containing two or more of the particle removal devices.

The residential air quality products industry was also not regulated by a government agency in the late 1990s, nor has the government published any guidelines or standards for use in determining how well an air cleaner works in removing pollutants from indoor air. However, standards for rating particle removal by air cleaners, both whole-house and portable, are published by two private trade associations. The Association of Home Appliance Manufacturers developed an American National Standards Institute-approved standard for portable air cleaners. Whole-house systems can be analyzed by "Standard 52-761" of the American Society of Heating, Refrigerating & Air Conditioning Engineers (ASHRAE), a trade group. Both standards estimate the effectiveness of an air-cleaning device in removing particles from indoor air.

One difficulty facing consumers is that air filtration standards focus only on particle removal. No standards exist to assess the comparative ability of air filters and purifiers to remove gaseous pollutants or radon—contaminants of increasing concern in the late 1990s. The removal of gaseous materials from indoor air can only be accomplished in those units containing adsorbent or reactive materials.

Like the water quality products industry, the manufacture and sale of air quality products was on the upswing in the late 1990s. Both industries benefited from highly publicized findings of contaminants in homes and communities. However, the air quality industry began its sharp increase in the early 1990s, meaning fewer companies were in the market than in the water quality market.

Another major difference between the two industries lies in the perceived utility of the products themselves. While questions were raised as to whether the water quality of the vast majority of Americans is poor enough to require residential purification, testing typically showed that the products performed as advertised, reducing or eliminating the presence of various contaminants. As of the late 1990s, that question of effectiveness had not been answered for many air quality products. For example, by the end of the twentieth century, the EPA had not taken a position on the value of home air cleaners, despite its recognition of the ill effects of air pollution on human health. Further, while standards exist for the quality of indoor air, standards for the products themselves are often difficult to compare across product lines.

BACKGROUND AND DEVELOPMENT

The water and air filtration and purification industries manufacture and sell systems and supplies that counter the effects of pollution and naturally occurring contaminants. Those effects range from the unhealthy and deadly to the aesthetic. Both industries have targeted the commercial and industrial markets for years—markets that are scrutinized by the EPA and the general public. More recent concerns about the safety of drinking water and the purity of indoor residential air drove an upswing in the retail market for those products. Both industries grew from being dominated by a few large manufacturers focusing on industrial and commercial applications to highly fragmented industries comprised of dozens of manufacturers, retailers, and distributors. Most were small businesses, all of whom vied for what appeared to be America's almost limitless appetite for contaminant-free living.

PUBLIC CONCERNS ABOUT WATER QUALITY

In the late 1990s, the water purification industry was confronted with a public concerned about water quality and prepared to spend money to eliminate contaminants. A 1999 consumer survey commissioned by the Water Quality Association (WQA), a trade group, revealed that the American public was increasingly suspicious of the tap water entering homes. Survey responses showed that three-quarters of consumers had some concern about their household water supply, and one in five consumers was dissatisfied with the quality of their water supply; one in three consumers felt that the water was not as safe as it should be. Despite these concerns, only one in four consumers reported ever having the water tested for contamination.

Consumer knowledge about water quality issues did not appear to be widespread. Forty-seven percent of respondents said that they wished they knew more about their household water supply; however, 23 percent said that they did not know how to obtain information. The survey results point to continued robust growth for the water quality industry. Among all respondents, adults between the ages of 18 and 44 were the most likely to believe household water was unsafe. Those consumers also are the least likely to know where to turn for information about their water. Increased reporting of water quality calamities in the 1990s, joined with the growing ubiquity of water purification devices in retail outlets, certainly had a great effect upon this consumer group.

The American consumer market appeared to be largely untapped by the industry in the 1990s. The WQA survey showed that due to increasing health concerns, 62 percent of consumers were using some sort of water treatment device (household water treatment or table-top pitchers), compared to 53 percent in 1997. Thirty-eight percent of consumers used a household water treatment device, compared to 32 percent in 1997 and 27 percent in 1995. Sales of "entry-level" devices, such as pour-through water carafes with filters, grew more robustly than any other type of water treatment device. The boom in entry-level devices demonstrates that the industry's marketing target has been met.

The bottled water market in the United States acts as a gauge for Americans' concerns with water quality; the bottled water market grew at an average 11-percent rate over the 10-year period from 1984 to 1994. The wholesale market for U.S. bottled water (nonsparkling) in 1984 was valued at about $700 million; in 1994, that market was valued at almost $1.9 billion. In gallons, the industry grew from about 800 million gallons consumed in 1984 to almost 2.3 billion gallons in 1994. In 1998, the Coca Cola Company announced its intention of entering the bottled water market, marking the first entry onto the market of one of the soft drink giants.

The growth of entry-level sales also has repercussions in the location of retail purchases. While 29 percent of Americans making water quality purchases in 1997 still purchased home water treatment devices from local water treatment dealers, department and discount stores grew in popularity as the site of purchase. Up from 7 percent in 1995, sales of water quality products at those stores tripled to 21 percent. As the industry offered more inexpensive products that required little expertise to install or maintain, accessibility through general retail outlets became possible.

In 1999, use of water treatment systems was at an all-time high. For the first time, according to the Water Quality Association, use of these systems caught up with the use of bottled water, and two-thirds of consumers used either home treatment systems, bottled water, or both.

Growing distrust of the water supply may have been unfounded or overstated for the large majority of Americans in the 1990s. Most Americans receive water from a public water system where it has already been tested and treated under regulations derived from the Safe Drinking Water Act of 1974. Only those who get water from other sources, such as private wells or small water systems serving a relatively small number of customers, could not be as certain of the quality of their water. Still, well-publicized breakdowns of even the largest water systems cast uncertainty into the consumers' collective consciousness. For example, in the mid-1990s more than a dozen communities in the Midwest were informed that their tap water had heightened concentrations of a weed killer. More than 100 people were killed by the waterborne contaminant cryptosporidia in Milwaukee in 1993. Further, in 1996, Washington, D.C., residents were given a "boil order" to combat unsafe bacteria levels.

Adding to Americans' suspicions were widely publicized findings and studies. In the summer of 1997, for example, the U.S. Geological Survey (USGS) asked U.S. and Canadian residents to aid in the scientific investigation of deformed frogs, toads, and salamanders. Citizens were encouraged to report sightings of abnormal and malformed amphibians they saw while outdoors. Whether the deformities arose from waterborne contaminants, and whether those contaminants could affect human health, had not been determined; however, it was known that amphibians are highly sensitive to alterations in the aquatic environment.

The Centers for Disease Control and Prevention (CDC) in Atlanta estimates that 1 million people annually develop illnesses due to U.S. drinking water and that nearly 1,000 people die as a result. The EPA also found water supplies falling below federal guidelines. A profile from the 1994 National Water Quality Inventory Report to Congress claimed that about 40 percent of surveyed rivers, lakes, and estuaries were not clean enough for basic uses such as fishing or swimming.

One study performed in 1995 by the National Resource Defense Council (NRDC) found that the tap water entering 80 million American homes contained significant levels of cancer-causing chemicals. The study found unsafe levels of arsenic, radon, and trihalomethanes.

A 1996 study by the Environmental Working Group (EWG) and the NRDC, using data compiled by the EPA, found that one in six Americans got water from a utility that had recent pollution problems. To compile the report, EWG and NRDC analyzed more than 16 million records submitted by public water suppliers to the EPA and state water agencies. A major finding of the report was "More than 45 million Americans in thousands of communities were served drinking water during 1994-1995 that was polluted with fecal matter, parasites, disease-causing microbes, radiation, pesticides, toxic chemicals, and lead [when related to] standards established under the federal Safe Drinking Water Act." The report also claimed that, during 1994 and 1995, more than 18,500 public water supplies reported at least one violation of a federal drinking water standard. Although the report received harsh criticism from water utilities and industry groups such as the American Water Works Association, it was widely publicized—and studied by Congress since it debated amendments to the Safe Drinking Water Act. The records were gathered in the Safe Drinking Water Information System, a computer database.

NATIONWIDE RESPONSES TO WATER QUALITY CONCERNS

American concerns about water quality were reflected in the actions of elected representatives. In October 1996, President Clinton announced an environmental initiative that allocated $45 million over 4 years for the U.S. Geological Survey to extend water quality testing to 75 cities, which increased the examining of 35 river basins and groundwater systems. The initiative also made data collected on the major rivers, water-supply watersheds, and drinking water wells available to the public on the Internet. Through the USGS Water Resources Data Web site, consumers can get real-time water data from 3,000 stations throughout the United States, daily streamflow reports from the National Water Information System, and records from the Water Quality Monitoring Network.

In addition, the amendment to the Safe Drinking Water Act of 1974, the Safe Drinking Water Act Amendment of 1996, created a revolving loan fund that will aid states in rebuilding and maintaining deteriorating water systems. That federal effort provided funds where the American public could see it in the form of a proposed budget giving every state at least $7 million. Up to $9.6 billion was authorized to be paid out to the states through the year 2003. Since fiscal 1994, President Clinton proposed $3 billion for that purpose in his budget requests; his administration's 1998 budget included $725 million earmarked to that end. States to receive the largest allocations are California, at $77 million; Texas, at $54 million; New

York, at $45 million; Massachusetts, at $27 million; and Illinois, at $25 million.

DETERIORATING AIR QUALITY

While the market for residential air cleaning products was already substantial and continued to grow in the late 1990s, fewer than 10 companies manufactured and marketed such products. With indoor air quality on the decline, however, that number was expected to increase, due in no small part to the well-publicized findings of agencies and scientists nationwide.

As the twentieth century draws to a close, scientific experiments detected a reliable connection between human health problems and dirty air. Epidemiologists estimate that the annual U.S. death toll from air pollution is 50,000—resulting from heart disease, asthma, bronchitis, stroke, and similar conditions. Faced with these figures, in 1977 the EPA proposed strengthening air pollution standards. The most comprehensive air pollution legislation is the Clean Air Act Amendment of 1970. Despite this law, approximately 121 million Americans live in areas where the air falls below health standards.

According to the EPA, the average American spends roughly 90 percent of his or her time indoors, where the air is more polluted than the outdoor air in even the largest and most industrialized cities. In the 1990s, the EPA called indoor air pollution one of the country's top five environmental issues. In 1998, the EPA estimated that more than 50 percent of homes and offices suffer from highly polluted indoor air. The agency estimates that such pollution costs Americans tens of billions of dollars a year in direct medical expenses and lost productivity. An estimated one in five Americans suffered allergy-related illness at some point during their lives, with indoor allergens responsible for a substantial number of those cases. Because of this, in 1993 the Institute of Medicine of the National Academy of Sciences urged a comprehensive effort to clean up the air in America's homes, schools, and businesses.

More findings in the 1990s made indoor air quality appear grim and in need of immediate relief. Along with AIDS and tuberculosis, asthma is one of the three chronic diseases with an increasing mortality rate. The National Institutes of Health call allergic disease one of America's most common and expensive health problems. Asthma and allergies alone cause over 130 million lost school days and 13.5 million lost work days each year. Further, indoor allergens are blamed for much of the acute asthma in adults under the age of 50, according to the National Academy of Science.

Amid such well-publicized breakdowns in air quality, the residential air products industry is expected to thrive. To do so, however, it must overcome certain concerns about its products as well as a less tangibly fouled medium than the one repaired by the water quality industry.

Air purifier sales did climb 11 percent in 1996 to $340 million, marking five years of consecutive sales growth, according to *HFN*. Retail sales accounted for the majority of the revenues at $275 million, while alternative distribution channels accounted for $65 million. Overall, the industry sold about 3.2 million units. Nonetheless, the industry's growth remained behind some projections that predicted revenues would expand by 30 to 40 percent in 1996. Still, some analysts believed air purifiers were among the most profitable small appliances since they have a 40-percent profit margin, according to *HFN*.

CURRENT CONDITIONS

WATER PRODUCTS SALES GROWTH

The 1990s saw phenomenal growth in the water quality products industry, and the upswing appeared to continue unabated as a new century begins. The public's concerns about water quality and aesthetics were widely held and widely publicized in the 1990s, and its willingness to purchase items claiming to rectify the problems at the spigot and throughout the house was on the rise. All types of water quality devices saw sales increases in that period; not surprisingly, more inexpensive entry-level products saw the greatest sales boom. Just as telling, consumers across all income brackets were more willing to purchase water quality equipment for the home. Water filter penetration increased from 27 percent in 1995 to 32 percent in 1997 to 38 percent in 1999, according to the National Consumer Water Quality Survey. Even with this growth, the industry still has plenty of room for expansion. Consequently, the outlook for water filtration devices remains bright, and *HFN* reported that about 20 percent of the U.S. population without water filters plans to purchase some kind of filtration device.

Predictions for growth in the water treatment industry were optimistic in the late 1990s. Revenue for residential water treatment products and systems, excluding bottled water sales, was valued at $1.01 billion in 1990. By the mid-1990s, that figure was $1.38 billion and was predicted to reach $2.32 billion by the year 2000.

The most significant legislation poised to have an effect on the water quality industry is the Safe Drinking Water Act Amendment of 1996. The Amendment applies more rigorous standards to drinking water sources and will pour billions of dollars into states to fund programs to improve local drinking water for the public. A large beneficiary of this was expected to be Culligan Water Technologies, the largest manufacturer of water purification and treatment products. The monetary benefits of the Amendment are expected to have an important impact on the industry as a whole as more money is available and public education on drinking water problems rise.

Another significant development in the industry is the growing availability of products for retail sale outside of locations normally associated with water treatment. As entry-level products are created and increased competition drives some prices down, more product niches will be marketed through department stores and other chain outlets. In 1997, a major hardware chain announced that it would carry a major brand of water testing kit that consumers could use themselves. The test is recommended to be performed up to four times per year depending on the source of water and the health needs of the individual.

In the late 1990s, the cost of water purification units varied greatly by method. The most inexpensive alternative, the carafe models, were priced from about $20 to $30, with some low-end models starting around $7. The pour-through model remained the fastest growing and best selling water filtration device in the late 1990s. The cost for filters ran from 50 cents to about $12. Faucet-mounted models, easily installed by the homeowner, had a cost from $15 to $55; replacement filters cost $10 to $15. Countertop models, attached to the faucet, cost anywhere from $40 to $300; filters for these ran as high as $95. The faucet model grew quickly in the late 1990s, accounting for 20 percent of all water filters sold. Culligan recently announced its plans to reintroduce its dual-filtration faucet-mounted models, which range in price from $24.99 to $39.99. These units guarantee that the levels of bacteria leaving the unit will not exceed the level of bacteria in the tap water as it enters the filter. Bacteria have actually been shown to multiply in household water systems, but this filter prevents that from occurring. These filters were introduced to limited markets in 1997, but improved marketing strategies have Culligan officials optimistic that the filters will be big sellers. Under-sink models, using 2 or 3 filter cartridges in a series and plumbed into the cold-water line, cost $45 to $500; filters ran from $11 to $100. Under-sink reverse osmosis models were very effective against a wide range of contaminants. They cost anywhere from $150 to over $1,000, and filters ran as high as $165.

With the strong penetration of pitcher water filters, manufacturers began to develop and launch new products with greater filtration capabilities and features in the late 1990s. Manufacturers created the new breed of water filters—removing more harmful microorganisms such as cryptosporidium, giardia, and cysts—to be portable and to monitor filter life electronically. For example, new portable filtration bottles have recently been introduced into the market. These units contain a filter, secured inside the top of the bottle, which improves taste and cuts down on odor and removes virtually all chlorine (99.8 percent), microscopic pathogens that cause gastro-intestinal illness, detergents, pesticides, industrial and agricultural wastes, and heavy metals. The 30 ounce bottles will filter 200 gallons, or more than 1,000 refills. Seychelle Environmental Technologies, Inc., makers of the bottle, predict sales of 175,000 units during the first 6 months on the market.

CONSUMER ACCEPTANCE OF AIR QUALITY PRODUCTS

In late 1997, a Riedl Marketing Group study indicated that approximately 15 percent of all U.S. households have some kind of air purification device. The study also found that 20 percent of the respondents without one expressed some interest in purchasing an air cleaner in 1998. Growth in the industry in the late 1990s was primarily in the portable market. Variety among portable machines grew greatly at that time, however, as consumers demanded larger and more powerful units. Thus, the general trend in the market at that time was toward larger, console-sized models. Because installation of a whole-house unit requires great expense and retrofitting of air-flow sources, consumers appeared to want to solve air quality problems room-by-room with the largest units available.

In the late 1990s, one indicator of the public's growing disenchantment with its indoor air could be seen in a battle of standards over the air in commercial establishments. Commercial indoor air quality is set by local code, often adopted from guidelines set out by the American Society of Heating, Refrigerating & Air Conditioning Engineers (ASHRAE). In 1997, ASHRAE proposed a new industry standard for ventilation. Its proposal carried great weight because its existing standard had become the most widely used and cited document for indoor air quality. The pro-

posals by ASHRAE were far more rigorous and far-ranging than those in place before. Of course, those standards, if adopted, will have no effect on residential air quality or products sold to consumers. However, the significant strengthening of the guidelines gave an indication of the changes occurring on air issues; Americans find indoor air quality unacceptable and are prepared to pay greatly to improve their commercial and residential environments.

A major issue facing some manufacturers of air quality products in the late 1990s was the creation of ozone, a lung irritant, in certain products, either as a deliberate step to aid in air cleaning or as a byproduct of the purification. In the late 1990s, the EPA was studying whether some products produced new pollutants or dispersed old ones. At least two manufacturers of portable units advertised that their products produced ozone to aid in removal of harmful gases; the EPA had not yet determined the possible health effects. Consumer confusion on the issue was high. For example, some marketing materials for products noted, without further explanation, that ozone is simply super-pure oxygen that occurs naturally on the planet. Certain advertising materials even compared the inhalation of ozone from a residential air purifier to the invigoration one feels after drinking water downstream from a waterfall.

Another technological concern for the industry was with studies showing that some electronic air cleaners themselves produce fine particulate material, or that filters and other devices remove particles from the environment and then re-emit gases and odors from the collected particles. In addition, some materials used in the manufacturing of air cleaners may themselves emit chemicals into indoor air; for example, formaldehyde may be emitted if particle board is used in the air cleaner housing. Another technological hurdle facing the air quality products industry in the late 1990s was many units' inability to remove certain odors, primarily cigarette odor, from indoor environments. While most models are able to remove the particles from smoke, most are unable to remove the gaseous elements of cigarette residue. Some units are designed to scent the air, leading homeowners to believe the odor has been eradicated. Ion generators also generated concern; studies showed a correlation between them and a heightened deposit of particles in the human lung.

Two new air quality products on the horizon may prove to further increase sales in the market. In late 1998, Clean Air Systems installed filtration modules designed to eliminate cigarette smoke at Richmond International Airport. These filter modules operate by filtering out smoke, particles, and gases while returning clean air to the immediate environment. These filters are twice as efficient as current filtration devices in absorbing 13 different chemical compounds found in cigarette smoke. Also in 1998, Environmental Elements Corporation was contracted by the EPA to develop a sterilizing filter capable of filtering more than 99 percent of microorganisms, including those which cause tuberculosis and Legionnaire's Disease. This filter would enhance the collection and destruction of such microorganisms that along with inorganic particles, contribute heavily to indoor air pollution. These new units will use electrically-created plasma, which effectively destroys microorganisms without using chemicals or heat. Medical facilities, especially hospitals, would greatly benefit from such technology.

INDUSTRY LEADERS

WATER QUALITY INDUSTRY

In the late 1990s, one company, Culligan Water Technologies, led the water purification and filtration industry and was followed at a long distance by other establishments that carved out portions of the market in particular product niches. Culligan Water Technologies, of Northbrook, Illinois, is a subsidiary of Astrum International Corporation. The company had net sales of $507.5 million for the fiscal year ending January 31, 1999, an increase of 36.3 percent over the previous year. Culligan manufactures water purification and treatment products for household, commercial, and industrial use. The company's products and services range from filters for tap water and household water softeners to advanced equipment and services for commercial and industrial applications. Culligan provides services in over 90 countries worldwide through a network of 1,400 sales and service centers.

Supporting its distribution network, Culligan maintains manufacturing facilities in the United States, Italy, Spain, and Canada. In the late 1990s, over a third of Culligan's revenues were from export and international sales. In addition, Culligan's licensed bottled water sales ranked fourth in the five-gallon bottled water market in the United States. In 1997, the company entered the consumer market selling filtration products directly to retailers. Culligan has been active in the water purification and treatment industry since 1936, and its brands are among the most recognized. Since the early 1980s, Culligan's residential water treatment systems have been installed in more than 3 million households in the United States, representing the largest installed base in the country, ac-

cording to the company. In 1988, Culligan became the first company to be certified by the independent National Sanitation Foundation under its standard for residential reverse osmosis drinking water systems.

As part of its distribution system, the company owns 26 Culligan dealers in North America, which had total revenues of approximately $70.5 million in 1997. The company-owned dealers are primarily located in major metropolitan markets, such as New York City, Los Angeles, Chicago, Houston, San Diego, and San Francisco. Since the beginning of 1997, the company-owned Dealer division made 11 acquisitions with aggregate revenues of over $19 million.

In 1997, Culligan created its new Consumer Market Division, which, through partnerships with other companies, sought quick access to niches of the retail market. The first products introduced by the division were faucet-mounted filters, which are sold through department stores. The division expanded its product line by aiming at the do-it-yourself market, selling under-counter systems, refrigerator water/ice maker filter systems, and a sediment and rust reduction whole-house filtration system. The Division also announced the introduction of a designer, glass-pitcher filtration system and two monitored faucet-mount systems. In 1997, Culligan entered into a marketing partnership with Health-O-Meter Products, Inc., the parent of Mr. Coffee, for plastic pour-through pitchers, with a major appliance manufacturer to provide a refrigerator water/ice maker filtration system, and a long-term agreement with Moen Inc. to develop Moen products incorporating Culligan water filtration assemblies.

Through its Everpure subsidiary, Culligan also markets point-of-use filtration systems for homes and recreational vehicles such as Winnebago, Fleetwood, and Airstream. In 1997, Culligan Water Technologies merged with Ametek Inc. of Paoli, Pennsylvania, a global manufacturer of electrical and electromechanical products and a producer of parts for the residential water treatment market.

Kinetico Inc. of Newbury, Ohio, was a leader in the production of under-counter reverse osmosis models in the late 1990s with approximate sales of $32 million. The privately held company employs 200 people and makes a line of products including a countertop filter model. Kinetico evolved from the Tangent Company, a small consulting design firm, eventually becoming a global organization of independent dealers, international distributors, and manufacturer representatives in more than 60 countries. The company uses a ceramic filter media developed by 3M Co., which Kinetico claims has proven very effective in the removal of microorganisms from water. Because of the success of the ceramic filter, Kinetico now uses it in many of its applications, including residential, commercial, and industrial products.

Another leader in the 1990s was Allegheny Teledyne Inc., the result of the merger between Teledyne Water Pik of Fort Collins, Colorado, and Allegheny Ludlum of Pittsburgh, Pennsylvania. With approximate annual sales of $3.9 billion in 1998, the company markets various products including a carafe model, a faucet-mounted model, and an under-sink model, as well as air purifiers in addition to its steel, industrial, and aerospace products. Allegheny Teledyne Inc. employs 21,500 people, an increase of 2.3 percent over 1997. The company's consumer division accounted for 7 percent of its overall revenues.

With more than 70 years of experience, privately held EcoWater Systems Inc. claims to be the oldest and largest manufacturer of residential water treatment equipment in the world. The firm, headquartered in Woodbury, Minnesota, is a composite of three former companies. One of these, the Lindsay Company, obtained the first patent for water conditioning in 1925. The Lindsay Company pioneered several industry firsts, such as automatic controls, high-capacity resin, console units, iron-free systems, and rust-proof fiberglass tanks. Lindsay became a member of the Marmon Group of companies in 1981 and, in 1983, purchased two other firms, after which the company was renamed EcoWater Systems in 1988. EcoWater is registered to the ISO 9001 Standard for Quality Systems and distributes its products through more than 1,400 independent water treatment dealers in the United States, Canada, Europe, Asia, and Africa. The parent company had sales of an estimated $6.03 billion in 1998.

Brita, manufactured by the Clorox Corporation of Oakland, California, was a leader in the countertop carafe market during the 1990s. The Brita unit is the most visibly successful of the carafe units and established an early lead in the brand-recognition battle. *HFN* reported that Brita controlled 60 percent of the water filter market by the late 1990s.

Aqua Care Systems, Inc., of Coral Springs, Florida, designs, manufactures, and markets filtration and water purification systems under subsidiaries KISS, Di-Tech Systems, and Midwest Water Technologies. Sales in 1998 topped $26.5 million, a one-year sales growth of 10.9 percent.

The booming water purification market also served to lure large companies known more for their expertise in other areas. Entering the water treatment

market in the late 1990s were appliance giant General Electric (GE) and Honeywell Inc., maker of thermostats and control products. GE officials expected water-softening and water-filtration products to become a $500-million business within five years. The company's new line was expected to include water-filtration and water-softening products, which the company called "SmartWater." According to GE, these systems allow homeowners to adjust the softness of the water throughout the home. Benefits, GE said, include prolonged life of water-using appliances and plumbing, cleaner dishes and clothing, and increased water-heater efficiency. The entrance of Honeywell Inc. into the water-purification market in 1997 was signaled by its purchase of Filtercold Inc., a small Arizona-based maker of water-purification systems with between $5 and $10 million in annual sales.

AIR QUALITY INDUSTRY

Honeywell Inc. was the leader in the air quality products industry in the late 1990s. Its Home and Building Control division is the division that manufactures and markets air quality systems. Sales for the division in 1998 were $3.4 billion. The company expanded its product line in 1996 with its acquisition of the Duracraft Corporation of Southborough, Massachusetts, a company with annual sales of about $180 million. The following year, Honeywell's Home and Building Control division also bought Phoenix Controls Corporation, which specializes in precision airflow systems. Total sales for Honeywell Inc. topped $8.4 billion for 1998, placing Honeywell at number 193 in the Fortune 500. They employed 57,000 people in 1998, an increase of 0.9 percent over 1997.

Other leaders in the industry include the Carrier Corporation of Farmington, Connecticut, a subsidiary of United Technologies Corp., and the Research Products Corporation of Madison, Wisconsin. Research Products employed 300 in the late 1990s with annual sales of $25 million.

AMERICA AND THE WORLD

WATER PRODUCTS SALES GROW ABROAD

The water purification industry has an international scope, in no small part due to the questionable quality of water worldwide. Sales of water purification products to the international community have grown. In 1994, 53 percent of industry members reported that more than 15 percent of revenues were derived from foreign sales. In addition, companies predict that foreign exports will continue to increase. In 1997, the Water Quality Association reported that approximately 44 percent of its members had a sales office outside the United States. Fifty-six percent indicated that they would acquire new or add to existing facilities outside the United States in the late 1990s. Even relatively small companies (those with revenues of less than $2 million annually) indicate they will open a sales office offshore.

AIR QUALITY PRODUCTS OVERSEAS

The air purification industry is expected to make large strides overseas as a new century begins. As America toiled to adhere to ever-increasing federal regulations on air pollution, nations around the world struggle with far worse pollution. Companies that focus on commercial applications of air filtration and purification equipment are expected to do the best overseas. Those firms concentrating on the residential market are expected to do well also, especially in nations with a burgeoning middle class.

RESEARCH AND TECHNOLOGY

WATER QUALITY INDUSTRY

In the late 1990s, research developments in the water purification industry ranged from the simple to the highly complex. All capitalized on America's fear of the water it drinks. On a local level, research that aided drinking water came from watershed management, which helped to keep water clean before becoming polluted. One example was in New York's purification of its water supply by microorganisms as the water percolated through the soil of the Catskills. Any municipality doubting the economic value of prevention rather than cure could look to New York's example: The city planned to spend $660 million to preserve that watershed; the alternative, a water treatment plant, would have cost $4 billion to build. On a national level, watershed management and source water protection was made a part of national policy in the Safe Drinking Water Act Amendment of 1996. The Amendment created a revolving fund that would aid states in keeping water supplies in good condition.

More high-technology research came from scientists with the Ernest Orlando Lawrence Berkeley National Laboratory (Berkeley Lab). Dr. Ashok Gadgil's UV Waterworks is a simple device that uses ultraviolet light to safely and cheaply disinfect water of the viruses and bacteria that causes cholera, typhoid,

dysentery, and other deadly diarrheal diseases. The strength of UV Waterworks lies in its differences from other ultraviolet-based water purifiers. The new system does not require pressurized water-delivery systems and electrical outlets to work. It uses gravity for water flow, allowing it to be used with any source of water; in addition, it only needs electricity for the UV light, which means it can be powered by a solar cell or a car battery. This ease of use offers a remarkably practical means of providing communities in developing nations with readily accessible supplies of safe drinking water.

In the UV system, passing water through the light inactivates the DNA of pathogens and purifies the water. The cost is estimated at about two cents per ton. It disinfects water at the rate of four gallons per minute, similar to the flow from a bathtub spout. In the late 1990s, a pilot project was being conducted in India; another was proposed for South Africa. Licensing of the technology is expected by EEG Inc. of Chicago; the company will have worldwide rights to the product except in India, where Urminus Industries Ltd. of Bombay holds the rights.

Another research development led to the addition of iodine to water to disinfect as well as purify. One Florida company, Pure H2O Bio-Technologies, notes that the addition of iodine leads to a higher "kill" rate for bacterial pathogens, which can cause a number of diseases such as cholera and cryptosporidiosis. Similar to chlorine in its ability to destroy microorganisms, iodine cannot react with organic compounds to produce any carcinogens. The heightened effectiveness against pathogens can be of some value to the average water drinker, but it can be a matter of life-and-death for those with impaired immune systems, such as AIDS or cancer patients.

AIR QUALITY INDUSTRY

In the late 1990s, interest was renewed in ultraviolet (UV) light technology for the control of bioaerosols, a general name for microbial contaminants including fungi, bacteria, and viruses. These contaminants (and byproducts) cause a wide range of adverse health effects ranging from mild effects such as headaches and fatigue to serious illnesses such as asthma and Legionnaire's disease. Because exposure to UV radiation can adversely affect health, the technology formerly was not widely accepted. In addition, cold temperatures and high air velocity can harm UV lamps. Research in the late 1990s suggests that the high intensity of UV lamps can be maintained in hostile environments. Thus, the technology can be used in mechanical ventilation systems, especially in whole-building cleaning.

FURTHER READING

"About Kinetico Incorporated." Newbury, Oh: Kinetico Quality Water Systems, 1999. Available from http://www.kinetico.com.

"Air Filtration Modules Let Smokers 'Indulge'." *Air Conditioning, Heating, & Refrigeration News,* 3 August 1998.

"Aqua Care Systems, Inc. Announces First Quarter Profit." *PR Newswire,* 13 April 1999.

Blackwood, Francy. "Exporting Clean Air Imports Millions in Revenues." *San Francisco Business Times,* 17 March 1997.

Censky, Peter. "Thirst for Clean Water Boosts Water-Filter Products." *Appliance,* January 1999.

"Clearing the Air in Bay Area Workplaces." *Tampa Bay Business Journal,* 28 October 1996.

"Consumer Use of Household Water Treatment at an All-Time High as Americans Remain Concerned About Quality." Lisle, IL: Water Quality Association, 16 March 1999.

Desilver, Drew. "Honeywell Plans to Increase Retail Focus." *Minneapolis/St. Paul City Business Journal,* 30 December 1996.

Dinell, David. "Vornado Targets Allergy Market with New Product." *San Francisco Business Journal,* 14 April 1997.

Eckhouse, Kim. "Culligan Expands Dual-Filtration Faucet-Mount Systems." *HFN,* 16 November 1998.

Eckhouse, Kim. "Next Level in Water Filtration." *HFN,* 19 January 1998.

"EcoWater Profile." Woodbury, MN: EcoWater Systems Inc., 1999. Available from http://www.ecowater.com.

"Environmental Elements Receives Indoor Air Filtration Research Contract from EPA." *PR Newswire,* 24 August 1998.

Ghahremani, Yasmin. "Troubled Waters in U.S. Homes: Study Says We're Drinking Cancer-Causing Chemicals." *CNN News,* 28 October 1995. Available from http://cnn.com/EARTH/9510/tap_water/index.html.

"Global Decline in Water Quality a Serious Problem, Say Researchers." *U.S. Water News Online,* July 1996. Available from http://www.uswaternews.com/archive/96/quality/declwatq.html.

Hamilton, Martha M. "Liquid Assets, Pure and Simple; Bottled, Filtered or Treated, Water Products Tap a Big Market." *The Washington Post,* 14 September 1996.

Hanania, Joseph. "Liquid Asset; The Right Filtration System Could Turn Your Hard Water Into Pure Pleasure." *Los Angeles Times,* 13 May 1997.

Hoover's Online. Austin, TX: The Reference Press, 1999. Available from http://www.hoovers.com.

Kerrigan, Karen. "Cleaning Up Indoor Air Carries Big Price Tag." *Washington Business Journal,* 11 November 1996.

Liu, Rea-Ting. "Cleaning the Air: Air-Cleaning Systems Find Wider Applications in Today's Facilities." Trade Press Publishing Corporation, 1997. Available from http://www.facilitiesnet.com/NS/NS3m7bb.html.

McLean, Bethany. "An Urge to Merge." *Fortune,* 13 January 1997.

McLoughlin, Bill. "Walking on Air." *HFN,* 24 November 1997.

Miller, Susan. "Filtration Firm as Pure Motives for IPO." *South Florida Business Journal,* 14 October 1996.

Murphy, H. Lee. "Culligan Moves Into Purifiers." *Advertising Age,* 1 July 1996.

O'Brien, Timothy L. "Rising Demand Buoys Water-Filter Makers." *Wall Street Journal,* 24 January 1994.

Patton, Carol. "Ametek Moves to Sharpen Its Edge." *Philadelphia Business Journal,* 19 May 1997.

Pinches, Kate. "Water-Filter Pitchers Offer Low-Cost Convenience." *Home Improvement Market,* January 1998.

"President Clinton to Increase Water Quality Monitoring." *U.S. Water News Online,* October 1996. Available from http://www.uswaternews.com/archive/96/quality/waterqual.html.

Redding, Rick. "GE Appliances Introduces Line of Water-Treatment Systems." *Business First,* 21 April 1997.

Romano, Jay. "Straining the Quality of Water." *The New York Times,* 10 November 1996.

"Safe Drinking Water Act Signed into Law." *U.S. Water News Online,* September 1996. Available from http://www.uswaternews.com/archive/96/policy/sdwalaw.html.

"S.E.C. Registration Statement Under the Securities Act of 1933, Culligan Water Technologies," 27 June 1997. Available from http://www.sec.gov/Archives/edgar/data/945382/0000950130-97-002994.txt.

Sellers, Pamela. "Air's Still Rising." *HFN,* 17 March 1997.

"Seychelle Introduces Revolutionary 'Bottom's UP' Filtration Bottle Nationwide." *PR Newswire,* 14 September 1998.

"Should You Use a Water Filter?" *Consumer Reports,* July 1997.

Stevens, William K. "How Much Is Nature Worth? For You, $33 Trillion." *The New York Times,* 20 May 1997.

"Study Raises Concerns Over Water Quality, Changes in Safe Drinking Water Act." *U.S. Water News Online,* June 1996. Available from http://www.uswaternews.com/archive/96/quality/sdwastdy.html.

"USGS Asks Public to Report Sightings of Deformed Frogs, Salamanders." *U.S. Water News Online,* July 1997. Available from http://www.uswaternews.com/archive/97/quality/usgask7.html.

"USGS—Water Resources Data." Reston, VA: U.S. Geological Survey, 1999. Available from http://h2o.er.usgs.gov/data.html.

"Vice President Releases State-by-State Safe Drinking Water Allocation Figures." *U.S. Water News Online,* July 1997. Available from http://www.uswaternews.com/archive/97/quality/vicpre7.html.

"Vital Living Products, Inc. D/B/A American Water Service Announces the Launch of Purtest Water Test at Participating Ace Hardware Stores." *PR Newswire,* 20 June 1997.

"Water Filtration Pouring in Sales." *HFN,* 13 April 1998.

Water Quality Association. *1997 National Consumer Water Quality Survey.* Lisle, IL: Water Quality Association, 1997.

———. *Statistical and Market Data: Point-Of-Use/Point-Of-Entry Water Quality Improvement Industry.* Lisle, IL: Water Quality Association, 1996.

Webber, Maura. "Concerns Over Water Quality Key to Firm's Prosperity." *Philadelphia Business Journal,* 11 November 1996.

Yarris, Lynn. "Berkeley Lab Scientists Win Two Discover Awards." Berkeley, CA: Ernest Orlando Lawrence Berkeley National Laboratory, 3 June 1996. Available from http://www.lbl.gov/Science-Articles/Archive/Discover-awards.html.

—Tim Eigo,
updated by Jeff Motluck and Wendy Mason

WEB DEVELOPERS

As Internet use expanded into mainstream society in the mid- to late 1990s, businesses and organizations realized that they could take advantage of the World Wide Web, using it as a means of promoting their products and services. Individuals also started creating Web pages for professional and recreational purposes; however, with the relatively high cost of Web design services, companies and organizations make up the largest segment of Web development market. Forrester Research Inc. reported that Web sites ranged in price from under $200,000 for a promotional site to $3.4 million for an online shopping site during the late 1990s. Simple home pages cost considerably less. Development fees depend on the size and features of the Web site. The average Web site ran $267,000 in the late 1990s, according to Forrester Research. In 1998, the industry's revenues totaled about $3 billion and by 2002 revenues are slated to reach $20 billion, according to International Data Corporation.

Although creating a Web site with minimal graphics and features requires little technical skill, more advanced, eye-catching pages benefit from knowledge of Internet programming languages such as HyperText Markup Language (HTML), Java, as well as new Web-design technologies. Therefore, numerous companies began offering Web site development services in the mid- to late 1990s. Forrester Research reported that there were about 40,000 Web developers in 1998. Some businesses focus exclusively on creating and hosting Web sites, whereas others offer it as a specialty service, hoping to cash in on the demand for Internet presence in addition to their other lines of work. The majority of dedicated Web developers are small businesses and a large share are single-person and home-based operations.

ORGANIZATION AND STRUCTURE

Generally, the goal of a Web site is to combine optimal functionality with a unique and stimulating visual display. To achieve this, clients must clearly inform developers of what purposes their Web sites will serve and what features and information they should include. In return, developers must indicate what they can accomplish given their tools and the current state of technology so that clients do not expect more than developers can reasonably deliver.

Once the site is developed, the developer may take on the role of a Web site custodian, often called a Webmaster, depending on the contract and on the content of the Web site. If a company or organization wishes to keep its site up-to-date, then such a service is indispensable, whether performed by the developer, a third-party maintenance service, or the client itself.

Ownership of the Web site or its parts also depends on the contract between the developer and client. Some developers retain rights to Web pages and their graphics, but many clients prefer to own the copyright themselves. Ownership can be ambiguous if not negotiated in advance since most sites include content and ideas provided by the client, but encoded and implanted by the developer. Hardware to support the site is usually a separate matter, often provided by third-party hosts. Very little legislation existed entering the late 1990s to guide clients and Web developers in these matters, so both parties eagerly await laws that will help avoid litigation stemming from ownership disputes.

Besides commissioning a Web site or purchasing it outright, organizations have two other options: renting a site or paying an initial fee and sharing the revenues the site generates. Renting is an economical method of getting on the Internet for companies with limited budgets, or companies looking to test the efficacy of having a Web site. Retailers planning to use Web sites for online commerce could benefit from paying a development fee, which may start at about $20,000, and then paying a percentage of its revenues to the developers. The latter option offers the client shared risk if the site fails to draw many sales.

While one developer can design simple Web sites consisting of a few pages, generally a whole team of Web developers must undertake the design of more complex sites such as online stores or magazines. When working on larger projects, developers usually divide up the labor by allocating specific tasks to specific developers: one developer composes graphics, another codes the functional aspects, and yet another prepares the encoded text. Furthermore, a project manager often coordinates and oversees the entire production of Web sites.

When creating a Web site, a developer typically uses HTML codes for the basic layout of the site. HTML codes indicate how the information should appear in a browser: centered, boldfaced, colored, and so forth. Each style feature is separately coded. For graphics, developers can place digital photographs and images on pages with HTML codes referencing the external graphics files. Dynamic Internet graphics can be developed through programming languages such as Sun Microsystems' Java or Microsoft's ActiveX. These languages allow the creation of active image applications—or applets—ones that rotate or change their form. Advanced Web-authoring tools aid Web site development by allowing developers to use other programming languages such as Visual Basic or C++, or by automating parts of the design process such as writing complex strings of commonly used HTML codes. For instance, a development tool might allow the designer to create a document using standard word processing techniques, which it converts to HTML. Leading software companies like Microsoft, International Business Machines Corp., and Adobe Systems Inc. all provide Web site development tools for professional and novice developers. However, as David Bicknell noted in *Computer Weekly,* many Web developers still find these tools cumbersome because they lack extensive support of HTML commands and contain circuitous editing interfaces. Instead, these de-velopers prefer simple text editors such as Microsoft's Notepad and Word Internet Assistant, according to Bicknell.

In 1995, as Web site development began to flourish as an industry, Kyle Shannon, co-founder of the Web-design firm Agency.Com Ltd., started the World Wide Web Artists Consortium (WWWAC) to serve the needs and interests of Web site developers. In 1996, the WWWAC had 500 members. The organization's focal points include advertising, digital imaging and graphics, electronic commerce, Internet law, and database integration.

The Internet Engineering Task Force (IETF) functions as an organization of vendors, designers, operators, and researchers concerned with the progress of Internet operation and development. Founded in 1986, the IETF consists of a series of work groups responsible for various aspects of Internet operation and architecture. The organization also played a key role in the development of Internet standards, but in 1996 the IETF ceded this responsibility because companies such as Netscape Communications Corp. and Microsoft Corp. continued to advance their Internet browser technology in different directions despite IETF standards, thereby launching mutually incompatible technology for browsing the World Wide Web. In 1996, the World Wide Web Consortium (W3C), an international group of Internet researchers—with the backing of both Netscape and Microsoft—started to assume responsibility for developing HTML and Web-authoring standards. With support from influential software manufacturers such as Abode, Apple Computer, Inc., Novell Inc., Netscape, and Microsoft, as well as from the IETF, W3C has a good chance of realizing its goal to create a more effective and uniform atmosphere on the World Wide Web. Founded in 1994, W3C strives to develop the Internet as an accessible and freely available worldwide medium, not dependent on proprietary features or specifications. The consortium is headed by Massachusetts Institute of Technology's Laboratory for Computer Science and the National Institute for Research in Computer Science and Control (INRIA), a public French research institute. In 1997, Tim Berners-Lee, the original author of HTML, served as the director of W3C.

BACKGROUND AND DEVELOPMENT

Prior to the advent of graphic Internet capabilities associated with the World Wide Web, the Internet offered little to the average person or even to companies. Scholars, businesses, and the U.S. military

TED NELSON,
XANADU VS. THE WEB

If the Internet and the World Wide Web had to be traced back to one man, it would inevitably fall on the shoulders of Ted Nelson. Although many different people have developed and designed the Web and the Internet as it is today, they would all agree their ideas were based in some way on Nelson's ideas and visions.

Nelson is credited as the inventor of hypertext, a term he coined in 1965, which is the basis for HTML, the language for designing Web pages. In 1960, Nelson began to envision computer networks as the repository of all human documentation, with notions of hyperlinked text and media, an almost unheard of concept at the time. From this original idea sprang the genesis for his pet project: Xanadu.

The Xanadu project and the current Web seem similar on the surface: an arena of knowledge and information; but the Web and Xanadu actually differ quite distinctly. Xanadu is not just a storage system or large-scale word processor, but a publishing system. Copyrighted materials could be sold in small amounts to be re-used without any special arrangement. Nelson has even written Xanadu to include its own detailed models for fine-grained ownership, sale, royalty, and storage payment.

The Xanadu usage model assumes a reader buying fragments from different publishers. At a high speed pace, the reader will be able to gather his information from all over the network. Whereas the Web permits links to one page, then a different link to another page, Xanadu would be able to link back and forth between like objects, and the links don't have to be created by the owner of the page. In other words, similar information would be linked together to allow the reader to be able to investigate their interests in full.

There are those that think his system sounds like the Web with payments, but that is not the case. His Xanadu is more along the lines of a world-wide book store, publishing company, and library, in which a reader can make "many-to-many micropayments," a charge of a fraction of a cent, to download fragments of publications and information. If the readers want information on beagles, they can go through this bookstore and download several sections from several different publications that are relevant to beagles; it's like having a research department in your PC.

Other Web pioneers, such as Tim Burners-Lee, the inventor of the World Wide Web, recognize Nelson as the visionary who made it all possible. However, Nelson does not feel today's Web is at all what he envisioned. "The World Wide Web is what we were trying to prevent: spaghetti hypertext and non-reusability." Nelson feels the Web is a broken version of his Xanadu; he even likened it to Karaoke singing. "Anybody can do it and that's why it's popular."

Knowing the Web will inevitably be around for a long time, Nelson is still attempting to work his Xanadu concept into the modern version of the Web. However, he is frustrated at what he has had to do to his original concept. Xanadu was completely unified, but Nelson has had to break it up in order to implement various parts into a model that will work within the structure of the Web.

Nelson finished a book in mid-1997, which is his "view of what I hope will someday be offered under the Xanadu name—but which I also hope will be done by anyone else who understands the Web's large-scale crumminess."

made up the primary users of Internet at this time. Use centered on exchange of information: posting text-only documents on browseable directory trees called gophers, and sending messages. However, in 1993 the graphical Web browser revolutionized the medium and helped launch the Internet into mainstream society in the United States and across the globe. The National Center for Supercomputing Applications at the University of Illinois Urbana-Champaign developed the first browser, Mosaic, and licensed it to Spyglass, Inc., which in turn licensed it to other companies.

As more consumers started to subscribe to Internet service providers such as America Online, Microsoft Network, and Netcom, businesses and organizations began to utilize the Internet for more than internal company and organization communication. They found that they could promote, and in some cases

deliver, their products and services via the World Wide Web. However, unless they had a technically savvy staff, they could not expect to create a very exciting, functional, and informative Web site. Therefore, companies and organizations outsourced this task to competent agencies or individuals familiar with Web page creation. In addition, many software companies such as Microsoft and Novell developed HTML editing applications to allow users to create their own Web pages with templates and coding tools. Older programs required some familiarity with HTML and only enabled HTML novices to create fairly generic pages based on templates or automated code generators known as "wizards." While newer programs made Web authoring easier, most still lacked capabilities for automated creation of original logos, graphics, and images that are common elements to Web pages. Hence, while Web developers may have started out by creating a basic, no-nonsense Web site, they must evolve alongside the technology and therefore must provide more advanced services and greater expertise in Web site design that commercial software cannot provide.

CURRENT CONDITIONS

The demand for Web developers in the late 1990s remained robust as companies and organizations continued to launch and upgrade their Web sites, creating an ongoing need for Web Developers in the mid- to late 1990s. While the initial slow growth of Internet commerce caused some consternation among businesses, the heightened growth of Internet commerce in the late 1990s reassured many companies that their Web sites were worth the investment. In 1998, sales of the Internet totaled $51.0 billion, including $43.0 billion in business-to-business sales and $8.0 billion in retail sales. While the $8.0 billion in retail sales represented only 1 percent of the total market, it reflected substantial growth of Internet commerce overall in that retail sales in 1996 reached only $1.1 billion. Moreover, all forms of Internet commerce are slated to skyrocket to $1.4 trillion by 2003, according to Forrester Research.

With the continued expansion of Internet use and Internet commerce, the Web development industry reaped $3 million in 1998 sales and International Data Corporation (IDC) predicts that the industry's revenues will jump to $20 billion by 2002. Moreover, about 40,000 companies and individuals provided Web development services in the late 1990s, according to Forrester Research. In the late 1990s, the average Web site cost about $267,000, while some ran over $3.4 million. In addition, *Business Marketing,* reported that Web developers raised their hourly fees in 1998 by as much as 17 percent above their fees in 1997 for programming and Web page designing. The fee hikes resulted in part from greater Web site overhead as well as from greater demands by companies seeking Web sites, according to *Business Marketing.* Nevertheless, fees for Web design remained somewhat lower in college towns such as Ann Arbor, Michigan; Boulder, Colorado; and Chapel Hill, North Carolina, in contrast to larger cities, because of the lower cost of doing business in these cities and the glut of Web developers.

The Web development industry experienced a spate of consolidations in the late 1990s, as a number of developers attempted to establish themselves as industry leaders. While there were about 40,000 Web developers overall, Forrester Research reports that only about 10-20 developers court major corporate accounts. In order to pique the curiosity of big companies, Web developers have merged to demonstrate that they are large and diverse enough to handle such accounts. For example, Web developers such as Agency.com, Razorfish, and US Web made a plethora of acquisitions in the late 1990s. Furthermore, the consolidation helps companies provide a wider array of services such as managing and maintaining Web sites, creating Web sites for Internet commerce, and solving security problems. In addition, a company such as ICC Technologies, which produces humidity control systems, acquired Web developers in an effort to diversify into the budding, lucrative industry.

Some organizations may view the Web site as a one-time investment, but more and more realize that more substantial sites require regular updating and enhancing to attract repeat visitors and keep up with the latest technological advances and fads. Consequently, demand for Web site developers continued to grow as more organizations wanted Web sites and more had their sites renovated. Some observers believe the visual appeal of a site decreases with each visit, thus, organizations need to revamp their Web sites periodically to ensure that the presentation appears fresh to returning visitors, according to a report by Guy Kawasaki in *Forbes.*

With the influx of Web sites and escalating competition online, developers often pay much attention to ensuring that their clients receive many "hits," or visitors selecting their pages are pleased with the success of their sites. Consequently, some developers employ dubious methods to achieve this, such as using a technique known as "keyword stuffing" or adding gratuitous or even irrelevant words to non-displaying HTML codes so that search engines will select the site more than they would without them, according to Laurie Flynn in *The New York Times.* In response, search engines have introduced various filters to avoid undue selection of Web sites.

In addition to advancing the industry, new Web design technology also creates problems for Web developers because it often excludes Web surfers who have older browsers, ones that do not support the latest HTML tags and extensions. On the other hand, by foregoing new technology, the Web developer may fail to make the site as functional as possible or fail to make it stand out. Web sites that flaunt new HTML advances without considering older browsers often receive complaints from users who attempted to access the site. Since this kind of a fiasco would devastate online commerce and hinder traffic at general Web sites, developers and clients may opt for constructing two Web sites: one for newer and one for older Web browsers. On the other hand, many Web developers simply choose a format compatible with antiquated Internet technology to avoid these problems; often they can encode compromises without resorting to dual sites. However, leading browser makers Netscape and Microsoft develop proprietary tags that create features to work only with their respective browsers. Hence, Netscape cannot support some features that Microsoft's Internet Explorer can and vice versa, causing further design problems for developers. Both companies agree in principle that some standards should be observed, and both are expected to comply with W3C standards in the future.

INDUSTRY LEADERS

USWeb went on an expansion spree in the late 1990s to become the industry's biggest player, according to *The New York Times.* Founded in 1995, USWeb averaged an acquisition a month during the late 1990s, buying its fifteenth Web developer, Seattle-based NSET, in 15 months in mid-1998. The company also announced its plans to buy another 10 Web developers in the coming year. USWeb specializes in helping businesses market themselves via the Internet, by designing Intranet, Extranet, Web sites, and Internet commerce systems. USWeb also courts major companies, boasting of 46 Fortune 100 companies. After the acquisitions, the company reported earning $280 million in combined sales and having 2,100 employees in 1998. Robert Shaw is the company's CEO.

According to the *Wall Street Journal,* Agency .Com Ltd. was another one of the leading Web site development firms in the late 1990s. Kyle Shannon and Chan Suh founded the firm in 1995 with only $80 and 2 employees. Based in New York, Agency.Com has successfully courted such major corporate clients as Metropolitan Life Insurance Co., American Express Co., Nike, and GTE. Shannon, chief creative officer of the company, attributes Agency.Com's outstanding performance to its sites' consistency and coherence, which center and ground visitors instead of bewildering them with an onslaught of superfluous images. In 1996, the advertising powerhouse, Omnicom Group, acquired Agency.Com for its Communicade division, its interactive marketing arm. In the following years, with strong corporate backing, Agency.Com acquired Online Magic, a Web-design company based in the United Kingdom with clients such as *The Economist* and Simon & Schuster, as well as Interactive Solutions and Spiral Media. In 1998, Agency.com continued its expansion by merging with Interactive Solutions. After the acquisitions, the company's annual sales totaled $80 million and Agency.Com employed 650 people in 1998.

Through acquisitions, Razorfish became one of the industry's leading companies in the late 1990s. After buying CHBI, Plastic, and Avalanche Systems, Razorfish has offices in London (CHBI Razorfish), San Francisco (Razorfish), and New York (Razorfish and Avalanche Systems). Found in 1994, New York-based Avalanche Systems Inc. has designed sites for Super Bowl XXX, NBC, VH-1, and Electra Records. With these acquisitions, Razorfish took a key step towards providing coast-to-coast service in the United States as well as in the globalization of the industry. The resulting company employed 140 workers and reported sales of $30 million for 1998. Razorfish's clients include the *Wall Street Journal,* Time Warner, Charles Schwab, and CBS. In 1999, the company went public in an effort to raise additional money for expansion.

WORK FORCE

Web site developers launch their careers from a host of backgrounds. Some started out as graphic designers, while others trained as computer programmers. Moreover, a significant contingent switched to Web site design from a multitude of unrelated fields. Knowledge of graphic design and computer programming facilitate Web site development, though many designers pick these skills up from Web-development literature or from college courses on HTML and Web site design. Furthermore, certain Web-authoring tools cater to novice programmers and require no familiarity with HTML or Java.

According to the *New York Times,* Web developers typically earn about $30,000 a year for HTML authoring and $100,000 a year for advanced programming using CGI and Perl—programming languages for advanced site functions such as image maps, forms, and database queries. Josh Bernhoff of Forrester Research estimated that the salary of HTML authors would rise by 10 percent and the salary of advanced programmers would increase by 20 percent between 1996 and 1998. However, long term job market projections remain uncertain because software producers such as Microsoft, Adobe, and Novell continue to refine programs to streamline and simplify Web authoring. As software automates Web development, skills such as HTML authoring could diminish in value, though technology of the late 1990s still could not obviate the need for advanced programming and graphic-design skills.

RESEARCH AND TECHNOLOGY

In the mid- to late 1990s, Web tool developers focused on products or creating Web sites without knowledge of HTML or Java. These tools forebode an era when Web developer would become an obsolete profession. As Web-authoring software becomes more user friendly and capable of creating high-quality sites, the role of Web developers decreases, unless they can provide value-added services or provide services that exceed the capabilities of commercial software.

Web developers, as well as the IETF and W3C, endeavored to create an Internet not bound to any one software company's proprietary tags or extensions, which causes headaches for developers, clients, and Internet users alike. In 1997, W3C introduced HTML 4.0 to replace its own version 3.2 as well as the IETF's HTML 3.0. HTML 4.0 was created so that Web developers could take advantage of state-of-the-art Web-authoring capabilities without the impediment of proprietary tags. In particular, the new version features enhanced frame functionality as well as a standard method for authors to embed graphics, objects, and scripts in documents. HTML 4.0 also has an expanded repertoire of characters and symbols, improving its amenability to use for scientific and international documents.

Emerging programming and Web-design tools of late 1990s included DHTML (Dynamic Hypertext Markup Language), cascading style sheets, scriplets, and XML (Extensible Markup Language). DHTML provides users with greater control than conventional HTML for positioning graphics, frames, and text on Web pages. This technology includes cascading style sheets, which give Web designers complete control over the placement of text, images, and audio files on Web sites. Microsoft created scriplets, which are reusable segments of DHTML code, to offer programmers some advantages over Java. Like Java applets, Web designers can use scriplets to develop dynamic Web pages, but with scriplets developers also can save and reuse parts of the code, such as the coding for navigation bars, according to *Computerworld.* XML is another permutation of HTML, which is also akin to SGML, a markup language used for defining structure and content descriptions of electronic documents. Consequently, with its text parsing, tree management, and formatting capabilities, XML creates electronically sorted and searchable Web pages.

FURTHER READING

Bicknell, David. "Web Developers Get Tooled Up." *Computer Weekly,* 4 July 1997, 16.

Carmichael, Matt. "College Towns See Lower Web Costs: Developers Offer Service with Less Overhead." *Business Marketing,* September 1998, 38.

———. "Survey: Developers' Hourly Fee Jump." *Business Marketing,* April 1998, 30.

Flynn, Laurie. "How Web Sites Are Stacking the Deck." *New York Times,* 11 November 1996.

Frost, Robin. "Net Interest: Web Design: More Than Just a Pretty Picture." *Wall Street Journal,* 31 October 1996, B6.

Gabriel, Trip. "Meteoric Rise of Web Site Designers." *New York Times,* 12 February 1996.

Gaudin, Sharon. "Microsoft Seeks to Woo Web Developers away from Java." *Computerworld,* 22 September 1997, 10.

Hise, Phaedra. "The Well-Managed Web Site." *Inc.,* October 1995.

Kawasaki, Guy. "Four Things to Ask Your Webmaster." *Forbes,* 6 May 1996, 126.

Mand, Adrienne. "Razorfish." *Mediaweek,* 18 February 1999, 22.

Moad, Jeff. "HTML Hodgepodge," 8 July 1996, 45.

Richtel, Matt. "Flurry of Mergers Signify Web Design Industry's Growth." *The New York Times,* 3 June 1998.

Stanek, William R., and John Garris. "DMTL." *PC Magazine,* 15 May 1998, 44.

Svanas, Galen. "URL That Is, Black Gold." *Brandweek,* 22 September 1997, 22.

Watson, Tom. "A Quiet Company with Huge Clients." *@NY,* February 1997. Available from http://www.avsi.com.

World Wide Web Consortium. "W3C Announces HTML 4.0," July 1997. Available from http://www.w3.org/Press/HTML4.

—Karl Heil

WIRELESS COMMUNICATIONS

Wireless communication involves the use of electromagnetic waves to transmit digital or analog information, such as sound, computer files, commands, and combinations thereof. Waves are generally produced and manipulated—changes of frequency and wavelength—by semiconductors and fall within the radio and microwave bands of the electromagnetic spectrum. Cellular phones, two-way pagers, wireless e-mail, and radio modems that enable computers to send and receive data are examples of recent products in the rapidly growing wireless communications field.

The wireless telecommunication services industry at the end of the 1990s was comprised largely of cellular telephone and paging services and a good number of personal communications service (PCS) networks. These various services allow customers with mobile telephones to send and receive calls to and from people with landline phones, pagers, or hand-held wireless phones. Wireless subscribers typically pay a monthly subscription fee plus an additional per-minute usage charge. According to the Cellular Telecommunications Industry Association (CTIA), at the beginning of 1999 there were an estimated 69 million mobile wireless subscribers generating about $33 billion per year. In addition, fixed wireless systems were growing in importance.

Like the rest of the telecommunications industry, the wireless industry was marked by significant turbulence as the 1990s drew to a close. The sweeping changes in the regulatory landscape brought about by the Telecommunications Reform Act of 1996, and the emergence of PCS systems as viable competition to cellular networks, promised lower costs and improved services to consumers and increased the stakes tremendously for industry players. A Yankee Group report predicts that the eventual value of the market will mushroom to more than $313.2 billion worldwide by 2002, up from $87.2 billion in 1996. Nonetheless, the huge capital investment required to build the networks necessary to be a big winner created the need for mergers, joint ventures, and other forms of strategic alliances.

In addition, in 1998 and 1999 the Federal Communications Commission (FCC) held auctions for licenses for more wireless channels at higher frequencies than those used by PCS for Local Multipoint Distribution Services (LMDS). The expectation was that these services would be used for wireless communication of video and data, including Internet access. Satellite-based global wireless systems was another burgeoning sector.

ORGANIZATION AND STRUCTURE

The FCC "sells air" by charging companies a fee to gain rights to a certain frequency. Beginning in 1994, for instance, the FCC auctioned off airspace for the new PCS technology and, in 1998 and 1999, it added licenses for LMDS. Such purchasers may, in turn, sell air to other parties for a profit. The FCC also regulates and sets guidelines for various aspects of the telecommunications industry, such as cellular telephone service.

The six wireless divisions identified by the FCC—which are by no means equal in size and scope—are commercial mobile radio services, domestic public fixed radio services, public mobile ser-

<hr/>

More On SUPERCONDUCTORS: A SECRET TO BETTER COVERAGE

Cell phone towers serve as base stations, repeaters, and intermediate connections for wireless phone transmissions. Rapid growth in cellular telephone usage created a corresponding need for more base station and repeater cell towers. The need for towers is most acute in locations where cell phone usage is highest, and where the respective land availability for tower sites is abysmally low. Co-located transmitters and receiver sites are also increasingly difficult to establish as the congestion from wireless communications increases, bringing noise and interference levels proportionally higher as well.

New breakthroughs in superconductor technology might offer some solutions to the congestion problems as research reveals that filters made from these new superconductive materials may be instrumental in reducing noise and interference to significant levels. High-performance superconductive filter systems installed at cell base stations were found to improve sensitivity and performance in both receivers and transmitters. In urban areas the superconductive filters improved reception by lowering the noise floor by 3 dB, and by greater levels in some cases. The filters permitted separations as high as 100 dB between bands. These improved levels of reliability lowered the blocked and dropped call rate by 40 percent. The superconductor technology improved not only transmission and reception quality, but also enabled co-leased towers to exist more easily in areas of increasingly limited space for locating tower sites.

vices, personal communications services, private land mobile radio services, private operational-fixed microwave services, and personal radio services.

COMMERCIAL MOBILE RADIO SERVICE

Commercial mobile radio service includes the cellular telephone industry. Cellular telephone systems use low-power radiotelephone transceivers. The cellular infrastructure in use in the United States at the end of the 1990s was largely analog, which uses a nominally continuous electrical signal to send and receive information. This differs from digital communications systems, which use digital signals to send and receive messages. Digital systems create virtually exact replicas of signals because they are fed through computers that assign binary codes—zeroes and ones—to each unit of information; analog systems create only very good copies of signals.

Geographic areas serviced by a cellular carrier are divided into small regions, sometimes only one mile across, called cells—hence the term "cellular." Because of cooperation within the industry, it is possible for the cellular service customers to be "handed off" from one service provider's antenna to another as the user passes from cell to cell.

The advantage of using a cellular system is "frequency reuse." Because the FCC grants a limited number of channels, or frequencies, to the cellular telephone service industry, it would be impossible to have only one, or even a few, transceivers in each service area. Multiple cells allow the same frequency to be used by many callers in the same service area. Furthermore, each cell can be subdivided into sectors, usually three, using directional antennas. As a result, a single service area can have thousands of callers communicating on several hundred designated channels.

DOMESTIC PUBLIC FIXED RADIO SERVICES

This category includes FM and AM radio. Other types of radio are short-wave, television, conventional microwave broadcasting, satellite systems, and communication systems for federal departments and agencies—in other words, internal electronic communication for branches of the military. This category is the area on the electromagnetic spectrum with the heaviest area of activity.

PUBLIC MOBILE SERVICES

Public mobile services includes pagers, air-to-ground service (such as aircraft-to-control tower communications), offshore service (for sailing vessels), and rural radio-telephone service.

PERSONAL COMMUNICATIONS SERVICE

Personal communications service or PCS is a departure from "traditional" wireless telecommunications that require high power and relatively large cells to accommodate phones moving rapidly through space in motor vehicles. PCS systems are digital and are maintained by a network of small transmitter-receiver antennas installed throughout a community—such as on buildings. The antennas are connected to a master telephone switch that is connected to a main telephone network. PCS systems use comparatively low-powered phones that operate at a higher radio frequency. As a result, the systems use smaller cells that allow a greater concentration of users. The net result of PCS differences is a cellular network with as much as 20 times the capacity of a standard cellular service area. This increased capacity allows PCS to spread costs over a potentially larger subscriber base. In addition, PCS phones weigh less and are cheaper to manufacture than their cellular counterparts. In 1996, PCS calling rates were running 15 to 20 percent lower than cellular in the same markets. PCS has the potential to allow a cellular user to utilize the same phone number for his landline and wireless communication devices so that other callers would not have to know his location before they called.

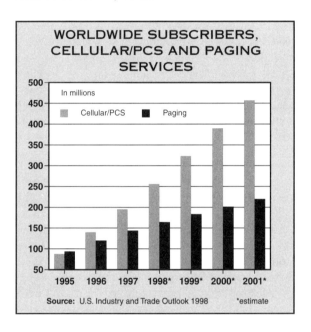

WORLDWIDE SUBSCRIBERS, CELLULAR/PCS AND PAGING SERVICES

In millions

■ Cellular/PCS ■ Paging

Source: U.S. Industry and Trade Outlook 1998   *estimate

PRIVATE LAND MOBILE RADIO SERVICE (PMR) AND PRIVATE OPERATIONAL-FIXED MICROWAVE SERVICES (OFS)

These two categories are rather difficult to distinguish; the principle difference is that the former is used exclusively by for-profit organizations and the latter more by nonprofit groups. Examples of PMR include dispatching radios used by taxis and two-way radios used by motion-picture studio employees. OFS was initially designated by the FCC for strictly nonprofit use and is used often by school systems; however, banks and other profit-making institutions often use it because of its low cost.

PERSONAL RADIO SERVICE

Created by the FCC in 1992, personal radio service is still in its infancy. This form of wireless communication includes video-on-demand, interactive polling, on-line shopping and banking, and other services classified under interactive video and data services (IVDS).

TELECOMMUNICATIONS REFORM ACT OF 1996

The Telecommunications Reform Act, signed into law February 8, 1996, swept away 62 years of regulation of the telecommunications industry. The legislation was intended to promote competition across the industry, thus resulting in the development of new technology, the creation of new business and new jobs, and ultimately lower prices. Local telephone companies (telcos), long-distance providers, wireless companies, and cable television operators would be free to offer any and all telecommunications services. Since all the major landline entities were already cellular providers, this did not have any immediate effect on the wireless industry, but the long-range goal of the major industry players was to provide "one stop shopping" for consumer's telecommunications needs. Mergers, acquisitions, and various kinds of joint ventures, which were already common in the wireless segment, began to change the shape of the broader telecommunications industry as companies tried to position themselves for future growth.

BACKGROUND AND DEVELOPMENT

The Detroit Police Department used the first mobile radio system on April 7, 1928. The spectrum for radio transmission was broadened seven years later to include FM, or frequency modulation, signals. FM transmission technology paved the way for the mobile radio systems that were widely used during World War II. After the war, American Telephone and Telegraph (AT&T)—which at that time held a virtual monopoly over phone service in America—introduced the Improved Mobile Telephone Service (IMTS), which made possible extremely limited cellular communication systems. The service was so restrictive that even by 1970, the Bell system in the city of New York could simultaneously sustain a total of only 12 mobile phone conversations.

Around 1980, under the guidance of AT&T, the first practical framework for mobile service in the United States, advanced mobile phone service (AMPS), was born. The FCC allocated space for AMPS in the Washington, D.C. test market, but it was not until 1983, in the Chicago and Baltimore markets, that companies provided relatively inexpensive, efficient consumer cellular service in the United States.

In the mid-1980s cellular service grew rapidly in the industrialized world with the implementation of different networking systems in North America, parts of Europe, and Japan. The first generation of technology quickly ran its course, expanding to the farthest reaches of the airspace spectrum allocated for it; this was particularly true in Europe, where in the mid- to late 1980s the second generation of mobile communications technology was born.

The first PCS licenses, for the 51 major trading areas in the United States, were auctioned off between December 1994 and March 1995. A total of 18 bidders won 99 licenses, generating $7.7 billion for the U.S. Treasury. Sprint Spectrum, an alliance of Sprint Corporation; Tele-Communications Inc.; the Comcast Corporation; and Cox Communications Inc. spent $2.1 billion for 29 licenses. AT&T Wireless took 21 licenses for $1.69 billion, and PrimeCo, a venture of AirTouch Communications; Bell Atlantic; NYNEX Corporation; and U.S. West Inc. spent $1.11 billion for 11 licenses.

Western Wireless Corp. launched its service in February 1996 in Honolulu and three western mainland cities. PrimeCo rolled out service in 16 cities in November 1996, and Sprint Spectrum was in 8 cities. AT&T Wireless, which was formed in 1994 when AT&T bought McCaw Cellular Communications, made major rollouts in 1997. The number of licenses purchased for each market put tremendous competitive pressure on everyone. Financial pressure was also great because of the cost of building the networks, along with the cost of the licenses. Moreover, many communities opposed the construction of the many transmitting towers necessary for the low-power networks. In addition, after purchasing these licenses, many PCS providers faced financial difficulty. The FCC, however, along with most industry observers, expected the investment to pay off bountifully within ten years.

In the late 1990s, PCS carriers began adopting new networks that included both wire and wireless technology. Known as the "hybrid approach," the blend of wire and wireless technology allows carriers to bypass the traditional stationary wireless local loop technology, according to *Telephony*. U. S. West and BellSouth were among the first companies to choose the hybrid approach for their services. Europe already has widely developed this kind of integrated network, and the Yankee Group predicts that by 2002 this market will grow to about $50 billion.

CURRENT CONDITIONS

As the twentieth century drew to a close, the wireless communications industry continued its explosive growth. In 1998 the industry experienced its greatest one-year increase in subscribers—25 percent, to more than 69 million—according to the Cellular Telecommunications Industry Association (CTIA). In 1985 there were only about 340,000 subscribers. Total revenue for service in 1998 was estimated at $33 billion, an increase of 20.4 percent over 1997. Capital expenditure also surged 31.3 percent, reaching a total cumulative investment of over $60 billion. At the same time, prices continued to fall. In 1998 the average monthly local wireless phone bill declined 7.8 percent to $39.43. Service also improved as more systems were converted to digital transmission and as carriers extended their reach geographically. AT&T Wireless unveiled a new rate plan, called Digital One, that eliminated roaming and long distance charges. Other companies that served wide geographic areas came out with similar plans. Acquiring such a national footprint was a major force behind the consolidation the industry began to experience.

In 1998 mergers and acquisitions in the U.S. telecommunications industry were valued at $234.8 billion, 4 times the figure for 1997. Among these were the merger of MCI and WorldCom, Ameritech and SBC Communications, AT&T and TCI, AT&T and British Telecom, and Bell Atlantic and GTE. All of these companies had significant wireless interests, although wireless may not have been the main driving force behind the deals. Mergers of specifically wireless carriers included AT&T with Vanguard Cellular and ALLTELL with 360 Communications. Early in 1999 the trend continued as AT&T made a deal for MediaOne Group, a major cable company, and Vodafone, the largest British wireless carrier agreed to acquire AirTouch, the second largest U.S. wireless carrier, for $66 billion. Assuming all regulatory hurdles were successfully passed, Vodafone AirTouch would be the world's largest wireless carrier—25 million subscribers. Industry analysts expected the trend toward consolidation to continue into the new century.

The consolidation had not had any obvious negative effect on the consumer by 1999. Indeed, prices continued to fall and services continued to improve. In some major U.S. cities, four or five—in some cases as many as seven—wireless carriers, some cellular and others PCS, competed for the customer. Pushed by competition from PCS, older cellular systems were being converted to digital formats, and companies were offering packages of value-added services such as voice-mail, caller ID, wireless e-mail, and news and information services, in addition to rate plans that eliminated roaming and long-distance charges in many areas.

A major focus of attention at the end of the 1990s was the wireless transmission of data. According to Brad Stevens of AT&T Wireless Data division, 1 million people were using wireless data applications in 1998. Allied Business Intelligence (ABI) produced a study that predicted a growth to 43 million wireless data subscribers by 2006 under its moderate forecast. The study's aggressive forecast had the growth to 88 million by 2006. The market research firm Dataquest predicted that wireless data revenue would grow from $460 million in 1999 to $3 billion in 2003.

One obstacle to growth lamented by some in the industry was the absence of an accepted standard, with U.S. companies split among GSM, TMDA, and CDMA. The emergence of a single standard was unlikely at least until the development of the third generation of mobile wireless technology, if even then. The technical issues were complex, which also made the job of selling wireless data services to nontechnical people difficult. Nevertheless, the increased business use of the Internet, in addition to the explosion of business use of data in general, made the data transmission market a priority for wireless carriers.

The FCC took an important step in advancing the cause of fixed wireless transmission of data, as opposed to mobile transmission by PCS and cellular services, when it held auctions for 986 licenses for Local Multipoint Distribution Services (LMDS). An LMDS system is capable of one-way and two-way broadband services—such as video programming, video conferencing, wireless local loop telephony, and high-speed data transmission such as Internet access. Such a system would consist of cells like mobile cellular and PCS systems except that the transmitting and receiving points must be stationary. The transmission rates can be much higher than is possible for mobile systems. Companies developing such systems were expected to compete with local telephone carriers and cable companies. In the 1998 auctions, 864 licenses were taken, covering more than 90 percent of the U.S. population, according to the FCC. A second auction was held in 1999 for the remaining licenses.

WNP Communications, the largest investor in the LMDS auction, bought 40 licenses in the 1998 auction, and Nextband, owned by Nextel and Nextlink Communications, bought 42 licenses. In January 1999 Nextlink, owned by cellular pioneer Craig McCaw, bought WNP and the other half of Nextband, thus giving Nextlink 95 percent of the LMDS licenses available in the United States.

Another positive development in the wireless industry was the emergence of new satellite-based com-

Wireless telephone communication has made it possible for people to communicate from anywhere. (Digital Stock.)

munications systems. Iridium, a joint venture of Motorola and several other telecom companies, began global commercial service in November 1998, enabling mobile telephone and pager service anywhere in the world. It used a system of 66 low earth orbit satellites. Globalstar Telecommunications, another partnership of telecom companies, including Qualcomm and Vodafone, expected to have its system of 48 satellites up and running by October 1999. A third direct competitor in this field, ICO Global, a London-based company, said it would begin service in the third quarter of 2000. The total global market for satellite-based phone service was estimated by Frank Guinard of Globalstar to be 30 million subscribers, which is twice the total capacity of these three systems. A study by Strategis Group, however, projected a market of 17 million subscribers by 2007.

A separate space race was underway for satellite-based data transmission. Leading ventures in this arena included Teledesic, started by Craig McCaw and Microsoft Chairman Bill Gates, and Astrolink, a joint venture of aerospace giant Lockheed Martin; TRW, a maker of electronics among other things; and Telecom Italia, a major European telecom company. Motorola dropped its Celestri satellite project to join the Teledesic effort. Hughes Electronics, a unit of Gen-

WIRELESS PRODUCTS AND SERVICES IN THE LATE 1990S

The following services and products illustrate how the "information skyway" is changing wireless communication in the late 1990s:

- Clipboards are being traded for electronic pads that can send and receive information from computers.
- Cellular phones are now being used as full-time, full-function phones, complete with voice mail and call forwarding, and as supercordless phones that automatically switch back to cordless phones when the user is in close proximity to the base station.
- Networks that enable pagers to send and receive messages are growing. Many pagers now have Web addresses for e-mail.
- Handsets and PDAs (personal digit assistants) are being connected to laptop computers to send faxes and e-mails, to access office databases wirelessly, and to support Internet access.
- Lithium ion batteries to increase telephone talk time (see Lithium Ion Batteries) are now available.
- A radio broadcast data system (RBDS) that displays news headlines, weather forecasts, and information on music being played on screens inside automobiles in operation.

eral Motors, began development of a similar project called Spaceway and planned to begin limited service in 2002 and full service in 2003. Both Teledesic and Astrolink expected to go into service in 2003. A study by Booz-Allen and Hamilton, a research and consulting company, projected that the global market for broadband communications would grow to almost $200 billion by 2005, and that satellite-based systems would capture 10-15 percent of that.

INDUSTRY LEADERS

In 1998 the largest wireless communication company in the United States was AT&T Wireless, with 9.1 million cellular and PCS subscribers, over 50 percent of whom were on a digital service. It had revenues in 1998 of $5.4 billion—an increase of 24.6 percent over the previous year. One of only a pair of companies with a national footprint, the other being Sprint PCS, it had assets on 120 U.S. cities.

AirTouch was the second largest, with 7.3 million subscribers in the United States in 1998. It also had subscribers in 12 other countries, giving it a total subscribership of almost 16 million. Its 1998 revenues were $5.2 billion, an increase of 44.2 percent. It is a partner in the Globalstar satellite project and in Qualcomm, a major manufacturer of wireless communications equipment. In 1999 it agreed to be acquired by Vodafone, which will make it the world's largest wireless carrier.

SBC Communications Inc. was the third leading wireless carrier in the United States in 1998. Its subsidiaries and units, such as Southwestern Bell and Cellular One, had 6.9 million subscribers in 16 states. It had agreed to acquire Comcast Cellular's operations, which would add another 850,000 subscribers, and Ameritech, another local Bell operating company, which would make it the second largest local phone company. SBC recorded 1998 sales of $28.8 billion.

Sprint PCS operated in 270 cities and claimed 1.7 million customers. It offered its personal communications services under several names: Sprint Spectrum, SprintCom, and PhillieCo. Sprint PCS reported 1998 revenues of $1.2 billion.

A "different kind of wireless company," Nextel began as a specialized mobile radio company providing services for taxi drivers, truckers, and other work groups. In 1991 it began to develop a digital network with an infusion of capital from Craig McCaw. In 1998 it served 2.04 million subscribers, primarily businesses. It posted 1998 revenues of $1.8 billion, an increase of 149.9 percent.

Lucent Technologies was involved in the emerging field of cellular digital packed data (CDPD), an area that promises advancement in the interface between telecommunications and the Internet. Lucent posted sales of $30.1 billion in 1998. Motorola makes cellular hardware, as does Mitsubishi Electronics America. Likewise Qualcomm Inc. develops, manufactures, markets, and licenses digital communications systems and products. There are a number of other strong companies offering either hardware, service, or both, including Samsung and U.S. Robotics.

AMERICA AND THE WORLD

As many of the major wireless service providers set their sights on expanding into the leading industrialized nations, some of the savviest visionaries were eyeing third world markets. Recognizing that half of the world's population lives more than 200 miles from the nearest telephone, many companies were striving to devise a blanket service that could deliver inexpensive wireless telephone service to every person on the globe. Even if a company could capture just one to two percent of the global marketplace, it would enjoy a subscriber base of 50 to 100 million people.

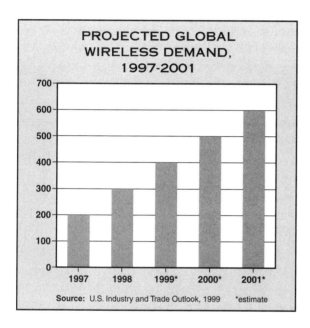

PROJECTED GLOBAL WIRELESS DEMAND, 1997-2001

Source: U.S. Industry and Trade Outlook, 1999   *estimate

To many observers the concept seemed logical. Although the United States boasted 58 telephones per 100 people, the telephone saturation rate in truly populous countries, such as China and Indonesia, was in the area of one percent. Furthermore, to achieve its high telecommunication rate, by 1992 the United States had invested the equivalent of $320 billion dollars in equipment to serve a population of only 250 million. For a fraction of that amount, some companies reasoned, a comprehensive global satellite network could be established that would put wireless telephone capabilities in the hands of every person in the world.

Such a system could potentially render comparatively expensive landline systems obsolete. Even phone users in the United States would be tempted to eliminate their local phone service in favor of a less-expensive, easier-to-use mobile phone system. Users could carry a phone in their pocket or on their wrist and either make calls or be reached at any destination. Similar thought processes had evoked visionary schemes like Iridium and Teledesic, which were scheduled to become fully operational shortly after the turn of the century. As evidence of its potential value, the Iridium project had attracted large investors

throughout China, the Middle East, Africa, Russia, and Latin America.

RESEARCH AND TECHNOLOGY

Wireless communication technology is advancing so rapidly that it is difficult to distinguish between the present and the future. Consumer acceptance of PCS was breathtakingly rapid but, with some uncertainty in the financial backing of PCS development, the timetable for widespread deployment of PCS was still in question. Also, new possibilities loomed for fixed wireless systems with the advent of LMDS.

AMPS, the analog system for U.S. cellular telecommunications, was being replaced by digital systems. Cellular telecommunications in the late 1990s had gone through two generations, of which AMPS represented the first; the third generation was being born in America and Europe where a variety of agencies under the European Commission acted as midwife. Their goal was to develop a third-generation mobile communications network, which would probably use cells of variable size, by 2000. This mixed-cell architecture, it was hoped, would help handle some of the technical areas of concern, such as "hand-off" when a user moves from one cell to another. In addition, there remained the problem, in the United States at least, of the competition among standards, primarily between GSM, which is nearly universal in Europe, and CDMA. Some analysts predicted an eventual convergence to one standard. But as Ulysses Black wrote at the conclusion of his book *Mobile and Wireless Networks,* which may be the closest thing around to a layman's guide to the new technology in telecommunications, "We know better than to say that these problems cannot be solved. So, as we say in the radio world, stay tuned, for more is yet to come."

FURTHER READING

"Airborne Information." *Fortune,* Winter 1997.

Bank, David, and Nicole Harris."Microsoft to Invest $500 Million in Nextel." *Wall Street Journal,* 11 May 1999.

Baker, Marci. "Calling For Capital." *Investment Dealers Digest,* 3 March 1997.

Black, Ulysses. *Mobile and Wireless Networks.* Upper Saddle River, NJ: Prentice Hall, 1996.

Blake, Pat. "Fixed or Mobile? How about Both?" *Telephony,* 1 June 1998.

Brodsky, Ira. "The Next Wave In Wireless: Selling Bulk Airtime." *Network World,* 31 March 1997.

Cane, Alan, and Louise Kehoe. "High-tech Deals Increase by 87%." *Financial Times USA Edition,* 26 January 1999.

Cole, Jeff. "GM's Hughes Puts Up Funds for Satellites." *Wall Street Journal,* 17 March 1999.

"D E F Auction Focus." *Telephony,* 17 February 1997.

Elstrom, Peter. "The Internet Space Race." *Business Week,* 1 June 1998.

———. "Sprint's Wireless High-Wire Act." *Business Week,* 3 March 1997.

Emmett, Arielle. "Paging FLEXes its Muscle: Market Revs up Telemetry Applications." *America's Network,* 1 November 1997.

Garg, Vijay K., and Joseph E. Wilkes. *Wireless and Personal Communications Systems.* Upper Saddle River, NJ: Prentice Hall, 1996.

Glosserman, Brad. "It's for You!" *Japan Times Weekly International Edition,* 21 December 1998.

Jones, Stephen S. "Redefining Wireless." *Wireless Review,* 15 March 1999.

Knox, Noelle. "MediaOne Accepts AT&T Takeover Offer." *AP Business Writer,* 3 May 1999.

"Lockheed Martin Leads Partnership for Satellite Broadband Network." *Associated Press Newswires,* 6 May 1999.

Malley, Chris. "The Wireless World." *Popular Science,* November 1995.

Mason, Charles. "Taking the Desktop to the Blacktop." *America's Network,* 1 March 1999.

——— "Satellites: The New Direct-to-Consumer Tool." *America's Network,* 15 September 1998.

Meyers, Jason. "Cellular Revisited." *Telephony,* 3 March 1997.

———. "Network Buildup." *Telephony,* 7 April 1997.

———. "Struggle for Survival: PCS Entrepreneurs Tread Dangerous Waters," 9 June 1997.

Nash, J. Madeleine. "Not in My Front Yard." *Time,* 4 November 1996.

O'Shea, Dan. "After the Discovery." *Telephony,* 31 March 1997.

Pappalardo, Denise."Nextlink Bets the Farm on Wireless." *Network World,* 25 January 1999.

"PCS Takes on Cellular." *Telephony,* 4 November 1996.

Reeves, Betsy. "Year in Review." *Wireless Review,* 1 December 1998.

Rhinds, Steve. "Globalstar to Break Even in First Year, Launch in October." *Dow Jones News Service,* 25 February 1999.

Schwartz, Nikki. "Lessons in Wireless Data." *Wireless Review,* 15 September 1998.

———. "Top 25 Wireless Carriers." *Wireless Review,* 1 December 1998.

"Shrinking Planet." *Fortune,* Technology Buyer's Guide Supplement, Winter 1997.

Strategis Group"World Mobile Satellite Telephony Subscribers Projected to Surpass 17 Million by 2007." Washington, D.C.: Strategis Group, 16 December 1998.

Sweeney, Dan. "Approaching Interoperability In Voice Networks." *Cellular Business,* March 1997.

Tyler, Hamilton. "Wireless Auctions: Sign of Times or Business Competition Killers?" *Computing Canada,* 31 March 1997.

U.S. Industry and Trade Outlook 1998. Washington, DC: McGraw-Hill and U.S. Department of Commerce, 1998.

Vittore, Vince. "LMDS Auctions Close with a Thud." *Telephony,* 6 April 1998.

"Warning: Sharp Growth Ahead." *Communications News,* May 1998.

—Judson Knight, updated by Karl Heil and
Howard Distelzweig

XML

INDUSTRY SNAPSHOT

Extensible Markup Language (XML), is a format used for documents exchanged over the Internet. Markup languages use "tags" to label particular parts of a document. For example, the name of the document might be placed between opening and closing tags. Many kinds of software applications work with documents that are organized using markup languages. The software then interprets the tags to determine how to display, print, or otherwise work with the document.

The prevalent format for distributing information over the World Wide Web has been Hypertext Markup Language (HTML). Like XML, HTML is derived from an older format called Standardized General Markup Language (SGML), which was in use before the Web existed. HTML is a small subset of SGML. It uses only about 70 tags, mainly to indicate how a document should be displayed or to link it to other documents. HTML is easy to learn, but not very flexible, and new tags are either defined by a time-consuming standards committee process or adopted unilaterally by a software developer to advance its own proprietary technologies. In contrast, XML is an open standard that allows the definition of as many tags as necessary. Once defined, the tags can be used to provide much richer information about a document, including attributes of its content as well as its format. Specialized tag sets make it easier to exchange data and get more relevant search results. Since the definitions of the tags come along with the document, the easy information exchange of the Web is preserved.

Software developers quickly perceived the potential of this technology, especially after it was en-

dorsed by the World Wide Web Consortium (W3C)—one of the major standards organizations for the Internet—in early 1998. Tools were built to generate XML, and Internet software began to incorporate XML support. As this process continues, XML is likely to have a major impact on the capabilities of the World Wide Web.

ORGANIZATION AND STRUCTURE

XML's tags are not primarily presentation-oriented, like those of HMTL. Rather, XML provides a way to define and use new tags that describe various elements of a document. Any elements that are opened and closed properly (using start and end tags) are considered "well-formed" and are acceptable. There can be an unlimited number of tags, including "nested" hierarchies (although not overlapping tags that do not nest properly). So, for example, a student's transcript might have tags indicating the student's name, student ID, and courses. Along with the transcript would come a Document Type Definition (DTD), a convention inherited from SGML, which describes how the document is organized. The document could be displayed in a Web browser or used with any other software capable of parsing it. (Parsing verifies the consistency between an XML document and its DTD.) The generic nature of XML lends itself to marking up database records and other structured information.

Since XML tags generally pertain to how information is organized, rather than how it is to be displayed, the same document may be presented in any number of ways. Different application software packages or scripts might produce HTML for a Web display, a Braille version, or a file formatted for printing, all from the same XML document.

XML is intended to complement HTML, not compete with it. But older HTML-based tools and applications are not compatible with the new technology. HTML conforms to a single DTD, so it does not provide this description with every document. Rather, HTML tools are built to this single specification. XML documents use tags that are not part of HTML's fixed set; at the same time, XML is actually stricter about syntax rules, such as tags being properly closed. Newer software is being developed to take advantage of XML's capabilities. Web browsers are now able to support XML, and HTML specifications allow mixing of the two formats in a single document. Electronic commerce, data interchange, and information discovery are becoming important applications of XML.

The DTDs, which describe the tags used in XML documents, can be provided in a number of ways. They can either be part of the document itself or reside in a separate file. Developers working with SGML have been generating application-specific DTDs for years, and many of these are available for public use. An XML convention called the "namespace" allows a document to reference a Universal Resource Locator (URL) address where a set of agreed-upon tag names has been published. Namespaces can be created by organizations, industries, hobbyist groups, companies, or any other entity with an interest in making a set of tags available for the type of data they work with. Using namespaces, information can be exchanged with all the capabilities inherent in XML and without generating confusion by inadvertent use of the same name in different ways.

All Web standards, including HTML and XML, are overseen by the W3C organization. W3C was founded in 1994 and is chaired by Tim Berners-Lee, who first conceived the World Wide Web and invented HTML. The W3C has more than 180 members, most of whom are commercial software developers. Standards discussions can be contentious because each company wants to gain a market advantage by distinguishing themselves, even as they recognize a need to maintain the interoperability that drives the Web. Often a company will develop a technology, propose it to the W3C as a standard, and then market it by announcing that it is soon to be W3C-endorsed. In practice, inclusion in the popular Netscape or Microsoft Internet Explorer browsers have been at least as critical as W3C endorsement for advancing a technology.

For XML, agreeing on tag sets is an important area for cooperation between software vendors and other XML users. By mid-1998, there were efforts to establish an overall tag clearinghouse to head off naming conflicts. "Webcasting" or "push technology" applications, in which an "active channel" of information is sent directly to a user over the Web rather than having the user traverse links, were early adopters of XML. DataChannel of Bellevue, Washington, a software company involved in Webcasting, formed the XML Active Content Technologies Council (X-ACT) in March 1998. Within a few months there were proposals that the council, consisting of software developers and users, should perhaps be chaired by a more neutral organization such as OASIS, a non-profit SGML/XML interest and advocacy group in Madison, Alabama. Other vendors questioned the necessity of such a move. (Also see the essay in this book entitled Push Technology.)

BACKGROUND AND DEVELOPMENT

HTML was one of the most important developments in the history of information technologies. By facilitating the explosion of the World Wide Web, it changed the way modern societies distribute information and do business; however, a few short years is a long time on the Internet. As the Web is expected to provide ever-increasing functionality, and users struggle to find relevant information in a vast global network, HTML is beginning to show its age. Broken links—a link that does not lead to an existing Web page—are proliferating, limited document formatting makes some types of applications difficult, and search engines are getting bogged down in the sheer volume of documents on the Internet. Many technologies are being developed to address one or more of these problems.

XML was created to improve methods of organizing and finding data. Since tags can be tailored to a particular type of information, it can be navigated more efficiently. If entire industries or other groups agree on a set of tags, then search tools can be built to provide more relevant results when applied to the group's data stores. More data validation can be done by the browser, and all forms of publishing, including Internet, paper, and CD-ROM, can be done from the same XML document.

Development of XML began in September 1996. The W3C formed an XML Working Group, chaired by Jon Bosak of Sun Microsystems, and this group issued several draft specifications for review and comment. In December 1997, Version 1.0 of the XML specification, written by Tim Bray, was issued as a W3C recommendation at a meeting of the SGML/ XML Conference in Washington, D.C. In February 1998, the W3C ratified XML as a standard.

The Extensible Style Language, XSL, describes how an XML document is formatted. XSL is a way to specify style sheets for XML documents, following the model of the Cascading Style Sheets used with HTML. Software vendors Microsoft, ArborText, and Inso submitted a proposal for XSL to the W3C in August 1997, and the W3C created an XSL Working Group. XSL Version 1.0 is expected to be approved by the W3C in the summer of 1999.

CURRENT CONDITIONS

Early applications of XML include the Channel Definition Format (CDF), developed by Microsoft and submitted to the W3C. The goal of the CDF is to standardize the format for information sent over active channels, so that users can receive information from multiple sources without being stymied by differences in proprietary push technologies. Utilized in Microsoft's Internet Explorer 4.0, CDF provides tags for specifying the channel, the information it provides, and the update schedule.

The Resource Description Framework (RDF) lets applications exchange information about data within a document, such as whether the data's position within the document is important, ratings for child protection, security and privacy, and intellectual property rights. The RDF consolidates several earlier efforts in the same area, such as Netscape's Meta Content Framework and Microsoft's XML-Data. Netscape has included the use of RDF in the 5.0 version of Navigator to store bookmarks, history information, and mail preferences.

In June 1998, software developers proposed that the Object Management Group (OMG), which includes major vendors such as IBM, Oracle, and Unisys, adopt XML as a standard format for exchanging data over the Internet between programming tools, applications, and data repositories. Plans to incorporate the standard in the IBM Visual Age Team Connection Enterprise Server, the Unisys Universal Repository, and the Microsoft Repository were announced. The OMG has also been involved in bringing XML into object-oriented application development tools and component repositories through their development of Extensible Metadata Interchange (XMI).

About... VOICE-BASED INTERNET CONNECTIONS

Voice Extensible Markup Language (VXML), already in the testing stages, promises to open the Internet to an estimated 58 percent of the population who do not have ready access to a computer. More importantly VXML will open new avenues of commercial convenience and communication by allowing consumers to comparison shop with a single telephone call to the Internet. There exist uncounted millions of people who fear using the Internet because of its complexity, and these individuals might also gain access through VXML-based telephone connections. Among the advantages of Internet shopping are the substantial discounts offered by vendors for merchandise and services purchased directly online, as well as the tax-free status of online commerce.

For airline travelers phone-based Internet ticketing would bring new efficiency. A traveler could locate the most convenient travel accommodations and then book a flight and reserve a car or a hotel room, all by dialing a single phone number to connect to the Internet. It would be easy to track packages through shippers' web sites. Tracking U.S. Mail and accessing postage rates would be simplified considerably. Language would never be a barrier, as users could select a preferred language before making an information request.

VXML-based Internet sites, already in the testing stages, will expand the character of the World Wide Web as a center for global commerce. Businesses that deal on the Web will experience significant expansion of their customer base overnight.

Open Financial Exchange (OFX) is a framework for data exchange among financial institutions and with their customers. By moving to XML, banks can allow their customers the ability to download account statements, pay bills electronically, and basically manage their finances online. Originally based on SGML, the format required some modifications, such as end tags, to be compatible with XML. It integrates formats used by Microsoft, Intuit (which provides the popular financial software package Quicken), and electronic banking vendor CheckFree.

XML/EDI is an effort to provide a standard XML electronic data interchange (EDI) format for such documents as invoices, loan applications, insurance claims, and other business forms. This requires compatibility with or gateways to existing EDI standards such as ANSI X12 and EDIFACT. Major EDI players such as IBM and GE, as well as start-up firms, are interested in XML/EDI and are cooperating under the auspices of a CommerceNet task force. Although Microsoft, Netscape, and IBM have representatives on the working group, none of the companies officially endorse the XML/EDI group. Furthermore, companies are concerned about having to transition away from existing EDI system investments, thus selling XML-based EDI systems will be a challenge until they can provide all the services currently available at propri-etary value-added networks (VANs).

A method for syndicating data for multiple uses on the Web is the Information and Content Exchange (ICE) protocol. It allows one company to provide con-tent to another through a content syndicated relation-ship. Business rules for the content and access rights to data can be enforced by using this protocol.

Specialized XML tags are also being developed in such fields as chemistry, astronomy, and geneal-ogy. Chemical Markup Language (CML), for exam-ple, provides a way of describing the structure of a molecule with advanced XML tags for the atoms, the bonds, and the isotopic constitution. A mathematics markup language will allow proper display and ma-nipulation of mathematical symbols and equations for the first time since the inception of the Web.

Software tools for displaying XML using Exten-sible Style Sheets have lagged somewhat behind the effort to develop XML tag sets. In mid-1998, Mi-crosoft released a preview of two XSL tools. One tool is a command-line utility that combines an XML doc-ument and an XSL style sheet to produce HTML out-put for display using a standard browser. The other tool employs Microsoft's proprietary ActiveX tech-nology to display XML directly.

INDUSTRY LEADERS

At a Seattle XML conference in March 1998, one month after adoption of the standard by the W3C, dozens of vendors announced new products. In the first year of XML's official existence, hundreds of SGML software packages have been updated to sup-port it. Some accommodation of the standard is also available in non-SGML word processing packages. The 4.0 versions of the major browsers, Netscape and Microsoft Internet Explorer, incorporate some XML features with extensive support for the format in the 5.0 versions.

Microsoft has been instrumental in the develop-ment of XML technology and tools. Internet Explorer

4.0 uses XML to schedule active channel information delivery and can process and display XML documents. Internet Explorer 5.0 supports XML 1.0, XSL, XML Document Object Model (DOM), and XML Name-spaces. Frontpage2000 also uses XML to support DOM, providing web developers with the ability to specify documents by category. The company is also making available its MSXML tool, which parses an XML document into a hierarchical tree and provides Java programming language methods for manipu-lating the resulting structure. Additionally, XML will be incorporated into Microsoft's upcoming Biz-Talk, which is used for building and maintaining e-commerce sites.

IBM has utilized 500 developers to create 17 XML technologies. Their proposal for XML Schema offers a way to overcome the limitations of DTDs by allowing data-typing so that information, such as a date or integer, can be tagged and identified. IBM, Motorola, Lucent, and AT&T have formed the Voice Extensible Markup Language Forum to develop fur-ther XML-based methods to access Web content by telephone. IBM has submitted Speech Markup Lan-guage (SpeechML), and Motorola has developed VoxML, an XML-based method for creating voice activated Web sites and automated call centers for conducting business, in what Motorola has called "v-commerce." Utilizing this technology, a person could phone a Web site, ask a question, and an XML-based search would deliver the text-to-voice informa-tion back over the telephone. IBM also plans to incor-porate xmLDAP, an XML technology that can query a company's directory services database through a proxy server that supports Lightweight Directory Ac-cess Protocol (LDAP), into the Extensible Query Lan-guage, which is being considered by the W3C.

XML is well suited for use with object-oriented databases (OODBs) due to its linking ability and hi-erarchical architecture. Poet Software Corporation has bundled a Content Management Suite with its OODB, allowing storage, manipulation, and navigation of XML and SGML, as well as HTML, text, graphics, audio, and video formats. Poet's product supports con-tent-based queries using XML tags. Object Design Inc.'s Excelon serves XML files to a browser and makes them available for return visits to the site by storing them in the server's cache memory.

DataChannel released its Channel Manager 2.0 and XML Parser 1.0 in March 1998. The package in-cluded utilities for managing XML-based push ser-vices and building Internet applications. It allows Mi-crosoft Word users to add a "Publish to Channel" option under Word's "Save As" menu item. This option automatically updates the channel via XML created from the Word document. Rio 3.1 is Data-Channel's latest XML-based web publishing system that uses ActiveX to add Metadata search ability and content saving in a browser.

Adobe is supporting XML in new versions of its FrameMaker and FrameMaker+SGML document creation packages. ArborText, a leading supplier of SGML software, accommodated XML in its Adept product, which is used for creating, maintaining, and managing documents, DTDs, and style sheets. In 1999 the company unveiled new technology that eliminates the use of DTDs in XML editing.

Interleaf and Microstar released their BladeRunner collaboration in December 1998. BladeRunner is an assembly engine for XML validation. It provides tree views, DTD checking, and assistance in recreating poorly structured XML documents. It will also allow data converted into components to be indexed, organized, and stored in a central repository.

Veo Systems Inc. of Mountain View, California, has released a reference library of common XML tags called Common Business Library (CBL), which will support Open Buying on the Internet (OBI), OFX, Open Trading Protocol (OTP), and ICE.

RESEARCH AND TECHNOLOGY

Like XML, dynamic HTML (DHTML) is an effort to improve on HTML, this time by allowing changing information to be presented to the user with fewer, slow full-document downloads. The DHTML specification allows scripts to access structured data such as XML under program control. DHTML was first released in Internet Explorer 4.0. The 5.0 version has increased the use of DHTML by making all the elements of a web page, such as graphics, text, buttons, and forms, dynamic. In addition, layout preferences will be retained by the browser for return visits to the page. DHTML, however, is taking hold more slowly than XML because of difficulties in reconciling different approaches by Netscape and Microsoft.

Another proposed improvement to the workings of the Web is Extensible Link Language (XLL). This would support simple links between documents like those currently used but also make possible names that are not dependent on the physical location of the data, bi-directional links, rings of links, and "transclusion," where linked documents appear to be part of the original document.

Several software vendors are developing ways to use XML as a "middleware" technology, tying together disparate resources over the web. Data-Channel's WebBroker software enables integration between Microsoft's Component Object Model, the competing Common Object Request Broker Architecture (CORBA), and databases using Structured Query Language (SQL). WebMethods introduced B2B ("business-to-business"), allowing firms to exchange data from Microsoft Excel spreadsheets and applications built with Java, JavaScript, C, C++, Visual Basic, and ActiveX. The latest version, 2.0, offers increased Open Database Connectivity and Java Database Connectivity support, as well as server-side XML data caching. In April 1998, Canadian vendor OmniMark shipped Konstructor 1.0, an XML-based middleware, capable of retrieving information from relational databases and assembling either SGML or XML documents. Lotus and Novell are planning support for XML in upcoming versions of their software suites. If implemented at both ends, XML could allow users who are sent an e-mail with an attached spreadsheet to read it even if their own spreadsheet application comes from a different vendor.

XML can make related data stores appear as a single "virtual database" (VDB). This allows searching for information in a structured way, delivering better results than keyword searches over the entire Web. Yahoo, a leading provider of hierarchically-organized directory information on the Web, is planning to use VDB technology to provide online comparison shopping. VDBs are also starting to be used in job recruitment applications.

The health care industry may be an important future user of XML technology. Sequoia Software Corporation has received a grant from the National Institute of Standards and Technology to work on an XML-based Master Patient Index prototype. A URL for each patient would lead to an XML document with that patient's medical history and other information. In May 1998, Sequoia and Azron, Inc. announced the addition of an XML generator to Azron's Electronic Medical Record handheld device, used to gather patient information. A standard way to access medical records from any location should greatly facilitate telemedicine and coordination of specialist care. A health care industry working group is developing Kona Architecture, an XML tag naming convention using the same vocabulary as existing medical information transfer protocols. (Also see the essay in this book entitled Telemedicine.)

A prerequisite for expanded electronic commerce and data interchange over the Web is secure transmission of sensitive financial and personal data. The W3C Digital Signature Initiative is working on XML-based security and authentication to make sure these needs are met. OBI is losing ground due to a greater acceptance of XML. Several companies are planning to release products that will utilize Commerce Extensible Markup Language (CXML) to define standards for Internet-based electronic commerce. Ariba's CXML, for example, is a set of 12 DTDs to support common E-Commerce transactions such as purchase orders, invoices, and change orders.

FURTHER READING

Babcock, Charles. "Will Servers Tag Along With XML?" *Inter@ctive Week Online,* 16 March 1999. Available from http://www.zdnet.com/intweek/.

Bremser, Wayne. "The Big 4.0." *Internet World,* January 1998.

Claymon, Deborah. "Tim Berners-Lee on XML and the W3C." *Red Herring,* July 1998.

Gardner, Dana. "Microsoft Lays Out Its Own Strategy For XML." *InfoWorld,* 19 October 1998.

Gonsalves, Antone. "XML Opens Object Tools to Web." *PC Week,* 22 June 1998.

———. "XML to Enable Component Sharing." *PC Week,* 2 November 1998.

Gottesman, Ben Z. "Why XML Matters." *PC Magazine,* 6 October 1998.

Hammond, Mark. "XML Adds Tagging Capabilities to Poet Database." *PC Week,* 18 May 1998.

Hannon, Brian. "Common Ground for Data Exchange." *PC Week,* 13 April 1998.

———. "A Promise of Better Data Exchange." *PC Week,* 15 June 1998.

———. "VDB Builds XML Virtual Databases." *PC Week,* 18 May 1998.

———. "XML Gains Momentum." *PC Week,* 30 March 1998.

———. "XML Gets Nod from the W3C." *PC Week,* 16 February 1998.

———. "XML Offers Data Cure." *PC Week,* 18 May 1998.

———. "XML Vendors Seek Tag Clearinghouse." *PC Week,* 20 April 1998.

Hannon, Brian, and Christy Walker. "XML Could Extend Groupware." *PC Week,* 15 June 1998.

Kaplan, Simone, and Brian Hannon. "Vendors Trumpet XML." *PC Week,* 5 October 1998.

Kerstetter, Jim. "XML Holds Promise As EDI Replacement." *PC Week,* 4 May 1998.

Mace, Scott, et al. "Weaving a Better Web." *Byte,* March 1998.

Moeller, Michael, and Mary Jo Foley. "Browser Battle Picks Up Steam." *PC Week,* 8 June 1998.

Nelson, Matthew. "3Com Paves the Way to Resellers." *InfoWorld,* 21 September 1998.

———. "Vendors Bet On Services, Standards." *InfoWorld,* 15 March 1999.

———. "Veo Systems Looks to Ensure I-Commerce, XML Interoperability." *InfoWorld,* 19 October 1998.

Nelson, Matthew, and Jeff Walsh. "Business to get XML Repository." *InfoWorld,* 3 August 1998.

Niccolai, James. "Sun, Netscape Announce XML Tool for Business Commerce." *InfoWorld,* 15 March 1999.

Orenstein, David. "Web Language That Tags Site Data Gains Industry Support." *Computerworld,* 11 January 1999.

Paul, Lauren Gibbons. "XML Standards Are Too Much of a Good Thing." *PC Week Online,* 12 April 1999. Available from http://www.zdnet.com/pcweek/.

Peterson, Scot. "XML Writes the Book." *PC Week,* 16 November 1998.

Rapoza, Jim. "IE 5.0 Reflects Language Advances." *PC Week,* 15 June 1998.

Rupley, Sebastian. "XML Starts to Live Up to Its Hype." *PC Magazine,* 7 April 1999.

Seltzer, Larry. "To Manage Content Relationships, Just Add ICE." *PC Week,* 16 November 1998.

Sikorski, Robert, and Richard Peters. "Turning the Big Five-O." *Science,* 16 October 1998.

———. "XML is Hatching." *Science,* 21 August 1998.

Sliwa, Carol, and David Orenstein. "IBM, Oracle Hop On XML Bandwagon." *Computerworld,* 16 November 1998.

Tweney, Dylan. "Net Prophet." *InfoWorld,* 19 October 1998.

Udell, Jon. "Extensible Markup Language." *Byte,* January 1998.

Walsh, Jeff. "IBM, W3C Advance XML Standards." *InfoWorld,* 22 February 1999.

———. "Sun, IBM to Trumpet XML Strategies At XTech." *InfoWorld,* 8 March 1999.

———. "XML Explodes onto the Scene: IBM Harnesses Language." *InfoWorld,* 30 November 1998.

"XML Tags Major Vendor Support." *PC Week,* 15 June 1998.

—Sherri Chasin Calvo, updated by David M. Lewon

YARD AND GARDEN PRODUCTS

Yard and garden care was one of the most popular pastimes in the United States in the late 1990s, and spending on yard and garden products is rising. In an article for the Associated Press, writer Alice Ann Love reported 1998 Department of Commerce figures which showed the average income for the estimated 270.3 million Americans rose 4.4 percent in 1998, up from $26,412 in 1997. Love noted that Steve Cochrane, an economist at Regional Financial Associates in West Chester, Pennsylvania, said of the rise, "It translates directly into buying power . . . There's money out there to spend." According to *American Demographics,* 25 percent of Americans gardened as a hobby. As such, products for yard and garden care have been increasing in sales and variety. Total retail sales in the late 1990s were approximately $22 billion, and expected to reach $28 billion by 2001. Americans were spending some of that increased income very willingly on their yards and gardens.

The yard and garden products industry was composed of manufacturers and wholesalers of tools, equipment, accessories, and out buildings, such as gazebos, conservatories and enclosed decks; growers of plant material and producers of seeds; retail stores and mail-order businesses; and consulting, planning, and landscaping services. Yard and garden products were available to consumers in general stores, home centers and hardware stores, as well as in specialty nurseries, greenhouses, and plant stores; direct-mail garden catalogs; and online shopping sites. In 1996 the *New York Times* ranked the outlets for yard and garden products. Garden centers and mass merchandisers were most popular, followed by hardware stores, supermarkets, feed/seed stores, home centers, and mail-order companies.

The market for outdoor power equipment (OPE) was expected to reach $7.7 billion by 1999, assuming an annual growth rate of about 5.6 percent. Manufacturers of lawn care equipment tend to also produce machinery for other industries and professional grade equipment. For example, Deere & Company produced lawn mowers and leaf blowers for the consumer retail market. The company also manufactured tractors, backhoe loaders, and harvesting machinery for the construction and agriculture markets. Other companies, such as Black & Decker, made edgers and trimmers, and also produced power tools. U.S. companies accounted for 95 percent of worldwide OPE sales. Lawn mowers represented the largest-selling OPE product line, accounting for 73 percent of U.S. OPE sales in the mid-1990s.

The market for garden tools and implements was predicted to grow at an annual rate of 3.2 percent to register sales of $3 billion by 1999. The market for soil and plant care tools, wheeled devices, and composters was rather fragmented in the late 1990s. No single company consequently maintained a large market share. This market did not carry strong brand loyalty, in general. Because the tools tended to be manufactured easily and inexpensively, new companies entered the market continuously. Yet some companies, including the well-known British company, Spear & Jackson, manufacturer of garden tools and implements since the late 1700s, continued to enjoy success at the high-end of the market, with a trusted reputation for the serious gardener.

Chemicals and pesticides were produced mainly by one of many subsidiaries of large chemical companies. This segment of the yard and garden products industry was experiencing slower growth in the late 1990s, mainly due to the increasing consumer trend toward "natural" gardening and lawn care. The industry was expected to achieve $1.9 billion in sales by 1999, up only 10.4 percent from 1994. Most of the sales in this segment, approximately 72 percent, came from the purchase of insecticides, with herbicides a distant second at 18 percent.

Plants and seeds were grown at large nurseries that catered to a national market, and at smaller local nurseries. Traditionally, consumers purchased flowers, vegetables, fruit trees, and plants at local nurseries or greenhouses. However, in the 1990s, mail order catalogues, supermarkets, mass retailers, and the Internet became increasingly popular ways for consumers to buy plants and seeds.

People in the United States by the late 1990s had established the habit of purchasing yard and garden supplies through a manufacturer's retail outlet chain such as Sears, K-Mart, and Ace or True Value Hardware, or through their local hardware stores. With the advent of home improvement superstores, such as Lowe's and Home Depot, more people began shopping at these outlets, which offered a large selection, low prices, and knowledgeable sales service. Home Depot offered weekly building classes for children, teaching the art and skill of building such items as birdhouses, small benches, and tables. This added incentive proved a successful market tool for that company.

BACKGROUND AND DEVELOPMENT

The maintenance of attractive yards and gardens was reserved for the aristocracy in the early nineteenth century. Functional gardens, on the other hand, were a necessary source of food for all classes. As time passed, and products became affordable and available, other classes began cultivating their yards for aesthetic purposes. In 1870 Elwood McGuire designed a machine used for push mowing. By 1885 the United States was building 50,000 lawnmowers each year. In the early twentieth century, push mowers were relatively common equipment for homeowners. As the United States became less agrarian and more urbanized in the mid-twentieth century, gardening became a hobby or avocation for many.

The development of grocery stores and supermarkets with efficient distribution channels for bringing fresh produce from across the country meant gardens were less necessary to provide food for families. During World War I and World War II, however, civilians were encouraged to plant "Victory Gardens" in order to supplement the national food supply. The popularity of the long-running, weekly televised program on the Public Television Broadcasting network that bore the name, "The Victory Garden," indicated that Americans continued to draw from the spirit of those war efforts, and continued to be fascinated by gardening.

In the early 1970s yard care and gardening experienced another surge, which coincided with the conservation of petroleum resources. The oil embargo and the subsequent energy crisis encouraged Americans to examine their patterns of energy consumption. This lead to a resurgence of growing food for personal use.

At the same time, the growing environmentalist movement emphasized a more natural, ecologically sound lifestyle. This was characterized by the consciousness of the interconnections between all living creatures, respect for the earth, and conservation of resources. The organic gardening movement, pioneered by individuals like J.I. Rodale, his son Robert Rodale, and Louis Bromfield, emphasized the use of compost rather than chemical fertilizers to deliver nutrients to plants and soil. Proponents of organic gardening also advocated natural pest control methods instead of powerful chemical pesticides.

Though the energy-consciousness and environmental trend of the early 1970s slowed as the oil shortage ended, the joys and pleasures of yard care and gardening continued to appeal to many who viewed the practice as a connection to the natural world. By the 1990s gardening was among the most popular hobbies of adult Americans. The 1995-96 *National Gardening Survey* reported 72 percent, or an estimated 72 million American households, participated in lawn and garden activities of some kind in 1995.

Environmental concerns as well as interest in gardening as a hobby helped shape trends in the yard and garden products industry in the early 1990s. For example, composting was good for the soil. Municipalities promoted it as a logical and viable alternative to discarding yard waste in landfills. By 1996 about 27 states had laws banning landfills entirely. In addition, U.S. Environmental Protection Agency (EPA) regulations passed in 1995 significantly impacted the outdoor power equipment segment of the industry. More stringent emissions requirements for lawn mowers,

*A **John Deere Lawn and Garden tractor in use**. (Courtesy of John Deere International.)*

garden tractors, rototillers, and chain saws forced manufacturers of these products to improve the fuel combustion of these products.

Other factors influenced the growth rate of the industry. In 1995, for example, the cold spring and dry summer combined with an increase in the number of retailers (and thus, decreased prices) to force industry sales into decline. The average household spent $303 on yard and garden products in 1995, compared to $342 in 1994. Concurrently, average spending on landscaping; indoor houseplants; herb, water, and container gardening; and raising transplants increased.

CURRENT CONDITIONS

According to the editors of *Roper Reports,* home ownership statistics were a strong indicator of the market for garden products. Low mortgage interest rates in the late 1990s helped many people purchase homes. These same people became concerned with landscaping and maintaining their yards and gardens. This led to continued success for the industry.

Many magazines helped consumers find their needed products and learn how to use them. These magazines included *Garden Design, Water Garden-*

Trends

A FIRM HOLD ON THE TRADITIONAL

Not all gardeners are swept away by the lure of technology—many are downright anti-computer. For these traditionalists, gardening is a tactile experience that involves a relationship with nature. They object to the need to be indoors that computers necessitate, and to the inability to carry them down to the garden for reference or curl up with one in the sunshine, as with a garden catalog or reference book. Further, some see the energy resources needed to operate the computer for help in gardening as wasteful.

While these traditionalists may well eschew the intrusion of computers into their gardening experience, electronic modes of delivering products, services, and information may open the door for a whole new breed of gardener, one that may not have been interested before such technology was widespread.

ing, *Organic Gardening, Country Living Gardener,* and special publications from various house- and garden-oriented magazines such as *Better Homes and Gardens,* with their *Garden, Deck, and Landscape Planner.* These publications emphasize the benefits of yard and garden care, and offer special features on composting, new machine and plant varieties, and decorative products. Smaller publications from gardening groups and societies, such as the newsletter-style publication of *The American Cottage Gardener,* produced under the auspices of the American Cottage Gardening Society, as well as its companion group, the American Dianthus Society, promoted the return of plant and flower species that had been prominent in earlier American gardens, especially in the nineteenth century. Such publications also enhanced communications among gardeners at geographic distances, enabling them to share advice and helpful hints for their gardens. These groups also increased interest in heirloom species of flowers, plants, fruits, and vegetables.

The late 1990s witnessed a continued interest in environmentally friendly products. With the increase in composting, more people purchased composting bins, chipper/shredders, and related products. Many companies produced watering kits and sprinkler systems that wasted less water than traditional methods. This was significant to the environmentally-driven concern to use less water. Gas-powered products featured lowered emissions, and companies

were exploring alternatives to pesticides and other chemicals.

Dr. Tim Rhodus of Ohio State University predicts opportunities for businesses offering customized services, post-sale customer follow-ups, and improved customer convenience. For example, businesses offering home delivery of plant materials and calls from a store representative after delivery could create satisfied customers, potentially leading to repeat business. Offering on-site soil testing or in-home garden planning services were expected to ensure appropriate plant choices. Questions about the amount of time the customer was willing to spend on yard maintenance also helped determine the proper plants and equipment. Rather than putting the burden on customers to educate themselves about yard and garden products, successful businesses would distinguish themselves from their competitors by offering educational opportunities at the point-of-sale. To do this, companies employed salespeople who were knowledgeable about plants and lawn care, and used technology to provide detailed, customized information on available products.

The yard and garden products industry was expected to succeed and expand in the twenty-first century, due to the generation of baby boomers who would be reaching upper-middle age and retirement age—the age group that traditionally spends the most time on lawn care and gardening. Interest in lawn care and gardening would likely increase sales of how-to books and gardening magazines, videos, and software, along with other products, notably, tools, compost, fertilizers, and other maintenance products.

INDUSTRY LEADERS

The leader in the pesticide market for many years was Monsanto Company, producer of Roundup and Ortho products. Continuing the trend of consolidation in the pesticide market, Monsanto signed a letter of intent to sell its lawn and garden division to Scotts Company. Scotts was set to acquire the Ortho and White Swan brands in the United States, plus three other Monsanto brands internationally, for $300 million. Monsanto retained production rights of Roundup products while Scotts marketed them under a long-term agreement.

The Scotts Company of Marysville, Ohio, had over 50 percent of the market share for do-it-yourself yard and garden products in the late 1990s. The company began in 1870 when Orlando McLean Scott bought the seed and hardware business that evolved into O.M. Scott & Sons. The company started with store sales and branched into mail order, specializing in grass seed for golf courses. Turf Builder, its flagship product, was a lawn fertilizer developed in 1928. It revolutionized lawn care by providing an alternative to manure. Scotts was purchased by ITT Corporation in 1971. In 1986 a management buyout made Scotts an independent private company. The company's sales continued to grow and it expanded through mergers and acquisitions of other companies in the lawn and garden business. In 1988 Scotts bought Hyponex, a leading potting soil producer; in 1995 it merged with Miracle-Gro, a successful maker of plant fertilizers. The Scotts Company began trading on the New York Stock Exchange in 1992.

Founded in 1893, Gardener's Supply Inc. of Burlington, Vermont, was the largest mail-order garden tool and supply company. Gardener's Supply planned to expand its wholesale operations to include nurseries and garden centers in order to retain its market position. Additionally, they planned to collaborate with other mail-order suppliers of high-quality plant materials and develop a corps of gardening experts acting as their product distributors. Smith & Hawken, founded in 1979 in Mill Valley, California, was another mail-order supplier of imported garden tools, clothing, garden furniture, and decorations. Acquired by CML Corporation in 1993, it also operated retail stores.

The Peaceful Valley Farm Supply of Grass Valley, California, was founded in 1976 in the midst of the environmental awareness movement. In their stated philosophy that appeared in their annual catalog, Peaceful Valley was, "dedicated to promoting sustainable agriculture by providing farmers and gardeners with cost-effective, state-of-the-art, organic growing supplies and the information and tools need to apply them." Among the mail-order offerings in their 1999 catalog were: vegetable seeds, including organic open-pollinated seed packs and bulk seeds; growing and propagating supplies, including soil blockers and growing containers; natural pest management supplies and solutions; tools; animal health products, and books.

The leader in the home improvement superstore category was Home Depot. In 1998 the company had $24.2 billion in sales and $1.2 billion in net income. Home Depot stores were usually contained in about 100,000 square feet and typically carried between 40,000 and 50,000 items, including yard and garden care equipment. The company prided itself on offering low prices, varied products, knowledge, and help to the do-it-yourself gardener. Other home improvement superstores that feature yard and garden equipment included 84 Lumber, Hechinger, and Lowe's. For those who preferred to shop at smaller stores, leaders included Ace Hardware, Servistar, and True Value. Yard and garden supplies could also be found in general retail stores such as Kmart, Ward's, Sears, and Wal-Mart.

Among the leaders in power tools manufacturing for yard and garden care in the late 1990s were Deere & Company followed by Toro Company. Other manufacturers included Tomkins, Homelite, Black & Decker Corporation, Snapper, Honda, and McCulloch. These companies produced equipment such as lawn mowers, chain saws, string trimmers, and leaf blowers.

Gardening enthusiasts could get information from many and varied sources, in addition to magazines, books and brochures. Television shows and Internet sites enjoyed the gardening boom, as well. HGTV, a division of E.W. Scripps Company, was the only national home and gardening cable channel, reaching 39 million cable households in the United States in the 1990s. That networks' programs included *Breaking Ground, The Gardener's Journal, Gardening by the Yard,* and *Joy of Gardening.* NBC's *Today* show, *Good Morning America* on ABC, and local talk shows around the United States offered gardening segments on their shows.

The Internet served as host to a wealth of information on gardening. GardenNet grouped categories, ranging from online shopping sites and catalogues, to planning a vacation to the world's best gardens. Most online garden sites provided more than just a place to buy. They offered the latest information in gardening techniques. Both SummerSun and Garden.com offered visitors not only products for sale, but information and guidance on design, tailoring ideas to the region of the country in which one lived. There were also many sites on gardening software and clubs for every flower imaginable.

Gardening enthusiasts in the United States cited the annual post-Christmas holiday mailings of seed catalogs as a key element in their passion. Along with federal tax forms, seed catalogs graced the often snow-covered mailboxes of those who otherwise only dreamed about spring. Companies that represented only a minute few of the thousands of seed & plant providers included Burpee; Mellinger's; Jackson & Perkins Roses & Gardens; Shepherd's Garden Seeds; White Flower Farms; Seed Savers Exchange, Heirloom Seeds & Gifts; and Johnny's Selected Seeds.

AMERICA AND THE WORLD

While some companies in the industry pursued international markets, for companies in the chemical and live plant business, costs of inspections and regulations overseas were often prohibitive. Many, such as Scotts, bought foreign companies as subsidiaries. Furthermore, Scotts was expected to get the edge on marketing products internationally when it acquired Monsanto's lawn and garden division. The sale included foreign brands such as Green Cross (Canada), Phostrogen (United Kingdom), and Defender (Australia). Moreover, lawn and garden supplies manufactured by U.S. companies were also entering foreign markets through retailers. Home Depot had several stores in Canada, and intended to expand into Puerto Rico and South America, should conditions prove amenable.

For equipment manufacturers, global distribution was easier. American companies sold lawn and garden equipment, as well as professional-use equipment, around the world. Foreign companies such as Honda, Hyundai, and Mitsubishi sold or distributed lawn-care products in the United States.

RESEARCH AND TECHNOLOGY

Research and technology affected the development of tools and equipment. *Appliance Manufacturer,* a trade journal covering the lawn and garden equipment industry, reported that the emphasis for outdoor garden products at the International Lawn, Garden, and Power Equipment Expo 96 was safety and ease of operation. Designs showed improvements in weight, balance, grip, and vibration, as well as in simplicity of use.

Interactive computer technology was a growing trend in this industry, but had not reached its full potential in the marketing of yard and garden products yet in the 1990s. Industry analysts expected that computer programs at retail centers would allow customers to input information about their particular yards or sites, as well as preferences for the amount of maintenance they wished to administer, in order to determine the best plant matches for their purposes. Such new systems of delivering customized information were expected to transform the retail experience and increase customer satisfaction. At the same time, collecting and analyzing this information would help retailers better track sales, improving their ability to meet the demands of a particular market. It would also

give them the ability to track what was sold to individuals, and create opportunities to send newsletters or mailings to advise customers when and how to care for their purchases.

Potential existed substantially, too, for using computer technology to educate homeowners about lawn care, gardening, and products. The Internet offered vast resources to home gardeners. Among them were zone-specific, up-to-date bulletins from local county extension services and the latest agricultural; and horticultural research from local land-grant universities. The Internet also held promise as a shopping vehicle for local nurseries and greenhouses, as well as for mail-order businesses. As it became possible to deliver video over the Internet, new opportunities would be available to provide instruction to customers for maintaining plants, building garden structures, creating compost, identifying insect pests, and installing irrigation systems, for example. These modes of delivering products, services, and information were expected to make gardening more accessible.

FURTHER READING

"The Black & Decker Corporation." *Hoover's Online,* 9 July 1998. Available from http://www.hoovers.com.

"Deere & Company." *Hoover's Online,* 9 July 1998. Available from http://www.hoovers.com.

Gallup Organization and National Gardening Association. *National Gardening Survey 1995-96.* Burlington, VT: Gallup Organization, 1996.

The Garden.com Home Page, 9 July 1998. Available from http://www.garden.com.

The GardenNet Home Page, 9 July 1998. Available from http://www.gardennet.com.

"Hands On: Trade Show of Outdoor Garden Equipment Puts Focus on User-Friendliness." *Appliance Manufacturer,* 1 October 1996.

"The Home Depot, Inc." *Hoover's Online,* 9 July 1998. Available from http://www.hoovers.com.

"Honda Motor Co., Ltd." *Hoover's Online,* 9 July 1998. Available from http://www.hoovers.com.

"Inch by Inch, Row by Row." *American Demographics,* April 1997.

Johnson, Sally. "Reaping What the Boomers Sow: Getting Down and Dirty in the Garden Is Big Business." *New York Times,* 28 September 1996.

Kelly, Joseph M. "Energy-Efficient Products, Pro Gear to Get Expo 97 Emphasis." *Home Improvement Market,* July 1997.

"Landfill Bans Spur Home Composting Programs." *World Wastes,* March 1996.

The Monsanto Home Page, 10 July 1998. Available from http://www.monsanto.com.

"Rules for Lawn Equipment." *New York Times,* 3 June 1995.

The SummerSun Home Page, 9 July 1998. Available from http://www.summersun.com.

"The Toro Company." *Hoover's Online,* 9 July 1998. Available from http://www.hoovers.com.

"TruServ Corporation." *Hoover's Online,* 10 July 1998. Available from http://www.hoovers.com.

"U.S. Home & Garden Chairman, Pres. & CEO-Interview." *Wall Street Corporate Reporter, Inc.,* 8 June 1998.

"U.S. Home & Garden, Inc." *Hoover's Online,* 9 July 1998. Available from http://www.hoovers.com.

The U.S. Lawn and Garden Market, August 1997. Available from http://www.findsvp.com/cgi-bin/Retrieve-Item.cgi?pub=LA477.

The U.S. Market for Lawn and Garden Outdoor Power Equipment, 9 July 1998. Available from http://www.findsvp.com.

The U.S. Market for Lawn and Garden Pesticides, 9 July 1998. Available from http://www.findsvp.com.

The U.S. Market for Lawn and Garden Tools and Implements, 9 July 1998. Available from http://www.findsvp.com.

Williams, Brian. "Storms Past, Scotts Finds Seeds of Change Yield a Blooming Success." *The Columbus Dispatch,* 27 July 1997.

—Joan Giglierano,
updated by Lisa Karl and Jane E. Spear

YEAR 2000 COMPLIANCE PRODUCTS AND SERVICES

INDUSTRY SNAPSHOT

January 1, 2000 is sometimes called "Black Saturday" because it was the first day since the dawn of the computing industry on which the year did not begin with the digits 19. As a result all computer programs worldwide that used a two-digit year field and assumed the value of 19 for the century—a convention that was until recently almost universal—were prone to "crash" or give erroneous results. Computer chips embedded in everything from VCRs to medical monitors became problematic in this regard.

Banks, utilities, the telecommunications industry, and businesses of all kinds predicted that their programs would be corrected before the deadline of December 31, 1999. For those that succeeded and brought their systems into compliance, a potential risk to data integrity lingered due to possible interactions with malfunctioning outside computers used by business partners and suppliers. Despite attempts to mitigate this risk through mutual technical support or contractual enforcement, the business world anticipated that the resulting rounds of finger pointing and litigation could cost 2 to 3 times as much as the original problem. Governments were forced to consider the potential for the failure of defense electronics, and the effects of economic upheaval and social disorder sparked by the disruption of critical systems, such as food distribution channels or electrical power systems. Preparations for the Year 2000, or "Y2K compliance," posed the biggest challenge ever faced by users of information technologies because intrinsic to Y2K compliance was the inflexible deadline.

ORGANIZATION AND STRUCTURE

Managers who recognized that due diligence was warranted in order for any business to survive the transition to the Year 2000, or "Y2K," acknowledged that the diagnosis of problematic systems was the first challenge. During the 1990s an industry rose quickly to bridge the gap to enable these businesses to survive the automated transition into the twenty-first century. The development of Y2K diagnostic hardware and software programs to isolate the vulnerability of systems was equally critical to the solution, as was the development of programs to correct the problems and create compliance. Consulting services sprang up rapidly, ranging from programming and system technologies to strategic business planning.

By the beginning of 1999, predictions of the total worldwide cost of the Y2K problem varied from about $50 billion to almost $4 trillion; the largest number of estimates hovered around the $300 billion mark. In an official report dated February 1999, the U.S. Senate called Y2K, "one of the most serious and potentially devastating events this nation has ever encountered. . . ." The most dire predictions came, not unexpectedly, from those vendors of Y2K compliance products, but for many the reality of Y2K surfaced as early as 1998 and 1999. For several months before the turn of the millenium, the year portion of expiration dates, project deadlines, and bond maturity dates entered the twenty-first century range for the first time in the history of electronic computing. The U.S. Office of Management and Budget predicted that the federal government would spend $5 billion between 1996 and 2000 to ensure Y2K compliance of its systems.

Some Y2K "bugs" in the federal system were isolated early—in 1998 and 1999—as preparations were underway in anticipation of October 1, 1999, the first day of fiscal year 2000. Similar bug detection occurred in most of the 50 United States, where July 1, 1999 signaled the start of fiscal year 2000. Some analysts predicted ever rising repair costs, in reaction to mounting unforeseen complications that pushed man-hour requirements for costly electronic technicians and systems professionals continually higher.

The factors that contributed to Y2K distinguished the problem from traditional crises of the past. First, the universal nature of the problem precluded reliance on standard contingency plans such as off-site backup systems, reciprocal agreements, and external assistance, because backup systems were equally susceptible to Y2K chaos. Next, the technological origin of the problem dictated that the most advanced industries—those most dependent upon computers and telecommunications—were at the greatest risk. Finally, the nature of the non-negotiable deadline to modify computer systems to accommodate the century change posed a problem that was unique in the computer industry, an environment where schedule slippage is normally accepted as a routine occurrence.

Companies that fixed their software when the Y2K issue initially surfaced had the luxury of treating Y2K like any standard project—it was time consuming and expensive, but relatively straightforward. Most allocated 5 to 25 percent of their information technology budget to the task from 1997 to 2000. Organizations that waited too long injected the complications of temporary solutions to be re-addressed at a later time, after the turn of the millenium. These temporary measures added to the cost of Y2K repairs, as the cost of outside help escalated rapidly with the approach of the year 2000. The Gartner Group consultants predicted in 1999 that 30 percent of companies worldwide would have at least one critical system fail as a result of inadequate preparations for Y2K.

Many managers were frustrated at the prospect of spending exorbitant resources on their computer systems just to ensure survival without gaining any improvement in productivity or functionality. Vendors attempted to capitalize on such attitudes by touting Y2K compliance as an incentive to purchase new hardware and software systems outright. By mid-1998, companies that had not already made significant progress on their Y2K compliance plan were advised to concentrate on system replacement rather than the more volatile project of comprehensive system repair. With nearly 30 percent of a typical corporate infor-

mation technology budget allocated to routine maintenance and repair, prudence would dictate the absorption of Y2K expense through an overall system upgrade to eliminate the dangers of Y2K failure and yield simultaneous enhancements. The Internal Revenue Service, for example, combined its Y2K effort with a plan to merge its 11 data centers into 2, replacing 17,000 workstations and 1,700 telecommunications circuits.

The potential price of Y2K failure was widely publicized. In a survey conducted by the Year 2000 Information Center, almost 70 percent of information technology professionals assessed Y2K as a very large or potentially fatal threat to organizations. Intercorporate lawsuits over missed deliveries or for delivery of non-compliant products threatened modern industry around the globe. Even minor disruptions of corporate services had the potential to generate lawsuits from other companies seeking to recover their own Y2K losses. Consumers could sue companies for loss or inconvenience. Stockholders and corporate directors could even sue their own companies for failure to address Y2K problems. Regardless of outcome, such lawsuits would inevitably drain corporate resources. The U.S. Senate Special Committee on the Year 2000 Technology Problem projected that the potential cost of law suits and legal judgements might run as high as $1 trillion.

The U.S. Securities and Exchange Commission passed a mandate requiring the disclosure of Y2K liabilities, and the Federal Depositors Insurance Corporation (FDIC) warned banks about the likelihood of litigation. Organizations received advice to establish proof of "due diligence" in addressing Y2K vulnerability. Some insurers offered "millennium insurance" at very high rates and with multiple loopholes. The projected need for retroactive repairs, updates of stopgap measures, on-going repairs of postponed updates of non-mission-critical systems, and unforeseen problems was augmented by the inevitable occurrence of February 29, 2000—leap year day would further complicate the circumstance of Y2K. Anticipation of an ongoing need for latent system repairs insured a future beyond the turn of the century for the fledgling Y2K industry.

BACKGROUND AND DEVELOPMENT

The first generation of computer programmers in the 1950s squeezed their code onto 80-column punch cards and worked with extremely limited computer memory. Every byte, or character, that could be conserved was important, and it seemed ridiculous at the time to waste two bytes of storage to designate the century. No one expected that the original code would still be used almost 50 years later. The two-digit calendar year entry was a programming convention. Although the early computer hardware was replaced long ago, a surprising number of old computer programs survived the ensuing 50 years. Technicians ported old software to new machines, enhanced the code, and used it as a framework to construct new systems. The retention of older programs was encouraged by "backward compatibility," an aspect of new machines that enabled companies to buy new hardware without replacing old software. Backward compatibility was a popular selling point among larger organizations that maintained huge installed databases. Consequently the two-digit year designation was a welcome convention until the pending change of the millenium loomed on the horizon.

Dates are crucial to business applications. Due dates, payment dates, birth dates, and expiration dates characterize transactions. On the average, dates show up about once in every 50 lines of code. Programs, in turn, consist of millions of lines of code, and companies run hundreds of programs in the course of doing business. With thousands of mainframe computers around the world, there were billions of lines of code to be examined for two-digit dates. Further complicating the problem was the lack of standards among early data processing professionals. Program naming conventions were a recent phenomenon. Early programmers, in contrast, referenced code variables in a variety of ways, often on whims. Dates with frivolous or unusual reference names such as "Fido" or "a98467" served to exacerbate Y2K repair.

In general, personal computer (PC) software was less critical to keeping world infrastructure working than mainframes, but because PCs were heavily used, the impact of Y2K non-compliance could not be ignored. While the newest versions of most popular operating systems and applications software were developed in consideration of Y2K compliance, older versions were not. Y2K hardware incompatibilities existed with all but the newest PCs, within an embedded memory chip called the BIOS. Individual appraisal of every machine remained the only method of BIOS assessment—even for many newer machines— because computers were often assembled from parts picked out of bins that frequently contained more than one manufacturing lot.

Organizations have tools that can be used to repair date problems that might arise in software. Commercial hardware and software may be upgraded or replaced with compliant versions. Two-digit calendar-year designators can be expanded to four digits or they may be re-coded in a way that allows the century information to be squeezed into the two-digit field. "Windowing" provides a temporary stopgap whereby years 0 through 30 are interpreted as 2000 through 2030, and years 31 through 99 are interpreted as 1931 through 1999. Other techniques included "year shifting" (subtracting a number such as 28 from all the dates), and "year interception" (detection, comparison, and replacement of the spurious dates with calculated corrections). Finally, there were the options of redeveloping the applications from scratch using four-digit year fields, or utilizing manual methods. Every technique offered advantages and disadvantages; some businesses chose to repair and some chose to postpone the problem. Most organizations approached the situation through a combination of techniques and systematically addressed the most critical programs first.

PIONEERS IN THE FIELD

Bob Bemer, one of the earliest programming gurus, helped to define the ASCII code, which allows different types of computers to exchange text information. He emerged from semi-retirement to tackle the Y2K situation with his company, BMR Software of Richardson, Texas. The BMR software package, called Vertex 2000, took a unique approach to the Y2K problem. Instead of expanding the date field "horizontally," going from two digits to four, Bemer's software took advantage of the fact that ASCII characters don't take up every last data bit in the space they are allotted. So the two-digit date field could be expanded "vertically," squeezing a code to denote the century into the extra space. The expanded characters are called "Bemer digits," or "bigits."

Bemer claimed that his solution could be implemented faster and less expensively; however, since programs adjusted with his method would run slower than before, this was only a temporary fix. Because Vertex 2000 worked not on the human-readable source code, but on the machine-readable object code, which results when a program is compiled, it was difficult to track and check using traditional systems engineering techniques.

Many programmers who know of Bemer and respect him as a visionary regard his solution as a very clever idea. However, in the final analysis the impact of the Vertex 2000 software package was limited by the same problem that plagues many Y2K efforts—it arrived too late.

CURRENT CONDITIONS

The jeopardy of Y2K non-compliance was not an issue confined to occurrences at midnight on December 31, 1999. As early as February of 1998, Federal Reserve Chairman Allan Greenspan said that the impact of the Y2K problem was evident in the economy because resources had been diverted. An estimated 40 percent of companies had already experienced Y2K problems by March 1998.

Organizations that were faced with the option of performing Y2K repairs in-house versus outsourcing the work to consultants, had to weigh the pros and cons. Consultants generate added cost and know less about any specific organization than do respective employees of the firm. Conversely, consultants have special expertise and their presence allows the regular staff to remain focused on running the business. Conditions were such by 1999 that Y2K software remedies were reasonably tested and sufficiently robust to arm consultants with effective tools.

The Federal Government, not among the leaders in Y2K preparation, accelerated its efforts considerably during the final months before the twentieth century. In June 1998 Congress allocated $3.9 billion for federal Y2K fixes, including a $1.6 billion emergency fund, for the Department of Defense, after the General Accounting Office warned that agencies would have to quadruple their repair rate in order to meet the deadline. The House Subcommittee on Government Management, Information and Technology, headed by Representative Stephen Horn, monitored the progress of federal agencies toward achieving Y2K compliance.

In mid-1998 an independent analysis of the Federal Aviation Administration (FAA) forecast a long-range completion date of 2009 for that agency. The FAA's Y2K chief, Ray Long, assured the public that mission-critical systems would comply by midnight on December 31, 1999, and pledged to be airborne at that time, on a commercial airplane, in order to demonstrate the safety of the nation's air travel systems. FAA further quelled public concern on Sunday morning, April 11, 1999, when administration officials successfully conducted a wide-scale test of Y2K system compliance. The experiment transpired at Denver International Airport in Colorado, the newest major airport in the nation. FAA administrator Jane Garvey, who made public her intention to join Long in the commercial airways at midnight on December 31, 1999, reported that FAA Y2K tests ran without major incident. . . . *New York Times* reporter Matthew Wald called the results "blissfully boring." According to

FAA statistics the administration maintains 423 mission-critical systems out of 627 total systems; only 151 of the mission-critical systems required Y2K modification. The FAA reported further that over 200 noncritical systems were either in compliance or had fixes in the offing by the April test date, with 88 percent of those fixes completed and the remaining systems scheduled for completion by June 1999.

The Social Security Administration (SSA) received an "A" rating in Y2K preparedness from Horn's subcommittee in May of 1998. The U.S. Treasury Department, which issues Social Security checks, assured that corresponding systems were in compliance as well.

As of June 1998, the Department of Defense (DOD) designated about 1,000 mission-critical systems to be repaired or replaced. Another 2,200 mission-critical systems remained under evaluation. This situation earned DOD a "D" rating under the subcommittee's evaluation criteria, which rated agencies on their overall progress. As the evaluation of DOD systems progressed, the ratio of non-compliant systems to total DOD systems increased, and the subcommittee lowered the rating even further.

Simulated failure testing of power systems, conducted under the guidance of the North American Electric Reliability Council in 1999, proved successful despite earlier commentary from *U.S. News and World Report* in December 1998, that an estimated 50 percent of U.S. utilities were not Y2K compliant. In March 1999 Michigan Consolidated Gas, Consumers Energy, and Detroit Edison alone reported spending a combined total of $48 million over a three-year period to insure Y2K compliance. Spokespeople for these and other U.S. utilities expressed optimism that power systems would bridge the gap into the new millenium without incident. Mock failures staged at key public utility companies across the United States on April 9, 1999 included simulation of voltage irregularities, telecommunication failures, and switching problems. Testers searched for latent faults that remained in on-line and back-up power systems. Council president, Michehl Gent, reported that the tests were useful in isolating the remaining problems. The drill was scheduled to recur on September 9, 1999. Other public services, like the California Highway Patrol, engaged in intensive investigation for faulty "embedded" chips that control machinery such as VCRs, car engines, and security devices. According to reports in 1999, the embedded chip problem was not of the magnitude originally suspected. According to Andy Kyte of the Gartner Group, as quoted by the *Sacramento Bee,* most of the embedded chips ". . .don't even know what planet they are on, much less care what date or time means." Almost all of the commercially and industrially used embedded chips that were susceptible to the Y2K bug were identified and replaced before they became a problem.

Various industry organizations undertook efforts to assist members in isolating and addressing Y2K problems under mutual cooperation. The Automotive Industry Action Group instituted a program whereby auto suppliers could become Y2K-certified by the Information Technology Association of America. The National Retail Federation and the Rx2000 Solutions Institute, which serves the health care industry, also instituted Y2K-compliance programs. The Mortgage Banks Association of America conducted industry-wide tests with mortgage service companies, credit bureaus, appraisers, insurance companies, the Federal Home Mortgage Corporation, and the Federal National Mortgage Association to insure Y2K readiness. The Bankers Forum 2000 met regularly and the Securities Industry Association scheduled Y2K interoperability testing for the second quarter of 1999. The FDIC anticipated completion of on-site visitation to all banks by June 1998, including assessments of 275 data processing companies and 12 major software companies.

Pre-Y2K surveys early in 1999 pinpointed key business arenas that lagged in compliance preparations. A survey of 44 major airlines by the International Air Transport Association, revealed that only 67 percent could anticipate full compliance by a target date of October 1, 1999. Earlier surveys, in 1998, held that over 30 percent of hospitals and 61 percent of small businesses had no Y2K plan at all. In anticipation of the unprepared, the poorly prepared, and the totally unpredictable, the insurance industry made preparations to protect itself against Y2K, from a less technical vantage. Insurance carriers around the world mailed letters to their policyholders to clarify that Y2K problems are exempt from coverage. Karen Ahearn of Erie Insurance Group defended the stance of the insurers, and explained that Y2K protection never fell under the protection of homeowner policies in particular, because the problem and its potential did not exist when most policies were written.

INDUSTRY LEADERS

Software vendors rushed to market with program applications to facilitate Y2K compliance. These hurried tools raised concerns about their own integrity.

As a result, analysts advised companies to give greatest consideration to those packages that were developed early in the course of the Y2K dilemma. Other applications that have had the chance to be improved and updated through several iterations are more highly recommended.

Most of the available tools were developed for COBOL programs running on IBM mainframes. They included Computer Associates' CA-Fix/2000 and CA-Accuchek, MainWare's Hourglass 2000, Isogon's SoftAudit/2000, ViaSoft's Bridge 2000, IBM's VisualAge 2000, and Cybermation's ESP Dateline 2000 Test Bench.

Another large category of tools were developed for PCs. These included Xpediter+ by Compuware, CACI's Restore 2000, and the Insight 2000 Toolkit by Software AG of North America. The scope of Y2K desktop tools varied widely. Some actually tested the BIOS chip. Others, such as Bindview Development's Netinventory, verified software version numbers against vendor listings of compliant versions. WRQ's Express 2000 ties into an enterprise software management tool to prioritize non-compliant program routines based on frequency of use. IST Development offered Y2K packages specifically for Microsoft Access; Excel and FoxPro; Lotus Approach and 1-2-3 spreadsheets; the Basic, Visual Basic, C, and C++ programming languages; and the dBase, Clipper, and Paradox databases.

Some compliance products examined data input from outside organizations in order to detect Y2K dependencies that might cause problems. These included OnMark 2000 by ViaSoft and Think 2000 by Thinking Tools. RescueWare, a product of Relativity Technologies Inc., looked at COBOL code and provided an analysis of what it did. The code was then converted into a newer language like C++, Visual Basic, or Java.

Government bureaus and agencies comprise a major market both for Y2K compliance tools and services. Among others, the federal General Services Administration (GSA) approved Check 2000 Client Server Version 3.0 for government purchase. The network utility was deployed at the U.S. Departments of Commerce and the Interior, to assess approximately 9,400 desktop computers. Douglas County, Nebraska, awarded a $2 million contract to New York-based Cognizant Technology Solutions to ensure the Y2K compliance of more than 4 million lines of code by March 1, 1999. The United States Agency for International Development, only 14 percent compliant by May 1998, awarded a $192 million Y2K contract to Computer Sciences Corporation for the replacement of one-half of the agency's 7,600 PCs. The contract provided for update of telecommunications networks, and the repair of "legacy software" systems that were originally developed for obsolete mainframe hardware.

WORK FORCE

The Y2K quandary created an employment boom among aging COBOL and FORTRAN programmers whose skills were previously considered obsolete. Masters of the mainframe and others who possessed in-depth familiarity with older programming languages commanded huge salaries, up to six figures and rising, as Y2K consultants. An employees market existed for skilled professionals, as organizations bid simultaneously for the services of a seriously limited number of expert employees to work on time-sensitive Y2K projects. At one point in 1998 there were 345,000 unfilled openings for Y2K workers, and that number continued to increase as many Y2K compliance projects moved into the more labor intensive repair and test phases. The employee shortage grew more critical as increasing numbers of organizations formulated Y2K policy.

In mid-1998, the Federal Office of Personnel Management instituted a policy allowing Federal retirees to return for Y2K work and collect their old salaries without forfeiting their current pension. Agencies were seeking to fill almost 400 Y2K positions, but found that many older employees preferred to work part-time and telecommute, and were not willing or able to put in the hours required to complete projects before the problem grew to critical proportions.

To boost the number of available Y2K programmers, employers were importing professionals from overseas, and the U.S. Senate approved a bill to expedite the process. Homegrown programmers were in demand as well. Y2K "boot camps" offered crash courses in COBOL to students of all ages. At the University of Maryland, a GI Bill-style program trained students in COBOL, sent them out to do Y2K work for two years at a Maryland business or state agency, and then offered them a four-year scholarship.

AMERICA AND THE WORLD

The world's financial systems are tightly linked through electronic commerce, and trillions of dollars change hands every day. Although Y2K repair was a major priority for the banking and securities industries in the United States, it has been less so in eastern countries, where companies were distracted by Asia's 1998 economic decline. Industry analysts were concerned that cautious trading, delays, or bad data in any part of the world's financial market could cause repercussions around the globe.

The defense establishment was addressing an even more pressing concern. The Pentagon embarked upon a formal cooperative program with other nuclear powers to share data about early warning signals, in order to avoid computer errors resulting in an accidental missile launch. The National Security Agency was concerned that hackers could exploit the confusion resulting from potential widespread systems failures. Overall, the Department of Defense was moving from thinking of Y2K as an information technology problem to regarding it as a national security issue, just as companies were making plans to ensure business survival.

The potential for worldwide computer failure was projected in a survey from Cap Gemini Group of Paris in November 1998, based on response from 1,700 businesses and government organizations surveyed in the United States and Europe. The Cap Gemini survey showed that the United States allocated a total of $655 billion dollars for Y2K repairs, and spent 61 percent of that total before the end of 1998. German organizations reported spending 52 percent of a total $82 billion allocated, while France spent 49 percent of $31 billion allocated. The United Kingdom, with $41 billion in funds allocated, reported that 47 percent of the funds were already spent. The Cap Gemini survey predicted at that time, allowing a three-month slippage margin, 58 percent of U.S. computers would comply by the midnight deadline of December 31, 1999. German respondents estimated that 78 percent of their computers would comply under the same circumstances, and the United Kingdom estimated 79 percent of their computers would be ready under the same criteria. All told only 60 percent of European respondents indicated that contingency plans were in place to counteract Y2K failure, while 98 percent of U.S. organizations reported contingency preparations. Also in November 1998, the Gartner Group of Stamford, Connecticut, reported that the Asian scene was in critical condition, with 50 percent of Japanese businesses projected to suffer critical failures over the Y2K bug, and 33 percent of Chinese systems projected for failure. These figures compared to a projected 15 percent of U.S. computers anticipated to experience critical failure. The final statistics could not be known with certainty because of potential liability for third-party damages. Many anticipated the potential of the Y2K bug to generate ripple effects throughout the global economy for three years or longer into the twenty-first century.

FURTHER READING

Brewin, Bob. "House Adds $1.6 Billion to DOD Y2K Funding." *Federal Computer Week,* 8 June 1998.

Brewin, Bob, and Heather Harreld. "Tension Mounts Over Y2K Problem." *Federal Computer Week,* 1 June 1998.

———. "US to Share Y2K Nuclear Data." *Federal Computer Week,* 8 June 1998.

Buchanan, Leigh. "Zero Zero Hour." *Inc. Technology,* 18 November 1997.

Coffee, Peter. "IT Faces the Year 2000 Facts." *PC Week,* 15 June 1998.

———. "Trials of the Century." *PC Week,* 13 April 1998.

"Cognizant Helps with Y2K Effort." *PC Week,* 9 March 1998.

Comarow, Avery. "Y2K Doesn't Bug Them." *U.S. News & World Report,* 23 November 1998.

"Cooperation Key to Y2K Efforts." *Federal Computer Week,* 15 June 1998.

DeJager, Peter, and Richard Bergeon. *Managing '00: Surviving the Year 2000 Computing Crisis.* New York: John Wiley and Sons, 1997.

DeJesus, Edmund X. "Solving for the Year 2000." *Byte,* January 1998.

———. "Year 2000 Survival Guide." *Byte,* July 1998.

Despeignes, Peronet. "Utilities Expect to be Set for Y2K." *Detroit News,* 7 March 1999.

Dornan, Bob. "Dornan on Rules and Regs." *Federal Computer Week,* 15 June 1998.

Duvall, Mel. "Year 2000 Solution Has Net Effect." *Interactive Week,* 1 June 1998.

"GAO Targets Army's Year 2000 Effort." *Federal Computer Week,* 15 June 1998.

Gibson, Stan. "Dear CEO: Your Stock Options Will Soon Be Junk." *PC Week,* 30 March 1998.

Gonsalves, Antone. "Y2K Tools for Users Playing Catch-up." *PC Week,* 13 April 1998.

Grose, Thomas K. "He Solved Rubik's Cube. Can He Fix Y2K?" *U.S. News & World Report,* 8 March 1999.

Hayashi, Alden M. "Millenium Bug Zapper." *Scientific American,* June 1998.

"Hospitals Lack Y2K Plans." *PC Week,* 22 June 1998.

The Information Technology Association of America. "ITAA's Year 2000 Outlook," 12 June 1998.

Johnston, Margaret. "New Automated Testing Tools Look Beyond Obvious." *Federal Computer Week,* 15 June 1998.

Levy, Steven. "Will the Bug Bite the Bull?" *Newsweek,* 4 May 1998.

Longman, Phillip J. "We May Be Nuts, But ..." *U.S. News & World Report,* 8 March 1999.

Madden, John. "Smaller Companies Run Big Y2K Risks." *PC Week,* 9 March 1998.

"The Millenium Bug." *The Economist,* 4 October 1997.

Morrow, James. "Y2K Kills Mr. Coffee! Who Should Pay?" *U.S. News & World Report,* 22 February 1999.

Neil, Stephanie. "2000 Reasons to Sue." *PC Week,* 9 March 1998.

———. "Y2K Ripple Effect." *PC Week,* 13 April 1998.

"OMB Releases Final Y2K Draft." *Federal Computer Week,* 15 June 1998.

Peyton, Carrie. "Fake Dilemmas, Real Concerns As Utilities Stage Test for 2000: Keeping Power On If Computers Fail." *Sacramento Bee,* 10 April 1999.

Rankin, Robert A. "Y2K Problems Inevitable, Senate Panel Says." *Detroit Free Press,* 24 February 1999.

"Repair, Replace, Retire." *Federal Computer Week,* 15 June 1998.

Shein, Esther. "Don't Forget to Factor in the Desktop." *PC Week,* 29 June 1998.

Stanglin, Douglas, and Ahmad Shaheen. "Year 2000 Time Bomb." *U.S. News and World Report,* 8 June 1998.

Surkan, Michael. "Network Management Enters Y2K Fray." *PC Week,* 23 March 1998.

Swett, Clint. "When the Cure Is Deadlier Than the Problem." *PC Week,* 15 June 1998.

———. "WRQ Puts Millenium Bug in Perspective." *PC Week,* 15 June 1998.

———. "Y2K Bugs Hidden in Chips: Experts Don't Expect a Technology Disaster." *Sacramento Bee,* 7 April 1999.

Taschek, John. "Sorry, No Y2K Happy Face Here." *PC Week,* 9 March 1998.

Tillett, L. Scott, and Brad Bass. "Y2K Costs Could Sap Clinton's Technology Budget Requests." *Federal Computer Week,* 1 June 1998.

Tillett, L. Scott, and Bob Brewin. "Administration Flunks Y2K Readiness Test." *Federal Computer Week,* 8 June 1998.

———. "GAO: Systems Will Miss Y2K Deadline." *Federal Computer Week,* 15 June 1998.

———. "House Moves to Head Off Y2K Snafu in Social Security." *Federal Computer Week,* 22 June 1998.

———. "House Strikes Compromise for Year 2000 Funding." *Federal Computer Week,* 29 June 1998.

———. "OMB Drops Three on Year 2000 Tier." *Federal Computer Week,* 8 June 1998.

Varon, Elana. "House Panel Matches $2.25B Y2K Funding." *Federal Computer Week,* 15 June 1998.

———. "IRS to Merge 11 Data Centers." *Federal Computer Week,* 22 June 1998.

———. "Techies Return." *Federal Computer Week,* 8 June 1998.

———. "USAID Picks CSC for Y2K Fix, Gear." *Federal Computer Week,* 8 June 1998.

Wald, Matthey L. "Air Traffic Control System Appears to Pass 2000 Test." *New York Times,* 12 April, 1999.

Wermiel, Jared. "Prepping for Year 2000." *PC Week,* 30 March 1998.

"Y2K Costs Still Underestimated." *PC Week,* 1 June 1998.

"Y2K and the Law." *PC Week,* 20 April 1998.

"Year 2000 Litigation." *PC Week,* 15 June 1998.

"Year 2000 Watch." *PC Week,* 2 March 1998 and 4 May 1998.

Yourdon, Edward, and Jennifer Yourdon. *Time Bomb 2000.* New York: Prentice Hall, 1998.

—Sherri Chasin Calvo, updated by Gloria Cooksey

Contributor Notes

Black, Virginia. Freelance writer and editor.

Bodine, Paul. Freelance writer and editor.

Brennan, Gerald E. Freelance writer living in Arcata, California; former editor of *HareLip*.

Brinker, Kaye. Freelance writer from Brooklyn Heights, New York; frequent contributor to *Bank Security Report*.

Burke, Anne. Freelance writer and editor.

Calvo, Sherri Chasin. Freelance writer; B.A. in Physics from Rutgers University and an M.B.A. in Information Systems from New York University; former newspaper reporter and editor.

Cook, Christopher M. Freelance writer and television producer from Ann Arbor, Michigan; a National Endowment for the Humanities journalist-in-residence at the University of Michigan in 1981-1982; contributes to *Hour Detroit Magazine* and *The Detroit Sunday Journal*.

Cooksey, Gloria. Freelance writer from Detroit, Michigan; earned a certificate in programming and operations from Data Control Institute and is certified as a network engineer; holds associate degrees in electronic communications and computer electronics and is licensed by the Federal Communications Commission to repair aircraft and marine communications equipment.

Crawford, Mark. Author of five books, professional writer and editor, consulting geologist, and songwriter from Madison, Wisconsin.

Deignan, Tom. Freelance writer; taught film, English, and American studies at St. John's University and The City University of New York.

DeShantz-Cook, Lisa. Freelance writer and editor.

di Lorenzi, Peter A. Ann Arbor, Michigan-based food and wine educator and consultant; M.A. in European history from the University of Michigan.

Distelzweig, Howard. Freelance writer and editor.

Eigo, Tim. Freelance business and law writer based in Phoenix, Arizona; M.A. from the University of Notre Dame and J.D. from the University of California, Hastings College of the Law.

Eldridge, Grant. Freelance writer and editor living in Pontiac, Michigan.

Fagan, Dave. Freelance journalist and business writer.

Gallagher, John. Journalist and freelance writer based in Detroit, Michigan; co-wrote *Walk Like a Giant, Sell Like a Madman* with Ralph R. Roberts in 1997.

Genaway, David C. Library Director Emeritus at Youngstown State University; founder of the National Conference on Integrated Online Library Systems; Ph.D. from the University of Minnesota.

Gerber, Judith. Full-time researcher and writer specializing in education, the arts, and political science; Bachelor's Degree in Psychology from U.C. Santa Cruz and Master's Degree in Public Administration from California State University; author of *Distinguished Women of the 20th Century*.

Giglierano, Joan. Business research analyst for American Electric Power and former business librarian based in Columbus, Ohio.

Gundersen, Linda. Freelance writer and editor from Doylestown, Pennsylvania.

Harding, Lauri. Freelance writer and editor.

Harper, Judith. Cincinnati-based developer and writer of technical manuals, articles, procedures, and training courses for print and online media; works with technology-based companies across the United States.

Hauser, Evelyn. Writer, researcher, and marketing consultant based in Arcata, California; M.A. from the College of Economics in Berlin, Germany.

Heil, Karl. Freelance writer; M.A. in linguistics from Eastern Michigan University.

Henderson, Tona. Freelance writer and business consultant based in State College, Pennsylvania; business librarian at Pennsylvania State University.

Hunt, Christopher. Freelance writer and web developer.

Jackson, Mike. Writer, documentary film producer, and cameraman living in New York; writes screenplays, short fiction, and freelance assignments.

James, Marinell. Freelance business writer.

Jensen, Susan. Freelance and short story writer located in California; adjunct college instructor of writing, literature, and education.

Karl, Lisa Musolf. Freelance writer, researcher, and editor based in the Chicago area; her work has appeared in *Parenting* magazine, *Baltimore Business Journal,* and *Orioles Magazine.*

Kasic, Christopher. Technical writer in the industrial process control and computer industry; he produces online- and HTML-help systems; his work has appeared in *Advance* and *Minnesota Technology.*

King, Brett Allan. Freelance writer and journalist living in Madrid, Spain.

Knight, Judson. Freelance writer from Atlanta, Georgia; partner in The Knight Agency, a firm specializing in literary representation and marketing.

Lawrie, Laura. Freelance writer, editor, and publishing consultant; managing editor of *American Behavioral Scientists.*

Levine, David. Freelance writer living in New York City; B.A. in journalism from the University of Wisconsin-Madison.

Levy, Dawn. Freelance science writer based in the San Francisco Bay area; former science writing intern for *Science* magazine and Stanford University; senior scientific editor for the J. David Gladstone Institutes at the University of California.

Levy, Marsha. Freelance writer and editor.

Lewis-Chapman, Lori. Freelance writer, editor, and proofreader living in Chicago.

Lewon, David M. Freelance writer and Web developer living in Auburn Hills, Michigan.

McInerney, Merry. Freelance writer and novelist from Ann Arbor, Michigan; her first novel, *Burning Down the House,* was published in 1994; her second novel, *Dog People,* was published in 1998.

McLaughlin, Cameron. Freelance writer and editor.

Nelson, Roxanne. Freelance writer and editor.

O'Donnell, Sandra E. Freelance writer; University of Michigan graduate.

Paulson, Linda. Freelance writer and editor.

Pennington-Boyce, Amy. Freelance writer and information researcher living in New Jersey.

Prady, Norman. Freelance writer and editor.

Roberts, Jeffrey. Technical communicator and freelance writer and editor; co-operates Point Productions, a company specializing in computer training and written communications with his partner Candy Zulkosky; B.A. in English from Indiana University and resides in northeastern Pennsylvania.

Rooks, Nancy. Freelance business writer based in Glenview, Illinois.

Sharp, Arthur G. Freelance business, education, and history writer; adjunct instructor at Naugatuck Valley Community-Technical College and Eastern Connecticut State University.

Shepherd, Ken. Freelance writer who teaches social science at Henry Ford Community College in Dearborn, Michigan.

Spear, Jane E. Canton, Ohio-based freelance writer and editor; graduate of St. John's College in Annapolis, Maryland.

Straub, Deborah Gillian. Grand Rapids, Michigan-based freelance writer and editor who has worked in reference book publishing for more than 20 years.

Wagner, Katherine B. Chicago-based freelance writer.

Weber, Will. Journalist, photographer, and freelance writer; director of "JOURNEYS International," a worldwide nature and culture exploration company; Ph.D. in Natural Resources from the University of Michigan.

Whittle, Janet. Feature writer and editor specializing in international business, industry analysis, and general business news and analysis; B.A. from Vassar College in political science and an M.A. in international studies from the University of Denver; has edited five books on international trade and business.

Wolfe, Joanne. Technical writer and editor; B.A.s in English and journalism from the University of Oregon; currently the editor-in-chief of *Wild Garden.*

Wood, Dorothy L. Freelance writer.

Woodward, Katherine. Freelance writer and editor.

Woodward, Nancy Hatch. Freelance writer and editor.

Yosifon, David. Reporter for the *Bay State Banner,* Boston's leading African American weekly; interests include literature, philosophy, and public transportation.

INDUSTRY INDEX

The Industry Index lists four-digit U.S. Standard Industrial Classification (SIC) codes, in numerical order, with the classification description following each code. The reference is followed by the page-number range(s) of relevant EEI essays.

SIC TO NAICS CONVERSION GUIDE

The following listing cross-references four-digit 1987 Standard Industrial Classification (SIC) codes, used in EEI, with 1998 North American Industry Classification System (NAICS) codes. Since the systems differ in specificity, some SIC categories correspond to more than one NAICS category.

AGRICULTURE, FORESTRY, & FISHING

0181   Ornamental Floriculture & Nursery Products *see* NAICS 111422: Floriculture Production; NAICS 111421: Nursery & Tree Production

0742   Veterinary Services for Animal Specialties *see* NAICS 54194: Veterinary Services

0752   Animal Specialty Services, Except Veterinary *see* NAICS 11521: Support Activities for Animal Production; NAICS 81291: Pet Care Services

CONSTRUCTION INDUSTRIES

1731   Electrical Work *see* NAICS 561621: Security Systems Services; NAICS 23531: Electrical Contractors

FOOD & KINDRED PRODUCTS

2032   Canned Specialties *see* NAICS 311422: Specialty Canning; NAICS 311999: All Other Miscellaneous Food Manufacturing

2047   Dog & Cat Food *see* NAICS 311111: Dog & Cat Food Manufacturing

2048   Prepared Feed & Feed Ingredients for Animals & Fowls, Except Dogs & Cats *see* NAICS 311611: Animal Slaughtering; NAICS 311119: Other Animal Food Manufacturing

2082   Malt Beverages *see* NAICS 31212: Breweries

2086   Bottled & Canned Soft Drinks & Carbonated Waters *see* NAICS 312111: Soft Drink Manufacturing; NAICS 312112: Bottled Water Manufacturing

2095   Roasted Coffee *see* NAICS 31192: Coffee & Tea Manufacturing; NAICS 311942: Spice & Extract Manufacturing

2099   Food Preparations, NEC *see* NAICS 311423: Dried & Dehydrated Food Manufacturing; NAICS 111998: All Other Miscellaneous Crop Farming; NAICS 31134: Non-chocolate Confectionery Manufacturing; NAICS 311911: Roasted Nuts & Peanut Butter Manufacturing; NAICS 311991: Perishable Prepared Food Manufacturing; NAICS 31183: Tortilla Manufacturing; NAICS 31192: Coffee & Tea Manufacturing; NAICS 311941: Mayonnaise, Dressing, & Other Prepared Sauce Manu-

facturing; NAICS 311942: Spice & Extract Manufacturing; NAICS 311999: All Other Miscellaneous Food Manufacturing

TOBACCO PRODUCTS

2111   Cigarettes *see* NAICS 312221: Cigarette Manufacturing

APPAREL & OTHER FINISHED PRODUCTS MADE FROM FABRICS & SIMILAR MATERIALS

2399   Fabricated Textile Products, NEC *see* NAICS 33636: Motor Vehicle Fabric Accessories & Seat Manufacturing; NAICS 315999: Other Apparel Accessories & Other Apparel Manufacturing; NAICS 314999: All Other Miscellaneous Textile Product Mills

PRINTING, PUBLISHING, & ALLIED INDUSTRIES

2741   Miscellaneous Publishing *see* NAICS 51114: Database & Directory Publishers; NAICS 51223: Music Publishers; NAICS 511199: All Other Publishers

CHEMICALS & ALLIED PRODUCTS

2821   Plastics Material Synthetic Resins, & Nonvulcanizable Elastomers *see* NAICS 325211: Plastics Material & Resin Manufacturing

2822   Synthetic Rubber *see* NAICS 325212: Synthetic Rubber Manufacturing

2833   Medicinal Chemicals & Botanical Products *see* NAICS 325411: Medicinal & Botanical Manufacturing

2834   Pharmaceutical Preparations *see* NAICS 325412: Pharmaceutical Preparation Manufacturing

2835   In Vitro & in Vivo Diagnostic Substances *see* NAICS 325412: Pharmaceutical Preparation Manufacturing; NAICS 325413: In-vitro Diagnostic Substance Manufacturing

2836   Biological Products, Except Diagnostic Substances *see* NAICS 325414: Biological Product Manufacturing

2841   Soaps & Other Detergents, Except Speciality Cleaners *see* NAICS 325611: Soap & Other Detergent Manufacturing

2842   Speciality Cleaning, Polishing, & Sanitary Preparations *see* NAICS 325612: Polish & Other Sanitation Good Manufacturing

2844   Perfumes, Cosmetics, & Other Toilet Preparations *see* NAICS 32562: Toilet Preparation Manufacturing; NAICS 325611: Soap & Other Detergent Manufacturing

2861   Gum & Wood Chemicals *see* NAICS 325191: Gum & Wood Chemical Manufacturing

2869   Industrial Organic Chemicals, NEC *see* NAICS 32511: Petrochemical Manufacturing; NAICS 325188: All Other Inorganic Chemical Manufacturing; NAICS 325193: Ethyl Alcohol Manufacturing; NAICS 32512: Industrial Gas Manufacturing; NAICS 325199: All Other Basic Organic Chemical Manufacturing

2873   Nitrogenous Fertilizers *see* NAICS 325311: Nitrogenous Fertilizer Manufacturing

2879   Pesticides & Agricultural Chemicals, NEC *see* NAICS 32532: Pesticide & Other Agricultural Chemical Manufacturing

STONE, CLAY, GLASS, & CONCRETE PRODUCTS

3264   Porcelain Electrical Supplies *see* NAICS 327113: Porcelain Electrical Supply Manufacturing

PRIMARY METALS INDUSTRIES

3357   Drawing & Insulating of Nonferrous Wire *see* NAICS 331319: Other Aluminum Rolling & Drawing; NAICS 331422: Copper Wire Drawing; NAICS 331491: Nonferrous Metal Rolling, Drawing, & Extruding; NAICS 335921: Fiber Optic Cable Manufacturing; NAICS 335929: Other Communication & Energy Wire Manufacturing

INDUSTRIAL & COMMERCIAL MACHINERY & COMPUTER EQUIPMENT

3524   Lawn & Garden Tractors & Home Lawn & Garden Equipment *see* NAICS 333112: Lawn & Garden Tractor & Home Lawn & Garden Equipment Manufacturing; NAICS 332212: Hand & Edge Tool Manufacturing

3535   Conveyors & Conveying Equipment *see* NAICS 333922: Conveyor & Conveying Equipment Manufacturing

3541   Machine Tools, Metal Cutting Type *see* NAICS 333512: Machine Tool Manufacturing

3542   Machine Tools, Metal Forming Type *see* NAICS 333513: Machine Tool Manufacturing

3559   Special Industry Machinery, NEC *see* NAICS 33322: Rubber & Plastics Industry Machinery Manufacturing; NAICS 333319: Other Commercial & Service Industry Machinery Manufacturing; NAICS 333295: Semiconductor Manufacturing Machinery; NAICS 333298: All Other Industrial Machinery Manufacturing

3564   Industrial & Commercial Fans & Blowers & Air Purification Equipment *see* NAICS 333411: Air Purification Equipment Manufacturing; NAICS 333412: Industrial & Commercial Fan & Blower Manufacturing

3569   General Industrial Machinery & Equipment, NEC *see* NAICS 333999: All Other General Purpose Machinery Manufacturing

3571   Electronic Computers *see* NAICS 334111: Electronic Computer Manufacturing

3572   Computer Storage Devices *see* NAICS 334112: Computer Storage Device Manufacturing

3575   Computer Terminals *see* NAICS 334113: Computer Terminal Manufacturing

3577   Computer Peripheral Equipment, NEC *see* NAICS 334119: Other Computer Peripheral Equipment Manufacturing

3589   Service Industry Machinery, NEC *see* NAICS 333319: Other Commercial & Service Industry Machinery Manufacturing

3599   Industrial & Commercial Machinery & Equipment, NEC *see* NAICS 336399: All Other Motor Vehicle Part Manufacturing; NAICS 332999: All Other Miscellaneous Fabricated Metal Product Manufacturing; NAICS 333319: Other Commercial & Service Industry Machinery Manufacturing; NAICS 33271: Machine Shops; NAICS 333999: All Other General Purpose Machinery Manufacturing

ELECTRONIC & OTHER ELECTRICAL EQUIPMENT & COMPONENTS, EXCEPT COMPUTER EQUIPMENT

3652   Phonograph Records & Prerecorded Audio Tapes & Disks *see* NAICS 334612: Prerecorded Compact Disc, Tape, & Record Reproducing; NAICS 51222: Integrated Record; Production/distribution

3661   Telephone & Telegraph Apparatus *see* NAICS 33421: Telephone Apparatus Manufacturing; NAICS 334416: Electronic Coil, Transformer, & Other Inductor Manufacturing; NAICS 334418: Printed Circuit/electronics Assembly Manufacturing

3663   Radio & Television Broadcasting & Communication Equipment *see* NAICS 33422: Radio & Television Broadcasting & Wireless Communications Equipment Manufacturing

3669   Communications Equipment, NEC *see* NAICS 33429: Other Communication Equipment Manufacturing

3674   Semiconductors & Related Devices *see* NAICS 334413: Semiconductor & Related Device Manufacturing

3679   Electronic Components, NEC *see* NAICS 33422: Radio & Television Broadcasting & Wireless Communications Equipment Manufacturing; NAICS 334418: Printed Circuit/electronics Assembly Manufacturing; NAICS 336322: Other Motor Vehicle Electrical & Electronic Equipment Manufacturing; NAICS 334419: Other Electronic Component Manufacturing

3691   Storage Batteries *see* NAICS 335911: Storage Battery Manufacturing

3699   Electrical Machinery, Equipment, & Supplies, NEC *see* NAICS 333319: Other Commercial & Service Industry Machinery Manufacturing; NAICS 333618: Other Engine Equipment Manufacturing; NAICS 334119: Other Computer Peripheral Equipment Manufacturing; Classify According to Function; NAICS 335129: Other Lighting Equipment Manufacturing; NAICS 335999: All Other Miscellaneous Electrical Equipment & Component Manufacturing

TRANSPORTATION EQUIPMENT

3714   Motor Vehicle Parts & Accessories *see* NAICS 336211: Motor Vehicle Body Manufacturing; NAICS 336312:

Gasoline Engine & Engine Parts Manufacturing; NAICS 336322: Other Motor Vehicle Electrical & Electronic Equipment Manufacturing; NAICS 33633: Motor Vehicle Steering & Suspension Components Manufacturing; NAICS 33634: Motor Vehicle Brake System Manufacturing; NAICS 33635: Motor Vehicle Transmission & Power Train Parts Manufacturing; NAICS 336399: All Other Motor Vehicle Parts Manufacturing

3731 Ship Building & Repairing *see* NAICS 336611: Ship Building & Repairing

3761 Guided Missiles & Space Vehicles *see* NAICS 336414: Guided Missile & Space Vehicle Manufacturing 3764

3769 Guided Missile Space Vehicle Parts & Auxiliary Equipment, NEC *see* NAICS 336419: Other Guided Missile & Space Vehicle Parts & Auxiliary Equipment Manufacturing

MEASURING, ANALYZING, & CONTROLLING INSTRUMENTS

3812 Search, Detection, Navigation, Guidance, Aeronautical & Nautical Systems & Instruments *see* NAICS 334511: Search, Detection, Navigation, Guidance, Aeronautical, & Nautical System & Instrument Manufacturing

3822 Automatic Controls for Regulating Residential & Commercial Environments & Appliances *see* NAICS 334512: Automatic Environmental Control Manufacturing for Regulating Residential, Commercial, & Appliance Use

3825 Instruments for Measuring & Testing of Electricity & Electrical Signals *see* NAICS 334416: Electronic Coil, Transformer, & Other Inductor Manufacturing; NAICS 334515: Instrument Manufacturing for Measuring & Testing Electricity & Electrical Signals

3827 Optical Instruments & Lenses *see* NAICS 333314: Optical Instrument & Lens Manufacturing

3829 Measuring & Controlling Devices, NEC *see* NAICS 339112: Surgical & Medical Instrument Manufacturing; NAICS 334519: Other Measuring & Controlling Device Manufacturing

3841 Surgical & Medical Instruments & Apparatus *see* NAICS 339112: Surgical & Medical Instrument Manufacturing

3845 Electromedical & Electrotherapeutic Apparatus *see* NAICS 334517: Irradiation Apparatus Manufacturing; NAICS 334510: Electromedical & Electrotherapeutic Apparatus Manufacturing

3851 Ophthalmic Goods *see* NAICS 339115: Ophthalmic Goods Manufacturing

3861 Photographic Equipment & Supplies *see* NAICS 333315: Photographic & Photocopying Equipment Manufacturing; NAICS 325992: Photographic Film, Paper, Plate & Chemical Manufacturing

MISCELLANEOUS MANUFACTURING INDUSTRIES

3944 Games, Toys, & Children's Vehicles, Except Dolls & Bicycles *see* NAICS 336991: Motorcycle, Bicycle & Parts Manufacturing; NAICS 339932: Game, Toy, & Children's Vehicle Manufacturing

3949 Sporting & Athletic Goods, NEC *see* NAICS 33992: Sporting & Athletic Good Manufacturing

TRANSPORTATION, COMMUNICATIONS, ELECTRIC, GAS, & SANITARY SERVICES

4512 Air Transportation, Scheduled *see* NAICS 481111: Scheduled Passenger Air Transportation; NAICS 481112: Scheduled Freight Air Transportation

4812 Radiotelephone Communications *see* NAICS 513321: Paging; NAICS 513322: Cellular & Other Wireless Telecommunications; NAICS 51333: Telecommunications Resellers

4813 Telephone Communications, Except Radiotelephone *see* NAICS 51331: Wired Telecommunications Carriers; NAICS 51333: Telecommunications Resellers

4841 Cable & Other Pay Television Services *see* NAICS 51321: Cable Networks; NAICS 51322: Cable & Other Program Distribution

4899 Communications Services, NEC *see* NAICS 513322: Cellular & Other Wireless Telecommunications; NAICS 51334: Satellite Telecommunications; NAICS 51339: Other Telecommunications

WHOLESALE TRADE

5043 Photographic Equipment & Supplies *see* NAICS 42141: Photographic Equipment & Supplies Wholesalers

5045 Computers & Computer Peripheral Equipment & Software *see* NAICS 42143: Computer & Computer Peripheral Equipment & Software Wholesalers; NAICS 44312: Computer & Software Stores - Retail

5065 Electronic Parts & Equipment, Not Elsewhere Classified *see* NAICS 42169: Other Electronic Parts & Equipment Wholesalers

5099 Durable Goods, NEC *see* NAICS 42199: Other Miscellaneous Durable Goods Wholesalers

5149 Groceries & Related Products, NEC *see* NAICS 42249: Other Grocery & Related Product Wholesalers

5199 Nondurable Goods, NEC *see* NAICS 54189: Other Services Related to Advertising; NAICS 42299: Other Miscellaneous Nondurable Goods Wholesalers

RETAIL TRADE

5261 Retail Nurseries, Lawn & Garden Supply Stores *see* NAICS 44422: Nursery & Garden Centers; NAICS 453998: All Other Miscellaneous Store Retailers; NAICS 44421: Outdoor Power Equipment Stores

5499 Miscellaneous Food Stores *see* NAICS 44521: Meat Markets; NAICS 722211: Limited-service Restaurants; NAICS 446191: Food Supplement Stores; NAICS 445299: All Other Specialty Food Stores

5521 Motor Vehicle Dealers *see* NAICS 44112: Used Car Dealers

5734 Computer & Computer Software Stores *see* NAICS 44312: Computer & Software Stores

5735 Record & Prerecorded Tape Stores *see* NAICS 45122: Prerecorded Tape, Compact Disc & Record Stores

5812 Eating & Drinking Places *see* NAICS 72211: Full-service Restaurants; NAICS 722211: Limited-service Restaurants; NAICS 722212: Cafeterias; NAICS 722213: Snack & Nonalcoholic Beverage Bars; NAICS 72231: Foodservice Contractors; NAICS 72232: Caterers; NAICS 71111: Theater Companies & Dinner Theaters

5941 Sporting Goods Stores & Bicycle Shops *see* NAICS 45111: Sporting Goods Stores

5942　Book Stores *see* NAICS 451211: Book Stores

5945　Hobby, Toy, & Game Shops *see* NAICS 45112: Hobby, Toy & Game Stores

5961　Catalog & Mail-order Houses *see* NAICS 45411: Electronic Shopping & Mail-order Houses

5963　Direct Selling Establishments *see* NAICS 72233: Mobile Caterers; NAICS 45439: Other Direct Selling Establishments

5999　Miscellaneous Retail Stores, NEC *see* NAICS 44612: Cosmetics, Beauty Supplies & Perfume Stores; NAICS 446199: All Other Health & Personal Care Stores; NAICS 45391: Pet & Pet Supplies Stores; NAICS 45392: Art Dealers; NAICS 443111: Household Appliance Stores; NAICS 443112: Radio, Television & Other Electronics Stores; NAICS 44831: Jewelry Stores; NAICS 453999: All Other Miscellaneous Store Retailers

FINANCE, INSURANCE, & REAL ESTATE

6159　Miscellaneous Business Credit Institutions *see* NAICS 52222: Sales Financing; NAICS 532: Included in Rental & Leasing Services Subsector by Type of Equipment & Method of Operation; NAICS 522293: International Trade Financing; NAICS 522298: All Other Nondepository Credit Intermediation

6162　Mortgage Bankers & Loan Correspondents *see* NAICS 522292: Real Estate Credit; NAICS 52239: Other Activities Related to Credit Intermediation

6163　Loan Brokers *see* NAICS 52231: Mortgage & Other Loan Brokers

6211　Security Brokers, Dealers, & Flotation Companies *see* NAICS 52311: Investment Banking & Securities Dealing; NAICS 52312: Securities Brokerage; NAICS 52391: Miscellaneous Intermediation; NAICS 523999: Miscellaneous Financial Investment Activities

6221　Commodity Contracts Brokers & Dealers *see* NAICS 52313: Commodity Contracts Dealing; NAICS 52314: Commodity Brokerage

6231　Security & Commodity Exchanges *see* NAICS 52321: Securities & Commodity Exchanges

6282　Investment Advice *see* NAICS 52392: Portfolio Management; NAICS 52393: Investment Advice

6289　Services Allied with the Exchange of Securities or Commodities, NEC *see* NAICS 523991: Trust, Fiduciary, & Custody Activities; NAICS 523999: Miscellaneous Financial Investment Activities

6311　Life Insurance *see* NAICS 524113: Direct Life Insurance Carriers; NAICS 52413: Reinsurance Carriers

6321　Accident & Health Insurance *see* NAICS 524114: Direct Health & Medical Insurance Carriers; NAICS 52519: Other Insurance Funds; NAICS 52413: Reinsurance Carriers

6331　Fire, Marine, & Casualty Insurance *see* NAICS 524126: Direct Property & Casualty Insurance Carriers; NAICS 52519: Other Insurance Funds; NAICS 52413: Reinsurance Carriers

6411　Insurance Agents, Brokers, & Service *see* NAICS 52421: Insurance Agencies & Brokerages; NAICS 524291: Claims Adjusters; NAICS 524292: Third Party Administrators for Insurance & Pension Funds; NAICS 524298: All Other Insurance Related Activities

6512　Operators of Nonresidential Buildings *see* NAICS 71131: Promoters of Performing Arts, Sports & Similar Events with Facilities; NAICS 53112: Lessors of Nonresidential Buildings

6513　Operators of Apartment Buildings *see* NAICS 53111: Lessors of Residential Buildings & Dwellings

6798　Real Estate Investment Trusts *see* NAICS 52593: Real Estate Investment Trusts

SERVICE INDUSTRIES

7011　Hotels & Motels *see* NAICS 72111: Hotels & Motels; NAICS 72112: Casino Hotels; NAICS 721191: Bed & Breakfast Inns; NAICS 721199: All Other Traveler Accommodation

7041　Organization Hotels & Lodging Houses, on Membership Basis *see* NAICS 72111: Hotels & Motels; NAICS 72131: Rooming & Boarding Houses

7231　Beauty Shops *see* NAICS 812112: Beauty Salons; NAICS 812113: Nail Salons; NAICS 611511: Cosmetology & Barber Schools

7319　Advertising, NEC *see* NAICS 481219: Other Nonscheduled Air Transportation; NAICS 54183: Media Buying Agencies; NAICS 54185: Display Advertising; NAICS 54187: Advertising Material Distribution Services; NAICS 54189: Other Services Related to Advertising

7361　Employment Agencies *see* NAICS 541612: Human Resources & Executive Search Consulting Services; NAICS 56131: Employment Placement Agencies

7363　Help Supply Services *see* NAICS 56132: Temporary Help Services; NAICS 56133: Employee Leasing Services

7371　Computer Programming Services *see* NAICS 541511: Custom Computer Programming Services

7372　Prepackaged Software *see* NAICS 51121: Software Publishers; NAICS 334611: Software Reproducing

7373　Computer Integrated Systems Design *see* NAICS 541512: Computer Systems Design Services

7374　Computer Processing & Data Preparation & Processing Services *see* NAICS 51421: Data Processing Services

7375　Information Retrieval Services *see* NAICS 514191: Online Information Services

7376　Computer Facilities Management Services *see* NAICS 541513: Computer Facilities Management Services

7377　Computer Rental & Leasing *see* NAICS 53242: Office Machinery & Equipment Rental & Leasing

7378　Computer Maintenance & Repair *see* NAICS 44312: Computer & Software Stores; NAICS 811212: Computer & Office Machine Repair & Maintenance

7379　Computer Related Services, NEC *see* NAICS 541512: Computer Systems Design Services; NAICS 541519: Other Computer Related Services

7381　Detective, Guard, & Armored Car Services *see* NAICS 561611: Investigation Services; NAICS 561612: Security Guards & Patrol Services; NAICS 561613: Armored Car Services

7382　Security Systems Services *see* NAICS 561621: Security Systems Services

7389　Business Services, NEC *see* NAICS 51224: Sound Recording Studios; NAICS 51229: Other Sound Recording Industries; NAICS 541199: All Other Legal Services; NAICS 81299: All Other Personal Services; NAICS 54137: Surveying & Mapping Services; NAICS 54141: Interior Design Services; NAICS 54142: Industrial Design Services; NAICS 54134: Drafting Services; NAICS 54149: Other Specialized Design Services; NAICS 54189: Other Services Related to Advertising; NAICS 54193: Translation & Interpretation Services; NAICS 54135: Building Inspection Services; NAICS

54199: All Other Professional, Scientific & Technical Services; NAICS 71141: Agents & Managers for Artists, Athletes, Entertainers & Other Public Figures; NAICS 561422: Telemarketing Bureaus; NAICS 561432: Private Mail Centers; NAICS 561439: Other Business Service Centers; NAICS 561491: Repossession Services; NAICS 56191: Packaging & Labeling Services; NAICS 56179: Other Services to Buildings & Dwellings; NAICS 561599: All Other Travel Arrangement & Reservation Services; NAICS 56192: Convention & Trade Show Organizers; NAICS 561591: Convention & Visitors Bureaus; NAICS 52232: Financial Transactions, Processing, Reserve & Clearing House Activities; NAICS 561499: All Other Business Support Services; NAICS 56199: All Other Support Services

7515 Passenger Car Leasing *see* NAICS 532112: Passenger Cars Leasing

7812 Motion Picture & Video Tape Production *see* NAICS 51211: Motion Picture & Video Production

7819 Services Allied to Motion Picture Production *see* NAICS 512191: Teleproduction & Other Post-production Services; NAICS 56131: Employment Placement Agencies; NAICS 53222: Formal Wear & Costumes Rental; NAICS 53249: Other Commercial & Industrial Machinery & Equipment Rental & Leasing; NAICS 541214: Payroll Services; NAICS 71151: Independent Artists, Writers, & Performers; NAICS 334612: Prerecorded Compact Disc , Tape, & Record Manufacturing; NAICS 512199: Other Motion Picture & Video Industries

7822 Motion Picture & Video Tape Distribution *see* NAICS 42199: Other Miscellaneous Durable Goods Wholesalers; NAICS 51212: Motion Picture & Video Distribution

7829 Services Allied to Motion Picture Distribution *see* NAICS 512199: Other Motion Picture & Video Industries; NAICS 51212: Motion Picture & Video Distribution

7832 Motion Picture Theaters, Except Drive-ins. *see* NAICS 512131: Motion Picture Theaters, Except Drive-in

7841 Video Tape Rental *see* NAICS 53223: Video Tapes & Disc Rental

7993 Coin Operated Amusement Devices *see* NAICS 71312: Amusement Arcades; NAICS 71329: Other Gambling Industries; NAICS 71399: All Other Amusement & Recreation Industries

7999 Amusement & Recreation Services, NEC *see* NAICS 561599: All Other Travel Arrangement & Reservation Services; NAICS 48799: Scenic & Sightseeing Transportation, Other; NAICS 71119: Other Performing Arts Companies; NAICS 711219: Other Spectator Sports; NAICS 71392: Skiing Facilities; NAICS 71394: Fitness & Recreational Sports Centers; NAICS 71321: Casinos; NAICS 71329: Other Gambling Industries; NAICS 71219: Nature Parks & Other Similar Institutions; NAICS 61162: Sports & Recreation Instruction; NAICS 532292: Recreational Goods Rental; NAICS 48711: Scenic & Sightseeing Transportation, Land; NAICS 48721: Scenic & Sightseeing Transportation, Water; NAICS 71399: All Other Amusement & Recreation Industries

8011 Offices & Clinics of Doctors of Medicine *see* NAICS 621493: Freestanding Ambulatory Surgical & Emergency Centers; NAICS 621491: HMO Medical Centers; NAICS 621112: Offices of Physicians, Mental Health Specialists; NAICS 621111: Offices of Physicians

8041 Offices & Clinics of Chiropractors *see* NAICS 62131: Offices of Chiropractors

8049 Offices & Clinics of Health Practitioners, NEC *see* NAICS 62133: Offices of Mental Health Practitioners; NAICS 62134: Offices of Physical, Occupational, & Speech Therapists & Audiologists; NAICS 621399: Offices of All Other Miscellaneous Health Practitioners

8059 Nursing & Personal Care Facilities, NEC *see* NAICS 623311: Continuing Care Retirement Communities; NAICS 62311: Nursing Care Facilities

8062 General Medical & Surgical Hospitals *see* NAICS 62211: General Medical & Surgical Hospitals

8071 Medical Laboratories *see* NAICS 621512: Diagnostic Imaging Centers; NAICS 621511: Medical Laboratories

8082 Home Health Care Services *see* NAICS 62161: Home Health Care Services

8099 Health & Allied Services, NEC *see* NAICS 621991: Blood & Organ Banks; NAICS 54143: Graphic Design Services; NAICS 541922: Commercial Photography; NAICS 62141: Family Planning Centers; NAICS 621999: All Other Miscellaneous Ambulatory Health Care Services

8211 Elementary & Secondary Schools *see* NAICS 61111: Elementary & Secondary Schools

8249 Vocational Schools, NEC *see* NAICS 611513: Apprenticeship Training; NAICS 611512: Flight Training; NAICS 611519: Other Technical & Trade Schools

8299 Schools & Educational Services, NEC *see* NAICS 48122: Nonscheduled speciality Air Transportation; NAICS 611512: Flight Training; NAICS 611692: Automobile Driving Schools; NAICS 61171: Educational Support Services; NAICS 611691: Exam Preparation & Tutoring; NAICS 61161: Fine Arts Schools; NAICS 61163: Language Schools; NAICS 61143: Professional & Management Development Training Schools; NAICS 611699: All Other Miscellaneous Schools & Instruction

8322 Individual & Family Social Services *see* NAICS 62411: Child & Youth Services; NAICS 62421: Community Food Services; NAICS 624229: Other Community Housing Services; NAICS 62423: Emergency & Other Relief Services; NAICS 62412: Services for the Elderly & Persons with Disabilities; NAICS 624221: Temporary Shelters; NAICS 92215: Parole Offices & Probation Offices; NAICS 62419: Other Individual & Family Services

8361 Residential Care *see* NAICS 623312: Homes for the Elderly; NAICS 62322: Residential Mental Health & Substance Abuse Facilities; NAICS 62399: Other Residential Care Facilities

8731 Commercial Physical & Biological Research *see* NAICS 54171: Research & Development in the Physical Sciences & Engineering Sciences; NAICS 54172: Research & Development in the Life Sciences

8732 Commercial Economic, Sociological, & Educational Research *see* NAICS 54173: Research & Development in the Social Sciences & Humanities; NAICS 54191: Marketing Research & Public Opinion Polling

8733 Noncommercial Research Organizations *see* NAICS 54171: Research & Development in the Physical Sciences & Engineering Sciences; NAICS 54172: Research & Development in the Life Sciences; NAICS 54173: Research & Development in the Social Sciences & Humanities

8742 Management Consulting Services *see* NAICS 541611: Administrative Management & General Management Consulting Services; NAICS 541612: Human Resources

& Executive Search Services; NAICS 541613: Marketing Consulting Services; NAICS 541614: Process, Physical, Distribution & Logistics Consulting Services

8748   Business Consulting Services, NEC *see* NAICS 61171: Educational Support Services; NAICS 541618: Other Management Consulting Services; NAICS 54169: Other Scientific & Technical Consulting Services

8999   Services, NEC *see* NAICS 71151: Independent Artists, Writers, & Performers; NAICS 51221: Record Production; NAICS 54169: Other Scientific & Technical Consulting Services; NAICS 51223: Music Publishers; NAICS 541612: Human Resources & Executive Search

Consulting Services; NAICS 514199: All Other Information Services; NAICS 54162: Environmental Consulting Services

PUBLIC ADMINISTRATION

9511   Air & Water Resource & Solid Waste Management *see* NAICS 92411: Air & Water Resource & Solid Waste Management

9512   Land, Mineral, Wildlife, & Forest Conservation *see* NAICS 92412: Land, Mineral, Wildlife, & Forest Conservation

NAICS TO SIC CONVERSION GUIDE

The following listing cross-references five- and six-digit 1998 North American Industry Classification System (NAICS) codes with the four-digit 1987 Standard Industrial Classification (SIC) codes used in EEI. Since the systems differ in specificity, some NAICS categories correspond to more than one SIC category.

AGRICULTURE, FORESTRY, FISHING, & HUNTING

111421 Nursery & Tree Production *see* SIC 0181: Ornamental Floriculture & Nursery Products; SIC 0811: Timber Tracts

111422 Floriculture Production *see* SIC 0181: Ornamental Floriculture & Nursery Products

111998 All Other Miscellaneous Crop Farming *see* SIC 0139: Field Crops, Except Cash Grains, NEC; SIC 0191: General Farms, Primarily Crop; SIC 0831: Forest Products; SIC 0919: Miscellaneous Marine Products; SIC 2099: Food Preparations, NEC

11521 Support Activities for Animal Production *see* SIC 0751: Livestock Services, Except Veterinary; SIC 0752: Animal Specialty Services, Except Veterinary; SIC 7699: Repair Services, NEC

CONSTRUCTION

23531 Electrical Contractors *see* SIC 1731: Electrical Work

FOOD MANUFACTURING

311111 Dog & Cat Food Manufacturing *see* SIC 2047: Dog & Cat Food

311119 Other Animal Food Manufacturing *see* SIC 2048: Prepared Feeds & Feed Ingredients for Animals & Fowls, Except Dogs & Cats

31134 Non-Chocolate Confectionery Manufacturing *see* SIC 2064: Candy & Other Confectionery Products; SIC 2067: Chewing Gum; SIC 2099: Food Preparations, NEC

311422 Specialty Canning *see* SIC 2032: Canned Specialties

311423 Dried & Dehydrated Food Manufacturing *see* SIC 2034: Dried & Dehydrated Fruits, Vegetables & Soup Mixes; SIC 2099: Food Preparation, NEC

311611 Animal Slaughtering *see* SIC 0751: Livestock Services, Except Veterinary; SIC 2011: Meat Packing Plants; SIC 2048: Prepared Feeds & Feed Ingredients for Animals & Fowls, Except Dogs & Cats

31183 Tortilla Manufacturing *see* SIC 2099: Food Preparations, NEC

311911 Roasted Nuts & Peanut Butter Manufacturing *see* SIC

2068: Salted & Roasted Nuts & Seeds; SIC 2099: Food Preparations, NEC

31192 Coffee & Tea Manufacturing *see* SIC 2043: Cereal Breakfast Foods; SIC 2095: Roasted Coffee; SIC 2099: Food Preparations, NEC

311941 Mayonnaise, Dressing & Other Prepared Sauce Manufacturing *see* SIC 2035: Pickled Fruits & Vegetables, Vegetable Seasonings, & Sauces & Salad Dressings; SIC 2099: Food Preparations, NEC

311942 Spice & Extract Manufacturing *see* SIC 2087: Flavoring Extracts & Flavoring Syrups; SIC 2095: Roasted Coffee; SIC 2099: Food Preparations, NEC; SIC 2899: Chemical Preparations, NEC

311991 Perishable Prepared Food Manufacturing *see* SIC 2099: Food Preparations, NEC

311999 All Other Miscellaneous Food Manufacturing *see* SIC 2015: Poultry Slaughtering & Processing; SIC 2032: Canned Specialties; SIC 2087: Flavoring Extracts & Flavoring Syrups; SIC 2099: Food Preparations, NEC

BEVERAGE & TOBACCO PRODUCT MANUFACTURING

312111 Soft Drink Manufacturing *see* SIC 2086: Bottled & Canned Soft Drinks & Carbonated Water

312112 Bottled Water Manufacturing *see* SIC 2086: Bottled & Canned Soft Drinks & Carbonated Water

31212 Breweries *see* SIC 2082: Malt Beverages

312221 Cigarette Manufacturing *see* SIC 2111: Cigarettes

TEXTILE PRODUCT MILLS

314999 All Other Miscellaneous Textile Product Mills *see* SIC 2299: Textile Goods, NEC; SIC 2395: Pleating, Decorative & Novelty Stitching, & Tucking for the Trade; SIC 2396: Automotive Trimmings, Apparel Findings, & Related Products; SIC 2399: Fabricated Textile Products, NEC

APPAREL MANUFACTURING

315999 Other Apparel Accessories & Other Apparel Manufacturing *see* SIC 2339: Women's, Misses', & Juniors' Outerwear, NEC; SIC 2385: Waterproof Outerwear; SIC

2387: Apparel Belts; SIC 2389: Apparel & Accessories, NEC; SIC 2396: Automotive Trimmings, Apparel Findings, & Related Products; SIC 2399: Fabricated Textile Products, NEC

CHEMICAL MANUFACTURING

32511 Petrochemical Manufacturing *see* SIC 2865: Cyclic Organic Crudes & Intermediates, & Organic Dyes & Pigments; SIC 2869: Industrial Organic Chemicals, NEC

32512 Industrial Gas Manufacturing *see* SIC 2813: Industrial Gases; SIC 2869: Industrial Organic Chemicals, NEC

325188 All Other Basic Inorganic Chemical Manufacturing *see* SIC 2819: Industrial Inorganic Chemicals, NEC; SIC 2869: Industrial Organic Chemicals, NEC

325191 Gum & Wood Chemical Manufacturing *see* SIC 2861: Gum & Wood Chemicals

325193 Ethyl Alcohol Manufacturing *see* SIC 2869: Industrial Organic Chemicals

325199 All Other Basic Organic Chemical Manufacturing *see* SIC 2869: Industrial Organic Chemicals, NEC; SIC 2899: Chemical & Chemical Preparations, NEC

325211 Plastics Material & Resin Manufacturing *see* SIC 2821: Plastics Materials, Synthetic & Resins, & Nonvulcanizable Elastomers

325212 Synthetic Rubber Manufacturing *see* SIC 2822: Synthetic Rubber

325311 Nitrogenous Fertilizer Manufacturing *see* SIC 2873: Nitrogenous Fertilizers

32532 Pesticide & Other Agricultural Chemical Manufacturing *see* SIC 2879: Pesticides & Agricultural Chemicals, NEC

325411 Medicinal & Botanical Manufacturing *see* SIC 2833: Medicinal Chemicals & Botanical Products

325412 Pharmaceutical Preparation Manufacturing *see* SIC 2834: Pharmaceutical Preparations; SIC 2835: In-Vitro & In-Vivo Diagnostic Substances

325413 In-Vitro Diagnostic Substance Manufacturing *see* SIC 2835: In-Vitro & In-Vivo Diagnostic Substances

325414 Biological Product Manufacturing *see* SIC 2836: Biological Products, Except Diagnostic Substance

325611 Soap & Other Detergent Manufacturing *see* SIC 2841: Soaps & Other Detergents, Except Specialty Cleaners; SIC 2844: Toilet Preparations

325612 Polish & Other Sanitation Good Manufacturing *see* SIC 2842: Specialty Cleaning, Polishing, & Sanitary Preparations

32562 Toilet Preparation Manufacturing *see* SIC 2844: Perfumes, Cosmetics, & Other Toilet Preparations

325992 Photographic Film, Paper, Plate & Chemical Manufacturing *see* SIC 3861: Photographic Equipment & Supplies

NONMETALLIC MINERAL PRODUCT MANUFACTURING

327113 Porcelain Electrical Supply Manufacturing *see* SIC 3264: Porcelain Electrical Supplies

PRIMARY METAL MANUFACTURING

331319 Other Aluminum Rolling & Drawing *see* SIC 3355: Aluminum Rolling & Drawing, NEC; SIC 3357: Drawing & Insulating of Nonferrous Wire

331422 Copper Wire Drawing *see* SIC 3357: Drawing & Insulating of Nonferrous Wire

331491 Nonferrous Metal Rolling, Drawing & Extruding *see* SIC 3356: Rolling, Drawing & Extruding of Nonferrous Metals, Except Copper & Aluminum; SIC 3357: Drawing & Insulating of Nonferrous Wire

FABRICATED METAL PRODUCT MANUFACTURING

332212 Hand & Edge Tool Manufacturing *see* SIC 3423: Hand & Edge Tools, Except Machine Tools & Handsaws; SIC 3523: Farm Machinery & Equipment; SIC 3524: Lawn & Garden Tractors & Home Lawn & Garden Equipment; SIC 3545: Cutting Tools, Machine Tools Accessories, & Machinist Precision Measuring Devices; SIC 3799: Transportation Equipment, NEC; SIC 3999: Manufacturing Industries, NEC

33271 Machine Shops *see* SIC 3599: Industrial & Commercial Machinery & Equipment, NEC

332999 All Other Miscellaneous Fabricated Metal Product Manufacturing *see* SIC 3291: Abrasive Products; SIC 3432: Plumbing Fixture Fittings & Trim; SIC 3494: Valves & Pipe Fittings, NEC; SIC 3497: Metal Foil & Leaf; SIC 3499: Fabricated Metal Products, NEC; SIC 3537: Industrial Trucks, Tractors, Trailers, & Stackers; SIC 3599: Industrial & Commercial Machinery & Equipment, NEC; SIC 3999: Manufacturing Industries, NEC

MACHINERY MANUFACTURING

333112 Lawn & Garden Tractor & Home Lawn & Garden Equipment Manufacturing *see* SIC 3524: Lawn & Garden Tractors & Home Lawn & Garden Equipment

33322 Rubber & Plastics Industry Machinery Manufacturing *see* SIC 3559: Special Industry Machinery, NEC

333295 Semiconductor Machinery Manufacturing *see* SIC 3559: Special Industry Machinery, NEC

333298 All Other Industrial Machinery Manufacturing *see* SIC 3559: Special Industry Machinery, NEC; SIC 3639: Household Appliances, NEC

333314 Optical Instrument & Lens Manufacturing *see* SIC 3827: Optical Instruments & Lenses

333315 Photographic & Photocopying Equipment Manufacturing *see* SIC 3861: Photographic Equipment & Supplies

333319 Other Commercial & Service Industry Machinery Manufacturing *see* SIC 3559: Special Industry Machinery, NEC; SIC 3589: Service Industry Machinery, NEC; SIC 3599: Industrial & Commercial Machinery & Equipment, NEC; SIC 3699: Electrical Machinery, Equipment & Supplies, NEC

333411 Air Purification Equipment Manufacturing *see* SIC 3564: Industrial & Commercial Fans & Blowers & Air Purification Equipment

333412 Industrial & Commercial Fan & Blower Manufacturing *see* SIC 3564: Industrial & Commercial Fans & Blowers & Air Purification Equipment

333512 Machine Tool Manufacturing *see* SIC 3541: Machine Tools, Metal Cutting Type

333513 Machine Tool Manufacturing *see* SIC 3542: Machine Tools, Metal Forming Type

333618 Other Engine Equipment Manufacturing *see* SIC 3519: Internal Combustion Engines, NEC; SIC 3699: Electrical Machinery, Equipment & Supplies, NEC

333922 Conveyor & Conveying Equipment Manufacturing *see* SIC 3523: Farm Machinery & Equipment; SIC 3535: Conveyors & Conveying Equipment

333999 All Other General Purpose Machinery Manufacturing *see* SIC 3599: Industrial & Commercial Machinery & Equipment, NEC; SIC 3569: General Industrial Machinery & Equipment, NEC

COMPUTER & ELECTRONIC PRODUCT MANUFACTURING

334111 Electronic Computer Manufacturing *see* SIC 3571: Electronic Computers

334112 Computer Storage Device Manufacturing *see* SIC 3572: Computer Storage Devices

334113 Computer Terminal Manufacturing *see* SIC 3575: Computer Terminals

334119 Other Computer Peripheral Equipment Manufacturing *see* SIC 3577: Computer Peripheral Equipment, NEC; SIC 3578: Calculating & Accounting Machines, Except Electronic Computers; SIC 3699: Electrical Machinery, Equipment & Supplies, NEC

33421 Telephone Apparatus Manufacturing *see* SIC 3661: Telephone & Telegraph Apparatus

33422 Radio & Television Broadcasting & Wireless Communications Equipment Manufacturing *see* SIC 3663: Radio & Television Broadcasting & Communication Equipment; SIC 3679: Electronic Components, NEC

33429 Other Communications Equipment Manufacturing *see* SIC 3669: Communications Equipment, NEC

334413 Semiconductor & Related Device Manufacturing *see* SIC 3674: Semiconductors & Related Devices

334416 Electronic Coil, Transformer, & Other Inductor Manufacturing *see* SIC 3661: Telephone & Telegraph Apparatus; SIC 3677: Electronic Coils, Transformers, & Other Inductors; SIC 3825: Instruments for Measuring & Testing of Electricity & Electrical Signals

334418 Printed Circuit/Electronics Assembly Manufacturing *see* SIC 3679: Electronic Components, NEC; SIC 3661: Telephone & Telegraph Apparatus

334419 Other Electronic Component Manufacturing *see* SIC 3679: Electronic Components, NEC

334510 Electromedical & Electrotherapeutic Apparatus Manufacturing *see* SIC 3842: Orthopedic, Prosthetic & Surgical Appliances & Supplies; SIC 3845: Electromedical & Electrotherapeutic Apparatus

334511 Search, Detection, Navigation, Guidance, Aeronautical, & Nautical System & Instrument Manufacturing *see* SIC 3812: Search, Detection, Navigation, Guidance, Aeronautical, & Nautical Systems & Instruments

334512 Automatic Environmental Control Manufacturing for Residential, Commercial & Appliance Use *see* SIC 3822: Automatic Controls for Regulating Residential & Commercial Environments & Appliances

334515 Instrument Manufacturing for Measuring & Testing Electricity & Electrical Signals *see* SIC 3825: Instruments for Measuring & Testing of Electricity & Electrical Signals

334517 Irradiation Apparatus Manufacturing *see* SIC 3844: X-Ray Apparatus & Tubes & Related Irradiation Apparatus; SIC 3845: Electromedical & Electrotherapeutic Apparatus

334519 Other Measuring & Controlling Device Manufacturing *see* SIC 3829: Measuring & Controlling Devices, NEC

334611 Software Reproducing *see* SIC 7372: Prepackaged Software

334612 Prerecorded Compact Disc , Tape, & Record Reproducing *see* SIC 3652: Phonograph Records & Prerecorded Audio Tapes & Disks; SIC 7819: Services Allied to Motion Picture Production

ELECTRICAL EQUIPMENT, APPLIANCE, & COMPONENT MANUFACTURING

335129 Other Lighting Equipment Manufacturing *see* SIC 3648: Lighting Equipment, NEC; SIC 3699: Electrical Machinery, Equipment, & Supplies, NEC

335911 Storage Battery Manufacturing *see* SIC 3691: Storage Batteries

335921 Fiber-Optic Cable Manufacturing *see* SIC 3357: Drawing & Insulating of Nonferrous Wire

335929 Other Communication & Energy Wire Manufacturing *see* SIC 3357: Drawing & Insulating of Nonferrous Wire

335999 All Other Miscellaneous Electrical Equipment & Component Manufacturing *see* SIC 3629: Electrical Industrial Apparatus, NEC; SIC 3699: Electrical Machinery, Equipment, & Supplies, NEC

TRANSPORTATION EQUIPMENT MANUFACTURING

336211 Motor Vehicle Body Manufacturing *see* SIC 3711: Motor Vehicles & Passenger Car Bodies; SIC 3713: Truck & Bus Bodies; SIC 3714: Motor Vehicle Parts & Accessories

336312 Gasoline Engine & Engine Parts Manufacturing *see* SIC 3714: Motor Vehicle Parts & Accessories

336322 Other Motor Vehicle Electrical & Electronic Equipment Manufacturing *see* SIC 3679: Electronic Components, NEC; SIC 3694: Electrical Equipment for Internal Combustion Engines; SIC 3714: Motor Vehicle Parts & Accessories

33633 Motor Vehicle Steering & Suspension Components Manufacturing *see* SIC 3714: Motor Vehicle Parts & Accessories

33634 Motor Vehicle Brake System Manufacturing *see* SIC 3292: Asbestos Products; SIC 3714: Motor Vehicle Parts & Accessories

33635 Motor Vehicle Transmission & Power Train Parts Manufacturing *see* SIC 3714: Motor Vehicle Parts & Accessories

33636 Motor Vehicle Fabric Accessories & Seat Manufacturing *see* SIC 2396: Automotive Trimmings, Apparel Findings, & Related Products; SIC 2399: Fabricated Textile Products, NEC; SIC 2531: Public Building & Related Furniture

336399 All Other Motor Vehicle Parts Manufacturing *see* SIC 3519: Internal Combustion Engines, NEC; SIC 3599: Industrial & Commercial Machinery & Equipment, NEC; SIC 3714: Motor Vehicle Parts & Accessories

336414 Guided Missile & Space Vehicle Manufacturing *see* SIC 3761: Guided Missiles & Space Vehicles

336415 Guided Missile & Space Vehicle Propulsion Unit & Propulsion Unit Parts Manufacturing *see* SIC 3764: Guided Missile & Space Vehicle Propulsion Units & Propulsion Unit Parts

336419 Other Guided Missile & Space Vehicle Parts & Auxiliary Equipment Manufacturing *see* SIC 3769: Guided Missile & Space Vehicle Parts & Auxiliary Equipment

336611 Ship Building & Repairing *see* SIC 3731: Ship Building & Repairing

336991   Motorcycle, Bicycle, & Parts Manufacturing *see* SIC 3944: Games, Toys, & Children's Vehicles, Except Dolls & Bicycles; SIC 3751: Motorcycles, Bicycles & Parts

MISCELLANEOUS MANUFACTURING

339111   Laboratory Apparatus & Furniture Manufacturing *see* SIC 3829: Measuring & Controlling Devices, NEC

339112   Surgical & Medical Instrument Manufacturing *see* SIC 3841: Surgical & Medical Instruments & Apparatus; SIC 3829: Measuring & Controlling Devices, NEC

339115   Ophthalmic Goods Manufacturing *see* SIC 3851: Opthalmic Goods; SIC 5995: Optical Goods Stores

33992   Sporting & Athletic Goods Manufacturing *see* SIC 3949: Sporting & Athletic Goods, NEC

339932   Game, Toy, & Children's Vehicle Manufacturing *see* SIC 3944: Games, Toys, & Children's Vehicles, Except Dolls & Bicycles

WHOLESALE TRADE

42141   Photographic Equipment & Supplies Wholesalers *see* SIC 5043: Photographic Equipment & Supplies

42143   Computer & Computer Peripheral Equipment & Software Wholesalers *see* SIC 5045: Computers & Computer Peripherals Equipment & Software

42169   Other Electronic Parts & Equipment Wholesalers *see* SIC 5065: Electronic Parts & Equipment, NEC

42199   Other Miscellaneous Durable Goods Wholesalers *see* SIC 5099: Durable Goods, NEC; SIC 7822: Motion Picture & Video Tape Distribution

42249   Other Grocery & Related Products Wholesalers *see* SIC 5149: Groceries & Related Products, NEC

42299   Other Miscellaneous Nondurable Goods Wholesalers *see* SIC 5199: Nondurable Goods, NEC

RETAIL TRADE

44112   Used Car Dealers *see* SIC 5521: Motor Vehicle Dealers, Used Only

443111   Household Appliance Stores *see* SIC 5722: Household Appliance Stores; SIC 5999: Miscellaneous Retail Stores, NEC; SIC 7623: Refrigeration & Air-Conditioning Service & Repair Shops; SIC 7629: Electrical & Electronic Repair Shops, NEC

443112   Radio, Television & Other Electronics Stores *see* SIC 5731: Radio, Television, & Consumer Electronics Stores; SIC 5999: Miscellaneous Retail Stores, NEC; SIC 7622: Radio & Television Repair Shops

44312   Computer & Software Stores *see* SIC 5045: Computers & Computer Peripheral Equipment & Software; SIC 7378: Computer Maintenance & Repair; SIC 5734: Computer & Computer Software Stores

44421   Outdoor Power Equipment Stores *see* SIC 5083: Farm & Garden Machinery & Equipment; SIC 5261: Retail Nurseries, Lawn & Garden Supply Stores

44422   Nursery & Garden Centers *see* SIC 5191: Farm Supplies; SIC 5193: Flowers, Nursery Stock, & Florists' Supplies; SIC 5261: Retail Nurseries, Lawn & Garden Supply Stores

44521   Meat Markets *see* SIC 5421: Meat & Fish Markets, Including Freezer Provisioners; SIC 5499: Miscellaneous Food Stores

445299   All Other Specialty Food Stores *see* SIC 5499: Miscellaneous Food Stores; SIC 5451: Dairy Products Stores

44612   Cosmetics, Beauty Supplies & Perfume Stores *see* SIC 5087: Service Establishment Equipment & Supplies; SIC 5999: Miscellaneous Retail Stores, NEC

446191   Food Supplement Stores *see* SIC 5499: Miscellaneous Food Stores

446199   All Other Health & Personal Care Stores *see* SIC 5047: Medical, Dental, & Hospital Equipment & Supplies; SIC 5999: Miscellaneous Retail Stores, NEC

44831   Jewelry Stores *see* SIC 5999: Miscellaneous Retailer, NEC; SIC 5944: Jewelry Stores

45111   Sporting Goods Stores *see* SIC 7699: Repair Shops & Related Services, NEC; SIC 5941: Sporting Goods Stores & Bicycle Shops

45112   Hobby, Toy & Game Stores *see* SIC 5945: Hobby, Toy, & Game Stores

451211   Book Stores *see* SIC 5942: Book Stores

45122   Prerecorded Tape, Compact Disc & Record Stores *see* SIC 5735: Record & Prerecorded Tape Stores

45391   Pet & Pet Supplies Stores *see* SIC 5999: Miscellaneous Retail Stores, NEC

45392   Art Dealers *see* SIC 5999: Miscellaneous Retail Stores, NEC

453999   All Other Miscellaneous Store Retailers *see* SIC 5999: Miscellaneous Retail Stores, NEC; SIC 5261: Retail Nurseries, Lawn & Garden Supply Stores

45411   Electronic Shopping & Mail-Order Houses *see* SIC 5961: Catalog & Mail-Order Houses

45439   Other Direct Selling Establishments *see* SIC 5421: Meat & Fish Markets, Including Freezer Provisioners; SIC 5963: Direct Selling Establishments

TRANSPORTATION & WAREHOUSING

481111   Scheduled Passenger Air Transportation *see* SIC 4512: Air Transportation, Scheduled

481112   Scheduled Freight Air Transportation *see* SIC 4512: Air Transportation, Scheduled

481219   Other Nonscheduled Air Transportation *see* SIC 7319: Advertising, NEC

48122   Nonscheduled Speciality Air Transportation *see* SIC 0721: Crop Planting, Cultivating, & Protecting; SIC 1382: Oil & Gas Field Exploration Services; SIC 4522: Air Transportation, Nonscheduled; SIC 7335: Commercial Photography; SIC 7997: Membership Sports & Recreation Clubs; SIC 8299: Schools & Educational Services, NEC; SIC 8713: Surveying Services

48711   Scenic & Sightseeing Transportation, Land *see* SIC 4119: Local Passenger Transportation, NEC; SIC 4789: Transportation Services, NEC; SIC 7999: Amusement & Recreation Services, NEC

48721   Scenic & Sightseeing Transportation, Water *see* SIC 4489: Water Transportation of Passengers, NEC; SIC 7999: Amusement & Recreation Services, NEC

48799   Scenic & Sightseeing Transportation, Other *see* SIC 4522: Air Transportation, Nonscheduled; SIC 7999: Amusement & Recreation Services, NEC

INFORMATION

51114   Database & Directory Publishers *see* SIC 2741: Miscellaneous Publishing

511199   All Other Publishers *see* SIC 2741: Miscellaneous Publishing

51121   Software Publishers *see* SIC 7372: Prepackaged Software

51211   Motion Picture & Video Production *see* SIC 7812: Motion Picture & Video Tape Production

51212   Motion Picture & Video Distribution *see* SIC 7822: Motion Picture & Video Tape Distribution; SIC 7829: Services Allied to Motion Picture Distribution

512131   Motion Picture Theaters, Except Drive-Ins *see* SIC 7832: Motion Picture Theaters, Except Drive-In

512191   Teleproduction & Other Post-Production Services *see* SIC 7819: Services Allied to Motion Picture Production

512199   Other Motion Picture & Video Industries *see* SIC 7819: Services Allied to Motion Picture Production; SIC 7829: Services Allied to Motion Picture Distribution

51221   Record Production *see* SIC 8999: Services, NEC

51222   Integrated Record Production/Distribution *see* SIC 3652: Phonograph Records & Prerecorded Audio Tapes & Disks

51223   Music Publishers *see* SIC 2731: Books: Publishing or Publishing & Printing; SIC 2741: Miscellaneous Publishing; SIC 8999: Services, NEC

51224   Sound Recording Studios *see* SIC 7389: Business Services, NEC

51229   Other Sound Recording Industries *see* SIC 7389: Business Services, NEC; SIC 7922: Theatrical Producers & Miscellaneous Theatrical Services

51321   Cable Networks *see* SIC 4841: Cable & Other Pay Television Services

51322   Cable & Other Program Distribution *see* SIC 4841: Cable & Other Pay Television Services

51331   Wired Telecommunications Carriers *see* SIC 4813: Telephone Communications, Except Radiotelephone; SIC 4822: Telegraph & Other Message Communications

513321   Paging *see* SIC 4812: Radiotelephone Communications

513322   Cellular & Other Wireless Telecommunications *see* SIC 4812: Radiotelephone Communications; SIC 4899: Communications Services, NEC

51333   Telecommunications Resellers *see* SIC 4812: Radio Communications; SIC 4813: Telephone Communications, Except Radiotelephone

51334   Satellite Telecommunications *see* SIC 4899: Communications Services, NEC

51339   Other Telecommunications *see* SIC 4899: Communications Services, NEC

514191   On-Line Information Services *see* SIC 7375: Information Retrieval Services

514199   All Other Information Services *see* SIC 8999: Services, NEC

51421   Data Processing Services *see* SIC 7374: Computer Processing & Data Preparation & Processing Services

FINANCE & INSURANCE

52222   Sales Financing *see* SIC 6141: Personal Credit Institutions; SIC 6153: Short-Term Business Credit Institutions, Except Agricultural; SIC 6159: Miscellaneous Business Credit Institutions

522292   Real Estate Credit *see* SIC 6162: Mortgage Bankers & Loan Correspondents

522293   International Trade Financing *see* SIC 6081: Branches & Agencies of Foreign Banks; SIC 6082: Foreign Trade & International Banking Institutions; SIC 6111: Federal & Federally-Sponsored Credit Agencies; SIC 6159: Miscellaneous Business Credit Institutions

522298   All Other Nondepository Credit Intermediation *see* SIC 5932: Used Merchandise Stores; SIC 6081: Branches &

Agencies of Foreign Banks; SIC 6111: Federal & Federally-Sponsored Credit Agencies; SIC 6153: Short-Term Business Credit Institutions, Except Agricultural; SIC 6159: Miscellaneous Business Credit Institutions

52231   Mortgage & Other Loan Brokers *see* SIC 6163: Loan Brokers

52232   Financial Transactions Processing, Reserve, & Clearing House Activities *see* SIC 6019: Central Reserve Depository Institutions, NEC; SIC 6099: Functions Related to Depository Banking, NEC; SIC 6153: Short-Term Business Credit Institutions, Except Agricultural; SIC 7389: Business Services, NEC

52239   Other Activities Related to Credit Intermediation *see* SIC 6099: Functions Related to Depository Banking, NEC; SIC 6162: Mortgage Bankers & Loan Correspondents

52311   Investment Banking & Securities Dealing *see* SIC 6211: Security Brokers, Dealers, & Flotation Companies

52312   Securities Brokerage *see* SIC 6211: Security Brokers, Dealers, & Flotation Companies

52313   Commodity Contracts Dealing *see* SIC 6099: Functions Related to depository Banking, NEC; SIC 6799: Investors, NEC; SIC 6221: Commodity Contracts Brokers & Dealers

52314   Commodity Brokerage *see* SIC 6221: Commodity Contracts Brokers & Dealers

52321   Securities & Commodity Exchanges *see* SIC 6231: Security & Commodity Exchanges

52391   Miscellaneous Intermediation *see* SIC 6211: Securities Brokers, Dealers & Flotation Companies; SIC 6799: Investors, NEC

52392   Portfolio Management *see* SIC 6282: Investment Advice; SIC 6371: Pension, Health, & Welfare Funds; SIC 6733: Trust, Except Educational, Religious, & Charitable; SIC 6799: Investors, NEC

52393   Investment Advice *see* SIC 6282: Investment Advice

523991   Trust, Fiduciary & Custody Activities *see* SIC 6021: National Commercial Banks; SIC 6022: State Commercial Banks; SIC 6091: Nondepository Trust Facilities; SIC 6099: Functions Related to Depository Banking, NEC; SIC 6289: Services Allied With the Exchange of Securities or Commodities, NEC; SIC 6733: Trusts, Except Educational, Religious, & Charitable

523999   Miscellaneous Financial Investment Activities *see* SIC 6099: Functions Related to Depository Banking, NEC; SIC 6211: Security Brokers, Dealers, & Flotation Companies; SIC 6289: Services Allied With the Exchange of Securities or Commodities, NEC; SIC 6799: Investors, NEC; SIC 6792: Oil Royalty Traders

524113   Direct Life Insurance Carriers *see* SIC 6311: Life Insurance

524114   Direct Health & Medical Insurance Carriers *see* SIC 6324: Hospital & Medical Service Plans; SIC 6321: Accident & Health Insurance

524126   Direct Property & Casualty Insurance Carriers *see* SIC 6331: Fire, Marine, & Casualty Insurance; SIC 6351: Surety Insurance

52413   Reinsurance Carriers *see* SIC 6311: Life Insurance; SIC 6321: Accident & Health Insurance; SIC 6324: Hospital & Medical Service Plans; SIC 6331: Fire, Marine, & Casualty Insurance; SIC 6351: Surety Insurance; SIC 6361: Title Insurance

52421   Insurance Agencies & Brokerages *see* SIC 6411: Insurance Agents, Brokers & Service

524291   Claims Adjusters *see* SIC 6411: Insurance Agents, Brokers & Service

524292   Third Party Administration for Insurance & Pension Funds *see* SIC 6371: Pension, Health, & Welfare Funds; SIC 6411: Insurance Agents, Brokers & Service

524298   All Other Insurance Related Activities *see* SIC 6411: Insurance Agents, Brokers & Service

52519   Other Insurance Funds *see* SIC 6321: Accident & Health Insurance; SIC 6324: Hospital & Medical Service Plans; SIC 6331: Fire, Marine, & Casualty Insurance; SIC 6733: Trusts, Except Educational, Religious, & Charitable

52593   Real Estate Investment Trusts *see* SIC 6798: Real Estate Investment Trusts

REAL ESTATE & RENTAL & LEASING

53111   Lessors of Residential Buildings & Dwellings *see* SIC 6513: Operators of Apartment Buildings; SIC 6514: Operators of Dwellings Other Than Apartment Buildings

53112   Lessors of Nonresidential Buildings *see* SIC 6512: Operators of Nonresidential Buildings

532112   Passenger Car Leasing *see* SIC 7515: Passenger Car Leasing

53222   Formal Wear & Costume Rental *see* SIC 7299: Miscellaneous Personal Services, NEC; SIC 7819: Services Allied to Motion Picture Production

53223   Video Tape & Disc Rental *see* SIC 7841: Video Tape Rental

532292   Recreational Goods Rental *see* SIC 7999: Amusement & Recreation Services, NEC

53242   Office Machinery & Equipment Rental & Leasing *see* SIC 7359: Equipment Rental & Leasing; SIC 7377: Computer Rental & Leasing

53249   Other Commercial & Industrial Machinery & Equipment Rental & Leasing *see* SIC 7352: Medical Equipment Rental & Leasing; SIC 7359: Equipment Rental & Leasing, NEC; SIC 7819: Services Allied to Motion Picture Production; SIC 7922: Theatrical Producers & Miscellaneous Theatrical Services

PROFESSIONAL, SCIENTIFIC, & TECHNICAL SERVICES

541199   All Other Legal Services *see* SIC 7389: Business Services, NEC

541214   Payroll Services *see* SIC 7819: Services Allied to Motion Picture Production; SIC 8721: Accounting, Auditing, & Bookkeeping Services

54134   Drafting Services *see* SIC 7389: Business Services, NEC

54135   Building Inspection Services *see* SIC 7389: Business Services, NEC

54137   Surveying & Mapping Services *see* SIC 7389: Business Services, NEC; SIC 8713: Surveying Services

54141   Interior Design Services *see* SIC 7389: Business Services, NEC

54142   Industrial Design Services *see* SIC 7389: Business Services, NEC

54143   Commercial Art & Graphic Design Services *see* SIC 7336: Commercial Art & Graphic Design; SIC 8099: Health & Allied Services, NEC

54149   Other Specialized Design Services *see* SIC 7389: Business Services, NEC

541511   Custom Computer Programming Services *see* SIC 7371: Computer Programming Services

541512   Computer Systems Design Services *see* SIC 7373: Computer Integrated Systems Design; SIC 7379: Computer Related Services, NEC

541513   Computer Facilities Management Services *see* SIC 7376: Computer Facilities Management Services

541519   Other Computer Related Services *see* SIC 7379: Computer Related Services, NEC

541611   Administrative Management & General Management Consulting Services *see* SIC 8742: Management Consulting Services

541612   Human Resources & Executive Search Consulting Services *see* SIC 8742: Management Consulting Services; SIC 7361: Employment Agencies; SIC 8999: Services, NEC

541613   Marketing Consulting Services *see* SIC 8742: Management Consulting Services

541614   Process, Physical, Distribution & Logistics Consulting Services *see* SIC 8742: Management Consulting Services

541618   Other Management Consulting Services *see* SIC 4731: Arrangement of Transportation of Freight & Cargo; SIC 8748: Business Consulting Services, NEC

54162   Environmental Consulting Services *see* SIC 8999: Services, NEC

54169   Other Scientific & Technical Consulting Services *see* SIC 0781: Landscape Counseling & Planning; SIC 8748: Business Consulting Services, NEC; SIC 8999: Services, NEC

54171   Research & Development in the Physical Sciences & Engineering Sciences *see* SIC 8731: Commercial Physical & Biological Research; SIC 8733: Noncommercial Research Organizations

54172   Research & Development in the Life Sciences *see* SIC 8731: Commercial Physical & Biological Research; SIC 8733: Noncommercial Research Organizations

54173   Research & Development in the Social Sciences & Humanities *see* SIC 8732: Commercial Economic, Sociological, & Educational Research; SIC 8733: Noncommercial Research Organizations

54183   Media Buying Agencies *see* SIC 7319: Advertising, NEC

54185   Display Advertising *see* SIC 7312: Outdoor Advertising Services; SIC 7319: Advertising, NEC

54187   Advertising Material Distribution Services *see* SIC 7319: Advertising, NEC

54189   Other Services Related to Advertising *see* SIC 7319: Advertising, NEC; SIC 5199: Nondurable Goods, NEC; SIC 7389: Business Services, NEC

54191   Marketing Research & Public Opinion Polling *see* SIC 8732: Commercial Economic, Sociological, & Educational Research

541922   Commercial Photography *see* SIC 7335: Commercial Photography; SIC 8099: Health & Allied Services, NEC

54193   Translation & Interpretation Services *see* SIC 7389: Business Services, NEC

54194   Veterinary Services *see* SIC 0741: Veterinary Services for Livestock; SIC 0742: Veterinary Services for Animal Specialties; SIC 8734: Testing Laboratories

54199   All Other Professional, Scientific & Technical Services *see* SIC 7389: Business Services

ADMINISTRATIVE & SUPPORT, WASTE MANAGEMENT & REMEDIATION SERVICES

56131   Employment Placement Agencies *see* SIC 7361: Employment Agencies; SIC 7819: Services Allied to Motion Pictures Production; SIC 7922: Theatrical Producers & Miscellaneous Theatrical Services

56132   Temporary Help Services *see* SIC 7363: Help Supply Services

56133   Employee Leasing Services *see* SIC 7363: Help Supply Services

561421   Telephone Answering Services *see* SIC 7389: Business Services, NEC

561422   Telemarketing Bureaus *see* SIC 7389: Business Services, NEC

561432   Private Mail Centers *see* SIC 7389: Business Services, NEC

561439   Other Business Service Centers *see* SIC 7334: Photocopying & Duplicating Services; SIC 7389: Business Services, NEC

561491   Repossession Services *see* SIC 7322: Adjustment & Collection; SIC 7389: Business Services, NEC

561499   All Other Business Support Services *see* SIC 7389: Business Services, NEC

561591   Convention & Visitors Bureaus *see* SIC 7389: Business Services, NEC

561599   All Other Travel Arrangement & Reservation Services *see* SIC 4729: Arrangement of Passenger Transportation, NEC; SIC 7389: Business Services, NEC; SIC 7999: Amusement & Recreation Services, NEC; SIC 8699: Membership Organizations, NEC

561611   Investigation Services *see* SIC 7381: Detective, Guard, & Armored Car Services

561612   Security Guards & Patrol Services *see* SIC 7381: Detective, Guard, & Armored Car Services

561613   Armored Car Services *see* SIC 7381: Detective, Guard, & Armored Car Services

561621   Security Systems Services *see* SIC 7382: Security Systems Services; SIC 1731: Electrical Work

56179   Other Services to Buildings & Dwellings *see* SIC 7389: Business Services, NEC; SIC 7699: Repair Shops & Related Services, NEC

56191   Packaging & Labeling Services *see* SIC 7389: Business Services, NEC

56192   Convention & Trade Show Organizers *see* SIC 7389: Business Services, NEC

56199   All Other Support Services *see* SIC 7389: Business Services, NEC

EDUCATIONAL SERVICES

61111   Elementary & Secondary Schools *see* SIC 8211: Elementary & Secondary Schools

61143   Professional & Management Development Training Schools *see* SIC 8299: Schools & Educational Services, NEC

611511   Cosmetology & Barber Schools *see* SIC 7231: Beauty Shops; SIC 7241: Barber Shops

611512   Flight Training *see* SIC 8249: Vocational Schools, NEC; SIC 8299: Schools & Educational Services, NEC

611513   Apprenticeship Training *see* SIC 8249: Vocational Schools, NEC

611519   Other Technical & Trade Schools *see* SIC 8249: Vocational Schools, NEC; SIC 8243: Data Processing Schools

61161   Fine Arts Schools *see* SIC 8299: Schools & Educational Services, NEC; SIC 7911: Dance Studios, Schools, & Halls

61162   Sports & Recreation Instruction *see* SIC 7999: Amusement & Recreation Services, NEC

61163   Language Schools *see* SIC 8299: Schools & Educational Services, NEC

611691   Exam Preparation & Tutoring *see* SIC 8299: Schools & Educational Services, NEC

611692   Automobile Driving Schools *see* SIC 8299: Schools & Educational Services, NEC

611699   All Other Miscellaneous Schools & Instruction *see* SIC 8299: Schools & Educational Services, NEC

61171   Educational Support Services *see* SIC 8299: Schools & Educational Services NEC; SIC 8748: Business Consulting Services, NEC

HEALTH CARE & SOCIAL ASSISTANCE

621111   Offices of Physicians *see* SIC 8011: Offices & Clinics of Doctors of Medicine; SIC 8031: Offices & Clinics of Doctors of Osteopathy

621112   Offices of Physicians, Mental Health Specialists *see* SIC 8011: Offices & Clinics of Doctors of Medicine; SIC 8031: Offices & Clinics of Doctors of Osteopathy

62131   Offices of Chiropractors *see* SIC 8041: Offices & Clinics of Chiropractors

62133   Offices of Mental Health Practitioners *see* SIC 8049: Offices & Clinics of Health Practitioners, NEC

62134   Offices of Physical, Occupational & Speech Therapists & Audiologists *see* SIC 8049: Offices & Clinics of Health Practitioners, NEC

621399   Offices of All Other Miscellaneous Health Practitioners *see* SIC 8049: Offices & Clinics of Health Practitioners, NEC

62141   Family Planning Centers *see* SIC 8093: Speciality Outpatient Facilities, NEC; SIC 8099: Health & Allied Services, NEC

621491   HMO Medical Centers *see* SIC 8011: Offices & Clinics of Doctors of Medicine

621493   Freestanding Ambulatory Surgical & Emergency Centers *see* SIC 8011: Offices & Clinics of Doctors of Medicine

621511   Medical Laboratories *see* SIC 8071: Medical Laboratories

621512   Diagnostic Imaging Centers *see* SIC 8071: Medical Laboratories

62161   Home Health Care Services *see* SIC 8082: Home Health Care Services

621991   Blood & Organ Banks *see* SIC 8099: Health & Allied Services, NEC

621999   All Other Miscellaneous Ambulatory Health Care Services *see* SIC 8099: Health & Allied Services, NEC

62211   General Medical & Surgical Hospitals *see* SIC 8062: General Medical & Surgical Hospitals; SIC 8069: Specialty Hospitals, Except Psychiatric

62311   Nursing Care Facilities *see* SIC 8051: Skilled Nursing Care Facilities; SIC 8052: Intermediate Care Facilities; SIC 8059: Nursing & Personal Care Facilities, NEC

62322   Residential Mental Health & Substance Abuse Facilities *see* SIC 8361: Residential Care

623311   Continuing Care Retirement Communities *see* SIC 8051: Skilled Nursing Care Facilities; SIC 8052: Intermediate Care Facilities; SIC 8059: Nursing & Personal Care Facilities, NEC

623312   Homes for the Elderly *see* SIC 8361: Residential Care

62399   Other Residential Care Facilities *see* SIC 8361: Residential Care

62411   Child & Youth Services *see* SIC 8322: Individual & Family Social Services; SIC 8641: Civic, Social, & Fraternal Organizations

62412   Services for the Elderly & Persons with Disabilities *see* SIC 8322: Individual & Family Social Services

62419   Other Individual & Family Services *see* SIC 8322: Individual & Family Social Services

62421   Community Food Services *see* SIC 8322: Individual & Family Social Services

624221   Temporary Shelters *see* SIC 8322: Individual & Family Social Services

624229   Other Community Housing Services *see* SIC 8322: Individual & Family Social Services

62423   Emergency & Other Relief Services *see* SIC 8322: Individual & Family Social Services

ARTS, ENTERTAINMENT, & RECREATION

71111   Theater Companies & Dinner Theaters *see* SIC 5812: Eating Places; SIC 7922: Theatrical Producers & Miscellaneous Theatrical Services

71119   Other Performing Arts Companies *see* SIC 7929: Bands, Orchestras, Actors, & Entertainment Groups; SIC 7999: Amusement & Recreation Services, NEC

711219   Other Spectator Sports *see* SIC 7941: Professional Sports Clubs & Promoters; SIC 7948: Racing, Including Track Operations; SIC 7999: Amusement & Recreation Services, NEC

71131   Promoters of Performing Arts, Sports & Similar Events with Facilities *see* SIC 6512: Operators of Nonresidential Buildings; SIC 7922: Theatrical Procedures & Miscellaneous Theatrical Services; SIC 7941: Professional Sports Clubs & Promoters

71141   Agents & Managers for Artists, Athletes, Entertainers & Other Public Figures *see* SIC 7389: Business Services, NEC; SIC 7922: Theatrical Producers & Miscellaneous Theatrical Services; SIC 7941: Professional Sports Clubs & Promoters

71151   Independent Artists, Writers, & Performers *see* SIC 7819: Services Allied to Motion Picture Production; SIC 7929: Bands, Orchestras, Actors, & Other Entertainers & Entertainment Services; SIC 8999: Services, NEC

71219   Nature Parks & Other Similar Institutions *see* SIC 7999: Amusement & Recreation Services, NEC; SIC 8422: Arboreta & Botanical & Zoological Gardens

71312   Amusement Arcades *see* SIC 7993: Coin-Operated Amusement Devices

71321   Casinos *see* SIC 7999: Amusement & Recreation Services, NEC

71329   Other Gambling Industries *see* SIC 7993: Coin-Operated Amusement Devices; SIC 7999: Amusement & Recreation Services, NEC

71392   Skiing Facilities *see* SIC 7999: Amusement & Recreation Services, NEC

71394   Fitness & Recreational Sports Centers *see* SIC 7991: Physical Fitness Facilities; SIC 7997: Membership Sports & Recreation Clubs; SIC 7999: Amusement & Recreation Services, NEC

71399   All Other Amusement & Recreation Industries *see* SIC 7911: Dance Studios, Schools, & Halls; SIC 7993: Amusement & Recreation Services, NEC; SIC 7997: Membership Sports & Recreation Clubs; SIC 7999: Amusement & Recreation Services, NEC

ACCOMMODATION & FOODSERVICES

72111   Hotels & Motels *see* SIC 7011: Hotels & Motels; SIC 7041: Organization Hotels & Lodging Houses, on Membership Basis

72112   Casino Hotels *see* SIC 7011: Hotels & Motels

721191   Bed & Breakfast Inns *see* SIC 7011: Hotels & Motels

721199   All Other Traveler Accommodation *see* SIC 7011: Hotels & Motels

72131   Rooming & Boarding Houses *see* SIC 7021: Rooming & Boarding Houses; SIC 7041: Organization Hotels & Lodging Houses, on Membership Basis

72211   Full-Service Restaurants *see* SIC 5812: Eating Places

722211   Limited-Service Restaurants *see* SIC 5812: Eating Places; SIC 5499: Miscellaneous Food Stores

722212   Cafeterias *see* SIC 5812: Eating Places

722213   Snack & Nonalcoholic Beverage Bars *see* SIC 5812: Eating Places; SIC 5461: Retail Bakeries

72231   Foodservice Contractors *see* SIC 5812: Eating Places

72232   Caterers *see* SIC 5812: Eating Places

72233   Mobile Caterers *see* SIC 5963: Direct Selling Establishments

OTHER SERVICES

811212   Computer & Office Machine Repair & Maintenance *see* SIC 7378: Computer Maintenance & Repair; SIC 7629: Electrical & Electronic Repair Shops, NEC; SIC 7699: Repair Shops & Related Services, NEC

812112   Beauty Salons *see* SIC 7231: Beauty Shops

812113   Nail Salons *see* SIC 7231: Beauty Shops

81291   Pet Care Services *see* SIC 0752: Animal Speciality Services, Except Veterinary

81299   All Other Personal Services *see* SIC 7299: Miscellaneous Personal Services, NEC; SIC 7389: Miscellaneous Business Services

PUBLIC ADMINISTRATION

92215   Parole Offices & Probation Offices *see* SIC 8322: Individual & Family Social Services

92411   Air & Water Resource & Solid Waste Management *see* SIC 9511: Air & Water Resource & Solid Waste Management

92412   Land, Mineral, Wildlife, & Forest Conservation *see* SIC 9512: Land, Mineral, Wildlife, & Forest Conservation

GENERAL INDEX

This index contains references to companies, associations, persons, government agencies, specific legislation, and terminology cited in the Encyclopedia of Emerging Industries. *Citations are followed by the page number(s) in which the term is discussed. Page references in italics refer to photos.*

A

A-Drive Corporation, 641

AAA, 179

AAAI, 66

AAHP, 396–97

Aames Financial Corporation, 444

AARP. *See* American Association of Retired Persons

ABA (American Bankers Association), 144

ABA (American Bar Association), 3

ABA (American Booksellers Association), 94, 97

Abbot Laboratories, 23, 25

ABC. *See* American Broadcasting Company

Abdominal exercises, 584

Abe, Takeshi, 21

Abercrombie and Kent, 715

ABI, 853

Abortion, adoption and, 255, 260

AboutWork, 805

ABS (Polymer). *See* Acrylonitrile-butadiene-styrene

Abseiling, 709

Absolute Software, 127–28

Absorption, active tuned mass, 485

A.C. Larocca Gourmet pizzas, 480

Academic achievement, in charter schools, 100, 101

Academic degrees, programs for, 27, 32

Academic standards, in vocational education programs, 29

Accelerated graphics port, 450

Accelerated Strategic Computing Initiative, 545, 547

Accelerometers
    in air bags, 411, 413
    development of, 410, 415, 416
    in silicon chips, 527

Access Media International, 209

Access NP, 821

Access to Medical Technology Act, 49

Accidents, traffic. *See* Traffic accidents

Accountants, in financial planning, 274, 275

Accounting firms. *See also* specific firms, e.g., Ernst & Young
    electronic sales and, 211

Accreditation (Education). *See also* Licenses
    of distance education programs, 31–32, 35

Accuwave, 324

ACE (American Council on Exercise), 581, 585

Ace Hardware, 864, 867

Acer Group, 216

Acetyl resins, in plastics, 588

Acetylene, polymers from, 587

ACLI, 283

ACM, 546

Acoustic holography, 317, 319

Acoustical engineering, *487*

Acoustical Solutions Inc., 487

Acoustics. *See* Sound

Acquired immunodeficiency syndrome. *See* AIDS (Disease)

Acquisitions and mergers
    of exercise product manufacturers, 582
    of ISPs, 209
    of lawn and garden product manufacturers, 868
    in managed care, 396
    risk management for, 643–46
    of specialty coffee companies, 703–4
    in telecommunications, 749–50, 752, 755–60, 851
    of wireless communications companies, 852, 854

Acrylonitrile-butadiene-styrene, 588

Active brake technology, 250

Active Control Experts, 14

Active matrix LCD, 786, 789

Active mufflers, 487, 488

Active noise cancellation, 485, 488

Active Services, 203

Active tuned mass absorbers, 485

Active Voice, 818

ActiveX, 844, 860, 861

ACTS, 6

Acupressure, 46, 469. *See also* Alternative medicine

Acupuncture, 48, 49
    analgesic properties of, 474
    in health spas, 312, 315
    new age products and, 469, 473

Adams Express Company, 664

Adamson, Steven, 656, 658

Adaptive Network Security Alliance, 122

ADC Telecommunications Inc., 269, 570

Adecco SA, 697

Ademco Security Group, 668

Adept Technology, 652

Agricultural industry
　genetic engineering in,　303, 305–9
　GIS systems for,　176, 177, 179
　information services for,　346
　machinery for,　863
　molecular design in,　427–29, 431
　new age products and,　469
　polymers in,　592
　produce and　(*See* Farm produce)
　robots in,　651
Agriculture, sustainable,　867
Agriculture Department.　*See* Department of Agriculture
Agro,　483
Ahearn, Karen,　875
AHPA,　491
AHPhA,　47
AI.　*See* Artificial intelligence
AICPA,　276
AID, on coffee production,　703
Aides
　home health,　327, 551
　nurses,　327, 331
AIDS (Disease),　**17–26.**　*See also* HIV (Viruses)
　drugs for,　18, 23, 24–25, 726
　gene therapy for,　306, 309
　molecular modeling for,　438
　origins of,　20–21
　oxygen therapy and,　537
　service organizations for,　18
　travel and,　714
AIDS vaccines,　21, 25
AIDSVAX,　21
AIG Risk Management, Inc.,　644, 646
AIIM International,　351, 356, 358
AIIP.　*See* Association of Independent Information Professionals
AIM Management Group,　466–67
AIMR,　276, 278
Air bag restraint systems,　**551–57**
　accelerometers for,　411, 413
　de-powered,　551, 552
　deaths from,　552–54
　development of,　410, 413, 415
　for heads,　555
　sensors for,　526, 554
　side-impact,　551–53, 556
Air cleaners
　electronic,　832, 833, 837
　portable,　831, 832, 837
　sales of,　836
Air collar restraints,　556
Air filters,　**831–35**
　in airports,　837–38
　ceramic,　838–39
　electret,　832
　electronic,　832
　mechanical,　832
　portable,　832
Air pollution
　environmental removal of,　242
　indoor　(*See* Indoor air pollution)
　risk management for,　645
　solar power and,　573
　from vehicle emissions,　38, 865–66
Air purification,　**831–42**

Air quality
　consumer awareness of,　831, 837
　deterioration of,　835–36
　products for,　832–33
　residential,　833
Air-to-ground communications,　656, 850
Air traffic control, virtual reality for,　815
Air walkers,　584
Aircraft industry
　flat panel displays for,　785, 788
　futures consulting for,　283
　holography in,　324
Airline industry
　smart cards for,　680
　specialty tourism and,　709, 710, 713, 714
　telephone services for,　761
　voice recognition systems for,　823, 828
　Y2K transition and,　874, 875
Airplanes
　autonomous,　527
　child safety seats in,　554
　deicing,　594
　fighter,　568
　jet,　487, 488
　mobile communications services for,　656, 850
　nanotechnology for,　413
　noise control and,　485–88
　positioning systems for,　659
　safety seats in,　551, 554
　supersonic,　488
Airport noise,　**485–89**
Airport Noise and Capacity Act of 1990,　486
Airport security services,　666
　biometrics for,　84, 87–88
Airports
　air filtration for,　837–38
　juice bars in,　634
　noise in,　**485–89**
　telemedicine for,　742
Airstream,　838
AirTouch Communications,　761, 852, 854
Akella, Annapoorna,　324
Akiyam, K.,　508
Akzo Nobel,　262
Alaimo, Dan,　793, 794
AlarmNet,　668
Alcatel Telecom,　269, 570, 658
Alcoholic beverages.　*See also* Beer
　vs. juice bars,　634
Alcohols, as alternative fuel,　42
Alcor Life Extension Foundation,　152–55
Aldrin, Buzz,　77
Aldus Software,　165
Ale,　132, 133
Alexander & Alexander Services,　646
Alfalfa, drugs from,　732
Alfred Murrah Federal Building, bombing,　665
Algae, micro, in nutritional supplements,　495, 497
Algorithms, for artificial intelligence,　71
Alibris,　502
Align Solutions Corporation,　738–39
All Sport,　599
Allefheny Ludlum,　839
Allegheny Teledyne Inc.,　839
Allen, Catherine,　682

ASHA. *See* American Seniors Housing Association
Ashkin, William, 34
ASHRAE, 833, 837
ASI. *See* Analytical Surveys, Inc.
ASICs, 673
Asimov, Isaac, 757
ASIS (American Society for Industrial Security), 663, 668
ASIS (American Society for Information Science), 347
ASOs, 18
Aspect Development Inc., 357
Aspen Laboratories, 237
ASRM. *See* American Society for Reproductive Medicine
Assembly lines, robotics for, 649–51
Asset management, 467, 643–44
Assigned risk pools, 644
Assisted living facilities, **1–7,** 200
Assisted reproductive technology. *See* Reproductive technology
Association for Computing Machinery, 546
Association for Financial Counseling and Planning Education, 276
Association for Investment Management and Research, 276, 278
Association of Executive Search Consultants, 621
Association of Home Appliance Manufacturers, 833
Association of Independent Information Professionals, 346–48
Association of Information and Image Management, 170
Association of Research Libraries, 450
Association of Telemedicine Service Providers, 743
Associations. *See also* names of specific associations
    commercial, 285
    garden, 866
    professional, 285, 800, 803
    trade, 285, 800, 803
    Web site development for, 843, 844
ASTC, 519
Asthma, increase of, 835
Astigmatism, lasers for, 508–12
ASTM, 334–35
Astra Hasle AB, 726
Astrolink, 658, 660, 853–54
Astronautics, **75–81**
Astronauts, telemedicine for, 742
Astronomy, XML for, 860
Astrum International Corporation, 838
Asymmetric digital subscriber line. *See* DSL
Asynchronous communications, 28, 267
Asynchronous Digital Subscriber Line. *See* DSL
A.T. Kearney Executive Search, 619, 621, 622
AT & T Corporation
    breakup of, 749–50, 756, 758–59
    computer network support from, 116, 117
    on elder day care, 202
    executive search services for, 621
    fiber optics and, 266
    infomercials for, 340
    Internet service by, 158, 361, 362, 364, 367
    in photonics, 568, 570
    in push technology, 628
    security for, 666
    software consulting for, 698
    in systems integration, 735
    in telemedicine, 745
    in telephone products & services, 760, 761
    toll-free numbers from, 388
    used computer equipment and, 781

in voice recognition systems, 823, 824, 829
in wireless communications, 720, 851, 852, 854
in XML development, 860
Atalla Security Products, 665
Atari, 449, 810
ATC, 13
ATE relays, 414
Athena Neuroscience, Inc., 436
Athletic clubs. *See* Health clubs
Athletic goods industry. *See* Sporting goods industry
Athletic shoes, 581, 584
Athletic training, 581, 583
    cross, 585
ATI, 706
ATM networks, 745, 759
ATMs. *See* Automated teller machines
Atom lasers, 374
ATR Interpreting Telecommunication Research, 829
ATSP, 743
AT&T Systems Leasing Corporation, 781
AT&T Wireless Services, 720, 851, 852, 854
Atwater Casino Group L.L.C., 292
Auctions
    online, 207
    of used computer equipment, 778, 781
Audio CDs, 515, 517–18
Audio messaging interface standard, 818
Audio recordings. *See* Sound recordings
Audiovisual computer. *See* Multimedia technology
Aureal Semiconductor, 453
Australian Holographics, 323
Authentication. *See also* Identification; Verification
    holography in, 317, 322
    push technology for, 628
    user, 126
Auto PC, 828
AutoAdvisor, 638
Autocad, 813
Autodesk, Inc., 127, 177, 813
Autogenic training, 46
Autoliv AB, 555, 556
Automated Fingerprint Identification System, 86, *664*
Automated Imaging Association, 527
Automated teller machines
    biometric identification for, 86
    security for, 664, 666, 669
    smart cards for, 680, 681
Automatic Data Processing, 229
Automatic pilots, artificial intelligence for, 67
Automation, industrial, **649–54**
Automatons, 650
Automobile dealers
    franchises for, 774
    used car superstores and, 772, 773
Automobile drivers
    education for, 551
    identification of, 90
Automobile financing, *vs.* leasing, 639–40
Automobile industry. *See also* Transportation industry
    captive finance divisions in, 637, 638
    child safety seats and, 337
    lasers for, 372
    robotics for, 649–52, 654
    used car superstores and (*See* Used cars)
    virtual communities for, 803

Y2K transition and, 875
Automobile leasing, **637–42**
    used cars and, 771, 772, 774
Automobile seats
    air bag injuries and, 552
    safety features of, 551, 555, 556
Automobile warranties, for used cars, 771
Automobiles
    armored, 663, 722
    artificial intelligence in, 70, 73
    electric, 41, 384, 385
    embedded systems for, 674
    gyroscopes for, 415, 416
    hybrid, 384, 385
    hydrogen fuel cell, *40*
    luxury, 640
    mobile satellite services for, 656
    online shopping for, 500, 504
    positioning systems for, 178–83, 372, 412, 659
    security for, 414
    semiconductors for, 671
    solar powered, 576
    used (*See* Used cars)
    voice systems for, 828
Automotive engineering
    advanced ceramics in, 14
    for alternative fuels, 37–41
    holography in, 319–20
    liquid metals in, 378
    nanotechnology for, 409, 410, 412, 413, 415
    plastics in, 587, 589, 591, 592
    semiconductors for, 673
    sensors for, 410–13, 523, 526
Automotive fuels. *See* Motor fuels
Automotive Industry Action Group, 875
Automotive Lease Guide, 640
Automotive Rentals Inc., 641
Automotive Service Association, 553
AutoNation, Inc, 771, 773, 774
Autonomous Technologies Corporation, 510
Avalanche Systems Inc., 847
Avalon (Computer), 545
Avatar, in virtual communities, 805
Aveda, 57
Aviation industry. *See* Aircraft industry
Aviation Safety and Capacity Expansion Act, 486
Avis Rent-a-Car, 147
Avon Products, 55, 56, 314, 491
AVRI, 826
Awareness Institute Reiki Certification, 315
AWE, 713, 714
AWWA, 835
AXENT Technologies, 125
Ayurvedic medicine, 312, 314, 473
Azido-deoxythymidine. *See* Zidovudine
Azron, Inc., 861
AZT. *See* Zidovudine

B

B. Dalton Bookseller, 96
BAA McArthur Glen, 534
Babe's Farm, 481
Babies R Us, 333–34
Baby Bells. *See* Regional Bell operating companies

Baby boom generation
    automobile leasing and, 639
    elder day care and, 199, 201
    health spas for, 312
    home health care and, 328
    infertility and, 255
    juice bars and, 633
    lawn and garden products for, 866
    nutritional supplements and, 482, 491
    outlet malls and, 534
    oxygen therapy and, 535
    retirement communities for, 3, 4
    specialty tourism for, 709, 714
Baby foods
    gourmet, 139
    infant formula, 305
    microwavable, 481
    natural, 472, 477, 480
    new age products and, 472
Baby products industry, **333–38**
Baby Superstore, 334
Babyak, Richard J., 616
Bacey, Mindy, 34
Bachelor's degrees, alternative programs for, 27, 32
Back pain
    alternative medicine for, 312, 474
    biosensors for, 414
Backroads, 715
Backup systems, 121, 666, 872
BackWeb Technologies, Inc., 625–29
Bacteria
    air filtration for, 840
    in bioremediation, 247
    in drinking water, 834
    drug resistant, 725–32
    in fruit juice, 633
    genetic mapping of, 730
    soil, 497
    water purification for, 840
Bacterial pneumonia, drugs for, 725
Bactericidal/permeability increasing protein, 731
Baekeland, Leo H., 589
Baez, Albert, 318
BAI, 251, 253
Baico, 555
Bailey, George, 441
Baird (Robert W.) & Company, 229
Baked products, 481–82, 632
    for pets, 561
Bakelite, 589
Bakelite Company, 590
Baker, James K., 827
Baker, Janet, 827
Bal-A-Vie, 314
Balaban, Naomi, 731
Balanced Budget Act, 327
Baldwin, Jerry, 704, 705
Ball Aerospace, 182
Balloons, sports and, 251, 712
Bananas, in fruit bar products, 631
Bandwidth technology
    development of, 117
    in digital imaging, 173
    fiber optic cable and, 265–67
    in parallel processing, 545

photonics and, 566, 567
push technology and, 626, 628, 629
in satellite television, 194, 198
in telemedicine, 744
Bank American Ventures, 203
Bank of America, 667
Bank One, 502
Bank One Stadium, 723
Bankers Life and Casualty, 328
Banking industry. *See also* Financial institutions; specific banks
in automobile leasing, 637, 638
biometric identification for, 86–87
consumer information from, 144, 145
financial planning and, 273, 275, 277
GIS systems for, 178, 181
information services for, 346
vs. mortgage companies, 441
mutual funds and, 466
online services in, 206, 210, 502
security services for, 664, 669
smart cards for, 680–83
systems integration for, 737
voice recognition systems for, 825
wireless communications for, 851
Y2K transition and, 871, 872, 876
Bankruptcy
gambling and, 289, 294
home mortgages and, 444
Banks
commercial, 442
mortgage, **441–46**
Bantron, 686
Bar codes
biological, 85
holography in, 319, 322
in MIS, 355
Bardeen, John, 674
Barkat, Eli, 628
Barlam, Steve, 203
Barley, in nonalcoholic beverages, 609
Barnes and Noble, 93–97
electronic publishing by, 221, 223
online marketing by, 208, 500, 502
in specialty coffee, 704
Barr, Gillian, 769
Barrier sensors, 665
Barror, Susan Bradford, 4
BarrTek, 769
Barry, Jim, 750, 751
Barry's Controls Aerospace, 485
Bars (Drinking establishments)
coffee, 702–5, 772
raw juice, **631–36**
Bartelstone, Roma, 202
Bartsch, Charles, 242
Bartz, Carol A., 813
Basch, Reva, 347
Base sequence
developments in, 305
in resistant bacteria, 728, 730
of *Staphylococcus aureus,* 730
in superdrug development, 730–31
BASF AG
in nutritional supplements, 491, 495, 496
in polymers, 591, 592

Bashaw, Matthew, 320
Basic Input Output System. *See* BIOS
Basketball, 404, 601
Baskin-Robbins Ice Cream, 140, 635
Bass Barbican NA, 605
Bass Beers Worldwide, 608
Batelle, Inc., 591
Bates, Ellen, 348
Bates Information Services, 348
Bateson, William, 304
Batteries
in electronic books, 223
liquid electrolyte, 381–82
lithium-ion, 216, **381–85,** 854
lithium-metal, 381–82, 385
nickel-cadmium *vs.* lithium, 216, 381, 382
for portable computers, 214–17, 381–84
rechargeable, **381–85**
recycling, 383
smart, 384
solar, 573, 574, 576–79
solid-state electrolyte, 381–82
window, 576
Bausch & Lomb Surgical, 509
Bay Networks, 745
Bayer AG, in polymers, 430, 591, 592
Bayer Corporation
in molecular modeling, 431
in nutritional supplements, 492
Bayer Faser GmbH, 592
B2B, 861
BBN, 435, 824
BCC. *See* Business Communications Company
BCI Company, 42
BDM International, 735, 738
Beacon Education Management, 100, 101, 105
Bear, John, 32
Bear, Stearns & Co., 292
Beard, James, 138
Bearings, advanced ceramic, 13
Beauticians, licensing, 315, 536
Beauty aids. *See* Health and beauty aids
Beauty salons, in health spas, 312, 313, 315
Bechtel Group, Inc., 246
Beck, Bernard, 819
Becker, Don, 545
Becker CPA Review, 33
Bedford, James H., 153–54
Bee pollen, in juice bar products, 632
Beepers (Pagers)
computer networks for, 849, 850, 854
displays for, 789
microwave applications in, 421
satellites for, 656, 657, 853
sensors for, 523, 524
services for, 759, 761
Beer. *See also* Breweries
ale, 132, 133
with espresso, 704
home-brewed, 131, 606
imported, 133
light, 606
near-, 606
nonalcoholic, **605–9**
specialty, **129–34**

Booksellers. *See also* specific booksellers, e.g., Amazon.com,
  Barnes and Noble
    desktop publishing and, 164
    independent, 93–95
    Internet based, 93, 95, 147–48, 208–9, 211
Bookstores
    in cybercafes, 157
    vs. electronic shopping, 502
    superstores, **93–98**
Boolean logic, *vs.* fuzzy logic, 69
Boost, 494
Booz-Allen and Hamilton, 854
Border Patrol (U.S.), on surveillance equipment, *721*
Borders, Louise, 96
Borders, Tom, 96
Borders Group Inc., 93–97
Borg-Warner, 663, 667
Boron
    in plastics, 587
    in semiconductors, 672
    in solar cells, 574
Bosak, Jon, 858
Bosco Products, 481
Bose, Satyendra Nath, 374
Bose Corporation, 487
Bose-Einstein condensation, 374
Boston Beer Company, 133, 134
Boston Computer Exchange, 781
Boston Consulting Group, 499, 501
Boswellia, in nutritional supplements, 497
Botanical supplements. *See* Dietary supplements
Bottled mineral water, 603, 607, 834
Bottles
    plastic, 588, 591
    recycling, 591
    security labels for, 668
Bourn Hall Clinic, 260
Bove, Albert, 537
Bovine somatotropin, 307, 428
Bowker, Gordon, 704, 705–6
Box office receipts. *See* Ticket sales
Boyce, Timothy, 3
Boyd Coffee, 702
Boyle, Tim, 385
BP. *See* British Petroleum Company
BP Pension Fund, 534
BPI, 731
BR Smoothie, 635
Braffman-Miller, Judith, 727
Brahmanism, in new age philosophy, 470
Braille, XML for, 858
Brain, cryopreservation of, 152–55
Brain cancer
    from cellular phones, 424
    gene therapy for, 309
Brainard, Paul, 165
Brakes
    active technology for, 250
    antiskid, 415
Brand name products
    mail-order sales of, 389
    nonalcoholic beverages and, 606, 608
    in online shopping, 503
    in outlet stores, 529
    in used car superstores, 771, 772

in water & air filtration, 831, 839
Branson, Richard, 460
Brass Eagle, 297–98
Brassica, anticancer properties of, 497
Brattain, Walter H., 674
Braun, Ferdinand, 673
Braun, Jerry, 298
Braun, Judith, 4, 202
Bray, Tim, 859
Breast feeding, products for, 333
Breathing exercises, 539
Breed Technologies, Inc., 415, 555
Breeding, genetic engineering in, 304
Bregman, Michael, 706–7
Brennan, Eric, 217–18
Breweries. *See also* Beer
    craft beer and, **129–34**
    nonalcoholic beer from, **605–9**
Brewpub beer. *See* Microbreweries
Bridge 2000, 875
Briefcases, for surveillance, 722
BrightAdvisor, 72
BrightResponse, 72
Brightware, 72
Brilliant, Larry, 802
Brilliant Media, 452
Brinkley, Joel, 786
Brinks, 663
Bristol-Meyers Squibb Company
    in endoscopy, 233
    in molecular design, 428
    in superdrug development, 726, 730
Britax, 334, 839
British Elastic Rope Sports Association, 249
British Petroleum Company, 576, 578, 667
British Sky Broadcasting, 195, 197
British Telecom
    in push technology, 628
    in voice mail systems, 821
    in wireless communications, 852
British Telecommunications PLC, 761
Broadband transmission. *See also* Transmission speed
    fiber optics and, 269
    in LMDS, 853
    vs. microwave transmission, 420
    satellites for, 655, 656
    for telephony, 755, 759
    wireless cable for, 421
Broadcasting
    educational, 30
    television (*See* Television broadcasting)
Brody, Jerry, *70, 71*
Brokers. *See also* Securities industry
    equipment, 778
    financial planning and, 274
    information (*See* Information services)
    insurance, 643
Bromfield, Louis, 864
Bronchoscopy, virtual, 812
Brookhaven Laboratories, 435, 436
Brooks Automation, Inc., 652
Brooks Brothers, 529, 531
Brookshire, J.J., 297
Brooktrout Technology Inc., 821
Brown, Arnold, 283

Brown, Greg, 56

Brown, Harrison, 282

Brown, Joy Louise, 257

Browner, Carol, 246

Brownfields, 242

Brownfields Economic Redevelopment Initiative, 243, 246

Bruce-Biggs, B., 283

Brunswick Corporation, 300

Bruskin-Goldring Research, 274

BSA, 127

BSAC, 414, 416

BT (Company), 759, 761

Buchannan, Bruce, 68

Buckland, Michael, 354

Buckler NA, 605

Buddhism, 470, 712

Budget Gourmet, 479

Budhraja, Vikram, 575–76

Buena Vista Home Movies, 186, 190

Bugging devices. *See* Eavesdropping

Build-to-order computers, 214, 217

Building. *See* Construction industry

Building Efficient Surface Transportation and Equity Act, 38

Bull CP8, 683

Bulletin Boards, Internet. *See* Computer bulletin boards

Bulletproof vests, 722

Bundling (Marketing), 146–47

Bungee Adventures Inc., 251, 253

Bungee jumping, 249–53

Bungee Safety Consultants, 253

Bureau Etudes Vision Stockplus, 527

Bureau of Labor Statistics. *See* U.S. Bureau of Labor Statistics

Burger Chef, 137

Burger King, 137, 140

Burglar alarms, 668

Burkett, Elinor, 20

Burlington Basket Company, 336

Burners-Lee, Tim, 222, 365, 844, 845, 858

Burnett, Leo, 147

Burnham, Bill, 277

Burns
    oxygen therapy for, 535, 537, 539
    polymers for, 594

Burpee Seeds, 868

Burroughs (Company), 544

Burton, Jack, 253

Burton, Kevin, 139

Burton, Tim, 111

Burton Snowboards, 252–53

Burwell, Helen, 347

Buses
    alternate fuel for, 37
    biometric identification of drivers, 90
    in specialty tourism, 710

Bush, George, on AIDS, 19, 21

Business Communications Company, 9, 12, 741, 743–44

Business ethics
    in coffee growing, 706
    in executive recruitment, 621
    for financial planners, 276
    in futures consulting, 284
    in infomercials, 340
    risk management and, 645
    for software consultants, 695

Business forecasting, consulting for, 285

Business information services, **345–50**
    virtual communities for, 800–801, 803

Business intelligence, surveillance for, 720, 721

Business losses, risk management for, 643

Business Machines Corporation, 202

Business planning, by futures consultants, **281–88**

Business Products Industry Association, 778

Business Software Alliance, 127

Business Technology Association, 778

Business-to-business market
    electronic, 205, 206, 210, 499, 500
    virtual communities for, 800
    Web sites and, 846

Business Vehicle Services, 637–38

Business Vision, 196

Bustillo, Maria, 261

Busy Body, 585

Butadiene
    polymers from, 587
    resins, 588

C

C. Everett Koop Institute, 743

C-band, for satellite services, 656

C++ programming language, 844, 861, 875

CA-Accucheck, 875

CA-Fix/2000, 875

Cable Competition and Consumer Protection Act, 421

Cable television
    deregulation of, 851
    fiber optics for, 265, 266, 268
    food channels, 136, 138
    for gardening, 867
    infomercials on, 340
    for Internet access, 196, 362, 366, 786–87
    photonics in, 567
    push technology for, 627
    vs. satellite broadcasting, 193, 194, 658
    telephone lines for, 752, 754
    wireless communications and, 853

Cables
    coaxial   (*See* Coaxial cables)
    fiber optic   (*See* Fiber optic cables)

Cablevision, 195

CACI, 875

CAD software.   *See also* Computer-aided design
    for nanotechnology, 410, 412, 416
    virtual reality in, 813

Cade, Mary, 599

Cade, Michael, 599, 600–601

Cafe Internet, 159

Cafe Kaldi, 159

Cafes, cyber, **157–61**

Caffe Tazza, 703

Caffeine, in nutritional supplements, 496

CAI, artificial intelligence in, 66

CAI Wireless Systems, 422, 424

CalArts, 111

Calcium
    in hot springs, 312
    in juice bar products, 631
    in nutritional supplements, 492, 497

Calculators, displays for, 786, 788

Caliber Learning Network, 33

Carpoint, 638

Carre, Kanon Bloch, 463, 466

Carrier Corporation, 839

Carrots, in fruit bar products, 631

Cars. *See* Automobiles

CarSource, 638

Cartography
artificial vision in, 66
digital, **175–84**
satellites for, 655, 659

Cartoons. *See* Caricatures and cartoons

Carwizard, 638

Casale, Frank, 695

Cascadian Farm, 472

Cascading Style Sheets, in XML, 859

Case, Stephen M., 366–67

Casino Control Act, 294

Casino Data Systems, 295

Casinos, **289–96.** *See also* Gambling industry

Casio, 172

Cassio Cassiopeia, 216

Castanet, 626–28

Castelle, 614

Castin-Silver, Harriet, 324

Casting, plastics, 588

CAT scan. *See* Computed tomography scan

Catalog companies. *See* Mail-order business

Catalysts
in anti-aging products, 58
for methanol, 589
molecular modeling of, 433, 436

Catalyzed electrochemical oxidation, 247

Cataracts, lasers for, 512

CatFinder, 561

Catheters
endoscopic technology in, 236, 237–38
micro, 237–38
multi channel, 237

Cathode ray tubes, in video displays, 783, 785–86, 790

Cathodes, in rechargeable batteries, 385

Catholic Charities, 203

Catholic HealthCare West, 49

Cattle, genetically engineered, 305, 306, 309

CAVE, 815

Cb Commercial Real Estate Group Inc., 297

CB radio. *See* Citizens band radio

CBL, 861

CBS, 787

CCDs. *See* Charge coupled devices

CCF, 284

CCRCs, **1–6**

CCTV. *See* Closed-circuit television

CD-interactive, 516

CD-ROMs. *See also* Optical storage devices
audio, 515, 517–18
catalogs, 388
desktop publishing of, 163, 164
double speed, 450
vs. DVDs, 187–89
extended architecture, 516
GIS systems on, 177
holography in, 322
infomercials for, 341
medical information on, 346
in multimedia computers, 447, 448, 451–53

photonics in, 566

publishing, 221–22 (*See also* Electronic publishing)

recordable, 515–16, 566

rental of, 792, 795

triple speed, 450

in used computer equipment, 780

video, 448–49

32X, 518

XA, 516

XML for, 858

CDB Infotek, 346, 348, 349

CDBG, 243–44

CDC 6600, 544

CDC (Centers for Disease Control). *See* Centers for Disease Control

CDC (Control Data Corporation), 544–45

CDF. *See* Channel definition format

CDLA, 778

CDNow, 207, 500

CDPD, 854, 855

CDTV, 449–50

Cedarlane Natural Foods, 480

Cefdinir, development of, 729

CEKN, 222

Cel animation, 108

Celanese, Hoechst, 433

Celebrities
as chefs, 136, 138, 300
endorsements by (*See* Endorsements (Advertising))
in infomercials, 340
nonalcoholic beverages and, 608

Celestial Seasonings, 57

Celestri (Satellite), 853

Cell Benesys, Inc., 309

Cell Genesis, Inc., 306

Cell Pathways, Inc., 431, 437

Cell Robotics, 373

Cellular digital packed data, 854, 855

Cellular One, 760, 854

Cellular Telecommunications Industry Association, 849, 852

Cellular telephones, 750, 761, 854
batteries for, 381, 383, 385
computer networks for, 759, 761, 849, 850–51, 855
eavesdropping on, 720, 721
health effects of, 424
microdisplays for, 784
microwave transmission for, 419, 421, 422
PDAs as, 213
satellites for, 657–58, 853
semiconductors for, 671, 676
sensors for, 524
solar power for, 573
telephony and, 755

Celluloid, 589

Cellulose
in alternative fuels, 42
nitrate, 589
polymers from, 593
in rechargeable batteries, 382

Celts, in new age philosophy, 470

Cement, molecular modeling of, 433

Cendant Corporation, 147

Censorship, smart cards and, 679–80

Census, GIS systems for, 183

Census Bureau. *See* U.S. Census Bureau

Clean Water Action Plan, 645
Cleaning agents, antibacterial products in, 61, 63
Cleaning (Maintenance), robotics for, 650
ClearSpeech, 488
Cleartype, 225
Clearview Cinema Group, 458, 459–60
CLECs, 760–61
Clement, Debbie, 828
Cleveland Clinic Foundation, 746
CLIA. *See* Clinical Laboratory Improvement Amendments
CLIA-88, 258–59
Client/server architecture
    consultants for, 694, 696
    in law enforcement, 355
    in MIS, 352, 357
    network support for, 116
    push technology for, 628
Clif Bar, 581
Climbing, mountain, 249–50, 252, 712, 714
Clinical Laboratory Improvement Amendments of 1988, 258–59
Clinical trials, of superdrugs, 726–31
Clinique, 54
Clinton, William
    on AIDS, 19, 21, 22
    on charter schools, 99, 102
    on education, 32
    on electronic commerce, 210, 501
    on environmental remediation, 241
    on gambling, 289, 293
    on genetic engineering, 303–4
    on human cloning, 260, 305
    on managed care, 395
    on Medicare reimbursements, 397
    on scientific research, 265
    on smart cards, 681
    on solar power, 575, 576
    on telecommunications, 756
    on video displays, 785, 787
    on water quality, 835
Clomiphene, for infertility, 259
Cloning, 303
    humans, 260, 305–6
    sheep, 305–7
Closed-circuit television, 665, 667, 719, 722, 723
    in telemedicine, 742
Clothing industry
    cross-marketing in, 145
    electronic sales in, 499, 502–3
    mail-order sales in, 387, 390
    outlet stores and, 530
    product licensing in, 406, 407–8
    protective clothing, 23, 722
    robotics for, 652
    sport clothes (*See* Sport clothes)
Club of Rome, 283
Clustering (Computers), 545–46, 548
CML (Chemical markup language), 860
CML Corporation, 867
CMOS transistors, 784
CMU. *See* Carnegie-Mellon University
CNET, 224
CNG, 38–39
CNIL, 148
CNW Marketing/Research, 640
Co-operative Insurance Society, 534

Coad, Peter, 696
Coad/Young methodology, 696
Coal, polymers from, 587
Coalition for Accountable Managed Care, 395
Coates, Joseph, 283
Coates & Jarratt, Inc., 285
Coatings
    advanced ceramic, 10–11
    microwave applications for, 419
    for plastics, 590
    plexiglas acrylic, 590
    polymer, 593, 594
    robotics in, 649, 651
Coaxial cables
    for Internet access, 362, 368
    in telemedicine, 741
Cobalt, in rechargeable batteries, 382
Cobb Theater, 458
COBOL, Y2K transition and, 875, 876
Coca-Cola Company
    advertising by, 147
    in bottled water, 834
    information management systems for, 356
    in new age products, 469, 472
    outlet stores and, 532
    in premium beverages, 597–99, 601, 602
    product licensing and, 406
Cochrane, Steve, 863
Cocoa, in specialty coffee, 702
Coconut milk, bacteria in, 633
Cod-liver oil, in nutritional supplements, 494
Coeur Business International, 354
Coffee
    augmented, 483
    bars, 702–5, 772
    cappuccino, 702
    carbonated, 704
    decaffeinated, 702
    espresso, 701, 702, 704
    flavored, 701, 702, 704
    ready-to-drink, 597, 600, 603
    specialty, **701–7**
Coffee Connection, 704
Coffee Group, 703
Coffee makers, 701, 702
Coffee People, Inc., 705
Coffee Republic, 706
Coffeehouses
    as cybercafes, 157, 158
    juice bars and, 631–33
    specialty coffee and, 701, 705
Cognex Corporation, 652
Cognition
    computer modeling of, 66
    vitamin E for, 496
Cognition (Company), 410
Cognizant Technology Solutions, 875
Cognos, Inc., 357
Cohen, Marshall, 502
Cohen-Esrey Real Estate Services Inc., 297
Coherent (Company), 512
Cohotin, Nicholas, 537
Cold light endoscopy, 234, 235
Cold molded plastics, 590
Coldwater Canyon, 531

Collage Video, 583

Collation, Elizabeth, 242

College degrees, programs for, 27, 32

College of American Pathologists, 259

Colleges. *See* Universities and colleges

Collins & Aikman, 556

Colonoscopes, 234

Color printers. *See* Printers (Computer)

ColorScript Laser 1000, 165

ColorSync Technology, 166

Colson, William E., 2, 5

Colson & Colson/Holiday Retirement Corp., 2, 3, 5, 6

Colt Protective Services, 667

Columbia/HCA Healthcare Corporation, 330, 744

Columbia Pictures, 186

Coma, oxygen therapy for, 539

CombiChem, Inc., 432, 436

Combinatorial analysis

    in molecular design, 429, 430

    in molecular modeling, 437

Comcast Corporation, 759, 852, 854

Comdisk Network Services, 116

CoMFA, 431

Comintern, 817

Commerce Department. *See* Department of Commerce

Commerce extensible markup language, 862

CommerceNet, 860

Commercial banks, in home mortgages, 442

Commercial paper, in mutual funds, 464

Commercial space services, **75–81**

Commercialization of Microsystems Conference, 412

Commission on Airline Safety and Security, 554

Commission on Recognition of Post-Secondary Education, 28

Commission on the Year 2000, 283

Commissions (Fees), for financial planners, 274–75

Commodities industry, consulting for, 273, 281

Commodity plastics, 588

Commodore Dynamic Total Vision, 449–50

Common Business Library, 861

Common Object Request Broker Architecture, 861

Communicable diseases, drug development for, **725–33**

Communication satellites, 77, 80, **655–61**

    frequencies for, 656

    global networks of, 855

    microwave transmission and, 419, 421

    in telemedicine, 741, 742

    in telephony, 755, 756, 762

    for television, 193, 195, 198, 655–56, 658, 660

    for wireless communications, 665–61, 849, 853

Communications. *See also* Telecommunications services

  industry

    air-to-ground, 656, 850

    asynchronous, 28, 267

    fiber optics for, 268

    security of, 125, 208

    synchronous (*See* Synchronous communications)

    two-way (*See* Two-way communication)

Communications & Space Euroconsult, 660

Communications networks. *See* Computer networks

Communities

    geographical, 800

    risk management for, 646

    solar powered, 577

    specialty tourism and, 712

    vertical industry, 800

    virtual, **799–807**

Community centers, adult day care in, 199, 200

Community colleges, in vocational education, 29

Community Development Block Grants, 243–44

Community gardens, 138, 864–65

Community Technology Institute, 820

Community Voice Mail, 820

Community Washington House, 4

Compact directional drilling, 247

Compact disc read-only memory. *See* CD-ROMs

Compaq 2015 C, *215*

Compaq Computer Corporation

    in computer security, 126–27

    DEC and, 216, 217, 738, 739

    in multimedia, 448, 452

    network support from, 115, 118

    in parallel processing, 547

    in portable computers, 214, *215,* 215–18

    in push technology, 628

    in security products, 665

    in video displays, 784, 786, 789

Compaq Plus, 214

Compaq Transportable, 214

Comparative molecular field analysis, 431

Compass Group, 622, 623

Competitive local-exchange carriers, 760–61

Competitive Technologies, Inc., 188

Complete Wellness Centers, Inc., 49–50

Complex programmable logic devices, 673

Composting, 865, 866

Comprehensive Environmental Response, Compensation and

  Liability Act. *See* CERCLA

Compressed air, vehicles, 41

Compressed natural gases, 38–39

CompuChem, 432

CompuCom Systems, 115

Compuplan, 777–78

CompuServe Corporation, 158, 361, 362, 367, 802

    America Online and, 368

    in electronic commerce, 206, 208

    in Internet development, 363

    push technology and, 625

Computational chemistry, in molecular modeling, 433, 435

Computed tomography scan, 322, 423

Computer-aided design. *See also* CAD software

    in GIS systems, 180

    mechanical, 813

    in molecular design, 431

    for nanotechnology, 410, 412, 416

    of plastics, 588–89

    in robotics, 652

    virtual reality for, 813

Computer-aided instruction, artificial intelligence in, 66

Computer-aided manufacturing

    of plastics, 588–89

    robotics for, 652

    virtual reality for, 813

Computer-aided medical diagnosis, artificial intelligence for, 65, 68–69

Computer animation, **107–13**

Computer Associates International, 84, 118, 357, 875

Computer-based training

    artificial intelligence in, 66

    for automobile leasing, 641

Computer bulletin boards, 799–800, 802, 804

Computer conferencing. *See* Teleconferencing
Computer crimes, 124–26, 504. *See also* Computer hackers;
  Software piracy
    cost of, *123,* 124–25
    hardware theft, 121–24, 127–28
    security for, 121–22
Computer Dealers and Lessors Association, 778
Computer Dealers Association, 778
Computer education
    classrooms for, 222
    consultants for, 693
    in cybercafes, 158
Computer Exchange, 781
Computer games
    3-D, 813
    artificial intelligence in, 69
    computer animation in, 108
    in cybercafes, 157, 159
    electronic sales of, 211
    mass marketing of, 403, 406
    in multimedia computers, 447
    superstores for, 94–95, 297
    in theater entertainment centers, 455
    in virtual reality, 811
Computer graphics. *See also* Graphics software
    in multimedia computers, 447, 450, 451
    parallel processing computers for, 544
    print services for, 611, 612
    in systems integration, 739
    in virtual communities, 800–802, 804, 805
    in virtual reality, 812–13
    in Web site development, 844, 845, 848
Computer hackers, 122, 123, 504, 876. *See also* Computer
  crimes
Computer hardware
    boards/cards (*See* Boards/cards (Computers))
    build-to-order, 214, 217
    encryption technology in, 665, 673
    lasers and, 373
    mail-order sales of, 387
    microwave applications in, 419
    in MIS, 352
    in molecular modeling, 435–36
    for multimedia, 448
    network support and, 115
    online shopping for, 206, 210–11, 499, 503
    in systems integration, 736, 737
    theft of, 121–24, 127–28
    for voice recognition, 827
Computer integration. *See* Systems integration
Computer languages. *See* Programming languages
Computer Leasing and Remarketing Association, 778–80
Computer Lessors Association, 778
Computer literacy, adult education for, 34
Computer Management Sciences, 697
Computer memory. *See also* Computer storage devices
    integrated, 677
    memory chips for, 672–73, 676
    random access (*See* Random access memory)
    read-only, 672–73
Computer Motion Inc., 237, 238, 652
Computer networks. *See also* Network computer
    Advance Intelligent Networking technology for, 762
    for beepers, 849, 850, 854
    fiber optics for, 265–67

gateways for, 352, 356–57
integration of (*See* Systems integration)
optical technology for, 519, 568
in parallel processing, 545
photonics for, 565
print services for, 611, 613, 616
security for, 665
smart cards for, 682, 683
support services for, **115–20**
synchronous communication and, 759
for telecommunications, 752, 755–56, 758–59, 761
in telemedicine, 741, 745
for telephony, 755
3D technology and, 811
Token Ring, 614
in virtual reality, 811
for wireless communications, 849, 852
Y2K transition and, 876
Computer peripherals. *See also* Modems; Printers (Computer)
    in desktop publishing, 167
    multifunction, 167, 613–14, 616
    for multimedia computers, 452
    used (*See* Used computer equipment)
Computer piracy. *See* Software piracy
Computer printers. *See* Printers (Computer)
Computer programming
    application (*See* Applications programming)
    Coad/Young methodology, 696
    consultants for, 694, 695
    development of, 696
    languages for (*See* Programming languages)
    in systems integration, 735, 736
Computer pulse transformers, 543
Computer Renaissance, 777, 780
Computer Science Corporation, 694, 697, 875–76
Computer security, **121–28,** 663–66
    biometrics for, 84–89
    for online shopping, 499, 504, 544
    smart cards for, 126–27, 682
    in systems integration, 739
    XML and, 859
Computer Security Institute, 89, 123
Computer services industry
    push technology for, 628
    software consulting in, **693–99**
Computer simulation
    in executive recruitment, 623
    in futures consulting, 281, 287
    of motion, 300, 458
    in noise control, 485
    parallel processing for, 543–45
    photonics and, 568
    virtual reality for, 810, 813, 814
Computer software
    animation (*See* Animation software)
    antivirus, 121, 123, 126–27, 627
    billing/invoicing, 351–52
    children's, 336
    consulting for, **693–99**
    cross-marketing, 143
    custom, 736
    database management, 780
    debugging, 666
    development of, 736–37
    educational (*See* Educational media)

lasers for, 371
machinery for, 863
plastics in, 587, 588, 591–93
professional employer organizations for, 229
robotics for, 652
time capsules and, 766
virtual reality for, 809
Consulting firms. *See also* Management consultants
for computer software, **693–99**
for executive recruitment, 619
for gardening, 863
for MIS, *356*
for molecular design, 430
for risk management, 643, 646
virtual communities for, 803
for Y2K transition, 871, 874
Consumer electronics. *See also* Electronics industry
flat panel displays for, 787
optical disks in, 515
solar powered, 576
Consumer Electronics Manufacturing Association, 750, 751
Consumer electronics stores. *See also* Electronics industry
multimedia computers in, 451
superstores for, 94–95
telephone products in, 750
Consumer Federation of America, 275
Consumer Healthcare Products Association, 491, 492
Consumer information
in banking, 144, 145
for infertility, 258
Internet and, 143, 146–48
in marketing, 143–49
Consumer Leasing Act of 1976, 638
Consumer preferences, analysis of, 143–44
Consumer Product Safety Act, 335
Consumer Product Safety Commission
on snowboarding, 252
on soaps, 61
on toys, 336
Consumer protection, infomercials and, 339
Consumer satisfaction. *See* Customer satisfaction
Consumers Bankers Association, 640
Consumers Energy, 874
Contact lenses, *vs.* laser surgery, 508, 509
Context (Linguistics), in voice recognition software, 824, 825
Continental Mills, 479
Continuing Care Retirement Communities, **1–6**
Continuum Electro-Optics, 374
Contraceptives, oral, 255, 260
Contrafund, 463
Control Data Corporation, 544–45
Control Module, Inc., 322
Convenience foods, 477, 479–82, 504
Convenience stores, 605, 634
Conversa. *See* Conversational Computing Corporation
Conversant, 827–28
Conversational Computing Corporation, 826
Convex Computer, 545, 547
Conxus, 819
Cook, William J., 657
Cookie files (Computer), 502
Cooks. *See* Chefs
Cooney, Robert, 298–99
Cooperative Home Care Associates, 331

Cooperative Research and Development Agreement, on advanced ceramics, 12–13
Coopers & Lybrand, L.L.P., 2, 697
Coors Beer
microbrews and, 129, 130, 132
non-alcoholic, 605, 607
Coors Ceramics, 13
Copper
indium gallium diselenide cells, 578
in liquid metal products, 379
in semiconductors, 671, 677
in time capsules, 766
Copper wire
amplifiers for, 265
vs. fiber optic cable, 265, 266, 567, 755, 762
Copying machines
digital, 614, 616
in multipurpose machines, 614, 616
vs. printers, 612
Copyright
for DVDs, 186
in electronic publishing, 222, 223, 501, 845
for multimedia, 448, 450
for software, 125, 127
for Web sites, 843
Coram Healthcare Corporation, 23, 330
CORBA, 861
Cordless telephones, 749, 750–51, 854
security for, 751
sensors for, 524
Corel Corporation
on artificial intelligence, 65
in multimedia, 451
online marketing by, 206
CorelDraw, 177
Coretese, Amy, 625
Corley, Buster, 300
CORMA, 431
Corn
for alternative fuels, 39, 41–42
genetic engineering of, 307–9
polymers from, 593
Corneal transplantation, 510, 512
Corneal ulcers, drugs for, 731
Corning Inc.
in fiber optics, 266, 268, 269
in photonics, 568, 569
Coronary artery bypass, 236, 237, 306
Corporate day care, 199–200, 202
Corporate Educational Services, 33
Corporate espionage, 720, 721
Corporate Protection Professionals, Inc., 666
Corporate sponsorship, of virtual communities, 800–801
Correctional institutions
biometric identification in, 88
data conversion and, 181
security for, 667
telemedicine and, 742, 744
Correspondence courses
for adults, 27–30
charter schools and, 104
Correspondence University (Ithaca, N.Y.), 30
Corriveau, Dave, 300
Corrosion, filtration for, 839
Cosco, 333

Crystnet, 435
CSC. *See* Computer Science Corporation
CSI. *See* Computer Security Institute
CTI (Computer-telephone integration), **755–64**
CTI Corporation, 562
CTI Information Systems, 818
CTIA, 849, 852
CTX International, 788
Cubist Pharmaceutical, 726, 728, 729–30
Cubix Corporation, 761
CUC International, 147
Cucina Holdings Inc., 703
Cuci's pizza, 480
Cucumbers, in juice bar products, 631
Cullen, Phil, 355
Culligan Water Technologies, 836, 838
Cultural tourism, 709, 711–14, 716
Culture
    in adult education, 34–35
    germ-conscious, 64
Cupaloy, 766
Cups, plastic drinking, 590
Curtiss Group, 622
Cushions, in passenger restraint systems, 556
Customer satisfaction
    with car dealerships, 773
    with managed care, 393, 395, 396
    with medical care, 48–49
    with used car superstores, 772, 774
    with used computer equipment, 780
    with voice mail systems, 819
    with water quality, 833
Cut-off switches, for air bags, 552–53
Cutting machines
    advanced ceramics for, 9
    lasers for, 373, 374
    liquid metals and, 378
Cuvelier, Chris, 634
CVM, 820
CVS, 473
1000CX Palmtop, 216
CXML, 862
Cxpediter+, 875
Cyanotech Corporation, 495, 497
Cyber-Times Software, 159
Cybercafes, **157–61**
CyberFlyer Technologies, 159
Cybermation, 875
CyberMondot Com, 803
CyberSage Corporation, 665
Cyberstar/Skybridge, 658, 660
Cybex, 582
Cycling, for exercise, 583, 584
Cymer, Inc., 373
Cyrix, 676
Cystoscopes, 234
Cysts, water purification for, 837
Czarnic, Tony, 429

D

Da Vinci, Leonardo, 66
Daewoo Electronics, 415–16
Dahr, Dietlef, 319

Daimler-Chrysler
    in auto leasing, 637, 639, 641
    IUCRC and, 416
Daimler-Chrysler Financial Corporation, 641
Dairy products, in beverages, 600, 603, 631
Daisy Manufacturing Company, 298
Daley Marketing Corporation, 779
Dallas Can!, 102
Dance, for exercise, 583
Danmount, 683
Dannenmaier, Silke, 828
Daptomycin, 728, 730
DARPA. *See* Advanced Research Projects Agency
Data cleaning, 356
Data compression
    in computer animation, 112
    holography in, 317
    microwave applications in, 421
    MPEG, 190, 195, 198, 451
    push technology for, 628
    in satellite television, 194, 195, 198
Data Connection Ltd., 818
Data encryption, 122, 124, 126
    of consumer information, 149
    hardware for, 665, 673
    for online shopping, 501
    push technology for, 628
    quantum technology and, 571
    on smart cards, 680
Data General Corporation, 746
Data Inc., 502
Data mining
    in marketing, 143, 144–45, 149
    in MIS, 352
    systems integration of, 735
Data processing, 565, 571. *See also* Computer programming
Data Protection Directive, 349
Data security. *See also* Computer security; Data encryption
    biometrics for, 84–89
    for online shopping, 499, 504, 544
    services for, **121–28,** 663–66
    smart cards for, 126–27, 682
    in systems integration, 739
    XML and, 859
Data transfer. *See* Electronic data interchange
Data transmission speed. *See* Transmission speed
Data warehousing, 352, 355
Database management systems, 176, 780
Database marketing, **143–50,** 352
    in mail-order companies, 387, 389, 391
Database searching
    by information brokers, 345
    push technology for, 625
    XML and, 858, 861
Databases
    artificial intelligence for, 65
    bibliographic (*See* Bibliographic databases)
    of chemical compounds, 434, 725–26
    corporate, 352–53
    for executive recruitment, 622–23
    full text, 345, 346, 349
    in futures consulting, 287
    of *Helicobacter pylori,* 730
    marketing of (*See* Database marketing)
    of medical records, 745

of molecular data, 436–37
in molecular design, 428–31
multiple access to, 354
on nutritional supplements, 494
object-oriented, 861
online, 206, 825
parallel processing of, 543–45, 548
of pets, 562, 563
of proteins, 436
relational (*See* Relational databases)
security for, **121–28,** 122–23
in specialty tourism, 710
in systems integration, 735
virtual, 803, 861
XML for, 857
Y2K transition and, 873
Datachannel, 860–61
Datamatics Management Services, 355
Datamonitor, 483
Dataquest Inc., 115
on multimedia, 447, 450–51
on portable computers, 216
on semiconductors, 676
on smart cards, 682
on wireless communications, 853
Datenschutz, 148
Dator, James, 282, 283, 286
Datta, Ashim, 425
Dave and Buster's, *299,* 300
David R. Marks International, 668
Davidson, Stuart, 811
Day care centers
for adults, **199–204**
for children (*See* Child day care)
corporate, 199–200, 202
intergenerational, 199
for pets, 559
DBMS, 176, 780
DBS television, **193–98**
DDHP, 321
De-alcoholization, of nonalcoholic beverages, 609
de Benedetti, Marco, 453
de la Riviere, Eric Le Proux, 660
De La Rue Card Systems, 683
De novo drug design, 434
De Serres, Frederick J., 242
de Turckheim, Maurice, 347
Deacidification, for preservation, 767
Dead, cryopreservation of, **151–56**
Deaf, voice recognition systems for, 824
Dean, Peter, 796
DeAndrea, Richard, 538
Death
from air bag systems, 552–54
cryopreservation and, 153
Debugging software, 666
DEC. *See* Digital Equipment Corporation
Decaffeinated coffee, 702
Decision making
futures consulting for, 282, 284–85
public, 284–85
risk management and, 643
Decision Resources, 492
Decision support systems, consultants for, 696

Decoders
MPEG, 190, 195, 198, 451
in satellite television, 194, 198
Decompression sickness, oxygen therapy for, 535, 536
Dede, Chris, 286
Dedicated Reader, 223
Deep Blue, 65, 69, *70,* 546, 547
Deep ion reactive etching, 414
Deere & Company, 356, 863, *865,* 867
Deerfield Manor Spa, 314
Deerfield Senior Day Centers, 203
Default (Finance)
in automobile leasing, 639
in home mortgages, 444
Defender (Brand name), 868
Defense Department. *See* Department of Defense
Defense industry
advanced ceramics for, 11
astronautics in, 75
biometric identification in, 86
displays for, 785, 787, 789
futures consulting for, 282
lasers for, 372
olfactory sensors for, 429
photonics and, 568
satellites for, 655, 659
security for, 663
sensors for, 429, 523–26
virtual reality for, 810, 812
Y2K transition and, 871, 874, 876
Defensor (Software), 665
DeFranco 7 Sons, 481
Degree of freedom, robotic, 653
Dehydration, beverages for, 601
Dehydroepiandrosterone, in anti-aging products, 53, 55–57
Deicing, of airplanes, 594
Deinococcus radiodurans, in bioremediation, 247
Dejanews, 804
DEKLAB Genetics Corporation, 305, 308
Del Webb Corporation, 3
Delbruck, Max, 304
Delfino, Erik, 613
Delicatessens, specialty coffee in, 701
Delivery of goods
electronic, 205, 206–7, 210, 348
infomercials and, 340
by mail-order companies, 387
for online shopping, 500, 503, 504
Delivery services
bicycle, 504
online shopping for, 206, 499, 500
Dell, Michael, 210, 389–90
Dell Computer Corporation
in mail-order sales, 389–90
online marketing by, 206, 208–11, 501, 505
in portable computers, 214, 216, 218
in sensing devices, 524
in voice recognition systems, 826
Deloitte & Touce, 697
Deloitte Consulting, 284
Delphi Automotive Systems, 828
Delta & Pine Land, 308
Delta 3 Rocket, 79
DeLuca, Anthony J., 246
Dementia, care for, 4, 200

Denisyuk, Yuri, 324
Denny's Restaurants, 319
Dental ceramics, 14
Dental insurance, 230, 396
Deodorizing cleansers, antibacterials in, 62
Deogun, Nikhil, 598–99
DeParle, Nancy-Ann Min, 327
Department of Agriculture
    on food safety, 135–36
    on genetic engineering, 303
    on new food products, 478
    on organic produce, 139
    on push technology, 627
    in telemedicine, 743
Department of Commerce
    on electronic commerce, 206, 208
    on genetic engineering, 303
    on satellite industries, 659
    on telemedicine, 743
    on Y2K compliance, 875
Department of Defense. *See also* Advanced Research Projects
  Agency
    on advanced ceramics, 12
    on environmental remediation, 244, 247
    on genetic engineering, 303
    in GIS development, 176
    in holography, 323
    Internet development and, 158, 363, 801
    on liquid metals, 379–80
    managed care for, 395
    parallel processing and, 547
    on push technology, 627
    in sensing devices, 525, 526
    systems integration for, 737
    in telemedicine, 745, 746
    in video displays, 785, 787
    in virtual reality, 810, 813
    on Y2K compliance, 874, 876
Department of Developmental Disabilities, 201
Department of Education, 28, 103
Department of Energy
    on advanced ceramics, 12, 13
    on alternative fuels, 40, 42
    on environmental remediation, 244, 247
    on genetic engineering, 303
    on lasers, 372
    on lithium batteries, 383, 384
    on microwave applications, 423
    parallel processing and, 545
    on solar power, 575–79
Department of Health and Human Services
    on AIDS, 18, 21, 24
    on fertility medicine, 259
    on genetic engineering, 303
    on home health care, 329
    on microwaves, 422
    on telemedicine, 742
Department of Housing and Urban Development, 243–44
Department of Labor
    on health occupations, 399
    on multimedia occupations, 452
Department of the Interior, 875
Department stores
    catalog sales by, 388–90
    dining in, 137

exercise products in, 585
oxygen therapy in, 540
security services for, 664
specialty coffee in, 701
video rentals in, 791, 794
water purification products in, 834
Depreciation, of leased automobiles, 639
Depression, herbal medicine for, 473–74
Deramus, Frank, 21
Deregulation, of telephone companies, 749–50, 752, 755–60, 851
Derickson, Sandra, 640
Dermatology, in telemedicine, 741, 746
Designed genetic change. *See* Genetic engineering
Desktop online analytical processing, 352
Desktop publishing, **163–68**
Desserts, 479, 481
Destination Spa Group, 314
Detectors. *See* Sensors
Detergents
    in drinking water, 837
    molecular modeling for, 438
    polymers in, 593
Detroit Diesel Corporation, 14
Detroit Edison, 874
Detroit Entertainment L.L.C., 292
Detroit Police Department, 851
Deutsche Telekom, 761, 762
Developer Design Corporation, 88
Developing countries
    AIDS in, 24
    alternative education for, 34
    Internet and, 34–35
    solar power for, 578
    specialty tourism and, 714
    used computer equipment for, 781
    water purification for, 840
    wireless communications for, 854–55
Developmental Disabilities Department. *See* Department of
  Developmental Disabilities
Devine, Brian, 560–61
Devol, George, 650
Devry, Inc., 33
Dewar, James, 153, 154
Dewars, in cryopreservation, 154, 155
Dewey, John, 29
DHA. *See* Omega-3 fatty acids
DHEA. *See* Dehydroepiandrosterone
DHTML, 848, 861
Di Giorno Rising Crust Pizza, 479
Diabetes, 373
    genetic engineering for, 305
Diabetic retinopathy, treatment for, 512, 539
Diageo, 482
Diagnostic imaging, transmission of, 741, 744, 746
Diagnostic tests
    for AIDS, *22, 23,* 24
    computer aided, 65, 68–69
    endoscopes for, 233–34, 237–38
    for eye diseases, 171
    home, *22, 23*
    for infertility, 258
    lasers for, 374
    molecular design in, 427
    nanotechnology for, 412

Pranactin, 234
telemedicine for, 741–42, 744
Dial, Tom, 163
Dial Corporation, 63–64
Dialog, Inc., 345, 347
Dialogic, 827
Diamond Data, 780
Diarrhea, water purification for, 840
Diedrick Coffee, 705
Diesel, Rudolph, 39
Diesel fuels, alternative, 39, 43
Dietary Supplement Health and Education Act of 1994, 54, 56, 492–94, 536
Dietary supplements, **491–98.** *See also* Vitamins
for AIDS, 20
anti-aging, 53–58
in cryopreservation, 151
in juice bar products, 631, 632, 634
in new age products, 470
oxygen therapy and, 535–37, 539
in premium beverages, 603
sales of, 55
Difusion, Inc., 629
DIG, 173
Digital Biometrics Inc., 89
Digital cameras, **169–74**
printers for, 615, 616
sensors for, 523, 524
for surveillance, 722, 723
Digital Cities, 225
Digital compression. *See* Data compression
Digital copying machines, 614, 616
Digital Equipment Corporation
in artificial intelligence, 118
Compaq merger, 69, 216, 217, 738
in GIS development, 177
in parallel processing, 546, 548
in printers, 616
in systems integration, 735, 739
Digital imaging, **169–74**
for maps, **175–83**
sensors for, 523, 524526
in telemedicine, 741, 745
in Web site development, 844
Digital Imaging Group, 173
Digital Information Sky Highway Network, 197
Digital integrated circuits, 416, 672, 676
Digital micromirror devices, 413, 415
Digital Millennium Copyright Act, 223
Digital multiplexing, 198
Digital One, 852
Digital Planet, 452
Digital projection international power display projector, 413
Digital scales, 319
Digital signal processors, 677, 751
Digital sound recordings
vs. analog, 447–48, 751
development of, 448–50
in high definition television, 783
optical disks for, 515
in theater entertainment centers, 458
THX system for, 461
Digital storage devices. *See* Computer storage devices
Digital switching. *See* Telecommunication switching equipment
Digital telephones, 720, 749–51

Digital television
regulation of, 784–87
semiconductors for, 787
video displays for, 783–84
vs. video rentals, 796
Digital video disks, **185–91,** 516
audio, 189, 190–91
vs. CDs, 187–89, 518
DVD-RAM, 518
holography in, 322
in multimedia computers, 447, 450, 451, 453
photonics in, 566
rental of, 792, 795, 796
Digits, Y2K transition and, 873
Dilute acid hydrolysis, for alternative fuels, 42
Dimensional Media Associates, 321, 322
Diners Club, 388
Dining, creative, **135–42**
Diode laser technology, 190
Diodes, light-emitting, 594, 790
Diploma mills, on the Internet, 31–32
DIRE, 414
DirecDuo, 195
DirecPC, 195, 660
Direct broadcast satellite television, **193–98**
Direct deposit services, security for, 665, 666, 669
Direct Digital Holographic Printer technology, 321
Direct mail. *See* Mail-order business
Direct marketing
infomercials for, **339–44**
of laser surgery, 510, 511
vs. mail-order sales, 388
Direct Marketing Association
on catalog sales, 388
on electronic commerce, 499, 501
on infomercials, 340
Direct response television. *See* Satellite television
DIRECTV, Inc., 193, 195, 196, 660
Disabled
toys for children, 336
voice recognition systems for, 824
Disaster planning, risk management for, 643, 645
Disaster relief, GIS systems for, 178
Disc Manufacturing Inc., 322
DISCO, 657
Discount stores. *See also* Retail stores
exercise equipment in, 583
nutritional supplements in, 492
outlets, **529–34**
pet supplies in, 562, 563
telephone products in, 750
water purification products in, 834
Discounts (Sales), for books, 93, 502
Discovery Channel
digital shows and, 786
Eco-Challenges, 712
specialty travel and, 713
Discovery Engine, 432
Discussion Group (Internet), 800–802, 804, 806
Diseases. *See also* specific diseases, e.g., AIDS (Disease)
chronic (*See* Chronic diseases)
communicable, **725–33**
diagnosis of (*See* Diagnostic tests)
genetic basis of, 730
genetic engineering for, 306–9

Downsizing
 computer consulting and, 693
 executive recruitment and, 620
 information services and, 345, 350
 security and, 665
Dragon Systems
 noise control products for, 488
 voice recognition systems by, 824–28
DragonDictate, 827
DRAM. *See* Dynamic random access memory
Drawing, in computer animation, 108, 111, 112
DreamWorks SKG
 in adult gaming, 299
 in computer animation, 110
 in DVD development, 188
 product licensing by, 403, 406, 407
DRENDEL, 68
Drew Medical Center, 745
Drexler Technology, 520–21
Dreyer's Grand Ice Cream, Inc., 704
Drilling
 compact directional, 247
 lasers for, 371
Drinking cups, plastic, 590
Drinking water, purification of, **831–42**
Driscoll, Elliott, 688
Drive-in restaurants, 137
Driver Employer Council of America, 228
Driver-Guide, 179
Drivers
 education, 551
 identification of, 90
 truck, 90, 228
Driver's Mart, 773
DRTV. *See* Satellite television
Drug approval, 726–27
Drug dealing, electronic surveillance and, 721
Drug industry. *See* Pharmaceutical industry
Drug resistance, by microorganisms, 725–32
Drugs
 for AIDS, 18, 23, 24–25, 726
 De novo design of, 434
 delivery systems for, 594
 development of, **725–33**
 vs. herbs, 474
 lead selection of, 726
 molecular design of, 427–31
 molecular modeling of, 433–38
 olfactory sensors for, 429
 smoking cessation, **685–91**
 use in sports, 582
Drugstores, nutritional supplements in, 491, 492
Druids, 470
Drying equipment, microwave applications in, 419
DSHEA. *See* Dietary Supplement Health and Education Act;
 Dietary Supplement Health and Education Act of 1994
DSI, 555
DSL
 in cybercafes, 160
 vs. fiber optic cable, 267, 567
 for Internet access, 368, 762
DSPs. *See* Digital signal processors
DTD. *See* Document type definition
DTP. *See* Desktop publishing
DuCoa LP, 495

Duke University, 801
Duke University Medical Center, 746
Dunkin' Donuts, 179
Dunn, Ashley, 739
Duo 210, 214–15
DuPont Company
 in environmental remediation, 241, 245
 in genetic engineering, 305
 in molecular modeling, 435, 436
 in parallel processing, 548
 in polymers, 591, 592
Duracell, 383
Duracraft Corporation, 839
Durrans, Brian, 769
Durwood, Stanley, 459
Dutta, Prabir, 579
DVD Forum, 186, 518, 519
DVD Video Group, 185, 187
DVDs. *See* Digital video disks
DWDM. *See* Multiplexing, wavelength division systems
Dye lasers, 372, 373
Dye sublimation printer, 612, 615
Dynamic Associates Inc., 423
Dynamic HTML, 848, 861
Dynamic random access memory, 520, 672, 675
Dynamics Essentials Inc., 495
Dyonics, 233
Dysentery, water purification for, 840

E

E. coli. *See* Escherichia coli
E-books. *See* Electronic publishing
e-DOCS, 826
E-Loan, 444
e-Steel, 800
E-Trainer, 585
E-zines, 165, 207, 221, 224
Eagle Point Software, 177
EAI. *See* Education Alternatives Inc.
Earls, Alan R., 736
Earth Day, 244
Earth Technology Corporation, 242, 244, 247
Earthbound Farm, 480
Earthquake Porter, 131
Earthquakes
 computer modeling of, 543
 sensors for, 414
Earth's Best, 472, 480
EarthWatch, 182, 713, 715
East Midlands Electricity, 738
Eastern philosophy
 in new age philosophy, 470
 tourism and, 712
Eastman, George, 590
Eastman Chemical, 591
Eastman Kodak Company
 in digital imaging, 171–73
 in holography, 323, 324
 in optical storage, 519
 in polymers, 590
Easy Photo, 171, 172
Eavesdropping, 720–23
eBay, 207
Ecco, 697

ECD, 577
Echinacea, supplemental, 482, 494
EchoSearch, 71
EchoStar Communications Corporation, 193, 196, 197
Economic development
    casinos and, 294
    futures consulting and, 282
    risk management for, 646
Economic Development Administration, 244
Ecotourism, 709, 711–14, 716, 717
Ecotourism Society, 712, 715
EcoWater Systems Inc., 839
ECS Telecommunications, 817
EDA. *See* Economic Development Administration
EDA-Bridge, 357
EDAP Technomed Group, 423
Eddie Bauer, 207, 391, 502
Edelson, Burton I., 661
EDFA. *See* Erbium-doped amplifiers
Edgar, David, 132
Edge Corporation, 451
EDI. *See* Electronic data interchange
EDIFACT, 859–60
Edison, Thomas, 674, 757
Edison Project, 100–101, 103, 104–5
Edison Technology Solutions, 575
Edleman, Cynthia, 562
Edmund's Web, 638
EDORAM. *See* Extended data output random access memory
EDS. *See* Electronic Data Systems Corporation
Education
    accreditation in, 31–32, 35
    adult, **27–36**
    centers, 33–34
    computer (*See* Computer education)
    distance (*See* Distance education)
    drivers, 551
    Internet and, 28, 31, 32–33
    privatization of, 99, 100
    special, 99–102
    tourism in, 709
    vocational, 27–29, 32
Education Alternatives Inc., 100, 103–4
Education Department. *See* Department of Education
Education Development Corporation, 33
Education Industry Group, 102
Educational broadcasting, in adult education, 30
Educational Development Corporation, 105
Educational media
    for children, 337
    electronic publishing of, 222, 225
    multimedia computers for, 447, 452
    virtual reality for, 809, 812, 814
    voice systems for, 819–20
Educational services industry, in adult education, 33–34
Educational television, in adult education, 28, 30
Edutainment, 450
Edwards, Anthony, 341
Edwards, Robert, 260
Edwards Theatres Circuit, 456, 458, 459
EEA, 424
EEG Inc., 840
EFX Elliptical Fitness Cross Trainer, 585
Egg (Human), donors, 262–63
EG&G Inc., 414, 415

EGT, 182
Ehrlich, Paul, 435
E.I. du Pont de Nemors & Company, 324, 590
EIA (Environmental Industry Association), 243
EIG, 102
800 telephone numbers, 388
84 Lumber, 867
Einstein, Albert, 372
Eisenberg, Daniel, 719
Ejection seats, for bungee jumping, 253
e4L, 343
El-Sum, Hussein, 318
Elbrus International, 546
Elderly. *See also* Aging
    day care for, **199–204**
    education for, 27
    exercise equipment for, 581
    health clubs for, 583–84
    home health care for, 328, 329–30
    housing for, **1–7**
    managed care and, 395
    nutritional supplements and, 494
    oxygen therapy for, 535, 537
    robot assistance for, 651
Electra Records, 847
Electric insulators
    ceramic, 10, 12
    plastic, 590
Electric power
    solar, **573–80**
    wind generated, 576
Electric utilities. *See also* Public utilities
    GIS systems for, 178
    MIS for, 355
    solar power and, 578
Electric vehicles, 41
    hybrid, 384, 385
Electrical engineering, in nanotechnology, 416
Electrical equipment and supplies
    advanced ceramics in, 10–11
    optical, 565, 567, 571
Electro-optical equipment, 565, 567, 571
Electroluminescence, polymers in, 593, 594
Electroluminescent display systems, 786, 789–90
Electromagnetic Energy Association, 424
Electromagnetic fields
    health effects of, 424
    photonics and, 565
    in wireless communications, 849
Electromagnetic levitation furnaces, 378
Electron beams, in holography, 318
Electron tubes, development of, 674
Electronic commerce, **205–12.** *See also* Electronic shopping
    in banking, 206, 210, 502
    business-to-business, 205, 206, 210, 499, 500
    consumer privacy and, 148–49
    cross-marketing in, 144, 146
    digital imaging for, 171
    growth of, 366
    infomercials for, 339, 342
    in investments, 466, 468
    MIS for, 351, 356
    multimedia computers for, 447
    product licensing in, 407
    risk management for, 644

security for, 208, 358, 681, 683
smart cards for, 681, 683
in software consulting, 699
virtual communities for, 800, 803–4, 806
Web site development for, 843, 844, 846, 847
wireless communications for, 851
XML and, 358, 858, 861–62
Y2K transition and, 876
Electronic components industry
advanced ceramics in, 9–12
microwave applications in, 419
molecular modeling for, 438
parallel processing computers in, 543
photonics and, 565
plastics in, 587, 591, 592
robotics for, 649, 652, 654
semiconductors for, 673
sensors for, 523
Electronic currency. *See* Electronic funds transfers
Electronic data interchange, 208, 859–60. *See also*
  Downloading
microwave applications in, 421
networks for (*See* Computer networks)
by satellite, 657
in telemedicine, 741, 744, 745
wireless communications for, 851, 853
XML and, 858
Electronic Data Systems Corporation
cross marketing by, 148
in systems integration, 735, 737–38
voice mail for, 821
Electronic Film System, 173
Electronic funds transfers
accounts for, 505
risk management for, 644
security for, 664
smart cards for, 679, 680, 683
Y2K transition and, 871, 872, 876
Electronic Industries Association, 527
Electronic ink, 225
Electronic mail systems
cybercafe access to, 157
development of, 802
EDI for, 208
intercepting, 721
junk mail on, 207, 627
MIME for, 818
in MIS, 351–52
print services for, 614
push technology for, 625, 627
telephone services for, 754, 820
virtual communities and, 799
viruses and, 123
voice systems for, 818, 820, 825
wireless communications for, 849, 852, 854
Electronic marketing, 206, 209–10, 501
in publishing, 209–10
by software consultants, 694
of specialty tourism, 710, 714, 715
of surveillance equipment, 719
of used computer equipment, 778–79
to virtual communities, 803–6
Electronic Media Survey, 499
Electronic numerical integrator and calculator, 67
Electronic Power Research Institute, 383

Electronic publishing, 165, **221–26**
desktop, 164, 165
of magazines, 165, 206, 207, 221, 224, 225
WWW for, 164
Xanandu project and, 845
XML for, 858
Electronic Retailing Association, 339–41, 343
Electronic Security Products, Inc., 668
Electronic shelf labels, for security, 719, 722
Electronic shopping, **499–506.** *See also* Electronic commerce
for automobiles, 500, 504
for bonds, 499, 500
for books, 93, 95, 147–48, 208–9, 211, 499, 502–3
for children's products, 334
for computers, 206, 210–11, 497, 503
credit card fraud in, 499, 501, 504
delivery services, 206, 499, 500
for executive recruitment, 623
for exercise products, 582
for food products, 477–78, 499, 503
for home mortgages, 444, 445
for infertility drugs, 258
infomercials for, 339, 342
for lawn and garden products, 863, 864, 867–68
in malls, 207, 499, 500, 503
for music, 207, 502, 503
for new age products, 471
for optical disks, 515
for oxygen therapy, 539
for securities, 277
smart cards for, 681, 683
for specialty coffee, 701
for specialty tourism, 710, 714–15
for stocks, 499, 500
for surveillance equipment, 719, 720
for used computer equipment, 778–79
virtual communities for, 800, 803–4, 806
Web site development for, 843
Electronic surveillance, 666–68, **719–24**
Electronic teaching methods. *See* Computer-based training
ElectroniCast Corporation, 270, 570
Electronics industry. *See also* Consumer electronics stores;
  specific electronics products
catalog sales in, 387, 390
micromachines in, 409
rechargeable batteries for, 381–82
Electronics Industry Association, 525
Electrostatic precipitation, for air filtration, 832
Elements (Beverage), 602
Elevators, embedded systems for, 674
Eli Lilly, 731
Ellio's Pockets, 479
Elliptical trainers, 585
Ellis, Michael J., 496
Ellison, Lawrence J., 738
Eloquent Technology, Inc., 825
Elsag Bailey Process Automation N.V., 651
Email. *See* Electronic mail systems
eMate, 215
Embargoes
oil, 39
Embedded systems, 674
semiconductors for, 671
Y2K transition and, 871, 873, 874–75

Everpure, 838
Everybook, 223
E.W. Blanch Holdings, Inc., 646
E.W. Scripps Company, 867
EWG, 834–35
eWorld, 804
Excel non-alcholic beer, 605, 607
Excimer lasers, for eye surgery, 508–11
Excise taxes
    environmental remediation and, 246
    nonalcoholic beverages and, 606
Excite (Search engine), 625
    in electronic commerce, 500
    virtual communities and, 805
Executive Car Leasing Company, 641
Executive Protection Associates, Inc., 666
Executive search firms, **619–23**
Executives, security for, 665, 666, 723
Exercise
    abdominal, 584
    aerobic (*See* Aerobic exercises)
    bicycles, 584, 585
    for body toning and sculpting, 583
    for cardiovascular health, 584–85
    centers (*See* Health clubs)
    dancing, 583
    in health spas, 311–13
    strengthening (*See* Strengthening exercises)
    stretches for, 313, 503
    videos, 582–84
Exercise equipment, **581–86**
    infomercials for, 339, 342
Exercise therapy, oxygen therapy and, 536
Exfoliation, in health spas, 315
Expeditions, 710, 712, 714, 715, 717
Expert systems
    artificial intelligence in, 66, 68, 69
    in futures consulting, 287
Explicitly parallel instructions computing, 546
Exploration
    space (*See* Space exploration)
    tourism, 710, 711
    underwater, 317, 319
Explore Zone, 812
Explorer 8, 657
Explosives
    detection of, 719, 722
    olfactory sensors for, 429
    robots for, 651, 653
Express 2000, 875
Extended data output random access memory, 672–73
Extended markup language. *See* XML
Extensible link language, 861
Extensible markup language. *See* XML
Extensible metadata interchange, 859
Extensible style sheets, for XML, 860
Extracorporeal electronic flash, 234, 235
Extractors, juice, 631–33
Extranets. *See also* Intranets
    designing, 847
    in MIS, 353, 354–55
    in online shopping, 500–501
    push technology for, 628
Extreme sports, **249–53,** 581, 711
Extrusion, of plastics, 588

Exxon Oil, 406
Eye diseases, digital imaging for, 171
Eye glasses
    vs. laser surgery, 508
    for surveillance, 722
    video, 668
Eye infections, drugs for, 731
Eye surgery, lasers for, 373, 375, **507–14**
Eyesight, artificial. *See* Artificial vision

F

FAA. *See* Federal Aviation Administration
Fabius, Laurent, 24
Fabric industry. *See* Textile industry
Face
    biometric identification of, 84–85, 87–88, 126
    in computer animation, 112
Face lift, lasers for, 373, 375
Facials
    in health spas, 312, 315
    oxygen therapy and, 538, 540
Factory outlets. *See* Outlet stores
Fadley, Charles, 319
Fair use (Copyright). *See also* Copyright
    of multimedia, 448, 450
Fairchild, Sherman, 178
Fairchild Semiconductor, 410, 680
Fakespace, 815
Falloposcopes, 237–38
False advertising, in infomercials, 339, 341
Family
    in elder day care, 201, 202
    entertainment for, 455, 458
    gambling resorts and, 293
    games for, 297
Family and Medical Leave Act, 645
Family medicine
    in managed care, 394
    smoking cessation and, 690
    voice systems for, 827
Famous Players, 457
Fannie Mae, 441, 442, 444, 446
Fantastick, 62
FANUC Ltd., 651–52
F.A.O. Schwartz, 336, 406
Farbenfabriken Bayer, 590
Farkas Berkowitz & Co., 245
Farm Act, 478
Farm produce
    availability of, 137
    new food products and, 478
    value-added, 477
Farmer, Fanny, 138
Farsightedness, lasers for, 508–9, 511, 512
Fashion Outlet, 531
Fast Ethernet, in computer clusters, 544
Fast food restaurants, 135, 137, 139
    juice bars in, 631
    product licensing in, 403, 405
    video rentals in, 796
Fat substitutes, 482
Fatty acids, omega-3, 482, 492
Fatty esters, in biofuels, 43

File servers. *See also* Computer networks; Network
 management software; Printer servers
  electronic sales of, 210
  parallel processing and, 545
  push technology and, 626
  support services for, 116
  for symmetric multiprocessing, 547
  in WANs, 363
Film
  photographic (*See* Photographic film)
  solar, 577, 578
  thin, 578, 594, 785
Film industry. *See* Motion picture industry
Films. *See* Motion pictures
Filtercold Inc., 839
Filtration
  air, **831–42**
  of drinking water, **831–42**
  dual, 836
  liquid metals in, 378
  membrane, 11, 831
  water, 831, 834, 836, 838, 839
Financial futures
  consulting for, **281–88**
  risk management for, 643, 646
Financial Information Privacy Act, 144
Financial institutions. *See also* names of specific banks and
 institutions
  in automobile leasing, 637, 638
  captive, 637, 638
  consumer information from, 144, 145, 148
  executive recruitment for, 619
  GIS systems for, 178
  in home mortgages, 441, 442
  online services by, 211, 502
  parallel processing computers in, 543
  push technology for, 629
  security for, 664
  smart cards for, 680–83
  XML for, 859, 862
  Y2K transition and, 871, 872, 876
Financial management
  information systems for, 354, 357
  software for, 277, 278, 463, 467
Financial planning, **273–79**
  mutual funds and, 465, 466
Financial Planning Association, 277
Find/SVP, 492
Findlay, John, 290
Fingerhut Companies, Inc., 342, 390
Fingerprints
  biometric identification of, 84, 86–88
  for computer security, 126–27
  vs. eye scans, 85
  scanners for, 89
Finkelstein, Richard, 352
Finnish baths. *See* Saunas
Fir, in aromatherapy, 474
Fire, Wind and Rain (Company), 577
Fire detectors, sensors for, 525
Firearms, in games, 298
Firewalls (Data security), 124–25, 127
The Firm, 583
FIRST, 126
First, Tom, 601

First Chicago NBD, 502
First National Bank and Trust Company, 445
First National Bank of Mason City, 445
First Team Sports, 253
First Union Corporation, 441, 443–45, 502
1st Books, 224
Fish oils, in nutritional supplements, 494
Fisher, George, 172
Fisher-Price, 333, 337
Fisher Scientific Company, 650
Fishing
  tours, 252, 712
  water quality and, 834
FiT TV, 342
Fitness centers. *See* Health clubs
Fitness equipment. *See* Exercise equipment
Fitness Products Council, 583, 584
Fixed rate mortgages, 442–43
Fixed satellite services, 656
Flash memory. *See* Computer memory
FlashPix, 173
Flat panel displays, 783, 785–89
Flatfoot Investigation and Protection Agency, 666
Flavoring essences
  in coffee, 701, 702, 704
  in premium beverages, 602, 603
Fleet Bank, 502
Fleet Financial Group, 445
Fleet management, leasing and, 638
Fleetwood, 838
Fleming, Alexander, 61, 727
Fleming, J. Ambrose, 674
Florey, Howard W., 727
Florida Fruit and Vegetable Association, 478
Florida International University, 602
Fluid dynamics, parallel processing computers in, 544
Fluoroquinolone, development of, 729
Fluoroware, 356
Flynn, Laurie, 846
FMCC. *See* Ford Motor Credit Company
FMR Corporation, 466
Foam rubber, in toys, 335
Folgers, 703
Folic acid, anticancer properties of, 496
Follicle stimulating hormone, 261–62
Follistim, for infertility, 262
Follitropin beta, for infertility, 262
Fonda, Jane, 583
Fonix Corporation, 828
Fonts
  desktop publishing and, 166
  in electronic publishing, 225
Food. *See also* Dietary supplements; Farm produce
  augmented, 479, 482, 483
  baby (*See* Baby foods)
  carryout, 137
  convenience, 477, 479–82, 504
  ethnic, 137–38, 477, 479–80
  frozen, 477, 479, 482
  fruit (*See* Fruit)
  genetically engineered, 303
  gourmet (*See* Gourmet food)
  high energy, 494, 496
  low-calorie, 479
  low-cholesterol, 479

low-fat, 479–81, 631, 632
mail-order sales of, 387
microwavable, 419, 425, 481, 482
natural (*See* Natural foods)
new age, 469, 472–73
new products, **477–84**
online shopping for, 477–78, 499, 503
organic (*See* Natural foods)
prepared, 135, 477, 479–82, 504
snacks, 479, 482
Food, Drug and Cosmetic Act, 54, 303, 492
Food additives
molecular design of, 427
as nutritional supplements, 492
Food and Drug Administration
on acupuncture needles, 474
on AIDS, 23, 24–25
on alternative medicine, 48
on antibacterial products, 61, 64
on artificial intelligence, 65
on artificial skin, 594
on cosmeceuticals, 54, 57
on endoscopy, 236
on ephedra, 494, 496
on fertility medicine, 258, 262
on food safety, 135–36
on genetic engineering, 303, 305, 307, 309
on herbal medicine, 474
on human cloning, 305–6
on insertable eye discs, 512
on juice bars, 633
on lasers, 372
on medical microwave applications, 420
on micromachines in medicine, 410
on new food products, 478
on nutraceuticals, 482
on nutritional supplements, 492, 493
on Olestra, 482
on ophthalmic lasers, 507–11
on oxygen therapy, 536, 537
on smoking cessation products, 686, 687
on superdrug development, 726–29
Food industry
cross-marketing in, 144
GIS systems for, 177
gourmet (*See* Gourmet food)
liquid metals in, 378
new products in, **477–84**
robotics for, 649, 654
safety in, 135–36
Food Marketing Institute, 478
Food Network, 136, 138
Food preservatives, 478
Food service. *See also* Restaurants
creative dining and, 135–41
in cybercafes, 158, 159
in elder day care, 199
in health spas, 311, 313, 315
information services for, 346
in juice bars, 631
in outlet malls, 532
in specialty tourism, 716
take-out, 477
in theater entertainment centers, 455, 458
in used car superstores, 772

workers, 140
Food stores. *See* Grocery trade
Food supplements. *See* Dietary supplements
Foodborne diseases, from fresh fruit juice, 633
Football, 601, 720
Ford, Gerald, 766
Ford, William Clay, Jr., 40
Ford Foundation, 820
Ford Motor Company
on alternative fuels, 40
in artificial intelligence, 70
in auto leasing, 637, 639, 640
cross marketing by, 148, 149
executive search services for, 622
holography by, 319–20
IP networks for, 763
in lithium batteries, 383
voice mail for, 821
Ford Motor Credit Company, 637, 641, 771
Forecasting
business, 285
weather (*See* Weather forecasting)
Foreign and Colonial Government Trust, 464
Foreign language translation software, 68, 72–73
voice recognition systems for, 823, 828, 829
Forensic sciences, computer animation in, 107, 109
Forest fire detection, sensors for, 525
Forestry products
for alternative fuels, 42
microwave applications in, 419
plastics in, 591
in semiconductors, 671
Formages, 504
Formaldehyde
indoor pollution from, 837
resistance to, 729
Formica Products Company, 590
Formichelli, Joseph, 217
Forrester, J.W., 283
Forrester Research Inc., 146
on electronic commerce, 206, 209, 500, 501
on financial planning, 277
on ISPs, 366, 368
on mortgages, 444
on new food products, 478
on smart cards, 679
on virtual communities, 803
on Web development, 843, 846, 847
FORTRAN, Y2K transition and, 876
Fortune 500 companies
executive recruitment for, 622
infomercials for, 341
MIS for, 354
risk management for, 644
security for, 667
systems integration for, 737
Web site development for, 847
Fortune City, 806
Forum of Incident Response and Security Teams, 126
Fossil fuels, *vs.* solar power, 575
Foundations (Endowments). *See also* names of specific
foundations, e.g., Ford Foundation
for AIDS, 18–19
for charter schools, 103

G

G. Heileman Brewing Company, 608
G Ball, *584*
Gabor, Dennis, 318–20, 324
Gadgil, Ashok, 840
Gagliardi, Anna, 346
Gagnard, James, 629
Galaxy IV, 659
Galena, in semiconductors, 673
Galileo Spacecraft, 77, 659, 660
Gallium
    arsenide in solar cells, 579
    in semiconductors, 672
Gallo, Robert, 24
Galoob Toys, 405
Gambling industry, **289–96**
Gambrius, 132
Game arcades, **297–302,** 458
Games
    card, 290
    computer (*See* Computer games)
    for gambling, 290, 291, 293
    safety devices for, 298
    video (*See* Video games)
Gamete intrafallopian transfer, 256–60
GameWorks, 299
Gamzon, Mel, 3
Gangrene, oxygen therapy for, 539
GAO. *See* General Accounting Office
Gap, Inc.
    charter schools and, 103
    fitness centers and, 581
    online marketing by, 207, 504
    outlet centers, 529
Gap insurance, 639
Garden equipment. *See* Lawn and garden equipment
Garden tractors, 865, *865*
Gardenburger, Inc., 480
Garden.com, 867
Gardening
    fertilizers for, 866, 867
    growth of, 863, 865
    organic, 864, 867
    on television, 867
GardenNet, 867
Gargarin, Yuri, 76
Garlic, in nutritional supplements, 492
Garnet lasers, 509
Gart Sports, 252, 582, 585
Gartner Group
    on electronic commerce, 501
    on information management systems, 351, 356
    on portable computers, 216
    on semiconductors, 676
    on used computer equipment, 779
    on Y2K compliance, 872, 874–75
Gas lasers, 372, 373
Gases, air filtration for, 833
Gasohol Competition Act, 37
Gasoline industry
    vs. alternate fuels, 37, 39, 40–41
    hazardous waste from, 241, 244
    recycling plastics for, 592

Gastrointestinal diseases
    drugs for, 730
    endoscopy for, 233, 234
Gastroscopes, 234
GATE, 35
Gates, William
    on artificial intelligence, 73
    on electronic publishing, 224
    on satellites, 658
    on wireless communications, 853
Gateway 2000 Inc., 214, 786
Gateways (Computer networks), in MIS, 352, 356–57
Gatorade, 599–602
GAV, 111–12
Gavilan Computer, 214
Gay men, tours for, 713
Gay Men's Health Crisis Center, 18
GBN, 283, 286
GC Companies, 458, 459
GE. *See* General Electric
GE Capital Auto Financial Services, 640, 641, 781
GE Plastics, 592
Geffen, David, 110, 406
GEICO, 644
Geistman, Bob, 796
Gemini mission, 76
Gemplus Card International, 682, 683
Gene sequence. *See* Base sequence
Gene therapy, 306, 308, 309
Genelabs Technologies, 431
Genelabs Technologies, i, 437
Genentech, Inc., 304–5
General Accounting Office
    on adult housing, 5
    on AIDS, 24
    on home health care, 329
    on managed care, 395
    on telemedicine, 743
    on Y2K compliance, 874
General Dynamics, 570
General Electric
    in air and water filtration, 839
    in artificial intelligence, 70
    as ISP, 363
    in photonics, 570
    in polymers, 590, 592
    in robotics, 650
General Foods Corporation, 481, 600, 703
General merchandise stores. *See* Department stores
General Mills, 404
General Motors Acceptance Corporation
    auto leasing and, 637, 641
    Mortgage, 443, 446
General Motors Corporation
    in auto leasing, 639
    in holography, 319, 323
    in lithium batteries, 383
    in micromachine development, 415
    in passenger restraint systems, 446, 554
    in robotics, 650, 651
    on safety devices, 553
    in satellites, 660
    in sensing devices, 526
    in systems integration, 737
    in wireless communications, 853–54

General Nutrition Corporation, 482, 495
General problem solver (Computer program language), 68
General Scanning, Inc., 322
General Services Administration, 875
General Wireless, 761
Generation X, juice bars and, 633
Genes
    recombinant, 304–5, 307
    terminator, 307
Genetech, Inc., 307–8, 428–29
Genetic code
    human, 305, 429, 434, 437, 548
    molecular design in, 430
    in nanotechnology, 156
    patents of, 304
Genetic disorders, 304, 306
Genetic engineering, **303–10**
    in bioremediation, 242, 247
    in drug development, 726, 731
    molecular design in, 427–29
    of mosquitoes, 497
Genetic mapping. *See* Chromosome mapping
Genetic screening, 263, 437
Genetics and IVF Institute, 262, 263–64
GEnie, 363
Genome Therapeutics, 726, 730
Gent, Michehl, 874
GEO satellites, 656
Geocities, 802, 804, 806
Geodesy, in digital mapping, 176
Geographic information systems, **175–84**
Geophysical instruments, holography in, 317, 319
Georgia Sweets, 481
Georgetown University, 527
GeoSystems Global, 180
Gerber Products, 333, 480
Gerber Scientific, Inc., 652
German Ministry of the Environment, 779
German Research Institute for Artificial Intelligence, 72–73
Germanium, in semiconductors, 673
Gerner, Karin, 298
Gerontology. *See also* Elderly
    growth of, 203
    home health care and, 329–30
Gerry Baby Products, 336
Gevalia Coffees, 703
Geyserville, 217
Giardia, water purification for, 837
Gibson, William, 809
Giddings & Lewis, 652
Giedecke & Devrient, 682
GIFT. *See* Gamete intrafallopian transfer
Gigabuys.com, 501
Gilder, George, 269, 759
Gillerlain, Sue, 707
Gingko
    in anti-aging products, 54, 56
    in nutritional supplements, 492
Gingrich, Newt, 284, 784
Ginnie Mae, 442
Ginsberg, Matthew, 69
Ginseng
    in beverage products, 599, 603, 632
    in nutritional supplements, 494
GIS. *See* Geographic information systems

Giusto, Randy, 217
Givenchy, 57
GIVF. *See* Genetics and IVF Institute
GKN Sinter Metals, 378
Glaser, Peter, 579
Glass
    in advanced ceramics, 10, 11
    in optical storage technology, 516
    in plastics, 587
    in semiconductors, 671
    sensors for, 665
    in time capsules, 766
Glass, Alastair, 270
Glasses, eye. *See* Eye glasses
Glaucoma, lasers for, 373, 512
Glaxo Welcome Inc.
    in AIDS research, 23–25
    in molecular design, 430
    in molecular modeling, 436
    in smoking cessation products, 687–90
Glenbridge Publishing, Ltd., 166
Glenco, 337
Glenn, John, 76, 77
Glick, Bernard R., 427
Global Alliance for Transnational Education, 35
Global Business Network, 283, 286
Global economy. *See also* International commerce
    futures consulting in, 281, 282, 284, 287
    risk management and, 647
Global Emergency Telemedicine System, 746
Global Hawk, 527
Global One, 761, 762
Global Positioning System
    satellites for, 175, 177–79, 182, 659, 660
    sensors for, 523
Global warming
    alternative fuels for, 37, 43
    risk management and, 645
    solar power and, 573, 575, 576
Globalization. *See* Global economy
Globalstar Telecommunications, 853, 854
GLOFLOW, 810
Gloria Jean, 705
Glossbrenner, Alfred, 347
Gloves, for virtual reality, 810, 814
Glucosamine, in nutritional supplements, 497
Glycerol, in cryopreservation, 154, 156
Glycolysis, for recycling plastics, 591
GM. *See* General Motors Corporation
GMAC. *See* General Motors Acceptance Corporation
GMER, 355
GMFANUC Robotics Corporation, 651
GNC. *See* General Nutrition Corporation
Gobi Inc., 451
Goddard, Robert, 76
Goddard, Valerie, 562
Goddard Space Flight Center, 79
Goggles, in virtual reality, 810, 812, 814
Gold Disk, 451
Goldberg, Emmanuel, 354
Golden, Hymie, 601
Golden Door, 314
Golden seal, in nutritional supplements, 493, 494
Goldin, Daniel, 77, 80–81

Visual Age Team Connection Enterprise Server,   859
in voice mail systems,   817
in voice recognition systems,   825–28
in Web development,   844
XML and,   859, 860
Y2K compliance and,   875
IBS.   *See* Institute for Brewing Studies
IC Sensor,   414, 415
Icat,   165
ICC Technologies,   846
ICCA,   737
ICE.   *See* Information and Content Exchange protocol
Ice climbing,   250
Ice cream,   481, 632, 704
ICF Kaiser International,   247
ICFP,   276
ICG Communications, Inc.,   367, 761
ICI,   463, 466
ICO Global,   853
ICON Health & Fitness,   582, 585
ICOS Corporation,   436
ICs.   *See* Integrated circuits
ICS Learning Systems,   33–34
ICSI.   *See* Intracystoplasmic sperm injection
ICTransducers,   410
IDC.   *See* International Data Corporation
Ideal Toy Company,   404
Idei Nobuyuki,   452–53
Identification
   biometrics for,   **83–91**
   of computer chips,   128
   computer security for,   121, 127
   fraudulent,   349
   holography for,   317, 322
   of pets,   562, 563
   push technology for,   628
   security for,   667
   smart cards for,   681, 683
   user,   126–27
Identification Technologies International Inc.,   85
IDT,   761
IDT-C6 microprocessor,   676
IEEE.   *See* Institute of Electrical and Electronics Engineers
IETF.   *See* Internet Engineering Task Force
IFTF,   282, 285
IGRA,   290
IGY,   76
IIP,   173
Il Giornale,   704, 705
Illumina, Inc.,   430
ILM.   *See* Industrial Light & Magic
ILS,   658
IMA,   448
iMac,   166
IMAGE (Company),   585
Imagek, Inc.,   173
ImagineCard,   683
Imaging systems
   computer generated,   66, 107, 109
   digital   (*See* Digital imaging)
   in drug development,   731
   in endoscopic technology,   233, 236–38
   holographic,   317, 318
   microwave applications in,   423
   in molecular design,   431

in molecular modeling,   437
print services for,   611
in telemedicine,   741, 746
thermal,   84
volumetric,   815
Imagyn Medical, Inc.,   237
Imation Corporation,   519
IMAX Corporation,   458–60
IMAX films,   457–59
IMC,   358
ImClone Systems Inc.,   436
Immersadesk,   815
Immersive Workbench,   815
Immigration, biometric identification for,   89–90
Immigration and Naturalization Service, on biometric
   identification,   89
Immunity
   juice for,   632
   vitamin E for,   496
   water purification and,   840
Immunizations.   *See also* Vaccines
   for travel,   717
Impaired vision, electronic publishing for,   222
Impotence, products for,   55–56, 492
Imprinted circuits,   672
Improved Mobile Telephone Service,   851
IMTS,   851
In-Line Retailer & Industry News,   253
In-line skating,   250, 253
In-Stat Research,   215, 818
In-store departments, for video rentals,   791–95
In vitro fertilization,   255–60, 263
Incense,   469, 475
Income funds.   *See* Mutual fund industry
Income tax, software consultants and,   695
Independent Computer Consultants Association,   737
Independent films, in theater entertainment centers,   456, 459
Independent living housing,   **1–7**
Independent practice association.   *See* Health maintenance
   organizations
Independent Publishers Association,   164
Independent study, in adult education,   28
Indian Gaming Regulatory Act of 1988,   290
Indians, American.   *See* Native Americans
Individual retirement accounts,   463, 466
Indole-3-Carbinol,   497
Indoor air pollution,   833, 835–37
Industrial automation,   **649–54**
Industrial development bonds, for environmental
   remediation,   244
Industrial Light & Magic,   109–11
Industrial Noise Control, Inc.,   487
Industrial pollution, environmental removal of,   241–47
Industrial robots,   649, 652
Industrial wastes, for alternative fuels,   41
Industry trends, consulting for,   **281–88**
Industry-University Cooperative Research Center,   416
Inertial navigation systems, micromachines for,   409
Infant formulas, genetically engineered,   305
Infants
   oxygen therapy for,   538
   products for   (*See* Baby products industry)
Infection
   drug development for,   **725–33**
   oxygen therapy for,   535, 537, 539

self, 644
for specialty tourism, 715
Insurance brokers, in risk management, 643
Insurance companies. *See also* Health insurance industry
AIDS and, 19
antibacterial products and, 62
captive, 644, 647
consumer information from, 144, 145
digital imaging for, 170
employee leasing and, 228
financial planning and, 274, 277
futures consulting for, 283
GIS systems for, 181
information services for, 346, 348
Internet access to, 647
mutual funds and, 466
security for, 723
Y2K transition and, 875
Insurance Institute for Highway Safety, on passenger restraint systems, 553
InsureSite, 644
Integrated circuits
analog, 416, 672, 676
application-specific, 673
in batteries, 384
ceramic, 10
development of, 674
digital, 672, 676
miniaturization of, 674
in nanotechnology, 409, 411–12, 415
on-chip, 410
photonics and, 565, 568, 571
semiconductors for, 671, 673
in telecommunications networks, 759
Integrated focal plane sensors, 527
Integrated services digital networks. *See* ISDN
Integrated Surgical Systems, 652
Intel Corporation
in artificial intelligence, 70
in computer security, 128
in digital imaging, 171, 172
in DVD development, 186
in multimedia, 448, 452
in parallel processing, 545, 546, 548
in portable computers, 217
in robotics, 652
in semiconductors, 672–77
in smart cards, 680, 683
in telemedicine, 745
in video displays, 784
in virtual reality, 804, 813
in voice mail systems, 819
in voice recognition systems, 825
Intellectual freedom, 679–80
Intellectual property
encryption of, 124
security for, 663
theft of, 719
XML for security, 859
IntelliChoice, 638
IntelliCorp, 72, 355–56
Intelligence, artificial. *See* Artificial intelligence
Intelliquest Research, 802
Intera Information Technologies Corporation, 177
Interactive Advantage, 116

Interactive Learning International Corporation, 641
Interactive media
in adult education, 28, 34
computer animation in, 108
DVDs for, 796
for exercise, 585
in games, 297
in gardening, 868
multimedia computers for, 448
optical storage for, 516
in push technology, 626
in telemedicine, 741, 742
in telephony, 755
in virtual reality, 811
wireless communications f, 851
Interactive Multimedia Association, 448
Interactive Solutions, 847
Interactive Systems Laboratories, 828
Interest rates, for home mortgages, 441–43
Interface Cybercafe, 159
Interferometry
holographic, 319
Mach-Zehnder heterodyne, 319
Intergraph Corporation, 181
Interim Healthcare, 331
Interim payment system (Medical care), 329
Interior decoration, computer animation in, 107
Interior Department. *See* Department of the Interior
Interlaced-scan technology, 784, 787
Interleaf, 861
Internal Revenue Service
on auto leasing, 640
on employee leasing, 227–30
on software consulting, 695
on Y2K compliance, 872
International Association for Financial Planning, 276–77
International Bibliographic Information on Dietary Supplements, 494
International Bodyguard Association, 668
International Business Machines. *See* IBM Corporation
International Coffee Organization, 707
International commerce
in executive recruitment, 619–22
futures consulting for, 286
Internet access and, 367–68
juice bars and, 634
in lawn and garden products, 868
mail-order companies and, 389
in motion pictures, 460
risk management for, 644
in satellite services, 657
in software consulting, 699
in specialty tourism, 716
in surveillance equipment, 720, 723
in systems integration, 739
in telemedicine, 746
telephony and, 761–62
in used computer equipment, 781–82
in water and air filtration, 839–40
wireless communications for, 854–55, *855*
Y2K transition and, 876–77
International Community College, 28
International Congress of Infectious Diseases, 725
International Council of Shopping Centers, 529, 534

Khermouch, Gerry, 632

Kick boxing, 583

Kidnapping, electronic surveillance for, 721

Kilby, Jack, 674, 680

Kill Real Estate Services, 301

Kilns, microwave, 419

Kimball, Ronald, 721

Kine and Company, 591

Kinetico Inc., 838

King, Julia, 739

Kingsbury Non-Alcoholic Beer, 608

Kinki University, time capsules and, 769

Kiosks

    for coffee, 702

    for computer use, **157–61,** 225–26

    for juice, 634

    for multimedia, 452

    for on-demand printing, 225–26

    sensors for, 524

    in used car sales, 771

Kirby Company, 319

KISS, 839

Kitchen products industry. *See* Housewares industry

Kiwifruit, in premium beverages, 603

Klement, Susan, 347

Kline & Company, 382

Kluck & Associates, 548

Klug, Michael, 321–22

Kmart

    electronic surveillance for, 722

    in exercise equipment, 585

    in infant and toddler products, 333, 334

    in lawn and garden products, 864, 867

    in new age products, 473

    in nutritional supplements, 492

    in pet products, 559, 560

    in video rentals & sales, 794

KMI, 267

Knickerbocker Toy Company, 337

Knight, Phil, 147

Knight Ridder, 224

Know Nutrajoint, 482

Knowledge

    in information services, 339, 350

    management systems, 351, 356

Knowledge-based systems. *See* Expert systems

Knowles, Malcolm Shepherd, 27

Knowlton, Ken, 108

Koblin, Beryl, 25

Koch, Jim, 133

Kockelman, John, 251, 253

Kockelman, Peter, 251, 253

Koen, Phil, 628

Kohlberg, Kravis, Roberts & Company, 458, 582

Komanduri, Ranga, 13

Komarove, Vladimir, 76

Kona Architecture, 861

Konover Property Trust Inc., 533

Konstructor, 861

Koopman, Marsha, 63

Korey, Mel, 342

Korn/Ferry International, 619, 621–23

KPMG Peat Marwik Thorne, 697

Kraft/General Foods, 481, 600

Kramer, Robert, 2

Kranitz, Michael, 639

Kroc, Ray, 147

Kroger Company, 791, 792, 795, 796

Krueger, Myron, 809, 810

Ku-band, for satellite services, 656

Kuhnau, Cynthia, 634

Kuhnau, Stephen, 634–35

Kurzweil, Ray, 73

Kurzweil Applied Intelligence, Inc., 488, 825–28

Kushner, Brian, 779, 781

Kutler, Jeffrey, 682

Kutnick, Robert, 537

KVANT, 577

Kyl Bill, 295

Kyocera Corporation, 13, 14

Kyte, Andy, 874–75

L

La Petite Boulangerie, 703

La Roche Posay, 56

Labels

    security, 668

    warning, 303, 308, 633

Labor Department. *See* Department of Labor

Labor productivity

    information management services and, 351

    risk management for, 645

Labor strikes, in professional sports, 404

Labor unions, teachers, 100–101

Laboratoires Homeopathiques de France, 50

Laboratories

    andrology, 258–59

    integrated systems for, 745

    MIS for, 354

    robotics for, 650

Laboratory for Integrated Medical Interface Technology, 815

Laboratory information management systems, 354

Labrador Ventures, 811

Lactic acid, polymers from, 591

LADARVision, 510

Lagasse, Emeril, 138

Lager, 132, 133, 608

Laidlaw Environmental Services Inc., 244, 246

LAM Conference, 377

Lancaster, Ian M., 317

Lancome, 54, 57, 491

Lande, David, 324

Lands End, Inc., 390, 502

Lands End Japan KK, 391

Landsat satellites, 77–79, 178

Landscape architecture, 863, 865

    virtual reality for, 809

Lane DeCamp, 521

Lang, Amanda, 626

Langenscheidt, Gustav, 29

Langhome Leasing, 641

Lanier, Jaron, 809, 810–11

LANs. *See* Local area networks

Lanxide Corporation, 378

Laparoscopes, in fertility medicine, 257

Laparoscopic surgery, 234

Laptop computers. *See* Portable computers

Large-screen televisions, 413, 785, 789

Larkin, Ronald H., 827

computer security and, 122–23
for crossover corporations, 144
for financial planners, 273, 275–76
for professional employer organizations, 229
Lehman Brothers Inc., 415
Leinenkugel Brewing Company, 132
Leisure industry. *See* Entertainment industry
Leisure World, 5
Leith, Emmett, 318, 324
Lemon juice, in sports beverages, 599
LendingTree, 444
Length of stay
in hospitals, 234
in nursing homes, 4
Lengyel, Jeff, 171
Lenius, Pat Natschle, 793
Lens Express, 510
LEO satellites, 656, 660
LEOMA, 372, 374
Leona Group, 103
Lernout & Hauspie, 825, 827
Lesbians, tours for, 713
Lesko, Matthew, 347
Lessin, Arlen R., 680
Levy, Stuart B., 63
Lexis-Nexis, 345–49
Lexmark, 616
Lexus Corporation, 340, 341
LeyCorp, 277
LG Chemical, 384
LG Group, 788
LHF, 50
Liability
environmental, 243, 244, 643, 645
insurance for, 644
product, 582, 645
risk management for, 643, 646
in specialty tourism, 715, 716
in telemedicine, 744
Libraries. *See also* Databases
electronic, 845
information services and, 345, 347–48, 350
MIS for, 352
of molecular data, 436–37
reference services in, 347
of toys, 335
Licensed products, **403–8**
beverages as, 599
for children, 334, 336
Licenses
adult education for, 33
for alternative medicine practitioners, 473
for beauticians, 536
for beverage technicians, 602
for chiropractors, 46
in computer consulting, 698
for financial planners, 273–76
for homeopathy practitioners, 47–48
for managed care organizations, 395
for massage therapists, 314–15
for molecular design data, 430
for naturopathic doctors, 48
for pharmaceutical products, 726
for private investigators, 723
software, 123, 127

for systems integration, 737
for telemedicine practice, 744, 746
for television broadcasting, 784
Licklider, J.C.R., 810
Life Care Service Corporation, 6
Life expectancy, *201*
Life Extension Buyers Club, 151
Life Extension Foundation, 151
Life insurance, AIDS and, 19
Life on Hold Trust, 155
Life sciences
genetic engineering and, 305
molecular modeling and, 436
Life Technologies, 171
Lifeforce, 540
LifeScience Corporation, 594
LifeStyles Condoms, 19
Light
in lasers, 372, 374
in photonics, 565, 566
sensors for, 524, 525
waves in holography, 318
Light beer, 606
Light-emitting diodes, 594, 790
Light therapy, 312
Lightweight Directory Access Protocol, 860
Ligon, Autsin, 771, 773
Limonta, Manuel, 308
LIMS, 354
Lincare Holdings Inc., 329, 330
Lincoln, Abraham, 664
Lindsay Company, 839
Linear image sensors, 526
Linear polypropylene, 589
Linezolid, development of, 729
Lingle, Ted, 703–4
Linseed-oil, polymers from, 593
Linux, 545, 547
Linvatec, 233
Lipacide PVB, 58
Lipton, 598, 601, 602
Liquefied petroleum gas
as alternative fuel, 38–39
from recycling, 592
Liquid crystal display. *See* LCD display
Liquid electrolyte batteries, 381–82
Liquid metals, **377–80**
Liquid nitrogen, in cryopreservation, 151
LiquidMetal, 379
Liquor stores, nonalcoholic beverages in, 605
Lisker, Joel, 86
LISP, in artificial intelligence, 67
Lisp Machines, Inc., 69
Listening, unauthorized. *See* Eavesdropping
Listerine, 62
Literacy, computer, 34
Lithium-ion batteries, 216, **381–85,** 854
Lithium-metal batteries, 381–82, 385
Lithium Technology, 385
Lithography, 516
in nanotechnology, 411, 412
Liti Holographics, 321
Litigation
AIDS-related, 21, 24
Y2K transition and, 872

Microelectromechanical systems. *See* Nanotechnology
Microendoscopy, 236
Microfiber disks, 520
Microfilms, in time capsules, 768
Microfluidic devices, 410
Microgravity
  effects of, 80
  liquid metals in, 377–79
Microkeratomes, 512
Micromachines. *See* Nanotechnology
Micromirror devices, 413, 415
Micron Technology Inc., 677
Micronutrients, 493–95
Microorganisms
  air filtration for, 838
  in bioremediation, 242
  in drinking water, 835, 840
  drug resistant, 725–32
  molecular design of, 427, 428
Microphones
  for eavesdropping, 722
  for sound quality, 488
Microprocessors
  chip-to-chip connections, 568
  development of, 674
  in digital imaging, 172
  encryption chips in, 673
  lasers for, 373
  memory chips for, 672–73
  micromachines for, 409, 414
  MMX, 676
  in multimedia computers, 448, 450, 453
  Pentium (*See* Pentium-based systems)
  photonics for, 565, 568
  in portable computers, 214, 217
  robotics for, 649, 651–52
  semiconductors for, 671–77
  single chip, 677
  in smart cards, 679, 682
  video, 410, 411, 413
Micropublishing, desktop publishing and, 163
Microsoft Corporation
  in artificial intelligence, 65, 73
  in auto leasing, 638
  in computer animation, 109, 110, 112
  cross marketing by, 148–49
  in digital imaging, 172, 173
  in digital television, 787
  in electronic commerce, 500
  in electronic publishing, 224–25
  holographic identification and, 320
  infomercials for, 340, 341
  in information management systems, 351, 354, 355
  in Internet printing, 614
  on Internet standards, 844
  as ISP (*See* Microsoft Network)
  in multimedia, 448–50, 453
  noise control products for, 488
  online marketing by, 206
  in optical storage, 518, 521
  in parallel processing, 545
  in push technology, 627–29
  in smart cards, 683
  in software consulting, 697, 698
  on software licensing, 127

  in systems integration, 738, 739
  in telemedicine, 745
  on video displays, 784
  in virtual reality, 814
  in voice mail systems, 819, 821
  in voice recognition systems, 825, 827, 828
  in Web development, 844, 847, 848
  in XML development, 358, 858–61
Microsoft Money, 278
Microsoft Network, 158, 361, 364, 366–68
Microsoft Windows
  biometric identification for, 86
  CE operating system, 213
  consultants for, 696
  in molecular modeling, 436
  for multimedia, 448
  print services for, 616
  smart cards for, 683
  in systems integration, 736, 739
  in telemedicine, 746
  virtual reality and, 813
  voice recognition for, 823, 825
Microsoft Word, 166, 167, 216
Microstar, 861
Microsurgery, 237, 238
Microsystems technology. *See* Nanotechnology
Microvalves, 414
Microwave amplification by stimulated emission of
  radiation, 372
Microwave antennas
  for satellite services, 362, 368
  for television, 194–95
  for wireless communications, 419, 421
Microwave Bypass Systems, Inc., 422
Microwave communication systems, in adult education, 28
Microwave equipment, **419–26.** *See also* Telecommunications
  equipment industry
  imaging systems, 423
  in networks, 759, 762
Microwave food products, 419, 425, 482
  baby foods, 481
Microwave Medical Corporation, 423
Microwave ovens, 419–23, 425
  semiconductors for, 671
Microwave Science, 425
MidasPlus, 431, 437
MIDI, 449
Midwest Water Technologies, 839
Midwifery, 473
Mileage, in automobile leasing, 639, 640
Military industry. *See* Defense industry
Milk
  in premium beverages, 600
  in specialty coffee, 702
Millenium Pharmaceuticals, 309
Millennium, time capsules and, 765
Miller, David A., 405
Miller, Gregg A., 562
Miller, Scott, 216
Miller Brewing Company, 129, 130, 132
  in non-alcoholic beer, 605, 606
Million Solar Roofs Initiative, 575
Mills Corporation, 530, 531, 533
Milstar program, 660
MIME, 818

Morinaga Nutritional Foods, 481
Morningstar Farms, 480
Morphing software, 112
Morre's Law, 683
Morrison Institute for Public Policy, 103
Morrison Knudsen Corporation, 246–47
Morse, Kitty, 140
Mortality. *See* Death
Mortgage-backed securities, 464
Mortgage Bankers Association, 441–43, 875
Mortgage banks, **441–46**
Mortgage brokers, 442
Mortgage Loan Corporation, 445
Mortgage.com, 444
Mortgages
    adjustable rate, 442–43
    fixed rate, 442–43
    home, **441–46,** 500
    low-cost, 446
    online shopping for, 499, 500
    refinancing, 443
    variable rate, 442–43
Morton International, 555
Mosaic (Software), 208, 845
Moschella, David, 784
Mosley, Brenda, 63
Mosquitoes, genetically engineered, 497
Mossberg, Tom, 520
Most, Bruce, 278
Motels. *See* Hotels and motels
Motion detectors, 665, 719, 722
Motion Picture Association of America, 455, 460
Motion picture industry
    cross-marketing in, 146
    DVDs and, 185–89
    product licensing in, 334, 403–7
Motion picture projectors, 372, 413
Motion picture theaters
    adult gaming and, 297
    in multiplex entertainment centers, **455–62**
    nanotechnology for, 413
    screens in, 459, 460
Motion pictures
    booking and distribution system, 457
    computer animation in, **107–13**
    holography in, 320
    IMAX films, 457–59
    independent, 456, 459
    optical storage of, 519
    in time capsules, 768
    video rentals of, 791–92, 795
Motion simulators, 300, 458
Motoman, Inc., 652
Motor fuels
    alternate, **37–43,** 573
    diesel, 39, 43
    sensors for, 410
Motor vehicles. *See also* Automobiles
    for alternative fuels, 37–41
    compressed air, 41
    flexible fuel, 40
    hydrogen fuel cell, *40*
    ultra low emission, 41
Motorola Inc.
    in artificial intelligence, 70

information management systems for, 353
IUCRC and, 416
in micromachine development, 409, 413, 415
in microwave applications, 419, 424
in parallel processing, 547
in robotics, 652
in satellites, 658, 660, 661
in semiconductors, 676, 677
in sensing devices, 524
in smart cards, 682
in video displays, 789
in voice mail systems, 819, 821
in voice recognition systems, 826
in wireless communications, 853, 854
in XML development, 860
Mountain bicycles, 249
Mountain Blue, 545
Mountain climbing
    equipment, 249–50, 252, 714
    tours, 712, 714
Mountain Travel, 713, 715
Mountain Travel-Sobek, 714
Mountain View, 72
Movement, robotic, 653
Movie Exchange, 792
Movie Gallery, 795
Movie theaters. *See* Motion picture theaters
MPAA, 455, 460
MPEG decoders, 190, 195, 198, 451
MPP. *See* Parallel processing
Mr. Clean, 62
MRDS, 354
MRI. *See* Magnetic resonance imaging
MSI. *See* Molecular Simulations Inc.
MSN. *See* Microsoft Network
MSNBC, 787
MST. *See* Nanotechnology
MTS, 714
MTV, product licensing by, 406
MTV Sports and Music Fest, 252
Mufflers, active, 487, 488
Mullis, Kary, 305
Multicase, Inc., 65
Multics Relational Data Store, 354
Multifunction peripherals, 167, 613–14, 616
Multilevel marketing, of nutritional supplements, 492
Multimedia software, **447–54,** 739
Multimedia technology, **447–54,** *449*
    in desktop publishing, 165
    DVDs as, 190–91
    in electronic publishing, 221–22
    in exercise products, 583
    optical storage and, 516, 519
    in push technology, 626
    superstores for, 94–95
    in telemedicine, 745
    voice systems for, 826
Multimedia Telecommunications Association, 756
Multinational corporations, consulting for, 286
Multipass C2500, 616
Multiple pregnancy, from fertility drugs, 256, 259, 261
Multiple sclerosis, oxygen therapy for, 539
Multiplex theater entertainment centers, **455–62**
Multiplexing
    digital, 198

National Association of Regulatory Utility Commissions, 756
National Association of Securities Dealers, 463, 464, 467
National Association of Temporary Staffing Services, 230
National Association of Theater Owners, 458
National Association on Data Processing & Liberty
  (France), 148
National Bank of Commerce, 230
National Basketball Association
  on premium beverages, 601
  product licensing and, 404
National Biofuels Program, 42
National Bodyguard Network, 666
National Book Network, 164
National Broadcasting Corporation. *See* NBC
National Cancer Institute
  on AIDS, 21, 24
  on smoking cessation, 685
National Car Rental, 738
National Center for Homeopathy, 48
National Center for Supercomputing Applications, 813, 815,
  845
National Certification Board for Therapeutic Massage and
  Bodywork, 314–15
National Coalition Against Gambling, 289
National Committee for Quality Assurance, 395
National Committee on Radiation Protection, 424
National Conference of Commissioners on Uniform State
  Laws, 639
National Council on Aging, 199
National Direct Corporation, 343
National Directory of Managed Care Organizations, 399
National Education Association, 99, 100
National Education Corporation, 33–34
National Exchange Carrier Association, 756
National Eye Institute, 508
National Flat Panel Display Initiative, 785, 788
National Football League
  on premium beverages, 601
  on surveillance equipment, 720
National Gambling Impact Commission, 293
National Geriatric Care Management Association, 202
National Gerontological Nursing Association, 4, 202
National Highway Traffic Safety Administration, 552–54
National Hockey League, 601
National Housing Agency, 2
National Human Resource Committee, Inc., 230
National Imaging and Mapping Agency, 179, 183
National Indian Gaming Association, 290, 294
National Infomercial Marketing Association, 339
National Information Infrastructure, 743
National Institute for Automotive Service Excellence, 774
National Institute for Research in Computer Science and
  Control, 844
National Institute of Justice, 124
National Institute of Standards and Technology
  on holographic technology, 324
  on lasers, 372
  on XML, 861
National Institute on Aging, 200–201
National Institute on Drug Abuse, 690
National Institutes of Health
  on AIDS, 18, 19, 23
  on air quality, 835
  on fertility medicine, 263
  on genetic engineering, 305

on lasers, 372
on microwave applications in medicine, 423
on molecular design, 430
on molecular modeling, 435
on nutritional supplements, 494, 496
on oxygen therapy, 536
on push technology, 627
on smoking cessation, 690
on virtual reality, 812
National Insurance Association of America, on AIDS, 17
National Investment Center, 2
National Library of Medicine, 346, 743
National Media Corporation, 340, 343
National Oceanic and Atmospheric Administration, 737
National Opinion Research Center, on gambling, 294
National Organic Standards Board, 478
National Park Scenic Overflight Concession Act, 486
National parks
  noise control and, 485, 486
  specialty tourism and, 710
National Prevention Information Network, 18
National Real Estate Investor, 3, 4
National Registry Inc., 86
National Renewable Energy Laboratory
  on alternative fuels, 38, 40
  on solar power, 576–78
National Research Council, on astronautics, 80–81
National Resource Defense Council, on water quality, 834–35
National Retail Federation, 875
National Rural Telecommunications Cooperative, 195
National Safe Kids Campaign, 334, 336–37
National Sanitation Foundation International, 832
National Science Foundation
  in Internet development, 363
  IUCRC and, 416
  in micromachine development, 410
  in parallel processing, 549
National Securities Market Improvement Act of 1997, 275
National security, computer security and, 122–23
National Security Agency, on Y2K compliance, 876
National Semiconductor Sensor Group, 410
National Solid Wastes Management Association, 243
National Tele-Immersion Initiative, 811
National Television Standards Committee, 786
National Transportation Safety Board, on child safety seats, 554
National Water Information System, 835
National Water Quality Inventory Report, 834
Nations Bank Corporation, 443, 502
Native Americans
  in gambling, 289, 290, 293
  new age philosophy and, 469, 470
  tourism and, 712
Natrol, 57
NATSS, 230
Natta, Guilio, 589
Natural Alternatives International, 495
Natural Dairy Products, 481
Natural disasters, risk management for, 643, 645
Natural foods
  anti-aging, 54
  antibacterial, 62
  for babies, 472, 477, 480
  coffee, 702–4
  growth of, 139
  juice bars, 631–32, 634

computer   (*See* Computer networks)

neural   (*See* Neural networks)

Neubauer, Richard A., 538–39

Neupogen, 428

Neur Navigational Corporation, 237

Neural Applications Corp., 71

Neural networks

artificial intelligence in, 66, 67, 69–71

holography in, 317

in marketing, 149, 391

in voice recognition systems, 828

Neurogaonkar, Ratnakar R., 324

Neurogen Corporation, 726, 730

Neurolabe, 815

Neurosurgery, virtual reality for, 812

Neurosuspension, 152–55

Neurpogen, 308

Neutering, 562, 563

Neuticles, 562

Neutrogena, 56, 57

New Age movement

beverages for, **597–604**

oxygen therapy and, 537

products and services for, **469–76**

tours for, 712

virtual communities for, 803

New Age Publishing and Retailing Alliance, 470

New Leaf distributors, 475

New Mexico State University, in parallel processing, 549

New optics, **565–72,** 762

New York Blood Center, on AIDS, 25

New York State Energy Research and Development
   Authority, 38–39

New Zealand Cryonics Society, 155

Newell, Allan, 67–68

NewLeaf, 308

Newquist, Deborah, 202

News agencies

online services by, 206, 346

push technology for, 625–29

wireless communications for, 852

News Corporation, 194, 198

News services. *See* News agencies

Newsgroups, 799–801

Newsletters, desktop publishing of, 163, 164

Newspapers

electronic, 206, 211, 222, 224, 625

from ISPs, 362

online shopping for, 499, 505

Newton, Isaac, 75

Nextband, 853

Nextel Communications, 761, 853

Nextlink Communications, 761, 853

NextWave Telecom, 761

Nexus, 416

NFL. *See* National Football League

NHK, 786

NHL, 601

NHRC, 230

NHTSA, 552–54

NIC (National Investment Center), 2

Nicabate, 689

Nickel

cadmium batteries, 216, 381, 382

in liquid metal products, 379

in optical storage technology, 516

Nickelodeon Theaters, 406

NicoDerm CQ, 686–88

Nicorette, 686–88

Nicotine

chewing gum, 685–87

substitute therapies, 685–90, *687*

Nicotine Anonymous, 690

Nicotrol, 688

Nidek, Inc., 507

Nieuwland, 577

NIGA, 290, 294

Night vision devices

sensors for, 523–27

for surveillance, 719, 721

NIH. *See* National Institutes of Health

NII, 743

Nike, 147, 503, 847

Nikoban, 686

NIMA International, 339

Nimbus CD International, 322

911 system, 757

Nintendo, 449, 814

Nippon Steel, 70

Nippon Telegraph & Telephone, 384–85

NiQuitin CQ, 689

Nissan Motor Acceptance Corporation, 641

Nissan Motor Corporation

in auto leasing, 641

in lithium batteries, 384

passenger restraint systems and, 554

virtual communities and, 805

NIST. *See* National Institute of Standards and Technology

Nitrogen, liquid, 151

NLM, 346, 743

NMAC, 641

NMR spectroscopy, 434

Noah's New York Bagels, Inc., 704

Noise Cancellation Technologies, Inc., 488

Noise control, **485–89,** 573

Noise Control Act, 486

Noise Control Technologies, 487

Nonalcoholic beverages, 403, 472, **605–9.** *See also* Coffee;
   Juice

Nonprofit organizations

charter schools as, 99, 100

in cryopreservation, 151, 152–53

in elder day care, 199–203

executive recruitment for, 622

in managed care, 395

virtual communities as, 800

Nonsurgical embryo selective thinning & transfer, 257

NordicTrack, 582, 585

Nordstrom Blend, 701, 704

Nordstrom Outlets, 531

Nortel. *See* Northern Telecom

North American Bungee Association, 249

North American Electric Reliability Council, 874

North American Graphic Arts Suppliers Association, 612

North American Securities Administrators Association, 276

North Atlantic Microwave Organization, 422

North Central Regional Educational Laboratory, 100

North Face, Inc., 252, 582

Northern Telecom, 117, 570, 749, 752–53, 761–63

in voice mail systems, 818, 821

Office of Fuel Development, 42
Office of Noise Abatement and Control Establishment Act of
    1996, 486
Office of Technology Assessment, 785–87
Offsite Data Services Ltd., 665–66
OFS, 851
OFX. *See* Open financial exchange
Oglethorpe University, 765, 767–69
Oil embargoes, 39
Oil industry. *See* Petroleum industry
Oil of Olay, 56–58
Oils
    animal, 43
    cod-liver, 494
    essential, 474
    fish, 494
    linseed, 593
    polymers from, 593
    vegetable, 39, 43
Ojasmit Holographics, 323
Oki Electric Industry Company, 86, 616
Oki Semiconductors, 682
Okidata Inc., 616
Oklahoma State University, on advanced ceramics, 13
OLAP, 352
Olestra, 482
Olfactory sensors, 429, 430
Olivetti Corporation, 453
Olson, H.F., 486
Olsten Corporation, 330, 697
Olympus Optical Company, 237
    in digital imaging, 172
    in endoscopy, 233, 236
    in optical storage, 519
    in sensing devices, 524, 527
O.M. Scott & Sons, 867
Omega-3 fatty acids, 482, 492
Omega Corporation, 667
Omega Tech, 482
OMG, 859
Omnibus Budget Reconciliation Act, 38
Omnibus Crime and Safe Streets Act, 720
OmniMark, 861
Omnipoint, 761
On-Line Communication Services Inc., 158
One Spirit, 471
1000CX Palmtop, 216
Online analytical processing, 352
Online auctions, 207
Online books. *See* Electronic publishing
Online business. *See* Electronic commerce
Online catalogs, 170, 205–6, 208–9
Online databases
    access to, 206
    voice systems for, 825
Online information services, 345, 346–47
Online Magic, 847
Online Medical Sales Network, 233
Online Originals, 224
Online shopping. *See* Electronic shopping
OnMark 2000, 875
Onnes, H. Kamerlingh, 153
Ono Pharmaceuticals Company, Ltd., 436
Onyx2 Infinite Reality Systems, 436, 812–13
OODBs, 860

OPEC, on oil production, 41
Open Buying on the Internet (Computer protocol), 861
Open financial exchange (Computer protocol), 859, 861
Open MP, 548
Open trading protocol, 861
Open University, 30, 35
OpenVision, 125
Operating systems (Computers). *See also* Microsoft Windows
    flash memory for, 673
    Mac, 739, 746, 823
    in systems integration, 735, 736
    Y2K transition and, 873
Operational-fixed microwave services, 851
Ophthalmic lasers, **507–14**
Opotek, Inc., 374
Oppenheimer, Roberta, 422
Opportunistic infections, in AIDS, 20
Optical data processing, in parallel processing, 546–47
Optical equipment
    lasers for, 374
    molecular modeling for, 438
    nanotechnology for, 412, 414
    photonics and, 565
    robotics for, 652
    signal processing and, 571
    switches, 762
Optical scanners
    artificial intelligence in, 71–72
    for biometric identification, 84–85
    in desktop publishing, 167
    in digital imaging, 169–71, 176
    for fingerprints, 89
    handheld, 452
    for high definition television, 784
    for holographic images, 324
    for information services, 285–87
    interlaced-scan, 784, 787
    lasers in, 371
    in multipurpose machines, 614, 616
    print services for, 611
    progressive-scan, 784, 787
    retinal, 85
    in security systems, 663
Optical sensors, **523–28**
Optical storage devices, **515–21**
    access speed of, 517, 518
    boards for, 515
    CD-ROM (*See* CD-ROMs)
    DRAM for, 520
    erasable, 515–16, 520, 566–67
    holography in, 519–20
    interactive, 516
    lasers for, 371
    magneto-optical, 519
    memory cards, 565
    for networks, 519, 568
    OROM, 520–21
    phase-change, 516
    photonics and, 565, 566
    recordable, 515–16, 566
    synchronous, 568
Optical Storage Technology Association, 188
Optico-electric equipment, 565, 567, 571
Optik, 237
Optimatch, 71

GENERAL INDEX

nutritional supplements and, 494
telemedicine and, 744–45
virtual reality and, 815
Physicists, in futures consulting, 286
Physiologic monitoring, telemedicine for, 742
Phytochemicals, as nutritional supplements, 492
Picture archiving systems, 744
Picture This (Software), 813
Piezoelectric ceramics, 13, 14
Piezoelectricity, in nanotechnology, 410
Pilgrimages, as tours, 712
Pillar Point Partners, 507
Pillsbury Company, 477, 482
Pilsner, 132, 133
Pine-Sol, 62, 64
Pinkerton, Alan, 228, 664
Pinkerton's National Detective Agency, 663, 664, 667
PINs. *See* Personal identification products
Pioneer Electronics, 186, 188, 189
Pioneer HiBred International, Inc., 305
Pioneer New Media Technologies, 519
Piper Jaffray, 277, 633
Pippen, Scottie, 599
Piracy (Software). *See* Software piracy
Pirelli, 269, 568, 569
Pitman, Isaac, 29
Pittsburgh Supercomputer Center, 549
Pittway Corporation, 668
Pixar Animation Studio, 107, 109, 110, 450, 452
PixTech Inc., 789
Pizza, frozen, 479
Pizza Hut, 140
Pizza restaurants, 137
Planar-Standish, 789
Planar Systems, Inc., 789
Planet Earth, 768
Planet Hollywood, 140, 459
Planet Smoothie, 633, 635
PlanGraphics, 177
Planned communities, for senior citizens, 3
Planning
    business, **281–88**
    financial (*See* Financial planning)
    strategic, 281, 284, 287
Plant Breeding International Cambridge, Ltd., 305
Plant extracts, in juice bar products, 632
Plants
    in bioremediation, 247
    CAD-CAM of, 588–89
    as drug sources, 725, 732
    genetically engineered, 303, 305–9, 427
    medicinal (*See* Medicinal plants)
    sales of, 863
Plasma
    display, 783, 786
    etching, 414
    genetically engineered, 306
Plasmids, in superdrug development, 728
Plastic containers, 588, 590, 591
Plastic surgery, 235, 373, 510
Plastic Systems, 847
Plastics
    antibacterial products and, 61, 63
    biodegradable, 591, 592
    cold molded, 590

commodity, 588
composites of, 587
disposable cups of, 590
for electric insulators, 590
engineering, 588, 591
liquid metals in, 378
microwave applications for, 419
molding of, 588–89
in optical storage technology, 516
packages of, 587, 588, 591
polymers (*See* Polymers)
preservation of, 767
recycling, 591–92
in semiconductors, 672
thermoplastic (*See* Thermoplastics)
thermosetting, 587, 591–92
in toys, 335
Platinum Technology, Inc., 72, 125
Platt, Charles, 152
Platt, Lewis E., 615, 738
Playback robots, 651
Playgrounds, in theater entertainment centers, 458
Playskool, 333
Playstation II, 107–8
Pleasant Company, 337
Plenitude, 56
Plexiglas acrylic coatings, 590
Plimpton, J.L., 250
PMH Caramanning, 637
PMR, 851
Pneumatic machinery, liquid metals in, 378
Pneumococcal pneumonia, drugs for, 727, 728
Pneumococus, drugs for, 727, 729
Pneumonia
    bacterial, 725
    pneumococcal, 727, 728
Pocketalk, 819
Poet Software Corporation, 860
Point-of-sale systems, displays for, 789
Point-of-service plans, *vs.* managed care, 393, 394, 396
Point-to-point communications equipment
    in adult education, 28
    satellites for, 658
PointCast, Inc., 625–29
Poisoning, by carbon monoxide, 535, 539
Polaroid
    in optical storage, 519
    in sensing devices, 524
    virtual communities and, 805
Polese, Kim, 628
Polhemus Inc., 813
Police. *See also* Law enforcement
    lasers for, 374
    MIS for, 355
    private investigators and, 723
    robots and, 651
    virtual reality for, 814
Polite Communications system, 628
Political risk, management of, 644
Polizzotto, Len, 85
Pollution
    air (*See* Air pollution)
    industrial, 241–47
    new age philosophy and, 470
    sensors for tracking, 523, 525

QVC, 339, 342
Qwest Communications International Inc., 760

R

Racetracks, gambling at, 289
Radar systems, 419, 568
Radial keratotomy, 508, 509
Radian International LLC, 245
Radio
    citizen band, 421
    dispatching, 851
    mobile (*See* Mobile communication systems)
    personal wireless, 851
    telephones, 850
Radio broadcast data system, 854
Radio frequency allocation
    for advanced mobile phone service, 851–52
    sales of, 757, 849–50
    for satellite services, 656
Radio frequency heating, 419
Radio frequency keratoplasty, 512
Radio modems, 849
Radio programs, product licensing in, 404
Radio Shack, 164
Radio stations
    in educational broadcasting, 30
    electromagnetic fields from, 424
    frequencies for, 850
    infomercials on, 342
Radio transmitters. *See also* Wireless communication systems
    for print services, 613
    solar powered, 574
    for telephony, 756
    for vehicle control, 650
Radioactive materials, robots for, 653
Radioactive wastes, ion exchangers for, 247
Radiography
    in telemedicine, 741, 744, 746
    voice systems for, 827
Radon, in drinking water, 834
Rafting (Sports)
    equipment for, 714
    tours, 710, 712, 717
    whitewater, 252, *711*
Railroad companies, 177, 178, 388
Rain forests, tours of, 715, 717
Rainbow Studios, 109, 112
Raisbeck Engineering, 486–87
Ralph Lauren Outlets, 533
RAM. *See* Random access memory
Ramada International Hotels and Resorts, 147
Ramnarayan, Sujata, 451
Ramoplanin, 728
Rancho La Puerta, 314
RAND Corporation
    in artificial intelligence, 69
    in futures consulting, 283–85
    origins of, 282
Randers, Jorgen, 283
Random access memory
    advanced architecture, 450
    dynamic, 520, 672, 675
    extended data output, 672–73
    holography in, 317

memory chips for, 672–73
    optical, 520
    static, 672
RAP cannula, 236, 237
RAP protein, 731
Rapaport, Richard, 659
Raptor Systems, 125
Raster, in GIS systems, 175–76
Raw juice bars, **631–36**
Raymond James & Associates, 229
Raymond Karsan Associates, 621
Raytheon Company
    in astronautics, 75, 78–79
    in GIS development, 182
    in microwave applications, 421–22
    in sensing devices, 525–27
    in video displays, 788
Razorfish, 846, 847
RBDS, 854
RBOCs. *See* Regional Bell operating companies
RCA Corporation, 786
RCN, 761
RCRA. *See* Resource Conservation and Recovery Act
RDA, in premium beverages, 600
RDF, 859
rDNA. *See* Recombinant DNA
Re-animation. *See* Cryopreservation
Read-only CD-ROMs. *See* CD-ROMs
Read-only memory, 672–73
Read-write CDs. *See* Recordable CDs
Ready Pac, 481
Ready Receptionist, 827
Ready-to-eat foods. *See* Convenience foods
ReadyCom, 818
Reagan, Ronald, 19, 20–21
Real estate business
    digital imaging for, 170
    financial planning and, 273
    GIS systems for, 182
    MIS for, 354
Real estate investment
    in retirement communities, 2–3
    trusts, 456, 530, 532, 533
Real-time systems
    in adult education, 28
    push technology for, 629
    in telemedicine, 741, 744
    for voice recognition, 827
RealAudio, 820
RealNetworks, 820
Reanimation Foundation, 151, 153
Rear projection displays, 788
Reason Public Policy Institute, 102, 104
Reasoning, artificial intelligence and, 65, 69
Rebarber, Theodore, 104
Receivers. *See also* Antennas
    in fiber optic technology, 267, 269
    in telemedicine, 745
Receptors, molecular modeling of, 436, 437
Rechargeable batteries, **381–85**
Reckitt & Coleman, 63–64
Recognition Systems, Inc., 84, 87
Recombinant DNA, in genetic engineering, 304–5, 307
Recombinant proteins, 304–6, 309
Recommended daily allowance, in premium beverages, 600

ReCompute, 779
Reconnaissance International, 317
Recordable CDs, 515–16, 566
Recording Industry Association of America, 191
Recording Industry Association of Japan, 191
Recording instruments. *See also* Sound recordings
    DVDs as, 185, 187–90
    for surveillance, 668, 720, 722
Recordings. *See* Sound recordings
Recreation agencies, 145, 294. *See also* Travel industry
Recreational Equipment, Inc., 252
Recreational vehicles, 573, 838
Recycling industry
    for batteries, 383
    hazardous waste and, 243, *245*
    new age philosophy and, 470
    for plastics, 591–92
    printer cartridges in, 615
    tires in, *245*
    used computer equipment in, 779
Red Book, 518
Red Rose Collection, 475
Redford, Robert, 459
Redhook Ale Brewery, 132, 133–34, 704, 706
Redstone, Sumner, 795
Redwood Microsystems, 414–15
Reebok, 585
Reed Elsevier, 349
Reference books, 221–22, 347
Reference services (Libraries), telephone, 347
Refinancing, 443
Reflection (Optics), in holography, 318
Reflective gratings, 520
Reflexology, 312, 315
Refractory materials, advanced ceramics in, 11–12
Regal Cinemas, 456, 458
Regional Bell operating companies, 749, 756, 758–61. *See also* specific companies
Regional Financial Associates, 863
Registered Financial Planners Institute, 277
Regulation, government. *See* Government regulation
Regulation M, 639
Regulators, pressure, 415
Rehabilitation, robotics for, 651
Reicher, Dan, 575
Reiki, in health spas, 312
Reimers, 540
Reinfetds, Juris, 126
Reinheitsgebot, 131
REIT. *See* Real estate investment, trusts
Rejuvenation, health spas for, 311, 313
Relational databases
    in MIS, 352, 354
    Multics Relational Data Store, 354
    parallel processing of, 543, 545
Relational online analytic processing, 352
Relationships, personal, Internet based, 805
Relativity Technologies Inc., 875
Relaxation techniques, 45–46
    in health spas, 311–13
Relays
    ATE, 414
    frame, 761
    micro, 410, 414
Relevant Knowledge Inc., 502

Reliance Group Holdings, Inc., 646
Reliance National, 646
ReliaStar Mortgage, 445
Religion, in new age philosophy, 469, 470, 474
Remediation, environmental. *See* Bioremediation
Remote access (Computers)
    print services for, 614, 616
    security for, 121, 122
Remote control, sensors for, 523
Remote sensing, 80, 180, 526
RenderMan, 110
Reneau, Inc., 540
Renewable resources
    alternative fuels as, 37, 41
    solar power, **573–80**
    wind power, 567
Repeaters (Electronics), for satellite services, 655–56
Repetitive strain injury, 644
Reporting software, 351–53
Repossession, of cars, 771
Reproductive technology, **255–64**
    endoscopic technology in, 237–38
Republic Industries, 774
RescueWare, 875
Research institutes, 283, 345. *See also* Information services
Research Products Corporation, 839
Resellers
    vs. build-to-order sales, 214
    of computer equipment, 778
    of Internet access, 362, 365
    value-added (*See* Value-added resellers)
Reservations (Tickets). *See* Ticket sales
Resins, in plastics, 588, 590, 591
Resistance exercise, equipment for, 581
Resolve (Brand name), 258
Resorts and spas, **311–16**
    classes in, 585
    exercise equipment for, 581, 582
    for gambling, **289–96**
    oxygen therapy in, 535, 538, 539–40
    for senior citizens, 1
    theme, 292
ReSource, 494
Resource Conservation and Recovery Act, 242–43, 383, 645
Resource description framework, 859
Respiratory diseases, oxygen therapy for, 535
Respiratory therapy. *See also* Oxygen therapy
    home, 327–30
    for smoking cessation, 686, 687
Responder (System), 820
Restaurants
    adult gaming and, 297, 300
    chain (*See* Chain restaurants)
    coffee, 705, 706
    creative dining in, **135–42**
    cybercafes as, **157–61**
    drive-in, 137
    fast food (*See* Fast food restaurants)
    gambling and, 290–91, 293
    juice bars in, 631, 634
    in outlet malls, 532
    in theater entertainment centers, 455
    in used car superstores, 772
Restoration, of art objects, 371
Restore 2000, 875

Rock climbing, 249–50, 253
Rockefeller Archive Center, 18
Rocket eBook, 223
Rockport, 503
Rockwell International Corporation
    in astronautics, 78
    in holography, 323
    in optical storage, 519
    in robotics, 651
    in sensing devices, 524, 526
Rodale, J.I., 864
Rodale, Robert, 864
Roebuck, Alvah, 388
Roentgen rays. *See* X-rays
Rogaine. *See* Minoxidil
Rogers, Adam, 659–60
Rohm & Haas Company, 435, 590
ROLAP, 352
Rolito, 250
Roller, Jeffrey, 741
Roller skates, 250
Rollerblade, Inc., 250, 253
Rollerblading, 250, 253
Rolm Corporation, 817
ROM, 672–73
Rome Laboratory, 569
Rome Reborn, 812
Ronco brand, 341, 342
Roosevelt, Eleanor, 766
Roosevelt, Theodore, 404
Rosedale, Mary, 330
Rosemont, 410
Rosen, Benjamin M., 738
Rosenberg, Philip S., 21
Rosengarten, David, 138
Roslin Institute, 305–6
Rotary Rocket Company, 77
RoTech Medical Corporation, 329
Roth, John A., 762–63
Rototillers, 865
Roulette, 290
Roundup (Pesticide), 307, 308, 866–67
Royal Canadian Mounted Police, on biometric identification, 84
Royalties, 164, 340
RSA Data Security Inc., 149
Rubber
    foam, 335
    in semiconductors, 671
Rubinstein, Seymour, 127
Ruby lasers, 372
RufNorth American, 554
Rugge, Sue, 347
Rum (Liquor), nonalcoholic, 609
Running, for exercise, 583
Rural areas
    telecommunications service for, 757, 761
    telemedicine for, 742, 743
Russell, Bertrand, 69
Russian Ministry of Atomic Energy, 577
Rust, filtration for, 839
Rust Environment & Infrastructure, 244, 247
Ruster, Allen, 170
RVs. *See* Recreational vehicles
Rx2000 Solutions Institute, 875
Ryan White Act of 1990, 19

S

S-band, for satellite services, 656
Saab, passenger restraint systems and, 553
Safaris, 710, 712, 714, 715, 717
Safe Drinking Water Act of 1974, 832, 834, 835
    amendment of 1996, 836, 840
Safeguard Health Enterprises, 398
Safeguard (Soap), 62
SafePak Corporation, 666, 669
Safety
    consultants, 228, 230
    public, 178, 663
    of specialty tourism, 716
    of toys, 334–36
    workplace, 228, 230, 644
Safety devices
    for extreme sports, 249, 250, 252, 253
    for games, 298
Safety-Kleen Corporation, 244, 246
SafetyLatch, 85, 89
Saffo, Paul, 523
Saflink Corporation, 85
Saft America, Inc., 384
Sage Group, on nutraceuticals, 482
Sailing, tours, 712, 717
Saks Fifth Avenue
    in electronic commerce, 503
    outlet centers, 529, 531
    security for, 667
Salad bars, 137, 632
Salads, pre-packaged, 480
Salaries. *See* Wages and salaries
Sales promotions, in mass marketing, 403, 406–7
Sales tax
    mail-order companies and, 389
    for online shopping, 210, 499–501
Salmonella, in fresh juice, 633
Salon.com, 225
Sam's Club, 492
Samsung, 652
Samuel Adams, 133
SAN. *See* Network-attached storage
San Andreas Brewing Company, 131
San Francisco AIDS Foundation, 18
San Marino Engineering Company, 38–39
San Migual NA, 605
Sanchez, Adalio, 217
Sand, in semiconductors, 672
Sandia National Laboratories
    in advanced ceramics, 12–13
    IUCRC and, 416
    in lasers, 374–75
    in lithium batteries, 385
    in micromachine development, 412
    parallel processing and, 545, 547
Sandoz, 688
Sandwiches, 479
Sanford C. Bernstein & Company, 394
Sanitation, in restaurants, 135–36
Santa Barbara Research Center, 527
Sanyo Electric
    in lithium batteries, 381, 384
    in optical storage, 519
    in solar power, 578

SAP-AG, 358
SAP software, 694, 696
Sapphire Group Inc., 355
Sapronov, Walt, 757
SAR, 568
Sara Lee, 479
Saranac-Matt Brewing Company, 608
Sarbanes, Paul S., 144
Sarcon Microsystems, 527
Sarnoff, David, 768
Sarnoff Corporation, 85
SART, 256, 259, 260
Sassaby, 57
SATAN (Security Analysis Tool for Auditing Networks), 128
Satellibild, 182
Satellite dish antennas, 193–95, *656*
Satellite Home Viewer Act, 194
Satellite Industry Association, 657
Satellite launch services industry, 75, 77–78, 182, **655–61**
Satellite television
    direct broadcast, **193–98**
    DSPs for, 677
    high power, 193, 195, 197
    infomercials on, 340
    microwave transmission of, 419
    satellites for, 193, 195, 198, 655–58, 660
    video displays for, 786
    vs. video rentals, 796
Satellites
    artificial (*See* Artificial satellites)
    communication (*See* Communication satellites)
    Landsat, 77–78, 178
    space (*See* Artificial satellites)
    weather, 523, 655, 659
Sato, T., 508
Saunas, in health spas, 312, 313
Savings
    medical accounts, 396
    personal, 273
    retirement, 278
Savings and loan associations, home mortgages from, 442
Saw palmetto, for prostate diseases, 494
Sawgrass Mills, 530, 533
Saxer Brewing Company, 132
SBA. *See* Small Business Administration
SBC Communications
    in DBS television, 196
    services by, 749, 753, 760
    in wireless communications, 852, 854
SBIR program, 416
SBIRS, 526
SBRC, 527
SCAA. *See* Specialty Coffee Association of America
Scales (Weighing instruments), digital, 319
Scanners, optical. *See* Optical scanners
Scarpa, James, 633, 634
Scentinel, 86
SCF. *See* Smart Card Forum
Schally, A.V., 259
Scheinman, Victor, 650
Schering-Plough Corporation
    in anti-aging products, 57
    in molecular design, 431
    in superdrug development, 726, 729, 730
Schima, Dave, 537

Schindler, Ross, *758*
Schless, David, 1
Schliesmann, Dick, 640
Schlumberger Electronic Transactions, 679, 681–83
Schneider, Cy, 404, 406
Schoenholt, Donald N., 704
Scholastic Corporation, 225
Scholastic Network, 225
Schonfield, Eric, 661
School districts, private management of, 100, 104
School funding, for charter schools, 99, 103–4
School-to-Work Opportunities Act, 29
Schools
    charter, **99–106**
    Internet access for, 362
    magnet, 101
    used computer equipment for, 779
Schraith, Jim, 214
Schultz, Howard, 704
Schuyler, Christine, 4
Schwartz, Peter, 282, 283
Schwartz, Richard, 629
Schwemmer, Geary, 323–24
Schwinn Bicycles, 582
SCIA, 680
Science. *See* specific sciences, e.g., Materials science, Cemistry, etc.
Science Applications International Corporation, 569
ScienceNet, 812
Scientific expeditions, in specialty tourism, 715
Scotch hose therapy, 312
Scott, Judith G., 229
Scott, Orlando McLean, 867
Scott, Tom, 601
Scott (O.M.) & Sons, 867
Scotts Company, 867, 868
Scowcroft, Bob, 473
Scrambling systems (Telecommunication), 666, 722
Scranton, Alec, 593
Scribner's Bookstore, 96
Scriplets, in Web site development, 848
Scripps (E.W.) Company, 867
Scripsit, 164
Scruggs, Richard, 739
Scuba diving
    equipment, 714
    tours, 710–12, 714, 717
SDDS, 460
Sea Launch (Satellite), 79
Sea Venture, 661
Seagate Software Company, 357
Seagate Technology Inc., 520
Search engines, Internet. *See* Internet search engines
Search strategies. *See* Database searching
Searle Company, 435
Sears, Richard, 388
Sears, Roebuck & Company, 158
    in exercise equipment, 582, 585
    history of, 388, 389
    infomercials for, 340, 341
    as ISP, 363
    in lawn and garden products, 864, 867
Seats
    automobile (*See* Automobile seats)
    belts, 551, 553, 555

microwave, 425, 665
  for miniaturization, 527
  motion, 665, 719, 722
  motor fuel, 410
  in nanotechnology, 414–16, 523, 524, 527
  for night vision, 523–27
  olfactory, 429, 430
  optical, **523–28**
  photon-type, 525
  pressure (*See* Pressure sensors)
  for printers, 524
  remote, 80, 180, 526
  for semiconductors, 524, 525, 528
  for telephones, 523, 524
  temperature, 525
  uncooled focal plane array, 525, 527
  for virtual reality, 814
  vision, 650, 652, 654
Sentient Networks, 117
Sentinel, 525
Sentry Technology Corporation, 722
Sequa, 555
Sequence robots, 651
Sequent Corporation, 545
Sequia Software Corporation, 358, 861
Serafini, Anthony, 304
Serono Laboratories, 256, 261–63
Serostim, for AIDS, 23
Servers
  file (*See* File servers)
  optical storage for, 520
  print, 611, 613–14, 616
  Web, 520, 614, 735–36
Service Merchandise, 585
Servistar, 867
Sex behavior, AIDS and, 22
Sex typing, sperm cells, 263–64
Seybold, Jonathan, 165
Seybold Seminars, 165
Seychelle Environmental Technologies, Inc., 837
SFNet, 158
SFSP, 277
SGI. *See* Silicon Graphics Inc.
SGMA. *See* Sporting Goods Manufacturers Association
SGML
  in Web site development, 848
  XML and, 857–60
SGS-Thomson, 682
Shakespeare & Co., 94
Shakey, 650
Shaklee Corporation, 57
Shakti Distributes, 475
Shannon, Kyle, 844, 847
Shapiro & Lobel, 640
Shareholders, 464, 465
Sharp Electronics Corporation
  in digital imaging, 172
  in multimedia, 452
  in optical storage, 519
  in video displays, 786, 788, 789
Sharp's (Beer), 605–7
Shasta Networks, 117
Shaw, Robert, 847
Shea, Biff, 329
Sheep, cloning, 305–7

Shell Chemical, 591
Shelter Island Risk Management Services, 646
Shen, Xiao A., 323
Shepard, Alan, 76
Shepard Poorman Communications Corporation, 170
Shepherds' Garden Seed, 868
Sher, Ron, 96
Shiatsu, 46, 469
Shichiku, 460
Shilts, Randy, 20
Ships, mobile satellite services for, 656
Shneiderman, Ben, 73
Shockley, William, 674
Shoes, athletic, 581, 584
Shon Dong-soo, 111–12
Shoplifting, surveillance for, 722
Shoplink, 503
Shopping, online. *See* Electronic shopping
Shopping malls. *See also* retail stores
  adult gaming and, 297, 301
  book sales from, 94
  gambling at, 289
  juice bars in, 633
  online, 207, 499, 500, 503
  outlet, **529–34**
  specialty coffee in, 705
Shorliffe, Edward, 68–69
Showers (Baths), Vichy, 312
SIA, 671, 673, 675
Sialon, in advanced ceramics, 10
Siegel, Benjamin "Bugsy," 290
Siegel, Larry, 531
Siegel, Zev, 704
Siemens Business Communications, 818
Siemens Company
  IUCRC and, 416
  in smart cards, 682
  in solar power, 576, 577–78
Siemens Computer Systems, 739
Siemens Corporate Research, 238
Siemens Nixdorf, 85
Siemens Rolm Communications Inc., 761
Siemens Solar Industries, 577–78
Sierra Club, 713
Sierra Nevada Brewing, 134
Sigmoidoscopes, 234
Sign making, robotics for, 652
Signal processing
  digital, 677, 751
  optical, 571
  sensors for, 525
Signature verification, 86, 88, 215
Sikorsky Aircraft, 485
S'il Vous Plait, 347
Silicon
  in advanced ceramics, 10
  carbide, 10
  nitride, 10
  pressure sensors, 410–11
  in solar cells, 574, 579
Silicon chips
  in airbags, 554
  in integrated circuits, 410
  micromachining, 409, 411, 527
  in molecular modeling, 437

Student achievement, in charter schools, 100
Student financial aid
    for adults, 35
    smart cards for loans, 681
Students, high risk, 101–2
Style sheets, extensible, 860
Stylus, for computer input, 215, 668
Stylus printers, 615
Styrofoam, for solar power storage, 579
Subaru, 552
Subprime lending rate, 443–44
Subscriptions
    in electronic publishing, 221, 223 (*See also* Membership)
    for information services, 347
    for Internet services, 362, 365
    for push technology, 625
    for virtual communities, 800
    for wireless communications, 849
Suda, Isamu, 153
Sudbury Systems, 817
Sugar, in beverage products, 599, 609
Sugarcane, as alternative fuel, 42
Suh, Chan, 847
Sulfa drugs, resistance to, 727, 729
Sulfur
    in gasoline, 40
    in hot springs, 312
Suminoto Pharmaceuticals Company, Ltd., 436
Sumitomo Metal Mining Company, 384, 578
Summer X Games, 252
SummerSun, 867
Summit, Roger, 347
Summit Environmental Group, 247
Summit Technology Inc., 507–11
Sun City, 3, 5
Sun City Squeeze, 635
Sun Microsystems, Inc.
    in desktop publishing, 165
    in information management systems, 358
    in molecular modeling, 434
    in multimedia, 450
    in parallel processing, 545
    in push technology, 628
    in smart cards, 683
    in systems integration, 738
    in telemedicine, 746
    in virtual reality, 811, 813, 814
    in Web development, 844
    in XML, 858
Sun Valley Squeeze, 602
Sundance Cinema, 459
Sundquist, Bruce, 397
Sunett, 481
Sunglasses, for surveillance, 722
Sunrise Educational Services, 105
Sunrise Technologies International, Inc., 509, 510–11
Sunscreening agents, 56
Sunsource International, 57
Super-twisted nematic screens, 785
Superatoms, in lasers, 374
Supercomputers, **543–49**
    in computer animation, 107
    history of, 544
    in molecular modeling, 436
    in virtual reality, 813

Superconductors
    ceramic, 10, 12, 14, 672
    in molecular modeling, 438
Superdrugs, **725–33**
Superfund. *See* CERCLA
Supermarkets
    children's products in, 333
    convenience foods in, 135, 139, 477
    holographic bar code readers in, 319
    juice bars in, 631
    lawn and garden products in, 863–64
    nonalcoholic beverages in, 605
    nutritional supplements in, 491
    pet supplies in, 561, 562
    prepared foods in, 135, 139
    smart cards for, 682
    specialty coffee in, 701, 702
    video rentals in, 791, 793–96
Supersonic aircraft, noise control of, 488
Superstores
    for adult gaming, 94–95, 297
    antitrust law and, 95
    baby, 333–34
    book, **93–98**
    music, **93–98**
    pet, 560–63
    used cars, 638, **771–75**
    video rental, 792–93
Support groups
    for smoking cessation, 686, 687, 690
    virtual communities for, 800
Supreme Court, on insurance for fertility medicine, 258
Surface Transportation Assistance Act, 38
Surgeon General's report, on physical activity, 581
Surgery
    antibiotics for, 729
    arthroscopic, 234
    computer animation in, 109
    endoscopic, **233–40**
    eye, 373, 375, **507–14**
    heart, 236, 237
    laparoscopic, 234
    lasers for (*See* Laser surgery)
    micro, 237, 238
    minimally invasive, 233, 235, 237
    nanotechnology for, 412
    neurological, 812
    plastic, 235, 373, 510
    robotics in, 235, 237, 238, 650, 652
    for tubal infertility, 256
    virtual reality technology in, 238, 812
Surgical equipment and supplies
    antibacterials in, 62
    endoscopes, 233
Surkan, Michael, 757
Surround sound systems
    in digital video discs, 190
    in multimedia computers, 453
    in speech recognition, 488
    in theater entertainment centers, 456, 458, 460
Surveillance, electronic. *See* Electronic surveillance
Survivor Stout, 131
Sushi, 138, 140
Sustainable agriculture, 867
Sustainable development, tourism and, 712

Sutherland, George, 282
Sutherland, Ivan, 810
Sutter Home Winery, Inc., 605, 607
SUVs, leasing of, 640
SVP, 347
Swanson's Foods, 139
Sweet, O. Robin, 139
Sweeteners, synthetic, 481
Swift-Eckerich, 479
Swiss Bank UBS, 738
Switches
    cross-bar, 758
    cut-off, 552–53
    optical, 762
    photonic, 570–71
    in semiconductors, 672
    sensors for, 524
    stored program control, 758
    in telecommunications networks, 757–59, 761, 762
SWOON, 805
Sybase Inc.
    in MIS, 351, 356–57
    in parallel processing, 545
    in software consulting, 697
Sylvan Learning Systems, Inc., 33
Symantec Corporation, 127
Symmetric multiprocessing, 547, 548
The Symposium, 283
Symyx Technologies, Inc., 430
Synchronous communications, in adult education, 28
Synchronous Optical Network, 568, 759, 762
Synechococcus, 497
Synercid, 729
Syngas fermentation, 42
Synrad, 374
Synthesis (Chemistry)
    molecular design for, **427–32**
    molecular modeling for, 433
Synthetic aperture radar, 568
Synthetic sweeteners, 481
Syrups, in specialty coffee, 702
Systems analysis, 281, 287
Systems integration, **735–40**
    with high definition television, 784, 786
    in robotics, 649
    in Web site development, 844
Systems security software, **121–28**

T

T1 communications, for Internet access, 362
Tabmint, 686
Tabulating Machines Company, 67
Tadiran Electronic Industries, 385
Tae Bo, 583
Tai chi, 469, 473, 585
TAIS. *See* Toshiba America Information Systems, Inc.
Takata, 556
Take-out food service, 477
Takeda, 491, 495, 496
TalkCity, 800, 802–4
Talkway, 804
Tamarack Storage Devices, 322
Tamgo, 165
Tan, Chung-Jen, *70, 71*

Tandem, 738
Tangent Company, 838–39
Tanger, Stanley, 531, 533
Tanger/Creighton, 531
Tanger Factory Outlet Centers Inc., 530, 531, 533
Tanimura & Antle, 480, 481
Tanner EDA, 410
Tappan, David, 585
Target, 334, 492, 583
Taste, water purification for, 832
Taste of Thai, 480
Taubman, A. Alfred, 103
Tax Equity and Fiscal Responsibility Act, 229
Tax-exempt securities, 464, 465
Tax-free exchanges, 466
Tax incentives, for environmental remediation, 244
Tax Reform Act, 229
Taxation
    captive insurance companies and, 647
    excise, 246, 606
    income, 695
    on Internet service, 362, 757
    sales (*See* Sales tax)
    state (*See* State taxation)
    on telecommunications services, 757
Taylor, Patrick, 117
TC-1 Labor Management System, 355
TCBY Enterprises Inc., 633, 635
TCI, 368, 759, 852
TDK Corporation, 383
Tea
    in coffee stores, 704
    green, 54
    herb, 599–602
    vs. nonalcoholic beverages, 607
    ready-to-drink, 597–99, 601–3, 701
Teacher certification, for charter schools, 99
Teachers' unions, charter schools and, 100–101
Team Corporation, 357
Team-Tidskapsler, 769
TEAM-UP, 575
TEC, 519
TechKnowledge, 746
Technical Reinvestment Program, 372
Technicolor Optical Disc Division, 322
Technolas GmbH, 509
Technology Applications Inc., 739
Technology Arts of Massachusetts, 750
Technology development
    futures consulting for, 282–85
    information services for, 349
Technology Evaluation Center (Japanese), 519
Technology Futures Inc., 285, 286
Technology in education, in adult education, 27–34
Technology Reinvestment Program, 372, 416
Tectrix, 582
Teddy bears, product licensing of, 404
TEFRA, 229
Tejin Limited, 436
Telco Communications Group, 760
Telcordia Technologies, 569
Tele Atlas, 182
Tele-Communications Inc., 368, 752, 852
Telecherics, 652
Telecom Italia, 853

Thomas, Bob, 641

Thomas & Betts, 382

Thomas Bros. Maps, 179

Thomas H. Lee Company, 560

Thompson-CFS, 811

Thomson Multimedia, 188, 518, 519

Thomson SA, 186

Thoreau, Henry David, 470

3Com Corporation

    fitness centers and, 581

    online marketing by, 206

    in sensing devices, 524

    in telemedicine, 745

3-D films

    computer animation in, 109, 111, 112

    IMAX for, 457–59

3D technology

    in computer games, 813

    in endoscopic technology, 236

    holography in, 317, 318, 320, 321

    immersive displays for, 813

    in molecular modeling, 433, 434

    in multimedia computers, 451

    in nanotechnology, 412

    networked, 811

    in optical storage technology, 519

    in television, 111, 815

    in virtual communities, 804

    in virtual reality, 809–14

    in x-rays, 322

Three-Five Systems, 789

3M Authentication Label, 320

3M Corporation

    in holography, 322

    in micromachine development, 412

    in optical storage, 518–19

    in smart materials, 320

    in water filtration, 838–39

360 Communications, 852

Threshold, 824

Thrift institutions, home mortgages from, 442

Thurber, Roger, 166

THX Digital surround system, 458, 460, 461

Thyssen AG, 651, 652

TI. *See* Texas Instruments

TI 1394 microprocessor, 676

TIB/Rendezvous, 629

Tibco, 629

Ticket sales

    electronic, 206, 210, 503

    holography for, 321

    nanotechnology for, 413

    in specialty tourism, 710, 714

    in theaters, 455–56, *457,* 459

    voice recognition systems for, 823, 828

Ticketmaster Online, 209, 221

Tilex, 62

Time capsules, **765–69**

Time Capsules, Inc., 767

Time division multiplexing system, 567

Time Life Music, 341

Time tracking, MIS for, 355

Time Warner Inc.

    in DVD development, 185–87, 189, 190

    in optical storage, 518, 519

    theaters, 460

Timken, H.H., 536

Tingley, Daniel, 591

Tires, recycling, *245*

TIS, 125

Tissues, cryopreservation of, 151, 153, 154

Titan Security, 668

Titanates, in advanced ceramics, 10

Titanium, in liquid metal products, 379

Title, Gary, 412

Titov, Gherman, 76

Titus, Dan, 633–34

Tivoli, 118

TL Technology, 88

TLC. *See* Laser Center, Inc.

TLC Capital Corporation, 511

TM (Transcendental meditation). *See* Meditation

TMA. *See* Toy Manufacturers Association

TMA Associates, 825

TMDA, 853

Tobacco, genetically engineered, 305

Tocotrienols, in nutritional supplements, 492

Toddlers, products for, **333–38,** 406

Toffler, Alvin, 283

Tofu, 481

Tofuti, 138

Toilet preparations industry

    anti-aging products and, 54–58

    vitamins in, 491

Token Ring networks, print services for, 614

Toll-free telephone numbers, mail-order companies and, 388

Toluene

    environmental removal of, 241

    polymers from, 587

Tomkins, 867

Tommee Tippee, 337

Toners (Xerography), 611–15

Tonka Corporation, 337

Tony the Tiger, 147

Tony's Pizza Service, 479

Tool and die industry, holography for, 317

Top Down Surround Sound, 488

Topical antibiotics, 728, 731

Toro Company, 867

Torrefazione Italia, 705

Torrent Networking Technologies, 117

Tort reform, risk management for, 645

Toshiba America Information Systems, Inc., 214–17

Toshiba Corporation

    in DVD development, 186, 187, 190

    in lithium batteries, 381, 384

    in multimedia, 452, 453

    in optical storage, 518, 519

    in semiconductors, 676

    in smart cards, 682

    in video displays, 788

Total New York Web site, 800

Touch

    in endoscopic technology, 238

    screens, 453, 771

    tone telephones, 817, 820

Tour guides (Persons), 710, 716

Tourist trade. *See also* Travel industry

    aerospace, 717

    environmental, 709, 711–14, 716, 717

specialty, **709–17**
Tours, package. *See* Package tours
Toussaint, Charles, 29
Tower Records, 499
Townes, Charles H., 372
Toxic waste management industry. *See* Hazardous waste
management industry
Toxicity, molecular modeling for, 435
Toxins, sensors for, 429, 430
Toy industry, **333–38,** 387
product licensing in, 404, 406–8
Toy Manufacturers Association, 334–36, 405
Toy stores, **333–38**
Toyota, 384, 641
Toys
safety of, 335
soft, 335, 404
Toys R Us, 333
TR Information Services, 348, 349
TRA. *See* Telecommunications Reform Act of 1996
Trace elements in nutrition, 493–95
TRACER, 247
Tracking systems
for pets, 562, 563
photonics in, 568
positioning systems for, 659
for security, 719
in space, 80
for surveillance, 722
for vehicles, 178–80, 182–83, 372, 412, 659
in virtual reality, 814
Tractors, garden, 865, *865*
Trade associations
futures consulting for, 285
virtual communities for, 800, 803
Trademarks, infringement services, 667
Traffic accidents
crash sensor for, 555
investigation of, 723
lasers for avoiding, 372
passenger restraint systems for, 551, 552
rear-end, 555
virtual reality for, 809
Traffic congestion, gambling and, 294
Traffic control, GIS systems for, 178
Training
autogenic, 46
computer based, 27, 641
employee (*See* Employee training)
for extreme sports, 249
obedience, 560
virtual reality for, 812
for voice recognition software, 824
Trampolines, for exercise, 583
Trans-Sensory Devices, 411
Trans-Time Inc., 155
Transcendental meditation. *See* Meditation
Transdermal medication, for smoking cessation, 685–89
Transducers, blood pressure, 410
Transformers, computer pulse, 543
TransG Seats, 556
Transgenic animals, 303, 305, 308, 309
molecular design of, 427, 429
Transgenic plants, 303, 306–9
molecular design of, 427, 429

Transistors
CMOS, 784
development of, 674
in semiconductors, 672, 677
Transit passes, holography for, 321
Translation software, 68, 72–73
voice recognition systems for, 823, 828, 829
Transmission Control Protocol/Internet Protocol, 762–63, 817
Transmission speed
holography and, 318
in optical storage technology, 517, 518, 520
of Pentium processors, 675–76
photonics for, 565–66
push technology and, 628
quantum technology and, 571
of supercomputers, 543
Transmitters
antennas (*See* Antennas)
in fiber optic technology, 267, 269
for holographic images, 324
radio, 574, 613, 650, 765
solar powered, 574
for surveillance equipment, 721, 722
Transnational corporations, futures consulting for, 286
Transparencies, printers for, 612
Transplantation
corneal, 510, 512
genetic engineering in, 303
organ, 235–36
Transponders, in satellite television, 194, 198
Transportable Remote Analyzer for Characterization and
Environmental Remediation, 247
Transportation. *See also* Vehicles
in elder day care, 199, 200, 202
GIS systems for, 178–80, 182–83, 372, 412, 659
micromachines for, 409
noise control, **485–89**
risks, 644
Transportation industry. *See also* Automobile industry
gambling and, 294
plastics in, 587, 592, 593
positioning systems for, 659
specialty tourism and, 709, 710
video displays for, 790
Transsoft Networks, 118
Transworld Telecommunications, 422, 424
Travel Advisories, 716
Travel agents, in specialty tourism, 710, 715
Travel Channel, 713
Travel industry
creative dining in, 136
cross-marketing in, 145
electronic sales in, 211
extreme sports and, 252
gambling and, 290–91, 294
online shopping in, 503
to remote destinations, 709, 710–11, 713, 715, 717
specialty tourism in, **709–17**
Travelers Group, 147
TRAVTEK, 179
Treadmills, 581, 582, 584, 585
Treasure Baskets To Go, 769
Treasury bills, in mutual funds, 464
Treasury Department
on push technology, 627

on smart cards, 680
on Y2K compliance, 874
Treatment Advocacy Center, 330
Trees, transgenic, 306
Trekking, 710, 712, 714, 717
Trends, consulting for, **281–88**
Trevelon Web, 710
TRI-W, 531
Triarc Companies, 598–600, 602, 603
Tribal Voice, 804, 806
Tribble (Software), 435
Tribune Company, 225
TRICAM-3, 238
Trichloroethylene, environmental removal of, 241
Tricolsan, 63
Trihalomethane, in drinking water, 834
TRILOGUE, 821
Trimble Navigation, 177
Tripos, Inc., 430, 431, 437
Trizec Hahn Development Corporation, 531
Trokel, Stephen L., 509
Tropicana, 601
Trotter, Company, 582
Trout, T. John, 324
Trovafloxacin, development of, 729
TRP, 372, 416
Truck drivers
    biometric identification of, 90
    as leased employees, 228
True Face Network, 84, 126
True Value Hardware, 864, 867
TrueWav RS fiber, 269
Trump, Donald, 294
Trump Hotels & Casino Resorts, 293, 294
Trust-Broker Security Suite, 665
Trusted Information Systems, 125
Trusts, in cryopreservation, 155
Truth, in artificial intelligence, 66
TRW Inc.
    on information management systems, 356
    in passenger restraint systems, 555
    in systems integration, 735, 738
    in wireless communications, 853
Tsiolkowvsky, Konstantin, 75, 76
TTFG, 285
Tuberculosis
    air filtration for, 838
    drugs for, 725, 727, 729
    oxygen therapy and, 537
    travel and, 714
Tubesing, Donald, 166
Tufts University, in superdrug development, 731
Turf Builder, 867
Turtle Beach Systems, 452
TV Navigator, 196
TWE. *See* The Washington House
Twenty-First Century Workforce Commission, 32
Twins, biometric identification of, 84, 85
Twinvideo, 238
Two-way communication
    on cable lines, 752
    microwave applications in, 420, 421
    mobile communications services for, 851
    in robotics, 651
Tyco International Ltd., 269, 663

Tyco Toys, 333, 337
Tyee Productions, 341
Tyers, Robert John, 250
Typesetting, desktop publishing for, 164–66
Typing patterns
    for biometric identification, 86, 126
Tyson Foods, 479

U

U-Spy, 722
UCC. *See* Uniform Commercial Code
UCLA. *See* University of California-Los Angeles
UCLA (Uniform Consumer Leases Act), 639
UCSF. *See* University of California-San Francisco
UGC Consulting, 177
UHCL, 286, 690
Ulcers
    corneal, 731
    peptic, 234, 493
ULEVs, 41
Ulitmate Xphoria, 494
Ultimate Technologies, Inc., 487
ULTRA, 525
Ultra low emission vehicles, 41
Ultrak, Inc., 722–23
Ultrak Europe, 723
Ultralife Batteries, 382
Ultraviolet radiation
    lasers and, 373
    in molecular design, 428
    screening, 56–57
    in water purification, 831, 840–41
UNAIDS, 21–24
Uncle Ben's Rice, 482
Uncooled focal plane array sensors, 525, 527
Uncooled Low-cost Technology Reinvestment Alliance, 525
Underground water, contaminated, 247
Underofler, John, 324
Undersea Hyperbaric Medical Society, 540
Underwater exploration, 317, 319
Underwriting. *See* Insurance
Unemployment compensation, professional employer
    organizations for, 229, 230
UNESCO, 34
Uniform Commercial Code, information services and, 349
Uniform Consumer Leases Act, 639
Uniform Resource Locators, 365, 858, 861
Unilever, 56, 57, 483
Unimates, 650
Unimation, 650
Uninsured persons, 395
Union of American Hebrew Congregations, 766
Union Tostadora, 483
Unions, labor, 100–101
Unisource, 761
Unisys Corporation
    in GIS development, 177
    in systems integration, 735, 738
    Universal Repository, 859
    in XML, 859
United Airlines, 148, 828
United Artists Theatre Circuit, 458, 459
United Fresh Fruit and Vegetable Association, 478
United Health Group, 398

U.S. Justice Department
  on DBS television, 194
  on systems integration, 736
  on telephone companies, 749–50, 756
  on theater chains, 457, 460
  on used computer equipment, 779–80
U.S. Naval Academy, on satellites, 659
U.S. Office of Management and Budget, on Y2K
  compliance, 871–72
U.S. Patent and Trademark Office
  on genetically engineered products, 304
  on holographic technology, 322
  on software licensing, 127
U.S. Pharmacopoeia, 492
U.S. Postal Service, 723
U.S. Robotics, 213, 216
U.S. Supreme Court, on patents for genetically engineered
  products, 305
U.S. West Communications Group, 761
U.S. West Inc., 749, 753, 754, 756–57, 852
US-ABC, 383
US Web, 846, 847
USA Networks, 342
USA Toy Library Association, 335
USAA, 644
USABC, 383, 384
USAC, 743
USACA, 12
USDA. *See* Department of Agriculture
Used cars
  leasing of, 638, 640
  superstores for, 638, **771–75**
Used computer equipment, **777–82**
USENET, 799, 801–2, 804
User interfaces (Computer)
  graphical (*See* Graphical user interface)
  in systems integration, 735
USGS, on water quality, 834, 835
USN Communications, 761
USPS, 723
USSB, 196–97
UTI, 487
Utilities. *See* Public utilities
Utility Photo Voltaic Group, 575
Utilization Review Accreditation Commission, 395
UV Waterworks, 840

V

V-8 splash tropical Blend Drink, 599–600
VA, on home health care, 329
Vacations, *vs.* specialty tourism, 709, 710
Vaccines
  for AIDS, 21, 25
  for *Helicobacter pylori,* 726
  for pets, 563
  polymers and, 594
  for resistant microbes, 728
  for smoking cessation, 690
  solar refrigeration of, 573
  for travel, 717
Vaegra, 492
Valence Technology, Inc., 385
Valenti, Jack, 455, 460
Value-added networks, 115–16, 208, 860

Value-added resellers
  of books, 211
  of computer equipment, 778
  of food, 477
  network support from, 115–16, 208
  in wireless communications, 852
Valves
  micro, 414
  proportional, 414
Van Allen radiation belts, 76
van den Berghe, Nicholas, 170
van Hedge Fund Advisors International Inc., 466
van Horn, Charles, 518
Vancomycin, microbial resistance to, 728, 729
Vanguard Cellular, 852
Vanguard Group, 463, 466
Vanguard (Satellite), 76
Vanilla, in specialty coffee, 702
Vanity Fair Outlets, 530
Vanity publishers, 223–24
VANs, 115–16, 208, 860
Vanston, John H., 285
Vanzura, Rick, 97
Variable rate mortgages, 442–43
Varicose veins, microwave treatment for, 423
Variflex, Inc., 253
VARoffice, 354
VARs. *See* Value-added resellers
Vasectomy, fertility medicine and, 257
VAX computers, in MIS, 354
VaxGen, Inc., 21
VCA. *See* Veterinary Centers of America
VCI (Voice Control Systems Inc.), 827
VCR. *See* Video cassette recorders
VCRs. *See* Video cassette recorders
VCS Security, Inc., 667
VDTs. *See* Video display terminals
Vector processing, 543
Vectors (Mathematics), in GIS systems, 175–76
Veg-O-Matic, 341
Vegetable juices
  bars for, **631–36**
  blends, 631
  in premium beverages, 601, 603
Vegetable oils, alternative fuels from, 39, 43
Vegetables
  in anti-aging products, 53
  cruciferous, 497
  prepared, 481
Vegetarian cookery
  baby foods, 472
  new products for, 480, 482, 632
Vegetarian restaurants, 138
Vehicle fleet management, leasing and, 638
Vehicles. *See also* Automobiles; Transportation
  electric, 41, 384, 385
  pollution from, 38, 865–66
  positioning systems for, 178–80, 182–83, 372, 412, 659
  radio controlled, 650
  recreational, 573, 838
  for specialty tourism, 709
  sport-utility, 640
Veit, Howard R., 397
Venom, molecular modeling of, 437
VENT, 715

Viisage Technology Inc., 85
Viking Space Probes, 77
Vincam Group, 229
Vincent, Donald, 651
Vinyl
    in plastics, 588
    in toys, 335, 336
Viramune, 25
Virgin Group, 460
Virtual Boy, 814
Virtual communities, **799–807**
Virtual databases, 803, 861
Virtual Reality Inc., 813
Virtual reality modeling language. *See* VRML
Virtual reality technology, **809–16**. *See also* VRML
    in games, 297, 299
    holography in, 319
    modeling language, 358
    in multimedia computers, 447
    parallel processing for, 545
    patient modeling in, 238
    in surgery, 238, 812
    in theater entertainment centers, 455, 458
    WWW and, 358
Virus diseases
    air filtration for, 840
    antibiotics for, 728
    drug development for, 726, 731–32
    water purification for, 840
Visa
    on biometric identification, 86
    on electronic commerce, 209
    holographic identification and, 320
    on smart cards, 679, 681, 682
Viselman, Ken, 406
Visiedo, Octavio, 103
Vision
    artificial, 66
    night (*See* Night vision devices)
    sensors, 650, 652, 654
Vision disorders
    electronic publishing for, 222
    surgery for, 373, 375, **507–14**
Vision Dome, 815
Visionics Corp., 85, 88
Visual Age 2000, 875
Visual basic (Computer language), 354, 844, 861, 875
Visualization (Mental images)
    by computers (*See* Computer simulation)
    in health spas, 313
    virtual reality for, 813
Visveshwara, Nadarasa, 538
Visx Inc., 507–11
Vitamin A, in premium beverages, 600
Vitamin B, in augmented food, 494
Vitamin C
    anticancer properties of, 496
    in juice bar products, 632
    in premium beverages, 600
    producers of, 496
    supplements, 491, 494
Vitamin E
    benefits of, 496
    natural *vs.* synthetics, 496
    producers of, 495

supplements, 491, 494
Vitamin Institute and Institute of Biochemistry, 493
Vitamin Superstore, 495–96
Vitamin World, 495
Vitamins, **491–98**. *See also* Dietary supplements
    in anti-aging products, 53–55
    antioxidant, 53–55
    in foods, 479, 482
    high-dosage, 537
    for infertility, 256
    in juice bar products, 631, 634
    natural *vs.* synthetics, 496
    in premium beverages, 603
    price fixing of, 495
    recommended daily allowance for, 600
    in skin care products, 491
Vixen, 214
VLSI Photonics, 568
VMX Inc., 817
Vocabulary, in voice recognition software, 824
VocalTec Communications, 761
Vocational education, for adults, 27–29, 32
Voctor Company, 186
Vodafone, 852–54
VODIS, 828
Voice changers, 719, 722
Voice Commander 99, 826
Voice Control Systems Inc., 827
Voice Extensible Markup Language. *See* VXML
Voice Extensible Markup Language Forum, 860
Voice File Recorder, 820
Voice Guardian, 826
Voice mail, **817–22**
    for cellular phones, 854
    in MIS, 352
    satellites for, 658
    services, 751
    telephony for, 755
    in virtual communities, 804
    wireless communications for, 852
Voice markup language, 826, 859, 860
Voice Message Exchange, 817
Voice recognition software, **823–29**
    artificial intelligence in, 66, 72–73
    for biometric identification, 85–86, 88
    continuous speech, 824–27
    development of, 488
    for dialing, 819
    discrete-word, 824, 825
    for driving instructions, 828
    DSPs for, 677
    in endoscopic technology, 238
    Internet based, 806, 821, 826, 859
    in multimedia computers, 447, 451
    in PDAs, 213
    real-time natural language, 827
    speaker dependent, 824
    in telemedicine, 745
    telephony and, 755
VoiceDialer, 827
VoicePad, 825, 827
VoicePlus, 827
VoicePro, 827
VoiceType, 825, 827
VoiceXpress, 825, 827

GENERAL INDEX

WorldCom Inc.
    in fiber optics, 269
    in Internet service provision, 361, 367
    in long-distance service, 759
    merger of, 752
    services by, 760
    in wireless communications, 852
WorldNet, 158, 361, 362, 364, 367
WorldPartners, 761
WorldView Service, 286
WORM drive, 515, 520, 566
Worthington Foods Inc., 480
Wow!, 364
WPI KOLL Asia Pacific Advisors, 301
WQA, 832–34
Wright, Debbra, 424
Wrinkle replacement, 373, 375
Wrist watches
    as phones, 384–85
    product licensing in, 404
Write-once, read-many drives, 515, 520, 566
Writers, in computer animation, 108
Writing, computer recognition of, 215
WRQ, 875
W3C. *See* World Wide Web Consortium
WTO (World Tourism Organization), 709, 715
WTO (World Trade Organization). *See* World Trade Organization
WWW. *See* World Wide Web
Wyatt, Pat, 407
Wyeth-Lederle, 728
Wynn, Stephen, 291, 294

X

X-34 satellite, 661
X-ACT, 858
X-rated films, renting, 792
X-rays
    crystallography (*See* Crystallography)
    holography in, 317–19, 322
    vs. microwave imaging, 423
    transmission of, 741, 744, 746
    in video displays, 790
Xanadu Project, 845
Xerox Corporation
    in artificial intelligence, 69
    in on-demand printing, 226
    in printers, 614, 616
    in sensing devices, 524
Xionics Document Technologies, 167
Xlibris, 224
XLL, 861
XMI, 859
XML, **857–62**
    EDI and, 859–60
    in MIS, 358
    in push technology, 627
    in Web site development, 848
XML Active Content Technologies Council, 858
xmLDAP, 860
XOMA Corporation, 731
Xoom, 806
XP robot, 650
XSL Working Group, 859

Xtenblade, 250
Xtra Secure, 86
Xylene, polymers from, 587

Y

Yager, Milan, 231
Yahoo!
    in cross marketing, 146
    in electronic commerce, 207, 500
    search engine, 625
    virtual communities and, 802, 804
    in XML development, 861
Yale University, in superdrug development, 731
Yamanouchi Pharmaceutical Company, 57
Yankee Group, 849, 852
Yard equipment. *See* Lawn and garden equipment
Yaskawa Electric Corporation, 651, 652
Yates, Dale, 781
Year 2000 Information Center, 872
Year 2000 transition (Computers), **871–78**
    consulting for, 693
    mass marketing of, 408
    risk management for, 643, 645
    securities industry and, 463, 468
    software consultants for, 696
Yeast, in nonalcoholic beverages, 606
Yellow Book, 518
Yellow pages, 500, 755
Yelmo Cineplex de Espana, 458
Yieldgard, 308
Y2K computer problem. *See* Year 2000 transition (Computers)
Yoga
    in health spas, 312
    new age products and, 469–71, 473, 475
    products for, 583, 585
    tourism, 709
Yogurt
    augmented, 483
    frozen, 632
    in juice bar products, 631, 632
    in premium beverages, 600
York, Anna Eliot, 30
Your Staff, 230
Yourdan, Ed, 695, 696
Yourdan, Inc., 696
Yovovich, B.G, 828

Z

Zadeh, Lotfi, 69
Zaffaroni, Alejandro c., 430
Zagam, 728
Zak Designs Inc., 408
Zaner, Laura O., 2
Zap-Tables, 481
Zdeblick, Mark, 415
Zebra Imaging, 320, 321–22
Zenith Electronics Corporation
    in DVD development, 188
    in multimedia, 452
    in video displays, 786, 788
Zeolites, in solar power storage, 579
Zero emission vehicles, 41